OXFORD COMMENTARIES ON INTERNATIONAL LAW

General Editors: *Professor Philip Alston*, Professor of International Law
at New York University, and *Professor Vaughan Lowe*, Chichele Professor
of Public International Law in the University of Oxford and Fellow of
All Souls College, Oxford.

The Convention on Cluster Munitions

A Commentary

This book has been developed in co-operation with the

The Convention on Cluster Munitions

A Commentary

Edited by

GRO NYSTUEN AND
STUART CASEY-MASLEN

OXFORD
UNIVERSITY PRESS

OXFORD
UNIVERSITY PRESS

Great Clarendon Street, Oxford OX2 6DP

Oxford University Press is a department of the University of Oxford.
It furthers the University's objective of excellence in research, scholarship,
and education by publishing worldwide in

Oxford New York

Auckland Cape Town Dar es Salaam Hong Kong Karachi
Kuala Lumpur Madrid Melbourne Mexico City Nairobi
New Delhi Shanghai Taipei Toronto

With offices in

Argentina Austria Brazil Chile Czech Republic France Greece
Guatemala Hungary Italy Japan Poland Portugal Singapore
South Korea Switzerland Thailand Turkey Ukraine Vietnam

Oxford is a registered trade mark of Oxford University Press
in the UK and in certain other countries

Published in the United States
by Oxford University Press Inc., New York

British Library Cataloguing in Publication Data

Data available

Library of Congress Cataloging-in-Publication Data

Data available

Typeset by Newgen Imaging Systems (P) Ltd., Chennai, India
Printed in Great Britain
on acid-free paper by
CPI Antony Rowe

ISBN 978–0–19–959900–4

1 3 5 7 9 10 8 6 4 2

Foreword

When, at some point in the future, I look back on my time as Norwegian Foreign Minister, one of the moments that will stand out most vividly is 30 May 2008 in Dublin, when the Convention on Cluster Munitions was adopted. I arrived in the city early that morning on a night flight from Greenland, having barely slept, in time to see for myself the final stages of the process leading up to the adoption of the Convention. I felt then—and still feel—tremendous joy, as well as respect and gratitude towards the many women and men who had worked so tirelessly for so long to give us that moment.

The adoption of the Convention on Cluster Munitions is the culmination of an 18-month-long intensive and inclusive diplomatic process to address the human suffering caused by cluster munitions. Technical, humanitarian, military and legal experts from States, international organizations and civil society had worked together to achieve a convention that would make a difference, in terms of both helping those already affected by these weapons and preventing more people from becoming victims in the future.

The development, adoption, signing and entry into force of the Convention are now milestones successfully passed. Ahead, starting with the first Meeting of States Parties, lie all the challenges of implementing the Convention, to ensure that its words are put into action. The partnerships between States, the United Nations, the International Committee of the Red Cross and the Cluster Munition Coalition that so successfully underpinned the Oslo Process will be key in ensuring that the Convention truly makes a difference for those affected.

There is still much work to be done. The prohibitions set out in the Convention must be reflected in national legal frameworks. Stockpiles must be destroyed, contaminated areas must be identified and cleared, and risk reduction programmes must be undertaken. The rights of victims to full social and economic inclusion together with adequate medical care and rehabilitation must be realized. International cooperation among the States Parties will be critical in ensuring timely implementation of these core provisions.

The Convention on Cluster Munitions was a response to an acute international humanitarian problem. Together with other instruments of humanitarian disarmament, such as the 1997 Anti-Personnel Mine Ban Convention, it will strengthen international humanitarian law and other frameworks for the protection of civilians.

This book is a legal commentary, but it should be read by all those with an interest in making the Convention a reality. The authors have all been involved in the development of the Convention, and they provide insight into and analysis of all of its provisions. I hope that this work will help the international community in the practical implementation of the Convention, and thus also help to ensure that the obligations set out therein are translated into reality on the ground.

Jonas Gahr Støre
Minister of Foreign Affairs
Oslo, June 2010

Preface

The Convention on Cluster Munitions was adopted by 107 States on 30 May 2008 at a specially convened diplomatic conference in Dublin, Ireland.[1] The Convention is a landmark achievement, not only for the States that negotiated it, but also for the Cluster Munition Coalition,[2] a network of several hundred non-governmental organizations (NGOs) worldwide; the International Committee of the Red Cross (ICRC);[3] and the United Nations (UN),[4] all of which campaigned effectively for a new international treaty to address comprehensively the problems caused by cluster munitions.[5]

The global campaign for the adoption of the Convention, which was based on the harm caused to civilian populations during and after use of cluster munitions, was followed by a determined push for its swift entry into force. One hundred and six States had signed the Convention by 25 May 2010, and the necessary level of ratifications or accessions (30) was secured on 16 February 2010, with the result that the Convention on Cluster Munitions entered into force as binding international law on 1 August 2010.

States adhering to the Convention must never under any circumstances use, develop, produce, acquire, stockpile, retain, or transfer cluster munitions. They are also generally prohibited from assisting, encouraging, or inducing anyone to undertake any activity prohibited by its provisions.

Each State is required—within eight years of becoming a party to the Convention—to destroy all stockpiled cluster munitions under its jurisdiction and control.[6] This deadline can be extended for an additional four years and further extensions of four years may also be granted in exceptional

---

[1] The Diplomatic Conference for the Adoption of a Convention on Cluster Munitions, held in Dublin on 18–30 May 2008. It is hereinafter referred to as the (Dublin) Diplomatic Conference.

[2] <http://www.stopclustermunitions.org>.

[3] <http://www.icrc.org/Web/Eng/siteeng0.nsf/htmlall/section-ihl-cluster-munition?OpenDocument>.

[4] Several UN agencies and bodies played an important role in promoting the adoption of the Convention, not least the UN Development Programme (UNDP) and the UN Children's Fund (UNICEF).

[5] Cluster munitions are generally explosive munitions that are dispersed or released from a 'parent' container that is launched, dropped, or fired from the ground, the air, or the sea. The definition of cluster munitions for the purposes of the Convention on Cluster Munitions and its scope are set out in its Articles 1 and 2 (see, further, the commentary on these provisions).

[6] See the commentary on Article 3 of the Convention.

circumstances. States may retain a limited number of cluster munitions and explosive submunitions for the development of and training in detection, clearance, or destruction techniques, or for the development of cluster munition counter-measures.

Each State must also clear its own territory or other territory it controls of cluster munition remnants (abandoned cluster munitions, failed cluster munitions, or unexploded submunitions or bomblets) within 10 years of becoming party to the Convention.[7] If a State is unable to do so, it may request extensions from a meeting of States Parties or a Review Conference for additional periods of up to five years at a time.

Far-reaching, and—for a treaty of international humanitarian law—unprecedented provisions are included on assistance for victims.[8] Each State Party that has cluster munition victims on its own or other territory under its control must provide for their medical care and physical rehabilitation, psychological support, and social and economic inclusion. Not only those who are killed or injured by cluster munitions are defined as 'cluster munition victims'; the term also extends to families and communities that have suffered socio-economic or other harm.[9]

As the ICRC has observed, on the basis of the Convention, 'cluster munitions will—like exploding and expanding bullets, chemical weapons, biological weapons, anti-personnel mines, weapons using undetectable fragments and blinding lasers—be regarded as weapons prohibited under IHL [international humanitarian law]'.[10] A new humanitarian norm has been created that may one day become customary law.

The aim and drafting of the Commentary

This Commentary seeks to explain the context and meaning of all of the Convention's provisions. The following experts, listed in alphabetical order, contributed texts to the Commentary:[11]

- Torfinn Rislaa Arntsen, Assistant Director General, Royal Ministry of Foreign Affairs, Norway; and member of the Norwegian Delegation to the Dublin Diplomatic Conference;

---

[7] See the commentary on Article 4 of the Convention.

[8] See the commentary on Article 5 of the Convention.

[9] See the commentary on Article 2, paragraph 1 of the Convention.

[10] 'The Convention on Cluster Munitions', Fact Sheet, ICRC, Geneva, November 2008.

[11] All of the contributors are writing in their personal capacity and the views expressed in the Commentary are therefore not those of the bodies or institutions for whom they work.

- John Borrie, Senior Researcher and Project Manager, United Nations Institute for Disarmament Research (UNIDIR), Geneva; and member of the UNIDIR Delegation to the Dublin Diplomatic Conference;
- Dr Théo Boutruche, Consultant on International Humanitarian Law;
- Dr Stuart Casey-Maslen, Senior Researcher, Geneva Academy of International Humanitarian Law and Human Rights; and Mine Action Editor, Landmine Monitor, Norwegian People's Aid;
- Professor Andrew Clapham, Director, Geneva Academy of International Humanitarian Law and Human Rights; and Professor of Public International Law at the Graduate Institute of International and Development Studies in Geneva;
- Bonnie Docherty, Lecturer, Harvard Law School; and Senior Researcher, Arms Division, Human Rights Watch, Washington, DC; and member of the Cluster Munition Coalition (CMC) delegation at the Dublin Diplomatic Conference;
- Tirza Leibowitz, Director of Advocacy, Survivor Corps, Washington, DC;
- Lou Maresca, Legal Adviser, Arms Unit, Legal Division, International Committee of the Red Cross (ICRC), Geneva; and member of the ICRC delegation at the Dublin Diplomatic Conference;
- Richard Moyes, Policy and Research Director, Action on Armed Violence, London; and Honorary Research Fellow in the Centre of Advanced International Studies at Exeter University; and member of the CMC delegation at the Dublin Diplomatic Conference;
- Thomas Nash, Coordinator, Cluster Munition Coalition; and member of the CMC delegation at the Dublin Diplomatic Conference;
- Professor Gro Nystuen, Associate Professor of international humanitarian law at the University of Oslo and the Norwegian Defence Staff University College; Senior Partner at International Law and Policy Institute, Oslo; and Head of the Legal Secretariat at the Dublin Diplomatic Conference;
- Dr Marcus Reiterer, Counsellor for Political Affairs, Austrian Embassy to the United States of America, Washington, DC; and member of the Austrian delegation at the Dublin Diplomatic Conference;[12]
- Declan Smyth, Deputy Legal Adviser, Department of Foreign Affairs of Ireland, and Chairman of the Irish National Committee on International

---

[12] Dr Reiterer served as the Friend of the President on Article 5 at the Dublin Diplomatic Conference.

Humanitarian Law; and member of the Irish delegation at the Dublin Diplomatic Conference; and

- Professor Virgil Wiebe, Associate Professor and Chair of the Department of Clinical Legal Education, University of St. Thomas School of Law, Minneapolis, MN.

Professor Charles Garraway, Department of Law, London School of Economics; Associate Fellow at Chatham House; and Visiting Fellow in the Department of Human Rights, University of Essex, Colchester reviewed the draft manuscript of the Commentary. In addition, the following experts reviewed drafts of the Commentary and provided suggestions to improve or add to the text:

- Mark Hiznay, Senior Researcher, Arms Division, Human Rights Watch, Washington, DC (Introduction and Article 1);
- Grethe Østern, Policy Adviser, Mine Action Department, Norwegian People's Aid, Oslo (Introduction, Title and Preamble and Articles 1–4);
- Steve Goose, Director, Arms Division, Human Rights Watch, Washington, DC (Articles 2 and 6–8);
- Colin King, Director, Colin King Associates (Article 3);
- Tamar Gabelnick, Treaty Implementation Director, International Campaign to Ban Landmines, Geneva (Articles 3 and 4);
- Vera Bohle, Evaluation and Disarmament Specialist, Geneva International Centre for Humanitarian Demining (Article 4);
- Lieutenant-Colonel Jim Burke, Adviser, Irish Defence Forces (Article 4);
- Eva Veble, Head, Mine Action Unit, Danish Church Aid (Article 4);
- Katleen Maes, Handicap International, Belgium (Article 5);
- Christophe Lanord, Consultant on International Humanitarian Law, and member of the Legal Secretariat at the Dublin Diplomatic Conference (Article 1, paragraph 3, and final clauses);
- Sherry Holbrook, former Legal Officer, Treaty Section of the UN Office of Legal Affairs (represented the UN Treaty Section in preliminary discussions and at the Dublin Diplomatic Conference serving as Facilitator and Legal Affairs Officer; currently Officer in the UN Office of the Special Adviser to the Secretary-General on Cyprus) (final clauses); and
- Maya Brehm, Researcher, United Nations Institute for Disarmament Research, Geneva (Article 21).

The review of all or part of the Commentary and the provision of comments or suggestions does not imply that these experts agree with any or all of the views expressed in the Commentary.

The layout of the Commentary

The introduction to the commentary discusses the development and use of cluster munitions and provides a historical overview of the legal regulation of the weapons and the negotiation of the Convention on Cluster Munitions.

The commentary on the Convention itself addresses first its title and pre-amble and then, separately but in sequential order, each of its Articles, with the respective commentary broken down into sub-paragraphs, where relevant. The commentary on each substantive provision also includes an overview of the relevant Article, a summary of the preparatory discussions, and details of the negotiation of the provisions. All paragraphs are numbered and accordingly cross-references, as well as the index at the end of the book, refer to para-graph, rather than page, numbering.[13]

The bibliography for the Commentary and a glossary of key terms and abbreviations is followed by the annexes. The first annex contains key pro-visions of international treaty law from the *1969 Vienna Convention on the Law of Treaties*;[14] subsequent annexes include documentation relating to the Convention on Cluster Munitions itself, including the Declaration that for-mally launched the 'Oslo Process', various drafts of the Convention and the proposals tabled formally at the Dublin Diplomatic Conference of May 2008, as well as the text of the Convention as adopted.

The principles of international treaty interpretation

The Commentary bases its interpretation of the Convention on the basic principles of treaty law,[15] notably the *1969 Vienna Convention on the Law of*

---

[13] e.g. §1.24 refers to the 24th numbered paragraph of the commentary on Article 1.

[14] Vienna Convention on the Law of Treaties, 1969, Done at Vienna on 23 May 1969. United Nations, Treaty Series, Vol. 1155, p. 331, available at: <http://treaties.un.org/doc/Treaties/1980/01/19800127%200052%20AM/Ch_XXIII _01p.pdf> (accessed 24 March 2010).

[15] For a more detailed discussion of international treaty law see, e.g., Aust, A., *Modern Treaty Law and Practice* (Cambridge: Cambridge University Press, 2007); de la Guardia, E., *Derecho de los tratados internacionales* (Buenos Aires: Abaco de Rodolfo Depalma, 1997); McNair, A., *Law of Treaties*, Second Edition (Oxford: Clarendon Press, 1961); Reuter, P., *Introduction au droit des traités*, Third Edition (Geneva: Publications de l'Institut Universitaire des Hautes Etudes

Treaties. General principles and methods for treaty interpretation are embodied in Articles 31 and 32 of the 1969 Vienna Convention.[16] The International Court of Justice (ICJ) has expressly affirmed that these provisions, which set out, respectively, the general rule and supplementary means of treaty interpretation, reflect customary law. Thus,

a treaty must be interpreted in good faith in accordance with the ordinary meaning to be given to its terms in their context and in the light of its object and purpose. Interpretation must be based above all upon the text of the treaty. As a supplementary measure recourse may be had to means of interpretation such as the preparatory work of the treaty and the circumstances of its conclusion.[17]

By virtue of Article 31, paragraph 3, any subsequent agreement or practice[18] relating to the treaty together with any relevant rules of international law must be considered together with the context.

Dr Gro Nystuen and Dr Stuart Casey-Maslen
Oslo
May 2010

Internationales—Genève, 1995); and Sinclair, I., *The Vienna Convention on the Law of Treaties,* Second Edition (Manchester: Manchester University Press, 1984).

[16] See Annex 1 for the text of the relevant Articles.

[17] Case concerning the Territorial Dispute (Libyan Arab Jamahiriya/Chad), *ICJ Reports 1994,* pp. 21–22.

[18] The International Law Commission has included, in a non-exhaustive list, the following acts as forms that State practice may take: 'treaties, decisions of international and national courts, national legislation, diplomatic correspondence, opinions of national legal advisers and the practice of international organisations'. Other categories could be policy statements, official manuals on legal questions, such as manuals of military law, executive decisions and practices, comments by governments on draft treaties produced by the International Law Commission, press releases, and resolutions relating to legal questions in the United Nations General Assembly. As far as cluster munitions are concerned, State practice also includes instructions to armed forces and their behaviour with respect to the weapons.

Donation of Royalties to the ICRC
Special Fund for the Disabled

All the royalties from this book are being donated to the International Committee of the Red Cross (ICRC) Special Fund for the Disabled. The Special Fund for the Disabled supports physical rehabilitation services in low-income countries. In 2009, it provided financial, material, technical, or training support to 63 rehabilitation centres in 30 countries.

For further information on the ICRC Special Fund for the Disabled, please contact the Fund's Director, Theo Verhoeff:

19, Avenue de la Paix
1202 Geneva
Switzerland

Tel: + 41 22 730 2357
Fax: + 41 22 730 3787

<http://www.icrc.org/fund-disabled>

Contents

Table of Cases

Eritrea Ethiopia Claims Commission

European Court of Human Rights

International Court of Justice

International Criminal Tribunal for Former Yugoslavia

Permanent Court of Justice

National Jurisdictions

Table of International Treaties and Conventions

Table of National Legislation

Table of National Legislation

Table of UN Resolutions

INTRODUCTION

Virgil Wiebe, John Borrie, and Declan Smyth[1]

Development and use of cluster munitions

Origin and development of cluster munitions

0.1 The precise origin of cluster munitions is the subject of debate. Research suggests that their development, at least conceptually, can be tracked as far back as the fifteenth century, to the time of Leonardo da Vinci. An inveterate weapons designer, da Vinci produced sketches of an exploding cannonball that would shatter into smaller bomblets[2] (although there is no evidence that

---

[1] Virgil Wiebe wrote the section, Development and Use of Cluster Munitions, and John Borrie wrote the section, The Negotiation of the Convention on Cluster Munitions, apart from the sub-section, Organization of the Diplomatic Conference: Basic Proposal, Rules of Procedure and Structure of Work, which was written by Declan Smyth.

[2] Marco Cianchi, *Leonardo da Vinci's Machines* (Becocci: 1988), p. 31, illustrations 36 and 38.

the design reached the production stage). Leonardo's reported rationale for the weapon foreshadowed the later design of some cluster munitions:

Leonardo realized that while the iron cannon ball is useful against large and immobile targets like fortresses, [it] is of little use against small, moving targets like advancing troops. Against these targets he thinks of using explosive cannon balls...which shatter on impact into many deadly fragments upon impact. He [Leonardo] comments: 'It is the most deadly machine that exists. And when the cannon ball falls the nucleus sets fire to the other balls, and the central ball explodes and shatters the others which catch fire in the time it takes to say a "Hail Mary". And it has an outer shell which encloses everything.'[3]

0.2 According to one authority, the British had come up with the idea of cluster bomb incendiaries in the 1914–1918 War.[4] The United States (US) Army Air Corps developed and produced explosive bomblets released directly from aircraft dispensers (similar to those defined by the Convention)[5] in the mid-1920s and refined their use during the 1939–1945 War in the South-west Pacific.[6] Further developments came in the 1950s and 1960s:

Compared to the bomb clusters of World War II, the cluster bombs of the 1960s embodied many advances. The little bombs, now called 'bomblets,' were smaller,

---

[3] *Ibid.*, p. 31.

[4] Eric Prokosch, *Technology of Killing: A Military and Political History of Antipersonnel Weapons* (London: Zed Books, 1995), p. 82.

[5] See, *infra*, the commentary on Article 2, paragraph 15.

[6] [Fragmentation bombs] are sometimes called personnel bombs, as they are designed for use against personnel targets, such as troops in action, on the march, in camp, or in unprotected cantonments. They are also effective against exposed personnel on the decks of ships, against airdromes, motor convoys, searchlights, field artillery units, antiaircraft batteries, and similar targets easily damaged or destroyed by fragments.... It has been found that the greatest number of men can be killed per unit weight by a bomb weighing about 25 pounds.

Air Service Tactical School, *Bombardment*, Government Printing Office, Washington, DC, 1926, pp. 11–12, cited in Rodman, M. K., *A War of Their Own: Bombers over the Southwest Pacific* (Alabama: Air University Press, Maxwell Air Force Base, 2005), p. 9.

While I was down at Langley I [then Captain George Kenney] developed this parachute bomb—this fragmentation bomb with a little parachute on it so that you would be able to get away from the thing at the time it exploded, and as soon as I got out there [SWPA] I got the 3,000 of those bombs that were left over from early testing—back about 1929 or 30 and which nobody wanted—they were stored in some forgotten warehouse.

General George C. Kenney, in interview by Colonel Marvin M. Stanley, 25 January 1967, transcript, 8, AFHRA, K 239.0512–747, quoted in Rodman, M. K., *A War of Their Own: Bombers over the Southwest Pacific, op. cit.*, p. 44. It is further reported that:

To facilitate the use of these weapons, [Lieutenant] Pappy Gunn 'came up with the "squirrel cage" for the B-25. This was a metal rack that looked just like a cage with columns of rods. It held parafrags [see, *infra*, §0.9] in fours stacked on top of the other, nose to tail. I recall that the cage carried about 200 23-pounders and the idea was that when you were over a target you toggled the whole lot.'

Cited in Rodman, *A War of Their Own: Bombers over the Southwest Pacific, op. cit.*, p. 45. See also Behrens, A., 'Secret Weapon', in Scutts, J. (ed.), *B-25 Mitchell at War* (London: Ian Allan, 1983), p. 51.

more numerous, and covered a wider area. They came in many varieties, including some employing the latest techniques of controlled fragmentation. They were scattered from 'dispensers' of various types, some of which were streamlined for carriage on high-speed jet aircraft. Many were interchangeable: different types of bomblets could be used with different dispensers, and vice versa. They could be used to attack multiple targets, wide-area targets, and small or moving targets which the pilot of a jet aircraft could not easily hit with a single munition.[7]

0.3 Developments in cluster munitions technology from the 1970s and into the present have largely focused on reducing the submunition failure rate through multiple fuzes, self-destruction mechanisms, and so-called sensor fuzing, in which each individual submunition is able to detect and target heat signatures and profiles. Efforts have also been made to target more accurately the main conventional munition from which submunitions are dispersed. Despite advances in technology, however, in some cases accuracy fell short of claims made by States and manufacturers, leading to scepticism about technological fixes to humanitarian concerns.

An overview of the use of cluster munitions

0.4 Any overview of the actual use of cluster munitions will doubtless not be comprehensive. Nonetheless, cluster munitions have certainly been used widely over the past seven decades and non-governmental organizations (NGOs) have attempted to document their use in detail. A report issued in 2009 by two international NGOs, Human Rights Watch and Landmine Action, affirms that cluster munitions:

have been used during armed conflict in 33 countries and disputed territories since the end of World War II, including Afghanistan, Albania, Angola, Azerbaijan, BiH [Bosnia-Herzegovina], Cambodia, Chad, Croatia, DRC [Democratic Republic of Congo], Eritrea, Ethiopia, Georgia, Grenada, Iraq, Israel, Kuwait, Lao PDR [Lao People's Democratic Republic, Laos], Lebanon, Montenegro, Saudi Arabia, Serbia, Sierra Leone, Sudan, Syria, Tajikistan, Uganda, Vietnam, and Zambia, as well as Chechnya, Falkland Islands/Malvinas, Kosovo, Nagorno-Karabakh, and Western Sahara. At least 14 government armed forces have used cluster munitions.[8]

---

[7] Eric Prokosch, *Technology of Killing, op. cit.*, pp. 82–83. Prokosch notes further (at p. 116) that:

The origins of modern cluster munitions are still surrounded in secrecy. A request in 1994 for the release under the Freedom of Information Act of sixteen technical reports on the development of cluster weapons in the 1950s and 1960s was denied.

[8] Human Rights Watch and Landmine Action, *Banning Cluster Munitions, Government Policy and Practice*, Mines Action Canada, Canada, May 2009, p. 13, available at: <http://www.lm.icbl.org/cm/2009/banning_cluster_munitions_2009.pdf> (accessed 5 March 2010).

Yet even this in-depth study has already been overtaken by new information. Later in 2009, evidence suggests that Morocco, which used cluster munitions in the Western Sahara region, also used cluster munitions in Mauritania at some time in the 1980s in its conflict with the Polisario Front.[9] There is also evidence that Libya has a previously unknown problem with unexploded submunitions.[10]

0.5 Given the lack of comprehensive knowledge of even the number of conflicts in which cluster munitions have been used, *a fortiori* no one knows to within even a reliable order of magnitude how many cluster munitions (parent munitions and/or submunitions) have been used in armed conflict, much less how many remain to be cleared.[11] Thus, according to the Belgian NGO, Handicap International, which undertook a study in the mid-2000s of global usage:

[s]ince their first deployment, tens of millions, perhaps hundreds of millions, of cluster submunitions have become the most deadly and persistent form of ERW [explosive remnants of war].[12]

0.6 The Germans dropped incendiary cluster munitions during the Spanish Civil War in 1937 and both Axis and Allied forces used cluster munitions in significant numbers during the 1939–1945 War. The massive use of cluster munitions during the conflict in South-east Asia in the 1960s and 1970s, and more recent use in Afghanistan, Iraq, and Lebanon, have tended to overshadow earlier use in the twentieth century. Nonetheless, the characteristics that would make cluster munitions a significant humanitarian concern were also manifest decades earlier.

0.7 In support of the Nationalist forces in the Spanish Civil War, German aircraft dropped conventional unitary bombs and incendiary cluster munitions on the Spanish town of Guernica on 26 April 1937.[13] This infamous raid

---

[9] See, e.g., Human Rights Watch, 'Timeline of Cluster Munition Use', Fact Sheet, April 2010.

[10] See, e.g., Bolger, D. P., *Americans at War: 1975–1986, An Era of Violent Peace* (Novato, CA: Presidio Press, 1988), p. 423.

[11] This includes a number of countries in which cluster munition have been used in military training.

[12] Handicap International, *Circle of Impact: The Fatal Footprint of Cluster Munitions on People and Communities* (Brussels: Handicap International, 2007), p. 9, available at: <http://www.stopclustermunitions.org/wp/wp-content/uploads/2009/02/circle-of-impact-may-07.pdf>.

[13] The German aircraft of the Condor legion conducted the raid in the following manner:

Su táctica consistió en arrojar primero bombas rompedoras ordinarias, luego racimos de pequeñas bombas incendiarias y simultáneamente, ametrallar al personal al descubierto, no sólo el que se encontraba en la ciudad, sino también en sus alrededores e incluso en las anteiglesias comarcales.

may not be the only one in which cluster munitions were used during that conflict.[14]

0.8 During the 1939–1945 War, perhaps the best known incident of the use of 'butterfly bombs' was the dropping of German SD-2 cluster munitions on the English port of Grimsby, England, on 13 June 1943. There are, however, reports of them being dropped on the town of Ipswich and the nearby RAF Wattisham airbase before that time.[15] *Stuka* dive bombers dropped cluster munitions on British troops evacuating by sea from the French port of Dunkirk in May 1940.[16] Germany also used SD-2 cluster munitions against Russian forces in 1941[17] and in 1943 along the Kursk gradient.[18] In October 2009, an 11-year-old boy found a butterfly bomb on the island of Malta; one such device had claimed the life of a 41-year-old man in 1981.[19] On 27 November 2009, a butterfly bomb was found by an oil company survey crew in Libya.

Martinez Bande, J. M., *Vizcaya. Monografías de la Guerra de España, No. 6* (Madrid: Libreria Editorial San Martin, 1971), pp. 107–108. An official translation is as follows:

> The tactics employed were to drop ordinary shells first, and then small incendiary cluster bombs, at the same time machine-gunning any villagers who had not yet reached cover—not only in the town itself, but also in its outlying districts and also around the neighbouring parishes.

Guernica Peace Museum <http://www.peacemuseumguernica.org/en/documentation/bombing-docu.html> (visited 17 August 2009).

[14] According to a recent account:

> [t]here was nothing new about the attack on Guernica. Other villages on the Basque front-lines, notably the town of Durango in late March, had been bombed in a similar fashion.

Corum, J. S., *Wolfrum von Richthofen: Master of the German Air War* (Lawrence, KS: University Press of Kansas, 2008), pp. 134–135.

[15] Jappy, M. J., *Danger UXB* (UK: Macmillan's Publisher's, 2001), pp. 155–175. Each SD-2 anti-personnel submunition weighed 2 kilograms, contained 225 grams of explosive, had a kill-radius of 25 metres, and an injury radius of 150 metres. Each was equipped with one of three fuses (impact, time delay, or motion-activated). The submunitions were packed 23 to a cylinder, which would open at a pre-set height to scatter the butterfly bombs. The bombs proved lethal on impact as well as long after impact, foreshadowing the effects of future cluster munitions. See *ibid.*, pp. 157–159; and also King, C., *Explosive Remnants of War: Submunitions and Other Unexploded Ordnance: A Study* (Geneva: ICRC, August 2000), pp. 10–11, Appendix B.

[16] Grant, R., 'The Stuka Terror', *Air Force Magazine,* November 2008, p. 68.

[17] Corum, J. S., *Wolfrum von Richthofen: Master of the German Air War, op. cit.*, p. 270. According to Corum, the SD-2 bomb:

> was first used in a large scale in the 1941 Soviet campaign and provided a huge increase in the Luftwaffe's effectiveness...when attacking ground troops or vehicles in the open. Since each SD-2 was a container of ninety-six bombs that covered an area of a few hundred meters, one aircraft dropping two or three of the canisters could effectively wipe out an entire Soviet road column.

[18] Human Rights Watch and Landmine Action, *Banning Cluster Munitions, op. cit.*, p. 14.

[19] Coster, K. B., 'Boy finds lethal WWII bomb in Qormi valley', *Times of Malta.com*, 29 October 2009, <http://www.timesofmalta.com/articles/view/20091029/local/boy-finds-lethal-wwii-bomb-in-qormi-valley> (accessed 24 March 2010).

Subsequent survey by an explosive ordnance disposal expert identified six more butterfly bombs.[20]

0.9 The Russian air force dropped RRAB-3 'Molotov bread basket' incendiary cluster munitions on Finland during the 'Winter War' in January 1940, and perhaps even earlier.[21] The Russian air force also used cluster munitions against German armour on the Eastern Front in 1943.[22] Beginning in September 1942, the US Army Air Corps made heavy use of the 23 pound 'parafrag bomb' in the South-west Pacific, a type of parachute-equipped bomblet delivered from dispenser racks and 'just as capable of killing ground troops as shredding exposed planes and equipment'.[23]

0.10 From the earliest use of these weapons, the characteristics that would later raise concerns about their spatial and temporal effects were apparent to observers. An early observer of the use of these weapons in Finland in 1940 noted their tendency for indiscriminate wide area effects:

> The very nature of this apparatus makes any question of accurate aiming quite out of the question: the object is the indiscriminate spraying of a wide area, and the effect can be seen after a raid in the numerous black patches on the snow where each bombs was dropped. Only a very few, in accordance with the laws of probability, strike buildings; but they make a wide area untenable by mere force of numbers. In fact, the 'Molotov bread basket' is the equivalent of the automatic gun for the infantryman.[24]

As for the lingering effects of unexploded submunitions, the 1943 attack on Grimsby involved more than 1,000 German SD-2 submunitions being dropped and it is reported that 'the majority of fatalities (47 of 61) occurred after, not during the attack'.[25] Already in the early 1940s, the US Army Air Corps faced problems with its parafrag bomblets, which got caught in trees

---

[20] Report by Jan-Ole Robertz, EOD Technical Advisor, Countermine Libya, 27 November 2009.

[21] 'Big Russian Bomb Holds Sixty Little Ones', *Popular Science,* July 1940, <http://blog.modern-mechanix.com/issue/?magname=PopularScience&magdate=7–1940> (accessed 28 July 2009); Langdon-Davies, J., *Finland: The First Total War* (London: George Rutledge & Sons, 1940), pp. 141, and 156–157.

[22] King, C., *Explosive Remnants of War: Submunitions and Other Unexploded Ordnance: A Study, op. cit.*, p. 10.

[23] Rodman, M. K., *A War of Their Own: Bombers over the Southwest Pacific, op. cit.*, pp. 44–45 and 47. The US also made extensive use of four-pound incendiary thermite bombs, 'designed to be carried in large numbers and spread over wide areas'. *Ibid.*, pp. 77–78.

[24] Langdon-Davies, J., *Finland: The First Total War, op. cit.*, p. 157.

[25] King, C. *Explosive Remnants of War: Submunitions and Other Unexploded Ordnance: A Study, op. cit.*, pp. 10–11.

or blinds [unexploded submunitions] resulted from being dropped from the wrong altitudes.[26]

0.11 During the 1950s, a few reports exist suggesting limited use by the US of air-dropped cluster munitions during the so-called 'police action' in Korea,[27] but the Korean War served more as an inspiration for the development of anti-personnel cluster munitions (in order to thwart large scale 'human waves') than as an actual theatre of use.[28]

0.12 During the conflict in South-east Asia, the US is believed to have dropped a total of nearly 400 million submunitions on Cambodia, Laos, and Vietnam.[29] Of these three countries, Laos absorbed the heaviest bombing

[26] 'Since the parafrags are likely to hang in trees and thus become duds, the 100lb parademo is substituted for the parafrag against such targets as aircraft and fuel dumps situated in wooded areas.' Headquarters V Bomber Command, Office of the Ordnance Officer, 'First Phase Recommendations on Bomb Loading for Various Primary Targets', 18 April 1944, 1, AFHRA, 732.804–1, cited in Rodman, M. K., *A War of Their Own: Bombers over the Southwest Pacific, op. cit.*, p. 103.

The statement as to duds among parachute (frag.) bombs is correct. The principal cause— release of parafrags from altitudes below 100 feet, which did not allow bomb fuzes sufficient time to arm completely.

Ibid., p. 123, citing the Assistant Chief of Air Staff, Intelligence, US Army Air Forces, 'Jap Opinion of AAF Bombing Tactics', *Informational Intelligence Summary*, No. 44–26, 20 August 1944, p. 4.

[27] According to US Navy records, on 8 October 1952, '[e]leven B-29s of the FEAF Bomber Command and 89 TF 77 aircraft struck the Kowon rail center. B-29s carried VT [proximity] fuzed 500 pound cluster bombs for effective flak suppression.' Department of the Navy, Naval Historical Center, 'Korean War: Chronology of U.S. Pacific Fleet Operations, September–December 1952', 21 June 2000, <http://www.history.navy.mil/wars/korea/chron52c.htm> (visited 30 July 2009). It is not clear if the term '500 pound cluster bomb' refers to a high explosive unitary bomb or a cluster munition. Another source claims that the US 'manufactured a copy of the SD2 for use during the Korean War and Vietnam War, designating it the M83 Butterfly Bomb.' 'US M-83 "Butterfly Bomb,"' <http://www.inert-ord.net/usa03a/usa6/bfly/index.html> (visited 30 July 2009). Corum notes that the 'U.S. Air Force found the SD-2 such an effective weapon that it copied and produced the bomb after the war; the SD-2 remained in the U.S. inventory as a standard munition into the 1960s.' Corum, J. S., *Wolfrum von Richthofen: Master of the German Air War, op. cit.*, p. 270.

[28] According to Simon Conway:

The most significant event in the development and subsequent use of cluster munitions was the Korean War—when American military might was challenged by an enemy that was technologically inferior but with inexhaustible supplies of manpower. US commanders confronted the nightmare of seeing their forces over-run by hordes of enemy soldiers. The result was a revolution in anti-personnel weapons with an emphasis on the production of large quantities of fast-flying lethal fragments over a wide area. . . . The war that cluster munitions were designed for was over by the time they had reached the stage of mass production.

Simon Conway, 'Cluster Munitions: Historical Overview of Use and Human Impacts', in International Committee of the Red Cross (ICRC), *Humanitarian, Military, Technical and Legal Challenges of Cluster Munitions, Montreux, Switzerland, 18 to 20 April 2007*, pp. 13–14.

[29] 'According to an analysis of US bombing data conducted by Handicap International, some 80,000 cluster munitions, containing 26 million submunitions, were dropped on Cambodia

with cluster munitions. On average, US forces flew one bombing run every eight minutes for nine years.[30] With more than 266 million submunitions dropped (based on records released by the US Government), cluster munitions comprise a significant portion of the bomb attacks from 1964 to 1973.[31] UXO Lao has estimated that up to 78 million unexploded 'bombies' (unexploded submunitions) remained in the ground as a result.[32] According to data provided by the US Embassy in Cambodia, 'between 1965 and 1975, 10% of the 150,000 air attacks on Cambodia employed various types of cluster bombs'.[33]

0.13 The 1970s saw use of cluster munitions in several other countries. In Zambia, remnants of cluster munitions used during that decade, including unexploded submunitions from air-dropped bombs, were found at Chikumbi and Shang'ombo in 2008–2009. In 1973, Israel used air-dropped cluster munitions against non-State armed group (NSAG) training camps near Damascus in Syria. In 1975–1988, Moroccan forces used artillery-fired and air-dropped cluster munitions against the Polisario Front in Western Sahara. In 1978, Israel used cluster munitions in southern Lebanon.[34]

0.14 Use expanded in the 1980s, especially in Afghanistan where between 1979 and 1989, Soviet forces used air-dropped and rocket-delivered cluster munitions on a wide scale. NSAGs also used rocket-delivered cluster munitions, but on a smaller scale. In 1982, Israel used cluster munitions against Syrian forces and NSAGs in Lebanon. That same year, United Kingdom

---

between 1969 and 1973; more than 414,000 cluster bombs, containing at least 260 million submunitions, were dropped on Laos between 1965 and 1973; and more than 296,000 cluster munitions, containing nearly 97 million submunitions, were dropped in Vietnam between 1965 and 1975.' See Human Rights Watch, *Cluster Munition Information Chart,* 17 July 2009, <http://www.hrw.org/en/news/2009/07/17/cluster-munition-information-chart>; and also 'The Unexploded Ordnance (UXO) Problem,' Lao National Unexploded Ordnance Programme (UXO Lao) <http://www.uxolao.org/uxo%20problem.html> (visited 19 August 2009).

[30] Lin, J., 'Shellshocked Laos', *Hobart Mercury* (Australia), 20 December 1996.

[31] *Lao National Unexploded Ordnance Programme 2008 Annual Report*, UXO Lao, Vientiane, 2009, p. 18, <http://www.uxolao.org/Download%20files/2008%20Annual%20Report.pdf>.

[32] In its 2006 report, UXO Lao put the total number at 288,485,886 used, with an estimated failure rate between 12 and 30%. Shane, K., 'Lao PDR', *Journal of Mine Action*, Winter 2006, <http://maic.jmu.edu/JOURNAL/10.2/profiles/laos/laos.htm>, citing email correspondence with John Dingley, UN Development Programme (UNDP), 9 November 2006.

[33] 'Cambodia National Level 1 Survey', 2002, <http://www.sac-na.org/pdf_text/cambodia/executive%20summary.htm>. According to the Cluster Munition Coalition (CMC):

An estimate based on US military databases states that 9,500 sorties in Cambodia delivered up to 87,000 air-dropped cluster munitions.

CMC, 'A History of Harm', <http://www.stopclustermunitions.org/the-problem/history-harm/> (visited 22 August 2009).

[34] Human Rights Watch, *Cluster Munition Information Chart,* 17 July 2009, *op. cit.*

(UK) forces dropped 107[35] BL-755 cluster bombs containing a total of 15,729 submunitions against Argentine positions on the Falkland Islands/Malvinas. In 1983, US Navy aircraft dropped 21 Rockeye cluster munitions during close air support operations in Grenada. That same year, US Navy aircraft dropped 12 CBU-59 and 28 Rockeye cluster munitions against Syrian air defence units near Beirut in Lebanon. In 1986–1987, French aircraft dropped cluster munitions on a Libyan airfield at Wadi Doum, in Chad. Libyan forces also used AO-1SCh and PTAB-2.5 submunitions against Chad.[36]

0.15 The 1990s witnessed a significant increase in the use of cluster munitions in terms both of the number of conflicts in which they were used and the number of States using them. In 1991, 'Saudi Arabian and US forces used artillery-delivered and air-dropped cluster munitions against Iraqi forces during the battle of Khafji' in Saudi Arabia.[37] In 1991, in Iraq and Kuwait, the 'US, France, and the UK dropped 61,000 cluster bombs containing some 20 million submunitions. The number of cluster munitions delivered by surface-launched artillery and rocket systems is not known, but an estimated 30 million or more dual purpose improved conventional munitions (DPICM) submunitions were used in the conflict.' In 1992–1994, PTAB submunitions were found in various locations in Angola. Submunitions were used during the same period in Nagorno-Karabakh, Azerbaijan, with submunition contamination identified 'in at least 162 locations' and 'in other parts of occupied Azerbaijan, adjacent to Nagorno-Karabakh'.[38]

0.16 In 1992–1995, Yugoslav forces and NSAGs used cluster munitions during the armed conflict in Bosnia and Herzegovina, where 'NATO aircraft [also] dropped two CBU-87 bombs'. During the 1992–1997 conflict in Tajikistan, unknown forces in the 'Civil War' used ShOAB and AO-2.5RT submunitions 'in the town of Gharm in the Rasht Valley'. In 1994–1996, Russian forces used cluster munitions against NSAGs in Chechnya. 'On May 2–3, 1995, an NSAG used Orkan M-87 multiple rocket launchers to conduct attacks in the city of Zagreb, [Croatia]. Additionally, the Croatian government claimed that Serb forces used BL-755 bombs in Sisak, Kutina, and along the Kupa River.' In 1996–1999, Sudanese government forces air dropped cluster munitions in southern Sudan, including Chilean-made PM-1 submunitions.[39]

---

[35] Or 106. The UK is not certain which figure is correct. See *Hansard*, 12 May 2000, Vol. 349, col. 512W, <http://www.hansard.millbanksystems.com/written_answers/2000/may/12/cluster-bombs#S6CV0349P0_20000512_CWA_175>.

[36] Human Rights Watch, *Cluster Munition Information Chart*, 17 July 2009, *op. cit.*

[37] *Ibid.*   [38] *Ibid.*   [39] *Ibid.*

0.17 In 1997, Nigerian ECOMOG (Economic Community of West African States Cease-fire Monitoring Group) peacekeepers used BLG-66 Beluga bombs on the eastern town of Kenema in Sierra Leone. In 1998, 'Ethiopia and Eritrea exchanged aerial cluster munition strikes. Ethiopia attacked Asmara airport, and Eritrea attacked Mekele airport. Ethiopia also dropped BL-755 bombs in Gash-Barka province in Eritrea.' In 1998–1999, 'Yugoslav forces used rocket-delivered cluster munitions in disputed border areas, and NATO forces carried out six aerial cluster munition strikes' in Albania. Sometime between 1998 and 2003, 'BL-755 bombs were used by unknown forces in Kasu village in Kabalo territory', in the Democratic Republic of the Congo. In 1999, it is reported that the 'US, UK, and Netherlands dropped 1,765 cluster bombs containing 295,000 submunitions' across what is now Serbia, Montenegro, and Kosovo.[40] In a failed attempt to kill Osama bin Laden in 1998, the US launched TLAM-D cruise missiles containing explosive submunitions on *al-Qaeda* training camps in Afghanistan.[41]

0.18 In 2001–2002, the 'US dropped 1,228 cluster bombs containing 248,056 submunitions' in Afghanistan. In 2003 in Iraq, the 'US and UK used nearly 13,000 cluster munitions, containing an estimated 1.8 to 2 million submunitions, in the three weeks of major combat.' Russian and Georgian forces both used cluster munitions during the August 2008 conflict in Georgia.[42]

0.19 Of particular note, cluster munitions were used extensively in south Lebanon in 2006. The UN Mine Action Coordination Centre of South Lebanon (MACC-SL) estimated that Israel used between 2.6 million and 4 million submunitions in its war with Hezbollah in July and August of 2006. Human Rights Watch received additional information from Israeli soldiers that pushed the estimates to between 3.2 and 4.6 million submunitions. The submunitions used were delivered by air-dropped bombs, artillery shells, and ground rockets. MACC-SL estimated that several hundred thousand unexploded submunitions were left behind.[43] As of December 2008, MACC-SL reported that 153,755 submunitions had been cleared through its efforts.[44] A

[40] *Ibid.*

[41] Kilian, M., '"The War Has Just Started": Terrorist Vows Revenge as the U.S. Stands Firm', *Chicago Tribune*, 22 August 1998, p. 1.

[42] Human Rights Watch, *Cluster Munition Information Chart, op. cit.* At some point during the decade, cluster munitions were also used in Uganda, as 'RBK-250/275 bombs and AO-1SCh submunitions have been found in the northern district of Gulu.' *Ibid.*

[43] See Human Rights Watch, *Flooding South Lebanon: Israel's Use of Cluster Munitions in Lebanon in July and August 2006*, Vol. 20, No. 2(E), February 2008, pp. 36–37.

[44] MACC-SL, 'November-December 2008 Report of the Mine Action Co-ordination Centre, South Lebanon', 18 December 2008, <http://www.maccsl.org/reports/Monthly%20 Reports/Monthly%202008/Monthly%20Report%20Nov-Dec%2008.pdf>, p. 6 (accessed 6

total of 265 civilians died or were injured as a result of unexploded submunitions between 14 August 2006 and 1 January 2009.[45] Human Rights Watch also reported that Hezbollah fired ground rockets containing at least 4,600 submunitions into Israel.[46] The massive use of cluster munitions by Israel in 2006 has been identified as a critical tipping point in efforts to prohibit cluster munitions.[47]

The negotiation of the Convention on Cluster Munitions[48]

0.20 Concern about the effects of cluster bombs on civilians, along with other anti-personnel weapons such as napalm, emerged in the late 1960s due to the use of these weapons in the war in South-east Asia.[49] This and related concerns about the impact of that and other conflicts contributed to international momentum for the development of two new protocols additional to the four *1949 Geneva Conventions*[50] in order to enhance the protection of civilians in armed conflict. The diplomatic conferences negotiating these protocols also lent consideration to weapon-specific measures, but agreement proved elusive and ultimately it was decided to adopt the two *1977 Additional Protocols*[51] without regulation of specific conventional weapons. Weapon-specific talks continued in a specially convened UN conference, which culminated in

August 2009). This does not include submunitions cleared by Hezbollah forces or by the civilian population.

[45] Civilian Cluster Bomb Victims Graph since 14 August 2006 up to 1 January 2009, <http://www.maccsl.org/reports/Victims/Victims.pdf> (visited 6 August 2009).

[46] Human Rights Watch, *Civilians under Assault: Hezbollah's Rocket Attacks on Israel in the 2006 War*, Vol. 19, No. 3(E), August 2007, pp. 44–46.   [47] See further, *infra*, §0.26.

[48] For a detailed history of international efforts to address the humanitarian impacts of cluster munitions culminating in the Convention on Cluster Munitions, see Borrie, J., *Unacceptable Harm: A history of how the international treaty banning cluster munitions was won* (Geneva: United Nations Institute for Disarmament Research/United Nations, 2009).

[49] Prokosch, E., *The Technology of Killing, op. cit.*

[50] Convention (I) for the Amelioration of the Condition of the Wounded and Sick in Armed Forces in the Field, Geneva, 12 August 1949; Convention (II) for the Amelioration of the Condition of Wounded, Sick and Shipwrecked Members of Armed Forces at Sea, Geneva, 12 August 1949; Convention (III) relative to the Treatment of Prisoners of War, Geneva, 12 August 1949; and Convention (IV) relative to the Protection of Civilian Persons in Time of War, Geneva, 12 August 1949.

[51] Protocol Additional to the Geneva Conventions of 12 August 1949, and relating to the Protection of Victims of International Armed Conflicts (Protocol I), 8 June 1977; and Protocol Additional to the Geneva Conventions of 12 August 1949, and relating to the Protection of Victims of Non-International Armed Conflicts (Protocol II), 8 June 1977.

the adoption in 1980 of the *Convention on Certain Conventional Weapons* (CCW).[52]

0.21 In 1974, a group of countries led by Sweden had called for the prohibition of a number of anti-personnel weapons including 'cluster warheads',[53] and these proposals were subsequently discussed during the remainder of the decade in the diplomatic conferences that resulted in the two *1977 Additional Protocols* and the CCW, as well as in meetings of experts convened by the International Committee of the Red Cross (ICRC) in Lucerne[54] and Lugano, Switzerland.[55] When the CCW was adopted in 1980, however, it contained no measures on cluster munitions. Further, despite accumulating evidence over the 1980s and 1990s of, particularly, the post-conflict impact on civilians of cluster munition use in places such as Afghanistan, Cambodia, Iraq, Kuwait, Laos, and Vietnam,[56] and following the North Atlantic Treaty Organization (NATO) air campaign against Federal Republic of Yugoslavia forces over the province of Kosovo in 1999,[57] States Parties to the CCW did not formally take up the issue at that time.

0.22 The achievement of the *1997 Anti-Personnel Mine Ban Convention*[58] led to an expansion of the international mine action sector,[59] and greater assessment of the post-conflict effects of failed or abandoned explosive weapons accompanied it.[60] The efforts of civil society and of the ICRC, in particular,

---

[52] Convention on Prohibitions or Restrictions on the Use of Certain Conventional Weapons Which May Be Deemed to Be Excessively Injurious or to Have Indiscriminate Effects, adopted in Geneva on 10 October 1980.

[53] 'Working Paper submitted by Egypt, Mexico, Norway, Sudan, Sweden, Switzerland and Yugoslavia to the Diplomatic Conference on the reaffirmation and development of international humanitarian law applicable in armed conflicts', CDDH/DT/2, 21 February 1974.

[54] ICRC, *Conference of Government Experts on the Use of Certain Conventional Weapons (Lucerne, 24 September–18 October 1974): Report* (Geneva: ICRC, 1975).

[55] ICRC, *Conference of Government Experts on the Use of Certain Conventional Weapons (Second Session – Lugano, 28 January–26 February 1976): Report* (Geneva: ICRC, 1976).

[56] See King, C., *Explosive Remnants of War: Submunitions and Other Unexploded Ordnance: A Study, op. cit.*

[57] See Human Rights Watch, *Ticking Time Bombs: NATO's use of cluster munitions in Yugoslavia*, Vol. 11, No. 6 (D), June 1999; and Maslen, S., *Explosive Remnants of War: Cluster Bombs and Landmines in Kosovo*, Revised Edition (Geneva: ICRC, June 2001).

[58] The formal title of this treaty is the Convention on the Prohibition of the Use, Stockpiling, Production and Transfer of Anti-Personnel Mines and on their Destruction.

[59] Mine action is the term used to describe efforts to address the threat from landmines and ERW. See, e.g., the International Mine Action Standards: IMAS 02.10: 'Guide for the Establishment of a Mine Action Programme', First Edition, 1 January 2003, available at <http://www. mineactionstandards.org/IMAS_archive/Final/IMAS%2002.10%20Guide%20for%20the%20 establishment%20of%20a%20mine%20action%20programme%20(First%20Edition).pdf>.

[60] Human Rights Watch and Landmine Action, *Banning Cluster Munitions, op. cit.*, p. 2.

heightened awareness among the international community about the hazards to civilians such explosive remnants of war (ERW)[61] cause—including submunitions. In late 2001, States Parties to the CCW agreed to negotiate a new protocol on ERW,[62] which was adopted in November 2003 as the Protocol on Explosive Remnants of War (*2003 Protocol V*). As a result of the particular hazards of unexploded submunitions relative to other kinds of ERW, discussions within the context of the CCW gave humanitarian actors a platform on which to draw attention to the impact of cluster munitions on civilians after conflict as well as at time of use, especially as the weapons were used again in Afghanistan in 2001–2002[63] and in Iraq in 2003.[64] Such use underlined problems associated with the accuracy and reliability of a weapon intended to saturate areas with explosive force, and increased disquiet among national policy-makers in a number of States Parties to the CCW, such as Norway.[65]

0.23 While *2003 Protocol V* adopted post-conflict measures generic to all weapons, including provisions regarding clearance, risk education for civilians, and information exchange relating to the use of munitions, it did not address the characteristic problems created by cluster munitions through any weapon-specific provisions, and the agreement is not retroactive in application.[66] Nevertheless, the issues around cluster munitions were kept alive in the CCW after 2003 in technical discussions revolving around what might constitute 'good' versus 'bad' submunitions, as well as in talks about the adequacy of existing humanitarian law rules governing their use. It was clear, however, that at that time several major military powers (and actual or potential cluster munition user or stockpiling nations) such as China, India, Israel, Pakistan, Russia, and the US firmly opposed negotiation of legally binding restrictions specific to cluster munitions.

---

[61] According to the definition in Article 2 of Protocol V on Explosive Remnants of War to the *Convention on Certain Conventional Weapons* (*2003 Protocol V*), ERW comprise abandoned explosive ordnance and unexploded ordnance, linked to an armed conflict. See further, *infra*, the commentary on Article 2, *esp.* §§2.184 *et seq.*

[62] 'Final Document of the Second Review Conference of the States Parties to the CCW, Geneva, December 11–21, 2001', UN doc. CCW/CONF.II/2.

[63] See, e.g., Human Rights Watch, *Fatally Flawed: Cluster Bombs and their use by the United States in Afghanistan*, Vol. 14, No. 7 (G), December 2002.

[64] See, e.g., Human Rights Watch, *Off Target: The conduct of the war and civilian casualties in Iraq* (Washington, DC: Human Rights Watch, 2003).

[65] See Petrova, M. H., *Small States and New Norms of Warfare*, EUI Working Papers MWP 2007/28 (San Domenico di Fiesole: European University Institute, 2007).

[66] See Maresca, L., 'A new protocol on explosive remnants of war: The history and negotiation of Protocol V to the 1980 Convention on Certain Conventional Weapons', *International Review of the Red Cross*, Vol. 86, No. 856, December 2004, pp. 815–835.

The emergence of the Oslo Process

0.24 On the margins of an international conference hosted in Ireland on the issue of ERW in April 2003, NGOs—mostly those involved in the anti-personnel mine ban movement—agreed to undertake sustained and coordinated campaigning against cluster munitions.[67] Correspondingly, a new NGO consortium, the Cluster Munition Coalition (CMC) was launched in November 2003 in The Hague.[68] 'The CMC was united behind a call for an immediate moratorium on the use of cluster munitions, an acknowledgement of States' responsibility for the explosive remnants they cause, and a commitment to provide resources to areas affected by ERW.'[69] With *2003 Protocol V* adopted shortly thereafter, the CMC's focus was really on cluster munitions. But, until 2006 the CMC's efforts made little headway in the CCW, with the focus of that multilateral process largely on efforts to achieve agreement of a protocol on 'mines other than anti-personnel mines'.[70]

0.25 More progress occurred at the national level in some countries. Norwegian elections in the autumn of 2005 resulted in a 'Red-Green' coalition of parties that made 'work for the introduction of an international ban on cluster bombs' part of its governing manifesto.[71] In June 2006, Norway declared a national moratorium on use of its stockpile of artillery-delivered cluster munitions until further testing in order to confirm whether they achieved levels of reliability matching their manufacturers' claims.[72] Meanwhile, among other

[67] The Irish Department for Foreign Affairs and Pax Christi Ireland hosted this conference, which was held on 23–25 April 2003. For information about the formal Dublin conference see *Explosive Remnants of War and Development—Voices from the Field: Conference Report, Dublin Castle, 23–25 April 2003.*

[68] Pax Christi Netherlands, *Conference Report: Cluster Munition Coalition International Launch Conference, 12–13 November 2003, The Hague, Netherlands.*

[69] Human Rights Watch and Landmine Action, *Banning Cluster Munitions, op. cit.*, p. 2.

[70] i.e. anti-vehicle mines. Continued use of the term 'mines other than anti-personnel mines' stemmed from previous work in the CCW in the context of Amended Protocol II. See, e.g., Maslen, S., *Commentaries on Arms Control Treaties, Volume I: The Convention on the Prohibition of the Use, Stockpiling, Production, and Transfer of Anti-Personnel Mines and on their Destruction*, Second Edition, Oxford Commentaries on International Law (Oxford: Oxford University Press, 2005), pp. 17–21, and §§2.44 *et seq.* Hereinafter, this work is referred to as the *Commentary on the 1997 Anti-Personnel Mine Ban Convention.*

[71] Office of the Norwegian Prime Minister, *The Soria Moria Declaration on International Policy* (in English, translated from Norwegian): <http://www.regjeringen.no/en/dep/smk/documents/Reports-and-action-plans/Rapporter/2005/The-Soria-Moria-Declaration-on-Internati.html?id=438515>.

[72] According to a statement of Norway in the *Convention on Certain Conventional Weapons* in June 2006:

In the process towards an international regulation prohibiting cluster munitions that may have unacceptable humanitarian effects, the Norwegian government has introduced a moratorium

national measures in a number of States,[73] Belgium had passed a national law prohibiting cluster munitions in February 2006, although it showed no inclination to play a lead role on trying to achieve a ban on the weapon in the CCW.[74]

0.26 In July 2006, conflict broke out in southern Lebanon between Hezbollah and Israel. As noted above,[75] both parties deployed cluster munitions during the 34-day conflict, and during the last few days of the conflict the Israeli Defence Forces fired massive quantities of ground-launched cluster munitions into southern Lebanon.[76] Israel's bombardment underlined both the humanitarian risks the weapons posed to civilians,[77] and soon revealed much higher submunition failure rates in operational use than the typical claims of manufacturers and the representatives of national militaries possessing them.[78]

0.27 The southern Lebanon conflict thus served to lend weight to the concerns of the CMC, the ICRC, the UN, and others about cluster munitions, as well as to increase support for the argument from some governments for weapon-specific measures internationally. In the context of the CCW, a growing number of its States Parties began to call for negotiation of a cluster munition-specific protocol—a prospect still opposed by several major military powers, which maintained that proper implementation of existing humanitarian law rules (perhaps combined with certain voluntary technical 'improvements' to submunitions such as self-destruct mechanisms intended to reduce failure rates) were sufficient. In view of the rejection by China, Russia, and others of the proposed protocol on 'mines other than anti-personnel mines' in late 2005, prospects for agreement to negotiate a robust

---

on Norwegian cluster munitions until these munitions have been further tested and a decision on their future is made.... It is imperative to start working, without further delay, towards an international ban on cluster munitions that cause unacceptable humanitarian problems.

Statement of Norway on ERW, *Convention on Certain Conventional Weapons*, 20 June 2006 (copy on file with the author).

[73] See, *infra*, §§0.167–0.169.

[74] See Petrova, M. H., *Small States and New Norms of Warfare*, *op. cit.*

[75] See, *supra*, §0.19.

[76] Rappaport, M., 'Israeli Defence Force commander: We fired more than a million cluster bombs in Lebanon', *Haaretz*, 12 September 2006.

[77] See Nash, T., *Foreseeable Harm: The use and impact of cluster munitions in Lebanon* (Landmine Action, London, 2006) and Human Rights Watch, *Flooding South Lebanon: Israel's Use of Cluster Munitions in Lebanon in July and August 2006* (Washington, DC: Human Rights Watch, February 2008).

[78] See, e.g., King, C., Dullum, O., and Østern, G., *M85—An Analysis of Reliability* (Oslo: Norwegian People's Aid, 2007).

legal instrument to curb the humanitarian impact of cluster munitions were hardly promising. Indeed, in the second half of 2006 Norway's Government began making plans for an international conference it would host to take up the prospect of a separate humanitarian treaty on cluster munitions.

0.28 The impending third review conference of the CCW (November 2006) was seen by many as a 'critical test of its ability to address a pressing humanitarian issue'.[79] The then-Secretary-General of the United Nations, Kofi Annan called for a 'freeze' on the use of cluster munitions in populated areas and for 'inaccurate and unreliable' cluster munitions to be destroyed.[80] Twenty-six States Parties to the CCW supported a proposal for a mandate to negotiate a specific protocol on cluster munitions.[81] But the proposal was rejected at the Review Conference, and States Parties were only able to agree on a weaker mandate to convene 'as a matter of urgency' further discussions on ERW in 2007.[82] The Review Conference's outcome left a number of governments involved feeling that the process had little potential to confront effectively the humanitarian hazards of cluster munitions. Its new ERW mandate stated little more than the obvious—that after adoption of the ERW protocol in 2003 and the subsequent Lebanon conflict, attention had turned to cluster munitions.

0.29 Norway's announcement on the penultimate day of the 2006 Review Conference was therefore regarded with considerable interest among governments, for varying reasons. Norway's Minister of Foreign Affairs, Jonas Gahr Støre, announced:

Norway will organise an international conference in Oslo to start a process towards an international ban on cluster munitions that have unacceptable humanitarian consequences...We must take advantage of the political will now evident in many countries to prohibit cluster munitions that cause unacceptable harm. The time is ripe to establish broad co-operation on a concerted effort to achieve a ban.[83]

---

[79] Human Rights Watch and Landmine Action, *Banning Cluster Munitions*, *op. cit.*, p. 3. The fact that attempts to negotiate a new protocol on mines other than anti-personnel mines (i.e. anti-vehicle mines) were not successful did not go unnoticed by several States.

[80] Secretary-General of the United Nations, 'Message to the Third Review Conference of the Convention on Certain Conventional Weapons', 7 November 2006.

[81] 'Proposal for a Mandate to Negotiate a Legally-Binding Instrument that Addresses the Humanitarian Concerns Posed by Cluster Munitions, Presented by Austria, Holy See, Ireland, Mexico, New Zealand, and Sweden', Third Review Conference of States Parties to the CCW, Geneva, 25 October 2006, UN doc. CCW/CONF.III/WP.1.

[82] 'Final Document of the Third Review Conference of the High Contracting Parties to the CCW', Geneva 7–17 November 2006, UN doc. CCW/CONF.III/11 (Part II), Decision 1.

[83] Norwegian Ministry of Foreign Affairs, 'Press Release: Norway takes the initiative for a ban on cluster munitions', No. 104/06, 17 November 2006 (copy on file with the author).

Some States, especially those supporting the proposal in the CCW for negotiation on cluster munitions, were positive, although any effort outside the UN was widely seen as a political risk. In contrast, Ronald Bettauer, the head of the US delegation to the CCW, said Washington was 'disappointed' with Norway, and claimed that the 'effort to go outside this framework is not healthy for the CCW' and would 'weaken the international humanitarian law' effort.[84]

The Oslo Conference on Cluster Munitions

0.30 Initially envisaged by the Norwegian Government as a gathering of fewer than 30 States, representatives of civil society and relevant international organizations, ultimately a total of 49 governments[85] as well as the UN, the ICRC, and the CMC participated in the Oslo Conference on Cluster Munitions (hereinafter, the 'Oslo Conference') on 22–23 February 2007. Participating governments included several cluster-munition-affected States as well as significant users or stockpilers of cluster munitions such as France, Germany, Japan, and the UK. The conference resulted in the issuing of the Oslo Declaration, which contained commitments to complete an international treaty by the end of 2008 to 'prohibit the use, production, transfer and stockpiling of cluster munitions that cause unacceptable harm to civilians' and to 'establish a framework for cooperation and assistance that ensures adequate provision of care and rehabilitation for survivors and their communities, clearance of contaminated areas, risk education and destruction of stockpiles of prohibited cluster munitions'.[86]

The Core Group

0.31 Between the 2006 CCW Review Conference and the Oslo Conference in February 2007, a 'core group' of interested States had

---

[84] Bettauer, R. J., 'Statement of the Head of the United States Delegation to the Closing Plenary Session of the Third CCW Review Conference', Geneva, 17 November 2006.

[85] The following 46 States endorsed the Oslo Declaration at the end of the Oslo Conference: Afghanistan, Angola, Argentina, Austria, Belgium, Bosnia and Herzegovina, Canada, Chile, Colombia, Croatia, Costa Rica, the Czech Republic, Denmark, Egypt, Finland, France, Germany, Guatemala, Holy See, Hungary, Iceland, Indonesia, Ireland, Italy, Jordan, Latvia, Lebanon, Liechtenstein, Lithuania, Luxembourg, Malta, Mexico, Mozambique, Netherlands, New Zealand, Norway, Peru, Portugal, Serbia, Slovakia, Slovenia, South Africa, Spain, Sweden, Switzerland, and the United Kingdom. Japan, Poland, and Romania withheld their endorsement of the Declaration at the conclusion of the Conference.

[86] Declaration, Oslo Conference on Cluster Munitions, 22–23 February 2007, contained in Annex 2 of this Commentary.

emerged in support of the Norwegian government initiative.[87] This move was inspired by the Ottawa Process, where, in the lead up to the negotiations on the *1997 Anti-Personnel Mine Ban Convention*, a similar core group of States had been one of several key driving forces. The core group in the Oslo Process consisted of Austria, Ireland, Mexico, New Zealand, Norway, Peru, and the Holy See.[88]

The Oslo Process

The Oslo Declaration

0.32 The Declaration of the Oslo Conference on Cluster Munitions (the 'Oslo Declaration') is the founding document of the so-called Oslo Process. Importantly for that process, the Oslo Declaration translated its stated concerns into a clear objective ('to effectively address the humanitarian concerns caused by cluster munitions'). Astutely, the Oslo Conference did not try to pre-negotiate key understandings crucial to achieving this—thereby allowing some States to defer their concerns about how the freestanding Oslo Process would fit in with the CCW, or what the eventual implications would be for their own stockpiles of cluster munitions. The obvious challenge would be about how to define 'cluster munitions that cause unacceptable harm to civilians',[89] which would be the subject of intensive debate in the course of 2007 and 2008 in the lead-up to the formal negotiations on a treaty which took place at a diplomatic conference in Dublin in May 2008.

0.33 The Oslo Declaration also made humanitarian concerns a central focus, as shown by the document's reference to measures such as clearance, stockpile destruction, victim assistance, and international cooperation, elements which ostensibly resembled those of the *1997 Anti-Personnel Mine Ban Convention*.[90] This increased the attractiveness of the Norwegian initiative to a large body of States not party to the CCW as well as in the developing world,

---

[87] See Borrie, J., *Unacceptable Harm, A History of How the Treaty to Ban Cluster Munitions Was Won* (New York and Geneva: UN and UNIDIR, 2009), pp. 162–163.

[88] Sweden was a part of the Core Group in the very beginning of the process, but withdrew soon after the Oslo Conference, see Nystuen, G., 'A New Treaty Banning Cluster Munitions: The Interplay between Disarmament Diplomacy and Humanitarian Requirements', in Baillet, C. (ed.), *Security: A Multidisciplinary Normative Approach* (Leiden/Boston: Brill, 2009), p. 144.

[89] The Oslo Declaration language has been described by the author in his history of the Oslo Process as 'masterfully ambiguous'. Borrie, J., *Unacceptable Harm, op. cit.*, p. xxiv.

[90] The tradition of unanimity for decision-making in the *Convention on Certain Conventional Weapons* means that it is very difficult to establish or restore a balance between military utility and the requirements of humanity when the use of a particular weapon system threatens the latter. Thus, the *Convention on Certain Conventional Weapons* tends to favour the status quo.

including some affected States. This in turn lent the Oslo Process additional humanitarian legitimacy.

0.34 The Oslo Declaration also created a concrete timetable for progress toward a legally binding instrument on cluster munitions, one not contingent on decision-making by consensus privileged in the *Convention on Certain Conventional Weapons*. Comprised initially of multilateral conferences in Lima (late May), Vienna (early December), and then Dublin (in 'early 2008'), as well as mentioning a European regional meeting to be held in Belgium, the Declaration timetable envisaged a legally binding instrument's adoption by the end of 2008 at the latest. Soon after this, it was also decided that one further meeting in Wellington (February 2008) would form part of the Oslo Process to set the stage for the Dublin negotiations. In the course of the Process, there would also be regional meetings and an important conference of States affected by cluster munitions held in Belgrade in October 2007.

The Oslo Process and the Convention on Certain Conventional Weapons

0.35 The emergence of the Oslo Process would spur on the efforts of certain States involved in both processes to achieve a negotiating mandate within the CCW by the end of 2007 despite the initiative started in Oslo.[91] For it became apparent that major possessors and producers of the weapons, such as China, Russia, and the US, all of which had shunned the Oslo Process and indicated concern about its ambitions, were now willing to show greater flexibility on such a negotiating mandate.[92]

0.36 As in dealing with anti-personnel mines in the 1990s, it had taken a freestanding international initiative outside the CCW to galvanize effective action. The difference this time was that instead of such a process *following* the adoption of an agreement by States Parties to the CCW (as with the Convention's *1996 Amended Protocol II*),[93] the Oslo Process and the CCW were working in parallel. Divisions between the two processes would not be neat, especially as a majority of the Convention's members had, by the end of 2007, become involved in the Oslo Process even while continuing to

[91] See Borrie, J., 'The "long year": Emerging international efforts to address the humanitarian impacts of cluster munitions, 2006–2007', *Yearbook of International Humanitarian Law*, Vol. 10 (2007), (Cambridge: T. M. C. Asser Press/Cambridge University Press, 2009), pp. 251–275.

[92] See, e.g., 'U.S. open to negotiations on cluster bombs but no ban', *Reuters*, Geneva, 18 June 2007.

[93] The formal title of this instrument is the Protocol on Prohibitions or Restrictions on the Use of Mines, Booby-Traps and Other Devices as amended on 3 May 1996 (Protocol II as amended on 3 May 1996 to the CCW).

participate in the much less ambitious talks under the CCW. Indeed, the 'core group' of States steering the Oslo Process continued to attend the sessions convened under the CCW.

0.37 The prospect for other countries, especially Australia, Canada, Japan, and most European NATO allies of the US, was that they would have to balance public concern and their commitment to the aspirations of the Oslo Declaration with the operational concerns of their military forces and the potential disapproval of their transatlantic ally. Their involvement in both processes might help to keep the Oslo Process's ambitions within acceptable bounds for them, and create pressure for agreement on lesser measures in the CCW in 2008 that would stand a chance of attracting those major users and producers of cluster munitions outside the Oslo Process.

0.38 Several important developments occurred during the period between the adoption of the Oslo Declaration and the Dublin negotiations 15 months later. The first real opportunity to wrestle collectively with substantive issues related to the content of a treaty on cluster munitions occurred at a meeting of experts convened by the ICRC in Montreux, Switzerland on 18–20 April 2007.[94] The Montreux meeting brought together both diplomatic and military experts from governments—including major military powers not participating in the Oslo Process—with humanitarian experts, including from international organizations and NGOs belonging to the CMC. In the course of the Montreux meeting it became apparent to an increasing number of diplomatic participants that suggested technical solutions (such as equipping submunitions with self-destruct features) would not prevent the problems cluster munitions cause.

0.39 Moreover, States arguing for continued retention and use of cluster munitions did not make a credible case for the legitimacy of the weapon in the face of contrasting perspectives from other governments, explosive ordnance disposal personnel, and civil society advocates of a ban. Not only were the military utility-centred positions (which usually trumped humanitarian considerations in discussions in the context of the CCW) found wanting in the face of empirical evidence of humanitarian harm, the Montreux meeting offered indications that the burden of proof was shifting from the shoulders of those trying to show the weapons caused 'unacceptable harm' to those claiming that cluster munitions did *not* do so.[95]

---

[94] See ICRC, *Humanitarian, Military, Technical and Legal Challenges of Cluster Munitions, Montreux, Switzerland, 18 to 20 April 2007.*

[95] For more on 'burden of proof' arguments see Rappert, B., and Moyes, R., 'The Prohibition of Cluster Munitions: Setting International Precedents for Defining Inhumanity', *Nonproliferation Review*, Vol. 16, No. 2 (July 2009), pp. 237–256.

0.40 Another significant development at the Montreux meeting was the unveiling of a 'non-paper' by Germany, later submitted to the CCW, which contained the draft text of a proposed new CCW protocol on cluster munitions.[96] Although welcomed as a sign of Germany's political commitment to the cluster munition issue, the proposal also drew sharp criticism from NGOs and some States for its perceived lack of ambition or clarity on key issues such as scope.[97]

The Lima Conference on Cluster Munitions

0.41 The first Chair's Discussion Text[98] of a treaty banning cluster munitions (the 'Lima Discussion Text')[99] was a sketch of what a treaty might look like, but was deliberately not referred to as a draft convention by the core group, because it was believed to be important not to start drafting and negotiations at this early stage. The text was designed to facilitate discussions on the key issues such as prohibitions and definitions. The text was issued prior to the next formal conference of the Oslo Process, held in Lima, Peru, on 23–25 May 2007. The Lima Conference on Cluster Munitions (the 'Lima Conference') attracted participation from 67 States,[100] 27 of which were participating in the Oslo Process for the first time and who were generally more concerned with the humanitarian problems posed by cluster munitions than ensuring exclusions for weapon systems (that many did not possess).

---

[96] Germany, 'Draft CCW Protocol on cluster munitions', UN doc. CCW/GGE/2007/WP.1, 1 May 2007.

[97] CMC, 'German proposal is not a basis for a new cluster munition treaty', Press release, Geneva, 27 April 2007.

[98] The chair's discussion texts, which were issued prior to the Lima and Vienna Conferences, were the result of discussions within the core group of States, taking into account the views of other States engaged in the Oslo Process.

[99] Chair's discussion text on a legally binding international instrument that will prohibit the use, production, transfer and stockpiling of cluster munitions that cause unacceptable harm to civilians, Lima, 23–25 May 2007.

[100] States participating in the Lima Conference were as follows: 14 from Africa (Angola, Burundi, Chad, Ghana, Guinea-Bissau, Lesotho, Liberia, Mauritania, Mozambique, Nigeria, Senegal, Tanzania, Uganda, and Zambia); 14 from the Americas (Argentina, Bolivia, Canada, Chile, Colombia, Costa Rica, Dominican Republic, Ecuador, Guatemala, Mexico, Panama, Paraguay, Peru, and Venezuela); eight from the Asia-Pacific (Australia, Bangladesh, Cambodia, Indonesia, Japan, Laos, New Zealand, and Thailand); 28 from Europe (Albania, Austria, Belgium, Bosnia and Herzegovina, Croatia, Czech Republic, Denmark, Estonia, Finland, France, Germany, Greece, Holy See, Hungary, Ireland, Italy, Lithuania, Luxembourg, Malta, the Netherlands, Norway, Poland, Portugal, Serbia, Slovakia, Spain, Switzerland, and the UK), and three from the Middle East (Egypt, Lebanon, and Yemen). See, e.g., Harrison, K., 'Report from the Lima Conference on Cluster Munitions, 23–25 May 2007', Women's International League for Peace and Freedom, p. 31.

0.42 While specific drafting of provisions was not discussed, the Lima Conference established the general framework and various elements of a future humanitarian treaty including the locations of its prohibitions, and measures on stockpile destruction, clearance of contaminated areas, and the victim assistance obligation.[101] On the whole, the Lima Conference went smoothly, although differences over the meeting's agenda showed that some countries, especially Australia, Canada, and many European members of NATO, were keen to settle the definition of 'cluster munitions that cause unacceptable harm to civilians' to their satisfaction as soon as possible. Some possessors of submunitions with self-destruct systems, for instance, believed these weapons should be excluded from any prohibition of cluster munitions that cause unacceptable harm to civilians.

The Vienna Conference on Cluster Munitions

0.43 At the next conference of the Oslo Process, held in Vienna, Austria, on 5–7 December 2007, the number of States attending had more than doubled to 138,[102] and again there was a strong CMC-led civil society contingent along with the ICRC and concerned UN bodies and agencies. Regional meetings in Costa Rica for Latin American States in September and for European nations in Brussels on 30 October, as well as a global conference of cluster-munition-affected States hosted by Serbia and UNDP in early October, had also served to bolster interest and attendance among States. Affected countries at the Belgrade Conference had endorsed the Oslo Process, which also saw several cluster munition survivors advocating for a strong humanitarian

---

[101] Human Rights Watch and Landmine Action, *Banning Cluster Munitions, op. cit.*, p. 4.

[102] States participating in the Vienna Conference were: Afghanistan, Albania, Algeria, Angola, Argentina, Armenia, Australia, Austria, Azerbaijan, Bangladesh, Belgium, Belize, Benin, Bolivia, Bosnia and Herzegovina, Brunei Darussalam, Bulgaria, Burkina Faso, Burundi, Cambodia, Cameroon, Canada, Chad, Chile, Colombia, Costa Rica, Côte d'Ivoire, Croatia, Cyprus, Czech Republic, Democratic Republic of Congo, Denmark, Djibouti, Dominican Republic, Ecuador, Egypt, El Salvador, Equatorial Guinea, Estonia, Ethiopia, Fiji, Finland, France, Gambia, Georgia, Germany, Ghana, Greece, Guatemala, Guinea, Guinea-Bissau, Holy See, Honduras, Hungary, Iceland, Indonesia, Iraq, Ireland, Italy, Jamaica, Japan, Jordan, Kazakhstan, Kenya, Kuwait, Kyrgyzstan, Laos, Latvia, Lebanon, Lesotho, Liberia, Liechtenstein, Lithuania, Luxembourg, Madagascar, Malawi, Malaysia, Mali, Malta, Mauritania, Mexico, Monaco, Montenegro, Morocco, Mozambique, Nepal, Netherlands, New Zealand, Nicaragua, Niger, Nigeria, Norway, Oman, Palau, Panama, Paraguay, Peru, Philippines, Poland, Portugal, Qatar, Romania, Samoa, San Marino, Sao Tome & Principe, Saudi Arabia, Senegal, Serbia, Seychelles, Sierra Leone, Slovakia, Slovenia, Somalia, South Africa, Spain, Sri Lanka, St. Kitts & Nevis, Sudan, Suriname, Swaziland, Sweden, Switzerland, Tajikistan, Tanzania, Thailand, the former Yugoslav Republic of Macedonia, Togo, Trinidad & Tobago, Turkey, Turkmenistan, Uganda, Ukraine, the UK, Uruguay, Venezuela, Vietnam, and Zambia. Source: Vienna Participants List from Austrian Ministry of Foreign Affairs (webpage discontinued; copy on file with author).

treaty as 'Ban Advocates'. The same week as the Vienna Conference on Cluster Munitions, Austria's parliament passed a national law outlawing cluster munitions as it defined them nationally.[103]

0.44 Austria, as chair of the Vienna Conference, tabled an updated discussion text reflecting the core group's revisions based on discussions at the Lima Conference.[104] Good progress was made in several substantive areas, in particular in building collective support for strong victim assistance and international cooperation and assistance measures. But the Vienna Conference also underlined that much work still needed to be done on the two most contentious issues emerging in the Oslo Process: how to define 'cluster munitions that cause unacceptable harm to civilians', and how to address 'interoperability',[105] especially the concern about joint military operations involving both States Parties and States not party to a future treaty outlawing cluster munitions. No general agreements emerged on possible solutions.

0.45 Of the two contentious issues, defining cluster munitions was to take centre stage at the Vienna Conference. As already noted, the Oslo Declaration had contained a commitment for States to 'prohibit the use, production, transfer and stockpiling of cluster munitions that cause unacceptable harm to civilians' and this categorical approach of defining and then banning had been maintained at the Lima Conference. The Vienna Discussion Text,[106] however, excluded the phrase 'that cause unacceptable harm to civilians' in Article 2 on definitions, which caused alarm among several countries. Some States reiterated their view that not all cluster munitions have unacceptable consequences for civilians. Other States disagreed, and a detailed report prepared by Norwegian defence scientists and NGOs entitled *M85—An Analysis of Reliability*[107] argued strongly (and persuasively, in the eyes of many national delegations present) that such a 'split-the-category' approach was inherently flawed and unlikely to be effective in addressing the risks to civilians posed by cluster munitions.

---

[103] 'Bundesgesetz über das Verbot von Streumunition' (NR: GP XXIII RV 232 AB 350 S. 42. BR: AB 7873 S.751.), *Austrian Federal Law Gazette* BGBl. I Nr. 12/2008, 7 January 2008, available at: <http://ris1.bka.gv.at/Appl/findbgbl.aspx?name=entwurf& format=html&docid=COO_202 6_100_2_367285>.   [104] Vienna Discussion Text of 14 November 2007.

[105] Interoperability, in general terms, refers to the ability of forces or agents of various States or international organizations to operate jointly in the performance of a task, mission, or operation. It has particular impact on the respective legal obligations of, and military relationship between, the armed forces of two or more States operating in a joint military alliance or operation. See further, *infra*, the commentary on Article 21, *esp.* §21.2.

[106] Vienna Discussion Text of 14 November 2007.

[107] King, C., Dullum, O., and Østern, G., *M85—An Analysis of Reliability, op. cit.*

0.46 The Vienna Conference did make useful progress in clarifying other aspects of the definition debate, including what should be exempted from the scope of the prohibition in Article 2 of the discussion text (which covered definitions). A common view emerged on less problematic exclusions from the definition, such as mines (already covered in other treaties),[108] and cluster munitions containing submunitions that emitted flare, smoke, and chaff rather than explosive submunitions. Proposals for exclusions for explosive submunitions based on reliability, low numbers contained in a single cluster munition, or sensor-fuzed technologies[109] did not, however, command wide support and would continue to be discussed at the next Oslo Process meeting in Wellington, New Zealand, from 18 to 22 February 2008.

0.47 The Meeting of States Parties to the CCW in November 2007, meanwhile, had achieved a mandate to 'negotiate a proposal to address urgently the humanitarian impact of cluster munitions, while striking a balance between military and humanitarian considerations'[110] with seven weeks of negotiations scheduled in Geneva in 2008. At the first week of these meetings in January, a number of States pushed hard—unsuccessfully as it turned out—for a working definition of cluster munitions. This would have raised the prospect of the States outside the Oslo Process being able to affect work on elaborating a definition at the Wellington Conference and Dublin Diplomatic Conference, because most governments would not want to develop two differing definitions of a cluster munition.[111]

The Wellington Conference on Cluster Munitions

0.48 The Wellington Conference on Cluster Munitions in February 2008 (hereinafter, the 'Wellington Conference') demonstrated more clearly the divisions in opinion regarding difficult issues such as defining what would be covered by the term cluster munitions and how interoperability would be addressed. In late 2007, a loose group of so-called 'like-minded' States

---

[108] See, *infra*, the commentary on Article 1, paragraph 3.

[109] These weapons use sensors and electronic micro-processors to identify and then attack targets, primarily vehicles, based on their heat-signature and profile. The use of the general term sensor-fuzed weapons should not be confused with the specific US CBU-97/CBU-105, which is often called the 'Sensor Fuzed Weapon'. See further, *infra*, §2.64.

[110] 'Report of the Meeting of the High Contracting Parties to the Convention on Prohibitions or Restrictions on the Use of Certain Conventional Weapons Which May Be Deemed to Be Excessively Injurious or to Have Indiscriminate Effects', UN doc. CCW/MSP/2007/5, 3 December 2007, p. 9.

[111] Although the definition of an anti-personnel mine differs somewhat between *1996 Amended Protocol II* and the *1997 Anti-Personnel Mine Ban Convention*. See, e.g., Maslen, S., *Commentary on the 1997 Anti-Personnel Mine Ban Convention, op. cit.*, §§2.1 *et seq.*

had emerged, many of them military allies of the US. The States associated with this group, however, were not necessarily 'like-minded' on many
issues of substance. Some were in favour of retaining many, if not all, of their
cluster munition arsenals, including the types of cluster munition shown to
be particularly hazardous to civilians, while others were not users of cluster
munitions and were not believed to have large stockpiles. In addition, many
of the 'like-minded' were concerned about interoperability with the US,
even though some of them were not US allies. Rather, the issue that served
to unite the 'like-minded' countries was concern about whether the Oslo
Process would safeguard their respective national proposals on issues such as
the definition of cluster munitions, a transition period for continued use, or
interoperability.[112]

0.49 Work proceeded on the basis of an evolving discussion text at the
Lima and Vienna conferences, in which core group States factored in proposals made in the meetings by various delegations according to their collective
assessment of how these views balanced out. This process differed from the
traditional approach used in forums like the CCW of negotiating on a roll-
ing text with square brackets around contentious points. The Wellington
Conference would be key to managing the Oslo Process's transition to a
treaty negotiation in Dublin and so, in late January 2008, New Zealand
made available a draft 'Convention text', an important psychological change
from the two earlier 'discussion' texts.[113] In addition, a draft Wellington
Conference Declaration was distributed: this echoed the Ottawa Process on
anti-personnel mines more than a decade before, in which each State participating in the Oslo Diplomatic Conference negotiations in September 1997
was required to subscribe to the June 1997 Brussels Declaration that set out
basic understandings.[114]

0.50 At the Wellington Conference, it became clear as soon as the conference began its discussions that some States, particularly those from the 'like-
minded' group, had come determined to get their proposals into the draft
Convention text. This was something the Conference's chair, Ambassador Don
MacKay, firmly resisted, referring to the plan agreed at the Oslo Conference
that textual negotiation was going to take place at the Diplomatic Conference
in Dublin and not before.

---

[112] For a more comprehensive description and analysis of the Wellington Conference, see Borrie,
J., *Unacceptable Harm, op. cit.*

[113] Draft Cluster Munitions Convention, 21 January 2008. See also Draft Cluster Munitions
Convention Explanatory Notes, 21 January 2008 and the Draft Wellington Declaration.

[114] See Maslen, S., *Commentary on the 1997 Anti-Personnel Mine Ban Convention, op. cit.*,
§§0.73–0.82.

0.51 Partly because of the tactics of the group of 15 or so 'like-minded' delegations, opposition to their desire for formal negotiation on their proposals before the Diplomatic Conference emerged among a range of States from various regions.[115] They advocated strongly that there should be no exclusion from the definition of a cluster munition under Article 2, paragraph 2(c) of the draft Convention text, and they also shared opposition to a transition period for cluster munition use.[116]

0.52 As it became clear that textual negotiation would not be undertaken in Wellington, the discussions turned to the status of a compendium paper.[117] The compendium was a document prepared by the Chair comprising all of the various non-papers presented in Wellington and which contained proposals to amend the draft Convention text. The issue revolved around whether the proposals in the compendium text would have equal status with the draft Convention text in Dublin.

0.53 Draft rules of procedure for the Diplomatic Conference[118] circulated on the penultimate day of work at the Wellington Conference stated that the draft Convention text 'shall constitute the basic proposal for consideration by the [Dublin] Conference'; the compendium proposals would count as 'other proposals', a distinction that could conceivably make a difference if the Diplomatic Conference resorted to voting, which some delegations feared might occur. Some argued that the draft Convention text was not an agreed document, and so there should be no difference in status between it and their proposals. The Chair's view, with support from many others, was that the draft Convention text possessed legitimacy, as it was the product of several rounds of talks in open format since early in the Oslo Process.[119]

---

[115] One member of the core group referred to them as the 'teetotal' States.

[116] The structure of the draft prohibition in Article 2(c) meant that anything defined as a cluster munition would be banned.

[117] See Compendium of Proposals submitted by Delegations during the Wellington Conference Addendum 1, <http://www.mfat.govt.nz/clustermunitionswellington/conference-documents/WCCM-Compendium-v2.pdf> (accessed 5 March 2010). Proposals by States were issued as formal papers at the Dublin Diplomatic Conference. Proposals by others, such as the ICRC, are included in Annex 6.

[118] The chief features of the draft Rules of Procedure were, namely, that only States that had subscribed to the Wellington Declaration were entitled to participate at the Diplomatic Conference (other States would be observers); that every effort should be made to reach general agreement but that where this was not possible provision was made for decision-making by two-thirds majority vote (the standard rule of decision making for the adoption of multilateral conventions); that NGOs would be observers with speaking rights; and that the Draft Cluster Munitions Convention would form the basic proposal before the Conference.

[119] The matter was resolved only on the final morning of the Conference when it was agreed that Ambassador McKay would transmit the Wellington Declaration (in which the draft Convention

0.54 In the end, the Wellington Declaration stated that States:

> also welcome the important work done by participants engaged in the cluster munitions process on the text of a draft Cluster Munitions Convention, dated 21 January 2008, which contains the essential elements identified above and decide to forward it as the basic proposal for consideration at the Dublin Diplomatic Conference, together with other relevant proposals including those contained in the compendium attached to this Declaration and those which may be put forward there.[120]

Some of the delegations who had wanted inclusion of text proposals already in Wellington linked their adherence to the Wellington Declaration with the understanding that the draft Convention text and compendium would—or should—have equal standing in Dublin. By the end of the first week of the Diplomatic Conference on 23 May 2008, 119 countries had supported the Wellington Declaration.[121] As it turned out, the status of the compendium did not become an issue in Dublin.[122]

The lead-up to the Diplomatic Conference

0.55 The Wellington Conference had ultimately succeeded in its objectives. The Conference also exposed differences in approach within the core group itself, with Norway becoming more active in promoting a position that differed from States seeking a total prohibition of all weapons with submunitions regardless of their technical features, such as Austria and Mexico. Meanwhile, by April, it was obvious that prospects for the CCW to address cluster munitions were at best uncertain in the face of few signs of flexibility from China, Russia, and others. Although it was negative in public statements to the Oslo Process and 'consulted' with its friends and allies in the lead-up to

---

text is established as the basic proposal) and the compendium of delegations' proposals attached to it to the Government of Ireland which, as host of the Diplomatic Conference, would treat the proposals set out in the compendium as proposals submitted in accordance with rule 31 of the draft Rules of Procedure, i.e. as 'other proposals'. This was accepted by the 'like-minded' and publicly confirmed by the Conference Chairman and the head of the Irish delegation (the Irish Government's nominee for President of the Diplomatic Conference) at the conclusion of the Wellington Conference.

[120] Declaration of the Wellington Conference on Cluster Munitions, 22 February 2008, <http://www.mfat.govt.nz/clustermunitionswellington/conference-documents/Wellington-declaration-final.pdf> (accessed 5 March 2010).

[121] List of countries subscribing to the Declaration of the Wellington Conference on Cluster Munitions (prepared by the New Zealand Ministry of Foreign Affairs and Trade), 23 May 2008, <http://www.clustermunitionsdublin.ie/pdf/Subscribing_23.5.08.pdf> (accessed 5 March 2010).

[122] List of countries subscribing to the Declaration of the Wellington Conference on Cluster Munitions (prepared by the New Zealand Ministry of Foreign Affairs and Trade), 23 May 2008, <http://www.clustermunitionsdublin.ie/pdf/Subscribing_23.5.08.pdf> (accessed 5 March 2010).

the Dublin negotiations it would not attend, a US Government internal policy review underway had months left to run, which further limited momentum in negotiations under the CCW.[123]

0.56 There was plenty of other activity in support of the Oslo Process in the final months leading up to the Dublin Conference. Bilateral consultations between core group States and others were increasing. Forty African states signed up to the Livingstone Declaration agreed in Zambia on 1 April in support of the Oslo Process and the adoption of a humanitarian treaty on cluster munitions.[124] Mexico hosted a conference of 22 Latin American and Caribbean states in Mexico City on 16–17 April 2008. On 23–24 April, the ICRC convened a workshop of around 10 ASEAN (Association of South East Asian Nation) States in Bangkok to engage them on cluster munition issues, which served to encourage Asian attendance at the Diplomatic Conference. And a Global Day of Action on 19 April 2008 coordinated by the CMC in more than 50 countries underlined civil society's advocacy efforts.[125]

Organization of the Diplomatic Conference: Basic Proposal, Rules of Procedure, and Structure of Work

0.57 As noted above, the Wellington Conference concluded with the adoption of the Wellington Declaration. By the terms of that Declaration the States concerned decided to forward the Wellington draft Convention text to the Dublin Diplomatic Conference as the basic proposal for consideration there, together with other relevant proposals made at Wellington as well as those that would be made in advance of, or at, Dublin.

0.58 Draft Rules of Procedure for the Diplomatic Conference were circulated to all delegations on the penultimate day of the Wellington Conference.[126] Developed by the core group, they were based on rules of procedure used at recent diplomatic conferences for the adoption of new instruments of international humanitarian law (in particular for the adoption of the Statute of the International Criminal Court[127] and of the *2005 Additional Protocol III* to the *1949 Geneva Conventions*). They also drew on the draft standard rules

---

[123] The US Secretary of Defense, Robert Gates, would eventually sign-off on a new policy on 'cluster munitions and unintended harm to civilians' on 19 June 2008. Available online at: <http://www.defenselink.mil/news/d20080709cmpolicy.pdf> (accessed 5 March 2010).

[124] Livingstone Declaration on Cluster Munitions, 1 April 2008, accessed at: <http://www.iss.co.za/dynamic/administration/file_manager/file_links/LIVINGSTONEDECL.PDF?link_id=19&slink_id=5859&link_type=12&slink_type=13&tmpl_id=3> (accessed 5 March 2010).

[125] Human Rights Watch and Landmine Action, *Banning Cluster Munitions, op. cit.*, p. 6.

[126] Subsequently published as Diplomatic Conference doc. CCM/2, 19 May 2008.

[127] UN doc. A/CONF.183/6 of 23 June 1998.

of procedure for UN Conferences[128] as well as the rules of procedure used for the Oslo Diplomatic Conference for the adoption of the *1997 Anti-Personnel Mine Ban Convention*.[129]

0.59 The principal features of the draft rules were the provisions concerning participants and observers (rules 1 and 2), the basic proposal (rule 30) and decision-making (rule 36). Only States that had subscribed to the Wellington Declaration would be invited to participate in the Conference, while other States, as well as intergovernmental and non-governmental organizations, would be invited to attend as observers. Rule 30 established the Wellington text as the basic proposal for the Diplomatic Conference.[130]

0.60 As host of the Diplomatic Conference, the Government of Ireland was determined to achieve the adoption of a Convention text by consensus. Paradoxically, the existence of a provision in the rules of procedure enabling the Conference to achieve its objective by vote, if necessary, was considered essential for this purpose as it encouraged delegations to find a compromise for fear that a vote might be called, which they could lose. (This is in contrast, for instance, to the Conference on Disarmament in which each member of the Conference has a veto on decision-making.) The draft Rules accordingly provided at rule 36, paragraph 1 that 'the Conference shall make its best endeavours to ensure that (its) work... is accomplished by general agreement' but, failing that, a decision on any matter of substance could be put to a vote.[131] A decision on a matter of substance put to a vote would require a two-thirds majority of those present and voting.[132]

0.61 In accordance with tradition at diplomatic conferences, the Government of Ireland, as host, nominated the President of the Conference (Ambassador Daithí O'Ceallaigh).[133] As Ambassador O'Ceallaigh was the

---

[128] UN doc. A/40/611 of 11 September 1985.

[129] Doc. APL/CRP 3 of 1 September 1997.

[130] The status of the Wellington text as the basic proposal would become relevant if and when voting were to take place at the Diplomatic Conference. When concern was expressed by a number of delegations about the status of other proposals made in Wellington the Government of Ireland, as host of the Diplomatic Conference, agreed to treat those proposals as proposals submitted in accordance with rule 31 (i.e. 'other proposals') and they were registered and published as such in advance of the Diplomatic Conference. However, only proposals made by States could be so treated: suggestions made by the ICRC and the CMC at Wellington could not be regarded as 'other proposals' under rule 31 because only States could subscribe to the Wellington Declaration and only such states could *participate* in the Diplomatic Conference (and therefore make proposals).

[131] Rule 36, paragraph 2.

[132] This reflects the generally applicable rule of international law, as provided at Article 9(2) of the *1969 Vienna Convention on the Law of Treaties* ('(t)he adoption of the text of a treaty at an international conference takes place by the vote of two thirds of the States present and voting, unless by the same majority they shall decide to apply a different rule').

[133] Then the Permanent Representative of Ireland to the UN in Geneva.

only candidate he was duly elected by acclamation at the opening plenary session on 19 May 2008. The Conference then formally adopted its agenda[134] and Rules of Procedure[135] by consensus and appointed eight Vice-Presidents.[136] Following this, Ambassador O'Ceallaigh set out how he proposed to organize the work of the Conference.[137] General statements were to be heard in Plenary while at the same time, given the relatively brief period available in which to achieve the objective of the Conference (just two weeks), consideration of individual articles of the draft Convention, together with relevant proposals for amendment, would begin in the Committee of the Whole[138] meeting in parallel.

0.62 Ambassador O'Ceallaigh explained that he did not intend to permit the introduction of text in square brackets into the draft Convention. Instead he proposed that where, following discussion, general agreement was recorded within the Committee of the Whole on the text of a provision of the draft Convention that text would be transmitted to the Plenary. If consensus on a particular provision were not possible in the Committee of the Whole the President would appoint a Friend to convene informal consultations in the search for agreement or would convene such consultations himself. Nothing would be formally agreed until everything was agreed in Plenary.

0.63 There had been some concern as to how non-governmental organizations, as observers, would be treated during the Conference and in particular whether they would have access to, and the right to speak at, all Conference meetings. The President explained that meetings of the Plenary and the

---

[134] 'Agenda', Diplomatic Conference doc. CCM/51, 19 May 2008.

[135] 'Rules of Procedure', Diplomatic Conference doc. CCM/52, 19 May 2008.

[136] The eight Vice-Presidents appointed by the Diplomatic Conference were the following: Ambassador Najla Riachi Assaker of Lebanon, Ambassador Jean-Francois Dobelle of France, Ambassador Juan Eduardo Eguiguren of Chile, Ambassador Mohamed Yahya Ould Sidi Haiba of Mauritania, Ambassador Steffen Kongstad of Norway, Ambassador Pablo Macedo of Mexico, Ms. Sheila Mweemba of Zambia, and Ambassador Sándor Rácz of Hungary.

[137] 'Summary Record of Opening Ceremony and First Session of the Plenary', Diplomatic Conference doc. CCM/SR/1, 18 June 2008.

[138] It is not usually possible to accomplish the work of a large international conference entirely in Plenary meetings, which are regarded as too cumbersome to carry out detailed preparation of the decisions to be taken at the conference. The annual General Assembly of the United Nations, for instance, allocates its work to six separate committees, all of which report to the Assembly in plenary. However, at a smaller conference with a relatively straightforward agenda, such as a diplomatic conference for the negotiation of a new convention, the conference may undertake detailed examination of a text while sitting as a committee of the whole. At such a conference general discussion and decision-making is reserved for the plenary. At the Dublin Diplomatic Conference provision was made for the Committee of the Whole at rule 50 of the Rules of Procedure. By convening it in parallel to the plenary, it was possible to hear general statements while simultaneously beginning work on the detailed examination of the draft Convention text.

Committee of the Whole would be open to participants and observers alike and that he expected the same to be the case with open-ended informal meetings. However where Friends chose to convene smaller informal meetings he acknowledged that the question of who to invite would be very much a matter for their judgement, although he pointed out that that judgement would inevitably be informed by the need to achieve the broadest possible agreement.

0.64 Ambassador O'Ceallaigh concluded his statement on the organization of the work of the Conference by stressing that a Convention text would be adopted at its conclusion: while he made it clear that he hoped this would be achieved by consensus, for which he would make every effort, the strong implication he conveyed to delegations was that he was prepared to submit a Convention text to the Conference for adoption by vote if necessary and that there was no question of reconvening the Conference at a later date. Knowledge of this intended course of action further encouraged all delegations to work for consensus.[139]

The negotiations at the Dublin Diplomatic Conference

0.65 From the first day of the Diplomatic Conference it was strikingly apparent that virtually all of the participating States at the Croke Park Stadium and Conference Centre[140] where the negotiations were taking place were genuinely seeking to agree on and adopt a treaty. Strong statements of resolve were made by Ireland's Foreign Minister, Micheál Martin, T.D.; the Secretary-General of the United Nations, Ban Ki-moon (in a video message); the President of the ICRC, Jakob Kellenberger, and Ad Melkert, Associate Administrator of UNDP.[141] There is no need here to give more than a general sense of how the Dublin negotiations progressed since the evolution of specific provisions of the Convention on Cluster Munitions is covered in detail in the main body of this Commentary. It is important to mention, however, that although there were controversies over definitions, associated concepts, and

---

[139] Thus, the President of the Diplomatic Conference stated his intention to:

adopt a Convention at the conclusion of this Conference. It's my hope that that Convention will be adopted by consensus, and as I've emphasised throughout my consultations, it's my intention to make every feasible effort to reach general agreement. But I want to underline once again: we will adopt a Convention by the end of next week.

Author's transcript; *cf.* Borrie, J., *Unacceptable Harm, op. cit.*, p. 267.

[140] <http://www.crokepark.ie/conference-centre>.

[141] Summary records of all of the formal sessions of the Dublin Diplomatic Conference were prepared by the Irish Department of Foreign Affairs. The summary records are available at the archives of the Irish Department of Foreign Affairs and through the website of the Diplomatic Conference at <http://www.clustermunitionsdublin.ie>.

military interoperability throughout the Oslo Process, excellent progress was quietly made in developing agreement on many of the substantive areas of a Convention text. These provisions included groundbreaking new standards on victim assistance, as well as for cluster munition clearance, stockpile storage and destruction, international assistance and cooperation, and transparency measures.

0.66 Differences still existed on issues like whether cluster munitions could be permitted for training and development purposes and the nature of provisions relating to the particular obligations of past user States. But most substantive issues were settled in the first week of the Diplomatic Conference under the auspices of Friends of the President that Ambassador O'Ceallaigh had appointed on various provisions.[142] Many of these provisions already showed lessons had been learned from the negotiation and implementation of previous multilateral agreements such as the *1997 Anti-Personnel Mine Ban Convention*, *2003 Protocol V*, and the UN Convention on the Rights of Persons with Disabilities. The Convention on Cluster Munitions, for example, contains broader provisions on victim assistance than those earlier agreements and has more robust transparency provisions than the *1997 Anti-Personnel Mine Ban Convention*.

0.67 Such advances were significant not least because they gave affected States and others in the developing world stakes in a successful outcome to the negotiations, and helped to ameliorate any perceived 'North-South' divide, which some had feared might occur. As for the 'like-minded', there appeared to be recognition among most that pursuit of their interests could be nuanced. As a consequence, certain delegations often prefaced their statements by reaffirming their commitment to the humanitarian aims of the Oslo Declaration. There were signs too that these countries were feeling domestic political pressure to promote a successful outcome. The CMC, in particular, had intensified its lobbying efforts in the lead-up to the Diplomatic Conference.

---

[142] Ambassador Caroline Millar of Australia served as a Friend of the President on the Preamble. Ambassador Christine Schraner Burgener of Switzerland served as a Friend of the President on 'interoperability'. Ambassador Don MacKay of New Zealand served as a Friend of the President on Article 2. Ambassador Steffen Kongstad of Norway served as a Friend of the President on Article 3. Lieutenant Colonel Jim Burke of the Irish Defence Forces served as a Friend of the President on Article 4. Mr. Markus Reiterer of Austria served as a Friend of the President on Article 5. Mr. Xolisa Mabhongo of South Africa served as a Friend of the President on Article 8. In addition, the delegation of Germany was asked to hold informal consultations on the possibility of transition periods and the delegation of Canada was asked to hold informal consultations on international cooperation and assistance.

0.68 An important target for civil society lobbying was the UK, which was a past user and, at the time, a possessor of cluster munitions, a NATO Member State, and a close ally of the US. Throughout the Diplomatic Conference, the UK's cluster munition policies and negotiating posture attracted major coverage in the British media and lobbying from British NGOs. A letter in *The Times* newspaper from several senior former British military generals on 19 May was especially significant and helped to further undermine military arguments for retaining weapons of humanitarian concern in the Oslo Process. In particular, the letter called for:

the Government of the United Kingdom to give up its remaining stocks of cluster munitions and agree the strongest possible ban on the weapon in the treaty negotiations in Dublin, starting today. Such a treaty will establish a new benchmark for the responsible projection of force in the modern world.[143]

Two days later, Gordon Brown's spokesperson announced that 'the Prime Minister had asked the Ministry of Defence to assess the remaining munitions to ensure there was no risk to civilians'.[144]

0.69 Although most of the rest of the draft Convention had taken shape by Tuesday of the second week of negotiations in Dublin—including a categorical prohibition on cluster munitions—at the end of that afternoon no solution had been found on interoperability, despite the intensive informal work led by Switzerland, as the 'Friend of the President' on this matter. President O'Ceallaigh told his Friends that he would resume direct responsibility for the draft Convention text, and announced to the Conference he would use the next 24 hours for bilateral consultations. The Irish carefully kept their concerns about interoperability to themselves: if the UK was not on board it might make it harder for other 'like-minded' States with stockpiles of cluster munitions and US alliance commitments to join—and those States were clearly anxious.

0.70 Having asked the UK for greater flexibility there was little more the President could do. On Tuesday night, as O'Ceallaigh and his team were in the midst of their consultations with individual delegations, a news story appeared on the website of the *Guardian* newspaper, which would be printed the next

[143] Letter from General Sir Hugh Beach, Field Marshal Lord Bramall, Major-General Patrick Cordingley, Lieutenant-General Sir Roderick Cordy-Simpson, Lieutenant-General Sir Jack Deverell, Major-General the Rev. Morgan Llewellyn, General Lord Ramsbotham, General Sir Michael Rose, and General Sir Rupert Smith, 'Cluster bombs don't work and must be banned', *The Times*, 19 May 2008.

[144] 10 Downing Street press briefing, 21 May 2008, 'cluster bombs', <http://www.number-10.gov.uk/output/Page15599.asp>.

morning.[145] It reported that the British Government was preparing to scrap Britain's entire arsenal of cluster munitions. This was confirmed the next day when Prime Minister Brown announced that:

In order to secure as strong a Convention as possible in the last hours of negotiation we have issued instructions that we should support a ban on all cluster bombs, including those currently in service by the UK.[146]

The announcement, in effect, signalled that Britain would buy into the Dublin outcome. But it was still by no means clear whether unanimous agreement on a treaty text in the Conference plenary would be possible.

0.71 On Wednesday morning (28 May), the President issued a complete draft Convention text, CCM/PT/15,[147] prepared during the night, and asked all delegations to seek instructions from their capitals on whether they could accept it.[148] The 'Presidency Paper' was based on the work in the Friends' consultations and the Committee of the Whole, rounded out with the President's take on solutions to the remaining issues following his bilateral meetings and drawing heavily on his team's judgement. However, some States still opposed on principle any Article 2, paragraph 2(c) exemption in the cluster munition definition. Moreover, several did not support a weight criterion being reinserted into the definition as part of cumulative criteria for exclusion. At the same time, some delegations would have to come to terms with the fact that 2(c) would exclude certain munitions using sensor-fuzed technologies from a ban.[149] On the other hand, cluster munitions as a category were to be clearly banned, and there were no transition periods on use that some States had wanted.

0.72 The conclusion the President and his team had drawn from their many bilateral discussions was that his Presidency Paper should not be changed further, lest the Dublin negotiations unravel. During the lunchtime on Wednesday, the Irish Presidency met with the African group and then the Latin Americans to promote this course of action. However, emerging from these meetings, it was still not certain that all of the States seeking a total

---

[145] Richard Norton-Taylor, 'UK ready to scrap killer cluster bombs: Ministers overrule opposition from military over controversial weapons', *Guardian*, 28 May 2008.

[146] 10 Downing Street, 'Breakthrough on cluster bombs draws closer', 28 May 2008, <http://www.number10.gov.uk/output/page15608.asp>.

[147] Initially, this paper was incorrectly numbered as PT/14, but this number had been reserved for a revised draft of Article 8.

[148] 'Presidency Paper: Draft Convention on Cluster Munitions', Diplomatic Conference doc. CCM/PT/15, 28 May 2008. The Presidency paper became available that morning.

[149] For explanation, see 'CMC Briefing Paper on the Convention on Cluster Munitions', July 2008; for details of sensor-fuzed weapons, see, *infra*, §2.64.

prohibition without exclusion would support the adoption of the Convention on the plenary floor.

0.73 The CMC's representatives were unhappy with the interoperability formulation, and wanted drafting changes in order to specify further the prohibition on assistance to prohibited activities by a State not party in Article 1 of the draft Convention. The CMC hoped to secure agreement from Canada and the UK—two countries that had been among the toughest on interoperability—and so persuade the President to amend the draft Convention text. Canada, however, said that it would not go along with further changes. O'Ceallaigh therefore told the CMC representatives that he would not make the changes they were proposing. Although the CMC was an observer rather a State participant in the negotiations, civil society support was important to the legitimacy of the Dublin outcome, and the CMC had been a crucial partner throughout the Oslo process. For their part, although unhappy about Article 21, paragraph 3, CMC campaigners realized that the strengths of other elements of the Presidency Paper far outweighed what it later described as the 'only stain on the fine fabric of the treaty text'.[150]

0.74 By now it was around five o'clock on Wednesday afternoon. The clock had been stopped and more than 100 delegations had been waiting for several hours for the last of the three language versions of the Presidency Paper (Spanish) to become available.[151] The President now had another outstanding problem to solve: Lebanon, a State affected by cluster munitions and an active and influential country among those seeking a total prohibition without exclusions, reiterated that it would not agree to the draft Convention unless the word 'strongly' was added to the provisions in Article 4 to give more weight to calls for assistance from past user states for clearance of cluster munition remnants and risk reduction education. The UK and others had earlier opposed this proposal.[152] The President conferred briefly with the relevant delegations, and the amendment was made.

---

[150] CMC, 'CMC Statement on the Agreement to Adopt the Cluster Munition Convention', delivered by Steve Goose, Human Rights Watch, CMC Co-Chair, 28 May 2008, Dublin Diplomatic Conference.

[151] Official documents at the Dublin Conference were produced in English, French, and Spanish.

[152] Lebanese Government authorities in Beirut insisted that the word 'strongly' be prefixed to 'encourage' in paragraph 4(a) of Article 4—a formulation of important symbolic value to some cluster munition affected countries. The UK apparently opposed this initially because the British Government saw little difference between 'encouraged' and 'strongly encouraged' in practical terms.

0.75 The President called the meeting to order and asked the Deputy Foreign Minister of Zambia, Fashion Phiri, who had just arrived in Dublin, to deliver his general statement to the Plenary. The President then informed the Conference:

The Presidency paper before us now represents my assessment at this point of where the best balance of interests and compromise consistent with the Oslo Declaration now lies. It is a package of elements that entails concession for all sides but remains nevertheless an extremely ambitious Convention text that meets the objectives we set ourselves in Oslo in February last year.

0.76 Zambia took the floor again, this time on behalf of the Africa Group, and made clear that African States could endorse the package, although they remained unhappy with certain elements of the text. Zambia sternly warned that if others opened up the text then the African States would reconsider. A cascade of endorsements ensued with New Zealand, Canada, Mexico, South Africa, Switzerland, France, the Philippines, and Indonesia echoing support for the text. Spotting his moment, Ambassador O'Ceallaigh intervened again to alter Article 4, paragraph 4 to make a 'correction' and insert the world 'strongly'. No delegation objected. More than two hours of statements endorsing the Convention on Cluster Munitions followed from States, international organizations, and the CMC. Finally, early that Wednesday evening, the decision was made to return to Croke Park on Friday to adopt formally the Convention on Cluster Munitions. The world now had a new humanitarian treaty categorically banning cluster munitions. On Friday 30 May 2008, 107 States returned to Croke Park to adopt the Convention on Cluster Munitions.[153]

---

[153] The following 107 States participated in the Dublin Conference: Albania, Argentina, Australia, Austria, Bahrain, Belgium, Belize, Benin, Bolivia, Bosnia and Herzegovina, Botswana, Brunei Darussalam, Bulgaria, Burkina Faso, Burundi, Cambodia, Cameroon, Canada, Chad, Chile, Comoros, Republic of the Congo, Cook Islands, Costa Rica, Côte d'Ivoire, Croatia, Czech Republic, Democratic Republic of the Congo, Denmark, Dominican Republic, Ecuador, El Salvador, Estonia, Fiji, Finland, France, Germany, Ghana, Guatemala, Guinea, Guinea-Bissau, Holy See, Honduras, Hungary, Iceland, Indonesia, Ireland, Italy, Jamaica, Japan, Kenya, Kyrgyzstan, Laos, Lebanon, Lesotho, Lithuania, Luxembourg, Madagascar, Malawi, Malaysia, Mali, Malta, Mauritania, Mexico, Moldova, Montenegro, Morocco, Mozambique, The Netherlands, New Zealand, Nicaragua, Niger, Nigeria, Norway, Palau, Panama, Papua New Guinea, Paraguay, Peru, Philippines, Portugal, Qatar, Samoa, San Marino, Sao Tome and Principe, Senegal, Serbia, Seychelles, Sierra Leone, Slovakia, Slovenia, South Africa, Spain, Sudan, Swaziland, Sweden, Switzerland, Tanzania, the former Yugoslav Republic of Macedonia, Timor-Leste, Togo, Uganda, the UK, Uruguay, Vanuatu, Venezuela, and Zambia. In addition, Colombia, Cyprus, Egypt, Eritrea, Ethiopia, Greece, Iraq, Kazakhstan, Kuwait, Latvia, Libyan Arab Jamahiriya, Oman, Poland, Romania, Saudi Arabia, Singapore, Thailand, Turkey, Ukraine, and Vietnam attended as observers. See 'Final Document', Diplomatic Conference doc. CCM/78, 30 May 2008.

COMMENTARY

The Title and Preamble of the Convention

Théo Boutruche, Stuart Casey-Maslen, Andrew Clapham, Thomas Nash, Markus Reiterer, and Declan Smyth[1]

[1] Théo Boutruche wrote the commentary on the eleventh, seventeenth, and twentieth preambular paragraphs; Andrew Clapham wrote the commentary on the twelfth preambular paragraph, Thomas Nash wrote the commentary on the second, fourth, and sixteenth preambular paragraphs, Markus Reiterer wrote the commentary on the sixth, seventh, eighth, ninth, and tenth preambular paragraphs, and Declan Smyth wrote the commentary on the first and third preambular paragraphs as well as on the negotiation of the preamble. The remaining commentary was written by Stuart Casey-Maslen.

The Convention on Cluster Munitions

The States Parties to this Convention,

Deeply concerned that civilian populations and individual civilians continue to bear the brunt of armed conflict,

Determined to put an end for all time to the suffering and casualties caused by cluster munitions at the time of their use, when they fail to function as intended or when they are abandoned,

Concerned that cluster munition remnants kill or maim civilians, including women and children, obstruct economic and social development, including through the loss of livelihood, impede post-conflict rehabilitation and reconstruction, delay or prevent the return of refugees and internally displaced persons, can negatively impact on national and international peace-building and humanitarian assistance efforts, and have other severe consequences that can persist for many years after use,

Deeply concerned also at the dangers presented by the large national stockpiles of cluster munitions retained for operational use and *determined* to ensure their rapid destruction,

Believing it necessary to contribute effectively in an efficient, coordinated manner to resolving the challenge of removing cluster munition remnants located throughout the world, and to ensure their destruction,

Determined also to ensure the full realisation of the rights of all cluster munition victims and *recognising* their inherent dignity,

Resolved to do their utmost in providing assistance to cluster munition victims, including medical care, rehabilitation and psychological support, as well as providing for their social and economic inclusion,

Recognising the need to provide age- and gender-sensitive assistance to cluster munition victims and to address the special needs of vulnerable groups,

Bearing in mind the Convention on the Rights of Persons with Disabilities which, *inter alia*, requires that States Parties to that Convention undertake to ensure and promote the full realisation of all human rights and fundamental freedoms of all persons with disabilities without discrimination of any kind on the basis of disability,

Mindful of the need to coordinate adequately efforts undertaken in various fora to address the rights and needs of victims of various types of weapons, and *resolved* to avoid discrimination among victims of various types of weapons,

Reaffirming that in cases not covered by this Convention or by other international agreements, civilians and combatants remain under the protection and authority of the principles of international law, derived from established custom, from the principles of humanity and from the dictates of public conscience,

Resolved also that armed groups distinct from the armed forces of a State shall not, under any circumstances, be permitted to engage in any activity prohibited to a State Party to this Convention,

Welcoming the very broad international support for the international norm prohibiting anti-personnel mines, enshrined in the 1997 Convention on the Prohibition of the Use, Stockpiling, Production and Transfer of Anti-Personnel Mines and on Their Destruction,

Welcoming also the adoption of the Protocol on Explosive Remnants of War, annexed to the Convention on Prohibitions or Restrictions on the

Use of Certain Conventional Weapons Which May be Deemed to be Excessively Injurious or to Have Indiscriminate Effects, and its entry into force on 12 November 2006, and *wishing* to enhance the protection of civilians from the effects of cluster munition remnants in post-conflict environments,

Bearing in mind also United Nations Security Council Resolution 1325 on women, peace and security and United Nations Security Council Resolution 1612 on children in armed conflict,

Welcoming further the steps taken nationally, regionally and globally in recent years aimed at prohibiting, restricting or suspending the use, stockpiling, production and transfer of cluster munitions,

Stressing the role of public conscience in furthering the principles of humanity as evidenced by the global call for an end to civilian suffering caused by cluster munitions and *recognising* the efforts to that end undertaken by the United Nations, the International Committee of the Red Cross, the Cluster Munition Coalition and numerous other non-governmental organisations around the world,

Reaffirming the Declaration of the Oslo Conference on Cluster Munitions, by which, *inter alia*, States recognised the grave consequences caused by the use of cluster munitions and committed themselves to conclude by 2008 a legally binding instrument that would prohibit the use, production, transfer and stockpiling of cluster munitions that cause unacceptable harm to civilians, and would establish a framework for cooperation and assistance that ensures adequate provision of care and rehabilitation for victims, clearance of contaminated areas, risk reduction education and destruction of stockpiles,

Emphasising the desirability of attracting the adherence of all States to this Convention, and *determined* to work strenuously towards the promotion of its universalisation and its full implementation,

Basing themselves on the principles and rules of international humanitarian law, in particular the principle that the right of parties to an armed conflict to choose methods or means of warfare is not unlimited, and the rules that the parties to a conflict shall at all times distinguish between the civilian population and combatants and between civilian objects and military objectives and accordingly direct their operations against military objectives only, that in the conduct of military operations constant care shall be taken to spare the civilian population, civilians and civilian objects and that the civilian population and individual civilians enjoy general protection against dangers arising from military operations,

HAVE AGREED as follows:

Overview

0.77 The simple title of the Convention on Cluster Munitions is a deliberate break with the practice of most other treaties outlawing conventional or non-conventional weapons, which have tended to be long. Its title does not refer to the core prohibitions set out in the Convention. The preamble covers a range of subjects, notably the humanitarian and developmental impacts underpinning the need for the treaty, the rights of those affected by cluster munitions, and the legal basis for the treaty. The preamble also identifies the main actions required to ensure the implementation of the Convention, contains references to key documents forming part of the 'Oslo Process',[2] and includes a paragraph addressing the application to non-State armed groups (NSAGs) of the core prohibitions set out in the Convention.

The Title of the Convention

The Convention on Cluster Munitions

0.78 The Convention's simple title was presented to the negotiating States by the President of the Dublin Diplomatic Conference in his consolidated text of 28 May 2008.[3] There were no formal negotiations on the title; although Hungary made a written proposal to rename the title of the draft Convention, this was not accepted.[4] The title of the Convention as adopted was deliberately short.[5] The title of the first draft of the Convention, the Lima Discussion Text, had referred to 'a legally binding international instrument that will prohibit the use, production, transfer and stockpiling of cluster munitions that cause unacceptable harm to civilians'.[6] The second draft, the Vienna Discussion

---

[2] See, *supra*, the Introduction (§§0.32 *et seq.*) for details of the Oslo Process.

[3] 'Presidency paper, *draft* Convention on Cluster Munitions', Diplomatic Conference doc. CCM/PT/15, 28 May 2008.

[4] Under Diplomatic Conference document 62 of 19 May 2008, Hungary had proposed to name the future treaty the 'Convention on the Prohibition of Cluster Munitions that Cause Unacceptable Harm to Civilians'.

[5] The core group discussed in January 2008 the desirability of a short title.

[6] Chair's discussion text on a legally binding international instrument that will prohibit the use, production, transfer and stockpiling of cluster munitions that cause unacceptable harm to civilians, Lima, 23–25 May 2007.

Text, however, did not include this language, nor did the Draft Cluster Munitions Convention submitted as the formal basis for negotiation at the Dublin Diplomatic Conference of May 2008.[7]

The preamble

0.79 The preamble of an international treaty typically sets out its purpose and the context of its adoption although there is no legal requirement that it do so,[8] nor even that a preamble be included.[9] Although not legally binding provisions, the content of the preamble can be usefully considered in an attempt to discern the object and purpose of the Convention.

Background to the preamble

0.80 The Lima Discussion Text did not contain draft preambular language. Four draft preambular paragraphs specifically addressing the issue of victims of cluster munitions were circulated as part of the Vienna Discussion Text. A complete draft preambular text, incorporating these paragraphs, was then developed by Ireland and considered by the core group at its meeting in Geneva on 10 and 11 January 2008. The Irish delegation chaired informal consultations during the February 2008 Wellington Conference[10] on most elements of the draft preamble (those paragraphs addressing victim issues were discussed by delegations at the consultations convened to consider Article 5).[11]

Negotiation of the preamble

0.81 A full draft preamble was included in the Draft Cluster Munitions Convention submitted by the Wellington Conference to the Dublin Diplomatic Conference as the formal negotiating text.[12] As no amendments

---

[7] See Draft Cluster Munitions Convention of 21 January 2008. The title of the Convention changed slightly in the formal draft of the Convention introduced as Diplomatic Conference doc. CCM/3 on 19 May 2008. In this document it was titled the Convention on Cluster Munitions. The reason for this amendment is not known.

[8] See, e.g., Aust, A., *Modern Treaty Law and Practice*, Second Edition (Cambridge: Cambridge University Press, 2007), pp. 425–426.

[9] Thus, e.g., the four *1949 Geneva Conventions* do not contain a preamble, but merely cite the conditions of their adoption.

[10] See, *supra*, §§0.48–0.54 for details of the Wellington Conference.

[11] See, *infra, esp.* the commentary on Article 2, paragraph 1.

[12] See Draft Cluster Munitions Convention of 21 January 2008 in Annex 5; see also 'Draft Convention on Cluster Munitions', Diplomatic Conference doc. CCM/3, 19 May 2008.

were to be made to the Draft Cluster Munitions Convention in advance of the Diplomatic Conference, where the consultations at the Wellington Conference had suggested likely agreement on the amendment of specific preambular text Ireland (acting in its national capacity) sought to capture this by submitting such text to the Diplomatic Conference as its own proposal for amendments.[13]

0.82 At the Diplomatic Conference, the President of the Conference, Ambassador O'Ceallaigh, asked Ambassador Caroline Millar of Australia to act as the Friend of the President on the preamble. She convened open-ended informal consultations on 26 May 2008 following which she issued a non-paper setting out a revised draft preamble. This text differed from the draft Convention text principally by the inclusion of additional text relating to assistance for cluster munition victims, the Martens' clause, non-State armed groups, and United Nations (UN) Security Council resolutions on women and children in armed conflict. A second non-paper, which corrected a small number of syntax errors, was issued on the morning of 27 May. This was then discussed at the Committee of the Whole at its meeting that afternoon following which some small editorial changes were made before its incorporation into the final draft Convention[14] presented to the Conference by the President on 28 May.

The States Parties

The States Parties to this Convention,

0.83 The term 'States Parties' is used in the *1969 Vienna Convention on the Law of Treaties,* and generally in multilateral treaties.[15] It was first inserted in the Draft Cluster Munitions Convention discussed at the February 2008 Wellington Conference and forwarded without amendment to the Dublin Diplomatic Conference.

---

[13] 'Proposal by Ireland for the amendment of the Preamble', Diplomatic Conference doc. CCM/4, 19 May 2008.

[14] 'Presidency Paper—*draft* Convention on Cluster Munitions', Diplomatic Conference doc. CCM/PT/15, 28 May 2008.

[15] The *Convention on Certain Conventional Weapons*, however, and other instruments of international humanitarian law tend to use the formulation 'High Contracting Parties'. (The formal title of this treaty is the Convention on Prohibitions or Restrictions on the Use of Certain Conventional Weapons Which May Be Deemed to Be Excessively Injurious or to Have Indiscriminate Effects, as amended on 21 December 2001. It is often shortened to the *Convention on Certain Conventional Weapons* or simply CCW.)

First preambular paragraph: the protection of civilians in armed conflict

> *Deeply concerned* that civilian populations and individual civilians continue to bear the brunt of armed conflict,

0.84 Increasingly in modern armed conflict the principal victims have been civilians, through death, injury, displacement, and the loss of both livelihood and property. This growing phenomenon was expressly recognized in 1999 by the UN Security Council, which stated 'its grave concern at the growing civilian toll of armed conflict and note(d) with distress that civilians now account for the vast majority of casualties in armed conflict and are increasingly directly targeted by combatants and armed elements'.[16]

0.85 Since 1999, the Secretary-General of the UN has provided regular, comprehensive reports to the Security Council on the issue of the protection of civilians in armed conflict, including recommendations for the improvement of their protection, many of which have been subsequently endorsed by Council resolution.[17] The effects of cluster munitions on civilian populations were specifically recognized by the Secretary-General for the first time in his 2007 report to the Council on civilians in armed conflict.[18] The first preambular paragraph of the Convention on Cluster Munitions situates the Convention firmly in the context of the broader objective of reducing the now widely recognized harm caused to civilians by armed conflict.

0.86 The first paragraph of the preamble to the draft Convention on Cluster Munitions expressed deep concern 'that civilian populations and individual civilians continue to suffer most from armed conflict'. During discussion of this paragraph in informal consultations at the Diplomatic Conference a small number of delegations proposed that the word 'most' be deleted from this paragraph. When this proved unacceptable to the majority, Ireland proposed that the phrase 'bear the brunt', which had recently been endorsed by all States at the Thirtieth International Conference of the Red Cross and Red Crescent Movement, be used instead.[19] The phrase was first used in this context by

---

[16] Statement by the President of the Security Council, UN doc. S/PRST/1999/6, 12 February 1999.

[17] See UN Security Council Resolutions 1265 (1999), 1296 (2000), 1674 (2006), and 1738 (2006).

[18] 'Report of the Secretary-General on the protection of civilians in armed conflict', UN doc. S/2007/643, 28 October 2007, §61 *et seq.* See also 'Report of the Secretary-General on the protection of civilians in armed conflict', UN doc. S/2009/277, 29 May 2009, para. 35.

[19] Resolution 3 (on the reaffirmation and implementation of international humanitarian law) of the Thirtieth International Conference of the Red Cross and Red Crescent Movement (Geneva, 26–30 November 2007) expressed deep concern that 'civilian populations and individual civilians

the Secretary-General of the UN when he recorded '[s]tark and disturbing evidence that civilians continue to bear the brunt of armed conflicts' in his 2004 report to the Security Council on the protection of civilians in armed conflict.[20]

Second preambular paragraph: the humanitarian impact of cluster munitions

> *Determined* to put an end for all time to the suffering and casualties caused by cluster munitions at the time of their use, when they fail to function as intended or when they are abandoned,

0.87 This paragraph describes the primary object and purpose of the Convention, which is to end the suffering and casualties caused by cluster munitions, both during and after attacks. The paragraph is drawn from the first preambular paragraph in the *1997 Anti-Personnel Mine Ban Convention* but the two elements of that single paragraph (first, the determination to end the harm, and second, the description of what this harm is) have been divided into two paragraphs in the Convention on Cluster Munitions.

0.88 The determination to 'put an end for all time' to the harm caused by cluster munitions stresses the definitive nature of the Convention's comprehensive prohibition—rather than a regulation, restriction, or partial prohibition of the weapon—as the appropriate solution. This can be compared, for example, to the preamble of *2003 Protocol V*,[21] which outlines the object of the instrument as the need to 'minimise the risks and effects of explosive remnants of war'.[22]

0.89 The paragraph refers to both the 'suffering' and the 'casualties' caused by cluster munitions. While the 'casualties' refer to the individuals who have suffered death or injury from cluster munitions, 'suffering' can be taken as a broader concept that encompasses also the other forms of harm that cluster munitions inflict: on individuals, their families, and communities, indirectly and directly, in terms of survival, health, livelihood, and development. The

---

continue to bear the brunt of armed conflicts and remain the main victims of violations of international humanitarian law committed by parties to an armed conflict.'

[20] 'Report of the Secretary-General to the Security Council on the protection of civilians in armed conflict', UN doc. S/2004/431, 28 May 2004, para. §3.

[21] The formal title of this instrument is the Protocol on Explosive Remnants of War of the Convention on Prohibitions or Restrictions on the Use of Certain Conventional Weapons Which May Be Deemed to Be Excessively Injurious or to Have Indiscriminate Effects, as amended on 21 December 2001.   [22] Preambular paragraph 2, *2003 Protocol V.*

Convention's definition of 'cluster munition victims'[23] reinforces this broad concept of the suffering experienced by people affected by cluster munitions.

0.90 Although a significant motivation for the prohibition on cluster munitions was the evidence gathered by non-governmental organizations (NGOs) and international organizations on the harm caused by the weapons to civilians,[24] this preambular paragraph is broader than the preceding or following one, as it implicitly encompasses also the harm caused to combatants. Thus, in line with the definition of a 'cluster munition victim', which itself includes military casualties, the paragraph reaffirms the purpose of the convention to prevent all harm from cluster munitions, whether experienced by civilian or military personnel.

0.91 The 'suffering and casualties' are attributed to three main causes: the actual attacks with cluster munitions ('at the time of their use'); the unexploded ordnance (UXO) from cluster munitions ('when they fail to function as intended'); and the abandoned explosive ordnance ('when they are abandoned'). Taken together, these distinct problems caused by cluster munitions can be considered the underlying rationale for the prohibition on the weapon category. A number of prohibitions on entire categories of weaponry have been justified either on the basis that they cause superfluous injury or unnecessary suffering (which was never argued for cluster munitions as part of the Oslo Process but had been raised as an issue in the 1970s),[25] or on the basis that they are inherently indiscriminate or disproportionate.[26] The Cluster Munition Coalition (CMC), for example, argued not that cluster munitions were inherently indiscriminate, but that they were 'prone to indiscriminate effects'.[27]

---

[23] See, *infra*, the commentary on Article 2, paragraph 1.

[24] According to Handicap International (HI), which reviewed available casualty data, 98% of recorded cluster munition casualties through 2006 were civilians. (This does not mean, of course, that this is an accurate representation of all submunition casualties.) The study confirmed a total of 13,306 victims—killed and injured—from cluster munitions. See HI, *Fatal Footprint: The Global Human Impact of Cluster Munitions*, Preliminary report, Brussels, November 2006.

[25] See, e.g., Borrie, J., *Unacceptable Harm: A history of how the international treaty banning cluster munitions was won, op. cit.*, p. 5, and *cf.* also *infra* the commentary on the twentieth preambular paragraph.

[26] But see, *infra*, §§0.136–0.137, which describes the Martić case before the International Criminal Tribunal for former Yugoslavia in which the judges determined that cluster munitions delivered by Orkan rocket in early May 1995 against Zagreb were indiscriminate weapons.

[27] The CMC call, updated following the February 2007 Oslo Conference, read as follows:

The Cluster Munition Coalition calls for the conclusion of an international treaty banning cluster munitions by 2008. Cluster munitions are understood to be unreliable and inaccurate weapons that are prone to indiscriminate use and that pose severe and lasting risks to civilians from unexploded submunitions.

CMC call as emailed by Thomas Nash, CMC Coordinator, to CMC members on 19 April 2007.

0.92 The preambular text circulated prior to the Wellington Conference did not recognize these distinct causes of harm from cluster munitions. During the first informal consultations on the Preamble in Wellington, the International Committee of the Red Cross (ICRC) and the CMC both called for an explicit recognition of the harm from cluster munitions during attacks as well as afterwards whether from UXO or from abandoned munitions.[28] The Irish proposal for the preamble that formed the basis for negotiations at the Diplomatic Conference in Dublin suggested some changes from the text discussed in Wellington, but did not refer to the distinct causes of harm from cluster munitions both during and after attacks as there was no consensus on this point at that time.[29]

Impact at time of use

0.93 The first means of harm identified in the second preambular paragraph is the suffering and casualties caused at time of use. The distribution of explosive force and fragmentation over a wide area was one of the technical characteristics of cluster munitions first identified as problematic. As noted above, in 1974 seven countries had submitted a proposal for a prohibition on 'cluster warheads' to a diplomatic conference in Geneva.[30] The rationale for this prohibition was entirely based on the impact of cluster munitions at the time of use, the working paper noting, for instance, that:

It would certainly be desirable to introduce a broad prohibition or restriction of use of fragmentation weapons which typically are employed against a very large area, with the substantial risk for indiscriminate effects that such use entails.

0.94 This theme continued in the consideration of cluster munitions within the *Convention on Certain Conventional Weapons*, where in a declaration at the Third Review Conference in 2006, 25 States recognized that in addition to prohibitions on certain types of cluster munitions, 'due to their tendenc[y] of having indiscriminate effects' an agreement should also 'prohibit the use of cluster munitions within concentrations of civilians'.[31]

---

[28] 'ICRC proposed text on the Preamble', contained in the Wellington Compendium; and the CMC, 'Observations by the Cluster Munition Coalition on the draft Convention on Cluster Munitions, dated 21 January 2008'.

[29] 'Proposal by Ireland for the amendment of the Preamble', Diplomatic Conference doc. CCM/4, 19 May 2008.

[30] Diplomatic Conference on the Reaffirmation and Development of International Humanitarian Law Applicable in Armed Conflicts, 'Working Paper CDDH/DT/2 submitted by Egypt, Mexico, Norway, Sudan, Sweden, Switzerland and Yugoslavia', 21 February 1974, p. 9. See, *supra*, the Introduction, at §0.21.

[31] See UN doc. CCW/CONF.III/WP.18. The declaration was endorsed by Austria, Belgium, Bosnia and Herzegovina, Croatia, Costa Rica, the Czech Republic, Denmark, Germany, Holy See,

The risk to civilians from cluster munitions at the time of use was a theme of concern throughout the Oslo Process; indeed, some States continued to argue that any cluster munitions not prohibited by the eventual treaty should be subject to an explicit prohibition against their use in populated areas.[32] Ultimately, the definition of 'cluster munitions' adopted in the Convention on Cluster Munitions identified, indirectly, 'indiscriminate area effect' as a fundamental characteristic of these weapons and this, combined with the risk from unexploded submunitions, is a key pillar supporting their prohibition.[33]

Impact from unexploded submunitions

0.95 The second pillar on which the prohibition is based is the risk to civilians from unexploded submunitions. Some risk of UXO is presented by all explosive weapons—as recognized by *2003 Protocol V*—but cluster munitions have been found to cause a particularly severe type of UXO threat, due to the large numbers of submunitions deployed, the complexity of their delivery (which increases the risk of unexploded submunitions, also called 'blinds'), their small size, the sensitivity of their fuzing systems, and the density of resultant contamination.[34]

0.96 Concerns over UXO were not the primary focus of the earliest articulations of public disquiet over cluster munitions (as evidenced by the 1974 working paper cited above, which does not even mention the UXO problem). By 1999, however, concerns over UXO had become the primary motivation for concern about the weapon.[35] The first international legal consideration of the weapon since the diplomatic conferences in 1974 and

Hungary, Ireland, Liechtenstein, Lithuania, Luxembourg, Malta, Mexico, New Zealand, Norway, Peru, Portugal, Serbia, Slovakia, Slovenia, Sweden, and Switzerland.

[32] Statements at the Lima Conference, 24 May 2007; and at the Vienna Conference, 6 December 2007 (all from Landmine Action notes; copies on file with the author).

[33] The preamble's recognition of the impact of cluster munitions 'at the time of their use' is thus significant and relates to the language in the definition of 'cluster munition' at Article 2, paragraph 2(c) whose *chapeau* prefacing to the list of characteristics required for a munition not to be considered a cluster munition reads:

A munition that, in order to avoid indiscriminate area effects and the risks posed by unexploded submunitions, has all of the following characteristics.

[34] See, e.g., J. Flanagan, UN Mine Action Service, 'ERW—Experience from field operations', UN doc. CCW/GGE/II/WP.13, July 2002.

[35] Human Rights Watch's call for a moratorium on cluster munitions following the bombing of Kosovo in 1999 referenced the area effect of cluster munitions, but was largely based on the post-conflict impact of unexploded submunitions. Similarly, concern over unexploded submunitions in South-east Asia had been the motivation for the call by the Mennonite Central Committee's call for a moratorium in 1999.

1976 took place within the broader discussion on ERW in the context of the CCW.[36]

0.97 Problems of UXO from cluster munitions had been specifically identified, among others, in Cambodia, the Lao People's Democratic Republic (Laos), and Vietnam following US bombardment during the Vietnam War; in the former Yugoslavia and in particular in Kosovo following the NATO bombardment in 1999; in Afghanistan during the US attack in 2001–2002; in Iraq in the Gulf War in 1991; and again in the US-led invasion in 2003.[37] As observed above,[38] the consequences of Israel's widespread use of the weapon in Lebanon in 2006 contributed significantly to the momentum towards a global ban on the weapon. Concern over UXO can also be seen in the context of developing legal norms to minimize the persistent harm to civilians caused by such weapons after the end of armed conflict, culminating in the Convention on Cluster Munitions.[39] Also relevant in the context of these developing norms are *1996 Amended Protocol II*, the *1997 Anti-Personnel Mine Ban Convention*, and *2003 Protocol V*.[40]

Impact from abandoned cluster munitions

0.98 Concerns over abandoned cluster munitions were not a major motivating factor in the development of the Convention on Cluster Munitions. Rather this reference reflects a generic concern that abandoned explosive weapons present a threat to the civilian population, as reflected in *2003 Protocol V*.[41] The reference to abandoned cluster munitions serves to rationalize the preamble's consideration of, especially, the post-conflict causes of harm from cluster munitions with the concept of 'cluster munition remnants', which, based on the Protocol V model, were defined in the Convention on Cluster Munitions

---

[36] Draft Mandate on Explosive Remnants of War for a Group of Governmental Experts, 'Final Document of the Second Review Conference of the 1980 Convention on Certain Conventional Weapons', UN doc. CCW/CONF.II/2, 11–21 December 2001.

[37] It was following the evidence of humanitarian harm from the use in Iraq in 2003 that NGOs came together to establish the Cluster Munition Coalition. See Human Rights Watch and Landmine Action, *Banning Cluster Munitions, op. cit.*, p. 2.

[38] See, *supra*, the Introduction to the Commentary, *esp.* §§0.19 and 0.26–0.27. In a similar vein, the Declaration of the Third Review Conference of the *Convention on Certain Conventional Weapons* noted: 'the foreseeable effects of explosive remnants of war on civilian populations as a factor to be considered in applying the international humanitarian law rules on proportionality in attack and precautions in attack'.

[39] See, e.g., Opening statement by Jakob Kellenberger, President of the ICRC, Dublin Diplomatic Conference, 19 May 2008.

[40] 'Final Document of the Third Review Conference of the Convention on Certain Conventional Weapons, Part II, Final Declaration', UN doc. CCW/CONF.III/11 (Part II), p. 4.

[41] *2003 Protocol V.*

as 'unexploded submunitions' and 'abandoned cluster munitions'.[42] However, the concern expressed here is not just linked to armed conflict, but is broader as munitions may be abandoned because of poor State control of their own munitions during peacetime.[43]

Third preambular paragraph: cluster munition remnants

> *Concerned* that cluster munition remnants kill or maim civilians, including women and children, obstruct economic and social development, including through the loss of livelihood, impede post-conflict rehabilitation and reconstruction, delay or prevent the return of refugees and internally displaced persons, can negatively impact on national and international peace-building and humanitarian assistance efforts, and have other severe consequences that can persist for many years after use,

0.99 The third preambular paragraph of the Convention is loosely based on the first preambular paragraph of the *1997 Anti-Personnel Mine Ban Convention*, which noted the negative effects of anti-personnel mines.[44] In expressing concern at the effects of cluster munition remnants[45] on civilians, this paragraph identifies one of the main factors motivating States in adopting the Convention.[46] In addition to death and injury caused to individual civilians by remnants these effects include long-term 'area denial', which is a consequence of the fear of unexploded submunitions. This fear acts to prevent or dissuade people from returning to their homes, land, and places of work in areas attacked by cluster munitions, as well as delaying reconstruction, a task

---

[42] See Article 2, paragraph 7, Convention on Cluster Munitions.

[43] Examples include abandoned cluster munitions in the Republic of Congo and arguably also Guinea-Bissau. See, e.g., International Campaign to Ban Landmines (ICBL), *Landmine Monitor Report 2008: Toward a Mine-Free World* (Ottawa: Mines Action Canada, 2008), pp. 295, 411, and 412.

[44] '*Determined* to put an end to the suffering and casualties caused by anti-personnel mines, that kill or maim hundreds of people every week, mostly innocent and defenceless civilians and especially children, obstruct economic development and reconstruction, inhibit the repatriation of refugees and internally displaced persons, and have other severe consequences for years after emplacement...'.

[45] Defined by Article 2, paragraph 7 as 'failed cluster munitions, abandoned cluster munitions, unexploded submunitions and unexploded bomblets'; see, *infra*, §§2.193 *et seq.*

[46] At the outset of the Oslo Process, Handicap International Belgium published two reports based on available data on casualties caused by cluster munitions: 'Fatal Footprint: the Global Human Impact of Cluster Munitions', November 2006 and 'Circle of Impact: The *Fatal Footprint* of Cluster Munitions on People and Communities', May 2007. These reports indicated that a very high proportion of recorded casualties from cluster munitions were civilians.

that must await the completion of often costly and time-consuming clearance operations.[47]

0.100 The third preambular paragraph developed from the second preambular paragraph of the Draft Cluster Munitions Convention of January 2008. In informal consultations chaired by the Friend of the President on the Preamble at the Diplomatic Conference in Dublin there was broad agreement to take up the suggestion first made at the Wellington Conference by the ICRC[48] that this draft paragraph should be subdivided into two new paragraphs to reflect the fact that while cluster munitions can continue to affect civilian populations for many years after use, they also have serious consequences for them at time of use.[49]

0.101 Accordingly, while the second preambular paragraph of the Convention identifies the three characteristics of cluster munitions and their use that give rise to adverse humanitarian consequences,[50] the third preambular paragraph focuses on the adverse long-term consequences of cluster munition remnants, particularly on peace-building, reconstruction, and development. It incorporates the reference to concerns at the impact of cluster munitions on 'international efforts to build peace and security', which had first been included in the third preambular paragraph of the Draft Cluster Munitions Convention.

Fourth preambular paragraph: stockpiled cluster munitions

> *Deeply concerned* also at the dangers presented by the large national stockpiles of cluster munitions retained for operational use and *determined* to ensure their rapid destruction,

0.102 This preambular paragraph is an important recognition of the rationale behind the obligation in the Convention on Cluster Munitions to destroy stockpiles of the weapons. It also reflects the widespread view among negotiating States that the Convention was a preventive as well as a responsive effort.[51] For instance, while Latin America was virtually unaffected by cluster

---

[47] An example of this indirect impact of cluster munition remnants is set out in a report published by Landmine Action shortly after the ceasefire in Lebanon in 2006: 'Foreseeable Harm: the use and impact of cluster munitions in Lebanon, 2006'.

[48] 'Comments of the International Committee of the Red Cross on the Wellington draft of a future cluster munitions convention', ICRC, 8 February 2008.   [49] See, *supra*, §§0.84 *et seq.*

[50] i.e. those resulting from use of cluster munitions that function as intended (i.e. explode on impact) as well as the persistent effects arising from unexploded submunitions and failed or abandoned cluster munitions (collectively known as 'cluster munition remnants').

[51] e.g., the agenda of the Belgrade Conference of States Affected by Cluster Munitions dealt with the issue of stockpile destruction in an agenda item entitled: 'Preventing Proliferation of Cluster Munitions'.

munition remnants and Africa was affected in a limited way—at least relative to its problem with landmines—countries in these regions consistently repeated their concern about the potential harm from cluster munitions should they be used in their regions. Thus, for example, Botswana noted during the negotiations at the Diplomatic Conference in Dublin that:

> while Botswana is not directly affected by this menace of cluster munitions, we have a serious concern regarding the possible proliferation of this type of weapon. . . . We note that, with billions of submunitions believed to be stockpiled in more than 70 countries, there is a need to avoid incidences of their transfer to other places, such as our own. Non-proliferation could, therefore, only be meaningfully achieved through the adoption of an international covenant which will be binding on all.[52]

0.103 The preamble's reference to the 'dangers presented by the large national stockpiles' is based on the consideration that the stockpiles of many, in particular European, countries involved in the negotiations reached into the millions of individual submunitions. The combined numbers of submunitions stockpiled by Germany, France, the Netherlands, and the United Kingdom (UK), for example, are estimated at more than 112 million.[53] The fact that the United States (US) alone is estimated to have a stockpile of at least 730 million submunitions[54] was also a major concern for participants in the Oslo Process.

0.104 The determination to ensure the 'rapid destruction' of cluster munitions provides the rationale for the obligation in the Convention to destroy all cluster munitions 'as soon as possible'. While the Convention allows States Parties to take up to eight years to complete the destruction of cluster munition stockpiles, and also includes the possibility of additional extensions to this deadline, the preamble emphasizes the requirement to fulfil the obligation 'as soon as possible'.[55]

Fifth preambular paragraph: efficient and coordinated clearance

> *Believing* it necessary to contribute effectively in an efficient, coordinated manner to resolving the challenge of removing cluster munition remnants located throughout the world, and to ensure their destruction,

0.105 Article 4 of the Convention on Cluster Munitions requires that each affected State Party clear and destroy all cluster munition remnants within 10 years of the treaty entering into force for it (although there is a possibility of requesting

---

[52] Statement of Botswana to the Plenary, Dublin Diplomatic Conference, 19 May 2008; see 'Summary Record of Second Session of the Plenary', Diplomatic Conference doc. CCM/SR/2, 18 June 2008.

[53] Human Rights Watch and Landmine Action, *Banning Cluster Munitions, op. cit.*, p. 20.

[54] *Ibid.*   [55] Article 3, paragraph 2, Convention on Cluster Munitions.

an extension from the Meeting of States Parties or a Review Conference of up to five years at a time). The fifth preambular paragraph sets out the States Parties' commitment to clearance of cluster munition remnants—and not merely in areas under the jurisdiction or control of States Parties—as well as to the manner in which clearance operations are to take place: in an 'efficient' and 'coordinated' manner through effective contribution by the States Parties.

0.106 With respect to efficiency, within the mine action sector in general,[56] and in the context of the *1997 Anti-Personnel Mine Ban Convention* in particular, significant efforts have been paid in recent years to improving the productivity of demining, which has been termed 'land release'.[57] As the International Mine Action Standards (IMAS) on land release state: 'on some occasions, land has been subjected to full clearance unnecessarily'.[58] Any land that is fully cleared but which proves not to have been contaminated with any explosive ordnance represents inefficiency and a potentially huge waste of resources for a national demining programme. Thus, there is now a better understanding that an array of techniques in addition to full clearance can enable suspected hazardous areas to be addressed efficiently and with a high degree of safety for both programme personnel and the intended beneficiaries. These techniques include better information gathering and verification, and greater use of high-quality non-technical[59] and technical survey.[60]

---

[56] Mine action is the term used to describe efforts to eliminate or reduce the impact of mines and explosive remnants of war. The UN definition comprises five core activities (also called 'pillars'): demining, mine/ERW risk education, victim assistance, stockpile destruction, and advocacy. See, e.g., IMAS 04.10: 'Glossary of mine action terms, definitions and abbreviations', Second Edition 1 January 2003, available at: <http://www.mineactionstandards.org>.

[57] See, e.g., ICBL, *Landmine Monitor Report 2009: Toward a Mine-Free World* (Ottawa: Mines Action Canada, 2009), <http://lm.icbl.org/index.php/publications/display?url=lm/2009/es/mine_action.html> (accessed 22 November 2009).

[58] IMAS 08.20: 'Land release', First Edition, New York, 10 June 2009, p. v, available at: <http://www.mineactionstandards.org>.

[59] Non-technical survey is defined by the relevant IMAS as survey which involves:

collecting and analysing new and/or existing information about a hazardous area. Its purpose is to confirm whether there is evidence of a hazard or not, to identify the type and extent of hazards within any hazardous area and to define, as far as is possible, the perimeter of the actual hazardous areas without physical intervention. A non-technical survey does not normally involve the use of clearance or verification assets. Exceptions occur when assets are used for the sole purpose of providing access for non-technical survey teams. The results from a non-technical survey can replace any previous data relating to the survey of an area.

IMAS 08.21: 'Non-Technical Survey', First Edition, New York, 10 June 2009, pp. 1–2.

[60] IMAS defines technical survey as:

a detailed intervention with clearance or verification assets into a CHA [confirmed hazardous area], or part of a CHA. It should confirm the presence of mines/ERW leading to the definition of one or more DHA [defined hazardous area] and may indicate the absence of mines/ERW which could allow land to be released when combined with other evidence.

IMAS 08.20: 'Land release', First Edition, *op. cit.*, p. 2.

0.107 Coordination—the 'harmonious functioning of different, inter-related mine action projects'—is a major challenge for all mine action programmes. The recommended approach to such programme management and coordination is through a two-tier structure: an inter-ministerial National Mine Action Authority that sets overall policy and strategy for the programme, and a mine action centre that conducts operational coordination, including tasking of clearance operations.[61]

0.108 An effective contribution to resolving the challenge of removing cluster munition remnants in affected countries and areas could be made in a number of ways. Donor States can do so by providing appropriate resources (human, technical, material, and financial) in a timely fashion. In turn, recipient States can ensure support is used swiftly and appropriately in accordance with defined priorities (whether humanitarian, social, or economic, or a mixture).

Sixth preambular paragraph: the rights of cluster munition victims

> *Determined* also to ensure the full realisation of the rights of all cluster munition victims and *recognising* their inherent dignity,

0.109 Preambular paragraphs six to ten set the stage for the Convention's focus on assisting cluster munition victims by highlighting the Convention's basic concepts for this topic: (a) a principled approach to victim assistance that is based on the rights of the victims and their dignity; (b) a commitment to provide victim assistance in a holistic manner covering its constituent elements, which include medical care, rehabilitation, psychological support, as well as social and economic inclusion; (c) sensitivity concerning the age and gender of the victims as well as the needs of vulnerable groups; (d) a reference to the Convention on the Rights of Persons with Disabilities; (e) the need for coordination with victim assistance work undertaken in various fora; and finally (f) the principle of non-discrimination.

0.110 Preambular paragraph 6 relates to the rights of all 'cluster munition victims', which in Article 2 are defined as meaning 'all persons who have been killed or suffered physical or psychological injury, economic loss, social marginalization or substantial impairment of the realization of their rights

---

[61] See, e.g., IMAS 02.10: 'Guide for the Establishment of a Mine Action Programme', First Edition, 1 January 2003, available at <http://www.mineactionstandards.org>; and Geneva International Centre for Humanitarian Demining (GICHD), *A Guide to Mine Action and Explosive Remnants of War*, Second Edition (Geneva: GICHD, 2007), *esp.* Chapter 10, available at: <http://www.gichd.org>.

caused by the use of cluster munitions. They include those persons directly impacted by cluster munitions as well as their affected families and communities.' Thus the determination to ensure the full realization of the rights of all cluster munition victims and recognizing their inherent dignity not only relates to those persons directly impacted by a cluster munition incident but also to their affected families and communities. In addition, the use of the term 'all' before 'persons' clarifies that victimization does not depend on the legal status of affected persons and hence covers persons who had suffered harm regardless of any status as citizens, migrants, refugees, internally displaced persons, etc.[62]

0.111 The formulation used in this preambular paragraph provides the first entry point of the so-called 'rights-based' approach to victim assistance; this approach essentially aims to prevent victims being seen as mere *objects* of treatment or charitable activities. The paragraph serves as a reminder that victims, as all other human beings or groups of human beings, are *subjects* or bearers of rights. This approach is parallel to the one taken in the Convention on the Rights of Persons with Disabilities, which the then-UN Secretary General, Kofi Annan, lauded as the 'dawn of a new era' for people with disabilities.[63] In the context of this preambular paragraph, it is noteworthy that the formulation chosen does not refer to 'human rights', but more generally to the 'rights' of cluster munition victims. The *full realisation of the rights* therefore relates not only to human rights as such, but also to other rights to which the victim is entitled.[64] The element of the full realization of victims' rights also mirrors one of the defining elements of victimization as contained in Article 2, paragraph 1, i.e. the 'substantial impairment of the realisation of their rights', which similarly and in striking contrast to preceding documents does not refer to fundamental or human rights, but rights in general.[65]

0.112 The recognition of the inherent dignity of human beings is an essential foundation of international human rights law. In addition to the second preambular paragraph of the UN Charter, the concept of human dignity has

---

[62] For a discussion of the term 'cluster munition victim' see, *infra*, the commentary on Article 2, paragraph 1.

[63] See UN, 'Lauding disability convention as "dawn of a new era," UN urges speedy ratification', Press release, <http://www.un.org/apps/news/story.asp?NewsID=20975&Cr=disab> (accessed 8 March 2010).

[64] On the distinction between human rights and other rights of a person, see also *infra* the commentary on Article 5. Insofar as rights other than human rights are concerned one may think of e.g. certain procedural rights in legal proceedings, such as access to certain information, etc.

[65] See, *infra*, the commentary on Article 2, paragraph 1, *esp.* §§2.26–2.28.

been most prominently employed in the first preambular paragraph of the *1948 Universal Declaration of Human Rights* and its Article 1. The Universal Declaration proclaims the recognition of the inherent dignity and equal and inalienable rights of all members of the human family as the foundation of freedom, justice, and peace in the world.[66] As cluster munition victims, many of whom are persons with disabilities, frequently face particular challenges in their societal lives and often face social (and sometimes legal) marginalization, preambular paragraph 6 serves an important reminder of their inherent dignity and rights.

Seventh preambular paragraph: the provision of assistance to cluster munition victims

> *Resolved* to do their utmost in providing assistance to cluster munition victims, including medical care, rehabilitation and psychological support, as well as providing for their social and economic inclusion,

0.113 Preambular paragraph 7 expresses the States Parties' resolve to 'do their utmost' to provide assistance to cluster munition victims. It also lists some of the constituent elements of this assistance, which include medical care, rehabilitation, and psychological support, as well as assistance for the social and economic inclusion of cluster munition victims. The resolve, thus expressed, mirrors the wide array of needs and rights of cluster munition victims. By consequence, the commitment expressed in the preambular paragraph, and elaborated in more detail in Article 5, signifies an holistic approach to the provision of victim assistance.[67]

0.114 In the Vienna Discussion Text[68] this paragraph also contained the nucleus of the eventual definition of cluster munition victims in as far as it relates to affected families and communities. Through the inclusion of this reference in Article 2, paragraph 1 it was no longer necessary to retain this reference in the preambular paragraph.

---

[66] Universal Declaration of Human Rights, adopted by the UN General Assembly in Resolution 217 A (III) of 10 December 1948. The full text of the first preambular paragraph reads as follows:

Whereas recognition of the inherent dignity and of the equal and inalienable rights of all members of the human family is the foundation of freedom, justice and peace in the world.

See also Article 1 of the declaration: 'All human beings are born free and equal in dignity and rights.'

[67] For a more detailed discussion see, *infra*, the commentary on Article 5.

[68] See Annex 4.

Eighth preambular paragraph: age and gender sensitivity

> *Recognising* the need to provide age- and gender-sensitive assistance to cluster munition victims and to address the special needs of vulnerable groups,

0.115 The main purpose of this preambular paragraph is to serve as a reminder that victim assistance needs to be carried out in a manner that is age- and gender-sensitive and should address the special needs of vulnerable groups.[69] This preambular paragraph should be considered in conjunction with preambular paragraph 15, which refers to UN Security Council resolutions 1325 on women, peace, and security, and 1612 on children in armed conflict.

0.116 According to data gathering and estimates by Handicap International (HI) a preponderance of casualties are men and boys: HI has found that some 84 per cent of cluster munition victims are male, while 27 per cent are young boys.[70] Some 40 per cent of cluster munition casualties concern children.[71] Yet, according to the ICRC, the implications of cluster munition incidents may often be worse for women and children than for men. For example, permanent disabilities in the perception of many societies render women unmarriageable. In addition, women are less likely to know about treatment, rehabilitation, and prosthetic services, and the manner in which services may be available often poses cultural and other impediments to women and children in need of assistance (e.g. through lack of privacy during examination and treatment or sex-separated accommodation, etc.).[72] Recognizing the need for age- and gender-sensitive assistance, therefore serves important practical purposes in order to remove existing barriers and aim at assistance that suits the needs of men, women, and children alike.

---

[69] For a brief introduction into the question of gender and cluster munitions see Women International League for Peace and Freedom, 'Cluster Munitions and Gender', 2008, <http://www.wilpf.int.ch/PDF/DisarmamentPDF/ClusterMunitions/SweClusterPublication.pdf> (visited 23 November 2009).

[70] HI, *Circle of Impact—the Fatal Footprint of Cluster Munitions on People and Communities* (Brussels: HI, 2007), available at: <http://en.handicapinternational.be>.

[71] See Women's International League for Peace and Freedom, 'Cluster Munitions and Gender', *op. cit.*

[72] *Cf.* ICRC, 'Women and War', p. 16, <http://www.peacewomen.org/ressources/Human_Rights/womenandwar08.pdf> (accessed 23 November 2009).

Ninth preambular paragraph: Convention on the Rights of Persons with Disabilities

> *Bearing in mind* the Convention on the Rights of Persons with Disabilities which, *inter alia*, requires that States Parties to that Convention undertake to ensure and promote the full realisation of all human rights and fundamental freedoms of all persons with disabilities without discrimination of any kind on the basis of disability,

0.117 Preambular paragraph 9 establishes a direct link to the *2006 Convention on the Rights of Persons with Disabilities* which had been adopted by the UN General Assembly some two months before the formal start of the Oslo Process in February 2007. Throughout the negotiation of the Convention on Cluster Munitions, the Convention on the Rights of Persons with Disabilities served as a source of inspiration for the elaboration of the victim assistance package. Yet, unlike preambular paragraphs 13 and 14, which, respectively, welcome the broad support for the *1997 Anti-Personnel Mine Ban Convention* and the adoption and entry into force of *2003 Protocol V*, preambular paragraph 9 merely *bears in mind* the Convention on the Rights of Persons with Disabilities. As at the time of the adoption of the Convention on Cluster Munitions not all negotiating States had fully clarified their position vis-à-vis the Convention on the Rights of Persons with Disabilities, it became necessary to use this compromise language, rather than any more positive and forthcoming formulation. Yet, the fact that the reference to the Convention was included in the preamble as well as the fact that the States Parties declared that they would bear it in mind, has an important bearing on the interpretation of the provisions of the Convention on Cluster Munitions as it forms part of the context that needs to be taken into consideration in that interpretation.[73]

0.118 The second part of this preambular paragraph reiterates the main content of the Convention on the Rights of Persons with Disabilities, which requires its States Parties to ensure and promote the full realization of all human rights and fundamental freedoms of all persons with disabilities without discrimination of any kind on the basis of disability. In the history of the Convention's negotiations this paragraph was the first to mention the principle of non-discrimination.[74] As this reference was deemed to be insufficient to address concerns related to the creation of a separate category of victims and the prevention of instances of discrimination, more specific

---

[73] *Cf.* Article 31, *1969 Vienna Convention on the Law of Treaties*, included in Annex 1.
[74] The reference to the Convention was first included in the Vienna Discussion Text.

elaborations of the principle of non-discrimination were included in the Convention.[75]

Tenth preambular paragraph: coordination of assistance to victims of weapons and non-discrimination

> *Mindful* of the need to coordinate adequately efforts undertaken in various fora to address the rights and needs of victims of various types of weapons, and resolved to avoid discrimination among victims of various types of weapons,

0.119 Preambular Paragraph 10 addresses two distinct, yet related issues. First, it highlights that victim assistance efforts are also undertaken in other fora than the Convention and expresses the need to coordinate these efforts; and second, it expresses the desire of the States Parties to avoid discrimination among victims of various types of weapons. During the negotiations of the victim assistance package both issues were discussed on various occasions. The question of non-discrimination and the wish not to create separate categories of victims that might receive differing levels of care was especially prominent during the Oslo Process.

0.120 Victim assistance efforts are currently carried out under a number of international agreements dealing with various types of weapons or explosive remnants of war, most notably according to Article 6, paragraph 3 of the *1997 Anti-Personnel Mine Ban Convention* and Article 8, paragraph 2 of *2003 Protocol V*. Both Conventions have refined their understandings of victim assistance through additional political declarations. In the case of the *1997 Anti-Personnel Mine Ban Convention*, the First and the Second Review Conferences held, respectively, in Nairobi, Kenya, in 2004, and in Cartagena, Columbia, in 2009, adopted the Nairobi Action Plan and the Cartagena Action Plan containing specific actions on victim assistance.

0.121 In a similar vein, and largely following the example of the Convention on Cluster Munitions' victim assistance package, States Parties to *2003 Protocol V* at their 2008 annual meeting adopted a Victim Assistance Action Plan with a set of concrete actions to be undertaken.[76] The *1997 Anti-Personnel Mine Ban Convention* also established a Standing Committee on Victim Assistance to guide the victim assistance activities under that treaty and provide a platform

---

[75] See Preambular Paragraph 10 and Article 5, paragraph 2(e) of the Convention.

[76] See Plan of Action on Victim Assistance, contained in Annex IV to the Final Document of the Second Conference of the High Contracting Parties to Protocol V on Explosive Remnants of War to the CCW, UN doc. CCW/P.V/CONF/2008/12 of 23 January 2009; available at: <http://www.unog.ch>.

for intersessional work on the topic. States Parties to *2003 Protocol V* have, since their first meeting in 2007, organized intersessional work through a coordinator for victim assistance appointed by the States Parties.

0.122 Work conducted within the auspices of the Convention on the Rights of Persons with Disabilities is also of great importance to victim assistance. Global victim assistance efforts are characterized by a multitude of actors: affected States, donor States, international institutions such as the UN; the ICRC; and an even bigger number of NGOs active on various levels such as the CMC, Survivor Corps (formerly known as Landmine Survivors Network), HI, *Licht für die Welt*, MSF, etc. This preambular paragraph highlights the fact that the better the work carried out under the various Conventions and fora and by the various actors is coordinated, the more improvement can be brought about on the ground for the lives of the victims. The paragraph thus expresses the sentiment that ensuring an efficient level of coordination is a joint responsibility by all for the benefit of the victims.[77]

0.123 During the negotiations of the Convention on Cluster Munitions many delegations expressed their support for the inclusion of a non-discrimination clause in the victim assistance package. In particular, the ICRC placed a special emphasis on the desire that the Convention should not be used to establish better treatment for cluster munition victims at the expense of other victims of armed conflict. The first reference to the principle of non-discrimination was contained in the Vienna Discussion Text's preambular paragraph on the Convention on the Rights of Persons with Disabilities, which itself aims at preventing discrimination on the ground of disability.

0.124 During the subsequent discussions it became evident that a more specific rule of non-discrimination needed to be included in the Convention. This rule is not referred to in this preambular paragraph but is contained in Article 5, paragraph 2(e), which provides that States Parties, in fulfilling their obligation under Article 5, paragraph 1, shall:

[n]ot discriminate against or among cluster munition victims, or between cluster munition victims and those who have suffered injuries or disabilities from other causes; differences in treatment should be based only on medical, rehabilitative, psychological or socio-economic needs.

The Convention's non-discrimination rule, therefore, does not only apply to instances of discrimination among cluster munition victims, but also more generally between cluster munition victims, other victims of armed violence,

---

[77] On the foregoing *cf.* Reiterer, M. A., 'Assistance to cluster munition victims: a major step towards humanitarian disarmament', in *Disarmament Forum 2009*, No. 4.

and persons who suffered injuries or disabilities from other causes. The Convention thus lays down a non-discrimination rule which is also relevant to the wider disability sector.

Eleventh preambular paragraph: 'Martens clause'

> *Reaffirming* that in cases not covered by this Convention or by other international agreements, civilians and combatants remain under the protection and authority of the principles of international law, derived from established custom, from the principles of humanity and from the dictates of public conscience,

0.125 This preambular paragraph restates the 'Martens clause' in its most contemporary wording, so named following a declaration by Professor von Martens, the Russian delegate at the Hague Peace Conferences in 1899. The formulation in this preambular paragraph is to be read in conjunction with the seventeenth preambular paragraph referring to the 'role of public conscience'.[78] The Martens clause was first included in the preamble of the 1899 Hague Convention II,[79] albeit with a slightly different formulation.[80] Although it originally sought to overcome the failure by delegates to agree on the question of the status of civilians who took up arms against an occupying force, the clause was then introduced in the Preamble of the *1907 Hague Convention IV*[81] and later included as a provision in the *1949 Geneva Conventions*[82] and in

---

[78] See further, *infra*, the commentary on the seventeenth preambular paragraph.

[79] The formal title of this treaty is Hague Convention (II) with Respect to the Laws and Customs of War on Land.

[80] The relevant paragraphs of the preamble reads as follows:

Until a more complete code of the laws of war is issued, the High Contracting Parties think it right to declare that in cases not included in the Regulations adopted by them, populations and belligerents remain under the protection and empire of the principles of international law, as they result from the usages established between civilized nations, from the laws of humanity and the requirements of the public conscience.

[81] The formal title of this treaty is Hague Convention (IV) respecting the Laws and Customs of War on Land. The restatement of the clause in the preamble reads as follows:

Until a more complete code of the laws of war has been issued, the High Contracting Parties deem it expedient to declare that, in cases not included in the Regulations adopted by them, the inhabitants and the belligerents remain under the protection and the rule of the principles of the law of nations, as they result from the usages established among civilized peoples, from the laws of humanity, and the dictates of the public conscience.

[82] The Martens Clause appears in all four *1949 Geneva Conventions*. See Article 63, paragraph 4, of Geneva Convention I, Article 62, paragraph 4, of Geneva Convention II, Article 142, paragraph 4, of Geneva Convention III, and Article 158, paragraph 4 of Geneva Convention IV. e.g.,

1977 Additional Protocol I.[83] The latter instrument contains the same wording as in the Convention on Cluster Munitions.

0.126 When considering the Martens clause in the context of the treaties governing the use of specific weapons, it is worth noting that the preamble of the CCW contains the same wording as the Convention on Cluster Munitions[84] whereas no such reference is found in the *1997 Anti-Personnel Mine Ban Convention*. The inclusion of such a preambular paragraph was first proposed by the Holy See during the Dublin Diplomatic Conference at informal consultations convened on 26 May 2008 by the Friend of the President on the Preamble, where it was accepted in broad terms (though subsequently it was amended slightly).[85] The term 'reaffirming' was preferred to 'confirming their determination'.[86] The text of the clause first appeared in an official document in the Presidency Paper of 28 May 2008[87] and was kept in the final text of the Convention.

0.127 The Martens clause means that no situation is outside the law. While this underlying logic seems widely recognized, various interpretations among scholars and lawyers as well as in State practice exist concerning the legal

Article 158, paragraph 4, in Part IV on 'Execution of the convention' reads as follows:

> The denunciation shall have effect only in respect of the denouncing Power. It shall in no way impair the obligations which the Parties to the conflict shall remain bound to fulfil by virtue of the principles of the law of nations, as they result from the usages established among civilized peoples, from the laws of humanity and the dictates of the public conscience.

[83] The formal title of this treaty is the Protocol Additional to the Geneva Conventions of 12 August 1949, and relating to the Protection of Victims of International Armed Conflicts. Article 1 paragraph 2 reads as follows:

> In cases not covered by this Protocol or by other international agreements, civilians and combatants remain under the protection and authority of the principles of international law derived from established custom, from the principles of humanity and from the dictates of public conscience.

[84] There are only a few slight differences. The preambular paragraph of the CCW reads as follows:

> Confirming their determination that in cases not covered by this Convention and its annexed Protocols or by other international agreements, the civilian population and the combatants shall at all times remain under the protection and authority of the principles of international law derived from established custom, from the principles of humanity and from the dictates of public conscience.

[85] The word 'applicable' placed before 'principles of international law' in the Friend of the President non-paper of 26 May 2008 was then deleted in the non-paper dated 27 May. See Friend of the President non-papers of 26 and 27 May 2008 (on file with the author).

[86] 'Proposal by the Holy See for amendment of the Preamble', not submitted as an official document to the Dublin Diplomatic Conference (on file with the author).

[87] 'Presidency Paper, *draft* Convention on Cluster Munitions', Diplomatic Conference doc. CCM/PT/15, 28 May 2008.

effects of the clause.[88] In its most restrictive reading, this clause would serve as an interpretative guideline when applying international humanitarian law rules. Commonly it is also construed as recalling the articulation between the two main sources of international law (custom and treaty law). Since treaties are not in place to regulate all situations and every issue, the Martens clause reiterates that customary law remains applicable.[89] This restatement of the scope of international humanitarian law is, however, rather superfluous given that such logic is inherent to international law and that treaties do not subsume or supersede customary law.[90]

0.128 A broader understanding of the Martens clause is that it rules out any *argumentum a contrario*, whereby a conduct which is not prohibited under international humanitarian law treaties would be *ipso facto* lawful. More broadly still, the text of the clause could be understood as introducing two other sources of international law, conferring a normative role to 'the principles of humanity' and 'the dictates of public conscience'.[91] Pleadings by States and dissenting opinions of several of the judges in the International Court of Justice's 1996 Advisory Opinion on the Legality of Nuclear Weapons illustrated the stark differences with regard to legal conceptions of the clause.[92] While the Court did not clarify the scope of the Martens clause in its advisory opinion,[93] the opinion shed light on its significance in the particular context of international humanitarian law governing the use of weapons. Notably, the Court claimed (though without adducing evidence) that the Martens clause 'has proved to be an effective means of addressing the rapid evolution of military technology'.[94]

---

[88] For an overview of those interpretations, see, e.g., Cassese, A., 'The Martens Clause: Half of a Loaf or Simply Pie in the Sky?', *European Journal of International Law*, Vol. 11, No. 1 (2000), pp. 129 *et seq.*

[89] Abi-Saab, G., 'The Specificities of Humanitarian Law', in Swinarski, C. (ed.), *Etudes et essais sur le droit international humanitaire et sur les principes de la Croix Rouge en l'honneur de Jean Pictet* (Dordrecht: Martinus Nijhoff, 1984), p. 275.

[90] This was clearly stated by the International Court of Justice in the Nicaragua case. See *Military and Paramilitary Activities in and against Nicaragua (Nicaragua v. United States of America), Merits, Judgment. ICJ Reports 1986*, p. 94, §176.

[91] For an extensive and thorough discussion on this issue see Cassese, A., 'The Martens Clause: Half of a Loaf or Simply Pie in the Sky?', *op. cit.*, pp. 193–208. Cassese concluded that 'no international or national court has propounded and acted upon the notion that there existed in the international community two additional and distinct sources of law, in addition to the treaty and custom processes' (p. 208).

[92] See *ibid.*, pp. 210–211, as well as Ticehurst, R., 'The Martens Clause and the Laws of Armed Conflict', *International Review of the Red Cross*, 1997, No. 317, pp. 125–134.

[93] See *Legality of the Threat or Use of Nuclear Weapons, Advisory Opinion, ICJ Reports 1996*, paragraphs 78, 84, and 87.   [94] *Ibid.*, paragraph 78.

0.129 Given the various interpretations of the legal implications of the Martens clause, one may question the value of this clause in the context of the Convention on Cluster Munitions. However, given the discussions as to the definition of a cluster munition, and the absence of any additional specific regulation[95] on those weapons excluded from the Convention's ambit on the basis that they meet the criteria set out in Article 2, paragraph 2(c), a particular value could be discerned in this area.[96] Thus, the explicit exception included for such weapons under the Convention does not *ipso facto* make the weapons inherently lawful, particularly if they prove to have similar adverse humanitarian consequences as cluster munitions. More generally, in the light of debate over the legality of cluster munitions even absent the Convention on Cluster Munitions, this clause recalls that the Convention is part of a broader and coherent legal framework as confirmed by the reference to the general principles in the Convention's preamble.[97]

Twelfth preambular paragraph: application of prohibitions to non-State armed groups

> *Resolved* also that armed groups distinct from the armed forces of a State shall not, under any circumstances, be permitted to engage in any activity prohibited to a State Party to this Convention,

0.130 This preambular paragraph describes the 'resolve' of States Parties to the Convention on Cluster Munitions not to allow non-State armed groups (NSAGs) to engage in any activity prohibited by the Convention. This refers particularly to the general prohibitions set out in Article 1,[98] namely on use, development, production, acquisition, stockpiling, retention, or transfer of cluster munitions, as defined.[99] In fact, use of cluster munitions by NSAGs has been relatively infrequent. Research by Human Rights Watch and Landmine Action in 2009 confirmed use by NSAGs of cluster munitions with only four States: Afghanistan, Bosnia and Herzegovina, Croatia, and Israel.[100]

---

[95] Beyond customary law and applicable treaty law, such as *1977 Additional Protocol I* or *2003 Protocol V*.

[96] For a detailed discussion of how the Martens Clause could be a relevant framework to address potential pitfalls stemming from a restrictive definition of cluster munitions under the Convention, see Di Ruzza, T., 'The Convention on Cluster Munitions: Towards a Balance between Humanitarian and Military Considerations?', *Military Law and the Law of War Review*, Vol. 47, Nos. 3–4 (2008), pp. 422–425.

[97] See further, *infra*, the commentary on the twentieth preambular paragraph.

[98] See further, *infra*, the commentary on Article 1, paragraph 1(a) of the Convention.

[99] See, *infra*, the commentary on Article 1, paragraphs 2 and 3, and Article 2 of the Convention.

[100] Human Rights Watch and Landmine Action, *Banning Cluster Munitions, op. cit.*, p. 13.

0.131 Preambular language on NSAGs did not appear in the draft Convention submitted to the Dublin Diplomatic Conference.[101] Draft language on NSAGs first appeared in a proposal for amendment of Article 1, tabled by the Philippines on the first day of the Conference:

3. This Convention shall also apply to situations resulting from conflicts referred to in Art. 1, paragraphs 1 to 6, of the Convention on Prohibitions or Restrictions on the Use of Certain Conventional Weapons Which May be Deemed to be Excessively Injurious or to have Indiscriminate Effects, as amended on 21 December 2001.

4. Armed groups that are distinct from the armed forces of a State shall not, under any circumstances, engage in any activity prohibited to a State Party under this Convention.[102]

0.132 The intent of the Philippines was to apply the Convention specifically to both international armed conflicts and armed conflicts of a non-international character, by reference to the extension of scope of the CCW, agreed by States Parties to that instrument in 2001. However, given the far broader language already included in Article 1 ('Each State Party undertakes never under any circumstances to …'), the effect might have been to narrow the scope of the Convention on Cluster Munitions.

0.133 In discussions at the Diplomatic Conference, Botswana called for the inclusion of language in the preamble 'referring to cooperation of non-state actors'. This proposal was supported by the Philippines, which declared that it would welcome language on the role of non-State actors either in the preamble or in Article 1. The inclusion of language on non-State actors in the preamble was also supported by Uganda.[103] Ultimately, the negotiating States agreed that similar language to that put forward by the Philippines should be included in the preamble.[104]

The implications of the preambular paragraph

0.134 There are a number of means by which a State Party could prevent an NSAG from engaging in conduct prohibited to a State Party to the Convention on Cluster Munitions. First and foremost, each State Party can

---

[101] See Draft Cluster Munitions Convention.

[102] 'Proposal by the Philippines for additional text to Article 1', Diplomatic Conference doc. CCM/56, 19 May 2008 (footnotes omitted).

[103] See 'Summary Record of Tenth Session of the Committee of the Whole', Diplomatic Conference doc. CCM/CW/SR/10, 18 June 2008; see also Human Rights Watch and Landmine Action, *Banning Cluster Munitions, op. cit.*, p. 46.

[104] Although the formulation was changed from an obligation of the groups themselves to one seemingly on States Parties to prevent NSAGs from undertaking a prohibited act.

respect its own obligations under Article 1, which include not transferring any cluster munitions to any NSAG. Second, it can adopt legislation, as sought by Article 9 of the Convention, which criminalizes possession or use of cluster munitions by any person within its jurisdiction or control (absent specific authority, for example, in the case of use or retention as permitted by Article 3 of the Convention).[105] Third, it can condemn any use of cluster munitions by any NSAG at any time.

0.135 Potentially, however, the impact of the Convention on NSAGs is relatively modest, given the limited recourse to these weapons that such entities have made in the last decades. As noted above, use has been reported by NGOs in only four conflicts. In Afghanistan, a non-State armed group, the Northern Alliance, used rocket-delivered cluster munitions during the civil war in the 1990s.[106] In Bosnia and Herzegovina, a Serb militia force used cluster munitions during the 1992–1995 conflict.[107] In Croatia, ethnic Serb forces delivered cluster munitions by Orkan rocket in early May 1995 against Zagreb. These cluster munition attacks were reported to have killed seven civilians and injured more than 200 others (see further below).[108] During the 2006 armed conflict in Lebanon, Hezbollah reportedly fired more than 100 Chinese-made Type-81 122mm cluster munition rockets into northern Israel.[109] Israel has said that it has since cleared all the UXO from these cluster attacks.[110]

0.136 Yet, despite the relatively scant practice of use by NSAGs, there has been a noted instance of an individual being held criminally responsible under international law for use by an NSAG of cluster munitions and for civilian deaths and injuries that resulted. In June 2007, Milan Martić was

---

[105] See, *infra*, the commentary on Article 3, paragraph 6 of the Convention.

[106] See CMC, 'Cluster Munitions in the Asia-Pacific Region', October 2008, prepared by Human Rights Watch; and Human Rights Watch and Landmine Action, *Banning Cluster Munitions, op. cit.*, p. 27.

[107] Human Rights Watch and Landmine Action, *Banning Cluster Munitions, op. cit.*, p. 45.

[108] In the mid-morning of 2 May 1995, troops of the self-styled Republic of Serbian Krajina launched several M-87 Orkan rockets that struck locations in Zagreb, including the main square, several shopping streets, a school, the village of Plešo near Zagreb airport, and the airport itself. Five persons, all civilians, were killed in these attacks, and at least 160 persons were severely injured. The following day, Zagreb was again hit by Orkan rockets. The areas hit were the Croatian National Theatre at Marshall Tito Square and a children's hospital, as well as another square. These attacks claimed two lives and injured 54 people. See Trial Chamber of the ICTY, 'Summary of Judgment for Milan Martić,' Press release, The Hague, 12 June 2007; and Human Rights Watch and Landmine Action, *Banning Cluster Munitions, op. cit.*, p. 66.

[109] Human Rights Watch, *Civilians Under Assault: Hezbollah's Rocket Attacks on Israel in the 2006 War*, Vol. 19, No. 3(E), August 2007, pp. 44–48, <http://www.hrw.org/sites/default/files/reports/iopt0807.pdf>. Hezbollah denied to the BBC that it had used cluster munitions. 'Hezbollah Denies Cluster Bomb Use', *BBC News*, 19 October 2006, <http://news.bbc.co.uk/2/hi/middle_east/6068154.stm> (both accessed 11 June 2009).

[110] Human Rights Watch and Landmine Action, *Banning Cluster Munitions, op. cit.*, p. 214.

convicted by the International Criminal Tribunal for the former Yugoslavia of war crimes and crimes against humanity and sentenced to 35 years' imprisonment. His crimes included the targeting of civilians in Zagreb using cluster munitions in early May 1995 in the two instances referred to above.[111]

0.137 According to the judgment of the tribunal:

The evidence shows that the M-87 Orkan was fired on 2 and 3 May 1995 from the Vojnic area, near Slavsko Polje, between 47 and 51 kilometres from Zagreb. However, the Trial Chamber notes in this respect that the weapon was fired from the extreme of its range. Moreover, the Trial Chamber notes the characteristics of the weapon, it being a non-guided high dispersion weapon. The Trial Chamber therefore concludes that the M-87 Orkan, by virtue of its characteristics and the firing range in this specific instance, was incapable of hitting specific targets. For these reasons, the Trial Chamber also finds that the M-87 Orkan is an indiscriminate weapon, the use of which in densely populated civilian areas, such as Zagreb, will result in the infliction of severe casualties. By 2 May 1995, the effects of firing the M-87 Orkan on Zagreb were known to those involved. Furthermore, before the decision was made to once again use this weapon on Zagreb on 3 May 1995, the full impact of using such an indiscriminate weapon was known beyond doubt as a result of the extensive media coverage on 2 May 1995 of the effects of the attack on Zagreb.[112]

0.138 Individual criminal liability for a member of an NSAG violating international humanitarian law regarding the protection of civilians is now enshrined in the *1998 Statute of the International Criminal Court*,[113] and there may be further crimes under customary international law that are not codified in this way.[114] In order for the International Criminal Court to obtain

[111] See also, e.g., Landmine Action UK, 'International Criminal Tribunal: Milan Martić guilty of indiscriminate use of cluster munitions in Zagreb war crime verdict', London, 12 June 2007; and Maslen, S. and Wiebe, V., *Cluster Munitions, A Survey of Legal Responses* (London: Landmine Action, March 2008), Chapter 6, <http://www.stopclustermunitions.org/wp/wp-content/uploads/2008/07/a-survey-of-legal-responses-lma.pdf> (accessed 8 March 2010) and Wiebe, V., 'For Whom the Little Bells Toll: Recent Judgments by International Tribunals on the Legality of Cluster Munitions', 35 *Pepperdine L. Rev.* 895 (2008), pp. 916–963.

[112] ICTY, Prosecutor v. Milan Martić, Judgment, Case No. IT-95–11-T, 12 June 2007, §463, p. 166, <http://www.icty.org/x/cases/martic/tjug/en/070612.pdf> (accessed 21 September 2009). In his subsequent appeal against conviction, Martić argued, *inter alia*, that the Court had erred in holding that the M-87 Orkan is an indiscriminate weapon. The Appeals Chamber dismissed his argument. See Prosecutor v. Milan Martić, Judgment, Case No. IT-95–11-A, 8 October 2008, paras. 239 *et seq.*, <http://www.icty.org/x/cases/martic/acjug/en/mar-aj081008e.pdf> (accessed 8 March 2010).

[113] See, e.g., Article 8, paragraph 2(c) (i) and (e) (i), *1998 Statute of the International Criminal Court*.

[114] Henckaerts, J.-M. and Doswald-Beck, L., *Customary International Humanitarian Law – Volume 1: Rules* (Cambridge: Cambridge University Press, 2005) at pp. 591–603, *esp.* pp. 599–601,

jurisdiction over the mere fact of using cluster munitions as a war crime *per se* the Statute of the Court would have to be amended in accordance with the amendment procedures.[115]

0.139 In fact this provision currently only applies to international armed conflicts, but at the time of any negotiated amendment it would be possible to amend the Article on war crimes so as to include prohibited weapons in situations of armed conflict of a non-international character, thus covering NSAGs. Such an extension of international criminal law would generate a war crime even where a member of an NSAG (or the armed forces of a State) uses cluster munitions 'proportionately' and against lawful military objectives.

0.140 If a State with jurisdiction over the specific actions of an NSAG has adopted legislation outlawing their use, a member of such an NSAG that possesses or uses cluster munitions will likely have violated national criminal law. But the imposition of international humanitarian law, human rights law, and international criminal law to an NSAG *qua* a distinct entity with international obligations is more complex.[116]

0.141 Lastly, it should be noted that the preamble refers to the resolve of States Parties that NSAGs 'shall not, under any circumstances, be permitted to engage' in any prohibited activity.[117] According to one commentator:

which deals with prohibited weapons and launching indiscriminate attacks:

> Launching indiscriminate attacks in non-international armed conflicts has been so frequently and vigorously condemned by the international community as to indicate the customary nature of this prohibition, which protects important values and is an offence under the legislation of numerous States.

Ibid., p. 601.

[115] See Article 8, paragraph 2(b) (xx) and Article 121. Belgium initially proposed an amendment that, if accepted, would have made it a war crime to use cluster munitions in international or non-international conflicts as prohibited in the Cluster Munitions Convention. This suggestion was removed in Belgium's revised proposal in response to concerns regarding the fact that the Convention had yet to enter into force. See 'Proposal of Belgium on amendments to Article 8 of the Rome Statute', reported by the Coalition for the International Criminal Court, <http://www.iccnow.org/?mod=belgianproposal> (accessed 15 December 2009).

[116] See Sivakumaran, S., 'Binding Armed Opposition Groups', *International and Comparative Law Quarterly*, Vol. 55 (2006) pp. 369–394; Sassòli, M., 'Transnational Armed Groups and International Humanitarian Law' (Harvard University: Program on Humanitarian Policy and Conflict Research, 2006); Clapham, A., 'Human rights obligations of non-state actors in conflict situations', *International Review of the Red Cross*, Vol. 88, No. 863 (2006), pp. 491–523; and Clapham, A., 'Extending International Criminal Law beyond the Individual to Corporations and Armed Opposition Groups', *Journal of International Criminal Justice*, Vol. 6 (2008), pp. 899–926.

[117] The language follows the wording included to cover the acts of NSAGs in the Optional Protocol to the Convention on the Rights of the Child on the involvement of children in armed conflict. For a discussion of the language used, see Clapham, A., *Human Rights Obligations of Non-State Actors* (Oxford: Oxford University Press, 2006), p. 75; and also UNICEF and Coalition to Stop

With its explicit reference to NSAGs, the convention also lays the groundwork for weapons treaties to address the behavior of more parties. Instead of merely relying on indirect clauses related to proliferation and use, it names NSAGs and suggests that the states in which they operate have a duty to limit their activities. By moving in the direction of more stringent IHL instruments, the Convention on Cluster Munitions could inspire future weapons treaties to go even further. Ultimately such treaties could impose both binding obligations on states parties to regulate NSAGs and responsibility on the groups themselves to control their own conduct.[118]

Thirteenth preambular paragraph: the norm prohibiting anti-personnel mines

Welcoming the very broad international support for the international norm prohibiting anti-personnel mines, enshrined in the 1997 Convention on the Prohibition of the Use, Stockpiling, Production and Transfer of Anti-Personnel Mines and on Their Destruction,

0.142 The prohibitions on the development, production, stockpiling, transfer, and use of anti-personnel mines,[119] enshrined in the *1997 Anti-Personnel Mine Ban Convention*,[120] is an important precedent for the Convention on Cluster Munitions and its own creation of a new international norm against cluster munitions. Indeed, many of the provisions included in the Convention on Cluster Munitions are drawn from, or inspired by, those set out in the *1997 Anti-Personnel Mine Ban Convention*.[121]

0.143 In launching the 'Ottawa Process' in October 1996, a freestanding process of treaty negotiation outside a UN-facilitated forum with the aim of outlawing anti-personnel mines, Canada had taken a diplomatic and political risk in pursuit of greater human security.[122] A total of 122 States signed the

the Use of Child Soldiers, *Guide to the Optional Protocol on the Involvement of Children in Armed Conflict* (New York: UNICEF, 2003), p. 17.

[118] Docherty, B., 'Breaking New Ground: The Convention on Cluster Munitions and the Evolution of International Humanitarian Law', *Human Rights Quarterly*, Vol. 31 (2009), p. 962.

[119] The proposed preambular language contained in the Draft Cluster Munitions Convention was slightly amended in the final text, replacing global support with 'very broad international support' and 'prohibiting the use of anti-personnel mines' with 'prohibiting anti-personnel mines'.

[120] The formal title of this treaty is the Convention on the Prohibition of the Use, Stockpiling, Production and Transfer of Anti-Personnel Mines and on Their Destruction.

[121] Under Article 1, paragraph 3 of the Convention, all landmines, including anti-personnel mines, are excluded from the purview of the Convention on the basis that they are regulated by other instruments of international law, notably the *1997 Anti-Personnel Mine Ban Convention*, *1980 Protocol II on mines, booby-traps and other devices*, and *1996 Amended Protocol II*.

[122] For details of the Ottawa Process, see, e.g., Cameron, M. L., Lawson, R., and Tomlin, B. (eds.), *To Walk without Fear: The Global Movement to Ban Landmines* (Ottawa: Oxford University

Convention when it was opened for signature on 3–4 December 1997, and by March 2010, 156 States—more than three-quarters of the world's nations—had become party to it.

0.144 The creation of the 'norm' against anti-personnel mines was deemed critical to modifying the behaviour of combatants. It was clear from the outset that certain major military powers would be unlikely to join the Convention in the short or medium term,[123] and with a ready supply of anti-personnel mines across conflict zones, stigmatizing the weapon was a key strategy for committed governments, the ICRC, and the NGOs making up the International Campaign to Ban Landmines. As a result of their collective efforts, since 2006, the only States confirmed to be using anti-personnel mines have been Myanmar and Russia, down from some 15 States a decade earlier.[124] A similar downward trend has been seen with respect to NSAGs.[125]

0.145 On 2 December 2009, the UN General Assembly adopted Resolution 64/56 on the Implementation of the Convention on the Prohibition of the Use, Stockpiling, Production and Transfer of Anti-personnel Mines and on Their Destruction.[126] The resolution was adopted by a recorded vote of 160 in favour to none against, with 18 abstentions.[127] Among those voting in favour were the following States not party to the *1997 Anti-Personnel Mine Ban Convention*: Armenia, Azerbaijan, Bahrain, China (which holds the world's largest stockpiles of anti-personnel mines), Finland (the only member of the European Union not a State Party), Georgia, Kazakhstan, Laos, Marshall Islands (a signatory), Micronesia, Mongolia, Morocco, Oman, Poland (a signatory), Singapore, Somalia, Sri Lanka, Tonga, and the United Arab Emirates.

0.146 Some have argued that at least certain aspects of the prohibition on anti-personnel mines are an emerging customary norm.[128] The ICRC's study of customary international humanitarian law, published in 2005, but based

---

Press, 31 December 1998). This represented a return to the traditional approach of elaborating new rules of international humanitarian law.

   [123] Notably, China, India, Pakistan, Russia, and the US.

   [124] See, e.g., the ban policy section of ICBL, *Landmine Monitor Report 2009: Toward a Mine-Free World* (Ottawa: Mines Action Canada, 2009), <http://lm.icbl.org/index.php/publications/display?url=lm/2009/es/ban.html> (accessed 8 March 2010).

   [125] Over the past 10 years, at least 59 NSAGs across 13 countries have committed to halt use of antipersonnel mines. See *ibid.*   [126] UN doc. A/64/391.

   [127] Cuba, the Democratic People's Republic of Korea, Egypt, India, Iran, Israel, Kyrgyzstan, Lebanon, Libya, Myanmar, Nepal, Pakistan, Republic of Korea, Russian Federation, Syria, United States, Uzbekistan, Vietnam. Of these, only Lebanon had signed the Convention on Cluster Munitions as of December 2009.

   [128] Most commentators affirm that a customary norm has not coalesced under international law. Professor Yoram Dinstein, e.g., observes that:

on research conducted over a period of several years prior to that, concluded that State practice 'appears to indicate that an obligation to eliminate anti-personnel mines is emerging'.[129] Writing in 2008, two ICRC experts concluded that:

from a strictly legal standpoint, the practice of states not party to the Mine Ban Treaty [the 1997 Anti-Personnel Mine Ban Convention] taken together is insufficient to conclude that these states consider themselves bound by a norm of customary law comprehensively prohibiting antipersonnel mines. However, much of their behaviour and statements give rise to an expectation that they will eventually, at some undetermined point in the future, fully adhere to the antipersonnel mine ban norm. At best, it can be said to be a 'universal-norm-in-waiting'.[130]

0.147 The primary advantage of customary international law over an international treaty is that whereas a treaty legally binds only those States which are parties to it, in most cases customary international law constrains all States,[131] even those that have not agreed to it.[132] Once a rule attains the status of customary international law,[133] States may not unilaterally repudiate it, and

With a view to elaborating clear norms of conduct in hostilities, a plethora of treaty provisions—each dealing with a chosen weapons—have been negotiated, signed, and ratified. Some of these treaty clauses (by no means all) have generated customary international law applicable to all states. Others (pre-eminently the repudiation of anti-personnel mines) remain binding only among Contracting Parties.

Dinstein, Y., 'Foreword' in Boothby, W. H., *Weapons and the Law of Armed Conflict* (Oxford: Oxford University Press, 2009), p. viii.

[129] Henckaerts, J.-M. and Doswald-Beck, L., *Customary International Humanitarian Law - Volume 1: Rules, op. cit.*, p. 283.

[130] Herby, P. and Lawand, K., 'Unacceptable Behavior: How Norms Are Established', in Williams, J., Goose, S. D., and Wareham, M. (eds.), *Banning Landmines—Disarmament, Citizen Diplomacy, and Human Security* (US: Rowman and Littlefield, 2008), p. 208.

[131] According to the international lawyer, Malcolm Shaw, 'where treaties reflect customary law, then non-parties are bound, not because it is a treaty provision but because it reaffirms a rule or rules of customary international law.'

Shaw, M. N., *International Law*, Fourth Edition (Cambridge: Cambridge University Press, 1997), p. 79.

[132] An important exception is a State that has attained the status of 'persistent objector' to a given rule, thereby refusing to accept the application of a specific customary law norm to itself. See Charney, J. I., 'The persistent objector rule and the development of customary international law', *British Yearbook of International Law*, Vol. 56, 1985, p. 2. Several States not party to the *1997 Anti-Personnel Mine Ban Convention* could credibly claim such status.

[133] International law recognizes the crystallization of norms of behaviour into customary rules binding on all States, irrespective of their adherence to specific international treaties. Indeed, for centuries, customary law was the predominant source of international law. Indeed, according to the Statute of the International Court of Justice, 'international custom, as evidence of a general practice accepted as law' is expressly recognized as one of the primary sources of international law along with international conventions and general principles of law. Statute of the International Court of Justice, Article 38(1), annexed to the UN Charter. Theodor Meron, however, affirms that general

newly emerging States will be deemed to accede to the rule as a condition of Statehood.[134]

0.148 To determine the existence of custom with regard to certain behaviour, it is necessary to identify 'a general recognition among States of a certain practice as obligatory'.[135] As generally accepted,[136] and, as clearly formulated by the Statute of the International Court of Justice,[137] the existence of customary international law demands two main elements: State practice (sometimes known under the Latin name *usus*) and *opinio juris sive necessitatis* (a belief that certain behaviour is required or prohibited by law).[138] This view is still predominant in State practice, literature, and court decisions, even though the question of how and when a norm can be seen as part of customary international law remains the subject of debate.

0.149 In practice, the burden of proving the existence of a customary rule falls on the one who asserts its existence.[139] Although it is acknowledged to be generally difficult to isolate the proof of *opinio juris* from State practice itself, jurisprudence has refused to accept this difficulty as an excuse removing the requirement of separate proof.[140] Having said that,

---

practice demonstrates custom and not *vice versa*, and points out that paragraph 102(2) of the *Third Restatement of the Foreign Relations Law of the United States* of 1987 provides 'more accurately', that customary international law 'results from a general and consistent practice of States which is followed by them from a sense of legal obligation'. Meron, T., *Human Rights and Humanitarian Norms as Customary Law* (Oxford: Clarendon Press, 1991), p. 3. See also Villiger, M. E., *Customary international law and treaties* (The Hague: Kluwer Law International, 1997), p. 15.

[134] See, e.g., Benesch, S. *et al.*, 'International Customary Law and Anti Personnel Landmines. Emergence of a New Customary Norm', Appendix in ICBL, *Landmine Monitor Report 1999: Toward a Mine-Free World* (US: Human Rights Watch, 1999), p. 1030.

[135] See Brownlie, I. *Principles of Public International Law*, Fifth Edition (Oxford: Clarendon Press, 1998), pp. 5–7.

[136] See for instance Rousseau, C., *Droit International Public*, Tome I (Paris: Sirey, 1970), pp. 315–325; Quoc Dinh, N., Dailler, P. and Pellet, A., *Droit International Public,* Sixth Edition (Paris: L.G.D.J, 1999), pp. 321–329; Bernhardt, R., 'Customary International Law', in Bernhardt, R. (ed.), *Encyclopaedia of Public International Law*, Vol. 1, 1992, p. 901.

[137] Article 38, paragraph 1(b).

[138] According to the work of Oppenheim, a custom is:

a clear and continuous habit of doing certain actions which has grown up under the aegis of the conviction that these actions are, according to international law, obligatory or right.

Jennings, R. and Watts, R. (eds.), *Oppenheim's International Law*, Ninth Edition (Oxford: Oxford University Press, 2008). In the corresponding French literature, State practice is defined as the material element (élément matériel) and *opinio juris* is the psychological constituent element of custom (élément psychologique).

[139] Brownlie, I., *Principles of Public International Law, op. cit.*, p. 11; Quoc Dinh, N., Dailler, P. and Pellet, A., *Droit International Public, op. cit.*, p. 330.

[140] Quoc Dinh, N., Dailler, P. and Pellet, A., *Droit International Public, op. cit.*, p. 330.

however, in many cases the International Court of Justice has been willing to assume the existence of an *opinio juris* on the basis of evidence of a general practice.[141] Without admitting that the mere repetition of conduct suffices in itself to prove the requisite *opinio juris*,[142] the Court has accepted on a number of occasions that solid proof of State practice evidences the *opinio juris*.[143] In other cases, the Court has adopted a more rigorous approach, calling for more positive evidence of the recognition of the validity of the rules in question.[144]

0.150 It may be that certain aspects of a customary norm against anti-personnel mines are emerging more rapidly than others. For while States not party to the Convention continue to stockpile far more anti-personnel mines than have been destroyed to date,[145] and several States either continue to use or produce anti-personnel mines (or reserve the right to do so) there is scant evidence of any transfer of anti-personnel mines. In 2009, *Landmine Monitor* concluded that for the past decade:

A *de facto* ban on the transfer of antipersonnel mines has been in effect since the mid-1990s; this prohibition is attributable to the mine ban movement and the stigma that the Mine Ban Treaty has attached to the weapon. Landmine Monitor has never conclusively documented any state-to-state transfers of antipersonnel mines. For the past decade, global trade in antipersonnel mines has consisted solely of a low-level of illicit and unacknowledged transfers.[146]

The proliferation of anti-personnel mines was the first aspect of the problem that the UN General Assembly sought to address, with a resolution calling for a moratorium on export in 1993.[147] Since then, the absence of any transfers or even of States defending their *right* to transfer anti-personnel mines has been notable.

0.151 The similarities between the Oslo Process on cluster munitions and the Ottawa Process on anti-personnel mines are notable. Both were launched

---

[141] Brownlie, I., *Principles of Public International Law, op. cit.*, p. 7.

[142] In the *North Sea Continental Shelf Cases*, the Court stated that: 'the frequency, or even habitual character of the acts is not in itself enough.' *ICJ Reports 1969*, para. 77, p. 44.

[143] See Quoc Dinh, N., Dailler, P. and Pellet, A., *Droit International Public, op. cit.*, p. 331. See *Interhandel Case, ICJ Reports 1959*, p. 27.

[144] See for instance the *Nicaragua Case* wherein the rule unanimously accepted was repeatedly violated but the Court noted that there was evidence of a considerable degree of agreement between the Parties as to the content of the customary international law relating to the non-use of force and non-intervention. *ICJ Reports 1986*, §184 *et seq.*

[145] See, e.g., the overview on ban policy contained in ICBL, *Landmine Monitor Report 2009: Toward a Mine-Free World, op. cit.*

[146] ICBL, *Landmine Monitor Report 2009: Toward a Mine-Free World, op. cit.*

[147] UN General Assembly Resolution 48K of 16 December 1993.

by a single State, supported by a core group of other States committed to a prohibition, and both resultant treaties were adopted by a Diplomatic Conference
convened outside the UN. John Borrie has also noted significant differences,
for example the fact that existing treaties within the UN already regulated
anti-personnel mines[148] whereas efforts to regulate cluster munitions were
ongoing while the Oslo Process was underway.[149] He affirms that:

> for most of those individuals building the Oslo process during its prologue and then
> steering the initiative for some of its course, the Ottawa process—for all of its appar-
> ent similarities—represented an example to learn from, and adapt, rather than follow
> too closely.[150]

0.152 It may take many years for the new norm prohibiting cluster munitions to crystallize as international custom. Similar to the norm against anti-
personnel mines, however, new use of cluster munitions by those States that
have not yet adhered to the Convention on Cluster Munitions will likely be
subject to greater international scrutiny and condemnation as a result of its
existence.

Fourteenth preambular paragraph: the protocol on explosive remnants of war

> *Welcoming* also the adoption of the Protocol on Explosive Remnants of War,
> annexed to the Convention on Prohibitions or Restrictions on the Use of
> Certain Conventional Weapons Which May be Deemed to be Excessively
> Injurious or to Have Indiscriminate Effects, and its entry into force on 12
> November 2006, and *wishing* to enhance the protection of civilians from
> the effects of cluster munition remnants in post-conflict environments,

0.153 This preambular paragraph welcomes the adoption and entry into
force of *2003 Protocol V.* Several provisions of the Convention on Cluster
Munitions are drawn from or inspired by those set out in *2003 Protocol V.* As
of March 2010, *2003 Protocol V* was the most recently adopted protocol of
the CCW. It requires parties to a conflict (whether in an international armed
conflict or an armed conflict of a non-international character) to reduce the

---

[148] *1980 Protocol II on mines, booby-traps and other devices* and *1996 Amended Protocol II.*

[149] Remarks at the launch of his 2009 work, *Unacceptable Harm.* However, it should be noted
that during the Ottawa Process a number of States sought to pursue a prohibition on the transfer of
anti-personnel mines in the Conference on Disarmament and further that *2003 Protocol V,* which
entered into force prior to the Convention on Cluster Munitions, addresses a part of the cluster
munitions problem.

[150] Borrie, J., *Unacceptable Harm: A history of how the international treaty banning cluster munitions was won* (Geneva: United Nations Institute for Disarmament Research, 2009), pp. 334–335.

dangers from explosive remnants of war (ERW).[151] As of 24 March 2010, 65 States were party to the Protocol.[152]

0.154 Specifically, the Protocol requires each party to an armed conflict to mark and clear ERW in territory they control after a conflict;[153] to provide technical, material, and financial assistance to facilitate the removal of ERW that result from its operations and which are located in areas it does not control;[154] to take 'all feasible precautions' to protect civilians from the effects of ERW;[155] and to record information on the explosive ordnance used by its armed forces and, after the end of active hostilities, to share that information with the other parties to the conflict and organizations engaged in ERW clearance or risk education programmes.[156] In addition to the obligations placed upon the parties to a conflict, all States Parties in a position to do so must provide assistance for the marking and clearance of ERW, risk education, and assistance for the care, rehabilitation and socio-economic reintegration of ERW victims.[157]

Fifteenth preambular paragraph: UN Security Council resolutions on women, peace, and security, and on children in armed conflict

> *Bearing in mind* also United Nations Security Council Resolution 1325 on women, peace and security and United Nations Security Council Resolution 1612 on children in armed conflict,

---

[151] ERW are defined as explosive ordnance that has been used or fired but which has failed to explode as intended (UXO) and stocks of explosive ordnance left behind on the battlefield (abandoned explosive ordnance). Such weapons include artillery shells, mortar shells, hand grenades, submunitions, and other similar weapons. The Protocol does not apply to the weapons covered by *1996 Amended Protocol II* (mines, booby traps and other devices). ICRC, 'Fact Sheet on the Convention on Certain Conventional Weapons', Geneva, March 2004.

[152] Albania, Australia, Austria, Belarus, Belgium, Bosnia and Herzegovina, Bulgaria, Canada, Chile, Costa Rica, Croatia, Cyprus, Czech Republic, Denmark, Ecuador, El Salvador, Estonia, Finland, France, Georgia, Germany, Guatemala, Guinea-Bissau, Holy See, Hungary, Iceland, India, Ireland, Italy, Jamaica, Latvia, Liberia, Liechtenstein, Lithuania, Luxembourg, the former Yugoslav Republic of Macedonia, Madagascar, Mali, Malta, Netherlands, New Zealand, Nicaragua, Norway, Pakistan, Paraguay, Peru, Portugal, Republic of Korea, Republic of Moldova, Qatar, Romania, Russian Federation, Senegal, Sierra Leone, Slovakia, Slovenia, Spain, Sweden, Switzerland, Tajikistan, Tunisia, Ukraine, United Arab Emirates, the United States of America, and Uruguay.   [153] Article 3, paragraph 2, *2003 Protocol V.*

[154] Article 3, paragraph 1, *2003 Protocol V.* Assistance can be provided directly to the party in control of the territory or through a third party such as the UN, international agencies, or NGOs.

[155] Article 5, *2003 Protocol V.* This may include the fencing and monitoring of territory contaminated with ERW, and the provision of warnings and risk education.

[156] Article 4, *2003 Protocol V.*

[157] *Cf.* Articles 7 and 8, *2003 Protocol V,* which deal, respectively, with assistance with respect to 'existing explosive remnants of war' (i.e. those existing when the Protocol entered into force for the relevant State Party), and broader cooperation and assistance.

0.155 This preambular paragraph notes the relevance of two landmark UN Security Council resolutions: 1325, adopted on 31 October 2000, on women, peace, and security, and 1612, adopted on 26 July 2005, on children in armed conflict.[158] The particular impact of cluster munitions on women and children was already highlighted in the third preambular paragraph to the Convention on Cluster Munitions, whereby States Parties expressed their concern that 'cluster munition remnants kill or maim civilians, including women and children …'.[159]

0.156 Resolution 1325 was the first resolution passed by the UN Security Council that 'specifically addresses the impact of war on women, and women's contributions to conflict resolution and sustainable peace.'[160] In contrast, the 2005 resolution on children in armed conflict had been preceded by numerous Council resolutions highlighting the plight of children in such situations.[161]

0.157 Preambular language on the two UN Security Council resolutions did not appear in the draft Convention submitted to the Dublin Diplomatic Conference,[162] nor in any of the formal proposals to amend the preamble tabled by negotiating States at the Conference itself. In the tenth session of the Committee of the Whole, Canada proposed that the preamble contain a reference to UN Security Council Resolution 1325 on the 'differential impact of conflict on different genders'. Norway supported the proposal, as did Argentina, South Africa, and Sweden.[163] Argentina added a suggestion

---

[158] Both resolutions were adopted unanimously.

[159] Third preambular paragraph. However, the draft text of the Convention submitted to the Dublin Diplomatic Conference referred to the determination of States Parties 'to put an end for all time to the suffering and casualties caused by the use of cluster munitions that kill or maim innocent and defenceless civilians and especially children', thus not highlighting the specific impact on women. See Draft Cluster Munitions Convention, Second preambular paragraph. Lesotho proposed including a reference to women in its suggested amendment to the draft paragraph:

> Aware/cognizant of other irreparable harm caused by the use of cluster munitions including to kill or maim innocent and defenceless civilians [and] especially women and children; obstruct economic development and reconstruction; delay or prevent the return of refugees and internally displaced persons and have other severe humanitarian consequences that can persist for many years after use.

'Proposal by Lesotho for the amendment of the Preamble', Diplomatic Conference doc. CCM/7, 19 May 2008.

[160] Women's International League for Peace and Freedom, 'PeaceWomen', <http://www.peacewomen.org/un/sc/1325.html> (accessed 4 June 2009).

[161] See, notably, UN Security Council Resolutions 1261 (1999) of 25 August 1999, 1314 (2000) of 11 August 2000, 1379 (2001) of 20 November 2001, 1460 (2003) of 30 January 2003, and 1539 (2004) of 22 April 2004.					[162] See Draft Cluster Munitions Convention.

[163] See 'Summary Record of Tenth Session of the Committee of the Whole', Diplomatic Conference doc. CCM/CW/SR/10, 18 June 2008.

to include a reference to children in armed conflict, which was supported in turn by Canada.[164] The text of the preambular paragraph first appeared in the Presidency Paper issued on 28 May 2008.[165] The text was unchanged in the text of the Convention as adopted.

0.158 The impact of armed conflict on women is an important—but not the only—theme addressed in UN Security Council Resolution 1325. According to the fourth preambular paragraph of the resolution, the Council expressed its concern that:

...civilians, particularly women and children, account for the vast majority of those adversely affected by armed conflict, including as refugees and internally displaced persons, and increasingly are targeted by combatants and armed elements, and recognizing the consequent impact this has on durable peace and reconciliation.

A general reference to the need to respect international humanitarian and human rights law protecting the rights of women and girls appears in the sixth preambular paragraph:

Reaffirming also the need to implement fully international humanitarian and human rights law that protects the rights of women and girls during and after conflicts.

0.159 There is no specific reference in either the preambular paragraphs or operative text of the resolution to the impact of cluster munitions, nor indeed to any specific weapons, but by its operative paragraph 9, the Council called upon:

...all parties to armed conflict to respect fully international law applicable to the rights and protection of women and girls, especially as civilians, in particular the obligations applicable to them under the Geneva Conventions of 1949 and the Additional Protocols thereto of 1977, the Refugee Convention of 1951 and the Protocol thereto of 1967, the Convention on the Elimination of All Forms of Discrimination against Women of 1979 and the Optional Protocol thereto of 1999 and the United Nations Convention on the Rights of the Child of 1989 and the two Optional Protocols thereto of 25 May 2000, and to bear in mind the relevant provisions of the Rome Statute of the International Criminal Court.

0.160 Available data suggests that women and girls are not the primary post-attack victims of unexploded submunitions,[166] but little data on those killed or injured during attacks is available. Thus, the final preambular paragraph of

---

[164] *Ibid.*

[165] 'Presidency Paper, *draft* Convention on Cluster Munitions', Diplomatic Conference Doc. CCM//PT/15, 28 May 2008.

[166] See, *supra*, the commentary on the eighth preambular paragraph, in §0.116.

Resolution 1325 refers to the 'need to consolidate data on the impact of armed conflict on women and girls'.

0.161 Children, however, are a major risk category as far as unexploded submunitions are concerned, typically at far greater risk of becoming casualties than are women.[167] Available data suggests that they formed more than half of all recorded submunition casualties in 2007,[168] and half of those in 2008.[169] Resolution 1612 is focused on the impact of armed conflict on children, whether as civilians or combatants. The resolution:

[s]trongly condemns the recruitment and use of child soldiers by parties to armed conflict in violation of international obligations applicable to them and all other violations and abuses committed against children in situations of armed conflict.[170]

0.162 Resolution 1612 is especially noteworthy because it established the UN-led Monitoring and Reporting Mechanism on Children and Armed Conflict ('the Mechanism') and its operational country-level Task Forces.[171] Indeed, according to one child rights advocacy body: 'With the adoption and implementation of Council Resolution 1612, the children and armed conflict...agenda became a hallmark of the Security Council's thematic work.'[172] The Mechanism and its Task Forces monitor and report on six grave violations:

- killing and maiming of children;

---

[167] Again, little data on those killed or injured during attacks is available, although in a notorious incident in Ethiopia in 2000, cluster bombs dropped by an Eritrean aircraft hit a school in Awder near the northern city of Mekele, reportedly killing 53 civilians, including 12 school children, and wounding another 105 civilians, including 42 school children. While Eritrea did acknowledge that one of its aircraft dropped cluster bombs in the vicinity of the Ayder School, it contended that this was an accident incidental to legitimate military operations, not a deliberate attack. See, e.g., Maslen, S. and Wiebe, V., *Cluster Munitions, A Survey of Legal Responses*, Landmine Action, March 2008, p. 9, citing Central Front (Eritrea v. Ethiopia), Ethiopia's Claim 2, Partial Award (Eritrea Ethiopia Claims Commission, 28 April 2004), *43 ILM 1275* (2004)(Partial Award), p. 1, accessed at: <http://www.pca-cpa.org/upload/files/ET%20Partial%20Award(1).pdf>.

[168] See 'Landmine/ERW/IED Casualties in 2007', in ICBL, *Landmine Monitor Report 2008*, <http://lm.icbl.org/index.php/publications/display?url=lm/2008/es/landmine_casualties_and_survivor_assistance.html#Landmine/ERW/IED_Casualties_in_2007> (accessed 17 June 2009).

[169] See ICBL, *Landmine Monitor Report 2009*, <http://lm.icbl.org/index.php/publications/display?url=lm/2009/es/mine_casualties.html>; *cf.* also, *supra*, the commentary on the eighth preambular paragraph, in §0.116. [170] Operative Paragraph 1.

[171] Operative Paragraphs 2 and 3; and see Watch List on Children in Armed Conflict, 'UN Security Council Resolution 1612 and Beyond: Strengthening Protection for Children in Armed Conflict', New York, May 2009, <http://watchlist.org/reports/pdf/PolicyPaper_09.pdf> (accessed 4 June 2009), p. 4. The establishment of the mechanism had earlier been proposed by the Security Council in Operative Paragraph 2 of its Resolution 1539, adopted unanimously on 22 April 2004.

[172] Watch List on Children in Armed Conflict, 'UN Security Council Resolution 1612 and Beyond: Strengthening Protection for Children in Armed Conflict', New York, May 2009, <http://watchlist.org/reports/pdf/PolicyPaper_09.pdf> (accessed 4 June 2009), p. 4.

- recruiting and using child soldiers;
- attacks against schools or hospitals;
- rape or other grave sexual violence against children;
- abduction of children; and
- denial of humanitarian access for children.

Thus, the use of cluster munitions against a school or, potentially, the killing or maiming of children as a result of either indiscriminate or disproportionate use of cluster munitions or even potentially through a wilful failure to clear unexploded submunitions, might meet the criteria set out under the resolution.

0.163 In order to ensure that grave violations reported through the Mechanism receive consistent and ongoing attention from the Security Council, Resolution 1612 also established the Security Council Working Group on Children and Armed Conflict (Working Group), the first of its kind. The Working Group is an official subsidiary body of the Council, and consists of all 15 Council Members. The Working Group is empowered to take concrete actions towards halting violations and holding perpetrators accountable, and also to make recommendations for concrete actions to the Security Council.

0.164 In August 2009, the Security Council adopted Resolution 1882, by which the Council noted its deep concern that:

children continue to account for a considerable number of casualties resulting from killing and maiming in armed conflicts including as a result of deliberate targeting, indiscriminate and excessive use of force, indiscriminate use of landmines, cluster munitions and other weapons...[173]

The resolution further asked the Secretary-General to 'include in the annexes to his reports on children and armed conflict those parties to armed conflict that engage, in contravention of applicable international law, in patterns of killing and maiming of children...in situations of armed conflict'.[174]

Sixteenth preambular paragraph: unilateral measures prohibiting cluster munitions

> *Welcoming* further the steps taken nationally, regionally and globally
> in recent years aimed at prohibiting, restricting or suspending the use,
> stockpiling, production and transfer of cluster munitions,

---

[173] UN Security Council Resolution 1882 of 4 August 2009, twelfth preambular paragraph.
[174] *Ibid.*, Operative Paragraph 3.

0.165 This language is based on a similar paragraph in the preamble to the *1997 Anti-Personnel Mine Ban Convention*. In 1993, a UN General Assembly resolution calling for a moratorium on the export of anti-personnel mines was adopted by consensus.[175] In 1995, the Assembly unanimously adopted a resolution calling for the eventual elimination of anti-personnel mines. By May 1996, when *1996 Amended Protocol II* was adopted, more than 40 States were supporting an international ban on anti-personnel mines, according to the ICRC.[176] In contrast, relatively few States had declared support for a ban on cluster munitions in advance of the negotiations at the Diplomatic Conference in Dublin in May 2008 and no consensus existed internationally even on the need to address the problem.

0.166 Nevertheless, a number of steps were taken towards the goal of curbing cluster munitions prior to the negotiation of the treaty. At the Third Review Conference of the CCW in November 2006, 26 States[177] supported a proposed negotiating mandate for a legally binding instrument 'that addresses the humanitarian concerns posed by cluster munitions'.[178] When this mandate was rejected, 25 States endorsed a joint declaration calling for an agreement that would prohibit the use of cluster munitions that 'pose serious humanitarian hazards because they are for example unreliable and/or inaccurate'.[179] In May 2007, at the Lima Conference on Cluster Munitions, Peru announced an initiative for a Latin American cluster-munition-free zone, which was supported by many States from the region.[180]

0.167 At national level, the Belgian parliament enacted a domestic prohibition on cluster munitions in February 2006, the first country to do

---

[175] UN General Assembly Resolution 48K of 16 December 1993.

[176] Maslen, S., *Commentary on the 1997 Anti-Personnel Mine Ban Convention, op. cit.*, §0.43.

[177] In its 'Daily update 7' from the review conference the CMC listed the 26 States supporting the mandate as: Argentina, Austria, Bosnia and Herzegovina, Chile, Costa Rica, Czech Republic, Denmark, Germany, Guatemala, Holy See, Hungary, Ireland, Liechtenstein, Lithuania, Luxembourg, Malta, Mexico, New Zealand, Peru, Portugal, Serbia, Slovakia, Slovenia, Spain, Sweden, and Switzerland. Belgium, Croatia, and Norway also signalled their commitment to negotiations during the Review Conference but did not support the negotiating mandate.

[178] The negotiating mandate is contained in UN doc. CCW/CONF.III/WP.1.

[179] The declaration is contained in UN doc. CCW/CONF.III/WP.18. It was endorsed by Austria, Belgium, Bosnia-Herzegovina, Croatia, Costa Rica, Czech Republic, Denmark, Germany, Holy See, Hungary, Ireland, Liechtenstein, Lithuania, Luxembourg, Malta, Mexico, New Zealand, Norway, Peru, Portugal, Serbia, Slovakia, Slovenia, Sweden, and Switzerland.

[180] Opening statement by Ambassador Gonzalo Gutierrez, Deputy Minister of Foreign Affairs, Peru, Lima Conference on Cluster Munitions, 23 May 2007.

so, as it had been for anti-personnel mines in 1995.[181] In October 2006, Luxembourg started work on a draft law prohibiting cluster munitions. This law was enacted in 2009 as part of Luxembourg's ratification of the Convention.[182] In December 2007 Austria passed a national law prohibiting cluster munitions.[183]

0.168 In 2004, Denmark adopted a temporary prohibition on the use of cluster munitions with a failure rate of more than 1 per cent.[184] In March 2005, Germany adopted a moratorium on the use of cluster munitions with a failure rate of more than 1 per cent.[185] In June 2006, Norway adopted a moratorium on use of cluster munitions pending review of its stockpile. This was extended in November 2006 to remain in effect until a new international treaty was in place.[186] In February 2007, Austria adopted a moratorium on the use of cluster munitions.[187] In June 2007, the Netherlands announced a temporary suspension of the use of cluster munitions.[188] In October 2007, Albania adopted a moratorium on the use

---

[181] Human Rights Watch and Landmine Action, *Banning Cluster Munitions, op. cit.*, p. 39.

[182] *Ibid.*, p. 112. 'Projet de lois portent approbation de la Convention sur les armes a sous-munitions ouverte a la signature a Oslo, le 3 decembre 2008' ('Draft legislation approving the Convention on Cluster Munitions open for signatures in Oslo, 3 December 2008'), No. 5981, Chambers of Deputies, Normal Session 2008–2009, 12 January 2009.

[183] Human Rights Watch and Landmine Action, *Banning Cluster Munitions, op. cit.*, p. 36. Statement of Austria, Vienna Conference, 5 December 2007.

[184] Human Rights Watch and Landmine Action, *Banning Cluster Munitions, op. cit.*, p. 68. Communication from the Danish Ministry of Defence, Division of International Law and Security Cooperation, to Pax Christi Netherlands, 16 February 2005.

[185] Human Rights Watch and Landmine Action, *Banning Cluster Munitions, op. cit.*, p. 78. It then noted that BL-755 cluster bombs were being phased out since 2001 due to an unacceptable dud rate and that the M26 cluster munition for the Multiple Launch Rocket System will not be used unless modernised. Statement by Amb. Volker Heinsberg, Permanent Representative to the Conference on Disarmament, on the Use and Reliability of Cluster Munitions, Working Group on ERW, Tenth Session of the CCW GGE, Geneva, 8 March 2005.

[186] Human Rights Watch and Landmine Action, *Banning Cluster Munitions, op. cit.*, pp. 135–136; and Norwegian Ministry of Foreign Affairs, 'Norway to take the lead in efforts to achieve an international ban on cluster munition', Press release, 3 November 2006, <http://www.regjeringen. no>; and 'Klasebomber laases ned' ('Cluster Bombs Locked Down'), *Aftenposten*, 3 November 2006, <http://www.aftenposten.no>.

[187] Human Rights Watch and Landmine Action, *Banning Cluster Munitions, op. cit.*, p. 36. Statement by Amb. Wolfgang Petritsch, Oslo Conference, 22 February 2007, <http://www. regjeringen.no>.

[188] Human Rights Watch and Landmine Action, *Banning Cluster Munitions, op. cit.*, p. 126; IKV Pax Christi, 'Netherlands suspends use of cluster munitions, but questions remain', Press release, 27 June 2007, <http://ikvpaxchristi.nl>; Corder, M., 'Dutch military ordered to stop using cluster

of cluster munitions,[189] joined by Hungary in November 2007,[190] Croatia in December 2007,[191] and Bulgaria[192] and Bosnia and Herzegovina[193] in February 2008.

0.169 Other national steps included Norway's destruction of its air-delivered cluster munitions in 2003;[194] the UK's withdrawal from service in March 2007 of its RBL-755 cluster bombs and M26 rockets, which it labelled 'dumb cluster munitions'.[195] States that opposed the Convention on Cluster Munitions had also taken steps nationally in advance of the treaty negotiation, notably the US, which in 2001 adopted a policy requiring cluster munitions acquired after 2005 to satisfy a failure rate of no more than 1 per cent.[196] In 2007, the US enacted a one-year legislative moratorium on exports of cluster munitions that did not meet the maximum

---

bombs until further notice', *Associated Press*, 26 June 2007; and 'Netherlands imposes moratorium on cluster bombs', *Xinhua*, 26 June 2007.

[189] Human Rights Watch and Landmine Action, *Banning Cluster Munitions, op. cit.*, p. 29; and the CMC, 'Survivors and States Join Forces Against Cluster Bombs', Press release, Belgrade, 4 October 2007.

[190] Human Rights Watch and Landmine Action, *Banning Cluster Munitions, op. cit.*, p. 90; and Ministry of Foreign Affairs of the Republic of Hungary, 'The Hungarian Government Introduced a National Ban on the Use of Cluster Munitions', <http://www.mfa.gov.hu>.

[191] Human Rights Watch and Landmine Action, *Banning Cluster Munitions, op. cit.*, p. 65. Statement of Croatia, Vienna Conference on Cluster Munitions, 5 December 2007. Notes by CMC/WILPF.

[192] Human Rights Watch and Landmine Action, *Banning Cluster Munitions, op. cit.*, p. 47; and Statement by Amb. Petko Draganov, Permanent Mission of Bulgaria to the UN, to the Conference on Disarmament, Geneva, 14 February 2008. He also urged the international community to negotiate such a legally binding instrument.

[193] Human Rights Watch and Landmine Action, *Banning Cluster Munitions, op. cit.*, p. 44. The decision was taken by the Council of Ministers and approved by the President. Harrison, K, 'Report from the Wellington Conference on Cluster Munitions, 18–22 February 2008', Women's International League for Peace and Freedom, p. 30.

[194] Human Rights Watch and Landmine Action, *Banning Cluster Munitions, op. cit.*, p. 134. Norway, 'National interpretation and implementation of International Humanitarian Law with regard to the risk of Explosive Remnants of War', Sixth Session of the CCW Group of Governmental Experts (GGE) on Explosive Remnants of War, Geneva, UN doc. CCW/GGE/VI/WG.1/WP.3, 24 November 2003. The paper stated that 'some countries may have self-imposed restrictions and policy that go further than the restrictions contained in the existing IHL. For the Norwegian Armed Forces, these restrictions i.a. imply that only air-delivered cluster bombs with a high reliability rate/self destruct mechanism may be used in international military operations.'

[195] Human Rights Watch and Landmine Action, *Banning Cluster Munitions, op. cit.*, p. 175; and Statement by Des Browne, Secretary of State for Defence, House of Commons, *Hansard* (London: HMSO, 15 December 2006), Column 1764, <http://www.publications.parliament.uk>.

[196] Human Rights Watch and Landmine Action, *Banning Cluster Munitions, op. cit.*, p. 251; and Secretary of Defence William Cohen, 'Memorandum for the Secretaries of the Military Departments, Subject: DOD Policy on Submunition Reliability (U)', 10 January 2001.

1 per cent failure rate and this export ban was made permanent in March 2009.[197]

Seventeenth preambular paragraph: the role of public conscience

Stressing the role of public conscience in furthering the principles of humanity as evidenced by the global call for an end to civilian suffering caused by cluster munitions and *recognising* the efforts to that end undertaken by the United Nations, the International Committee of the Red Cross, the Cluster Munition Coalition and numerous other non-governmental organisations around the world,

0.170 This preambular paragraph elaborates on the role played by civil society and more generally the public conscience in the process leading to the adoption of the Convention on Cluster Munitions. Although there may not have been explicit linkage in the negotiations between this paragraph and the one restating the Martens clause, both are closely linked.[198] Unlike the latter paragraph, this one was included in the Draft Cluster Munitions Convention of January 2008 and remained unchanged throughout the negotiations at the Diplomatic Conference in Dublin.[199] This preambular paragraph draws on the unprecedented recognition of the campaigning work by civil society in a similar paragraph of the preamble of the *1997 Anti-Personnel Mine Ban Convention*.

0.171 The wording of this preambular paragraph is interesting if put into perspective with the construction of the Martens clause. While this clause places 'the principles of humanity' and 'the dictates of public conscience' on an equal footing,[200] this paragraph spells out the interaction between the two: the public conscience plays a role in advancing the principles of humanity. This elaboration views the public conscience as a means to put forward the demands of humanity in relation to a given weapon that would not respect these principles.

---

[197] Human Rights Watch and Landmine Action, *Banning Cluster Munitions*, *op. cit.*, p. 251; and Making omnibus appropriations for the fiscal year ending September 30, 2009, and for other purposes (H.R.1105), 111th Congress, 2009, <http://Thomas.loc.gov>. Section 7056 deals with the export of cluster munitions. [198] See, *supra*, §§0.125 *et seq.*

[199] The only attempt to modify this preambular paragraph came from the UK in its proposal for amendment of the preamble of 19 May 2008. The amendment concerned the deletion of the word 'global' to qualify the call for an end to civilian suffering caused by cluster munitions. This might have been motivated by the will to mirror the same preambular paragraph contained in the *1997 Anti-Personnel Mine Ban Convention* where there is no reference to this term. See 'Proposal by the United Kingdom for the amendment of the Preamble', Diplomatic Conference doc. CCM/6, 19 May 2008.

[200] Be they interpretative guidelines, notions inspiring the development of international humanitarian law, or sources of law.

0.172 There are many references to the notion of humanity in the international legal regulation of weapons,[201] including with respect to the prohibition of a specific weapon.[202] While the border between legal considerations and morals could be difficult to discern, the Convention on Cluster Munitions and previously the *1997 Anti-Personnel Mine Ban Convention* clearly illustrate the dynamic role public conscience and civil society can play in the process of adopting a prohibition on specific weapons.

0.173 It is worth noting that the first specific recognition in this preambular paragraph concerns the efforts undertaken by the UN even though the Convention was negotiated outside UN auspices. Such reference was absent in the similar paragraph of the *1997 Anti-Personnel Mine Ban Convention*. In 2006, the Secretary-General of the UN stressed the 'atrocious, inhumane effects of cluster munitions' and urged States Parties to the CCW 'to make full use of this framework to devise effective norms that will reduce and ultimately eliminate the horrendous humanitarian and development impact of these weapons'.[203] UN efforts include active participation in attempts to regulate cluster munitions such as the work of the UN Mine Action Team (UNMAT) on substantive issues within the CCW framework or the Oslo Process[204] and activities on the ground by various UN bodies.[205]

---

[201] The 1976 US Air Force Pamphlet holds that:

completing the principle of necessity and implicitly contained within it is the principle of humanity which forbids the infliction of suffering, injury or destruction not actually necessary for the accomplishment of legitimate military purposes. The principle of humanity results in a specific prohibition against unnecessary suffering…

See 'International Law—The Conduct of Armed Conflict and Air Operations', *Air Force Pamphlet 110–31*, US Department of the Air Force, 1976, §§1–3 (a) (2).

[202] The preamble of the Saint Petersburg 1868 Declaration Renouncing the Use, in Time of War, of Explosive Projectiles Under 400 Grammes Weight stated that: 'employment of arms which uselessly aggravate the sufferings of disabled men, or render their death inevitable…would, therefore, be contrary to the laws of humanity'.

[203] Secretary-General of the United Nations, 'Message to the third Review Conference of the Convention on Certain Conventional Weapons', UN doc. SG/SM/10720, 7 November 2006.

[204] See e.g.: UNMAT statement on humanitarian impact of cluster munitions at the CCW Group of Governmental Experts, Geneva, June 2007; UNMAT statement on legal issues concerning cluster munitions to the CCW Group of Governmental Experts, Geneva, June 2007; and UNMAT statement regarding the clearance of cluster munitions at the Lima Conference, May 2007, available at: <http://www.mineaction.org/overview.asp?o=1324&status_flag=L&rand=0.5885431> (accessed 8 March 2010).

[205] In her opening address on behalf of UNMAT at the February 2008 Wellington Conference, UNICEF's Deputy Executive Director stressed that the UN-system contributes in a variety of ways. She stated:

Our extensive experience on the ground and at global level in providing both risk reduction education and assistance to survivors is complemented by UNDP and UNMAS's technical

0.174 The specific reference to the work of the ICRC in an international treaty is no novelty. Provisions in the *1949 Geneva Conventions*[206] and their *1977 Additional Protocols*[207] attribute a formal role to the ICRC as an impartial humanitarian body. What may be new is the recognition of the ICRC's work in the preamble of a Convention. Under its general mandate to assist victims of war, the ICRC works to minimize the impact of armed conflict, including the consequences of cluster munitions, on the civilian population. As for the involvement of the ICRC in the attempts to regulate those weapons, it dates back as far as the first initiatives in this regard. The ICRC used its expertise both legally and in the field to document the effects of cluster munitions[208] and address the various challenges posed by those weapons.[209]

0.175 As the preamble to the *1997 Anti-Personnel Mine Ban Convention* recognized the campaigning role of the International Campaign to Ban Landmines (ICBL),[210] so the corresponding preambular paragraph of the Convention on Cluster Munitions refers to the work of the CMC. This paragraph undoubtedly benefited from the momentum created by the action and recognition of the ICBL during the development of the *1997 Anti-Personnel Mine Ban Convention*. The CMC campaigned for a comprehensive prohibition on cluster munitions and, since the adoption of the Convention on Cluster Munitions, has worked to promote universal adherence to and full implementation of this treaty. Its work, as well as the work of other NGOs, was acknowledged throughout the Oslo Process. The Declaration of the Wellington Conference specifically referred to their active support. In this regard, and in the continuation of the process undertaken to ban anti-personnel mines beforehand, the Convention on Cluster Munitions is partly the result of a

expertise and support to cluster munitions-affected countries. The Office for the Coordination of Humanitarian Affairs, the Office for Disarmament Affairs, the UN Institute for Disarmament Research, UNHCR, OHCHR, WFP and six other UN bodies also contribute to addressing the obstacles to humanitarian access and development caused by cluster munitions and to preventing humanitarian crises.

[206] See, e.g., common Article 3.

[207] See, e.g., Article 5, paragraph 3, *1977 Additional Protocol I*, and Article 24, *1977 Additional Protocol II*.

[208] See Maslen, S., *Cluster Bombs and Landmines in Kosovo: Explosive Remnants of War* (Geneva: ICRC, 2001), available at: <http://www.icrc.org/web/eng/siteeng0.nsf/htmlall/explosive-remnants-of-war-brochure-311201?opendocument> (accessed 8 March 2010).

[209] In 2007, the ICRC hosted an Expert Meeting to look at the various challenges of cluster munitions. See *Humanitarian, Military, Technical and legal Challenges of Cluster Munitions, Expert Meeting – Montreux, Switzerland, 18–20 April 2007*, ICRC, available at: <http://www.icrc.org/web/eng/siteeng0.nsf/html/p0915> (accessed 8 March 2010); and see also *supra* §0.36.

[210] Maslen, S., *Commentary on the 1997 Anti-Personnel Mine Ban Convention, op. cit.*, §0.125 and fn. 56.

collective effort of various organizations reflecting a certain form of public conscience against cluster munitions.

Eighteenth preambular paragraph: the Oslo Declaration

> *Reaffirming* the Declaration of the Oslo Conference on Cluster Munitions, by which, *inter alia*, States recognised the grave consequences caused by the use of cluster munitions and committed themselves to conclude by 2008 a legally binding instrument that would prohibit the use, production, transfer and stockpiling of cluster munitions that cause unacceptable harm to civilians, and would establish a framework for cooperation and assistance that ensures adequate provision of care and rehabilitation for victims, clearance of contaminated areas, risk reduction education and destruction of stockpiles,

0.176 The Oslo Conference on Cluster Munitions was convened by the Government of Norway and took place on 22 to 23 February 2007. Forty-nine States attended the Conference, together with several UN programmes and specialized agencies, the ICRC, and a number of NGOs. At the conclusion of the Conference, 46 of the 49 States endorsed the Oslo Declaration,[211] which expressly recognized 'the grave consequences caused by the use of cluster munitions and the need for immediate action' to address them. It marked the commencement of the 'Oslo Process' which would culminate in the adoption of the Convention on 30 May 2008 and its opening for signature five months later in Oslo.[212]

0.177 The States that endorsed the Oslo Declaration committed themselves to a number of actions, including the conclusion of 'a legally binding international instrument that will ... prohibit the use, production, transfer and stockpiling of cluster munitions that cause unacceptable harm to civilians, and establish a framework for cooperation and assistance that ensures adequate provision of care and rehabilitation to survivors and their communities, clearance of contaminated areas, risk education and destruction of stockpiles of prohibited cluster munitions'. The reaffirmation of the Declaration in the preamble of the Convention serves as an acknowledgement of the central

---

[211] The following 46 States endorsed the Oslo Declaration: Afghanistan, Angola, Argentina, Austria, Belgium, Bosnia and Herzegovina, Canada, Chile, Colombia, Croatia, Costa Rica, the Czech Republic, Denmark, Egypt, Finland, France, Germany, Guatemala, Holy See, Hungary, Iceland, Indonesia, Ireland, Italy, Jordan, Latvia, Lebanon, Liechtenstein, Lithuania, Luxembourg, Malta, Mexico, Mozambique, Netherlands, New Zealand, Norway, Peru, Portugal, Serbia, Slovakia, Slovenia, South Africa, Spain, Sweden, Switzerland and the UK. Japan, Poland, and Romania withheld their endorsement of the Declaration at the conclusion of the Conference.

[212] For a detailed history of the Oslo Process, see generally Borrie, J., *Unacceptable Harm*, *op. cit.*

role of the process that was set in train by the Oslo Conference on Cluster Munitions 15 months earlier.

Nineteenth preambular paragraph: universalization and implementation of the Convention on Cluster Munitions

> Emphasising the desirability of attracting the adherence of all States to this Convention, and *determined* to work strenuously towards the promotion of its universalisation and its full implementation,

0.178 The desire for universality of adherence to the Convention is an obvious aim for States Parties. A similar paragraph was contained in the *1997 Anti-Personnel Mine Ban Convention*, and although the negotiations leading up to its inclusion in that instrument were fractious,[213] this was not the case in the Convention on Cluster Munitions. The proposal for such a paragraph was first made by Ireland in its broader proposal to the Diplomatic Conference for amendment of the preamble:

Emphasising the desirability of attracting the adherence of all States to this Convention, and determined to work strenuously towards the promotion of its universalisation.[214]

The only change in the final text was to add 'and its full implementation' at the end of the paragraph during the Diplomatic Conference negotiations.[215] This is significant as it suggests a collective endeavour to ensure that full implementation of the Convention and not merely an individual State responsibility.

0.179 The preambular paragraph should be read in conjunction with Article 21, paragraph 1 of the Convention on Cluster Munitions, which provides that:

Each State Party shall encourage States not party to this Convention to ratify, accept, approve or accede to this Convention, with the goal of attracting the adherence of all States to this Convention.[216]

---

[213] This was due to the explicit references to where such efforts at universalization should be made. Maslen reports that:

France was especially determined that a future role of the Conference on Disarmament in the elimination of anti-personnel mines be explicitly recognized and had included a paragraph to that effect in its proposal for the preamble introduced at the Oslo Diplomatic Conference. Less contentious were the references to the United Nations and the Review Conferences of the CCW.

Maslen, S., *Commentary on the 1997 Anti-Personnel Mine Ban Convention, op. cit.*, §0.129 [footnotes omitted].

[214] 'Proposal by Ireland for the amendment of the Preamble', Diplomatic Conference doc. CCM/4, 19 May 2008.   [215] This was at the suggestion of the Philippines.

[216] See, *infra*, the commentary on this provision.

In contrast to the corresponding paragraph in the *1997 Anti-Personnel Mine Ban Convention*, however, neither Article 21, paragraph 1, nor the present preambular paragraph indicates in which fora, or by which means, promotion of adherence should take place.[217]

Twentieth preambular paragraph: the principles and rules of international humanitarian law

> *Basing* themselves on the principles and rules of international humanitarian law, in particular the principle that the right of parties to an armed conflict to choose methods or means of warfare is not unlimited, and the rules that the parties to a conflict shall at all times distinguish between the civilian population and combatants and between civilian objects and military objectives and accordingly direct their operations against military objectives only, that in the conduct of military operations constant care shall be taken to spare the civilian population, civilians and civilian objects and that the civilian population and individual civilians enjoy general protection against dangers arising from military operations,

0.180 Similar to the *1997 Anti-Personnel Mine Ban Convention*, the Convention on Cluster Munitions can be seen as having a hybrid nature that mixes elements of international humanitarian law and disarmament law.[218] This final paragraph of the preamble explicitly places the Convention on Cluster Munitions within the framework of international humanitarian law whereas its link to disarmament law implicitly stems from the fourth preambular paragraph and substantive provisions on the development, production, stockpiling and transfer of cluster munitions. One may argue that the Convention primarily derives from a humanitarian imperative given that the main driving force of the Oslo Process was the impact of cluster munitions on civilians.[219]

---

[217] Although Article 21, paragraph 2 provides that:

Each State Party shall notify the governments of all States not party to this Convention, referred to in paragraph 3 of this Article, of its obligations under this Convention, shall promote the norms it establishes and shall make its best efforts to discourage States not party to this Convention from using cluster munitions.

[218] In its statement to the closing plenary, Norway, reflecting on the Oslo Process, remarked that it had taken a 'humanitarian approach to disarmament'. See, e.g., 'Summary Record of Fourth Session of the Plenary and Closing Ceremony of the Conference', Diplomatic Conference doc. CCM/SR/4, 18 June 2008; *cf.* also Borrie, J., *Unacceptable Harm, op. cit.*, p. 314.

[219] The ICRC stated, e.g., that 'the starting-point of the Convention was international humanitarian law rather than an arms control approach'. See 'Summary Record of Eleventh Session of the Committee of the Whole', Diplomatic Conference doc. CCM/CW/SR/11, 18 June 2008, p. 8.

0.181 Furthermore, this paragraph illustrates the dual normative structure of international humanitarian law governing the use of weapons combining general principles and rules on the one hand, and specific norms on particular weapons on the other hand.[220] The issue arises when considering the proper articulation between those two types of norms and when determining 'how far the definite prohibitions are only specific expressions or materializations of the general prohibitory provision'.[221]

0.182 While some may argue that the reference to general principles of international humanitarian law in the Convention on Cluster Munitions merely results from the repetition of a similar formula, almost as a standard clause, in the preamble of treaties on weapons,[222] in fact this preambular paragraph has significant value. This paragraph not only serves to aid interpretation of certain terms but also links the Convention with existing principles and rules of international humanitarian law. This is relevant, for example, when considering the question of whether cluster munitions are inherently indiscriminate, an issue which is closely linked to that of the definition of cluster munitions under the Convention.[223] Of course, suggesting that cluster munitions are indiscriminate *per se* would mean that past uses amounted to violations of international humanitarian law,[224] an implication to which many States would have objected.[225]

0.183 The negotiation of this preambular paragraph aimed to ensure that relevant international humanitarian law norms with regard to cluster munitions were coherently reflected. The corresponding paragraph in the Draft Cluster Munitions Convention of January 2008 was slightly different from

---

[220] On this dual structure, see, e.g., Cassese, A., 'Means of Warfare: The Traditional and The New Law', *op. cit.*, p. 161; Solf, W. A., 'Weapons, Prohibited', in Bernhardt, R. (ed.), *Encyclopaedia of Public International Law*, Vol. 4 (Amsterdam: North-Holland, 2000), p. 1437.

[221] Oeter, S., 'Methods and Means of Combat', in Fleck, D. (ed.), *The Handbook of Humanitarian Law of Armed Conflicts* (Oxford: Oxford University Press, 2004), p. 114.

[222] In this regard, Cassese refers to 'a phenomenon of "viscosity" of legal notions and phrases, that frequently occurs in legislative drafting'. Cassese, A., 'Weapons causing unnecessary suffering: are they prohibited?', *Rivista di diritto internazionale*, Vol. 58, 1975, p. 23.

[223] See further *infra* the commentary on Article 2, paragraph 2.

[224] On the same discussion with regard to landmines, *cf.* Maslen, S., and Herby, P., 'An international ban on anti-personnel mines: History and negotiation of the "Ottawa treaty"', *International Review of the Red Cross*, No. 325, 1998, pp. 693–713.

[225] Thus, the wording of the 2007 Draft CCW Protocol on Cluster Munitions submitted by Germany was not kept. The preamble of this text read as follows:

Recognizing that cluster munitions, due to their indiscriminate effects and high risk of becoming explosive remnants of war, are of serious humanitarian concern during and after armed conflict.

See Draft CCW Protocol on Cluster Munitions submitted by Germany, UN doc. CCW/GGE/2007/WP.1.

the one finally adopted.[226] The most significant difference was the absence of the mention of certain rules and principles of international humanitarian law. Ireland's proposal to the Diplomatic Conference to amend the preamble was to replace the word 'guided' by 'basing themselves' using the same phrasing as the preamble to the *1997 Anti-Personnel Mine Ban Convention*. Most notably, it added a reference to other rules of international humanitarian law.[227] Following the decision by the President of the Conference to leave the discussions to the end of the negotiations, this proposal was discussed on 27 May 2008 at the thirteenth session of the Committee of the Whole.[228]

0.184 When addressing the significance of this final paragraph and the proper relationship between the Convention on Cluster Munitions and the general principles and rules contained in the preamble, the case of the *1997 Anti-Personnel Mine Ban Convention* is an interesting one. While the former refers to principles and rules aimed at protecting civilians, the preambular paragraph on general principles of the 1997 Convention also mentions the principle that prohibits the employment in armed conflicts of weapons, projectiles, and means and methods of warfare of a nature to cause superfluous injury or unnecessary suffering. It could therefore be argued that this principle served as a legal rationale to prohibit the use of anti-personnel mines,[229] and that this was not

---

[226] The paragraph in the preamble of the Draft Convention reads as follows:

Guided by the principle of international humanitarian law that the right of parties to an armed conflict to choose methods or means of warfare is not unlimited, and in particular on the general rule that parties to a conflict must at all times distinguish between the civilian population and combatants and between civilian objects and military objectives and accordingly direct their operations against military objectives only.

[227] See 'Proposal by Ireland for the amendment of the Preamble', Diplomatic Conference doc. CCM/4, 19 May 2008. The new paragraph reads as follows:

Basing themselves on the rules of international humanitarian law that the right of parties to an armed conflict to choose methods or means of warfare is not unlimited, that the parties to a conflict shall at all times distinguish between the civilian population and combatants and between civilian objects and military objectives and accordingly direct their operations only against military objectives, *that in the conduct of military operations constant care shall be taken to spare the civilian population, civilians and civilian objects and that the civilian population and individual civilians enjoy general protection against dangers arising from military operations,'* (original emphasis).

See also Friend of the President non-papers of 26 and 27 May 2008 (copies on file with the author).

[228] 'Summary Record of Thirteenth Session of the Committee of the Whole', Diplomatic Conference doc. CCM/CW/SR/13, 18 June 2008.

[229] See Henckaerts, J.-M. and Doswald-Beck, L., *Customary International Humanitarian Law— Volume 1: Rules, op. cit.*, p. 241. In addition to the discussion in the context of the ICRC's SIrUS Project (*cf.* Coupland, R. M., 'Abhorrent weapons and superfluous injury or unnecessary suffering: from field surgery to law', *British Medical Journal*, Vol. 315, 1997, p. 1450), see ICRC, *Les armes*

the case in the Convention on Cluster Munitions. On the other hand, effects of anti-personnel fragmentation weapons towards combatants already raised concern in the past vis-à-vis the prohibition of unnecessary suffering.[230]

0.185 The discussions on the final paragraph during the conference led to a broadening of the reference to norms of international humanitarian law. With a view to also contributing to solving the issue of additional provisions governing the relationship with other treaties, the Netherlands suggested to include further principles of international humanitarian law, by changing the first line of the paragraph as stated in the Draft Cluster Munitions Convention to read as follows:

basing themselves upon already existing rules and norms of international humanitarian law, including the principle (delete international humanitarian law) that the right of parties to an armed conflict to choose methods or means of warfare is not unlimited (…).[231]

To stress the importance of the principles at stake Mexico proposed to use 'particularly' instead of 'including'.[232] To avoid redundancy, Austria suggested deleting the words 'already existing'.[233] Following those discussions, the phrasing adopted in the Presidency Paper draft Convention on Cluster Munitions of 28 May 2008[234] referred both to 'principles and rules of international humanitarian law' and spelled out the relevant norms on which the Convention is based. Also worth noting is the use of the term 'principle' concerning the absence of an unlimited right to choose means and methods of warfare whereas the other norms are referred to as 'rules'. This was done in order to separate the very general principle from more concrete rules which were to follow.

---

de nature à causer des maux superflus ou à frapper sans discrimination, Rapport sur les travaux d'un groupe d'experts, ICRC, Geneva, 1973, p. 79, para. 247; Coupland, R. M., 'Antipersonnel Mines: Why a Ban?', *Community Eye Health Journal*, Vol. 10, 1997, No. 23, pp. 33–35, and Sommaruga, C., 'Does the nature of mine injuries also justify a total ban?', *Landmines: Demining News from the United Nations*, Vol. 1.4, September 1996, p. 11.

[230] A Working Paper submitted to the Diplomatic Conference in 1974 specifically referred to 'cluster warheads with bomblets which act through the ejection of a great number of small calibred fragments or pellets' and called for their prohibition of use on the basis of both the principle against causing superfluous injury or unnecessary suffering, and the prohibition on indiscriminate attacks. See *Working Paper submitted by Egypt, Mexico, Norway, Sudan, Sweden, Switzerland and Yugoslavia to the Diplomatic Conference on the reaffirmation and development of international humanitarian law applicable in armed conflict*, CDDH/DT/2, 21 February 1974, pp. 8–9 (on file with the author). On this example, *cf.* also Borrie, J., *Unacceptable Harm, op. cit.*, pp. 5–6.

[231] See 'Summary Record of Thirteen Session of the Committee of the Whole', *op. cit.*, p. 4.

[232] *Ibid.* [233] *Ibid.*

[234] Presidency Paper, *draft* Convention on Cluster Munitions, *op. cit.*

0.186 The final paragraph details the norms of international humanitarian law that serve as a basis for the regulation of cluster munitions. While the Draft Convention of January 2008 only referred to two general norms— the 'principle' of the absence of an unlimited right to choose weapons and the 'general rule' of distinction— Ireland proposed adding the rules of international humanitarian law whereby 'in the conduct of military operations constant care shall be taken to spare the civilian population, civilians and civilian objects and that the civilian population and individual civilians enjoy general protection against dangers arising from military operations'.[235] The desire to protect civilians against the effects of cluster munitions is the primary *raison d'être* of the Convention.[236]

0.187 Article 22 of the *1907 Hague Regulations* lays down the principle that 'the right of belligerents to adopt means of injuring the enemy is not unlimited'. *1977 Additional Protocol I* restates this principle in a broader scope: 'In any armed conflict, the right of the Parties to the conflict to choose methods or means of warfare is not unlimited.'[237] The 'means of warfare' refer to the weapons, arms, or projectiles, whereas the 'methods' relate to the way in which weapons are used.[238] Those terms ultimately cover the two issues that may arise when considering the legality of the use of a weapon and are fully relevant for cluster munitions: either those weapons are inherently indiscriminate or they are used in an indiscriminate manner in certain circumstances. While this vague principle does not carry much effect in itself, it may be read as a reaffirmation of the principle of military necessity limiting the conduct of warfare, including for means and methods of warfare. In this regard the principle of the absence of unlimited choice, likewise the principle of humanity, serves as structural element of international humanitarian law from which sub-principles developed[239] as well as norms on specific weapons.

0.188 The rule of distinction is one of the most fundamental tenets of international humanitarian law. It aims at protecting both civilians and civilian objects. The final paragraph restates this rule as contained in *1977 Additional Protocol I*.[240] It holds that:

the parties to a conflict shall at all times distinguish between the civilian population and combatants and between civilian objects and military objectives and accordingly direct their operations against military objectives only.

[235] See 'Proposal by Ireland for the amendment of the Preamble', *op. cit.*

[236] See the first, third, and fourteenth preambular paragraphs of the Convention on Cluster Munitions.   [237] See Article 35, paragraph 1.

[238] Sandoz, Y., Swinarski, C., and Zimmermann, B. (eds.), *Commentary on the Additional Protocols of 8 June 1977 to the Geneva Conventions of 12 August 1949, op. cit.*, p. 498, §1402.

[239] Oeter, S., 'Methods and Means of Combat', in Fleck, D. (ed.), *The Handbook of Humanitarian Law of Armed Conflicts, op. cit.*, p. 112.   [240] Article 48.

This general rule is materialized through more specific rules, notably the prohibition of indiscriminate attacks, which is of a customary nature, applicable in both international and non-international armed conflict.[241]

0.189 With regard to weapons, it is consequently prohibited to use means of warfare that are indiscriminate and such use is considered to constitute an indiscriminate attack. According to Article 51, paragraph 4 of *1977 Additional Protocol I* indiscriminate attacks are *inter alia* those:

(b) which employ a method or means of combat which cannot be directed at a specific military objective; or (c) which employ a method or means of combat the effects of which cannot be limited as required by international humanitarian law; and consequently which, in each such case, are of a nature to strike military objectives and civilians or civilian objects without distinction.

0.190 The potential for cluster munitions to have extensive indiscriminate effects served as the main incentive to campaign for an international ban.[242] In his opening speech to the Diplomatic Conference, the Minister for Foreign Affairs of Ireland, Mr. Micheál Martin, noted that:

there was broad consensus that cluster munitions may be indiscriminate at the time of use and that their high failure rate created a hazard of unexploded ordnance for civilians in post-conflict environments.[243]

Also of importance is that under the law on the conduct of hostilities, even when an attack is directed at a clear military objective, such an attack is prohibited as being indiscriminate if it is expected to cause incidental loss of civilian life, injury to civilians, damage to civilian objects, or a combination thereof, which would be excessive in relation to the concrete and direct military advantage anticipated.[244] This is a codification of the principle of proportionality.

0.191 The rule 'that in the conduct of military operations constant care shall be taken to spare the civilian population, civilians and civilian objects' constitutes the precautions in attack that are to be respected by a party to a conflict. It first appeared in Article 2 of 1907 Hague Convention IX with Respect to Bombardments by Naval Forces in Time of War. The wording 'constant care' is taken from *1977 Additional Protocol I*.[245] The general principle complements the principle of distinction by encompassing a series of more specific

---

[241] See Rule 11, in Henckaerts, J-M. and Doswald-Beck, L. (eds.), *Customary International Humanitarian Law—Volume 1: Rules*, *op. cit.*

[242] See e.g., Statement of Mozambique, 'Summary Record of Opening Ceremony and First Session of the Plenary', Diplomatic Conference doc. CCM/SR/1, 18 June 2008, p. 5.

[243] See 'Summary Record of Opening Ceremony and First Session of the Plenary', *op. cit.*, p. 1.

[244] See, e.g., Article 51, paragraph 5(b) of *1977 Additional Protocol I*.

[245] See Article 57, paragraph 1 of *1977 Additional Protocol I*.

obligations, notably in the application to weapons, whereby 'each party to the conflict must take all feasible precautions in the choice of means and methods of warfare with a view to avoiding, and in any event to minimizing, incidental loss of civilian life, injury to civilians and damage to civilian objects'.[246]

0.192 This reference to the rule of 'constant care to spare the civilian population, civilians and civilian objects' is unprecedented in the preamble of a treaty on weapons. This is notable as within the context of the work of the Group of Governmental Experts established by States Parties to the CCW, only half of respondent States identified the particular principle of 'constant care to spare the civilian population, civilians and civilian objects' when asked to identify existing principles of international humanitarian law applicable to the use of force during an armed conflict which they considered to be relevant to the use of munitions, including submunitions, that may become ERW.[247]

0.193 Of particular importance in the list of 'rules' contained in the twentieth preambular paragraph is the last one, the norm 'that the civilian population and individual civilians enjoy general protection against dangers arising from military operations'. This was added, together with the rule of constant care, in the Ireland's proposal to the Diplomatic Conference to amend the preamble.[248] The rule of the general protection against the effects of hostilities is a restatement from Article 51, paragraph 1, of *1977 Additional Protocol I.* The other paragraphs of this provision spell out detailed rules, including the prohibition on indiscriminate attacks, to 'give effect' to the general protection of the civilian population and individual civilians against the dangers arising from military operations. This rather neglected rule of the general protection against the effects of hostilities may be the most significant element of the last paragraph of the preamble as it sets out a broad protection for the civilians against the effects of hostilities that goes beyond the attacks themselves.

---

[246] See Article 57, paragraph 2(a)(ii), of *1977 Additional Protocol I.* See also the other paragraphs of Article 57.

[247] See McCormack, T., Mtharu, P. B., and Finnin, S., *Report on States Parties' Responses to the Questionnaire: International Humanitarian Law and Explosive Remnants of War,* Asia Pacific Centre for Military Law, University of Melbourne Law School, March 2006, p. 7.

[248] See 'Proposal by Ireland for the amendment of the Preamble', *op. cit.*

Article 1. General obligations and scope of application

Virgil Wiebe,[1] Declan Smyth, and Stuart Casey-Maslen[2]

Article 1—General obligations and scope of application

1. Each State Party undertakes never under any circumstances to:

(a) Use cluster munitions;

(b) Develop, produce, otherwise acquire, stockpile, retain or transfer to anyone, directly or indirectly, cluster munitions;

(c) Assist, encourage or induce anyone to engage in any activity prohibited to a State Party under this Convention.

2. Paragraph 1 of this Article applies, *mutatis mutandis*, to explosive bomblets that are specifically designed to be dispersed or released from dispensers affixed to aircraft.

3. This Convention does not apply to mines.

[1] The author wishes to thank Arianna Halper for invaluable research assistance.

[2] Virgil Wiebe wrote the commentary on the negotiation of Article 1 and paragraph 1; Declan Smyth wrote the commentary on Article 1, paragraph 2, and Stuart Casey-Maslen wrote the commentary on Article 1, paragraph 3, based on a draft by Christophe Lanord.

Overview of the Article

1.1 Article 1, and particularly its paragraph 1, can be considered the core of the Convention on Cluster Munitions. Article 1 lays down broad prohibitions whereby States Parties undertake 'never under any circumstances' to use, develop, produce, otherwise acquire, stockpile, retain, or transfer to anyone, directly or indirectly, all cluster munitions as defined by the Convention.[3] It also prohibits States Parties from assisting, encouraging, or inducing anyone to engage in any activity prohibited under the Convention. The provision reflects the aim of the 2007 Oslo Declaration,[4] where 46 States committed themselves to:

[c]onclude by 2008 a legally binding international instrument that will…prohibit the use, production, transfer and stockpiling of cluster munitions that cause unacceptable harm to civilians.[5]

---

[3] See, *infra*, the commentary on Article 1, paragraph 3, and on Article 2.

[4] 'Declaration, Oslo Conference on Cluster Munitions, 22–23 February 2007', contained in Annex 2 to this Commentary.

[5] Norwegian Ministry of Foreign Affairs, '46 Countries endorsed Oslo-declaration', <http://www.regjeringen.no/en/dep/ud/selected-topics/Humanitarian-efforts/46-countries-endorsed-Oslo-declaration.html?id=455360>; and Norwegian Ministry of Foreign Affairs, 'Cluster munitions to be banned by 2008', *Press release No. 21/07*, 23 February 2007, <http://www.regjeringen.no/en/dep/ud/press/News/2007/Cluster-munitions-to-be-banned-by-2008.html?id=454942> (both visited 20 May 2009).

1.2 The phrase 'never under any circumstances' means that the prohibitions in Article 1 apply at all times, including peacetime, internal disturbances and tensions, and situations of armed conflict.[6]

1.3 The Convention regulates the behaviour of States.[7] While Article 1 does not seek to regulate directly the actions of non-State armed groups (NSAGs), the two references in Article 1 to 'anyone' clearly encompass members of such groups.[8] Moreover, State Parties are obliged to prohibit to individuals and entities the acts that are prohibited to States Parties under Article 1.[9] States Parties also specify their resolve, in a preambular paragraph, whereby 'armed groups distinct from the armed forces of a State shall not, under any circumstances, be permitted to engage in any activity prohibited to a State Party to this Convention'.[10]

1.4 The object of the prohibition in paragraph 1 of Article 1 is 'cluster munitions'. Paragraph 2 of Article 1 serves to prohibit the use, production, development, acquisition, stockpiling, retention, and transfer of 'explosive bomblets',[11] as well as assisting, encouraging, or inducing others to engage in such activity. The nature and effect of explosive bomblets are very similar to those of explosive submunitions[12] but specific provision is made for such bomblets because, as they are released or dispersed from a dispenser fixed to an aircraft rather than from another munition, it was feared that they would not fall within the Convention's definition of a cluster munition.[13]

1.5 Under Article 1, paragraph 3, the Convention—and therefore its prohibitions—does not apply to any mines.[14] Certain anti-vehicle and

---

[6] *Cf.*, e.g., Krutzsch, W., and Trapp, R., *A Commentary on the Chemical Weapons Convention* (The Netherlands: Martinus Nijhoff Publishers, 1994), pp. 12–13; and Maslen, S., *Commentaries on Arms Control Treaties, Volume I: The Convention on the Prohibition of the Use, Stockpiling, Production, and Transfer of Anti-Personnel Mines and on their Destruction*, Second Edition, Oxford Commentaries on International Law (Oxford: Oxford University Press, 2005), §§1.4–1.8. Hereinafter, this work is referred to as the *Commentary on the 1997 Anti-Personnel Mine Ban Convention*.

[7] See, *supra*, §0.83 on the opening of the preamble: 'The States Parties to this Convention'.

[8] Paragraph 1(b) and (c). *Cf.*, *infra*, §1.59.

[9] Article 9; see, *infra*, the commentary in §§9.46 *et seq.*

[10] See, *supra*, the commentary on the twelfth preambular paragraph.

[11] An 'explosive bomblet' is defined in Article 2, paragraph 13, as 'a conventional munition, weighing less than 20 kilograms, which is not self-propelled and which, in order to perform its task, is dispersed or released by a dispenser, and is designed to function by detonating an explosive charge prior to, on or after impact'. A 'dispenser' is defined by Article 2, paragraph 15, as 'a container that is designed to disperse or release explosive bomblets and which is affixed to an aircraft at the time of dispersal or release'.

[12] It should be noted that prior to the adoption of the Convention colloquially the terms 'submunition' and 'bomblet' were used interchangeably, particularly in military circles. The Convention introduces a clear legal distinction between 'explosive submunitions' and 'explosive bomblets'.

[13] See further, *infra*, §§1.82–1.88.   [14] Article 1, paragraph 3.

anti-personnel mines can be delivered from a dispenser or container and might otherwise be prohibited but for this exclusion.[15] These weapons are addressed by other instruments of international law, as discussed below.[16]

Preparatory discussions and negotiations

1.6 Three issues arising in the preparatory discussions and formal negotiations that led to the agreement on Article 1 of the Convention on Cluster Munitions merit brief attention at the outset.[17] While these three issues were resolved in other Articles or ultimately not addressed at all in the Convention, States initially proposed and debated them in the context of Article 1. Those issues are as follows: (1) How would cluster munitions be defined, in light of the Oslo Declaration calling for prohibitions on cluster munitions 'that cause unacceptable harm to civilians'?;[18] (2) Would there be transition periods before all or some of the core Article 1 obligations entered into full legal force?;[19] and (3) How would the issue of 'interoperability'[20] with States not party to the Convention be resolved?[21] Additional issues emerged in the course of the negotiations and were resolved with less debate, such as the inclusion within the ambit of Article 1 of explosive bomblets[22] and issues relating to non-State armed groups (NSAGs).

Cluster munitions 'that cause unacceptable harm to civilians'

1.7 The Oslo Declaration had called for the imposition of prohibitions on use, production, transfer, and stockpiling of 'cluster munitions that cause

[15] Article 2 defines a 'mine' as 'a munition designed to be placed under, on or near the ground or other surface area and to be exploded by the presence, proximity or contact of a person or a vehicle'. Article 2, paragraph 12.

[16] See, *infra*, the commentary on Article 1, paragraph 3 (§§1.89–1.91); see also, *supra*, the commentary on the thirteenth preambular paragraph.

[17] The background discussions and negotiating history of each paragraph of Article 1 are then presented and immediately followed by commentary on each paragraph.

[18] The definition of a cluster munition is addressed by Article 2.

[19] As indicated *infra* in §§1.14–1.17, proponents of transition periods were unsuccessful.

[20] Interoperability can be explained in general terms as 'the ability of forces or agents of various States or international organisations to operate jointly in the performance of a task, mission, or operation'. See, *infra*, the commentary on Article 21, *esp.* in §21.2.

[21] Interoperability is covered by Article 21, a provision dedicated to relations with States not party to this Convention.

[22] These issues are addressed *infra* in §1.82 and in the commentary on Article 3.

unacceptable harm to civilians'.[23] Intentionally imprecise, the ambiguity of this phrase served to attract a wider number of States to the discussions.[24] The phrase is not formally defined in the treaty, nor was it ultimately contained in any of its articles, although it is included in the eighteenth preambular paragraph that refers to the Oslo Declaration. As the discussions unfolded, two approaches to resolving this ambiguity emerged: the 'split cluster munitions into categories' approach, and the 'define and ban' approach.[25]

1.8 The Lima Discussion Text[26] embodied what became the 'split cluster munitions into categories' approach. It included a single paragraph for Article 1 which would have introduced prohibitions on specifically defined cluster munitions 'because of their unacceptable harm to civilians and civilian objects during and after use'.[27] Article 2 of that draft text defined the weapons systems that would be 'considered prohibited cluster munitions under this treaty'. The draft would not have prohibited systems with explosive submunitions 'designed to, manually or automatically, aim, detect and engage point targets'.[28] This approach would have created two classes of cluster munitions: i.e. cluster munitions prohibited by the Convention and those not prohibited.[29]

[23] For a detailed history of the formulation of the Oslo Declaration, see Borrie, J., *Unacceptable Harm: A History of How the Treaty to Ban Cluster Munitions Was Won* (New York and Geneva: UN and UN Institute for Disarmament Research, 2009), pp. 121–157. See *esp.* p. 154 for the breadth of early interpretations of the phrase by different States.

[24] The Oslo Declaration might be read to imply that certain cluster munitions might cause *acceptable harm* to civilians, presumably those which either through their use or design accord with the general principles of international humanitarian law. To those arguing that *all* cluster munitions caused unacceptable harm (particularly those that had been used in combat up to that date), the phrase could be interpreted as calling for a complete ban. The ambiguity created space for negotiations amongst a broader range of players, from smaller States without any such munitions in their arsenals to large producers and users.   [25] Borrie, J., *Unacceptable Harm, op. cit.*, p. 146.

[26] Chair's discussion text on a legally binding international instrument that will prohibit the use, production, transfer and stockpiling of cluster munitions that cause unacceptable harm to civilians, Lima, 23–25 May 2007.

[27] Article 1, Lima Discussion Text, contained in Annex 3 to this Commentary.

[28] Article 2, Lima Discussion Text. The draft article reads as follows:

The following weapons systems shall be considered prohibited cluster munitions under this treaty:

Air carried dispersal systems or air delivered, surface or sub-surface launched containers, that are designed to disperse explosive sub-munitions intended to detonate following separation from the container or dispenser, unless they are designed to, manually or automatically, aim, detect and engage point targets, or are meant for smoke or flaring, or unless their use is regulated or prohibited under other treaties.

[29] The ICRC, e.g., had proposed to ban 'inaccurate and unreliable' cluster munitions. The definition in the Lima text sought to encompass this notion without using it as an actual definition of cluster munitions. See, e.g., Borrie, J., *Unacceptable Harm, op. cit.*, pp. 168–169.

1.9 The views of States at the Lima Conference on Cluster Munitions (the 'Lima Conference') on the scope of the weapons to be covered by the prohibition are said to have 'ranged across a spectrum of those advocating a total ban of all and any cluster munitions, those wishing to draw a line between unacceptable cluster munitions and those which can be used responsibly without endangering civilians, and those advocating a more limited ban exempting cluster munitions with self-destruct mechanisms and certain failure rates'.[30]

1.10 In the Vienna Discussion Text,[31] prepared for the December 2007 Vienna Conference,[32] the draft Article 1 took the 'define and ban' approach, which included a prohibition of all 'cluster munitions' as defined. Under this approach the term 'unacceptable harm to civilians and civilian objects' would be explained only indirectly, by defining what cluster munitions are—or are not—under Article 2, paragraph 2. This approach eventually prevailed, with language of the Vienna Discussion Text for Article 1, paragraph 1,[33] carried through verbatim to the Draft Convention submitted to the May 2008

---

[30] Harrison, K., 'Report from the Lima Conference on Cluster Munitions, 23–25 May 2007', Women's International League for Peace and Freedom. See also Handicap International, 'In Brief: Update From Lima Conference, May 24 2007', available at <http://www.handicap-international. us/our-fight-against-landmines-and-cluster-bombs/in-brief>; and Tice, S., 'Cluster Munitions: The Ban Process', *Journal of Mine Action*, Summer 2008, <http://maic.jmu.edu/JOURNAL/12.1/ sp/tice/tice.htm> (both accessed 1 February 2010). e.g., France took the position that some cluster munitions would be prohibited and others authorized. Permanent Mission of France to the Conference on Disarmament, 'Intervention de la délégation française concernant la définition des armes à sous munitions, Conférence de Lima, Lima, 24 mai 2007', <http://www.delegfrance-cd-geneve.org/declarations/ssdos_decl_sous_munitions/definition_lima24050/.htm>. See also Permanent Mission of France to the Conference on Disarmament, 'French non-paper on Cluster munitions', 19 April 2007, <http://www.delegfrance-cd-geneve.org/declarations/ssdos_decl_sous_munitions/non-pap-ENG.htm> (both visited 1 February 2010), proposing characteristics of 'prohibited cluster munitions' and 'authorised cluster munitions'. It is further reported that: 'States in favor of...exemptions [for large categories of submunitions] included Australia, Denmark, Finland, France, Germany, Japan, Poland, and the United Kingdom.' Goose, S. D., 'Cluster Munitions: Ban Them', *Arms Control Today*, January/February 2008, <http://www. armscontrol.org/act/2008_01–02/goose> (accessed 21 March 2010).

[31] Vienna Discussion Text of 14 November 2007, included in Annex 4 to this Commentary.

[32] See, *supra*, §§0.43–0.46 for a summary of the Vienna Conference.

[33] The text was as follows:

Article 1 – General obligations and scope of application
Each State Party undertakes never under any circumstances to:
a) Use cluster munitions.
b) Develop, produce, otherwise acquire, stockpile, retain or transfer to anyone, directly or indirectly, cluster munitions.
c) Assist, encourage or induce anyone to engage in any activity prohibited to a State Party under this Convention.

Vienna Discussion Text.

Diplomatic Conference in Dublin[34] and into the final text of the Convention it adopted.[35]

1.11 The controversy between the two approaches was not resolved until Dublin. Some States were concerned that newer versions of cluster munitions containing explosive submunitions equipped with point target detection would be banned under the treaty, and still others sought to retain older versions of cluster munitions.[36] Several States, including Austria, Cambodia, Ghana, Indonesia, and Mexico, are said to have 'supported more all-encompassing definitions that made no allowances for any weapons that employ explosive submunitions'.[37]

1.12 The definition of cluster munitions in the Vienna Discussion Text omitted any proposal of what weapons systems would—and would not—be covered by the Convention, leaving ellipses in Article 2, paragraph 2(c) to indicate the need for further elaboration.[38] While the discussions at the Vienna

---

[34] Article 1, paragraph 1, Draft Cluster Munitions Convention, contained in Annex 5 to this Commentary.

[35] Article 1, paragraph 1. It has since been argued that this shift to a 'precautionary approach' potentially represented a significant shift in the negotiation of international arms control agreements, i.e. that the burden of proof shifted from States having to argue what types of munitions should be ruled out of bounds, to having to argue what weapons should be allowed. Rappert, B., and Moyes, R., 'The Prohibition of Cluster Munitions: Setting International Precedents for Defining Inhumanity,' *Nonproliferation Review*, Vol. 16, No. 2, July 2009, pp. 237, 238, and 245–246. At p. 247, Rappert and Moyes argue that:

> [F]or small states with minimal diplomatic resources and technical expertise, requiring exclusions to be 'argued in' enabled them to actively participate in a critical area of the process. They did not need to substantiate what should be prohibited. Throughout the Oslo Process, a variety of states—including Indonesia, Botswana, Cambodia, Fiji, Guatemala, Zambia, Ghana, Jamaica, Lebanon, and the Cook Islands—drew on considerations such as the history of humanitarian problems with cluster munitions to argue that specific proposed exemptions or exclusions based on factors such as failure rates, 'direct fire' capacity, and limits on the number of submunitions had not been sufficiently demonstrated.

[36] Borrie, J., 'How the Cluster Munition Ban was Won: Oslo Treaty Negotiations Conclude in Dublin', *Disarmament Diplomacy*, Summer 2008. According to Borrie:

> France, Germany, Japan, the Netherlands and the UK [were] especially active. This group included countries like Finland, Japan and Slovakia, which appeared deeply attached to retaining many, if not all, of their cluster munition arsenals including the types of cluster munition demonstrated to be particularly problematic. It also included countries such as Australia and Canada…The first major concern was that an eventual ban on cluster munitions causing unacceptable harm would encapsulate weapons they possessed (or would like to possess) which have submunitions that use sensor-fusing technologies to detect and engage individual targets.

See also Borrie, J., *Unacceptable Harm, op. cit.*, pp. 206–208, and 266–275.

[37] Rappert, B., and Moyes, R., 'The Prohibition of Cluster Munitions: Setting International Precedents for Defining Inhumanity', *op. cit.*, p. 245.

[38] Article 2, paragraph 2, Vienna Discussion Text. The commentary attached to the Vienna Discussion Text described the process as follows:

Conference certainly did not resolve the issue of what constituted 'unacceptable harm to civilians and civilian objects', they did attempt to move those discussions out of Article 1 and into Article 2 of the Convention.[39] Following the Conference, the core group of States driving the Oslo Process produced a Draft Cluster Munitions Convention in January 2008. This was done in advance of the Wellington Conference due to be held in February 2008.[40] Following the approach of the Vienna Discussion Text, the Draft Convention applied the prohibitions to all cluster munitions, while leaving the definition of just what the term 'cluster munitions' meant for further negotiations.[41]

1.13 Discussions continued at the February 2008 Wellington Conference. The Draft Convention issued in January was forwarded unchanged to the Diplomatic Conference as the formal basis for negotiation.[42] A 'Compendium of Proposals' was also produced to allow States to present their proposals that they felt had not been adequately considered in the Draft Convention.[43] Several of those proposals called for prohibitions in Article 1 to be placed on cluster munitions or submunitions 'as defined in Article 2',[44] thereby attempting to preserve the distinction between 'acceptable' and 'unacceptable' cluster munitions.[45] This debate was renewed at the Diplomatic Conference. Despite

There were other proposals to exclude sub-munitions that aim, detect and engage point targets, and some States proposed to exclude cluster munitions which contain fewer than a specified number of explosive sub-munitions, sub-munitions with self destruct or self deactivation or other failsafe mechanisms, explosive sub-munitions with a tested failure rate of less than a specified percentage, and that the age of the sub-munition should be relevant. Some other States opposed some or all of these elements, with some proposing a comprehensive prohibition on all cluster munitions.

Article 2: Definitions, Vienna Discussion Text Explanatory Annex, 14 November 2007.

[39] See Borrie, J., *Unacceptable Harm, op. cit.,* pp. 187–188.

[40] See, *supra*, §§0.48–0.54 for details of the Wellington Conference.

[41] Draft Cluster Munitions Convention, 21 January 2008.

[42] It became a conference document at the Diplomatic Conference. 'Draft Convention on Cluster Munitions', Diplomatic Conference doc. CCM/3, 19 May 2008.

[43] Compendium of Proposals Submitted by Delegations during the Wellington Conference (hereinafter, the 'Wellington Compendium'), contained in Annex 6 to this Commentary.

[44] See, e.g., French and Swiss proposals calling for prohibitions on 'cluster munitions as defined in article 2', Wellington Compendium, Addendum 1, p. 6; and UK proposal calling for prohibitions on 'submunitions as defined in Article 2b'. *Ibid.*, pp. 6–7. The Wellington Compendium is included in Annex 6 to this Commentary.

[45] In the Wellington Compendium (at p. 8), Australia, Canada, Denmark, Finland, France, Germany, Italy, Japan, Netherlands, and the UK included a draft definition, prefaced by the following statement:

The following text was developed in response to discussions on cluster munition definitions and captures significant issues requiring further consideration in order to develop an agreed definition of 'cluster munitions that cause unacceptable harm to civilians'. This text is

a number of proposed amendments to the Draft Convention,[46] the approach taken in the Draft Convention ultimately prevailed, although not until the final day of active negotiations.[47] The definition of what constitute 'cluster munitions' (and therefore what were covered by the Article 1 prohibitions) was resolved in the negotiations around Article 2, paragraph 2.[48]

Transition periods

1.14 An issue raised early[49] in the process and only resolved on the final day of active negotiations at the Diplomatic Conference was that of a transition period on the prohibitions on use, production, and transfer of cluster munitions following entry into force. States in favour of such transition periods argued that time was needed to develop alternative weapons systems in national defence capabilities. Such an approach would encourage States possessing the weapons to adhere to the treaty sooner rather than later and force them to develop concrete plans to make cluster munitions obsolete.[50] States and civil society groups who opposed such transition periods argued that such an approach would undermine

proposed for inclusion in the Compendium to be attached to, and which is understood to have equal status with, the Draft Convention.

[46] 'Proposal by France for the amendment of Article 1', Diplomatic Conference doc. CCM 11, 19 May 2008, calling for prohibitions on 'cluster munitions **as defined in Article 2**' (original emphasis); 'Proposal by Switzerland for the amendment of Article 1', Diplomatic Conference doc. CCM 12, 19 May 2008; and 'Proposal by the United Kingdom for the amendment of Article 1', Diplomatic Conference doc. CCM 13, 19 May 2009, calling for prohibitions on '**sub-munitions as defined in Article 2b**' (original emphasis).

[47] 'Presidency Paper, *draft* Convention on Cluster Munitions', Diplomatic Conference doc. CCM/PT/15, 28 May 2008.   [48] See, *infra*, the commentary on Article 2, paragraph 2.

[49] See e.g. UK statement made at Oslo in February 2007:

[W]e agree with others that the conclusion of a legally binding instrument is our aspiration and that in common with other such agreements a transition period will be required in the final instrument itself.

Final Statement by Ambassador John Duncan, UK Ambassador for Multilateral Arms Control and Disarmament, Oslo Conference on Cluster Munitions, 22–23 February 2007, <http://ukunarmscontrol.fco.gov.uk/resources/en/pdf/pdf1/postgv_statementatosloconference> (accessed 8 March 2010).

[50] In a draft protocol first advocated at a meeting of experts convened by the ICRC in April 2007 at Montreux (and later submitted as a working paper at the CCW in May 2007), Germany proposed a transition period allowing for use:

It is prohibited in all circumstances to use any cluster munitions as defined in Article 2 [...] years after this Protocol enters into force for the respective High Contracting Party. . . . Pending the entry into force of the prohibition under the first sentence of this paragraph, the respective High Contracting Party undertakes to use cluster munitions only as a last resort if no other type of munition is available to reach the desired military advantage.

UN doc. CCW/GGE/2007/WP.1 1 May 2007, p. 7. At the Montreux meeting, transition periods of up 10 years were discussed. ICRC, *Humanitarian, Military, Technical And Legal Challenges Of*

the Convention: if cluster munitions were worthy of being banned due to the excessive harm they caused to civilians, allowing them to be used, produced, or transferred, for example, for a set period of years seemed difficult to justify and would frustrate the object and purpose of the Convention.

1.15 At the February 2008 Wellington Conference, the UK stated that

if transition periods are agreed, Article 1 is the right place to include them. There is an argument that in the real world of delivering an improvement to those whose communities are affected by Cluster Munitions, rather than having no commitment from possessing states at all, it would be better to put in place a structured plan for the removal from service of weapons systems.[51]

In contrast, on 1 April 2008 at the conclusion of the Livingstone Conference on Cluster Munitions,[52] 39 African States declared that a 'prohibition should be total and immediate from the convention's entry into force in order to prevent further suffering'.[53] The view of the Cluster Munition Coalition (CMC) was that 'any treaty on cluster munitions must include... [n]o provision for a transition period on the prohibition on use, production and transfer [and] [n]o geographic exceptions for the prohibition on use, production and transfer'.[54]

1.16 The Dublin Diplomatic Conference rejected transition periods. While a number of States argued vigorously for transition periods, a significant majority of States opposed them. On behalf of the participating African States, Zambia restated its opposition to transition periods based upon the Livingstone Declaration.[55] Several other States[56] made it clear at the outset of the Diplomatic Conference that they opposed transition periods, particularly

---

Cluster Munitions, Expert Meeting, Montreux, Switzerland, 18 to 20 April 2007, ICRC, Geneva, 2007, pp. 77–78.

[51] Statement by Ambassador John Duncan, UK Ambassador for Multilateral Arms Control and Disarmament, Wellington Conference, 18 February 2008, paragraph 14. The UK delegation included such a proposal in the Wellington Compendium:

For the purposes of this Convention, Article 1 does not come in to force until [x] years after entry in to [*sic*] force of the Convention.

Wellington Compendium, p. 7. The UK renewed this proposal at the Diplomatic Conference; see fn. 58 *infra*.

[52] For details of the Conference, see e.g. the report by the CMC, available at: <http://www.stopclustermunitions.org/wp/wp-content/uploads/2008/05/report-on-livingston-conference-31-march-1-april.pdf> (accessed 8 March 2010).

[53] Livingstone Declaration on Cluster Munitions, 1 April 2008, para. 14, available at: <http://www.issafrica.org/uploads/LIVINGSTONEDECL.PDF> (accessed 8 March 2010).

[54] CMC, '(Revised) Observations by the Cluster Munition Coalition on the Draft Cluster Munitions Convention, dated 21 January 2008', p. 13 (Annex A).

[55] See 'Summary Record of Opening Ceremony and First Session of the Plenary', Diplomatic Conference doc. CCM/SR/1, 18 June 2008, pp. 4–5.

[56] Argentina, Guatemala, Indonesia, Malta, and Venezuela.

with respect to use.[57] In contrast, both Japan and the UK tabled proposals for transition periods to be included in Article 1, though without suggesting a specific time period. Japan's proposals were limited to transition periods on use only and in the form of country-specific declarations, while the UK proposal would have applied to Article 1 in its entirety and to all States Parties.[58]

1.17 At the end of the first week of negotiations, five States in a session of the Committee of the Whole sought to preserve the possibility of including transition periods by postponing final discussions on the issue. In response, more than 50 States expressed opposition to any transition periods. Further discussion the following Monday (26 May), resulted in no change of position.[59] In announcing and defending the President's draft text on 28 May 2008, Ambassador O'Ceallaigh simply stated that: 'There will be no transition period for use of cluster munitions.'[60]

'Interoperability' and assisting, encouraging, or inducing prohibited activities

1.18 The issue of 'interoperability', and specifically the participation by States Parties in joint military operations (including those mandated by

---

[57] 'Summary Record of First Session of the Committee of the Whole', Diplomatic Conference doc. CCM/CW/SR/1, 18 June 2008, pp. 1–3.

[58] Japan suggested two alternatives:

Any State Party may declare at the time of the deposit of its instruments of ratification, acceptance, approval or accession that, while implementing paragraph 1 of this Article, it will continue to use, only when strictly necessary, cluster munitions for a limited period of time not exceeding [x] years from the entry into force of this Convention for that State Party...

or

In the event that a State Party determines that it cannot immediately comply with paragraph 1 (a) of this Article, it may declare at the time of the deposit of its instruments of ratification, acceptance, approval or accession that it will defer compliance with paragraph 1 (a) of this Article for a period not to exceed [X] years from the entry into force of this Convention for that State Party. During this period, a State Party may use cluster munitions only when strictly necessary.

Proposal by Japan for the amendment of Article 1, Diplomatic Conference doc. CCM/10, 19 May 2008. The UK proposed more direct and sweeping language, the same it had put forward at the Wellington Conference:

For the purposes of this Convention, Article 1 does not come in to force until [x] years after entry in to force of the Convention.

'Proposal by the United Kingdom for the amendment of Article 1', Diplomatic Conference doc. CCM/14, 19 May 2008.

[59] 'Summary Record of Eighth Session of the Committee of the Whole', Diplomatic Conference doc. CCM/CW/SR/8, 18 June 2008, pp. 5–7; Summary Record of Eleventh Session of the Committee of the Whole'; Diplomatic Conference doc. CCM/CW/SR/11, 18 June 2008, p. 11.

[60] 'Summary Record of Fifteenth Session of the Committee of the Whole', Diplomatic Conference doc. CCM/CW/SR/15, 18 June 2008, p. 2.

the United Nations (UN) Security Council), with States not party to the Convention on Cluster Munitions, proved to be a major point of contention in the final negotiations of Article 1 from the beginning of the Diplomatic Conference until the final day of negotiations. Several States were concerned that military cooperation with States not party could generate criminal liability for their personnel as well as responsibility for the States Parties, or that through such military cooperation they might risk being accused of assisting, encouraging, or inducing the use of cluster munitions.[61] In opposing specific language addressing interoperability, other States and civil society groups looked to the *1997 Anti-Personnel Mine Ban Convention* as a model for how such issues had been addressed previously without the need for a separate article.

1.19 Until the negotiations at the Dublin Diplomatic Conference in May 2008, most of the debate centred on proposals to amend the text of Article 1. Resolution was, however, reached through the creation of additional provisions in Article 21 on Relations with States not party to this Convention.[62] Following the formal adoption of the Convention on 30 May 2008, a number of States addressed interoperability directly in their statements. Norway declared that: 'Regarding Article 21 in the Convention we note that delegations from all regions agree that this convention does not hinder future international military operations, even if some participating states may not be party to the convention';[63] Canada 'regarded it as an essential element to legally protect joint military operations, which actually strengthened the Convention'; and Hungary 'welcomed Article 21 of the Convention as an appropriate solution to safeguard peacekeeping and humanitarian operations'.[64]

1.20 Other States criticized Article 21 or sought to limit its reach following the formal adoption of the Convention on 30 May 2008. Argentina maintained the view that while 'it was part of the necessary consensus', it 'should not appear in the Convention, on the basis that this Article generates uncertainty without contributing to the aims of the Convention'; Venezuela 'was unhappy with the provision on interoperability, which it regarded as undermining the spirit and

---

[61] The US, a major possessor, producer, user, and exporter of cluster munitions, had made it clear that it would not be participating in the Oslo Process. US allies had been especially alerted to the potential difficulties with military cooperation with States not party and the effect this may have on military operations in the future.

[62] See the commentary on the negotiating history of Article 21 for details of these discussions in §§21.14 *et seq.*

[63] Statement 30 May 2008 by Norway, <http://www.regjeringen.no/nb/dep/ud/dep/org/avdelinger/avdeling_fn/avdelingsdirektor-steffen-kongstad/taler-og-artikler/2008/cluster_munition.html?id=516100> (accessed 1 March 2010).

[64] 'Summary Record of Fourth Session of the Plenary and Closing Ceremony of the Conference', Diplomatic Conference doc. CCM/SR/4, 18 June 2008, pp. 2–3.

purpose of the Convention'; Costa Rica 'would have preferred . . . more rigour in Article 21'; and Zambia 'expressed its understanding that Article 21 would not create a loophole for States Parties to allow the indefinite stockpiling and transit of cluster munitions on their territories'.[65] Iceland stated that 'Article 21 of the Convention dealt with particular concerns regarding joint military operations with States not party, without allowing for departure from the specific obligations of the Convention.'[66] The interaction between Article 1 and Article 21 is discussed further below.[67]

Paragraph 1

Each State Party undertakes never under any circumstances to:

(a) Use cluster munitions;

(b) Develop, produce, otherwise acquire, stockpile, retain or transfer to anyone, directly or indirectly, cluster munitions;

(c) Assist, encourage or induce anyone to engage in any activity prohibited to a State Party under this Convention.

Preparatory discussions and negotiations

1.21 Article 1, paragraph 1 of the Convention is very similar in content to Article 1 of the *1997 Anti-Personnel Mine Ban Convention*,[68] which in turn drew

---

[65] *Ibid.*, pp. 3–7.

[66] Statement by the Government of Iceland upon the adoption of the Convention on Cluster Munitions, Dublin, 30 May 2008, available at: <http://www.clustermunitionsdublin.ie/pdf/IcelandStatementGE.pdf> (accessed 8 March 2010). Iceland further stated that:

While the article sets out an appeal to States which are not parties to join the regime of the Convention, it recognizes the need for continuing cooperation in what is hoped will be a short transition period. This intention is captured clearly in paragraph 3 of the Article which should not be read as entitling States Parties to avoid their specific obligations under the Convention for this limited purpose. The decision to reinforce this position by listing some examples in paragraph 4 cannot therefore be interpreted to allow departures in other respects.

[67] See, *infra*, §§1.62 *et seq.* and §§21.13 *et seq.*

[68] The formal title of this treaty is the Convention on the Prohibition of the Use, Stockpiling, Production and Transfer of Anti-Personnel Mines and on Their Destruction. Article 1, paragraph 1 reads as follows:

Each State Party undertakes never under any circumstances:

a. To use anti-personnel mines;

b. To develop, produce, otherwise acquire, stockpile, retain or transfer to anyone, directly or indirectly, anti-personnel mines;

c. To assist, encourage or induce, in any way, anyone to engage in any activity prohibited to a State Party under this Convention.

heavily upon the language of Article 1, paragraph 1 of the *1993 Chemical Weapons Convention.*[69] The earliest 'discussion text' of the treaty, the Lima Discussion Text,[70] contained all four prohibitions referred to in the Oslo Declaration (production, stockpiling, transfer, and use),[71] and was reported to be 'largely modelled' on what is laid down in Article 1 of the *1997 Anti-Personnel Mine Ban Convention.*[72] As in that Convention, the Lima Discussion Text also prohibited the related activities of acquisition and retention of cluster munitions and banned assisting, encouraging, or inducing anyone to engage in prohibited activities.

1.22 The Convention as adopted differed in three main ways from the Lima Discussion Text. First, the negotiating States removed the opening phrase of Article 1, paragraph 1—'Because of their unacceptable harm to civilians and civilian objects during and after use,'—and referenced it instead in a preambular paragraph (the eighteenth). Second, they applied the prohibitions to all cluster munitions, as opposed to 'cluster munitions as defined in article 2', by arriving at a definition of cluster munitions that excluded weapons with specific, multiple safety features.[73] Finally, they removed the phrase 'in any way' from paragraph 1(c).[74]

1.23 At the Diplomatic Conference in Dublin, the Philippines proposed adding the scope provisions found in *2003 Protocol V* of the *Convention on*

---

[69] The formal title of this treaty is the Convention on the Prohibition of the Development, Production, Stockpiling and Use of Chemical Weapons and on their Destruction. Article 1, paragraph 1 reads as follows:

Each State Party to this Convention undertakes never under any circumstances:

    (a) To develop, produce, otherwise acquire, stockpile or retain chemical weapons, or transfer, directly or indirectly, chemical weapons to anyone;

    (b) To use chemical weapons;

    (c) To engage in any military preparations to use chemical weapons;

    (d) To assist, encourage or induce, in any way, anyone to engage in any activity prohibited to a State Party under this Convention.

[70] See Annex 3 to this Commentary.

[71] Article 1 of the Lima Discussion Text read as follows:

Article 1—General obligations and scope of application

Because of their unacceptable harm to civilians and civilian objects during and after use, each State Party undertakes never under any circumstances:

    a) To use cluster munitions as defined in Article 2.

    b) To develop, produce, otherwise acquire, stockpile, retain or transfer to anyone, directly or indirectly, cluster munitions as defined in Article 2.

    c) To assist, encourage or induce, in any way, anyone to engage in any activity prohibited to a State Party under this convention.

[72] Cluster Munition Coalition (CMC), 'Report on the Lima Conference on Cluster Munitions and Next Steps', undated, p. 1.

[73] See, *supra*, §§1.10–1.12, for a review of these changes.

[74] See, *infra*, §1.62 for a brief discussion of the reasons for the deletion of the phrase.

Certain Conventional Weapons (CCW),[75] which specifically apply in situations of armed conflict.[76] A desire to encompass acts by NSAGs may have motivated the proposal, as the Philippines included in it an additional paragraph on NSAGs.[77] The proposal's supporters claimed it supplemented the 'under any circumstances' language by stating that the treaty would 'also apply' to such conflict situations.[78] Clearly, however, situations of armed conflict are covered by the wording 'never under any circumstances' but the language would have created confusion about the meaning of this latter term. The proposal was not adopted.

Commentary

The comprehensive nature of the obligations

1.24 While the text of Article 1 of the Convention draws heavily upon the 1997 *Anti-Personnel Mine Ban Convention*, its title differs by adding the phrase 'and scope of application' after 'General obligations'. The term 'Scope of Application' is normally reserved for treaties addressing international humanitarian law, which apply particularly to situations of armed conflict, while other treaties are not so restricted. Nevertheless, the meaning of the entire title 'General obligations and scope of application' of Article 1 is made clear in the first line of the article, where each State Party 'undertakes never under any circumstances'.

---

[75] The formal title of this treaty is the Convention on Prohibitions or Restrictions on the Use of Certain Conventional Weapons Which May Be Deemed to Be Excessively Injurious or to Have Indiscriminate Effects, as amended on 21 December 2001.

[76] 'This Convention shall also apply to situations resulting from conflicts referred to in Art. 1, paragraphs 1 to 6, of the Convention on Prohibitions or Restrictions on the Use of Certain Conventional Weapons Which May Be Deemed to Be Excessively Injurious or to Have Indiscriminate Effects, as amended on 21 December 2001', referencing Article 1, paragraph 3, of *2003 Protocol V*. 'Proposal by Philippines for additional text to Article 1', Diplomatic Conference doc. CCM/56, 19 May 2008.

[77] Drawing on text in Article 4, paragraph 1 of the 2000 Optional Protocol to the Convention on the Rights of the Child on the involvement of children in armed conflict, the Philippines proposed addressing NSAGs in the Convention on Cluster Munitions in the following way:

Armed groups that are distinct from the armed forces of a State shall not, under any circumstances, engage in any activity prohibited to a State Party under this Convention.

'Proposal by Philippines for additional text to Article 1', Diplomatic Conference doc. CCM/56, 19 May 2008.

As noted *supra* in §1.3, the issue of NSAGs was ultimately addressed in the twelfth preambular paragraph of the Convention.

[78] Philippine Campaign to Ban Landmines Task Force on Cluster Munitions, 'Proposal for Coverage of Non-State Armed Groups under Art. 1 on General Obligations and Scope of Application', 12 May 2008.

1.25 With respect to the text of Article 1, paragraph 1 that served as the basis of negotiations at the Diplomatic Conference (and which was not thereafter altered), the explanatory notes of the Draft Convention on Cluster Munitions stated that:

The scope of application of the treaty is 'never under any circumstances', meaning that application of the treaty is not limited to any situation of armed conflict but applies at all times. The provision thus is largely similar to corresponding provisions in the Biological Weapons Convention, the Chemical Weapons Convention and the Anti-Personnel Mine Ban Treaty.[79]

1.26 These prohibitions on cluster munitions under the Convention are immediate and, *prima facie*, comprehensive. Consonant with the scope of application, cluster munitions may not be used at any time: in attack or defence, in times of peace, during internal disturbances or tensions, or during armed conflict, even in situations of supreme emergency threatening the survival of the nation. In addition, the wording 'any circumstances' covers all actions by a State Party wherever it exercises jurisdiction, whether geographically (within or outside its own territory) or over persons. A leading commentary on the *1993 Chemical Weapons Convention* states that the wording 'undertakes never under any circumstances' 'emphasizes the comprehensive and totally binding nature of the prohibitions' set forth and that:

This relates to the geographical scope of these prohibitions: They have a universal dimension, which means they extend to all activities of States Parties everywhere.[80]

The prohibition on use

1.27 Under Article 1, each State Party undertakes never under any circumstances to use cluster munitions.[81] This prohibition certainly encompasses any new employment of cluster munitions or explosive bomblets, other than

---

[79] Draft Cluster Munitions Convention Explanatory Notes, Wellington, 21 January 2008.

[80] Krutzsch, W., and Trapp, R., *A Commentary on the Chemical Weapons Convention, op. cit.*, p. 12. It goes on to state that:

The wording excludes any justification for such activity, whether for self-defence in the case of attack with those weapons or in other exceptional circumstances. The wording covers all intents and purposes for such activities, independent of the character of the armed conflict, whether an international or non-international one, whether the parties involved had recognized themselves or whether or not it is a civil strive [*sic*]. *Ibid.,* p. 13, footnotes omitted.

[81] Additionally, nothing in Article 21(3) on *Relations with States not party to this Convention* 'shall authorise a State Party: (c) To itself use cluster munitions, or (d) To expressly request the use of cluster munitions in cases where the choice of munitions used is within its exclusive control.' Article 21, paragraph 4.

in strict accord with the purposes permitted under Article 3, paragraph 6 of the Convention on Cluster Munitions, i.e. 'the development of and training in cluster munition and explosive submunition detection, clearance or destruction techniques, or for the development of cluster munition countermeasures'.[82]

1.28 The Convention does not, however, explicitly define the term 'use'. One might suggest that any act of employing a weapon consistent with its general purpose constitutes usage. A common dictionary definition of the term is as follows: 'To put into practice or operation; to carry into action or effect; to employ or make use of (an article, etc.), esp. for a profitable end or purpose; to utilize, turn to account; to work, employ, or manage (an implement, instrument, etc.); to manipulate, operate, or handle, esp. to some useful or desired end.'[83] The verbs used in the official French (*employer*) and Spanish (*emplear*) versions of the treaty text translate directly to English as 'employ'.

1.29 Further, other defined terms in the Convention help to illuminate the meaning of the term. According to a portion of Article 2(4),[84] a 'failed cluster munition' means 'a cluster munition that has been fired, dropped, launched, projected or otherwise delivered and which should have dispersed or released its explosive submunitions', implying that use includes firing,[85] dropping,[86]

---

[82] Article 3, paragraph 8 requires States Parties retaining, acquiring, or transferring cluster munitions or explosive submunitions in accordance with paragraphs 6 and 7 of the article to submit a detailed report 'on the planned and actual *use* of these cluster munitions' (emphasis added).

[83] *Oxford English Dictionary*, Oxford University Press, CD-ROM Version 3.1, 2004.
As Maslen recognized with respect to landmines:

> This suggests that the ordinary meaning of the term is not necessarily a single act, as is the emplacement of an anti-personnel mine, but can be something that takes place over a period of time.

Maslen, S., *Commentary on the 1997 Anti-Personnel Mine Ban Convention*, §1.19.

[84] See, *infra*, the commentary on Article 2, paragraph 4 in §§2.167 *et seq.*

[85] Among definitions of 'fire' is '[t]o detonate the main explosive charge by means of a firing system'. A firing system is a '[s]ystem designed to actuate an explosive, electric or other train, in order to cause the explosion of a charge.' *United Kingdom Glossary of Joint and Multinational Terms and Definitions*, Joint Doctrine Publication 0–01.1, Seventh Edition, June 2006, pp. F-3, F-5, <http://www.mod.uk/NR/rdonlyres/E8750509-B7D1-4BC6-8AEE-8A4868E2DA21/0/JDP0011Ed7.pdf> (accessed 8 March 2010). 'Firing' often refers to the use of ground-to-ground missiles. See, e.g., Scheffran, J., 'Missiles in conflict: the issue of missiles in all its complexity', *Disarmament Forum*, Vol. 1, 2007, p. 11 ('Hezbollah militia fired almost 4,000 missiles from Lebanese territory, causing serious damage and 43 deaths in the densely populated Galilee region in northern Israel.')

[86] 'Dropping' refers to the use of air-to-ground cluster munitions delivered by aircraft. 'Regardless of its type or purpose, dropped ordnance is dispensed from an aircraft.' US Army, Marine Corps, Navy, Air Force, *UXO: Multi-Service Tactics, Techniques, and Procedures for Unexploded Explosive Ordnance Operations*, FM 3–100.38, MCRP 3–17.2B, NTTP 3–02.4.1, AFTTP(I) 3–2.12, August

launching,[87] projecting,[88] otherwise delivering cluster munitions,[89] as well as dispersing or releasing[90] explosive submunitions. Article 2, paragraphs 3, 5, 13, and 15 of the Convention also use the terms 'dispersed' and 'released' in referring to the employment of explosive submunitions and explosive bomblets.

2005, p. A-1. See also *UK Glossary of Joint and Multinational Terms, op. cit.,* p. A-15 ('airdrop: Delivery of personnel or cargo from aircraft in flight.').

[87] The 'launching' of cluster munitions can take place from air to ground or from ground to ground. For instance a launcher is defined as a 'structural device designed to support and hold a missile in position for firing.' *UK Glossary of Joint and Multinational Terms, op. cit.,* p. L-4. The Hague Declaration of 1899 referred to 'the launching of projectiles and explosives from balloons.' Declaration (IV, 1), to Prohibit, for the Term of Five Years, the Launching of Projectiles and Explosives from Balloons, and Other Methods of Similar Nature, The Hague, 29 July 1899. In describing a test of a Joint Standoff Weapon loaded with submunitions from the CBU-97/CBU-105 Sensor Fuzed Weapon aboard an F-16 aircraft, a US defence industry trade publication reported that the 'weapon was launched 10 miles from its target and managed to hit seven of eight ground targets in its initial test.' 'US – Third JSOW Variant Tested Oct 18,' *Aviation Week & Space Technology,* 18 October 1999. Further, the term 'Multiple Launch Rocket System' covers a multitude of ground-based weapons systems that can fire rockets with loaded with submunitions. See, e.g., *MLRS Multiple Launch Rocket System, US,* <http://www.army-technology.com/projects/mlrs/> (visited 14 August 2009); Andrei Chang, 'Sudan obtains advanced Chinese MLRS,' *UPI Asia,* 10 July 2009, <http://www.upiasia.com/Security/2009/07/09/sudan_obtains_advanced_chinese_mlrs/1455/>; and *Weishi (WS-1/-2) Multiple Launch Rocket Systems,* <http://www.sinodefence.com/army/mrl/weishi.asp> (site updated 31 December 2008).

[88] 'Projection' ordinarily refers to ordnance dispersed by ground-based munitions systems like rockets or missiles. 'Projected ordnance can be projectiles, mortars, rockets, rifle grenades, or guided missiles.' *US Army, Marine Corps, Navy, Air Force, UXO. Multi-Service Tactics, op. cit.,* p. A-2. It can also cover firing from artillery cannons. See, e.g., *MSTA-S 2S19 152mm Self Propelled Howitzer, Russia,* <http://www.army-technology.com/projects/mstas/> (visited 14 August 2009).

[89] 'Deliver' has been used to describe the use of cluster munitions from aircraft:

JSOW [Joint Standoff Weapon] is an accurate, adverse-weather, glide munition, which was successfully employed in Kosovo and Iraq in 1999. The [US] Air Force will use it to deliver cluster munitions that seek and destroy armored and soft targets at ranges up to 40 nautical miles.

Prepared Statement of General Michael E. Ryan Chief of Staff Department of the Air Force before the [US] Senate Armed Services Committee, March 1, 2000. Deliver can also mean 'employ.'

[90] The verbs 'released' and 'expended' have been used to describe air launched cluster munition use. The US military has used the term 'air-dispensed submunitions' to refer to submunitions released from larger canisters. See, e.g., US Army, Marine Corps, Navy, Combat Air Forces, *UXO: Multiservice Procedures for Operations in an Unexploded Ordnance Environment,* FM 100–38, MCRP 4–5.1, NWP TP 3–02.4.1, ACCPAM 10–752, PACAFPAM 10–752, USAFEPAM 10–752, July 1996, pp. C-2, E-1, <http://www.dtic.mil/doctrine/jel/service_pubs/uxo.pdf>. One definition of release is: 'In air armament, the intentional separation of a free-fall aircraft store, from its suspension equipment, for purposes of employment of the store.' *UK Glossary of Joint and Multinational Terms, op. cit.,* p. R-10.

1.30 In certain circumstances, the wilful failure to clear and destroy all cluster munition remnants located in areas under a State Party's jurisdiction or control 'as soon as possible' as required by Article 4 might constitute use.[91] For example, a State Party might decide to retain a cluster munition contaminated area near a border with a neighbour it considered possibly hostile to use it as a *de facto* minefield. Prohibited use could also include the act of failing to mark a contaminated area under a State Party's jurisdiction or control for the purpose of luring enemy forces into the area for the purpose of force attrition. Subsequent State practice, including any relevant statements attached to ratification and discussions and decisions at the Meeting of States Parties, may clarify these points.

1.31 In contrast, taking actions such as channelling one's own forces around known areas containing unexploded submunitions in order to protect those forces does not constitute 'use'. Likewise, a State Party taking action to identify and mark cluster munition contaminated areas under its jurisdiction or control, as required by Article 4, paragraph 2, is not to be considered 'use' notwithstanding the fact that such marking might be identified by current or potential enemy forces as a military obstacle.

1.32 More difficult is the potential situation where a State Party seeks to take military advantage of a cluster munition contaminated area outside its jurisdiction or control and where it did not create the hazard.[92] During the negotiation process, the only recorded comment on this point was that of the CMC, which urged that:

States should make clear either through additional treaty text or through the diplomatic record that 'use' is not just new deployment of cluster munitions, but also

---

[91] *Cf.*, e.g., Venezuela's statement in the context of the *1997 Anti-Personnel Mine Ban Convention* that it needed to maintain minefields to protect its bases against intrusion by non-State armed groups from neighbouring Colombia. See e.g. ICBL, *Landmine Monitor Report 2009, Toward a Mine-Free World* (Ottawa: Mines Action Canada, 2009), Venezuela country report, section on use, <http://lm.icbl.org/index.php/publications/display?act=submit&pqs_year=2009&pqs_type=lm&pqs_report=venezuela> (accessed 8 March 2010).

[92] An obstacle is defined in US military doctrine as '[a]ny obstruction designed or employed to disrupt, fix, turn, or block the movement of an opposing force, and to impose additional losses in personnel, time, and equipment on the opposing force. Obstacles can be natural, manmade, or a combination of both.' *UXO: Multi-Service Tactics, op. cit.*, pp. 6–7. 'Once emplaced, minefields and unexploded ordnance hazards are lethal and unable to distinguish between friend and foe. . . . UXO hazard areas are treated as obstacles.' US Joint Chiefs of Staff, *Joint Doctrine for Barriers, Obstacles, and Mine Warfare*, Joint Pub, 3–15, 24 February 1999, pp. III-6 to III-7. For a discussion of the differences between minefields and areas contaminated with submunitions, see, e.g., Borrie, J., *Unacceptable Harm, op. cit.*, p. 113.

encompasses the intentional gaining of military or strategic advantages from areas previously contaminated.[93]

Paragraph 1(b)

> Each State Party undertakes never under any circumstances to: [...] Develop, produce, otherwise acquire, stockpile, retain or transfer to anyone, directly or indirectly, cluster munitions;

Direct or indirect commission of prohibited activities

1.33 Paragraph 1(b) of Article 1 prohibits the development, production, acquisition by other means, stockpiling, retention and transfer of cluster munitions to anyone, whether directly or indirectly. The phrase 'directly or indirectly' modifies each of the six verbs in the sub-paragraph (b). While one might argue that the phrase modifies only the verb closest to it (i.e. transfer), a comparison of similar language in related treaties supports the broader reading. In contrast, Article I, paragraph 1(a), of the *1993 Chemical Weapons Convention* states that:

> Each State Party to this Convention undertakes never under any circumstances to develop, produce, otherwise acquire, stockpile or retain chemical weapons, or transfer, directly or indirectly, chemical weapons to anyone.

1.34 The prohibition under that Convention 'is limited to direct or indirect transfer and not the proceeding activities in the clause'.[94] The clear delineation between the first five undertakings (to not develop, produce, otherwise acquire, stockpile or retain) and the last undertaking (to not transfer) by placement of the words 'chemical weapons' makes clear that 'directly or indirectly' was meant to modify only 'transfer' in that usage. Under Article 1, Paragraph 1(2) of the *1997 Anti-Personnel Mine Ban Convention*, 'each State Party undertakes never under any circumstances to develop, produce, otherwise acquire, stockpile, retain or transfer to anyone, directly or indirectly, anti-personnel mines'. This language is identical to that found in the Convention on Cluster Munitions. The words 'directly or indirectly' have

---

[93] CMC, '(Revised) Observations by the Cluster Munition Coalition on the Draft Cluster Munitions Convention, dated 21 January 2008', p. 2.

[94] Maslen, S., *Commentary on the 1997 Anti-Personnel Mine Ban Convention, op. cit.*, §1.32, fn. 65.

similarly been understood in the *1997 Anti-Personnel Mine Ban Convention* to apply to all six verbs.[95]

1.35 The prohibition on indirect as well as direct actions means that the reach of the prohibitions is broad, and is intended to prevent flawed interpretations aiming at circumventions of the prohibitions. Indirectly means 'second-hand, in a roundabout way... [,] by implication, obliquely, circumlocutorily, periphrastically'.[96]

The prohibition on development

1.36 States Parties undertake never under any circumstances to develop, directly or indirectly, cluster munitions.[97] The term 'develop' is not defined in the Convention. To develop something is 'to cause [it] to grow or come into active existence or operation'.[98] In the context of the *1993 Chemical Weapons Convention*, '"develop" is by virtue of its purpose, the preparation of the production of chemical weapons as distinct from permitted research'.[99] This prohibited objective might also materialize and become obvious through specific equipment used and methods applied.[100] The ambit of the Convention on Cluster Munitions is broader than the *1993 Chemical Weapons Convention*, however, as it encompasses a prohibition on indirect as well as direct development. The Norwegian Government, in its explanatory note to national implementing legislation, stated that:

[i]t is presumed that the development of cluster munitions covers the process up to production.[101]

---

[95] Maslen, S. *Commentary on the 1997 Anti-Personnel Mine Ban Convention, op. cit., esp.* §§1.32 and 1.42. The Danish parliamentary resolution calling for ratification of the Convention on Cluster Munitions contains a contrary interpretation, commenting on Article 1 as follows:

The ban on cluster munitions involves banning the use, development, manufacture, acquisition, stockpiling, retention, and indirect and direct transfer of cluster munitions to others.

B 60 Forslag til folketingsbeslutning om Danmarks godkendelse af konventionen om klyngeammunition undertegnet den 4. december 2008 i Oslo, §3.3, 19 November 2009, <http://pp.ft.dk/samling/20091/beslutningsforslag/B60/som_fremsat.htm> (accessed 15 March 2010).

[96] '[I]ndirectly *adverb*', in Lindberg, C. A. (ed.), *The Oxford American Thesaurus of Current English*, OUP, 1999; and *Oxford Reference Online*, OUP, 4 July 2009, <http://www.oxfordreference.com/views/ENTRY.html?subview=Main&entry=t22.e7178>.

[97] Additionally, nothing in Article 21, paragraph 3 on *Relations with States not party to this Convention* 'shall authorise a State Party: (a) To develop... cluster munitions.' Article 21, paragraph 4, Convention on Cluster Munitions.

[98] *Oxford English Dictionary*, Oxford University Press, CD-ROM Version 3.1, 2004.

[99] Krutzsch, W., and Trapp, R., *A Commentary on the Chemical Weapons Convention, op. cit.*, p. 13.   [100] *Ibid.*

[101] Excerpts from Proposition No. 7 (2008–2009) to the Odelsting on a Bill relating to the implementation of the Convention on Cluster Munitions in Norwegian law,

1.37 Maslen commented on indirect development in the context of the *1997 Anti-Personnel Mine Ban Convention*:

This would seemingly cover development of anti-personnel mines by offshore corporations or companies providing funding for research and development in non-Party States, seeking to avoid the reach of national legislation within the jurisdiction. A State Party may not commission, provide funding, or issue licenses for such activities, and, in accordance with Article 9 of the Convention, should ensure that it has taken all appropriate measures to prevent or suppress the development of anti-personnel mines by persons or territory under its jurisdiction or control.[102]

1.38 The development of components[103] that might be used in cluster munitions as well as in weapons not prohibited under the Convention raises interpretive challenges. Developing multi-use components with the intent that the designs of such components be used in cluster munitions would violate the Convention, although such development raises difficult evidentiary challenges in proving the requisite intent.[104]

1.39 As the process of developing weapons often involves multiple stages of testing or production, at some stages a weapon might well be considered prohibited if the process were stopped at those points.[105] Using the example of Article 2, paragraph 2(c), weapons which possess all five listed characteristics (e.g. each submunition must be equipped with an electronic self-destruction mechanism) are not considered cluster munitions. In development, an explosive submunition might not yet be equipped with an electronic self-destruction mechanism for the purpose of testing other features of the submunition, thus making it prohibited at that stage. If such development or testing is not intended to lead to the production of cluster munitions, it is not prohibited under the Convention.

---

para. 4.2.2 (17 October 2008), <http://www.stopclustermunitions.org/wp/wp-content/uploads/2009/02/norwegian-national-legislation-on-cluster-munitions.pdf>. For the original Norwegian, see Ot.prp. nr. 7 (2008–2009), available at <http://www.regjeringen.no/pages/2118118/PDFS/OTP200820090007000DDDPDFS.pdf> (both accessed 8 March 2010).

[102] Maslen, S., *Commentary on the 1997 Anti-Personnel Mine Ban Convention, op. cit.*, §1.32.

[103] A non-exhaustive list of components of cluster munitions is provided in the commentary, *infra*, on the prohibition on production (§1.43).

[104] See also, *infra*, §§1.72 *et seq.* on investment as assistance.

[105] Excerpts from Proposition No. 7 (2008–2009) to the Odelsting on a Bill relating to the implementation of the Convention on Cluster Munitions in Norwegian law, *op. cit*, para. 4.2.2.

The prohibition on production

1.40 Under Article 1, paragraph 1(b), States Parties undertake never under any circumstances to produce, directly or indirectly, cluster munitions.[106] The prohibition on production is effective immediately upon entry into force and is not subject to any exception.

1.41 The term 'produce' is not defined in the Convention. There is a certain overlap between the concept of development and the concept of production. Using both terms decreases the scope for circumventing the prohibition, notwithstanding that the two concepts have separate meaning; development normally taking place before production. To produce something is 'to bring (a thing) into existence from its raw materials or elements, or as the result of a process'.[107] The official French text of the Convention translates 'produce' as *produire*. One State Party, Luxembourg, does not use the word *produire* in implementing legislation, but rather uses the word *fabriquer*.[108] The word *fabriquer* may be translated in English as 'to make, to produce, to manufacture'.[109]

1.42 As with the *1997 Anti-Personnel Mine Ban Convention*, the prohibition is on indirect as well as direct production. According to a commentary of that Convention:

[T]he prohibition on the production of anti-personnel mines encompasses indirect as well as direct production, which would encompass the licensing of foreign companies to produce anti-personnel mines or components intended to be employed in anti-personnel mines.[110]

As discussed above with respect to the prohibition on development, care must be taken in the production of any submunitions to ensure that they are covered by the prohibitions in the Convention on Cluster Munitions.

1.43 Cluster munitions, if examined closely, can be broken down into a series of individual components. These are often produced by a variety of manufacturers. There is no list in the Convention of all 'components' of cluster

[106] Additionally, nothing in Article 21(3) on *Relations with States not party to this Convention* 'shall authorise a State Party: (a) To...produce...cluster munitions.' Article 21, paragraph 4, Convention on Cluster Munitions.

[107] *Oxford English Dictionary*, Oxford University Press, CD-ROM Version 3.1, 2004.

[108] Loi du 4 juin 2009 portant approbation de la Convention sur les armes à sous-munitions, ouverte à la signature à Oslo le 3 décembre 2008, Doc. parl. 5981; sess. ord. 2008–2009, Article 2, p. 2038.

[109] Larousse online dictionary, <http://www.larousse.fr/dictionnaires/francais-anglais/fabriquer> (visited 8 March 2010).

[110] Maslen, S., *Commentary on the 1997 Anti-Personnel Mine Ban Convention*, *op. cit.*, §1.34.

munitions, although key parts, notably explosive submunitions, are listed in Article 2. The Convention, does, however, commit States Parties to 'never under any circumstances [....] develop, produce, otherwise acquire, stockpile, retain or transfer to anyone, directly or indirectly, cluster munitions'. Thus, both development and production of components designed for cluster munitions are covered by the prohibition. Such components might be:

- The canister or dispenser,
- The ejection system (the mechanism that expels the submunitions from the canister),
- The explosive submunitions,
- The detonation mechanism or fuse for both the main weapon and the submunitions,
- The propulsion system (e.g. base bleed, rocket engine), and
- The guidance system (the mechanism that guides the main weapon or the submunitions towards their target area).

Some of these are mentioned in Article 2, while others are not. This commentary does not attempt to provide an exhaustive list of what might constitute components of cluster munitions.

1.44 The production of components of cluster munitions which potentially have multiple uses in other products is more problematic. In Luxembourg's national implementing legislation it is stated that:

Aux termes des articles 1 et 2 de la Convention, il est interdit... de fabriquer, [ou] d'assembler des pièces préfabriquées en arme complète... des armes à sousmunitions ou des sous-munitions explosives.[111]

In English, the provision may be translated as:

Pursuant to the terms of article 1 and 2 of the Convention, it is prohibited... to manufacture [or] to assemble prefabricated pieces into complete weapons... of cluster munitions or explosive submunitions.

The Luxembourg legislation therefore bans (1) the manufacture of cluster munitions; (2) their assembly from pre-fabricated parts; (3) the manufacture of explosive submunitions; and (4) the assembly of explosive submunitions from pre-fabricated parts.[112]

---

[111] Loi du 4 juin 2009 portant approbation de la Convention sur les armes à sous-munitions, ouverte à la signature à Oslo le 3 décembre 2008, Doc. parl. 5981; sess. ord. 2008–2009, Article 2, p. 2038.

[112] Article 2 of the law apparently bans the production of explosive bomblets implicitly, by referencing Articles 1 and 2 of the Convention.

1.45 The Norwegian Government, in its explanatory note to the national implementing legislation, also addressed the question of the production of components, including multiple use components:

In addition to production of the complete weapon, the prohibition on production applies to production of components of cluster munitions. Thus, depending on the circumstances, the production of components that can be used in the production of cluster munitions may be covered by the prohibition. The question is how far-removed the component is from the final product, i.e. the cluster munition. If it is clear that the component can only be used in the production of cluster munitions, the production of such components is covered by the prohibition. In such cases, it is clear what the product is to be used for, and it is difficult to envisage it as having alternative uses. Other components, such as explosives or chemicals that can be used for many purposes other than the production of cluster munitions, do not, however, fall within the scope of the prohibition as long as it is not clear that the final use for which they are intended is the production of cluster munitions. The same must apply to multi-purpose materiel, for example a container that can also be used for cluster munitions or other munitions that do not fall within the scope of the prohibition, as long as the intended final use is unclear.[113]

The end use of multiple-use components might be addressed through export controls.

1.46 Licensing the production of cluster munitions by foreign companies constitutes indirect production. According to *Banning Cluster Munitions, Government Policy and Practice*, a 2009 report by two nongovernmental organizations (NGOs), '[m]any states have licensed the production of cluster munitions to companies in other states'.[114] The report cites numerous examples. The South Korean firm Poongsan licensed the Pakistan Ordnance Factories in November 2004 to co-produce dual purpose improved conventional munition (DPICM) projectiles in Pakistan.[115] Israel Military Industries has licensed companies in Argentina, Germany, India, Romania, Switzerland, Turkey, the UK, and the US to produce or assemble DPICM submunitions.[116] US manufacturers licensed a Dutch firm, Eurometaal NV, in the late 1980s to produce 155mm artillery DPICM projectiles. Eurometaal shared production with a Turkish firm, MKEK beginning in 1994, but closed production

---

[113] Excerpts from Proposition No. 7 (2008–2009) to the Odelsting on a Bill relating to the implementation of the Convention on Cluster Munitions in Norwegian law, *op. cit.*

[114] Human Rights Watch and Landmine Action, *Banning Cluster Munitions, Government Policy and Practice* (Ottawa: Mines Action Canada, May 2009), p. 18.

[115] *Ibid.*, pp. 18, 225 (footnotes omitted).   [116] *Ibid.*, pp. 18, 179, 215 (footnotes omitted).

capacity in 2002.[117] The US 'concluded a licensing agreement with South Korea in 2001 for production' of DPICM submunitions.[118] The US has also licensed production of DPICM artillery projectiles to Turkey.[119]

1.47 The investment in firms producing or assembling cluster munitions or producing or assembling key components may also be prohibited. The issue is addressed below in the section on assistance.[120]

Prohibition on acquisition

1.48 Under Article 1, paragraph 1(b), States Parties undertake never under any circumstances to otherwise acquire, directly or indirectly, cluster munitions.[121] This covers the acquisition of cluster munitions other than through production of the weapons, such as, for example, by purchasing, borrowing, stealing, or embezzling cluster munitions. The aim is to ensure that all forms of acquisition are covered by the Convention. Furthermore, when acquiring weapons systems, a State Party is obliged to assess the munitions to ensure that the characteristics of the munitions do not violate the Convention.[122] As the definition of what is and is not a cluster munition relies greatly on technical requirements,[123] great care must be taken in the acquisition of

---

[117] *Ibid.,* pp. 128, 248 (footnotes omitted).

[118] *Ibid.,* p. 218 (footnotes omitted).   [119] *Ibid.,* p. 260.

[120] See, *infra*, §§1.72 *et seq.*, for further discussion on investment as assistance to prohibited acts.

[121] Additionally, nothing in Article 21(3) on *Relations with States not party to this Convention* 'shall authorise a State Party: (a) To...otherwise acquire...cluster munitions.' Article 21, paragraph 4.

[122] *See* Article 36, *1977 Additional Protocol I*. 'This obligation applies to purchasing [weapons]. There are far more countries purchasing weapons than countries manufacturing weapons, and the former may be Parties to the Protocol, while the latter, who conceive, develop, manufacture and sell the weapon may not yet be. Whatever the case may be, the purchaser should not blindly depend on the attitude of the seller or the manufacturer, but should proceed itself to evaluate the use of the weapon in question with regard to the provisions of the Protocol or any other rule of international law which applies to it.' *Commentary on Additional Protocols I and II of 8 June 1977, op. cit.,* p. 426.

[123] According to Article 2, paragraph 2(c), a cluster munition is not a 'munition that, in order to avoid indiscriminate area effects and the risks posed by unexploded submunitions, has all of the following characteristics:

(i)   Each munition contains fewer than ten explosive submunitions;
(ii) Each explosive submunition weighs more than four kilograms;
(iii) Each explosive submunition is designed to detect and engage a single target object;
(iv) Each explosive submunition is equipped with an electronic self-destruction mechanism;
(v)   Each explosive submunition is equipped with an electronic self-deactivating feature.'

See also, *infra*, the commentary on Article 2, paragraph 2.

new weapons.[124] Whether States Parties should consider not only technical requirements but also the expected or foreseeable effects of munitions that might be acquired is a point of unresolved contention.[125]

1.49 The term 'acquire' is not defined in the Convention. To acquire ordinarily means 'to receive, or get as one's own (without reference to the manner), to come into possession of'.[126] While the prohibition on the acquisition of cluster munitions appears to be absolute in Article 1, there is a limited exception allowing acquisition and retention for 'the development of and training in cluster munition and explosive submunition detection, clearance or destruction techniques, or for the development of cluster munition counter-measures'. However, the 'amount of explosive submunitions retained or acquired shall not exceed the minimum number absolutely necessary for these purposes'.[127]

Prohibitions on stockpiling and retention

1.50 Under Article 1, paragraph 1(b), States Parties undertake never under any circumstances to stockpile or retain, directly or indirectly, cluster munitions.[128] There is a certain overlap between the concepts of stockpiling and retention. The prohibition on stockpiling is subject to a certain deadline for destruction of stocks. The prohibition on retention is subject to an exception regarding cluster munitions used for certain purposes such as training mine clearance personnel.[129]

The prohibition on stockpiling

1.51 The Convention does not define the verb 'to stockpile'. The term ordinarily means 'to accumulate a stock of (something); spec. to build up a stock of . . . weapons . . . ,'[130] while a stockpile is defined as 'A reserve or store of goods or commodities, esp. one accumulated in anticipation of shortage or market

---

[124] See Sandoz, Y. *et al.*, *Commentary on the Additional Protocols I and II of 8 June 1977, op. cit.*, p. 426:

> [T]he purchaser should not blindly depend on the attitude of the seller or the manufacturer, but should proceed itself to evaluate the use of the weapon in question with regard to the provisions of the Protocol or any other rule of international law which applies to it.

[125] See, *infra*, the commentary on Article 2, paragraph 2(c).

[126] *Oxford English Dictionary*, Oxford University Press, CD-ROM Version 3.1, 2004.

[127] See, *infra*, the commentary on Article 3, paragraph 6.

[128] The ambit of the obligation on States Parties to destroy stockpiles of cluster munitions is addressed in the commentary on Article 3. In addition, nothing in Article 21(3) on *Relations with States not party to this Convention* 'shall authorise a State Party: (b) To itself stockpile . . . cluster munitions'. Article 21, paragraph 4.

[129] See, *infra*, the commentary on Article 3, paragraph 6.

[130] *Oxford English Dictionary*, Oxford University Press, CD-ROM Version 3.1, 2004.

fluctuation; An accumulation of ... weapons.'[131] The Convention applies to all cluster munitions held in stocks.[132]

1.52 Publicly available data on numbers of clusters munitions in stockpiles capture only some of the global total. In 2009, seven signatories were said to be holding about 672,000 cluster munitions containing more than 115 million submunitions, which were pending destruction.[133] Six non-signatory States held cluster munitions containing at least 745 million submunitions.[134] According to Human Rights Watch, as of December 2009, 87 countries had stockpiled cluster munitions and/or dispenser systems. The organization classified global stockpiles into weapon types and countries that have held or currently hold those weapons.[135] According to research by two NGOs, as of May 2009:

Countries that are no longer thought to have stockpiles include [Convention] signatories Australia, Honduras, Mali, and Spain, and non-signatories Argentina and Iraq. Spain completed its stockpile destruction program in March 2009.[136]

The stockpiling of foreign cluster munitions

1.53 A number of signatory States have expressed the view that the storage of cluster munitions by a foreign power in national territory is prohibited under Article 1 of the Convention[137] or that 'storage of cluster munitions by a state not party within the territory of a state party would weaken the effects of

---

[131] *Ibid.*

[132] See, *infra*, the commentary on Article 3 for further details of the obligation to destroy stockpiles of cluster munitions.

[133] Human Rights Watch and Landmine Action, *Banning Cluster Munitions, op. cit.,* p. 20. The UK: 38.7 million; Germany: 33 million; Netherlands: 26 million; France: 14.9 million; Norway: 3.1 million; Austria: 798,336; and Slovenia: 52,920.

[134] *Banning Cluster Munitions, op. cit.,* p. 20. The US: 730 million; Bahrain: 6.1 million; Jordan: 3.1 million; Morocco: 2.5 million; Egypt: 2.2 million; and Saudi Arabia: 1.2 million. At the August 2009 Group of Governmental Experts meeting of the *Convention on Certain Conventional Weapons*, the Russian representatives stated that 'the Russian Federation had acquired a huge stockpile of cluster munitions', apparently referring to legacy weapons acquired after the fall of the Soviet Union. Katie Harrison, 'Update from the CCW, Tuesday 18 August 2009: More of the Same,' *Landmine Action*, undated.

[135] Human Rights Watch, *Cluster Munition Information Chart*, December 2009.

[136] Human Rights Watch and Landmine Action, *Banning Cluster Munitions, op. cit.*, p. 20.

[137] Letter from Juan Manuel Gomez Robledo, Undersecretary for Multilateral Affairs and Human Rights, Mexico to Stephen Goose, Executive Director, Arms Division, Human Rights Watch, 10 March 2009, available at: <http://lm.icbl.org/cm/2009/countries/pdf/Mexico%20MFA%20Cluster%20Response%203.2009.pdf>. Letter from Amb. Saviour F. Borg, Permanent Mission of the Republic of Malta to the UN in New York to Stephen Goose, Human Rights Watch, 2 March 2009. Letter from the Permanent Mission of Lebanon to the UN in Geneva to Human Rights Watch, 10 February 2009. Letter from Dr. Petio Petev, Bulgarian Ministry of Foreign Affairs to Stephen Goose, Human Rights Watch, 25 February 2009.

the convention'.[138] This position may be somewhat at odds with Article 3, paragraph 1, which states that 'Each State Party shall, in accordance with national regulations, separate all cluster munitions under its *jurisdiction and control* from munitions retained for operational use and mark them for the purpose of destruction.'[139] The language implies that stockpiles of cluster munitions in the jurisdiction but not under the control of a State Party are exempt from the destruction requirements of Article 3, paragraph 2. Additionally, Article 21, paragraph 4(b) states that '[n]othing in paragraph 3 of this Article shall authorise a State Party...(b) To *itself* stockpile or transfer cluster munitions' (emphasis added). This issue is discussed below in the respective commentary on these provisions.

The prohibition on retention

1.54 To 'retain' is ordinarily defined as 'to keep hold or possession of; to continue having or keeping'.[140] It is potentially a broad concept.[141] While stockpiling suggests accumulation and build-up, retention might be viewed as holding on to weapons already acquired. Holding on to weapons acquired through an amnesty or by coming into control of stockpiles formerly held by others might be included in retention. Japan's proposal during the Wellington Conference and then again during the Diplomatic Conference to replace the term 'retain' with 'own, possess' did not attract support from the negotiating States.[142] In its implementing legislation, Japan uses the terms 'possess' and

---

[138] See 'Intervention de son Excellence Monsieur Marcel Ranjeva, Ministre des Affaires Etrangeres, Republique de Madagascar, Ceremonie de Signature de la Convention Internationale Sur Les Armes a Sous Munitions', Oslo, 3 December 2008, <http://www.clusterconvention.org/pages/pages_i/documents/Madagascar312.pdf> (accessed 8 March 2010). The Minister of Foreign Affairs of Madagascar further stated that:

[N]ous tenons à exprimer, que l'acceptation du transit d'armes à sous-munitions sur le territoire d'un Etat Partie, et du stockage d'armes à sous-munitions par un Etat non Partie sur le territoire d'un Etat Partie, sont de manière à affaiblir les effets escomptés de la Convention.

[139] Article 3, paragraph 1 (emphasis added).
[140] *Oxford English Dictionary*, Oxford University Press, CD-ROM Version 3.1, 2004.
[141] To the extent that 'stockpile' might be narrowly read to address keeping reserves held in the event of a shortage or emergency, the inclusion of 'retain' clearly addresses those objects being held or possessed more generally.
[142] '[W]e suggest an idea to replace the word "retain" with "own, possess" in order to strengthen the provision. In our understanding, the word "retain" implies "keeping cluster munitions for a certain period of time." On the other hand, the wording of "own, possess" does not have such a "time factor" and means a fact that those cluster munitions actually "belong to" the countries which own or possess them; therefore this wording is stronger.' Statement of Japan, Wellington Conference, undated but February 2008, <http://www.mfat.govt.nz/clustermunitionswellington/conference-documents/Japan.pdf>(accessed 8 March 2010). See also 'Proposal by Japan for the amendment of Article 1', Diplomatic Conference doc. CCM/10, 19 May 2008.

'possession'.[143] Likewise, a person who 'possesses, retains, or stockpiles a cluster munition' is considered under New Zealand's implementing legislation to have committed an offence.[144]

1.55 As with respect to acquisition, Article 3, paragraph 6 lays down a limited exception to the general prohibition on retention for 'the development of and training in cluster munition and explosive submunition detection, clearance or destruction techniques, or for the development of cluster munition counter-measures'. However, the 'amount of explosive submunitions retained or acquired shall not exceed the minimum number absolutely necessary for these purposes'.[145] States Parties have incorporated these exceptions into national implementing legislation.[146] These exceptions apply explicitly to cluster munitions only and not to explosive bomblets or dispensers.

Prohibition on transfer

1.56 Under Article 1, paragraph 1(b), States Parties undertake never under any circumstances to transfer, directly or indirectly, cluster munitions to anyone.[147] The prohibition is immediate and the only exceptions to the prohibition are set out in Article 3, paragraphs 6 and 7.[148]

---

[143] Act on the Prohibition of the Production of Cluster Munitions and the Regulation of the Possession of Cluster Munitions, Chap. 3 (Japan, August 2009).

[144] Cluster Munitions Prohibition Act 2009, Act 2009 No. 68, Part 2, Clause 10(1)(c) and (4), <http://www.legislation.govt.nz/act/public/2009/0068/latest/DLM2171615.html> (accessed 25 March 2010). The offences laid down are a prison term not exceeding seven years or a fine not exceeding $500,000, or both, for possessing, retaining, or stockpiling cluster munitions.

[145] See, *infra*, the commentary on Article 3, paragraph 6.

[146] See, e.g., New Zealand's implementing legislation:

(1) Despite section 10(1), an officer does not commit an offence by using, acquiring, possessing, retaining, or transferring an authorised cluster munition if he or she is doing so—(a) in the course of his or her employment or duties; and (b) for the purposes of developing, or training persons in, techniques of cluster munition detection, clearance, or destruction; and (c) in compliance with any notice given under section 15 [ministerial notice requirements for cluster munition acquisition].

Cluster Munitions Prohibition Act 2009, *op. cit.*, Clause 11.

[147] Additionally, nothing in Article 21(3) on *Relations with States not party to this Convention* 'shall authorise a State Party: (b) To itself stockpile or transfer cluster munitions' Article 21, paragraph 4.

[148] Under Article 3, paragraph 6, it is permitted to transfer a limited number of cluster munitions (not exceeding the 'minimum number absolutely necessary') for the purposes of 'development of and training in cluster munition and explosive submunition detection, clearance or destruction techniques, or for the development of cluster munition counter-measures'. Under Article 3, paragraph 7, it is permitted to transfer cluster munitions for the purpose of destruction. See, *infra*, the commentary on these provisions.

1.57 Information about the actual extent of international trade in cluster munitions is not publicly available. According to research by two NGOs published in 2009:

[w]hile the true scope of the global trade in cluster munitions is difficult to ascertain due to lack of official information, at least 15 countries have transferred more than 50 types of cluster munitions to at least 60 other countries.[149]

1.58 The term 'transfer' is defined in Article 2, paragraph 8 of the Convention as follows:[150]

Transfer involves, in addition to the physical movement of cluster munitions into or from national territory, the transfer of title to and control over cluster munitions, but does not involve the transfer of territory containing cluster munition remnants.[151]

The meaning of the term transfer is discussed under Article 2, paragraph 8 of this commentary.

1.59 'Anyone' means 'anybody, any person'.[152] 'Anyone' includes States, whether or not party to the convention; organisations or companies;[153] as well

---

[149] Human Rights Watch and Landmine Action, *Banning Cluster Munitions, op. cit.*, p. 23. For additional details, see pp. 23–24 and specific information in the country sections of that report.

[150] The definition is taken almost verbatim from Article 2, paragraph 4 of the *1997 Anti-Personnel Mine Ban Convention*, with 'cluster munitions' being substituted for 'anti-personnel mines' and 'cluster munition remnants' being substitute for 'emplaced anti-personnel mines'. That definition in turn was taken nearly verbatim from Article 2, paragraph 15 of *1996 CCW Amended Protocol II*, with 'anti-personnel mines' being substituted for 'mines'.

[151] According to Article 31, paragraph 4 of the *1969 Vienna Convention on the Law of Treaties*:

A special meaning shall be given to a term if it is established that the parties so intended.

Among negotiating States, only Ireland formally proposed a slightly different definition of transfer for consideration:

'Transfer' means the physical movement of cluster munitions into or from national territory or the transfer of title to or control over cluster munitions, but does not include the transfer of territory containing cluster munition remnants.

'Proposal by Ireland for the amendment of Article 2,' Diplomatic Conference doc. CCM 25, 19 May 2008, p. 2.

[152] *Oxford English Dictionary*, Oxford University Press, CD-ROM Version 3.1, 2004.

[153] Thus, Luxembourg's implementing legislation has interpreted 'anyone' to include juridical as well as natural persons:

'Art. 2. Aux termes des articles 1 et 2 de la Convention, il est interdit à toute personne physique ou morale de mettre au point, de fabriquer, d'assembler des pièces préfabriquées en arme complète, de transformer, de réparer, d'acquérir, de vendre, d'utiliser, de détenir, de transporter, de transférer, de stocker ou de conserver des armes à sous-munitions ou des sous-munitions explosives.'

('Art 2. It is prohibited to any person or legal entity, within the terms of Articles 1 and 2 of the Convention, to develop, produce, assemble prefabricated pieces of cluster munitions into complete weapons, to alter, repair, acquire, sell, use, possess, transport, transfer, stockpile, or retain cluster munitions or explosive submunitions.').

as a person or a group of persons (irrespective of citizenship), including non-State armed groups.[154]

1.60 The transfer of key components of cluster munitions is also prohibited. The same limitations that apply to production and development regarding components apply. The transfer of multiple use components, when the intent of that transfer is to result in the assembly of production of cluster munitions, is prohibited.[155] For example, components which could be used in both cluster munitions as well as non-prohibited products would be electronic self-destruction mechanisms specified in Article 2, paragraph 2(c)(iv). A possessor or producer of such multiple use components who transfers such components when they know or should know such components will be used to produce cluster munitions violates the prohibition on transfer.[156]

Permitting transit of cluster munitions across the
territory of a State Party

1.61 More complex is the question of transit of cluster munitions across, above or through the territory of a State Party. Subsequent to the negotiations, a number of signatory States expressed the view that such transit was prohibited. At least one State has expressed the contrary view that there is a distinction between transfer and transit and that transit of cluster munitions that remain the property of a third party is not prohibited under the Convention.[157]

Paragraph 1(c)

Each State Party undertakes never under any circumstances to: [...]
Assist, encourage or induce anyone to engage in any activity prohibited
to a State Party under this Convention

---

[154] Krutzsch, W., and Trapp, R., *A Commentary on the Chemical Weapons Convention, op. cit.*, p. 18. According to Human Rights Watch, '"anyone" includes states parties, States not party, and non-state actors such as armed rebel groups, private companies, and individuals.' Docherty, B., 'Staying True to the Ban on Cluster Munitions: Understanding the Prohibition on Assistance in the Convention on Cluster Munitions', Human Rights Watch, June 2009, p. 5.

[155] Such a prohibition on the transfer of key components of cluster munitions might also be considered a prohibition on assistance in the production of cluster munitions.

[156] States Parties may consider end-user requirements for such situations.

[157] Bulgaria, Lebanon, Malta, Mexico, South Africa, and Zambia expressed the view that transit is prohibited in response to an inquiry from Human Rights Watch in early 2009. The Netherlands took the contrary view in response to the same inquiry. For a more detailed discussion of this issue, see, *infra*, §2.198.

The prohibition on assisting, encouraging, or inducing prohibited activities

1.62 In accordance with Article 1, paragraph 1(c), each State Party undertakes never under any circumstance to assist, encourage, or induce anyone to engage in any activity prohibited to a State Party under this Convention. This language was drawn nearly verbatim from Article 1, paragraph 1(c) of the *1997 Anti-Personnel Mine Ban Convention*. The only difference is that the phrase 'in any way' follows the word induce in that Convention, but is omitted from the Convention. This omission does not alter the scope of the prohibition. It is redundant language that could potentially create uncertainty about the scope of other provisions containing prohibitions not referring to the term 'in any way'. The inclusion of Article 21—Relations with States not party to this Convention—and in particular its paragraphs 3 and 4, complicates the issue of what does and does not constitute assistance.[158]

1.63 A State Party is prohibited from providing assistance, encouragement and inducement 'to anyone'.[159] Stemming from the *1993 Convention on Chemical Weapons*, this wording was chosen in order to emphasize the ban on assistance. The three concepts are not defined in the Convention. It is, however, clear from the wording of Article 1, paragraph 1(c) that assistance, encouragement, and inducement are prohibited with regard not only to use, but also development, production, acquisition, stockpiling, retention, and transfer.

1.64 Article 1, paragraph 1 of the Convention, together with its subparagraph (c) makes it clear that States Parties will have violated the Convention whether they have themselves used, developed etc., cluster munitions, or just assisted 'anyone' to do so. The prohibition against assisting, etc., thus applies only to States Parties, but both States not Party and other entities, as well as States Parties, are covered by the term 'anyone'.

1.65 The concept of assistance in international law is not clearly defined. International rules on State responsibility might, however, provide some insight into the concept. Article 16 of the draft articles on Responsibility of States for Internationally Wrongful Acts states that:

A State which aids or assists another State in the commission of an internationally wrongful act by the latter is internationally responsible for doing so if:

(a) that State does so with knowledge of the circumstances of the internationally wrongful act; and

---

[158] See the commentary on Article 21 for the relevant negotiating history on this provision and a review of its impact on the obligations of States Parties.　　　[159] See, *supra*, §1.59.

(b) the act would be internationally wrongful if committed by that State.[160]

Only States that are party to the Convention are bound by the prohibitions laid down in the Convention. For a State not Party it would not be an 'internationally wrongful act' to, as a point of departure, use, produce, etc., cluster munitions. Therefore, the articles on Responsibility of States for Internationally Wrongful Acts would only be directly applicable to assistance to violations committed by States Parties. However, in determining the general content of 'assistance', the Articles may be helpful.[161]

1.66 The commentary by the International Law Commission suggests that Article 16 limits the scope of responsibility for assistance in three ways. 'First, the relevant State organ or agency providing aid or assistance must be aware of the circumstances making the conduct' of the assisted State or party internationally wrongful. 'The second requirement is that the aid or assistance must be given with a view to facilitating the commission of the wrongful act, and must actually do so.'[162] Finally, 'it is a necessary requirement for the responsibility of an assisting State that the conduct in question, if attributable to the assisting State, would have constituted a breach of its own international obligations'.[163]

1.67 It seems to follow that the threshold for 'assistance' is relatively high. The first requirement is that the assisting State must have had knowledge about the act that constitutes (or, for States not Party, would have constituted) the violation of the Convention. The second requirement, however, according to the Commentary on Article 16, is that the assisting State must have had an intention of assisting someone in conducting such an unlawful act and must also have succeeded in contributing significantly to the commission of the act.

1.68 Assist is not defined in the Convention. To 'assist' in general parlance means 'to help, aid: a. a person in doing something ... b. a person in

---

[160] Article 16, International Law Commission (ILC), *Draft articles on Responsibility of States for Internationally Wrongful Acts, with commentaries 2001,* UN, 2008, p. 65.

[161] The draft articles also only address aiding or assisting other *States,* whereas the Convention addresses assisting, encouraging, or inducing *anyone.*

[162] ILC, *Draft articles on Responsibility of States, op. cit.,* p. 66 (Commentary on Article 16, paragraphs 3 and 5). 'There is no requirement that the aid or assistance should have been essential to the performance of the internationally wrongful act; it is sufficient if it contributed significantly to that act.' *Ibid.*

[163] ILC, *Draft articles on Responsibility of States, op. cit.,* p. 66 (Commentary on Article 16, paragraph 6). The commentary on Part IV (of which Article 16 is a part) recognizes 'the possibility that the same conduct may be internationally wrongful so far as one State is concerned but not for another State having regard to its own international obligations.' *Ibid.,* p. 65 (Commentary on Part IV, paragraph 8). See below for further discussion of interoperability.

necessity; c. an action, process, or result. To second, support; to succour, relieve; to further, promote.'[164] A commentary on the corresponding provision of the *1993 Chemical Weapons Convention* states that assistance 'can be given by material or intellectual support...but also financial resources, technological-scientific know-how or provision of specialised personnel, military instructions, etc. to anybody who is resolved to commit such prohibited activity or by support in the concealment of such activities'.[165]

1.69 The content of 'encourage' and 'induce' is even less clear than 'assist' from an international law point of view. To 'encourage' means generally to 'embolden, make confident; to incite, induce, instigate; in weaker sense, to recommend, advise; to stimulate (persons or personal efforts) by assistance, reward, or expressions of favour or approval; also, in bad sense, to abet'.[166] To 'induce' means generally to 'To lead (a person), by persuasion or some influence or motive that acts upon the will, to...some action, condition, belief, etc.; to lead on, move, influence, prevail upon (any one) to do something. a. Of persons, personal action, influence, etc.'[167]

1.70 It would seem that the act of encouragement in Article 1, paragraph 1(c) would have to be undertaken by a State Party with a view to generating violations of the Convention. Otherwise, a variety of acts or omissions by a State Party may be perceived as encouragement to such violations without having been intended so. Likewise, inducement by a State Party would have to be undertaken with a view to generate violations of the Convention. Moreover, inducement would perhaps imply that the violation actually would have to happen, thus having a stricter scope than encouragement. A commentary on the corresponding provision in the *1993 Chemical Weapons Convention* states that the prohibition on encouraging or inducing 'means contributing to the emergence of resolve of anybody to commit a prohibited activity by instigating, promising assistance, etc'.[168]

[164] *Oxford English Dictionary*, Oxford University Press, CD-ROM Version 3.1, 2004.

[165] See Krutzsch, W., and Trapp, R., *A Commentary on the Chemical Weapons Convention, op. cit.*, p. 17. According to Human Rights Watch, '[a]ssistance should be understood as any act or omission that proximately contributes to anyone's engagement in an activity prohibited to a state party under the convention.' Bonnie Docherty, 'Staying True to the Ban on Cluster Munitions: Understanding the Prohibition on Assistance in the Convention on Cluster Munitions,' Human Rights Watch, June 2009, pp. 5–6.

[166] *Oxford English Dictionary*, Oxford University Press, CD-ROM Version 3.1, 2004.

[167] *Ibid.* See Krutzsch, W., and Trapp, R., *A Commentary on the Chemical Weapons Convention, op. cit.*, p. 17.

[168] See Krutzsch, W., and Trapp, R., *A Commentary on the Chemical Weapons Convention, op. cit.*, p. 17.

1.71 The criminal law concepts of 'aiding and abetting' also illuminate the meaning of assistance. To 'abet' means 'to aid, encourage, or assist (someone), esp. in the commission of a crime.'[169] Someone who is actually or constructively present at and aids and abets in the commission of a crime can be held liable as a principal. On the other hand, an accessory is 'one who procures, counsels, commands, or abets the principal, and is absent when the latter commits the crime [accessory before the fact], or who, after the crime has been committed, receives, relieves, comforts, or assists the perpetrator [accessory after the fact]'.[170] The Convention clearly prohibits States' actions that fall either into (1) the category of a principle aider, encourager or inducer, or (2) an 'accessory before the fact' to prohibited activities. The Convention might also prohibit actions that could be characterized as 'accessorial after the fact' when such 'assistance given by one State to another after the latter has committed an internationally wrongful act may amount to the adoption of that act by the former State'.[171]

Assistance, encouragement and inducement, and financial investment in firms producing cluster munitions

1.72 Does investment in firms producing cluster munitions constitute assistance, encouragement, or inducement? This issue was raised by the CMC during the Oslo Process but no proposals to this effect were submitted by any of the negotiating States in Dublin. Considering the very wide scope of Article 1, paragraph 1(c), covering not only assistance, but also encouragement and inducement, States Parties may interpret the Convention to this effect. At the Diplomatic Conference after negotiations had formally ended but prior to the closing ceremony, the CMC called for States to put on the diplomatic record that 'the prohibition on assistance in Article 1, paragraph 1(c) includes a *prohibition on investments*

---

[169] *Black's Law Dictionary* (Eighth Edition, 2004).

In connection with the principal in the second degree or accessory before the fact, the terms 'aid' and 'abet' are frequently used interchangeably, although they are not synonymous. To 'aid' is to assist or help another. To 'abet' means, literally, to bait or excite, as in the case of an animal. In its legal sense, it means to encourage, advise, or instigate the commission of a crime.

Charles E. Torcia, *Wharton's Criminal Law* §29, at 181 (Fifteenth Edition, 1993) cited in *Black's Law Dictionary* (Eighth Edition, 2004).

[170] F. C. Amendola, *et al.*, 22 *Corpus Juris Secundum, Criminal Law* §165. 'Under some authority, accessory conduct is no longer recognized as conduct making one a party.' *Ibid.*

[171] ILC, *Draft articles on Responsibility of States, op. cit.*, p. 65 (Commentary on Part IV, paragraph 9), *citing* Article 11, Conduct acknowledged and adopted by a State as its own.

in cluster munitions producers'.[172] No State made such a statement, but several States subsequently responded to inquiries on this issue by Human Rights Watch:

[S]everal signatories to the Convention on Cluster Munitions have expressed their views on the issue of financial investment in acts prohibited by the convention. Mexico stated that 'investment for the production of cluster munitions is also prohibited by the Convention.' Lebanon stated that financing and investment in cluster munition production or transfer is prohibited. Bulgaria noted that while a ban on investment in cluster munition production is not explicit in the text of the convention, it would need to be 'considered in light of the general prohibition on the development and production of cluster munitions.' The Netherlands said that investment in production of cluster munitions runs counter to the spirit of, but is not banned by, the convention.[173]

Lebanon's position is quite explicit, stating that investment in firms that produce cluster munitions, as well as investment in companies that provide financing to producers, is prohibited.[174] Additionally, Laos has stated that it 'is of the view that . . . the investment of [*sic*] cluster munitions should be banned'.[175] Mexico has a similar understanding of the purview of the Convention.[176]

---

[172] Understandings for the Diplomatic Record, 28 May 2008, 8:00. In a position paper distributed at the Dublin Diplomatic Conference, the CMC stated that it believes that:

the prohibition on assistance includes a prohibition on investments in cluster munitions. . . . Financing and investment are active choices, based on clear assessment of the company and its plans. Investing in a cluster munitions producer is a choice to support the production of these weapons that cause unacceptable harm. . . . A ban on investments in cluster munitions will stem capital flows from signatory countries towards cluster munitions producing or trading companies.

CMC, 'Investment in Civilian Suffering to be Halted by Future Cluster Munitions Convention', CMC Policy Paper, undated.

[173] Human Rights Watch and Landmine Action, *Banning Cluster Munitions, op. cit.,* pp. 20–21 (footnotes omitted).

[174] 'It is the understanding of the Government of Lebanon that Article /1/ paragraph (c) of the Convention prohibits the investment in entities engaged in the production or transfer of cluster munitions or investment in any company that provides financing to such entities. In the view of Lebanon "assistance" as stipulated in Article /1/ paragraph (c) includes investment in entities engaged in the production or transfer of cluster munitions and is thus prohibited under the Convention.' Letter to Human Rights Watch from the Permanent Mission of Lebanon to the UN Office in Geneva, 10 February 2009.

[175] Letter from Saleumxay Kommasith, Director General, Department of International Affairs, Ministry of Foreign Affairs, Lao PDR, to Human Rights Watch, 25 February 2009.

[176] '[I]t is Mexico's opinion that investment for the production of cluster munitions is also prohibited by the Convention.' Letter from Juan Manuel Gomez Robledo, Undersecretary of Multilateral Affairs and Human Rights to Stephen Goose, Human Rights Watch, 4 March 2009.

1.73 Several States have addressed the issue of investment in national implementing legislation. New Zealand prohibits intentional or knowing investment in the development or production of cluster munitions.[177] Luxembourg has explicitly prohibited such investments under national legislation.[178] Ireland has prohibited the investment of public monies in companies producing prohibited munitions.[179]

1.74 In addition, State Party practice may be instructive. Following the signing of the Convention, the Norwegian Ministry of Finance followed the recommendation of its pension fund's ethics council and withdrew its investments from Textron, a company manufacturing a cluster munition.[180] This disinvestment decision followed on an earlier decision in 2005 to withdraw from investments in cluster munitions producers as well as the producers of key components of cluster munitions. In June 2005, the ethics council (now called the Council on Ethics for the Government Pension Fund—Global)[181] recommended excluding producers of key components of cluster munitions from Norwegian government pension fund investment.[182]

---

[177] 'A person commits an offence who provides or invests funds with the intention that the funds be used, or knowing that they are to be used, in the development or production of cluster munitions.' Cluster Munitions Prohibition Act 2009, *op. cit.*, Part 2, Clause 10(2).

[178] The Luxembourg law reads as follows: 'Art. 3. Il est interdit à toute personne physique ou morale de financer, en connaissance de cause, des armes à sous-munitions ou des sous-munitions explosives.' ('It is prohibited to any person or legal entity to knowingly finance cluster munitions or explosive submunitions.') Loi du 4 juin 2009 portant approbation de la Convention sur les armes à sous-munitions, ouverte à la signature à Oslo le 3 décembre 2008, <http://www.chd.lu/wps/PA_1_084AIVIMRA06I4325L10000000/FTSShowAttachment?mime=application%2fpdf&id=998826&fn=998826.pdf> (accessed 8 March 2010).

[179] Cluster Munitions and Anti-Personnel Mines Act 2008, Sections 11–15.

[180] 'Textron has become the latest defence firm to be blacklisted by Norway's $380 billion Government Pension Fund-Global (GPFG), the largest of Norway's sovereign wealth funds.... "Textron produces cluster weapons, which are banned pursuant to the Convention on Cluster Munitions," [Norway's finance minister, Kristin] Halvorsen, said: "We cannot participate in the funding of this type of production." ... "The Ethics Council said it finds it appropriate to base future recommendations of exclusion on the definitions provided in the cluster munitions convention," the council statement said.' O'Dwyer, G., 'Defense Stocks and Ethics', *Defense News*, 2 March 2009, p. 26. See also Norway Ministry of Finance, 'Cluster weapons manufacturer excluded from the Government Pension Fund—Global', Press release no. 14/209, 30 January 2009, <http://www.regjeringen.no/en/dep/fin/press-center/Press-releases/2009/cluster-weapons-manufacturer-excluded-fr.html?id=543105> (accessed 8 March 2010). For additional history on disinvestment from companies producing cluster munitions, see Human Rights Watch and Landmine Action, *Banning Cluster Munitions, op. cit.*, pp. 18–19.

[181] <http://www.regjeringen.no/en/sub/styrer-rad-utvalg/ethics_council.html?id=434879> (accessed 8 March 2010).

[182] The Advisory Council 'has recommended excluding companies which are involved in production of key components for such cluster weapons. Such components may typically be the bomb canister as well as the bomblets which constitute the ammunition, in addition to other parts which

Such decisions are made on the basis of established ethical guidelines that require the '[n]egative screening of companies from the investment universe that either themselves, or through entities they control produce weapons that through normal use may violate fundamental humanitarian principles'. These decisions on disinvestment from cluster munitions producers were thus not based on an interpretation of the scope of Article 1, paragraph 1(c) on assistance etc., as they were based on guidelines adopted four years prior to the adoption of the Convention on Cluster Munitions. The Textron exclusion, which came after the adoption of the Convention, was thus based on the scope of the definition of a cluster munition in Article 2, not on the scope of Article 1, paragraph 1(c).

1.75 The question of whether 'assist, encourage or induce' in Article 1, paragraph 1(c) of the *1997 Anti-Personnel Mine Ban Convention* could be interpreted to include investments was, however, discussed in Norway by a Government appointed Advisory Council on International Law in 2001. Its mandate was to determine whether investments through the Petroleum Fund could constitute a breach of Norway's international legal obligations. The Commission recommended to the Ministry of Finance that the Singaporean company (Singapore Technologies) be excluded from the Fund's investment universe, 'because any investment in such a company could constitute a violation of the complicity provision in the Mine

are essential for the functioning of the weapon.' The Advisory Council on Ethics for the Norwegian Government Petroleum Fund, Recommendation of 16 June 2005 on the exclusion of companies involved in production of cluster munitions, p. 2, <http://www.regjeringen.no/pages/1661742/Tilrådning%20klasevåpen%20eng%2015%20juni%202005.pdf> (accessed 8 March 2010):

> Even the small explosive devices or bomblets are of course key components in a cluster munition. They consist, inter alia, of the explosives themselves, the surrounding canister and a detonation mechanism or fuse that makes the explosive charge detonate. These are also key components. The canister that contains bomblets is, as a rule, specially designed for this purpose and must therefore be regarded as a key component of a cluster munition. It also consists of several sub-components.
>
> All canisters have a mechanism or a fuse that makes the canister open and drop the smaller explosive devices. In many cases, both the canister and the bomblets have guidance mechanisms that make it possible to steer them towards the target and ensure that they strike at the correct angle. Such guidance mechanisms make it possible to drop cluster bombs from great heights and therefore avoid anti-aircraft fire. They may therefore also be considered as key components. *Ibid.*, p. 3

The Norwegian Ministry of Finance subsequently excluded cluster munition producers who either confirmed they did produce the weapons or did not respond to inquiries. Norway Ministry of Finance, A Further Eight Companies Excluded from the Petroleum Fund, Press Release No. 57/205, 2 September 2005, <http://www.regjeringen.no/en/archive/Bondeviks-2nd-Government/ministry-of-finance/Nyheter-og-pressemeldinger/2005/a_further_eight_companies_excluded.html?id=256695> (accessed 8 March 2010).

Ban Convention (Article 1(1)(c))'.[183] The following discussion of Article 1, paragraph 1(c) was contained in the recommendation:

The provision in article 1 (1) (c) says nothing about which forms of assistance etc. that are meant to be covered. The provision is widely formulated and must be presumed to be intended to cover all forms of assistance. [....] The question is whether investments in Singapore Technologies Engineering (STE) can be perceived as assisting within the meaning of the convention. [....] According to the rules of the Petroleum Fund, the fund cannot acquire more than 3% ownership of an individual company. [....] It can, however, hardly be demanded that the investment shall be of a specific amount in order for it to be covered by the Convention. According to article 31 of the Vienna Convention on the Law of Treaties, a convention shall be interpreted in accordance with its wording and in compliance with the object and purpose of the convention. Neither the wording of the convention nor its purpose supports such a restrictive interpretation.

Furthermore, the prohibition against assistance is not limited to cover only new offers of shares, in order for the company to be supplied with 'new' capital. According to the Advisory Commission's view, the point is that any investment of money in a company can be regarded as a form of support to the company even though the sums, relatively speaking, are low. The mere fact that the Petroleum Fund invests at all in a company, could, for example, contribute to other states and investors following suit. And even if an investment in a company was so modest that it probably would not reach the threshold of the prohibition on states to 'assist' in landmine production, this would probably nevertheless be covered by the alternatives 'encourage or induce in any way'. To own shares in Singapore Technologies Engineering as long as the company (or its subsidiary) continues to produce anti-personnel mines, can, according to the view of the Advisory Commission, therefore be affected by the accessory provision in article 1 (1) (c).[184]

1.76 In 2007, before the Convention was negotiated, Belgium enacted a law prohibiting investment in submunitions.[185] The law bans 'the financing of companies under Belgian law or foreign law that produce, use, repair, distribute, import, export, store or transport anti-personnel mines and/or

---

[183] Nystuen, G., 'Investment policies and arms production – experiences from the Norwegian Pension Fund-Global', in Borrie, J. and Martin Randin, V. (eds.), *Thinking Outside the Box in Multilateral Disarmament and Arms Control Negotiations* (Geneva: UNIDIR, 2006).

[184] <http://www.regjeringen.no/en/dep/fin/Selected-topics/the-government-pension-fund/responsible-investments/Advisory-Commission-Documents/Advisory-Commission.html?id=413581> (accessed 1 March 2010).

[185] Loi interdisant le financement de la fabrication, de l'utilisation ou de la détention de mines antipersonnel et de sous-munitions, F. 2007 — 1661 [C – 2007/03169], 20 March 2007, published in Belge Moniteur, 26 April 2007, available at <http://www.moniteur.be>.

sub-munitions in the meaning of this law, and with regard to the spreading thereof'. Financing is defined to include 'all forms of financial support, namely credits, bank guarantees and the acquisition of financial instruments issued by that company'. The law also called upon the government to publish a list 'i) of the companies that are shown to carry out an activity in contravention of the previous sentence; ii) of the companies that own a majority share in the companies covered by part i) and iii) the institutions for collective investment that hold financial instruments of companies covered by parts i) and ii)'.[186] At the time of writing, the list of companies had not been published.[187]

1.77 The *1997 Anti-Personnel Mine Ban Convention* contains similar language on assistance and its interpretation may provide insight in how States Parties to the Convention on Cluster Munitions may be expected to behave. Despite relevant practice, however, with respect to the corresponding provisions in the Convention on Cluster Munitions, there is not yet sufficient State practice to draw any firm conclusions on whether or not investment in production is covered by 'assist, encourage or induce'. On the other hand, there seems to be sufficient State practice to assert that such an interpretation cannot be excluded.

1.78 While the Danish parliament determined that implementing legislation beyond simple ratification was not necessary,[188] its defence committee has engaged Government ministries on implementing policies, including the question of investment.[189] The Government assessed that 'by acceding to the Convention it will be prohibited for the Danish government, including municipalities, under certain circumstances to invest in companies that are mainly producing or trading in cluster munitions'.[190] The minority on the defence committee called upon the Government to clarify that position by

---

[186] Loi interdisant le financement de la fabrication, de l'utilisation ou de la détention de mines antipersonnel et de sous-munitions, *op. cit.*. English translation taken from Netwerk Vlaanderen vzw & IKV Pax Christi, *Belgium no longer an international frontrunner*, 12 February 2010, p. 2.

[187] Civil society groups in early 2010 called upon the Government to publish the list and to use the Convention definition of cluster munitions in doing so. *Ibid.*

[188] B 60 Forslag til folketingsbeslutning om Danmarks godkendelse af konventionen om klyngeammunition undertegnet den 4. december 2008 i Oslo, § 2, 19 November 2009, <http://pp.ft.dk/samling/20091/beslutningsforslag/B60/som_fremsat.htm>. The parliament voted in favour of ratification on 17 December 2009, <http://www.ft.dk/dokumenter/tingdok.aspx?/samling/20091/beslutningsforslag/b60/som_vedtaget.htm>, and deposited ratification at the UN on 12 February 2010. CMC, 'Denmark ratifies landmark convention banning cluster munitions', Press release, 12 February 2010, <http://www.stopclustermunitions.org/media/press-releases/?id=2038> (accessed 1 March 2010).

[189] Betænkning afgivet af Forsvarsudvalget den 10 december 2009, Betænkning over Forslag til folketingsbeslutning om Danmarks godkendelse af convention (Report submitted by the Defense Committee of 10 December 2009), <http://www.ft.dk/dokumenter/tingdok.aspx?/samling/20091/beslutningsforslag/b60/bilag/6/790705/index.htm>.   [190] *Ibid.*, §4.

providing investors with a list of cluster munitions manufacturers, as well as investigating the possibility of an 'outright ban' on investments.[191]

1.79 The Danish Ministry of Economy and Trade issued a report in January 2010 addressing three issues: (1) whether the Belgium Government had created a list of companies as a result of its ban on investments (the Belgium Government had not yet done so); (2) to what extent creating such a list would be acceptable under the WTO (concluding that creating such a list would be possible under existing WTO rules, because the WTO has never adopted a treaty on investment, and investment related provisions of existing WTO agreements—TRIMs, or Trade Related Investment Measures—do not apply to cluster munitions); and (3) any other problems associated with drawing up a list of companies as an investment ban (concluding that while European Union rules on free movement of capital should be considered, such a ban could be justified in terms of public policy). The report nonetheless goes on to suggest that active and socially responsible investment strategies by institutional investors such as pension funds may be more successful in curbing cluster munition production and that creating ban lists may be counterproductive. That is, by investing in companies in which cluster munition production is a small percentage of their overall business, investors may be able to persuade them to cease the munitions production.[192]

1.80 Equally at issue is the question of investment in firms that produce multi-use key components, i.e. components which are essential for the functioning of cluster munitions but which are also components in non-prohibited munitions. Investment in the production of such components may be acceptable if sufficient assurances are made by the manufacturer that the end use of their components will not be the production of cluster munitions. The

---

[191] *Ibid.*

[192] Afklaring af spørgsmål fra Forsvarsudvalget vedr. forslag til folketingsbeslutning om forbud mod investeringer i, produktion af og handel med klyngevåben (B 173), Okonomi og Erhvervministeriet, Forsvarsudvalget 2009–10, FOU alm. del Bilag 45, Offentligt, 11 January 2010, <http://www.ft.dk/dokumenter/tingdok.aspx?/samling/20091/almdel/fou/bilag/45/783692/index.htm> (accessed 20 March 2010). An exclusion list could limit the freedom of investors but the report notes that most Danish pension funds already adopt an ethical investment policy and private investors seek to profile themselves by investing responsibly. The report warns that legislation may curb this type of investments and unintentionally limit efforts to invest responsibly. The UN Principles for Responsible Investment (UNPRI) promote active ownership as the main strategy for responsible investment. The report cautions that Danish investors might not be able to follow the UN's recommendations of an active ownership strategy with regard to companies listed on the exclusion list. It should be left to the investors to choose between active ownership and disinvestment only in cases where active ownership is unsuccessful. The report notes that it can be extremely difficult to draft an objective list of companies, because cluster munition production often makes up only a small part of a large company's production. *Ibid.*

commentary on the draft articles on State Responsibility provides helpful insight:

a State providing financial or other aid to another State should not be required to assume the risk that the latter will divert the aid for purposes which may be internationally unlawful. Thus, it is necessary to establish a close connection between the action of the assisting, directing or coercing State on the one hand and that of the State committing the internationally wrongful act on the other. Thus, ... the former State should be aware of the circumstances of the internationally wrongful act in question, and establish a specific causal link between that act and the conduct of the assisting, directing or coercing State.[193]

Practice by States Parties prohibiting investment in cluster munition production will help to clarify the issue.

Assistance and Article 21[194]

1.81 There is a close link between Article 1, paragraph 1(c) on assistance and Article 21 on interoperability. Article 21 was negotiated and adopted due to concern that military cooperation with States not party to the Convention might constitute assistance in contravention of Article 1. Article 21 must be read in concert with Article 1, as it says 'notwithstanding the provisions of Article 1 ... and in accordance with international law, States Parties, their military personnel or nationals, may engage in military cooperation and operations with States not party to this Convention that might engage in activities prohibited to a State Party'.[195] The impact of Article 21 on interpreting Article 1, paragraph 1(c) is discussed in detail in the commentary on Article 21.

Paragraph 2

Paragraph 1 of this Article applies, *mutatis mutandis*, to explosive bomblets that are specifically designed to be dispersed or released from dispensers affixed to aircraft.

---

[193] *Draft articles on Responsibility of States for Internationally Wrongful Acts, with commentaries 2001, op. cit.*, p. 65.

A State providing material or financial assistance or aid to another State does not normally assume the risk that its assistance or aid may be used to carry out an internationally wrongful act. If the assisting or aiding State is unaware of the circumstances in which its aid or assistance is intended to be used by the other State, it bears no international responsibility.

Commentary on Article 16, paragraph 4, p. 66.

[194] For a fuller discussion of the issue, see, *infra*, the commentary on Article 21.

[195] Article 21, paragraph 3.

Preparatory discussions and negotiations

1.82 The proposal to prohibit explosive bomblets—munitions contained in dispensers fixed to aircraft—was first made by Ireland at the Wellington Conference. Ireland argued that as the area effects of these bomblets and the humanitarian consequences of their use are essentially the same as those of explosive submunitions they should also be prohibited, and stated that failure to do so could open a loophole in the Convention.[196] Ireland feared that even though these weapons resemble submunitions, because explosive bomblets are not part of a larger ('parent') munition they would not fall within the definition of a cluster munition. It asserted that without an express prohibition of explosive bomblets a clear incentive would exist for weapons manufacturers to develop more advanced systems for dispersal from fixed dispensers of munitions that would escape the treaty's purview. There was even concern that submunitions removed from cluster munitions prohibited by the Convention might in the future be diverted for use in specially adapted dispensers.

1.83 No provision addressing explosive bomblets was made in the Draft Cluster Munitions Convention that formed the basis of the negotiation of the Convention. At the Dublin Diplomatic Conference, Ireland formally proposed the amendment of the draft Convention text to provide that 'dispensers, affixed to an aerial platform and designed to disperse or release explosive bomblets, are subject to the same provisions as cluster munitions'.[197] An accompanying proposal for the amendment of Article 2 provided draft definitions of 'explosive bomblet' and 'unexploded explosive bomblet'.[198] While there was broad support at the Conference for the objective of the proposed prohibition, Canada, Spain, and the UK noted that they would have to consider the proposed definitions carefully.[199] Informal consultations were then conducted

---

[196] These systems are already in existence and some have been used in armed conflict in the past, such as the SUU-13/A, used by the US during the Vietnam War. The SUU-13/A was a dispenser in the form of a rectangular box attached to an aircraft's undercarriage that ejected its submunitions straight down from 40 ports in the bottom of the box. The SUU-14/A resembled a bundle of six pipes strapped together, fixed with a cap at the front. Submunitions were ejected from the rear by pistons located in the front of each tube. The British-made JP-233 bomblet dispenser was used extensively by Royal Air Force Tornado bombers during the first Gulf War against Iraqi airfields but has since been withdrawn from service by the UK. See also, *supra*, §0.2.

[197] 'Proposal by Ireland for the amendment of Article 1', Diplomatic Conference doc. CCM/15, 19 May 2008.

[198] 'Proposal by Ireland for the amendment of Article 2', Diplomatic Conference doc. CCM 25, 19 May 2008.

[199] The UK in particular was concerned to assess what implications the proposal had for its CRV-7/M-73 system. This is a so-called 'direct fire' munition fired from rocket pods mounted on helicopters. Each rocket pod can carry 19 CRV-7/M261 rockets, each of which contains nine M-73

between Ireland, as proposer, and these delegations. Following these consultations changes were made to the proposed definitions of 'explosive bomblet' and 'unexploded bomblet' and a new draft definition of a dispenser elaborated.[200] For the purpose of clarity the focus of the proposal became the explosive bomblets themselves rather than the dispenser.

1.84 On 28 May 2008, the President of the Conference introduced his consolidated draft Convention Text[201] which provided that paragraph 1 of Article 1 'applies, *mutatis mutandis,* to explosive bomblets that are specifically designed to be dispersed or released from dispensers affixed to aircraft'.[202] This text was included in the Convention as Article 1, paragraph 2.

Commentary

1.85 Explosive bomblets are weapons similar in effect to submunitions but do not fall within the definition of a cluster munition as they are dispersed or released from dispensers affixed to an aircraft, and not from a larger ('parent') munition. The legal effect of paragraph 2 of Article 1 is that each State Party undertakes never under any circumstances to:

(a) use explosive bomblets that are specifically designed to be dispersed or released from dispensers affixed to aircraft;
(b) develop, produce, otherwise acquire, stockpile, retain or transfer to anyone, directly or indirectly, such explosive bomblets; or
(c) assist, encourage, or induce anyone to engage in any activity involving explosive bomblets and which is prohibited to a State Party under the Convention.

1.86 Paragraph 2 does not expressly provide that other provisions of the Convention applicable to cluster munitions also apply, *mutatis mutandis* (i.e. with the necessary changes having been made), to explosive bomblets. A number of other provisions of the Convention apply nevertheless. Article 4 requires that clearance and destruction operations be carried out in respect of 'cluster munition contaminated areas', which are areas containing 'cluster munition remnants'.[203] The latter are defined as including 'unexploded

---

submunitions. At the time the UK was arguing for the exclusion of 'direct fire' systems from the definition of a cluster munition under Article 2 (*cf., infra,* §2.75).

[200] See, *infra,* the commentary on Article 2. The relevant definitions exclude 'self-propelled' munitions weighing less than 20 kilograms.

[201] 'Presidency Paper, *draft* Convention on Cluster Munitions', Diplomatic Conference doc. CCM/PT/15, 28 May 2008.   [202] At Article 1, paragraph 2.

[203] See, *infra,* the commentary on Article 4, paragraph 1.

bomblets'.[204] Likewise, Article 6, paragraph 4, obliges States Parties in a position to do so to provide assistance in the clearance and destruction of cluster munition remnants generally. Article 9 requires States Parties to take all appropriate measures to implement the Convention, including the imposition of penal sanctions to prevent and suppress any prohibited activity, and this applies to activities involving explosive bomblets just as it does to cluster munitions.[205] With respect to Article 5, national overseas development aid programmes for the assistance of victims of munitions do not generally distinguish between types of munitions and the provision of assistance is not generally dependent on the nature of the munition involved. Victims of explosive bomblets are therefore just as likely to benefit from such programmes as cluster munition victims, notwithstanding the absence of an express obligation under Article 5 to assist the former.

1.87 The Convention does not expressly require the destruction of explosive bomblet stocks under Article 3, nor does it expressly require annual reports under Article 7 in respect of stocks of explosive bomblets and of progress towards their destruction. Similarly, the limited exceptions for retention found in Article 3, paragraph 6 and for transfer found in Article 3, paragraph 7 do not expressly apply to explosive bomblets. These omissions are to a large extent an oversight, explained by the fact that the Diplomatic Conference was able to agree only at the very end of its work that explosive bomblets should be addressed by the Convention at all.

1.88 As noted above,[206] the provisions of the Convention concerning explosive bomblets are intended to pre-empt a potentially very large loophole that might have been exploited in the future had these weapons not also been prohibited. However, insofar as any existing stocks of explosive bomblets are concerned, as the Convention prohibits their retention, stockpile and transfer, a State Party would appear to be required to destroy whatever stocks it possesses immediately prior to entry into force of the Convention in order to avoid finding itself in violation of these obligations. This could be the effect of a literal reading of Article 3, which does not expressly apply to explosive bomblets.[207] However, the circumstances of the conclusion of the

---

[204] See, *infra*, the commentary on Article 2.

[205] See, e.g., Section 6(1) of Ireland's Cluster Munitions and Anti-Personnel Mines Act 2008, which provides that 'a person who (a) uses, (b) develops or produces, (c) acquires, (d) possesses or retains, or (e) transfers to any person, a cluster munition or explosive bomblet is guilty of an offence.'   [206] See, *supra*, §1.4.

[207] Arguably a literal reading of the text leads to a result that is 'manifestly absurd or unreasonable' within the meaning of Article 32 of the *Vienna Convention on the Law of Treaties*, which would then permit recourse to supplementary means of interpretation 'including the preparatory work

Convention suggest that this is an oversight. The better interpretation of the Convention would be that as stockpiling of explosive bomblets explicitly is banned, an obligation to destroy them implicitly follows. It seems likely that this will become a topic under discussions on stockpile destruction at Meetings of States Parties and other Convention-related meetings and conferences.[208]

Paragraph 3

This Convention does not apply to mines.

Preparatory discussions and negotiations

1.89 Based on discussions at the Lima and Vienna conferences, the Draft Cluster Munitions Convention introduced language that specifically excluded landmines.[209] According to the commentary accompanying the draft, the paragraph:

specifies that the present Convention does not regulate mines as defined in Article 2 (1) of Amended Protocol II to the CCW, reflecting the discussion at the Lima and

---

of the treaty and the circumstances of its conclusion' in order to interpret the Convention. The President of the Dublin Conference, Ambassador O'Ceallaigh, stated that the inclusion of paragraph 2 of Article 1 in the final President's draft text:

addressed the anomaly relating to bomblets released from dispensers attached to aircraft. These look and behave like submunitions but they are not, since they do not come from a larger munition. Both informal and bilateral consultations had shown that it was considered important to address this issue at this stage, in order to avoid the Convention's obligations being circumvented by the use of such systems.

Cf. 'Summary Record of Fifteenth Session of the Committee of the Whole', Diplomatic Conference doc. CCM/CW/SR/15, 18 June 2008, p. 2.

[208] During the Diplomatic Conference, at the Meeting of the Committee of the Whole immediately preceding the Plenary Meeting at which participating States agreed to adopt the Convention, the ICRC 'encouraged States to make clear in their statements upon adoption that destruction obligations also apply to bomblets from dispensers'. Summary Record of Sixteenth Session of the Committee of the Whole, Diplomatic Conference doc. CCM/CW/SR/16, 18 June 2008, p. 9.

[209] 'This Convention does not apply to "mines" as defined by the Protocol on Prohibitions or Restrictions on the Use of Mines, Booby-Traps and Other Devices, as amended on 3 May 1996, annexed to the Convention on Prohibitions or Restrictions on the Use of Certain Conventional Weapons which may be Deemed to be Excessively Injurious or to have Indiscriminate Effects.'
Article 1, paragraph 2, Draft Cluster Munitions Convention.

Vienna Conferences. This means that neither anti-vehicle mines[210] nor anti-personnel mines fall under the scope of application of this Convention.[211]

1.90 During the Diplomatic Conference, the drafters simplified the language to state that 'this Convention does apply to mines',[212] adding a definition of 'mine' that includes all landmines, whether anti-personnel or anti-vehicle.[213] The definition of the term 'mine' was taken verbatim from the *1997 Anti-Personnel Mine Ban Convention*.[214] The simplification of language stemmed from discussions led by Ambassador Christine Schraner Burgener of Switzerland, who served as a Friend of the President at the Diplomatic Conference.[215] Although the focus of her consultations was the issue of interoperability and issues related to the scope of application of the Convention, she introduced a significant redrafting of the part of Article 1 related to the exclusion of mines when reporting to the Committee of the Whole. No State formally proposed such a re-writing, but it improved the clarity of the text.[216] In introducing the modified language, Ambassador O'Ceallaigh, the President of the Conference, said that 'Paragraph 3 had been amended in response to an objection to the reference to mines being framed by the Convention on Certain Conventional Weapons.'[217] He further noted that the paragraph 'now refers to mines' and that the definition of a mine 'is identical to that of the Anti-Personnel Mine Ban Convention'.[218]

---

[210] At the Wellington Conference, the CMC called for the inclusion of remotely delivered anti-vehicle mines in the negotiation of the Convention on Cluster Munitions as 'they are inadequately regulated elsewhere'. CMC, '(Revised) Observations by the Cluster Munition Coalition on the Draft Cluster Munitions Convention, dated 21 January 2008', p. 2. This argument did not attract the support of negotiating States.

[211] Draft Cluster Munitions Convention Explanatory Notes, 21 January 2008.

[212] Article 1, paragraph 3.   [213] Article 2, paragraph 12.

[214] Under Article 2, paragraph 2 of the *1997 Anti-Personnel Mine Ban Convention*:

'Mine' means a munition designed to be placed under, on or near the ground or other surface area and to be exploded by the presence, proximity or contact of a person or a vehicle.

This definition varies slightly from that found in the *1996 CCW Amended Protocol II*, Article 2, paragraph 1:

'Mine' means a munition placed under, on or near the ground or other surface area and designed to be exploded by the presence, proximity or contact of a person or vehicle.

[215] See Diplomatic Conference docs. CCM/CW/SR/1 and CCM/CW/SR/9.

[216] Presidential text delivered on 28 May 2008 at 10am; see 'Summary Record of Fourteenth Session of the Committee of the Whole', Diplomatic Conference doc. CCM/CW/SR/14, 18 June 2008; and 'Summary Record of Fifteenth Session of the Committee of the Whole', *op. cit.*

[217] 'Summary Record of Twelfth Session of the Committee of the Whole', Diplomatic Conference doc. CCM/CW/SR/12, 18 June 2008.   [218] *Ibid.*

Commentary

1.91 By virtue of paragraph 3 of Article 1, all landmines, whether anti-personnel or anti-vehicle, are excluded from the purview of the Convention. Thus, a munition that contains landmines as submunitions is regulated by customary international law as well as other instruments of international law, notably, where applicable, the *1997 Anti-Personnel Mine Ban Convention*, *1980 Protocol II on mines, booby-traps and other devices*, and *1996 Amended Protocol II*.

Article 2. Definitions

Bonnie Docherty, Lou Maresca, Richard Moyes, and
Markus Reiterer[1]

Article 2—Definitions

For the purposes of this Convention:

1. **'Cluster munition victims'** means all persons who have been killed or
suffered physical or psychological injury, economic loss, social marginalisation or substantial impairment of the realisation of their rights caused by the
use of cluster munitions. They include those persons directly impacted by
cluster munitions as well as their affected families and communities;

2. **'Cluster munition'** means a conventional munition that is designed
to disperse or release explosive submunitions each weighing less than 20
kilograms, and includes those explosive submunitions. It does not mean
the following:

(a) A munition or submunition designed to dispense flares, smoke,
pyrotechnics or chaff; or a munition designed exclusively for an air
defence role;

(b) A munition or submunition designed to produce electrical or electronic effects;

(c) A munition that, in order to avoid indiscriminate area effects and
the risks posed by unexploded submunitions, has all of the following
characteristics:

(i) Each munition contains fewer than ten explosive submunitions;

(ii) Each explosive submunition weighs more than four kilograms;

(iii) Each explosive submunition is designed to detect and engage a
single target object;

(iv) Each explosive submunition is equipped with an electronic self-
destruction mechanism;

(v) Each explosive submunition is equipped with an electronic self-
deactivating feature;

---

[1] Markus Reiterer wrote the commentary on paragraph 1, Richard Moyes wrote the commentary
on paragraphs 2–3, Lou Maresca wrote the commentary on paragraphs 4–7 and 15, and Bonnie
Docherty wrote the overview, preparatory discussions, and negotiating history of the 'other' definitions as well as the commentary on paragraphs 8–14.

3. '**Explosive submunition**' means a conventional munition that in order to perform its task is dispersed or released by a cluster munition and is designed to function by detonating an explosive charge prior to, on or after impact;

4. '**Failed cluster munition**' means a cluster munition that has been fired, dropped, launched, projected or otherwise delivered and which should have dispersed or released its explosive submunitions but failed to do so;

5. '**Unexploded submunition**' means an explosive submunition that has been dispersed or released by, or otherwise separated from, a cluster munition and has failed to explode as intended;

6. '**Abandoned cluster munitions**' means cluster munitions or explosive submunitions that have not been used and that have been left behind or dumped, and that are no longer under the control of the party that left them behind or dumped them. They may or may not have been prepared for use;

7. '**Cluster munition remnants**' means failed cluster munitions, abandoned cluster munitions, unexploded submunitions and unexploded bomblets;

8. '**Transfer**' involves, in addition to the physical movement of cluster munitions into or from national territory, the transfer of title to and control over cluster munitions, but does not involve the transfer of territory containing cluster munition remnants;

9. '**Self-destruction mechanism**' means an incorporated automatically-functioning mechanism which is in addition to the primary initiating mechanism of the munition and which secures the destruction of the munition into which it is incorporated;

10. '**Self-deactivating**' means automatically rendering a munition inoperable by means of the irreversible exhaustion of a component, for example a battery, that is essential to the operation of the munition;

11. '**Cluster munition contaminated area**' means an area known or suspected to contain cluster munition remnants;

12. '**Mine**' means a munition designed to be placed under, on or near the ground or other surface area and to be exploded by the presence, proximity or contact of a person or a vehicle;

13. '**Explosive bomblet**' means a conventional munition, weighing less than 20 kilograms, which is not self-propelled and which, in order to perform its task, is dispersed or released by a dispenser, and is designed to function by detonating an explosive charge prior to, on or after impact;

14. '**Dispenser**' means a container that is designed to disperse or release explosive bomblets and which is affixed to an aircraft at the time of dispersal or release;

15. '**Unexploded bomblet**' means an explosive bomblet that has been dispersed, released or otherwise separated from a dispenser and has failed to explode as intended.

Overview of the Article

2.1 Article 2 sets out a number of definitions 'for the purposes of this Convention'.[2] Two of these definitions were derived either verbatim or with slight modification from the *1997 Anti-Personnel Mine Ban Convention*:[3] specifically 'mine' and 'transfer'.[4] Others were adapted from related definitions in *1996 Amended Protocol II*[5] and *2003 Protocol V*[6] annexed to the *Convention on Certain Conventional Weapons* (CCW).[7] However, the definitions of cluster munition victims, and of cluster munition, explosive submunition, explosive bomblet, and dispenser were largely elaborated within the negotiation of the Convention on Cluster Munitions itself.

Preparatory discussions and negotiations

2.2 Preparatory discussions and the negotiations of Article 2 were generally divided into three 'streams': one focusing on the definition of cluster munition victims (paragraph 1),[8] the second on the definition of cluster munition (paragraphs 2 and 3),[9] and the third on 'other' definitions (the remaining

---

[2] This implies that they may not have a wider impact on international law, including the use of these terms in other treaties that may govern cluster munitions or even other weapons.

[3] The formal title of this treaty is the Convention on the Prohibition of the Use, Stockpiling, Production and Transfer of Anti-Personnel Mines and on Their Destruction.

[4] Although the definition of transfer in the *1997 Anti-Personnel Mine Ban Convention* was itself taken from *1996 Amended Protocol II* to the *1980 Convention on Certain Conventional Weapons*.

[5] The formal title of this instrument is the Protocol on Prohibitions or Restrictions on the Use of Mines, Booby-Traps and Other Devices as amended on 3 May 1996. The definitions of self-destruction mechanism and self-deactivating are taken from the Protocol.

[6] *2003 Protocol V*. The definition of abandoned cluster munition is adapted from the definition of abandoned explosive ordnance in Article 2, paragraph 3 of the Protocol.

[7] The Convention on Prohibitions or Restrictions on the Use of Certain Conventional Weapons Which May Be Deemed to Be Excessively Injurious or to Have Indiscriminate Effects, as amended on 21 December 2001 (CCW).

[8] The definition of 'cluster munition victims' was generally discussed as an integral part of the victim assistance package which encompassed Article 5 itself, the relevant parts of the preamble, as well as other pertinent parts of the Convention text. In the course of the conferences held in Lima, Belgrade, Brussels, and Vienna the call for the Convention to include a definition of the term was made regularly with the result that the Draft Cluster Munitions Convention presented to the Wellington Conference defined, for the first time, those covered by cluster munition victims. Some elements of the definition, however, had been introduced into the Oslo Process at a fairly early stage.

[9] From the Lima Discussion Text, through the Vienna Discussion Text of November 2007, the February 2008 Wellington Conference, and the Dublin Diplomatic Conference, drafts of Article 1 presented prohibitions on the use, production, stockpiling, and transfer of 'cluster munitions' as a whole category. Discussions regarding the definition of 'cluster munition' therefore provided the

definitions, i.e. paragraphs 4–15).[10] The definition of 'cluster munition', and certain related definitions such as that of 'explosive submunition' were closely linked to the General Obligations and Scope of the Convention as articulated in Article 1.

2.3 There remain other terms within the Convention, including those used within certain definitions themselves, which would have warranted further clarification. These include terms such as 'assist', 'in a position to do so', and 'air defence role'.[11] Given differing interpretations among States, however, negotiating a definition of some of these terms might have proved contentious.

Cluster munition victims

Paragraph 1

> **'Cluster munition victims'** means all persons who have been killed or suffered physical or psychological injury, economic loss, social marginalisation or substantial impairment of the realisation of their rights caused by the use of cluster munitions. They include those persons directly impacted by cluster munitions as well as their affected families and communities;

Overview

2.4 The definition of 'cluster munition victim' sets the stage for the Convention's victim assistance provisions in Article 5. On a technical level it determines the group of people to whom States are obliged to provide victim assistance. More broadly, it informs the essence of victim assistance, for assistance to individuals killed or physically injured by the weapon will be different from assistance to others in the family or community who have not been physically injured by the weapons, but who are nonetheless significantly affected by them. The definition is broad, enumerating harm beyond physical

---

primary mechanism for determining how wide-ranging or narrow these prohibitions would be in practice (i.e. what specific existing weapons and possible future weapons would be subject to the prohibitions in Article 1).

[10] The 'other' definitions had implications for Article 1 (transfer, mine, dispenser, and explosive bomblet), the main definition of cluster munition in Article 2 ('self-destruction mechanism' and 'self-deactivating'), and Article 4 regarding clearance of cluster munition remnants. Many of the drafts for these definitions drew initially on those contained in *1996 Amended Protocol II*, the *1997 Anti-Personnel Mine Ban Convention*, and *2003 Protocol V*.

[11] For a brief discussion of this provision see, *infra*, §§2.95, 2.104, and 2.117–2.118.

injury to include psychological suffering, economic loss, social marginalization, and impairment of the realization of rights. As is seen in the commentary on Article 5, the substantive obligation to provide victim assistance has to respond to all those different types of harm.

Preparatory discussions

2.5 As noted above, the definition of cluster munition victims was generally discussed as an integral part of the victim assistance package which encompassed Article 5 itself.[12] In the course of the conferences in Lima, Belgrade, Brussels, and Vienna[13] there were regular calls for a definition of the term cluster munition victims to be included. This was done for the first time in the Draft Cluster Munitions Convention presented to the Wellington Conference. Some elements of the definition, however, had been introduced into the Oslo Process at a fairly early stage, as discussed below.

2.6 The Oslo Declaration committed the participating States to the establishment of 'a framework for cooperation and assistance that ensures adequate provision of care and rehabilitation to survivors and their communities'.[14] The drafters of the Vienna Discussion Text—while not introducing a definition of cluster munition victims proper—wished to highlight a broad understanding of victims by including a preambular paragraph referring to 'victims of cluster munitions, which inter alia include the persons directly affected, their families and communities'.[15] This formulation reflected discussions on victim assistance that had previously taken place in Lima, Belgrade, and Brussels.

2.7 At the end of the European Conference on Cluster Munitions held in Brussels on 31 October 2007, the rapporteur of the victim assistance session was able to report that:

there was a general understanding that victim assistance is a broad and comprehensive concept, which should use as a starting point, but also as a constant reference point the needs and rights of victims. [...] Already the term victim as such is to be understood broadly, i.e. encompassing the survivor as such—the victim of the direct impact, but also other victimized persons, including family and affected communities.[16]

---

[12] See, *infra*, the commentary on Article 5.

[13] See, *supra*, the Introduction to this Commentary for a description of these conferences.

[14] See Oslo Declaration, paragraph 1(ii).

[15] See Vienna Discussion Text, first preambular paragraph.

[16] Summary on the Victim Assistance discussion, European Regional Conference on Cluster Munitions Brussels, 31 October 2007, Rapporteur: Markus Reiterer, Austria, available at: <http://www.diplomatie.be/en/pdf/reiter.pdf> (accessed 8 March 2010).

This principled approach was essentially supported during the Vienna Conference and formed part of what the President of the Vienna Conference, Ambassador Wolfgang Petritsch, called the *Vienna Consensus* on victim assistance, which reinforced the endeavours to establish victim assistance as 'a key legal obligation of the same quality as the other main building blocks of the future treaty'[17] and hence work towards a definition of the term 'cluster munition victims'.

2.8 The Draft Cluster Munitions Convention for the first time contained a draft definition of cluster munition victims, which was placed as the first definition of Article 2 thereby highlighting the importance attached to the humanitarian cause pursued by the Oslo Process.[18] The definition contained in the draft Convention read as follows:

'**Cluster munition victims**' means persons who have suffered physical or psychological injury, economic loss, social marginalisation or substantial impairment of the realisation of their rights caused by the use of cluster munitions. They include those persons directly impacted by cluster munitions as well as their families and communities.

The draft essentially followed the assumption that any victim assistance provision would have to use as a starting and constant reference point the needs and rights of the victims. While the definition highlights the injury or loss incurred by a victim of cluster munitions, Article 5 concentrates on how best to respond to the needs arising from such injury or loss. The draft definition sought to paint a realistic picture of victimization by portraying the defining factors that lead to the assumption that a particular person in fact has become a victim of the weapon.

2.9 The draft definition built on the discussions outlined above and the description of the term 'mine victim' as contained in Paragraph 64 of the so-called Review Document adopted at the 2004 Nairobi Summit on a Mine-Free World, which states:

It is now generally accepted that victims include those who either individually or collectively have suffered physical or psychological injury, economic loss or substantial

---

[17] Closing Remarks by Ambassador Wolfgang Petritsch at the end of the Vienna Conference. During the Conference, Spain—among others—stated that there was a need to define who is entitled to the rights outlined in the Article on victim assistance and the preamble in order to facilitate the provision of international cooperation and assistance and to provide a sense of direction for assistance. See Harrison, K., 'Report of the Vienna Conference on Cluster Munitions, 5–7 December 2007', Women's International League for Peace and Freedom, January 2008, <http://www.wilpf.int.ch/disarmament/clustermunitions/ViennaConference/viennareport.htm> (accessed 8 March 2010).

[18] The decision on the draft text and its placement of the definition was made during a meeting of the core group States in early January 2008 following an informal proposal by Austria.

impairment of their fundamental rights through acts or omissions related to mine utilization.[19]

The definition in the Draft Cluster Munitions Convention also drew on the definition of 'victims of gross violations of international human rights law and serious violations of international humanitarian law', contained in the Basic Principles and Guidelines on the Right to a Remedy and Reparation for Victims of Gross Violations of International Human Rights Law and Serious Violations of International Humanitarian Law.[20] That definition reads as follows:

For purposes of the present document, victims are persons who individually or collectively suffered harm, including physical or mental injury, emotional suffering, economic loss or substantial impairment of their fundamental rights, through acts or omissions that constitute gross violations of international human rights law, or serious violations of international humanitarian law. Where appropriate, and in accordance with domestic law, the term 'victim' also includes the immediate family or dependants of the direct victim and persons who have suffered harm in intervening to assist victims in distress or to prevent victimization.[21]

2.10 The Draft Cluster Munitions Convention signified two major developments as compared to the texts mentioned above. First, in addition to the concepts of physical and psychological injury, and economic loss or substantial impairment of the realization of rights, the draft text also included the concept of social marginalization as a form of victimization of a person. Second, the draft text developed the idea contained in the phrase 'either individually or collectively have suffered' by introducing a specific reference to the families and communities of persons directly impacted by cluster munitions.

2.11 This draft definition did not remain without criticism. During the Wellington Conference Switzerland proposed to delete the entire definition, expressing concern that the inclusion of a definition might facilitate discrimination against victims of other weapons or explosive remnants of war.

---

[19] See Nairobi Summit on a Mine-free World, Review of the Operation and Status of the Convention on the Prohibition of the Use, Stockpiling and Production and Transfer of Anti-Personnel Mines and on their Destruction: 1999–2004, contained in doc. APLC/CONF/2004/5, paragraph 64.

[20] The Guidelines were adopted by the UN General Assembly in its Resolution 60/147 of 16 December 2005.

[21] Basic Principles and Guidelines on the Right to a Remedy and Reparation for Victims of Gross Violations of International Human Rights Law and Serious Violations of International Humanitarian Law.

Switzerland argued that:

the present wording of Article 5 and 2 inappropriately reinforces the notion that 'cluster munition victims' should be considered a separate group. This contradicts one of the essential principles of victim assistance, namely the principle of non-discrimination.[22]

The delegation of the United Kingdom (UK) saw 'a certain logic' in the Swiss proposal not to include a definition of the term in the treaty text, but concluded that 'it might be legally more prudent' to have one. The main concerns expressed by the UK, however, related to the broadness of some elements of the definition, i.e. the reference to families and communities as well as social marginalization and the substantial impairment of the realization of the victims' rights. In addition, the UK raised the question whether the definition should cover both civilians and military personnel.[23]

2.12 The subsequent discussions concentrated primarily on the question of including families and communities under the definition of cluster munition victims. Guatemala rightly pointed out that already the Oslo Declaration referred to the 'survivors and their communities'; it further argued that the text of the treaty would fall short of the Oslo Declaration, if such a reference were not included.[24] Croatia supported the inclusion of families and communities as this 'reflects the reality on the ground'.[25] Similarly, the delegations of the Lao People's Democratic Republic (Laos), Morocco, Norway, Canada, and the Cluster Munition Coalition (CMC) expressly supported the reference to families and communities.

2.13 While the Wellington Conference did not make any changes to the draft text as such, two proposals relating to the definition of cluster munition victims were included in the Compendium: the Swiss proposal to delete the definition, and a proposal by the UK reflecting its concerns as described above.[26] The UK proposal did not mention either social marginalization or the impairment of the realization of rights, and endeavoured to avoid the concern expressed as to families and communities by replacing the definition's second sentence by the following formulation: 'cluster munition victims include such

[22] See Statement on Victim Assistance by Ambassador Beat Nobs, Wellington Conference, 20 February 2008, available at: <http://www.mfat.govt.nz/clustermunitionswellington/conference-documents/statements.php> (accessed 25 March 2010). *Cf.* also 'Proposal by Switzerland for the amendment of Article 2', Diplomatic Conference doc. CCM/21, 19 May 2008.

[23] See Statement of the UK, Wellington Conference, 20 February 2008, available at *ibid.*

[24] See Intervención de la delegación de Guatemala, Articulo 5: 'Asistencia a las Victimas', 20 February 2008, available at *ibid.*   [25] See Statement of Croatia, available at *ibid.*

[26] See, *supra*, §2.11.

persons directly impacted by cluster munitions'.[27] By stating that victims *include* persons directly impacted, however, the UK signalled that also other entities than those individuals could be regarded as victims of cluster munitions.

Negotiations

2.14 While the preparatory work as well as the negotiations in Dublin focused mostly on the text of Article 5 of the draft Convention, the definition was the subject of a number of informal discussions undertaken at the Diplomatic Conference by the Friend of the President on Victim Assistance with interested delegations. The Swiss delegation signalled its readiness to lift its objection against the definition as a whole, but wished to see the inclusion of clear language aimed at preventing discrimination among victims of different weapons and explosive remnants of war. Switzerland's concern was essentially solved by introducing a provision that later became Article 5, paragraph 2(e), and was supported by a significant number of delegations as well as the International Committee of the Red Cross (ICRC).

Families and Communities

2.15 The question of the reference to families and communities was also discussed in informal consultations held by the Friend of the President on Victim Assistance and two open-ended consultations convened during the first week of the Diplomatic Conference. Still the broadness of the concept remained at the centre of discussions, which were held in a constructive and cooperative spirit by all participating delegations.

2.16 At the outset of the consultations the UK stated that it was 'broadly happy' with the draft definition, but still expressed concerns about the broadness of the concepts of family and community. The UK therefore suggested additional wording at the end of the second sentence to limit the scope of the families and communities to those in areas affected by cluster munitions. The UK proposal read as follows:

They include those persons directly impacted by cluster munitions, as well as their families and communities *in areas affected by cluster munitions*.[28]

---

[27] See Wellington Compendium (included in Annex 6 to this Commentary), p. 13. The full text of the definition of cluster munition victims as proposed by the UK read as follows:

'Cluster Munition Victims' means any persons who have suffered physical or psychological injury or economic loss, caused by the use of cluster munitions; cluster munition victims include such persons directly impacted by cluster munitions.

[28] Suggestion made orally by the UK delegate during informal consultations on victim assistance on 21 May 2008. The UK's suggestion was supported, among others, by Madagascar.

2.17 In reaction, a number of delegations expressed scepticism about the introduction of a territorial approach to the victim definition, noting that victims often have to move away from affected areas[29] and that 'persons, families and communities that are really affected need to receive assistance regardless of territory'.[30] This point was also reiterated by Croatia, which stated:

What is clear is that people, who have been victimized, whether they remain or leave an area or are forced to move about, must receive assistance.[31]

2.18 While the Friend of the President acknowledged the concerns expressed by the UK and others concerning the broadness of the concepts, he also reiterated the problems relating to a geographical limitation of the victim definition. To avoid these problems he suggested formulating a material rather than geographic limitation. The Canadian delegation during the first meeting of the Committee of the Whole on victim assistance had already proposed to solve this problem by adding after the terms 'families and communities' at the end of the definition's second sentence the phrase 'that have been materially and demonstrably affected by cluster munitions'.[32] While this proposal provided a general direction in which a solution to the problem was eventually found, the formulation itself was criticized as being highly limited and overly subjective.[33] Finally, Australia supported by Argentina, Belgium, Canada, France, Germany, and others proposed simply to include the term 'affected' before 'families and communities'; this suggestion was subsequently accepted so that the final version of the last sentence reads:

They include those persons directly impacted by cluster munitions as well as their affected families and communities.

Persons killed; irrelevance of the victims' status

2.19 The Philippines raised two further issues relating to the definition. First, it proposed a clarification whereby the death of persons as a result of the use of cluster munitions would also be covered by the definition.

---

[29] Statement of Laos during informal consultations on victim assistance on 21 May 2008.

[30] Statement of Norway during informal consultations on victim assistance on 21 May 2008, which was then supported by among others, Belgium, Chile, Croatia, Guatemala, New Zealand, and the CMC.

[31] Statement of Croatia during informal consultations on victim assistance on 21 May 2008.

[32] See 'Summary Record of Second Session of the Committee of the Whole', Diplomatic Conference doc. CCM/CW/SR/2, 18 June 2008.

[33] Observations by the International Federation of Red Cross and Red Crescent Societies and the UN Mine Action Service during informal consultations on victim assistance on 21 May 2008.

Second, it suggested that it be expressly clarified that 'migrants under the jurisdiction and control of an affected State' would fall under the ambit of the definition.[34]

2.20 With respect to the first suggestion, the Philippines argued that specific rules of international humanitarian law are relevant in cases of death as a result of weapon use and therefore this element would need to be reflected in the definition. Although it was argued that death caused by cluster munitions could be regarded as the most severe form of physical injury and would therefore already be covered by the definition,[35] a short discussion revealed broad support for this proposal so that the phrase 'who have been killed' was included in the draft definition after the term 'persons'. The inclusion of this phrase also shows the significance of the broadening of the definition to include families and communities: while assistance to *persons who have been killed* would be devoid of meaning were the definition only to take into consideration individuals, the inclusion also of families and communities in the definition makes it clear that the victim assistance obligation is also relevant for those whose victimization is the result of the demise of one of its members.

2.21 The second proposal by the Philippines relating to migrants was initially discussed in a series of informal bilateral consultations conducted by the Friend of the President and settled during the second open-ended consultations on victim assistance that took place on 22 May 2008. It was argued that this proposal created the risk of establishing a shopping list of a potentially unlimited number of groupings such as migrants, refugees, internally displaced persons, nationals of a State Party, nationals of States not party, etc. The definition, however, from the outset was intended to be all-embracing and non-discriminatory.[36] Finally, the Philippines supported by Croatia and Serbia proposed to solve this issue by inserting the term 'all' before 'persons' in the definition's first sentence.

---

[34] See 'Proposal by Philippines for the amendment of Article 2', Diplomatic Conference doc. CCM/57, 19 May 2008. The proposal read as follows:

'**Cluster munition victims**' means persons who have suffered *death*, physical or psychological injury, economic loss, social marginalization or substantial impairment of the realization of their rights caused by the use of cluster munitions. They include those persons directly impacted by cluster munitions as well as their families and communities and also *migrants under the jurisdiction and control of an affected State*. (*original emphasis*.)

[35] Remarks by the Friend of the President during informal consultations on victim assistance on 21 May 2008.

[36] This view was also supported by the Office of the High Commissioner for Refugees (UNHCR). Statement of UNHCR during informal consultations on victim assistance on 22 May 2008.

2.22 With these amendments the informal consultations reached a common understanding on the following definition, which subsequently was formally adopted by the Conference:

'**Cluster munition victims**' means all persons who have been killed or suffered physical or psychological injury, economic loss, social marginalisation or substantial impairment of the realisation of their rights caused by the use of cluster munitions. They include those persons directly impacted by cluster munitions as well as their affected families and communities.

In introducing the Non-Paper containing this definition to the Committee of the Whole the Friend of the President specifically referred to the formulation 'all persons' as clarifying that the definition covers all persons 'who had suffered harm regardless of their status as migrants, refugees, Internally Displaced Persons, etc'.[37]

Commentary

2.23 The definition of cluster munition victims contains the defining elements of victimization caused by the use of cluster munitions and in doing so paints a realistic picture of the effects the use of such munitions may have on individuals as well as families and communities. The history of the negotiations as described above reveals a number of principles which were followed during the negotiations: pursuit of a broad approach by including the various 'circles' of victims[38] in the definition; reflecting as accurately as possible the reality of victimization; and irrelevance of status of the victim.

'all persons'

2.24 The use of the term *all persons* in the definition makes clear that any person irrespective of his/her status has to be regarded as a cluster munition victim if the defining elements contained in the definition's first sentence apply, i.e. that he/she has been killed or suffered physical or psychological injury, economic loss, social marginalization or substantial impairment of the realization of their rights caused by the use of cluster munitions. This interpretation, which already derives from the ordinary meaning of the term, is also confirmed by the negotiating history. As described above, the word 'all' had been inserted to ensure that all persons 'who had suffered harm regardless of their status as migrants, refugees, Internally Displaced Persons, etc.' are to be

---

[37] See 'Summary Record of Eighth Session of the Committee of the Whole', Diplomatic Conference doc. CCM/CW/SR/8, 18 June 2008 (*cf.* discussion on Article 5).

[38] i.e. the affected individual, family, and community.

regarded as cluster munition victims. The definition also makes it clear that there is no difference as to whether a person was a civilian or a combatant at the time he/she became a cluster munition victim.

'killed or suffered physical or psychological injury, economic loss, social marginalisation or substantial impairment of the realisation of their rights'

2.25 This formulation lists the defining elements of victimization: in addition to the more obvious elements of death or physical or psychological injury that lead to the qualification as victims, these defining elements also include other less obvious, yet serious elements: economic loss, social marginalization, or substantial impairment of the realization of rights. The use of the term 'or' between the various defining elements makes clear that it is sufficient that only one of those elements needs to apply in a given case in order for a person to fall under the scope of the definition. It is not necessary therefore to have suffered physical or psychological harm plus economic loss, social marginalization, or substantial impairment of the realization of rights: either of these elements is sufficient as long as its occurrence is caused by the use of cluster munitions. Economic loss and social marginalization are common factors of victimization. For example, suffering from a disability in many societies leads to social stigmatization of the individual in question as well as his/her family or often larger community.

2.26 The formulation 'substantial impairment of the realization of their rights' in essence is a further development of the formulations used in both the Nairobi Review Document and the Guidelines adopted by the UN General Assembly: substantial impairment of their fundamental rights. There are two main distinctions, as discussed below.

2.27 First, Article 2, paragraph 1 does not refer to an impairment of rights, but an impairment of the realization of rights. In doing so, the text defines more precisely the subject of impairment by acknowledging that the main problem for victims is not so much an impairment of the rights as such—which regularly continue to be the same before and after the use of cluster munitions—but the impediment to actually realize those rights. For example, while in a democratic society victims and 'non-victims' have a right to vote in elections, it might be much harder for a cluster munition victim actually to participate in the vote which may be, for instance, the result of a physiological barrier (e.g. victim has lost sight through cluster munition use) or the land denial caused by cluster munition use makes it extremely difficult to have access to a voting station.

2.28 Second, Article 2, paragraph 1 does not restrict impairment to only fundamental rights, but covers rights in general. This provision is, therefore, broader than merely covering those rights which might be deemed fundamental, such as the right to life, the prohibition of torture, or the right to freedom of movement. Any subjective right, not just fundamental rights, of the person in question may be the object of the substantial impairment.

'caused by the use of cluster munitions'

2.29 This formulation clarifies that the detrimental effects enumerated in the definition need to be caused by the use of cluster munitions. In other words there needs to be a causal link between the use of the weapon and the occurrence of the detrimental effect to establish victimisation in the meaning of Article 2, paragraph 1. Not all detrimental effects related to the use of cluster munitions qualify for victimization. This formulation essentially functions as a crucial qualifier and puts necessary limits to the broadness of the definition.

'affected families and communities'

2.30 According to the second sentence of the definition not only the individual human being falls under the ambit of the definition of cluster munition victim, but also affected families and communities, thus going beyond the scope of application of the Convention on the Rights of Persons with Disabilities which does not apply to persons other than those with disabilities themselves.[39] The inclusion of these concepts in the definition was at the centre of negotiations on the definition, as some delegations expressed the concern that these concepts were overly broad.

2.31 The formulation adopted clarifies that in order to fall under the definition of a cluster munition victim a family or community needs to be affected in reality by the use of cluster munitions. As the second sentence of the definition commences with the phrase 'They include', it clearly refers back to the term 'persons' contained in the definition's first sentence. Hence, families and communities have to undergo any of the adverse effects enumerated in the definition to qualify as a victim: in other words, in order for a family or community to qualify as victim it needs to have suffered from either psychological injury, economic loss, social marginalization, or substantial impairment of the realization of their rights caused by the use of cluster munitions. Death or physical injury as such might seem not to be directly applicable when victimization relates to families or communities, however the death or physical

---

[39] Article 1, UN Convention on the Rights of Persons with Disabilities.

injury of a family or community member may result in psychological injury, economic loss, social marginalization, or substantial impairment of the realization of their rights caused by the use of cluster munitions and therefore lead to victimization of the family or community.

2.32 In the absence of an internationally agreed definition of the terms family or community, it is to be assumed that in fulfilling its obligation vis-à-vis families and communities as cluster munition victims the respective State Party will have a rather wide margin of appreciation and that the question who belongs to a certain family or community will eventually have to be clarified through the internal legal order of the respective State Party. The situation is similar to, for example, the use of the term 'family member' in Article 37 of the *1961 Vienna Convention on Diplomatic Relations*, which also contains no definition of the term and hence leaves a wide margin of appreciation to each State Party.

The definition of a cluster munition

Overview

2.33 The definition of cluster munition delineates the technological category that is subject to the prohibitions contained in Article 1 and subject to obligations and provisions throughout the treaty. In general terms, a cluster munition means a conventional munition designed to disperse or release explosive submunitions—conventional munitions dispersed and released by cluster munitions and which are designed to detonate an explosive charge before, upon, or following impact, typically with the target object or the ground[40]— each weighing less than 20 kilograms. However, a series of exclusions set out in sub-paragraphs (a) to (c) restricts the weapons that are captured by the general definition in the *chapeau* of Article 2, paragraph 2. The scope of the prohibition is also limited by Article 1, paragraph 3, which stipulates that the Convention does not apply to 'mines'. In contrast, at least the core prohibitions of the Convention are applied *mutatis mutandis* to explosive bomblets, under Article 1, paragraph 2.[41]

---

[40] See, *infra*, the commentary on Article 2, paragraph 3 for detailed commentary on the definition of explosive submunition.

[41] This means that the production, stockpiling, transfer, and use of explosive bomblets is prohibited even though they do not fall within the definition of a cluster munition set out in Article 2, paragraph 2.

2.34 The Convention would appear to prohibit all conventional weapons with explosive submunitions that had been evidenced, at the time of the negotiations, as resulting in civilian casualties either at the time of their use or subsequently.[42] For certain types of submunition-based weapons, the definition has both effects-based and technical requirements to determine their permissibility. Where numbers are used in the definition they arguably facilitate a clear determination of what falls inside or outside the definition.[43]

2.35 The main definition and sub-paragraph (a) both exclude from prohibition certain systems that employ submunitions and that are weapons in the common usage of the term, or which might be considered or used as weapons (e.g. weapons with submunitions weighing more than 20 kilograms and air-defence weapons.) No further technical requirements are demanded of weapons excluded through the main definition or at sub-paragraph (a). Sub-paragraphs (a) and (b) also exclude from prohibition other military systems that are not weapons in the common usage of the term but that may be used to create illuminating, obscuring, or diversionary effects. As described above, however, the greatest focus in negotiations was on sub-paragraph (c).

2.36 Sub-paragraph (c) provides a statement of the problematic effects that should be avoided in order to warrant exclusion from prohibition: 'indiscriminate area effects and the risks posed by unexploded submunitions'. This formulation should be read in conjunction with the preamble wherein the intent of the Convention is said to be, *inter alia*, 'to put an end for all time to the suffering and casualties caused by cluster munitions at the time of their use, when they fail to function as intended or when they are abandoned'. Thus the problematic humanitarian effects of cluster munitions are understood to be both 'indiscriminate area effects' at time of use as well as 'risks posed by unexploded submunitions' if they 'fail to function as intended' as well as the general risk posed by all explosive weapons if they are left abandoned in the post-conflict environment.

---

[42] e.g., all munitions listed on the Human Rights Watch chart 'Overview of a Dirty Dozen Cluster Munitions' are prohibited under the Convention (<http://www.hrw.org/sites/default/files/related_material/munitionChart0806.pdf>, accessed 8 March 2010). However, there have also been criticisms that the definition allows some types of weapons with submunitions to continue to be used and that the definition is based in part on 'numbers' that must to some extent be arbitrary. See, e.g., Statements of Chile and Spain, 'Summary Record of Eleventh Session of the Committee of the Whole', Diplomatic Conference doc. CCM/CW/SR/11, 18 June 2008.

[43] It might, however, be noted that the general concept of a cluster munition, as a weapon with multiple submunitions, is based on the numerical distinction between 'one' and 'more than one' as much as on the subsidiary relationship of the submunitions to the container.

2.37 In order to avoid both 'indiscriminate area effects and the risks posed by unexploded submunitions' the munition must have five technical characteristics relating to: the number of submunitions, the minimum weight of the submunitions, the capacity of individual submunitions to detect and engage targets, and the presence of both electronic self-destruct and self-deactivation features. Taken together these characteristics should reduce sufficiently the likelihood of these munitions creating a significant humanitarian problem.

2.38 The technical characteristics listed in paragraph 2(c) (i) to (v) can exclude a weapon from being defined as a cluster munition and thereby from prohibition. However, weapons that meet the technical characteristics but that when used are found to generate 'indiscriminate area effects or risks posed by unexploded submunitions' because the technical characteristics do not function as intended could be examined within the context of the Convention, for example at the Meeting of States Parties or a Review Conference. The explicitly stated intent of the exclusion in the *chapeau* of Article 2, paragraph 2(c) necessitates the effective functioning of the technical characteristics. If, for example, a weapon excluded under paragraph 2(c) turned out to have self-destruct mechanisms that did not work, it may no longer be justified to exclude it from the prohibition. Such an interpretation is supported by statements by Austria, Lebanon, Malta, and the CMC during the negotiation of the Convention[44] and implicitly supported in other proposals.[45]

Preparatory discussions

2.39 Article 2, paragraph 2 was a focus of extensive discussions during all of the preparatory meetings for the Dublin Diplomatic Conference, and during the final negotiations. The February 2007 Oslo Conference brought together States most of which had previously indicated support for prohibitions on at least certain types of cluster munitions. During this conference a number of States called for a ban on 'all cluster munitions', while others expressed a clear

---

[44] 'Summary Record of Eleventh Session of the Committee of the Whole', Diplomatic Conference doc. CCM/CW/SR/11, 18 June 2008. Austria 'considered that effects-based language should be adopted. This should be complemented by a reporting requirement on new weapons and their effects in Article 7.' Lebanon stated that Article 2, paragraph 2(c) 'must comply with the highest humanitarian standards, and contain safeguards for the review of exemptions at Review Conferences.'

[45] See 'Proposal by France for the amendment of Article 2', Diplomatic Conference doc. CCM/20, 19 May 2008. As noted *infra* in §2.72, the French proposal made reference to a review mechanism that would allow the parameters of the definition to be considered again by States Parties 'no later than 5 years after entry into force' in line with the treaty's provisions regarding Review Conferences.

sense that only certain types might warrant prohibition. Other participants noted that what might count as 'all cluster munitions' would be dependent upon how a future treaty would define this term.[46]

2.40 The outcome document of this meeting, the Oslo Declaration, committed States to conclude by 2008 a legally binding international instrument that would 'prohibit the use, production, transfer and stockpiling of cluster munitions that cause unacceptable harm to civilians'.[47] However, there was no commonly accepted definition of a cluster munition and no common agreement as to how the categories of 'cluster munition' and 'cluster munitions that cause unacceptable harm to civilians' related to each other. The lack of a commonly agreed or accepted definition at the outset of the Oslo Process led to some tough negotiations.

2.41 The diversity of possible definitions was reflected in a paper prepared by the Geneva International Centre for Humanitarian Demining (GICHD) in June 2007,[48] which listed definitions and descriptions of cluster munitions and related terms that had been adopted or proposed by different bodies. Such definitions and descriptions varied in both basic terms and structures. Some linked the term cluster munitions to the container whereas others applied the term to the container and its submunitions as a system. Some made explicit statements about the delivery system for the weapons and others described how the submunitions would create an effect within the target area. The GICHD paper illustrated the numerous possible approaches to defining what was—and what was not—a cluster munition for the purpose of the future Convention.

2.42 A persistent discussion within the preparatory meetings leading to the Dublin Diplomatic Conference was the extent to which the clause 'that cause unacceptable harm to civilians' necessitated a category distinct from 'cluster munitions'. A number of States suggested a distinction between 'cluster munitions' and 'cluster munitions that cause unacceptable harm to civilians'.[49] Yet, despite the importance of the latter term to the structure of the negotiations,

[46] Oslo Conference on Cluster Munitions, 22 February 2007 (Landmine Action notes; copy on file with author).

[47] Declaration of the Oslo Conference on Cluster Munitions of 23 February 2007. The wording appeared to favour a more selective approach to the prohibition of weapons that might be considered cluster munitions.

[48] See 'Overview of Existing and Proposed Definitions, Submitted by the Geneva International Centre for Humanitarian Demining (GICHD)', UN doc. CCW/GGE/2007/WP.5, Geneva, 12 June 2007.

[49] Statements made at the Lima Conference, 24 May 2007 (Landmine Action notes; copy on file with author).

no State chose to delineate what might be considered acceptable harm.[50] The subsequent debate also reflected a number of themes that were to be discussed in later meetings of the Oslo Process, notably:

- the possibility of limiting the number of submunitions;
- the need to establish 'reliability' and 'accuracy' criteria for any weapon to be exempted from the ambit of the future convention;
- the potential utility of self-destruct mechanisms and self-neutralization mechanisms;
- the questionable utility of testing reliability rates as an indicator of combat performance;
- the potential prohibition on use in populated areas of any cluster munitions not prohibited by the convention; and
- that the burden of proof was on those seeking exclusions from prohibition to justify their claims.[51]

Although certain States endorsed particular technical characteristics as providing grounds for confidence that humanitarian problems would be avoided or sufficiently reduced in the future, there was little done to interrogate the relationship between certain technologies and the actual or likely outcomes for civilians during and after conflict. A significant exception to this was an analysis undertaken by Norwegian People's Aid, the Norwegian Defence Research Establishment, and Colin King Associates into the reliability of M85 submunitions both in testing and operational conditions.[52]

2.43 The Lima Discussion Text already included a categorical prohibition on the use, production, stockpiling, and transfer of cluster munitions under Article 1. Article 2 of that text stated that 'the following weapons systems shall be considered prohibited cluster munitions under this treaty':

Air carried dispersal systems or air delivered, surface or sub-surface launched containers, that are designed to disperse explosive sub-munitions intended to detonate following separation from the container or dispenser, unless they are designed to, manually or automatically, aim, detect and engage point targets, or are meant for smoke or flaring, or unless their use is regulated or prohibited under other treaties.

---

[50] Indeed, on 19 February 2008 during the Wellington Conference, Zambia stated:

If any form of harm is acceptable, it would be interesting to see those of us advocating for a partial ban to volunteer themselves as examples for all of us to see just how acceptable harm is.

Available at: <http://www.mfat.govt.nz/clustermunitionswellington/conference-documents/Zambia-definitions.pdf>.

[51] Landmine Action notes; copy on file with author.

[52] King, C., Dullum, O., and Østern, G., *M85—An Analysis of Reliability* (Oslo: Norwegian People's Aid, 2007), see also §2.56.

2.44 The definition of cluster munition presented in the Lima Discussion Text provided an initial indication of how the Oslo Declaration language of 'cluster munitions that cause unacceptable harm to civilians' might be interpreted. In Article 1, it adopted prohibitions on the use, production, and stockpiling of cluster munitions as a defined category of weapons. It then presented a broad definition of cluster munitions, including air-carried 'dispensers' as well as 'containers', but recognized that certain items that might fall under the principal definition should not be subject to prohibition. This definition excluded from prohibition systems that produce smoke or flare effects. It also excluded systems with submunitions designed to 'aim, detect and engage point targets'. With respect to such systems, however, the definition applied no further controls that might be expected to limit their propensity to become unexploded ordnance (UXO). It is also important to note that the definition in the Lima text considered cluster munitions to be the 'dispersal system', i.e. the dispenser or container, rather than the combination of both container and submunitions that was adopted in subsequent definitions.[53]

2.45 The definition also excluded from prohibition weapons subject to regulation or prohibition under other treaties. Such a formulation was intended to avoid problems caused by the category of cluster munitions overlapping with other weapon categories, such as remotely delivered landmines. It was also noted, however, that the general rules of international humanitarian law regulate all weapons.[54] At a more specific level this approach would have created the potential for weapons initially prohibited under the Convention on Cluster Munitions to later fall outside the scope of the prohibition if subject to regulation under another legal instrument. Subsequent draft texts excluded mines explicitly from the scope of the treaty rather than as a component of the definition of cluster munition.

2.46 Discussions of the definition at the May 2007 Lima Conference were chaired by Ambassador Don MacKay of New Zealand, who would subsequently chair discussions on definitions at the Vienna Conference, serve as President of the Wellington Conference on Cluster Munitions, and act as Friend of the President on definitions at the Dublin Diplomatic Conference. In introducing the definition in the Lima Discussion Text, MacKay highlighted to participants that while the definition related to

[53] From the Vienna Discussion Text onwards, a cluster munition was deemed to comprise both the container and its submunitions.
[54] Statements on definitions of the CMC and the ICRC, Lima Conference, 24 May 2007 (Landmine Action notes; copy on file with author).

cluster munitions as a whole category, certain weapons with submunitions were not prohibited.[55]

2.47 Some States explicitly argued that the Lima definition was too broad and would prohibit weapons without justification, while others argued that the definition was not wide enough or pressed for a 'total ban'.[56] The definition proposed in the Lima Discussion Text was similar in its implications for current weapon systems to the one ultimately adopted in the Convention. In many respects the definition was reinforced during the course of the Oslo Process, in particular in the way that the exclusion for weapons that detect and engage so-called 'point targets' was drafted. However, in some other areas the definition was to become less comprehensive, by providing exemptions for submunitions over a certain weight and for so-called 'air-defence' systems. It has been argued that the strengthening of the definition was facilitated in part by the influence of the revised structure of a definition, presented at the December 2007 Vienna Conference, on the subsequent discussions and negotiations.[57]

2.48 Thus, the Vienna Discussion Text[58] presented a wholesale restructuring of the definition into the form that was to shape the subsequent negotiations. Rather than stipulating the precise boundaries of what was and was not a cluster munition, the Vienna text introduced a broad definition but left open three serial lines for systems that should not be subject to prohibition (see below). Structured in this way, the text invited States to argue into the text systems that should be considered 'acceptable' against a categorical presumption that such systems cause 'unacceptable harm':

'**Cluster munition**' means a munition that is designed to disperse or release explosive sub-munitions, and includes those explosive sub-munitions. It does not mean the following:

(a) ...
(b) ...
(c) ...

2.49 Significantly, cluster munitions were now defined as 'munitions' that comprised both a container and the submunitions it contained. This served

---

[55] Introduction by Ambassador Don MacKay, Lima Conference, 24 May 2007 (Landmine Action notes; copy on file with author).

[56] Landmine Action notes; copy on file with author.

[57] Rappert, B., and Moyes, R., 'The Prohibition of Cluster Munitions: Setting International Precedents for Defining Inhumanity', *Nonproliferation Review*, Vol. 16.2, July 2009.

[58] The Vienna Discussion Text of 14 November 2007 is included in Annex 4 to this Commentary.

to clarify certain elements of the text by ensuring that any prohibitions that applied to 'cluster munitions' applied to both the containers and the submunition contents of those containers. However, this approach also produced challenges, notably its apparent exclusion of systems that used dispensers affixed to aircraft (which could not readily be considered 'munitions'),[59] and risks of circularity in the definition of cluster munition and explosive submunition. The definition also now used the phrase 'dispersed or released', a phrase previously used in a definition of cluster munitions contained in a paper circulated by UN agencies for discussions in the context of the CCW,[60] and that describes both active and passive mechanisms by which the submunitions may separate from the container.

2.50 In addition to the definition of cluster munition in the Vienna Discussion Text there was a definition of the term 'explosive sub-munitions':

'**Explosive sub-munitions**' means munitions that in order to perform their task separate from a parent munition and are designed to function by detonating an explosive charge prior to, on or immediately after impact.

This definition drew on a NATO definition of a submunition as 'any munition that, to perform its task, separates from a parent munition',[61] a definition also followed in the International Mine Action Standards (IMAS) glossary of mine action terms, definitions, and abbreviations.[62] The second part of the definition drew upon elements of definition developed in the context of the CCW. The *Declaration on Cluster Munitions* endorsed by 25 States at the Third Review Conference of the CCW (17 November 2006) referred to cluster munitions as being 'designed to eject sub-munitions containing explosives designed to detonate on, prior to, or immediately after impact...' A similar formulation had been used by the UK in a statement to the CCW on 13 November 2006.[63]

2.51 An 'Explanatory Annex' to the Vienna Discussion Text presented a summary of different elements that had been proposed during the Lima

---

[59] This implication of the Vienna Discussion Text definition was raised by the GICHD during the Vienna Conference on 6 December 2007 (Landmine Action notes; copy on file with author).

[60] See UNMAS, UNDP and UNICEF, 'Proposed definitions for cluster munitions and submunitions', UN doc. CCW/GGE/X/WG.1/WP.3, 8 March 2005.

[61] NATO Glossary of Terms and Definitions, AAP-6 (2009), 2-S-14, available at: <http://www.nato.int/docu/stanag/aap006/aap6.htm> (accessed 8 March 2010).

[62] IMAS 04.10: 'Glossary of mine action terms, definitions and abbreviations', Second Edition, 1 January 2003, available at <http://www.mineactionstandards.org> (accessed 8 March 2010).

[63] Statement by Ambassador John Duncan on Cluster Munitions, Third Review Conference of the CCW, Geneva, 13 November 2006.

Conference as offering possible grounds for systems being excluded from prohibition:

Article 2: Definitions

At the Lima Meeting there appeared to be broad agreement that land-mines would be excluded from the definition of 'cluster munition' since they are already covered by other treaties. Some States also proposed that one or more of the following should be excluded: flare, smoke and chaff munitions and sub-munitions that are inert post impact. There were other proposals to exclude sub-munitions that aim, detect and engage point targets, and some States proposed to exclude cluster muni-tions which contain fewer than a specified number of explosive sub-mu-nitions, sub-munitions with self destruct or self deactivation or other failsafe mechanisms, explosive sub-munitions with a tested failure rate of less than a specified percentage, and that the age of the sub-munition should be relevant. Some other States opposed some or all of these ele-ments, with some proposing a comprehensive prohibition on all cluster munitions.

2.52 During the Vienna Conference, the Friend of the Chair on Definitions adopted a process of work to consider in turn the different characteristics proposed as a basis for exclusion from prohibition. In line with the order in which these characteristics were listed in the Explanatory Annex, this process of consideration would start with characteristics that were considered to be the least contentious; that is to say, it would start with those characteristics that might be expected to have the lowest risk of allowing submunition-based weapons with 'unacceptable' humanitarian effects to escape prohibition. Yet, despite the structure proposed by the Chair, the discussion of definitions in Vienna was again wide-ranging. Only a few States spoke explicitly in favour of excluding systems that dis-pensed flares, smoke, or chaff; landmines; or systems that deployed electri-cal devices.[64]

2.53 As had occurred at the Lima Conference, a number of States raised concerns that the approach being taken to defining a cluster munition was not in accordance with their understanding of the Oslo Declaration, while a few made reference to a perception that discussing the technological extent of the prohibition under the definition of a 'cluster munition' seemed to prejudge the process leading to a categorical prohibition.[65] By contrast, other States, including a number affected by cluster munition remnants, argued broadly

---

[64] Landmine Action notes; copy on file with author.   [65] *Ibid.*

in favour of the categorical approach to prohibition and urged against further exclusions.[66]

2.54 Germany provided a detailed presentation of a 'step-by-step' proposal it had introduced in the context of the CCW in May 2007 as a draft Protocol VI to that treaty. This proposal took a three-stage approach: a prohibition on so-called inaccurate and unreliable cluster munitions; a phase-out period for so-called accurate and reliable cluster munitions; and an eventual replacement of cluster munitions with 'alternative munitions'.[67]

2.55 The ICRC noted that the terms 'inaccurate and unreliable', which it had itself used to articulate the problems of cluster munitions, were being widely used by States and offered some points of clarification on these terms. It noted that while the language was neither legal nor technical, it considered that the terms applied to 'all cluster munitions used to date'. The ICRC went on to suggest that of the criteria proposed by States, so-called sensor fuzing, increased reliability measures, and limitations on numbers, if adopted cumulatively, seemed to offer a better degree of civilian protection than most other proposals. However, the ICRC also noted that the burden of proof was on those calling for such exclusions, and that this should relate to how munitions functioned in reality not just under ideal test conditions.[68]

2.56 The Vienna Conference also saw the publication of an influential report and a detailed presentation of research on the performance of M85 submunitions in both test conditions and operational use.[69] A DPICM-type submunition[70] with a mechanical self-destruct mechanism, the M85 (or variants) was in the arsenals of a number of States taking part in the negotiations, including Austria, Norway, Switzerland and the UK. While Austria and Norway had both imposed a moratorium, several States had already resolved internally to exempt such weapons from prohibition. The grounds offered for such an exemption were either the presence of a self-destruct mechanism (or more generally a 'fail-safe' mechanism) or a stipulation that submunitions

---

[66] *Ibid.*

[67] Draft CCW Protocol on Cluster Munitions submitted by Germany, 2007 Session of the CCW Group of Governmental Experts on Cluster Munitions, UN doc. CCW/GGE/2007/WP.1, Geneva, 1 May 2007.

[68] Harrison, K., 'Report of the Vienna Conference on Cluster Munitions, 5–7 December 2007', Women's International League for Peace and Freedom, January 2008, <http://www.wilpf.int.ch/disarmament/clustermunitions/ViennaConference/viennareport.htm> (accessed 8 March 2010).

[69] King, C., Dullum, O., and Østern, G., *M85: An Analysis of Reliability, op. cit.*

[70] Dual-purpose improved conventional munitions. See, e.g., GICHD, *A Guide to Cluster Munitions*, Second Edition, Geneva, 2009, pp. 10–11, 13, 17.

meeting certain reliability criteria should not be prohibited. The latter was generally expressed in terms of the proportion of submunitions failing to detonate as designed during test firings.

2.57 The research presented during the Vienna Conference showed not only that M85 submunitions had fallen below specified reliability benchmarks in test conditions, but that in operational use there were indications of significantly higher failure rates. The significance of this was two-fold: on the one hand there was evidence that munitions with self-destruct mechanisms could still present a post-conflict humanitarian threat, and on the other hand it called into question the possibility of using testing as a basis for meaningful regulation.

2.58 The report also rejected the concept of 'non-dangerous duds', by which certain States had argued that any submunitions left unexploded that had not 'armed' should not be considered within calculations of reliability because they did not present a significant civilian risk.[71]

2.59 In addition to challenging a number of specific technical arguments that were of central importance to discussion of what should, or should not, be prohibited, the M85 report set a high standard for evidence and analysis linked to actual testing and combat data.

2.60 The discussions at the Vienna Conference allowed the definition of cluster munitions to be further developed in the Draft Cluster Munition Convention prepared in advance of the Wellington Conference, while maintaining the same overall structure.[72] This text excluded 'mines' from prohibition, not by amending the definition of a cluster munition but through an amendment to the scope of the Convention as expressed in Article 1, paragraph 2:

This Convention does not apply to 'mines' as defined by the Protocol on Prohibitions or Restrictions on the Use of Mines, Booby-Traps and Other Devices, as amended on 3 May 1996, annexed to the Convention on Prohibitions or Restrictions on the Use of Certain Conventional Weapons which may be Deemed to be Excessively Injurious or to have Indiscriminate Effects.[73]

---

[71] See the use of the term 'dangerous duds' in the proposal, 'Draft CCW Protocol on Cluster Munitions submitted by Germany', 2007 Session of the CCW Group of Governmental Experts on Cluster Munitions, CCW/GGE/2007/WP.1, Geneva, 1 May 2007.

[72] Draft Cluster Munitions Convention of 21 January 2008.

[73] On 6 December 2007, during the Vienna Conference, the CMC had questioned whether remotely delivered anti-vehicle mines dispersed from a container should be excluded from definition as cluster munitions and asked delegations to consider whether these weapons might not cause unacceptable harm to civilians.

2.61 Under the definition of cluster munition in Article 2, paragraph 2, there were now exclusions accepted for systems 'designed to dispense flares, smoke, pyrotechnics or chaff', and for systems 'designed to produce electrical or electronic effects':

'Cluster munition' means a munition that is designed to disperse or release explosive sub-munitions, and includes those explosive sub-munitions. It does not mean the following:

(a) a munition or sub-munition designed to dispense flares, smoke, pyrotechnics or chaff;

(b) a munition or sub-munition designed to produce electrical or electronic effects;

(c) …

This left sub-paragraph (c) open for the possible insertion of further characteristics that might warrant exclusion from prohibition.

2.62 The definition of 'explosive sub-munitions' in the Draft Cluster Munition Convention remained unchanged from the Vienna text:

'**Explosive sub-munitions**' means munitions that in order to perform their task separate from a parent munition and are designed to function by detonating an explosive charge prior to, on or after impact.

2.63 Discussions at the Wellington Conference continued the process of work established in Vienna of considering certain characteristics as a basis for exclusion, proceeding from those that might be considered least contentious. Having excluded essentially 'non-weapon' systems after the discussion in Vienna, consideration now came to systems that employed submunitions designed to detect and engage specific targets.[74]

2.64 A number of States taking part in negotiations had sensor-fuzed munitions in their arsenals or were in the process of procuring such munitions. These weapons use sensors and electronic micro-processors to identify and then attack targets, primarily vehicles, based on their heat-signature and profile. Detonation of the munition is initiated by an electrical current from the depletion of a battery integral to the submunition. Such systems generally create an explosively formed projectile that is fired down onto the target from a significant stand-off distance, without creating the lateral fragmentation at ground level that has typically been used in submunitions in order to create an anti-personnel effect. Through this combination of targeting specific objects

---

[74] Introduction by Ambassador Don MacKay, Wellington Conference, 19 February 2008 (Landmine Action notes; copy on file with author).

and limited use of lateral fragmentation, these systems differed from systems that scattered submunitions randomly. While the sensors of the submunitions search for targets within a 'footprint' area on the ground, the application of physical force within that footprint is much more narrowly defined than that created by the broad scattering of traditional explosive submunitions.[75]

2.65 The munitions of this type in service with negotiating States also contained electronic self-destruct and self-deactivation systems. Electronic self-destruct mechanisms were different to the mechanical self-destruct mechanisms employed on submunitions such as the M85 because they were not reliant on the functioning of moving parts after the submunition had armed. Furthermore, electronic self-deactivation mechanisms depleted the battery normally required to initiate detonation of the main explosive charge and were therefore held to render any unexploded submunitions less susceptible to detonation as a result of physical contact.

2.66 It was argued that such systems were more reliable than mechanical mechanisms because circuitry could be tested during production and munition storage providing an elevated level of quality control.[76] In addition, these self-destruct mechanisms were supposed to function in the air before the submunition struck the ground, which might further limit unpredictability resulting from the effects of ground conditions on the mechanical systems designed to operate after impact. Whereas the self-destruct mechanism on impact-fuzed systems such as the M85 were 'back-up' mechanisms designed to operate if the submunition failed to function as designed, in sensor-fuzed systems the self-destruct mechanism operates where no valid target is identified by the sensor system. This is not necessarily a result of a failure in the system but may simply be because no valid targets are present in the area being

---

[75] See, e.g., the entries 'GIWS DM 702 SMArt 155 ammunition system' and 'Bofors/Giat Industries 155mm Bonus sensor-fuzed munition' in Ness, L. and Williams, A. G. (eds.), *Jane's Ammunition Handbook 2006–2007* (UK: Jane's Information Group, November 2006), pp. 657–658, and 649–650; see also Rheinmetall Defence press releases on SMArt 155 (01/07/2008), <http://www.rheinmetall-defence.com/index.php?fid=4504&qid=&qpage=0&lang=3& query=SMArt%20155>, and (10/03/2005), <http://www.rheinmetall-defence.com/index. php?lang=3&fid=3241>; and also UK Ministry of Defence, 'New precision "search and destroy" anti-armour weapon', News release, 19 November 2007; and Jane's Information Group, '155mm Bofors Trajectory Correctable Munition (Sweden), Field artillery', <http://www.janes.com/ articles/Janes-Ammunition-Handbook/155-mm-Bofors-Trajectory-Correctable-Munition-Sweden.html> (all accessed 8 March 2010).

[76] See, e.g., Presentation by Colin King to the Vienna Conference on Cluster Munitions, 6 December 2007; the discussion on definitions at the Wellington Conference, 19 February 2008 (Landmine Action notes; copy on file with author); and US Defense Science Board Task Force on Munitions System Reliability, September 2005, *Munitions System Reliability*, Office of the Under Secretary of Defense for Acquisition, Technology and Logistics, Washington, DC, 20301–3140.

searched by the sensors. These considerations are among a number of others that differentiate such systems from cluster munitions of the DPICM type and are likely to affect system reliability.[77]

2.67 In addition to these features of electronic fuzing, the sensor-fuzed systems in the arsenals of negotiating States at the time were all limited to two relatively large submunitions in each container munition (by contrast the US 'Sensor Fuzed Weapon'[78] contained a total of 40 individual explosive submunitions, often described as 'skeets'). The limitation on numbers has a bearing on both the area-effect of the munition at the time of use and the likely level of UXO contamination that would result from each munition being fired. These munitions contained in combination—and in many cases in the most reliable available form—many features that States had proposed independently as possible grounds for exclusion from prohibition. Thus, if such features in combination were not sufficient grounds to avoid prohibition, it was difficult to see how they could be adopted individually as a basis for exclusion.

2.68 The discussion of sensor-fuzed munitions at the Wellington Conference began with a statement by one State in which it argued that these were not 'area weapons' and also that they had a number of cumulative safeguards, including self-destruct and self-neutralization features, which meant they were sufficiently different from cluster munitions as commonly understood not to warrant prohibition.[79] During the course of the subsequent discussion a number of other States spoke positively about a possible exclusion for sensor-fuzed munitions.[80] However, a significant body of States raised concerns about such an approach. Two States stated that the cost of these systems would mean the Convention would penalize those that could not afford them. Another State noted difficulties in defining 'point' and 'area' targets, and expressed scepticism about safeguards such as self-destruct and self-neutralization mechanisms in practice, while a fourth State questioned reliance on 'unproven technical safeguards'.[81] The CMC raised concerns about the wide area covered by some of these munitions and emphasized that the burden of proof was on the advocates of these weapons to demonstrate suf-

---

[77] The report *M85: An analysis of reliability* (*op. cit.*) provides an analysis of such factors at Section 4.4: 'Failure Analysis'. While it does not compare the susceptibility of different systems to these factors, the typology it presents would provide a useful framework for analysis.

[78] US CBU-97/CBU-105.

[79] Statement of Germany, Wellington Conference, 19 February 2008 (Landmine Action notes; copy on file with author).

[80] Discussions on definitions at the Wellington Conference, 19 February 2008 (Landmine Action notes; copy on file with author).

[81] Landmine Action notes; copy on file with author.

ficient safeguards for humanitarian protection.[82] The ICRC raised concerns that the devolution of certain targeting decisions to automated systems raised other legal concerns.[83] Statements opposing any further exclusions from the definition of a cluster munition were made by some 20 States.[84]

2.69 While the plenary discussions in Wellington were effectively locked between those in favour of an exclusion (at the very least) for submunitions that detect and engage individual targets and those that were not, certain States continued to argue for exemptions for weapons on other grounds. The formal proposals submitted during the course of the Wellington Conference provide an indication of the range of exclusions still being sought.

2.70 The discussion of the definition in Wellington saw a number of formal proposals put forward by States. These were incorporated into the 'Compendium' attached to the Wellington Declaration, and became official documents during the Diplomatic Conference. While some of these papers proposed actual changes to the treaty text, others were more discursive. For example, a joint proposal by Australia, Canada, Denmark, Finland, Germany, Italy, Japan, the Netherlands, and the UK (which later became Conference document CCM/17 in Dublin) listed characteristics, which 'either individually or in some combination' were put forward as being potential descriptors of those cluster munitions that do not cause unacceptable harm to civilians. It went on to list 'sensor fuzing', 'fail-safe systems' (such as mechanical or electronic self-destruct, self-neutralization and self-deactivation mechanisms), 'restrictions on the numbers of submunitions', 'delivery by direct fire', 'failure rates', and 'accuracy' (in terms of delivery of the cluster munition to the target area). Further, this paper linked the scope of the definition to the possible need for transition periods (either with respect to Article 1 as a whole or to Article 1 as it would relate to certain subsets of prohibited cluster munitions.)

2.71 While that paper sought to maintain a broad menu of options for exclusion, individual States argued for different specific limitations on the scope of technology that would be prohibited. Japan submitted a proposal that weapons with fewer than 10 submunitions would fall outside the scope of the treaty and that reliable 'or' accurate cluster munitions should not be prohibited.[85] Germany proposed a more comprehensive definition that would

---

[82] Statement of the CMC, Wellington Conference, 19 February 2008 (Landmine Action notes; copy on file with author).

[83] Statement of the ICRC, Wellington Conference, 19 February 2008 (Landmine Action notes; copy on file with author).

[84] Discussions on definitions at the Wellington Conference, 19 February 2008 (Landmine Action notes; copy on file with author). [85] Became Diplomatic Conference doc. CCM/18.

exclude from prohibition only weapons with fewer than 10 submunitions each designed 'to engage point targets within a predefined area' and also incorporating self-destruct and self-deactivation mechanisms. However, their proposal also foresaw a sub-paragraph (d), implying that this might not be the extent of the exclusions from prohibition.[86]

2.72 France proposed that the term 'cluster munition' should refer specifically to the 'container' or 'carrier' rather than to the weapon system inclusive of its submunitions. It suggested that weapons with fewer than 10 submunitions should be excluded from prohibition. It also proposed different options for an additional exclusion at a sub-paragraph (d) for a munition 'designed to engage within a pre-defined area in a reliable and accurate manner' or 'that fulfils a combination of precise criteria regarding reliability and accuracy'. Beyond these exclusions, the French text proposed an additional definition of a 'carrier-container' which specifically listed artillery shells, air bombs, and guided or unguided missiles (potentially leaving open questions as to whether submunitions delivered by rockets or mortars would fall within the scope of the treaty.) The proposed definition of carrier-container also included dispensers that would remain attached to an aircraft during use unless these were for the delivery of 'direct fire munitions', this latter exclusion so as to avoid prohibiting 'rocket pods'. The French proposal made reference to a review mechanism that would allow the parameters of the definition to be considered again by States Parties 'no later than 5 years after entry into force' in line with the treaty's draft provisions regarding review conferences.[87]

2.73 Switzerland also proposed that 'cluster munition' should refer to the 'container' or 'carrier' rather than to the weapon system inclusive of its submunitions. It proposed excluding under Article 2, paragraph 2(c) only weapons that were 'designed to engage a point target within a pre-defined area' and which were also equipped with self-destruct, self-neutralization, 'or' self-deactivation mechanisms. The Swiss proposal followed the French definition of a 'carrier container' but proposed an alternative option for excluding rocket pods by requiring that dispensers be 'designed to dispense submunitions in a single act'.[88]

2.74 The UK proposed that the term cluster munition refer to a 'carrier container' and argued that weapons with less than a certain—undefined—number

[86] Became Diplomatic Conference doc. CCM/19.

[87] Became 'Proposal by France for the amendment of Article 2', Diplomatic Conference doc. CCM/20, 19 May 2008.

[88] Became 'Proposal by Switzerland for the amendment of Article 2', Diplomatic Conference doc. CCM/21, 19 May 2008.

of submunitions should fall outside the scope of the treaty. The UK proposal emphasized that this referred to 'conventional' munitions out of apparent concern that the process might inadvertently prohibit nuclear weapons. The UK sought to define cluster munitions in general as weapons 'designed to dispense conventional explosive submunitions over a pre-defined area', which seemed to be at odds with other proposals that used similar language to articulate specific exclusions from definition as a cluster munition. Indeed, the same UK document proposed an exclusion from prohibition for weapons 'designed to deliver effects within a pre-defined area'. Further to this they proposed exclusions for 'munitions that incorporate a failsafe system', for 'direct fire weapons' or those 'designed to deliver effects . . . on a point target'.[89]

2.75 The UK was one of a number of States that called for a blanket exclusion from prohibition for so-called 'direct fire' weapons (such as cluster munition variants of the Hydra and CRV-7 rockets used by attack helicopters). Such weapons were argued to be more accurate than other cluster munitions because the operator had a 'line of sight' to the target. However, questions were raised by the CMC and others regarding the relevance of such a characteristic to the area-effect of the cluster munition or of the likely risk of UXO being generated. Discussion of an exclusion for 'direct fire' munitions persisted into the negotiations in Dublin but gained little traction.

2.76 In a more discursive proposal, Sweden noted that one 'essential feature' in exclusions from prohibition should be 'the existence of an electrical fail safe system which must embrace both self destruct (SD) *and* self-deactivation (SDA) mechanisms'. They noted that 'the rationale for electrical systems is that batteries always discharge and render the munitions inoperable in the self-deactivating phase'. Sweden also suggested that these features should be cumulative with an 'internal guidance system—including sensors—to aid accuracy'.[90]

2.77 Peru proposed a general exclusion in Article 2, paragraph 2(c), to exclude from prohibition munitions or submunitions that have 'technical characteristics that allow to limit [*sic*] the area affected and reduce the risk of UXO contamination'.[91] Although this proposal did not delineate the characteristics that would be required, the idea of linking specific technical characteristics to

---

[89] Became 'Proposal by the United Kingdom for the amendment of Article 2', Diplomatic Conference doc. CCM/23, 19 May 2008.

[90] Became 'Proposal by Sweden for the amendment of Article 2', Diplomatic Conference doc. CCM/26, 19 May 2008.

[91] Became 'Proposal by Peru for the amendment of Article 2', Diplomatic Conference doc. CCM/24, 19 May 2008.

a statement of the effects being sought was picked up again during the negotiations at the Diplomatic Conference with the inclusion of an 'effects-based'
chapeau statement in Article 2, paragraph 2(c).

2.78 Ireland[92] proposed an amendment to the definition of 'explosive submunition' so as to link these directly to the main definition of a cluster munition as opposed to a 'parent munition'. Such a proposal did away with the
apparent need for a definition of a 'carrier container' as distinct from a 'cluster
munition'. This proposal was picked up, in a modified form, in the development of the definition of explosive submunition in the negotiations in Dublin.
Ireland also proposed a definition of 'explosive bomblet' as 'a munition which
in order to perform its task is dispersed or separated from a dispenser, affixed
to an aerial platform, and is designed to function by detonating an explosive
charge prior to, on or after impact'.

2.79 Similar to Ireland's proposal, the ICRC argued that the definition
of 'explosive submunition' be amended to refer to those being 'dispersed
or released from a cluster munition'.[93] This ensured that, in the terms 'dispersed or released', the relationship between a cluster munition and the
explosive submunitions was expressed in the same terms in both parts of the
definitions.

Negotiations

2.80 The document that carried the Draft Cluster Munitions Convention
from the Wellington Conference to the Diplomatic Conference in Dublin was
the Wellington Declaration, which States were required to endorse in order to
be full participants in the negotiations. The Wellington Declaration used the
language of the Oslo Declaration regarding a prohibition on 'cluster munitions that cause unacceptable harm to civilians':

States met in Wellington from February 18 to 22, 2008, to pursue an enduring solution to the grave humanitarian consequences caused by the use of cluster munitions.
They are convinced that this solution must include the conclusion in 2008 of a legally

---

[92] Became 'Proposal by Ireland for the amendment of Article 2', Diplomatic Conference doc.
CCM/25, 19 May 2008. Under the Irish proposal:

'**Explosive sub-munition**' means a munition that in order to perform its task separates from
a **cluster** munition and is designed to function by detonating an explosive charge prior to, on
or after impact.

[93] According to the ICRC paper included in the Wellington Compendium:

'Explosive sub-munitions' means munitions that in order to perform their task are **dispersed
or released** from a cluster munition and are designed to function by detonating an explosive
charge prior to, on or after impact.

binding international instrument prohibiting cluster munitions that cause unaccept-able harm to civilians. In that spirit they affirm that the essential elements of such an instrument should include:

• A prohibition on the use, production, transfer and stockpiling of cluster munitions that cause unacceptable harm to civilians... [94]

2.81 The text of the Draft Cluster Munitions Convention was submitted unchanged by the Wellington Conference to the Diplomatic Conference to serve as the basis for negotiations. Although there were to be changes made in almost all sections of the definition of cluster munition, discussion focused on paragraph 2(c) of Article 2. This discussion was broadly polarized between those States arguing for language to be inserted that would allow certain weapons to be excluded from prohibition and others arguing for the deletion of this sub-paragraph.

2.82 A significant number of those States seeking to exclude or exempt[95] particular weapon types from prohibition continued to refer to the phrase 'unacceptable harm' as used in the Oslo Declaration and the Wellington Declaration as a basis for expecting that certain weapons with submunitions would not be prohibited.[96] Some of these States sought initially to promote the discursive listing of a wide range of technologies as a possible basis for exclu-sions or exemptions contained in Conference document CCM/17.[97] However as the negotiations progressed, the emphasis shifted towards those endorsing a set of cumulative technical provisions. By contrast, those arguing for the dele-tion of Article 2, paragraph 2(c) often expressed scepticism that technological features could be relied upon to avoid the humanitarian problems associated with cluster munitions.[98]

2.83 With divergent views expressed in the opening session of the Committee of the Whole, the President of the Conference, Ambassador O'Ceallaigh appointed Ambassador Don MacKay of New Zealand to act as Friend of the President, to convene informal discussions on Article 2 and if

[94] Declaration of the Wellington Conference on Cluster Munitions, 22 February 2008.

[95] As these terms were used by the CMC, an 'exempted' technology would still be a cluster munition. This echoed debates over whether the treaty should distinguish between prohibited and allowed cluster munitions. By contrast, an 'excluded' technology was held to be similar to a clus-ter munition, but also sufficiently different to warrant falling outside the definition of that term. These distinctions are implicit in the CMC document, 'Dublin Diplomatic Conference on Cluster Munitions 2008—Lobbying Guide' (London: CMC, 2008).

[96] Australia, Canada, France, the Netherlands, Norway, and the UK. See, e.g., 'Summary Record of First Session of the Committee of the Whole', Diplomatic Conference doc. CCM/CW/SR/1, 18 June 2008, p. 4.

[97] Bulgaria, Denmark, Italy, Japan, South Africa, Sweden, and the UK. *Ibid.*, pp. 4, 5, 6.

[98] Indonesia supported by Guatemala, Jamaica, Mexico, and Venezuela. *Ibid.*, p. 5.

a text was not informally agreed to 'submit the proposal that he considered best'.[99] The informal consultations were structured first to consider whether certain technical characteristics might individually be considered sufficient to warrant weapons falling under the main definition being excluded from prohibition. The Friend of the President circulated an informal paper containing 'Elements for discussion in relation to (c)', which listed the following:

- A munition or sub-munition designed to locate and engage a point target within a pre-defined area (i.e. sensor fusing, multiple or single)
- A munition or sub-munition that is delivered by direct fire (i.e. line-of-sight fire)
- A munition or sub-munition that otherwise meets accuracy requirements, in terms of delivery of the munition and sub-munition to the target area
- A munition that contains less than ... sub-munitions (i.e. limited numbers of sub-munitions per cluster munition)
- A sub-munition that contains electronic fail-safe mechanisms (self destruct and/or self-deactivation)
- A sub-munition that contains mechanical fail-safe mechanisms (self destruct and/or self-neutralization)
- A sub-munition that meets prescribed reliability/failure rates
- A sub-munition that otherwise meets reliability requirements, in terms of not leaving unacceptable quantities of hazardous unexploded ordnance (UXO)
- Any other elements that States may wish to propose.

2.84 The paper also noted the need to 'future-proof' the definition, which was taken to mean that any exclusion at paragraph 2(c) should not allow the same problematic effects experienced in the past to be repeated with other similar weapons in the future. This paper noted that these elements might be discussed in combination (i.e. cumulatively) as well as individually. This list did not explicitly make reference to the weight of submunitions or to air-defence systems, both of which were addressed during subsequent negotiations and included in the definition ultimately adopted.

2.85 With many States expressing scepticism of technical characteristics individually, discussion proceeded to consider whether characteristics taken cumulatively might provide grounds for confidence that 'unacceptable harm'

---

[99] 'Summary Record of First Session of the Committee of the Whole', *op. cit.*

would not result from the use of these weapons.[100] In order to structure discussion of these cumulative options the Friend of the President circulated an informal paper of 'Proposals that have been made on cumulative lists of criteria'. This contained eight options, labelled A to H, of cumulative technical characteristics for a possible exclusion at paragraph 2(c). Each option contained between two and five bullet points drawn in the main from the specific elements that had been listed individually in the first informal paper. Throughout the informal discussions, the technical characteristics, both individually and in combinations, were considered in relation to their relevance to the negative humanitarian effects that were associated with cluster munitions.[101]

2.86 Formal proposals made by States during the Wellington Conference and compiled into the Compendium were also circulated individually as formal documents of the Diplomatic Conference. Furthermore, a number of formal proposals on the definition of cluster munition and explosive submunition were circulated at the very start of the Diplomatic Conference. Slovakia argued that sub-paragraph (c) should exclude submunitions with a failure rate of 'not more than 1%' and which also had some sort of self-destruct, self-deactivation, or self-neutralization feature.[102]

2.87 Spain followed a number of the proposals submitted in Wellington in arguing that cluster munition should refer solely to the 'carrier container'.[103] The Spanish proposal advocated an exclusion from prohibition in sub-paragraph (c) for weapons with submunitions equipped with 'a self-safe mechanism that, combined with the normal function mechanism, guarantees that the number of remaining dangerous duds that can cause harm to non-combatants is in practice equal to zero'. By using the term 'dangerous duds', however, this proposal returned to criteria that had been widely criticized during previous meetings. Other terms such as 'guarantee... in practice' raised significant concerns about how such a definition would be implemented. In addition to these technical characteristics, the Spanish proposal argued that any submunitions

---

[100] See Ambassador Don MacKay's report on this process, contained in 'Summary Record of Ninth Session of the Committee of the Whole', Diplomatic Conference doc. CCM/CW/SR/9, 18 June 2008.

[101] Ambassador MacKay reported later that:

An effects-based approach had been taken in the informal consultations, where the proposed elements had been measured both singly and cumulatively against the need for accuracy and reliability.

'Summary Record of Ninth Session of the Committee of the Whole', *op. cit.*

[102] 'Proposal by Slovakia for the amendment of Article 2', Diplomatic Conference doc. CCM/64, 19 May 2008.

[103] 'Proposal by Spain for the amendment of Article 2', Diplomatic Conference doc. CCM/67, 19 May 2008.

excluded in sub-paragraph (c) should be 'painted and marked in order to distinguish it from the terrain and to warn about their dangerousness'.

2.88 The Czech Republic proposed excluding 'landmines' from the Convention in Article 2, paragraph 2(c) (rather than through Article 1) and also proposed an additional sub-paragraph (d) that would exclude from prohibition weapons with fewer than ten submunitions each equipped with self-destruct 'and/or' self-deactivation mechanisms.[104] In addition, the Czech Republic proposed stipulating that the term 'explosive submunitions' refer only to submunitions that would explode 'immediately' after impact, a stipulation that seemed also to be concerned to exclude remotely delivered landmines from prohibition.

2.89 On 21 May, Norway circulated a proposal that suggested excluding at sub-paragraph (c) munitions with submunitions that met a number of cumulative criteria. In these criteria, and also in the main definition, the Norwegian proposal used thresholds based on weight to further define a cluster munition:

'Cluster munition' means a munition that is designed to disperse or release explosive sub-munitions each weighing less than 20 kilograms, and includes those explosive sub-munitions. It does not mean the following:

a) a munition or sub-munition designed to dispense flares, smoke, pyrotechnic or chaff effects.
b) a munition or sub-munition designed to produce electrical or electronic effects;
c) a munition with sub-munitions each weighing more than five kilograms, designed to seek, detect and engage point targets, and equipped with electronic self destruct and self deactivation mechanisms.

The introduction of the upper submunition weight threshold of 20 kilograms in the main definition went on to be adopted in the final definition of a cluster munition. The cumulative list of criteria presented at sub-paragraph (c) is similar to that contained in the final definition, though there were to be further developments in drafting, the addition of a limitation on submunition numbers and, very importantly, the addition of a *chapeau* at sub-paragraph (c) that links the technical characteristics to the effects of humanitarian concern. The lower weight limit of a minimum of five kilograms for permitted explosive submunitions was also to be lowered to four kilograms in the final stages of negotiation.

---

[104] 'Proposal by Slovakia for the amendment of Article 2', Diplomatic Conference doc. CCM/68, 19 May 2008.

2.90 But while the Norwegian proposal began to establish some support for a set of cumulative criteria at sub-paragraph (c), the only alternative position commanding support from a range of countries was for the removal of the sub-paragraph altogether. In a formal proposal tabled jointly, Argentina, Chile, Costa Rica, the Dominican Republic, Ecuador, Guatemala, Guinea, Honduras, Mexico, Nicaragua, Panama, Peru, Uruguay, and Zambia all called for the deletion of Article 2, paragraph 2(c).[105] In a subsequent session of the Committee of the Whole, on 26 May, Austria, Benin, Botswana, Burkina Faso, Burundi, the Democratic Republic of Congo, Ghana, Guinea, Laos, Nigeria, Panama, Senegal, Sierra Leone, and Venezuela, all expressed support for the deletion of the sub-paragraph.[106]

2.91 Against this backdrop, on 22 May, a Friend of the President's 'Paper on Definition of a "Cluster Munition"' was circulated. This effectively summarized the position as a choice between the deletion of 2(c) and a set of cumulative criteria at 2(c) which were linked to a statement of the negative effects that were the basis for considering cluster munitions unacceptable. This summary paper did not, however, adopt the weight-based criteria proposed by Norway.

'Cluster munition' means a munition that is designed to disperse or release explosive sub-munitions, and includes those explosive sub-munitions. It does not mean the following:

a) a munition or sub-munition designed to dispense flares, smoke, pyrotechnics or chaff or air defence systems;

b) a munition or sub-munition designed to produce electrical or electronic effects;

c) a munition that has all of the following characteristics to minimise its area effect and the risk of unexploded ordnance contamination from its use:

    a) each munition contains fewer than 10 sub-munitions;

    b) each sub-munition is designed to locate and engage a point-target within a pre-defined area;

    c) each sub-munition is equipped with an electronic self-destruction mechanism;

    d) each submunition is equipped with an electronic self-deactivating feature.

The Friend of the President's Paper introduced for the first time a *chapeau* at 2(c). This provided a mechanism for linking the technical

---

[105] 'Proposal by Argentina, Ecuador, Guatemala, Uruguay, Dominican Republic, Mexico, Nicaragua, Panama, Peru, Costa Rica, Chile, Honduras, Zambia and Guinea for the amendment of Article 5', Diplomatic Conference doc. CCM/71, 21 May 2008.

[106] 'Summary Record of Eleventh Session of the Committee of the Whole', Diplomatic Conference doc. CCM/CW/SR/11, 18 June 2008.

characteristics that might be held to justify an exclusion from prohibition with the problematic effects that needed to be avoided. This *chapeau* would be further developed during the course of the negotiations to establish a new precedent for defining weapons in relation to their problematic characteristics.

2.92 Also on 22 May, Canada circulated a formal proposal supporting the inclusion of effects-based language in the *chapeau* of paragraph 2(c) but which sought to modify the specific text of that *chapeau*. The Canadian proposal also called for the removal of the proposed limitation based on the number of submunitions.[107] Canada had expressed on several occasions a preference to avoid numbers that must necessarily be arbitrary.

2.93 On 23 May, the UK circulated a proposal that continued to argue for wide exemptions for systems such as the M85.[108] Elements of this proposal were now substantially at odds with the broad direction of the definition debate. The paper proposed blanket exemptions from prohibition for 'direct fire' munitions, for any munition with fewer than 10 submunitions, and for any submunitions equipped with a self-destruct mechanism. There were no statements in support of the UK proposal.

2.94 On 23 May, a revised 'Chair's Discussion Paper' was circulated which further developed the paper of the previous day based on the subsequent discussions.[109] It incorporated the weight-based criteria proposed by Norway, modified the language of the *chapeau* at paragraph 2(c) and amended the terminology for self-destruction and self-deactivation features:

'Cluster munition' means a munition that is designed to disperse or release explosive sub-munitions each weighing less than 20 kilograms, and includes those explosive sub-munitions. It does not mean the following:

a) a munition or sub-munition designed to dispense flares, smoke, pyrotechnics or chaff; or air defence systems;
b) a munition or sub-munition designed to produce electrical or electronic effects;
c) a munition that has the following characteristics to limit its area effect and reduce the risk of unexploded ordnance contamination from its use:

   a.) each munition contains fewer than 10 sub-munitions;
   b.) each sub-munition weighs more than five kilograms;

---

[107] 'Proposal by Canada for the amendment of Article 2', Diplomatic Conference doc. CCM/74, 22 May 2008.

[108] 'Proposal by the United Kingdom for the amendment of Article 2', Diplomatic Conference doc. CCM75, 23 May 2008.

[109] Report of Ambassador Don MacKay, in 'Summary Record of Ninth Session of the Committee of the Whole', Diplomatic Conference doc. CCM/CW/SR/9, 18 June 2008.

c.) each sub-munition is designed to locate and engage a point-target within a pre-defined area;

d.) each sub-munition is equipped with an electronic self-destruct mechanism;

e.) each submunition is equipped with an electronic self-deactivating mechanism.

In presenting this paper to the Committee of the Whole, Ambassador Don MacKay 'emphasised that the discussion paper was not an agreed text, but represented the Friend of the President's own assessment of possible language for Article 2(c), if it is to exist. Fundamental differences remained on an Article 2(c) and whether or not it should be included. A formal proposal had been made for its deletion.'[110]

2.95 At the beginning of the second week of negotiations, States remained broadly polarized between those seeking certain exclusions at Article 2, paragraph 2(c) and those favouring the deletion of the sub-paragraph. However, the discussion paper circulated by the Chair was receiving some support from both sides of this divide. Among those favouring additional provisions at paragraph 2(c), Australia, Canada, France, Germany, the Netherlands, Norway, Sweden, and Switzerland were all broadly supportive of the direction of the Chair's paper. Among those calling for deletion of the sub-paragraph, many indicated some degree of support for the Chair's text or an openness to continue discussions along these lines.[111] A significant number of States spoke critically of the inclusion of an exemption for 'air defence systems' proposed by the UK to be included in paragraph 2(a),[112] including Argentina, Botswana, Costa Rica, Norway, and Panama.[113]

2.96 A number of States also sought further evidence or proof to justify claims that weapons excluded at paragraph 2(c) would not cause 'unacceptable harm' to civilians.[114] Austria and Lebanon, supported by Malta, argued that any weapons excluded under the sub-paragraph should be subject to scrutiny and their status in relation to the Convention reviewed in the future. Canada also implicitly supported such a position in arguing that, 'it is incumbent on States to monitor the use and results of weapon develop-

---

[110] 'Summary Record of Ninth Session of the Committee of the Whole', Diplomatic Conference doc. CCM/CW/SR/9, 18 June 2008.

[111] Argentina, Austria, Burkina Faso, Burundi, Chile, DR Congo, Ghana, Guatemala, Guinea, Lebanon, Mexico, Nigeria, Senegal, Sierra Leone, Uruguay, and Zambia.

[112] See, *infra*, §§2.104 and 2.117–2.118.

[113] 'Summary Record of Eleventh Session of the Committee of the Whole', Diplomatic Conference doc. CCM/CW/SR/11, 18 June 2008.

[114] Democratic Republic of Congo, Jamaica, and Laos.

ment' and reminded States 'of the possibility of amending the Convention by a two-thirds majority. States will have the opportunity in the annual meetings of States Parties and in the Review Conference to adjust to future developments.'[115]

2.97 On 26 May, as a supplement to their earlier proposal, Norway circulated an 'Explanatory note' providing further analysis of the thinking behind using weight as one of a number of cumulative criteria.[116] It summarized these in the following terms:

The proposed weight limit will in practice eliminate up to 99% of all cluster munitions currently in stocks, and all existing cluster munitions that have ever been used in war.

A weight based criteria is robust. It is easy to understand, easy to verify and in practice almost impossible to circumvent.

The proposed weight limit will allow for weapons that do not cause the problem we aim to address, and will prohibit those that inherently cause such problems.

A weight limit for point target sub-munitions would automatically reduce the total numbers of sub-munitions that could physically fit into any parent munition. This will substantially reduce the problem of unexploded ordnance.

A weight limit for such point target sub-munition would safeguard against a future miniaturization (and resulting increase in numbers). This will prevent a repetition of the very problems we seek to address with this treaty.

Larger sub-munitions are easier to detect, less sensitive to handle and thus easier to clear. This will reduce the risk for civilian accidents due to inadvertent contact with unexploded ordnance.

2.98 As a summary of the implications of the weight criteria, the 'Explanatory note' stated:

1. More than 20 kilograms per submunitions—excluded from the scope of the convention
2. Between 5 and 20 kilograms per sub-munition—excluded under the condition that they meet strict requirements of single target, self destruct and self-deactivation
3. Less than 5 kilograms per submunition—categorically prohibited.

In addition to these explanations based on perceived humanitarian considerations, the upper weight limit proposed by Norway had the effect of excluding France's KRISS anti-runway submunitions from the scope of the Convention.

---

[115] 'Summary Record of Eleventh Session of the Committee of the Whole', *op. cit.*
[116] See *ibid.*

During discussions of the definition on 26 May in the Committee of the Whole, France expressed 'full support' for the weight criterion proposed by Norway.[117]

2.99 A proposal by Spain on 27 May was the last formal proposal submitted on the main definition of cluster munition during the negotiations.[118] It adopted the effects-based *chapeau* introducing sub-paragraph (c) but proposed vaguely defined exclusion for munitions with 'sub-munitions which only address the area encompassed by the intended military objective'[119] in addition to requiring the presence of electronic self-destruction and self-deactivation mechanisms.

2.100 In addition to the discussion of the main definition of 'cluster munition' were parallel, ongoing discussions of terms integral to this definition. These included the definition of 'explosive submunition' and such terms as 'point target', 'self-destruct devices', 'self-deactivation', and 'self-neutralisation'.

2.101 On 23 May a revised definition of an explosive submunition was circulated by the Friend of the President on 'other' definitions.[120] Very similar to that in the Draft Convention, this definition was for 'explosive submunition' in the singular rather than in the plural. It defined an explosive submunition as separating 'from' a cluster munition as opposed to from a 'parent munition'.[121] Three days later, a further revised definition was circulated by the Friend of the President on 'other' definitions.[122] This version inserted explicit reference to a 'conventional' munition and changed the term 'separates from' to 'dispersed or released by' to describe the relationship between explosive submunitions and cluster munitions as had been proposed in Wellington by the ICRC. This latter change created coherence of language between the definition of explosive submunition and that of cluster munition. The term dispersed and released 'by' was preferred to 'from' because the latter emphasized more strongly a distinction between 'cluster munition' and 'explosive submunitions' whereas the

---

[117] 'Summary Record of Eleventh Session of the Committee of the Whole', Diplomatic Conference doc. CCM/CW/SR/11, 18 June 2008.

[118] 'Proposal by Spain for the amendment of Article 2', Diplomatic Conference doc. CCM/76.

[119] The proposal referred to the definition of 'military objective' contained in *1980 Protocol III on Incendiary Weapons* (Protocol III on Prohibitions or Restrictions on the Use of Incendiary Weapons to the CCW).

[120] 'Informal Paper—Friend of the President on definitions other than that of a "Cluster Munition" and a "Cluster Munitions Victim"', 23 May 2008, 13:00.

[121] '"Explosive submunition" means a munition that in order to perform its task separates from a cluster munition and is designed to function by detonating an explosive charge prior to, on or after impact.'

[122] 'Informal Paper—Friend of the President on definitions other than that of a "Cluster Munition" and a "Cluster Munitions Victim"', 26 May 2008, 15:30.

definition of cluster munition explicitly included the explosive submunitions. This definition of explosive submunition was adopted in the final Convention text:

'Explosive submunition' means a conventional munition that in order to perform its task is dispersed or released by a cluster munition and is designed to function by detonating an explosive charge prior to, on or after impact.

By defining the term 'explosive submunition' in relation to a 'cluster munition', space was also created for the existence of 'submunitions' that were used in other systems not defined as cluster munitions (for example, those systems that might be excluded from prohibition either due to the weight criteria in the main definition, or through the characteristics described at 2(a)–(c)).

2.102 With proposed definitions of a cluster munition making reference to weapons that would 'engage a point target', on 26 May an informal paper circulated by the Friend of the President on 'other definitions'[123] noted the NATO definition of a 'point target' as a 'target that requires the accurate placement of bomb or fire'. Later in the day a revised paper summarized the state of the debate over the definition of this term:[124]

Two approaches were discussed. One was to define 'point target'. The other was to use alternative language in Article 2c. that would avoid the need to define 'point target'.

1. 'Point target' means a target that requires the accurate placement of bomb or fire on a single object.[125]

2. 2.c.b. Each submunition is designed to detect and engage a single target object.

The second of these options was adopted in the final text of the Convention.

2.103 On 28 May 2008, the 'Presidency Paper, *draft* Convention on Cluster Munitions' (Conference document CCM/PT/15) was circulated. The definitions in this paper were to be adopted without further change. The definition of explosive submunition was unchanged from that circulated by the Friend of the President on 26 May. However, the definition of cluster munition had been subject to a number of adjustments from the 'Chair's Discussion Paper' of 23 May.

---

[123] 'Informal Paper—Friend of the President on definitions other than that of a "Cluster Munition" and a "Cluster Munitions Victim"', 26 May 2008, 11:00.

[124] 'Informal Paper—Friend of the President on definitions other than that of a "Cluster Munition" and a "Cluster Munitions Victim"—Approaches to the need to define "point target" arising from the language in Article 2c b', 26 May 2008, 15:30.

[125] The addition of the phrase 'on a single object' came from a suggestion by Canada.

2.104 It was now clarified that 'cluster munition' meant a 'conventional munition'.[126] While the lack of a definition for 'air defence' remained a weakness, the wording of the exclusion for air-defence systems had been improved through a stipulation that such systems should be 'designed exclusively' for such a role. The minimum weight limit at sub-paragraph (c) (ii) had been reduced from five kilograms to four kilograms, a change that went in the direction of widening the scope of the exclusion although no open discussions explained the implications or reasoning behind this. The phrase 'point-target within a pre-defined area' was replaced with 'a single target object', reflecting the discussions that had taken place on this. The term 'self-deactivating mechanism' was replaced with the term 'self-deactivating feature'.

2.105 The *chapeau* at sub-paragraph (c) had been significantly reworded. Whereas the discussion text of 23 May stipulated that the technical characteristics were 'to limit' area effect and 'reduce' the risk of UXO, the new *chapeau* brought in more absolute language and, by introducing the term 'indiscriminate area effects', linked the *chapeau* to terminology in other areas of international humanitarian law. Following a suggestion by Germany, the original intent of the *chapeau* was clarified that a munition must have 'all' of the technical characteristics at (c)(i) to (v) in order not to be considered a cluster munition.[127]

2.106 A final change of note was that all of the serial lines under sub-paragraph (c) now referred to 'explosive submunitions' where previously they had referred simply to submunitions. This is problematic because it creates a logical flaw in the definition. Serials (i) to (v) refer to the characteristics of weapons that are not cluster munitions due to the characteristics of their 'explosive submunitions', yet 'explosive submunitions' are subsequently defined as components of a 'cluster munition'. It is thus not logically coherent that these weapons are not cluster munitions but also have explosive submunitions. This problem did not exist in the Chair's text of 23 May because the serial items under sub-paragraph (c) referred simply to 'submunitions'. The Summary Record of the Committee of the Whole for 26 May 2008 attributes the proposal to use the term 'explosive submunitions' in the sub-paragraph to Germany.[128] Notwithstanding this technical inconsistency, it is clear that it does not alter the meaning of the definition, and that cluster munitions including their explosive submunitions are prohibited unless they fulfil the five technical criteria in Article 2, paragraph 2(c)(i)–(v). The issue was identified and

---

[126] 'Conventional munition' means that it is not a nuclear, chemical, or biological munition.
[127] 'Summary Record of Eleventh Session of the Committee of the Whole', Diplomatic Conference doc. CCM/CW/SR/11, 18 June 2008.   [128] *Ibid.*

raised by the CMC prior to adoption of the Convention, but it was too late to reopen the text for anything but editorial changes.

2.107 In presenting the text, the President of the Conference, Ambassador O'Ceallaigh, noted that 'a restrictive effects-based definition had been used which would prohibit the vast majority of submunition-based weapons systems existing in the world today, and all of those which have been used'.[129] On recommending the text for adoption the President described 'an extremely ambitious Convention text' and noted that that 'the headline definition of a "cluster munition" will lead to the prohibition of all cluster munitions that cause unacceptable harm to civilians and that it prohibits all cluster munitions ever used in armed conflict. For many states represented this will involve the removal of all cluster munitions from national stocks.'[130]

2.108 The far-reaching scope of the definition was widely recognized by States as a very good result, although a number of States would have preferred a definition with no exclusions whatsoever.[131] Civil society also recognized the strength of the definition. ICRC welcomed the definitions as 'comprehensive'.[132] The CMC stated that 'the draft Convention outcome far exceeded the expectations of nearly everyone. The prohibition contained therein was more comprehensive than that of the Mine Ban Treaty: not just some cluster munitions but all were prohibited; no distinction was made between good and bad cluster munitions.' It noted further that: 'The exclusion in Article 2(c) applied to munitions that do not have the same effects as cluster munitions, that is, that do not have wide area and excessive unexploded ordnance effects.'[133]

Paragraph 2

'Cluster munition' means a conventional munition that is designed to disperse or release explosive submunitions each weighing less than

---

[129] 'Summary Record of Fifteenth Session of the Committee of the Whole', Diplomatic Conference doc. CCM/CW/SR/15, 18 June 2008.

[130] 'Summary Record of Fifteenth Session of the Committee of the Whole', Diplomatic Conference doc. CCM/CW/SR/16, 18 June 2008.

[131] e.g. Costa Rica noted that they would have preferred a broader definition, and Argentina expressed a need to remain watchful regarding the humanitarian impact of any weapons excluded under sub-paragraph (c). The latter view was also expressed by the CMC on the adoption of the Convention, see 'Summary Record of Fourth Session of the Plenary and Closing Ceremony of the Conference', Diplomatic Conference doc. CCM/SR/4, 18 June 2008.   [132] *Ibid.*

[133] *Ibid.*

20 kilograms, and includes those explosive submunitions. It does not mean the following:

(a) A munition or submunition designed to dispense flares, smoke, pyrotechnics or chaff; or a munition designed exclusively for an air defence role;

(b) A munition or submunition designed to produce electrical or electronic effects;

(c) A munition that, in order to avoid indiscriminate area effects and the risks posed by unexploded submunitions, has all of the following characteristics:

(i) Each munition contains fewer than ten explosive submunitions;

(ii) Each explosive submunition weighs more than four kilograms;

(iii) Each explosive submunition is designed to detect and engage a single target object;

(iv) Each explosive submunition is equipped with an electronic self-destruction mechanism;

(v) Each explosive submunition is equipped with an electronic self-deactivating feature;

Commentary

Conventional munition

2.109 Cluster munitions are defined as 'conventional' munitions, thus clarifying that the Convention is not concerned with nuclear, chemical, or biological weapons that may use submunitions. Without such clarification, certain nuclear weapons that have multiple submunition warheads might have fallen under the definition of cluster munitions.

2.110 Defining a cluster munition as a 'munition' distinguishes it from the proposals made during the negotiations to define a cluster munition as a 'carrier container'. This formulation, introduced in the Vienna Discussion Text, makes it clear that the term cluster munition refers to the whole weapon system, not simply a component or delivery mechanism. However, by using the term 'munition' it opened up the requirement for a separate definition in order to capture those weapons that used a dispenser that remained affixed to an aircraft. For more discussion, see the commentary below on the phrase 'and includes those submunitions'[134] as well as those discussing the definitions of 'explosive bomblet'[135] and 'dispenser'.[136]

---

[134] §2.115.   [135] §§2.223–2.228.   [136] §§2.229–2.236.

Disperse or release

2.111 The phrase 'disperse or release' acknowledges that the mechanism by which explosive submunitions (or explosive bomblets) are separated from the container or dispenser can be either active or passive. That is to say, that the submunitions may be actively propelled from the container or may simply fall from the container due to the removal of some barrier to their movement.

Explosive submunition

2.112 Explosive submunitions are defined at Article 2, paragraph 3 as follows:

3. '**Explosive submunition**' means a conventional munition that in order to perform its task is dispersed or released by a cluster munition and is designed to function by detonating an explosive charge prior to, on or after impact;

This definition is discussed further below.

Weighing less than 20 kilograms

2.113 The upper weight limit of 20 kilograms in the first part of the definition provides a broad basis for weapons with submunitions not to be considered cluster munitions. The Convention does not therefore apply to any weapons with submunitions weighing 20 kilograms or more.

2.114 The CMC noted during the Diplomatic Conference that a high upper weight limit might be necessary to distinguish submunitions from other aircraft bombs deployed from bomb racks.[137] While most weapons commonly considered cluster munitions have submunitions weighing significantly less than 20 kilograms it was significant in the context of the negotiations that this component of the definition served to exclude from prohibition the French Apache,[138] an anti-runway system that employs ten KRISS submunitions, each weighing approximately 50 kilograms.[139]

---

[137] Statement of the CMC, Friend of the President's Informal Consultations on Definitions, Diplomatic Conference, 21 May 2008.

[138] APACHE (*Arme Propulsée Antipiste à Charges Ejectables*) is a cruise missile system that dispenses KRISS anti-runway submunitions. See, e.g., Hewson, R., *Jane's Air-Launched Weapons*, Issue 53, Jane's Information Group, Coulsdon, UK, 2009, pp. 234–239; see also FAS, Military Analysis Network, 'APACHE', <http://www.fas.org/man/dod-101/sys/missile/row/apache.htm> (visited 28 October 2009).

[139] Forecast International 2005, 'Ordnance & Munitions Forecast, Kill Runway Improved Submunition—Archived 12/2006', <http://www.forecastinternational.com/archive/or/vm0492.doc> (accessed 28 October 2009).

And includes those explosive submunitions

2.115 This phrase was introduced in the Vienna Discussion Text and serves to define cluster munitions as both the container and its submunitions. This was in contrast to the Lima Discussion Text and a number of proposals that sought to define a cluster munition as a 'container', and thus by implication a component of a weapon system rather than the weapon system itself.

A munition or submunition designed to produce flares,
smoke, pyrotechnics, or chaff

2.116 Systems that use explosive submunitions but which are designed to produce flares, smoke, pyrotechnics, or chaff are excluded from prohibition. Systems designed for these purposes are not primarily weapons designed to kill or wound people or to damage military objects but rather are intended to create illuminating, communicative, obscuring, or diversionary effects. They may be used to 'mark' targets on the ground or may serve as counter-measure systems to protect vehicles from attack. Submunitions employed in such systems may use an explosive charge in order to create these effects and so, without this clarification, these systems might be held to fall under the definition of a cluster munition and so be prohibited. While such systems may not primarily be intended for use against personnel, the border line between these functions can be blurred. For example, white phosphorous can be used both to create smoke and as an incendiary weapon.

A munition designed exclusively for an air-defence role

2.117 Unlike systems for producing 'flares, smoke, pyrotechnics or chaff', munitions 'designed exclusively for an air-defence role' are primarily weapons for use against aircraft. It is a potential weakness of the definition in the Convention that this phrase is not subject to further specific definition.[140] During the negotiations in Dublin, the UK raised the concern that certain air-defence weapons might inadvertently be prohibited, despite being quite different from cluster munitions as generally understood.[141] The specific weapons of concern to the UK were understood to be its 'Starstreak' missiles, generally

---

[140] A number of States (including Argentina, Botswana, Costa Rica, Norway, and Panama) were critical of the inclusion of this provision or called for further definition of this term within the negotiations. See 'Summary Record of Eleventh Session of the Committee of the Whole', Diplomatic Conference doc. CCM/CW/SR/11, 18 June 2008.

[141] Statement of the UK, Meeting of the Friend of the Chair on Definitions, Diplomatic Conference, 21 May 2008.

considered an air-to-air or ground-to-air weapon that uses three explosive submunitions.[142]

2.118 The UK noted on a number of occasions, and it was clarified by the chair of the informal discussions, that the term 'air defence' referred to 'ground-to-air' weapons that resulted in 'effects in the air' rather than on the ground.[143] The term 'air-defence role' should not therefore be interpreted as allowing so-called 'anti-runway' munitions that, it might be argued, are used to defend pre-emptively against aerial attack. The interpretation presented here is further supported by the fact that a Chair's discussion text produced in the context of the CCW presented munitions 'designed for an air-defence role' and munitions 'designed primarily or exclusively as anti-runway munitions' as two distinct items on the same list.[144] It is notable that the exclusion from prohibition only applies to systems 'designed exclusively' for this role, and therefore any systems that were developed to provide both ground-to-air and ground-to-ground capability, and falling under the broader definition of a cluster munition, would be prohibited.

Submunitions designed to produce electrical or electronic effects

2.119 Systems with submunitions that produce electrical or electronic effects may be used as radio-jammers to disrupt communications equipment or in other 'counter-measure' functions. Such systems are not primarily weapons designed to kill or wound people or to damage military objects.

---

[142] See, UK Army website 'Starstreak High Velocity Missile', <http://www.army.mod.uk/equipment/artillery-air-defence/1509.aspx> (accessed 29 January 2010) and Frontier India, 'Starstreak missiles', 29 January 2009, <http://frontierindia.net/uks-starstreak-high-velocity-missile-system-to-get-extended-life> (visited 29 October 2009). An online report from Jane's has suggested that the next generation of Starstreak missile would also be able to engage 'light armoured vehicles' in addition to aircraft. See <http://www.janes.com/events/exhibitions/dsei2007/sections/daily/day1/starstreak-ii-sighted.shtml> (accessed 29 January 2010). Furthermore, the manufacturer's literature also promotes its utility against 'surface targets such as Armoured Personnel Carriers (APCs), static installations or terrorist platforms' (Thales Air Defence Limited, STARSTREAK: Lightweight Multiple Launcher (LML), ref: 05/2005—LML). Given that the definition in Article 2 excluded from prohibition only munitions 'designed exclusively for an air-defence role' such a development would likely render these weapons prohibited. Furthermore, since the test of legality relates to their design, it would be the process of weapons planning, development, and testing that determines the permissibility of the weapons rather than the stated plans for use of those stockpiling these weapons.

[143] *Ibid.*, and Statement of the UK, Friend of the President's Informal Consultations on Definitions, Diplomatic Conference, 21 May 2008.

[144] Chair's informal draft discussion text for the September 2008 Group of Governmental Experts to the *Convention on Certain Conventional Weapons*, 5 September 2008.

To avoid indiscriminate area effects and to avoid the risk posed by
unexploded submunitions

2.120 The *chapeau* clause introducing sub-paragraph (c) of Article 2, paragraph 2 articulates the problematic humanitarian effects that are considered
defining features of cluster munitions and which must be avoided—for any
weapons with explosive submunitions weighing less than 20 kilograms and
that are not designed exclusively for air defence—to be considered permissible. The *chapeau* provides a statement of the problematic effects that the
subsequent technical characteristics are intended, cumulatively, to avoid. It
therefore provides both a justification for the exclusion of weapons that meet
these technical criteria and also a potential mechanism for determining if these
technical criteria function as intended.[145] By linking the definition of what is
prohibited to the humanitarian effects that are the basis for prohibition, this
chapeau is an important legal innovation. While cluster munitions are not
defined as being 'designed' to create these problematic effects, paragraph 2(c)
stipulates that munitions must be designed positively to avoid these effects if
they are not to be prohibited.

2.121 The phrase 'to avoid' is made problematic by being applied equally
to both 'indiscriminate area effects' and 'risks posed by unexploded submunitions'. As explained in further detail below, some risk from UXO cannot be
wholly avoided in explosive munitions. Absent any qualification on the level of
'risks posed by unexploded submunitions' that must be avoided, it is difficult
to read 'avoid' in that context as being absolute; rather it needs to be understood as more akin to 'greatly limit'. By contrast, 'indiscriminate' attacks are
subject to absolute prohibition under *1977 Additional Protocol I*[146] and hence
it is reasonable here to assume that the term 'to avoid' should be read in an
absolute sense (i.e. indiscriminate area effects are not allowed).

Indiscriminate area effects

2.122 'Indiscriminate area effects' can be understood to represent a problematic characteristic of cluster munitions 'at the time of their use'[147] and are
distinct from the pattern of UXO contamination that may be found after

---

[145] Statements of Austria and Lebanon, supported by Malta, reported in 'Summary Record
of Eleventh Session of the Committee of the Whole', Diplomatic Conference doc. CCM/CW/
SR/11, 18 June 2008. See also Statement of the CMC in 'Summary Record of Fourth Session of
the Plenary and Closing Ceremony of the Conference', Diplomatic Conference doc. CCM/SR/4,
18 June 2008. *Cf.* also, *supra*, §2.38.

[146] The formal title of this treaty is the Protocol Additional to the Geneva Conventions of
12 August 1949, and relating to the Protection of Victims of International Armed Conflicts.

[147] Second preambular paragraph.

use.[148] 'Indiscriminate area effect' refers to the so-called 'footprint' within which cluster munitions scatter individual explosive munitions randomly. The term 'indiscriminate area effects' is not defined in the Convention, but can be further understood both by reference to the specific technical characteristics held as necessary to avoid such effects and by consideration of other legal instruments that make use of similar terms. Of particular relevance would be Article 51, paragraphs 4 and 5, of *1977 Additional Protocol I* which prohibits indiscriminate attacks and describe such attacks. The description of indiscriminate attacks as those that 'are of a nature to strike military objectives and civilians or civilian objects without distinction'[149] and the specific identification as indiscriminate of attacks 'by bombardment by any methods or means which treats as a single military objective a number of clearly separated and distinct military objectives located in a city, town, village or other area containing a similar concentration of civilians or civilian objects'[150] have particular bearing on the concept of 'indiscriminate area effects'. The detailed definition of what technologies are prohibited under the Convention on Cluster Munitions should serve to influence interpretation of these general rules as they relate to the distribution of explosive force and fragmentation across areas.

2.123 Of the cumulative characteristics that are necessary to avoid the humanitarian problems indicated under the paragraph 2(c) *chapeau*, points (i) to (iii) are related, *inter alia*, to the aim to avoid 'indiscriminate area effects'. These technical characteristics serve to calibrate how such effects are to be understood. Paragraph 2(c) (iii) requires the individual submunitions to detect and engage a 'single target object'. Such a 'target object' should be a vehicle, artillery piece, or other such distinct item. It is prohibited, therefore, to use weapons where the explosive submunitions are scattered and distribute explosive force and fragmentation randomly across an area. This represents a substantial functional distinction between weapons excluded from prohibition at paragraph 2(c) and cluster munitions. This obligation not to distribute explosive force and fragmentation randomly across an area is further strengthened by sub-paragraph (c), points (i) and (ii).[151]

---

[148] This distinction is clear from the fact that 'indiscriminate area effect' and 'risk of unexploded submunitions' are presented separately as problematic characteristics.

[149] Article 51, paragraph 4, of *1977 Additional Protocol I*.

[150] Article 51, paragraph 5, of *1977 Additional Protocol I*.

[151] Sub-paragraph (c)(i) serves to limit the number of submunitions permissible in accordance with points (ii) to (v) that can be delivered by a single container munition. Point (ii) seeks to prevent the miniaturization of permissible submunitions and hence the miniaturization of the whole weapon system in a way that would effectively subvert the intent of point (i) by allowing large numbers of such munitions to be launched at once. These provisions both also work to strengthen

2.124 None of the characteristics intended to avoid indiscriminate area effects relates to the accuracy of the container or dispenser. So 'indiscriminate area effects' are *not* considered to result primarily from the risk of 'area effects' from submunitions being deployed in the wrong place. Rather 'indiscriminate area effects' are wholly considered to result from the use of multiple explosive items to distribute explosive force and fragmentation randomly across a pre-defined area, which was a key purpose and salient design feature of cluster munitions. Article 2, paragraph 2(c)(i) and (ii) may further suggest that 'indiscriminate area effects' can result from submunitions that detect and engage single object targets if these weapons are used in large quantities.

2.125 Prior to the Oslo Process, concern regarding the 'area effect' of cluster munitions had led some States to call for a prohibition on certain types of cluster munitions, combined with a 'prohibition on the use of cluster munitions in areas of civilian concentration'.[152] This call was also echoed during the Oslo Process.[153] The Convention on Cluster Munitions adopts a prohibition on a defined category of technology but has no rules or regulations governing technologies that are not subject to that prohibition. However, any munitions excluded under paragraph 2(c) must still be used in accordance with the rules of international humanitarian law governing attacks,[154] and the mere fact that these weapons are not prohibited under the terms of paragraph 2(c) does not mean that they are necessarily appropriate for use in areas of civilian concentration. With respect to weapons designed to detect and engage individual targets, the CMC raised the concern during the Oslo Process that such weapons cannot themselves distinguish between military objectives on the one hand, and civilians and civilian objects on the other.[155]

---

the obligations at points (iii) and (iv) that are specifically intended to avoid risks from UXO. While the Convention's comprehensive prohibition rules out the saturation of an area with submunitions, taken together these two additional provisions provide limitations on the capacity for an individual munition to deploy submunitions in an area even if they detect and engage single target objects.

[152] Declaration on Cluster Munitions, Third Review Conference of the States Parties to the CCW, Geneva, UN doc. CCW/CONF.III/WP.18, 17 November 2006, endorsed by 25 States.

[153] Statements of Italy, the Netherlands, and Switzerland, Lima Conference, 24 May 2007; and Statements of France and Switzerland, Vienna Conference, 6 December 2007 (all from Landmine Action notes; copy on file with author).

[154] This was specifically noted by Canada in a statement to the Wellington Conference on 19 February 2008 (Landmine Action notes; copy on file with author).

[155] Statement CMC on Definitions, Wellington Conference, 19 February 2008 (Landmine Action notes; copy on file with author).

To avoid the risk posed by unexploded submunitions

2.126 In addition to avoiding 'indiscriminate area effects', weapons that fall outside the definition of a cluster munition at paragraph 2 (c) must also avoid creating 'risks posed by unexploded submunitions'. It is widely recognized that the use of any type of explosive ordnance will create some level of UXO risk. Efforts to minimize these risks focus on reducing the likelihood of individual items being left unexploded and on reducing the susceptibility of any such unexploded items to subsequent accidental detonation. Through cumulative technical criteria, paragraph 2(c) establishes the level of precaution that must be taken in order to reduce the risk of unexploded submunitions to an acceptable level.

2.127 Of the cumulative characteristics necessary to avoid the humanitarian problems indicated in the sub-paragraph (c) *chapeau*, points (i), (ii), (iv), and (v) relate *inter alia* to avoiding 'risks posed by unexploded submunitions'. The limitation on numbers serves to reduce the likelihood of items being left unexploded while the minimum weight requirement was argued by Norway as serving, among other things, to prevent miniaturization that would facilitate use in greater numbers in the future. The requirements of (iv) and (v) are both wholly concerned with reducing UXO risk. It should also be noted that current submunition-based weapons designed to detect and engage individual target objects are designed to detonate in the air, a feature that substantially removes variations in ground conditions from factors likely to influence reliability.

i. Each munition contains fewer than ten explosive submunitions

2.128 Munitions with 10 or more explosive submunitions cannot be excluded from prohibition under paragraph 2(c). Limitations on the number of submunitions that could be delivered in a single container were discussed extensively as offering potential to reduce the humanitarian risk presented by cluster munitions. Certain States put forward proposals that the number of submunitions, on its own and usually set at '10 or more', should determine whether or not a munition is considered a cluster munition.[156] Such proposals were significantly more permissive that the final definition, which requires munitions with fewer than ten submunitions to meet a number of other criteria to enhance civilian protection.

---

[156] See, e.g., the papers formally submitted at the Diplomatic Conference by Japan (doc. CCM/18), France (doc. CCM/20), and the UK (doc. CCM/23).

2.129 The number of submunitions does have a direct bearing on the likely level of UXO threat that will be created by a single cluster munition; the greater the number of submunitions, the greater the likelihood of one or more of the submunitions failing to explode as intended. This same relationship makes it logically problematic to regulate cluster munitions according to a submunition percentage failure rate without linking this percentage to the number of submunitions. Limiting the number of submunitions also has a bearing on the likelihood of a munition creating an 'indiscriminate area effect', even where each of those submunitions is 'designed to detect and engage a single target object'.

2.130 There are, however, certain munitions where the relationship between the 'cluster munition' and its 'submunitions' is not straightforward. The CBU-97/CBU-105 'Sensor Fuzed Weapon', which is prohibited under the Convention on Cluster Munitions, contains 10 BLU-108 units, each of which in turn dispenses four explosive devices (commonly called 'skeets' or 'warheads' by the manufacturers) that have the capacity to detect and engage single object targets. In this situation the individual so-called skeets are the 'explosive submunitions' under the terms of the Convention because they match the description of 'explosive submunition' whereas the BLU-108 taken as a whole does not.[157] On the other hand, the BLU-108 should not itself be considered a 'cluster munition' where it is used as a component of the CBU-97/CBU-105 but rather to be part of the mechanism by which the cluster munition actively disperses the submunitions.

ii. Each explosive submunition weighs more than four kilograms

2.131 As noted above, the minimum weight requirement for submunitions serves to prevent miniaturization of submunitions considered acceptable under other criteria and hence reduces the likelihood of such submunitions being deployed in such quantities that they might still create the problematic effects associated with cluster munitions in the past. It was also argued that smaller submunitions are more likely to be handled and engaged with by civilian populations and that larger munitions may be less sensitive and therefore less problematic to clear.[158] The characteristic was derived from a Norwegian

---

[157] It is the 'skeets' rather than the BLU-108 that are designed primarily 'to function by detonating *an* explosive charge' prior to impact [*emphasis added on the singular*].

[158] Norway, 'How to address the humanitarian effects of unacceptable cluster munitions: Explanatory note on the Norwegian informal proposal based on weight criterion to Art 2 on definitions, presented 21 May 2008', Diplomatic Conference, 26 May 2008.

proposal,[159] but in the final stages of the negotiations the weight limit was reduced from five kilograms to four kilograms.[160] A proposal for decreasing the weight limit to three kilograms had been informally presented to the Irish Presidency, and a proposal for four kilograms was presented as a compromise.

iii. Each explosive submunition is designed to detect and engage a single target object

2.132 The requirement that each explosive submunition be designed to detect and engage a single target object is the most critical distinguishing feature for weapons with submunitions that are not considered cluster munitions under paragraph 2(c). While the other technical criteria can all be held to limit the effects associated with cluster munitions, this requires munitions to function in a way that is arguably very different to cluster munitions as commonly understood. Submunitions generally held to fulfil this requirement to 'detect and engage a single target object' include the German SMArt 155 or the French/Swedish BONUS, and the 'skeet' warheads deployed via BLU-108 from the US CBU-97/CBU-105 Sensor Fuzed Weapon.[161] The legal status of these submunitions is, however, not only dependent on these capacities, but also on the other cumulative characteristics relating to their weight, electronic self-destruct and self-neutralization mechanisms and the number deployed in each container. These submunitions all use combinations of infrared and other sensors to identify certain types of object and then engage this target while still in the air, by detonating to create an explosively formed projectile.[162] As a result, the explosive force of the submunitions is generally directed downwards and narrowly onto the target object without the lateral anti-personnel effects at ground level associated with traditional impact-fuzed cluster munitions.

2.133 Weapons that detect and engage targets in this way are often referred to in general as sensor-fuzed weapons.[163] Certain of these weapons are unitary munitions (i.e. they do not use submunitions) and so do not fall under the

---

[159] Norway, 'Informal proposal based on weight criterion to Art 2 on definitions', Diplomatic Conference, 21 May 2008.

[160] Thus, the four skeets deployed by the CBU-97/CBU-105 'Sensor Fuzed Weapon', each of which weighs three kilograms, would not fall within this exception.

[161] See, e.g., Jane's, '155 mm Bonus sensor-fuzed munition (International), Field artillery', <http://www.janes.com/articles/Janes-Ammunition-Handbook/155-mm-Bonus-sensor-fuzed-munition-International.html> (accessed 29 October 2009); also regarding SmART 155 <http://www.rheinmetall-defence.com/index.php?lang=3&fid=3241> (accessed 29 January 2010); and regarding the Sensor Fuzed Weapon <http://www.textrondefense.com/products/airlaunched/sfw.htm> (accessed 29 January 2010).   [162] See *ibid.*

[163] The use of the general term sensor-fuzed munitions should not be confused with the specific US CBU-97/CBU-105, which is often called the 'Sensor Fuzed Weapon'.

Convention on Cluster Munitions at all. Others, such as the US CBU-97/ CBU-105 with 'skeet' submunitions, do fall under the Convention and are prohibited due to the number of submunitions (40) and the weight of these submunitions (less than four kilograms). Thus, the Convention does not offer a blanket exclusion for sensor-fuzed munitions as a category but splits that category into prohibited and not-prohibited variants. The only such weapon system thought not to be prohibited by the Convention on Cluster Munitions and that had been used in combat at the time of the Convention's negotiation was the US SADARM system.[164] This system was used by US forces in Iraq in 2003. No civilian casualties had been presented as resulting from this specific system at the time of the Dublin negotiations though Human Rights Watch in an analysis of the conflict in Iraq noted that further research would be needed 'to determine the weapon's humanitarian effects'.[165]

2.134 Munitions such as SMArt 155 and BONUS, and the 'skeet' explosive submunitions of the BLU-108 do not distinguish between military objectives and civilian objects but rather are programmed to identify as targets objects that fit profiles of heat and shape associated with certain military objects (typically armoured fighting vehicles). It is not known what analysis has been done of how such profiles compare with the profiles of objects commonly in civilian use (such as different types of civilian vehicles, generators, and other heat sources) or how susceptible such submunitions are to identifying objects commonly in civilian use as targets. While certain types of weapons with submunitions that 'detect and engage individual target objects' are excluded from prohibition under the Convention, they are nonetheless still subject to the general rules of international humanitarian law that govern attacks. Any limitations of such systems in distinguishing between objects that may be in civilian use and objectives that may be in military use might limit circumstances in which they can lawfully be used. For example, the likelihood of an attack being lawful in a desert situation where a party is attacking an area full only of military vehicles is greater than for an attack in a populated area where military vehicles are interspersed with vehicles in civilian use.

2.135 The phrase 'detect and engage' is not defined further in the Convention. The Lima Discussion Text provided an exclusion for certain

---

[164] The US Sensor Fuzed Weapon was also used by US forces in Iraq but it is prohibited under the Convention on Cluster Munitions due to the weight and number of submunitions that it employs in an individual cluster munition. SMArt 155 and BONUS are not thought to be prohibited under the technical criteria in Article 2, paragraph 2(c), of the Convention but they had not been used in combat at the time of the negotiations.

[165] Human Rights Watch, *Off Target—The Conduct of the War and Civilian Casualties in Iraq* (Washington, DC: Human Rights Watch, 2003), pp. 84–85.

weapons with submunitions 'designed to, manually or automatically, aim, detect and engage point targets'. In contrast, a number of proposals in Wellington referred only to weapons 'designed to engage' certain targets. The requirement that the submunitions 'detect' the target establishes a greater sense of autonomous targeting within the submunition itself and suggests that the force of the submunition is to be applied to the single target object directly.

2.136 This sense of the term engage is linked to the phrase 'single target object'. During the negotiations this term was adopted in preference to the term 'point target', which was already defined by NATO as 'a target that requires the accurate placement of bombs or fire'. This definition did not seem practical as a legal definition. Instead, by requiring a 'target object' the sense is given that what is being referred to are anti-vehicle or anti-*matériel* weapons, rather than anti-personnel weapons. Furthermore, by requiring each submunition to engage a 'single' target object the sense is further given that the explosive force of the submunition should be directed at and limited to the individual target object.

iv. Each explosive submunition is equipped with an electronic self-destruction mechanism

2.137 In this context, a self-destruction mechanism is intended to automatically destroy the submunition in the event that it fails to detect a single target object or, having detected such an object, fails to 'engage' it in a way that results in the destruction of the submunition. Thus in terms of the analysis above of 'risks posed by unexploded submunitions', the self-destruction mechanism works to reduce the likelihood of a submunition being left unexploded after use. A self-destruction mechanism is defined at Article 2, paragraph 9 as:

'Self-destruction mechanism' means an incorporated automatically-functioning mechanism which is in addition to the primary initiating mechanism of the munition and which secures the destruction of the munition into which it is incorporated.

There is no specific definition of 'an electronic self-destruction mechanism'. During the preparatory discussions and negotiation of Article 2 it was noted that electronic self-destruction mechanisms were preferable to mechanical self-destruction mechanisms because they were both more reliable and more amenable to in-service reliability testing.[166]

---

[166] See, *supra*, §§2.65–2.66. An electronic self-destruction mechanism should be understood as one that is initiated by electronic processing and uses an electrical current to detonate the munition

v. Each explosive submunition is equipped with an electronic self-deactivating feature

2.138 There is no specific definition of an 'electronic' self-deactivating feature in the Convention. In this context, a self-deactivating feature is intended to render an unexploded submunition incapable of functioning.[167] Thus, in terms of the analysis above of 'risks posed by unexploded submunitions', a self-deactivation feature works to reduce the threat posed by any submunition that has been left unexploded. A self-deactivating mechanism is defined in Article 2, paragraph 10 as follows:

'Self-deactivating' means automatically rendering a munition inoperable by means of the irreversible exhaustion of a component, for example a battery, that is essential to the operation of the munition.

Paragraph 3

'**Explosive submunition**' means a conventional munition that in order to perform its task is dispersed or released by a cluster munition and is designed to function by detonating an explosive charge prior to, on or after impact;

Commentary

2.139 Explosive submunitions are conventional munitions[168] that are dispersed and released by cluster munitions and which are designed to detonate an explosive charge before, upon, or following impact, typically with the target object or the ground. Different types of cluster munition have contained from fewer than 10 up to several hundred explosive submunitions in a single

---

(rather than the physical movement of a firing-pin into a detonator, as with a mechanical self-destruction mechanism).

[167] During the preparations of the Convention the relative advantages of electronic mechanisms were noted in a presentation by Colin King to the Vienna Conference on Cluster Munitions, 6 December 2007 and elsewhere.

[168] Thus, as in the main definition of cluster munition, the definition of explosive submunition clarifies that this is not encompassing nuclear, chemical, or biological weapons. A munition is not defined in the Convention but is defined by NATO to mean:

A complete device charged with explosives, propellants, pyrotechnics, initiating composition or chemical, biological, radiological or nuclear material, for use in military operations, including demolitions.

NATO STANAG AAP-6 (2009), p. 2-M-11.

container. When the cluster munition opens, the submunitions inside are generally scattered over the area below. Explosive submunitions have often consisted of a body formed of high explosive encased in metal, and a structure or mechanism for orienting and stabilizing the submunition in the air (sometimes also serving to arm the munition). Submunitions may have a wide range of further characteristics relating to the type of targets they are designed to attack, their methods of arming and detonation, and the presence or absence of further features intended to reduce the risks of their creating UXO contamination.[169]

2.140 Considerations of target type have seen submunitions with combinations of pre-formed fragmentation around the outer casing (to create an anti-personnel effect), a shaped charge at the forward end (to create an anti-armour effect), and an incendiary lining (to create a further anti-*matériel* effect). Methods of arming may use the spin of the submunition in the air or the inertia of certain components under acceleration. Among other methods, detonation may be initiated through the inertia of a firing pin under rapid deceleration of the submunition or stress applied to a piezo-electric[170] crystal. Some more recent submunitions have been fitted with self-destruct mechanisms, so-called self-neutralization mechanisms, and self-deactivation mechanisms in an effort to reduce the likelihood of UXO being produced as well as to reduce the threat of any items that are left unexploded.[171]

'Other definitions' (paragraphs 4–15)

Overview

2.141 The remaining 12 definitions in Article 2—the so-called 'other definitions'—were far less controversial during the Oslo Process than the first three, but they play an important role in clarifying the meaning of the Convention on Cluster Munitions. Several deal with terms used in Article 1 on General Obligations and Scope of Application. The definition of transfer (paragraph 8) spells out what the prohibition on transfer encompasses while the definition of mine (paragraph 12) describes a weapon not covered by the

---

[169] See, e.g., GICHD, *A Guide to Cluster Munitions*, Second Edition, *op. cit.*

[170] Piezo-electric refers to 'electric polarization in a substance resulting from the application of mechanical stress.' See, e.g., *Oxford English Dictionary*, CD-ROM Version 3.1, Oxford University Press, 2004.

[171] For a detailed analysis of one particular type, see King, C., Dullum, O., and Østern, G., *M85—An Analysis of Reliability*, *op. cit.*

Convention. Paragraphs 13 and 14 work with Article 1, paragraph 2 to help close a loophole that would have meant the Convention did not apply to explosive bomblets launched from dispensers. The definitions of self-destruction mechanism and self-deactivating (paragraphs 9 and 10) relate to Article 2, paragraph 2, helping to elucidate the definition of cluster munition. Finally, six definitions articulate the parameters of the provisions related to clearance. They include the definitions of cluster munition remnants and its components (paragraphs 4–7 and 15) and of cluster munition contaminated area (paragraph 11).

Preparatory discussions

2.142 While Article 2, paragraphs 1 to 3 were the subject of more discussion during the Oslo Process, the other 12 definitions, ultimately articulated in paragraphs 4 to 15, developed alongside them. None of these definitions appeared in the Lima Discussion Text, which only provided a preliminary definition of cluster munition.[172] At the May 2007 Lima Conference, one State noted the need to define other terms, such as explosive submunition, abandoned submunition, and cluster munition remnants existing at the time of entry into force.[173] Another State called for a definition of transfer, an activity banned under Article 1.[174] There was no formal discussion of the content of these proposed definitions, however.

2.143 The Vienna Discussion Text responded to the call to define terms related to cluster munitions that become threats as ERW. In that text, unexploded cluster munitions referred to cluster munitions that were prepared for use and used yet failed to explode as intended. Abandoned cluster munitions referred to unused cluster munitions that were 'discarded or dumped' by a party and were no longer under the control of that party. The text used the overarching term cluster munition remnants to encompass the two categories just mentioned.[175] Cluster munition remnants replaced the Lima Discussion Text's use of 'unexploded ordnance from cluster munitions' in the Articles on

---

[172] Article 2, Lima Discussion Text. The text left some terms, such as transfer, undefined and used a variety of different terms for the words that would eventually be added to the list of definitions. Articles 4 and 7, e.g., used the term 'unexploded ordnance from cluster munitions' to refer to what the Convention on Cluster Munitions would call 'cluster munition remnants'.

[173] Statement at the Lima Conference, 24 May 2007 (Landmine Action notes; copy on file with author).   [174] *Ibid.*; and Article 1(b), Lima Discussion Text.

[175] The Vienna Discussion Text defined these terms as follows:

'Unexploded cluster munitions' means cluster munitions that have been primed, fused, armed, or otherwise prepared for use and used. They may have been fired, dropped, launched or projected, and should have exploded but failed to do so.

clearance, international cooperation and assistance, and transparency.[176] All three definitions drew heavily from Article 2 of *2003 Protocol V.*[177]

 2.144 The Vienna Discussion Text also added a definition of transfer. The definition read:

'Transfer' means the physical movement of cluster munitions into or from national territory or the transfer of title to or control over cluster munitions, but does not include the transfer of territory containing cluster munition remnants.[178]

It included the main elements of the definition of transfer in the *1997 Anti-Personnel Mine Ban Convention* but changed their presentation. The *1997 Anti-Personnel Mine Ban Convention* states that: '"Transfer" involves, *in addition to* the physical movement . . . , the transfer of title . . . and control . . .'.[179] The Vienna Discussion Text was arguably clearer than its predecessor. It specified that transfer meant *either* physical movement *or* transfer of title and control. The *1997 Anti-Personnel Mine Ban Convention*, by contrast, left open for debate whether transfer meant *either* physical movement *or* transfer of title and control or whether it meant there had to be both physical movement *and* transfer of title and control to be transfer.[180] The structure of the definition of transfer would be discussed again during the May 2008 Diplomatic Conference in Dublin.

 2.145 The Explanatory Annex to the Vienna Discussion Text made clear that the new Convention would not cover landmines because they were governed by other treaties.[181] The Annex listed them as one of several exclusions to the definition of cluster munition. The text, however, did not define mine.

'Abandoned cluster munitions' means cluster munitions that have not been used and that have been discarded or dumped, and that are no longer under the control of the party that discarded or dumped them. Abandoned cluster munitions may or may not have been prepared for use.

 'Cluster munition remnants' means unexploded cluster munitions and abandoned cluster munitions.

Article 2, Vienna Discussion Text.

 [176] Article 4, paragraph 1, Article 5, paragraph 5(a), and Article 7, paragraph 1(c), Lima Discussion Text; and Article 4, paragraph 1, Article 6, paragraphs 4 and 5, and Article 7, paragraph 1(e) and (i), Vienna Discussion Text.

 [177] The most notable difference between the definitions in the Vienna Discussion Text and those in *2003 Protocol V* was that the former did not include the phrases 'used *in an armed conflict*' and 'party *to an armed conflict*' (*emphasis added*). The removal of the reference to armed conflict meant that the terms arguably applied to a wider range of circumstances. *Cp.* Article 2, Vienna Discussion Text, with Article 2, paragraphs 2 and 3, *2003 Protocol V.*

 [178] Article 2, Vienna Discussion Text.

 [179] Article 2, paragraph 4, *1997 Anti-Personnel Mine Ban Convention* (*emphasis added*).

 [180] For further discussion of this distinction, see, *infra*, the commentary on Article 2, paragraph 8 in §2.197.   [181] Explanatory Annex, Vienna Discussion Text.

2.146 At the December 2007 Vienna Conference, discussion on the other definitions was again limited but some participants made relevant statements. Regarding the Vienna Discussion Text's definition of transfer, the CMC argued that it should make clear that transit of cluster munitions through national territory is explicitly prohibited.[182] The ICRC, concerned about ambiguities in the definition of unexploded cluster munition, suggested the development of a definition for unexploded submunitions.[183] One State called for a definition for contaminated field; the Vienna Discussion Text used a variety of undefined terms for that concept.[184] Several States expressed support for the Explanatory Annex's exclusion of mines although they did not address how to define mine.[185] Finally, the GICHD noted a possible loophole in the Convention—submunitions released from a dispenser affixed to an aircraft, instead of from a cluster munition.[186] States would seek to close this loophole at the Diplomatic Conference in part by adding definitions to Article 2.

2.147 The Draft Cluster Munitions Convention made only small changes to the other definitions in the Vienna Discussion Text. Most notably it clarified that '"[u]nexploded cluster munitions" includes both unexploded parent munitions and unexploded explosive sub-munitions'.[187] It also, in Article 1, made the first effort to define mine, combining the definition with a statement of its exclusion from the scope of the Convention. It said the definition of mines would be the same as that in *1996 Amended Protocol II*.[188]

2.148 At the Wellington Conference, Chair of the Conference Don MacKay of New Zealand set the other definitions aside to focus on the more controversial definition of cluster munition.[189] There were, however,

---

[182] Statement of the CMC, Vienna Conference, 6 December 2007 (Landmine Action notes; copy on file with author).

[183] Comments of the ICRC to the Vienna Discussion Text, December 2007 (copy on file with author).

[184] Statement at the Vienna Conference, 6 December 2007 (Landmine Action notes; copy on file with author). See, e.g., Article 4, paragraph 6(b)(iii) ('contaminated areas'), and Article 7, paragraph 1(i) ('areas identified to be contaminated by cluster munition remnants'), Vienna Discussion Text.

[185] Statements at the Vienna Conference, 6 December 2007 (Landmine Action notes; copy on file with author).

[186] Statement of the GICHD, Vienna Conference, 6 December 2007 (Landmine Action notes; copy on file with author).

[187] Article 2, Draft Cluster Munitions Convention. The other two changes were minor wording revisions that caused no change in meaning.

[188] Article 1, paragraph 2, Draft Cluster Munitions Convention.

[189] MacKay also moved discussions of cluster munition victim to the sessions on Article 5 on victim assistance.

significant proposals for other definitions. The ICRC proposed a structure for Article 2 that included a definition for unexploded explosive submunitions and introduced the concept of failed cluster munitions.[190] Several government statements on other definitions were also made in the main hall. While there was no dispute that the new Convention should not apply to mines, two States objected to defining the weapons with reference to *1996 Amended Protocol II*, to which they were not a party.[191] One State also suggested defining cluster munition areas as 'areas which are dangerous due to the suspected presence of cluster munitions'.[192]

2.149 Despite the limited attention paid to these definitions during the Wellington Conference, the Wellington Compendium, which would be forwarded to the Diplomatic Conference in Dublin, included six related proposals. Several sought to clarify the definition of cluster munition remnants and its components. Following the ICRC proposal mentioned above, Ireland proposed deleting the definition of unexploded cluster munitions and replacing it with failed cluster munition and unexploded explosive submunition. Failed cluster munition referred to a cluster munition that suffered a catastrophic failure, in other words that was delivered but failed to disperse or release its submunitions. Unexploded explosive submunition meant an explosive submunition that had separated from a cluster munition but 'failed to explode as intended'. Ireland's proposal updated the definition of cluster munition remnants accordingly.[193] The ICRC's suggestion noted earlier was also recorded in the Compendium.[194]

---

[190] Comments of the ICRC on the Wellington draft of a future cluster munitions convention, 8 February 2008 (copy on file with author).

[191] Statements at the Wellington Conference, 18 February 2008 (Landmine Action notes; copy on file with author).

[192] Statement at the Wellington Conference, 18 February 2008 (Landmine Action notes; copy on file with author).

[193] The proposal stated:

'Failed cluster munition' means a cluster munition that has been fired, dropped, launched, projected or otherwise delivered and which should have dispersed or released its explosive submunitions but failed to do so;

'Unexploded explosive submunition' means an explosive submunition which has been released dispersed or otherwise separated from a cluster munition and has failed to explode as intended;...

'Cluster munition remnants' means *failed cluster munitions*, abandoned cluster munitions, *unexploded explosive submunitions and unexploded explosive bomblets*.

'Article 2: Definitions', Wellington Compendium, p. 14 (*emphasis removed*). Ireland resubmitted this proposal at the Diplomatic Conference (Com/25).

[194] 'Article 2: Definitions', Wellington Compendium, p. 12. The major difference was that the Irish definition of cluster munition remnants encompassed, as discussed below, unexploded explosive bomblets.

2.150 France and Germany also proposed revisions to the definitions related to cluster munition remnants but took theirs almost verbatim from *2003 Protocol V*.[195] Like Ireland and the ICRC, they dispensed with unexploded cluster munition and added a definition of unexploded submunition although they did not address the category of failed cluster munitions.[196] They also proposed a revised definition of abandoned explosive cluster munition and a new one of existing explosive remnants of submunitions.[197] They designed the latter to accompany a proposal they made for a provision on user State responsibility for clearance of unexploded submunitions that pre-dated entry into force of the Convention.[198] The French and German proposal updated the definition of cluster munition remnants to cover unexploded submunitions and abandoned explosive cluster munitions.[199]

2.151 The Wellington Compendium included a second set of proposals that sought to address the loophole GICHD had pointed out in Vienna regarding munitions released from a dispenser. Ireland defined the term explosive bomblet as 'a munition which in order to perform its task is dispersed or separated from a dispenser, affixed to an aerial platform, and is designed to function by detonating an explosive charge prior to, on or after impact'. These

---

[195] Article 2, paragraphs 2–5, *2003 Protocol V.* The only changes adapted the *2003 Protocol V* definitions to cluster munitions and submunitions, by, for example, replacing the term ordnance with the latter terms.

[196] France and Germany defined unexploded submunition as an 'explosive sub-munition that has been primed, fused, armed, or otherwise prepared for use and used in an armed conflict. It may have been fired, dropped, launched or projected and should have exploded but failed to do so'. 'Article 2: Definitions', Wellington Compendium, pp. 12–13. They resubmitted this proposal at the Diplomatic Conference as 'Proposal by France and Germany for the amendment of Article 2', Diplomatic Conference doc. CCM/22, 19 May 2008.

[197] According to the proposal by France and Germany:

'Abandoned explosive cluster-munition' means explosive cluster-munition that has not been used during an armed conflict, that has been left behind or dumped by a party to an armed conflict and which is no longer under control of the party that left it behind. Abandoned explosive cluster-munitions may or may not have been primed, fused, armed or otherwise prepared for use;...

'Existing explosive remnants of sub-munitions' means unexploded submunitions and abandoned explosive cluster-munitions that existed prior to the entry into force of this Convention for the State party on whose territory it exists.

'Article 2: Definitions', Wellington Compendium, pp. 12–13.

[198] The French and German proposal to the Diplomatic Conference noted the relationship between the definition of existing explosive remnants of submunitions and their user State responsibility proposal. See 'Proposal by France and Germany for additional text', Diplomatic Conference doc. CCM/47, 19 May 2008. For further discussion of user State responsibility, see, *infra*, the commentary on Article 4, paragraph 4 and Article 6, paragraph 4.

[199] 'Article 2: Definitions', Wellington Compendium, pp. 12–13; and 'Proposal by France and Germany for the amendment of Article 2', Diplomatic Conference doc. CCM/22, 19 May 2008.

munitions were not covered by the definition of explosive submunitions. Explosive submunitions are released from cluster munitions, which, unlike dispensers, are a type of munition. Explosive bomblets pose the same threat to civilians as explosive submunitions, however, because they have an area effect and are prone to leaving behind UXO. Ireland included unexploded explosive bomblets under its revised definition of cluster munition remnants.[200]

2.152 France and Switzerland adopted a different approach to the dispenser problem in separate proposals in the Wellington Compendium. They listed dispensers as a type of cluster munition. France described a cluster munition as a type of carrier-container and defined carrier-container, in part, as 'a dispenser, affixed to an aircraft, which is not designed to dispense direct-fire munitions'.[201] Switzerland offered two options for the description of dispenser within the definition of carrier-container. Option one stated a dispenser was 'affixed to an aircraft, which is designed to dispense multiple sub-munitions in a single act'. Option two was identical to France's proposal.[202]

2.153 Finally, Indonesia formalized its proposal on cluster munition areas in the Wellington Compendium. It defined them as 'areas which are dangerous due to the presence or suspected presence of cluster munitions'.[203]

Negotiations

2.154 While efforts to finalize the definition of cluster munition dominated negotiations of Article 2 at the Diplomatic Conference, Friend of the President on Definitions Don MacKay asked Lieutenant-Colonel Jim Burke of Ireland to convene informal meetings devoted to the other definitions. During these discussions, several definitions were added to those in the Draft Cluster Munitions Convention and others were revised. The meetings also

---

[200] 'Article 2: Definitions', Wellington Compendium, p. 14. Ireland resubmitted this proposal at the Diplomatic Conference as: 'Proposal by Ireland for the amendment of Article 2', Diplomatic Conference doc. CCM/25, 19 May 2008.

[201] 'Article 2: Definitions', Wellington Compendium, p. 10. France resubmitted this proposal at the Diplomatic Conference as: 'Proposal by France for the amendment of Article 2', Diplomatic Conference doc. CCM/20, 19 May 2008.

[202] 'Article 2: Definitions', Wellington Compendium, p. 11. Switzerland resubmitted this proposal at the Diplomatic Conference as: 'Proposal by Switzerland for the amendment of Article 2', Diplomatic Conference doc. CCM/21, 19 May 2008. At the Diplomatic Conference, Spain would submit a proposal that incorporated the French provision and Swiss option two on dispenser. 'Proposal by Spain for the amendment of Article 2', Diplomatic Conference doc. CCM/67, 19 May 2008.

[203] 'Article 2: Definitions', Wellington Compendium, p. 15. Indonesia resubmitted this proposal at the Diplomatic Conference as: 'Proposal by Indonesia for the amendment of Article 2', Diplomatic Conference doc. CCM/27, 19 May 2008.

addressed the definition of explosive submunition, the negotiation of which is discussed above.[204]

2.155 Participants in these meetings discussed the various proposals from the Wellington Compendium that had been resubmitted at the Diplomatic Conference. The Draft Cluster Munitions Convention had used the term unexploded cluster munitions to encompass both parent munitions and sub-munitions that were used but did not explode. The ICRC explained that that term was inappropriate because cluster munitions merely release submunitions and are not designed to explode themselves.[205] Ireland and the ICRC both suggested as an alternative dividing that term into failed cluster munition and unexploded submunition.[206] There was no public disagreement with this point. The Convention on Cluster Munitions did not reflect the French and German proposal based on *2003 Protocol V*; the negotiating States preferred to include the Irish proposal almost verbatim.[207]

2.156 Abandoned cluster munition received similarly brief attention. The GICHD suggested changing 'discarded' to 'left behind' to encompass more passive abandonment.[208] The final version of the definition used 'left behind'. It also added the phrase 'or explosive submunitions' to ensure it encompassed caches of individual submunitions as well as the parent cluster munitions.[209]

2.157 Negotiators generally supported the Wellington Compendium proposals for the Convention on Cluster Munitions to cover explosive bomblets. Ireland called on States to cover dispensers with explosive bomblets under Article 1 and to define the terms in Article 2.[210] Expressing support for the Irish proposal, one State said the French and Swiss alternatives relating to

[204] See, *supra*, the commentary on preparatory discussions and negotiations of Article 2 in §§2.39 *et seq.*

[205] Statement of the ICRC, Friend of the President's Discussions on Definitions, Diplomatic Conference, 21 May 2008 (Landmine Action notes; copy on file with author).

[206] See 'Article 2: Definitions', Wellington Compendium, pp. 12 and 14. Ireland resubmitted its proposal in Dublin as: 'Proposal of Ireland for the amendment of Article 2', Diplomatic Conference doc. CCM/25, 19 May 2008. The ICRC did not have standing to resubmit its proposal at the Diplomatic Conference because only States were eligible to do so.

[207] Article 2, paragraphs 4 and 5. The only notable change in the Convention was to remove the word 'explosive' from the phrase 'unexploded explosive submunition'.

[208] Statement of GICHD, Friend of the President's Discussions on Definitions, Diplomatic Conference, 21 May 2008 (Landmine Action notes; copy on file with author).

[209] Article 2, paragraph 6.

[210] Statement of Ireland, 'Summary Record of First Session of the Committee of the Whole', Diplomatic Conference doc. CCM/CW/SR/1, 18 June 2008, p. 2; and Statement of Ireland, Friend of the President's Discussions on Definitions, Diplomatic Conference, 21 May 2008 (Landmine Action notes; copy on file with author).

carrier-containers were too complicated.[211] The Convention on Cluster Munitions ultimately included in the definition both dispenser and explosive bomblet. Dispenser, defined for the first time at the Diplomatic Conference, meant a container 'affixed to an aircraft' that released explosive bomblets.[212] The definition of explosive bomblet, based on Ireland's original proposal in the Wellington Compendium, was expanded to add a weight requirement of less than 20 kilograms and to specify that it was not self-propelled. In addition, the phrase 'was separated' was changed to 'released'.[213] The Convention also defined unexploded bomblet, making only minor revisions to the Irish proposal.[214] To cover all of the different types of ERW now listed in the Convention, cluster munition remnants was redefined to include 'failed cluster munitions, abandoned cluster munitions, unexploded submunitions and unexploded bomblets'.[215]

2.158 The final proposal for Article 2 in the Wellington Compendium was Indonesia's proposal to define cluster munition area. Participants at the Diplomatic Conference generally supported adding this term in the list of definitions,[216] but made several amendments to Indonesia's original language in the Compendium. One State proposed changing cluster munitions to cluster munition remnants.[217] The ICRC suggested removing the phrase 'which are dangerous', even though it came from the *1997 Anti-Personnel Mine Ban Convention*, because it was too subjective.[218] Ultimately, language suggested by the CMC served as the basis for the final definition, which read 'an area known or suspected to contain cluster munition remnants'.[219]

[211] Statement at the Friend of the President's Discussions on Definitions, Diplomatic Conference, 21 May 2008 (Landmine Action notes; copy on file with author).

[212] Article 2, paragraph 14.

[213] *Cp.* Article 2: Definitions', Wellington Compendium, p. 14; and 'Proposal of Ireland for the amendment of Article 2', Diplomatic Conference doc. CCM/25, 19 May 2008, with Article 2, paragraph 13.

[214] *Cp.* Article 2: Definitions', Wellington Compendium, p. 14; and 'Proposal of Ireland for the amendment of Article 2', *op. cit.*, with Article 2, paragraph 15. The only major modification was to remove the phrase 'affixed to an aerial platform' after dispenser because dispenser was defined separately. It also changed the term from unexploded explosive bomblet to unexploded bomblet and made a couple of small wording amendments.   [215] Article 2, paragraph 7.

[216] Statements at the Friend of the President's Discussions on Definitions, Diplomatic Conference, 21 May 2008 (Landmine Action notes; copy on file with author).

[217] Statement at the Friend of the President's Discussions on Definitions, Diplomatic Conference, 21 May 2008 (Landmine Action notes; copy on file with author).

[218] Statement of the ICRC, Friend of the President's Discussions on Definitions, Diplomatic Conference, 21 May 2008 (Landmine Action notes; copy on file with author).

[219] Statement of the CMC, Friend of the President's Discussions on Definitions, Diplomatic Conference, 21 May 2008 (Landmine Action notes; copy on file with author).

2.159 Although not discussed in Wellington, transfer was modified some-what during the negotiations of Article 2 in Dublin.[220] Some States objected to the fact that the definition in the Draft Cluster Munitions Convention differed from those in the *1997 Anti-Personnel Mine Ban Convention* and *1996 Amended Protocol II*.[221] On 22 May, Norway therefore proposed a new definition almost identical to those in the earlier treaties.[222] The ICRC expressed concern that the 'in addition to' formulation of past instruments would lead to confusion about whether transfer required both physical movement and transfer of title and control, or required only one or the other.[223] At the Committee of the Whole on 26 May, Jim Burke, who was chairing the discussions on the other definitions, noted that it would be difficult to achieve consensus on this topic. Ultimately the Convention on Cluster Munitions adopted verbatim the language from the *1997 Anti-Personnel Mine Ban Convention* and *1996 Amended Protocol II*.

2.160 As the definition of cluster munition evolved during the Diplomatic Conference, it became clear that definitions of self-destruction mechanism and self-deactivating needed to be added to the text of the Convention.[224] Spain made the first proposal, drawing language directly from *1996 Amended Protocol II* and defining the terms as follows:

'Self-destruction mechanism' means an incorporated or externally attached automatically-functioning mechanism which secures the destruction of the mechanism into which it is incorporated or to which it is attached.

---

[220] In addition to the debate discussed in the text above, one State asked that the definition of transfer be clarified to prohibit the recipient of a transfer from forwarding cluster munitions to a third party unless for destruction, but its proposal did not advance. Statement at the Committee of the Whole, Diplomatic Conference, 19 May 2008 (Landmine Action notes; copy on file with author). The CMC also reiterated its call for explicit clarification that transfer encompasses transit. Statement of the CMC, Friend of the President's Discussions on Definitions, Diplomatic Conference, 21 May 2008 (Landmine Action notes; copy on file with author).

[221] Statements at the Friend of the President's Discussions on Definitions, Diplomatic Conference, 21 May 2008 (Landmine Action notes; copy on file with author). See Article 2, paragraph 4, *1997 Anti-Personnel Mine Ban Convention*; and Article 2, paragraph 15, *1996 Amended Protocol II*.

[222] 'Proposal by Norway for the amendment of Article 2', Diplomatic Conference doc. CCM/73, 22 May 2008. The only difference was that the Norwegian proposal replaced the two uses of 'involves' with 'means' and 'include'. Norway received support from several States. Statements at the Friend of the President's Discussions on Definitions, Diplomatic Conference, 22 May 2008 (Landmine Action notes; copy on file with author).

[223] Statement of the ICRC, Friend of the President's Discussions on Definitions, Diplomatic Conference, 22 May 2008 (Landmine Action notes; copy on file with author).

[224] For further discussion of the introduction of self-destruction mechanism and self-deactivating in the definition of cluster munition, see, *supra*, the commentary on Article 2, paragraph 2.

'Self-deactivating' means automatically rendering a munition inoperable by means of the irreversible exhaustion of a component, for example a battery, that is essential to the operation of the munition.[225]

2.161 Three days later, Norway offered an alternative proposal that it said sought to strengthen the definitions in *1996 Amended Protocol II*. Its proposal stated:

'Self-destruct mechanism' means a mechanism that physically destroys the warhead in the event that it does not function as intended and thus leav[es] no unexploded objects behind;

'Self-deactivation mechanism' means a mechanism that drains the sub-munition of the energy required to bring it to detonation and thus render[s] the remaining unexploded object safe to handle and safe in any incidental contact.[226]

Norway's definition of self-destruct mechanism did not address whether the mechanism was incorporated into the munition and put more emphasis on effects, i.e., 'leaving no unexploded objects behind'. Besides turning the adjective self-deactivating into the noun self-deactivation mechanism, Norway's definition of the latter again focused on effects, i.e., 'rendering the remaining unexploded object safe to handle'.

2.162 The Norwegian proposal attracted some support, but other participants in the negotiations objected to its approach. Several States said they were willing to adopt the Norwegian version although one suggested adding 'is designed to' before 'destroy' and 'drain' in order to cover mechanisms that functioned improperly.[227] ICRC welcomed the effort to clarifying the language in *1996 Amended Protocol II*; however, it questioned the use of the new term warhead and suggested using explosive ordnance from *2003 Protocol V* instead.[228]

2.163 Concerns centred on the last phrase of self-deactivation mechanism. One State said civilians often find creative ways to use UXO so UXO never reaches the level of being entirely safe to handle.[229] Another noted that it is

---

[225] 'Proposal by Spain for the amendment of Article 2', Diplomatic Conference doc. CCM/67, 19 May 2008.

[226] 'Proposal by Norway for the amendment of Article 2', Diplomatic Conference doc. CCM/72, 22 May 2008.

[227] Statements at the Friend of the President's Discussions on Definitions, Diplomatic Conference, 22 May 2008 (Landmine Action notes; copy on file with author).

[228] Statement of the ICRC, Friend of the President's Discussions on Definitions, Diplomatic Conference, 22 May 2008 (Landmine Action notes; copy on file with author).

[229] Statement at the Friend of the President's Discussions on Definitions, Diplomatic Conference, 22 May 2008 (Landmine Action notes; copy on file with author).

problematic from a mine action perspective to describe UXO as safe to handle.[230] At least four States said they preferred the existing version in *1996 Amended Protocol II*.[231]

2.164 In the end the States rejected Norway's proposals and adopted the approach of *1996 Amended Protocol II*. The definition of self-deactivating was identical to that in the Protocol. The definition of self-destruction mechanism took out references to being 'externally attached' and clarified that such a mechanism was 'in addition the primary initiating mechanism of the munition'.[232]

2.165 Finally, States discussed the insertion of a definition of mine. In the Draft Cluster Munitions Convention, mine had been defined in Article 1 by reference to the definition in *1996 Amended Protocol II*.[233] Indonesia reiterated its earlier objection to that approach in the first meeting of the Committee of the Whole and proposed replacing it with the language of the *1997 Anti-Personnel Mine Ban Convention*.[234] The final text of the Convention on Cluster Munitions adopted Indonesia's suggestion. It moved the definition of mine to Article 2 and used the definition of the *1997 Anti-Personnel Mine Ban Convention*.[235]

2.166 Article 2 changed dramatically over the course of the Oslo Process not only because of debate about the first three definitions but also because of the addition and evolution of the other 12. Some of the final definitions, notably transfer, self-deactivating, and mine, reproduced the language of earlier treaties verbatim. Others, such as the components of cluster munition remnants, self-destruction mechanism, and cluster munition contaminated area, followed the approach of earlier treaties but sharpened the precedent or tailored it to the needs of this new Convention. Still others, in particular explosive bomblet and dispenser, emerged to deal with areas previously unaddressed in international law. While the first three definitions of Article 2 determined the scope of some of the core obligations of the Convention, the other definitions made its provisions clearer and more precise.

---

[230] Statement at the Friend of the President's Discussions on Definitions, Diplomatic Conference, 22 May 2008 (Landmine Action notes; copy on file with author).

[231] Statements at the Friend of the President's Discussions on Definitions, Diplomatic Conference, 22 May 2008 (Landmine Action notes; copy on file with author).

[232] Article 2, paragraphs 9 and 10.

[233] Article 1, paragraph 2, Draft Cluster Munitions Convention.

[234] Statement of Indonesia, 'Summary Record of the First Session of the Committee of the Whole', Diplomatic Conference doc. CCM/CW/SR/1, 18 June 2008, p. 4. The definitions of mine in *1996 Amended Protocol II* and the *1997 Anti-Personnel Mine Ban Convention* are identical except that the latter inserts the phrase 'designed to be' before 'placed' and 'exploded'. Article 2, paragraph 1, *1996 Amended Protocol II*; and Article 2, paragraph 2, *1997 Anti-Personnel Mine Ban Convention*. [235] Article 2, paragraph 12.

Paragraph 4

'**Failed cluster munition**' means a cluster munition that has been fired, dropped, launched, projected or otherwise delivered and which should have dispersed or released its explosive submunitions but failed to do so;

Commentary

2.167 A failed cluster munition is one of four types of cluster munition remnants.[236] Its definition covers the case where a cluster munition fails to open and release the explosive submunitions it contains. Such a situation is often referred to as a catastrophic failure. When a cluster munition falls to the ground intact, it may break open on impact scattering submunitions in the immediate area of the crash. These submunitions may not have armed themselves as they have not been released or dispersed. However, they remain a danger to civilians and could explode if they are disturbed, manipulated, or tampered with.

2.168 A failed cluster munition must first and foremost meet the requirements of Article 2, paragraph 2 to establish that it is a cluster munition for the purposes of the Convention. In addition, the weapon must have been fired, dropped, launched, projected, or otherwise delivered. In other words, the munition must have been used.[237] These terms are not specifically defined in the Convention, but they generally describe the methods by which air- or ground-launch systems deliver cluster munitions. They are also key criteria for distinguishing a failed cluster munition from an abandoned cluster munition.

2.169 The main characteristic of a failed cluster munition is that it has been unable—for whatever reason—to release or disperse the explosive submunitions it is carrying. As a result, it threatens civilians and is included in the definition of cluster munition remnants. The clearance of failed cluster munitions is essential, and as a component of cluster munition remnants, it is governed by the obligations and deadlines laid out in Article 4 of the Convention. Articles 6 and 7 also establish obligations regarding failed cluster munitions as a type of cluster munition remnant. Article 6, paragraph 4 obliges each State Party in a position to do so to provide assistance for the clearance of cluster munition remnants. Article 7, paragraph 1(i) requires a State Party to report on the status and progress of programmes for the

---

[236] See, *infra*, the commentary on Article 2, paragraph 7 in §§2.193 *et seq.*
[237] See, *supra*, the commentary in §§1.27 *et seq.* for a discussion of use.

clearance and destruction of all types of cluster munition remnants, including failed cluster munitions.[238]

2.170 The term failed cluster munition and the other terms in the definition of cluster munition remnants were developed to ensure that the Convention, and particularly Article 4 on the clearance of cluster munition remnants, clearly applied to the different circumstances in which cluster munitions pose a danger to civilians. As explained below in more detail,[239] ambiguities in a number of draft definitions raised concerns that important aspects of the cluster munitions problem would not be covered by the obligations being proposed in the drafts of the Convention.

2.171 The Lima Discussion Text did not specify if it applied to a cluster munition that failed to release or disperse its submunitions. It did not specifically include or define concepts such as failed cluster munitions and unexploded cluster munitions. Although the Lima Discussion Text required each State Party 'to clear all unexploded ordnance from cluster munitions in areas under its jurisdiction and control...',[240] the scope of this obligation was ambiguous. The requirement to clear UXO originating from cluster munitions would almost certainly apply to unexploded submunitions that had been released and failed to explode as intended (the most obvious form of UXO), but it was less clear to what extent it also encompassed cluster munitions that had failed to open and remained intact when hitting the ground.[241]

2.172 While the Vienna Discussion Text set out the first definitions for unexploded cluster munitions, abandoned cluster munitions, and cluster munition remnants, it did not completely clarify the situation on failed cluster munitions. At first glance, failed cluster munitions would appear to be integrated into the definition of unexploded cluster munitions.[242] However, the definition stated that unexploded cluster munitions 'should have exploded but failed to do so'. This sentence created confusion because it is the submunition, and not the cluster munition itself, that is expected to explode.[243]

---

[238] See Article 4; Article 6, paragraph 4; and Article 7, paragraph 1(i).

[239] See, *infra*, the commentary on Article 2, paragraph 5 in §§.2.180–2.182.

[240] Article 4, paragraph 1, Lima Discussion Text.

[241] Most definitions of UXO require that the munition be used or prepared for use. See, e.g., Article 2, paragraph 2, *2003 Protocol V*.

[242] The Vienna Discussion text defined unexploded cluster munitions as follows:

Unexploded cluster munitions means cluster munitions that have been primed, fused, armed, or otherwise prepared for use and used. They may have been fired, dropped, launched or projected, and should have exploded but failed to do so.

Article 2, Vienna Discussion Text.

[243] A similar point was made by Human Rights Watch in its paper, 'Observations on the Cluster Munition Convention Discussion Text', p. 2, circulated in advance of the Vienna Conference.

2.173 There was an attempt to clarify this matter in the Draft Cluster Munitions Convention. This text added a sentence to the definition in the Vienna Discussion Text to specify that the definition 'includes both unexploded parent munitions [i.e., failed cluster munitions] and unexploded submunitions'.[244] Concerns remained about the ambiguity of the definition, however, which led the ICRC to suggest a different structure for Article 2.[245] It proposed that the definition of unexploded cluster munition be changed to failed cluster munition and that a definition of unexploded explosive submunition be added to Article 2.[246] It also proposed that both of these concepts be included in the definition of cluster munition remnants to indicate that both were covered by the Convention.[247] The CMC supported this restructuring.[248]

2.174 Ireland subsequently submitted a proposal on Article 2 for the Wellington Compendium that included the ICRC's suggestions as well as additional elements to ensure that Article 2 was comprehensive.[249] It resubmitted it at the May 2008 Diplomatic Conference in Dublin. The Irish proposal

Failed cluster munitions also did not appear to be covered in the definition of an abandoned cluster munition as that definition indicates that an abandoned cluster munition is a cluster munition that has not been used. Article 2, Vienna Discussion Text.

[244] The Explanatory Notes to the Draft Cluster Munitions Convention affirmed this understanding. 'Draft Cluster Munitions Convention Explanatory Notes', 21 January 2008, p. 2. For full text, see Annex 5 to this Commentary.

[245] The ICRC believed that the Article might be read as encompassing only failed cluster munitions, not individual submunitions that failed to explode as intended after release. Both the Vienna Discussion Text and Draft Cluster Munitions Convention defined unexploded cluster munitions first and foremost as cluster munitions, not submunitions. The Draft Cluster Munitions Convention tried to clarify the scope of the definition with its new last sentence, but it did not specify if it encompassed unexploded explosive submunitions separated from the parent munition or only those that were still a component of the parent munition. In addition, both the ICRC and the CMC were concerned about the use of the phrase parent munition because this term was not defined in the text and its meaning might not be generally understood. 'Comments of the International Committee of the Red Cross on the Wellington draft of a future cluster munitions convention', *op. cit.*, p. 2; and 'Observations by the Cluster Munitions Coalition on the Draft Cluster Munitions Convention, dated 21 January 2008', p. 3.

[246] The ICRC proposed the following definition:

'Failed cluster munitions' means cluster munitions that have been fired, dropped, launched, projected or otherwise delivered and which should have dispersed or released their explosive submunitions but failed to do so.

'Comments of the International Committee of the Red Cross on the Wellington draft of a future cluster munitions convention', *op. cit.*, p. 2. [247] *Ibid.*

[248] 'Observations by the Cluster Munitions Coalition on the Draft Cluster Munitions Convention, dated 21 January 2008', p. 3.

[249] In addition to the changes proposed by the ICRC, the Irish proposal included definitions for explosive bomblet and unexploded explosive bomblet. 'Article 2: Definitions', Wellington Compendium, p. 13.

included the following definition of failed cluster munition:

'Failed cluster munition' means a cluster munition that has been fired, dropped, launched, projected or otherwise delivered and which should have dispersed or released its explosive submunitions but failed to do so.[250]

The language proposed in this definition received broad support in both the informal consultations on definitions and the plenary sessions of the Dublin negotiations. The final text of the Convention adopted it verbatim.

Paragraph 5

'Unexploded submunition' means an explosive submunition that has been dispersed or released by, or otherwise separated from, a cluster munition and has failed to explode as intended;

Commentary

2.175 Unexploded submunitions are generally regarded as a principal feature of the cluster munition problem. The large numbers of submunitions released when cluster munitions are used and the significant quantities that often fail to explode as intended can quickly contaminate wide swathes of land. Unexploded submunitions have been a high proportion, and sometimes the bulk, of the UXO threat in countries where cluster munitions have been used.

2.176 The definition of unexploded submunition is intended to ensure that the Convention's obligations clearly apply to those submunitions that have separated from the cluster munition container but have not exploded. Unexploded submunition is a component of cluster munition remnants and as such its definition has particular relevance for Article 4 of the Convention as well as some provisions in Articles 6 and 7.[251]

2.177 Three elements must be present for a munition to qualify as an unexploded submunition. First, the munition in question must be an explosive submunition as defined in Article 2, paragraph 3 of the Convention. Second, the explosive submunition must have been dispersed, released, or otherwise separated from the cluster munition container. Finally, the explosive submunition must have failed to explode as intended.

---

[250] 'Proposal by Ireland for the amendment of Article 2', Diplomatic Conference doc. CCM/25, 19 May 2008.

[251] See, e.g., Article 4; Article 6, paragraphs 4 and 6; and Article 7, paragraph 1(c), (h), and (i).

2.178 The Convention does not specifically define the terms dispersed, released, and otherwise separated. Thus, they are to be understood in accordance with their everyday meaning taking into account the context in which they are used. The main notion underlying these terms in this case is that the submunitions are no longer physically contained in but are now independent of the cluster munition.

2.179 The phrase 'failed to explode as intended' is meant to take into account that there are different ways through which the detonation of an explosive submunition can be initiated. Many models are designed to detonate following impact on a hard surface. Others explode after a time-delay. This distinction is highlighted in the definition of explosive submunition where it refers to munitions 'designed to function by detonating an explosive charge prior to, on or after impact'. The main consequence of 'failed to explode as intended' is that submunitions designed to explode after a time delay would not be considered unexploded submunitions during the period that their detonation was intentionally delayed but would become an unexploded submunition once that time period had expired.[252]

2.180 Like failed cluster munition, the definition of unexploded submunition was a rather late addition to Article 2. The Lima and Vienna discussion texts and the Draft Cluster Munitions Convention did not contain a specific definition for unexploded submunition. Instead, the definition of unexploded cluster munitions appeared to encompass the concept. The ICRC noted a lack of clarity at the Vienna Conference, however:

We have some concern that several definitions in Article 2 may be ambiguous and cause confusion as States implement their obligations. For example, we feel that it is unclear whether the definition of 'unexploded cluster munitions' encompasses submunitions which have been dispersed and failed to explode as intended (unexploded submunitions). It might be read as describing only a cluster munition which had been delivered but failed to disperse its submunitions. This can, for example, have implications on how a State interprets the clearance obligations in subsequent articles.[253]

2.181 To overcome these concerns, the ICRC proposed that a separate definition of unexploded submunitions be added to the draft Convention.[254] Such a definition was not, however, included in Article 2 of the Draft Cluster Munitions Convention which served as the basis for negotiations at the

---

[252] Several spin-armed BLU-63 submunition variants, e.g., were time-delayed. King, C., *Explosive Remnants of War: A Study on submunitions and other unexploded ordnance* (Geneva: ICRC, August 2000), pp. I-1 and I-2.

[253] Comments of the ICRC to the Vienna Discussion Text, *op. cit.*   [254] *Ibid.*

Diplomatic Conference. Nevertheless, it was a component of the Irish and ICRC proposals to restructure Article 2 that were annexed as a compendium to the Wellington Declaration and forwarded to the Diplomatic Conference, with support from the CMC.[255] At the negotiations, France and Germany also submitted a proposal to amend Article 2 that included a definition of unexploded submunition based on *2003 Protocol V*.[256]

2.182 Following informal discussions at the Diplomatic Conference, the Friend of the President on Article 2 circulated several papers suggesting possible language for definitions including that of unexploded explosive submunition. This language closely followed the Irish proposal. Overall, the elements of this definition were not contentious or the subject of extensive debate in the informal discussions or the Committee of the Whole. The most significant change to occur in the final text of the Convention was the deletion of the term 'explosive' in the main heading.[257]

Paragraph 6

> **'Abandoned cluster munitions'** means cluster munitions or explosive submunitions that have not been used and that have been left behind or dumped, and that are no longer under the control of the party that left them behind or dumped them. They may or may not have been prepared for use;

Commentary

2.183 A central feature of failed cluster munitions and unexploded submunitions is that the weapons have been used. In the case of failed cluster

---

[255] The proposal of Ireland defined an unexploded explosive submunition as: 'an explosive submunition which has been released dispersed or otherwise separated from a cluster munition and has failed to explode as intended'. 'Proposal by Ireland for the amendment of Article 2', Diplomatic Confernce doc. CCM/25, 19 May 2008. The ICRC used nearly identical wording in its submission for the compendium attached to the Wellington Declaration but defined these weapons in the plural, i.e., unexploded explosive submunitions. 'Article 2: Definitions', Wellington Compendium, p. 12. The elements of the two definitions, however, are the same. See also 'Observations by the Cluster Munitions Coalition on the Draft Cluster Munitions Convention, dated 21 January 2008', p. 3.

[256] 'Proposal by France and Germany for the amendment of Article 2', Diplomatic Conference doc. CCM/22, 19 May 2008. This proposal states:

> Unexploded sub-munition means explosive submunition that has been primed, fused, armed, or otherwise prepared for use and used in an armed conflict. It may have been fired, dropped, launched or projected and should have exploded but failed to do so.

[257] Thus the term defined became 'unexploded submunition'. See 'Informal Paper, Friend of the President on Article 2', 26 May 2008.

munitions, they have been fired, launched, or otherwise delivered, and if they are unexploded submunitions, they have separated from the cluster munition container. As such, neither term covers the situation in which stockpiles of cluster munitions have been left behind on the battlefield or at a military base and not used. In addition, the terms may not be seen to include situations where the aircraft of a party to a conflict has dumped its cluster munitions prior to returning to its base for landing—as sometimes occurs when an aircraft returns to an aircraft carrier at sea.[258] The definition of abandoned cluster munitions would fill this gap.

2.184 The concept of abandoned explosive ordnance is a rather new addition to international humanitarian law. It was first proposed and adopted in the context of *2003 Protocol V*. As noted in an early paper proposing the framework for an ERW protocol, as no definition of abandoned explosive ordnance existed, one would need to be developed during the Protocol's negotiation.[259] As a result, the definition of abandoned cluster munitions in the Convention on Cluster Munitions borrows a number of concepts from the Protocol.[260]

2.185 To qualify as abandoned cluster munitions, weapons must first meet the definition of cluster munition or explosive submunition.[261] As mentioned above, one of the main features of abandoned cluster munitions is that they have not been used, which helps clarify that the definition is not intended to encompass munitions that have been used and failed to explode (i.e., failed cluster munitions or unexploded submunitions). Rather, it is meant to cover cluster munition stockpiles or even individual cluster munitions that may have been left or discarded by a party to the conflict. Such weapons can be found on the battlefield, around military positions, and in or near military bases and depots.

---

[258] See, e.g., BBC, 'Nato dumps bombs in Adriatic', 16 May 1999, <http://news.bbc.co.uk/2/hi/americas/344929.stm>; and Norton-Taylor, R., 'Italian fishermen strike over lethal haul', *Guardian*, 15 May 1999, <http://www.guardian.co.uk/world/1999/may/15/richardnortontaylor1> (both accessed 29 October 2009).

[259] 'ERW Framework Paper: Possible structure for an ERW instrument', UN doc. CCW/GGE/IV/WG.1/WP.1, 28 February 2003. Most instruments and operational standards only defined unexploded ordnance.

[260] Article 2(3) of *2003 Protocol V* defines abandoned explosive ordnance as:

explosive ordnance that has not been used during an armed conflict, that has been left behind or dumped by a party to an armed conflict, and which is no longer under control of the party that left it behind or dumped it. Abandoned explosive ordnance may or may not have been primed, fused, armed or otherwise prepared for use.

[261] 'Abandoned cluster munitions' should be read to include abandoned bomblets and their dispensers, including where the bomblets are still inside the dispensers. The definition of cluster munition remnants does not formally cover bomblets and their dispensers where these have been abandoned (either as part of stockpiles, or potentially where aircraft carrying such systems have crashed in territory now controlled by another State) and remain intact.

2.186 Another element of this definition is that the weapons have been left or dumped by a party to the conflict. The terms 'left behind or dumped' indicate that a cluster munition can become abandoned through the passive or active conduct of a State Party or a party to the conflict. In this respect, the definition of abandoned cluster munition would encompass instances where a party moves from an area or position and leaves behind a stock of cluster munitions as well as situations where the party actively discards the weapons. An additional element of this definition is that the weapons are no longer under the control of the party that left them behind or dumped them. This criterion is meant clearly to reflect that the munitions are indeed abandoned.

2.187 Both large and small stockpiles of cluster munitions are, in principle, covered by the definition as there is no requirement that the stocks be a particular size or that they contain a minimum number of munitions. Although the definition is phrased in the plural, it would be logical that individual cluster munitions are also covered even if they are not amassed in a stockpile. First, small numbers of munitions, even individual munitions, can be left at temporary military positions. Second, cluster munitions are likely to be discarded individually and not in large numbers. Finally, a different understanding on the scope of this definition would mean that an individual cluster munition that had been abandoned would not be covered by Article 4 as it would not meet any of the requirements to be a cluster munition remnant. This reading would be contrary to the object and purpose of the Convention.

2.188 The definition also explicitly includes explosive submunitions that have not been used but have been left behind or dumped by a party to the conflict. It would thus cover situations where a dumped cluster munition broke open exposing or spilling the explosive submunitions contained inside. It would also include instances where explosive submunitions spilled or otherwise separated from an abandoned stockpiled cluster munition due to corrosion, ageing, or other factors. Although these submunitions had separated from the cluster munition, it might be argued they did not meet the definition of an unexploded submunition because they had not been used or failed to explode as intended. The reference to explosive submunitions in this definition helps ensure that the Convention covers the variety of scenarios where cluster munitions and explosive submunitions could pose a danger to civilians.

2.189 Finally, the last sentence of the definition indicates that cluster munitions and explosive submunitions that may or may not have been prepared for use qualify as an abandoned cluster munition. It is meant to clarify that such weapons need not be armed, fuzed, or otherwise ready for use. A similar clarification is found in the definition of abandoned explosive ordnance in Article 2 of *2003 Protocol V.* It was included in that instrument in response to discussions on whether it was necessary for the protocol to encompass weapons that had not yet been prepared for use, on the basis that they did not pose an immediate danger to civilians. Clearance organizations stressed that it was essential for the Protocol to include all explosive munitions, whether or not prepared for use, in light of the fact that such weapons would still need to be cleared as part of their operations.[262] They also highlighted that such weapons are a danger as civilians will often tamper with them to extract explosives or metal.

2.190 Abandoned cluster munitions, like failed cluster munitions and unexploded submunitions, fall under the definition of cluster munition remnants. Therefore obligations related to clearance, clearance assistance, and clearance reporting in Articles 4, 6, and 7, respectively, apply to this type of munition.

2.191 The need for a definition of abandoned cluster munition was realized early in the Oslo Process. A formulation of this term appeared in Article 2 of the Vienna Discussion Text which defined abandoned cluster munitions as:

cluster munitions that have not been used and that have been discarded or dumped, and that are no longer under the control of the party that discarded or dumped them. Abandoned cluster munitions may or may not have been prepared for use.[263]

With the exception of one editorial adjustment, this definition was left unchanged in the Draft Cluster Munitions Convention.[264] Overall, the definition was not contentious at this stage, and there was only one proposal for its amendment in the Wellington Compendium.[265]

2.192 At the Diplomatic Conference, the definition underwent several minor modifications in the informal discussions hosted by the Friend of the President on Definitions. The term 'discarded' was replaced by 'left behind' and 'or explosive

---

[262] Maresca, L., 'A new protocol on explosive remnants of war: The history and negotiation of Protocol V to the 1980 Convention on Certain Conventional Weapons', *International Review of the Red Cross*, Vol. 86, December 2004, p. 825.   [263] Article 2, Vienna Discussion Text.

[264] The second sentence of the definition was changed to read: '*They* may or may not have been prepared for use' (*emphasis added to indicate change*).

[265] Drawing almost verbatim from *2003 Protocol V*'s definition of abandoned explosive ordnance, France and Germany jointly proposed the following definition:

'Abandoned explosive cluster munition' means explosive cluster-munition that has not been used during an armed conflict, that has been left behind or dumped by a party to an armed conflict and which is no longer under control of the party that left it behind. Abandoned explosive cluster-munitions may or may not have been primed, fused, armed or otherwise prepared for me [*sic*].

This proposal was later submitted to the Diplomatic Conference as: 'Proposal by France and Germany for the amendment of Article 2', Diplomatic Conference doc. CCM/22, 19 May 2008. See also Article 2, paragraph 3, *2003 Protocol V.*

submunitions' was inserted after 'cluster munitions' at the start of the first sentence. This latter change was intended to ensure that individual submunitions that escaped from a left or discarded cluster munition would fall under the definition.[266] With these changes the definition moved to the President's Text and was agreed to by the Committee of the Whole without further amendment.

Paragraph 7

'Cluster munition remnants' means failed cluster munitions, abandoned cluster munitions, unexploded submunitions and unexploded bomblets;

Commentary

2.193 The phrase cluster munition remnants was developed to provide an umbrella term encompassing the four main forms in which cluster munitions can generally be found in conflict-affected areas: failed cluster munitions, abandoned cluster munitions, unexploded submunitions, and unexploded bomblets.[267] To qualify as a cluster munition remnant, an object must meet the requirements of one of these categories. While cluster munition remnants is not a term with technical or operational implications, its use in the Convention makes it easier to follow and understand the relevant obligations, particularly in Article 4 on Clearance and Destruction of Cluster Munition Remnants and Risk Reduction Education. It also has a bearing on the comprehension and application of the preamble of the Convention, the definitions of transfer and cluster munition contaminated area, Article 6 (international cooperation and assistance), Article 7 (transparency measures), and Article 11 (Meetings of States Parties). The term cluster munition remnants did not previously exist in any instrument but is influenced by the approach to the definition of ERW taken in *2003 Protocol V*.[268]

2.194 The definition of cluster munition remnants evolved along with that of other definitions related to the post-conflict dangers of cluster munitions.[269]

---

[266] This addition was motivated by reports of Italian fisherman finding individual submunitions in their nets. See, *supra*, fn. to §2.183.

[267] See the commentary on Article 2, paragraphs 4, 5, 6, and 15.

[268] The *2003 Protocol V* definition of explosive remnants of war is simply: 'Explosive remnants of war means unexploded ordnance and abandoned explosive ordnance.' Article 2, paragraph 4, *2003 Protocol V*.

[269] Namely, along with the definitions of failed cluster munitions, abandoned cluster munitions, unexploded submunitions, and unexploded bomblets. See, *supra*, the commentary on preparatory discussions and negotiations of Article 2, paragraphs 4–15 in §§2.142 *et seq*.

The Vienna Discussion Text and Draft Cluster Munitions Convention defined the term as 'unexploded cluster munitions and abandoned cluster munitions'.[270] In the Wellington Compendium, Ireland proposed a definition that encompassed 'failed cluster munitions, abandoned cluster munitions, unexploded explosive submunitions and unexploded explosive bomblets'.[271] The ICRC submitted a similar proposal, but it did not include the concept of unexploded explosive bomblets.[272]

2.195 At the Diplomatic Conference, the Friend of the President's first informal paper proposed a definition comparable to the ones submitted by Ireland and the ICRC in the compendium attached to the Wellington Declaration:

Cluster munition remnants means *failed cluster munitions*, abandoned cluster munitions and *unexploded explosive submunitions*.[273]

This wording changed slightly when it was decided to delete 'explosive' from the heading 'unexploded explosive submunitions'. The amendment was more editorial than substantive as the term had also been removed from the title of the definition of unexploded submunition.[274]

2.196 A second change occurred once it was decided that the Convention would require definitions for explosive bomblet and unexploded bomblet.[275]

---

[270] Article 2, Vienna Discussion Text; and Article 2, Draft Cluster Munitions Convention.

[271] 'Article 2: Definitions', Wellington Compendium, p. 14. The proposal was resubmitted to the Diplomatic Conference as: 'Proposal by Ireland for the amendment of Article 2', Diplomatic Conference doc. CCM/25, 19 May 2008.

[272] 'Article 2: Definitions', Wellington Compendium, p. 12. The Irish and ICRC proposals were similar in that they extended the types of weapons encompassed by the concept of cluster munition remnants. A joint proposal by France and Germany suggested amendments to some terminology in the definition of cluster munition remnants. Their proposal stated:

'Explosive remnants of cluster munitions' means unexploded submunitions and abandoned explosive cluster munitions.

Their proposal also included a definition of 'existing explosive remnants of sub-munitions', which related to a proposal on user State responsibility for clearance and was a new concept that appeared to suggest that the Convention should draw distinctions between new and existing remnants. 'Article 2: Definitions', Wellington Compendium, pp. 12–13; and 'Proposal by France and Germany for the amendment of Article 2', Diplomatic Conference doc. CCM/22, 19 May 2008. See also, *supra*, the commentary on preparatory discussions and negotiations of Article 2, paragraphs 4–15 in §§2.142 *et seq.*

[273] 'Informal Paper—Friend of the President on Article 2: Definitions other than that of a "Cluster Munition" and a "Cluster Munition Victim"', 23 May 2008, 13:00 (*emphasis in original to indicate new or amended text*).

[274] The use of the term explosive in the heading of the unexploded explosive submunition definition was generally considered unnecessary as the definition began: 'Unexploded explosive submunition means an explosive submunition...'.

[275] The negotiation of these definitions is discussed *supra* in the commentary in §§2.151–2.152 and §2.157.

With agreement on these definitions, it was evident that the definition of cluster munition remnants needed to be broadened to reflect this development. Thus, in his final informal paper the Friend of the President proposed that unexploded bomblets be added to the definition of cluster munition remnants.[276] With this amendment the definition went into the President's Text and was adopted.

Paragraph 8

'Transfer' involves, in addition to the physical movement of cluster munitions into or from national territory, the transfer of title to and control over cluster munitions, but does not involve the transfer of territory containing cluster munition remnants;

Commentary

2.197 The definition of transfer addresses the relocation of cluster munitions across State borders and changes in their ownership. As a result, it clearly covers the import and export of cluster munitions by sale or through provision of military assistance. Because it links its initial phrases with 'in addition to' instead of merely 'or', however, the definition raises serious questions of interpretation. It could mean that either movement across borders *or* transfer of title and control is sufficient to constitute transfer. In that case, if a State Party allowed a State not party to deliver cluster munitions to a military base it is hosting on its territory, it would violate the prohibition on transfer, which is articulated in Article 1, paragraph 1(b). Many States have interpreted the virtually identical definition of transfer in the *1997 Anti-Personnel Mine Ban Convention* in this way.[277] Alternatively the definition could mean that there

---

[276] The Friend of the President's definition read as follows: 'Cluster munition remnants means failed cluster munitions, abandoned cluster munitions, unexploded bomblets and unexploded submunitions.'

[277] The definitions in the Convention on Cluster Munitions and *1997 Anti-Personnel Mine Ban Convention* only differ in that cluster munitions and cluster munition remnants replace anti-personnel mines and emplaced anti-personnel mines. See Article 2, paragraph 4, *1997 Anti-Personnel Mine Ban Convention*. According to a commentary on the *1997 Anti-Personnel Mine Ban Convention*, 'although State practice is divergent, transfer appears to be either the physical movement of anti-personnel mines into or from national territory, or the transfer of title to and control over the mines'. Maslen, S., *Commentaries on Arms Control Treaties, Volume I: The Convention on the Prohibition of the Use, Stockpiling, Production, and Transfer of Anti-Personnel Mines and on their Destruction*, Second Edition, Oxford Commentaries on International Law (Oxford: Oxford University Press, 2005), §2.61. Maslen notes that this approach accommodates both common definitions of transfer, i.e., 'to convey from one place . . . to another' and to 'convey . . . by deed or legal process'.

must be physical movement across borders *and* a handover of title and control for transfer to occur. This reading restricts the scope of the provision and would primarily cover sales and foreign aid. Regardless of the interpretation, a passing of title must always be accompanied by a passing of control to amount to transfer.

2.198 Transfer can also be understood to encompass transit, i.e., the movement of cluster munitions across a State's territory whether by land, across territorial waters, or through airspace. During the Oslo Process, the CMC repeatedly argued that transfer should be read as encompassing transit. According to the Summary Records from the Diplomatic Conference, for example, the CMC stated that 'it was the clear understanding of all States that the definition of "transfer" encompassed the transit of cluster munitions through a State Party's territory'.[278] Since the Convention opened for signature in December 2008, several States, including Bulgaria, Burkina Faso, Ecuador, Lebanon, Malta, Mexico, and South Africa, have publicly stated their view that transit is prohibited.[279]

2.199 The second half of the definition of transfer creates an exclusion. It states that transfer 'does not involve the transfer of territory containing cluster munition remnants'.[280] The prohibition on transfer in Article 1, paragraph 1(b) seeks to end the proliferation of weapons and the spread of use. A change in control of an area contaminated with cluster munition remnants does not interfere with that goal, and therefore the Convention did not have to include it under the prohibition on disarmament or humanitarian grounds. The exclusion does not give a State Party an incentive to acquire contaminated territories to obtain potentially usable abandoned cluster munitions because it would also assume the obligation to clear them.

---

[278] Statement of the CMC, 'Summary Record of Eleventh Session of the Committee of the Whole', Diplomatic Conference doc. CCM/CW/SR/11, 18 June 2008, p. 10. See also Statement of the CMC, Friend of the President's Discussions on Definitions, Diplomatic Conference, 21 May 2008 (Landmine Action notes; copy on file with author); and Statement of the CMC, Vienna Conference, 6 December 2007 (Landmine Action notes; copy on file with author).

[279] Human Rights Watch and Landmine Action wrote letters to all signatories of the Convention on Cluster Munitions, inquiring about their understandings of the Convention, including the issue of transit. Lebanon and South Africa stated that they believed the prohibition on transfer encompassed transit. The others listed above wrote, or said in public statements in different contexts, that transit was banned but did not specify if it was prohibited as a form of transfer or as a form of assistance with activities prohibited by the Convention. In addition, Madagascar has said permitting transit would weaken the Convention, and Zambia wrote that transit is banned as a form of assistance. Of those States that responded to the inquiries of Human Rights Watch and Landmine Action, only the Netherlands specifically said that transit was permitted. Human Rights Watch and Landmine Action, *Banning Cluster Munitions: Government Policy and Practice* (Ottawa: Mines Action Canada, 2009), pp. 24–25.   [280] Article 2, paragraph 8.

It allows, however, a State Party to take control of a territory that it wishes to help clear. Without the exclusion in the definition of transfer, the Convention would prohibit a State Party from acquiring for any reason new territory that happens to be affected by cluster munitions. Public international law, not the Convention on Cluster Munitions, should govern the legality of the acquisition of territory.

2.200   The term transfer appears in two places in the Convention on Cluster Munitions. Article 1, paragraph 1(b) makes the prohibition on transfer one of the core obligations of the Convention. That provision establishes the absolute nature of the ban by stating that transfer is prohibited 'under any circumstances' and 'to anyone, directly or indirectly'.[281] Transfer is the only activity prohibited by the Convention that is defined. The term also appears in Article 3, which permits 'the transfer of cluster munitions to another State Party for the purpose of destruction', for the 'development of and training in cluster munition and explosive submunition detection, clearance or destruction techniques, or for the development of cluster munition counter-measures'.[282] States Parties must report on the details of any such transfers.[283] While allowing transfer of cluster munitions for destruction was largely uncontroversial, during the negotiating process many States challenged allowing transfer for training and development purposes.[284]

2.201   The definition of transfer received only a little attention before the Diplomatic Conference. At the Lima Conference, one State listed it among several terms that might need to be defined in the Convention,[285] and a preliminary definition was added in the Vienna Discussion Text. That version read:

'Transfer' means the physical movement of cluster munitions into or from national territory or the transfer of title to or control over cluster munitions, but does not include the transfer of territory containing cluster munition remnants.[286]

---

[281] Article 1, paragraph 1(b). For further discussion of this provision, see, *supra*, the commentary on Article 1 in §§1.33–1.35 and 1.56 *et seq*.   [282] Article 3, paragraphs 6–7.

[283] Article 3, paragraph 8.

[284] The Vienna Discussion Text contained the first reference to transferring cluster munitions 'for the purpose of destruction'. Article 3, paragraph 6, Vienna Discussion Text. The provision remained unchanged in the Draft Cluster Munitions Convention, but the Convention on Cluster Munitions modified the destruction phrase so that only transfer 'to another State Party' was allowed. This change ensured that cluster munitions are delivered only to a State with an obligation to destroy them. Over the objections of some, the Convention also added permission to transfer cluster munitions for training and development purposes. Article 3, paragraphs 6–7. For further discussion of these provisions and their negotiation history, see, *infra*, the commentary on Article 3.

[285] Statement at the Lima Conference, 27 May 2007 (Landmine Action notes; copy on file with author).   [286] Article 2, Vienna Discussion Text.

It drew much of its language from the *1997 Anti-Personnel Mine Ban Convention* and *1996 Amended Protocol II* but organized it somewhat differently.[287]

2.202 During the Diplomatic Conference, several States expressed a desire to use the same language as other treaties. One State noted that this approach would be consistent with past documents and 'avoid legal confusion'.[288] In response, Norway introduced alternative language; its formal proposal structured the provision like the corresponding definitions in the *1997 Anti-Personnel Mine Ban Convention* and *1996 Amended Protocol II*, beginning it with '*in addition to* the physical movement of cluster munitions into or from national territory'.[289] The ICRC expressed concern, saying that that formulation had led to 'years of debate' in the landmine context. It said that the wording did not make clear whether transfer required both physical movement *and* a change of title and control, or only one or the other.[290] Despite the lack of clarity, the final version of the definition adopted Norway's amendment. It also replaced 'means' and 'includes' with 'involves', thus making its language effectively the same as that in the *1997 Anti-Personnel Mine Ban Convention* and *1996 Amended Protocol II*.[291]

Paragraph 9

'Self-destruction mechanism' means an incorporated automatically-functioning mechanism which is in addition to the primary initiating

---

[287] Article 2, paragraph 4, *1997 Anti-Personnel Mine Ban Convention*; and Article 2, paragraph 15, *1996 Amended Protocol II*. The *1997 Anti-Personnel Mine Ban Convention*'s definition reads:

'Transfer' involves, in addition to the physical movement of anti-personnel mines into or from national territory, the transfer of title to and control over the mines, but does not involve the transfer of territory containing emplaced anti-personnel mines.

1996 Amended Protocol II has the same definition except that it does not include 'anti-personnel'.

[288] Statement at the Friend of the President's Discussions on Definitions, Diplomatic Conference, 21 May 2008 (Landmine Action notes; copy on file with author).

[289] 'Proposal by Norway for the Amendment of Article 2', Diplomatic Conference doc. CCM/73, 22 May 2008 (*emphasis added to indicate changes*).

[290] Statement of the ICRC, Friend of the President's Discussions on Definitions, Diplomatic Conference, 22 May 2008 (Landmine Action notes; copy on file with author).

[291] The only difference in the definitions of transfer in these three treaties is the weapon the definitions apply to, i.e., cluster munitions, anti-personnel mines, or mines. Article 2, paragraph 8; Article 2, paragraph 4, *1997 Anti-Personnel Mine Ban Convention*; and Article 2, paragraph 15, *1996 Amended Protocol II*.

mechanism of the munition and which secures the destruction of the
munition into which it is incorporated;

Commentary

2.203 Article 2, paragraph 9 uses technical and objective language to define
a self-destruction mechanism as a device intended to decrease the number
of unexploded submunitions and thus the harm they cause. The definition
states that it is 'an incorporated automatically-functioning mechanism', which
means it must be a component of a munition and operate without human
or other intervention. If the mechanism functions as designed, the munition
destroys itself independently.

2.204 The definition adds two requirements to that basic criterion. First,
the mechanism must be 'in addition to the primary initiating mechanism
of the munition'. This phrase clarifies that it serves as a secondary system.
Second, it 'secures the destruction of the munition into which it is incorporated'. In other words, it must achieve a certain goal, i.e., to eliminate an explosive
submunition that failed to detonate on impact. The definition uses 'secures
the destruction' rather than 'is designed to secure'.[292] Although presumably
it was not intended, the definition literally suggests that a device is not a self-
destruction mechanism if it fails to function, even if it was designed to destroy
its munition and meets all the other criteria.[293]

2.205 The term self-destruction mechanism appears only once in the
Convention. Article 2, paragraph 2(c)(iv) states: 'Each explosive submunition is
equipped with an electronic self-destruction mechanism.'[294] That sub-paragraph
presents one of five cumulative characteristics a weapon must have to fall under
Article 2, paragraph 2(c)'s narrow exclusion to cluster munition. To reduce the
'risks posed by unexploded submunitions', the self-destruction mechanism backs
up an explosive submunition's primary initiating mechanism and is in turn backed
up by an electronic self-deactivating feature.[295] The provision further narrows the
type of self-destruction mechanism by stating that it must be electronic, which, at
least one expert has said, increases its chance of functioning properly.[296]

[292] Article 2, paragraph 9.
[293] Two States identified this problem with another version of the definition, but States did not
adjust the final version that appeared in the Convention itself accordingly. Statements at the Friend
of the President's Discussions on Definitions, Diplomatic Conference, 22 May 2008 (Landmine
Action notes; copy on file with author).
[294] Article 2, paragraph 2(c) (iv). See also, *supra*, the commentary on Article 2, paragraph 2(c).
[295] Article 2, paragraph 2.
[296] Statement by Colin King, Friend of the President's Discussion on Definitions, Diplomatic
Conference, 22 May 2008 (Landmine Action notes; copy on file with author).

2.206 States first highlighted the relevance of self-destruction mechanisms to the definition of cluster munition at the Lima Conference, and the discussion continued during each of the subsequent Oslo Process meetings. They saw the mechanisms as tools for reducing the 'unacceptable' harm of the weapons.[297] Although some States initially argued that submunitions with self-destruction mechanisms should not be banned, other States and the CMC countered that the mechanisms were insufficient by themselves because they often failed in conflict.[298] The latter view ultimately prevailed. States also rejected the proposition to exclude certain weapons from the definition of cluster munition based on their failure rate, which a self-destruction mechanism could lower, because it is impossible to determine an accurate rate for conflict situations in testing environments.[299]

2.207 Despite these lengthy discussions, States began considering language for the definition of self-destruction mechanism only during final negotiations at the Diplomatic Conference. Spain noted that the term was already well defined in international law and proposed borrowing verbatim the definition of *1996 Amended Protocol II*, which states:

'Self-destruction mechanism' means an incorporated or externally attached automatically-functioning mechanism which secures the destruction of the munition into which it is incorporated or to which it is attached.[300]

[297] In the Oslo Declaration, States committed to 'prohibit the use, production, transfer and stockpiling of cluster munitions that cause unacceptable harm to civilians'. Oslo Declaration of 23 February 2007, point 1(i). During the negotiation process that followed, many States reiterated that they had agreed to ban only cluster munitions that cause unacceptable harm, not all cluster munitions. They therefore sought to determine the boundaries of that class of weapons.

[298] As noted above, an influential report released at the Vienna Conference documented how the M85, a submunition with a self-destruction mechanism widely touted as a weapon that would not result in significant UXO contamination, had a much higher failure rate than the 1% advertised by manufacturers. The report found that the M85 used by Israel in south Lebanon had a failure rate of about 10% under combat conditions. King, C., Dullum, O., and Østern, G., *M85—An Analysis of Reliability, op. cit.*, p. 15. See, *supra*, the commentary on preparatory discussions of Article 2 paragraph 2 in §2.56.

[299] For an analysis of the discrepancy between failure rates in tests and in combat, see King, C., Dullum, O., and Østern, G., m85—An Analysis of Reliability, op. cit., p. 34. For further discussion of the debate over the definition of cluster munition, see, *supra,* the commentary on preparatory discussions and negotiations of Article 2, paragraph 2 in §§2.39 *et seq.*

[300] Statement of Spain, Friend of the President's Discussion on Definitions, Diplomatic Conference, 20 May 2008 (Landmine Action notes; copy on file with author); 'Proposal by Spain for the Amendment of Article 2', Diplomatic Conference doc. CCM/67, 19 May 2008; and 'Proposal by Spain for the Amendment of Article 2', Diplomatic Conference doc. CCM/76, 27 May 2008. See also Article 2, paragraph 10, *1996 Amended Protocol II*. France independently proposed a definition of a 'self safe mechanism', which could be a self-destruction mechanism, but States did not ultimately use that term or adopt that definition. 'Proposal by France for the Amendment of Article 2', Diplomatic Conference doc. CCM/20, 19 May 2008.

2.208 Norway said it sought to build on existing models and proposed defining the term as 'a mechanism that physically destroys the warhead in the event that it does not function as intended and thus leav[es] no unexploded objects behind'.[301] Norway's version focused on the desired effects of the mechanism—destroying the warhead and leaving no unexploded submunitions—rather than the technical characteristics of the device. Several States objected to this proposal, stating that they preferred to use an already accepted definition.[302] Ultimately the Convention's final definition drew on that in *1996 Amended Protocol II* and refined it. It removed references to 'externally attached' and clarified that a self-destruction mechanism was a secondary device 'in addition to the primary initiating mechanism of the munition'.[303]

Paragraph 10

'**Self-deactivating**' means automatically rendering a munition inoperable by means of the irreversible exhaustion of a component, for example a battery, that is essential to the operation of the munition;

Commentary

2.209 The definition of self-deactivating adopts a technical and objective approach similar to that of the definition of self-destruction mechanism, and it too relates to efforts to decrease the harm of unexploded submunitions.[304] To be self-deactivating, a feature must render a munition 'inoperable' so that it can no longer detonate even if disturbed, and it must do so 'automatically', i.e., independently and without outside intervention. It accomplishes this end 'by means of the irreversible exhaustion of a component, for example a battery, that is essential to the operation of the munition'.[305] The component must be

---

[301] Statement of Norway, Friend of the President's Discussion on Definitions, Diplomatic Conference, 22 May 2008 (Landmine Action notes; copy on file with author); and 'Proposal by Norway for the Amendment of Article 2', Diplomatic Conference doc. CCM/72, 22 May 2008.

[302] Statements at the Friend of the President's Discussion on Definitions, Diplomatic Conference, 22 May 2008 (Landmine Action notes; copy on file with author).

[303] *Cp.* Article 2, paragraph 9, with Article 2, paragraph 10, *1996 Amended Protocol II.*

[304] Self-destruction mechanism is defined as a noun, and self-deactivating as an adjective. The former is a term for a specific technical tool, while the latter refers to a process that can be accomplished by various devices.

[305] Article 2, paragraph 10. As with self-destruction mechanism, self-deactivating does not include the phrase 'designed to', which could be literally interpreted to mean that a self-deactivating feature that failed would not fall under the definition. This understanding, however, is presumably the unintended result of an oversight in drafting.

essential to the workings of the munition in order to ensure that the munition cannot function after the component's exhaustion when it is no longer appropriate for it to do so. While the definition allows for a range of components, including those yet to be invented, it singles out batteries as the most common components that can lose their charge and self-deactivate.

2.210 Irreversibility guarantees that the inoperability is permanent and the munition cannot become dangerous again. Like a self-destruction mechanism, a self-deactivating feature serves the purpose of removing the threat of an unexploded submunition. While the former works by detonating a weapon shortly after it has failed, however, the latter realizes its goal not by exploding the weapon but by making sure that, after a certain point, it is incapable of exploding.

2.211 The term self-deactivating is used only once in the Convention, in Article 2, paragraph 2(c)(v), which provides that: 'Each explosive submunition is equipped with an electronic self-deactivating feature.'[306] This subparagraph presents one of five cumulative criteria necessary to meet the narrow exclusion to the definition of cluster munition.[307] It seeks to eliminate the danger of an unexploded submunition in a situation where both primary and secondary fuzing mechanisms have failed. That provision limits the feature even more than the definition of self-deactivating by requiring that it be electronic. Self-deactivating features generally are electronic because a mechanical mechanism can be neutralized but not exhausted.

2.212 States debated throughout the Oslo Process whether weapons excluded under the definition of cluster munition should be required to have a self-deactivating feature, but they did not discuss a formal definition of the term until the Diplomatic Conference. None of the discussion texts offered draft language.

2.213 During the Diplomatic Conference, Spain suggested adopting the definition used in *1996 Amended Protocol II*,[308] and Norway supported drafting a new one. Norway's proposal stated that:

'Self-deactivation mechanism' means a mechanism that drains the sub-munition of the energy required to bring it to detonation and thus rendering the remaining unexploded object safe to handle and safe in any incidental contact.[309]

---

[306] Article 2, paragraph 2(c)(v). See also, *supra*, the commentary on Article 2, paragraph 2(c).

[307] Article 2, paragraph 2(c).

[308] 'Proposal by Spain for the amendment of Article 2', Diplomatic Conference doc. CCM/76, 27 May 2008. France independently proposed a definition of a 'self safe' mechanism, which could be a self-deactivation mechanism, but States did not ultimately use that term or adopt that definition. 'Proposal by France for the amendment of Article 2', Diplomatic Conference doc. CCM/20, 19 May 2008.

[309] 'Proposal by Norway for the amendment of Article 2', Diplomatic Conference doc. CCM/72, 22 May 2008.

While Norway said it sought to 'strengthen' *1996 Amended Protocol II*'s definition,[310] the second part of its proposal describing the effects of the mechanism attracted criticism. One State, for example, expressed concern about the difficulty of meeting the standard of 'rendering the... object... safe in any incidental contact' because a self-deactivating mechanism could not be expected to protect against all unsafe acts, such as civilians taking submunitions apart for explosives.[311] Another added that it was problematic to describe a piece of UXO as 'safe to handle';[312] indeed, explosive ordnance disposal standards strongly oppose anything that could encourage an untrained civilian to handle ordnance. Some States said more generally that they preferred to use *1996 Amended Protocol II*'s version because it had already been accepted internationally.[313] In the end, States rejected Norway's proposal and adopted Spain's, which used verbatim the language of *1996 Amended Protocol II*'s definition.[314]

Paragraph 11

'**Cluster munition contaminated area**' means an area known or suspected to contain cluster munition remnants;

Commentary

2.214 The definition of cluster munition contaminated area delineates what territory is unsafe and needs to be checked for contamination which, if any is found, must be cleared and destroyed in accordance with Article 4. To be considered a 'cluster munition contaminated area', it is sufficient that an area contain any cluster munition remnants, in other words failed cluster munitions, abandoned cluster munitions, unexploded submunitions, or unexploded bomblets.[315]

2.215 The presence of these remnants can be either 'known or suspected'.[316] This phrase ensures that the definition covers most possible contaminated areas. Immediately after a strike, it can be difficult to determine for certain if

---

[310] Statement of Norway, Friend of the President's Discussions on Definitions, Diplomatic Conference, 22 May 2008 (Landmine Action notes; copy on file with author).

[311] Statement at the Friend of the President's Discussion on Definitions, Diplomatic Conference, 22 May 2008 (Landmine Action notes; copy on file with author).   [312] *Ibid.*

[313] Statements at the Friend of the President's Discussion on Definitions, Diplomatic Conference, 22 May 2008 (Landmine Action notes; copy on file with author).

[314] See Article 2, paragraph 12, *1996 Amended Protocol II* and Article 2, paragraph 10.

[315] Article 2, paragraph 7.   [316] Article 2, paragraph 11.

cluster munition remnants litter a field or not, especially if the submunitions have penetrated a soft surface. The Convention does not require an absolute determination because, given its humanitarian purpose, precautions must be taken with any area that is potentially contaminated in order to protect civilians.[317]

2.216 The term cluster munition contaminated area is used primarily in relation to clearance and risk reduction education. Article 4, paragraph 1 of the Convention obliges each State Party 'to clear and destroy, or ensure the clearance and destruction of, cluster munition remnants located in cluster munition contaminated areas under its jurisdiction or control'.[318] Article 4, paragraph 2 requires the State Party to 'mak[e] every effort to identify all' such areas, take 'all feasible steps to ensure' they are 'perimeter-marked, monitored and protected', and conduct risk reduction education for civilians 'living in or around' the areas.[319] Article 7, which governs transparency measures, mandates related reports on 'the size and location of all cluster munition contaminated areas under [a State Party's] jurisdiction or control', the size and location of areas cleared, and measures to warn civilians living in the areas.[320] The definition clarifies the areas to which certain of the Convention's obligations apply.

2.217 A definition of cluster munition contaminated area was first proposed only in the Wellington Compendium, but discussion of the need for such a term began at the Vienna Conference. At that meeting, one State suggested the phrase contaminated field, and the Vienna Discussion Text used a variety of terms to capture the concept, including contaminated areas.[321] In the

---

[317] The International Mine Action Standards (IMAS) definition of hazardous area uses similar language to that of the Convention's definition of cluster munition contaminated area. It defines hazardous area as: 'a generic term for an area not in productive use due to the perceived or actual presence of **mines** or **ERW**.' IMAS 04.10: 'Glossary of Mine Action Terms, Definitions and Abbreviations', Second Edition, 1 January 2003, available at: <http://www.mineactionstandards. org>.

[318] Article 4, paragraph 1.

[319] Article 4, paragraph 2(a), (c), and (e). For further discussion of these clearance obligations, see, *infra*, the commentary on Article 4, paragraph 2.

[320] Article 7, paragraph 1(h), (i), and (j). For further discussions of transparency provisions, see the commentary on Article 7, paragraph 1.

[321] Statement at the Vienna Conference, 6 December 2007 (Landmine Action notes; copy on file with author). Using a related term, the Vienna Discussion Text required applications for clearance extensions to address '[c]ircumstances which impede the ability of the State Party to destroy all the cluster munition remnants in *contaminated areas*'. Article 4, paragraph 6(b)(iii), Vienna Discussion Text (*emphasis added*). That phrase was changed to 'areas under its jurisdiction or control' in the Draft Cluster Munitions Convention (Article 4, paragraph 6(b)(iii)) and appears that way in the final text of the Convention (Article 4, paragraph 6(g)). In the Vienna Discussion Text, other provisions that ultimately used cluster munition contaminated area instead employed phrases such as

Wellington Compendium, Indonesia formally proposed a definition, drawn almost verbatim from the *1997 Anti-Personnel Mine Ban Convention*, stating, 'Cluster munitions areas mean areas which are dangerous due to the presence or suspected presence of cluster munitions.'[322] The ICRC noted that use of the subjective word dangerous in the definition was problematic because it required a determination of what was dangerous.[323] The final version removed that word and changed cluster munitions to cluster munition remnants,[324] which meant that areas containing unexploded bomblets would be covered by the definition and areas containing stockpiles under destruction would not be. The Convention on Cluster Munitions also added the word contaminated to the term itself, characterizing such areas as dangerous and pointing to the need to clear them.[325]

Paragraph 12

> 'Mine' means a munition designed to be placed under, on or near the ground or other surface area and to be exploded by the presence, proximity or contact of a person or a vehicle;

'areas under its jurisdiction or control' (Article 4, paragraphs 1 and 2(c)); 'affected areas' (Article 7, paragraph 1(e)), or 'areas identified to be contaminated by cluster munition remnants' (Article 7, paragraph 1(i)). The Draft Cluster Munitions Convention followed an approach similar to the Vienna Discussion Texts see, e.g., Article 4, paragraphs 1 and 2(c), and Article 7, paragraph 1(e), Draft Cluster Munitions Convention.

[322] 'Article 2: Definitions', Wellington Compendium, p. 15. Indonesia resubmitted its proposal as: 'Proposal by Indonesia for the Amendment of Article 2', Diplomatic Conference doc. CCM/27, 19 May 2008. The only differences between Indonesia's proposal and the definition in the *1997 Anti-Personnel Mine Ban Convention* are that the cluster munition version is plural and that it uses the term cluster munition contaminated areas rather than mined area. *Cf.* Article 2, paragraph 5, *1997 Anti-Personnel Mine Ban Convention*. The *1997 Anti-Personnel Mine Ban Convention*'s definition is a modified version of the definition of mined area in *1996 Amended Protocol II*, which states, '"mined area" is an area which is dangerous due to the presence of mines'. Article 2, paragraph 8, *1996 Amended Protocol II*. The *1997 Anti-Personnel Mine Ban Convention* added the important element of 'suspected presence'.

[323] Statement of the ICRC, Friend of the President's Discussion on Definitions, Diplomatic Conference, 21 May 2008 (Landmine Action notes; copy on file with author).

[324] One State suggested this amendment. Statement at the Friend of the President's Discussion on Definitions, Diplomatic Conference, 21 May 2008 (Landmine Action notes; copy on file with author).

[325] The Oxford English Dictionary defines 'contaminated' as 'defiled, sullied, or infected by contact, esp. with noxious substances'. Cluster munition contaminated areas are littered with harmful cluster munition remnants that prevent civilians from safely occupying the land or tending their farms. *Oxford English Dictionary*, Oxford University Press, CD-ROM Version 3.1, 2004.

Commentary

2.218 The definition of mine clarifies the differences between this weapon and an explosive submunition. Drawn completely from the *1997 Anti-Personnel Mine Ban Convention*,[326] it has two elements. The first relates to how a mine is used. It states that a mine is 'designed to be placed under, on or near the ground or other surface area'. The second element describes how the munition can be detonated. It states that a mine is 'designed to be . . . exploded by the presence, proximity or contact of a person or vehicle'. The term mine only appears once in the Convention on Cluster Munitions. Article 1, paragraph 3 states: 'This Convention does not apply to mines.'[327]

2.219 Mines are distinguishable from explosive submunitions on both counts. The latter are not 'placed'; they are 'dispersed or released by a cluster munition'. Submunitions are also designed to explode 'prior to, on or after impact', rather than primarily on contact from a person or vehicle. While unexploded submunitions resemble *de facto* landmines because people can set them off by disturbing them after strikes, these weapons have failed and are not operating as intended.

2.220 While States clearly expressed their desire to exclude mines from the Convention from the beginning of the Oslo Process, the means of doing so gradually evolved. The Explanatory Annex to the Vienna Discussion Text noted, 'At the Lima Conference there appeared to be broad agreement that landmines would be excluded from the definition of "cluster munition" since they are already covered by other treaties.'[328] The Vienna Discussion Text itself did not include any mention of mines, but several States reiterated the positions expressed in Lima at the Vienna Conference.[329]

2.221 In its Article 1, paragraph 2, the Draft Cluster Munitions Convention stated that the Convention did not apply to mines as defined in *1996 Amended Protocol II*.[330] The text combined the scope of application and the definition in a provision outside of Article 2 on definitions.

---

[326] See Article 2, paragraph 2, *1997 Anti-Personnel Mine Ban Convention*.

[327] Article 1, paragraph 3. See also, *supra*, the commentary on Article 1, paragraph 3.

[328] The Annex then listed other possible exclusions, some of which were later included in Article 2, paragraph 2, suggesting that the Convention should exclude mines under the definition of cluster munition. The final Convention did not adopt this approach. Explanatory Annex, Vienna Discussion Text.

[329] Statements at the Vienna Conference, 6 December 2007 (Landmine Action notes; copy on file with author).

[330] Article 1, paragraph 2, Draft Cluster Munitions Convention; and Article 2, paragraph 1, *1996 Amended Protocol II*. *1996 Amended Protocol II* has a similar definition of mine to that in the final Convention on Cluster Munitions except that it does not include the words 'designed to be'.

2.222 During the Wellington Conference and the Dublin Diplomatic Conference, Indonesia objected to the reference to *1996 Amended Protocol II* because it was not a party to that instrument and proposed replacing it with language from the *1997 Anti-Personnel Mine Ban Convention*.[331] The final Convention split the provision on scope of application and definition, adopted the previously accepted *1997 Anti-Personnel Mine Ban Convention* wording for the latter, and placed it in Article 2.

Paragraph 13

> 'Explosive bomblet' means a conventional munition, weighing less than 20 kilograms, which is not self-propelled and which, in order to perform its task, is dispersed or released by a dispenser, and is designed to function by detonating an explosive charge prior to, on or after impact;

Commentary

2.223 The definition of explosive bomblet captures weapons that resemble explosive submunitions but are delivered in a different way. The Convention uses similar language to describe the two weapons and their means of operating. Both are 'conventional munitions' and are 'designed to function by detonating an explosive charge prior to, on or after impact'.[332] The inclusion of the phrase 'designed to' is important because it ensures a munition that otherwise fits the definition is still an explosive submunition or bomblet even if it fails to detonate as intended. Although explosive submunitions do not by definition have a weight requirement, the definition of cluster munition refers to them as 'weighing less than 20 kilograms', and the definition of explosive bomblet adopts the same specification.[333]

2.224 Submunitions and bomblets are distinguishable because the latter are 'dispersed or released by a dispenser', which according to Article 2,

---

[331] Statement of Indonesia, 'Summary Record of First Session of the Committee of the Whole', Diplomatic Conference doc. CCM/CW/SR/1, 18 June 2008.

[332] Article 2, paragraphs 3 (explosive submunition) and 13 (explosive bomblet).

[333] Article 2, paragraphs 2 (cluster munition) and 13 (explosive bomblet). Explosive bomblets, however, are not subject to some of the same limitations as explosive submunitions because the definition of dispenser does not enumerate exclusions comparable to those enumerated in the definition of cluster munition in paragraph 2(a-c). Therefore, if dispensers were developed that had some of the characteristics in sub-paragraphs a through c, the explosive bomblets they carried would be banned by the Convention.

paragraph 14, is a container affixed to an aircraft.[334] Submunitions, by contrast, are dispersed or released by cluster munitions, typically bombs, artillery projectiles, rockets, or missiles.[335] While no other treaty has defined explosive bomblet, in common usage the term had previously meant an air-dropped submunition, and sometimes any kind of submunition.[336] In the context of the Convention on Cluster Munitions, it still refers to a weapon released in the air but has a much narrower meaning.

2.225 The term explosive bomblet appears in Articles 1 and 2. Article 1, paragraph 2 states, 'Paragraph 1 of this Article applies, *mutatis mutandis*, to explosive bomblets that are specifically designed to be dispersed or released from dispensers affixed to aircraft.'[337] It means that the core prohibitions of the Convention apply to explosive bomblets. Given that, as described above, explosive submunitions and explosive bomblets are designed to explode in the same way, they are prone to the same malfunctions and can cause comparable humanitarian harm. They also have similar area effects. Therefore, the Convention bans them both.[338]

2.226 The only other use of explosive bomblet is in Article 2. In that Article, the definitions of dispenser, which is 'designed to disperse or release explosive bomblets', and unexploded bomblet, which is a failed explosive bomblet, also use the term.[339] The failure to mention explosive bomblets in other Articles of the Convention suggests that some obligations, such as

---

[334] Article 2, paragraphs 13 and 14.   [335] Article 2, paragraph 3.

[336] The IMAS definition of bomblet simply states 'see submunition'. IMAS 04.10, 'Glossary of mine action terms, definitions and abbreviations', *op. cit.*, p. 4, definition 3.22. The IMAS definition of submunition is 'any munition that to perform its task, separates from a parent munition [or] . . . mines or munitions that form part of a CBU, artillery shell or missile payload'. *Ibid*, definition 3.255. See also Prosecutor *v.* Martic, Case No. IT-95–11-T, Judgment, paragraph 462 (12 June 2007) ('The M-87 Orkan is a non-guided projectile, the primary military use of which is to target soldiers and armoured vehicles. Each rocket may contain either a cluster warhead with 288 so-called bomblets or 24 anti-tank shells.'); and Prosecutor *v.* Martic, Case No. IT-95–11-A, Appeals Judgment, paragraph 247 (8 October 2008).

[337] Article 1, paragraph 2. For further discussion of this provision, see, *supra*, the commentary on Article 1, paragraph 2.

[338] Ireland argued that explosive bomblets and explosive submunitions should be regulated in the same way when proposing that the Convention apply to explosive bomblets. Statement of Ireland, Committee of the Whole, Diplomatic Conference, 19 May 2008 (Landmine Action notes; copy on file with author).

[339] Article 2, paragraphs 14 (dispenser) and 15 (unexploded bomblet). The definitions of dispenser and explosive bomblet are somewhat circular as they both define themselves with regard to their relationship to the other. Dispensers are containers that release explosive bomblets and explosive bomblets are conventional munitions released by dispensers. Only other parts of the definitions clarify their meaning. The terms cluster munition and explosive submunition have a similar problem.

those related to victim assistance and transparency, may not take them into account. The Commentary discusses the implications of this in greater depth elsewhere.[340]

2.227 Most of the discussions surrounding explosive bomblets occurred late in the Oslo Process.[341] At the Vienna Conference, the GICHD warned that, if left unaddressed, munitions released from a dispenser might become a potential loophole,[342] but States did not take up the issue in detail until the Diplomatic Conference. There they considered an Irish proposal, published first in the Wellington Compendium and resubmitted in Dublin, which defined explosive bomblet as 'a munition, which in order to perform its task is dispersed or separated from a dispenser, affixed to an aerial platform, and is designed to function by detonating an explosive charge prior to, on or after impact'.[343] An accompanying proposal for Article 1 stated that dispensers with explosive bomblets were 'subject to the same provisions as cluster munitions'.[344]

2.228 The final version of the definition of explosive bomblet generally resembled the Irish proposal, but it made a few amendments. To parallel more closely the definition of explosive submunition, it modified munition with 'conventional', replaced 'separated from' with 'released by', and inserted a weight requirement. It also removed the phrase 'affixed to an aerial platform' because dispenser had been defined in another paragraph. Finally it clarified that an explosive bomblet is 'not self-propelled'. Ireland's related proposal for Article 1, paragraph 2 was also modified in the text of the Convention to the language discussed above.

Paragraph 14

'**Dispenser**' means a container that is designed to disperse or release explosive bomblets and which is affixed to an aircraft at the time of dispersal or release;

---

[340] See, *supra*, the commentary on Article 1, paragraph 2 in §§1.85 *et seq.* and on Article 3 in §3.3.

[341] See also, *supra*, the commentary on Article 1 in §§1.82–1.83.

[342] Statement of GICHD, Vienna Conference, 6 December 2007 (Landmine Action notes; copy on file with author).

[343] 'Article 2: Definitions', Wellington Compendium, p. 14; and 'Proposal by Ireland for the Amendment of Article 2', Diplomatic Conference doc. CCM/25, 19 May 2008.

[344] 'Dispensers, affixed to an aerial platform and designed to disperse or release explosive bomblets, are subject to the same provisions as cluster munitions.' 'Proposal by Ireland for the Amendment of Article 1', Diplomatic Conference doc. CCM/15, 19 May 2008.

Commentary

2.229 The definition of dispenser clarifies the nature of an explosive bomblet's delivery system. The first part of the definition explains the form and purpose of a dispenser. It is 'a container that is designed to disperse or release explosive bomblets'.[345] The phrase uses the words 'is designed to' because such a container is still a dispenser even if it fails to function. The second half of the definition describes the key feature that distinguishes a dispenser in the context of the Convention, namely it is 'affixed to an aircraft'. Since it needs only to be affixed 'at the time of dispersal or release', later loss or jettisoning does not change its status.[346]

2.230 While a dispenser disperses or releases smaller munitions like a cluster munition does, it differs in three significant ways. It is considered a container not a munition, it carries explosive bomblets rather than explosive submunitions, and it is an attachment to an aircraft instead of an independent unit.[347]

2.231 Articles 1 and 2 both have references to dispensers. Article 1, paragraph 2 states, 'Paragraph 1 of this Article applies, *mutatis mutandis*, to explosive bomblets that are specifically designed to be dispersed or released from dispensers affixed to aircraft.'[348] The use of the term in that provision reinforces the primary distinction between explosive bomblets and explosive submunitions, i.e., their delivery system, but it is redundant. Explosive bomblets, as defined in Article 2, paragraph 13, are always carried in dispensers, and a dispenser is always affixed to an aircraft.

2.232 The term also appears in the definitions of explosive bomblet in Article 2, which is a munition that is 'dispersed or released by a dispenser', and unexploded bomblet, an explosive bomblet that has been delivered by a dispenser and failed.[349] The word dispenser is unnecessary in the latter definition because an unexploded bomblet is a type of explosive bomblet and all explosive bomblets are dispersed from dispensers; however, its inclusion does not undermine the definition in any way.

---

[345] Article 2, paragraph 14.   [346] *Ibid.*

[347] *Cp.* Article 2, paragraph 14, with Article 2, paragraph 2.

[348] Article 1, paragraph 2. For further discussion of this provision, see, *supra*, the commentary on Article 1, paragraph 2 in §§1.85 *et seq.*

[349] Article 2, paragraphs 13 (explosive bomblet) and 15 (unexploded bomblet). As explained, *supra*, in a footnote to the commentary on the definition of explosive bomblet in §2.226, the definitions of dispenser and explosive bomblet are somewhat circular as they both define themselves with regard to their relationship to the other. Only other parts of the definitions clarify their meaning.

2.233 There were several proposed uses and definitions of the term dispenser during the Oslo Process. In its definition of cluster munition, the Lima Discussion Text referred to a 'container or dispenser' from which explosive submunitions separated. It did not, however, define dispenser so it is unclear if it was intended to mean a unit attached to an aircraft.[350] The term did not appear in the Vienna Discussion Text, but at the Vienna Conference, as noted above, GICHD warned that munitions released from a dispenser might represent a potential loophole.[351]

2.234 The Wellington Compendium included three potential definitions of dispenser for Article 2. France proposed defining carrier-container, a term it had inserted in the definition of cluster munition, as:

a) a conventional munition that may be [an] artillery shell, air bomb, guided or unguided missile or,

b) a dispenser, affixed to an aircraft, which is not designed to dispense direct-fire munitions.[352]

Switzerland supported the French proposal as one option and proposed as a second: 'a dispenser, affixed to an aircraft, which is not designed to dispense multiple sub-munitions in a single act'.[353] In the same document, Ireland did not define dispenser separately but described it as being 'affixed to an aerial platform' in its definition of explosive bomblet.[354]

2.235 At the Diplomatic Conference, States considered these formulations. Spain put forward a new proposal for Article 2, which contained France's

---

[350] Article 2, Lima Discussion Text. At the Lima Conference, the CMC called for a definition of container but did not mention dispensers. Statement of the CMC, Lima Conference, 27 May 2007 (Landmine Action notes; copy on file with author).

[351] Statement of the GICHD, Vienna Conference, 6 December 2007 (Landmine Action notes; copy on file with author); and see, *supra*, the commentary on preparatory discussions for the other definitions in §2.146.

[352] 'Article 2: Definitions', Wellington Compendium, p. 10. France resubmitted its proposal as: 'Proposal by France for Amendment of Article 2', Diplomatic Conference doc. CCM/20, 19 May 2008. States had lengthy debates about the issue of direct-fire munitions because several States wanted to exclude these munitions from the definition of cluster munition. As a result, France excluded them from the definition of dispenser in its proposal. The final Convention on Cluster Munitions, however, covers direct-fire munitions.

[353] 'Article 2: Definitions', Wellington Compendium, p. 11. Switzerland resubmitted its proposal as: 'Proposal by Switzerland for the Amendment of Article 2', Diplomatic Conference doc. CCM/21, 19 May 2008.

[354] 'Article 2: Definitions', Wellington Compendium, p. 14. Ireland resubmitted its proposal as: 'Proposal by Ireland for the Amendment of Article 2', Diplomatic Conference doc. CCM/25, 19 May 2008.

definition of dispenser.[355] Ireland resubmitted its Article 2 proposal and supplemented it with a proposal for Article 1, paragraph 2 that described but did not officially define the term:

Dispensers, affixed to an aerial platform and designed to disperse or release explosive bomblets, are subject to the same provisions as cluster munitions.[356]

2.236 Ultimately, the Convention adopted a definition of dispenser that is separate from that of cluster munition. It highlights the shared characteristic of these proposals (it is 'affixed to an aircraft') while drawing on the Irish idea that it must be 'designed to disperse or release explosive bomblets'. It also clarified that a dispenser is a container and need only be affixed 'at the time of dispersal or release'. The Convention changed the focus of Article 1, paragraph 2 to explosive bomblets because it is they, not the inert dispenser, which pose a threat to civilians. As mentioned above, however, it retained a mention of dispenser in that provision.[357]

Paragraph 15

'**Unexploded bomblet**' means an explosive bomblet that has been dispersed, released or otherwise separated from a dispenser and has failed to explode as intended.

Commentary

2.237 As discussed above,[358] a definition of explosive bomblets was added to Article 2 at a late stage of the negotiations. Explosive bomblets differ from explosive submunitions in that they are delivered directly from a dispenser attached to an aircraft as opposed to being dispersed or released from a bomb, shell, rocket, or missile that has been dropped or fired. Despite the different mode of delivery, explosive bomblets raise the same concerns as explosive submunitions from a technical and humanitarian point of view.

---

[355] 'Proposal by Spain for the Amendment of Article 2', Diplomatic Conference doc. CCM/67, 19 May 2008. A later Spanish proposal did not include this definition because it omitted the term carrier-container, under which dispenser was defined. See 'Proposal by Spain for the Amendment of Article 2', Diplomatic Conference doc. CCM/76, 27 May 2008.

[356] 'Proposal by Ireland for the amendment of Article 2', Diplomatic Conference doc. CCM/25, 19 May 2008; and 'Proposal by Ireland for the Amendment of Article 1', Diplomatic Conference doc. CCM/15, 19 May 2008.

[357] Article 1, paragraph 2. See also, *supra*, the commentary on Article 2, paragraph 14 in §2.231.   [358] See, *supra*, the commentary on Article 2, paragraph 13 in §§2.227–2.228.

2.238 The concept of unexploded bomblet was added to Article 2 to ensure that the Convention applied to explosive bomblets when they fail to explode as intended and thus become a danger to those living in conflict-affected areas. Like failed cluster munitions, abandoned cluster munitions, and unexploded submunitions, unexploded bomblets are a constituent element of cluster munition remnants and are therefore covered by the clearance obligations of Article 4. They are also covered by clearance-related provisions in Articles 6 and 7.[359]

2.239 The definition of unexploded bomblet has direct links to several other Article 2 definitions, namely unexploded submunition, explosive bomblet, and dispenser. As a result, it shares a number of terms and elements and has few new or specific features. For example, like an unexploded submunition, an unexploded bomblet must have 'failed to explode as intended'.[360] In addition, it must meet the criteria for an explosive bomblet that has 'separated from a dispenser'.[361]

2.240 Unexploded bomblets were not specifically discussed in the early stages of the Convention's development. There was no definition of the term in the Lima Discussion Text, the Vienna Discussion Text, or the Draft Cluster Munitions Convention. Later in the Oslo Process, it was generally assumed that these bomblets would be covered by the definitions of explosive submunition and unexploded submunition due to the fact that several proposals for the definition of a cluster munition included the phrase carrier/container,[362] which would have covered direct dispensing systems. As negotiations advanced on the definition of cluster munition and the concept of carrier/container fell aside, however, it became clear that explosive bomblets and unexploded bomblets would need distinct definitions.[363]

2.241 A definition for unexploded explosive bomblet was first proposed by Ireland in its submission to the Wellington Compendium. It suggested the following wording:

'Unexploded explosive bomblet' means an explosive bomblet which has been released dispersed or otherwise separated from a dispenser, affixed to an aerial platform, and has failed to explode as intended.[364]

---

[359] See, e.g., Article 4; Article 6, paragraphs 4 and 6; and Article 7, paragraph 1(c), (h), and (i).
[360] Article 2, paragraphs 5 and 15.   [361] Article 2, paragraphs 13–15.
[362] See, e.g., 'Proposal by France for the amendment of Article 2', Diplomatic Conference doc. CCM/20, 19 May 2008; 'Proposal by Switzerland for the amendment of Article 2', Diplomatic Conference doc. CCM/21, 19 May 2008; 'Proposal by the United Kingdom for the amendment of Article 2', Diplomatic Conference doc. CCM/23, 19 May 2008; and 'Proposal by Spain for the amendment of Article 2', Diplomatic Conference doc. CCM/67, 19 May 2008.
[363] The term dispenser would also need to be defined.
[364] 'Article 2: Definitions', Wellington Compendium, p. 14.

Ireland formally resubmitted the proposal at the Diplomatic Conference.

2.242 The main changes to the Irish definition of unexploded bomblet in Dublin were the deletion of the phrase 'affixed to an aerial platform' and the removal of 'explosive' from the definition's heading. The phrase 'affixed to an aerial platform' was deemed unnecessary in light of the inclusion of a definition for 'dispenser'. The removal of 'explosive' from the heading was mainly editorial in light of the definition's direct link to the definition of 'explosive bomblet'. With these changes the definition was included in the President's Text and subsequently adopted.

Article 3. Storage and stockpile destruction

Declan Smyth

Article 3—Storage and stockpile destruction

1. Each State Party shall, in accordance with national regulations, separate all cluster munitions under its jurisdiction and control from munitions retained for operational use and mark them for the purpose of destruction.

2. Each State Party undertakes to destroy or ensure the destruction of all cluster munitions referred to in paragraph 1 of this Article as soon as possible but not later than eight years after the entry into force of this Convention for that State Party. Each State Party undertakes to ensure that destruction methods comply with applicable international standards for protecting public health and the environment.

3. If a State Party believes that it will be unable to destroy or ensure the destruction of all cluster munitions referred to in paragraph 1 of this Article within eight years of entry into force of this Convention for that State Party it may submit a request to a Meeting of States Parties or a Review Conference for an extension of the deadline for completing the destruction of such cluster munitions by a period of up to four years. A State Party may, in exceptional circumstances, request additional extensions of up to four years. The requested extensions shall not exceed the number of years strictly necessary for that State Party to complete its obligations under paragraph 2 of this Article.

4. Each request for an extension shall set out:

(a) The duration of the proposed extension;

(b) A detailed explanation of the proposed extension, including the financial and technical means available to or required by the State Party for the destruction of all cluster munitions referred to in paragraph 1 of this Article and, where applicable, the exceptional circumstances justifying it;

(c) A plan for how and when stockpile destruction will be completed;

(d) The quantity and type of cluster munitions and explosive submunitions held at the entry into force of this Convention for that State Party and any additional cluster munitions or explosive submunitions discovered after such entry into force;

(e) The quantity and type of cluster munitions and explosive submunitions destroyed during the period referred to in paragraph 2 of this Article; and

(f) The quantity and type of cluster munitions and explosive submunitions remaining to be destroyed during the proposed extension and the annual destruction rate expected to be achieved.

5. The Meeting of States Parties or the Review Conference shall, taking into consideration the factors referred to in paragraph 4 of this Article, assess the request and decide by a majority of votes of States Parties present and voting whether to grant the request for an extension. The States Parties may decide to grant a shorter extension than that requested and may propose benchmarks for the extension, as appropriate. A request for an extension shall be submitted a minimum of nine months prior to the Meeting of States Parties or the Review Conference at which it is to be considered.

6. Notwithstanding the provisions of Article 1 of this Convention, the retention or acquisition of a limited number of cluster munitions and explosive submunitions for the development of and training in cluster munition and explosive submunition detection, clearance or destruction techniques, or for the development of cluster munition counter-measures, is permitted. The amount of explosive submunitions retained or acquired shall not exceed the minimum number absolutely necessary for these purposes.

7. Notwithstanding the provisions of Article 1 of this Convention, the transfer of cluster munitions to another State Party for the purpose of destruction, as well as for the purposes described in paragraph 6 of this Article, is permitted.

8. States Parties retaining, acquiring or transferring cluster munitions or explosive submunitions for the purposes described in paragraphs 6 and 7 of this Article shall submit a detailed report on the planned and actual use of these cluster munitions and explosive submunitions and their type, quantity and lot numbers. If cluster munitions or explosive submunitions are transferred to another State Party for these purposes, the report shall include reference to the receiving party. Such a report shall be prepared for each year during which a State Party retained, acquired or transferred cluster munitions or explosive submunitions and shall be submitted to the Secretary-General of the United Nations no later than 30 April of the following year.

Overview of the Article

3.1 At the time of the negotiations a very large group of States was believed to possess cluster munitions,[1] which made the inclusion of a disarmament element

---

[1] In April 2007, Human Rights Watch listed the following 75 States as countries that stockpile cluster munitions: Algeria, Angola, Argentina, Austria, Azerbaijan, Bahrain, Belarus, Belgium, Bosnia and Herzegovina, Brazil, Bulgaria, Canada, Chile, China, Croatia, Cuba, Czech Republic, Denmark, Egypt, Eritrea, Ethiopia, Finland, France, Georgia, Germany, Greece, Guinea, Guinea Bissau, Honduras, Hungary, India, Indonesia, Iran, Iraq, Israel, Italy, Japan, Jordan, Kazakhstan, Kuwait, Libya, Moldova, Mongolia, Morocco, Netherlands, Nigeria, Norway, North Korea, Oman, Pakistan, Poland, Portugal, Republic of Korea, Romania, Russia, Saudi Arabia, Serbia, Singapore, Slovakia, South Africa, Spain, Sudan, Sweden, Switzerland, Syria, Thailand, Turkey, Turkmenistan, Ukraine, United Arab Emirates, United Kingdom, United States of America, Uzbekistan, Yemen and Zimbabwe (Human Rights Watch, 'At a Glance: Global Overview of Cluster Munition Policy and Practice', at: <http://www.landmineaction.org/resources/HRW%20 Dirty%20Dozen%20Mega%20Chart.pdf> (accessed 29 October 2009)). A June 2009 publication by Human Rights Watch and Landmine Action lists a further 10 States as currently or formerly stockpiling cluster munitions: Australia, Colombia, Estonia, Mali, Montenegro, Peru, Qatar, Slovenia, Sri Lanka, and Uganda (Human Rights Watch and Landmine Action, *Banning Cluster Munitions: Government Policy and Practice*, Mines Action Canada, Ottawa, May 2009 (hereinafter, *Banning Cluster Munitions*)). The same publication, however, noted that: 'Countries that are no longer thought to have stockpiles include [Convention] signatories Australia, Honduras, Mali, and

in the Convention on Cluster Munitions inevitable. This disarmament element consists of the general obligation imposed by Article 1, paragraph 1 'never under any circumstances to...acquire, stockpile (or) retain...cluster munitions' together with the duty under Article 3 to destroy stockpiles. These provisions support the Convention's core obligation 'never under any circumstances to...use cluster munitions' by ensuring that cluster munitions will not be available for use in the future. A disarmament element was also regarded as essential to prevent the future proliferation of cluster munitions to States not party to the Convention. It reflects similar obligations imposed by the *1993 Chemical Weapons Convention*[2] and the *1997 Anti-Personnel Mine Ban Convention*.[3]

3.2 Accordingly the fourth preambular paragraph of the Convention expresses deep concern 'at the dangers presented by the large national stockpiles of cluster munitions retained for operational use' and the determination of States Parties 'to ensure their rapid destruction'. This objective is to be met by Article 3, which regulates storage and destruction of cluster munition stocks.[4] It requires a State Party to separate all cluster munitions under its jurisdiction and control from stocks of other munitions. A State Party may retain the minimum number of cluster munitions or explosive submunitions absolutely necessary for the purposes of developing techniques for detection, clearance and destruction, or counter-measures. All other stocks must be marked for destruction and, as soon as possible but not later than eight years after entry into force for the State Party concerned, must be destroyed, either by the State Party itself or on its behalf in another State Party. If unable to meet this deadline a State Party may seek an extension of up to four years, and, in exceptional circumstances, an extension may be renewed.

3.3 Perhaps surprisingly, Article 3 does not directly address stocks of 'explosive bomblets'.[5] This is partly explained by the fact that the Dublin Diplomatic

Spain, and non-signatories Argentina and Iraq. Spain completed its stockpile destruction program in March 2009.'

<http://www.stopclustermunitions.org/wp/wp-content/uploads/2009/06/how-big-is-the-problem-120609.pdf>.

[2] The formal title of this treaty is the Convention on the Prohibition of the Development, Production, Stockpiling and Use of Chemical Weapons and on their Destruction.

[3] The formal title of this treaty is the Convention on the Prohibition of the Use, Stockpiling, Production and Transfer of Anti-Personnel Mines and on Their Destruction.

[4] Article 4 on the other hand regulates the clearance and destruction of cluster munition remnants, i.e. those that have been used or abandoned.

[5] The nature and effect of 'explosive bomblets', which are prohibited by Article 1(2) of the Convention, are very similar to those of explosive submunitions but specific provision is made for them because, as they are released or dispersed from a dispenser fixed to an aircraft rather than from another munition, they do not come within the Convention's definition of a cluster munition. See, *supra*, §§1.4, and 1.82 *et seq.*

Conference was able to agree only at the very end of its work that explosive bomblets should be addressed by the Convention at all. The provisions of the Convention concerning explosive bomblets are intended to pre-empt a potentially very large problem that might have arisen in the future as a consequence of prohibiting cluster munitions and those provisions are therefore limited to prohibitions on use, development, production, acquisition, stockpiling, retention, and transfer. However, insofar as any existing stocks of explosive bomblets are concerned, as the Convention prohibits their retention and transfer, a State Party must necessarily destroy whatever stocks it possesses in order to avoid violating these obligations. As these obligations not to retain or transfer explosive bomblets are not expressly qualified by Article 3 in the way that similar obligations concerning cluster munitions are (i.e. destroy as soon as possible but no later than eight years following adherence to the Convention), as of writing it appears quite possible that the Meeting of States Parties may be asked to consider whether also to interpret the rules set out in Article 3 as applying also to the destruction of explosive bomblets.

Preparatory discussions

3.4 Stockpile destruction was specifically identified in the February 2007 Oslo Declaration as a key element of the legally binding instrument that States committed themselves to conclude by 2008. Each of the draft Convention texts beginning with the Lima Discussion Text[6] contained a provision on destruction of cluster munition stockpiles. Although the *1993 Chemical Weapons Convention* and *1997 Anti-Personnel Mine Ban Convention* served as templates for the Convention on Cluster Munitions, there are nevertheless significant differences in the respective obligations concerning destruction of stockpiles.

3.5 Several important issues arose during the course of the negotiation of Article 3, in particular the time period in which the process of destruction of stocks must be completed and, given the considerable technical and logistical challenges of ensuring safe destruction of cluster munitions, whether there should be provision for the extension of this period if necessary. A number of delegations proposed retaining some stocks of cluster munitions or explosive submunitions for the purposes of developing clearance and disposal capabilities and of training personnel in these. The scope of application of Article 3

---

[6] Chair's discussion text on a legally binding international instrument that will prohibit the use, production, transfer and stockpiling of cluster munitions that cause unacceptable harm to civilians, Lima, 23–25 May 2007. The Lima Discussion Text is included in Annex 3 to this Commentary.

was also an important issue in the discussions. These matters were ultimately resolved only at the conclusion of negotiations at the Diplomatic Conference.

3.6 Article 3 of the Lima Discussion Text[7] required separation of cluster munitions from stocks of other munitions and their storage in separate stockpiles for the purpose of destruction (no similar obligation was imposed by the *1993 Chemical Weapons Convention* or the *1997 Anti-Personnel Mine Ban Convention*). The State Party would be required to 'destroy or ensure destruction' of these stocks 'as soon as possible but not later than six years after entry into force' of the Convention with respect to that State Party. The Lima text also made provision entitling a State Party unable to meet the deadline to request a meeting of States Parties or a Review Conference to agree to extend it for a period of up to 10 years, and to request a renewal of such an extension. No provision was made for the retention of stocks for training and development purposes.

3.7 A small number of changes were made to the text for the Vienna Conference. The Vienna Discussion Text[8] included a requirement that 'destruction methods comply with applicable international standards for protecting public health and the environment'.[9] Importantly, it also made provision permitting the transfer of cluster munitions for the purposes of destruction, notwithstanding the general prohibition on transfer set out at Article 1(1) of the Convention.[10] This reflected the likelihood that a small number of States or private concerns will develop a comparative advantage in the destruction of stocks and that, for some States Parties, the expense and technical difficulty of developing their own programmes may in fact serve to delay prompt destruction. The Vienna text also removed the provision in the Lima Discussion Text that enabled extensions of the deadline to be renewed.

3.8 Only minor drafting changes were made to the text of Article 3 for the February 2008 Wellington Conference.[11] No changes were made to any part of the Draft Cluster Munitions Convention[12] at the Wellington Conference, which forwarded it to the Diplomatic Conference as the negotiating text.

---

[7] Chair's discussion text on a legally binding international instrument that will prohibit the use, production, transfer and stockpiling of cluster munitions that cause unacceptable harm to civilians, Lima, 23–25 May 2007.   [8] Vienna Discussion Text of 14 November 2007.

[9] Article 3, paragraph 2, Vienna Discussion Text.

[10] Article 3, paragraph 6, Vienna Discussion Text.

[11] Principally the requirement in paragraph 1 that each State Party 'undertakes to separate cluster munitions from stocks for potential use' was changed to read '[e]ach State Party undertakes to remove all cluster munitions from stockpiles of munitions retained for operational use'. See, *supra*, §§0.46–0.54 for details of the Wellington Conference.

[12] The text of the Draft Cluster Munitions Convention is contained in Annex 5 to this Commentary.

Accordingly, insofar as Article 3 was concerned, in almost all respects the draft text of the Convention on which negotiations began in Dublin was the same as that discussed in Vienna.

Negotiations

3.9 At the Diplomatic Conference several formal proposals for the amendment of Article 3 were made. A group of States led by Australia proposed the retention of a 'limited number' of cluster munitions for the purposes of developing techniques for detection, clearance, and destruction, and for training in these techniques. They also proposed permitting transfer of cluster munitions for these purposes.[13] Both the United Kingdom (UK)[14] and Peru[15] formally proposed that the deadline for destruction of cluster munitions be increased from six years to ten.

3.10 Article 3 was discussed during the first meeting of the Committee of the Whole on 19 May 2008. Canada, Slovakia, and the UK expressed concern that the formulation of draft Article 3, paragraph 1 suggested that separate facilities should be built or maintained for cluster munitions removed from stocks and that this would be both expensive and unnecessary. Slovakia submitted a formal proposal for the amendment of paragraph 1 that would simply require a State Party 'to clearly designate all cluster munitions in its stockpiles for the purposes of destruction'.[16] The timeframe within which destruction of stocks should be completed and the question of retention of stocks for training purposes remained contentious.[17]

3.11 These issues were ultimately resolved in the subsequent informal consultations undertaken by Ambassador Steffen Kongstad of Norway, who acted as Friend of the President on Article 3. The text that emerged from

---

[13] 'Proposal by Australia, Denmark, Finland, France, Germany, Italy, Japan, Slovakia, Sweden, Switzerland and the United Kingdom for the amendment of Article 3', Diplomatic Conference doc. CCM/28, 19 May 2008.

[14] 'Proposal by the United Kingdom for the amendment of Article 3', Diplomatic Conference doc. CCM/29, 19 May 2008.

[15] 'Proposal by Peru for the amendment of Article 3', Diplomatic Conference doc. CCM/30, 19 May 2008.

[16] 'Proposal by Slovakia for the amendment of Article 3', Diplomatic Conference doc. CCM/65, 19 May 2008

[17] For instance, the Cluster Munition Coalition (CMC) opposed proposals for retention of stocks, arguing that detection and clearance techniques could be developed and practised without the need for 'live' munitions. They also argued that if such retention were to be permitted it should be accompanied by stringent reporting requirements.

these efforts and that was subsequently adopted by the Conference provided a deadline of eight years from the time of entry into force for each State Party within which it must complete destruction of its stocks. (The *1997 Anti-Personnel Mine Ban Convention* requires destruction within four years of entry into force of the Convention for the State Party concerned[18] while the *1993 Chemical Weapons Convention* requires destruction within 10 years of general entry into force.[19])

3.12 The final text of Article 3 also enables the Meeting of States Parties or a Review Conference to agree to extensions of the eight-year deadline in individual cases by up to four years upon request, and to further extensions 'in exceptional circumstances' of up to four more years. No similar provision is made in the *1997 Anti-Personnel Mine Ban Convention* although one extension is permitted under the terms of the *1993 Chemical Weapons Convention.*[20]

3.13 The Diplomatic Conference added a number of additional details to be submitted in support of a request for an extension.[21] The final text also provided for the retention of 'a limited number of cluster munitions and explosive submunitions for the development of and training in cluster munition and explosive submunition detection, clearance or destruction techniques, or for the development of cluster munition counter-measures'.[22] The quantity of explosive submunitions concerned is not to exceed 'the minimum number absolutely necessary for these purposes'.[23] Notwithstanding the general prohibition on transfers set out in Article 1, paragraph 1(b), transfers of cluster munitions are permitted for the purposes of destruction itself and for developing and practising detection, clearance, and destruction techniques, and counter-measures. Such transfers are subject to detailed reporting requirements.[24]

Relationship to other Articles of the Convention

3.14 It was widely acknowledged from the outset of the Oslo Process that for some States the technical difficulty and expense of ensuring the destruction of cluster munition stocks could serve to delay or prevent adherence to the Convention and that the provision of assistance would therefore be an

---

[18] Article 4, *1997 Anti-Personnel Mine Ban Convention*.
[19] Article IV, paragraph 6, *1993 Chemical Weapons Convention* and Part IV (A) of the Verification Annex, §17.
[20] *1993 Chemical Weapons Convention*, Part IV (A) of the Verification Annex, §26.
[21] Article 3, paragraph 4(a)–(f).   [22] Article 3, paragraph 6.   [23] *Ibid.*
[24] Article 3, paragraph 8.

important element in achieving the Convention's objectives. Indeed the Oslo Declaration committed participating States to conclude a legally binding international instrument that, *inter alia*, established 'a framework for cooperation and assistance that ensures…destruction of stockpiles of prohibited cluster munitions'. Article 6, paragraph 5 of the Convention therefore requires that '[e]ach State Party in a position to do so shall provide assistance for the destruction of stockpiled cluster munitions…'[25]

3.15 In the interests of transparency, Article 7 of the Convention requires each State Party to report certain information to the Secretary-General of the United Nations within 180 days of entry into force of the Convention, and annually thereafter. This information is circulated by the Secretary-General to all States Parties. It includes information on the total of all cluster munitions, including explosive submunitions, under the jurisdiction and control of a State Party, to include a breakdown of their type, quantity, and, if possible, lot numbers;[26] the status and progress of programmes for the destruction of cluster munitions, including details of the methods to be used; the location of destruction sites and the safety and environmental standards to be observed;[27] on the types and quantities of cluster munitions and explosive submunitions actually destroyed;[28] and on any stockpiles discovered after reported completion of the destruction programme.[29]

3.16 There is a complex relationship between Articles 1, 3, and 21. Pursuant to Article 1 a State Party undertakes never under any circumstances, *inter alia*, to stockpile or retain cluster munitions. Article 3 requires it to destroy or ensure destruction of cluster munitions under its 'jurisdiction and control' within a limited timeframe. Whether therefore Article 3 applies to stockpiles of cluster munitions owned or possessed by a State not party to the Convention but located on the territory of a State Party will depend on whether these munitions are understood to be under the latter's jurisdiction and control. The stockpiling of cluster munitions by a State not party to the Convention on the territory of a State Party is most likely to arise in the context of military cooperation or operations between such States, a matter regulated by Article 21. Paragraph 2 of that Article requires a State Party engaged in military cooperation and operations with States not party, *inter alia*, to 'promote the norms' established by the Convention and to 'make its best efforts to discourage States not party to (the) Convention from using cluster munitions'.

---

[25] See further, *infra*, the commentary on this provision.
[26] Article 7, paragraph 1(b).   [27] Article 7, paragraph 1(e).
[28] Article 7, paragraph 1(f).   [29] Article 7, paragraph 1(g).

3.17 Paragraph 3 of Article 21 provides that:

Notwithstanding the provisions of Article 1 ... and in accordance with international law, States Parties, their military personnel or nationals, may engage in military cooperation and operations with States not party to this Convention that might engage in activities prohibited to a State Party.

3.18 Paragraph 4 of Article 21 provides that the preceding paragraph shall not be interpreted as authorizing a State Party, *inter alia*, to 'itself stockpile ... cluster munitions'.[30] Whether this provision places the stockpiling of cluster munitions by a State not party to the Convention on the territory of a State Party, done within the framework of military cooperation or operations, beyond the scope of Article 1, paragraph 1(c), which prohibits States Parties from assisting in stockpiling, is considered elsewhere.[31] It is, however, difficult to reconcile a State Party's continued acquiescence in the stockpiling of cluster munitions on its territory by a State not party, even if they remain under the jurisdiction and control of the latter, with the former's obligation under Article 21, paragraph 2, to make its best efforts to discourage the latter from using cluster munitions.

Paragraph 1

> Each State Party shall, in accordance with national regulations, separate all cluster munitions under its jurisdiction and control from munitions retained for operational use and mark them for the purpose of destruction.

3.19 The obligations imposed on a State Party by Article 3 apply to 'all cluster munitions under its jurisdiction and control'.[32] Paragraph 1 requires separation of cluster munitions under the 'jurisdiction and control' of a State Party from munitions retained for operational purposes and their marking for destruction. Paragraph 2 of Article 3 (which sets out a State's Parties obligations with respect to the destruction of cluster munitions) addresses 'cluster munitions referred to in paragraph 1', i.e. to cluster munitions under the jurisdiction and control of the State Party. Paragraph 3 likewise is concerned with 'cluster munitions referred to in paragraph 1'.

3.20 The formulation 'jurisdiction and control' differs from that employed by the corresponding provisions of the *1993 Chemical Weapons Convention* ('all chemical weapons owned or possessed by a State Party, or that are located

---

[30] Article 21, paragraph 4 (b).
[31] See, *infra*, the commentary on Article 21, paragraph 3, esp. §§21.72 *et seq.*
[32] Article 3, paragraph 1.

in any place under its jurisdiction or control')³³ and the *1997 Anti-Personnel Mine Ban Convention* ('all stockpiled anti-personnel mines it owns or possesses, or that are under its jurisdiction or control').³⁴ The criteria of ownership and possession were not cited in any of the drafts of Article 3 elaborated during the Oslo Process. The most striking difference between Article 3 and its counterparts in the *Chemical Weapons* and *Anti-Personnel Mine Ban Conventions* (and indeed Article 4 of the Convention on Cluster Munitions itself) is that the former refers to 'jurisdiction *and* control' while the others use the formulation 'jurisdiction *or* control'. In fact the form of words adopted for Article 3 in the Convention is undoubtedly the result of a clerical error that occurred during the preparation of a composite text towards the end of the Diplomatic Conference.³⁵ However, as will be seen below, it is submitted that the formulation does not substantially affect the scope of the obligation to destroy cluster munition stocks.

3.21 It must first be understood what is meant by the formulation '*jurisdiction and control*' in order to determine what cluster munitions fall within the scope of Article 3 and, in particular, whether Article 3 applies to cluster munitions belonging to a State not party to the Convention that are stored or stockpiled on the territory of a State Party.³⁶ It is important also to consider the application of Article 3 to a State Party's own cluster munitions that

---

³³ Article IV, paragraph 1 of the *1993 Chemical Weapons Convention*.

³⁴ Article 4 of the *1997 Anti-Personnel Mine Ban Convention*.

³⁵ The Lima and Vienna Discussion Texts and the Draft Cluster Munitions Convention referred to cluster munitions under the 'jurisdiction *or* control' of States Parties. This term was also used in successive informal discussion texts developed by the Friend of the President for Article 3 on 21, 22, and 25 May 2008. Following agreement within the Committee of the Whole the text was then revised by the Conference Secretariat for the purposes of ensuring consistent use of terminology throughout the whole draft Convention text. This revised text was then reissued as Presidency Text CCM/PT/13 of 26 May for transmission to the Plenary. The formulation 'jurisdiction *and* control' first appears here, albeit in strikethrough in paragraph 2 only. It was intended to move the phrase to paragraph 1 in order to clarify that the cluster munitions addressed by that paragraph are the same cluster munitions addressed by the rest of the Article, i.e. that the cluster munitions to be removed from munitions retained for operational use are the same as those to be destroyed. However, due to a clerical error, the phrase was not inserted as intended in paragraph 1. A correction was then issued but this used the phrase 'jurisdiction *or* control' (CCM/PT/13 Corr. (27 May 2008)). This is turn was objected to by a number of delegations who insisted that the phrase agreed had been 'jurisdiction *and* control'. The latter phrase was then restored to the text in CCM/PT/15 (the draft Convention text put to the Conference on 28 May) and the Convention text as adopted (CCM 77). The French and Spanish texts of Conference doc. CCM/77 also use the phrase 'jurisdiction *and* control'.

³⁶ A complicating factor here is that the terms *jurisdiction* and *control* are not used in a consistent manner throughout the Convention text. Article 3 applies to 'all cluster munitions under [the] jurisdiction and control' of a State Party. Article 4 concerns 'areas' under its 'jurisdiction or control'. Article 9 is directed to 'persons or . . . territory under its jurisdiction or control.'

may be stored or stockpiled outside its territory. The question of whether a State Party is prohibited under the Convention from permitting a State not party to stockpile cluster munitions on its territory (as distinct from ensuring their destruction if they are so stockpiled) is considered in the commentary on Articles 1 and 21.

The concepts of jurisdiction and control

3.22 Although not defined by the Convention, *jurisdiction* is a widely understood concept in international law. It is an essential incident of a State's sovereignty, enabling the lawful exercise of its authority and power by means of executive, legislative, and judicial action. Sovereignty and jurisdiction are not co-extensive but, as the Permanent Court of Justice noted in the *Lotus* case, a State's 'title to exercise jurisdiction rests in its sovereignty'.[37] Jurisdiction is primarily territorial in nature (i.e. a State exercises jurisdiction throughout its sovereign territory) but the generally recognized principles of international law also permit States to exercise jurisdiction extraterritorially in certain circumstances.[38] However, in order to exercise its jurisdiction a State must first assert its jurisdiction. As Oppenheim notes, international law 'determines the permissible limits of a state's jurisdiction in the various forms it may take, while [the internal law of the State] prescribes the extent to which, and the manner in which, the state in fact asserts its jurisdiction'.[39]

3.23 There are in international law several instances of derogation from the jurisdiction of a State on its own territory, such as sovereign and diplomatic immunities.[40] There are also circumstances in which derogation from the territorial jurisdiction of a State is granted by way of concession or waiver,

---

[37] PCIJ Reports, Series A, No. 10, p. 15.

[38] For instance, under the *flag State principle* a State exercises jurisdiction on ships and aircraft registered in that State. The *nationality principle* allows a State to exercise its jurisdiction over certain offences committed abroad by its own nationals, such as murder. Other bases for the exercise of jurisdiction extraterritorially include the *passive personality*, *security* and *universality principles*. For a thorough discussion of jurisdiction in international law generally see Jennings, R. and Watts, R. (eds.), *Oppenheim's International Law*, Ninth Edition, Vol. 1, Part 1 (Oxford: Oxford University Press, 2008), pp. 456 *et seq.*; Brownlie, I., *Principles of Public International Law*, Sixth Edition (Oxford: Oxford University Press, 2003), pp. 297 *et seq.*; and Shaw, M. N., *International Law*, Third Edition (Cambridge: Cambridge University Press, 1994), pp. 393 *et seq.*

[39] Jennings, R. and Watts, R. (eds.), *Oppenheim's International Law*, Ninth Edition, Vol. 1, Part 1, *op. cit.*, pp. 456–457.

[40] e.g., the *1961 Vienna Convention on Diplomatic Relations* provides that a diplomatic agent of the sending State shall enjoy immunity from the criminal jurisdiction of the receiving State, as well as from its civil jurisdiction with certain exceptions. Article 31, paragraph 1, 1961 *Vienna Convention on Diplomatic Relations*.

such as in the case of the armed forces of one State stationed on the territory of another in time of peace. While the law regulating the exercise of jurisdiction by sending and receiving States in respect of a visiting force is subject to some uncertainty, Brownlie cites as the 'most satisfactory in principle' an approach based on the rationale of the judgment in the *Schooner Exchange* case.[41] This establishes in favour of the visiting force 'an implied waiver by the receiving state of the exercise of any powers which would seriously affect the integrity and efficiency of the force'.[42] Oppenheim notes that for visiting forces the consent of the State 'to receive the force on its territory implies the grant of at least sufficient immunity from local jurisdiction as not to interfere with the effective performance by the force of the functions in respect of which the consent was given'.[43]

3.24 Whether regarded as a waiver of local jurisdiction or immunity from it, absent variation by special agreement[44] these interpretations suggest that the sending State will be entitled to exercise jurisdiction over the visiting force sufficient to ensure its integrity and effectiveness, including over any munitions it may stockpile on the territory of the receiving State. This presumption of immunity from local jurisdiction is supported by the *2004 UN Convention on Jurisdictional Immunities of States and Their Property*, which protects certain specific categories of property of a State from the jurisdiction of the courts of another State, including 'property of a military character or used or intended for use for military purposes'.[45]

3.25 The term *control* is not defined by the Convention. There are 20 separate occurrences of it in the text of the Convention on Cluster Munitions and it is not used in a consistent manner. Unlike the term 'jurisdiction' however, 'control' has no broadly understood, single meaning in international law and

---

[41] The Schooner Exchange *v.* McFadden (1812) 7 *Cranch* 116.

[42] See Brownlie, I., *Principles of Public International Law*, *op. cit.*, p. 359.

[43] Jennings, R. and Watts, R. (eds.), *Oppenheim's International Law*, Ninth Edition, *op. cit.*, p. 1158.

[44] The legal status of visiting forces is nowadays often set down by treaty, at least in part. These treaties tend to regulate in particular the conditions for the exercise of criminal jurisdiction over visiting forces by the sending and receiving States. For instance, the *1951 NATO Status of Forces Agreement (SOFA)* regulates the exercise of criminal, disciplinary, and civil jurisdiction by sending and receiving States with respect to persons, primarily members of the sending State force, members of its civilian component, and persons subject to the military law of the sending State. It does not regulate jurisdiction over property. The preamble to the *SOFA* provides that the conditions under which the forces of one State serve in the territory of the other, 'in so far as such conditions are not laid down by the present Agreement, will continue to be the subject of separate arrangements between the Parties concerned...' Accordingly, whether the receiving State exercises jurisdiction over the sending State's property, including munitions, would seem to depend on the existence of such separate arrangements, if any.   [45] Articles 19 and 21, paragraph 1(b).

its interpretation will depend to a large extent on the context in which it is used. For instance 'control of territory' clearly entails physical control of an area which may or may not be within the territorial jurisdiction of the State concerned. In contrast, when used in the context of persons or property the term 'control' may have a different meaning again. 'Control of persons' may relate to the exercise of authority or power over them. 'Control over property' may mean possession, legal title, use, or the exercise of power. In each case it may also mean jurisdiction itself.[46]

Scope of application of Article 3

3.26 Article 3 applies to the cluster munitions under the 'jurisdiction and control' of a State Party. A State Party's own cluster munitions, whether stockpiled on its territory or offshore on board its naval vessels, will be under its jurisdiction and control and will therefore come within the terms of Article 3. In addition, where, as part of the deployment abroad of a visiting force, a State Party has stockpiled cluster munitions on the territory of another State, absent a special arrangement to the contrary between them, as noted above[47] these munitions will enjoy a presumption of immunity from the jurisdiction of the receiving State and, as they will therefore fall within the jurisdiction and control of the sending State Party, they will be subject to the destruction obligations imposed on that State Party by Article 3. Conversely, Article 3 will not apply to cluster munitions stockpiled on the territory of a State Party that remain under the jurisdiction and control of a State not party to the Convention. As indicated above,[48] however, whether a State Party is entitled to permit such stockpiling on its territory is addressed by Articles 1 and 21.

3.27 It seems very unlikely that a State will exercise either jurisdiction or control over cluster munitions, but not both. Such a situation might be considered to arise were one State to make cluster munitions available for use by

---

[46] For instance, the International Court of Justice, in its Advisory Opinion on the Legal Consequences of the Construction of a Wall in the Occupied Palestinian Territory (24 July 2004), endorsed the view that Israel's *control* of the Occupied Palestinian Territories established its 'effective jurisdiction' over them for the purposes of the Covenant on Civil and Political Rights and engaged Israel's responsibility under that instrument in respect of acts committed there by it or on its behalf (§110). The UN Human Rights Committee has interpreted the term 'a person... subject to (the) jurisdiction' of a State Party (Article 2, paragraph 1 of the Covenant on Civil and Political Rights) as meaning any person 'within the power or effective control of that State Party, even if not situated within the territory of that State Party' (*General Comment No. 31—The Nature of the General Legal Obligation Imposed on States Parties to the Covenant*, UN doc. CCPR/C/21/Rev.1/Add.13, 26 May 2004). See also the Decision of the Grand Chamber of the European Court of Human Rights in the Bankovic *et al. v.* Belgium *et al.* case (12 December 2001).

[47] See, *supra*, §3.23.   [48] See, *supra*, §3.18.

another but retain for itself title to, and jurisdiction over, those munitions. Even here, however, the limited control the latter might exercise is likely to be subject to the ultimate control of the former, who may choose at any moment to withdraw the right to use or retain them. It seems improbable that the latter State could in such circumstance be described as exercising 'control' over them within the meaning of that term for the purposes of Article 3. Moreover, if the latter is a State Party it would be prohibited by Article 1 from using, acquiring, or possessing cluster munitions. If the former State is a State Party and the latter is not, the obligation of good faith implementation of treaties[49] means that, upon adherence to the Convention, it is not open to a State Party to assign jurisdiction and/or control over its cluster munition stocks to a State not party to the Convention in order to avoid its Article 3 storage and destruction obligations.[50] Furthermore, it is inconceivable that any State not party to the Convention would arrange to stockpile its own cluster munitions on the territory of a State Party if there were any possibility that this might entail their destruction by the latter pursuant to Article 3.

3.28 Finally, although Article 3 requires a State Party to destroy or ensure destruction of 'all' cluster munitions under its jurisdiction and control, it must be interpreted subject to Article 3, paragraph 6, which provides that:

[n]otwithstanding the provisions of Article 1 of this Convention, the retention or acquisition of a limited number of cluster munitions and explosive submunitions for the development of and training in cluster munition and explosive submunition detection, clearance or destruction techniques, or for the development of cluster munition counter-measures, is permitted.[51]

Obligation to separate and mark for destruction

3.29 Paragraph 1 of Article 3 requires a State Party to 'separate all cluster munitions under its jurisdiction and control from munitions retained for operational use and mark them for the purpose of destruction'. The purpose of this obligation is to ensure that, pending their destruction, cluster munitions do not inadvertently find their way into stocks of munitions that will be used. As noted above,[52] it was agreed at the Diplomatic Conference that there is no need for States to maintain or build separate facilities for the storage of cluster munitions removed from stocks. However, they should be kept separate from

---

[49] See Article 26, *1969 Vienna Convention on the Law of Treaties*.

[50] This would in any event also entail a violation of the prohibition in Article 1, paragraph 1(c) on the transfer of cluster munitions.   [51] See, *infra*, §§3.51–3.52.

[52] See, *supra*, §3.9.

stocks of munitions intended for use in military operations, including training for such operations.

3.30 The term 'mark for the purpose of destruction' is not defined and must therefore be interpreted by reference to the object and purpose of the Convention.[53] In this context the relevant purpose is to ensure that, pending their destruction, cluster munitions should not be confused with other munitions and risk the possibility of being used, however inadvertently. The marking of munitions is ordinarily carried out at the time of their manufacture and may be done by way of laser, head-stamping, engraving, colour-coding, or stencilling of the munitions themselves. Munition packaging (steel or wooden crates, for example) may also be marked. Best practice would suggest that cluster munitions intended for destruction as well as explosive submunitions (where stored separately), together with their packaging, be marked with visible, permanent inscriptions to the extent possible.[54]

3.31 The obligation to separate cluster munitions from other munitions and to mark them for destruction is to be carried out 'in accordance with national regulations'. This clause, which was added to the text during the course of the Diplomatic Conference, is largely superfluous in that it is clearly a matter for each State Party to take whatever measures may be necessary within its own legal system to meet its obligations under Article 3, paragraph 1. For instance it may be necessary to adopt or amend national law to permit the movement and storage of munitions intended for destruction or the construction and operation of facilities to carry out the process of industrial scale destruction of munitions (planning permission, etc.). The clause is not intended to permit a State Party to argue that pre-existing national regulation prevents or prohibits the separation of cluster munitions from stocks of other munitions and/or their destruction.

Paragraph 2

> Each State Party undertakes to destroy or ensure the destruction of all cluster munitions referred to in paragraph 1 of this Article as soon as possible but not later than eight years after the entry into force of this Convention for that State Party. Each State Party undertakes to ensure

---

[53] See Article 31, paragraph 1, *1969 Vienna Convention on the Law of Treaties*.

[54] See, for instance, Chapter I—Best Practice Guide on Ammunition Marking, Registration and Record-Keeping in the *OSCE Handbook of Best Practices on Conventional Ammunition*, September 2008 (<http://www.osce.org/item/32978.html>, accessed 29 October 2009).

that destruction methods comply with applicable international standards for protecting public health and the environment.

Obligation to destroy or ensure destruction

3.32 The Convention does not define the term 'destroy' but, having regard to its object and purpose, the obligation to destroy or ensure destruction of a State Party's cluster munitions is ultimately intended to ensure that these munitions are never used. The Oxford English Dictionary defines 'to destroy' as: 'To undo, break into useless pieces, or reduce into a useless form, consume, or dissolve (any material structure or object).'[55] Accordingly the term 'destroy' should be interpreted to mean to damage beyond repair or to render permanently unusable.

3.33 Paragraph 2 of Article 3 requires each State Party to 'destroy or ensure the destruction of all cluster munitions' under its jurisdiction and control. The term 'cluster munition' is defined by Article 2, paragraph 2 as meaning 'a conventional munition that is designed to disperse or release explosive submunitions each weighing less than 20 kilograms, and includes those explosive submunitions'. Accordingly both explosive submunitions and the larger ('parent') munition from which they are dispensed come within the scope of the obligation to destroy or ensure destruction. As will be seen below,[56] while destruction processes such as disassembly and cryofracture provide for the possibility of recovery of materials from a munition, in order to meet the obligation to destroy a munition the process concerned must ensure that any materials concerned cannot be used again as a cluster munition. It will not be sufficient simply to remove the explosive submunitions from the larger munition, destroy the former but retain the latter for some other purpose. The fact that the larger munition 'is designed to disperse or release explosive submunitions' within the terms of the definition of a cluster munition means that a State Party must render it incapable of doing so if it is to meet its obligation to destroy stockpiled cluster munitions.

3.34 It was acknowledged from the outset of the Oslo Process that in many cases the destruction of cluster munition stocks could be technically complex, expensive, and time-consuming (far more so than the destruction of most anti-personnel mines, for instance). Moreover, at the time of the negotiations, many States lacked the munition destruction capacity to dispose of cluster munitions and indicated that they would require assistance. The scale of the

---

[55] *Oxford English Dictionary*, Oxford University Press, CD-ROM Version 3.1, 2004.
[56] *Cf., infra*, §§3.40–3.42.

undertaking, involving the destruction of tens of millions of stockpiled explosive submunitions, was widely recognized.[57]

'as soon as possible but not later than eight years'

3.35 Each State Party is obliged to destroy or ensure destruction of its cluster munition stocks 'as soon as possible but not later than eight years' after entry into force of the Convention with respect to that State Party. Work on the preparation of a destruction programme should therefore begin immediately after the Convention enters into force for a State possessing cluster munitions.

3.36 It can be expected that a State Party's progress toward meeting its stockpile destruction obligation will be closely monitored by other States Parties and interested observers by reference to the annual reports required under Article 7 of the Convention. These reports must set out details of the total of all cluster munitions, including explosive submunitions, under a State Party's jurisdiction and control, including particulars of type, quantity, and, if possible, lot numbers;[58] the status and progress of programmes developed by a State Party for the destruction of its cluster munitions, including details of the methods used, the location of destruction sites, and the safety and environmental standards observed;[59] and the types and quantities of cluster munitions and explosive submunitions actually destroyed.[60]

---

[57] According to information compiled by the CMC, of the 107 States participating at the Diplomatic Conference 43 had stockpiles (Argentina, Australia, Austria, Bahrain, Belgium, Bosnia and Herzegovina, Bulgaria, Canada, Chile, Croatia, Czech Republic, Denmark, Estonia, Finland, France, Germany, Guinea, Guinea Bissau, Honduras, Hungary, Indonesia, Italy, Japan, Mali, Moldova, Montenegro, Morocco, the Netherlands, Nigeria, Norway, Peru, Portugal, Qatar, Serbia, Slovakia, Slovenia, South Africa, Spain, Sudan, Sweden, Switzerland, Uganda, and the UK). Another 17 States with stockpiles attended the Diplomatic Conference as observers (Colombia, Egypt, Eritrea, Ethiopia, Greece, Iraq, Kazakhstan, Kuwait, Libya, Oman, Poland, Romania, Saudi Arabia, Singapore, Thailand, Turkey, and Ukraine). See <http://www.stopclustermunitions.org/wp/wp-content/uploads/2009/06/how-big-is-the-problem-120609.pdf> 25 July 2009).

According to a statement made by its delegation at the June 2009 Berlin Conference on the Destruction of Cluster Munitions, Germany alone intends to destroy upwards of 50 million explosive submunitions by 2015. Statement by Thomas Frisch, 'German National Stockpile Destruction Programme', Berlin Conference, 25 June 2009, available at: <http://www.berlin-ccm-conference.org/menu/conference-documents/> (accessed 29 October 2009). The Ministry of Defence in Norway has announced that it will destroy all of its stockpiled cluster munitions before the end of 2010. See Ministry of Defence, 'Focus on Afghanistan and the Army', Press release, 11 May 2010, http://www.regjeringen.no/nb/dep/fd/pressesenter/pressemeldinger/2010/Fokus-pa-Afghanistan-og-Haren.html?id=604440> (accessed 27 May 2010).

[58] Article 7, paragraph 1(b).   [59] Article 7, paragraph 1(e).
[60] Article 7, paragraph 1(f).

3.37 Reports submitted under Article 7 enable a State Party to draw attention to any financial or logistical difficulties anticipated or encountered in the preparation and conduct of a programme of destruction. It is reasonable to assume at this juncture that a State Party unable to complete the destruction process within eight years and therefore in need of an extension of its deadline, will have to demonstrate to a meeting of States Parties that genuine efforts to meet the original deadline were made, including the early commencement of preparations for destruction.

International standards for protecting public health and the environment

3.38 Options for the destruction of cluster munitions will be limited by practical and legal considerations. While practical considerations will include such matters as the size of stockpiles and the technical and financial means available to a State Party, the destruction process will also be subject to applicable legal rules, in particular those concerning the protection of public health and the environment. The latter will be relevant in view of the fact that many munitions contain hazardous materials and toxic chemicals which, if allowed to leach, particularly into ground water, will cause pollution and may seriously harm human drinking water supplies. Some may be carcinogenic. These pollutants include heavy metals such as lead, copper, barium, beryllium, magnesium, copper, and cadmium; and chemical compounds used in explosives and propellants such as trinitrotoluene (TNT), Royal Demolition Explosive (RDX), nitro-glycerine, dinitrotoluene (DNT), and diphenylamine.

3.39 Paragraph 2 of Article 3 requires that States Parties 'ensure that destruction methods comply with applicable international standards for protecting public health and the environment'. There are no internationally recognized general standards for the destruction of cluster munitions *per se* such as exist in the case of landmines.[61] A range of relevant international instruments may nevertheless apply. For instance, dumping munitions at sea is prohibited for States Parties to the *1972 London Convention*[62] (and under the 1996 Protocol that supersedes it) as is the incineration of munitions at sea by a subsequent amendment.[63] These instruments may be supplemented by applicable

---

   [61] IMAS 11.10: 'Guide for Stockpile Destruction', *op. cit.*
   [62] *Convention on the Prevention of Marine Pollution by Dumping of Wastes and Other Matter*, done at the International Maritime Organisation, London, and at Mexico City, Moscow and Washington on 29 December 1972.   [63] Amendments adopted on 12 October 1978.

regional instruments.[64] The *1989 Basel Convention* regulates the international movement of hazardous waste,[65] while agreements such as the *1957 European Agreement concerning the International Carriage of Dangerous Goods by Road*, based on the *United Nations Recommendations on the Transport of Dangerous Goods*,[66] regulate the international transport of dangerous goods, including explosives and munitions, within Europe. The *1998 Aarhus Protocols to the 1979 UNECE Convention on Long-range Transboundary Air Pollution*[67] *(on Persistent Organic Pollutants*[68] and *on Heavy Metals*[69]) set legally binding limits on the emission of certain toxins and heavy metals for installations that burn, *inter alia*, hazardous wastes, including some chemical compounds used in munitions. It will be for each State Party to determine on a case-by-case basis the applicable international standards in preparing and executing destruction programmes.

Destruction methods

3.40 A number of methods exist for the destruction of cluster munitions and the choice of method will be guided by consideration of factors such as suitability of the munition concerned for a particular method, likely cost, local capacity, quantities of munitions to be destroyed, physical condition of the munitions concerned and available technical expertise, as well as applicable environmental, health and safety laws and regulations. While there are not at present standards for the destruction of cluster munitions analogous to the IMAS, the following methods of destruction[70] are likely to be considered, separately or in combination, by States Parties in meeting their obligations under Article 3:

- detonation or incineration (either in the open air or in a closed environment, such as underground in disused mines);

[64] For instance incineration and dumping of munitions at sea is prohibited in the North East Atlantic by Article 4 of the *Convention for the Protection of the Marine Environment of the North-East Atlantic*, done at Paris on 22 September 1992 (the 'OSPAR Convention') and in the Baltic Sea by Articles 10 and 11 of the *Convention on the Protection of the Marine Environment of the Baltic Sea Area*, done at Helsinki on 9 April 1992.

[65] *Convention on the Control of Transboundary Movements of Hazardous Wastes and their Disposal*, done at Basel, 22 March 1989.

[66] *Recommendations on the transport of dangerous goods: model regulations*, Twelfth Revised Edition, New York, 2001, UN doc. ST/SG/AC.10/1/Rev.12.

[67] Done at Geneva on 13 November 1979.

[68] Done at Aarhus on 24 June 1998.   [69] Done at Aarhus on 24 June 1998.

[70] For a discussion of destruction methods see 'Best Practice Guide on the Destruction of Conventional Ammunition' in the *OSCE Handbook of Best Practices on Conventional Ammunition*, September 2008 (<http://www.osce.org/item/32978.html>); and Geneva International Centre for Humanitarian Demining, *A Guide to Cluster Munitions*, Second Edition, June 2009 (<http://www.gichd.org/gichd-publications/guide-to-cluster-munitions/>), both accessed 29 October 2009.

- disassembly (either manually or mechanically); and
- cryofracture/cryogenic fracturing (this process involves freezing a munition in liquid nitrogen, crushing it to expose its explosive component, which is then ignited, followed by recovery of the metal scrap).

Destruction programmes may involve a combination of several, or even all, of these methods.

3.41 National detonation or manual disassembly programmes will be sufficient for many States Parties whose stockpiles consist of less sophisticated weapon systems. Mechanical disassembly and cryofracture on the other hand are advanced and expensive industrial processes and for many developing States, in particular, they may be beyond their current expertise or resources.

3.42 Where advanced processes are regarded as necessary for the destruction of stocks held by some developing States the progress of their destruction programmes may depend on how cooperation and assistance among States Parties for the destruction of cluster munitions stocks is developed under Article 6 of the Convention. For instance, while in some cases it may be appropriate to arrange for the transfer of stocks from States currently lacking facilities or expertise for the destruction of cluster munitions in the most efficient or environmentally sound manner to States in which this task can be carried out, the expense of such transfers may be great, the munitions may not be in sufficiently large quantities to justify transfer or they may be too unsafe to move. Alternatives may therefore have to be considered, including the development of regional destruction facilities or national capacity. However, at this remove it appears likely that the more advanced processes will be unnecessary for stocks of cluster munitions held by most developing countries. Indeed, there are clear advantages to destruction locally where this is appropriate: it should keep costs low, will reduce security risks associated with the transport of munitions and will assist in developing national capacity. These issues are likely to be addressed by future Meetings of States Parties within the framework of Article 6.[71]

---

[71] Even in advance of the Convention's entry into force, at the time of writing a number of States have begun the process of stockpile destruction and one (Spain) announced completion of the process in March 2009. Austria, Belgium, Canada, Colombia, France, Germany, the Netherlands, Norway, Switzerland, and the UK are reported to have begun destruction of cluster munition stockpiles. *Cf.* Publication summarizing the Berlin Conference on the Destruction of Cluster Munitions, Berlin, 25–26 June 2009, <http://www.berlin-ccm-conference.org/fileadmin/pdf/CCM_Berlin/CCM-Berlin-CompletePublication-Aug2009.pdf> (accessed 12 March 2010). According to a Norwegian Ministry of Defence press release of 7 May 2009, the destruction of Norway's stocks of cluster munitions had begun by means of closed detonation at a disused copper mine at Løkken Verk in Trøndelag.

Paragraphs 3, 4, and 5

3. If a State Party believes that it will be unable to destroy or ensure the destruction of all cluster munitions referred to in paragraph 1 of this Article within eight years of entry into force of this Convention for that State Party it may submit a request to a Meeting of States Parties or a Review Conference for an extension of the deadline for completing the destruction of such cluster munitions by a period of up to four years. A State Party may, in exceptional circumstances, request additional extensions of up to four years. The requested extensions shall not exceed the number of years strictly necessary for that State Party to complete its obligations under paragraph 2 of this Article.

4. Each request for an extension shall set out:

(a) The duration of the proposed extension;

(b) A detailed explanation of the proposed extension, including the financial and technical means available to or required by the State Party for the destruction of all cluster munitions referred to in paragraph 1 of this Article and, where applicable, the exceptional circumstances justifying it;

(c) A plan for how and when stockpile destruction will be completed;

(d) The quantity and type of cluster munitions and explosive submunitions held at the entry into force of this Convention for that State Party and any additional cluster munitions or explosive submunitions discovered after such entry into force;

(e) The quantity and type of cluster munitions and explosive submunitions destroyed during the period referred to in paragraph 2 of this Article; and

(f) The quantity and type of cluster munitions and explosive submunitions remaining to be destroyed during the proposed extension and the annual destruction rate expected to be achieved.

5. The Meeting of States Parties or the Review Conference shall, taking into consideration the factors referred to in paragraph 4 of this Article, assess the request and decide by a majority of votes of States Parties present and voting whether to grant the request for an extension. The States Parties may decide to grant a shorter extension than that requested and may propose benchmarks for the extension, as appropriate. A request for an extension shall be submitted a minimum of nine months prior to the Meeting of States Parties or the Review Conference at which it is to be considered.

Requests for an extension

3.43 Unlike the *1997 Anti-Personnel Mine Ban Convention*, the Convention on Cluster Munitions makes provision for the extension of the applicable deadline for the destruction of stockpiles. In this respect the approach taken is closer to the *1993 Chemical Weapons Convention*, which permits extension for a period not to exceed 15 years after the entry into force of that Convention.[72] As noted above,[73] provision for extensions was made in the Lima Discussion Text but subsequent texts, including the basic proposal for the Diplomatic Conference, omitted any such reference.

3.44 Article 3, paragraph 3 permits a State Party to make a request to the Meeting of States Parties or a Review Conference for an extension of the eight-year period for up to four years if it 'believes that it will be unable to destroy or ensure the destruction of all cluster munitions' under its jurisdiction and control within that period. In 'exceptional circumstances' a State Party may make a request for 'additional extensions' of up to four years. In accordance with Article 3, paragraph 4, a State Party seeking a first extension shall set out in its request details of the proposed duration of the extension,[74] a detailed explanation of the proposed extension, including the financial and technical means available to or required by it for the destruction of all cluster munitions under its jurisdiction and control,[75] a plan for the completion of stockpile destruction within the proposed extension period, including a detailed account of the financial and technical means available to, or required by, it to implement the plan, the quantity and type of munitions remaining to be destroyed, and the anticipated annual rate of destruction.[76] Where a State Party seeks an additional extension it must also provide a detailed explanation of the 'exceptional circumstances justifying it'.[77]

3.45 A concern was expressed during the negotiations that the reference in Article 3, paragraph 4(b) to 'financial means' may require the divulgence of information that will be commercially sensitive where a programme for destruction is put out to competitive tender, or that might even be unlawful.[78] The Friend of the President, however, assured States that what is sought by the term is merely an overview of financial requirements: the provision is not intended to undermine tendering procedures.[79]

---

[72] *1993 Chemical Weapons Convention*, Part IV (A) of the Verification Annex, §26.

[73] See, *supra*, §3.6.   [74] Article 3, paragraph 4(a).   [75] Article 3, paragraph 4(b).

[76] Article 3, paragraph 4(c)–(f).   [77] Article 3, paragraph 4(b).

[78] Under European Community law, for instance.

[79] *Cf.* 'Summary Record of Eleventh Session of Committee of the Whole', Diplomatic Conference doc. CCM/CW/SR/11, 18 June 2008.

3.46 Given the detailed reporting obligations imposed on States Parties by the Convention it should be relatively straightforward to monitor progress toward destruction of stockpiles within the eight-year period. Article 7, paragraph 1 requires annual reports that set out, *inter alia*, the details of all cluster munitions, including explosive submunitions, under the jurisdiction and control of a State Party, including details of their type, quantity and, if possible, lot numbers,[80] the status and progress of destruction programmes and detailed itemisations of the numbers and types of cluster munitions destroyed and of those remaining on hand.[81] These reports, which are transmitted to all States Parties by the Secretary-General of the United Nations, are likely to be the subject of consideration at the Meeting of States Parties[82] and it seems reasonable to assume that peer pressure, as well as programmes of international cooperation and assistance developed within the framework of Article 6, will serve to minimize the need for extensions.

3.47 Pursuant to Article 3, paragraph 5, a request for an extension is to be submitted a minimum of nine months prior to the Meeting of States Parties or the Review Conference at which it will be considered. Although the Meeting of States Parties is, pursuant to Article 11, paragraph 1, to take place 'regularly' there is no strict requirement that they be convened annually after the first Review Conference.[83] Pursuant to Article 12, the first Review Conference shall be convened by the Secretary-General of the United Nations five years after entry into force of the Convention, and thereafter at the request of one or more States Parties at an interval of no less than five years. The experience of many similar treaties suggests that States Parties will meet annually whether or not strictly required. However, the first of the eight-year deadlines for the completion of stockpile destruction will expire after the period during which annual meetings of States Parties and the first Review Conference are automatically mandated.

3.48 Article 3, paragraph 5 provides that the Meeting of States Parties or the Review Conference to which a request for extension is made shall assess the request and decide by a majority of votes of States Parties present and voting whether to grant the request. At this remove, and given the general inclination of States to seek to avoid votes on such matters where possible, it seems likely

---

[80] Article 7, paragraph 1(b). [81] Article 7, paragraph 1(e).

[82] Article 11, paragraph 1 provides that:

States Parties shall meet regularly in order to consider and, where necessary, take decisions in respect of any matter with regard to the application or implementation of this Convention, including... [m]atters arising from the reports submitted under the provisions of this Convention...

[83] Article 11, paragraph 2.

that every effort will be made to reach such decisions by consensus. Certainly this is the experience to date in the case of the first requests submitted to the Meeting of States Parties to the *1997 Anti-Personnel Mine Ban Convention* for extensions to the requirement for the destruction of mines in mined areas under Article 5 of that Convention.

3.49 Article 3, paragraph 5 allows the Meeting of States Parties or the Review Conference to which a request for extension is made to grant a shorter extension period than that sought, or to propose benchmarks. Provision for the latter is the result of a suggestion made at the Dublin Diplomatic Conference in informal consultations conducted by the Friend of the President. Benchmarks are targets or milestones to be met at regular intervals in completing the destruction process, such as an annual agreed rate of destruction.

3.50 Although not expressly provided for it is possible also that a Meeting of States Parties or a Review Conference might seek to impose conditions upon granting an extension. For instance, while the procedure for making and approving requests for extensions for stockpile destruction is very similar to that which applies in respect of clearance and destruction of cluster munition contaminated areas under Article 4 (and indeed clearance of mined areas under Article 5 of the *1997 Anti-Personnel Mine Ban Convention*), stockpiles are clearly capable of transfer to another State Party in a way that contaminated areas are not. It seems possible at this remove therefore that the Meeting of States Parties might either enquire as to why transfer of stockpiles for the purpose of destruction was not contemplated earlier, or it may consider granting an extension subject to the condition that the stockpiles concerned be transferred to a State Party with a demonstrated capacity for destruction. The (to date limited) experience of the treatment of requests for extensions under the *1997 Anti-Personnel Mine Ban Convention* would suggest that, in granting extensions, conditions can be imposed by the Meeting of States Parties. This is a simple reflection of bargaining power: a State Party that fails to obtain an extension will find itself in violation of the Convention and so must be prepared to accept an extension on whatever terms are available to it.[84]

---

[84] See, e.g., the 'Decisions on the request submitted by the United Kingdom for an extension of the deadline for completing the destruction of anti-personnel mines in accordance with Article 5 of the Convention', Ninth Meeting of the States Parties, 28 November 2008. In granting the 10-year extension sought it effectively requires the UK, *inter alia*, to provide, in addition to its Article 7 reporting requirements, 'regular reports on the following elements: establishment of a National Mine Action Authority and other implementation bodies; establishment of the necessary regulatory framework; progress on contracts let and budgets made available; progress in clearance; Environmental, ecological and technical assessments undertaken'. See Decisions of the Ninth Meeting of States Parties on Article 5 deadline Extension Requests, <http://www.

Paragraph 6

Notwithstanding the provisions of Article 1 of this Convention, the retention or acquisition of a limited number of cluster munitions and explosive submunitions for the development of and training in cluster munition and explosive submunition detection, clearance or destruction techniques, or for the development of cluster munition counter-measures, is permitted. The amount of explosive submunitions retained or acquired shall not exceed the minimum number absolutely necessary for these purposes.

Retention or acquisition of a limited number of cluster munitions and explosive submunitions

3.51 Although Article 1, paragraph 1(b) of the Convention prohibits the retention or acquisition of cluster munitions by a State Party, that provision is subject to paragraph 6 of Article 3, which provides that retention or acquisition 'of a limited number of cluster munitions and explosive submunitions for the development of and training in cluster munition and explosive submunition detection, clearance or destruction techniques, or for the development of cluster munition counter-measures, is permitted'.[85] As noted above,[86] the necessity for retention or acquisition of cluster munitions was a contentious issue throughout the negotiations. Although ultimately conceded, it was in turn made subject to the condition that 'the amount of explosive submunitions retained or acquired shall not exceed the minimum number absolutely necessary for these purposes'. This stipulation reflects the approach adopted by the *1997 Anti-Personnel Mine Ban Convention*[87] where a widely diverging practice with respect to retention is evident. While this may be replicated in the case of cluster munitions[88] it is possible also that a process of peer pressure

---

apminebanconvention.org/meetings-of-the-states-parties/9msp/what-was-decided/article-5-extension-requests-analysis-of-requests/> (accessed 29 October 2009).

[85] It might be noted here that while retention or acquisition of cluster munitions in accordance with paragraph 6 is permitted 'notwithstanding the provisions of Article 1', although it is not expressly stated the provisions of paragraph 2 of Article 3, which require a State Party to destroy or ensure the destruction of all cluster munitions under its jurisdiction and control, are clearly also subject to paragraph 6. [86] See, *supra*, §§3.5–3.8.

[87] Article 3(1) of that Convention provides that 'Notwithstanding the general obligations under Article 1, the retention or transfer of a number of anti-personnel mines for the development of and training in mine detection, mine clearance, or mine destruction techniques is permitted. The amount of such mines shall not exceed the minimum number absolutely necessary for the above-mentioned purposes.'

[88] According to the publication authored by Human Rights Watch and Landmine Action, *Banning Cluster Munitions (op. cit.)*, Spain, which has announced the completion of its programme

exercised at the Meeting of States Parties, informed by the detailed annual reports required to be submitted in accordance with paragraph 8, will serve to limit what can be regarded as 'the minimum number absolutely necessary'.

3.52 Paragraph 8 of Article 3 requires the submission of a detailed report concerning the retention or acquisition of submunitions, see below under 'Reporting obligations'.

Paragraph 7

> Notwithstanding the provisions of Article 1 of this Convention, the transfer of cluster munitions to another State Party for the purpose of destruction, as well as for the purposes described in paragraph 6 of this Article, is permitted.

Transfers

3.53 Paragraph 7 of Article 3 permits transfers of cluster munitions and explosive submunitions, notwithstanding the general prohibition on transfers imposed by Article 1. Such transfers are permitted only for the purposes of ensuring the destruction of the cluster munitions concerned in accordance with paragraph 2, or to enable a State Party to acquire a limited number of cluster munitions and explosive submunitions for the development of and training in detection, clearance or destruction techniques, or for the development of cluster munition counter-measures, in accordance with paragraph 6. Transfers for the latter purpose shall not exceed the minimum number absolutely necessary.[89] Transfers may only be made to another State Party.

Paragraph 8

> States Parties retaining, acquiring or transferring cluster munitions or explosive submunitions for the purposes described in paragraphs 6 and 7 of this Article shall submit a detailed report on the planned and actual use of these cluster munitions and explosive submunitions and their

---

for the destruction of stockpiles, intends to retain 836 cluster munitions (containing 28,615 submunitions) for the purposes of training and testing countermeasures. In contrast, at the Berlin Conference on Stockpile Destruction (25–26 June 2009), both Austria and Norway stated their intention to retain no cluster munitions at all upon completion of their stockpile destruction programmes.

[89] Article 3, paragraph 6.

type, quantity and lot numbers. If cluster munitions or explosive submunitions are transferred to another State Party for these purposes, the report shall include reference to the receiving party. Such a report shall be prepared for each year during which a State Party retained, acquired or transferred cluster munitions or explosive submunitions and shall be submitted to the Secretary-General of the United Nations no later than 30 April of the following year.

Reporting obligations

3.54 A State Party retaining or acquiring cluster munitions or submunitions in accordance with paragraph 6 must submit a detailed report to the Secretary-General of the United Nations. Such a report must provide details of the planned and actual use of the cluster munitions and explosive submunitions; their type, quantity, and lot numbers; and the identity of the receiving party. For each year thereafter in which a State Party that retains or has acquired cluster munitions or explosive submunitions retains them, that State Party must submit a similar report to the Secretary-General no later than 30 April of the following year.

3.55 A State Party making a transfer of cluster munitions and explosive submunitions in accordance with paragraph 7 must submit a detailed report concerning the transfer to the Secretary-General of the United Nations pursuant to paragraph 8. This report must set out particulars of the planned and actual use of the cluster munitions and explosive submunitions; their type, quantity and lot numbers; and the identity of the receiving party. Likewise the State Party receiving the transfer (i.e. acquiring cluster munitions or explosive submunitions for training and development purposes in accordance with paragraph 6, or for destruction in accordance with paragraph 7) must make a similar report, setting out details of the planned and actual use (including destruction) of the cluster munitions and explosive submunitions, and their type, quantity, and lot numbers. For each year thereafter in which the State Party that has received the transfer retains these cluster munitions and explosive submunitions that State Party must submit a similar report to the Secretary-General no later than 30 April of the following year.

3.56 The reporting obligations contained in Article 3 constitute increased control and transparency with regard to retained, transferred and acquired submunitions compared to the corresponding provisions in the *Anti-Personnel Mine Convention*. While not expressly stated, given the purpose of ensuring transparency with regard to transfers under Article 3, paragraph 7, it is expected that the Secretary-General of the United Nations will circulate the reports received under Article 3, paragraph 8 to all States Parties in the manner required by reports submitted pursuant to Article 7 (and indeed by the corresponding provision of the *1997 Anti-Personnel Mine Ban Convention*).[90] Certainly no provision of the Convention prohibits him from doing so.

[90] Article 7, paragraph 1(d), *1997 Anti-Personnel Mine Ban Convention*.

Article 4. Clearance and destruction of cluster munition remnants and risk reduction education

Stuart Casey-Maslen

Article 4—Clearance and destruction of cluster munition remnants and risk reduction education

1. Each State Party undertakes to clear and destroy, or ensure the clearance and destruction of, cluster munition remnants located in cluster munition contaminated areas under its jurisdiction or control, as follows:

(a) Where cluster munition remnants are located in areas under its jurisdiction or control at the date of entry into force of this Convention for that State Party, such clearance and destruction shall be completed as soon as possible but not later than ten years from that date;

(b) Where, after entry into force of this Convention for that State Party, cluster munitions have become cluster munition remnants located in areas under its jurisdiction or control, such clearance and destruction must be completed as soon as possible but not later than ten years after the end of the active hostilities during which such cluster munitions became cluster munition remnants; and

(c) Upon fulfilling either of its obligations set out in sub-paragraphs (a) and (b) of this paragraph, that State Party shall make a declaration of compliance to the next Meeting of States Parties.

2. In fulfilling its obligations under paragraph 1 of this Article, each State Party shall take the following measures as soon as possible, taking into consideration the provisions of Article 6 of this Convention regarding international cooperation and assistance:

(a) Survey, assess and record the threat posed by cluster munition remnants, making every effort to identify all cluster munition contaminated areas under its jurisdiction or control;

(b) Assess and prioritise needs in terms of marking, protection of civilians, clearance and destruction, and take steps to mobilise resources and develop a national plan to carry out these activities, building, where appropriate, upon existing structures, experiences and methodologies;

(c) Take all feasible steps to ensure that all cluster munition contaminated areas under its jurisdiction or control are perimeter-marked, monitored and protected by fencing or other means to ensure the effective exclusion of civilians. Warning signs based on methods of marking readily recognisable by the affected community should be utilised in the marking of suspected hazardous areas. Signs and other hazardous area boundary markers should, as far as possible, be visible, legible, durable and resistant to environmental effects and should clearly identify which side of the marked boundary is considered to be within the cluster munition contaminated areas and which side is considered to be safe;

(d)　Clear and destroy all cluster munition remnants located in areas under its jurisdiction or control; and

(e)　Conduct risk reduction education to ensure awareness among civilians living in or around cluster munition contaminated areas of the risks posed by such remnants.

3.　In conducting the activities referred to in paragraph 2 of this Article, each State Party shall take into account international standards, including the International Mine Action Standards (IMAS).

4.　This paragraph shall apply in cases in which cluster munitions have been used or abandoned by one State Party prior to entry into force of this Convention for that State Party and have become cluster munition remnants that are located in areas under the jurisdiction or control of another State Party at the time of entry into force of this Convention for the latter.

(a)　In such cases, upon entry into force of this Convention for both States Parties, the former State Party is strongly encouraged to provide, *inter alia*, technical, financial, material or human resources assistance to the latter State Party, either bilaterally or through a mutually agreed third party, including through the United Nations system or other relevant organisations, to facilitate the marking, clearance and destruction of such cluster munition remnants.

(b)　Such assistance shall include, where available, information on types and quantities of the cluster munitions used, precise locations of cluster munition strikes and areas in which cluster munition remnants are known to be located.

5.　If a State Party believes that it will be unable to clear and destroy or ensure the clearance and destruction of all cluster munition remnants referred to in paragraph 1 of this Article within ten years of the entry into force of this Convention for that State Party, it may submit a request to a Meeting of States Parties or a Review Conference for an extension of the deadline for completing the clearance and destruction of such cluster munition remnants by a period of up to five years. The requested extension shall not exceed the number of years strictly necessary for that State Party to complete its obligations under paragraph 1 of this Article.

6. A request for an extension shall be submitted to a Meeting of States Parties or a Review Conference prior to the expiry of the time period referred to in paragraph 1 of this Article for that State Party. Each request shall be submitted a minimum of nine months prior to the Meeting of States Parties or Review Conference at which it is to be considered. Each request shall set out:

(a) The duration of the proposed extension;

(b) A detailed explanation of the reasons for the proposed extension, including the financial and technical means available to and required by the State Party for the clearance and destruction of all cluster munition remnants during the proposed extension;

(c) The preparation of future work and the status of work already conducted under national clearance and demining programmes during the initial ten year period referred to in paragraph 1 of this Article and any subsequent extensions;

(d) The total area containing cluster munition remnants at the time of entry into force of this Convention for that State Party and any additional areas containing cluster munition remnants discovered after such entry into force;

(e) The total area containing cluster munition remnants cleared since entry into force of this Convention;

(f) The total area containing cluster munition remnants remaining to be cleared during the proposed extension;

(g) The circumstances that have impeded the ability of the State Party to destroy all cluster munition remnants located in areas under its jurisdiction or control during the initial ten year period referred to in paragraph 1 of this Article, and those that may impede this ability during the proposed extension;

(h) The humanitarian, social, economic and environmental implications of the proposed extension; and

(i) Any other information relevant to the request for the proposed extension.

7. The Meeting of States Parties or the Review Conference shall, taking into consideration the factors referred to in paragraph 6 of this Article, including, *inter alia*, the quantities of cluster munition remnants reported, assess the request and decide by a majority of votes of States Parties present and voting whether to grant the request for an extension. The States Parties may decide to grant a shorter extension than that requested and may propose benchmarks for the extension, as appropriate.

8. Such an extension may be renewed by a period of up to five years upon the submission of a new request, in accordance with paragraphs 5, 6 and 7 of this Article. In requesting a further extension a State Party shall submit relevant additional information on what has been undertaken during the previous extension granted pursuant to this Article.

Overview of the Article

4.1 Article 4 sets out the obligations upon affected States Parties to free contaminated land of cluster munition remnants. Under Article 4 each State is required to clear and destroy cluster munition remnants on territory under its jurisdiction or control within 10 years of becoming party to the Convention.[1] Cluster munition remnants are defined in Article 2 to mean the following:[2]

- Failed cluster munitions (where cluster munitions are dropped or fired but a dispenser fails to disperse the submunitions as intended);[3]
- Abandoned cluster munitions (where unused cluster munitions have been left behind or dumped, and are no longer under the control of the party that left them behind or dumped them);[4]
- Unexploded submunitions (where submunitions have landed, but have failed to explode as intended);[5] and
- Unexploded bomblets (where explosive bomblets have been dropped from a fixed-wing dispenser but have failed to explode as intended).[6]

4.2 If, after a State becomes a party to the Convention, cluster munitions are used in areas under its jurisdiction or control and become cluster munition remnants, the affected State is allowed up to 10 years after the end of active hostilities to complete clearance and destruction operations.[7] In addition, where a State that later becomes party to the Convention used cluster munitions against another State Party before entry into force of the Convention for this latter State, the State that used the cluster munitions is 'strongly encouraged' to provide assistance for the marking, clearance, and destruction of such cluster munition remnants, including, where available, information on types and quantities of the cluster munitions used, precise locations of cluster

---

[1] Article 4, paragraph 1.

[2] See further, *supra*, the commentary on the definition of cluster munition remnants contained in Article 2, paragraph 7 in §§2.193 *et seq*.

[3] See, *supra*, the commentary on the definition in Article 2, paragraph 4.

[4] See, *supra*, the commentary on the definition in Article 2, paragraph 6.

[5] See, *supra*, the commentary on the definition in Article 2, paragraph 5.

[6] See, *supra*, the commentary on the definition in Article 2, paragraph 15.

[7] Article 4, paragraph 1(b).

munition strikes, and areas in which cluster munition remnants are known to be located.[8]

4.3 In fulfilling its Article 4 clearance and destruction obligations, an affected State Party is obliged to do the following 'as soon as possible':

- Survey, assess, and record the threat, making every effort to identify all contaminated areas under its jurisdiction or control;
- Assess and prioritise needs for marking, the protection of civilians, and clearance and destruction of cluster munition remnants;
- Take 'all feasible steps' to perimeter-mark, monitor and fence hazardous areas;
- Conduct risk reduction education to ensure civilians living in or around affected areas are aware of the risks;
- Take steps to mobilise the necessary resources; and
- Develop a national plan, building, where appropriate, upon existing structures, experiences, and methodologies.[9]

In doing so, each State Party must take into account international standards, including the International Mine Action Standards (IMAS).[10]

4.4 Upon completion of its Article 4 clearance and destruction obligations, a State Party is required to make a declaration of compliance to the next Meeting of States Parties.[11] If, however, a State is unable to meet its 10-year deadline for clearance and destruction of cluster munition remnants, it may request extensions from the Meeting of States Parties or a Review Conference for additional periods of up to five years at a time.[12]

Relationship to other Articles of the Convention

4.5 Article 4 has relevance for, and is to be interpreted in conjunction with, many other provisions in the Convention. The definition of cluster munition remnants, the subject of the obligations under Article 4, is set out in Article 2, paragraphs 4–7 and 15. The definition of 'cluster munition contaminated area', particularly relevant for paragraphs 1 and 2 of Article 4, is set out in Article 2, paragraph 11. Article 2, paragraph 8 clarifies that the definition of transfer does not encompass the transfer of territory containing cluster munition remnants. As noted in the *chapeau* to Article 4, paragraph

---

[8] Article 4, paragraph 4(a) and (b).   [9] Article 4, paragraph 2.
[10] Article 4, paragraph 3.   [11] Article 4, paragraph 1(c).
[12] Article 4, paragraphs 5–8.

2, there is a link between the clearance and destruction of cluster munition remnants and international cooperation and assistance as set out in Article 6. Article 6, paragraph 4 refers specifically to Article 4, paragraph 4 and notes that a State Party's international assistance and cooperation obligations related to clearance are in addition to the special responsibility user States have to assist with clearance of contamination they caused in the past. Article 7, especially paragraph 1(h)–(j) and (m), requires transparency reporting on issues related to the implementation of Article 4. Article 9 requires that States Parties take measures to implement the Convention, which includes the obligations under Article 4. Article 11, paragraph 1(f) and Article 12, paragraph 2(c) specifically provide for the Meeting of States Parties and Review Conferences, respectively, to consider a formal request by a State Party for an extension to its deadline for the clearance and destruction of cluster munition remnants, as set out in Article 4, paragraphs 5–8.

Preparatory discussions

4.6 The motivation for clearance of cluster munition remnants is set out in the preamble to the Convention on Cluster Munitions, whereby States Parties express their concern that:

... cluster munition remnants kill or maim civilians, including women and children, obstruct economic and social development, including through the loss of livelihood, impede post-conflict rehabilitation and reconstruction, delay or prevent the return of refugees and internally displaced persons, can negatively impact on national and international peace-building and humanitarian assistance efforts, and have other severe consequences that can persist for many years after use.[13]

4.7 Article 4 draws on the content and drafting of two other major instruments of international humanitarian law: the *1997 Anti-Personnel Mine Ban Convention*[14] and Protocol V on explosive remnants of war of the *Convention on Certain Conventional Weapons (2003 Protocol V)*.[15] The *1997 Anti-Personnel Mine Ban Convention* requires that a State clear all anti-personnel mines in mined areas under its jurisdiction or control within 10 years of becoming

---

[13] Third preambular paragraph.

[14] The formal title of this treaty is the Convention on the Prohibition of the Use, Stockpiling, Production and Transfer of Anti-Personnel Mines and on Their Destruction.

[15] The formal title of this treaty is the Convention on Prohibitions or Restrictions on the Use of Certain Conventional Weapons Which May Be Deemed to Be Excessively Injurious or to Have Indiscriminate Effects, as amended on 21 December 2001.

party to that treaty, and the drafting of Article 4 of the Convention on Cluster Munitions was strongly influenced by both the framing of the obligation in that Convention and subsequent experiences in its implementation.[16] The corresponding obligation under the *1997 Anti-Personnel Mine Ban Convention* includes anti-personnel mines dispersed from a cluster munition.[17] As set out in Article 1, paragraph 3, of the Convention on Cluster Munitions, all mines are specifically excluded from the Convention's ambit.[18]

   4.8 A requirement to clear areas contaminated with explosive remnants of war, including abandoned or unexploded cluster munitions, was laid down in *2003 Protocol V*.[19] However, no deadline was set down by the Protocol, other than merely to require that each State Party shall clear, remove, or destroy such devices in affected territories under its control 'as soon as feasible'.[20] It also limited the obligation to explosive remnants of war resulting from armed

---

   [16] Article 5, *1997 Anti-Personnel Mine Ban Convention*.

   [17] One well-known cluster munition type that disperses mines is the Gator mine system, developed and used by the United States of America (US). The Gator system contains a mix of BLU-91/B antivehicle and BLU-92/B anti-personnel mines. (See, e.g., GlobalSecurity.org, 'Gator Mine System', <http://www.globalsecurity.org/military/systems/munitions/gator.htm>, accessed 15 March 2009.) According to Landmine Monitor, Gator mines were 'undoubtedly' the mine-type most widely used by the US during the 1991 Gulf War:

> Declassified Army documents hint at the problems U.S. scatterable mines caused in 1991 when U.S. troops stormed Iraqi defenses so rapidly that they inadvertently penetrated their own 'live' minefields. A U.S. Army memorandum states: 'The purpose of this message is to remind all XVIII ABN Corps soldiers to leave unexploded mines alone.... XVIII ABN Corps has suffered several severe injuries as a result of unexploded munitions being disturbed.... Coalition aircraft and enemy AAA have littered Corps area of operations with dangerous unexploded ammunition.... Due to rapid Allied advance, activated Gator minefields could be encountered. Gator mines... have been used to mine airfields, MSRS, approaches and bridges, and assembly areas.... Extreme caution must be exercised in moving/maneuvering through areas where air strikes have been conducted.'

'Message Information Update, Subject: Unexploded Munitions', ARCENT, XVIII Corps, 28 February 1991, cited in International Campaign to Ban Landmines (ICBL), *Landmine Monitor Report 1999, Toward a Mine-Free World*, Human Rights Watch, Washington DC, April 1999, <http://www.icbl.org/lm/1999/usa.html> (accessed 15 March 2009).

   [18] The decision specifically to exclude anti-personnel mines dispersed by cluster munitions from the purview of the Convention on Cluster Munitions (see, *supra*, §§1.4 and 1.83–1.85) is explained by their prohibition under the *1997 Anti-Personnel Mine Ban Convention*. Anti-vehicle mines are also excluded from the Convention on Cluster Munitions, as the negotiating States did not wish to extend the prohibition to these weapons, even when limiting such a prohibition to those dispersed by cluster munitions.

   [19] According to Article 3, paragraph 2 of *2003 Protocol V*:

> After the cessation of active hostilities and as soon as feasible, each High Contracting Party and party to an armed conflict shall mark and clear, remove or destroy explosive remnants of war in affected territories under its control.

   [20] The use of the term 'feasible' in this provision is not defined, but Article 5, paragraph 1, of the Protocol stipulates that:

conflicts after the entry into force of the Protocol for a concerned State. In the context of the Convention on Cluster Munitions, the need to clear areas contaminated with cluster munitions was first identified in the 2007 Oslo Declaration, which recognized 'the grave consequences caused by the use of cluster munitions' and affirmed the commitment of states to, *inter alia*, 'establish a framework for cooperation and assistance that ensures...clearance of contaminated areas [and] risk education'.[21] The concern to ensure clearance of cluster munition contamination was initially reflected in the draft text included in the Lima Discussion Text. The text, which followed to a significant extent the corresponding provision in the *1997 Anti-Personnel Mine Ban Convention*, contained many of the elements ultimately adopted, but focused only on unexploded ordnance (UXO) and did not seem to cover abandoned or failed cluster munitions.

4.9 The Vienna Discussion Text of 14 November 2007 further elaborated many of the elements ultimately adopted in the Convention. The draft provision, now entitled 'Clearance and destruction of cluster munition remnants', differed notably from the final text by virtue of the shorter deadline proposed for the completion of clearance operations—five years[22] instead of the 10 years ultimately included.[23] A new element appeared in Article 4, paragraph 4 of the Vienna Discussion Text and served as a building block for the Convention's final version. This paragraph created an obligation for a State that later becomes party to the Convention and that used cluster munitions against another State Party prior to entry into force of the Convention. In the Vienna Discussion Text, the obligation was set down as follows:

Where cluster munition remnants were delivered by a State Party before entry into force of this Convention to territory now under the jurisdiction or control of another

High Contracting Parties and parties to an armed conflict shall take all feasible precautions in the territory under their control affected by explosive remnants of war to protect the civilian population, individual civilians and civilian objects from the risks and effects of explosive remnants of war. Feasible precautions are those precautions which are practicable or practicably possible, taking into account all circumstances ruling at the time, including humanitarian and military considerations...

[21] Oslo Declaration, 23 February 2007, point 1(ii).

[22] See Article 4, paragraph 1, Vienna Discussion Text of 14 November 2007 (see Annex 4 of this Commentary).

[23] A proposal by the United Kingdom (UK) at the Dublin Diplomatic Conference suggested the 10-year deadline. It also sought to limit the obligation to those cluster munition remnants posing a 'humanitarian threat'. Diplomatic Conference doc. CCM/33, 19 May 2008, Article 4, paragraph 1. On 23 May 2009, the Friend of the President for clearance and destruction of cluster munition remnants, announced that based on informal consultations with States, his draft paper had raised the deadline to 10 years.

State Party to this Convention, the former State Party shall provide bilaterally, inter alia, technical, financial, material or human resources assistance to facilitate the marking, clearance and destruction of such cluster munition remnants.[24]

4.10 In many ways, the drafting of paragraph 4 was sharpened in the Draft Cluster Munitions Convention of January 2008.[25] It added a clause specifying through whom the assistance would be given.[26] It clarified that the obligation covered abandoned as well as used cluster munitions. Most important, the Draft Cluster Munitions Convention added a sentence requiring those States Parties that decide to give assistance to provide information on the number, type, and location of the cluster munitions they used or abandoned. During negotiations at the Diplomatic Conference in Dublin, States made no major objections to the latter requirement, which was by then set out as sub-paragraph (b). The words 'shall include' remained in sub-paragraph (b) rather than being softened. Such information, which can only come from States that used or abandoned cluster munitions, can greatly facilitate clearance efforts.

Negotiations

4.11 The text of Article 4, paragraph 4 as adopted in the Convention on Cluster Munitions is the same as the text in the Draft Cluster Munitions Convention except for three changes. First, the final text was restructured from a single paragraph into a *chapeau* with two sub-paragraphs. Second, following a proposal by Ireland,[27] the Friend of the President added the phrase 'where available', qualifying the provision of information; he explained that such information might not always be available because historically there was no obligation for States to retain it.

4.12 Finally, while absolute language—'shall provide'—was used in the Draft Cluster Munitions Convention, after lengthy debate at the Diplomatic Conference,[28] the language in what had become paragraph 4(a) was at the

---

[24] Article 4, paragraph 4, Vienna Discussion Text.

[25] Article 4, paragraph 4, Draft Cluster Munitions Convention of 21 January 2008 (see Annex 5 of this Commentary).

[26] Assistance can be provided 'either bilaterally or through a mutually agreed third party, including through the United Nations system or other relevant organisations'. Article 4, paragraph 4, Draft Cluster Munitions Convention; and Article 4, paragraph 4(a).

[27] 'Proposal by Ireland for the amendment of Article 4', Diplomatic Conference doc. CCM/31, 19 May 2008.

[28] Italy tabled a proposal at the Dublin Diplomatic Conference to delete the provision. See 'Proposal by Italy for the amendment of Article 4', Diplomatic Conference doc. CCM/34, 19 May 2008. France and Germany jointly proposed to preserve but amend the provision. Their proposal

very last moment amended to 'strongly encouraged to provide'.[29] Despite this change, Article 4, paragraph 4 is the first provision in a weapons treaty to place responsibility on a State Party to assist with clearance of explosive remnants of war left by its munitions before the treaty enters into force for it.

4.13 The Draft Convention on Cluster Munitions also contained an obligation of a State Party to clear and destroy any cluster munitions that may become remnants on its territory after it becomes party to the Convention,[30] as follows:

Where, after entry into force of this Convention for that State Party, cluster munitions have become cluster munition remnants located in areas under its jurisdiction or control, such clearance and destruction must be completed as soon as possible but no later than 5 years after such cluster munitions became cluster munition remnants.[31]

The final text adopted in Dublin delayed the deadline to 10 years, thereby bringing it into line with the general obligation for clearance and destruction, although the time period only begins to elapse once the active hostilities which resulted in cluster munition remnants have ended.[32]

4.14 A second area in which the negotiation of the Article broadened the scope of an obligation was in the area of risk education, termed 'risk reduction education' in the Convention on Cluster Munitions. As noted above, the Oslo

---

would have narrowed the scope of the provision by only referring to assistance in the form of information, qualifying States Parties with 'in a position to do so', and changing 'shall provide' to 'are invited to make available, without delay after the cessation of active hostilities and as far as practicable, subject to these parties' legitimate security interests, such information ...' 'Proposal by France and Germany for additional text', Diplomatic Conference doc. CCM/47, 19 May 2008. These proposals received support from, *inter alia*, Australia, Canada, Japan, and the UK. In formal and informal sessions in Dublin, several States, including Lebanon, Cambodia, Guatemala, Mexico, and Venezuela, argued strongly in favour of the provision, which was ultimately preserved although in a weaker form. See, e.g., 'Summary Record of Second Session of the Committee of the Whole', Diplomatic Conference doc. CCM/CW/SR/2, 18 June 2008, p. 3.

[29] See, *supra*, §0.74.

[30] The Vienna Discussion Text had drawn on *2003 Protocol V* when describing the obligation of a State to clear and destroy any cluster munitions that may become remnants on its territory after it becomes party to the Convention. According to draft Article 4, paragraph 2, a State Party would only have been required to do the following:

As soon as feasible after entry into force of this Convention, each State Party that has been affected in the past or may be affected in the future by cluster munition use shall ... (d) clear and destroy all cluster munition remnants within its jurisdiction.

Thus, the intention was not to set a specific deadline for clearance and destruction of cluster munition remnants within the jurisdiction of a State Party and, further, not even to require clearance of affected areas that might fall under the control of the State after the Convention's entry into force.

[31] Article 4, paragraph 1(b), Draft Cluster Munitions Convention.

[32] Article 4, paragraph 1(b), Convention on Cluster Munitions. See the commentary on this provision *infra*.

Declaration had referred to the need to include risk education in the future convention.[33] The Vienna Discussion Text had followed the approach taken in the *1997 Anti-Personnel Mine Ban Convention*, which situated an obligation regarding risk education only as one of international cooperation and assistance:

Each State Party in a position to do so shall provide assistance for . . . risk education and cluster munitions awareness activities.[34]

4.15 The text of the Draft Cluster Munitions Convention included an obligation in Article 4, whereby each State Party 'shall as soon as possible', taking into consideration the provisions of the convention regarding international cooperation and assistance:

Conduct risk education to ensure awareness among civilians living in or around areas in which cluster munition remnants are located of the risks posed by such remnants.[35]

Only minor drafting changes were made to this proposed text at the Dublin Diplomatic Conference. However, to reflect the addition to the content of the Article, its title was also amended to include a reference to risk reduction education. Finally, the negotiations in Dublin also added the obligation, not present in either of the formal draft texts, to make a formal declaration of compliance with either of the main clearance obligations at the meeting of States Parties following the completion of clearance and destruction operations.[36]

4.16 At the Diplomatic Conference, four formal proposals were tabled for amendment to the Draft Cluster Munitions Convention: by Ireland,[37] a joint proposal by France and Germany,[38] by the UK,[39] and by Italy.[40] The proposal by Ireland sought to reflect the discussions at the Wellington Conference, while the other three proposals largely sought to limit the scope of one or more of the paragraphs contained in the Draft Cluster Munitions Convention, in

---

[33] This reference was reiterated in the Declaration of the Wellington Conference of 22 February 2008.   [34] Article 6, paragraph 8, Vienna Discussion Text.

[35] Article 4, paragraph 2(e), Draft Cluster Munitions Convention.

[36] Ireland put forward the proposal for this addition. See Diplomatic Conference doc. CCM/31, 19 May 2008, Article 4, paragraph 1(c).

[37] 'Proposal by Ireland for the amendment of Article 4', Diplomatic Conference doc. CCM/31, 19 May 2008.

[38] 'Proposal by France and Germany for the amendment of Article 4', Diplomatic Conference doc. CCM/32, 19 May 2008.

[39] 'Proposal by the United Kingdom for the amendment of Article 4', Diplomatic Conference doc. CCM/33, 19 May 2008.

[40] 'Proposal by Italy for the amendment of Article 4', Diplomatic Conference doc. CCM/34, 19 May 2008.

particular with respect to the responsibility of former users.[41] Informal consultations on Article 4 at the Conference were chaired by Lieutenant-Colonel Jim Burke of Ireland, who served as the Friend of the President for clearance and destruction of cluster munition remnants.

Paragraph 1

Each State Party undertakes to clear and destroy, or ensure the clearance and destruction of, cluster munition remnants located in cluster munition contaminated areas under its jurisdiction or control, as follows:

(a) Where cluster munition remnants are located in areas under its jurisdiction or control at the date of entry into force of this Convention for that State Party, such clearance and destruction shall be completed as soon as possible but not later than ten years from that date;

(b) Where, after entry into force of this Convention for that State Party, cluster munitions have become cluster munition remnants located in areas under its jurisdiction or control, such clearance and destruction must be completed as soon as possible but not later than ten years after the end of the active hostilities during which such cluster munitions became cluster munition remnants; and

(c) Upon fulfilling either of its obligations set out in sub-paragraphs (a) and (b) of this paragraph, that State Party shall make a declaration of compliance to the next Meeting of States Parties.

Commentary

4.17 This paragraph contains a series of significant obligations centred on the clearance and destruction of cluster munitions that have been used or abandoned. Each State undertakes to destroy or ensure the destruction of cluster munition remnants located in areas under its jurisdiction or control as soon as possible but not later than 10 years after becoming party to the Convention in the case of existing contamination, and 10 years after the end of active hostilities for any subsequent contamination.[42] Thus, an affected State depositing its instrument of ratification (or accession) will have around ten and a half years to complete the necessary clearance in accordance with

---

[41] *Cf.* CCM/32. The UK also sought to restrict the obligation to clear and destroy cluster munition remnants to those 'that pose a humanitarian threat'. *Cf.* CCM/33.

[42] Thus, contamination arising after entry into force on territory under the jurisdiction or control of a State Party must seemingly occur within the context of an armed conflict for this additional deadline to be relevant.

Article 4, paragraph 1(a), although it also undertakes to complete the requisite clearance 'as soon as possible'. In case of contamination following entry into force, it does not matter whether cluster munitions are used or abandoned by a State or non-State armed group.[43]

4.18 Paragraph 1 follows the logic of the corresponding obligations with respect to anti-personnel mines laid down by Article 5 of the *1997 Anti-Personnel Mine Ban Convention*, but it differs in a number of respects from that provision. The basic deadline set for completion of clearance operations for existing contamination—10 years—is the same in both treaties, but the Convention on Cluster Munitions adds a specific obligation—and deadline— to clear and destroy cluster munitions that may become remnants following entry into force of the treaty for any State Party.[44] It also adds a formal obliga- tion to make a 'declaration of compliance' to the Meeting of States Parties that follows completion of clearance operations.[45]

Clearance and destruction

4.19 The Convention on Cluster Munitions requires both clearance and destruction of cluster munition remnants,[46] indicating that the definition of clearance for the purposes of Article 4 does not include destruction.[47] Neither 'clearance' nor 'destruction' is, however, formally defined.[48]

---

[43] The overwhelming majority of use of cluster munitions has been by States, but use by non- State armed entities has also occurred. In this regard, see, *supra*, the commentary on the twelfth preambular paragraph in §§0.130 *et seq.*

[44] In a small number of cases, States Parties to the *1997 Anti-Personnel Mine Ban Convention* have become contaminated with anti-personnel mines after its respective entry into force. In 2007, e.g., this concerned The Gambia, apparently as a spill-over from the violence in the Casamance region of Senegal. See ICBL, *Landmine Monitor Report 2008, Toward a Mine-Free World* (Ottawa: Mines Action Canada, 2008), p. 19.

[45] At the Diplomatic Conference, the Friend of the President for clearance and destruction of cluster munition remnants announced on 23 May 2008 that based on informal consultations with States, his draft paper had suggested including this obligation. See 'Summary Record of Ninth Session of the Committee of the Whole', Diplomatic Conference doc. CCM/CW/SR/9, 18 June 2008. It has become accepted practice under the *1997 Anti-Personnel Mine Ban Convention* for a formerly affected State Party to make such a declaration upon completion of clearance operations, and this has been endorsed by a Meeting of the States Parties, but it is not a formal treaty require- ment. See Final Report of the Seventh Meeting of States Parties, Annex IV: Proposed Voluntary Declaration of Completion of Article 5 Obligations, doc. APLC/MSP.7/2006/5, 17 January 2007, pp. 8 (§28), and 68.

[46] Article 5 of the *1997 Anti-Personnel Mine Ban Convention* refers only to the destruction of anti-personnel mines.

[47] In contrast, the 2007 Oslo Declaration referred only to the need for 'clearance of contami- nated areas'.

[48] The fifth preambular paragraph of the Convention on Cluster Munitions declares that States Parties believe it 'necessary to contribute effectively in an efficient, coordinated manner to resolving

4.20 In mine action (the collective name for the range of activities which aim to reduce the social, economic, and environmental impact of mines and explosive remnants of war, including cluster munition remnants),[49] the term usually applied to the process of making a contaminated area safe from explosive ordnance is clearance, which is in turn part of the broader process of demining.[50] Clearance is defined by the International Mine Action Standards (IMAS) as 'tasks or actions to reduce or eliminate the Explosive Ordnance (EO) hazards from a specified area'.[51] The reference to 'reduction' of the hazards, however, would tend to suggest—erroneously according to a leading authority—that the IMAS might accept less than total removal of explosive hazards.[52]

4.21 The obligation to 'destroy' cluster munition remnants comes from the realm of disarmament. This makes it explicit that cleared cluster munition remnants must not only be removed from the ground, they must also be rendered inoperable, although there is no obligation to destroy them *in situ*.[53]

4.22 Mine action organizations generally refer to clearance of ERW as battle area clearance (BAC) or explosive ordnance disposal (EOD). According

the challenge of removing cluster munition remnants located throughout the world, and to ensure their destruction'.

[49] It is normal to speak of the five 'pillars' or 'complementary groups of activities' of mine action: risk education; demining; victim assistance; stockpile destruction; and advocacy against the use of anti-personnel mines and cluster munitions. The definition in the International Mine Action Standards as of March 2009 needed updating to take account of the Convention on Cluster Munitions. See IMAS 04:10: 'Glossary of mine action terms, definitions and abbreviations', Second Edition, January 2003 (as amended), Definition 3.158, available at: <http://www.mineactionstandards.org/imas.htm>.

[50] According to the International Mine Action Standards (IMAS), demining refers to 'activities which lead to the removal of mine and ERW hazards, including technical survey, mapping, clearance, marking, post-clearance documentation, community mine action liaison and the handover of cleared land. Demining may be carried out by different types of organisations, such as NGOs, commercial companies, national mine action teams or military units. Demining may be emergency-based or developmental... [I]n IMAS standards and guides, mine and ERW clearance is considered to be just one part of the demining process.' IMAS 04:10: 'Glossary of mine action terms, definitions and abbreviations', *op. cit.*, Definition 3.53.   [51] *Ibid.*, Definition 3.33.

[52] Email from Faiz Paktian, Head of Standards and Quality Management, Geneva International Centre for Humanitarian Demining (GICHD), Geneva, 19 March 2009. He notes that the relevant IMAS on clearance requirements states that: 'Land shall be accepted as "cleared" when the demining organisation has ensured the removal and/or destruction of all mine and ERW hazards from the specified area to the specified depth.' IMAS 09.10: 'Clearance requirements', Second Edition, 1 January 2003, Section 4, p. 1, available at: <http://www.mineactionstandards.org> (accessed 5 April 2009).

[53] In fact, the sensitivity of many submunition fuzes means that destruction by detonation *in situ* is the safest method. In some countries, however, untrained personnel have been required to pick up and carry submunitions for destruction elsewhere, sometimes with deadly consequences. See, e.g., GICHD, *A Guide to Cluster Munitions*, Second Edition, Geneva, June 2009, p. 60.

to the IMAS, BAC is 'the systematic and controlled clearance of hazardous areas where the risk is known not to include mines'.[54] With respect to BAC of unexploded submunitions or bomblets, operations are normally subdivided into two categories: surface (or visual) clearance, and sub-surface clearance. According to the Geneva International Centre for Humanitarian Demining (GICHD), surface clearance:

has been used on several occasions after conflict as a quick and effective means to remove the immediate hazard in an area, i.e. the visible threat. In many emergency response scenarios this is the kind of clearance methodology employed although it is hazard and terrain dependent. For example, it may be particularly appropriate in urban areas or on rocky hard ground where unexploded submunitions are lying on or above the surface. Surface clearance will normally include both the ground and also above it, e.g. in trees, fencing and/or caught in urban constructions.[55]

4.23 The GICHD further notes that visual search may be supported in vegetation by relevant detection instruments, such as a magnetometer.[56] A magnetometer operates on the principle of magnetic fluxgate.[57] This principle is described as follows:

The fluxgate consists of two sensors separated by a fixed distance and mechanically aligned. In the absence of a ferromagnetic material, the earth magnetic flux is the

---

[54] IMAS 09.11: 'Battle Area Clearance (BAC)', First Edition, 1 September 2007, p. v. One view of the relationship between the two disciplines is that BAC focuses on locating the explosive hazard, which then leads to an EOD task. Others view BAC (and indeed mine clearance) as a subset of EOD. EOD is defined under the IMAS as

the detection, identification, evaluation, render safe, recovery and disposal of EO. EOD may be undertaken:

a) as a routine part of mine clearance operations, upon discovery of ERW;
b) to dispose of ERW discovered outside hazardous areas, (this may be a single item of ERW, or a larger number inside a specific area); or
c) to dispose of EO which has become hazardous by deterioration, damage or attempted destruction.

IMAS 04.10: 'Glossary of mine action terms, definitions and abbreviations', *op. cit.*, Definition 3.90.

[55] GICHD, *A Guide to Cluster Munitions*, Second Edition, Geneva, May 2009, p. 60.

[56] Thus, some operators further classify surface clearance into visual clearance or instrument-assisted visual clearance. Where there is vegetation that might obscure an unexploded submunition or bomblet, using a UXO detector may prevent a demining accident.

[57] Popular UXO detectors include the off-the-shelf *GA magnetic detectors* manufactured by the US company, Schonstedt (see, e.g., <http://www.schonstedt.com/index.cfm?page=GA-72-Cdreadmore>), which have been used to detect unexploded submunitions in numerous cluster munition affected countries and territories, including Azerbaijan, Georgia, Kosovo, and Lebanon. Any object containing ferromagnetic materials (iron, steel and alloys) is detected. The detection range is greatly dependent on the mass and orientation of the target, ranging from a couple of centimetres to several metres.

same at both sensors, therefore the fluxgate output is zero. When an object close to the bottom sensor alters the earth magnetic flux due to its own magnetic field, the balance of the gate is altered, producing a measurable output.[58]

4.24 At some point, cluster munition strike areas should normally be cleared using a sub-surface instrument search if this is not done initially (unless the nature of the surface makes it obvious that contamination will not be located below the surface, e.g. in the case of asphalt or concrete). Again, for sub-surface search a metal detector, a magnetometer,[59] or a large-loop detector,[60] may be used.[61] Once a signal is found, the area is carefully excavated, typically using a small trowel, until the item has been identified. If it proves to be an unexploded submunition or bomblet, a small donor charge will normally be placed to blow up the weapon.[62]

4.25 In contrast with the corresponding core provision in the *1997 Anti-Personnel Mine Ban Convention*, the text of Article 4, paragraph 1, of the Convention on Cluster Munitions does not explicitly require that 'all' cluster munition remnants be cleared and destroyed.[63] There are four issues that should be considered here—first, the requisite depth of clearance; second, at what point to stop clearing a cluster munition strike area; third, respect for international standards for clearance and destruction: and four, whether it

---

[58] GICHD, *Detectors and Personal Protective Equipment Catalogue 2009*, Geneva, January 2009, p. 161. In contrast, a metal detector uses electromagnetic induction to detect metal.

[59] Some quality assurance personnel in Lebanon have, however, questioned the reliability of certain magnetometers for sub-surface submunition detection.

[60] Large-loop detectors apply the eddy current pulse induction principle for the detection of metal components in ERW. The Ebinger Large Loop Technology UPEX 740 M, e.g., has been used for BAC operations in Afghanistan, Angola, Cambodia, France, Kosovo, Lao People's Democratic Republic, the UK, and Vietnam. GICHD, *Detectors and Personal Protective Equipment Catalogue 2009*, Geneva, January 2009, p. 116. See also <http://www.ebingergmbh.com>.

[61] According to one authority, sub-surface search:

should initially be carried out with standard metal/mine detectors e.g. pulse induction. This should detect the great majority of buried remnants (to about 45 centimetres depth). Thereafter magnetometer search can be used as a verification measure and to detect deeply buried remnants. Magnetometers are expensive to acquire and require special skills to operate and interpret correctly. Magnetometers detect peaks in magnetic field strength rather than the object itself. Use of magnetometers in inappropriate circumstances or by inadequately trained personnel can lead and has lead to avoidable casualties. This capability will not always be available to a clearance operation.

Email from Lt.-Col. Jim Burke, Adviser, Irish Defence Forces, 7 October 2009.

[62] As noted *supra* (§4.21), in certain circumstances, and depending on the munition, an item may be moved to another site for later destruction.

[63] Though a corresponding provision in paragraph 2(d) of the Article lays down the requirement to '[c]lear and destroy all cluster munition remnants located in areas under its jurisdiction or control'.

is possible to retain cluster munition remnants in accordance with Article 3, paragraph 6.

4.26 With respect to the first of these issues, it should be borne in mind that clearance operations only seek to locate and destroy cluster munitions up to a certain specified depth. According to the GICHD, 'the extent and the depth of clearance should be decided by national authorities based on the particular situation they are facing'. The IMAS on BAC states the following:

If a battlefield requires sub-surface clearance, the specified depth of clearance shall be determined by the tasking authority and may be developed through the use of a technical survey, or from other reliable information which establishes the depth of the ERW hazards expected in the area and an assessment of the future intended land use. In the absence of reliable information on the depth of ERW hazard, a default depth for clearance should be established by the tasking authority...

As examples, the typical default depth for sub-surface clearance in Kosovo is 50 centimetres and in Lebanon is 20 centimetres, based on estimated munition ground penetration depths. In the Lao People's Democratic Republic (Laos), the munition depths vary widely and a pragmatic default depth of 25 centimetres has been established based on the most common (agricultural) land use.[64]

4.27 With respect to the second issue, that of when to stop clearance, the GICHD suggests a standard be set, 'for example to search 25–50 metres past the last submunition found by a clearance (to cover "fade-out")'.[65] A cluster strike leaves what is known as a 'footprint', which covers the area impacted by up to several hundred individual detonations, caused by the explosion of submunitions dispersed from the cluster munition. The footprint is usually in an ellipse pattern, covering the entry (or beginning of the strike zone) and the 'fade-out' (the end of the strike zone).[66]

4.28 Third, with respect to applicable international standards, Article 4 requires that States Parties to the Convention on Cluster Munitions 'take into account' international standards, including the IMAS, but, therefore, they do not have to follow them to the letter.[67] Indeed, it is noted in the

---

[64] IMAS 09.11: 'Battle Area Clearance (BAC)', First Edition, 1 September 2007, p. 3.

[65] In Lebanon, e.g., applicable standards require that clearance continue 50 metres past the last submunition found.

[66] GICHD, *A Guide to Cluster Munitions*, Second Edition, Geneva, June 2009, p. 62. See also Clark, C., 'The Convention on Cluster Munitions: considering implementation from a battle area clearance perspective' in *Disarmament Forum*, No. 1 (Geneva: United Nations Institute for Disarmament Research, 2010).

[67] See, *infra*, the commentary on paragraph 3 of this Article (*esp.* §§4.83 *et seq.*) for further details on the content of the IMAS pertaining to clearance of cluster munition remnants.

IMAS that:

IMAS assists National Mine Action Authorities (NMAA) to establish national standards and national SOPs by establishing a frame of reference, which can be used, or adapted for use, as a national standard.[68]

Ensure the clearance and destruction of cluster munition remnants

4.29 The phrase 'or ensure the clearance and destruction of' demonstrates that, in addition to using its own demining assets, such as engineers from its own armed forces, a State Party may call on the services of others—the military or demining forces of another State, demining NGOs, or commercial demining companies, for instance—to carry out the necessary operations. This occurs frequently, with Georgia, Laos, Lebanon, and Serbia, among others, benefiting from foreign clearance capacity in addition to using its own staff and equipment.[69]

Cluster munition remnants

4.30 As noted above, cluster munition remnants are defined under Article 2, paragraph 7 to include the following:[70]

- Failed cluster munitions;[71]
- Abandoned cluster munitions;[72]
- Unexploded submunitions;[73] and
- Unexploded bomblets.[74]

Failed cluster munitions

4.31 Failed cluster munitions are cluster munitions that are dropped or fired but whose dispensers fail to disperse the submunitions as intended. There are a number of factors that explain why after being dropped or fired a cluster munition dispenser fails to disperse the submunitions as intended. These

---

[68] IMAS 01.10: 'Guide for the application of International Mine Action Standards (IMAS)', Second Edition, 1 January 2003, p. 2 (Section 5).

[69] In 2008, for instance, Landmine Monitor reported that in August, Russia's state demining agency EMERCOM began clearance of unexploded submunitions at Niš airport in Serbia, with funding from the Russian government. ICBL, *Landmine Monitor Report 2008, op. cit.*, p. 622.

[70] See, *supra*, the commentary on the definition of cluster munition remnants (§§2.193 *et seq.*).

[71] See, *supra*, the definition in Article 2, paragraph 4, and the accompanying commentary.

[72] See, *supra*, the definition in Article 2, paragraph 6, and the accompanying commentary.

[73] See, *supra*, the definition in Article 2, paragraph 5, and the accompanying commentary.

[74] See, *supra*, the definition in Article 2, paragraph 15, and the accompanying commentary.

include poor manufacture, dropping of a cluster munition at too low an alti-
tude, and the age of the cluster munition.[75]

Abandoned cluster munitions

4.32 Abandoned cluster munitions are unused cluster munitions that have
been left behind or dumped and that are no longer under the control of the
party that left them behind or dumped them.[76] For example, contamination
from stockpiled cluster munitions was among large quantities of other ordnance after NATO planes had bombed a Yugoslav army (VJ) ammunition
storage area at Goles in Kosovo in 1999:

> Over a period of four and a half months in 2000, the clearance organisation BACTEC
> destroyed more than 6,500 items of UXO at this location (despite KFOR units already
> having worked on the site.) These items included aircraft bombs, high explosive pro-
> jectiles, air-to-air missiles, rockets and mines as well as British manufactured (but
> apparently VJ stockpiled) BL755 cluster munitions.[77]

4.33 There is also a problem of unused cluster munitions that are not technically abandoned but which are encountered in ammunition storage areas
that a State Party is not actively maintaining, guarding, or which it has simply forgotten about. This has occurred in several States, such as Angola,[78]

---

[75] A report by Landmine Action on the use by Israel of cluster munitions in Lebanon in August
2006 depicts a CBU 58B cluster bomb found near Nabatiyeh, which:

> displayed complete failure. Presumably after failing to open properly during delivery virtu-
> ally none of the submunitions have dispersed, armed or exploded. The 1-year U.S. warranty
> for the cluster bomb was also visible on the side of the container, having expired in July
> 1974.

Nash, T., *Foreseeable Harm, The use and impact of cluster munitions in Lebanon: 2006* (London:
Landmine Action, October 2006), p. 10.

[76] 'Abandoned cluster munitions' should arguably be read to include abandoned 'bomblets' and
their dispensers, including where the bomblets are still inside the dispensers. The definition of
'cluster munition remnants' does not formally cover bomblets and their dispensers where these have
been abandoned (either as part of stockpiles, or potentially where aircraft carrying such systems
have crashed in territory now controlled by another state). This oversight could be addressed by the
Meeting of States Parties recognizing that the term 'abandoned cluster munitions' should be read
to include abandoned 'bomblets' and their dispensers, including where the bomblets are still inside
the dispensers.

[77] Moyes, R., *Cluster munitions in Kosovo: Analysis of use, contamination and casualties*
(London: Landmine Action, February 2007), p. 45, <http://www.landmineaction.org/resources/
LMAKosovoFinal.pdf >(accessed 25 March 2010).

[78] HALO Trust reports that it has Weapons and Ammunition Disposal (WAD) teams working in support of the Angolan Air Force and Army to destroy the considerable stocks of weapons and ammunition that were amassed during the Civil War. By November 2007 HALO's team
had destroyed more than 500 tonnes of ammunition and over 20,000 Small Arms and Light
Weapons. The majority of ammunition destroyed was made up of aircraft bombs but includes

Guinea-Bissau,[79] and the Republic of Congo.[80] There is a clear overlap with Article 3 of the Convention on Cluster Munitions, as these cluster munitions should usually be considered stockpiles. However, should an 'undesired explosive event'[81] occur in an ammunition storage area, it is probable that the cluster munitions and/or explosive submunitions should be considered failed cluster munitions or unexploded submunitions.[82] It is likely, as one authority has noted, that after an explosion any such submunitions would be unexploded submunitions as they were 'dispersed or released by, or otherwise separated from, a cluster munition and had failed to explode as intended'.[83] The difference will have practical implications for the disposal method selected.[84]

Unexploded submunitions and bomblets

4.34 By far, the greatest clearance challenge is with unexploded submunitions and bomblets. Unexploded submunitions are submunitions that have landed after being dispersed from the cluster munition container but have failed to explode as intended. Unexploded bomblets are explosive bomblets that have been dropped from a fixed-wing dispenser but have similarly failed to explode as intended. No one knows how many unexploded submunitions and bomblets remain to be cleared worldwide, but they certainly number in the many millions.

4.35 According to the GICHD, submunition 'failure rates' are dependent on a number of factors, including:

- design (i.e. failures in design or assembly);
- length and condition of storage (e.g. the working parts have deteriorated over time);

---

guided missiles and cluster bombs. HALO Trust, 'Angola', <http://www.halotrust.org/angola. html#wad> (accessed 18 March 2009).

[79] Landmine Action, 'Guinea-Bissau, 2007 Activities', London, April 2008.

[80] Mines Advisory Group (MAG) reports that in the Republic of Congo: 'Just 500 metres from Brazzaville International Airport, 26 hectares of land are heavily contaminated with bombs, cluster munitions, grenades and mines, as a result of a depot explosion more than 10 years ago. Detonations occur each year on this site, as community members encroach further onto the contaminated land to sustain a livelihood.' MAG, *Eliminating the legacy of conflict, Annual Review 2008*, Manchester, pp. 12–13.

[81] See, e.g., GICHD, *Explosive Remnants of War (ERW), Undesired Explosive Events in Ammunition Storage Areas*, Geneva, November 2002.

[82] e.g., in a report on their clearance activities in Guinea-Bissau in 2007, Landmine Action depict unexploded PTAB 2.5 submunitions still within their cluster munition container that was ejected by an explosion at the Bra armoury in the capital, Bissau, during the 1998–1999 Civil War. Landmine Action, 'Guinea-Bissau, 2007 Activities', Unpublished report, London, April 2008.

[83] Email from Lt.-Col. Jim Burke, Adviser, Irish Defence Forces, 7 October 2009.

[84] Email from Vera Bohle, Evaluation and Disarmament Specialist, GICHD, 20 August 2009.

- drop height, angle, attitude and velocity (e.g. too high, too low, too slow, too fast);
- vegetation (e.g. heavy, dense, or soft);
- ground conditions at the impact area (e.g. soft, hilly, or wet); and
- interaction (e.g. the effects of collisions, blast, and fragmentation from other submunitions or bomblets).[85]

The sensitivity of fuzing and the general unpredictability of unexploded ammunition mean that these weapons should be treated with extreme caution:

There are many individual factors and combinations which may influence whether a submunition will explode as designed or not. Also, submunition duds may be left in a highly dangerous state, partially or fully armed and often damaged. There are many instances of submunitions being moved several times, and then exploding on the last move. These weapons are extremely unpredictable. In essence, however, all submunitions are inherently dangerous once released from the delivery system and armed, and should be treated as such.[86]

Cluster munition contaminated areas under a State Party's jurisdiction or control

4.36 The term 'cluster munition contaminated area' is defined by Article 2, paragraph 11, to mean an area 'known or suspected to contain cluster munition remnants'.[87] It is not specified how such a suspicion can arise or how it can then be discounted.[88] It is a broad term, potentially

---

[85] GICHD, *A Guide to Cluster Munitions,* Second Edition, June 2009, pp. 25–26.
[86] GICHD, *A Guide to Cluster Munitions,* First Edition, November 2007, p. 30.
[87] See, *supra,* the commentary on this provision.
[88] In mine action, much discussion over recent years has centred on the concept of land release. According to the IMAS on land release, e.g.:

A principal objective of mine action is to remove the explosive hazards (landmines and explosive remnants of war (ERW)) from areas where they have been laid or abandoned. Mine action operations have typically employed demining assets to do this, such as manual clearance teams, explosive detection animals and mechanical systems, either individually or in combination. These methods have resulted in thousands of square kilometres of land being released back to communities for productive use. However, on some occasions, land has been subjected to full clearance unnecessarily.

While some of the operational principles of survey and clearance have been well understood and used by many mine action operators, inadequate or inaccurate survey can exaggerate the mines/ERW problem. In addition, survey data needs to be reviewed over time as more information becomes available particularly as communities become established and land use further developed in the aftermath of conflict. An objective of mine action is to define, re-define and clear land that is contaminated by mines/ERW.

encompassing military training areas, which would thereby include a number of States whose contamination does not result from any armed conflict.[89]

4.37 Further, the full global extent of contamination from cluster munition remnants was not known as of writing.[90] At least 25 States and three disputed territories are believed to be affected to some degree: Afghanistan, Angola, Argentina,[91] Azerbaijan, Bosnia and Herzegovina, Chad, Cambodia, Croatia, the Democratic Republic of Congo, Georgia, Guinea-Bissau, Iraq, Kuwait, Laos, Lebanon, Mauritania, Montenegro, Russia, Serbia, Syria, Sudan, Tajikistan, Uganda, the UK,[92] Vietnam, and Zambia, along with Kosovo, Nagorno-Karabakh, and Western Sahara.[93] In addition, the situation is unclear in at least a further 10 States where cluster munitions are believed or reported to have been used or abandoned since the 1940s: the Republic of Congo, Eritrea, Ethiopia, Grenada, Israel,[94] Libya, Malta, Saudi Arabia, Sierra Leone, and Yemen.[95]

The scope of the obligation: 'jurisdiction or control'

4.38 The undertaking accepted by each State Party is to destroy or ensure the destruction of 'cluster munition remnants located in cluster munition contaminated areas under its jurisdiction or control'.[96] Neither 'jurisdiction' nor 'control' is defined in the Convention on Cluster Munitions, although the

---

IMAS 08.20: 'Land release', First Edition, 10 June 2009, p. v, available at: <http://www.mineactionstandards.org>.

[89] e.g., Chile, Jordan, the Netherlands, Norway and others are believed to have unexploded submunitions as a result of use of cluster munitions in training exercises rather than as a result of armed conflict.

[90] For details of alleged use, see, *supra*, the Introduction to this Commentary.

[91] Argentina and the UK are engaged in a sovereignty dispute regarding the Falklands Islands/Malvinas, which are affected by unexploded submunitions. See, e.g., ICBL, *Landmine Monitor Report 2008*, *op. cit.*, p. 1070.

[92] Argentina and the UK are engaged in a sovereignty dispute regarding the Falklands Islands/Malvinas, which are affected by unexploded submunitions. See *ibid*.

[93] Presentation by Stuart Casey-Maslen, Mine Action Editor, Landmine Monitor, to Norwegian People's Aid (NPA) 2009 Operations Meeting in Lebanon, 26 February 2009.

[94] According to research by Human Rights Watch, Israel claims to have cleared all the cluster munition remnants from its territory that resulted from use by Hezbollah in the armed conflict in Lebanon in August 2006. See Human Rights Watch and Landmine Action, *Banning Cluster Munitions*, *op. cit.*, p. 214.

[95] Presentation to NPA Operations Meeting in Lebanon, 26 February 2009, *op. cit.*, and subsequent research.

[96] The distinction with the formulation in Article 3 of the Convention on Cluster Munitions (jurisdiction *and* control) is clearly significant. See, further, the commentary on this provision, *supra*, in §§3.22 *et seq*.

words appear also in Articles 3,[97] 5, 6, 7, and 9, but both terms have been used widely in international law, including in earlier international disarmament and humanitarian law texts. The terms are discussed in turn below.

4.39 The concept and reach of jurisdiction is described in the commentary on Article 3.[98] A State's jurisdiction clearly covers all of its sovereign territory, whether metropolitan or non-metropolitan.[99]

4.40 The language employed in defining the scope of the obligation in Article 4 of the Convention on Cluster Munitions was adapted from the *1997 Anti-Personnel Mine Ban Convention*, which in turn was amended from the *1993 Chemical Weapons Convention*.[100] Article 1, paragraph 2, of the *1993 Chemical Weapons Convention* provides that:

> Each State Party undertakes to destroy chemical weapons it owns or possesses, or that are located in any place under its jurisdiction or control, in accordance with the provisions of this Convention.[101]

According to a commentary of the 1993 Convention, the provision 'compels States Parties to use jurisdiction with regard to natural and legal persons on its territory, in other places under the jurisdiction outside the territory and on vessels flying its flag or on aircraft registered under the national law, to implement the destruction obligation'.[102] Thus, the jurisdictional competence of a State is 'primarily territorial', encompassing metropolitan and non-metropolitan areas.

The meaning of control

4.41 The term 'control' was similarly taken from the corresponding provisions in the *1997 Anti-Personnel Mine Ban Convention* and the *1993 Chemical*

---

[97] One significant difference between Articles 3 and 4 is that in the case of Article 4 *either* jurisdiction *or* control is sufficient for the purpose of constituting the obligation to destroy cluster munition remnants, whereas in Article 3 both jurisdiction and control are required for the obligation to destroy stockpiles to apply.

[98] *Cf., supra*, §§3.22 *et seq.* It should be noted, however, that in Article 4, jurisdiction is over 'areas' whereas in Article 3 jurisdiction is over the 'stockpiles' of cluster munitions themselves.

[99] See, e.g., Mann, F. A., 'The Doctrine of International Jurisdiction Revisited After Twenty Years', *RdC* 111 (1964-I), p. 20; and Mann, F. A., 'The Doctrine of Jurisdiction in International Law', *RdC* 186 (1984-III), p. 41.

[100] The formal title of this treaty is the Convention on the Prohibition of the Development, Production, Stockpiling and Use of Chemical Weapons and on their Destruction.

[101] The text of the 1993 Convention is available on the website of The Organisation for the Prohibition of Chemical Weapons (the Convention's implementing body), at: <http://www.opcw.org/chemical-weapons-convention/>.

[102] Krutzsch, W., and Trapp, R., *A Commentary on the Chemical Weapons Convention* (The Netherlands: Martinus Nijhoff Publishers, 1 July 1994), p. 16.

Weapons Convention.[103] According to the commentary of the latter Convention referred to above, the term 'means places over which the State Party exercises factual power or authority, in particular occupied territories. Such places may belong to another State but have an extraterritorial status, or belong to the international parts of the globe. In cases in which the legal status of a place is disputed, for instance in an occupied territory, the State Party actually exercising the control is addressed by this provision.'[104] Thus, control refers primarily to areas outside the jurisdictional competence of the State that are nonetheless within its control.

4.42 The situation is, however, further complicated when a State Party is participating in an international military alliance with other States at least one of which is not party to the Convention on Cluster Munitions, and the alliance operates under the aegis of an intergovernmental organization.[105] Under international law, many intergovernmental organizations, such as the UN or the North Atlantic Treaty Organization (NATO), enjoy a legal personality that is distinct from that of its member States.[106] These and other organizations sometimes undertake collective military action or engage in peacekeeping operations in which they may come to exercise control over territory that is contaminated with cluster munition remnants. The question is therefore to what extent the personnel of a State Party will engage the responsibility of that State Party to conduct clearance of cluster munition remnants in accordance with Article 4.

4.43 As Professor John Cerone has noted, 'While the lines of responsibility are relatively clear when states act in an individual capacity, the issue of

---

[103] *Cf.* Article 5, paragraph 1, *1997 Anti-Personnel Mine Ban Convention*; and Article 1, paragraph 2, *1993 Chemical Weapons Convention*.

[104] Krutzsch, W. and Trapp, R., *A Commentary on the Chemical Weapons Convention, op. cit.*, pp. 16–17.

[105] There is, as yet, no international, legally binding definition of what constitutes an intergovernmental organization. In 2003, at its 55th session the International Law Commission provisionally adopted a draft article whereby: '... the term "international organization" refers to an organization established by a treaty or other instrument governed by international law and possessing its own international legal personality. International organizations may include as members, in addition to States, other entities'. (Official Records of the General Assembly, Fifty-eighth Session, Supplement No. 10 (A/58/10), chap. IV, sect. C, §53.) Simply put, therefore an intergovernmental organization (IGO) is an organization comprised primarily of states (often referred to as member states), but which may also include other intergovernmental organizations. IGOs are established by international treaty, which provides the IGO with an international legal personality.

[106] Wilde, R., 'Enhancing Accountability at the International Level: The Tension between International Organization and Member State Responsibility and the Underlying Issues at Stake', *Journal of International and Comparative Law*, No. 416, 2006, p. 401. See, also, International Court of Justice, Advisory Opinion, 'Reparation for Injuries Suffered in the Service of the United Nations', 11 April 1949, <http://www.icj-cij.org/docket/files/4/1835.pdf>.

attribution becomes more complex in the context of collective action, particularly in light of the range of circumstances in which states may conduct collective operations'.[107] According to draft Article 5 on the Responsibility of International Organizations (Conduct of organs or agents placed at the disposal of an international organization by a State or another international organization), also adopted in May 2004:

The conduct of an organ of a state or an organ or agent of an international organization that is placed at the disposal of another international organization shall be considered under international law an act of the latter organization if the organization exercises effective control over that conduct.

4.44 Thus, determining who has effective control over the military force or forces is critical to any determination of responsibility. But as Professor Cerone has observed:

States may simply deploy military forces jointly or through 'coalitions of the willing', which may or may not have separate legal personality. They may also contribute troops to UN or NATO forces in which operations are under the command and control of these organizations. Or they may deploy forces together with other states acting pursuant to a UN mandate, while retaining command and control. In these situations, chains of command may or may not be unified, states may or may not retain control over their contributed troops, and the lines of attribution may be muddled as a result.[108]

He concludes that, given the

complex array of possibilities, the issue of attribution must be assessed in light of the particular features of each operation. In general, the conduct of a state's military forces will be attributable to that state while those forces are acting in their national capacity. However, if troops are fully seconded to an intergovernmental organization, or another entity with separate international legal personality, such that they are acting on behalf of that organization or entity and are no longer acting on behalf of their state of nationality, then their conduct may no longer be attributable to their state of nationality.[109]

4.45 This leads to an assessment of whether this international responsibility is exclusive to the intergovernmental organization or complementary to the international responsibility of the States contributing military personnel. In

---

[107] Remarks of Professor John Cerone at the 31st San Remo Round Table on Current Problems of International Humanitarian Law, 'Peace operations and the complementarity of human rights law and international humanitarian law', San Remo, Italy, 14 September 2008.

[108] *Ibid.*

[109] *Ibid.*

line with the principles set out above, the UN Special Rapporteur refers to the commentary on draft Article 57 on State responsibility, whereby:

if a State seconds officials to an international organization so that they act as organs or officials of the organization, their conduct will be attributable to the organization, not the sending State.[110]

4.46 Similarly, the UN Secretariat has stated that:

The principle of attribution of the conduct of a peacekeeping force to the United Nations is premised on the assumption that the operation in question is conducted under United Nations command and control, and thus has the legal status of a United Nations subsidiary organ. In authorized chapter VII operations conducted under national command and control, the conduct of the operation is imputable to the state or states conducting the operation. In joint operations, namely, those conducted by a United Nations peacekeeping operation and an operation conducted under national or regional command and control, international responsibility lies where effective command and control is vested and practically exercised.[111]

4.47 Unfortunately, the situation is not always so clear-cut. Thus, Professor Cerone suggests that given the fact contributing States often retain a significant degree of control over their troops, those troops 'may be operating in both capacities simultaneously, in which case their conduct may be attributable to their sending state as well as to the intergovernmental organization through which they have been deployed'.[112] He concedes, though, that this is not the position taken by the landmark judgment of the European Court of Human Rights in the *Behrami* case, decided in May 2007.[113] The case concerned responsibility for the death of Gadaf Behrami, and the serious injury to his 10-year-old brother, Bekim, as a result of cluster munitions dropped by NATO forces during the 1999 conflict between the organization and the former Federal Republic of Yugoslavia and which had not been cleared.

---

[110] Official Records of the General Assembly, Fifty-sixth session, Supplement No. 10 and corrigendum (A/56/10 and Corr.1), Chap. IV, Sect. E.2, §3 of the commentary, p. 361, cited by UN Special Rapporteur, 'Second report on responsibility of international organizations', UN doc. A/CN.4/541, p. 15.

[111] See 'Responsibility of international organizations, Comments and observations received from international organizations', UN doc. A/CN.4/545, 25 June 2004, p. 18; see also paragraphs 17–18 of the Secretary-General's report, UN doc. A/51/389.

[112] Remarks of Professor John Cerone at the 31st San Remo Round Table on Current Problems of International Humanitarian Law, *op. cit.*

[113] Behrami *v.* France (European Court on Human Rights, Application No. 71412/01), admissibility decision 2 May 2007.

4.48 In 2000, the two boys accidentally detonated an unexploded submunition. A UN report observed that a French Officer from the Kosovo Force (KFOR, a NATO military force) had accepted that KFOR had been aware of the presence of unexploded submunitions in their area of responsibility for months, but that their clearance was not a high priority. Before the European Court of Human Rights, Agim Behrami complained under Article 2 (the right to life) of the *1950 European Convention on Human Rights*, on his own behalf and on behalf of his son Gadaf Behrami, about the latter's death. It was submitted that the incident took place because of the failure of French KFOR troops to mark and/or clear the unexploded submunitions, which those troops knew to be present on that site.[114]

4.49 The Court held, however, that 'the impugned acts and omissions of KFOR and UNMIK cannot be attributed to the respondent States and, moreover, did not take place on the territory of those States or by virtue of a decision of their authorities'.[115] Accordingly, given that neither NATO/KFOR nor the UN/UNMIK is a party to the European Convention, the Court concluded that the complaints 'must be declared incompatible *ratione personae* with the provisions of the Convention'.[116]

4.50 The logic of the judgment in the *Behrami* case, which has been hotly debated and also strongly criticized by a number of commentators,[117] has nonetheless been followed in subsequent judicial decisions. For example, a 2008 case in the Netherlands concerned the failure of the Dutch battalion of the UN force in Bosnia and Herzegovina (DutchBat) to protect civilians in the town of Srebrenica from summary execution and other exactions committed by Serb forces. The Netherlands District Court of

---

[114] Their father initially complained that France had not respected UN Security Council Resolution 1244 of 10 June 1999. Resolution 1244 required KFOR to supervise demining 'until the international civil presence can, as appropriate, take over responsibility for this task'. Operative Paragraph 9(e), UN Security Council Resolution 1244 of 10 June 1999.

[115] Behrami *v.* France (Application No. 71412/01) Judgment, paragraph 151.

[116] *Ibid.*, paragraph 152.

[117] See, e.g., Milanovic, M., and Papic, T., 'As Bad as it Gets: The European Court of Human Rights' Behrami and Saramati Decision and General International Law', *International and Comparative Law Quarterly*, Vol. 57, 2008. According to Cerone:

> The Behrami judgment of the European Court of Human Rights misapplies [the applicable] rules in several ways. Most significantly, the Court concluded that because it had found the conduct at issue attributable to the UN, it could not be attributable to the sending state. It thus failed to recognize that the same conduct may be attributable both to an international organization and to a sending state.

Remarks of Professor John Cerone at the 31st San Remo Round Table on Current Problems of International Humanitarian Law, *op. cit.*

The Hague concluded in September 2008 that if a State made available armed forces to the UN and placed them under the 'command and control' of the organization, the actions of those armed forces were attributable to the UN alone.[118] The decision to recognize the UN's immunity from prosecution in the case was confirmed by the Court of Appeal on 30 March 2010, although the Court stated that the Netherlands did not enjoy such immunity.[119]

4.51 Although the conclusion differed, the approach taken in the *Behrami* case was followed in the *Al-Jedda* case, decided by the UK's House of Lords in 2007. The Law Lords considered an appeal by Mr Al-Jedda from a decision by the Court of Appeal, protesting his detention by British troops in Iraq. The majority of the Lords in their 12 December judgment agreed with Lord Bingham that:

> At no time did the US or the UK disclaim responsibility for the conduct of their forces or the UN accept it. It cannot realistically be said that US and UK forces were under the effective command and control of the UN, or that UK forces were under such command and control when they detained the appellant.[120]

4.52 In sum, in the context of the Convention on Cluster Munitions, jurisdiction over an area means any area that falls within the sovereign territory of a State Party, including both metropolitan and overseas territories. Control means areas that fall outside a State Party's sovereign territory but over which they exercise effective, sustained control[121] through physical occupation by their armed forces or other means.[122]

---

[118] HN *v*. The Netherlands (Ministry of Defence and Ministry of Foreign Affairs), District Court of The Hague, September 2008, paragraphs 4.8 and 4.11.

[119] See, e.g., Gerechtshof's-Gravenhage (Dutch Court of Appeal), 'Mothers of Srebrenica cannot sue UN for compensatory damages', News release, The Hague, 30 March 2010, <http://www. rechtspraak.nl/Actualiteiten/Mothers+of+Srebrenica+cannot+sue+UN+for+compensatory+dam ages.htm> (accessed 1 April 2010).

[120] R (on the application of Al-Jedda) (FC) (Appellant) *v*. Secretary of State for Defence (Respondent), UK House of Lords, December 2007, paragraph 23.

[121] Clearance of an area of cluster munition remnants is time-consuming, and requires safe working conditions and the appropriate equipment if it is to be conducted to humanitarian standards. Realistically, therefore, transitory control cannot be sufficient to found an international legal responsibility for clearance under Article 4.

[122] According to a 2004 Advisory Opinion by the International Court of Justice (ICJ), e.g., the West Bank remains occupied (in legal terms), notwithstanding the establishment of the Palestinian Authority and its mandate over certain areas:

> The territories situated between the Green Line... and the former eastern boundary of Palestine under the Mandate were occupied by Israel in 1967 during the armed conflict between Israel and Jordan. Under customary international law, these were therefore occupied territories in which Israel had the status of occupying Power. Subsequent events in these territories, as

4.53 In contrast to Article 3, either jurisdiction *or* control is sufficient for a State Party to hold legal obligations over contaminated areas. In addition, areas under the control of a State Party may correspond to some or all of the sovereign territory of another State Party, meaning that two States Parties may each have co-existing legal obligations over the same contaminated areas. In the case of a multinational military operation operating under the aegis of an intergovernmental organization and involving at least one State Party to the Convention on Cluster Munitions, the factors that determine whether a State Party is bound to implement Article 4 and destroy cluster munition remnants 'as soon as possible' will be whether that State Party has effective control over an area containing cluster munition remnants.

Cluster munitions becoming remnants after entry into force for a State Party

4.54 Sub-paragraph (b) of paragraph 1 recognizes that subsequent contamination may occur following entry into force of the convention for any State (whether as a result of use by a State not party or even a State Party to the Convention on Cluster Munitions in violation of its obligations, including the affected State Party itself, using cluster munitions on territory under its jurisdiction or control). As noted above, the affected State Party is given up to 10 years after the end of active hostilities in which cluster munitions were used to complete clearance and destruction operations.[123]

4.55 The phrase 'the end of active hostilities' is not formally defined in the Convention on Cluster Munitions or elsewhere in international humanitarian law.[124] A similar phrase was used in *1949 Geneva Convention III*,[125] dealing with the repatriation of prisoners of war, and again in the *1977 Additional*

---

described in paragraphs 75 to 77 above, have done nothing to alter this situation. All these territories (including East Jerusalem) remain occupied territories and Israel has continued to have the status of occupying Power.

ICJ, 'Legal Consequences of the Construction of a Wall in the Occupied Palestinian Territory', Advisory Opinion, 2004, *ICJ Report 2004*, at para. 78, available at: <http://www.icj-cij.org/docket/files/131/1671.pdf> (accessed 1 March 2010). For a contrary view on the situation in the Occupied Territories, see, e.g., Benvenisti, E., 'Responsibility for the Protection of Human Rights under the Interim Israeli Palestinians Agreements', 28 *Is. L. Rev.* 297 (1994), p. 312.

[123] Article 4, paragraph 1(b).

[124] In addition to its use in *1949 Geneva Convention III* and *1977 Additional Protocol I*, this or a similar phrase is used in Articles 7, paragraph 3(a) and 9 of *1980 Protocol II on Mines* and Article 9, paragraphs 2 and 10, paragraph 1 of *1996 Amended Protocol II on Mines*, as well as in Article 3, paragraph 4 of *2003 Protocol V on Explosive Remnants of War*, which applies 'after the cessation of active hostilities and as soon as feasible'.

[125] Convention (III) relative to the Treatment of Prisoners of War, Geneva, 12 August 1949.

Protocol I,[126] *inter alia* in Article 33 on missing persons. According to the commentary of the provision published by the ICRC:

As regards the absolute limit of the 'end of active hostilities', virtually the same expression can be found in the Geneva Conventions, though only in one place.[127] The Commentary in French on the Third Convention equates the end of active hostilities with a cease-fire... (though this term is not mentioned in the English text), underlining the fact that hostilities 'could cease without any peace treaty, or even armistice'... In fact, the meaning of the expression 'active hostilities' is no different in this context from that of the expression 'hostilities'. In both cases it refers to armed hostilities.[128]

Declaration of compliance

4.56 Sub-paragraph (c) requires that in either of the two scenarios outlined in sub-paragraphs (a) and (b) of Article 4, paragraph 1, the affected State Party must make a declaration of compliance to the next Meeting of States Parties. Should completion of clearance and destruction operations occur prior to a Review Conference, although the Convention does not explicitly require it, presumably it would be expected that a declaration of compliance would nonetheless be made to that conference.[129] Should additional contamination occur following such a declaration of compliance, presumably a new declaration

[126] Protocol Additional to the Geneva Conventions of 12 August 1949, and relating to the Protection of Victims of International Armed Conflicts (Protocol I), 8 June 1977.

[127] Article 118, paragraph 1, *1949 Geneva Convention III*. 'The French text is identical (la fin des hostilités actives); in the English version there is a slight difference: 'the cessation of active hostilities' instead of 'the end of active hostilities'. On the other hand, Article 17, paragraph 4, of the First Convention and Article 130, paragraph 3, of the Fourth Convention use the same expression in French: 'dès que les circonstances le permettront et au plus tard à la fin des hostilités'. In the English text they are different in wording: First Convention: 'As soon as circumstances permit, and at the latest at the end of hostilities'; Fourth Convention: 'as soon as circumstances permit, and not later than the close of hostilities'.

[128] Sandoz Y., Swinarski C., Zimmermann B. (eds.), *Commentary on the Additional Protocols of 8 June 1977 to the Geneva Conventions of 12 August 1949* (Geneva: ICRC/Martinus Nijhoff Publishers, 1986), §1238.

[129] The proposed voluntary declaration of completion of clearance of anti-personnel mines in mined areas under a State Party's jurisdiction or control put forward by Guatemala and the International Committee of the Red Cross for the *1997 Anti-Personnel Mine Ban Convention* was as follows:

State declares that it has destroyed/ensured the destruction of all anti-personnel mines in areas under its jurisdiction or control in which anti-personnel mines were known or suspected to be emplaced, in accordance with Article 5 of the Convention.

State declares that it completed this obligation on [date].

See Final Report of the Seventh Meeting of States Parties, Annex IV: Proposed Voluntary Declaration of Completion of Article 5 Obligations, doc. APLC/MSP.7/2006/5, 17 January 2007, p. 68.

will be made, following the approach taken by States Parties to the *1997 Anti-Personnel Mine Ban Convention*.[130]

Paragraph 2

In fulfilling its obligations under paragraph 1 of this Article, each State Party shall take the following measures as soon as possible, taking into consideration the provisions of Article 6 of this Convention regarding international cooperation and assistance:

(a) Survey, assess and record the threat posed by cluster munition remnants, making every effort to identify all cluster munition contaminated areas under its jurisdiction or control;

(b) Assess and prioritise needs in terms of marking, protection of civilians, clearance and destruction, and take steps to mobilise resources and develop a national plan to carry out these activities, building, where appropriate, upon existing structures, experiences and methodologies;

(c) Take all feasible steps to ensure that all cluster munition contaminated areas under its jurisdiction or control are perimeter-marked, monitored and protected by fencing or other means to ensure the effective exclusion of civilians. Warning signs based on methods of marking readily recognisable by the affected community should be utilised in the marking of suspected hazardous areas. Signs and other hazardous area boundary markers should, as far as possible, be visible, legible, durable and resistant to environmental effects and should clearly identify which side of the marked boundary is considered to

---

[130] In 2006, States Parties to the *1997 Anti-Personnel Mine Ban Convention* adopted a Proposed Voluntary Declaration of Completion of Article 5 Obligations, which included provision for how to address new contamination found after a declaration of compliance with Article 5 had been made:

In the event that previously unknown mined areas are discovered after this date, State will:

(i) report such mined areas in accordance with its obligations under Article 7 and may voluntarily share such information through any other informal means such as the Intersessional Work Programme, including the Standing Committee meetings;

(ii) ensure the effective exclusion of civilians in accordance with Article 5; and

(iii) destroy or ensure the destruction of all anti-personnel mines in these mined areas as a matter of urgent priority, making its needs for assistance known to other States Parties, as appropriate.

Final Report of the Seventh Meeting of States Parties, Annex IV: Proposed Voluntary Declaration of Completion of Article 5 Obligations, doc. APLC/MSP.7/2006/5, 17 January 2007, p. 68.

be within the cluster munition contaminated areas and which side is considered to be safe;

(d) Clear and destroy all cluster munition remnants located in areas under its jurisdiction or control; and

(e) Conduct risk reduction education to ensure awareness among civilians living in or around cluster munition contaminated areas of the risks posed by such remnants.

4.57 This paragraph, which builds on and develops a similar, albeit shorter, provision contained in *2003 Protocol V*,[131] sets out in more detail the set of 'demining' obligations that lead to the clearance and destruction of cluster munition remnants.[132] These can be summarized as follows:

- Survey, assess and record the threat from cluster munition remnants, making every effort to identify all contaminated areas under its jurisdiction or control;
- Assess and prioritize needs for marking, protection of civilians, clearance and destruction;
- Take steps to mobilize resources for these operations;
- Develop a national plan, building, where appropriate, upon existing structures, experiences, and methodologies.
- Take 'all feasible steps' to perimeter-mark, monitor, and fence hazardous areas;
- Conduct risk reduction education to ensure civilians living in or around cluster-munition-contaminated areas are aware of the risks; and

---

[131] According to Article 3, paragraph 3, of *2003 Protocol V*:

After the cessation of active hostilities and as soon as feasible, each High Contracting Party and party to an armed conflict shall take the following measures in affected territories under its control, to reduce the risks posed by explosive remnants of war:

(a) survey and assess the threat posed by explosive remnants of war;

(b) assess and prioritize needs and practicability in terms of marking and clearance, removal or destruction;

(c) mark and clear, remove or destroy explosive remnants of war;

(d) take steps to mobilize resources to carry out these activities.

[132] According to the IMAS, demining refers to:

activities which lead to the removal of mine and ERW hazards, including technical survey, mapping, clearance, marking, post-clearance documentation, community mine action liaison and the handover of cleared land... [I]n IMAS standards and guides, mine and ERW clearance is considered to be just one part of the demining process.

IMAS 04:10: 'Glossary of mine action terms, definitions and abbreviations', *op. cit.*, Definition 3.53.

- Clear and destroy all cluster munition remnants.[133]

4.58 In accordance with paragraph 3, in carrying out these activities each affected State Party is required to 'take into account' international standards, including the IMAS.[134] In addition, an affected State Party must do so 'taking into consideration' the provisions of Article 6 of the Convention on international cooperation and assistance.[135] Each activity or set of related activities is considered in turn.

Survey, assessment, and recording of the threat

4.59 Sub-paragraph (a) requires that each State Party survey, assess, and record the threat posed by cluster munition remnants, 'making every effort to identify all cluster munition contaminated areas under its jurisdiction or control'. This provision is more comprehensive than the similar provision in *2003 Protocol V*.[136] It is also considerably more specific than the corresponding provision in the *1997 Anti-Personnel Mine Ban Convention*, which more generally requires States Parties to 'make every effort to identify all areas under its jurisdiction or control in which anti-personnel mines are known or suspected to be emplaced...'.[137]

4.60 International standards similarly stress the importance of identifying where explosive hazards, including cluster munition remnants, are located. Thus, according to the IMAS, should the decision be taken to develop a national mine action programme, it will be necessary to conduct a 'comprehensive assessment' of the affected country, known as a General Mine Action Assessment (GMAA).[138] Where one is not already ongoing or completed, existing programmes should also begin the GMAA process as early as possible.

4.61 The aim of the GMAA is to:

- assess the scale and impact of the mine/ERW problem on the country and individual communities;
- investigate all reported and/or suspected areas of contamination, quantities and types of explosive hazards; and

---

[133] The ordering of the sub-paragraphs largely follows the logical sequence of events in chronological order, save for the placement of risk reduction education after the obligation to clear and destroy all cluster munition remnants.

[134] Article 4, paragraph 3. See, *infra*, the commentary on this provision.

[135] See, *infra*, the commentary on Article 6, in particular with respect to paragraphs 1–6 and 9–12.

[136] Under Article 3, paragraph 3 of *2003 Protocol V*, States Parties are only required 'as soon as feasible' to 'survey and assess the threat posed by explosive remnants of war'. The amendments were proposed by Ireland at the outset of the Dublin Diplomatic Conference. 'Proposal by Ireland for the amendment of Article 4', Diplomatic Conference doc. CCM/31, 19 May 2008.

[137] Article 5, paragraph 2, *1997 Anti-Personnel Mine Ban Convention*.

[138] See IMAS 08.10: 'General mine action assessment', Second Edition, 1 January 2003.

- collect general information such as the security situation, terrain, soil characteristics, climate, routes, infrastructure, and local support facilities.

In addition, the GMAA process 'gathers information on national capabilities and potential to address the problem, and the need for external assistance including financial, human skills, material and information. The information collected should be sufficient to enable priorities to be established or updated and plans to be developed. It is a continuous process.'[139]

4.62 National surveys of areas contaminated with cluster munition remnants have been conducted in a number of affected countries, such as Laos,[140] Serbia,[141] or, partially, in Vietnam.[142] Surveys will typically identify not only the existence of contaminated areas, but also assess[143] the human, social, and economic impact of cluster munition remnants (see the

---

[139] According to the IMAS, a GMAA is 'the continuous process by which a comprehensive inventory can be obtained of all reported and/or suspected locations of mine or ERW contamination, the quantities and types of explosive hazards, and information on local soil characteristics, vegetation and climate; and assessment of the scale and impact of the landmine and ERW problem on the individual, community and country'. IMAS 04.10: 'Glossary of mine action terms, definitions and abbreviations', *op. cit.*, Definition 3.101.

[140] See Handicap International, 'Living with UXO: Final Report National Survey on the Socio-Economic Impact of UXO in Lao PDR', Vientiane, 1997.

[141] A survey of cluster munition remnants by Norwegian People's Aid in 2007–2009 found that:

> Cluster bombs were used in 105 deployment zones during the NATO intervention in 1999. Four types of sub-munitions were used, the total number of sub-munitions dropped was around 37,000 and of these, an estimated 2,500 are left unexploded in the ground. Immediately after the bombing Serb military forces undertook surface clearance in a number of areas, but no data is available on this clearance. Since then humanitarian clearance has been undertaken in around 4 km² with around 250 unexploded submunitions cleared... The total suspected hazard area covers 30.7 km² in 16 municipalities, an area around the size of New Belgrade. Accidents recorded to date have resulted in 191 victims, 31 fatal and 160 suffering injuries. More than 88,000 people live close to hazard areas in 28 local communities.

NPA, 'Scale of cluster bomb problem in Serbia revealed for first time', Press Conference, Belgrade, 10 March 2009, <http://www.npaid.org/?module=Articles;action=Article.publicShow;ID=7727> (accessed 22 March 2009).

[142] According to its website, since 2001, the Information Management and Mine Action Programs (iMMAP) of Veterans for America (VFA) has worked with the Vietnamese Ministry of Defence to coordinate with the Technology Centre for Bomb & Mine Disposal (BOMICEN), Engineering Command, to design and implement a Vietnam Unexploded Ordnance/Landmine Impact Assessment and Rapid Technical Response Project. 'The project's goal is to define the nature and scope of unexploded ordnance (UXO) and landmine contaminated areas in Vietnam and its adverse social and economic consequences through the execution of a UXO/landmine survey and impact assessment down to commune level.' VFA, 'VFA's Programs in Vietnam', <http://www.veteransforamerica.org/our-programs/post-conflict-rehabilitation/vfas-programs-in-vietnam> (accessed 22 March 2009).

[143] For the purposes of the IMAS on General Mine Action Assessment, 'an "assessment" defines a "continually refined process of information gathering and evaluation", whereas a "survey"

commentary on sub-paragraph (b) below). Owing to the risk of exaggerating the extent of contamination,[144] these 'impact' surveys are increasingly being complemented by a so-called non-technical survey,[145] as well as a subsequent technical survey,[146] in order to identify more precisely and accurately the contaminated areas.[147]

is a distinct operational task capable of being contracted.' IMAS 08.10: 'General mine action assessment', Second Edition, 1 January 2003, p. v.

[144] Thus, e.g., an Analysing Group of States Parties to the *1997 Anti-Personnel Mine Ban Convention*, tasked to conduct an analysis of requests for extensions to Article 5 deadlines for clearance of mined areas, noted in a number of instances that impact surveys had overestimated the extent of contamination. e.g., in the case of Chad, the Group stated that: 'The findings of the LIS inaccurately identified/estimated the extent of the challenge.' Analysis of the Request Submitted by Chad for an Extension of the Deadline for Completing the Destruction of Anti-Personnel Mines in Accordance with Article 5 of the Convention, Submitted by the President of the Eighth Meeting of the States Parties on behalf of the States Parties mandated to analyse requests for extensions, doc. APLC/MSP.9/2008/WP.30, 19 November 2008, paragraph 5, <http://www.apminebanconvention.org/fileadmin/pdf/mbc/clearing-mined-areas/art5_extensions/countries/9MSP-ext-analysis-Chad-en.pdf> (accessed 22 March 2009). Similarly, in the case of Senegal, the Analysing Group noted that, 'if the LIS [Landmine Impact Survey] as in other cases grossly overestimated the true size of the challenge, the outcomes of general and technical survey efforts may be the potential for Senegal to complete implementation sooner than by 1 March 2016'. Doc. APLC/MSP.9/2008/WP.14, 30 October 2008, paragraph 3. With respect to Thailand it was stated by the Analysing Group that: 'The LIS grossly overestimated the area known or suspected to contain mines and it was impossible and illogical for Thailand to initiate an effective mine clearance plan based upon areas identified by the LIS.' Doc. APLC/MSP.9/2008/WP.8, 9 October 2008, paragraph 2.

[145] Non-technical survey is a recent term which describes the verification of suspected hazardous areas, but without the use of clearance assets, such as demining machines, manual deminers, or mine/explosives detection dogs. According to the IMAS on land release:

> The term 'Non-technical Survey' describes an important survey activity which involves collecting and analysing new and/or existing information about a hazardous area. Its purpose is to confirm whether there is evidence of a hazard or not, to identify the type and extent of hazards within any hazardous area and to define, as far as is possible, the perimeter of the actual hazardous areas without physical intervention. A non-technical survey does not normally involve the use of clearance or verification assets. Exceptions occur when assets are used for the sole purpose of providing access for non-technical survey teams. The results from a non-technical survey can replace any previous data relating to the survey of an area.

IMAS 08.20: 'Land release', First Edition, 10 June 2009, pp. 1–2.

[146] Technical survey is the use of clearance assets or mine-protected vehicles to confirm and then reduce a suspected hazardous area to the actual perimeters of the minefield or ERW area. According to the IMAS on land release:

> The term 'Technical Survey' describes a detailed intervention with clearance or verification assets into a CHA, or part of a CHA. It should confirm the presence of mines/ERW leading to the definition of one or more DHA and may indicate the absence of mines/ERW which could allow land to be released when combined with other evidence.

IMAS 08.20: 'Land release', First Edition, 10 June 2009, p. 2.

[147] It is reported that: 'Land release principles are also applicable to battle areas, including areas affected by cluster munition remnants, but procedures tailored to battle areas are to be elaborated in a separate IMAS.' See ICBL, *Landmine Monitor Report 2009, op. cit.*, p. 42, fn. 46.

4.63 The reference to assessment of the threat covers not only the need to analyse the results of surveys of contamination, it also requires that existing data (such as data on the use of cluster munitions) be reviewed in order to identify likely hazardous areas. The reference to recording the threat is a logical consequence of any survey or assessment, and presumably includes storage of the data in a secure format and location, whether electronically or in hard copy (or preferably both).[148]

Assessing and prioritizing needs

4.64 Sub-paragraph (b) is also based on similar provisions in *2003 Protocol V*.[149] It contains three separate obligations, the first of which is to assess and prioritize needs in terms of marking, protection of civilians, clearance, and destruction.

4.65 This first obligation in sub-paragraph (b) demands that priorities be set to assess needs. The formulation of the obligation does not, however, provide guidance on how these priorities should be determined. Criteria to prioritize action with respect to contaminated areas might include the following:

- The location of casualties within the last 12 months or other period;
- Areas to which refugees or the internally displaced are planning or likely to return;
- Fertile agricultural land in food insecure areas; or
- Areas in which reconstruction or development projects are planned.

Developing a national plan

4.66 The result of assessment both of the threat and of needs should lead naturally into planning. The second obligation under sub-paragraph (b) is to develop a national plan to carry out marking, the protection of civilians, and clearance and destruction of cluster munition remnants, 'building, where appropriate, upon existing structures, experiences and methodologies'.[150]

---

[148] See, e.g., GICHD, *A Guide to Cluster Munitions*, First Edition, November 2007, Chapter 4.

[149] Article 3, paragraph 3(b) and (d) require States Parties to: 'assess and prioritize needs and practicability in terms of marking and clearance, removal or destruction', and to 'take steps to mobilize resources to carry out these activities.'

[150] This language was added by Ireland at the outset of the Diplomatic Conference. 'Proposal by Ireland for the amendment of Article 4', Diplomatic Conference doc. CCM/31, 19 May 2008. Its intent is not clear, unless it is to indicate that where a State is engaged in a demining programme to address landmine contamination, a separate coordination and management structure is not desirable. Surely, it is not intended to stifle innovations and testing that seek to improve clearance efficiency.

4.67 According to the IMAS, 'a General Mine Action Assessment Planning for mine action requires accurate and timely information on the form, scale and impact of the risk posed by mines and Explosive Remnants of War (ERW). Such information will come from local information, surveys and assessment missions and ongoing local mine action projects and tasks.'[151]

4.68 The plan does not have to be for a specific duration. Typically, an action or work plan will be annual in duration (normally over a calendar year), whereas a strategic plan will be for three to five years (although it can be longer). The obligation only talks of a single national plan; in reality, however, both forms of plan will usually be required in the case of a State with significant contamination.

4.69 As noted in the *chapeau* to Article 4, paragraph 2, there is a clear link with Article 6 on international cooperation and assistance. Under Article 6, paragraph 11, an affected State Party 'may, with the purpose of developing a national action plan, request the United Nations system, regional organisations, other States Parties or other competent intergovernmental or non-governmental institutions to assist its authorities to determine, inter alia: (a) The nature and extent of cluster munition remnants located in areas under its jurisdiction or control; . . . [and] (c) The time estimated as necessary to clear and destroy all cluster munition remnants located in areas under its jurisdiction or control.'

Resource mobilization

4.70 The third obligation under sub-paragraph (b) is to 'take steps to mobilise resources'.[152] The term should be understood broadly, to include not just financial but also material (i.e. demining and personal protective equipment), political, technological,[153] and human resources for coordination, management, and implementation of clearance and related activities.[154] Resource mobilization, which will take place at national and sub-regional level,[155] as

---

[151] IMAS 08.10: 'General mine action assessment', *op. cit.*, p. v.

[152] A similar provision was included in Article 3, paragraph 3(d), *2003 Protocol V.*

[153] Under Article 11, paragraph 1, of the Convention on Cluster Munitions, 'The States Parties shall meet regularly in order to consider and, where necessary, take decisions in respect of any matter with regard to the application or implementation of this Convention, including: . . . (d) The development of technologies to clear cluster munition remnants.'

[154] See Article 4, paragraph 4(a) for the provision calling for any State to provide resources for clearance operations where that State used cluster munitions prior to becoming party to the Convention on Cluster Munitions against another State, which is a party or which subsequently becomes one.

[155] Article 7, paragraph 1(m) on transparency measures implicitly stresses the importance of national support for clearance of cluster munition remnants, requiring that affected States Parties report on:

well as, in many cases, at international level, is one of the enabling activities of mine action.[156] Article 6, paragraph 11 also notes that an affected State Party may ask for assistance to determine the financial, technological, and human resources required for the implementation of the plan.

Marking and fencing hazardous areas

4.71 Sub-paragraph (c) requires States Parties to take 'all feasible steps'[157] to ensure that 'all cluster munition contaminated areas under its jurisdiction or control are perimeter-marked, monitored and protected by fencing or other means to ensure the effective exclusion of civilians'. This provision, which corresponds to Article 5 (2) of the *1997 Anti-Personnel Mine Ban Convention*, is adapted from language in the non-binding Technical Annex to *2003 Protocol V*.[158]

4.72 The provision in sub-paragraph (c) further requires that warning signs 'based on methods of marking readily recognisable by the affected community' should be used to mark suspected hazardous areas. 'Signs and other hazardous area boundary markers should, as far as possible, be visible, legible, durable and resistant to environmental effects and should clearly identify which side of the marked boundary is considered to be within the cluster munition contaminated areas and which side is considered to be safe.'[159]

4.73 As noted in the relevant IMAS,[160] mine and other explosive ordnance hazards are marked to provide a clear and unambiguous warning of danger to the local population. Marking of contaminated areas tends to be carried out either immediately prior to clearance (often called 'temporary marking') or in situations where formal clearance is unlikely to occur for a considerable time, often measured in years (sometimes rather misleadingly referred to as 'permanent marking').[161] Fencing of contaminated areas, where it is possible to do so, involves installing a physical barrier to reduce the risk of unintentional entry into hazardous areas.[162]

The amount of national resources, including financial, material or in kind, allocated to the implementation of Articles 3, 4 and 5 of this Convention.

Sub-paragraph (n) requires reporting on international cooperation and assistance.

[156] See the definition of mine action contained in IMAS 04.10: 'Glossary of mine action terms, definitions and abbreviations', *op. cit.*, Definition 3.158.

[157] Thus, e.g., long-term marking of areas suspected to contain cluster munition remnants may not be feasible where contamination is significant or widespread.

[158] Article 2(h), Technical Annex to *2003 Protocol V*.

[159] This language is identical to Article 2(i), Technical Annex to *2003 Protocol V*. It was proposed by Ireland at the outset of the Dublin Diplomatic Conference. 'Proposal by Ireland for the amendment of Article 4', Diplomatic Conference doc. CCM/31, 19 May 2008.

[160] IMAS 08.40: 'Marking mine and UXO hazards', Second Edition, 1 January 2003, p. v.

[161] Markings need to be maintained and replaced, owing to climate, destruction, or theft of warning signs.

[162] GICHD, *A Guide to Cluster Munitions*, Second Edition, June 2009, pp. 74 *et seq.*

4.74 According to the GICHD, marking 'can and does save lives. It should be borne in mind, however, that evidence exists that marking will not be successful in reducing risk-taking if the local population is impoverished.'[163] The GICHD further suggests that fencing should be used selectively, for reasons of cost as well as because fencing can be—and often is—removed by the local population and used for other purposes:

Fencing can be usefully erected around military installations or heavily UXO/submunition-contaminated sites close to heavily populated areas. It is recommended that such fenced areas be guarded. In Kosovo, for example, although UXO-affected sites were marked with specific warning signs (differing from those used to mark mined areas), permanent fencing is only used today in Lukare (Pristina) around a previous ammunition storage depot and military barracks.[164]

Risk reduction education

4.75 Under sub-paragraph (e),[165] States Parties are required to conduct 'risk reduction education to ensure awareness among civilians living in or around cluster munition contaminated areas of the risks posed by such remnants'.[166] Thus, the Convention on Cluster Munitions introduces a new term to the mine action sector: risk reduction education.[167] Previously the terms mine awareness,[168] mine risk education,[169] or simply risk education[170]

---

[163] GICHD, *A Guide to Cluster Munitions*, First Edition, November 2007, p. 59.

[164] GICHD, *A Guide to Cluster Munitions*, First Edition, November 2007, p. 59.

[165] Logically, this provision should precede the obligation to conduct clearance and destruction operations, set out in sub-paragraph (d).

[166] According to the Technical Annex to *2003 Protocol V*:

Warnings and risk education should be provided to the affected civilian population which comprises civilians living in or around areas containing explosive remnants of war and civilians who transit such areas.

Technical Annex, Article 2(d), *2003 Protocol V.*

[167] The addition of the word 'reduction' was proposed by Ireland at the outset of the Diplomatic Conference. 'Proposal by Ireland for the amendment of Article 4', Diplomatic Conference doc. CCM/31, 19 May 2008. At the Wellington Conference it was decided not to amend the text in advance of Dublin. However, as progress had been made on Article 4 in discussions chaired by Ireland, Ireland proposed to capture this progress in the form of a 'national proposal'. In effect, CCM/31 is a revised 'Chair's Paper' arising from the Wellington Conference.

[168] See, e.g., Article 6, paragraph 3, *1997 Anti-Personnel Mine Ban Convention.*

[169] This term is used by the IMAS. See, e.g., IMAS 07.11: 'Guide for the management of mine risk education', First Edition, 23 December 2003.

[170] See, e.g., Article 5, *2003 Protocol V*, and Article 2 of the Technical Annex to the Protocol. The term has also been used by the Landmine Monitor since its annual report in 2008. See ICBL, *Landmine Monitor Report 2008*, *op. cit.*, pp. 31 *et seq.*

had been used by international treaties or standards.[171] There is no specific requirement under paragraph 2 of Article 4 to conduct an assessment of the need for risk reduction education or to prioritize those needs.[172] There is also no specific requirement under the Convention to provide assistance to conduct risk reduction education, although, paradoxically, Article 6, paragraph 5 requires States Parties to 'provide assistance to identify, assess and prioritise needs and practical measures in terms of marking, risk reduction education, protection of civilians and clearance and destruction as provided in Article 4 of this Convention'.

4.76 The relevant IMAS on mine risk education (MRE)[173] defines the term as 'activities which seek to reduce the risk of injury from mines/ERW by raising awareness and promoting behavioural change including public information dissemination,[174] education and training,[175] and community mine action

---

[171] For a useful summary and comparison of the risk education provisions in *1996 Amended Protocol II* and *2003 Protocol V*, the *1997 Anti-Personnel Mine Ban Convention*, and the Convention on Cluster Munitions, *cf.* the unpublished paper by Gustavo Laurie of UNMAS: Laurie, G., 'An analysis of Mine Risk Education provisions in mine action-related treaties', undated but 2008.

[172] *Cf.* Article 4, paragraph 2(b).

[173] According to the IMAS, MRE is one of the five components of mine action. The others are: demining, victim assistance, advocacy to stigmatise the use of landmines and support a total ban on anti-personnel landmines, and stockpile destruction. As of March 2010, the IMAS on MRE were being reviewed and, as part of this process, were likely to be reduced to a single, consolidated IMAS that would include reference to the obligations under the Convention on Cluster Munitions.

[174] Public information dissemination refers to public information activities that seek to reduce the risk of injury from mines and ERW by raising awareness of the risk to individuals and communities, and by promoting behavioural change. It is primarily a one-way form of communication transmitted through mass media. This may provide relevant information and advice in a cost-effective and timely manner. In an emergency post-conflict situation, due to time constraints and lack of accurate data, public information dissemination is often the most practical means of communicating safety information to reduce risk. IMAS 07.11: 'Guide for the management of mine risk education', First Edition, 23 December 2003, p. 3.

[175] Education and training is a two-way process, which involves the imparting and acquiring of knowledge, attitude and practice through teaching and learning. Education and training activities may be conducted in formal and non-formal environments. This may include teacher-to-child education in schools, parent-to-children and children-to-parent education in the home, child-to-child education, peer-to-peer education in work and recreational environments, landmine safety training for humanitarian aid workers and the incorporation of landmine safety messages in regular occupational health and safety practices. IMAS 07.11: 'Guide for the management of mine risk education', First Edition, 23 December 2003, p. 4.

liaison.[176,177] In addition, the term mine risk reduction is defined as 'those actions which lessen the probability and/or severity of physical injury to people, property or the environment . . . [178] Mine risk reduction can be achieved by physical measures such as clearance, fencing or marking, or through behavioural changes brought about by MRE.'[179]

4.77 Although one of the five 'pillars' of mine action, the extent to which risk education is effective in reducing the number of new casualties is not universally agreed.[180] Indeed, the limitations of the approach are implicitly recognized by the formulation in sub-paragraph (e), which only sees awareness-raising as the aim of risk reduction education.[181] Most experts agree that behavioural change—whereby those living in affected areas should act to minimize the risk to themselves and their families and communities—is an integral component of efforts to reduce casualties from ERW or mines. The IMAS on MRE note that risk education 'should not normally

[176] Community liaison refers to the system and processes used to exchange information between national authorities, mine action organizations and communities on the presence of mines and explosive remnants of war, and of their potential risk. It enables communities to be informed when a demining activity is planned to take place, the nature and duration of the task, and the exact locations of areas that have been marked or cleared. Beyond demining, community liaison can support relief and development interventions that reduce the risk to affected communities. IMAS 07.11: 'Guide for the management of mine risk education', *op. cit.*, p. 4; see also GICHD, *A Guide to Cluster Munitions*, Second Edition, June 2009, p. 81.

[177] IMAS 04.10: 'Glossary of mine action terms, definitions and abbreviations', *op. cit.*, Definition 3.168

[178] In March 2008, participants at a meeting of experts on the future of risk education (RE), jointly organized by the GICHD and UNICEF, agreed that RE 'continued to be an important component of broader risk reduction efforts, and that the sector had become increasingly professional. However, participants also recognized that many RE projects continued to be poorly designed or implemented, and failed to make the requisite changes for sustainable and integrated programming.' ICBL, *Landmine Monitor Report 2008*, *op. cit.*, p. 33.

[179] IMAS 04.10: 'Glossary of mine action terms, definitions and abbreviations', *op. cit.*, Definition 3.169.

[180] According to Landmine Monitor:

In 2008 UNICEF observed some challenges for RE [risk education]. Most importantly, it noted that considerable awareness-raising had occurred, but this and the often basic messages disseminated had not led to sustained behavioral change. UNICEF also saw the need to adapt RE provision to changing country situations as they evolve from emergency to development phases. This was hampered, however, by the absence of data and standardized evaluations to demonstrate RE effectiveness, and by the fact that RE was often seen as a marginal activity in comparison with other mine action components.

ICBL, *Landmine Monitor Report 2008: Toward a Mine-Free World*, *op. cit.*, p. 33.

[181] In contrast, Article 6, paragraph 11(d) refers to the need for international cooperation and assistance in support of risk reduction education programmes and awareness activities 'to reduce the incidence of injuries or deaths caused by cluster munition remnants'.

be a stand-alone activity. It is an integral part of mine action planning and implementation.'[182]

4.78 According to a document adopted by the First Review Conference of States Parties to the *1997 Anti-Personnel Mine Ban Convention*:

Since the Convention was established, the field of mine risk education (MRE) has evolved to become more standardised and professional. It is now accepted that MRE should be incorporated into broader mine action programmes, ensuring an effective two-way information exchange both to ensure the effectiveness of MRE programmes and to obtain information from affected communities to support mine clearance priority-setting. It has been stressed that MRE programmes should include a clear communications strategy, targeting a variety of different audiences in a manner that takes age and gender into consideration, as well as social, economic, political and geographical factors. It has been emphasised that a careful assessment of needs should be carried out. For example, needs assessments may overcome a tendency to focus on MRE activities on children, which are not necessarily the category most at-risk, and challenge the assumption that, simply because a State Party is affected by landmines, an MRE programme is necessary or appropriate. In addition, it has been emphasised that effective monitoring and evaluation systems need to be developed to continuously measure mine risks and the impact of programmes on reducing risk.[183]

Clearance and destruction

4.79 Under Paragraph 2(d), each affected State Party is required to clear and destroy all cluster munition remnants located in areas under its jurisdiction or control 'as soon as possible'.[184] According to Article 7, paragraph 1(i), affected States Parties are required to report on the following:

The status and progress of programmes for the clearance and destruction of all types and quantities of cluster munition remnants cleared and destroyed in accordance with Article 4 of this Convention, to include the size and location of the cluster munition contaminated area cleared and a breakdown of the quantity of each type of cluster munition remnant cleared and destroyed.

---

[182] IMAS 07.11: 'Guide for the management of mine risk education', *op. cit.*, p. 3.

[183] Final Report of the *1997 Anti-Personnel Mine Ban Convention*, Part II: Review of the Operation and Status of the Convention on the Prohibition of the Use, Stockpiling, Production and Transfer of Antipersonnel Mines and on Their Destruction: 1999–2004, doc. APLC/CONF/2004/5, 9 February 2005, p. 23 (#49), available at: <http://www.nairobisummit.org/fileadmin/pdf/review_conference/documents/final_report/RC_Final_Report_en.pdf> (accessed 1 March 2010).

[184] Similar, albeit weaker provisions were included in Article 3, paragraph 3(c), *2003 Protocol V*, whereby States Parties are required to 'mark and clear, remove or destroy explosive remnants of war'.

The link with Articles 6 and 7

4.80 As noted in the *chapeau* to Article 4, paragraph 2, there is a link between the clearance and destruction of cluster munition remnants and international cooperation and assistance. Although the ultimate responsibility for clearance lies with the affected State Party, in some cases international support is critical to the success of implementation of its obligations under Article 4 (as well as other provisions in the Convention, notably in Article 3 with respect to stockpile destruction). Thus, according to Article 6, paragraph 4:

In addition to any obligations it may have pursuant to paragraph 4 of Article 4 of this Convention, each State Party in a position to do so shall provide assistance for clearance and destruction of cluster munition remnants and information concerning various means and technologies related to clearance of cluster munitions, as well as lists of experts, expert agencies or national points of contact on clearance and destruction of cluster munition remnants and related activities.

4.81 According to paragraph 5 of Article 6:

Each State Party in a position to do so shall provide assistance . . . to identify, assess and prioritise needs and practical measures in terms of marking, risk reduction education, protection of civilians and clearance and destruction as provided in Article 4 of this Convention.

4.82 In addition, according to Article 7, paragraph 1(c), States Parties are required to report on the technical characteristics of each type of cluster munition produced prior to their becoming party to the Convention on Cluster Munitions:

to the extent known, and those currently owned or possessed by it, giving, where reasonably possible, such categories of information as may facilitate identification and clearance of cluster munitions; at a minimum, this information shall include the dimensions, fusing, explosive content, metallic content, colour photographs and other information that may facilitate the clearance of cluster munition remnants.

Paragraph 3

> In conducting the activities referred to in paragraph 2 of this Article, each State Party shall take into account international standards, including the International Mine Action Standards (IMAS).

4.83 According to paragraph 3, in conducting the activities referred to in paragraph 2, 'each State Party shall take into account international standards, including the International Mine Action Standards (IMAS)'. Although the relevant international standards are not limited to the IMAS, these are the primary framework of reference for the clearance and destruction of cluster munition remnants and related activities.

4.84 The IMAS[185] define themselves as 'documents developed by the UN on behalf of the international community, which aim to improve safety and efficiency in mine action by providing guidance, by establishing principles and, in some cases, by defining international requirements and specifications'.[186] There are many such standards that are potentially relevant to the implementation of Article 4, particularly:

- IMAS 02.10: Guide to the Establishment of a Mine Action Programme,
- IMAS 04.10: Glossary of mine action terms, definitions and abbreviations,
- IMAS 07.10: Guide for the Management of Demining Operations,
- IMAS 07.11: Guide for the Management of Mine Risk Education,
- IMAS 07.41: Monitoring of MRE Programmes,
- IMAS 08.10: General Mine Action Assessment,
- IMAS 08.20 Land Release,
- IMAS 08.21 Non-technical Survey,
- IMAS 08.22 Technical Survey,
- IMAS 08.30: Post-clearance Documentation,
- IMAS 08.40: Marking of Hazards,
- IMAS 08.50: Data Collection and Needs Assessment for MRE,
- IMAS 09.10: Clearance Requirements,
- IMAS 09.11: Battle Area Clearance,
- IMAS 09.20: Guidelines for Post Clearance Sampling,
- IMAS 09.30: Explosive Ordnance Disposal,
- IMAS 09.50: Mechanical Demining,
- IMAS 10.10: S&OH General Principles,
- IMAS 10.20: Demining Worksite Safety,
- IMAS 10.30: Personal Protection Equipment,
- IMAS 10.40: Medical Support to Demining Operations,
- IMAS 10.50: Storage, Transportation and Handling of Explosives,
- IMAS 10.60: Reporting and Investigation of Demining Incidents,

---

[185] All IMAS are available at:<http:// www.mineactionstandards.org/imas.htm>.

[186] IMAS 04.10: 'Glossary of mine action terms, definitions and abbreviations', *op. cit.*, Definition 3.133. *Cf.* also IMAS 01.10: 'Guide for the application of International Mine Action Standards (IMAS)', Second Edition, 1 January 2003.

- IMAS 10.70: Safety & Occupational Health—Protection of the Environment,
- IMAS 12.10: Planning for MRE Programmes,
- IMAS 12.20: Implementation of MRE Programmes,
- IMAS 14.10: Guide for the evaluation of Mine Action Intervention, and
- IMAS 14.20: Evaluation of MRE Programmes.[187]

4.85 Other relevant international standards would include environmental standards for the protection of wildlife (though these would not override the obligation to conduct clearance and destruction operations),[188] and others might indirectly govern clearance operations, for example where machines or other methods used for the destruction of anti-personnel submunitions cause significant damage to the soil,[189] property, or other infrastructure.[190] For instance, although the area is not affected by cluster munition remnants,

---

[187] As noted, *supra*, as of March 2010, the IMAS on MRE were being reviewed and, as part of this process, were likely to be reduced to a single, consolidated IMAS.

[188] Council Directive 79/409/EEC on the conservation of wild birds, commonly referred to as the Birds Directive, is the European Union's oldest piece of nature legislation and one of the most important, creating a comprehensive scheme of protection for all wild bird species naturally occurring in the Union. It was adopted unanimously by the Members States in 1979 as a response to increasing concern about the declines in Europe's wild bird populations resulting from pollution, loss of habitats, as well as unsustainable use. See <http://ec.europa.eu/environment/nature/legislation/birdsdirective/index_en.htm>. The text of the Birds Directive is found at: <http://eur-lex.europa.eu/LexUriServ/LexUriServ.do?uri=CELEX:31979L0409:EN:HTML>.

[189] Though see also in this regard, IMAS 10.70: 'Safety & occupational health—Protection of the environment', First Edition, 1 October 2007. According to this IMAS (pp. 3–4):

Where mechanical operations involve the removal of vegetation, or occur on ground that may be subject to erosion, the NMAA should specify the requirements and the measures that the demining organisations shall take to ensure the regeneration of vegetation and to limit erosion... Such measures may include:

a) Re-seeding and re-planting (e.g. grass, trees, ground cover);

b) Return of processed soils to the effected site (Soils that have been mechanically sifted, or gone through remediation, etc.);

c) Planting or construction of wind barriers;

d) Preparation of drainage systems;

e) Performing the mechanical operation in a period when the soil and vegetations is less vulnerable; and

f) Avoiding deep tracks by using proper equipment.

[190] According to IMAS 10.70 (p. 4):

Mines and Explosive Remnants of War (ERW) should be disposed of in a manner that minimises environmental impact and without creating damage to property or infrastructure. If mines or ERW must be destroyed in situ and there is a risk to property or infrastructure, protective works shall be used. If, even with protective works, there is still a risk of damage to

Denmark has noted with respect to its obligations under the *1997 Anti-Personnel Mine Ban Convention* that mine clearance on the Skallingen peninsula might affect rare bird colonies.[191] Denmark has reported that Skallingen is protected by several international directives and conventions, including the Ramsar environmental convention.[192] Similar concerns with respect to the effects of clearance on the Falkland Islands, which are contaminated with both mines and cluster munition remnants, have been expressed by the UK.[193]

Paragraph 4

This paragraph shall apply in cases in which cluster munitions have been used or abandoned by one State Party prior to entry into force of this Convention for that State Party and have become cluster munition remnants that are located in areas under the jurisdiction or control of another State Party at the time of entry into force of this Convention for the latter.

(a) In such cases, upon entry into force of this Convention for both States Parties, the former State Party is strongly encouraged to provide, inter alia, technical, financial, material or human resources assistance to the latter State Party, either bilaterally or through a mutually agreed third party, including through the United Nations system or other relevant organisations, to facilitate the marking, clearance and destruction of such cluster munition remnants.

(b) Such assistance shall include, where available, information on types and quantities of the cluster munitions used, precise locations of cluster munition strikes and areas in which cluster munition remnants are known to be located.

property or infrastructure, the NMAA [National Mine Action Authority], local authorities and local communities shall be consulted about the operation.

[191] See Denmark Article 5 deadline Extension Request, 27 March 2008, Form C.4, available at: <http://www.apminebanconvention.org/background-status-of-the-convention/clearing-mined-areas/42-states-parties-in-the-process-of-implementing-article-5/denmark/> (accessed 1 March 2010).

[192] Letter from Jakob Karlshøj, Ministry of Transport, to His Royal Highness Prince Mired Raad Al-Hussein of Jordan, President of the Eighth Meeting of the States Parties, 27 March 2008. The Convention on Wetlands, signed in Ramsar, Iran, in 1971, is an intergovernmental treaty which provides the framework for national action and international cooperation for the conservation and wise use of wetlands and their resources. There were 159 States Parties as of March 2009, with 1,833 wetland sites, totalling 1.7 million square kilometres, designated for inclusion in the Ramsar List of Wetlands of International Importance. See <http://www.ramsar.org/>.

[193] See UK Article 5 deadline Extension Request, 30 May 2008, pp. 3, 12, 18–19, 23–24, and the Annex, <http://www.apminebanconvention.org/background-status-of-the-convention/clearing-mined-areas/42-states-parties-in-the-process-of-implementing-article-5/united-kingdom/> (accessed 1 March 2010).

4.86 This paragraph is one of the most innovative provisions of the Convention on Cluster Munitions. No previous weapons treaty includes a comparable provision seeking to hold States responsible for assisting clearance of munitions that they used or abandoned *before* the treaty entered into force for them. Because of its precedent-setting nature, the paragraph was one of the most difficult on which to agree. During both formal meetings and the informal sessions chaired by the Friend of the President for Article 4, some States objected to the provision's retroactive character while others argued user States should be held responsible for practical and moral reasons.[194]

4.87 Article 4, paragraph 4 stipulates that when a State that later becomes party to the Convention either used cluster munitions or abandoned them on the territory of another State Party, the State that used or abandoned the cluster munitions is 'strongly encouraged' to provide assistance for the marking, clearance, and destruction of the resultant cluster munition remnants. The language employed is in the form of an exhortation rather than an unfettered legal obligation. It applies to use on areas under the jurisdiction or control of an affected State before both the user State and the affected State become party to the Convention on Cluster Munitions.[195]

---

[194] Italy had formally proposed the deletion of the provision in its paper submitted to the Dublin Diplomatic Conference. 'Proposal by Italy for the amendment of Article 4', Diplomatic Conference doc. CCM/34, 19 May 2008. At the Conference, Canada and Japan supported this proposed deletion. See 'Summary Record of Second Session of the Committee of the Whole', Diplomatic Conference doc. CCM/CW/SR/2, 18 June 2008, p. 2; and 'Summary Record of Ninth Session of the Committee of the Whole', 23 May 2009, Diplomatic Conference doc. CCM/CW/SR/9, 18 June 2008, p. 4. In formal and informal sessions in Dublin, other States, such as Lebanon, Cambodia, Guatemala, Mexico, and Venezuela, pressed to keep a strong version of the provision. See, e.g., 'Summary Record of Second Session of the Committee of the Whole', *op. cit.*, p. 3. The provision was ultimately preserved, although in a less strict form than originally proposed. For more details of the debate over and evolution of this provision, see the commentary on preparatory discussions and negotiations of Article 4 in §§4.9–4.12.

[195] When ratifying the Convention on 3 December 2008, the Holy See observed in point 4 of its declaration that:

> Article 4.4 highlights moral responsibility in cases where cluster munitions have been used or abandoned and have became cluster munitions remnants prior to the entry into force of the Convention. State responsibility should be given effective expression in the area of cooperation and assistance.

Holy See, Ratification Declaration, 3 December 2008, <http://www.unog.ch/80256EDD006B8954/ (httpAssets)/42E72A73A7F63697C125756D003EAD09/$file/HolySee.pdf> (accessed 26 May 2010). *Cf.* also Article 6, paragraph 6, which provides that:

> Where, after entry into force of this Convention, cluster munitions have become cluster munition remnants located in areas under the jurisdiction or control of a State Party, each State Party in a position to do so shall urgently provide emergency assistance to the affected State Party.

4.88 The provision lists a variety of types of assistance that a user State can choose to give. It can render assistance through the provision of, *inter alia*, technical support, funding, relevant equipment (e.g., detectors or personal protective equipment),[196] or personnel. Article 6, paragraph 2 lays out a similar list of options with which any State Party can seek to meet its international cooperation and assistance obligations for clearance, although that paragraph does not specifically mention human resources.[197] Assistance can be provided directly or through a third party, such as the UN.[198]

4.89 While paragraph 4(a) strongly encourages user States to provide assistance for clearance, paragraph 4(b) obligates those who choose to render assistance to provide, where available,[199] information on types and quantities of the cluster munitions used, precise locations of cluster munition strikes, and areas in which cluster munition remnants are known to be located. Specifically highlighting the need to provide detailed data on strikes and abandoned munitions clarifies and potentially broadens the scope of Article 4, paragraph 4. Such information is critical to facilitate clearance, yet user States, the only States with the information, have not always provided it. In October 2006, for example, a representative of the UN Mine Action Coordination Centre–South Lebanon said:

The main obstacle for the clearance operations is that we lack good reference information from the Israeli government on the locations they hit with clusters and the quantities.[200]

Lack of information was still negatively affecting MACC SL's clearance operations two years later, in October 2008.[201] Clearance operators in other conflicts have faced similar difficulties in obtaining accurate information about cluster munition strikes.[202] Paragraph 4(b) seeks to address that problem.

---

[196] Presumably explosives detection dogs would fall under this item.

[197] Article 6, paragraph 2.

[198] See, e.g., Article 3, paragraph 1, and Article 4, paragraph 2, *2003 Protocol V.*

[199] The term 'where available' was added because in some cases, especially when use occurred a long time ago, States Parties that had formerly used cluster munitions might not have the relevant information.

[200] Government of Lebanon, 'Higher Relief Commission Daily Situation Report No. 78', 19 October 2006, available at: <http://www.lebanonundersiege.gov.lb/images_Browse/00000649_situation%20report%2078.doc> (accessed 1 March 2010).

[201] Mine Action Coordination Centre–South Lebanon, *Quarterly Report: July-September 2008*, 20 October 2008, p. 1.

[202] See, e.g., Human Rights Watch, *A Dying Practice: Use of Cluster Munitions by Russia and Georgia in August 2008*, April 2009, p. 76; and Human Rights Watch, *Fatally Flawed: Cluster Bombs and Their Use by the United States in Afghanistan*, Vol. 14, No. 7(G), December 2002, pp. 37–38.

Paragraph 5

If a State Party believes that it will be unable to clear and destroy or ensure the clearance and destruction of all cluster munition remnants referred to in paragraph 1 of this Article within ten years of the entry into force of this Convention for that State Party, it may submit a request to a Meeting of States Parties or a Review Conference for an extension of the deadline for completing the clearance and destruction of such cluster munition remnants by a period of up to five years. The requested extension shall not exceed the number of years strictly necessary for that State Party to complete its obligations under paragraph 1 of this Article.

4.90 Each State, in accordance with Article 4, paragraph 1, 'undertakes to clear and destroy, or ensure the clearance and destruction of, cluster munition remnants located in cluster munition contaminated areas under its jurisdiction or control' as soon as possible but not later than 10 years after becoming party to the Convention, or, in the case of contamination from cluster munition remnants that occurs in an armed conflict after that time, within 10 years of the end of active hostilities in which cluster munitions were used or abandoned. Understanding, however, that certain States Parties might not be able to meet these deadlines—primarily owing to the extent of contamination—States Parties are given the possibility under Article 4, paragraph 5, to request an extension of the deadline for a period of up to five years. The period requested must not exceed the number of years 'strictly necessary' for the completion of clearance obligations under paragraph 1 of Article 4.

4.91 To be able to request an extension period, a State Party must simply believe that it will be unable to meet the deadline set down in Article 4, paragraph 1. *Prima facie*, this is a purely subjective assessment; there is no need for any rationale to support it, although the content of the written request is governed by Article 4, paragraph 6 discussed below. Moreover, the inability of the State Party to meet the deadline may be entirely due to its own fault; this will not preclude it from being permitted to submit a request. Any exacerbating factors will, of course, be relevant to the application for an extension period. The mechanism also gives States Parties the opportunity to call attention to unaddressed needs in accordance with the obligations to provide assistance under Article 6.

Paragraph 6

A request for an extension shall be submitted to a Meeting of States Parties or a Review Conference prior to the expiry of the time period referred to in paragraph 1 of this Article for that State Party. Each request shall be submitted a minimum of nine months prior to the Meeting of States Parties or Review Conference at which it is to be considered. Each request shall set out:

(a) The duration of the proposed extension;

(b) A detailed explanation of the reasons for the proposed extension, including the financial and technical means available to and required by the State Party for the clearance and destruction of all cluster munition remnants during the proposed extension;

(c) The preparation of future work and the status of work already conducted under national clearance and demining programmes during the initial ten year period referred to in paragraph 1 of this Article and any subsequent extensions;

(d) The total area containing cluster munition remnants at the time of entry into force of this Convention for that State Party and any additional areas containing cluster munition remnants discovered after such entry into force;

(e) The total area containing cluster munition remnants cleared since entry into force of this Convention;

(f) The total area containing cluster munition remnants remaining to be cleared during the proposed extension;

(g) The circumstances that have impeded the ability of the State Party to destroy all cluster munition remnants located in areas under its jurisdiction or control during the initial ten year period referred to in paragraph 1 of this Article, and those that may impede this ability during the proposed extension;

(h) The humanitarian, social, economic and environmental implications of the proposed extension; and

(i) Any other information relevant to the request for the proposed extension.

4.92 In accordance with paragraph 6, an affected State Party that seeks an extension period must apply for it no later than the last Meeting of States Parties or Review Conference before its deadline elapses. In addition, a request must be submitted at least nine months prior to the relevant meeting or conference.

4.93 A detailed set of requirements is laid down for the content of the request.[203] These requirements are cumulative; each of the following must therefore be addressed in the request:

- The period of the extension requested;

---

[203] The list is longer and more specific than the one required by Article 5, paragraph 4, of the *1997 Anti-Personnel Mine Ban Convention* for the purposes of that treaty.

- A detailed explanation of the reasons for the proposed extension.[204] This must include available funding and technical means for the clearance and destruction of all cluster munition remnants during the proposed extension;
- Plans for future work;
- Progress in national clearance and demining programmes during the initial 10-year period (and any subsequent extensions);
- Total area contaminated by cluster munition remnants upon becoming a State Party and any additional areas discovered subsequently;
- Total area cleared of cluster munition remnants since becoming a State Party;
- Total contaminated area remaining to be cleared during the proposed extension;
- The circumstances that have prevented full compliance with clearance and destruction obligations during the initial 10-year period, as well as any relevant circumstances that may impede a State Party's ability to comply fully during the proposed extension;
- The humanitarian, social, economic and environmental implications of the proposed extension; and
- Any other information relevant to the request for the proposed extension.

Paragraph 7

The Meeting of States Parties or the Review Conference shall, taking into consideration the factors referred to in paragraph 6 of this Article, including, inter alia, the quantities of cluster munition remnants reported, assess the request and decide by a majority of votes of States Parties present and voting whether to grant the request for an extension. The States Parties may decide to grant a shorter extension than that requested and may propose benchmarks for the extension, as appropriate.

4.94 The Review Conference or the Meeting of States Parties that assesses the request must take account of the information submitted by the State Party seeking the extension period. The specific reference to the 'quantities of cluster munition remnants reported' suggests that the extent of both the contamination and progress in clearance will be relevant factors in the determination of States Parties.

---

[204] The distinction between this requirement and the obligation to set out 'The circumstances that have impeded the ability of the State Party to destroy all cluster munition remnants located in areas under its jurisdiction or control during the initial ten year period . . .' is not clear.

4.95 The States Parties are required to 'assess the request' at the meeting or Review Conference and decide by a majority of votes of the States Parties present and voting whether to grant the request for an extension. It is unlikely that a well-founded request for an extension would be refused. If it were, how-ever, once the 10-year deadline had elapsed, the State Party would be in viola-tion of its undertakings under the Convention.

4.96 Given doubt in the case of the *1997 Anti-Personnel Mine Ban Convention* as to whether the States Parties could agree to a shorter extension period than that requested, the paragraph makes it explicit that this option is possible. It is also possible for States Parties to set 'benchmarks' for the extension, 'as appro-priate'. The term benchmark is not defined in the Convention, although it is ordinarily defined as a 'point of reference; a criterion, touchstone'.[205] In this context, it means a set of yardsticks or targets that the requesting State Party is expected to meet during the extension period. Possible benchmarks might be clearance of a specific region or area, the conduct of a survey, or the provision of a certain level of resources by a stipulated deadline.

Paragraph 8

> Such an extension may be renewed by a period of up to five years upon the submission of a new request, in accordance with paragraphs 5, 6 and 7 of this Article. In requesting a further extension a State Party shall submit relevant additional information on what has been undertaken during the previous extension granted pursuant to this Article.

4.97 A State Party that is heavily contaminated may request more than one extension period. Each request for a further extension period, which must again fulfil the requirements set out in paragraphs 5–7 of this article, may presumably seek a shorter or longer period than the previous one (as long as no single period exceeds five years). The request must also be accompanied by 'relevant additional information' on what has been undertaken during the pre-vious extension period. This will ensure that the other States Parties are able to exercise a degree of ongoing supervision of the State Party's commitment to fully meeting its obligations.

---

[205] *Oxford English Dictionary*, Oxford University Press, CD-ROM Version 3.1, 2004. The ety-mology of the word is from surveying of land in which a surveyor's mark is cut in some durable material, such as a rock, wall, gate-pillar, or face of a building.

Article 5. Victim assistance

Markus Reiterer and Tirza Leibowitz[1]

Article 5—Victim assistance

1. Each State Party with respect to cluster munition victims in areas under its jurisdiction or control shall, in accordance with applicable international humanitarian and human rights law, adequately provide age- and gender-sensitive assistance, including medical care, rehabilitation and psychological support, as well as provide for their social and economic inclusion. Each State Party shall make every effort to collect reliable relevant data with respect to cluster munition victims.

2. In fulfilling its obligations under paragraph 1 of this Article each State Party shall:

(a) Assess the needs of cluster munition victims;

(b) Develop, implement and enforce any necessary national laws and policies;

(c) Develop a national plan and budget, including timeframes to carry out these activities, with a view to incorporating them within the existing national disability, development and human rights frameworks and mechanisms, while respecting the specific role and contribution of relevant actors;

(d) Take steps to mobilise national and international resources;

(e) Not discriminate against or among cluster munition victims, or between cluster munition victims and those who have suffered injuries or disabilities from other causes; differences in treatment should be based only on medical, rehabilitative, psychological or socio-economic needs;

(f) Closely consult with and actively involve cluster munition victims and their representative organisations;

(g) Designate a focal point within the government for coordination of matters relating to the implementation of this Article; and

(h) Strive to incorporate relevant guidelines and good practices including in the areas of medical care, rehabilitation and psychological support, as well as social and economic inclusion.

[1] The authors wish to thank Tracey Begley for her invaluable assistance in documenting the negotiation meetings.

Overview of the Article

5.1 Victim assistance in the Convention on Cluster Munitions should be seen as a package of measures with Article 5 at its heart. It allocates clear responsibility to each State Party to adequately provide age- and gender-sensitive assistance to cluster munition victims in areas under its jurisdiction or control. That assistance includes medical care, rehabilitation and psychological support, as well as provision for their social and economic inclusion. It also sets out in detail how a State Party is to implement these obligations. As such, the provision represents a major step forward as compared to the first breakthrough on victim assistance in treaties governing weapons, in the *1997 Anti-Personnel Mine Ban Convention*,[2] which contained only two references to victims: in the preamble and in a paragraph on international cooperation and assistance.[3]

Preparatory discussions

5.2 The history of the negotiations of the Convention's victim assistance package[4] is remarkably different from most other international negotiations: traditional negotiations often follow an approach where one aims high at the beginning and finally settles for the point of convergence, which usually is much lower than what was at the table initially. The negotiation of the victim assistance package constitutes a rare case of 'negotiating upwards', i.e. commencing in a fairly humble manner and finally reaching clearer and more

---

[2] The formal title of this treaty is the Convention on the Prohibition of the Use, Stockpiling, Production and Transfer of Anti-Personnel Mines and on their Destruction.

[3] Article 6, paragraph 3.

[4] This commentary on Article 5 focuses on the preparatory discussions and negotiations of the overall victim assistance package; the preparatory discussions and negotiations of the definition of 'cluster munition victims' has been described *supra* in §§2.4 *et seq.*

stringent outcomes. A contributing factor to this upward movement was the role that civil society played alongside negotiating States. The Cluster Munition Coalition (CMC), led in this issue by Survivor Corps and Handicap International, advocated for strong victim assistance provisions. The participation of Ban Advocates, campaigning for the ban and for victim assistance from first-hand experience of the devastating effects of cluster munitions, helped bring the issue to the fore and garner almost universal support.

5.3 The February 2007 Oslo Declaration had already referred to victim assistance: paragraph 1 of the Declaration, which determined the main objectives of the Convention to be negotiated, had included the issue of cooperation and assistance, which encompassed victim assistance. Paragraph 1(ii) of the Declaration states its aim as being to:

establish a framework for cooperation and assistance that ensures adequate provision of care and rehabilitation to survivors and their communities, clearance of contaminated areas, risk education and destruction of stockpiles of prohibited cluster munitions.

The Oslo Declaration, which was designed as a declaration of political intent, necessarily had to be short and to provide a framework, rather than enunciate legal obligations formulated in treaty language. It is primarily for this reason that the language used in sub-paragraph (ii) might in retrospect appear rather dense, mixing concepts which in the final outcome would appear distinct from each other.

5.4 Most notably, the Oslo Declaration refers to *survivors* rather than *victims*—the term employed and defined in the final treaty text; secondly it refers to survivors and their *communities* without mentioning the *families* of survivors—an important clarification that has been included in the definition of cluster munition victims—and finally, it relates to victim assistance in reference to establishing a framework for cooperation and assistance. This last point was modelled on Article 6 of the *1997 Anti-Personnel Mine Ban Convention*, which regulates how cooperation with and assistance to affected States carrying out their obligations under that Convention should be effected.

5.5 But the final text of the Convention on Cluster Munitions went a decisive step further by separating the obligation of States to victims in areas under their jurisdiction or control to provide adequate assistance from the obligation for States in a position to do so to provide international cooperation and assistance. These and other clarifications and developments now contained in the Convention were the result of intensive negotiations between the Oslo Conference in February 2007 and the adoption of the treaty text at the Dublin

Diplomatic Conference in May 2008. They were, though, firmly rooted in the Oslo Declaration and the decade-long experience gained through the application of the *1997 Anti-Personnel Mine Ban Convention*.

5.6 The inclusion of provisions on assisting the victims of specific weapons or explosive remnants of war in international disarmament agreements is a fairly young phenomenon: the first ever international treaty to do so was the *1997 Anti-Personnel Mine Ban Convention* which in its Article 6, paragraph 3 provides the following:

> Each State Party in a position to do so shall provide assistance for the care and rehabilitation, and social and economic reintegration, of mine victims and for mine awareness programs. Such assistance may be provided, inter alia, through the United Nations system, international, regional or national organizations or institutions, the International Committee of the Red Cross, national Red Cross and Red Crescent societies and their International Federation, non-governmental organizations, or on a bilateral basis.

This approach has also been introduced into the framework of the *Convention on Certain Conventional Weapons*:[5] Article 8 of its Protocol V on Explosive Remnants of War (*2003 Protocol V*) employs parallel language to that contained in the *1997 Anti-Personnel Mine Ban Convention*.[6]

5.7 In particular in the framework of the *1997 Anti-Personnel Mine Ban Convention*, Article 6, paragraph 3—although laying down legal obligations only for States 'in a position to do so' and mixing two distinct concepts[7]—has proven to be of enormous practical importance, both in the lives of survivors, their families, and communities, and in the overall implementation efforts of that Convention.[8] Article 6, paragraph 3 essentially served as a basis that enabled and initiated systematic work under the *1997 Anti-Personnel Mine Ban Convention* relating to victim assistance. Thus, States Parties created a Standing Committee on Victim Assistance that has worked towards better understanding of the issues at hand, including

---

[5] The formal title of this treaty is the Convention on Prohibitions or Restrictions on the Use of Certain Conventional Weapons Which May Be Deemed to Be Excessively Injurious or to Have Indiscriminate Effects, as amended on 21 December 2001.

[6] At the 2008 Meeting of States Parties to *2003 Protocol V*, the States Parties went a decisive step further, by adopting a Protocol V Action Plan on Victim Assistance.

[7] i.e. victim assistance and mine risk education.

[8] The decade-long efforts on victim assistance were the subject of a conference organized by Austria in 2007; the proceedings of this Conference provide a good overview of the work done and remaining challenges, see 'Assisting Landmine Survivors—A Decade of Efforts, The Vienna Symposium', available at: <http://www.apminebanconvention.org/tenth-anniversary> (accessed 1 March 2010).

deepening knowledge, exchanging ideas, and disseminating best practices. It also keeps a watchful eye on the implementation of the victim assistance provision, establishing a workable methodology for a quite complex field of activity. States Parties also further refined the victim assistance provisions of the *1997 Anti-Personnel Mine Ban Convention*, through the Nairobi Action Plan, which, although not legally binding, aimed to establish more concrete actions to assist the victims. In addition, the Convention's Implementation Support Unit established an important project to support implementation processes in States Parties with responsibility for significant numbers of mine victims.[9]

5.8 Including a provision on victim assistance in the *1997 Anti-Personnel Mine Ban Convention* was by no means easy: none of the first three drafts of that Convention referred to victim assistance and only after lengthy debates at the Diplomatic Conference in Oslo was a final compromise reached with a number of donor governments that had expressed concern 'about the financial ramifications of such an obligation'.[10] Hence, 'seeing that an international instrument prohibiting a conventional weapon would also address the needs of those who had fallen victim to the weapon was a hard fought victory'.[11] In doing so, the negotiators of the *1997 Anti-Personnel Mine Ban Convention* had taken a step of historic significance, which provided an important starting point for the elaboration of the victim assistance package of the Convention on Cluster Munitions.[12]

5.9 One of the main lessons of implementing Article 6, paragraph 3 of the *1997 Anti-Personnel Mine Ban Convention* also relates to the fact that often

[9] On victim assistance work undertaken in the framework of the *1997 Anti-Personnel Mine Ban Convention* see, e.g., Brinkert, K., 'Making sense out of the Anti-Personnel Mine Ban Convention's obligation to landmine victims': <http://www.apminebanconvention.org/fileadmin/pdf/publications/VA_Paper_Brinkert_JMA_31Mar2006.pdf> (accessed 1 March 2010).

[10] Maslen, S., *Commentaries on Arms Control Treaties, Volume I: The Convention on the Prohibition of the Use, Stockpiling, Production, and Transfer of Anti-Personnel Mines and on their Destruction,* Second Edition, Oxford Commentaries on International Law (Oxford: Oxford University Press, 2005), §6.9.

[11] Brinkert, K., 'Making sense out of the Anti-Personnel Mine Ban Convention's obligation to landmine victims', *op. cit.*

[12] At the same time, the difficulties in reaching the compromise contained in the *1997 Anti-Personnel Mine Ban Convention* were not forgotten and informed the approach taken for the negotiations on the Convention. Discussions with former negotiators of, and campaigners for, the *1997 Anti-Personnel Mine Ban Convention* which Markus Reiterer held in his capacity as negotiator focusing on victim assistance indicated that a cautious approach to the topic was warranted in order to avoid reactions that could have been detrimental to the overall outcome. Based on these considerations, an iterative approach was taken that resulted in considerable progress being made throughout the 14 months of work on the Convention on Cluster Munitions.

persons 'directly impacted by mines are a sub-group of larger communities of persons with injuries and disabilities'.[13] In other words: while the Convention on Cluster Munitions and the UN Convention on the Rights of Persons with Disabilities (CRPD) differ in scope, a direct link exists between the victim assistance work under the Convention and the overall disability sector. Timely for the negotiations of the Convention on Cluster Munitions was the fact that the CRPD had been adopted by the UN General Assembly on 13 December 2006, i.e. two months before the Oslo Conference. The adoption of the CRPD and its subsequent opening for signature on 30 March 2007 (i.e. two months before the first substantive meeting of the Oslo Process in Lima), put additional focus on the rights and needs of persons with disabilities.

5.10 The CRPD itself marks a 'paradigm shift' in attitudes vis-à-vis persons with disabilities: rather than being viewed (as often was and is the case) as *objects* of charity, rehabilitation, medical treatment, etc., the CRPD perceives persons with disabilities as *subjects* of the law, i.e. bearers of rights, and in particular human rights. As cluster munition victims are often themselves persons with disabilities, the link between the Convention on Cluster Munitions and the CRPD is evident. Consequently, and although not all States at the time of negotiations had fully clarified their position on the CRPD, the concepts and approaches enshrined in that Convention substantially informed the negotiations of the Convention on Cluster Munitions.

The Lima Conference

5.11 The victim assistance package contained in the Lima Discussion Text,[14] prepared for the Lima Conference on 23–25 May 2007, was to a large extent the product of two seemingly mutually exclusive desires: first, a considerable degree of caution was required given the history of the victim assistance negotiations for the *1997 Anti-Personnel Mine Ban Convention*; and second—as demanded by a number of States and civil society—the new Convention should strengthen and clarify the obligations of States vis-à-vis cluster munition victims.

5.12 In order to strengthen victim assistance in the future Convention, the Lima Discussion Text dedicated a separate paragraph to victim assistance.

---

[13] 'Review of the operation and status of the Convention on the Prohibition of the Use, Stockpiling, Production and Transfer of Anti-Personnel Mines and on their Destruction 1999–2004' (Part II of the Final Report of the First Review Conference of the States Parties), paragraph 65.

[14] Chair's discussion text on a legally binding international instrument that will prohibit the use, production, transfer and stockpiling of cluster munitions that cause unacceptable harm to civilians, Lima, 23–25 May 2007. See Annex 3 to this Commentary.

This represented significant progress compared to the *1997 Anti-Personnel Mine Ban Convention* where victim assistance is addressed as part of the Article dealing with international cooperation and assistance. In addition, the Lima Text included a distinct article on victim assistance. In doing so, the Lima text took the first step to separate the concept of national obligations to provide victim assistance from the concept of providing (international) assistance for victim assistance.

5.13 Article 6 of the Lima Text read as follows:

1. Each State Party shall, in accordance with applicable international human rights standards, endeavour to take steps such as providing medical care and rehabilitation as well as facilitating social and economic reintegration of victims of cluster munitions, in order to ensure the full realisation of their human rights and respect for their inherent dignity.

2. Each State Party in a position to do so shall provide assistance for the care and rehabilitation, and social and economic reintegration of victims and for cluster munition awareness programs. Such assistance may be provided, inter alia, through the United Nations system, international, regional or national organizations or institutions, the International Committee of the Red Cross, national Red Cross and Red Crescent societies and their International Federation, non-governmental organizations, or on a bilateral basis.

In addition to creating a distinct provision on victim assistance and aiming at conceptual clarification, the Lima Discussion Text included other noteworthy developments. First, it established a direct link to international human rights standards. While the relationship between human rights and victim assistance that directly deals with human beings seems rather obvious, expressly spelling out that link in the draft text was a major step forward. Few disarmament treaties relate to victims at all, and none had ever included a reference to their rights. Second, the draft aimed to establish an obligation which was not qualified by the terms 'in a position to do so'. The omission of these words, however, would come at the price of creating an obligation to 'endeavour to take steps' rather than actually achieving certain results, or undertaking specific activities.

5.14 Discussions at the Lima Conference showed broad agreement that victim assistance should be a core provision of the new treaty contained in a separate Article, should employ a rights-based approach, and that it should relate not only to directly impacted individuals.[15] Although no new text was

[15] *Cf.* CMC, 'CMC Report on the Lima Conference and Next Steps', available at: <http://www.stopclustermunitions.org/wp/wp-content/uploads/2008/05/cmc-report-on-the-lima-conference-23-25-may.pdf >(accessed 1 March 2010).

presented to or developed by the two following meetings, i.e. the meeting of affected States organized by Serbia in Belgrade on 3–4 October 2007 and the regional European meeting organized by Belgium in Brussels on 31 October 2007, these meetings also helped to foster a common understanding of the future victim assistance package.

The Belgrade meeting of States affected by cluster munitions

5.15 The Belgrade meeting of States affected by cluster munitions was of particular importance in shaping the conceptual framework of the victim assistance package to be included in the future Convention. Not only was the sentiment that victim assistance needed to be one of the main building blocks of the future Convention strengthened, the meeting also showed the willingness of affected States to commit themselves to take a primary role in the victim assistance efforts under the future Convention. The facilitator of the victim assistance discussions at the Belgrade Conference in summarizing the discussions was, hence, able to declare that there was a general understanding among participants at the Belgrade meeting that the State on whose territory the victims are, should adequately provide assistance to cluster munition victims.[16] This was an important commitment on the part of affected States, a commitment that clearly needed to be cushioned by appropriate undertakings by possible donor States to provide international cooperation and assistance for victim assistance.

5.16 In recognizing this dichotomy the Belgrade Conference laid a main building block for the final architecture of the victim assistance package, i.e. a substantial commitment of those States with victims in areas under their jurisdiction or control, and a parallel commitment on behalf of possible donor States to support these efforts. This approach is also warranted by some practical considerations. First, it is the territorial State that is best placed to assist the victims. Second, an obligation to assist victims is also closely linked to every State's responsibility for the well-being of its citizens. Third, victim assistance should usually be incorporated into existing structures, e.g. medical and social services, the economic system of a State, etc. And finally, as affected States are often among the poorest in the world, a fair degree of support by the international community is needed to enable the best possible assistance to be provided to cluster munition victims. The Belgrade Conference also witnessed a number of statements addressing the

---

[16] Oral summary by Markus Reiterer, acting as facilitator of the victim assistance discussions at the Belgrade meeting.

role of the State that had actually used cluster munitions against another State and thereby caused individuals to become cluster munition victims. In raising this issue some delegations also demanded reparations for injury incurred through the use of cluster munitions by another State. The sensitivity of this issue, however, could have proven detrimental for the way forward on victim assistance. The facilitator of the victim assistance discussions in Belgrade therefore urged participants to focus on the humanitarian aspects of the victim assistance package.

The Brussels European Regional Conference on Cluster Munitions

5.17 At the October 2007 Brussels Conference, States from across Europe met primarily to discuss two issues of high importance for the Cluster Munition Convention process: stockpile destruction and victim assistance. As the last meeting before the Vienna Conference, the next formal Oslo Process meeting after Lima, the Brussels Conference provided an important opportunity to further develop a joint understanding of what the victim assistance package should look like. Following the discussions at the Brussels Conference, the rapporteur on victim assistance, Markus Reiterer of Austria, provided a summary in which he stated, *inter alia*, that:

[t]here is unequivocal support that a new instrument on cluster munitions will have to contain clear and comprehensive provisions on assistance to victims of cluster munitions.[17]

He also stated that there was:

a general understanding that victim assistance is a broad and comprehensive concept, which should use as a starting point, but also as a constant reference point the needs and rights of victims. Already the term *victim* as such is to be understood broadly, *i.e.* encompassing the survivor as such—the victim of the direct impact, but also other victimized persons, including family and affected communities.[18]

5.18 In the assessment of the rapporteur, the Brussels Conference also supported the basic approach taken during the Belgrade Conference whereby:

While assistance to victims is the primary responsibility of the State on whose territory the victims are, it is quite evident that this responsibility needs to be mirrored by a clear commitment of those States who are able to do so, to cooperate and support assistance and victims.[19]

---

[17] Summary of the Victim Assistance Discussion, European Regional Conference on Cluster Munitions, Brussels, 31 October 2007, rapporteur: Markus Reiterer; at: <http://www.diplomatie.be/en/pdf/reiter.pdf> (accessed 1 March 2010 but page no longer available). [18] *Ibid.*
[19] *Ibid.*

On the issue of human rights the rapporteur stated that:

[t]he rights of the victims—and in particular their human rights—are fundamental to adequately assist victims. Therefore, human rights and the rights-based approach to victim assistance are crucially important. The recent Convention on the Rights of Persons with Disabilities will be of crucial importance in formulating the legal and policy framework for victim assistance. The new instrument should therefore also refer to this Convention as well as other applicable human rights standards.

5.19 A number of delegations raised concerns relating to the fact that also other international agreements deal with victim assistance (i.e. the *1997 Anti-Personnel Mine Ban Convention* and *2003 Protocol V*) and that some type of coordination was necessary in order to prevent overlap, waste of scarce resources, and duplication of efforts. The rapporteur in his summary also remarked on this issue and called for coordination among all relevant actors.[20]

5.20 The Brussels meeting was also characterized by a discussion of the issue of non-discrimination. In its presentation, the ICRC stated:

it must be highlighted that the measures in the area of victim assistance taken as part of the implementation of a future treaty must not be implemented so as to discriminate against other war wounded or those injured by other weapons.[21]

This observation was shared by an increasing number of delegations during the Brussels conference and subsequently in the further negotiations of the Convention. On this issue, the rapporteur remarked that as a basic approach 'all victims should receive the best possible care', irrespective of whether they have been injured by an anti-personnel mine, ERW, or cluster munitions.[22]

The Vienna Conference on Cluster Munitions

5.21 Based on the discussions held at the conferences in Lima, Belgrade, and Brussels, the drafters of the Vienna Discussion Text[23] presented under the responsibility of the Conference's president, Ambassador Wolfgang Petritsch of Austria, were able to submit an improved version of a victim assistance package. This new version contained four preambular paragraphs highlighting various issues of importance to victim assistance, a new version

---

[20] *Ibid.*

[21] Statement by Louis Maresca, ICRC, 'Assistance for the victims of cluster munitions: The perspective of the International Committee of the Red Cross', Brussels Conference, at: <http://www.diplomatie.be/en/pdf/maresca.pdf> (accessed 1 March 2010).

[22] Summary of the Victim Assistance Discussion, European Regional Conference on Cluster Munitions, Brussels, 31 October 2007, *op. cit.*

[23] Vienna Discussion Text of 14 November 2007.

of a separate article on victim assistance (Article 5), a new paragraph (paragraph 8) contained in Article 6 on international cooperation and assistance, and a new sub-paragraph (paragraph 7(j)) contained in Article 7 on transparency reporting.

5.22 The package as presented to the Vienna Conference for discussion attempted to respond to various calls and concerns expressed in the course of earlier discussions and endeavoured to strengthen the obligation to adequately provide assistance. It thereby embarked on six main improvements as compared to the Lima Discussion Text.

1. **Establishment of an unqualified legal obligation**
   Article 5, paragraph 1 of the Vienna Discussion Text required '[e]ach State Party with respect to victims of cluster munitions in areas under its jurisdiction or control' to adequately provide assistance to cluster munition victims. This obligation is not qualified by the terms 'in a position to do so', thereby increasing the stringency of the obligation.

2. **A clear distinction between the responsibilities of States with cluster munition victims in areas under their jurisdiction or control and the commitments by possible donor states**
   Whereas Article 5, paragraph 1 relates to the first group of States, the obligations of possible donor States would be under the commitment to provide international cooperation and assistance. For this second group of States[24] the qualifier 'in a position to do so' still applies.

3. **Comprehensive understanding of victim assistance and the term victim**
   While Article 5, paragraph 1 lists the basic building blocks of victim assistance, i.e. medical care and rehabilitation, psychological support and social and economic inclusion, the first preambular paragraph highlights that the term 'victims of cluster munitions' not only relates to the person directly affected but also to their families and communities.

4. **Unequivocal link to human rights**
   The link to human rights has been expressed in various layers. Most notably, Article 5, paragraph 1 itself requires that victim assistance shall be provided 'in accordance with applicable international human rights standards'. Second, preambular paragraph 2 expresses the States determination 'to ensure the full realisation of the rights of victims of cluster munitions,

---

[24] Although there will be an overlap between these two groups, as some States Parties will be in a position to provide international cooperation and assistance, while themselves having obligations under Article 5.

and recognizing their inherent dignity'. Third, preambular paragraph 3 refers to the UN Convention on the Rights of Persons with Disabilities.

5. Incorporation of the principle of non-discrimination

In order to address concerns raised by the ICRC and some delegations, the Vienna Discussion Text also included a reference to the principle of non-discrimination by highlighting in its fourth preambular paragraph the CRPD's prohibition of discrimination of any kind on the basis of disability.

6. Establishment of a requirement to report on the implementation of the victim assistance provisions

Recognizing the victim assistance package's character as one of the main building blocks of the new Convention, it was necessary to include a provision on transparency reporting relating to victim assistance.

5.23 The victim assistance package contained in the Vienna Discussion Text was received favourably by delegations. Almost 30 delegations took the floor in a very constructive discussion and—as expressed by Afghanistan— this discussion displayed an *'overwhelming consensus'* on the victim assistance concepts contained in the draft text.[25] Moreover, the conference, in the words of its President, heard 'convincing demands to further strengthen the text'. He continued by stating that: 'Clearly victim assistance will be a key legal obligation of the same quality as the other main building blocks of the future treaty.' He called this important outcome the 'Vienna Consensus on victim assistance'.[26]

5.24 Several suggestions were made to further strengthen the text, *inter alia*: the elaboration of a definition of the term cluster munition victim; the issue of non-discrimination, which so far had only been contained in the preamble; the formulation of additional guidance as to how the obligation to provide victim assistance should be implemented (e.g. through the establishment of national plans, strategies, and objectives); the inclusion of victims in

---

[25] Statement of Afghanistan, Vienna Conference, 6 December 2008. For a concise report on the deliberations of the Vienna Conference, see Harrison, K., 'Report from the Vienna Conference on Cluster Munitions, 5–7 December 2008', Women's International League for Peace and Freedom, available at: <http://www.wilpf.int.ch/disarmament/custermnitions/ViennaConference/viennareport.htm#_Toc188777781> (accessed 1 March 2010).

[26] Statement by Ambassador Wolfgang Petritsch, President of the Vienna Conference on Cluster Munitions. See also report of Amb. Petritsch to the Wellington Conference on Cluster Munitions. The CMC report on the Vienna Conference notes the following: 'The victim assistance discussion demonstrated commitment and consensus among states to the provision outlined in the Vienna Discussion Text.'

CMC, 'Report on the Vienna Conference on Cluster Munitions', 21 December 2007.

decision-making; including a reference to age- and gender-sensitivity; and the improvement of the reporting requirement relating to victim assistance.[27]

The Wellington Conference on Cluster Munitions

5.25 The Draft Convention on Cluster Munitions, prepared for the Wellington Conference, only included one, albeit significant, change to the victim assistance package: a proposed definition of the term 'cluster munition victim', which read as follows:

'**Cluster munition victims**' means persons who have suffered physical or psychological injury, economic loss, social marginalisation or substantial impairment of the realisation of their rights caused by the use of cluster munitions. They include those persons directly impacted by cluster munitions as well as their families and communities.

Apart from the discussions of the new definition which are dealt with in the commentary on Article 2,[28] the victim assistance work of the Wellington Conference concentrated on a number of main issues as discussed below.[29]

Non-discrimination

5.26 The principle of non-discrimination, which had already been discussed at the Vienna Conference on Cluster Munitions, figured quite prominently at the Wellington Conference. A number of delegations highlighted the importance of a reference to the principle of non-discrimination in the future text.[30] Some delegations, such as that of the ICRC, expressed concern that the wording already employed by the draft Convention (i.e. a reference to the principle of non-discrimination in the preambular paragraph concerning the CRPD) would not be sufficient to prevent discrimination from occurring. The ICRC, consequently, proposed alternative language for Article 5, paragraph 2 which read as follows:

In fulfilling its obligations under paragraph 1 of this Article each State Party shall make no distinction with respect to other victims of armed conflict on any grounds

[27] See CMC, 'Report on the Vienna Conference on Cluster Munitions', *op. cit.*

[28] See, *supra*, the commentary on Article 2, paragraph 1.

[29] For a concise report on the Wellington Conference, see, e.g., Harrison, K, 'Report from the Wellington Conference on Cluster Munitions, 18–22 February 2008', Women's International League for Peace and Freedom, pp. 24 *et seq.*, available at: <http://www.wilpf.int.ch/PDF/DisarmamentPDF/ClusterMunitions/Report_Wellington.pdf> (accessed 1 March 2010).

[30] Those delegations included Albania, Australia, Bangladesh, Canada, Croatia, the Lao People's Democratic Republic (Laos), New Zealand, Norway, Morocco, the United Kingdom (UK), the UN Mine Action Team, and the CMC.

other than medical ones or the rehabilitative, psychological or social-economic needs of the victim. States Parties shall also endeavour to implement the relevant profession-al guidelines and best practices in the care, treatment, support and socio-economic inclusion of victims.[31]

This proposal was supported, *inter alia*, by Canada.[32] An alternative proposal was put forward by Switzerland:

> In fulfilling its obligations under paragraph 1, each State Party shall ensure that there is no discrimination between cluster munition victims and those who have suffered injuries or who live with disabilities resulting from other circumstances.[33]

5.27 Both proposals suggested formulations that sought to establish a norm of non-discrimination to be embodied in the victim assistance package, albeit with differing elements: whereas the ICRC proposals focused on the preven-tion of discrimination between the specific victims of cluster munitions on the one hand and war victims in general on the other, the Swiss proposal also related the non-discrimination rule to disabilities resulting from other causes. At the same time, whereas the Swiss proposal did not envisage the possibility of some (legitimate) differentiation in treatment, the ICRC proposal aimed at relating differences in treatment to possibly differing needs of victims in terms of medical care, psychological support, or in relation to social and economic needs of the victims. The ICRC thinking on that issue, hence, had the advan-tage of acknowledging a relationship between the non-discrimination rule and the needs of the victim; this, finally, became an important element in over-coming concerns that the principle of non-discrimination could be misused as a justification for non-fulfilment of the victim assistance obligations.

Modalities for the implementation of Article 5, paragraph 1

5.28 Already at the Vienna Conference a number of requests to provide fur-ther guidance on how to implement the victim assistance obligation had been made. Paragraph 2 as contained in the Draft Cluster Munitions Convention presented to the Wellington Conference by several delegations was deemed insufficient. The main suggestions concerned the establishment or adaptation of national plans, policies, and frameworks to deal with assistance to cluster munition victims or making available appropriate budgets.[34]

---

[31] See Compendium of proposals submitted by delegations during the Wellington Conference (the Wellington Compendium), Addendum 1, p. 24 (see Annex 6).

[32] *Cf.* Statement by the head of the Canadian delegation, Earl Turcotte.

[33] Wellington Compendium, p. 23.

[34] On the above elements, statements were made *inter alia* by Belgium, Cambodia, Laos, Norway, and Spain.

5.29 Another important issue concerned the inclusion of cluster munition victims in decision-making.[35] This principle is based on the internationally recognized human right to participate in decision-making processes affecting one's life, which is established in the International Bill of Human Rights, and lately in the Convention on the Rights of Persons with Disabilities. Similar language was adopted in the Convention on Cluster Munitions itself.[36] A number of delegations also suggested ensuring that victim assistance would be provided in an age- and gender-sensitive manner.[37] Both elements were later included in the final text of the Convention.

5.30 Two additional issues were raised at the Wellington Conference. First, the suggestion was made to include a reference to victim assistance in Article 9 on national implementation measures.[38] Second, Bangladesh and the CMC suggested including victim assistance in Article 1 on General Obligations and Scope of the Convention. Neither of the two proposals was ultimately included in the Convention.[39]

'Under its jurisdiction or control'

5.31 During the Wellington Conference certain delegations expressed unease in relation to the approach that States should provide assistance with respect to cluster munition victims in areas under their jurisdiction or control. In particular, the United Kingdom (UK) had concerns with this concept and suggested alternative language according to which a State would only have been obliged to provide assistance to victims 'injured in its own territory'.[40]

---

[35] This issue was raised by, among others, Bangladesh, Belgium, Cambodia, Chile, Croatia, Guatemala, Morocco, Spain, Switzerland, and the CMC.

[36] *Universal Declaration of Human Rights*, Article 21; *International Covenant on Civil and Political Rights*, Article 25; Convention on the Rights of Persons with Disabilities, Article 4.

[37] This suggestion was put forward, *inter alia*, by Norway, Spain, and the UN Mine Action Team.   [38] *Cf.* Statements of Cambodia and the CMC.

[39] These two proposals did not receive sufficient support for further elaboration. The main reason for this might be seen in the fact that neither would have added value in legal terms.

[40] The entire UK proposal read as follows:

1. Each State Party with respect to cluster munitions victims injured in its own territory shall, in accordance with national laws and practices, provide for their medical care and treatment. Each State Party shall make every effort to collect reliable relevant data with respect to victims of cluster munitions.

2. In fulfilling its obligation under paragraph 1 of this Article each State Party shall ensure that the measures adopted are in accordance with fundamental human rights principles, including non-discrimination, and shall take into consideration relevant guidelines and good practices in the areas of medical care and treatment.

See Wellington Compendium, p. 24. It may be noted that this approach would have led to a result where—by way of an entirely theoretical example—say Iraq would have been obliged to provide assistance to a UK soldier injured in Iraq by a cluster munition employed by UK troops, even if the

In addition to the practical problems of implementation resulting from such a concept, this proposal essentially contradicted the basic approach employed throughout the entire discussions of the victim assistance package, i.e. that victim assistance should be undertaken according to the rights and needs of victims and not the place of injury.

5.32 No textual changes were made to any elements of the Draft Cluster Munitions Convention, which was forwarded to the Dublin Diplomatic Conference as the basis for formal negotiations. However, suggestions made during the Wellington Conference were incorporated into the so-called Compendium of proposals that was also passed on to the Dublin Conference.

Negotiations

5.33 The negotiations at the Dublin Diplomatic Conference had to find solutions to the following main issues: the definition of cluster munition victims, an appropriate wording for the non-discrimination rule that would prohibit discrimination without serving as a justification for non-fulfilment of victim assistance obligations, and the formulation of additional guidance on how to implement the main victim assistance obligation. In addition, an unforeseen problem occurred relating to national human rights frameworks.

The first discussion in the Committee of the Whole

5.34 The first thorough reading of Article 5 took place at the meeting of the Committee of the Whole on 20 May 2008, marked by a constructive atmosphere but a multitude of calls for further improvements of the text, in particular as far as the modalities for the implementation of the overall victim assistance obligation were concerned.[41] This initiative to provide more guidance for the actual implementation of the obligation under Article 5, paragraph 1 was led by a number of predominantly Latin American States drawing substantially from a proposal elaborated by representatives of civil society. During the Committee of the Whole meeting, Argentina, Costa Rica,

---

soldier were subsequently brought back to the UK. The UK proposal did not meet with substantial support.

[41] *Cf.* 'Summary Record of Second Session of the Committee of the Whole', Diplomatic Conference doc. CCM/CW/SR/2, 18 June 2008, pp. 4 *et seq.*

Guatemala, Mexico, and Peru (among others) indicated that they were preparing a proposal to that effect. This proposal was later circulated as Conference document CCM/70[42] and included a number of suggestions concerning the principle of non-discrimination; full and effective participation of victims; the development and implementation of national laws, policies, and action plans; resource mobilization; and the designation of national focal points. This proposal constituted the backbone of what later became paragraph 2 of Article 5.

5.35 In addition to the issues mentioned above, the Philippines brought up the question of user responsibility by arguing for the insertion of a new paragraph which would address the international responsibility of user States towards victim assistance for the past use of cluster munitions. The Philippines proposed the following wording:

> When a State Party, before entry into force of the Convention for it, has used or abandoned cluster munitions in areas under the jurisdiction or control of another State Party, the former State Party shall have the responsibility to help the latter State Party in addressing the requirements of victim assistance as delineated in Article 5(1).[43]

5.36 This notion was supported by the Lao People's Democratic Republic (Laos). A discussion of user responsibility could have lead to an undue politicization of the debate on a topic that had hitherto profited from its predominantly humanitarian character. The President of the Conference, in a move to preserve the humanitarian character of the debate, advised the Committee of the Whole without entering into any substantive discussion of the proposition that 'any issues of international cooperation and assistance' would be dealt with under Article 6.[44] Subsequently, the issue of user responsibility only resurfaced rather briefly during the discussions on victim assistance.

5.37 At the end of the meeting of the Committee of the Whole, the President of the Conference appointed Markus Reiterer of Austria as Friend of the President on Victim Assistance and mandated him to carry out consultations with a view to search for text for Article 5, text for the definition of cluster munition victims, and relevant draft preambular paragraphs.[45] The Friend of the President subsequently undertook a series of informal bilateral consultations as well as two rounds of consultations open to all interested participants

---

[42] 'Proposal by Argentina, Ecuador, Guatemala, Uruguay, Dominican Republic, Mexico, Nicaragua, Panama, Peru, Costa Rica, Chile, Honduras, Zambia and Guinea for the amendment of Article 5' Diplomatic Conference doc. CCM/70, 21 May 2008.

[43] See 'Proposal by the Philippines for the amendment of Article 5', Diplomatic Conference doc. CCM/58, 19 May 2008.

[44] See 'Summary Record of Second Session of the Committee of the Whole', *op. cit.*, p. 7.

[45] *Ibid.*, p. 8.

of the Conference. These consultations focused on finding solutions for the outstanding issues, including the definition of cluster munition victims,[46] the question of non-discrimination, the reference to international human rights and humanitarian law, and the further development of guidance for the implementation of the victim assistance obligation.

The non-discrimination rule

5.38 The discussions on the non-discrimination rule sought to find suitable wording that would adequately address concerns about creating a new category of victims to the detriment of others. At the same time, it was important to link the rule to the needs of the victims in order to avoid the non-discrimination rule being used as a justification for non-compliance with the victim assistance obligation following an (inappropriate) interpretation that as long as all types of victims and other persons with disabilities would be treated in an equally appalling manner, no discrimination would occur.

5.39 At the outset of consultations in Dublin there were essentially three proposals on the table addressing non-discrimination: (1) the ICRC proposal according to which no distinction should be made between cluster munition victims and 'with respect to other victims of armed conflict on any grounds other than medical ones or the rehabilitative, psychological or social-economic needs of the victim'; (2) the Swiss proposal obliging States Parties to 'ensure that there is no discrimination between cluster munition victims and those who have suffered injuries or who live with disabilities resulting from other circumstances'; and (3) the proposal contained in Conference document CCM/70 presented by Argentina and others simply to include a reference to human rights law and principles, including non-discrimination in Article 5, paragraph 1.

5.40 Whereas the ICRC proposal had the disadvantage of restricting the non-discrimination rule only to war victims and not taking into account other persons with disabilities or injuries, it had the distinct advantage of linking non-discrimination to the needs of victims. In contrast, the Swiss proposal also related the non-discrimination rule to disabilities resulting from other causes, but did not establish a link to the needs of the victims. The third proposal had the advantage of being short and concise, but seemed to lack the necessary precision.

---

[46] For a review of discussions leading to the definition of the term 'cluster munition victim' See, *supra,* the commentary on Article 2, paragraph 1.

5.41 The discussions during the first open-ended consultations on 21 May 2008, while not yet leading to conclusive results, provided clarity on how the concept of non-discrimination in the context of victim assistance was understood by the negotiating parties; i.e. that non-discrimination should encompass not only war victims but also other persons with similar problems and it should establish a link to the needs of the victims. Based on these discussions and the input provided through the Swiss and the ICRC proposal respectively, the Friend of the President submitted an informal draft of the victim assistance package, including the non-discrimination rule for the second round of open-ended consultations on 22 May 2008. He suggested the following wording on non-discrimination:

[States should n]ot discriminate among cluster munition victims, or between cluster munition victims and those who have suffered injuries or disabilities from other causes; differences in treatment should be based only on medical, rehabilitative, psychological or socio-economic needs.[47]

Following a proposal made by Guatemala the words 'against or' were inserted into the proposal before 'among cluster munition victims'.[48] The text as amended by the Guatemalan proposal was accepted after brief discussion and was included in the final version of Article 5 paragraph 2(e).

International humanitarian and human rights law

5.42 Whereas a reference to international human rights standards had already been contained in the Vienna Discussion Text and found widespread support during the Vienna Conference, the idea of including a reference to international humanitarian law was first officially proposed by the Philippines at the Diplomatic Conference. The proposal sought the inclusion of a reference to international humanitarian law after human rights law in the first sentence of Article 5, paragraph 2 and read as follows:

Each State Party with respect to cluster munitions victims in areas under its jurisdiction or control shall, in accordance with international human rights law **and international humanitarian law**, adequately provide for their medical care and rehabilitation, psychological support and social and economic inclusion.[49]

5.43 During the first round of open-ended consultations the proposal by the Philippines was supported by Switzerland, the ICRC, and a number

---

[47] See informal non-paper presented by the Friend of the President.
[48] *Cf.* Oral statement of Guatemala during the informal consultations on 22 May 2008.
[49] Emphasis in the original; see Diplomatic Conference doc. CCM/58.

of other delegations,[50] but the UK expressed reservations. The UK basically argued that international humanitarian law only applies in a very specific set of circumstances and that the new Convention on Cluster Munitions should create new rules of international humanitarian law. Thus, the use of the wording 'in accordance with' might—so the argument went—be construed as restricting assistance to be given. The UK, during the second open-ended consultations proposed to replace 'in accordance with' by 'taking into account'.[51] This suggestion was countered by the argument that international humanitarian and human rights law as *law* is binding and needs to be applied *in toto* rather than just merely taken into account.[52]

5.44 As regards the reference to international human rights law, the Holy See during the first round of open-ended consultations raised a question concerning the fact that not all parties to the Convention on Cluster Munitions would necessarily be party to other human rights conventions, in particular the CRPD.[53] The Friend of the President explained that 'in accordance with' international law would necessarily have to be understood as a reference to international legal obligations binding on the respective party in question. As a consequence, if a State did not ratify the CRPD, it would not become binding to this State through a mere commitment to act in accordance with international obligations.[54]

5.45 In order to find a compromise to overcome the concerns raised by the UK and the Holy See and that would be suitable to all negotiating partners, the Friend of the President in his non-paper prepared for the second round of open ended consultations proposed adding the term 'applicable' before the reference to international human rights and humanitarian law so that victim assistance would need to be provided in accordance with *applicable* international humanitarian and human rights law. In introducing this proposal, the Friend of the President explained that for any international norm to be binding on a State it would have to fulfil the three-fold test required under international law of being applicable *ratione personae, ratione materiae,* and *ratione tempore.* The use of the term 'applicable' serves as a mere clarification of this rule.[55] Following a final round of discussions and various textual suggestions, the approach outlined by the Friend of the President was accepted.

---

[50] Those delegations included Argentina and Chile.

[51] Oral statement of the UK during the informal consultations on 22 May 2008.

[52] Oral statement of the ICRC during the informal consultations on 22 May 2008.

[53] Oral statement of Holy See during the informal consultations on 22 May 2008.

[54] Oral statement of Markus Reiterer during the informal consultations on 22 May 2008.

[55] *Ibid.*

Age- and gender-sensitive victim assistance

5.46 Already during the Wellington Conference the UN Mine Action Team (UNMAT)[56] had proposed to clarify that victim assistance should be carried out in an 'age- and gender appropriate' manner.[57] During the informal open-ended consultations, Norway proposed to include the concept of gender sensitivity. As age- and gender-sensitivity are relevant for all areas of victim assistance it was decided that these concepts should be referred to in Article 5, paragraph 1 of the Convention, which obliges relevant States Parties to 'adequately provide age- and gender-sensitive assistance'. These concepts are also included in the eighth preambular paragraph, which recognizes 'the need to provide age- and gender-sensitive assistance to cluster munition victims and to address the special needs of vulnerable groups'.[58]

Additional guidance on implementing the core victim assistance obligations

5.47 The formulation of additional guidance on implementing the obligation under Article 5, paragraph 1 was primarily based on the proposal made by Argentina and a group of States and introduced to the informal consultations by Guatemala.[59] The proposal drew considerable inspiration from work carried out by the CMC and in particular Survivor Corps and Handicap International,[60] and largely sought to generate concrete benchmarks for how best to implement the core victim assistance obligations.

5.48 In large part, the consultations concerning Article 5, paragraph 2 focused on structuring the guidance given and finding the most appropriate language that would strike a balance between the required stringency of the norm and the need for some flexibility to allow for adaptability to the respective national circumstances. The logic finally applied in paragraph 2 encompasses needs assessment, the creation and operationalization of the necessary legal framework, the development of budgets and plans, the dedication of a focal point, and the mobilization of national and international resources. Most importantly, it also includes the principles of both inclusion of victims in decision-making and non-discrimination, and refers to the integration of

---

[56] UNMAT is the informal grouping at both international and national levels of the UN bodies and agencies most involved in mine action.   [57] See Wellington Compendium, p. 24.

[58] See, *supra,* the commentary on this preambular paragraph, in §§0.115 *et seq.*

[59] *Cf.* Oral statement by Guatemala during the informal consultations on 21 May 2008.

[60] Formerly, Landmine Survivors Network.

victim assistance efforts into existing national development, disability, and human rights frameworks.

5.49 In the course of the consultations the question was raised as to whether the entire introductory phrase of paragraph 2 ('In fulfilling its obligations under paragraph 1 of this Article each State Party shall...') should be qualified by the insertion of a phrase like 'as appropriate' or 'as necessary' to allow for a level of flexibility. Paragraph 2 finally took a more nuanced approach, by only employing qualifiers where they were necessary (e.g. the use of the term 'necessary' in sub-paragraph (b) and not using them where they could have had an undue diminishing effect, such as in relation to the rule of non-discrimination.

Existing national disability, development, and human rights frameworks

5.50 Already the proposal contained in Conference document CCM/70 referred to the approach of incorporating victim assistance efforts into existing disability, development, and human rights frameworks and mechanisms.[61] Early in the consultations the Holy See had pointed to difficulties in relation to the reference to 'human rights frameworks', which could be understood as referring to the UN Convention on the Rights of Persons with Disabilities, which the Holy See has neither signed nor ratified due to concerns *inter alia* relating to abortion and reproductive rights.[62] Paragraph 2 as a whole, however, was intended to establish rules for the implementation of the obligation under paragraph 1 by and within States. The intention of this particular phrase was to provide for incorporation of victim assistance efforts into existing structures of the respective State. Hence, the Friend of the President proposed to specify that the term 'national' should be inserted before 'referring to disability, development and human rights frameworks and mechanisms' and thereby clarify that it was not to be understood as a reference to international mechanisms. This did not, however, satisfy the Holy See's concern, so a major part of the

---

[61] See Diplomatic Conference doc. CCM/70. The relevant part of the proposal read as follows:

In fulfilling its obligations under paragraph 1 of this Article each State Party shall: (a) assess the needs of victims, take steps to mobilise national and international resources and develop a national plan including the time estimated to carry out these activities, with a view to incorporating it within existing disability, development and human rights frameworks and mechanisms.

[62] *Cf.* Oral statement by Holy See during the informal consultations on 21 May 2008. *Cf.* also di Ruzza, T., 'The Convention on Cluster Munitions: Towards a Balance between Humanitarian and Military Considerations?', *Military Law and the Law of War Review*, Vol. 47, Nos. 3–4 (2008), pp. 406 *et seq.* and 432.

second round of informal open-ended consultations was devoted to finding a solution to this issue.

5.51 During these consultations the UK argued that the language referring to national laws and policies and the relevant existing mechanisms and frameworks would 'overplay the role of the State' and that 'one would need to balance between the law of the State and the role of the NGO community, many of whom cherish their independence from the State'.[63] The Friend of the President therefore suggested adding the phrase 'while respecting their specific role and contribution' after the reference to 'existing national disability, development and human rights frameworks and mechanisms'. Although the representative of the CMC declared that the NGO community would not see 'the language as restricting our independence'[64] and a number of delegations questioned the need for this language,[65] the delegations of the UK and the Holy See insisted on such a reference. The formulation finally adopted in subparagraph (c) reads as follows:

Develop a national plan and budget, including timeframes to carry out these activities, with a view to incorporating them within the existing national disability, development and human rights frameworks and mechanisms, while respecting the specific role and contribution of relevant actors.

5.52 Finally, in a 'Declaration attached to the Holy See instrument of ratification to the Convention on Cluster Munition' the Holy See affirmed that States should be 'mindful that this broader assistance must be respectful of the right to life from the moment of conception to natural death, in order to conform to the fundamental principles of respect for human life, and ensure the recognition of human dignity'. Moreover, the Holy See restated 'its understanding and interpretation of article 5.2(c), where the Convention recognizes "the specific role and contribution of relevant actors": when a State Party develops a national plan and budget to carry out assistance activities according to the Convention "with a view to incorporating them within the existing national disability, development and human rights frameworks and mechanisms", it shall guarantee the pluralism that is inherent in any democratic society and the diversity of relevant non-governmental actors'.[66]

---

[63] *Cf.* Oral statement by UK during the informal consultations on 22 May 2008.

[64] *Cf.* Oral statement by CMC during the informal consultations on 21 May 2008.

[65] These delegations included, *inter alia*, Croatia and New Zealand.

[66] See Declaration attached to the Holy See instrument of ratification to the Convention on Cluster Munition, at <http://treaties.un.org/Pages/ViewDetails.aspx?src=TREATY&mtdsg_no=XXVI-6&chapter=26&lang=en>(accessed 1 March 2010).

Reaching agreement

5.53 During the second round of open-ended consultations on 22 May 2008, the negotiators managed to find solutions for the outstanding issues referred to above. Towards the end of the consultations, the Philippines again brought up the issue of user responsibility. Consistent with the ruling of the President this issue was referred to the discussions under Article 6 on international cooperation and assistance. Subsequently, the Friend of the President submitted to the President of the Conference a non-paper containing the negotiated texts of Article 2, paragraph 1; Article 5; and the relevant preambular paragraphs. This text was forwarded to the Committee of the Whole during its meeting on 23 May 2008, where it was strongly supported.[67] The President concluded the meeting by proposing to forward the text to plenary as a Presidency Text; there were no objection to this proposal.

5.54 Although at times celebrated as ground-breaking and historic, it has to be borne in mind that the victim assistance package of the Convention is firmly rooted in the experience gained and progress made through the victim assistance work under the *1997 Anti-Personnel Mine Ban Convention*, without which the result would not have been possible. In that sense:

> [the] victim assistance package is not a radically new invention; on the contrary, the package is the (initial) culmination of efforts: it can be seen as the logical consequence—if not codification—of the work undertaken and lessons learned in implementing the victim assistance provision of the 1997 Anti-Personnel Mine Ban Convention.[68]

Commentary

5.55 The main obligation to provide assistance to cluster munition victims is expressed in Article 5, paragraph 1, which provides that:

> [e]ach State Party with respect to cluster munition victims in areas under its jurisdiction or control shall, in accordance with applicable international humanitarian and

---

[67] The following delegations declared their strong satisfaction with the agreement reached on victim assistance: Austria, Belgium, Bosnia and Herzegovina, Burundi, Cambodia, Canada, Chad, Chile, Cook Islands, Croatia, Dominican Republic, Ecuador, Fiji, France, Germany, Ghana, Guatemala, Guinea, Guinea-Bissau, Iraq, Lebanon, Madagascar, Mali, Montenegro, Mozambique, Nigeria, Senegal, Serbia, Sierra Leone, Spain, Sudan, Sweden, Switzerland, Thailand, Uganda, the UK, Vanuatu, Venezuela, and Zambia, as well as the Office of the UN High Commissioner for Refugees, and the CMC. See 'Summary Record of Eighth Session of the Committee of the Whole' Diplomatic Conference doc. CCM/CW/SR/8, 18 June 2008, pp. 7 *et seq.*

[68] *Cf.* Reiterer, M. A., 'Assistance to Cluster Munition Victims: a major step towards humanitarian disarmament', in *Disarmament Forum*, No. 1 (Geneva: United Nations Institute for Disarmament Research, 2010).

human rights law, adequately provide age- and gender-sensitive assistance, including medical care, rehabilitation and psychological support, as well as provide for their social and economic inclusion.

5.56 The breadth and depth of the development in this area can be highlighted by comparing this provision with its precursor in the *1997 Anti-Personnel Mine Ban Convention* (Article 6, paragraph 3), which qualifies an obligation to 'provide assistance for the care and rehabilitation, and social and economic reintegration, of mine victims' by limiting it to States Parties 'in a position to do so'.[69] In contrast, Article 5 of the Convention on Cluster Munitions sets unequivocal obligations on each State Party with cluster munition victims in areas under its jurisdiction or control and clearly provides what action is required and on whose behalf.[70] Indeed, the comprehensive nature of the provision ensures that victim assistance is established as an obligation of the same legal relevance and value as the Convention's other major obligations.[71]

For whom? The definition of 'cluster munition victims'

5.57 The first main feature of the Convention's victim assistance package is the definition of the term 'cluster munition victims', which covers 'all persons who have been killed or suffered physical or psychological injury, economic loss, social marginalisation or substantial impairment of the realisation of their rights caused by the use of cluster munitions'. The definition further clarifies that victims 'include those persons directly impacted by cluster munitions as well as their affected families and communities'.[72] The definition is intentionally broad, mirroring the circumstances that are characteristic of the impact of cluster munitions: the broad effects on families

---

[69] The term 'in a position to do so' is not defined in the Convention on Cluster Munitions. For an overview of the Convention's victim assistance package see, e.g., Reiterer, M. A., 'Assistance to Cluster Munition Victims: a major step towards humanitarian disarmament', *op. cit.*

[70] *Cp.* Statement by the Friend of the President on Victim Assistance, Markus Reiterer, delivered one week after the adoption of the Convention during the 2008 intersessional Standing Committee on Victim Assistance of the *1997 Anti-Personnel Mine Ban Convention*, <http://www.apminebanconvention.org/fileadmin/pdf/mbc/IWP/SC_june08/Speeches-VA/SCVA-OtherMatters-6June08-Austria-en.pdf> (accessed 1 March 2010).

[71] The significance of the Convention's approach to victim assistance is also enhanced by the fact that for the first time a treaty dealing with disarmament issues creates a direct link to human rights by stipulating that States Parties shall 'adequately provide' assistance to cluster munition victims in accordance with international human rights law. The way Article 5 is drafted, however, makes it clear that it does not create an individual entitlement of specific victims to receive a certain treatment, compensation, etc. Article 5 does not create a subjective right of a victim (as a human rights instrument would do); it creates an obligation for specific States.   [72] Article 2, paragraph 1.

and communities, the harm beyond physical injury, and the burden on the realization of rights.

Who bears responsibility for victim assistance?

5.58   Compared to the victim assistance provision of the *1997 Anti-Personnel Mine Ban Convention*, Article 5 of the Convention on Cluster Munitions represents a major step forward in clarifying who bears responsibility for assisting the victims of cluster munitions.[73] Article 5 identifies clearly who bears the responsibility vis-à-vis cluster munition victims. It also sets out a much clearer conceptual framework and embodies a substantially more stringent legal obligation than that contained in the *1997 Anti-Personnel Mine Ban Convention* by requiring each State Party to provide the assistance required with respect to cluster munition victims 'in areas under its jurisdiction or control'. It is important to note that it is *either* jurisdiction *or* control that is necessary, not the occurrence of both elements at the same time.[74]

What assistance should be provided?

5.59   Under Article 5, the relevant States Parties are obliged to 'adequately provide age- and gender-sensitive assistance', including medical care, rehabilitation, and psychological support, as well as to promote the social and economic inclusion of victims. The various terms used are important: the term 'adequately' ensures a certain level of flexibility in the actual provision of victim assistance—setting assistance in relation to prevailing circumstances, needs, and capacities. The terms age-sensitive and gender-sensitive highlight the need for assistance to take age and gender into account in the provision of assistance. And further, Article 5, paragraph 1 lists the constituent elements of victim assistance: medical care (which encompasses emergency and ongoing medical care), rehabilitation, psychological support (the importance of and need for which is often underestimated), and finally the elements of inclusion of victims in social and economic life.

---

[73] The approach taken by the *1997 Anti-Personnel Mine Ban Convention* glossed over this question by essentially making it a commitment for each State in a position to do so to provide assistance to victims. In practice that means that the *1997 Anti-Personnel Mine Ban Convention* combines the commitments by affected States and those of possible donor States to provide assistance for the care and rehabilitation, and social and economic reintegration, of mine victims. This approach has the distinct disadvantage of qualifying the commitments of both possible donors and affected States with the phrase 'in a position to do so'.

[74] For a more detailed discussion of the concepts of jurisdiction and control see, *supra*, the commentary on Articles 3 and 4 pertaining to this issue and, *infra*, §5.65.

Guidance for implementing the victim assistance package

5.60 Article 5 concludes by setting out a non-exhaustive list of elements that provide the modalities for the implementation of victim assistance. The text of this provision was intended to provide sufficient guidance to States while at the same time avoiding being overly prescriptive. One of the victim assistance issues discussed most intensively during the Oslo Process was the question of non-discrimination: in drafting the relevant provisions it was deemed essential to ensure the best possible assistance to cluster munition victims, but not at the expense of other victims of armed conflict.

5.61 In other words, the new provision was to be crafted in a way which would not allow it to be construed as creating a new category of victims enjoying 'preferential' treatment. In response, Article 5, paragraph 2(e) prohibits discrimination against and among cluster munition victims as well as between cluster munition victims and those who have suffered injuries or disabilities from other causes. To avoid the risk that such a broad clause could be interpreted as an excuse for inactivity (on the basis of the maxim that as long as everyone is treated in the same insufficient manner, no discrimination occurs), the second sentence specifies that differences in treatment should be related only to the actual needs of the cluster munition victims.

Structure of the victim assistance package

5.62 Article 5 is the heart of victim assistance, with additional provisions clarifying the rights-based approach at the basis of victim assistance (preamble), a definition of 'victim' (Article 2, paragraph 1), guidance on international cooperation and assistance (Article 6, paragraph 7), and transparency measures and reporting (Article 7, paragraph 1(k)). Article 5 is divided into content and implementation measures. Paragraph 1 determines the content of victim assistance: the actual legal obligation and its scope of application, the areas it covers, and its shared roots with humanitarian and human rights law. Paragraph 2 deals mainly with implementation measures: steps to be taken at the process level, but which also directly influence the content.

Type of legal obligation: 'Each State Party . . . shall . . . provide . . . assistance'

5.63 The *1997 Anti-Personnel Mine Ban Convention*'s instruction that 'Each State Party in a position to do so shall provide assistance'[75] became in

---

[75] Article 6, paragraph 3, *1997 Anti-Personnel Mine Ban Convention*.

the Convention on Cluster Munitions two separate obligations. As in the *1997 Anti-Personnel Mine Ban Convention*, so here State Parties 'in a position to do so' should assist each other in addressing the needs of victims, as required by Article 6, paragraph 7, in the context of international cooperation and assistance. However, in the context of a State which has victims in territories under its jurisdiction or control, '[e]ach State Party [...] shall [...] provide [...] assistance' to these victims.

5.64   The qualifier 'in a position to do so' was dropped, reflecting an evolution in the understanding of victim assistance from an issue that belongs to the realm of international cooperation between States in a position to provide assistance, to one that primarily rests within each State towards victims in that State. The 2004 Nairobi Report had already recognized that 'the ultimate responsibility for victim assistance rests with each State Party within which there are landmine survivors and other mine victims. This is logical given that it is the basic responsibility of each State to ensure the well-being of its citizens.'[76] The Convention on Cluster Munitions translates this understanding into a legal obligation.

Scope of application—'with respect to cluster munition victims in areas under its jurisdiction or control'

5.65   *Jurisdiction or control* and *jurisdiction and control* mark the boundaries of States' obligations throughout this Convention.[77] A State Party's obligation to provide victim assistance pertains to victims (as defined in Article 2 paragraph 1) who are physically located within the jurisdiction or control of a State, without regard to where they were actually affected. An attempt at a narrower scope of obligation, that recognizes a State's obligation only towards victims who were affected in areas under its jurisdiction or control, was rejected during the negotiations.[78] Basing the obligation of States Parties to guarantee the human rights of individuals on the ground of present jurisdiction rather than the locale of past grievance is consistent with the core of victim assistance, which is guaranteeing victims' rights within the broader national mechanisms of disability, development, and human rights.[79] Other examples exist in international human rights law that support this thrust.[80]

---

[76] 'Nairobi Report', *op. cit.*, paragraph 81.
[77] See Articles 3, 4, 5, 6, and 9. For a full analysis, see the relevant commentary on Articles 3 and 4.   [78] See, *supra*, the discussion of this issue during the negotiations, in §5.42.
[79] See Article 5, paragraph 2(c).
[80] See, e.g., Article 1 of the European Convention on Human Rights:

The High Contracting Parties shall secure to everyone within their jurisdiction the rights and freedoms defined in Section I of this Convention.

'In accordance with applicable international humanitarian and human rights law'

5.66 Negotiating States showed overwhelming support for explicitly affirming the link between disarmament and human rights and consequently the Convention refers to human rights in three places: first, the preamble expresses States Parties' determination to ensure the 'full realisation' of the rights of all cluster munition victims and recognizes their inherent dignity; second, the preamble bears in mind the UN Convention on the Rights of Persons with Disabilities; and third—and perhaps most importantly—Article 5 stipulates that victim assistance shall be provided 'in accordance with applicable international humanitarian and human rights law'. The Convention on Cluster Munitions thus upholds and promotes the human rights of survivors and other victims. The Convention embodies a rights-based approach to victim assistance, i.e. an approach that takes as a reference point not only the needs of victims, but also their rights.

5.67 That victim assistance 'is more than just a medical or rehabilitation issue—it is also a human rights issue' was already recognized by States Parties to the *1997 Anti-Personnel Mine Ban Convention*.[81] The preamble to the Convention on Cluster Munitions sets the stage for a human rights-based framework for victim assistance by citing States Parties' determination to 'ensure the full realisation of the rights of all cluster munition victims'. Article 5, paragraph 1, which establishes that victim assistance will be provided 'in accordance with applicable international humanitarian and human rights law', confirms this link.

5.68 It is important to note that the formulation 'in accordance with applicable international [...] law' does not bear a restriction as to the source of the law. Consequently relevant norms of international humanitarian and human rights law may be derived from all sources of international law, be they international treaties, international customary law[82] or general principles of law.[83]

5.69 Relevant humanitarian law relates to the body of international law that protects civilians in wartime and its aftermath, including the *1949 Geneva Conventions* and their three *Additional Protocols*. Articles related to the protection of the wounded and sick and medical and relief personnel, and to

---

[81] Nairobi Report, *op. cit.*, para. 68.

[82] On customary law in the realm of international humanitarian law, see Henckaerts, J.-M., Doswald-Beck, L. (eds.), *Customary International Humanitarian Law—Volume 1: Rules* (Cambridge: ICRC/Cambridge University Press, 2005).

[83] *Cf.* Article 38, Statute of the International Court of Justice.

obligations of the occupying power towards civilians, are examples of provisions relevant in the context of victim assistance.

5.70 The nature of cluster munitions is that their impact continues beyond armed conflict. Accordingly, the essence of victim assistance exceeds medical and other urgent treatment and aims to enable victims' full and equal participation in society. Humanitarian law can therefore be only part of the answer. Reference to human rights law in this Article aptly complements the reference to humanitarian law. In principle, all norms established within the realm of international human rights law may be relevant for victim assistance; this includes norms promoting equality and non-discrimination, economic, social, and cultural rights, and civil and political rights, as well as those protecting the rights of marginalized groups, such as persons with disabilities, women, and children.

5.71 The CRPD is of particular importance and is consequently referred to specifically in the ninth preambular paragraph of the Convention.[84] The CRPD sets the global standard for equality, inclusion, and full participation of persons with disabilities in society and respect for their dignity and autonomy, and guides States Parties on how to guarantee persons with disabilities enjoyment of the full range of civil, political, economic, social, and cultural rights.

5.72 As the 2004 Nairobi Report had already recognized, steps to assist mine victims should be viewed as part of a State's progress in promoting the rights of persons with disabilities. Individuals impacted by landmines 'are a sub-group of larger communities of persons with injuries and disabilities'.[85] Persons with disabilities face stigma and physical and attitudinal barriers that prevent their full inclusion in society. The remedy lies in changing attitudes and removing barriers. The CRPD provides comprehensive guidance on how to create that fundamental change. Thus, implementation of victim assistance gains detail and direction by viewing it through the lens of the human rights standard applying to persons with disabilities in general.

5.73 As noted above, the term *applicable* in the phrase *in accordance with applicable humanitarian and human rights law* was inserted during the negotiations in Dublin to provide additional clarification.[86] In order for a norm of international law to be 'applicable' it needs to be applicable *ratione personae* (the norm is binding on the State in question), *ratione temporis* (the norm's temporal scope of application is fulfilled), and *ratione materiae* (the matter at

---

[84] See, *supra*, the commentary on preambular paragraph 9 in §§0.117 *et seq.*

[85] Nairobi Report, *op. cit.*, paragraph 65; see also paragraph 66.

[86] *Cf. supra* §§5.42–45.

hand falls within the material scope of the treaty).[87] Accordingly, treaties to which a State has not given its consent to be bound do not as a rule create obligations for that State. However, norms contained in a treaty may develop into customary international law and thus have a binding effect even on States not party to that particular treaty.[88] In addition, international courts and tribunals have resorted to non-binding instruments (including a treaty that is not binding on a given State) for the interpretation of a State's obligations under a treaty to which it is bound, when the latter treaty is silent or lacking precision.[89]

The content of victim assistance: 'adequately provide... assistance including medical care, rehabilitation, and psychological support as well as... social and economic inclusion'

5.74 The victim assistance provision of the *1997 Anti-Personnel Mine Ban Convention*, though brief compared to the one adopted in the Convention on Cluster Munitions, addresses both the short- and long-term impact caused by the weapon. 'Medical care and rehabilitation' are the immediate necessary responses to an injury, but assistance in 'social and economic reintegration' are as necessary to enable victims to reclaim their place in society.[90]

5.75 Early on in its implementation, States Parties to the *1997 Anti-Personnel Mine Ban Convention* developed a common understanding of the priorities deriving from these four pillars (medical care, rehabilitation, and economic and social reintegration), to include: collecting accurate and up-to-date data in order to understand the extent of the challenge; emergency and continuing medical care; physical rehabilitation; psychological support and social reintegration; economic reintegration; and the establishment, enforcement and implementation of relevant laws and public policies.[91] It is interesting to note how these evolved within the negotiation of the Convention on Cluster Munitions.

---

[87] On the insertion of the term 'applicable' see, *supra*, the commentary on the negotiations during the Diplomatic Conference, *esp.* §5.45.

[88] An early example of such a transformation of treaty norms into norms of customary international law occurred in relation to the *Regulations Concerning the Laws and Customs of War on Land* contained in the Annex to the Hague Convention (IV) Respecting the Laws and Customs of War on Land of October 18, 1907; *cf.* Neuhold, H., Hummer, W., Schreuer, C. (eds.), *Handbuch des Völkerrechts*, Fourth Edition (Vienna: Manz Verlag, 2004), Vol. 1, pp. 38 and 541 *et seq.*

[89] See, e.g., the European Court of Human Rights' decision in Demir and Baykara *v.* Turkey, application no. 34503/97, 12 November 2008 [GC], *esp.* paragraphs 65–78.

[90] Article 6, paragraph 3, *1997 Anti-Personnel Mine Ban Convention*.

[91] Nairobi Report, *op. cit.*, paragraph 69.

5.76 Medical care and rehabilitation resurfaced in the same formulation. Economic and social *reintegration* turned into economic and social *inclusion*, in line with the accepted rights-based terminology used, for example, in the CRPD. One of the fundamental principles running throughout that treaty is full participation and inclusion in society.[92] While *integration* connotes a division between society—the 'integrator'—and a survivor whose challenge it is to reintegrate, *inclusion* lends itself better to the idea that society should be structured in a way which is inclusive of all its members. Psychological support, not expressly mentioned in the *1997 Anti-Personnel Mine Ban Convention* text, and understood by States as residing under the element of social reintegration, became an independent element of victim assistance, testifying to the importance attributed to it in the recovery of cluster munition victims. And the elements of data collection, and laws and public policies, each turned into a stand-alone component, also indicating the importance attributed to them by negotiating States.

5.77 The qualifier *adequately* was inserted immediately preceding the list of victim assistance elements: 'Each State Party...shall...adequately provide...assistance including medical care', etc. The term *adequately* serves a dual purpose: establishing a standard of quality and responsiveness to the needs and rights of victims while at the same time allowing States Parties a margin of flexibility to tailor victim assistance to the national context.

5.78 One of the biggest challenges that States have continuously grappled with during the years of implementation of the *1997 Anti-Personnel Mine Ban Convention* has been how to define the necessary components of each of these pillars (if they can at all be defined in ways which will apply universally). Certainly the treaty itself cannot quantify what must exist in medical care, rehabilitation, or economic and social inclusion for a State Party to have fulfilled its obligation. But even the detailed guidance documents developed from year to year in the Meetings of States Parties of the *1997 Anti-Personnel Mine Ban Convention* did not produce a clear standard for what should exist in each of the areas. Instead, they prescribed the enhancement of capacity, in particular in the areas of medical care and rehabilitation: more competent surgical management, more trained first-aid responders, better equipment and infrastructure of clinics, more trained rehabilitation specialists.[93] Another avenue for clarifying the content of victim assistance took the form of guidelines development on specific components of victim assistance.[94]

---

[92] Articles 3, 19, 24, and 26, CRPD.

[93] Nairobi Report, *op. cit.*, paragraphs 72–75.

[94] e.g. Landmine Survivors' Network's 'Surviving Limb Loss, Life after Injury: A rehabilitation manual for the injured and their helpers', the ICRC's 'Care in the Field for Victims of Weapons

5.79 Still, the knotty issue of 'quantification' of victim assistance, and its influence on the possibility of measuring progress, have repeatedly been raised in discussions between civil society and States Parties to the *1997 Anti-Personnel Mine Ban Convention*.[95] The Convention on Cluster Munitions deals with this issue by significantly strengthening the ability to hold States accountable for implementation, mainly through prescribing implementation measures, which appear under paragraph 2 of Article 5, as discussed below.

5.80 With respect to *economic and social inclusion*, mine and cluster munition survivors underscore economic and social marginalization as one of the most devastating long-term effects of mine and cluster munition use. Harm does not stop at physical injury. Consequences of mine and cluster munition use include social stigma; new physical limits experienced by individuals hurt by these weapons which limit their opportunity to return to work or find a new way of subsistence; inaccessibility of workplaces and of vocational training programmes; lack of access to schools, which decreases the opportunity for economic inclusion in the long run; and lack of access to public spaces and services in general. Consequently, victim assistance translates into helping dismantle stigmas, providing a support net that guarantees an adequate standard of living, creating opportunities for return to work or for new gainful enterprises, and ensuring accessibility to public places and services with particular focus on schools, workplaces, and health services.

5.81 The term *psychological support* refers to a range of methodologies of psychosocial support promoting recovery, including both professional mental health services (which in many countries are lacking and in some are almost wholly absent), and peer support. Peer support, conducted by other survivors who have gone through a process of recovery, has become a staple methodology promoted by survivor organizations[96] and is practised in many countries to assist victims in overcoming their trauma. The example of, and guidance by,

of War', the World Health Organization's 'Prosthetics and Orthotics Services in Developing Countries', and the World Rehabilitation Fund's 'Guidelines for Socio-Economic Integration of Landmine Survivors'.

[95] See, e.g., ICBL interventions on victim assistance at the Ninth Meeting of States Parties of the *1997 Anti-Personnel Mine Ban Convention* (November 2008), at <http://www.apminebanconvention.org/fileadmin/pdf/mbc/MSP/9MSP/day5/9MSP-Item12d-28Nov2008-ICBL-LM.pdf> and <http://www.apminebanconvention.org/fileadmin/pdf/mbc/MSP/9MSP/day5/9MSP-Item12d-28Nov2008-ICBL.pdf >(both accessed 1 March 2010).

[96] See, e.g., Afghan Landmine Survivors Organization at <http://www.afghanlandminesurvivors.org/index.php?page=home>; Survivor Corps' peer support methodology at <http://www.survivorcorps.org/NetCommunity/Page.aspx?pid=304>; and Uganda Landmine Survivors Association at <http://uganda-survivors.org/about> (all accessed 1 March 2010).

someone who shares similar experiences and is living life to the fullest has been found a powerful tool in assisting victims through their path to recovery.

Age and gender: 'provide age- and gender-sensitive assistance'

5.82 Article 5, paragraph 1 on age- and gender-sensitive assistance should be read together with preambular paragraph 10 which cites 'the need to provide age- and gender-sensitive assistance to cluster munition victims and to address the special needs of vulnerable groups'. While women constitute only 5 to 10 per cent of mine or cluster munition victims, they face multiple barriers to recovery and inclusion in society, necessitating a tailored response that ensures women an equal opportunity to recovery and inclusion.[97] Children do constitute a large sub-group among those hurt or killed by ERW—about one third of the total number of casualties—and their path towards recovery and inclusion in society is under double jeopardy on account of being children.[98]

5.83 The highlighting of women's and children's rights as part of the larger group whose rights are being protected has not always been the case in international human rights treaties. With few exceptions, the International Covenant on Social, Economic and Cultural Rights (ICESCR) and the International Covenant on Civil and Political Rights (ICCPR) address themselves mainly to 'men and women', with no differentiation except where the issue is specific to women, such as prohibiting the carrying out of a death sentence with regard to a pregnant woman.[99] Similarly, as a rule children are mentioned in relation to rights or obligations of their parents, for example when affirming the liberty of parents to ensure moral and religious education for their children.[100]

5.84 Targeted address of the rights of women and children came with the Convention on the Elimination of All Forms of Discrimination against Women, and the Convention on the Rights of the Child. These treaties, respectively, note the concern that despite existing human rights treaties, discrimination against women continues to be pervasive, and children are in need of extra protection of their rights.

---

[97] For a more detailed explanation see, e.g., the fact sheet prepared by the Swiss Campaign to Ban Landmines, at <http://www.scbl-gender.ch/index.php?id=233> (accessed 1 March 2010).

[98] See, e.g., the figures on women and children cited in Annex IV of the Nairobi Report; and the Landmine Monitor factsheet on Landmines and Children, June 2008, available at: <http://lm.icbl.org/index.php/LM/Our-Research-Products/Factsheets> (accessed 1 March 2010).

[99] Article 6, paragraph 5, International Covenant on Civil and Political Rights. An interesting exception is the Article 7(a)(1) in the ICESCR on the right to work, which highlights the importance of guaranteeing women equal conditions of work as men.

[100] Article 18, paragraph 3, International Covenant on Civil and Political Rights.

5.85 Much debate occurred in the negotiations on the CRPD on how to reflect the recognition that women and children are doubly prone to discrimination. A dual approach was eventually applied. An Article on each issue— women with disabilities and children with disabilities—lays down the need for special measures to counter the added discrimination they face, and guiding principles on how to uphold their rights, for example the best interests of children as a primary consideration. Parallel to that, wherever a right covered in the Convention is pertinent to women (and girls) or to children, specific mention is made of the corresponding obligation to ensure their rights are protected. In such a manner particular mention is made of women or children (or both) in the Articles on access to justice; freedom from exploitation, violence and abuse; health; and adequate standard of living and social protection.[101]

5.86 The 2004 Nairobi Action Plan already underscored the necessity of giving attention to gender and age in order to guarantee that women and children draw maximum benefit from the provision of victim assistance.[102] This approach is now incorporated in the Convention on Cluster Munitions. By addressing age and gender in Article 5, paragraph 1, the Convention on Cluster Munitions appropriately establishes age and gender considerations as a core issue that informs all parts of victim assistance. The term *age- and gender- sensitive assistance* encapsulates the concept of an active duty to ensure that the assistance does in fact achieve substantive equality, among others by way of accommodations. The CRPD uses similar terms: *gender- and age-sensitive assistance and support* in the context of freedom from exploitation, violence or abuse; and *age-appropriate accommodations* in the context of access to justice.[103]

Data collection: 'make every effort to collect reliable data'

5.87 In order to provide comprehensive assistance, the existence of reliable data on the number of victims and the types of injuries, as well as a grasp of the needs of victims and the gaps in their fulfilment is crucial. As basic as this demand is, many States Parties to the *1997 Anti-Personnel Mine Ban Convention* lack accurate data even on the number of landmine victims. Others have collected that data, but due to a fragmented system, this data,

---

[101] Article 13; Article 16, paragraphs 1, 2, 4, and 5; Article 25; and Article 28(b), CRPD.
[102] Nairobi Action Plan, *op. cit.*, Action 35:

Ensure that, in all victim assistance efforts, emphasis is given to age and gender considerations and to mine victims who are subject to multiple forms of discrimination.

[103] Articles 16, paragraphs 1 and 2, and Article 13, paragraph 1, respectively, CRPD.

often aggregated as part of injury surveillance, may not reach health and social affairs agencies. Still others are not making the data available to the public.[104] The Convention on Cluster Munitions reaffirms the importance of data collection by its explicit reference at the end of Article 5, paragraph 1.

5.88 Reading this provision in light of the corresponding guidance in the CRPD enriches the understanding of States' obligation in this context. Collection of data is not an end in itself. In fact its technical nature could unwittingly allow States to digress from the real issue at hand, which is their obligation to demonstrate concrete progress on the ground, and instead dwell on the hardships of collecting data. It can also fortify over-medicalization of disability. For these reasons the Article on data collection which originally had appeared at the beginning of the CRPD drafts was eventually moved to the end. The final version of CRPD's Article 31 on *Statistics and Data Collection* clarifies that data collection must be approached as a *means*. It is justified by enabling States 'to formulate and implement policies to give effect' to that Convention and to 'identify and address the barriers faced by persons with disabilities in exercising their rights'. The process of collecting and maintaining data must ensure confidentiality and respect for privacy of the persons to whom it pertains.[105] It is clear both from the CRPD and from the Convention on Cluster Munitions that data should go beyond the numbers of individuals injured and killed, and address the wider ramifications of cluster munition use, such as measureable aspects of long-term recovery, and the economic impact on individuals and communities.

Concretizing the obligation: needs assessment, national plan, budget, timeframes, and mobilizing resources

5.89 Up until to the beginning of the Dublin Diplomatic Conference, the drafts of the Convention on Cluster Munitions contained only limited references to implementation measures. With a view to strengthening this aspect of victim assistance, civil society undertook a number of initiatives. Addressing the text of the then-Draft Convention, Survivor Corps, a leading civil society organization on victim assistance, reasoned as follows:

Lack of states' accountability has been one of the greatest challenges to progress in victim assistance under the 1997 Anti-Personnel Mine Ban Convention. However, the current draft cluster munitions treaty text *has not progressed* significantly compared

---

[104] See the summary of Data Collection in Landmine Monitor's 2009 Report, at <http://lm.icbl.org/index.php/publications/display?url=lm/2009/es/mine_casualties.html#data_collection> (accessed 1 March 2010).   [105] Article 31, CRPD.

with the 1997 Anti-Personnel Mine Ban Convention in terms of tangible and verifiable obligations. While it does create an obligation to report annually on provision of victim assistance, even that obligation does not articulate what specifically must be reported. If no progress is made, an opportunity to make a real difference in the lives of survivors and affected communities will have been lost.

Taking the Wellington draft as a base, we suggest stronger, more detailed provisions on developing and implementing measurable national plans. There should be a clear articulation of measurability in implementation and reporting, just as there are such provisions with regard to other core obligations of the treaty.

Our highest priority is adding language that would make it possible to monitor implementation, i.e. requires States to create national plans with priorities and a time frame, and to report on progress in implementation of the programs under the national plans.[106]

This position was taken up by the CMC, and adopted by key negotiating States, including many affected States. Subsequently, during the Dublin Diplomatic Conference a whole section—what is now Article 5, paragraph 2—was added to the draft Convention.[107]

5.90 Paragraphs 2(a), (c), and (d) establish implementation measures. Together they form a list of implementing activities that are indispensible to successful provision of victim assistance. An assessment of needs enables an effective intervention (sub-paragraph (a)). A national plan, budget, and timeframe are the most basic components of a successful victim assistance programme (sub-paragraph (c)). True to the rationale that motivated the addition of paragraph 2, these activities can be monitored: Has the State Party in question conducted a needs assessment? Is there a national plan in place? Has a budget been allocated to carry out the activities of the national plan? If not, what has the State Party done to mobilize national or international resources (sub-paragraph (d))?

5.91 The actions foreseen in this provision are no strangers to this Convention. They are used to guide implementation measures of the other treaty obligations as well. Needs assessment, development of a national plan, and resource mobilization all appear as essential steps in implementing the obligation to clear and destroy cluster munition remnants as required by Article 4 ('*Assess* and prioritise *needs* in terms of marking, protection of civilians, clearance and destruction, and *take steps to mobilise*

---

[106] Survivor Corps, 'Improving Language on Victim Assistance in the Cluster Munitions Treaty', May 2008 (copy on file with the author).

[107] On the history of the preparatory discussions and negotiations See, *supra*, §§5.10 *et seq*.

resources and *develop a national plan* to carry out these activities...').[108] The importance of attaching a timeframe to the fulfilment of a treaty obligation is familiar from Article 6 on international cooperation, which enables a State Party to ask for assistance to 'determine... [t]he time estimated as necessary to clear and destroy all cluster munition remnants'.[109] Consistency is increased across the Convention on Cluster Munitions by applying similar forms of implementation measures to the different treaty obligations.

5.92 Even as States Parties are required to create a plan and allocate a budget, the content of the plan and the size of the budget are left for each State Party to determine, as long as these guarantee that each concerned State Party 'adequately provide[s]' victim assistance. It was assumed that the measurable benchmarks contained in paragraph 2 of Article 5 increase clarity as to States' obligations and provide a lever for holding States accountable to fulfilling these obligations, while not being overly prescriptive.

Aligning efforts and mechanisms

5.93 The guidance provided by sub-paragraphs (c) and (g) of paragraph 2 is key to refining the conceptualization of victim assistance and resolving questions about its implementation: Will successful victim assistance programmes be ones that target cluster munition victims only? Is it legal, or viable, to generate preferential treatment for cluster munitions survivors only, in the areas that go to the root of social and economic rights, such as health, employment and education? For example, can a State adopt legislation that provides a right to health services to this group only, while discounting other groups facing similar obstacles to receiving basic health services?

5.94 The answers lie in paragraph 2(c) and (g), which establishes the following:

In fulfilling its obligations under paragraph 1 of this Article each State Party shall:

(c) Develop a national plan and budget... with a view to incorporating them within the existing national disability, development and human rights frameworks and mechanisms...

(g) Designate a focal point within the government for coordination of matters relating to the implementation of this Article;

---

[108] Article 4, paragraph 2(b).   [109] Article 6, paragraph 11(c).

Incorporation within existing mechanisms

5.95 Victim assistance aims to provide victims with the core social and economic rights, such as adequate medical care, an adequate standard of living, employment and education as part of social and economic inclusion. However, these rights may be lacking for most of the population in many cluster munition-affected countries. How then to reconcile between this reality and the treaty's explicit requirement of States Parties to provide victim assistance? Furthermore, considering that cluster munition victims are a subgroup within the community of persons with disabilities, and since many barriers that cluster munition victims face are common to other marginalized groups as well (e.g. persons living in poverty and persons with disabilities), what would be the most effective way to address these barriers?

5.96 The guidance provided by Article 5, paragraph 2(c) is vital. Victim assistance activities should be developed 'with a view to incorporating them within the existing national disability, development and human rights frameworks and mechanisms...'. Thus, the scarcity or inadequacy of medical care for cluster munition victims must be addressed as part of steps that improve the general health system. Poverty experienced by many cluster munition victims must be addressed through the wider lens of development programmes for broader populations. And the inaccessibility of vocational training centres to victims will be best solved through a strong human rights mechanism applying to persons with disabilities, and the mandating of a universal standard of accessibility for these and other types of public places and services.

5.97 Nonetheless, it does not suffice only to incorporate victim assistance into broader frameworks. Steps targeting cluster munition victims are necessary where, because of their particular circumstances, they are denied access to the necessary services. Rural and remote areas are often contaminated more than other areas with remnants of weapons, giving rise to a concentration of large numbers of victims. The same areas usually lack health and social services that are provided in more central areas in a given country. Victim assistance therefore means guaranteeing services to victims living in rural and remote areas by developing services and making them available in those areas, creating effective means of transportation to service centres, or a combination of both. Cluster munition victims will sustain certain types of injuries, necessitating a specific kind of emergency care and long-term services. Particular steps may have to be taken to guarantee that this set of services is available to the victims.

5.98 A complete concept of victim assistance can thus be formulated as follows. While victims' rights should be ensured through programmes advancing the rights of broader groups within the national context, programmes specifically targeting victims' services should be provided where needed to ensure access to services provided to the public.[110] In other words: assistance to mine victims should be viewed as a part of a country's overall public health and social services systems and human rights frameworks. However, within those general systems, deliberate care must be taken to ensure that landmine victims and other persons with disability receive the same opportunities in life: health care, social services, a life-sustaining income, education, and participation in the community, as every other sector of a society.[111]

5.99 Another important facet of incorporating victim assistance within broader national schemes is the level of State ownership towards victim assistance. In order to fulfil its victim assistance obligations it is not sufficient for a State Party merely to allow an international organization to operate a service for cluster munition victims, a service that is here today but may disappear once the organization pulls out. Only by mandating incorporation into broader national frameworks, which requires States Parties to assume ownership over the services and responsibility towards victims, will long-lasting and fundamental change be achieved.

5.100 The CRPD itself points in a similar direction, calling for the advancing of the rights of a certain group within a broader context in order to enhance sustainability. It emphasizes, for example, 'the importance of mainstreaming disability issues as an integral part of relevant strategies of sustainable development', and, from the other side, that 'international cooperation, including international development programmes, is inclusive of and accessible to persons with disabilities'.[112]

5.101 The CRPD, representing the human rights standard pertaining to persons with disabilities, which include cluster munition survivors, and containing an 'explicit social development dimension',[113] is an especially appropriate framework through which to implement victim assistance. Passing the various areas of victim assistance through the corresponding disability, development, and human rights framework provided by the CRPD helps to clarify how victim assistance should look. For example, medical care, a familiar victim assistance pillar, corresponds to the right to health. The CRPD provides

---

[110] Guiding Principles for Victim Assistance, compiled by the working group on victim assistance of the ICBL (2007), at <http://www.icbl.org/index.php/icbl/content/view/full/21843> (accessed 1 March 2010).   [111] Nairobi Report, *op. cit.*, para 66.

[112] Preamble (g) and Article 32, paragraph 1(a), CRPD.

[113] 'Report of the Secretary-General on the follow-up to the implementation of the outcome of the World Summit for Social Development and of the twenty-fourth special session of the General Assembly', *op. cit.*

important guidance on the right to health that is highly relevant for victim assistance. It includes a call for health care that is accessible to persons with disabilities, making it available as closely as possible to people's communities, and ensuring that informed consent forms the basis of all care. Victim assistance action therefore should incorporate these elements.

5.102 Similarly, economic inclusion corresponds to the right to work and employment. As provided by the CRPD, full inclusion of survivors and persons with disabilities in the open labour market is a guiding principle, from which the obligations to ensure accessibility of workplaces and of general vocational centres, and access to general vocational programmes, are derived.

Designation of a governmental focal point

5.103 A prerequisite to achieving the necessary level of coordination between different national mechanisms is, as Article 5, paragraph 2(g) instructs, the designation of a governmental focal point. The role of the focal point is the 'coordination of matters relating to the implementation of this Article'. The CRPD also foresees the designation:

of one or more focal points within government for matters relating to the implementation of the present Convention, and [...] the establishment or designation of a coordination mechanism within government to facilitate related action in different sectors and at different levels.[114]

Given the many overlapping areas between victim assistance and the promotion of the rights of persons with disabilities, the establishment of governmental focal points to guarantee a two-way mutually beneficial influence between the treaties is all the more compelling.

Development of laws and policies

5.104 Developing, implementing, and enforcing any necessary national laws and policies, as mandated by Article 5 paragraph 2(g), is an essential step towards providing victim assistance that is human rights-based and connected with the broader frameworks of disability, development and human rights. If it is to be anchored in, and influence, the system's level, victim assistance will have to appear in the form of laws and policies. Laws are the appropriate vehicle for creating change at the system's level, such as health, education, employment, or social affairs systems. Policies, more flexible by nature, could serve as a vehicle specifically to target cluster munition victims, and even specific groups among them, where the targeted approach is necessary, such

---

[114] Article 33, paragraph 1, CRPD.

as policies targeting victims who live in rural and remote areas where services are scarce.

5.105 The corresponding requirement in the CRPD is helpful better to understand the scope of this obligation. Article 4, paragraph 2 requires its States Parties:

(a) To adopt all appropriate legislative, administrative and other measures for the implementation of the rights recognized in the present Convention;

(b) To take all appropriate measures, including legislation, to modify or abolish existing laws, regulations, customs and practices that constitute discrimination against persons with disabilities;

(c) To take into account the protection and promotion of the human rights of persons with disabilities in all policies and programmes;

(d) To refrain from engaging in any act or practice that is inconsistent with the present Convention and to ensure that public authorities and institutions act in conformity with the present Convention;

(e) To take all appropriate measures to eliminate discrimination on the basis of disability by any person, organization or private enterprise.

The guidance gleaned from this is two-fold. On the *process* level, laws, policies, customs, practices, and programmes should be carefully analysed, in some cases abolished or amended, and in other cases developed. On the *substance* level, since victim assistance and the promotion of the rights of persons with disabilities share many common elements, an effective way to counter marginalization of cluster munition victims is to apply this scrutiny to law, policy, and practice relating to persons with disabilities.

Fundamental principle: Consultation with and involvement of victims in decision-making and implementation

5.106 The obligation in Article paragraph 2(f) to 'closely consult with and actively involve cluster munition victims and their representative organizations' reflects the right to participate in decision-making processes affecting one's life. Those experiencing victimization are most suited to articulate their needs, and their opinion is crucial to the way the needs will be addressed and their rights recognized.

5.107 The language closely follows the formulation of this right in the CRPD, and the principle is certainly common: exclusion from decision-making processes has always been a symptom of exclusion from society in general. The answer to such exclusion comes in the form of a fundamental principle of inclusion in decision-making processes. Article 4, paragraph 3, of the CRPD points at the important junctions where such consultation should take place:

In the development and implementation of legislation and policies to implement the present Convention, and in other decision-making processes concerning issues relating to persons with disabilities, States Parties shall closely consult with and actively involve persons with disabilities, including children with disabilities, through their representative organizations.

Accordingly, consultation with and involvement of cluster munition victims should take place in every process that potentially will affect their lives, both on the global and domestic levels, and in issues directly related to implementation of the treaty and beyond.

Fundamental principle: Non-discrimination

5.108 Preferential treatment to a group of individuals, to the exclusion or detriment of others, though all share the same needs and face similar barriers, is a familiar occurrence in many countries. An example of this phenomenon is the accordance of benefits to individuals injured in conflict-related activities, rather than to all persons with disabilities with similar needs and facing similar barriers.

5.109 Article 5, paragraph 2(e) clarifies the non-exclusive nature of victim assistance prescribed in the treaty. The non-discrimination clause aims at avoiding the creation of a preferred group, i.e. cluster munition victims, among other groups with similar needs. Victim assistance should be provided in a way that narrows the gap between groups in society who are all entitled to rights and whose needs, and the barriers they face, may be similar. In determining how this is to be done, the guidance provided in paragraph 2 is key: incorporate victim assistance into broader national mechanisms thereby influencing these broader mechanisms, which in turn will have an effect on other individuals and groups with similar needs. Thus, the chances increase of victim assistance becoming a vehicle for change for much larger groups than cluster munition victims only.

5.110 The second half of paragraph 2(e), instructing that 'differences in treatment should be based only on medical, rehabilitative, psychological or socio-economic needs' is familiar from other instruments of international humanitarian law. For example, an occupying power is required to provide medical care to civilians in that area, and at the same time not to discriminate in the provision of this treatment and ensure that the sole consideration is the medical one.[115] The reference to differentiation in treatment based (only) on the *needs* of victims removes this clause from the detrimental sphere of relativism, in which States could claim fulfilment of the non-discrimination obligation by refraining from providing the services to any group. Instead, the provision makes clear that States Parties have to address the needs of victims, and at the same time do so without discrimination towards other groups.

Best practices

5.111 Article 5, paragraph 2(h) requires States Parties to:

(s)trive to incorporate relevant guidelines and good practices including in the areas of medical care, rehabilitation and psychological support, as well as social and economic inclusion.

The strength of this requirement lies less in its level of obligation, which is advisory, but rather in the idea that it reflects: a condition for achieving quality victim assistance is the incorporation of guidelines and good practices in all areas of victim assistance.[116]

---

[115] See, e.g., Article 3, *1977 Additional Protocol I*.
[116] See, *supra*, fn. 94 for examples of guidelines and best practices.

Article 6. International cooperation and assistance

Bonnie Docherty and Richard Moyes[1]

Article 6—International cooperation and assistance

1. In fulfilling its obligations under this Convention each State Party has the right to seek and receive assistance.

2. Each State Party in a position to do so shall provide technical, material and financial assistance to States Parties affected by cluster munitions, aimed at the implementation of the obligations of this Convention. Such assistance may be provided, *inter alia*, through the United Nations system, international, regional or national organisations or institutions, non-governmental organisations or institutions, or on a bilateral basis.

3. Each State Party undertakes to facilitate and shall have the right to participate in the fullest possible exchange of equipment and scientific and technological information concerning the implementation of this Convention. The States Parties shall not impose undue restrictions on the provision and receipt of clearance and other such equipment and related technological information for humanitarian purposes.

4. In addition to any obligations it may have pursuant to paragraph 4 of Article 4 of this Convention, each State Party in a position to do so shall provide assistance for clearance and destruction of cluster munition remnants and information concerning various means and technologies related to clearance of cluster munitions, as well as lists of experts, expert agencies or national points of contact on clearance and destruction of cluster munition remnants and related activities.

5. Each State Party in a position to do so shall provide assistance for the destruction of stockpiled cluster munitions, and shall also provide assistance to identify, assess and prioritise needs and practical measures in terms of marking, risk reduction education, protection of civilians and clearance and destruction as provided in Article 4 of this Convention.

6. Where, after entry into force of this Convention, cluster munitions have become cluster munition remnants located in areas under the jurisdiction or control of a State Party, each State Party in a position to do so shall urgently provide emergency assistance to the affected State Party.

[1] Bonnie Docherty wrote the overview, preparatory discussion and negotiation history, and the commentary on paragraphs 4–7. Richard Moyes wrote the commentary on paragraphs 1–3 and 8–12.

7. Each State Party in a position to do so shall provide assistance for the implementation of the obligations referred to in Article 5 of this Convention to adequately provide age- and gender-sensitive assistance, including medical care, rehabilitation and psychological support, as well as provide for social and economic inclusion of cluster munition victims. Such assistance may be provided, *inter alia*, through the United Nations system, international, regional or national organisations or institutions, the International Committee of the Red Cross, national Red Cross and Red Crescent Societies and their International Federation, non-governmental organisations or on a bilateral basis.

8. Each State Party in a position to do so shall provide assistance to contribute to the economic and social recovery needed as a result of cluster munition use in affected States Parties.

9. Each State Party in a position to do so may contribute to relevant trust funds in order to facilitate the provision of assistance under this Article.

10. Each State Party that seeks and receives assistance shall take all appropriate measures in order to facilitate the timely and effective implementation of this Convention, including facilitation of the entry and exit of personnel, materiel and equipment, in a manner consistent with national laws and regulations, taking into consideration international best practices.

11. Each State Party may, with the purpose of developing a national action plan, request the United Nations system, regional organisations, other States Parties or other competent intergovernmental or non-governmental institutions to assist its authorities to determine, *inter alia*:

(a) The nature and extent of cluster munition remnants located in areas under its jurisdiction or control;

(b) The financial, technological and human resources required for the implementation of the plan;

(c) The time estimated as necessary to clear and destroy all cluster munition remnants located in areas under its jurisdiction or control;

(d) Risk reduction education programmes and awareness activities to reduce the incidence of injuries or deaths caused by cluster munition remnants;

(e) Assistance to cluster munition victims; and

(f) The coordination relationship between the government of the State Party concerned and the relevant governmental, intergovernmental or non-governmental entities that will work in the implementation of the plan.

12. States Parties giving and receiving assistance under the provisions of this Article shall cooperate with a view to ensuring the full and prompt implementation of agreed assistance programmes.

Overview of the Article

6.1 Article 6 lays out the Convention's obligations related to international cooperation and assistance. It applies to all States Parties, including not only users, producers, stockpilers, and affected countries, but also States Parties that do not fit into one of those categories. Most of the paragraphs are directed at States Parties 'in a position to do so', which limits the obligations to a certain extent.[2] Some States during the Oslo Process had proposed removing that phrase and making assistance under Article 6 completely obligatory for all States, but that idea was rejected because consensus seemed too difficult to achieve.[3] The qualification means that the majority of international cooperation and assistance will likely come from nations that have greater resources, but given the range of assistance that can be given, all States are arguably in a position to contribute in some way.

6.2 Article 6 establishes that every State Party has the right to 'seek and receive assistance'[4] and lists a variety of types of assistance that other States Parties must provide. States Parties must assist with the primary positive obligations of the Convention on Cluster Munitions: stockpile destruction, clearance and destruction of cluster munition remnants, and victim assistance.[5] The mandated assistance goes beyond that, however, to include:

- 'technical, material and financial assistance' designed to help implement the Convention,[6]
- exchange of 'equipment and scientific and technological information',[7]

---

[2] Article 6, paragraphs 2 and 4–9.

[3] Two States made such a proposal at the Wellington Conference in February 2008, but the Chair of the session said he thought it would be difficult to compel States Parties to assist. Statements at the Wellington Conference, 21 February 2008 (Landmine Action notes; copy on file with author). Botswana reiterated the proposal during the May 2008 Diplomatic Conference in Dublin and received support from Ethiopia, South Africa, and Zambia. 'Summary Record of Second Session of the Committee of the Whole', Diplomatic Conference doc. CCM/CW/SR/2, 18 June 2008, pp. 8 and 10–11.

[4] Article 6, paragraph 1.

[5] Article 6, paragraphs 4, 5, and 7.

[6] Article 6, paragraph 2.

[7] Article 6, paragraph 3.

- assistance for assessing needs and measures related to marking, risk reduction education, and protection of civilians,[8]
- emergency assistance if cluster munitions are used again in the future,[9] and
- assistance for economic and social recovery.[10]

States Parties may also request assistance from other States or organizations in developing national action plans.[11] Donor States Parties have the option to make contributions through trust funds.[12] States Parties that receive assistance must facilitate implementation of the Convention by removing hurdles to assistance.[13]

6.3 The inclusion of an Article on international cooperation and assistance serves multiple purposes. It advances the humanitarian goals of the Convention—ridding the world of cluster munitions and the harm they cause—by requiring assistance with many activities that minimize the civilian suffering caused by the weapons.[14] It also promotes disarmament aims by mandating assistance for stockpile destruction.[15] On a more practical level, the Article helps ensure that States Parties can meet their positive obligations to destroy stockpiles, clear cluster munition remnants, and assist victims. This assistance thus reduces the burdens of the Convention on Cluster Munitions on stockpiling and affected States and makes them more willing to become party to it. Finally, the Article spreads the costs of dealing with the problems of cluster munitions.

6.4 Previous treaties served as models for Article 6, but its final version encompasses much more than its predecessors. In the *1997 Anti-Personnel Mine Ban Convention,*[16] *1996 Amended Protocol II*, and *2003 Protocol V*,[17] the

---

[8] Article 6, paragraph 5.   [9] Article 6, paragraph 6.   [10] Article 6, paragraph 8.
[11] Article 6, paragraph 11.   [12] Article 6, paragraph 9.
[13] Article 6, paragraphs 10 and 12.

[14] The preamble of the Convention describes its humanitarian goal as: 'put[ting] an end for all time to the suffering and casualties caused by cluster munitions at the time of their use, when they fail to function as intended or when they are abandoned.' Second preambular paragraph.

[15] The preamble of the Convention expresses States Parties' concern with 'the dangers presented by the large national stockpiles of cluster munitions retained for operational use and [their determination] to ensure their rapid destruction.' Fourth preambular paragraph.

[16] The formal title of this treaty is the Convention on the Prohibition of the Use, Stockpiling, Production and Transfer of Anti-Personnel Mines and on Their Destruction.

[17] Amended Protocol II on Mines, Booby-Traps and Other Devices (*1996 Amended Protocol II*) and Protocol V on Explosive Remnants of War (*2003 Protocol V*) of the *1980 Convention on Certain Conventional Weapons*. The formal title of the *1980 Convention on Certain Conventional Weapons* is the Convention on Prohibitions or Restrictions on the Use of Certain Conventional Weapons Which May Be Deemed to Be Excessively Injurious or to have Indiscriminate Effects, as amended on 21 December 2001.

international cooperation and assistance Articles include provisions on clearance, stockpile destruction, and/or victim assistance.[18] The Convention on Cluster Munitions adds obligations to provide other types of assistance, such as assistance for emergencies and social and economic recovery.[19] It also augments several provisions, by, for example, enumerating more forms of victim assistance and referencing user State responsibility for clearance.[20] During the Oslo Process, States repeatedly emphasized the importance of international cooperation and assistance,[21] and they continued to amend Article 6 until late in the negotiations at the Diplomatic Conference in Dublin. Virtually every change they made broadened the scope of the obligations and pushed international weapons law in new, increasingly humanitarian directions.

Preparatory discussions

6.5 States considered international cooperation and assistance a key element of the future Convention from the very beginning of the Oslo Process. The Oslo Declaration highlighted the need for cooperation and assistance for victims, clearance, risk education, and stockpile destruction. By signing on to the Declaration, States committed to conclude a legally binding instrument that would 'establish a framework for cooperation and assistance that ensures adequate provision of care and rehabilitation to survivors and their communities, clearance of contaminated areas, risk education and destruction of stockpiles of prohibited cluster munitions'.[22] States also spoke of cooperation and assistance in statements made at the February 2007 Oslo Conference.[23] Several States emphasized that affected and developing States would need help to meet any obligations the future Convention would establish.[24] States' dedication to this issue would continue throughout the preparatory discussions

---

[18] Article 6, paragraphs 4, 5, and 3, *1997 Anti-Personnel Mine Ban Convention*; Article 11, paragraphs 2–3, *1996 Amended Protocol II*; and Article 8, paragraphs 4 and 7, *2003 Protocol V*.

[19] Article 6, paragraphs 6 and 8.   [20] Article 6, paragraphs 7 and 4.

[21] See, e.g., Statement of Zambia on behalf of 39 African States, 'Summary Record of Opening Ceremony and First Session of the Plenary', Diplomatic Conference doc. CCM/SR/1, 18 June 2008, p. 5; and Statements of Timor-Leste and Thailand, 'Summary Record of Second Session of the Plenary', Diplomatic Conference doc. CCM/SR/2, 18 June 2008, pp. 2, 4.

[22] Oslo Declaration of 23 February 2007, point 1(ii). For full text, see Annex 2 to this Commentary. See also 'Addressing the Humanitarian Impacts of Cluster Munitions: Key Issues', Background Paper to the Oslo Conference on Cluster Munitions, 22–23 February 2007, <http://www.clusterconvention.org/pages/pages_vi/vib_opdoc_backgrpaper.html> (accessed 6 February 2010).   [23] See, *supra*, §0.30 for details of the Conference.

[24] Statements at the Oslo Conference, 22 February 2007; and Statement at the Oslo Conference, 23 February 2007 (all from Landmine Action notes; copy on file with author).

and negotiations until adoption of the Convention on Cluster Munitions 15 months later.

6.6 The Lima Discussion Text[25] laid out the basic elements of international cooperation and assistance in a stand-alone Article that would grow broader and more demanding with each draft that followed.[26] (While numbered Article 5 in the Lima text, the Article would change places in the Vienna Discussion Text with the one devoted to victim assistance and become Article 6, its final nomenclature in the Convention on Cluster Munitions.) The Lima Article's six paragraphs:

- established the 'right to seek and receive assistance';
- established the duty to facilitate exchange of equipment, material, and information and the right to participate in that exchange;
- obliged States Parties in a position to do so to provide assistance for clearance;
- obliged States Parties in a position to do so to provide assistance for stockpile destruction;
- allowed States Parties to request help with developing national programmes from intergovernmental, governmental, and non-governmental organizations; and
- required donor and recipient States to cooperate to ensure implementation of assistance programmes.[27]

International cooperation and assistance also figured in Article 6 of the Lima Discussion Text (later Article 5), which created victim assistance obligations.[28] Article 11 made international cooperation a topic of discussion at Meetings of States Parties, with a provision that would remain almost the same throughout the Oslo Process.[29]

6.7 The Lima Discussion Text drew heavily on Article 6 of the *1997 Anti-Personnel Mine Ban Convention*. All of the Lima text's paragraphs on

---

[25] Chair's discussion text on a legally binding international instrument that will prohibit the use, production, transfer and stockpiling of cluster munitions that cause unacceptable harm to civilians, Lima, 23–25 May 2007. For full text, see Annex 3 to this Commentary.

[26] Article 5, Lima Discussion Text.   [27] *Ibid.*

[28] Article 6, Lima Discussion Text.

[29] Article 11, paragraph 1(c), Lima Discussion Text. Between the Lima Conference and the adoption of the Convention on Cluster Munitions, the *chapeau* added the italicized words:

The States Parties shall meet regularly in order to consider *and, where necessary take decisions in respect of any matter* with regard to the application or the implementation of this Convention.

Cp. Article 11, paragraph 1, Lima Discussion Text, with Article 11, paragraph 1. See, *infra*, the commentary on Article 11.

international cooperation and assistance appear in the *1997 Anti-Personnel Mine Ban Convention* with essentially the same language.[30] There were only two notable differences between the two documents. First, the Lima text placed the *1997 Anti-Personnel Mine Ban Convention*'s requirement to provide international assistance to victims in a separate Article on victim assistance.[31] Second, the Lima text did not explicitly offer States Parties the option to provide clearance assistance by contributing to a trust fund.[32] Later versions of the international assistance Article for cluster munitions would add paragraphs on victim assistance and trust funds although use different language.[33] They would also move far beyond the *1997 Anti-Personnel Mine Ban Convention*, establishing additional and more demanding obligations for international cooperation and assistance.

6.8 At the May 2007 Lima Conference,[34] States renewed their support for including provisions on international cooperation and assistance. Donor and developing countries alike stressed the importance of international cooperation and assistance, with the latter reiterating that most affected States would need outside help to deal with the problems caused by cluster munitions.[35] One State, for example, said that countries with limited resources would find it difficult to meet their obligations without assistance and that the Article could ultimately affect its decision to ratify.[36] The discussions in Lima also gave initial indications of issues that would become more important in later meetings of the Oslo Process. Another State called for an obligation to be placed on user States to clear unexploded submunitions and for the creation of a United

---

[30] Article 6, *1997 Anti-Personnel Mine Ban Convention*. Some similar language can be found in *2003 Protocol V*. For example, Article 7, paragraph 1 establishes the right to seek and receive assistance, and Article 8, paragraph 4 has a related provision on the exchange of 'equipment, material, and scientific and technological information'. Article 7, paragraph 1, and Article 8, paragraph 4, *2003 Protocol V*. The *1993 Chemical Weapons Convention* also includes a related paragraph stating:

> Each State Party undertakes to facilitate, and shall have the right to participate in, the fullest possible exchange of equipment, material and scientific and technological information concerning means of protection against chemical weapons.

Article 10, paragraph 3, Convention on the Prohibition of the Development, Production, Stockpiling and Use of Chemical Weapons and on their Destruction (*1993 Chemical Weapons Convention*).

[31] Article 6, Lima Discussion Text; and Article 6, paragraph 3, *1997 Anti-Personnel Mine Ban Convention*. [32] *Cf.* Article 6, paragraph 4, *1997 Anti-Personnel Mine Ban Convention*.

[33] Article 6, paragraphs 7 and 9.

[34] See, *supra*, §§0.41–0.42 for details of the Conference.

[35] Statements at the Lima Conference, 23 and 24 May 2007 (Landmine Action notes; copy on file with author).

[36] Statement at the Lima Conference, 24 May 2007 (Landmine Action notes; copy on file with author).

Nations (UN) trust fund for assistance.[37] The UN Development Programme (UNDP) and the Cluster Munition Coalition (CMC) supported assigning special responsibility to user States to help with clearance and to share information, and they argued for inclusion of a provision on international assistance for victims in the international cooperation and assistance Article.[38]

6.9 The Vienna Discussion Text responded to some of the interventions made in Lima.[39] In Article 6, paragraph 4 on assistance for clearance, it addressed the call for user State responsibility by amending the opening phrase to:

Each State Party in a position to do so *and in particular a State Party that has used cluster munitions on the territory of another State Party* shall provide assistance for clearance.[40]

No precedent for such an obligation existed in past weapons treaties. This paragraph also included a new requirement to provide assistance in the form of information on clearance technologies and experts.[41] In paragraph 8 of the same Article, the Vienna text established an obligation for States Parties to help affected States that, under the dramatically revised Article on victim assistance (now Article 5), assumed primary responsibility to care for victims.[42] The paragraph was based on similar ones in the *1997 Anti-Personnel Mine Ban Convention* and *2003 Protocol V*,[43] but it added 'psychological support' to the list of types of assistance.[44] Finally, the Vienna text inserted a paragraph 9 allowing States Parties 'in a position to do so' to contribute to trust funds for assistance.[45] While the *1997 Anti-Personnel Mine Ban Convention* mentions a voluntary UN trust fund,[46] the cluster munition trust fund provision borrowed its more general language from *2003 Protocol V*.[47] It differed, however, because it changed the Protocol's obligatory '*shall* contribute' to the voluntary '*may* contribute'.[48]

---

[37] *Ibid.*

[38] Statements of UNDP and the CMC, Lima Conference, 24 May 2007 (Landmine Action notes; copy on file with author).

[39] Vienna Discussion Text of 14 November 2007. For full text, see Annex 4 to this Commentary.

[40] Article 6, paragraph 4, Vienna Discussion Text *(emphasis added to indicate changes)*.

[41] *Ibid.*   [42] Article 6, paragraph 8, and Article 5, Vienna Discussion Text.

[43] Article 6, paragraph 3, *1997 Anti-Personnel Mine Ban Convention*; and Article 8, paragraph 2, *2003 Protocol V*.   [44] Article 6, paragraph 8, Vienna Discussion Text.

[45] Article 6, paragraph 9, Vienna Discussion Text.

[46] Article 6, paragraph 4, *1997 Anti-Personnel Mine Ban Convention*.

[47] Article 8, paragraph 3, *2003 Protocol V*.

[48] *Cp.* Article 6, paragraph 9, Vienna Discussion Text, with Article 8, paragraph 3, *2003 Protocol V (emphasis added)*.

6.10 The Vienna Discussion Text also made some amendments and additions related to topics that had not attracted public attention at the Lima Conference. The first paragraph of Article 6 on the right to seek and receive assistance excised the final phrase, which came from the *1997 Anti-Personnel Mine Ban Convention* and which had qualified the right with 'where feasible, from other States Parties to the extent possible'.[49] A new paragraph 2 obliged all States Parties in a position to do so to 'provide technical, material and financial assistance to States Parties affected by cluster munitions'.[50] A new paragraph 6 required assistance to assess needs and measures for marking contaminated areas, clearing cluster munition remnants, and protecting civilians generally.[51] These two new paragraphs were related, but not identical, to paragraphs in *2003 Protocol V*.[52] Each change either introduced a new obligation or made an existing one broader.[53]

6.11 During discussions of the international cooperation and assistance Article (now Article 6) at the December 2007 Vienna Conference,[54] the controversy over user State responsibility emerged. A number of developing States, as well as UNDP and the CMC, stressed the importance of such a provision.[55] One State asserted that user States bear a moral as well as legal responsibility, especially to provide assistance to victims.[56] In contrast, another State argued that such a provision would be difficult to implement and could hold States responsible for munitions left 40 to 50 years ago. It suggested looking at the model of Article 3, paragraph 1 of *2003 Protocol V* instead.[57] That Article, however, did not assign responsibility for ordnance that pre-dated the instrument, and user States were obliged only to provide assistance 'where feasible'.[58] The discussion about user State responsibility would become increasingly contentious over the course of the Oslo Process.

---

[49] Article 6, paragraph 1, Vienna Discussion Text; and Article 6, paragraph 1, *1997 Anti-Personnel Mine Ban Convention*.   [50] Article 6, paragraph 2, Vienna Discussion Text.

[51] Article 6, paragraph 6, Vienna Discussion Text.

[52] See Article 3, paragraph 5, *2003 Protocol V* (mandating 'technical, financial, material and human resources assistance'); and Article 8, paragraph 1, *2003 Protocol V* (mandating assistance for marking, clearance and risk education, not assessment of these activities).

[53] The Vienna Discussion Text also added a reference to Article 6 in Article 4 on clearance. It required States Parties to take certain measures, 'taking into consideration the provisions of Article 6 of this Convention regarding international cooperation and assistance'. Article 4, paragraph 2, Vienna Discussion Text. This provision would remain unchanged in the Convention on Cluster Munitions.   [54] See, *supra*, §§0.43–0.46 for details of the Conference.

[55] Statements at the Vienna Conference, 7 December 2007 (Landmine Action notes; copy on file with author).

[56] Statement at the Vienna Conference, 7 December 2007 (Landmine Action notes; copy on file with author).   [57] *Ibid.*

[58] Article 3, paragraph 1, *2003 Protocol V*.

6.12 While continuing to recognize the importance of international cooperation and assistance, donor States began to highlight the obligations of recipient States, foreshadowing a major debate that would occur during final negotiations at the Diplomatic Conference in Dublin. One State encouraged affected States to allocate their resources as effectively as possible and to exempt donor States from taxes and duties for clearance equipment.[59] Another State noted that affected States have a duty to manage and control remediation programmes because they know their own needs.[60] Other topics States discussed at the Vienna Conference included the trust fund paragraph[61] and a proposal to provide assistance for clearance training for peacekeepers.[62]

6.13 The Draft Cluster Munitions Convention of January 2008,[63] which was distributed before the Wellington Conference, for the most part broadened the scope of draft Article 6 compared to the earlier Lima and Vienna discussion texts. New paragraph 6 obliged States Parties in a position to do so 'urgently [to] provide emergency assistance to the affected State Party' if cluster munitions were used after entry into force of the Convention.[64] New paragraph 8 obliged States Parties in a position to do so to 'provide assistance to contribute to the economic and social recovery needed as a result of cluster munition use in affected States Parties'.[65] These two paragraphs required assistance for different situations and different needs than previous drafts and most previous weapons treaties.[66]

6.14 In addition to inserting new provisions, the Draft Cluster Munitions Convention amended the wording of those that had been included in the prior discussion texts. It substituted the phrase directly placing obligations on user States with: 'In addition to any obligations [a State Party] may have pursuant to paragraph 4 of Article 4 of this Convention.'[67] Article 4, paragraph 4 had

---

[59] Statement at the Vienna Conference, 7 December 2007 (Landmine Action notes; copy on file with author). [60] *Ibid.*

[61] There were two States particularly wary of the addition of paragraph 9 on trust funds. Statements at the Vienna Conference, 7 December 2007 (Landmine Action notes; copy on file with author).

[62] Two States called for clearance training for peacekeepers. Statements at the Vienna Conference, 7 December 2007 (Landmine Action notes; copy on file with author).

[63] Draft Cluster Munitions Convention of 21 January 2008. For full text, see Annex 5 to this Commentary. [64] Article 6, paragraph 6, Draft Cluster Munitions Convention.

[65] Article 6, paragraph 8, Draft Cluster Munitions Convention.

[66] The *1993 Chemical Weapons Convention*, however, allows for and establishes a process for provision of emergency assistance. Article 10, paragraphs 6–11, *1993 Chemical Weapons Convention*.

[67] Article 6, paragraph 4, Draft Cluster Munitions Convention.

become the primary provision on user State responsibility for clearance.[68] The draft Convention's Explanatory Notes explained:

Many delegations have highlighted the central role of this Article for the implementation of the Convention and especially supported the language regarding the assistance that shall be provided by each State Party in a position to do so, as well as the State Party that has used cluster munitions on the territory of another State Party. This obligation on the latter is already explicit in Article 4, paragraph 4, and is also referred to in paragraph 4 of Article 6.[69]

The Notes thus clarified that the Draft Cluster Munitions Convention's revisions reflected reorganization of the treaty not abandonment of the principle of user State responsibility.

6.15 Other amendments to Article 6 sharpened the Draft Cluster Munitions Convention. In the victim assistance paragraph, the draft replaced 'social and economic *reintegration*' with 'social and economic *inclusion*'.[70] This change reflected a growing understanding that every person (irrespective of, for example, disability) should be able to access equally and participate fully in any activity or service in their community, and it expanded the provision's coverage by encompassing victims who were not necessarily integrated beforehand.[71] The text merged the paragraphs on stockpile destruction and assessment of measures related to marking, protection of civilians, and clearance.[72] It added risk education to the latter list of humanitarian activities for which certain assistance was to be provided; in the process, it removed risk education from the victim assistance paragraph.[73] It also honed and clarified the language of paragraph 10, which allowed States Parties to seek help with developing national action plans from States and organizations.[74]

6.16 As at the Vienna Conference, at the February 2008 Wellington Conference[75] several States commented on user State responsibility during discussions on international cooperation and assistance. Some States argued that user States had both a legal and a moral obligation to assist with clearance

---

[68] Article 4, paragraph 4, Draft Cluster Munitions Convention.

[69] 'Draft Cluster Munitions Convention: Explanatory Notes', 21 January 2008, p. 4. For full text, see Annex 5 to this Commentary.

[70] Article 6, paragraph 7, Draft Cluster Munitions Convention *(emphasis added)*.

[71] The new language also emphasized the burden on society to be inclusive rather than the division between victim and society that needs to be overcome for integration. For further discussion of the difference between reintegration and inclusion, see, *supra*, the commentary on Article 5, in §5.48.   [72] Article 6, paragraph 5, Draft Cluster Munitions Convention.

[73] Article 6, paragraphs 5 and 7, Draft Cluster Munitions Convention; and Article 6, paragraph 8, Vienna Discussion Text.

[74] Article 6, paragraph 10, Draft Cluster Munitions Convention.

[75] See, *supra*, §§0.48–0.54 for details of the Conference.

of the land they contaminated. Others argued that all States should bear responsibility, and two States suggested that discussing user State responsibility would cause disharmony in the negotiations.[76]

6.17 During Article 6 discussions at the Wellington Conference, States raised a few other concerns that would not lead to changes in the text of the future Convention. As stated above, two States called for international cooperation and assistance to be obligatory for all States, not just those in a position to do so.[77] The Chair of the meeting responded that it would not be easy to compel States to help.[78] Several States proposed adding assistance for livelihood in the victim assistance provision.[79] Two States reiterated the desire for assistance to provide clearance training for peacekeepers.[80]

6.18 The Wellington Declaration, adopted at the end of the Conference, highlighted the value States continued to place on international cooperation and assistance as they prepared for formal negotiations in Dublin. It listed two 'essential elements' of the new instrument. First, the instrument must prohibit use, production, transfer, and stockpiling of cluster munitions. Second, it must establish '[a] framework for cooperation and assistance that ensures adequate provision of care and rehabilitation to survivors and their communities, clearance of contaminated areas, risk education, and destruction of stockpiles'.[81]

6.19 The compendium of proposals attached to the Draft Cluster Munitions Convention that was forwarded to the Diplomatic Conference (the Wellington Compendium) included four proposals related to Article 6. Sponsoring States would resubmit each of them as formal proposals to the Diplomatic Conference in Dublin. Denmark, France, Germany, and Sweden proposed a new paragraph—then called 9 (bis)—placing obligations on recipient States to facilitate assistance.[82] This proposal would turn out to be the most controversial one during Article 6 discussions in Dublin. The UK sought to reinsert the qualifying language of paragraph 1 on the right to seek and receive assistance by concluding the paragraph with: 'where feasible, from other

---

[76] Statements at the Wellington Conference, 21 February 2008 (Landmine Action notes; copy on file with author). [77] *Ibid.*

[78] Statement of the Chair of the Conference, Wellington Conference, 21 February 2008 (Landmine Action notes; copy on file with author).

[79] Statements at the Wellington Conference, 21 February 2008 (Landmine Action notes; copy on file with author). [80] *Ibid.*

[81] Declaration of the Wellington Conference on Cluster Munitions. For full text, see Annex 7 to this Commentary.

[82] 'Article 6: International Cooperation and Assistance', Wellington Compendium, *op. cit.*, p. 24; and 'Proposal by Denmark, France, Germany and Sweden for the amendment of Article 6', Diplomatic Conference doc. CCM/37, 19 May 2008. For full text of the Wellington Compendium, see Annex 6 to this Commentary.

States Parties to the extent possible'. It also suggested cutting the paragraph on assistance for economic and social recovery and adding the word 'coordination' before 'relationship' in paragraph 9(f).[83] With the exception of the last insertion, States would ultimately reject the UK's proposals for Article 6. Italy sought the deletion of the mention of Article 4, paragraph 4, but its proposal also failed.[84] Finally France and Germany proposed significantly softening the user State responsibility provision and placing it in either Article 4 or 'preferably' in Article 6.[85] An amended version of the provision would ultimately be included in Article 4, paragraph 4, but the French and German model was not accepted.

Negotiations

6.20 In the Diplomatic Conference, discussions on international cooperation and assistance centred on two issues: the obligations of recipient States and user State responsibility. Provisions related to both appear in the final text of the Convention. As proposed in the Wellington Compendium, paragraph 9(bis), which dealt with the former issue, read:

Each State Party that receives assistance shall take all appropriate measures in order to facilitate the timely and effective implementation thereof, including by collecting and releasing all relevant data and information, by granting favourable entry and visa regimes for international personnel involved in assistance programmes, and by ensuring the unimpeded import of relevant material and equipment free of financial and administrative burdens.[86]

At the 20 May 2008 meeting of the Committee of the Whole, paragraph 9(bis) received some initial support, including from Canada, Germany, Ghana,

---

[83] 'Article 6: International Cooperation and Assistance', Wellington Compendium, pp. 24–26; and 'Proposal by the United Kingdom for the amendment of Article 6', Diplomatic Conference doc. CCM/38, 19 May 2008.

[84] 'Article 6: International Cooperation and Assistance', Wellington Compendium, p. 26; and 'Proposal by Italy for the amendment of Article 6', Diplomatic Conference doc. CCM/39, 19 May 2008.

[85] 'Additional Text Proposals', Wellington Compendium, pp. 31–32; and 'Proposal by France and Germany for additional text', Diplomatic Conference doc. CCM/47, 19 May 2008. Under this proposal, States Parties were 'invited to make [information] available [to the affected State Party], without delay after the cessation of active hostilities and as far as practicable, subject to these parties' legitimate security interests'.

[86] 'Article 6: International Cooperation and Assistance', Wellington Compendium, p. 24. See also 'Proposal by Denmark, France, Germany and Sweden for the amendment of Article 6', Diplomatic Conference doc. CCM/37, 19 May 2008.

and the Netherlands, but Argentina and South Africa raised some concerns, especially whether it would require changing national laws.[87] President of the Conference Dáithí O'Ceallaigh included the Wellington Compendium's version in a 23 May non-paper, only changing 'receives' to '*seeks and* receives'.[88]

6.21 The non-paper's paragraph 9(bis) dominated discussion of Article 6 at the 26 May meeting of the Committee of the Whole. A large number of States, primarily affected or developing States, spoke against the provision. They expressed concern that the paragraph included too much detail and would interfere with State sovereignty by requiring them to change national laws. Mexico, Sierra Leone, and the UK described the non-paper's language as 'over-prescriptive'.[89] Indonesia proposed cutting the paragraph after the word 'implementation' and leaving the details to bilateral agreements between donors and recipients.[90] This idea received support from Botswana, Cambodia, Chile, Ethiopia, Lesotho, the Philippines, South Africa, Sudan, Uganda, Venezuela, and Zambia.[91] Several donor countries, notably Canada, Germany, the Netherlands, and Sweden, adopted the opposite position.[92] The Netherlands, for example, described the details as 'essential elements'.[93] At the end of the discussion, Canada proposed replacing the details with the phrase: 'including facilitating the entry of personnel, materiel and equipment in a manner consistent with national laws'.[94] After Chile, Guinea, and Mexico voiced

[87] Statements of Argentina, Canada, Germany, Ghana, the Netherlands, and South Africa, 'Summary Record of Second Session of the Committee of the Whole', *op. cit.*, pp. 9–10.

[88] Article 6, paragraph 9(bis), 'Non-Paper Circulated by the President: Possible Amendments to Article 6', 23 May 2008 (*emphasis added to indicate change*). The non-paper actually says 'or' not 'and', but the President explained that that was a mistake and corrected it orally in the Committee of the Whole. Statement of the President of the Conference, 'Summary Record of Tenth Session of the Committee of the Whole', Diplomatic Conference doc. CCM/CW/SR/10, 18 June 2008, p. 3.

[89] Statements of Mexico, Sierra Leone, and the UK, 'Summary Record of Tenth Session of Committee of the Whole', *op. cit.*, p. 5.

[90] Statement of Indonesia, 'Summary Record of Tenth Session of Committee of the Whole', *op. cit.*, p. 4.

[91] Statements of Botswana, Cambodia, Chile, Ethiopia, Lesotho, the Philippines, South Africa, Sudan, Uganda, Venezuela, and Zambia, 'Summary Record of Tenth Session of Committee of the Whole', *op. cit.*, pp. 4–5. South Africa, supported by Mexico, also wanted to cut the paragraph at that place, but it suggested as an alternative adding the phrase 'in accordance with national laws and policies'. Statements of Mexico and South Africa, 'Summary Record of Tenth Session of Committee of the Whole', *op. cit.*, p. 5.

[92] Statements of Canada, Germany, the Netherlands, and Sweden, 'Summary Record of Tenth Session of Committee of the Whole', *op. cit.*, pp. 4–5.

[93] Statement of the Netherlands, 'Summary Record of Tenth Session of Committee of the Whole', *op. cit.*, p. 4.

[94] Statement of Canada, 'Summary Record of Tenth Session of Committee of the Whole', *op. cit.*, p. 5.

their support, the President asked Canada to hold bilateral consultations to refine the proposal.[95]

6.22 The debate continued at the next meeting of the Committee of the Whole on 27 May, where Canada submitted a new version of paragraph 9(bis). It read:

Each State Party that seeks and receives assistance shall take all appropriate measures in order to facilitate the timely and effective implementation of the Convention, including facilitation of the entry of personnel, materiel and equipment, in a manner consistent with national laws and regulations and international best practices.[96]

6.23 The remaining discussion centred around the phrase 'international best practices' because some States feared it would still oblige them to amend national laws.[97] Canada explained that national laws would predominate over international best practices and that there would be no legal requirement to change national laws.[98] South Africa proposed changing the phrase to 'and where necessary consider international best practices'.[99] The next day, Canada reported through President O'Ceallaigh that it had produced a new draft that was acceptable to all States.[100] The final version of the paragraph, which became Article 6, paragraph 10 in the Convention on Cluster Munitions, added 'and exit' after 'entry' and changed the final phrase to 'taking into consideration international best practices'.[101]

---

[95] Statements of Chile, Guinea, Mexico, and the President of the Conference, 'Summary Record of Tenth Session of Committee of the Whole', *op. cit.*, pp. 5–6.

[96] Statement of the President of the Conference, 'Summary Record of Thirteenth Session of the Committee of the Whole', Diplomatic Conference doc. CCM/CW/SR/13, 18 June 2008, p. 1.

[97] Several States expressed concern about the proposal and demanded clarification. Indonesia reiterated its call to stop after 'implementation'; the Philippines echoed that position and said that paragraph 11 was sufficient. Cameroon, Laos, Serbia, and Switzerland, by contrast, supported Canada's version of paragraph 9(bis). Several other countries, including Albania, Australia, Germany, and the Netherlands, said they were not happy with the proposal but could accept it. Statements of Albania, Australia, Cameroon, Germany, Indonesia, Laos, the Netherlands, the Philippines, Serbia, and Switzerland, 'Summary Record of Thirteenth Session of the Committee of the Whole', *op. cit.*, pp. 2–3.

[98] Statement of Canada, 'Summary Record of Thirteenth Session of the Committee of the Whole', *op. cit.*, p. 2.

[99] Statement of South Africa, 'Summary Record of Thirteenth Session of the Committee of the Whole', *op. cit.*, p. 3.

[100] Statement of the President of the Conference, 'Summary Record of Fifteenth Session of the Committee of the Whole', Diplomatic Conference doc. CCM/CW/SR/15, 18 June 2008, p. 2.

[101] Article 6, paragraph 10.

6.24 The Dublin negotiations produced one other noteworthy amendment to Article 6.[102] Austria suggested inserting language into the victim assistance paragraph (paragraph 7) referring to Article 5. It read: 'Each State Party in a position to do so shall provide assistance *for the implementation of the obligations referred to in Article 5 of this Convention to adequately provide age- and gender-sensitive assistance, including …*'.[103] The proposal received support from several States, including Albania, Canada, Ethiopia, and Switzerland.[104] This change reinforced the strong provision of Article 5 and emphasized the need for assistance that is sensitive to specific victims.

6.25 User State responsibility also remained contentious at the Diplomatic Conference although most of the debate occurred during discussions surrounding Article 4, where the main provision was placed. In the Committee of the Whole meeting on Article 6 on 20 May, at least four States—Chad, the Democratic Republic of Congo, Lesotho, and Zambia—called for imposing responsibility for victim assistance on user States,[105] but the Convention as adopted did not include such a requirement. It did, however, retain the phrase in Article 6, paragraph 4 cross-referring to Article 4.[106]

---

[102] Most other amendments to Article 6 from the Draft Cluster Munitions Convention to the final Convention on Cluster Munitions were small. They included (with amendments in italics):

- Paragraph 3: changing 'provision of clearance equipment' to 'provision *and receipt* of clearance *and other such* equipment';
- Paragraph 4: changing 'clearance' and 'clearance *and destruction*';
- Paragraph 10: changing 'United Nations' to 'United Nations *system*';
- Paragraph 10(d): changing 'risk education programmes' to 'risk *reduction* education programmes'; and
- Paragraph 10(f): changing 'relationship' to '*coordination* relationship'.

[103] The President reported this proposal to the Committee of the Whole. Statement of the President of the Conference, 'Summary Record of Thirteenth Session of the Committee of the Whole', *op. cit.*, p. 1 (*emphasis added to indicate changes*). Similar language about age- and gender-sensitive assistance would also be included in the Preamble to the Convention. See, *supra*, the commentary on the eighth preambular paragraph.

[104] Statements of Canada and Ethiopia, 'Summary Record of Tenth Session of the Committee of the Whole', *op. cit.*, p. 5; and Statements of Albania and Switzerland, 'Summary Record of Thirteenth Session of the Committee of the Whole', *op. cit.*, pp. 2–3.

[105] Statements of Chad, the Democratic Republic of Congo, Lesotho, and Zambia, 'Summary Record of Second Session of the Committee of the Whole', Diplomatic Conference doc. CCM/CW/SR/2, 18 June 2008, pp. 10–11. On 26 May, the Philippines also said it attached 'great importance' to Article 4, paragraph 4. Statement of the Philippines, 'Summary Record of Tenth Session of the Committee of the Whole', *op. cit.*, p. 3.

[106] Article 6, paragraph 4. Other proposals made during the Diplomatic Conference failed. The Philippines proposed adding references to migrants and the International Organization for Migration in the victim assistance paragraph. Statement of the Philippines, 'Summary Record of Second Session of the Committee of the Whole', *op. cit.*, p. 9. Several States, including Botswana, Ethiopia, and South Africa, called for making international cooperation and assistance obligatory. Botswana said that a failure to do so would hinder developing States from meeting their obligations

6.26 Over the course of the Oslo Process, the final Article on internation-al cooperation and assistance had expanded dramatically and grown more demanding. Six paragraphs had been added since the Lima Discussion Text. A robust paragraph on victim assistance paralleled the groundbreaking require-ments set out in Article 5.[107] Other new provisions established: a general obligation to provide 'technical, material and financial assistance' to affected States; more specific obligations to provide assistance for assessment of civil-ian protection measures, emergencies, and economic and social recovery; and the possibility of contributing to assistance through trust funds.[108] Another paragraph placed obligations on States receiving aid to facilitate the provision of assistance.[109] Significant amendments to the relevant provisions in the Lima text included: the removal of qualifications from the right to seek and receive assistance; a reference to user State responsibility for clearance; and an obliga-tion to provide information related to clearance.[110]

6.27 Several States acknowledged the significance of this accomplish-ment in statements after the adoption of the Convention in Dublin.[111] Austria described the Articles on international cooperation and assistance and victim assistance as 'exceptional provisions', which would 'set new standards in international humanitarian law'.[112] Cambodia stated that international cooperation and assistance was 'essential to achieving the ambitions of the text'.[113] Samoa described Article 6 as one of the Articles 'central to the development of international humanitarian law'.[114] States had both accomplished the goal articulated in the Oslo Declaration, of creating a 'framework for cooperation and assistance' and set an important precedent for future treaties.

---

under the treaty. Statements of Botswana, Ethiopia, and South Africa, 'Summary Record of Second Session of the Committee of the Whole', *op. cit.*, pp. 8–11. Indonesia once more raised the issue of assistance for training in clearance of cluster munition remnants in preparation for peacekeeping operations. Statement of Indonesia, 'Summary Record of Second Session of the Committee of the Whole', *op. cit.*, p. 9.

[107] Article 6, paragraph 7.   [108] Article 6, paragraphs 2, 5, 6, 8, and 9.
[109] Article 6, paragraph 10.   [110] Article 6, paragraphs 1 and 4.

[111] Several States had also highlighted the importance of international cooperation and assist-ance in opening statements to the Diplomatic Conference. Statement of Zambia on behalf of 39 African States, 'Summary Record of Opening Ceremony and First Session of the Plenary', *op. cit.*, p. 5; and Statement of Thailand, 'Summary Record of Second Session of Plenary', *op. cit.*, p. 4.

[112] Statement of Austria, 'Summary Record of Sixteenth Session of the Committee of the Whole', Diplomatic Conference doc. CCM/CW/SR/16, 18 June 2008, p. 4.

[113] Statement of Cambodia, 'Summary Record of Fourth Session of the Plenary and Closing Ceremony of the Conference', Diplomatic Conference doc. CCM/SR/4, 18 June 2008, p. 3.

[114] Statement of Samoa, 'Summary Record of Sixteenth Session of the Committee of the Whole', *op. cit.*, p. 5.

Paragraph 1

In fulfilling its obligations under this Convention each State Party has the right to seek and receive assistance.

Commentary

6.28 Each State Party has the right to seek and receive assistance from the wider international community in support of its efforts to implement the Convention. Paragraph 1 draws on the text of corresponding provisions in the *1997 Anti-Personnel Mine Ban Convention*[115] and *2003 Protocol V.*[116] The Convention on Cluster Munitions broadens the nature of the obligation compared to the language of the *1997 Anti-Personnel Mine Ban Convention* by omitting the qualifying phrases 'where feasible' and 'to the extent possible'. Similarly, it does not use the phrase 'where appropriate' from *2003 Protocol V.* Given that resources for assistance are finite,[117] the purpose of those earlier phrases was apparently to limit the obligation on State Parties to provide assistance to other States Parties exerting this right. The formulation was confusing, however, as in both the *1997 Anti-Personnel Mine Ban Convention* and *2003 Protocol V* the phrases seemed to limit the right of States to seek and receive assistance.[118]

6.29 The Convention on Cluster Munitions establishes that the right to seek and receive assistance is unqualified, but articulating a right does not in itself determine whether assistance will be received or given or at what level. Under Article 6, paragraphs 2, 4, 5, 6, 7, 8, and 9, the obligation on States Parties to provide assistance applies only if they are 'in a position to do so'. As

---

[115] Article 6, paragraph 1 of the *1997 Anti-Personnel Mine Ban Convention* states: 'In fulfilling its obligations under this Convention each State Party has the right to seek and receive assistance, where feasible, from other States Parties to the extent possible.'

[116] Article 7, paragraph 1 of *2003 Protocol V* states:

Each High Contracting Party has the right to seek and receive assistance, where appropriate, from other High Contracting Parties, from states non-party and relevant international organisations and institutions in dealing with the problems posed by existing explosive remnants of war.

[117] See Maslen, S., *Commentaries on Arms Control Treaties, Volume I: The Convention on the Prohibition of the Use, Stockpiling, Production, and Transfer of Anti-Personnel Mines and on their Destruction*, Second Edition, Oxford Commentaries on International Law (Oxford: Oxford University Press, 2005), §§6.11 and 6.12.

[118] In the case of the *1997 Anti-Personnel Mine Ban Convention*, e.g., it is unclear why the 'feasibility' of the assistance being received should condition the right of the State Party to receive that assistance.

explained below, however, in most cases States Parties are arguably in a position to provide some form of assistance.[119]

6.30 Article 6, paragraph 1 is also broad because it does not specify from whom States Parties have the right to seek and receive assistance. The *1997 Anti-Personnel Mine Ban Convention* stipulates that the right applies only to relationships with other States Parties. *2003 Protocol V* does not contain that limitation, listing several possible sources of assistance: High Contracting Parties, States not party, and relevant international organizations and institutions.[120] The Convention on Cluster Munitions adopts the latter approach although it does not enumerate particular bodies.

6.31 The first phrase of Article 6, paragraph 1 links the right to seek and receive assistance with the duty to fulfil the Convention's obligations. In other words, a State Party can only invoke the right if it needs assistance to implement the Convention. The provision follows the formulation of the *1997 Anti-Personnel Mine Ban Convention*, copying the opening language of that treaty's corresponding provision.[121] It takes a broader approach than *2003 Protocol V*, which ties the right merely to 'problems posed by existing explosive remnants of war'.[122]

6.32 The first draft of this paragraph in the Oslo Process was taken verbatim from the *1997 Anti-Personnel Mine Ban Convention*.[123] The Vienna Discussion Text removed the qualifying phrase 'where feasible, from other States Parties to the extent possible'.[124] During the Wellington Conference, the UK noted that the removal of this language might be problematic and proposed reinserting the phrase at the Diplomatic Conference.[125] Its proposal failed, however, and the paragraph remained unchanged through to the adoption of the Convention.

Paragraph 2

Each State Party in a position to do so shall provide technical, material and financial assistance to States Parties affected by cluster munitions,

---

[119] See, *infra*, the commentary on Article 6, paragraph 2 in §§6.36–6.37.
[120] Article 6, paragraph 1, *1997 Anti-Personnel Mine Ban Convention*; and Article 7, paragraph 1, *2003 Protocol V*.   [121] Article 6, paragraph 1, *1997 Anti-Personnel Mine Ban Convention*.
[122] Article 7, paragraph 1, *2003 Protocol V*.
[123] Article 5, paragraph 1, Lima Discussion Text; and Article 6, paragraph 1, *1997 Anti-Personnel Mine Ban Convention*.   [124] Article 6, paragraph 1, Vienna Discussion Text.
[125] 'Proposal by the United Kingdom for the amendment of Article 6', Diplomatic Conference doc. CCM/38, 19 May 2008.

aimed at the implementation of the obligations of this Convention. Such assistance may be provided, *inter alia*, through the United Nations system, international, regional or national organisations or institutions, non-governmental organisations or institutions, or on a bilateral basis.

Commentary

6.33 Elaborating on the assistance States Parties have a right to seek and receive, paragraph 2 of Article 6 lays out the general obligation of States Parties to provide assistance to States Parties that are 'affected' by cluster munitions. It delineates the basic forms of assistance, which can be technical, material, or financial, and suggests channels through which assistance may be provided. The paragraph, which did not come from the *1997 Anti-Personnel Mine Ban Convention*, first appeared in the Vienna Discussion Text.[126] It remained virtually unchanged in the final text of the Convention on Cluster Munitions.[127]

6.34 While all States Parties have a right to seek and receive assistance to facilitate implementation of the Convention, paragraph 2 notes that the general obligation to provide assistance is to those States Parties that are 'affected' by cluster munitions. That term, which is not defined in the Convention on Cluster Munitions, commonly refers to States Parties in which cluster munitions have been used and that, as a result, are contaminated with cluster munition remnants and have duties toward cluster munition victims. While the reference to affected States appears to be a limitation on the responsibility to provide assistance, there are other specific provisions under Article 6, in particular the obligation in paragraph 5 to provide assistance for stockpile destruction, that require assistance even if the recipient State is not 'affected by cluster munitions' in the common usage of that term.

6.35 Article 6 establishes specific obligations to provide assistance relating to clearance and destruction of cluster munition remnants (paragraph 4); destruction of stockpiled cluster munitions (paragraph 5); identification, assessment, and prioritization of marking, risk education, civilian protection measures, and clearance and destruction (paragraph 5); emergency situations (paragraph 6); victim assistance (paragraph 7); and social and economic recovery needed as a result of cluster munition use (paragraph 8). Underpinning and extending beyond these enumerated areas, paragraph 2 frames a general responsibility to help States Parties affected by cluster munitions fulfil all of the Convention's obligations.

[126] Article 6, paragraph 2, Vienna Discussion Text.
[127] The only change was that 'Each State Party' replaced 'All States Parties'. Article 6, paragraph 2.

'In a position to do so'

6.36 The obligation to provide assistance is limited to those States Parties 'in a position to do so'. This qualifying phrase is repeated in paragraphs 4, 5, 6, 7, 8, and 9 and recognizes that resources for assistance are finite. The implication of this qualifier will be that each State Party must make the determination of whether or not it is 'in a position to do so'. This same phrase conditions the obligation to provide assistance in *2003 Protocol V, 1997 Anti-Personnel Mine Ban Convention*, and *1996 Amended Protocol II*.[128]

6.37 During the preparatory discussions for the Convention on Cluster Munitions at least two States expressed their concern that the phrase 'in a position to do so' implied that these obligations were voluntary.[129] However, given the strong political (if not legally binding) impact of this provision as well as the wide range of forms that assistance can take, it may be understood that not providing some form of assistance should be the exception to the rule. These factors suggest that the onus is on those States Parties not providing assistance to justify that it is because they are not 'in a position to do so' rather than because they decline to help. States may assist in so many ways that they should virtually always be 'in a position to do so'.[130]

'Technical, material, and financial assistance'

6.38 Paragraph 2 stipulates that assistance may be technical, material, and financial. It can include information or technical advice, materials or equipment needed to implement relevant work (for example, unexploded ordnance (UXO) detectors or personal protective equipment), or funding for projects or activities that work toward implementation of the Convention. The variety of the forms of assistance that can be provided means that assistance need not only be a preserve of wealthy States Parties.

6.39 The recent history of mine action provides examples of the different forms of assistance that have been given in support of the comparable humanitarian provisions of the *1997 Anti-Personnel Mine Ban Convention*.[131]

---

[128] Article 7, paragraph 2, and Article 8, paragraph 3, *2003 Protocol V*; Article 6, paragraphs 3–5, *1997 Anti-Personnel Mine Ban Convention*; and Article 11, paragraph 3, *1996 Amended Protocol II*.

[129] Statements at the Wellington Conference, 21 February 2008 (Landmine Action notes; copy on file with author).

[130] States Parties could explicitly express their evaluation that they are not in a position to provide assistance in their report on international cooperation and assistance under Article 7, paragraph 1(n).

[131] Mine action is defined by the UN as including five core components: mine risk education, demining, victim assistance, stockpile destruction, and advocacy to ban anti-personnel mines. See IMAS 04.10: 'Glossary of Mine Action Terms, Definitions and Abbreviations', Second Edition,

The bulk of international assistance for mine action, however, continues to be provided in the form of financial support. In 2008, 23 countries and the European Commission provided about US$517.8 million (€351.7 million) in international funding to at least 53 States for mine action.[132] According to *Landmine Monitor Report 2009*, States have contributed $4.27 billion in international assistance to mine action between 1992 and 2008.[133]

Channels for the provision of assistance

6.40 Paragraph 2 provides a non-exhaustive list of channels for the provision of assistance. This list is similar to those set out in the *1997 Anti-Personnel Mine Ban Convention* and in Article 6, paragraph 7 of the Convention on Cluster Munitions.[134] Rather than referring to specific organizations, the general formulation in Article 6, paragraph 2 indicates that organizations and institutions operating at a range of geographic levels can all be appropriate partners in the provision of assistance.

6.41 The ongoing international work of mine action illustrates the important roles for institutions of the UN system. Many UN departments, agencies, programmes, and funds play significant roles in mine action in order to 'ensure an effective, proactive and coordinated response' to the problems of mines and explosive remnants of war (ERW).[135] In turn, different agencies of the UN system, such as UNDP and the UN Children's Fund (UNICEF), have important roles in more specific elements of mine action.

6.42 International, regional, and national institutions and non-governmental organizations (NGOs) also contribute to protecting civilians from the detritus of war. International organizations, such as the International Committee of the Red Cross (ICRC), have actively addressed problems of mines and ERW, in particular through their work with victims and survivors of explosive weapons incidents. Regional organizations have also played a significant role. For example, the Organization of American States (OAS) through its mine action programme has sought to assist OAS Member

1 January 2003. This definition might be broadened to encompass advocacy to ban cluster munitions and support universalization of the relevant treaties.

[132] These figures represent the highest yearly total to date. International Campaign to Ban Landmines (ICBL), *Landmine Monitor Report 2009: Toward a Mine-Free World*, (Ottawa: Mines Action Canada, 2009), p. 78. In contrast, national funding for mine action totalled $108.7 million, often in the form of in-kind contributions from the government. *Ibid.*, p. 79.

[133] *Ibid.*, p. 78.

[134] See Article 6, paragraphs 3 and 4, *1997 Anti-Personnel Mine Ban Convention*; and Article 6, paragraph 7.

[135] See, e.g., the UNMAS-managed website E-MINE (Electronic Mine Information Network), <http://www.mineaction.org/overview.asp?o=22> (accessed 1 March 2010).

States in addressing such problems at a national level.[136] In addition, a large number of NGOs implement projects across the whole range of activities that can be considered assistance within this framework. These NGOs include organizations specializing in the removal of explosive hazards, training in risk education, or extending assistance to victims, as well as more generalist organizations that address such problems as part of their broader framework of operations. Such organizations include both commercial companies and charities.

6.43 While paragraph 2 highlights that direct State-to-State assistance is not the only appropriate mechanism for support to an affected State, it concludes by noting that assistance on a 'bilateral basis' is also an option. The term assistance itself suggests that such provision should be made in a spirit of cooperation, which is further emphasized in paragraph 12.[137]

Paragraph 3

Each State Party undertakes to facilitate and shall have the right to participate in the fullest possible exchange of equipment and scientific and technological information concerning the implementation of this Convention. The States Parties shall not impose undue restrictions on the provision and receipt of clearance and other such equipment and related technological information for humanitarian purposes.

Commentary

6.44 Paragraph 3 establishes a general responsibility to 'facilitate' and a 'right to participate in' the exchange of equipment and information relevant to the implementation of the Convention. Reinforcing the underlying humanitarian object of the Convention, the paragraph prohibits 'undue restrictions' on such an exchange if it is made for 'humanitarian purposes'. States Parties must consider this purpose when they evaluate the implications of allowing others access to technologies and information. The prohibition on interfering with assistance may apply to the exchange of equipment and information not only between States Parties but also between States Parties and organizations

---

[136] Organization of American States, 'Demining', <http://www.oas.org/en/topics/demining.asp> (accessed 1 March 2010).

[137] For further discussion, see commentary, *infra*, on Article 6, paragraph 12.

implementing activities that support the humanitarian purposes of the Convention.[138]

6.45 This paragraph imposes an obligation on all States Parties, including those that give assistance and those that receive it. It deals with an exchange of equipment and information, which inherently implies the involvement of at least two parties. It also refers to 'provision *and* receipt' of equipment and information. Paragraph 3 relates to two other provisions of Article 6 that govern the interaction of donor and recipient states. Paragraph 12 adopts a similar cooperative approach, requiring all States Parties to work together to ensure implementation of assistance programmes.[139] Paragraph 10, like the second sentence of paragraph 3, prohibits interference with the transfer of assistance.[140]

6.46 Paragraph 3 closely follows the language of the *1997 Anti-Personnel Mine Ban Convention*,[141] which in turn draws on the language of *1996 Amended Protocol II*,[142] the *1993 Chemical Weapons Convention*,[143] and the *1972 Biological Weapons Convention*.[144] It does not adopt the more restricted formulation of the corresponding provision in *2003 Protocol V*,[145] which limits the exchange to equipment, material, and information necessary for the implementation of its provisions. The Oslo Process made only minor changes to the original version of the paragraph in the Lima Discussion Text, which was essentially identical to that in the *1997 Anti-Personnel Mine Ban*

---

[138] The second part of the paragraph does not stipulate that the bodies receiving 'clearance and other such equipment' are necessarily States.

[139] For more information, see commentary, *infra*, on Article 6, paragraph 12.

[140] For more information, see commentary, *infra*, on Article 6, paragraph 10.

[141] Article 6, paragraph 2, of the *1997 Anti-Personnel Mine Ban Convention* states:

Each State Party undertakes to facilitate and shall have the right to participate in the fullest possible exchange of equipment, material and scientific and technological information concerning the implementation of this Convention. The States Parties shall not impose undue restrictions on the provision of mine clearance equipment and related technological information for humanitarian purposes.

[142] Article 11, paragraph 1, *1996 Amended Protocol II*.

[143] Article 10, paragraph 3, *1993 Chemical Weapons Convention*.

[144] Article 10, paragraph 1, Convention on the Prohibition of the Development, Production and Stockpiling of Bacteriological (Biological) and Toxin Weapons and on their Destruction (*1972 Biological Weapons Convention*).

[145] Article 8, paragraph 4, of *2003 Protocol V* provides that:

Each High Contracting Party shall have the right to participate in the fullest possible exchange of equipment, material and scientific and technological information other than weapons related technology, necessary for the implementation of this Protocol. High Contracting Parties undertake to facilitate such exchanges in accordance with national legislation and shall not impose undue restrictions on the provision of clearance equipment and related technological information for humanitarian purposes.

Convention.[146] Consistent with the cooperative approach of Article 6, however, the Diplomatic Conference changed 'provision of . . . equipment and . . . information' to 'provision and receipt'.

Paragraph 4

> In addition to any obligations it may have pursuant to paragraph 4 of Article 4 of this Convention, each State Party in a position to do so shall provide assistance for clearance and destruction of cluster munition remnants and information concerning various means and technologies related to clearance of cluster munitions, as well as lists of experts, expert agencies or national points of contact on clearance and destruction of cluster munition remnants and related activities.

Commentary

6.47 Paragraph 4 establishes an obligation to provide assistance for clearance activities. Like many other paragraphs in Article 6, the obligation applies only to those States Parties 'in a position to do so'. The clearance obligations laid out in Article 4 could be burdensome for some affected States, particularly those, such as Laos, with the most heavily contaminated areas.[147] By ensuring that those States will receive international assistance for clearance, this paragraph aims to help them meet their obligations. It serves a humanitarian purpose by reducing the number of cluster munition remnants that threaten civilians and advances universalization by making it less burdensome for affected States to join the Convention.

6.48 The paragraph is modelled on corresponding provisions in the *1997 Anti-Personnel Mine Ban Convention*, which in turn drew on *1996 Amended Protocol II*.[148] It merges two *1997 Anti-Personnel Mine Ban Convention*

---

[146] Article 5, paragraph 2, Lima Discussion Text; and Article 6, paragraph 2, *1997 Anti-Personnel Mine Ban Convention*. The only difference between these two provisions was that the Lima Discussion Text deleted 'mine' before 'clearance equipment'.

[147] The United States (US) is reported to have dropped about 270 million submunitions on Laos in the 1960s and 1970s. Although, according to *Landmine Monitor*, the exact extent of its contaminated areas is unknown, a 1997 study found 15 of the country's then 18 provinces were affected by submunitions and other ERW. Almost half of the ERW cleared over the past 12 years have been submunitions. ICBL, *Landmine Monitor Report 2009, op. cit.*, p. 974.

[148] Article 6, paragraphs 4 and 6, *1997 Anti-Personnel Mine Ban Convention*; and Article 11, paragraphs 3 and 4, *1996 Amended Protocol II*. *2003 Protocol V* also requires assistance for clearance, but it uses different language. See Article 3, paragraph 5, and Article 7, *2003 Protocol V*.

paragraphs,[149] bringing a clause about providing information on how to clear cluster munitions into the paragraph on clearance assistance. Article 6, paragraph 4 of the Convention on Cluster Munitions adds a reference to user State responsibility and encompasses destruction, as well as clearance, of cluster munition remnants. It also removes language outlining through which bodies assistance for clearance can be provided. Paragraph 4 remained largely the same after the Vienna Discussion Text, with the exception of revisions to a phrase on user State responsibility, which are discussed below.

User State responsibility for clearance

6.49 The opening phrase of Article 6, paragraph 4 refers to paragraph 4 of Article 4, the central provision on user State responsibility for clearance. This latter provision 'strongly encourages' States Parties that used cluster munitions before the Convention enters into force to provide assistance, such as 'technical, financial, material or human resources assistance', to affected States Parties for clearance.[150] User States that choose to assist must provide information on the types, locations, and numbers of cluster munitions used.[151] As discussed in the commentary on Article 4, it is a groundbreaking provision that sets a precedent in international humanitarian law.[152] The reference to it in Article 6 has the potential to influence future Articles on international cooperation and assistance.

6.50 User State responsibility in general is designed to advance the humanitarian goals of the Convention by decreasing the number of cluster munition remnants and to turn a moral duty to take responsibility for one's own actions into a legal one.[153] The user State responsibility provision in Article 6, paragraph 4 serves two further purposes. First, by referencing Article 4, it reinforces the user State responsibility provision in that Article. It emphasizes the importance of the special responsibility user States bear for clearance. Second,

---

[149] Article 6, paragraph 4 (on clearance), and Article 6, paragraph 6 (on provision of clearance information), *1997 Anti-Personnel Mine Ban Convention*. *1996 Amended Protocol II* and *2003 Protocol V* also have similar provisions on the obligation to provide information related to clearance. Article 11, paragraph 2, *1996 Amended Protocol II*; and Article 8, paragraph 5, *2003 Protocol V*.

[150] Article 4, paragraph 4(a).   [151] Article 4, paragraph 4(b).

[152] See, *supra*, the commentary on Article 4 in §§4.86 *et seq.*

[153] Human Rights Watch and Harvard Law School detailed the case for user State responsibility in a briefing paper distributed at the Wellington Conference. See Human Rights Watch International Human Rights Clinic, 'User State Responsibility for Cluster Munition Clearance: Memorandum to Delegates of the Wellington Conference on Cluster Munitions', 19 February 2008, <http://www.hrw.org/sites/default/files/related_material/arms0208.pdf> (accessed 29 October 2009).

it clarifies that a State Party's obligations under Article 6, paragraph 4 are 'in addition to any obligations it may have pursuant to paragraph 4 of Article 4'.[154] In other words, user States cannot argue that meeting their Article 4 obligations are sufficient to meet their Article 6 obligations. Similarly they cannot say that they have met their Article 4 obligations by providing assistance under Article 6.

6.51 The opening phrase of paragraph 4 was one of the most controversial during discussions of Article 6. The Vienna Discussion Text was the first to mention user State responsibility, stating that 'each State Party in a position to do so *and in particular a State Party that has used cluster munitions on the territory of another State Party* shall provide assistance for clearance'.[155] The Draft Cluster Munitions Convention changed that wording to the way it appears in the final text of the Convention.[156] Many stockpiling States adamantly opposed the inclusion of any such responsibility, saying that it could implicate cluster munitions left decades ago and that all States should share the burden of clearance.[157] Several affected and developing States strongly supported it, arguing that they needed extra assistance and that user States bore a moral responsibility to help.[158] While the provision in Article 4 was somewhat softened during the final negotiations in Dublin ('shall' was changed to 'are strongly encouraged'),[159] the reference in Article 6 remained unchanged despite a proposal to delete it.

Obligation to assist with clearance and destruction

6.52 The first obligation under Article 6, paragraph 4 is for States Parties in a position to do so to 'provide assistance for clearance and destruction of cluster munition remnants'.[160] Under Article 4, the primary responsibility for clearance rests with affected States Parties, but Article 6 ensures they will receive international assistance to meet their 10-year deadline for clearance. To fulfil their Article 4 obligations, affected States Parties must: survey, assess, and record the threat; prioritize needs; mobilize resources and develop a national

---

[154] Article 6, paragraph 4.

[155] Article 6, paragraph 4, Vienna Discussion Text (*emphasis added*).

[156] Article 6, paragraph 4, Draft Cluster Munitions Convention.

[157] Statements at the Wellington Conference, 21 February 2008 (Landmine Action notes; copy on file with author). Some States expressed similar opposition to user State responsibility during discussions of Article 4, paragraph 4 both in the preparatory discussions on that provision and at the Diplomatic Conference itself. For more information, see, *supra*, the commentary on Article 4 in §§4.9–4.12.

[158] Statements at the Vienna Conference, 7 December 2007; and at the Wellington Conference, 21 February 2008 (all from Landmine Action notes; copy on file with author).

[159] Article 4, paragraph 4.   [160] Article 6, paragraph 4.

plan; take precautions to ensure contaminated areas are marked and monitored; and clear and destroy all cluster munition remnants.[161] Article 6, paragraph 4 requires other States Parties to provide assistance for these activities.

6.53 Paragraph 4 does not specify what types of assistance States Parties must provide, but clues can be gleaned from elsewhere in the Convention. Article 6, paragraph 2 provides some guidelines, requiring States Parties in a position to do so to provide 'technical, material and financial assistance' to affected States Parties.[162] Financial assistance has received particular attention in the landmine context. While technical, material, and financial assistance are all valuable, the list is not exhaustive. Human resources and information—both types of assistance that Article 4 strongly encourages user States to provide—are also useful.[163] Strike data, including the locations, numbers, and types of cluster munitions used, is especially critical for efficient clearance. It expedites the process by helping deminers to identify contaminated areas, to estimate how many remnants need to be cleared, and to prepare to work with specific submunition types.[164]

6.54 The obligation to provide clearance assistance remained almost the same throughout the Oslo Process. The primary change was to add the words 'and destruction' after clearance in the final text of the Convention.[165] This amendment ensures that States Parties assist not only with removal of cluster munition remnants but also with rendering them inoperable.[166] It parallels affected States' obligations under Article 4 to 'clear and destroy, or ensure the clearance and destruction of, cluster munition remnants'.[167] The words 'and destruction' were also added in paragraph 4 of Article 6 to the obligation to provide lists of experts and points of contact on clearance.[168]

---

[161] Article 4, paragraphs 1 and 2. See also, *supra*, the commentary on Article 4, paragraphs 1 and 2. [162] Article 6, paragraph 2.

[163] See Article 4, paragraph 4.

[164] For more information on deminers' need for clearance information, see, e.g., Human Rights Watch, *A Dying Practice: Use of Cluster Munitions by Russia and Georgia in August 2008*, April 2009, p. 76, <http://www.hrw.org/en/reports/2009/04/14/dying-practice-0>; Human Rights Watch, *Flooding South Lebanon: Israel's Use of Cluster Munitions in Lebanon in July and August 2006*, Vol. 20, No. 2(E), February 2008, pp. 91–92, <http://www.hrw.org/en/reports/2008/02/16/flooding-south-lebanon-0>; and Human Rights Watch, *Fatally Flawed: Cluster Bombs and Their Use by the United States in Afghanistan*, Vol. 14, No. 7(G), December 2002, pp. 37–38, <http://www.hrw.org/reports/2002/us-afghanistan/> (all accessed 29 June 2010).

[165] This phrase did not appear in any of the discussion texts or the Draft Cluster Munitions Convention.

[166] For more discussion of these terms see, *supra*, the commentary on Article 4.

[167] Article 4, paragraph 1. [168] Article 6, paragraph 4.

Obligation to provide information on how to
clear cluster munitions

6.55 Paragraph 4 contains an additional obligation for States Parties in a position to do so to provide information related to how to clear cluster munitions. It requires provision of information on 'means and technologies' of clearance and lists of 'experts, expert agencies or national points of contact on clearance and destruction' that affected States can consult.[169] The obligation concerns general information about clearance rather than data on specific strikes. Such information is important for affected States Parties, which bear the responsibility for ensuring their territory is free of cluster munition remnants, and for the clearance organizations that work in those countries.

6.56 Similar provisions appear in *2003 Protocol V*, the *1997 Anti-Personnel Mine Ban Convention*, and *1996 Amended Protocol II*,[170] but none was included in the Lima Discussion Text. Drafters of the Vienna Discussion Text added it at the suggestion of one State.[171] The provision in the Convention on Cluster Munitions differs from its predecessors in part because the earlier treaties dictated that the information should be provided to a UN mine clearance database. The new Convention removes that detail, likely because no such master database exists for cluster munitions. Presumably, under the Convention, information goes directly to other States Parties.

Paragraph 5

Each State Party in a position to do so shall provide assistance for the destruction of stockpiled cluster munitions, and shall also provide assistance to identify, assess and prioritise needs and practical measures in terms of marking, risk reduction education, protection of civilians and clearance and destruction as provided in Article 4 of this Convention.

Commentary

6.57 Paragraph 5 lays out obligations regarding stockpile destruction and identification, assessment, and prioritization of measures for the protection of

---

[169] *Ibid.*

[170] Article 8, paragraph 5, *2003 Protocol V*; Article 6, paragraph 6, *1997 Anti-Personnel Mine Ban Convention*; and Article 11, paragraph 2, *1996 Amended Protocol II*.

[171] Statement at the Vienna Conference, 7 December 2007 (Landmine Action notes; copy on file with author).

civilians.[172] The two obligations, both drawn from past treaties, are unrelated; they provide assistance for different parties, activities, and purposes. Assistance for stockpile destruction first appeared in the Lima Discussion Text,[173] and assistance for assessing measures for the protection of civilians in the Vienna Discussion Text.[174] The Draft Cluster Munitions Convention combined them into one.[175] The reasons behind the merger are unclear because States did not address these individually uncontroversial provisions during negotiations. Putting them in the same paragraph, however, does not affect the obligations they establish.

Obligation to assist with stockpile destruction

6.58 The first half of paragraph 5 obliges States Parties in a position to do so to 'provide assistance for the destruction of stockpiled cluster munitions'.[176] Although it does not explicitly state so, the paragraph clearly relates to Article 3 on Storage and Stockpile Destruction.[177] Article 3 requires States Parties to destroy their stockpiles within eight years,[178] and Article 6, paragraph 5 will help stockpilers meet that obligation. In this case, the assistance provision advances the disarmament objective of the Convention on Cluster Munitions. It could also encourage stockpiling States to join the Convention because they can receive help with destruction. Unlike affected States, most stockpilers (though by no means all) are developed countries with more financial resources,[179] but destruction is potentially expensive and the obligation under Article 3 could deter them from becoming States Parties. Bringing such States on board and under the obligations of the Convention is important because any State with an arsenal of cluster munitions is a potential user.

6.59 This part of paragraph 5 does not specify what forms the assistance can take, but the technical, material, and financial assistance referenced in paragraph 2 is almost certainly required.[180] Technical information educates stockpiling States about the safest and most cost-effective means of destruction, while in-kind donations of material allow stockpilers to share the tools of destruction. Financial assistance is also valuable. In the landmine context,

---

[172] Article 6, paragraph 5.   [173] Article 5, paragraph 4, Lima Discussion Text.
[174] Article 6, paragraph 6, Vienna Discussion Text.
[175] Article 6, paragraph 5, Draft Cluster Munitions Convention.
[176] Article 6, paragraph 5.
[177] For further discussion of Article 3, see, *supra*, the commentary on Article 3.
[178] Article 3, paragraph 2.
[179] For a list of States believed to stockpile cluster munitions, see, e.g., Human Rights Watch, 'Cluster Munition Information Chart', 20 November 2009, <http://www.hrw.org/en/news/2009/07/17/cluster-munition-information-chart>(accessed 1 March 2010) .
[180] Article 6, paragraph 2.

most international assistance goes toward mine clearance rather than stockpile destruction,[181] and the same may occur with cluster munitions. Nonetheless, destroying cluster munitions can be more expensive than destroying mines so stockpiling States may need more financial assistance.[182]

6.60 This provision was uncontroversial during the Oslo Process. States ultimately accepted the original wording articulated in the Lima Discussion Text.[183] Beyond acknowledging the need to help cluster munition stockpilers,[184] States devoted little public discussion to the topic. The language for this provision was drawn from directly from the *1997 Anti-Personnel Mine Ban Convention*.[185]

Obligation to assist with identification, assessment, and prioritization of measures to protect civilians

6.61 The second half of paragraph 5 requires States Parties in a position to do so to assist with the assessment of measures to address the threat to civilians caused by cluster munition contamination. Specifically they must 'provide assistance to identify, assess and prioritise needs and practical measures'.[186] This provision helps affected States Parties to meet their obligations under Article 4, paragraph 2(b) by providing assistance to determine civilian

---

[181] 'The experience of implementing the AP Mine Ban Convention has shown that, while a large number of States Parties have stepped up to provide assistance in destroying emplaced mines, only a few have provided support for the destruction of stockpiled anti-personnel mines.' Brinkert, K., Director of the Anti-Personnel Mine Ban Convention Implementation Support Unit, 'Lessons learned from the AP Mine Ban Convention for the destruction and retention of cluster munitions in accordance with the Convention on Cluster Munitions', Berlin Conference on the Destruction of Cluster Munitions, 25–26 June 2009, p. 4, <http://www.berlin-ccm-conference.org/menu/conference-documents/> (accessed 1 March 2010). For a list of States that have provided assistance for stockpile destruction under Article 6, paragraph 5 of the *1997 Anti-Personnel Mine Ban Convention*, see *ibid.*, Table 4, p. 9.

[182] 'Stockpile destruction of cluster munitions is not analogous to the destruction of anti-personnel mines under the Ottawa Treaty because cluster munitions are more complex and their destruction is more expensive.' Peter Courtney-Green, NATO Maintenance and Supply Agency, 'Technical Aspects of Cluster Munitions Stockpile Destruction', Berlin Conference on the Destruction of Cluster Munitions, 25–26 June 2009, p. 2, <http://www.berlin-ccm-conference.org/menu/conference-documents/> (accessed 1 March 2010).

[183] The Vienna Discussion Text changed the paragraph to read 'assistance for the *clearance and* destruction of stockpiled cluster munitions'. Article 6, paragraph 5, Vienna Discussion Text. Drafters may have inserted 'clearance' in order to cover abandoned stockpiles. Abandoned stockpiles, however, are covered under other provisions relating to clearance of cluster munition remnants, which include 'abandoned cluster munitions'. For clearance provisions, see Article 4; for the definition of 'abandoned cluster munitions', see Article 2, paragraph 7. Therefore the addition was unnecessary and removed.

[184] See, e.g., Statement at the Lima Conference, 24 May 2007 (Landmine Action notes; copy on file with author). [185] Article 6, paragraph 5, *1997 Anti-Personnel Mine Ban Convention*.

[186] Article 6, paragraph 5.

protection needs, but it does not require assistance with any measures themselves.[187] Unlike assistance with stockpile destruction, this kind of assistance helps affected, not stockpiling States, and for humanitarian, not disarmament reasons.

6.62 The 'needs and practical measures' mentioned in paragraph 5 concern actions designed to reduce civilian casualties from cluster munition remnants. The provision lists 'marking, risk reduction education, protection of civilians and clearance and destruction'.[188] Marking helps keep civilians away from dangerous areas. Risk reduction education alerts civilians to the dangers of handling cluster munition remnants or working in areas that are contaminated. Protection of civilians, a more general, overarching phrase, encompasses any safety measures including those not listed. Clearance and destruction remove the threat itself. The same types of assistance required for direct clearance are necessary for assessment of these enumerated actions. Technical knowledge, equipment, money, human resources, and information on cluster munition strikes can all facilitate efforts to prevent harm to civilians.

6.63 Neither the *1997 Anti-Personnel Mine Ban Convention* nor *1996 Amended Protocol II* includes a comparable provision. *2003 Protocol V* contains a loosely related provision requiring direct assistance for 'marking and clearance, removal or destruction of explosive remnants of war, and for risk education',[189] but not for assessment of those activities. The cluster munition version of this provision first appeared in the Vienna Discussion Text[190] and went through the Oslo Process with little discussion. There were only two notable changes. First, as noted above, it was merged with the provision on assistance for stockpile destruction in the Draft Cluster Munitions Convention. Second, risk education was moved from the victim assistance provision to this paragraph in the Draft Cluster Munitions Convention; the final Convention changed the term to 'risk reduction education'.[191]

Paragraph 6

Where, after entry into force of this Convention, cluster munitions have
become cluster munition remnants located in areas under the jurisdiction

---

[187] Article 4, paragraph 2(b). See also commentary, *supra*, on Article 4, paragraph 2. Article 4, paragraph 2(e) requires States Parties to conduct risk reduction education, but the Article does not mention risk reduction education under its assessment and prioritization provision.

[188] Article 6, paragraph 5.   [189] Article 8, paragraph 1, *2003 Protocol V.*

[190] Article 6, paragraph 6, Vienna Discussion Text.

[191] Article 6, paragraph 5, Draft Cluster Munitions Convention; and Article 6, paragraph 5.

or control of a State Party, each State Party in a position to do so shall
urgently provide emergency assistance to the affected State Party.

Commentary

6.64 Paragraph 6 obligates States Parties in a position to do so to provide
emergency assistance in the case of future use of cluster munitions.[192] While
States did not specifically propose including such a provision during public
discussions, drafters of the Draft Cluster Munitions Convention introduced
in Wellington added it. There was little discussion of the provision in formal
meetings. The provision has no precedent in the *1997 Anti-Personnel Mine
Ban Convention*, but there is a provision requiring emergency assistance in
the *1993 Chemical Weapons Convention*.[193] It also follows logically from the
humanitarian purpose of the Convention on Cluster Munitions; in the preamble, States Parties express determination to 'put an end for all time to the
suffering and casualties caused by cluster munitions'.[194] Emergency assistance
is crucial to achieving that goal.

Scope of the obligation

6.65 The obligation in paragraph 6 applies only in cases where cluster munitions are used after entry into force of the Convention on Cluster Munitions.[195]
The Convention treats new contamination as a more pressing problem than
existing contamination because cluster munition remnants cause more civilian casualties immediately after a conflict than they do subsequently. In the
first three months after the 2006 conflict between Israel and Hezbollah,
for example, there were between 50 and 60 civilian casualties from cluster
munition remnants per month in Lebanon; after that, the monthly numbers
dropped to 20 or fewer.[196] The time constraint—i.e., to provide assistance

---

[192] Article 6, paragraph 6.

[193] Article 10, paragraphs 6–11, *1993 Chemical Weapons Convention*.

[194] Second preambular paragraph.

[195] States not party to the Convention are the most likely users, but States Parties could also
potentially violate the prohibition on use. *Cf.* Article 4, paragraph 4 (addressing cluster munitions
used before entry into force).

[196] Mine Action Co-ordination Centre–South Lebanon, 'Civilian Cluster Bomb Victims since
14 August 2006 up to 01 January 2009', <http://www.maccsl.org/reports/Victims/Victims.pdf>
(chart in '320 Casualties as at January 01, 2009', available at: <http://www.maccsl.org/War%20
2006.htm>) (both accessed 1 October 2009, but website no longer functioning). Similar statistics
came out of the 2003 conflict in Iraq. Al-Hilla General Teaching Hospital reported 221 injuries
in the first 11 days after a US cluster munition attack and attributed most of those to unexploded
submunitions; between May and August it reported an additional 32 civilian casualties from unexploded submunitions. Human Rights Watch, *Off Target: The Conduct of the War and Civilian*

'urgently'—is the only one in Article 6. It requires that donor States prioritize emergency assistance in crisis situations. The remaining provisions of Article 6, by contrast, lay out obligations involving assistance for pre-existing as well as potential future cluster munition contamination.

6.66 Paragraph 6 also explicitly narrows the recipients of assistance to States Parties that are affected by use. The provision only applies to cluster munition remnants 'located in areas under the jurisdiction or control of a State Party'. It concludes by stating that the assistance must be provided to the 'affected State Party'.[197] Thus, a donor State Party is under no obligation to provide assistance to States not party to the Convention on Cluster Munitions, even if they have been the targets of cluster munition use. The paragraph defines affected States Parties as States that have 'jurisdiction or control' over contaminated territory, words borrowed from Article 4 on clearance and destruction and Article 5 on victim assistance.[198] The use of parallel language is appropriate since much emergency assistance relates primarily to activities described in those Articles. Paragraph 6 is one of only three provisions of Article 6 that specify the recipient of assistance (although in most cases, except for stockpile destruction, it would be an affected State that needs assistance).[199]

Character of emergency assistance

6.67 Paragraph 6 requires States Parties in a position to do so 'urgently [to] provide emergency assistance to the affected State Party'.[200] It does not define emergency assistance, but such assistance should be understood as supporting certain types of activities that are crucial in the days, weeks, and months after a conflict in which cluster munitions are used. These activities strive to reduce civilian casualties, which occur in greater numbers during those early periods.

6.68 There are several kinds of activities that could fit this description. For example, risk reduction education protects civilians, and particularly children, by warning them that cluster munition remnants are deadly.[201] It teaches

---

Casualties in Iraq (New York: Human Rights Watch, 2003), pp. 128–129, <http://www.hrw.org/en/node/12207/section/1>.

[197] Article 6, paragraph 6.

[198] For further discussion of these terms see, *supra*, the commentary on Articles 3, 4, and 5.

[199] The other provisions are Article 6, paragraphs 2 and 8, both of which mention affected States Parties. [200] Article 6, paragraph 6.

[201] 'In the emergency phase, [mine risk education] is a valuable means of protection where clearance assets cannot cope with the amount of work and the impact of population on tasks.' 'Clearance of Cluster Munitions Based on Experience in Lebanon', TNMA [Technical Notes for Mine Action] 09.30/06, Version 1.0, January 2008, available at <http://www.mineactionstandards. org>. The CMC noted during the Wellington Conference that 'emergency, as well as longer-term

people to identify cluster munition remnants and not to approach, play with, or attempt to clear them. Marking prevents civilians, such as farmers, from unknowingly entering contaminated areas where they could be maimed or killed.[202] Early clearance targets areas most frequented by civilians. Deminers generally prioritize schools and hospitals, homes and main roads, farms, and less populated areas in that order, striving to save lives first and then to prevent socio-economic harm.[203] It is sometimes recommended to concentrate on contamination above the ground in the initial stages of an emergency, leaving sub-surface clearance for later. Emergency medical care for victims can prevent the deaths of those injured by cluster munitions.

6.69 Paragraph 6 does not specify what form emergency assistance for these types of activities should take. As with paragraphs 4 and 5, technical, material, financial, human, and informational assistance are valuable.[204] In the case of Lebanon, for example, States provided emergency financial assistance for cluster munition clearance amounting to $68.8 million in 2006.[205] This paragraph explicitly requires, however, only that States Parties provide emergency assistance urgently.[206] In emergency situations, the speed of the assistance can be as important as the form it takes.

Paragraph 7

Each State Party in a position to do so shall provide assistance for the implementation of the obligations referred to in Article 5 of this Convention to adequately provide age- and gender-sensitive assistance, including medical care, rehabilitation and psychological support, as well as provide for social and economic inclusion of cluster munition victims.

---

risk education ... substantially reduces civilian casualties.' CMC, 'Intervention on Clearance', February 2008, <http://www.mfat.govt.nz/clustermunitionswellington/conference-documents/CMC-statement-clearance.pdf> (accessed 29 June 2009, but website no longer functioning). See also generally UNICEF and Geneva International Centre for Humanitarian Demining (GICHD), 'Emergency Mine Risk Education', IMAS Mine Risk Education Best Practice Guidebook 9, Geneva, 2005, available at <http://www.mineactionstandards.org>.

[202] 'The marking of mine and ERW hazards is undertaken to provide a clear and unambiguous warning of danger to the local population.' GICHD, *A Guide to International Mine Action Standards* (Geneva: GICHD, 2006), p. 56; and Chapter 6 in GICHD, *A Guide to Cluster Munitions*, Second Edition (Geneva: GICHD, 2009), both available at <http://www.gichd.org>.

[203] See, e.g., Human Rights Watch, *Flooding South Lebanon: Israel's Use of Cluster Munitions in Lebanon in July and August 2006, op. cit.*, p. 83.

[204] See, *supra*, the commentary on Article 6, paragraphs 4 and 5 in *esp.* §§6.53 and 6.59.

[205] ICBL, *Landmine Monitor Report 2008: Toward a Mine-Free World* (Ottawa: Mines Action Canada, 2008), p. 58.   [206] Article 6, paragraph 6.

Such assistance may be provided, *inter alia*, through the United Nations system, international, regional or national organisations or institutions, the International Committee of the Red Cross, national Red Cross and Red Crescent Societies and their International Federation, non-governmental organisations or on a bilateral basis.

Commentary

6.70 This paragraph obliges States Parties in a position to do so to provide assistance for victim assistance. It is based on similar paragraphs in the *1997 Anti-Personnel Mine Ban Convention* and *2003 Protocol V*[207] but is more specific. It originally appeared as a separate Article in the Lima Discussion Text,[208] but when the Vienna Discussion Text created a stand-alone Article on affected States' victim assistance obligations, the international assistance provision was moved to Article 6.[209] States continued to discuss and amend it through the Diplomatic Conference in Dublin, adding the reference to Article 5 and 'age- and gender-sensitive assistance' in the final stages of the negotiations.[210]

6.71 Paragraph 7 is closely linked to Article 5, from which it draws much of its language.[211] Its specific reference to Article 5 reinforces the importance of the victim assistance obligations of that Article. Paragraph 7 also serves a humanitarian purpose itself because it supports the provision of assistance to victims. Finally, it seeks to ensure that affected States Parties will be able to meet their Article 5 obligations and thus be more willing to join the Convention.

Obligation to assist victims

6.72 Paragraph 7 obliges States Parties to 'provide assistance for the implementation of the obligations referred to in Article 5'.[212] Because it requires assistance for implementation, rather than direct assistance with victim assistance, it suggests more clearly than the other paragraphs of Article 6 that affected States will remain primarily responsible for implementation. The specific duties of affected States for this remedial measure are outlined in Article 5.[213] Like most other provisions in Article 6, paragraph 7 does not specify types of assistance, but it presumably encompasses both financial and in-kind support.

---

[207] Article 6, paragraph 3, *1997 Anti-Personnel Mine Ban Convention*; and Article 8, paragraph 2, *2003 Protocol V.* [208] Article 6, Lima Discussion Text.

[209] Article 6, Vienna Discussion Text. The Vienna text devoted Article 5 to victim assistance.

[210] See, *supra*, the commentary on preparatory discussions and negotiations of Article 6.

[211] See Article 5, paragraph 1. [212] Article 6, paragraph 7.

[213] Article 5. See also, *supra*, the commentary on Article 5.

6.73 The care that paragraph 7 seeks to support will both medically aid people harmed by cluster munitions and ensure their places in society. The victim assistance it describes includes 'medical care, rehabilitation and psychological support, as well as … social and economic inclusion of cluster munition victims'.[214] The addition of psychological support, which did not appear in the *1997 Anti-Personnel Mine Ban Convention* or *2003 Protocol V*, broadens the obligation. The same applies to changing 'reintegration' to 'inclusion'. The latter change reflected a growing understanding that every person (irrespective of for example disability) should be able to access equally and participate fully in any activity or service in his or her community. Inclusion covers victims even if they were not integrated into society before becoming victims. Paragraph 7 also tailors assistance to particular groups of victims, requiring it to be 'age- and gender-sensitive'. Austria suggested inserting that phrase during the Diplomatic Conference,[215] and other States agreed to the proposal. All of the language describing the kind of care to be assisted is drawn directly from Article 5.[216] As defined in Article 2, paragraph 1, cluster munition victim includes individuals injured or killed, affected families, and communities.[217]

6.74 According to paragraph 7, States Parties can provide assistance for victim assistance bilaterally or through a non-exhaustive list of organizations. Most of the groups are the same as those enumerated in Article 6, paragraph 2: 'the United Nations system, international, regional or national organizations or institutions, [and] non-governmental organizations'.[218] Paragraph 7, however, also includes the ICRC and the national Red Cross and Red Crescent Societies. These bodies are known for their humanitarian aid programmes so they are a logical addition to a list related to victim assistance. The ICRC, for example, runs or supports more than 70 rehabilitation centres around the world helping victims of landmines and ERW; in addition to medical care and physical rehabilitation, the organization provides physical rehabilitation equipment (such as prostheses and crutches), training, and funding.[219] It is unclear why only two paragraphs of Article 6

[214] Article 6, paragraph 7.

[215] The President of the Conference reported on Austria's proposal in the Committee of the Whole. Statement of the President of the Conference, 'Summary Record of Thirteenth Session of the Committee of the Whole', *op. cit.*, p. 1.

[216] Article 5, paragraph 1. For further discussion of Article 5's obligations, see, *supra*, commentary on Article 5.

[217] Article 2, paragraph 1. For further discussion of the definition of cluster munition victim, see, *supra*, the commentary on Article 2, paragraph 1.

[218] See commentary on Article 6, paragraph 2, *supra*, at §§6.40–6.43.

[219] ICRC, 'Physical Rehabilitation', undated, <http://www.icrc.org/web/eng/siteeng0.nsf/htmlall/section_physical_rehabilitation?opendocument>; ICRC, 'ICRC Special Fund for the

list organizations through which assistance can be provided, but a possible explanation is that paragraph 2 could be viewed as an overarching paragraph that relates to more technical paragraphs, such as those on clearance and stockpile destruction.[220]

Paragraph 8

Each State Party in a position to do so shall provide assistance to contribute to the economic and social recovery needed as a result of cluster munition use in affected States Parties.

Commentary

6.75 Recognizing the wide range of harm that may be caused by cluster munitions, paragraph 8 establishes an obligation for States Parties to provide assistance to address the social and economic effects of these weapons. Paragraph 8 was introduced in the Draft Cluster Munitions Convention and remained unchanged in the final text of the Convention. Paragraph 7 establishes an obligation to promote the social and economic inclusion of cluster munition victims in their communities. Paragraph 8 is concerned with economic and social recovery at a more general level.

6.76 Cluster munitions are known for interfering with livelihoods as well as costing lives. Cluster munition remnants often litter farms and fields for months or years and thus impede agricultural activities. After Israel used a very large number of cluster munitions in south Lebanon during the conflict in 2006, especially during the last few days of fighting, the UN Food and Agricultural Organization reported that at least 26 per cent of the largely agrarian region's agricultural land had been contaminated.[221] As in other affected States, farmers there were faced with the choice of risking their lives to cultivate their fields or sacrificing their harvest and not having enough food for their family. After each of the four major conflicts in which States have used cluster munitions over the past decade—Afghanistan (2001–2002), Iraq

---

Disabled', <http://www.icrc.org/WEB/DOC/sitesfd0.nsf/htmlall/sfd-projects>; and ICRC, *Caring for Landmine Victims* (Geneva: ICRC, 2005), <http://www.icrc.org/Web/Eng/siteeng0.nsf/htmlall/p0863/$File/ICRC_002_0863.PDF> (all accessed 29 October 2009).

[220] See Article 6, paragraph 2.
[221] Human Rights Watch, *Flooding South Lebanon: Israel's Use of Cluster Munitions in Lebanon in July and August 2006, op. cit.*, p. 78.

(2003), Lebanon (2006), and Georgia (2008), researchers documented socio-economic effects.[222]

6.77 Paragraph 8 allows for a very broad reading of what assistance for economic and social recovery encompasses. As is true for other provisions of Article 6, technical, material, and financial support are all appropriate in this context. Development programmes tailored to helping communities affected by cluster munitions would serve to advance economic and social recovery. For example, in some places, such as Cambodia and Laos, the economic benefits of scrap metal collection have led to accidents from UXO, including cluster munition remnants. Community development programmes might work to reduce the economic incentives to take risks with cluster munition remnants.[223] Like paragraphs 2 and 6, paragraph 8 explicitly limits the obligation to providing assistance to other affected States Parties, not to all affected States.

Paragraph 9

Each State Party in a position to do so may contribute to relevant trust funds in order to facilitate the provision of assistance under this Article.

Commentary

6.78 Paragraph 9 affirms that States Parties' contributions to certain trust funds may be considered assistance in accordance with their obligations under this Article. The provision is superficially based on Article 8, paragraph 3 of *2003 Protocol V*.[224] Paragraph 9 is essentially a more general formulation of the explicit reference in Article 6, paragraph 4 of the *1997 Anti-Personnel Mine*

---

[222] See, e.g., Human Rights Watch, *A Dying Practice: Use of Cluster Munitions by Russia and Georgia in August 2008, op. cit.*, pp. 52, 62–63; Human Rights Watch, *Flooding South Lebanon: Israel's Use of Cluster Munitions in Lebanon in July and August 2006, op. cit.*, pp. 78–81; Human Rights Watch, *Off Target: The Conduct of War and Civilian Casualties in Iraq, op. cit.*, p. 110; and Human Rights Watch, *Fatally Flawed: Cluster Bombs and Their Use by the United States in Afghanistan, op. cit.*, pp. 28–29.

[223] See Moyes, R., *Tampering: the deliberate handling and use of live ordnance in Cambodia* (Phnom Penh: Handicap International Belgium, Mines Advisory Group, Norwegian People's Aid, 2004), <http://www.stopclustermunitions.org/wp/wp-content/uploads/2008/07/tampering-npa.pdf>; and GICHD, *A study of scrap metal collection in Lao PDR*, (Geneva: GICHD, 2005), available at: <http://www.gichd.org> (both accessed 1 March 2010).

[224] 'Each High Contracting Party in a position to do so shall contribute to trust funds within the United Nations system, as well as other relevant trust funds, to facilitate the provision of assistance under this Protocol.' Article 8, paragraph 3, *2003 Protocol V*. This formulation highlights in particular the relevance of trust funds within the UN system, but most significantly it makes provision of assistance through trust funds an obligation in its own right.

Ban Convention to certain trust funds as possible channels by which States Parties may assist mine clearance and related activities. The trust fund provision of the Convention on Cluster Munitions was introduced in the Vienna Discussion Text and remained unchanged in the Convention as adopted.[225]

6.79 A trust fund serves as a mechanism through which States Parties can provide financial assistance with only limited engagement in the prioritization or practical planning of the use of that assistance and with limited bureaucratic commitment. During the Oslo Process, UNMAS encouraged 'un-earmarked' donations[226] to trust funds because they can facilitate assistance in response to emergencies.[227] Unlike the corresponding provisions in the *1997 Anti-Personnel Mine Ban Convention* and *2003 Protocol V*, Article 6, paragraph 9 of the Convention on Cluster Munitions does not name possible trust funds, such as those administered by the UN. In order to be 'relevant' under this Convention's provision, a trust fund would have to help provide the kind of assistance referred to elsewhere in Article 6.

Paragraph 10

> Each State Party that seeks and receives assistance shall take all appropriate measures in order to facilitate the timely and effective implementation of this Convention, including facilitation of the entry and exit of personnel, materiel and equipment, in a manner consistent with national laws and regulations, taking into consideration international best practices.

Commentary

6.80 While most provisions of Article 6 are directed at States Parties that provide assistance, paragraph 10 establishes an obligation on States Parties that seek and receive assistance to 'take all appropriate measures ... to facilitate the timely and effective implementation' of the Convention. The paragraph highlights facilitating 'the entry and exit of personnel, materiel and equipment' as one possible appropriate measure, but it does not include an

---

[225] Article 6, paragraph 9, Vienna Discussion Text. A comma after 'trust funds' was deleted between the Vienna Discussion Text and the Draft Cluster Munitions Convention, but it had no grammatical or legal significance.

[226] Un-earmarked funds are not required to be used for a specific purpose, programme, or project.

[227] Statement of UNMAS, Vienna Conference, 7 December 2007 (Landmine Action notes; copy on file with author).

exhaustive list.[228] According to the provision, in deciding what measures to take, States Parties must consider international best practices. For example, States receiving assistance have sometimes waived customs and other taxation charges on the importation of equipment for clearance operations. The paragraph makes clear, however, that the obligation to facilitate implementation of the Convention and the consideration of international best practices must be 'consistent with', not supersede 'national laws and regulations'.

6.81 Paragraph 10 relates to two others in Article 6. It generalizes an obligation of paragraph 3, which in its second part prohibits States Parties from imposing 'undue restrictions on the provision and receipt of clearance and other such equipment and related technological information for humanitarian purposes'.[229] It also works together with paragraph 12, which requires donor and recipient States Parties to cooperate on implementation.[230] Paragraph 10 elaborates on recipient States' duties in cooperation, thus responding to concerns that paragraph 12 was too vague to influence practice.

6.82 Paragraph 10, which has no precedent in the *1997 Anti-Personnel Mine Ban Convention* or *2003 Protocol V*, was the most contentious component of the negotiations of Article 6 during the Diplomatic Conference in Dublin. An initial version, proposed by four States at the Wellington Conference and included in the Wellington Compendium, set out a longer list of appropriate measures and no mention of national law.[231] Traditional donor States pushed for the paragraph in an effort to improve efficiency of humanitarian programmes. Other, primarily affected or developing States expressed concern that the proposed provision would require them to amend national laws and would thus undermine State sovereignty. The final text enumerated only one appropriate measure, clarified the role of international best practices, and stressed the importance of national law.[232]

---

[228] An early proposal for the paragraph listed as several appropriate measures: 'collecting and releasing all relevant data and information, . . . granting favourable entry and visa regimes for international personnel involved in assistance programmes, and . . . ensuring the unimpeded import of relevant material and equipment free of financial and administrative burdens'. 'Article 6: International Cooperation and Assistance', Wellington Compendium, p. 24; 'Proposal by Denmark, France, Germany and Sweden for the amendment of Article 6', Diplomatic Conference doc. CCM/37, 19 May 2008.　　　　　　　　　　　　　　　　　　　　[229] Article 6, paragraph 3.

[230] Article 6, paragraph 12.

[231] 'Article 6: International Cooperation and Assistance', Wellington Compendium, p. 24; and 'Proposal by Denmark, France, Germany and Sweden for the amendment of Article 6', Diplomatic Conference doc. CCM/37, 19 May 2008.

[232] For further discussion of the debate surrounding Article 6, paragraph 10 (then paragraph 9(bis)), see, *supra*, §§6.19–6.23.

Paragraph 11

Each State Party may, with the purpose of developing a national action plan, request the United Nations system, regional organisations, other States Parties or other competent intergovernmental or non-governmental institutions to assist its authorities to determine, *inter alia*:

(a) The nature and extent of cluster munition remnants located in areas under its jurisdiction or control;

(b) The financial, technological and human resources required for the implementation of the plan;

(c) The time estimated as necessary to clear and destroy all cluster munition remnants located in areas under its jurisdiction or control;

(d) Risk reduction education programmes and awareness activities to reduce the incidence of injuries or deaths caused by cluster munition remnants;

(e) Assistance to cluster munition victims; and

(f) The coordination relationship between the government of the State Party concerned and the relevant governmental, intergovernmental or non-governmental entities that will work in the implementation of the plan.

Commentary

6.83 Paragraph 11 encourages affected States Parties to request assistance for the development of national action plans to address the problems caused by cluster munitions. While paragraphs 4, 5, 6, 7, and 8 require States Parties in a position to do so to provide assistance for certain activities, paragraph 11 allows States Parties to seek assistance to approach these activities through an integrated national plan. Paragraph 11 indicates that States Parties may ask for help from a range of bodies, including UN institutions or other intergovernmental organizations, regional organizations, States Parties, and NGOs.[233]

6.84 When developing their national action plans, States Parties may seek advice on a range of subjects, including those listed in sub-paragraphs (a) to (f). Several of the sub-paragraphs touch on topics related to obligations under the Convention on Cluster Munitions, including the obligations to clear cluster munition remnants, conduct risk reduction education, and provide victim

---

[233] Maslen notes with respect to the *1997 Anti-Personnel Mine Ban Convention* that this list of mechanisms for the provision of assistance does not preclude the possibility of a State Party seeking assistance elsewhere, for example from a commercial company. Maslen, S., *Commentary on the 1997 Anti-Personnel Mine Ban Convention, op. cit.,* §6.37.

assistance.[234] Two other sub-paragraphs, those dealing with available resources and coordination relationships, relate to implementation of the national plan rather than the Convention as a whole.[235] This list of areas about which States Parties may seek information should not be considered exhaustive, however. It does not explicitly address key issues such as the development of national legislation and destruction of stockpiles, and the phrase '*inter alia*' precedes it. Like the corresponding provision in the *1997 Anti-Personnel Mine Ban Convention*, paragraph 11 of Article 6 does not stipulate the type of assistance to be provided, but it most likely includes 'technical advice and assistance, whether through an assessment mission or longer-term secondment of qualified staff to a mine-affected State, for example within a national mine action centre'.[236]

6.85 Effective coordination and management are widely considered essential to the success of a mine action programme and should be a component of a national action plan.[237] In many cases, a distinct entity within the government of the affected State—with technical or advisory support from UN institutions, other partner organizations, or governments—assumes responsibility for such a programme. While frequently termed a mine action coordination centre or mine action centre, this type of institution usually has a mandate that covers cluster munitions as well as landmines.[238] It plays an important role in liaising between operational concerns and the development of national policies at the political level, creating national plans for dealing with the effects of weapons, and monitoring compliance with international and national standards.

6.86 Paragraph 11, which evolved gradually during the Oslo Process, was adapted with several minor modifications from Article 6, paragraph 7 of the *1997 Anti-Personnel Mine Ban Convention*.[239] While the *chapeau* in the latter

---

[234] Article 6, paragraph 11 (a), (c), (d), and (e).   [235] Article 6, paragraph 11 (b) and (f).

[236] Maslen, S., *Commentary on the 1997 Anti-Personnel Mine Ban Convention, op. cit.*, §6.54.

[237] ICBL, *Landmine Monitor Report 2008, op. cit.*, p. 21.

[238] Despite their names, such centres generally do not limit themselves to working on landmines. The Mine Action Coordination Centre-South Lebanon, for example, actively coordinated clearance of unexploded submunitions after Israel littered the south Lebanon with them in 2006. See, e.g., Human Rights Watch, *Flooding South Lebanon: Israel's Use of Cluster Munitions in Lebanon in July and August 2006, op. cit.*, p. 84. Similarly, the UN Mine Action Coordination Centre in Kosovo coordinated response to landmines, unexploded cluster munition remnants, and explosive remnants of war. See Moyes, R., *Cluster munitions in Kosovo: Analysis of use, contamination and casualties* (London: Landmine Action, 2007).

[239] The *1997 Anti-Personnel Mine Ban Convention* provision reads:

States Parties may request the United Nations, regional organizations, other States Parties or other competent intergovernmental or non-governmental fora to assist its authorities in the elaboration of a national demining program to determine, inter alia:

a. The extent and scope of the anti-personnel mine problem;

refers to 'elaboration of a national demining program', that in the Convention on Cluster Munitions describes 'develop[ment] of a national action plan'. This change clarifies that the purpose of the assistance is to establish a plan that encompasses not just clearance of cluster munition remnants but the full range of activities necessary to respond to the problems caused by cluster munitions.[240]

6.87 Other differences that appear in Article 6, paragraph 11 of the Convention on Cluster Munitions sharpen the provision. Paragraph 11(a) changes the *1997 Anti-Personnel Mine Ban Convention*'s tautological 'extent and scope' to 'nature and extent'.[241] The latter implies a requirement to understand not only the geographic distribution of contamination, but also more qualitative aspects relating to the types of munitions comprising the contamination. Paragraph 11(f) clarifies the corresponding language of the *1997 Anti-Personnel Mine Ban Convention*[242] by noting that it is specifically the 'coordination relationship' between the affected State Party and the implementing partners that is being determined here, not the wider relationship between these entities.

Paragraph 12

> States Parties giving and receiving assistance under the provisions of this Article shall cooperate with a view to ensuring the full and prompt implementation of agreed assistance programmes.

b. The financial, technological and human resources that are required for the implementation of the program;

c. The estimated number of years necessary to destroy all anti-personnel mines in mined areas under the jurisdiction or control of the concerned State Party;

d. Mine awareness activities to reduce the incidence of mine-related injuries or deaths;

e. Assistance to mine victims;

f. The relationship between the Government of the concerned State Party and the relevant governmental, inter-governmental or non-governmental entities that will work in the implementation of the program.

Article 6, paragraph 7, *1997 Anti-Personnel Mine Ban Convention*.

[240] The broadening of this phrase reflects how the term 'demining programme' has been understood in the context of the *1997 Anti-Personnel Mine Ban Convention*. Maslen notes that 'Although [Article 6,] paragraph 7 [of the *1997 Anti-Personnel Mine Ban Convention*] refers to only a "demining programme", . . . the programme goes beyond demining to include other components of mine action.' Maslen, S., *Commentary on the 1997 Anti-Personnel Mine Ban Convention, op. cit.*, §6.52.

[241] Article 6, paragraph 11(a); and Article 6, paragraph 7(a), *1997 Anti-Personnel Mine Ban Convention*. [242] Article 6, paragraph 7(f), *1997 Anti-Personnel Mine Ban Convention*.

Commentary

6.88 Unlike most provisions of Article 6, paragraph 12 imposes obligations on both donor and recipient States Parties. It requires them to work together to implement assistance programmes fully and promptly. Appearing at the end of the Article on international cooperation and assistance, it serves as a reminder of the cooperative approach the Convention on Cluster Munitions takes toward implementation.[243] States Parties are required to assist their counterparts to ensure the Convention's obligations are met.

6.89 Paragraph 12 does not specify what form cooperation should take, but other related provisions of Article 6 offer possibilities. Paragraph 3, which refers to an 'exchange' and 'the provision and receipt' of equipment and information, also requires two-way cooperation. In particular, it specifies that States Parties must not 'impose undue restrictions' on the exchange of equipment or information.[244] Paragraph 10 similarly obliges recipient States Parties to smooth 'the entry and exit of personnel, materiel and equipment' as one 'appropriate measure' to facilitate implementation of the Convention in a 'timely and effective' manner.[245]

6.90 The Lima Discussion Text copied the provision verbatim from Article 6, paragraph 8 of the *1997 Anti-Personnel Mine Ban Convention*, and it remained virtually unchanged through the Oslo Process.[246] The comparable paragraph of the *1997 Anti-Personnel Mine Ban Convention* originated in a German proposal. It sought to ensure that the recipients of assistance take active steps to facilitate the timely and cost-free entry of personnel and equipment to implement relevant humanitarian projects.[247] During negotiations of the *1997 Anti-Personnel Mine Ban Convention*, Germany had proposed the following language:

Each State Party receiving assistance under the provisions of this article shall cooperate with a view to ensuring the full and prompt implementation of agreed assistance

---

[243] The Convention on Cluster Munitions also adopts a cooperative approach to compliance. See, *infra*, the commentary on Article 8.

[244] For further discussion, see, *supra*, the commentary on Article 6, paragraph 3.

[245] For further discussion, see, *supra*, the commentary on Article 6, paragraph 10.

[246] Article 5, paragraph 6, Lima Discussion Text; and Article 6, paragraph 8, *1997 Anti-Personnel Mine Ban Convention*. The only difference from the Lima Discussion Text is that the Convention on Cluster Munitions changed 'Each State Party' to 'States Parties'. This change was made in Article 6, paragraph 11 of the Draft Cluster Munitions Convention.

[247] Maslen, S., *Commentary on the 1997 Anti-Personnel Mine Ban Convention, op. cit.*, §6.56. Maslen noted that during the negotiation of the *1997 Anti-Personnel Mine Ban Convention* a proposal by Germany referred indirectly 'to problems which sometimes have been encountered in importing mine clearance equipment. Customs formalities and duties have not been greatly appreciated by donor States, as these have been unnecessarily time-consuming and expensive.'

programmes. It shall in particular effectively assist seconded experts, provide its own contribution in good time and ensure immediate and cost-free customs clearance of all material supplied on behalf of the assisting party.[248]

The second half of this proposal was ultimately dropped, and the opening phrase was changed from 'Each State Party receiving assistance' to 'Each State Party giving and receiving assistance'. During negotiations of the Convention on Cluster Munitions, some States Parties again raised concerns about obstacles to the implementation of assistance programmes and argued that more specific legal provisions were necessary. As a result, paragraph 10, imposing an explicit obligation on recipient States Parties, was inserted to supplement paragraph 12.

---

[248] Proposal of Germany, Oslo Diplomatic Conference doc. APL/CW.23, 2 September 1997.

Article 7. Transparency measures

Bonnie Docherty

Article 7—Transparency measures

1. Each State Party shall report to the Secretary-General of the United Nations as soon as practicable, and in any event not later than 180 days after the entry into force of this Convention for that State Party, on:

(a) The national implementation measures referred to in Article 9 of this Convention;

(b) The total of all cluster munitions, including explosive submunitions, referred to in paragraph 1 of Article 3 of this Convention, to include a breakdown of their type, quantity and, if possible, lot numbers of each type;

(c) The technical characteristics of each type of cluster munition produced by that State Party prior to entry into force of this Convention for it, to the extent known, and those currently owned or possessed by it, giving, where reasonably possible, such categories of information as may facilitate identification and clearance of cluster munitions; at a minimum, this information shall include the dimensions, fusing, explosive content, metallic content, colour photographs and other information that may facilitate the clearance of cluster munition remnants;

(d) The status and progress of programmes for the conversion or decommissioning of production facilities for cluster munitions;

(e) The status and progress of programmes for the destruction, in accordance with Article 3 of this Convention, of cluster munitions, including explosive submunitions, with details of the methods that will be used in destruction, the location of all destruction sites and the applicable safety and environmental standards to be observed;

(f) The types and quantities of cluster munitions, including explosive submunitions, destroyed in accordance with Article 3 of this Convention, including details of the methods of destruction used, the location of the destruction sites and the applicable safety and environmental standards observed;

(g) Stockpiles of cluster munitions, including explosive submunitions, discovered after reported completion of the programme referred to in sub-paragraph (e) of this paragraph, and plans for their destruction in accordance with Article 3 of this Convention;

(h) To the extent possible, the size and location of all cluster munition contaminated areas under its jurisdiction or control, to include as much detail as possible regarding the type and quantity of each type of cluster munition remnant in each such area and when they were used;

(i) The status and progress of programmes for the clearance and destruction of all types and quantities of cluster munition remnants cleared and destroyed in accordance with Article 4 of this Convention, to include the size and location of the cluster munition contaminated area cleared and a breakdown of the quantity of each type of cluster munition remnant cleared and destroyed;

(j) The measures taken to provide risk reduction education and, in particular, an immediate and effective warning to civilians living in cluster munition contaminated areas under its jurisdiction or control;

(k) The status and progress of implementation of its obligations under Article 5 of this Convention to adequately provide age- and gender-sensitive assistance, including medical care, rehabilitation and psychological support, as well as provide for social and economic inclusion of cluster munition victims and to collect reliable relevant data with respect to cluster munition victims;

(l) The name and contact details of the institutions mandated to provide information and to carry out the measures described in this paragraph;

(m) The amount of national resources, including financial, material or in kind, allocated to the implementation of Articles 3, 4 and 5 of this Convention; and

(n) The amounts, types and destinations of international cooperation and assistance provided under Article 6 of this Convention.

2. The information provided in accordance with paragraph 1 of this Article shall be updated by the States Parties annually, covering the previous calendar year, and reported to the Secretary-General of the United Nations not later than 30 April of each year.

3. The Secretary-General of the United Nations shall transmit all such reports received to the States Parties.

Overview of the Article

7.1 Article 7 establishes transparency measures for States Parties to the Convention on Cluster Munitions. The Article obliges each State Party to submit an initial report within 180 days of the Convention's entry into force for it, followed by annual reports with updated information on the previous calendar year. Each State Party must submit its reports to the Secretary-General of the United Nations (UN), who in turn will transmit them to other States Parties. The Article mandates reports on 14 subjects, most of which relate to States Parties' positive obligations under the Convention, particularly those laid out in Articles 3 to 6. The list of enumerated subjects includes stockpile destruction, clearance, risk reduction education, victim assistance, and international cooperation and assistance.

7.2 As was made clear in discussions during the Oslo Process, States intended Article 7 to promote compliance with the Convention on Cluster Munitions and to serve as a confidence-building measure.[1] Information provided under Article 7 will help States work together to achieve the Convention's goals. When a State Party falls short of its obligations under the Convention, reports

---

[1] See, e.g., Statement of the Cluster Munition Coalition (CMC), Oslo Conference on Cluster Munitions, 23 February 2007; and Statements at the Lima Conference, 25 May 2007 (all from Landmine Action notes; copy on file with author).

can reveal what challenges it faces and what kind of international assistance it needs to overcome obstacles. In addition, reports facilitate an exchange of information that can enable States Parties to learn from each other. For example, States Parties can adapt or improve on another State's programmes or use its technical data to identify cluster munitions and contaminated areas.

7.3 As an added benefit, by revealing information about its progress in implementing the Convention, a State Party allows others to monitor its actions. Assuming that the reports are made available to the public,[2] civil society can serve as an important watchdog that tracks the conduct of States Parties. Ultimately, Article 7 advances both the disarmament and humanitarian aims of the Convention by promoting compliance with obligations related to stockpile destruction and remedial measures.

7.4 While other weapons instruments include reporting and verification requirements,[3] Article 7 of the *1997 Anti-Personnel Mine Ban Convention*[4] was the most direct model for Article 7 of the Convention on Cluster Munitions. Transparency has played a critical role in ensuring States Parties meet their obligations under the *1997 Anti-Personnel Mine Ban Convention* and has helped the International Campaign to Ban Landmines (ICBL) to produce the *Landmine Monitor*, the annual analysis of, *inter alia*, State implementation of that treaty.[5] Article 7 of the Convention on Cluster Munitions takes transparency even further. It builds on precedent for transparency measures, supplementing it with reporting requirements on newly discovered stockpiles, victim assistance, national points of contact, national resources, and international cooperation and assistance.[6] Thus Article 7 will not only promote compliance

---

[2] As will be explained in the commentary on Article 7, paragraph 3 (*infra*, §7.68), the Article does not explicitly require that the reports be made public, but precedent under the *1997 Anti-Personnel Mine Ban Convention* suggests they will be.

[3] See, e.g., Article 3 and Parts IVA and V of Annex on Implementation and Verification, Convention on the Prohibition of the Development, Production, Stockpiling and Use of Chemical Weapons and on their Destruction (*1993 Chemical Weapons Convention*); Article 9 and paragraph 1 Technical Annex, Protocol on Prohibitions or Restrictions on the Use of Mines, Booby-Traps and Other Devices as amended on 3 May 1996 (*1996 Amended Protocol II*) to the *Convention on Certain Conventional Weapons*; and Article 4 and paragraph 1, Technical Annex, Protocol V on Explosive Remnants of War (*2003 Protocol V*) to the *Convention on Certain Conventional Weapons*. The formal title of the *Convention on Certain Conventional Weapons* is the Convention on Prohibitions or Restrictions on the Use of Certain Conventional Weapons Which May Be Deemed to Be Excessively Injurious or to Have Indiscriminate Effects, as amended on 21 December 2001.

[4] The formal title of this treaty is the Convention on the Prohibition of the Use, Stockpiling, Production and Transfer of Anti-Personnel Mines and on Their Destruction.

[5] Current and past *Landmine Monitor* reports are available at: <http://lm.icbl.org/>.

[6] Article 7, paragraph 1(g) and (k)–(n).

with the Convention on Cluster Munitions, it may also set a new baseline for transparency measures in future humanitarian and disarmament treaties.

Preparatory discussions

7.5 Although the Oslo Declaration did not include a specific reference to the issue, the need for transparency measures was recognized from the outset of the Oslo Process. One State and the Cluster Munition Coalition (CMC) highlighted its importance in interventions at the Oslo Conference on Cluster Munitions in February 2007.[7] Following the model of the *1997 Anti-Personnel Mine Ban Convention*, the Lima Discussion Text[8] contained a stand-alone Article devoted to transparency.[9] Although States engaged in less discussion on this Article than on some other draft provisions, they broadened its scope in each draft text and through the final week of negotiations.

7.6 The Lima Discussion Text established the framework for Article 7 on transparency measures. It required each State Party to report to the UN Secretary-General on certain matters within 180 days of entry into force for that State Party.[10] It also obliged each State Party to submit annual updates.[11] The Secretary-General in turn was tasked with transmitting the reports to other parties to the Convention.[12] In its Article 11, the Lima Discussion Text also made State transparency reports a subject of discussion at the regular Meetings of States Parties.[13] The framework language of these Articles, drawn directly from the *1997 Anti-Personnel Mine Ban Convention*,[14] remained unchanged throughout the Oslo Process.

7.7 The list of matters to be reported on, by contrast, continued to evolve during the Oslo Process. The Lima Discussion Text enumerated eight subjects that States would be required to report on:

- national implementation measures,

---

[7] Statements at the Oslo Conference, 23 February 2007 (Landmine Action notes; copy on file with author). The CMC stated its view that the current lack of transparency on cluster munitions made it very important to include transparency measures in the future Convention. See, *supra*, §0.30 for details of the Conference.

[8] Chair's discussion text on a legally binding international instrument that will prohibit the use, production, transfer and stockpiling of cluster munitions that cause unacceptable harm to civilians, Lima, 23–25 May 2007. For full text, see Annex 3 to this Commentary.

[9] Article 7, Lima Discussion Text.   [10] Article 7, paragraph 1, Lima Discussion Text.
[11] Article 7, paragraph 2, Lima Discussion Text.
[12] Article 7, paragraph 3, Lima Discussion Text.
[13] Article 11, paragraph 1(b), Lima Discussion Text.
[14] Article 7 and Article 11, *1997 Anti-Personnel Mine Ban Convention*.

- stockpiles of cluster munitions,
- the location of contaminated areas and details of the cluster munitions used,
- the status of programmes for 'conversion or de-commissioning of production facilities for cluster munitions',
- the status of programmes for stockpile destruction,
- the types and quantities of stockpiled cluster munitions destroyed,
- the technical characteristics of stockpiled cluster munitions, and
- warnings to the population about contaminated areas.[15]

7.8 Many paragraphs of the Lima Discussion Text's Article 7 laid down the details on which each State Party needed to report. All would appear in some version in the final text of the Convention. The Lima Discussion Text's list drew heavily on Article 7 of the *1997 Anti-Personnel Mine Ban Convention*, but the text did not include a requirement to report on clearance.[16]

7.9 During the discussions at the May 2007 Lima Conference,[17] several States and observers emphasized the importance of the proposed transparency Article, both to facilitate compliance with the Convention and to serve as a confidence-building measure.[18] The CMC highlighted transparency's practical value for illuminating obstacles to compliance and States Parties' needs for assistance.[19] While a number of States and the CMC saw the *1997 Anti-Personnel Mine Ban Convention* as a good starting point, other States argued that the provisions in that treaty could be improved upon.[20] Few specifics were discussed during the Lima Conference, but several States argued that transparency was a necessary precondition for allowing retention of cluster munitions for training purposes.[21] The CMC emphasized the need for robust

---

[15] Article 7, paragraph 1(a)–(h), Lima Discussion Text. The Lima text also did not include the *1997 Anti-Personnel Mine Ban Convention*'s requirement for transparency related to munitions retained for training because the Lima text did not include a provision allowing such retention. Comparable provisions on retention and associated transparency would ultimately be added to Article 3 of the Convention on Cluster Munitions. *Cp.* Article 7, paragraph 1(f) and (g), *1997 Anti-Personnel Mine Ban Convention*; and Article 3, paragraphs 6–8.

[16] Article 7, paragraph 1(f) and (g), *1997 Anti-Personnel Mine Ban Convention*.

[17] See, *supra*, §§ 0.41–0.42 for details of the Conference.

[18] Statements at the Lima Conference, 25 May 2007 (Landmine Action notes; copy on file with author).

[19] Statement of the CMC, Lima Conference, 25 May 2007. See also Statement of the International Committee of the Red Cross (ICRC), Lima Conference, 25 May 2007 (both from Landmine Action notes; copy on file with author).

[20] Statements at the Lima Conference, 25 May 2007 (Landmine Action notes; copy on file with author).

[21] Statements at the Lima Conference, 24 May 2007 (Landmine Action notes; copy on file with author).

paragraphs on reporting and added that all reports should be made public in order to allow independent monitoring.[22]

7.10 The Vienna Discussion Text[23] added four new subjects of transparency and removed one. First, Article 7, paragraph 1(c) obliged each State Party to report on, '[t]o the extent possible, all other cluster munitions that are stockpiled on its territory'.[24] This provision covered foreign stockpiles, i.e., those that were located on a State Party's territory but possessed by another State. It related to Article 3 of the Vienna Discussion Text, which required States Parties to destroy or ensure destruction of stockpiles 'under its jurisdiction *or* control' and presumably covered foreign stockpiles.[25] Second, drawing on some of the language from the *1997 Anti-Personnel Mine Ban Convention*, Article 7, paragraph 1(h) created a reporting requirement for 'the types and quantities of all cluster munitions cleared and destroyed'.[26] Third, Article 7, paragraph 1(j) obliged each State Party to report on measures it had taken to assist victims.[27] Finally, Article 7, paragraph 1(k) established a duty for each State Party to provide contact details of the institutions that would fulfil the obligations of the Article and the Convention.[28] This information was designed to allow follow-up to the reports. Although there had been no public pressure to do so at the Lima Conference, the Vienna Discussion Text for no clear reason removed the obligation to report on the types and numbers of stockpiled cluster munitions that were destroyed.[29] Other changes to the Article were minor and primarily involved insertion of the newly defined term cluster munition remnants in appropriate places.[30]

---

[22] Statement of the CMC, Lima Conference, 25 May 2007 (Landmine Action notes; copy on file with author).

[23] Vienna Discussion Text of 14 November 2007. For full text, see Annex 4 to this Commentary. [24] Article 7, paragraph 1(c), Vienna Discussion Text.

[25] Article 3, paragraph 2, Vienna Discussion Text (*emphasis added*). In the final text of the Convention, the 'or' in Article 3 was changed to 'and'. The amendment raised questions about whether the Convention obliged States Parties to ensure destruction of foreign stockpiles. For further discussion, see, *supra*, the commentary on Article 3. The change in Article 3 could help explain why this paragraph of Article 7 was ultimately cut in the Convention on Cluster Munitions.

[26] Article 7, paragraph 1(g), *1997 Anti-Personnel Mine Ban Convention*; and Article 7, paragraph 1(h), Vienna Discussion Text. [27] Article 7, paragraph 1(j), Vienna Discussion Text.

[28] Article 7, paragraph 1(k), Vienna Discussion Text.

[29] See Article 7, paragraph 1(f), Lima Discussion Text.

[30] Article 7, paragraph 1(e) and (i), Vienna Discussion Text. For the definition of cluster munition remnants initially proposed, see Article 2, Vienna Discussion Text. The only other amendments were to remove 'as defined by Article 2' after the term cluster munition in Article 7, paragraph 1(b), (f), and (g), Vienna Discussion Text.

7.11 During formal discussions at the Vienna Conference in December 2007,[31] States did not comment on any of these changes, but several proposed expanding Article 7's transparency measures further.[32] Most notably, a number of States called for reports on international cooperation and assistance provided under Article 6. One State highlighted the importance of tracking spending and the outcomes of assistance.[33] Another called for both donors and recipients to be transparent about the use of assistance money.[34] Observer groups made additional contributions to the discussions on Article 7. The International Committee of the Red Cross (ICRC) expressed its support for the Vienna Discussion Text's addition of reporting requirements on victim assistance, and the CMC said that States Parties should collect data on cluster munition survivors and their needs and priorities.[35] The CMC also reiterated its call for making reports available to the public, including non-governmental organizations (NGOs) and cluster munition survivors, emphasizing the need for objective monitoring of the treaty. It noted that civil society, through the *Landmine Monitor*, serves as the 'watchdog' of the *1997 Anti-Personnel Mine Ban Convention* and that it could serve the same role for the Convention on Cluster Munitions.[36]

7.12 The Draft Cluster Munitions Convention,[37] prepared for the February 2008 Wellington Conference,[38] preserved most of the provisions of the Vienna Discussion Text's Article 7. It also added a number of disarmament measures and amended existing humanitarian reporting requirements. According to the draft Convention's Explanatory Notes: 'During the discussions held in Vienna, a growing support for transparency was evident.'[39] In particular, the Explanatory Notes underlined the need to distinguish between destroyed stockpiles and cleared and destroyed cluster munition remnants.[40] As a result, the Draft Cluster Munitions Convention again included the requirement

---

[31] See, *supra*, §§0.43–0.46 for details of the Conference.

[32] Statements at the Vienna Conference, 5 and 7 December 2007 (Landmine Action notes; copy on file with author).

[33] Statement at the Vienna Conference, 7 December 2007 (Landmine Action notes; copy on file with author). [34] *Ibid.*

[35] Statements of the ICRC and the CMC, Vienna Conference, 7 December 2007 (Landmine Action notes; copy on file with author). While seeking clarification on the details required, one State supported submitting victim assistance information to the UN Secretary-General. Statement at the Vienna Conference, 6 December 2007 (Landmine Action notes; copy on file with author).

[36] Statement of the CMC, Vienna Conference, 7 December 2007 (Landmine Action notes; copy on file with author).

[37] Draft Cluster Munitions Convention of 21 January 2008. For full text, see Annex 5 to this Commentary. [38] See, *supra*, §§0.48–0.54 for details of the Conference.

[39] 'Draft Cluster Munitions Convention Explanatory Notes', 21 January 2008, p. 5. For full text, see Annex 5 to this Commentary. [40] *Ibid.*

that each State Party report on the types and quantities of stockpiled cluster munitions that it destroyed, as well as on remnants cleared and destroyed. Modified somewhat from the Lima Discussion Text, the relevant paragraph mandated not merely 'a breakdown of the quantity of each type of cluster munition destroyed' but also 'details of the methods of destruction used, the location of the destruction sites and the applicable safety and environmental standards observed'.[41] Since the provision still demanded general information on types and quantities, this amendment established additional, not just different, reporting obligations.

7.13 As mentioned in the Explanatory Notes, the Draft Cluster Munitions Convention also added an obligation to be transparent about stockpiles discovered after a State Party has destroyed its originally known stockpiles.[42] Although this paragraph had no precedent in the text of the *1997 Anti-Personnel Mine Ban Convention*, it drew on the experience of implementing that treaty.[43] Several States had discovered sometimes significant stockpiles of anti-personnel mines under their jurisdiction or control after they had, ostensibly, completed stockpile destruction. The Draft Cluster Munitions Convention's paragraph on newly discovered stockpiles sought to advance the disarmament aim of the new Convention by helping to ensure that newly discovered stockpiles did not fall under a loophole and remain in State arsenals. Despite calls at the Vienna Conference for reporting on international cooperation and assistance, the Draft Cluster Munitions Convention did not insert a related provision.

7.14 The draft Convention made substantive changes to one provision, expanding the paragraph on reporting on warnings about contaminated areas, which had been taken from the *1997 Anti-Personnel Mine Ban Convention*. Reflecting a new obligation in Article 4, paragraph 2(e), it now covered broader 'measures taken to provide risk education' as well as 'an immediate and effective warning'.[44] At the same time, the draft narrowed the target audience making it clearer and more specific. It replaced 'population' with 'civilians living in areas under [the State Party's] jurisdiction or control in which

---

[41] *Cp*. Article 7, paragraph 1(f), Lima Discussion Text; and Article 7, paragraph 1(h), Draft Cluster Munitions Convention.

[42] 'Draft Cluster Munitions Convention Explanatory Notes', *op. cit.*, p. 5; and Article 7, paragraph 1(i), Draft Cluster Munitions Convention.

[43] For more discussion of how States Parties to the *1997 Anti-Personnel Mine Ban Convention* have dealt with reporting on newly discovered stockpiles, see, *infra*, the commentary on Article 7, paragraph 1(g) in §7.47.

[44] Article 4, paragraph 2(e), and Article 7, paragraph 1(k), Draft Cluster Munitions Convention.

cluster munition remnants are located'.[45] The Explanatory Notes to the draft text highlighted this change.[46] The Draft Cluster Munitions Convention also tightened the language of several other paragraphs without substantively changing their meaning.[47]

7.15 During discussions about the Draft Cluster Munitions Convention at the February 2008 Wellington Conference, objections to certain provisions, especially related to stockpile reporting, started to emerge. Several States wanted to delete paragraph 1(c) requiring transparency about foreign stockpiles. One State argued it obliged States Parties to report on stockpiles over which they had no jurisdiction or control, and another State emphasized the same difficulty. The Chair of the session responded that States Parties only had to report 'to the extent possible'.[48] The first State also proposed deleting the paragraph on the status of programmes for stockpile destruction, arguing the Convention should include only a paragraph on the types and quantities of stockpiles destroyed.[49] The CMC, by contrast, expressed its support for all of the paragraphs on stockpile reporting and asked that the paragraph on newly discovered stockpiles require information on the destruction as well as the existence of those stockpiles.[50]

7.16 Although it originated in the *1997 Anti-Personnel Mine Ban Convention* and Lima Discussion Text, the paragraph on the status of programmes for converting or decommissioning production facilities also drew criticism.[51] Two States questioned whether monitoring private facilities served the Oslo Process's humanitarian goals.[52] Another State responded that private ownership presented no obstacle to reporting and that similar provisions existed in other disarmament instruments, notably the *1997 Anti-Personnel Mine Ban Convention*.[53] The CMC stated that it was surprised by the proposal to remove

---

[45] Article 7, paragraph 1(k), Draft Cluster Munitions Convention.

[46] 'Draft Cluster Munitions Convention Explanatory Notes', *op. cit.*, p. 5.

[47] Article 7, paragraph 1(a), (g), (j), and (m), Draft Cluster Munitions Convention.

[48] Article 7, paragraph 1(c), Draft Cluster Munitions Convention; and Statements at the Wellington Conference, 21 February 2008 (Landmine Action notes; copy on file with author).

[49] Article 7, paragraph 1(g), Draft Cluster Munitions Convention; and Statement at the Wellington Conference, 21 February 2008 (Landmine Action notes; copy on file with author).

[50] Statement of the CMC, Wellington Conference, 21 February 2008 (Landmine Action notes; copy on file with author).

[51] Article 7, paragraph 1(f), Draft Cluster Munitions Convention; Article 7, paragraph 1(d), Lima Discussion Text; and Article 7, paragraph 1(e), *1997 Anti-Personnel Mine Ban Convention*.

[52] Statements at the Wellington Conference, 21 February 2008 (Landmine Action notes; copy on file with author).

[53] Statement at the Wellington Conference, 21 February 2008 (Landmine Action notes; copy on file with author).

the provision because States Parties should make sure that there is no ability to produce cluster munitions in the future.[54]

7.17   States generally offered support for transparency on other topics. They renewed their calls for reporting on international cooperation and assistance. One State described the need for accountability for both donors and recipients.[55] Several States endorsed the inclusion of victim assistance reporting.[56] Finally, a number of States highlighted the importance of transparency with regard to cluster munitions retained for training purposes, arguing for specific reporting to be required on that subject,[57] a suggestion that States would take up again at the Dublin Diplomatic Conference in May 2008.

7.18   States also discussed procedural matters related to transparency at the Wellington Conference. Two called for a simpler, less burdensome process for States Parties largely unaffected by cluster munitions.[58] One of these also asked for clarification that reports not be required after States had met their obligations.[59] The CMC again raised the issue of requiring States Parties to make their reports public so that independent watchdogs could ensure that the reports matched reality.[60] The Convention on Cluster Munitions ultimately included none of these proposals.

Negotiations

7.19   States continued to add to and refine Article 7 during formal negotiations at the Diplomatic Conference. Transparency for retention of stockpiles

---

[54] Statement of the CMC, Wellington Conference, 21 February 2008 (Landmine Action notes; copy on file with author).

[55] Statement at the Wellington Conference, 21 February 2008 (Landmine Action notes; copy on file with author).

[56] Statements at the Wellington Conference, 20 February 2008 (Landmine Action notes; copy on file with author). The CMC called for including survivor perspectives in victim assistance reporting.

[57] Statements at the Wellington Conference, 21 February 2008 (Landmine Action notes; copy on file with author).   [58] *Ibid.*

[59] Statement at the Wellington Conference, 21 February 2008 (Landmine Action notes; copy on file with author). In the context of the *1997 Anti-Personnel Mine Ban Convention*, the UN has included a cover page form to expedite reporting for States Parties for whom the information to be provided in one or some of the reporting forms is the same as in past reports. Therefore, when using the cover page, only forms that contain new information would need to be submitted. See UN Office at Geneva (UNOG), 'Disarmament: Article 7 reporting forms', <http://www.unog.ch/80256EE600585943/(httpPages)/2B050F75A5100D47C12573E800670E42?OpenDocument> (accessed 26 March 2010).

[60] Statement of the CMC, Wellington Conference, 21 February 2008 (Landmine Action notes; copy on file with author). The CMC also urged States to submit voluntary reports before entry into force.

for training purposes was the first related topic addressed in the Committee of the Whole. Australia said a reporting requirement might help resolve the debate over retention, and several States expressed a willingness to allow it as long as the Convention required transparency.[61] A group of eight States resubmitted a proposal for language on this topic, which had originally appeared in the Compendium of Proposals attached to the Wellington Declaration (the Wellington Compendium).[62] It proposed mandating transparency on 'the total number, types and locations of cluster munitions kept under the provision of paragraph 6 of Article 3'.[63] While the *1997 Anti-Personnel Mine Ban Convention* required States to release this information in paragraph 1(d) of its Article 7 on transparency measures, the Convention on Cluster Munitions ultimately included its comparable, yet more detailed, provision in paragraph 8 of Article 3 on Storage and Stockpile Destruction.[64]

7.20 States proposed and succeeded in adding two new paragraphs to Article 7. Belgium suggested requiring each State Party to report on national resources allocated to meeting its treaty obligations. With the exception of endorsement from the CMC, the Committee of the Whole did not devote any discussion to the idea, and it was included in the final Convention.[65] Paragraph 1(m) reads: 'The amount of national resources, including financial, material or in kind, allocated to the implementation of Articles 3, 4 and 5 of this Convention.'[66] Addressing a subject raised on a number of occasions during the Oslo Process, Belgium renewed the call for reports on international cooperation and assistance. Again this proposal succeeded without any further discussion other than support expressed by the CMC.[67] Paragraph 1(n) reads: 'The amounts, types and destinations of international cooperation and assistance provided under Article 6 of this Convention.'[68] Both of these additions set legal precedent for future weapons treaties.

---

[61] Statement of Australia, 'Summary Record of Third Session of the Committee of the Whole', Diplomatic Conference doc. CCM/CW/SR/3, 18 June 2008, p. 3; and Statements of Fiji, Italy, Portugal, Senegal, and the CMC, 'Summary Record of First Session of the Committee of the Whole', Diplomatic Conference doc. CCM/CW/SR/1, 18 June 2008, pp. 7–8.

[62] For full text of the Wellington Compendium, see Annex 6 to this Commentary.

[63] 'Proposal by Australia, Denmark, France, Germany, Italy, Sweden, Switzerland and UK for the Amendment of Article 7', Diplomatic Conference doc. CCM/40, 19 May 2008; and 'Article 7: International Cooperation and Assistance', Wellington Compendium, pp. 26–28.

[64] Article 7, paragraph 1(d), *1997 Anti-Personnel Mine Ban Convention*; and Article 3, paragraph 8.

[65] Statements of Belgium and the CMC, 'Summary Record of Third Session of the Committee of the Whole', *op. cit.*, pp. 2–3.   [66] Article 7, paragraph 1(m).

[67] Statements of Belgium and the CMC, 'Summary Record of Third Session of the Committee of the Whole', *op. cit.*, pp. 2–3.   [68] Article 7, paragraph 1(n).

7.21 In response to debate over the controversial definition of cluster munitions in Article 2, paragraph 2(c), Austria called for an Article 7 reporting requirement on 'new weapons and their effects'. States were trying to determine what weapons with submunitions the definition would exclude on the basis that they did not cause the same humanitarian harm as those that would be prohibited by the Convention. Malta seconded Austria's proposal, saying it would 'safeguard the limits of the exemptions'.[69] This initiative on mandating reports on weapons not banned by the treaty ultimately failed.

7.22 The most significant amendments to existing paragraphs were to those governing clearance and victim assistance. In paragraph 1(i), drafters rewrote a requirement to report on the 'types and quantities of all cluster munition remnants cleared and destroyed' to parallel more closely the reporting requirements on the 'status and progress of programmes' for decommissioning of production facilities and stockpile destruction. The final version reads, with changes noted in italics:

The status and progress of programmes for the clearance and destruction of all types and quantities of cluster munition remnants cleared and destroyed in accordance with Article 4 of this Convention, to include the size and location of the cluster munition contaminated area cleared and a breakdown of the quantity of each type of cluster munition remnant cleared and destroyed.[70]

The change, made at the CMC's suggestion, obliges each State Party to provide more information than previously proposed.[71]

7.23 The paragraph on victim assistance reporting adopted a similar 'status and progress of programmes' format and also inserted additional language from Article 5. The final version demands transparency with regard to the character of the assistance ('age- and gender-sensitive') as well as its type ('medical care, rehabilitation and psychological support' and 'social and economic inclusion of cluster munition victims').[72] The amendments, another suggestion by the CMC, not only make Article 7's provisions more consistent with the Convention's substantive obligations but also clarify that each State

---

[69] Statements of Austria and Malta, 'Summary Record of Eleventh Session of the Committee of the Whole', Diplomatic Conference doc. CCM/CW/SR/11, 18 June 2008, p. 5. For more information on the debate surrounding Article 2, paragraph 2(c), see, *supra,* the commentary on Article 2.

[70] Article 7, paragraph 1(i).

[71] Statement of the CMC, 'Summary Record of Third Session of the Committee of the Whole', *op. cit.*, pp. 2–3.

[72] Article 7, paragraph 1(k). The paragraph also clarified that the 'reliable relevant data' States Parties are required to collect must be 'with respect to cluster munition victims'.

Party must report on the progress of programmes and reinforce the importance of certain kinds of victim assistance.[73]

7.24 Several smaller proposals for sharpening Article 7 were implemented with minimal discussion. Four paragraphs that required reports on stockpiles of cluster munitions added the phrase 'including explosive submunitions'.[74] Although arguably unnecessary since the final definition of cluster munition encompasses the term explosive submunitions, the insertions emphasize that point.[75] Paragraph 1(c) on technical characteristics clarified that information on 'cluster munitions produced' referred to those weapons produced before entry into force because, of course, the Convention bans production after its entry into force for each State Party.[76] References to reports on the status of disarmament programmes in paragraphs 1(d) and (e) were expanded to include the progress of these programmes.[77] Adopting a CMC suggestion, paragraph 1(g) mandated transparency not only on newly discovered stockpiles of cluster munitions but also on plans for their destruction.[78] Finally, in two places, a new obligation to report on the size of cluster munition contaminated areas supplemented the requirement to report on their locations.[79]

7.25 Article 7 of the Convention on Cluster Munitions is narrower than the provisions on transparency proposed in the Draft Cluster Munitions Convention in two ways. First, the paragraph explicitly requiring reporting on foreign stockpiles was not included in the Convention as adopted. Although not formally discussed in Dublin, as mentioned above, some States had objected to the provision in Wellington. The reporting obligation, however, extends to foreign stockpiles under the reporting State's jurisdiction and control as

---

[73] Statement of the CMC, 'Summary Record of Third Session of the Committee of the Whole', *op. cit.*, pp. 2–3.

[74] Article 7, paragraph 1(b), (e), (f), and (g). Belgium, supported by the CMC, proposed these amendments. Statements by Belgium and the CMC, 'Summary Record of Third Session of the Committee of the Whole', *op. cit.*, p. 1.

[75] At the last meeting of the Committee of the Whole, the ICRC noted that the Article 7 should be read to require reports on explosive bomblets too. Statement of the ICRC, Sixteenth Session of Committee of the Whole, Diplomatic Conference, 28 May 2008 (Landmine Action notes; copy on file with author). For more information on explosive bomblets, see, *supra*, the commentary on Article 1, paragraph 2, and Article 2, paragraph 13.   [76] Article 7, paragraph 1(c).

[77] Article 7, paragraph 1(d) and (e).

[78] Article 7, paragraph 1(g); and Statement of the CMC, 'Summary Record of Third Session of the Committee of the Whole', *op. cit.*, p. 2.

[79] Article 7, paragraph 1(h) and (i). Belgium, Canada, and the CMC supported this change. Statements by Belgium, Canada, and the CMC, 'Summary Record of Third Session of the Committee of the Whole', *op. cit.*, pp. 1, 3. The same sub-paragraphs—(h) and (i)—inserted the newly defined term cluster munition contaminated area. See also, *supra*, the commentary on Article 2, paragraph 11.

specified in Article 3(1). Second, paragraph 1(b) replaced the reference to 'stockpiled cluster munitions owned or possessed by it, or under its jurisdiction or control' with a cross-reference to Article 3, paragraph 1.[80] This change was noteworthy because the latter provision was amended at the last minute, largely due to a typographical error, to refer to stockpiles under a State Party's 'jurisdiction *and* control', instead of 'jurisdiction *or* control', thus potentially narrowing its coverage.[81]

7.26 In sum, despite these exceptions, for the most part, Article 7 was broadened during the Oslo Process. It built on the *1997 Anti-Personnel Mine Ban Convention*, its main source, while clarifying and expanding on the language of some of its provisions. It also added paragraphs unprecedented in weapons treaties on:

- stockpiles discovered after destruction of known stockpiles,
- victim assistance,
- national points of contact,
- national resources allocated for implementation, and
- international cooperation and assistance.[82]

These transparency requirements should provide valuable information on the progress of implementation of the Convention on Cluster Munitions and have the potential to increase States Parties' compliance with their obligations.

Paragraph 1

Each State Party shall report to the Secretary-General of the United Nations as soon as practicable, and in any event not later than 180 days after the entry into force of this Convention for that State Party, on:

(a) The national implementation measures referred to in Article 9 of this Convention;

(b) The total of all cluster munitions, including explosive submunitions, referred to in paragraph 1 of Article 3 of this Convention, to include a breakdown of their type, quantity and, if possible, lot numbers of each type;

(c) The technical characteristics of each type of cluster munition produced by that State Party prior to entry into force of this Convention for

---

[80] Article 7, paragraph 1(b), Draft Cluster Munitions Convention.

[81] For information on the last-minute change to the text of Article 3, see, *supra*, §3.20 and *esp.* fn. 35.   [82] Article 7, paragraph 1(g) and (k)–(n).

it, to the extent known, and those currently owned or possessed by it, giving, where reasonably possible, such categories of information as may facilitate identification and clearance of cluster munitions; at a minimum, this information shall include the dimensions, fusing, explosive content, metallic content, colour photographs and other information that may facilitate the clearance of cluster munition remnants;

(d) The status and progress of programmes for the conversion or decommissioning of production facilities for cluster munitions;

(e) The status and progress of programmes for the destruction, in accordance with Article 3 of this Convention, of cluster munitions, including explosive submunitions, with details of the methods that will be used in destruction, the location of all destruction sites and the applicable safety and environmental standards to be observed;

(f) The types and quantities of cluster munitions, including explosive submunitions, destroyed in accordance with Article 3 of this Convention, including details of the methods of destruction used, the location of the destruction sites and the applicable safety and environmental standards observed;

(g) Stockpiles of cluster munitions, including explosive submunitions, discovered after reported completion of the programme referred to in sub-paragraph (e) of this paragraph, and plans for their destruction in accordance with Article 3 of this Convention;

(h) To the extent possible, the size and location of all cluster munition contaminated areas under its jurisdiction or control, to include as much detail as possible regarding the type and quantity of each type of cluster munition remnant in each such area and when they were used;

(i) The status and progress of programmes for the clearance and destruction of all types and quantities of cluster munition remnants cleared and destroyed in accordance with Article 4 of this Convention, to include the size and location of the cluster munition contaminated area cleared and a breakdown of the quantity of each type of cluster munition remnant cleared and destroyed;

(j) The measures taken to provide risk reduction education and, in particular, an immediate and effective warning to civilians living in cluster munition contaminated areas under its jurisdiction or control;

(k) The status and progress of implementation of its obligations under Article 5 of this Convention to adequately provide age- and gender-sensitive assistance, including medical care, rehabilitation and psychological support, as well as provide for social and economic inclusion of cluster munition victims and to collect reliable relevant data with respect to cluster munition victims;

(l) The name and contact details of the institutions mandated to provide information and to carry out the measures described in this paragraph;

(m) The amount of national resources, including financial, material or in kind, allocated to the implementation of Articles 3, 4 and 5 of this Convention; and

(n) The amounts, types and destinations of international cooperation and assistance provided under Article 6 of this Convention.

Overview and *chapeau*

7.27   Paragraph 1 is the heart of Article 7 because it lists all of the topics on which a State Party must report.[83] Its *chapeau* lays out the guidelines for submission of an initial report. The *chapeau* takes verbatim from the language of Article 7, paragraph 1 of the *1997 Anti-Personnel Mine Ban Convention*, with which States Parties have largely complied.[84] According to the *Landmine Monitor Report 2009*, the compliance rate for submission of initial reports was 98 per cent.[85] The *chapeau* first appeared in the Lima Discussion Text and remained unchanged throughout the Oslo Process.[86]

7.28   There are three components of the *chapeau*. First, it uses the word 'shall' indicating that the transparency measures it enumerates are mandatory. Second, it sets a deadline for each State Party's initial report, which must be submitted 'as soon as practicable' but 'not later than 180 days after the entry into force of this Convention for that State Party'. While the paragraph lays out a lengthy list of information required, the State Party has about one year after depositing its instrument of ratification or accession to compile the material for the report because entry into force takes some six months and Article 7 allows States Parties a further six months to submit their reports. This schedule should give a State Party ample time to meet its obligation. Finally, the *chapeau* involves the UN in the transparency process, stating that each State Party must submit its report to the Secretary-General.[87] Although States negotiated

---

[83]   There is also the possibility that the Meeting of States Parties of the Convention on Cluster Munitions may agree to adopt or amend a reporting form to facilitate voluntary reporting on certain issues, e.g., foreign stockpiling of cluster munitions on the territory of a State Party but not under the latter's jurisdiction and control. A voluntary reporting form (Form J) was added within the context of the *1997 Anti-Personnel Mine Ban Convention*, for instance, with respect to support for victim assistance and the provision of international cooperation and assistance. Another form was adapted for newly discovered stockpiles. See, *infra*, §7.47.

[84]   Article 7, paragraph 1, *1997 Anti-Personnel Mine Ban Convention*.

[85]   International Campaign to Ban Landmines (ICBL), *Landmine Monitor Report 2009: Toward a Mine Free World* (Ottawa: Mines Action Canada, 2009), p. 22.

[86]   Article 7, paragraph 1, Lima Discussion Text.   [87]   Article 7, paragraph 1.

the Convention on Cluster Munitions outside a UN forum, as had occurred in the case of the *1997 Anti-Personnel Mine Ban Convention*, the organization will be called on to serve many administrative roles in its implementation.[88]

Paragraph 1(a): national implementation measures

7.29 Paragraph 1(a) obliges each State Party to report on the national implementation measures required by Article 9 of the Convention.[89] The paragraph, which has identical language to the *1997 Anti-Personnel Mine Ban Convention*, first appeared in the Lima Discussion Text and remained unchanged throughout the Oslo Process.[90] While Article 9 highlights the requirement to provide for penal sanctions for violations, a State Party must adopt 'all appropriate legal, administrative and other measures to implement this Convention'.[91] For example, in addition to passing its Cluster Munitions and Anti-Personnel Mines Act 2008, Ireland has announced taking other steps toward implementation, such as 'amendment of military doctrine and training, review of Ireland's policy on international peacekeeping and the deployment overseas of the Defence Forces, and integration into Irish Aid programmes of funding for assistance with clearance and destruction of cluster munitions and for their victims'.[92] Consistent with Article 9, States Parties must report on implementation measures for all their obligations—negative and positive—in the Convention.[93]

7.30 Reports on national implementation measures serve several purposes. They allow States Parties to compare models of implementation, which they can adapt for their own national circumstances or reject as inadequate. The reports can also influence interpretation of the Convention by producing a record of State policy and practice.[94] Finally they have the potential to increase compliance with Article 9 by encouraging individual States Parties to pass measures and subjecting those measures to international review.

[88] The UN Secretary-General will, for example, convene the Meeting of States Parties and Review Conferences and serves as the Convention's depository. Articles 11, 12, and 22.

[89] Article 7, paragraph 1(a).

[90] Article 7, paragraph 1(a), *1997 Anti-Personnel Mine Ban Convention*; and Article 7, paragraph 1(a), Lima Discussion Text. [91] Article 9.

[92] Department of Foreign Affairs of Ireland, 'Note on the Measures Taken by Ireland to Implement Article 21 of the Convention on Cluster Munitions', 11 March 2009, p. 1, attached to Letter from Ambassador Dáithí O'Ceallaigh, Permanent Mission of Ireland to the UN in Geneva, to Thomas Nash, Coordinator, CMC, 16 March 2009.

[93] See, *infra*, the commentary on Article 9.

[94] The *1969 Vienna Convention on the Law of Treaties* lists 'subsequent practice in the application of the treaty' as one element to take into account when interpreting a treaty. Article 31, paragraph 3(b), *1969 Vienna Convention on the Law of Treaties*.

Paragraph 1(b): stockpiles of cluster munitions

7.31 Each State Party must report on the total number of cluster munitions it stockpiles, breaking down that information by 'type, quantity and, if possible, lot numbers of each type'.[95] The Lima Discussion Text adopted language on stockpiles from the *1997 Anti-Personnel Mine Ban Convention*,[96] but it was changed and arguably narrowed with no formal discussion during the negotiations in Dublin. As originally worded, the provision applied to 'all stockpiled cluster munitions as defined in Article 2 owned or possessed by it, or under its jurisdiction or control'.[97] The Convention on Cluster Munitions amended the language to 'all cluster munitions, including explosive submunitions, referred to in paragraph 1 of Article 3'.[98] By defining the category of weapons by reference to Article 3, paragraph 1, the Convention limits required reporting to 'cluster munitions under [a State Party's] jurisdiction and control'.[99] The change could be significant because, as discussed above, the Convention removed a separate paragraph explicitly requiring reports on foreign stockpiles in its final version.[100] According to the text as adopted, State Parties have an obligation to report on foreign stockpiles that are considered to be under their 'jurisdiction *and* control', as opposed to stockpiles that are under 'jurisdiction *or* control'.

7.32 The information required by paragraph 1(b) establishes what stockpiles of cluster munitions a new State Party has when it joins the treaty and thus what weapons it needs to destroy. Other States and organizations can use this baseline to monitor a State Party's progress of destruction and encourage it to meet its obligation to destroy all stockpiles as soon as possible. The paragraph has the added benefit of providing information for research on past proliferation of cluster munitions.

Paragraph 1(c): technical characteristics

7.33 The Convention on Cluster Munitions requires each State Party to provide information on the technical characteristics of cluster munitions that it previously produced and those that it currently stockpiles.[101] Like the

---

[95] Article 7, paragraph 1(b).

[96] *Cp.* Article 7, paragraph 1(b), *1997 Anti-Personnel Mine Ban Convention*; and Article 7, paragraph 1(b), Lima Discussion Text.   [97] Article 7, paragraph 1(b), Lima Discussion Text.

[98] Article 7, paragraph 1(b).

[99] Article 3, paragraph 1. See also, *supra*, the commentary on Article 3, paragraph 1, especially the ambit of the phrase 'jurisdiction and control' in §§3.22 *et seq.*

[100] The phrase 'including explosive submunitions' was also added in Article 7, paragraph 1(b) after 'all cluster munitions' during the Diplomatic Conference.

[101] Article 7, paragraph 1(c).

previous two paragraphs, this one originally appeared in the Lima Discussion Text, which merely adapted to cluster munitions the wording of the *1997 Anti-Personnel Mine Ban Convention*'s corresponding provision.[102] There was no public discussion of this provision, and the only amendment to it occurred during the Diplomatic Conference. After the word 'produced', paragraph 1(c) added 'by that State Party prior to entry into force of this Convention for it'.[103] The change does not significantly alter the provision's meaning. Instead it clarifies that the paragraph refers not to current production—which would make no sense since the Convention prohibits all production—but to past production.

7.34 In addition to explaining to what cluster munitions it applies, paragraph 1(c) provides a detailed list of what technical characteristics a State Party must report. It states that 'at a minimum, this information shall include the dimensions, fusing, explosive content, metallic content, colour photographs and other information that may facilitate the clearance of cluster munition remnants'. The paragraph specifies that it intends the information to help with the 'identification and clearance of cluster munitions', and the provision of each type of technical characteristic advances that goal.[104] Information on appearance, such as dimensions and colour photographs, will help people recognize cluster munitions in stockpiles or their remnants on the ground. Details about fuzing and explosive content are essential to assist the safe destruction of cluster munitions and their remnants. An awareness of the metallic content will help deminers determine what technology they need to locate cluster munition remnants, particularly those that have penetrated the surface of the ground. Details about weight are also a relevant technical characteristic, as weight is one of the criteria defining cluster munitions in Article 2.[105]

7.35 Despite its specificity, the paragraph qualifies the reporting requirement with two phrases: 'to the extent known' and 'where reasonably possible'.[106] The former phrase may have been necessary because a State Party will not always have detailed information about weapons produced years or decades ago. The latter phrase, which applies to current stockpiles, seems unnecessary in some circumstances because States often have access to details about their arsenals. For States engaged in an armed conflict or which have recently emerged from one, however, providing such detail may be difficult. Thus the

---

[102] Article 7, paragraph 1(h), *1997 Anti-Personnel Mine Ban Convention*; and Article 7, paragraph 1(g), Lima Discussion Text.   [103] Article 7, paragraph 1(c).
[104] *Ibid.*   [105] See Article 2, paragraph 2.
[106] Article 7, paragraph 1(c).

phrase 'where reasonably possible' may reflect a real-world situation rather than represent a loophole.

7.36 Paragraph 1(c) serves primarily an information-sharing function. It has the potential to help States to identify weapons found in their stockpiles and affected States to clear cluster munitions safely and effectively as the Convention on Cluster Munitions obliges them to do. Indirectly it enhances reports under paragraph 1(b) by providing more details about cluster munition stockpiles.

Paragraph 1(d): programmes for conversion or decommissioning of production facilities

7.37 Paragraph 1(d) requires each State Party to report on 'the status and progress of programmes for the conversion of decommissioning of production facilities for cluster munitions'.[107] It first appeared in the Lima Discussion Text, adapted almost verbatim from the *1997 Anti-Personnel Mine Ban Convention*.[108] As noted above,[109] there were calls for its deletion but in the Convention as adopted the paragraph was maintained and in fact broadened. The wording was changed from 'status' to 'status and progress', which suggests that a State Party has to demonstrate its programmes are moving forward.[110]

7.38 The concern with production facilities stems from Article 1, paragraph 1(b)'s prohibition on production.[111] The Convention on Cluster Munitions does not elaborate on that prohibition, nor does it explicitly establish an obligation to convert or decommission existing facilities. The existence of paragraph 1(d) of Article 7, however, implies that States Parties are required to convert or decommission. Paragraph 1(d) does not specify whether its reporting requirement applies to private as well as government production facilities, but as evidenced by the discussion at the Wellington Conference, States have interpreted the term facilities as encompassing both.[112] The paragraph also does not clarify whether, to be covered, a facility must produce whole cluster munitions or can produce their components. Given the intent behind the paragraph—to end the production of cluster munitions, it seems

---

[107] Article 7, paragraph 1(d).

[108] Article 7, paragraph 1(e), *1997 Anti-Personnel Mine Ban Convention*; and Article 7, paragraph 1(d), Lima Discussion Text.   [109] See, *supra*, §7.16.

[110] Article 7, paragraph 1(f), Draft Cluster Munitions Convention; and Article 7, paragraph 1(d).

[111] Article 1, paragraph 1(b). According to this provision: 'Each State Party undertakes never under any circumstances to:...produce...cluster munitions.'

[112] See Statements at the Wellington Conference, 21 February 2008 (Landmine Action notes; copy on file with author).

that programmes should be designed to shut down or convert the production even of components destined for cluster munitions.

7.39 Paragraph 1(d)'s reporting requirement promotes fulfilment of the implicit obligation it creates to eliminate production facilities. Reporting can reveal challenges a State Party is facing in achieving full conversion or decommissioning and needs for assistance it may have. Sharing information about programmes also presents opportunities for States Parties to learn implementation strategies from each other. Finally, by mandating that a State Party has transparent programmes and report on their progress, the paragraph encourages it to meet its obligations and allows outside monitoring of compliance.

Paragraph 1(e): programmes for stockpile destruction

7.40 Following the format of the previous paragraph, paragraph 1(e) requires reports on the 'status and progress' of stockpile destruction programmes.[113] The original version in the Lima Discussion Text borrowed the principle from Article 7, paragraph 1(f) of the *1997 Anti-Personnel Mine Ban Convention*, but only took that sub-paragraph's language on stockpile destruction, excising references in this provision to clearance programmes.[114] There was little discussion of and only minor wording amendments to the paragraph through most of the Oslo Process. At the Diplomatic Conference, 'status' was changed to 'status and progress' and 'including explosive submunitions' was inserted after cluster munitions.[115]

7.41 While other paragraphs in Article 7, paragraph 1 deal with stockpiles and their destruction, this one focuses on reports related to programmes. It implicitly requires each State Party to have a plan for destruction, an obligation not articulated elsewhere in the Convention. As in paragraph 1(d), the focus on progress puts pressure on a State Party not only to design a programme but also to implement it.[116] The paragraph also specifies that each State Party must report on 'details of the methods that will be used in destruction, the location of all destruction sites and the applicable safety and environmental standards to be observed'.[117] Compelling transparency on such details presses each State Party to develop a thorough plan and to pay attention to the care with which it is implemented.

---

[113] Article 7, paragraph 1(e).

[114] Article 7, paragraph 1(f), *1997 Anti-Personnel Mine Ban Convention*; and Article 7, paragraph 1(e), Lima Discussion Text.   [115] Article 7, paragraph 1(e).

[116] See, *supra*, the commentary on Article 7, paragraph 1(d) in §7.37.

[117] Article 7, paragraph 1(e).

7.42 As it has a similar structure to Article 7, paragraph 1(d), the reporting requirement on stockpile destruction programmes serves similar ends to those discussed in the commentary on decommissioning programmes.[118] It exposes challenges and needs. It provides information on model programmes on which other States Parties can draw. Lastly, it promotes implementation by facilitating monitoring.

Paragraph 1(f): stockpiles destroyed

7.43 Each State Party must provide details about the stockpiled cluster munitions, including explosive submunitions, that it destroys in accordance with Article 3 of the Convention.[119] This paragraph evolved over the course of the Oslo Process. The *1997 Anti-Personnel Mine Ban Convention* also requires information on stockpile destruction, and its provision served as a model for that in the Lima Discussion Text.[120] The Vienna Discussion Text, however, omitted the paragraph. The Draft Cluster Munitions Convention reinserted it, but instead of only requiring information on types and quantities of cluster munitions destroyed, it also required 'details of the methods of destruction used, the location of the destruction sites and the applicable safety and environmental standards observed'.[121] That language came from the paragraph on stockpile destruction programmes.[122] The only change that occurred during the Diplomatic Conference was the addition of the phrase 'including explosive submunitions'.[123]

7.44 Paragraph 1(f) requires reporting on two sets of information related to destruction. First, it calls for data on the types and quantities of cluster munitions destroyed. This requirement corresponds to Article 7, paragraph 1(b), which sets a baseline with respect to existing stockpiles.[124] Second, it calls for information on the process of destruction. As mentioned above, that obligation parallels the one in paragraph 1(e) on destruction programmes.[125]

7.45 Reports on the progress of stockpile destruction, combined with the baseline set in paragraph 1(b), allow for independent tracking of compliance with Article 3. A report that demonstrates little progress can illuminate the

---

[118] See, *supra*, the commentary on Article 7, paragraph 1(d) in §7.39.

[119] Article 7, paragraph 1(f).

[120] Article 7, paragraph 1(f), *1997 Anti-Personnel Mine Ban Convention*; and Article 7, paragraph 1(f), Lima Discussion Text.

[121] Article 7, paragraph 1(h), Draft Cluster Munitions Convention.

[122] Article 7, paragraph 1(g), Draft Cluster Munitions Convention.

[123] Article 7, paragraph 1(f).

[124] Article 7, paragraph 1(b) and (f).   [125] Article 7, paragraph 1(e) and (f).

challenges a State Party faces and reveal its need for assistance or expose a possible lack of political will. This transparency obligation also encourages a State Party to meet its destruction deadline and to do so with care. Finally, as with several previous paragraphs, information sharing on the destruction process provides other States Parties with model programmes they can consider adopting or improving.[126]

Paragraph 1(g): newly discovered stockpiles

7.46 Article 7 obliges each State Party to report not only on existing stockpiles but also on ones discovered after it has destroyed all initially known stockpiles in accordance with Article 3.[127] The Draft Cluster Munitions Convention was the first Oslo Process document to include such a provision.[128] At the CMC's urging, it was amended in the Convention as adopted to encompass information on destruction plans as well as on the stockpiles themselves.[129]

7.47 The inclusion of this reporting requirement sets precedent for future weapons treaties, although the idea behind it came from experience with the *1997 Anti-Personnel Mine Ban Convention*. The principle appeared in the *2004 Nairobi Action Plan*, which was adopted as a five-year plan of action by States Parties at the First Review Conference of the *1997 Anti-Personnel Mine Ban Convention*.[130] In 2008, the Eighth Meeting of States Parties of that treaty adopted a modified model form for Article 7 reports that includes questions about stockpiles discovered and destroyed after the deadline for destruction has passed.[131]

7.48 Article 3 of the Convention on Cluster Munitions does not include a provision explaining how to deal with newly discovered stockpiles, but

---

[126] See, *supra*, the commentary on Article 7, paragraph 1(a), (d), and (e) in §§7.30, 7.39, and 7.42. [127] Article 7, paragraph 1(g); and Article 3.

[128] Article 7, paragraph 1(i), Draft Cluster Munitions Convention.

[129] 'Statement of the CMC, Summary Record of the Third Session of the Committee of the Whole', *op. cit.*, p. 1; and Article 7, paragraph 1(g). The paragraph also added the phrase 'including explosive submunitions' after 'cluster munitions' as the Convention had in paragraphs 1(b), (e), and (f).

[130] Action 15 of the Nairobi Action Plan states:

All States Parties will:... [w]hen **previously unknown stockpiles** are discovered after stockpile destruction deadlines have passed, report such discoveries in accordance with their obligations under Article 7, take advantage of other informal means to share such information and destroy these mines as a matter of urgent priority.

'Ending the Suffering Caused by Anti-Personnel Mines: Nairobi Action Plan 2005–2009', Nairobi Summit on a Mine-Free World, 29 November–3 December 2004, doc. APLC/CONF/2004/5, 9 February 2005, p. 3.

[131] Eighth Meeting of the States Parties of the *1997 Anti-Personnel Mine Ban Convention*, Final Report, doc. APLC/MSP.8/2007/6, 30 January 2008, pp. 7 and 58 (Annex II).

Article 7, paragraph 1(g) implies that there is a duty to destroy them. It does not specify what information about these stockpiles is required, but it would logically mirror the information on known stockpiles required under paragraph 1(b), which includes 'a breakdown of their type, quantity and if, possible, lot numbers of each type'.[132] Rather than refer to 'the status and progress of programmes' as other paragraphs do, it mentions 'plans'. The lack of specificity may lead States Parties to provide less specific information on their progress, but the intent behind the words seems to be the same.

7.49 The details required in paragraph 1(g)'s reporting provide both baseline data and a plan for dealing with the newly discovered stockpiles, parallelling paragraphs 1(b) and (e) on known stockpiles.[133] In addition, transparency on the subject should help to identify associated challenges and needs. This paragraph also helps to close a loophole in Article 3 on stockpile destruction by encouraging States Parties to take action on discovered stockpiles. It does not establish a timeline for destruction, but the fact that the Convention on Cluster Munitions prohibits all stockpiling suggests that timely destruction is appropriate.[134] The ICBL has urged States Parties to the *1997 Anti-Personnel Mine Ban Convention* to destroy newly discovered stockpiles of anti-personnel mines 'no later than one year after discovery'.[135]

Paragraph 1(h): cluster munition contaminated areas

7.50 The first paragraph on transparency measures for clearance obliges each State Party to report on 'all cluster munition contaminated areas under its jurisdiction or control'.[136] The Convention earlier defines cluster munition contaminated area as 'an area known or suspected to contain cluster munition remnants'.[137] The language of paragraph 1(h) comes from the *1997 Anti-Personnel Mine Ban Convention* and was introduced in the Lima Discussion Text.[138] Most of the amendments to the wording came as the preparatory

---

[132] Article 7, paragraph 1(b).   [133] Article 7, paragraph 1(b), (e), and (g).

[134] See Article 1, paragraph 1(b) banning stockpiling.

[135] According to the *Landmine Monitor Report 2004*, which reviewed landmine policy and practice before the First Review Conference and the Nairobi Action Plan:

> The ICBL has stressed the importance of timely destruction of these newly found mines, no later than one year after discovery, and has urged complete transparency about numbers and types discovered and the destruction process.

ICBL, *Landmine Monitor Report 2004: Toward a Mine-Free World* (New York: Human Rights Watch, 2004), p. 15.

[136] Article 7, paragraph 1(h).   [137] Article 2, paragraph 11.

[138] Article 7, paragraph 1(c), *1997 Anti-Personnel Mine Ban Convention*; and Article 7, paragraph 1(c), Lima Discussion Text.

texts defined more terms. For example, the Lima Discussion Text's 'areas that contain, or are suspected to contain, unexploded ordnance from cluster munitions' became 'areas that contain, or are suspected to contain, cluster munition remnants' in the Vienna Discussion Text and was ultimately shortened to 'cluster munition contaminated areas' in the Convention as adopted.[139] The most substantive change occurred at the Diplomatic Conference in Dublin in response to Belgian and Canadian proposals supported by the CMC: 'location' was changed to 'size and location'.[140]

7.51 Paragraph 1(h) specifies different types of data for which transparency is required. Each State Party must report on cluster munition contaminated areas under its 'jurisdiction or control' because those are the places to which it would have access and of which it would thus have knowledge. It must disclose information related to each area, specifically its size and location.[141] Each State Party is also required to provide 'as much detail as possible' about the contents of each area, including 'the type and quantity of each type of cluster munition remnant in such area and when they were used'. The phrase 'to the extent possible' qualifies the reporting requirement and, because of its vague nature, has the potential to narrow the scope of the provision.[142] Arguably it is difficult for a State to be aware of all contaminated areas within its jurisdiction or control, but the term cluster munition contaminated area already limits the report to 'known or suspected' areas and thus does not hold it responsible for areas that it neither knows about nor suspects.[143]

7.52 Paragraph 1(h) serves a significant humanitarian function. The information reported on is essential for warning civilians of danger zones and types of deadly objects, which is required by Article 4, paragraph 2(e), and implicitly mandated by Article 7, paragraph 1(j).[144] It also facilitates clearance, one of the Convention's major remedial measures and an obligation under Article 4.[145] Clearance professionals need information both on areas and on the type and

[139] Article 7, paragraph 1(c), Lima Discussion Text; Article 7, paragraph 1(e), Vienna Discussion Text; and Article 7, paragraph 1(h).

[140] Article 7, paragraph 1(h). Statements of Belgium, Canada, and the CMC, 'Summary Record of Third Session of the Committee of the Whole', *op. cit.*, pp. 1, 3.

[141] The inclusion of the obligation in the Convention on Cluster Munitions to report on estimated size of contaminated areas is an important lesson from the implementation of the *1997 Anti-Personnel Mine Ban Convention*, which required States Parties to report only on the location of suspected or confirmed mined areas. See, e.g., the mine action overviews in ICBL, *Landmine Monitor Report 2009, op. cit.*; and ICBL, *Landmine Monitor Report 2008: Toward a Mine-Free World* (Ottawa: Mines Action Canada, 2008).   [142] Article 7, paragraph 1(h).

[143] Article 2, paragraph 11.

[144] Article 4, paragraph 2(e); and Article 7, paragraph 1(j).

[145] States Parties must clear cluster munition contaminated areas in their territory within 10 years or apply for an extension. See, *supra*, the commentary on Article 4, paragraph 1.

quantity of cluster munition remnants. It is less clear why the date of use is important, except that it gives clearance professionals information about the age of the remnants and would provide evidence of any alleged use prohibited by the Convention. As with most other paragraphs in Article 7, this one also has the potential to promote compliance. It provides a baseline for how much area needs to be cleared and how many cluster munition remnants must be destroyed against which progress can be measured.

Paragraph 1(i): clearance programmes

7.53 Paragraph 1(i) obliges each State Party to report on the status and progress of its clearance programmes.[146] While the *1997 Anti-Personnel Mine Ban Convention* includes a provision on clearance programmes, its language is significantly different and was not included in the Lima Discussion Text.[147] The Vienna Discussion Text added a paragraph requiring transparency about the types and quantities of cleared cluster munitions, but it did not mention programmes.[148] The paragraph was changed dramatically during the Diplomatic Conference negotiations when it adapted the previous version to the 'status and progress' format of paragraphs 1(d) and (e).[149]

7.54 Much of the commentary above on the similarly formatted paragraphs—particularly 1(d) and (e)—applies here.[150] Paragraph 1(i) relates to Article 4's obligation for affected States to clear contaminated areas within 10 years, yet it adds an implicit obligation, not enumerated in Article 4, to develop a clearance programme. The inclusion of the phrase 'status and progress' suggests that the programme must not only exist but also be progressing. The provision also requires detailed information, including 'the size and location of the cluster munition contaminated area cleared and a breakdown of the quantity of each type of cluster munition remnant cleared and destroyed'.[151]

---

[146] Article 7, paragraph 1(i).

[147] Article 7, paragraph (f), *1997 Anti-Personnel Mine Ban Convention*.

[148] Article 7, paragraph 1(h), Vienna Discussion Text. The version in the Draft Cluster Munitions Convention changed cluster munition to cluster munition remnants and deleted the phrase 'after entry into force of this Convention for that State Party'. The latter phrase was unnecessary because the timeline is clarified in Article 4. Article 7, paragraph 1(j), Draft Cluster Munitions Convention.   [149] Article 7, paragraph 1(i); and see Article 7, paragraphs 1(d) and (e).

[150] See, *supra*, the commentary on Article 7, paragraphs 1(d) and (e).

[151] Article 7, paragraph 1(i). The inclusion of the obligation in the Convention on Cluster Munitions to report on size of contaminated areas cleared is a further important lesson from the implementation of the *1997 Anti-Personnel Mine Ban Convention*. With regard to destruction of mines, that treaty required States Parties to report only on the number and type of anti-personnel mines destroyed by mine clearance operations, which is of limited value in tracking progress in many States Parties. Article 7, paragraph 1(g), *1997 Anti-Personnel Mine Ban Convention*.

7.55 One of the primary purposes of this provision appears to be promoting implementation. It allows for monitoring by requiring the release of information on the progress of clearance. It works in conjunction with paragraph 1(h), which provides baseline data on contaminated areas.[152] If progress is slow, reports can help to identify challenges and needs for assistance. Because its structure was changed to encompass reporting on a State Party's clearance programme, the paragraph also provides information that other States can use when designing their own programmes. Finally, because it includes the size and location of contaminated areas among the details required, it helps to advance the humanitarian aims of the treaty by mandating reporting on which areas have been cleared and thus are safe.

Paragraph 1(j): risk reduction education

7.56 This paragraph obliges each State Party to report on the provision of both risk reduction education and immediate warnings of the dangers of cluster munition contamination.[153] The Lima Discussion Text borrowed language from the *1997 Anti-Personnel Mine Ban Convention* about providing an 'immediate and effective warning',[154] but the provision evolved over the course of the Oslo Process. The Draft Cluster Munitions Convention added a requirement to report on risk reduction education in order to reflect insertion of a new duty to conduct such education in Article 4, paragraph 2(e).[155] It also clarified the audience for the risk reduction education and warnings, changing it from the more general 'population' to 'civilians living in areas under its jurisdiction or control in which cluster munition remnants are located'.[156] The only additional amendment in the final Convention was the replacement of the end of the latter phrase with the newly defined term cluster munition contaminated area.[157]

7.57 This paragraph's reports deal with two kinds of awareness-raising. Risk reduction education measures refer to long-term programmes established to alert civilians to the dangers of cluster munition remnants. 'Immediate and effective' warnings address the pressing need for awareness in the initial

---

[152] See, *supra*, the commentary on Article 7, paragraph 1(h).

[153] Article 7, paragraph 1(j).

[154] Article 7, paragraph 1(i), *1997 Anti-Personnel Mine Ban Convention*; and Article 7, paragraph 1(h), Lima Discussion Text.

[155] Article 4, paragraph 2(e), and Article 7, paragraph 1(k), Draft Cluster Munitions Convention. The *1997 Anti-Personnel Mine Ban Convention* did not include an obligation to provide risk reduction education or an explicit obligation to provide immediate and effective warnings.

[156] Article 7, paragraph 1(k), Draft Cluster Munitions Convention.

[157] Article 7, paragraph 1(j).

aftermath of use of cluster munitions and may be less formal.[158] In both cases, States, clearance professionals, and UN agencies or NGOs can disseminate their message through a variety of media, including posters, leaflets, and television or radio announcements.[159] Education and training are also important but generally involve more complicated, long-term programmes.[160] Rather than addressing the whole population of a State, paragraph 1(j) narrows its focus to civilians who live in the vicinity of contaminated areas because they are the most affected as well as to areas under a State Party's jurisdiction or control because a State Party should bear responsibility for contamination only on its own territory or on territory it controls.[161]

7.58 This reporting requirement advances the Convention's humanitarian goals by encouraging awareness programmes. In particular, it will help reduce civilian casualties by promoting compliance with the obligation to provide risk reduction education in Article 4, paragraph 2(e).[162] Transparency will help to identify challenges and needs for assistance in cases where a State Party fails to live up to its obligation. A sharing of information on awareness measures will give States Parties models to assist them in designing their own programmes.

Paragraph 1(k): victim assistance

7.59 The reporting requirement in this paragraph is part of a groundbreaking package of victim assistance provisions spread throughout the Convention

---

[158] The Technical Annex of *2003 Protocol V* differentiates between warnings and risk education. It defines warnings as 'the punctual provision of cautionary information to the civilian population, intended to minimise risks caused by explosive remnants of war in affected territories.' It states that:

> [r]isk education to the civilian population should consist of risk education programmes to facilitate information exchange between affected communities, government authorities and humanitarian organizations so that affected communities are informed about the threat from explosive remnants of war. Risk education programmes are usually a long term activity.

Technical Annex, paragraph 2, *2003 Protocol V*. The International Mine Action Standards (IMAS) define mine risk education as:

> activities which seek to reduce the risk of injury from mines/Explosive Remnants of War (ERW) by raising awareness and promoting behavioural change; including public information dissemination, education and training, and community mine action liaison.

IMAS 12.20: 'Implementation of Mine Risk Education Programmes and Projects', First Edition, 23 December 2003, p. 1. See also IMAS 12.10: 'Planning for mine risk education programmes and projects', First Edition, 23 December 2003.
[159] IMAS 12.20: 'Implementation of Mine Risk Education Programmes and Projects', *op. cit.*, p. 2. [160] *Ibid.*, p. 3.
[161] Article 7, paragraph 1(j). [162] See Article 4, paragraph 2(e).

on Cluster Munitions.[163] Because it establishes no specific victim assistance duties with respect to victims under a State Party's jurisdiction, the *1997 Anti-Personnel Mine Ban Convention* does not include a comparable paragraph. A version of the provision was inserted in the Vienna Discussion Text as Article 5 on victim assistance started to take shape and to place obligations on affected States.[164] Article 5 listed what types of assistance each affected State Party had to provide to its victims. Negotiations at the Diplomatic Conference and the evolution of Article 5 led to significant changes. Article 7, paragraph 1(k) was reworked to fit the 'status and progress' format discussed above with regard to paragraphs 1(d), (e), and (i), and to reinforce that, under Article 5, assistance must be 'age- and gender-sensitive'.[165] To reflect the language of Article 5, the type of data each State Party must collect was also made more specific by revising it from 'reliable relevant data' to 'reliable relevant data with respect to cluster munition victims'.[166]

7.60 Paragraph 1(k) relates very closely to Article 5. Its wording comes directly from Article 5, paragraph 1, therefore reinforcing that provision as well as requiring reporting on it. In addition to clarifying that the assistance must be 'age- and gender-sensitive', it enumerates types of assistance, including 'medical care, rehabilitation and psychological support, as well as ... social and economic inclusion of cluster munition victims'.[167] The data required under paragraph 1(k) will inform the type of assistance provided, ideally with input from the victims themselves. As discussed above, the reference to 'status and progress' implies that each State Party must not only have a victim assistance programme in place, but that it must move forward with its implementation.[168]

7.61 Victim assistance reporting, like many provisions of Article 7, paragraph 1 serves multiple purposes. It encourages implementation, advances humanitarian aims, and highlights the challenges faced by and needs of affected States Parties.

Paragraph 1(l): national contacts

7.62 Each State Party is required to provide details about institutions responsible for its implementation of the Convention.[169] This provision,

---

[163] See also the preamble; Article 2, paragraph 1; Article 5; and Article 6, paragraph 7.
[164] Article 5, and Article 7, paragraph 1(j), Vienna Discussion Text.
[165] Article 5, paragraph 1; and Article 7, paragraph 1(d), (e), and (i).
[166] Article 5, paragraph 1; and Article 7, paragraph 1(k).
[167] Article 5, paragraph 1; and Article 7, paragraph 1(k).
[168] For a discussion of other similar provisions, see, *supra*, the commentary on Article 7, paragraph 1(d), (e), and (i).   [169] Article 7, paragraph 1(l).

which did not appear in the *1997 Anti-Personnel Mine Ban Convention* or the Lima Discussion Text, was introduced in the Vienna Discussion Text.[170] It was shortened in the Draft Cluster Munitions Convention, bringing it more into line with the other paragraphs of Article 7, paragraph 1.[171] This version appeared in the final Convention. The paragraph requires name and contact details for two types of institutions: those assigned to fulfil the reporting requirements of Article 7, and those responsible for implementing the measures on which States Parties must report.[172] These contact details allow interested parties to follow up on the reports required under Article 7. They know to which institution they should talk if a State Party does not provide the required information to the UN Secretary-General. These parties can also seek further information to supplement the reports submitted in order to learn, for example, about model programmes they might wish to adopt.

Paragraph 1(m): national resources

7.63 This reporting obligation requires each State Party to specify the amount of resources it has dedicated to implementation of three key Articles of the Convention.[173] It has no precedent in the *1997 Anti-Personnel Mine Ban Convention* and was added only during final negotiations at the Diplomatic Conference.[174] The paragraph requires information on a range of resources, 'including financial, material or in kind', that are allocated for implementation of Article 3 on stockpile destruction, Article 4 on clearance and risk reduction education, and Article 5 on victim assistance.[175] In other words, it calls for data on the amount of resources set aside for implementing the programmes reported on elsewhere in Article 7. Such reports can show when a State Party does not have enough resources and thus needs international cooperation and assistance to meet its obligations under the Convention. It can also facilitate

---

[170] Article 7, paragraph 1(k), Vienna Discussion Text.
[171] Article 7, paragraph 1(m), Draft Cluster Munitions Convention. The Vienna Discussion Text had framed the provision as an additional piece of information rather than one of a series of topics on which States Parties must report. It stated:

> In addition, each State Party shall provide the name and contact details of the institutions mandated to provide information as described in this Article and of the institutions mandated to carry out the measures described in this Article.

Article 7, paragraph 1(k), Vienna Discussion Text.
[172] Article 7, paragraph 1(l).   [173] Article 7, paragraph 1(m).
[174] Belgium proposed its inclusion and received support from the CMC. Statements of Belgium and the CMC, 'Summary Record of Third Session of the Committee of the Whole', *op. cit.*, pp. 2–3.   [175] Article 7, paragraph 1(m).

monitoring of a State Party's commitment to implementation by illuminating whether it has devoted sufficient resources.

Paragraph 1(n): international cooperation and assistance

7.64 While past treaties, including the *1997 Anti-Personnel Mine Ban Convention*, have required States Parties to provide cooperation and assistance to support implementation efforts, the Convention on Cluster Munitions goes a step further, requiring them to report on it.[176] This paragraph does not appear in the *1997 Anti-Personnel Mine Ban Convention* and was only added during the Diplomatic Conference after repeated calls by States at the conferences in Vienna and Wellington and at the Diplomatic Conference in Dublin itself.[177] It obliges each State Party to provide information on the cooperation and assistance it is giving under Article 6, which mandates help with a range of implementation measures, including stockpile destruction, clearance, and victim assistance.[178] Each State Party must report on three pieces of information: the 'amounts, types and destinations of international cooperation and assistance'.[179] Notably, it does not require the recipient State to be transparent about how it uses this assistance despite proposals that it should do so.[180]

7.65 Paragraph 1(n) helps ensure effective international cooperation and assistance. Paragraph 1(n) is closely linked with 1(m), which mandates reports on national resources allocated for implementation and should reveal which States Parties need assistance and what kind they need.[181] The latter information, combined with paragraph 1(n)'s breakdown by 'amounts, types and destinations', will facilitate provision of the best kind of assistance. In addition, reporting on international cooperation and assistance will allow States Parties

---

[176] Article 7, paragraph 1(n).

[177] See, e.g., Statements at the Vienna Conference, 7 December 2007; and at the Wellington Conference, 21 February 2008 (all from Landmine Action notes; copy on file with author). During the Diplomatic Conference, Belgium called again for inclusion of a requirement to report on international cooperation and assistance and received support from the CMC. Statements by Belgium and the CMC, 'Summary Record of Third Session of the Committee of the Whole', *op. cit.*, pp. 2–3.

[178] See, e.g., Article 6, paragraphs 4, 5, and 7. For further discussion of these obligations, see, *supra*, the commentary on Article 6.   [179] Article 7, paragraph 1(n).

[180] See, e.g., Statement at the Vienna Conference, 7 December 2007; and at the Wellington Conference, 21 February 2008 (all from Landmine Action notes; copy on file with author). Article 6, paragraph 12 requires donor and recipient States to cooperate on implementation, thereby placing a duty on the recipient State, but it does not oblige such a State to provide information on how it uses the assistance.

[181] Paragraph 1(m) literally only requires a State Party to report the amount of resources it has allocated, but the paragraph's enumeration of types of resources implies that the State Party should break down that amount by those categories. Article 7, paragraph 1(m).

to coordinate their support, avoid duplication, and make sure that all needs are covered. Finally, paragraph 1(n) encourages a State Party to donate assistance because others will be monitoring its support.

Paragraph 2

> The information provided in accordance with paragraph 1 of this Article shall be updated by the States Parties annually, covering the previous calendar year, and reported to the Secretary-General of the United Nations not later than 30 April of each year.

7.66 Paragraph 2 requires each State Party to provide annual reports updating the information it provided under paragraph 1.[182] The language for this provision is drawn from the *1997 Anti-Personnel Mine Ban Convention* and was subject only to minor style edits during the Oslo Process.[183] It clarifies that a State Party must not only produce an initial report but also provide a new one on the subjects listed in paragraph 1 every year. It specifies that the reports are due on 30 April following the calendar year being reported on, the same day as laid down by the *1997 Anti-Personnel Mine Ban Convention*. Because the treaties require some overlapping information, this correspondence will ease the burden of reporting.[184] As with paragraph 1, this provision involves the UN by requiring the Secretary-General to be the recipient of all information. Annual reports facilitate monitoring because States Parties and other observers can track a State Party's progress or lack thereof. They in turn help ensure that each State Party meets its obligations and deadlines under the Convention on Cluster Munitions.

Paragraph 3

> The Secretary-General of the United Nations shall transmit all such reports received to the States Parties.

---

[182] Article 7, paragraph 2.

[183] Article 7, paragraph 2, *1997 Anti-Personnel Mine Ban Convention*.

[184] Compliance with this provision of the *1997 Anti-Personnel Mine Ban Convention*, however, has not been high. According to *Landmine Monitor Report 2009*:

> As of the end of August 2009, only 88 States Parties had submitted annual updates for calendar year 2008. A total of 64 states had not submitted updates. This equates to a compliance rate of 58%, a rate that will likely go up somewhat in the coming months. The compliance rate for annual updates has been dropping steadily in recent years.

ICBL, *Landmine Monitor Report 2009, op. cit.*, pp. 22–23.

7.67 The final paragraph of Article 7 requires the UN Secretary-General to transmit all the reports he or she receives to other States Parties.[185] It is identical to Article 7, paragraph 3 of the *1997 Anti-Personnel Mine Ban Convention* and remained unchanged throughout the Oslo Process.[186] It shows that the States Parties to the Convention on Cluster Munitions intend that the Convention's reports reach a broader audience than just the UN.

7.68 The CMC repeatedly called for the paragraph to specify that the reports are to be made public, but the final version does not address the matter.[187] It does not guarantee publication but also does not prohibit it. The UN has posted the Article 7 reports of the *1997 Anti-Personnel Mine Ban Convention* and Article 10 reports on *2003 Protocol V* on the internet, where they are available to the public, so it is likely it will follow the same procedure with respect to the Convention on Cluster Munitions.[188]

7.69 Although paragraph 3 does not establish a timeline for the Secretary-General to pass on the reports he or she receives, their timely transmission will allow States Parties and others to monitor each State Party's compliance both with Article 7 and the Convention as a whole. Assuming the reports become publicly available, civil society can serve as an additional, important watchdog. Transmission also facilitates the exchange of ideas about how best to implement the Convention and allows States Parties to identify where they need to provide international cooperation and assistance.

---

[185] Article 7, paragraph 3.

[186] Article 7, paragraph 3, *1997 Anti-Personnel Mine Ban Convention*.

[187] Statements of the CMC, Lima Conference, 25 May 2007; Vienna Conference, 7 December 2007; and Wellington Conference, 21 February 2008 (all from Landmine Action notes; copy on file with author).

[188] Article 7 reports for the *1997 Anti-Personnel Mine Ban Convention* are available on the disarmament section of the website of the UN Office at Geneva at: <http://www.unog.ch/80256EE600585943/(httpPages)/A5378B203CBE9B8CC12573E7006380FA?OpenDocument>. Article 10 reports for *2003 Protocol V* are also available on the disarmament section of the website of the UN Office at Geneva at: <http://www.unog.ch/80256EE600585943/(httpPages)/B84B4C205835421DC12574230039C42E?OpenDocument> (both accessed 1 March 2010).

Article 8. Facilitation and clarification of compliance

Bonnie Docherty

Article 8—Facilitation and clarification of compliance

1. The States Parties agree to consult and cooperate with each other regarding the implementation of the provisions of this Convention and to work together in a spirit of cooperation to facilitate compliance by States Parties with their obligations under this Convention.

2. If one or more States Parties wish to clarify and seek to resolve questions relating to a matter of compliance with the provisions of this Convention by another State Party, it may submit, through the Secretary-General of the United Nations, a Request for Clarification of that matter to that State Party. Such a request shall be accompanied by all appropriate information. Each State Party shall refrain from unfounded Requests for Clarification, care being taken to avoid abuse. A State Party that receives a Request for Clarification shall provide, through the Secretary-General of the United Nations, within 28 days to the requesting State Party all information that would assist in clarifying the matter.

3. If the requesting State Party does not receive a response through the Secretary-General of the United Nations within that time period, or deems the response to the Request for Clarification to be unsatisfactory, it may submit the matter through the Secretary-General of the United Nations to the next Meeting of States Parties. The Secretary-General of the United Nations shall transmit the submission, accompanied by all appropriate information pertaining to the Request for Clarification, to all States Parties. All such information shall be presented to the requested State Party which shall have the right to respond.

4. Pending the convening of any Meeting of States Parties, any of the States Parties concerned may request the Secretary-General of the United Nations to exercise his or her good offices to facilitate the clarification requested.

5. Where a matter has been submitted to it pursuant to paragraph 3 of this Article, the Meeting of States Parties shall first determine whether to consider that matter further, taking into account all information submitted by the States Parties concerned. If it does so determine, the Meeting of States Parties may suggest to the States Parties concerned ways and means further to clarify or resolve the matter under consideration, including the

initiation of appropriate procedures in conformity with international law. In circumstances where the issue at hand is determined to be due to circumstances beyond the control of the requested State Party, the Meeting of States Parties may recommend appropriate measures, including the use of cooperative measures referred to in Article 6 of this Convention.

6. In addition to the procedures provided for in paragraphs 2 to 5 of this Article, the Meeting of States Parties may decide to adopt such other general procedures or specific mechanisms for clarification of compliance, including facts, and resolution of instances of non-compliance with the provisions of this Convention as it deems appropriate.

Overview of the Article

8.1 Article 8 establishes the compliance mechanism for the Convention on Cluster Munitions. Its title indicates that States intended it both to facilitate compliance and to help clarify issues associated with the implementation of the Convention's provisions. Article 8 is one of three Articles that create systems to ensure States Parties meet the positive and negative obligations laid out elsewhere in the Convention, but it adopts a different approach. Article 9 requires each State Party to take measures to implement the Convention at the national level while Article 8 works at the international level. Article 10 explains how States Parties shall resolve disputes about the 'interpretation or application of this Convention'.[1] Article 8, by contrast, involves a potentially less adversarial process to address interpretive or factual questions.

---

[1] Article 10, paragraph 1.

8.2 The underlying principle of Article 8 is cooperative compliance. This approach, as noted by one expert, 'assumes goodwill on the part of all States Parties and emphasizes resolution of issues in a non-confrontational manner and assistance to help States Parties to meet their obligations rather than criticism for failing to do so'.[2] In Article 8, paragraph 1, States Parties agree to collaborate to facilitate compliance; they must 'consult and cooperate' on implementation and 'work together in a spirit of cooperation'.[3] The next four paragraphs of the Article lay out a formal procedure to which States Parties may turn if they have questions about compliance that they cannot deal with informally. Initially, they may address the problem with the help of the Secretary-General of the United Nations (UN).[4] If that fails to produce a satisfactory result, they have the option to appeal to the Meeting of States Parties, which may offer advice to clarify or resolve the matter.[5] The procedure has certain limitations because it requires neither the Meeting of States Parties to provide recommendations nor the concerned States Parties to accept them. Nevertheless, it is based on accepted legal precedent.

8.3 Article 8 draws heavily on the corresponding compliance provisions of the *1997 Anti-Personnel Mine Ban Convention* but is considerably shorter. While negotiations of the provisions in the 1997 treaty were heated,[6] having that treaty's language to follow made the negotiations of Article 8 generally short and smooth during the Oslo Process on cluster munitions. Article 8 of the Convention on Cluster Munitions took its first four paragraphs virtually verbatim from the *1997 Anti-Personnel Mine Ban Convention*.[7] Paragraph 5 merged two paragraphs from that treaty.[8] Only paragraph 6, which allows States Parties to develop additional compliance mechanisms in the future, is completely new. Article 11 of Protocol V on Explosive Remnants of War of

---

[2] Goose, S. D., 'Goodwill Yields Good Results: Cooperative Compliance and the Mine Ban Treaty,' in Williams, J., Goose, S. D., and Wareham, W. (eds.), *Banning Landmines: Disarmament, Citizen Diplomacy, and Human Security* (US: Rowman and Littlefield, 2008), p. 106.

[3] Article 8, paragraph 1.   [4] Article 8, paragraph 2.

[5] Article 8, paragraphs 3 and 5.

[6] Maslen, S., *Commentaries on Arms Control Treaties, Volume I: The Convention on the Prohibition of the Use, Stockpiling, Production, and Transfer of Anti-Personnel Mines and on their Destruction*, Second Edition, Oxford Commentaries on International Law (Oxford: Oxford University Press, 2005), §§8.1 *et seq*. (Hereinafter, this work is referred to as the *Commentary on the 1997 Anti-Personnel Mine Ban Convention*.)

[7] See Article 8, paragraphs 1–4, Convention on the Prohibition of the Use, Stockpiling, Production and Transfer of Anti-Personnel Mines and on Their Destruction (*1997 Anti-Personnel Mine Ban Convention*).

[8] Article 8, paragraphs 6 and 19, *1997 Anti-Personnel Mine Ban Convention*.

the *Convention on Certain Conventional Weapons*[9] (*2003 Protocol V*) similarly emphasizes cooperation.[10]

8.4 The compliance Article of the Convention on Cluster Munitions differs from that of the *1997 Anti-Personnel Mine Ban Convention* in three ways. First, it removes all references to the fact-finding missions that the Meeting of States Parties of the 1997 treaty may authorize.[11] Second, it does not lay out a decision-making process for any Meeting of States Parties that is asked to consider a compliance issue.[12] Third, it does not explicitly allow States Parties to convene a Special Meeting of States Parties to deal with compliance issues.[13] States Parties to the *1997 Anti-Personnel Mine Ban Convention* have yet to invoke the more formal aspects of Article 8, however, so the Convention on Cluster Munitions is essentially streamlining an unused mechanism.[14] Furthermore, paragraph 6 allows the Meeting of States Parties to 'adopt such other general procedures or specific mechanisms for clarification of compliance . . . and resolution of instances of non-compliance'.[15] Paragraph 6 means the Meeting of States Parties has the freedom to import the mechanisms of the *1997 Anti-Personnel Mine Ban Convention* or to create new ones. This paragraph allows States Parties to broaden and elaborate on the original compliance mechanism should they choose to in the future.

Preparatory discussions

8.5 Compared to the negotiations of Article 8 of the *1997 Anti-Personnel Mine Ban Convention*, negotiations of Article 8 of the Convention on Cluster

---

[9] The formal title of this treaty is the Convention on Prohibitions or Restrictions on the Use of Certain Conventional Weapons Which May Be Deemed to Be Excessively Injurious or to Have Indiscriminate Effects, as amended on 21 December 2001.

[10] Article 11, paragraph 2, Protocol V on Explosive Remnants of War (*2003 Protocol V*).

[11] The *1997 Anti-Personnel Mine Ban Convention* allows the Meeting of States Parties to authorize fact-finding missions to clarify matters of compliance. It lays out a detailed process for such a mission, addressing *inter alia* the appointment of experts, the responsibilities of the State Party being investigated, the final report to the Meeting of States Parties, and the Meeting's response. Article 8, paragraphs 8–18, *1997 Anti-Personnel Mine Ban Convention*.

[12] Article 8, paragraphs 6 and 20, *1997 Anti-Personnel Mine Ban Convention*.

[13] Article 8, paragraph 5, *1997 Anti-Personnel Mine Ban Convention*.

[14] Despite the underlying principle of cooperative compliance, in the view of one commentator some States Parties still seem to feel that it is 'against the aura of good feeling that surrounds the [*1997 Anti-Personnel Mine Ban Convention*]' formally to invoke Article 8. Goose, S. D., 'Goodwill Yields Good Results: Cooperative Compliance and the Mine Ban Treaty,' in *op. cit.*, p. 108 (noting that States Parties have yet to invoke Article 8 of the *1997 Anti-Personnel Mine Ban Convention*).

[15] Article 8, paragraph 6.

Munitions were characterized by limited, generally uncontentious discussions. According to one commentator, 'Article 8 [of the *1997 Anti-Personnel Mine Ban Convention*]...was one of the hardest provisions to agree on as the negotiating position of certain States on the twin issues of verification and compliance were often far apart'.[16] Indeed, that author claimed that the divide 'at times appeared like a chasm'.[17] Some States wanted to follow the strict verification approach used in disarmament law,[18] while others preferred the less rigid model common in international humanitarian law.[19] During the process to create the Convention on Cluster Munitions, States used the compromise reached in the *1997 Anti-Personnel Mine Ban Convention* as a starting point and accepted changes without extensive debate.[20]

---

[16] Maslen, S., *Commentary on the 1997 Anti-Personnel Mine Ban Convention, op. cit.*, §8.1.

[17] *Ibid.* For more information on the negotiations of Article 8 of the *1997 Anti-Personnel Mine Ban Convention*, see, e.g., Goose, S. D., 'Goodwill Yields Good Results: Cooperative Compliance and the Mine Ban Treaty,' in *op. cit.*, pp. 106–108.

[18] While the *1997 Anti-Personnel Mine Ban Convention* borrows some of the principles of its compliance Article from the *1993 Chemical Weapons Convention*, the latter disarmament treaty has a much more detailed verification mechanism. Articles 9 and 12 and Annex on Implementation and Verification, Convention on the Prohibition of the Development, Production, Stockpiling and Use of Chemical Weapons and on their Destruction, 13 January 1993 (*1993 Chemical Weapons Convention*).

[19] The *1949 Geneva Conventions*, e.g., provide few details on the steps to be followed in resolving questions of compliance. A party to a conflict may request an inquiry into alleged violations and must agree on an inquiry procedure with other parties to the conflict. If they cannot reach an agreement, they should pick an 'umpire' to choose a procedure. Finally, '[o]nce the violation has been established, the Parties to the conflict shall put an end to it and shall repress it with the least possible delay'. See, e.g., Article 149, Geneva Convention Relative to the Protection of Civilian Persons in Time of War of August 12, 1949. Article 90 of the *1977 Protocol I* to the *1949 Geneva Conventions* establishes an International Fact-Finding Commission, which has the power, *inter alia*, to investigate grave breaches or serious violations of the Geneva Conventions and the Protocol. Article 90, Protocol Additional the Geneva Conventions of 12 August 1949, and relating to the Protection of Victims of International Armed Conflicts, 8 June 1977 (*1977 Additional Protocol I*). While created under international humanitarian law, the Commission arguably resembles the more formal type of investigative body found in disarmament law. States, however, have never requested an inquiry from the Commission. Garraway, C., 'The International Fact-Finding Commission', *Commonwealth Law Bulletin*, Vol. 34, No. 4 (December 2008), pp. 813, 814.

[20] Goose writes of the compromise,

> The negotiators [of the *1997 Anti-Personnel Mine Ban Convention*] worked to strike a balance that would bring as many countries on board as possible while still providing meaningful measures to gauge and induce compliance. The final language reflects the view that complete verification of prohibitions on antipersonnel mines is an impossible task, and therefore an unachievable regime should not be attempted. A less ambitious regime was accepted because the antipersonnel mine is not like a weapon of mass destruction, where states must be concerned about a sudden, militarily devastating attack.

Goose, S. D., 'Goodwill Yields Good Results: Cooperative Compliance and the Mine Ban Treaty', in *op. cit.*, p. 107.

8.6 While compliance attracted little attention during the Oslo Conference that initiated the process to create a new Convention,[21] the Lima Discussion Text[22] included a separate Article on Facilitation and Clarification of Compliance. Article 8 of the draft text included five paragraphs, the first four of which were drawn verbatim from the *1997 Anti-Personnel Mine Ban Convention*. They laid out:

- an agreement 'to consult and cooperate' regarding implementation of the Convention and 'to work together in a spirit of cooperation to facilitate compliance';
- the process for submitting a Request for Clarification to another State Party;
- the process for forwarding the Request to the next Meeting of States Parties if the requested State Party submits no response or an unsatisfactory one; and
- the option to request the UN Secretary-General to help facilitate clarification of compliance pending the Meeting of States Parties.[23]

8.7 A new fifth paragraph allowed the Meeting of States Parties to 'consider and approve further procedures and mechanisms for determining instances of non-compliance with the provisions of this Convention and on the steps that may be taken in such instances'.[24] The Lima Discussion Text excluded all references to the fact-finding missions described in the *1997 Anti-Personnel Mine Ban Convention*, but paragraph 5 opened the door for States Parties to consider mechanisms such as that one in the future. The Lima Discussion Text's Article 8 also notably excluded the provisions found in the *1997 Anti-Personnel Mine Ban Convention* on the role of the Meeting of States Parties, the option to call for a Special Meeting of States Parties, and the requirements for decision-making.[25]

---

[21] One State cited compliance as an element to include in the future Convention. The CMC highlighted transparency and compliance as two elements it did not hear discussed during the Oslo Conference. Statements at the Oslo Conference on Cluster Munitions, 23 February 2007 (Landmine Action notes; copy on file with author). See, *supra*, §0.30 for details of the Conference.

[22] Chair's discussion text on a legally binding international instrument that will prohibit the use, production, transfer and stockpiling of cluster munitions that cause unacceptable harm to civilians, Lima, 23–25 May 2007. For full text, see Annex 3 to this Commentary.

[23] Article 8, paragraphs 1–4, Lima Discussion Text.

[24] Article 8, paragraph 5, Lima Discussion Text.

[25] *Cp.* Article 8, Lima Discussion Text, with Article 8, paragraphs 5–20, *1997 Anti-Personnel Mine Ban Convention*.

8.8 Reinforcing Article 8, Article 11, paragraph 1(e) in the Lima Discussion Text listed States Parties' Article 8 submissions as one of the matters to be discussed at the annual Meetings of States Parties. The *chapeau* of Article 11 required States Parties to 'meet regularly in order to consider any matter with regard to the application or implementation of this Convention'.[26] It remained unchanged in the Convention on Cluster Munitions except that, beginning with the Vienna Discussion Text,[27] it added the phrase 'and, where necessary, take decisions in respect of any matter'.[28]

8.9 Much of the discussion of Article 8 at the May 2007 Lima Conference[29] centred on a comparison of the Lima Discussion Text and the *1997 Anti-Personnel Mine Ban Convention*. Praising the parts borrowed from the *1997 Anti-Personnel Mine Ban Convention*, speakers supported the emphasis on 'a spirit of cooperation'.[30] Addressing the Lima Discussion Text's omission of any reference to fact-finding missions, the Cluster Munition Coalition (CMC) noted that perhaps it made sense to exclude them because they had never been used.[31] Others were more critical of the Lima Discussion Text. The International Committee of the Red Cross (ICRC) said it was premature to drop the fact-finding mechanism,[32] and one State said the Convention on Cluster Munitions should adopt the whole Article on compliance from the *1997 Anti-Personnel Mine Ban Convention*, specifically the provision allowing a Special Meeting of States Parties to be convened.[33] Another State called for the future Convention to build on the compliance provisions of the *1997 Anti-Personnel Mine Ban Convention* and *2003 Protocol V*.[34] While not objecting to the new paragraph 5, which allowed States Parties to approve additional mechanisms, some criticized

---

[26] Article 11, paragraph 1(e), Lima Discussion Text.

[27] Vienna Discussion Text of 14 November 2007. For full text, see Annex 4 to this Commentary.

[28] Article 11, paragraph 1, Vienna Discussion Text. The Vienna Discussion Text and Draft Cluster Munitions Convention required States Parties to discuss matters related to 'interpretation, application or implementation of this Convention', but the Convention on Cluster Munitions cut the word 'interpretation'. Article 11, paragraph 1, Vienna Discussion Text; and Article 11, paragraph 1, Draft Cluster Munitions Convention. See further, *infra*, the commentary on Article 11.

[29] See, *supra*, §§0.41–0.42 for details of the Conference.

[30] Statements at the Lima Conference, 25 May 2007 (Landmine Action notes; copy on file with author).

[31] Statement of the CMC, Lima Conference, 25 May 2007 (Landmine Action notes; copy on file with author).

[32] Statement of the ICRC, Lima Conference, 25 May 2007 (Landmine Action notes; copy on file with author).

[33] Statement at the Lima Conference, 25 May 2007 (Landmine Action notes; copy on file with author).   [34] *Ibid.*

it as being too vague.[35] Two States and the CMC noted the need to supplement a compliance Article with Article 9 on National Implementation Measures.[36]

8.10 The Vienna Discussion Text left the first four paragraphs of Article 8 virtually the same,[37] but in response to calls for stronger and more specific provisions, it replaced the Lima Discussion Text's paragraph 5 with new paragraphs 5 and 6. The new paragraph 5 drew on Article 8, paragraphs 6 and 19 of the *1997 Anti-Personnel Mine Ban Convention*.[38] It set up a two-step role for the Meeting of States Parties if it received a Request for Clarification. First, the States Parties would have to decide whether to address the matter, and second, they could 'suggest…ways and means further to clarify or resolve the matter under consideration'.[39] Unlike the *1997 Anti-Personnel Mine Ban Convention*, the paragraph did not detail the requirements for decision-making.[40] Article 8, paragraph 6 of the Vienna Discussion Text allowed the Meeting of States Parties to 'decide to adopt such other general procedures for clarification and resolution of instances of non-compliance with the provisions of this Convention as it deems appropriate'.[41] This version differed from the Lima Discussion Text's Article 8, paragraph 5. While that paragraph addressed mechanisms for 'determining instances of non-compliance' and for dealing with them, the corresponding paragraph in the Vienna text focused on 'clarification and resolution' of identified instances.[42]

8.11 Discussion at the December 2007 Vienna Conference[43] focused on ways to monitor compliance. One State emphasized that civil society should play the same monitoring role as it had with the *1997 Anti-Personnel Mine Ban Convention*, if it received the consent of the State concerned.[44] Another called for provisions on fact-finding missions, even if in an abbreviated format, to

---

[35] Statements at the Lima Conference, 25 May 2007 (Landmine Action notes; copy on file with author). [36] *Ibid.*

[37] Article 8, paragraphs 1–4, Vienna Discussion Text. The only small change was that in paragraph 2 'questions relating to compliance' was changed to 'questions relating to a matter of compliance'.

[38] Article 8, paragraph 5, Vienna Discussion Text; and Article 8, paragraphs 6 and 19, *1997 Anti-Personnel Mine Ban Convention*. [39] Article 8, paragraph 5, Vienna Discussion Text.

[40] The *1997 Anti-Personnel Mine Ban Convention* requires States Parties to 'make every effort' to reach a decision by consensus. If they fail, they must decide the first step by a majority of those present and voting and the second step by a two-thirds majority of those present and voting. Article 8, paragraphs 6 and 20, *1997 Anti-Personnel Mine Ban Convention*.

[41] Article 8, paragraph 6, Vienna Discussion Text.

[42] Article 8, paragraph 5, Lima Discussion Text; and Article 8, paragraph 6, Vienna Discussion Text. [43] See, *supra*, §§0.43–0.46 for details of the Conference.

[44] Statement at the Vienna Conference, 7 December 2007 (Landmine Action notes; copy on file with author).

provide a tool for promoting compliance.[45] The CMC reiterated that these provisions were only a 'paper requirement' in the *1997 Anti-Personnel Mine Ban Convention*, but it praised the new paragraph 6 allowing States Parties to adopt additional 'procedures for clarification and resolution' in the future. While supportive of the cooperative compliance approach, with regard to paragraph 5, it urged States to elaborate on 'ways and means' to clarify or resolve a situation that they could recommend to the concerned States Parties.[46]

   8.12 Article 8 did not change between the Vienna Discussion Text and the Draft Cluster Munitions Convention,[47] yet discussions on the Article continued at the February 2008 Wellington Conference.[48] States reiterated the importance of the cooperative approach.[49] One State stressed the need for a partnership and asked that the language be clarified to emphasize the role of all States Parties in promoting compliance.[50] Another State called for provisions articulating a preference for consensus inserted in the text of the future Convention.[51] Similar provisions appear in Article 8, paragraphs 6 and 20, of the *1997 Anti-Personnel Mine Ban Convention*, which require the Meeting of States Parties to 'make every effort' to reach consensus when making decisions about whether to consider a Request for Clarification and what recommendations to make.[52] A third State supported the call for clarification of the decision-making process.[53]

   8.13 Other participants at the Wellington Conference pushed for Article 8 to include further details about the compliance mechanism. One State said the future Convention would be ineffective without a strong compliance mechanism and asked for more elaborate procedures, such as a subsidiary body. At

---

[45] *Ibid.*

[46] Statement of the CMC, Vienna Conference, 7 December 2007 (Landmine Action notes; copy on file with author). The previous day the CMC had also argued that the general obligations of Article 1 should include humanitarian as well as disarmament provisions in order to clarify that compliance applies to both types of provisions.

[47] Draft Cluster Munitions Convention of 21 January 2008. For full text, see Annex 5 to this Commentary.   [48] See, *supra*, §§0.48–0.54 for details of the Conference.

[49] The CMC also said it agreed with the cooperative approach of the *1997 Anti-Personnel Mine Ban Convention* and Draft Cluster Munitions Convention. Statement of the CMC, Wellington Conference, 21 February 2008 (Landmine Action notes; copy on file with author).

[50] Statement at the Wellington Conference, 21 February 2008 (Landmine Action notes; copy on file with author).   [51] *Ibid.*

[52] If the Meeting fails to reach consensus, States Parties will consider a matter if a majority of those present and voting support doing so and will make recommendations to the concerned States Parties if two-thirds of those present and voting are in favour of them. Article 8, paragraphs 6 and 20, *1997 Anti-Personnel Mine Ban Convention*.

[53] Statement at the Wellington Conference, 21 February 2008 (Landmine Action notes; copy on file with author).

the same time, however, it distinguished between compliance and dispute set-tlement; the latter it explained was between two States and looked to the past while the former should be non-adversarial and look to the future.[54] Also seek-ing increased specificity, the CMC said that it would be useful for the future if States discussed then what means they would use to resolve compliance matters brought to their attention. The CMC further encouraged States to consider possible formal and informal procedures that could be adopted under paragraph 6.[55]

8.14 The United Kingdom (UK) made the only formal proposal to amend the Draft Cluster Munitions Convention in the Compendium attached to the Wellington Declaration (the Wellington Compendium) and resubmitted it at the May 2008 Diplomatic Conference in Dublin. It preserved paragraphs 1 to 5 of Article 8 of the Draft Cluster Munitions Convention but sought to delete paragraph 6, which allowed States Parties to develop other compliance mechanisms at a later date. It also proposed that references be added to provisions in the *1997 Anti-Personnel Mine Ban Convention*, including those establishing a decision-making process and allowing States Parties to call a Special Meeting of States Parties to address compliance issues.[56]

Negotiations

8.15 Discussion of Article 8 at the Dublin Diplomatic Conference was lim-ited. The President of the Conference, Dáithí O'Ceallaigh, appointed Xolisa Mabhongo of South Africa as Friend of the President on Compliance,[57] and Mabhongo held the majority of the conversations on Article 8 informally. States had few opportunities to comment on the draft Article in the Committee of the Whole. Argentina expressed the most concern about the draft Article, claiming that the existing language 'over-simplif[ied] procedures' of the *1997 Anti-Personnel Mine Ban Convention*, although it noted that 'verification mis-

---

[54] *Ibid.*

[55] Statement of the CMC, Wellington Conference, 21 February 2008 (Landmine Action notes; copy on file with author).

[56] 'Article 8: Facilitation and Clarification of Compliance', Wellington Compendium, p, 28; and 'Proposal by the United Kingdom for the Amendment of Article 8', Diplomatic Conference doc. CCM/42, 19 May 2008. For full text of the Wellington Compendium, see Annex 6 to this Commentary.

[57] Statement of the President of the Conference, 'Summary Record of Third Session of the Committee of the Whole', Diplomatic Conference doc. CCM/CW/SR/3, 18 June 2008, p. 4.

sions might not occur in practice'.[58] Indonesia supported the Article as drafted but wanted provisions on Special Meetings of States Parties added.[59] These States were echoing the comments of others at previous conferences. In the end, most efforts to amend the text, such as the calls to have a more detailed compliance mechanism, to allow Special Meetings, and to clarify the decision-making process in the text of the Convention, failed.

8.16 The Convention on Cluster Munitions as adopted differed from the draft Convention submitted to the Wellington Conference in only two notable ways.[60] Paragraph 6 allowed the Meeting of States Parties 'to adopt such other general procedures *or specific mechanisms* for clarification of compliance, *including facts*'.[61] Although not discussed in the Committee of the Whole, the first change, the reference to 'specific mechanisms', presumably allows the Meeting of States Parties to develop mechanisms designed for particular situations. The second change, the addition of 'including facts', seems to allow such a Meeting to address factual disputes related to compliance as well as differences of opinions about interpretation of the Convention.

8.17 On the whole, Article 8 grew both sharper and broader over the course of the Oslo Process. The end result had a simpler mechanism for compliance than Article 8 of the *1997 Anti-Personnel Mine Ban Convention* because it cut provisions related to Special Meetings and fact-finding missions. States Parties, however, have formally invoked neither of these compliance provisions (nor any others) in the first 10 years following entry into force of the *1997 Anti-Personnel Mine Ban Convention*,[62] and even the first draft of Article 8 in the Lima Discussion Text did not include them. Between the Lima Discussion Text and the Convention on Cluster Munitions, the mandate of the Meeting of States Parties to address claims of non-compliance became clearer and a paragraph explicitly leaving open the door for States Parties to develop additional compliance mechanisms was refined. While vague, the latter paragraph not only allows for the extension of this Convention's

---

[58] Statement of Argentina, 'Summary Record of Third Session of the Committee of the Whole', *op. cit.*, p. 3. The CMC again noted that 'a reference to fact-finding missions was possible' but that States Parties had not invoked them under the *1997 Anti-Personnel Mine Ban Convention*. Statement of the CMC, 'Summary Record of Third Session of the Committee of the Whole', *op. cit.*, p. 3.

[59] Statement of Indonesia, 'Summary Record of Third Session of the Committee of the Whole', *op. cit.*, p. 3.

[60] A typographical error that had somehow escaped notice through the Oslo Process was also corrected in paragraph 5: the reference to Article 5 on victim assistance in Article 8, paragraph 5 was changed to Article 6 on international cooperation and assistance.

[61] Article 8, paragraph 6 (*emphasis added to indicate changed language*).

[62] Goose, S. D., 'Goodwill Yields Good Results: Cooperative Compliance and the Mine Ban Treaty', in *op. cit.*, p. 108.

compliance provisions, but also sets a precedent for other weapons treaties in the future.

Paragraph 1

> The States Parties agree to consult and cooperate with each other regarding the implementation of the provisions of this Convention and to work together in a spirit of cooperation to facilitate compliance by States Parties with their obligations under this Convention.

8.18 The first paragraph of Article 8 lays out the underlying approach of the whole Article, i.e., cooperative compliance. The paragraph is identical to Article 8, paragraph 1 of the *1997 Anti-Personnel Mine Ban Convention* and follows the principle behind Article 11, paragraph 2 of *2003 Protocol V*.[63] It remained unchanged throughout the Oslo Process, and many participants in the process made statements describing this approach as key to the success of compliance.[64] The paragraph opens, 'The States Parties agree', thereby highlighting from the outset that it creates a system approved by all States Parties. This phrase contrasts with provisions in the rest of the Convention, which frequently open 'Each State Party shall', a phrase that imposes a legal obligation. The paragraph then explains that States Parties must both 'consult', i.e., seek each other's advice and opinion, and 'cooperate', i.e., act collectively for a common purpose.[65] Finally, the provision requires that States Parties 'work together in a spirit of cooperation'.[66] All of this language emphasizes the decision of States Parties to collaborate and distinguishes the Article from Article 10 on the settlement of more adversarial disputes.[67]

---

[63] Article 8, paragraph 1, *1997 Anti-Personnel Mine Ban Convention*; and Article 11, paragraph 2, *2003 Protocol V.* The latter provision states that:

> The High Contracting Parties undertake to consult each other and to co-operate with each other bilaterally, through the Secretary-General of the United Nations or through other appropriate international procedures, to resolve any problems that may arise with regard to the interpretation and application of the provisions of this Protocol.

[64] Statements at the Lima Conference, 25 May 2007; and at the Wellington Conference, 21 February 2008 (all from Landmine Action notes; copy on file with author).

[65] Article 8, paragraph 1. According to the Oxford English Dictionary 'consult with' means 'to take counsel *with*; to seek advice from' and 'cooperate' means 'to work together, act in conjunction (*with* another person or thing, *to* an end or purpose, or *in* a work)' (*emphasis in original*). *Oxford English Dictionary*, Oxford University Press, CD-ROM Version 3.1, 2004.

[66] Article 8, paragraph 1.

[67] One State emphasized the need to distinguish Articles 8 and 10. Statement at the Wellington Conference, 21 February 2008 (Landmine Action notes; copy on file with author).

8.19 Paragraph 1 also explains on which general issues States Parties are required to cooperate. First they must consult and cooperate 'regarding the implementation' of the Convention, in other words how States Parties operationalize the instrument's provisions. States Parties must further work together 'to facilitate compliance' with the Convention.[68] This phrase does more than mandate that they put provisions into practice domestically; it requires that they do so in a way that fulfils their obligations under the Convention. Discussing the parallel paragraph of the *1997 Anti-Personnel Mine Ban Convention*, one commentator argues that that paragraph requires States Parties to pursue compliance on their own before turning to the formal mechanism described below.[69] More generally, paragraph 1 sets a cooperative tone for the rest of Article 8.

Paragraph 2

> If one or more States Parties wish to clarify and seek to resolve questions relating to a matter of compliance with the provisions of this Convention by another State Party, it may submit, through the Secretary-General of the United Nations, a Request for Clarification of that matter to that State Party. Such a request shall be accompanied by all appropriate information. Each State Party shall refrain from unfounded Requests for Clarification, care being taken to avoid abuse. A State Party that receives a Request for Clarification shall provide, through the Secretary-General of the United Nations, within 28 days to the requesting State Party all information that would assist in clarifying the matter.

8.20 Paragraph 2, which is essentially identical to the one in the *1997 Anti-Personnel Mine Ban Convention* and which went virtually unchanged through the Oslo Process,[70] establishes the first step of the formal compliance mechanism of the Convention on Cluster Munitions. In some cases, one or more States Parties may 'wish to clarify and seek to resolve questions relating to a matter of compliance'.[71] A State Party might wish for guidance on a difference in treaty interpretation or a determination of whether another State Party has violated its obligations. While States Parties are likely to turn to

---

[68] Article 8, paragraph 1.

[69] Maslen, S., *Commentary on the 1997 Anti-Personnel Mine Ban Convention, op. cit.*, §8.18.

[70] The only difference is that the *1997 Anti-Personnel Mine Ban Convention* and Lima Discussion Text referred to 'compliance' rather than 'a matter of compliance'. *Cp.* Article 8, paragraph 2, *1997 Anti-Personnel Mine Ban Convention* and Article 8, paragraph 2, Lima Discussion Text, with Article 8, paragraph 2.   [71] Article 8, paragraph 2.

this mechanism only if less formal discussions have failed,[72] the paragraph preserves Article 8, paragraph 1's spirit of cooperation. It provides for the filing of a Request for Clarification rather than an adversarial accusation of non-compliance (although the act of formally requesting clarification would likely be seen as an unfriendly gesture by the requested State Party).

8.21 The lengthy paragraph outlines the procedure a State Party may follow if it wishes clarification regarding another State Party's conduct. The first State Party can submit, through the Secretary-General of the UN, a Request for Clarification, which the Secretary-General in turn will forward to the State Party whose conduct is being questioned. The former must submit 'all appropriate information', which could include such documents as Article 7 reports from the latter, civil society reports of non-compliance, or other sources of knowledge. Once it receives a Request for Clarification, the requested State Party has 28 days to respond and must similarly provide, through the Secretary-General, all relevant information.[73] The Secretary-General serves as an important intermediary in the formal process, which likely only started because informal discussions broke down.

8.22 Paragraph 2 requires each State Party to 'refrain from unfounded Requests for Clarification' thereby encouraging States Parties to bring forward only their most serious concerns.[74] Lack of use rather than abuse of the provision, however, has been the experience of the *1997 Anti-Personnel Mine Ban Convention*. In fact, civil society and some States have on a number of occasions urged States Parties to start invoking this neglected mechanism 'whenever appropriate, and not to only use it in the most dire situations'.[75] While compliance with the *1997 Anti-Personnel Mine Ban Convention* is said to have been 'exemplary', in part because of pressure from civil society monitoring, States Parties have generally approached it in an *ad hoc* way instead of relying on the Article 8 system.[76]

---

[72] Maslen, S., *Commentary on the 1997 Anti-Personnel Mine Ban Convention, op. cit.*, §8.18.

[73] Article 8, paragraph 2. [74] *Ibid.*

[75] Maslen, S., *Commentary on the 1997 Anti-Personnel Mine Ban Convention, op. cit.*, §8.25 (quoting the International Campaign to Ban Landmines (ICBL)). Between 2000 and 2002, Canada and others worked to develop an agreement to operationalize Article 8, but States Parties rejected the creation of even informal compliance measures. Goose, S. D., 'Goodwill Yields Good Results: Cooperative Compliance and the Mine Ban Treaty,' in *op. cit.*, pp. 109–110.

[76] Goose, S. D., 'Goodwill Yields Good Results: Cooperative Compliance and the Mine Ban Treaty,' in *op. cit.*, pp. 108–110, 121. On 1 March 2008, however, three States Parties (Belarus, Greece, and Turkey) failed to meet their stockpile destruction deadlines under the Convention, and as of March 2010, two years later, all three remained in serious violation of it. See ICBL, *Landmine Monitor 2009: Toward a Mine Free World* (Ottawa: Mines Action Canada, 2009), p. 17; and ICBL, 'Anti-Landmine Treaty Working, Lives and Limbs Saved', Press release, 12 November 2009,

Paragraph 3

> If the requesting State Party does not receive a response through the Secretary-General of the United Nations within that time period, or deems the response to the Request for Clarification to be unsatisfactory, it may submit the matter through the Secretary-General of the United Nations to the next Meeting of States Parties. The Secretary-General of the United Nations shall transmit the submission, accompanied by all appropriate information pertaining to the Request for Clarification, to all States Parties. All such information shall be presented to the requested State Party which shall have the right to respond.

8.23 Paragraph 3, again identical to the corresponding provision in the *1997 Anti-Personnel Mine Ban Convention*[77] and also unchanged through the Oslo Process, lays out the next step of the process should the first step fail to produce an adequate response. It applies if the requested State Party produces no response to a Request for Clarification or provides an 'unsatisfactory' one. In that case, the requesting State Party may turn, through the Secretary-General of the UN, to the Meeting of States Parties.[78] According to Article 11 of the Convention on Cluster Munitions, States Parties must convene a Meeting annually until the first Review Conference in order to consider a range of matters, including submissions under Article 8.[79] In preparation for the Meeting, the UN Secretary-General will forward all relevant documents to the States Parties.[80] The paragraph does not specify if the documents will be made public or only distributed to States Parties. Since States Parties may invite representatives of civil society, the ICRC, the UN, and other organizations to their Meetings[81] and the paragraph does not require the materials be kept secret, it is reasonable to argue that these groups should have access to them.[82] The requested State Party retains its right to respond although the paragraph does not provide any details for how it should do so.[83]

<http://www.lm.icbl.org/index.php/LM/Press-Room/Press-Releases/LM09_Press_Release_English> (accessed 1 March 2010).

[77] Article 8, paragraph 3, *1997 Anti-Personnel Mine Ban Convention*.

[78] Article 8, paragraph 3.   [79] Article 11, paragraph 1(e).

[80] Article 8, paragraph 3.   [81] Article 11, paragraph 3.

[82] Article 8, paragraph 2 similarly does not specify if initial Requests for Clarification need be kept confidential.

[83] Article 8, paragraph 3. See also Maslen, S., *Commentary on the 1997 Anti-Personnel Mine Ban Convention, op. cit.*, §8.38.

Paragraph 4

> Pending the convening of any Meeting of States Parties, any of the States
> Parties concerned may request the Secretary-General of the United
> Nations to exercise his or her good offices to facilitate the clarification
> requested.

8.24 Under paragraph 4, concerned States Parties may ask the UN
Secretary-General to intervene in a matter of compliance before the next
Meeting of States Parties. Like the preceding paragraphs, this paragraph is
drawn verbatim from the *1997 Anti-Personnel Mine Ban Convention*[84] and was
not changed during the Oslo Process. Either requesting or requested States
Parties may ask the Secretary-General to 'exercise his or her good offices to
facilitate the clarification requested'.[85] The paragraph is relatively vague and
does not specify what kind of steps the Secretary-General could take to facilitate clarification. Nevertheless, this part of the mechanism exemplifies the
responsibilities placed on the UN to help to implement the Convention on
Cluster Munitions even though States negotiated the instrument in an independent forum outside of that organization.

8.25 While an equivalent provision also appears in the *1997 Anti-Personnel
Mine Ban Convention*, paragraph 4 is particularly important to the Convention
on Cluster Munitions because, unlike its predecessor, the Convention does
not allow for the convening of a Special Meeting of States Parties to address
issues of compliance.[86] During the Oslo Process, some States called for such
a provision to be included, but their proposals failed.[87] Thus an appeal to the
Secretary-General of the UN is the only way to expedite a clarification of
compliance.

---

[84] Article 8, paragraph 4, *1997 Anti-Personnel Mine Ban Convention*.
[85] Article 8, paragraph 4.
[86] In the *1997 Anti-Personnel Mine Ban Convention*, the requesting State Party 'may propose
through the Secretary-General of the United Nations the convening of a Special Meeting of the
States Parties to consider the matter [of compliance]'. The Secretary-General then forwards all
relevant materials to the other States Parties, and if one-third of them favour a Special Meeting,
it will be convened within another 14 days. Article 8, paragraph 5, *1997 Anti-Personnel Mine Ban
Convention*.
[87] See, e.g., Statement at the Lima Conference, 25 May 2007 (Landmine Action notes; copy on file
with author); 'Article 8: Facilitation and Clarification of Compliance', Wellington Compendium,
p. 28; 'Proposal by the United Kingdom for the Amendment of Article 8', Diplomatic Conference
doc. CCM/42, 19 May 2008; and Statement of Indonesia, 'Summary Record of Third Session of
the Committee of the Whole', *op. cit.*, p. 3.

Paragraph 5

Where a matter has been submitted to it pursuant to paragraph 3 of this Article, the Meeting of States Parties shall first determine whether to consider that matter further, taking into account all information submitted by the States Parties concerned. If it does so determine, the Meeting of States Parties may suggest to the States Parties concerned ways and means further to clarify or resolve the matter under consideration, including the initiation of appropriate procedures in conformity with international law. In circumstances where the issue at hand is determined to be due to circumstances beyond the control of the requested State Party, the Meeting of States Parties may recommend appropriate measures, including the use of cooperative measures referred to in Article 6 of this Convention.

8.26 Paragraph 5 lays out the role of the Meeting of States Parties in compliance. It did not appear in the Lima Discussion Text but was added in the Vienna Discussion Text and remained essentially the same in the Convention on Cluster Munitions.[88] It merges key elements of Article 8, paragraphs 6 and 19, of the *1997 Anti-Personnel Mine Ban Convention*, which establish a two-step process for the Meeting of States Parties to follow.[89] According to Article 8 of the Convention on Cluster Munitions, when it receives a submission related to a Request for Clarification, the Meeting must first decide 'whether to consider that matter further'.[90] The paragraph obliges it to take into account all the evidence and to make a specific determination. The Meeting cannot, therefore, just ignore the submission although the provision does not require it to consider the matter further.

8.27 If the Meeting of States Parties decides to proceed, in a second step it 'may suggest to the States Parties concerned [i.e., both requesting and requested States Parties] ways and means further to clarify or resolve the matter'. For example, the Meeting of States Parties can recommend 'the initiation of appropriate procedures in conformity with international law'.[91] One possible international legal procedure could be an appeal to the International Court of Justice for an advisory opinion on a question of treaty interpretation.[92] One

---

[88] Article 8, paragraph 5, Vienna Discussion Text. As mentioned earlier, the only change in paragraph 5 between the Draft Cluster Munitions Convention and the Convention on Cluster Munitions was the correction of a typographical error that changed the reference to Article 5 to a reference to Article 6. *Cp.* Article 8, paragraph 5, Draft Cluster Munitions Convention, with Article 8, paragraph 5.

[89] Article 8, paragraphs 6 and 19, *1997 Anti-Personnel Mine Ban Convention*.

[90] Article 8, paragraph 5.   [91] *Ibid.*

[92] Writing about the corresponding provision of the *1997 Anti-Personnel Mine Ban Convention*, Maslen mentions an International Court of Justice advisory opinion as one potentially appropriate

State and the CMC called for more specific options to be drafted, or at least for discussions to be held that could be reflected in the summary records and that could be referred to later. No such discussions took place.[93] This second step has limited force. The Meeting of States Parties is not obliged to propose ways and means, and even if it does make recommendations, the paragraph does not require concerned States Parties to follow them.

8.28 The paragraph allows for the possibility that a State Party may fail to comply with the Convention 'due to circumstances beyond [its] control'.[94] In such cases, the Meeting of States Parties has the option to 'recommend appropriate measures, including the use of cooperative measures referred to in Article 6 of this Convention'.[95] The reference to international cooperation and assistance highlights that the goal of Article 8 is for States Parties to collaborate to achieve the Convention's ends, not to expose and punish violators.

8.29 While drawing much of its language from the *1997 Anti-Personnel Mine Ban Convention*, Article 8, paragraph 5 of the Convention on Cluster Munitions does not address how the Meeting of States Parties should reach decisions. Paragraphs 6 and 20 of the *1997 Anti-Personnel Mine Ban Convention* require States Parties to 'make every effort' to reach consensus; if they fail, support from a majority of those present and voting is necessary to consider a compliance matter, and support from two-thirds is necessary to offer recommendations on ways and means to clarify and resolve the matter.[96] As noted above, the UK sought to add provisions on decision-making to the Convention on Cluster Munitions but failed.[97]

Paragraph 6

> In addition to the procedures provided for in paragraphs 2 to 5 of this Article, the Meeting of States Parties may decide to adopt such other general procedures or specific mechanisms for clarification of compliance, including facts, and resolution of instances of non-compliance with the provisions of this Convention as it deems appropriate.

procedure. Maslen, S., *Commentary on the 1997 Anti-Personnel Mine Ban Convention, op. cit.*, §8.70.

[93] Statement of the CMC, Vienna Conference, 7 December 2007; and Statements at the Wellington Conference, 21 February 2008 (all from Landmine Action notes; copy on file with author). [94] Article 8, paragraph 5.

[95] *Ibid.* [96] Article 8, paragraphs 6 and 20, *1997 Anti-Personnel Mine Ban Convention*.

[97] 'Article 8: Facilitation and Clarification of Compliance', Wellington Compendium, p, 28; and 'Proposal by the United Kingdom for the Amendment of Article 8', Diplomatic Conference doc. CCM/42, 19 May 2008.

8.30 The innovative final paragraph of Article 8 enables the Meeting of States Parties to develop alternative compliance mechanisms. A related but somewhat different version of the provision appeared in the Lima Discussion Text.[98] The Vienna Discussion Text adopted new language that formed the basis for the paragraph in the Convention on Cluster Munitions, which made only two changes.[99] The final version allows the Meeting of States Parties to adopt 'specific mechanisms for clarification' as well as general procedures and specifies that 'clarification of compliance' can include facts.[100]

8.31 While this paragraph does not establish any obligations, it allows the Meeting of States Parties to create a wide range of new ways to deal with matters of compliance. It can adopt general procedures that would be broadly applicable or specific mechanisms for certain situations. It can address clarifications related to either treaty interpretation or factual disagreements. Finally it can develop alternatives for both 'clarification of compliance' and 'resolution of instances of non-compliance'.[101] Some participants in the Oslo Process wanted Article 8 to be more detailed.[102] While paragraph 6 is itself rather vague, it opens the door to the addition of any type of supplementary mechanism, even the rejected idea of fact-finding missions, at a later date.

---

[98] Article 8, paragraph 5, Lima Discussion Text.
[99] Article 8, paragraph 6, Vienna Discussion Text; and Article 8, paragraph 6.
[100] Article 8, paragraph 6.   [101] *Ibid.*
[102] Statements at the Lima Conference, 25 May 2007; at the Vienna Conference, 7 December 2007; and at the Wellington Conference, 21 February 2008 (all from Landmine Action notes; copy on file with author); and *cf.* also Statements of Argentina and Indonesia, 'Summary Record of Third Session of the Committee of the Whole', *op. cit.*, p. 3.

Article 9. National implementation measures

Lou Maresca[1]

Article 9—National implementation measures

Each State Party shall take all appropriate legal, administrative and other measures to implement this Convention, including the imposition of penal sanctions to prevent and suppress any activity prohibited to a State Party under this Convention undertaken by persons or on territory under its jurisdiction or control.

Overview of the Article

9.1 Article 9 sets out the obligation for each State Party to take action to ensure that the requirements of the Convention are implemented at national level. Such action is clearly necessary if the goals of the Convention are to be achieved. Under the Article, a State Party is required to take all appropriate steps to ensure the implementation of the Convention by its officials, agencies, and armed forces, as well as to ensure its respect by persons or on territory under its jurisdiction or control. This includes the adoption of measures, including penal sanctions, to prevent and suppress acts prohibited by the Convention as well as measures to ensure that the Convention's positive requirements are fulfilled.

---

[1] The sections, Measures to implement this Convention and Key areas of national implementation, were contributed by Gro Nystuen.

9.2 The Article recognizes that the Convention's implementation will necessitate a variety of domestic measures and actions. For example, the imposition of penal sanctions to prevent and suppress prohibited activity is likely to require the amendment of existing penal law or the adoption of new legislation specifically for this purpose. Likewise, a regulatory and administrative framework must be in place to allow activities such as clearance, stockpile destruction, and victim assistance to occur and to ensure they are accomplished to the standards set out in the Convention's provisions. This will likely require the development and/or adoption of a variety of regulations, administrative orders, policies, and programmes. In addition, and in light of the nature of the Convention and its implications for a State's armed forces, the manuals, directives, policies, and training applicable to military personnel may also need adjustment.

Preparatory discussions

9.3 It was agreed early in the Oslo Process that a treaty prohibiting cluster munitions would contain provisions intended to ensure national implementation of the relevant obligations. All relevant previous international law instruments prohibiting or regulating the use of certain weapons included such provisions, although they often varied in scope and substance.[2] There had also been calls in other international fora for domestic action to prevent and suppress the harm caused by cluster munitions, prior to the Oslo Process.[3]

---

[2] In particular, the Convention on the Prohibition of the Use, Stockpiling, Production and Transfer of Anti-personnel Mines and on Their Destruction (*1997 Anti-Personnel Mine Ban Convention*); the Protocol on Prohibitions, or Restrictions on the Use of Mines, Booby-Traps and Other Devices as amended on 3 May 1996 (*1996 Amended Protocol II*) annexed to the Convention on prohibitions or Restrictions on the Use of Certain Conventional Weapons Which May be Deemed to be Excessively Injurious or to Have Indiscriminate Effects (*1980 Convention on Certain Conventional Weapons*); the Convention on the Prohibition of the Development, Production and Stockpiling of Bacteriological (Biological) and Toxin Weapons and on Their Destruction (*1972 Biological Weapons Convention*); and the Convention on the Prohibition of the Development, Production Stockpiling and Use of Chemical Weapons and on Their Destruction (*1993 Chemical Weapons Convention*).

[3] See, e.g., Human Rights Watch, 'Memorandum to CCW Delegates: Essential Elements for Reducing the Civilian Harm of Cluster Munitions, paper prepared for the Convention on Certain Conventional Weapons Group of Governmental Experts on Explosive Remnants of War, November 8–19, 2004'; Draft CCW Protocol on Cluster Munitions (submitted by Germany), UN doc. CCW/GGE/2007/WP.1; and Paper of the Cluster Munitions Coalition on the elements of a new treaty, distributed at Regional Civil Society Forum on Cluster Munitions, 22 May 2007.

9.4 A first version of Article 9 was included in the Lima Discussion Text. This provision was nearly identical to the provision on national implementation found in the *1997 Anti-Personnel Mine Ban Convention*.[4] Like that treaty, the Lima Discussion Text required each State to take all appropriate measures, including the imposition of penal sanctions, to prevent and suppress the occurrence of any prohibited activity.[5]

9.5 The language of the Lima Discussion Text was changed slightly in the Vienna Discussion Text[6] prepared in advance of the December 2007 Vienna Conference on Cluster Munitions. In an effort to clarify its scope, in particular what was meant by 'persons or on territory under its jurisdiction or control', the Vienna Discussion Text amended Article 9 as follows:

Each State Party shall take all appropriate legal, administrative and other measures, including the imposition of penal sanctions, to prevent and suppress any activity prohibited to a State Party under this Convention *undertaken anywhere by natural persons possessing its nationality, or by any natural or legal person anywhere on its territory or in any place under its jurisdiction or control* (Emphasis added.) .

9.6 Following the discussion at the Vienna Conference, however, a decision was made by the core group to return to the original language of the Lima text. Thus, Article 9 of the Draft Cluster Munitions Convention, prepared for the Wellington Conference, closely followed the Lima Discussion Text and, as a result, the *1997 Anti-Personnel Mine Ban Convention*.[7] The explanation for returning to the language of the Lima text was outlined in the explanatory note accompanying the draft convention.

---

[4] The difference was that Article 9 of the Lima Discussion Text began 'Each State shall take...' whereas the text of the *1997 Anti-Personnel Mine Ban Convention* begins 'Each State Party shall take...'

[5] Chair's discussion text on a legally binding international instrument that will prohibit the use, production, transfer and stockpiling of cluster munitions that cause unacceptable harm to civilians, Lima, 23–25 May 2007; see Annex 3 to this Commentary. Article 9 of the Lima Discussion Text provided that:

Each State shall take all appropriate legal, administrative and other measures, including the imposition of penal sanctions, to prevent and suppress any activity prohibited to a State Party under this Convention undertaken by persons or on territory under its jurisdiction or control.

[6] Vienna Discussion Text of 14 November 2007.

[7] Article 9, Draft Convention on Cluster Munitions:

Each State Party shall take all appropriate legal, administrative and other measures, including the imposition of penal sanctions, to prevent and suppress any activity prohibited to a State Party under this Convention undertaken by persons or on territory under its jurisdiction or control.

At the Vienna Conference, several delegations expressed concern regarding potential incompatibilities with existing national legal systems. This concern also related to the scope of jurisdiction based on nationality envisioned in the text. This Article has now been amended to replicate the equivalent provision in the Anti-Personnel Mine Ban Treaty, to clarify that national implementation measures shall be undertaken in accordance with a State Party's existing national legislative framework.[8]

9.7 In addition to these developments, there were calls during the Oslo Process to strengthen and add additional elements to Article 9. Prior to the Vienna Conference, Human Rights Watch proposed that the Vienna Discussion Text include language to encourage States to enact new, comprehensive legislation to implement the Convention domestically, and asked that there be a deadline for the adoption of national implementation measures.[9] The Cluster Munition Coalition (CMC) made similar proposals going into the Wellington Conference.[10]

9.8 No proposals were made to change Article 9 in the Compendium of Proposals attached to the Wellington Declaration. Thus, Article 9 as contained in the Draft Cluster Munitions Convention went forward as the only basis for negotiation at the Dublin Diplomatic Conference.

Negotiations

9.9 Negotiations on Article 9 at the Diplomatic Conference were not particularly contentious. The most significant change to its contents was in response to a proposal submitted by the Philippines to amend Article 9 as follows:

Each State Party shall take all appropriate legal, administrative and other measures **to implement this Convention,** including the imposition of penal sanctions, to prevent

---

[8] Draft Cluster Munitions Convention Explanatory Note, 21 January 2008 , p. 5.

[9] Human Rights Watch, 'Human Rights Watch Observations on the Cluster Munitions Convention discussion text circulated in advance of the Vienna Convention on Cluster Munitions', December 2007, p. 5.

[10] In addition to the two points made by Human Rights Watch, the CMC asked that:

The national measures article should include a paragraph demanding States Parties to take appropriate legal, administrative and other measures to ensure the human rights of cluster munition victims, other war victims and persons with disabilities in line with other national human rights and development frameworks and mechanisms.

CMC, 'Observations by the Cluster Munitions Coalition on the Draft Cluster Munitions Convention, dated 21 January 2008', undated, pp. 10–11.

and suppress any activity prohibited to a State Party under this Convention undertaken by persons or on territory under its jurisdiction or control.[11]

The Presidency text submitted to the Plenary closely followed the Philippines' suggestion and added to it by deleting the comma after 'penal sanctions'.[12] The Presidency text was included in the draft Convention submitted to the Committee of the Whole and was subsequently adopted by the Conference.

Commentary

9.10 The effective implementation of the Convention at national level is of fundamental importance if the instrument is to achieve its goal of ending the death, injury, and suffering caused by cluster munitions. Domestic action to fulfil and ensure compliance with the Convention's obligations is an inherent element of the general principle of international law whereby: 'Every treaty in force is binding upon the parties to it and must be performed by them in good faith.'[13] Article 9 reflects this aspect of *pacta sunt servanda* by specifically requiring each State Party to take all appropriate legal, administrative, and other measures to implement the Convention.

9.11 There are two important features of Article 9. The first is that Article 9 requires each State Party to take all 'appropriate legal, administrative and other *measures to implement*' the full range of the Convention's obligations. This includes not only the Convention's core prohibitions but also its positive requirements. Second, Article 9 requires that States specifically impose *penal sanctions* for activities prohibited to States, carried out by 'persons or on territory under its jurisdiction or control'.[14]

---

[11] 'Proposal by Philippines for the amendment of Article 9', Diplomatic Conference doc. CCM/60, 19 May 2008 (original emphasis).

[12] 'Presidency Text transmitted to the Plenary—Article 9', Diplomatic Conference doc. CCM/PT/8, 22 May 2008.   [13] Article 26, *1969 Vienna Convention on the Law of Treaties*.

[14] This specific requirement to take domestic measures to implement all aspects of the Convention is similar to the approach taken by the *1993 Chemical Weapons Convention*, Article VII, paragraph 1 of which states:

> Each State Party shall, in accordance with its constitutional processes, adopt the necessary measures to implement its obligations under this Convention. In particular, it shall:
>
> (a) Prohibit natural and legal persons anywhere on its territory or in any other place under its jurisdiction as recognized by international law from undertaking any activity prohibited to a State Party under this Convention, including enacting penal legislation with respect to such activity;
>
> (b) Not permit in any place under its control any activity prohibited to a State Party under this Convention; and

9.12 As a result of the changes made at the Diplomatic Conference, the scope of this provision is broader than the corresponding provisions of other notable international treaties on weapons. The relevant provisions of the *1997 Anti-Personnel Mine Ban Convention* and the *1972 Biological Weapons Convention* only specify that a State must take measures to prevent and suppress prohibited activities and do not mention the implementation of positive obligations.[15] Similarly, *1996 Amended Protocol II* also contains an obligation to take 'appropriate measures' to prevent and suppress violations and also includes a specific requirement for the State Party's armed forces to train its personnel and issue military instructions and procedures so as to ensure that its soldiers comply with its provisions.[16] While a requirement to take additional measures to implement fully these instruments would continue to apply under the principle of *pacta sunt servanda*, the explicitly broader approach of the Convention on Cluster Munitions is a useful restatement and reminder of general international law in this area.

9.13 Article 9 entails that the domestic implementation of the Convention will likely require the development and adoption of a variety of measures as indicated by the phrase 'legal, administrative and other measures'. Such measures would include national laws, administrative orders and regulations, departmental policies, civil programmes, and military instructions. The nature and scope of the measures eventually adopted for a particular obligation are, to a large extent, left to the discretion of the State Party. The Convention does, however, specify that the measures taken must include the imposition of penal sanctions to prevent and suppress violations.

9.14 As indicated above, the national measures developed by a State Party will need to target a range of obligations and activities covered by the Convention. These include the Convention's main prohibitions in Article 1[17] as well as measures to implement the Convention's positive obligations, in particular Article 3 (Storage and stockpile destruction); Article 4 (Clearance and destruction of cluster munition remnants and risk reduction education); Article 5 (Victim assistance); Article 6 (International cooperation and assistance); Article 7 (Transparency measures); and Article 21 (Relations with States not party to this Convention).

(c) Extend its penal legislation enacted under subparagraph (a) to any activity prohibited to a State Party under this Convention undertaken anywhere by natural persons, possessing its nationality, in conformity with international law.

[15] See Article 9 of the *1997 Anti-Personnel Mine Ban Convention* and Article 4 of the *1972 Biological Weapons Convention*.   [16] Article 14 (1) and (3), *1996 Amended Protocol II*.
[17] See, *infra*, the commentary on legal, administrative, and other measures in §§9.20–9.23.

The term 'appropriate'

9.15 The requirement that measures to implement the Convention must be 'appropriate' applies to both the necessary legal, administrative, and other measures to ensure the positive implementation of the Convention as well as to the imposition of penal sanctions. This follows from the word 'including', which indicates that penal sanctions are part of the 'appropriate legal administrative and other measures'.

9.16 The term 'appropriate' is not defined in the instrument and there was little discussion of it during the Article's evolution. On its face, the term would appear to give a significant degree of freedom to a State Party to choose the kinds of measures required to implement the Convention's provisions. Such discretion would seem fitting given the different legal and regulatory systems of States and the different types of provisions and obligations contained in the Convention.[18] In some jurisdictions, the provisions of international treaties are given domestic effect as an immediate consequence of the State's ratification of the instrument, whereas in others, States may enact legislation simply stating that the Convention shall apply directly as national law. In other jurisdictions the particular obligations laid down in the Convention will need to be transposed into national legislation in order for those legal and other rules to take effect vis-à-vis natural persons and private and public entities within that State.

9.17 The term 'appropriate' may also be understood as encompassing such measures as are considered 'necessary' for the purpose of giving effect to the Convention for each State Party. Legislative or administrative measures dealing with stockpile destruction would, for example, not be required for States Parties without stockpiles. This would also flow from the principle of *pacta sunt servanda* as well as the general definition of 'appropriate' as 'specially fitted or suitable, proper'.[19] The term 'appropriate' moreover implies that the measures taken by a State Party must be consistent with the objectives of the instrument and allow for the full implementation of the provision in question. As a result, measures which ran counter to the goals of the Convention, which fell short of the standards it sets or which were disproportionate would not be permitted.

9.18 Several human rights treaties also use the term 'appropriate' in provisions on national implementation and highlight these two aspects of the word.

---

[18] *Cf.* also, S. Maslen, *Commentaries on Arms Control Treaties, Volume 1: The Convention on the Prohibition of the Use, Stockpiling, Production, and Transfer of Anti-Personnel Mines and on their Destruction* (Oxford: Oxford University Press, 2005), §§9.15 *et seq.*

[19] *Oxford English Dictionary*, Oxford University Press, CD-ROM Version 3.1, 2004.

The *1989 Convention on the Rights of the Child*, for example, requires that 'States Parties shall undertake all appropriate legislative, administrative, and other measures for the implementation of the rights recognized in the present Convention.'[20] In addition, the *1966 International Covenant on Economic, Social and Cultural Rights* employs similar language obliging States Parties to:

take steps, individually and through international assistance and co-operation, especially economic and technical, to the maximum of its available resources, with a view to achieving progressively the full realization of the rights recognized in the present Covenant by all appropriate means, including particularly the adoption of legislative measures.[21]

9.19 In its general comment on the nature of States Parties' obligations under the Covenant, the Committee on Economic, Social and Cultural Rights highlights the various aspects of the term 'appropriate' as mentioned above. The Committee specifies that: 'by all appropriate means, the Covenant adopts a broad and flexible approach which enables the particularities of the legal and administrative systems of each State, as well as other relevant considerations, to be taken into account'.[22] It also noted that this flexibility coexists with an obligation to use all the means at the disposal of the State to give effect to the rights recognized in the Covenant. Finally, the Committee affirms that:

Although the precise method by which Covenant rights are given effect in national law is a matter for each State party to decide, the means used should be appropriate in the sense of producing results which are consistent with the full discharge of its obligations by the State party.[23]

Legal, administrative, and other measures

9.20 As discussed earlier, the Convention on Cluster Munitions contains a variety of positive and negative obligations that will require implementation

---

[20] Article 4.

[21] Article 2(1), *1966 International Covenant on Economic, Social and Cultural Rights*. The United Nations Convention on the Rights of Persons with Disabilities uses similar language requiring States Parties in Article 4(a): 'To adopt all appropriate legislative, administrative and other measures for the implementation of the rights recognized in the present Convention.' Article 4(b) also requires States Parties: 'To take all appropriate measures, including legislation, to modify or abolish existing laws, regulations, customs and practices that constitute discrimination against persons with disabilities.'

[22] Committee on Economic, Social and Cultural Rights, 'Substantive Issues Arising in the Implementation of the International Covenant on Economic, Social and Cultural Rights, General Comment No. 9, The domestic application of the Covenant', UN doc. E/C.12/1998/24, CESCR, 3 December 1998, paragraph 1.   [23] *Ibid.*, paragraph 5.

at the national level.[24] Executing these requirements will, in many instances, necessitate a mix of domestic laws, regulations, orders, policies, programmes, and other actions. The Convention does not specify the kind of action that a State must take in the implementation of a particular provision but provides, more generally, that legal, administrative, and other measures must be taken.

9.21 The phrase 'legal measures' is not defined in the Convention, but it can be generally understood to encompass national legislation, decrees, and regulations that have the force of law. Most legal systems employ both legislation and regulatory rules to control or govern conduct. In many contexts, regulations may, like legislation, be reviewed and enforced by courts and include penalties for violation.

9.22 The term 'administrative measures', also not defined in the Convention, could be generally understood as orders, procedures, policies, budgets or allocation of funds, or instructions issued by the executive, including ministries, and other public institutions.

9.23 The phrase 'other measures' is not clarified in the Convention nor was it discussed in the negotiations or in the evolution of Article 9. From the context of its use in Article 9, however, it is clear that this is a 'catch all'-provision and encompasses any measures which are neither legal nor administrative in nature, but which are nevertheless necessary to implement the Convention. Yet, it should be recognized that the line between administrative and other measures is not a clear-cut one and specific actions may fall into either category.

Measures to implement this Convention

9.24 The obligations under the Convention must be implemented through 'legal', 'administrative' or 'other' measures. It is thus not a requirement that legislation is adopted for the purpose of implementing the Convention's positive obligations, but States have in some cases used national legislation to do so. Administrative and other measures are generally used to execute obligations that do not require the adoption of specific legislation as well as to 'operationalise' aspects of a national law.

9.25 The national law adopted by Austria, for example, requires that existing stocks of cluster munitions must be reported to the Federal Ministry of Defence and Sports within one month after the law's entry into force and that these stocks must be destroyed within three years.[25] There has also been

---

[24] See, *supra*, §9.14.
[25] Section 4 of the Federal Law on the Prohibition of Cluster Munitions, as amended 7 May 2009, Federal Law Gazette I No. 41/2009 (No.:GP XXIII RV 75 AB 101 p. 17. BR: AB 8094 p. 768).

relevant practice in other treaties on weapons. Such an approach has, for example, also been used to execute provisions of the *1997 Anti-Personnel Mine Ban Convention*. The national laws of France[26] and Spain[27] established deadlines for the destruction of their anti-personnel mine stockpiles. The French law also established a national commission for the elimination of anti-personnel mines and requires that specific information be provided for the preparation of the national reports required by Article 7 of the Convention. In addition to making violations of the *1997 Anti-Personnel Mine Ban Convention* criminal offences under national law, the 2003 Anti-personnel Mine Act of Zambia, created the Zambian Mine Action Centre and established it as the principal body responsible for the clearance of anti-personnel mines and mine action activities within the country.[28] A commentary of the *1997 Anti-Personnel Mine Ban Convention* identifies a number of administrative measures taken by the UK government in its implementation of that instrument.[29]

Key areas of national implementation[30]

9.26 In implementing the prohibitions in *Article 1*, it is not necessarily sufficient to impose penal sanctions for individuals carrying out acts prohibited under the Convention. Also rewriting of military doctrine, and where appropriate; changing military training procedures and rewriting military manuals and policies may be necessary. It may also be necessary to take measures to ensure permanent termination of production or development of cluster munitions.

9.27 *Article 2*, which lays down definitions for the purposes of the Convention, does not in itself necessitate specific measures, but it is clear that these definitions are binding in the sense that a State Party cannot adopt legislation or other measures that go below the standard set in Article 2. On the

---

[26] Article 3, Law No. 98–564 of 8 July 1998 on the elimination of anti-personnel mines (France); Article 3.

[27] Article 3, Law No. 33/1998 of 5 October 1998 on the total prohibition of anti-personnel mines and weapons having a similar effect.

[28] Act No. 16 of 2003, 'Prohibition of Anti-personnel Mines Act, 2003', date of assent, 11 December 2003.

[29] These include: organizing stockpile destruction and/or concluding the relevant contracts; issuing clear commands to all troops on the new responsibilities regarding anti-personnel mines; rewriting military doctrine, where appropriate; changing military training procedures and rewriting military manuals, Maslen, S., *Commentary on the 1997 Anti-Personnel Mine Ban Convention*, *op. cit.*, §9.20.

[30] This section is not intended to be a guide to the content of national legislation, but it identifies some of the key issues that would typically need to be covered in domestic implementation measures.

other hand, States can, if they wish, ban more weapons than those defined as cluster munitions, or they can undertake more comprehensive obligations towards victims than required in the Convention, or carry out destruction or clearing before the deadlines.

9.28 The implementation of the obligations in *Article 3* requires that States Parties with stored or stockpiled cluster munitions must adopt measures that will ensure the separation of cluster munitions from other munitions, as well as for the destruction of cluster munitions. Such 'measures' will typically be plans and policies as well as instructions from the national defence authorities. Other necessary measures will typically be allocation of financial and other resources for this purpose through the adoption of national budgets. Similarly, as national laws prohibiting cluster munitions will often contain exceptions allowing the use and stockpiling of a limited number of cluster munitions for training purposes in accordance with Article 3, a mechanism to authorize and monitor this activity could be developed by administrative action.

9.29 The obligations in *Article 4* to clear contaminated areas will likewise require that States, in which there are such areas, must develop national plans and policies, and allocate financial and other resources, for identifying con-taminated areas, marking such areas, and clearing them in accordance with the provisions in Article 4.

9.30 In *Article 5* on victim assistance, the nature of legal, administrative and other measures are described in more detail; *inter alia* as 'develop, imple-ment and enforce any necessary laws and policies', development of a national plan and budget, taking steps to mobilize resources, and designation of a focal point within the government for implementation of victim assistance. The implication of Article 9 in this context appears to be that in case the measures described in Article 5 itself should prove inadequate to implement the victim assistance obligations as defined in Article 5 (1), also measures other than those listed in Article 5 (2) must be undertaken.

9.31 Under *Article 6*, States Parties 'in a position to do so' must take meas-ures, including technical and financial measures, to cooperate with or assist other States Parties with regard to facilitate implementing the Convention. Such measures may consist of, in addition to technical or financial support, for example bilateral or multilateral agreements on assistance or cooperation with regard to obligations such as stockpile destruction, clearance, or victim assistance.

9.32 States Parties must also take measures with regard to the reporting obligations in *Article 7*. The reporting must cover all of the obligations in the Convention, including the obligations to 'take measures' under Article 9. In practice, the reporting obligations cover the responsibilities of a number of different public organs or ministries within areas such as foreign affairs, defence, development aid, interior affairs including justice and legislation, health and social services, finance, and education. It would therefore seem appropriate to determine a responsible authority for coordination of the reporting obligations under Article 7. In most countries it is probably not necessary to adopt legislation to identify an authority responsible for preparing and filing Article 7 reports.

9.33 Any action to be taken under *Article 8* on facilitation and clarification of compliance would normally be taken by ministries of foreign affairs as part of their ordinary responsibilities. Unlike the corresponding Article 8 in the *1997 Anti-Personnel Mine Ban Convention*, Article 8 in the Convention on Cluster Munitions does not necessitate national legislation providing for privileges and immunities of members of fact-finding missions, as such fact-finding missions were not included in the treaty.

9.34 Article 21, paragraph 1 requires that States Parties take measures to encourage States that are not party to accede to the Convention with the aim of its full universalization. Such measures could be developing national policies for promoting accession to the Convention in bilateral and multilateral fora. Also, such measures could be the funding of national, regional, or international meetings on the Convention aiming at encouraging more States to become party. Moreover, Article 21, paragraph 2 specifies that States Parties shall promote the norms of the Convention and discourage States not party from using cluster munitions. This too requires national policies on taking these matters up with States not party. The responsibility for developing and carrying out routines for notifying States not party, with whom States Parties participate in military cooperation and operations, of its obligations under the Convention on Cluster Munitions, would typically fall to the national defence authorities.

Imposition of penal sanctions

9.35 Article 9 specifically requires that the measures taken to implement the Convention include the imposition of penal sanctions to prevent and suppress violations. As mentioned above, a State has a certain degree of discretion in how it chooses to implement specific provisions. However, establishing penal sanctions, as required by Article 9, will normally necessitate the amendment of existing penal law or the adoption of a new law specifically for this purpose.[31]

---

[31] However, this would not be necessary if a State already has in place national legislation criminalizing the range of actions prohibited by the Convention on Cluster Munitions. The International Committee of the Red Cross (ICRC) has prepared a model law to assist common law States in

9.36 Generally, such legislation will, at a minimum, need to establish the actions prohibited by Article 1 of the Convention as offences and create penalties proportionate to the seriousness of the violation.[32] Specifically, the law will need to prohibit and penalize the use of cluster munitions as well as the direct and indirect development, production, acquisition, stockpiling, retention, and transfer of these weapons.[33] In addition, assisting, encouraging, or inducing any of these acts will also need to be prohibited and subject to penal sanction.[34]

9.37 The Convention on Cluster Munitions does not specify penalties for violations. The primary indicator in this regard is that the penal sanctions instituted by a State Party must prevent and suppress prohibited activity. While the specific penalties foreseen in national law are by and large left to the discretion of the State Party, in order to be effective in preventing and suppressing violations the sanctions adopted must be severe enough to ensure that any existing or continuing activity violating the Convention is ended and deter violations from occurring in the future. States that have adopted penal legislation on cluster munitions have generally treated violations as serious offences. Luxembourg, for example, has established a penalty of five to 10 years in prison and a fine of €25,000 to €1 million for violation of its national law. For serious violation of the main prohibitions, Ireland has instituted a penalty of imprisonment not exceeding 10 years and/or a fine not exceeding €1 million for conviction on indictment.[35] The 2009 Cluster Munitions Prohibition Act of New Zealand outlines a term of imprisonment not exceeding seven years and a fine of up to NZ$500,000.[36] The law also explicitly allows the creation of regulations for the purpose of implementing the Convention and prescribing offences for non-compliance. The penalty for an offence against a regulation is a fine not exceeding NZ$5,000.[37]

developing national legislation to prevent and suppress violations of the Convention (available at: <http://www.icrc.org>). The model law may also be of use for civil law States to ensure that all aspects of the Convention are covered in national measures.

[32] *Cf.* also, *supra*, §9.17.

[33] However, several provisions of the Convention allow exceptions to the instrument's main prohibitions. Domestic legislation and regulations will have to take account of these exceptions as they have implications for the scope of criminal liability. See, e.g., Article 3, paragraph 6.

[34] Generally, States accomplish this by including specific provisions in the legislation under consideration criminalizing such acts, see, e.g., Ireland's Cluster Munitions and Anti-personnel Mine Bill 2008, Part 2, Section 6, paragraph 2. If they are not specifically included in such a law, these acts are often normally covered by a State's existing legislation on aiding and abetting the commission of offences.

[35] The Irish national law also has a lesser penalty for summary conviction of no more than 12 months and/or a fine not exceeding €5,000 on summary conviction.

[36] Cluster Munition Prohibition Act 2009, Section 10(4).   [37] *Ibid.*, Section 19(1).

9.38 In addition to the direct commission of prohibited acts, national penal legislation or other provisions of national criminal law will normally also cover aiding and abetting prohibited conduct. Article 21, paragraphs 3 and 4, however, allows the military personnel and nationals of States Parties to engage in military cooperation and operations with a State that is not a party to the Convention even though that non-party State may use, develop, produce, acquire, stockpile, retain, or transfer cluster munitions.

9.39 Several States Parties to the Convention have included provisions in their national legislation to implement this aspect of Article 21. The 2009 Cluster Munitions Prohibition Act of New Zealand, for example, provides that a member of the New Zealand Armed Forces does not violate the Act 'merely by engaging, in the course of his or her duties, in operations, exercises, or other military activities with the armed forces of a State that is not a party to the Convention and that has the capability to engage in conduct prohibited by Section 10(1)'.[38] The national law adopted by Ireland contains a provision which seeks to exclude criminal responsibility for certain acts linked to a military or UN operation which may be construed as constituting assisting, encouraging, or inducing prohibited activity.[39] Clause 9 of the UK's Cluster Munitions (Prohibitions) Bill provides a defence where the 'person's conduct took place in the course of, or for the purpose of, an international military operation or an international military co-operation activity'. In contrast, the national laws of Austria and Luxembourg, for example, do not include such provisions.

Jurisdiction or control

9.40 The phrase 'persons or on territory under its jurisdiction or control' in Article 9 outlines the scope of the penal measures required by the Convention to prevent and suppress prohibited activity. The concepts of 'jurisdiction' and 'control' have particular meanings under international law, as discussed above.[40]

9.41 In Article 9 the terms 'jurisdiction or control' pertain to *persons* and *territory*. The phrase 'persons *or* on territory under its jurisdiction or control' (emphasis added) has been used in other treaties on weapons. It entails that penal sanctions must apply both to *acts carried out by persons* under a State

---

[38] See Clause 11(6) of the Act. Clause 10(1) establishes the conduct prohibited by the law.
[39] See Section 7(4) of the Cluster Munitions and Anti-personnel Mines Act 2008.
[40] *Cf.*, *supra*, the commentary on Article 3, in §§3.22 *et seq.*

Party's jurisdiction or control and to *acts carried out on territory* under its jurisdiction or control.[41]

9.42 Whereas, for example, the clearing obligations laid down in Article 4 apply to contaminated areas 'under jurisdiction or control', the obligations in Article 9 are limited to 'territory' and 'persons'. A State's territory is normally clearly defined.[42] It would, first and foremost, encompass the geographic area within the borders of the State. It also follows from international law that a State's territory include its territorial waters and airspace and that offences committed on ships and aircrafts on the high seas are also considered to be committed on the territory of the vessel's flag State.[43]

9.43 The reference in Article 9 to 'jurisdiction or control' over *territory* makes the question of *extraterritorial application* (as a result of the scope of 'jurisdiction'—see discussion pertaining to Article 4) less relevant with regard to defining the obligations. Penal sanctions shall, however, according to Article 9, apply to *persons* under a State's jurisdiction or control, which to a certain extent means even when they are not present in the territory of the State. The principle of nationality and domestic legislation normally define the scope of this 'extraterritorial' jurisdiction. While nearly all States recognize jurisdiction based on nationality for offences committed abroad, there are differences in how and in what circumstances States exercise such jurisdiction.[44] The current language of Article 9 is meant to take this into account and allow for the exercise of extraterritorial jurisdiction consistent with national law and practice.

9.44 The reference to 'persons ' that are only under a State's '*control*' is also largely irrelevant when discussing the imposition of penal sanctions. It

---

[41] Thus, Article 9 does not require the imposition of penal sanctions for acts committed by a foreigner abroad, although it does not prevent States from doing so. For the purpose of enforcement jurisdiction, however, there must be a 'jurisdictional link', e.g. if a criminal act is committed by a foreigner abroad, the perpetrator would have to be present on the territory of a State Party in order for the State to exercise criminal jurisdiction over that person. The same would be the case if jurisdiction rested on the fact that a victim of the use of cluster munitions abroad was a national of the enforcing State (the passive personality principle). If a prohibited act was committed by one of its nationals abroad, that State Party would likely have established jurisdiction over an offence applying the nationality principle.. However, some States may in such cases apply the principle of double criminality, requiring that the criminal act was committed on the territory of another State having established the penal provisions envisaged in Article 9 in its national legislation.

[42] See, e.g., Cassese, A., *International Law*, Second Edition (Oxford: Oxford University Press, 2005), pp. 81–83.

[43] See, e.g., Cassese, A., *International Criminal Law* (Oxford: Oxford University Press, 2003), p. 279.

[44] See Shaw, M., *International Law* (Cambridge: Cambridge University Press, 2008), pp. 659–666.

would seem highly unlikely (and inconsistent with rule of law principles) that a State would impose penal sanctions on anyone without having some form of jurisdiction.

9.45 Article 9 does not limit States' right to assume broader jurisdiction with regard to penal legislation. The Article sets out the minimum requirements.[45]

'Persons'

9.46 The Convention does not specify if 'persons' is meant to include not only individuals (i.e. natural persons) but also entities such as corporations and companies (i.e. legal persons). As mentioned above, the Vienna Discussion Text was clearer on this point by using the phrase 'by any natural or legal person'.[46] However, this phrasing was not adopted and it was decided that such issues should be addressed within the domestic legal context. Nevertheless, a number of States have provisions in their legal codes whereby companies, corporations, and other such entities can be held criminally liable for acts prohibited by national law and regulations.[47] The extent to which legal persons as such may be held liable for prohibited conduct will normally depend on the national law within States Parties.

9.47 It is clear that the obligation to impose penal sanctions to prevent and suppress prohibited acts also applies to such *conduct* when committed by a legal person, for example by a company incorporated under the law of that State. The prohibitions on the development, acquisition, production, and transfer of cluster munitions would only be effective if the conduct of legal persons was covered. Although direct application of Article 9 penal

---

[45] Practice in this area can already be seen in the national legislation of a number of States Parties. The national law of New Zealand, e.g., provides that its law 'applies to all acts done or omitted in New Zealand' and to all acts done or omitted outside New Zealand by—(a) a New Zealand citizen; (b) a person who is ordinarily a resident in New Zealand but not the citizen of any State; (c) a member of the armed forces; or (d) a body corporate, or a corporation sole, incorporated in New Zealand, Cluster Munitions Prohibition Act, Section 9 (1) and (2). See also Norwegian Penal Law (of 1902) §12(3). The Cluster Munitions and Anti-personnel Mines Act of Ireland is more limited in this regard as it specifies that it applies to offences committed outside the State only if the act (a) is committed on board an Irish ship; (b) is committed on an aircraft registered in the State; or (c) is committed by a member of the Defence Forces, *cf.* Cluster Munitions and Anti-Personnel Mines Act 2008, Section 6 (3). The national law of Luxembourg makes no reference to extraterritorial application. Specific reference would be required for the law to apply outside the territory of Luxembourg. See Luxembourg Penal Code Article 4.   [46] See, *supra*, §§9.5–9.6.

[47] *Cf.*, e.g., Diskant, E. B., 'Comparative Corporate Criminal Liability: Exploring the Uniquely American Doctrine Through Comparative Criminal Procedure', 118 *Yale L.J.* 126 (2008), available at: <http://www.yalelawjournal.org/the-yale-law-journal/content-pages/comparative-corporate-criminal-liability:-exploring-the-uniquely-american-doctrine-through-comparative-criminal-procedure/> (accessed 12 March 2010).

sanctions to legal persons is a matter for national law, the relevant sanctions could be imposed on natural persons with liability for the act committed by the legal entity. As discussed below, some States have established criminal liability for legal persons, as distinct from the personal criminal liability of natural persons who are responsible for the conduct of that legal person under domestic law. The question of corporate criminal liability was discussed at length in the negotiations on the 1999 Convention for the Suppression of the Financing of Terrorism. As a result, States Parties were given a wide range of options to implement sanctions on legal persons, taking into account the variations in national criminal legislation prevailing at the time.[48]

9.48 Some States had (by March 2010) adopted legislation whereby a company or corporate body can explicitly be guilty of an offence and may be held liable and punished for engaging in prohibited activity.[49] Other States have incorporated penal sanctions for legal persons as a general part of their domestic legislation and thus the prohibitions laid down in the relevant legislation apply automatically to legal as well as natural persons.[50]

9.49 Penal sanctions established by national law will generally apply to a State's military personnel involved in an international military alliance or combined operation.[51] Without prejudice to applicable rules on privileges and immunities, national penal sanctions will also apply to a foreign State's military forces present on the territory of a State Party (visiting forces). This is clearly the case for military personnel conducting operations under the command

---

[48] Article 5 of the Convention reads:

1. Each State Party, in accordance with its domestic legal principles, shall take the necessary measures to enable a legal entity located in its territory or organized under its laws to be held liable when a person responsible for the management or control of that legal entity has, in that capacity, committed an offence set forth in article 2. Such liability may be criminal, civil or administrative.

2. Such liability is incurred without prejudice to the criminal liability of individuals having committed the offences.

3. Each State Party shall ensure, in particular, that legal entities liable in accordance with paragraph 1 above are subject to effective, proportionate and dissuasive criminal, civil or administrative sanctions. Such sanctions may include monetary sanctions.

[49] See e.g., Section 1(3) of Austria's Federal Law on the Prohibition of Cluster Munitions, Federal Law Gazette, No. 12 12/2008. The national laws of Ireland, Luxembourg and New Zealand also have provisions addressing this issue.

[50] E.g., under Section 18(c) of Ireland's 2005 Interpretation Act, '"Person" shall be read as importing a body corporate (whether a corporation aggregate or a corporation sole) and an unincorporated body of persons, as well as an individual.'

[51] See, e.g., Standing Rules of Engagement for US Forces, Chairman of the Joint Chiefs of Staff Instruction, CJCS1.01A, 15 Jan. 2000. p. A-2.

and control of the UN.[52] However, as described in the commentary below on Article 21,[53] a troop-contributing State maintains criminal jurisdiction over its forces abroad, but does not exercise jurisdiction over the function or mission of an international operation within a separate chain of command. It is for the operation, as an international subject, to decide what acts are within the function and mission of the operation and to refer to the sending State the exercise of criminal jurisdiction over potential misconduct.

9.50 Concerns about the potential for criminal liability for the acts of military personnel engaged in operations with States not party to the Convention on Cluster Munitions led to the elaboration of Article 21. As mentioned above, to address this element at the national level, some domestic laws have incorporated provisions limiting the potential for penal liability for certain roles or actions undertaken by their military officials which may raise concern under the Convention.

---

[52] See Secretary-General's Bulletin, Observance by United Nations forces of international humanitarian law, UN doc. ST/SGB/1999/13, Section 2 (Application of national law) provides:

> The present provisions do not constitute an exhaustive list of principles and rules of international humanitarian law binding upon military personnel, and do not prejudice the application thereof, nor do they replace the national laws by which military personnel remain bound throughout the operation.

[53] *Cf., infra*, §§21.61–21.71.

Article 10. Settlement of disputes

Stuart Casey-Maslen

Article 10—Settlement of disputes

1. When a dispute arises between two or more States Parties relating to the interpretation or application of this Convention, the States Parties concerned shall consult together with a view to the expeditious settlement of the dispute by negotiation or by other peaceful means of their choice, including recourse to the Meeting of States Parties and referral to the International Court of Justice in conformity with the Statute of the Court.

2. The Meeting of States Parties may contribute to the settlement of the dispute by whatever means it deems appropriate, including offering its good offices, calling upon the States Parties concerned to start the settlement procedure of their choice and recommending a time-limit for any agreed procedure.

Overview of the Article

10.1 Article 10 establishes the process by which disputes[1] between two or more States Parties regarding the interpretation or application[2] of the

---

[1] A 'dispute' has been defined by the Permanent Court of International Justice as 'a disagreement on a point of law or fact, a conflict of legal views or interests between persons'. *Mavrommatis* case, Permanent Court of International Justice, 1924, Ser. A, No. 2, pp. 11–12. A more recent statement by the International Court of Justice (ICJ) suggested that a dispute 'is a disagreement on a point of law, a conflict of legal views or interests between parties'. Case Concerning East Timor (Portugal *v.* Australia), *ICJ Reports 1995*, pp. 90, 99, cited by Clark, R. S., 'Article 119—Settlement of Disputes', in Triffterer, O. (ed.), *Commentary on the Rome Statute of the International Criminal Court: Observers' Notes, Article by Article* (Baden-Baden: Nomos Verlagsgesellschaft, 1999), pp. 1242–1243.

[2] As has been remarked:

Treaties give rise to numerous disputes about their interpretation or application. Although the two terms are usually mentioned in the same breath, strictly speaking when the meaning is clear the text is applied; when it is not clear, it has to be interpreted.

Convention on Cluster Munitions are to be settled. Although not explicit in the provision, this process would seem to be complementary to the provisions of Article 8, which deals with facilitation and clarification of compliance.[3] If, for example, a State Party that had invoked the provisions of Article 8 against another State Party, and either was not satisfied with the outcome, it would appear possible for Article 10 to be invoked.

10.2 Article 10 seeks the peaceful and expeditious resolution of any such disputes, where possible through consultation and negotiation. A Meeting of States Parties may play an important role in identifying either a resolution of the dispute or the means by which resolution may be reached. The States Parties concerned may also, *inter alia*, seek to refer the dispute to the International Court of Justice (ICJ) for settlement.[4]

Preparatory discussions and negotiations

10.3 Article 10 draws on the corresponding compliance provisions of the *1997 Anti-Personnel Mine Ban Convention*, but makes a number of notable changes. The Lima Discussion text took the first two paragraphs verbatim from the corresponding provision in the *1997 Anti-Personnel Mine Ban Convention*, but deleted entirely the third and final paragraph which referred to the provision on facilitation and clarification of compliance (Article 8 of that Convention):[5]

1. The States Parties shall consult and cooperate with each other to settle any dispute that may arise with regard to the application or the interpretation of this Convention. Each State Party may bring any such dispute before the Meeting of the States Parties.

2. The Meeting of the States Parties may contribute to the settlement of the dispute by whatever means it deems appropriate, including offering its good offices, calling

---

Aust, *Modern Treaty Law and Practice* (Cambridge: Cambridge University Press, 2000), p. 285, citing Lord McNair, *Law of Treaties*, p. 365.

[3] See, *supra*, the commentary on this provision, *esp.* §§8.1, 8.18, and 8.27.

[4] The ICJ was established by the Charter of the United Nations (UN) as the UN's principal judicial organ. The Statute of the ICJ is annexed to the UN Charter, of which it forms an integral part. According to Article 96 of the UN Charter:

1. The General Assembly or the Security Council may request the International Court of Justice to give an advisory opinion on any legal question.

2. Other organs of the United Nations and specialized agencies, which may at any time be so authorized by the General Assembly, may also request advisory opinions of the Court on legal questions arising within the scope of their activities.

[5] 'This Article is without prejudice to the provisions of the Convention on facilitation and clarification of compliance.' Article 10, paragraph 3, *1997 Anti-Personnel Mine Ban Convention*.

upon the States Parties to a dispute to start the settlement procedure of their choice and recommending a time-limit for any agreed procedure.

10.4 During the May 2007 Lima Conference, it was suggested to include a reference to the ICJ. Following the Lima Conference, the draft provision was amended in the Vienna Discussion Text to reflect this and the text of draft Article 10 subsequently remained unchanged through to the adoption of the Convention.[6]

Paragraph 1

When a dispute arises between two or more States Parties relating to the interpretation or application of this Convention, the States Parties concerned shall consult together with a view to the expeditious settlement of the dispute by negotiation or by other peaceful means of their choice, including recourse to the Meeting of States Parties and referral to the International Court of Justice in conformity with the Statute of the Court.

10.5 Paragraph 1 applies to any dispute between two or more States Parties and which relates to the interpretation or application of the Convention. It requires the States Parties concerned to 'consult together' with a view to the 'expeditious settlement of the dispute'. The means to be used must be pacific but a non-exhaustive list of possibilities is laid down.[7] These include, notably, negotiation (presumably directly between the States Parties concerned), 'recourse' to the Meeting of States Parties, and referral to the ICJ 'in conformity with the Statute of the Court'.

10.6 The role of Meetings of States Parties would appear to be formally limited to disputes surrounding the 'application' of the Convention. Article 11 refers specifically to submissions of States Parties under Article 10, but the

---

[6] The Explanatory Notes accompanying the Draft Cluster Munitions Convention of January 2008 state that :

Several States noted at the Vienna Conference that reference of a dispute to the International Court of Justice would require mutual consent of the Parties. This is already reflected in paragraph 1, which refers to other peaceful means 'of their choice', and also says 'in conformity with the Statute of the Court'.

[7] The UN Charter requires parties to 'any dispute, the continuance of which is likely to endanger the maintenance of international peace and security' to seek a pacific settlement by 'negotiation, enquiry, mediation, conciliation, arbitration, judicial settlement, resort to regional agencies or arrangements, or other peaceful means of their own choice'. Article 33, UN Charter.

chapeau of that reference states that:

The States Parties shall meet regularly in order to consider and, where necessary, take decisions in respect of any matter with regard to the application or implementation of this Convention.[8]

Thus, it does not seem that a Meeting of States Parties has a specific mandate to consider, let alone take a decision, regarding the interpretation of any of the Convention's provisions.[9]

10.7 One significant issue of both interpretation and application for the Meeting of States Parties, which may or may not be the subject of a dispute, is the question of whether explosive bomblets are subject to the stockpile destruction requirements of Article 3 of the Convention.[10] Another may be the precise implications for interoperability of paragraphs 3 and 4 of Article 21 on military cooperation and operations between States Parties and States not party to the Convention,[11] including whether a declaration made by a State Party actually constitutes a reservation to the treaty.[12]

Paragraph 2

> The Meeting of States Parties may contribute to the settlement of the dispute by whatever means it deems appropriate, including offering its good offices, calling upon the States Parties concerned to start the settlement procedure of their choice and recommending a time-limit for any agreed procedure,

10.8 Under paragraph 2, the Meeting of States Parties may contribute to the settlement of any dispute 'by whatever means it deems appropriate'. This includes, but is not limited to, offering its 'good offices' and calling upon the States Parties to a dispute 'to start the settlement procedure of their choice and recommending a time-limit for any agreed procedure'. This provision is taken verbatim from the *1997 Anti-Personnel Mine Ban Convention*, which itself drew heavily on the corresponding provision in the *1993 Chemical*

---

[8] Article 11, paragraph 1.

[9] In practice, the Meeting of States Parties will adopt decisions that will, directly or indirectly, interpret the Convention. This has certainly been the experience of similar meetings in the context of the *1997 Anti-Personnel Mine Ban Convention*, which has, e.g., adopted an understanding relating to the 'minimum number absolutely necessary' of anti-personnel mines retained for training in mine detection or clearance under Article 3 of that Convention.

[10] See, *supra*, the commentary on Article 3, *esp.* §3.3.

[11] See, *infra*, the commentary on Article 21, *esp.* §21.11.

[12] See, *infra*, the commentary on Article 19.

Weapons Convention. To date, no occasion within the lifetime of the *1997 Anti-Personnel Mine Ban Convention* has resulted in such a role for a Meeting of States Parties.

10.9 The language of the paragraph indicates that the Meeting of States Parties of the Convention on Cluster Munitions does not have the authority to impose a settlement on the parties to the dispute, although they could of course agree, in advance or *ex post*, to accept a decision of the Meeting as binding upon them.[13]

---

[13] See also Krutzsch, W., and Trapp, R., *A Commentary on the Chemical Weapons Convention* (The Netherlands: Martinus Nijhoff Publishers, 1994), p. 236.

Article 11. Meetings of States Parties

Stuart Casey-Maslen

Article 11—Meetings of States Parties

1. The States Parties shall meet regularly in order to consider and, where necessary, take decisions in respect of any matter with regard to the application or implementation of this Convention, including:

(a) The operation and status of this Convention;

(b) Matters arising from the reports submitted under the provisions of this Convention;

(c) International cooperation and assistance in accordance with Article 6 of this Convention;

(d) The development of technologies to clear cluster munition remnants;

(e) Submissions of States Parties under Articles 8 and 10 of this Convention; and

(f) Submissions of States Parties as provided for in Articles 3 and 4 of this Convention.

2. The first Meeting of States Parties shall be convened by the Secretary-General of the United Nations within one year of entry into force of this Convention. The subsequent meetings shall be convened by the Secretary-General of the United Nations annually until the first Review Conference.

3. States not party to this Convention, as well as the United Nations, other relevant international organisations or institutions, regional organisations, the International Committee of the Red Cross, the International Federation of Red Cross and Red Crescent Societies and relevant non-governmental organisations may be invited to attend these meetings as observers in accordance with the agreed rules of procedure.

Overview of the Article

11.1 Article 11 covers 'regular' meetings of States Parties, which are authorized to consider, and if necessary take decisions, in respect of any matter regarding the 'application or implementation' of the Convention. A non-exhaustive list of issues that the Meeting of States Parties may address includes the following:

- matters arising from reports submitted in accordance with the provisions of the Convention;
- the development of technologies to clear cluster munition remnants;
- a request for an extension of the deadline for stockpile destruction of cluster munitions[1] or clearance and destruction of cluster munition remnants;[2]
- the provision of international cooperation and assistance in accordance with Article 6;
- requests for clarification of compliance in accordance with Article 8;
- support for dispute settlement between two or more States Parties in accordance with Article 10; and, more generally,
- the operation and status of the Convention.

11.2 The first Meeting of States Parties is to be convened by the Secretary-General of the United Nations (UN) within one year of entry into force. Subsequent meetings are to be convened annually until the first review conference, which in accordance with Article 12, will occur five years after entry into force of the Convention. The review conference will then determine the frequency of subsequent meetings. States not party, as well as the UN, other 'relevant' international organizations or institutions, regional organizations, the International Committee of the Red Cross, the International Federation of Red Cross and Red Crescent Societies, and relevant non-governmental

---

[1] In accordance with Article 3.   [2] In accordance with Article 4.

organizations 'may be invited to attend all meetings of States Parties as observers'.

11.3 The provision does not refer to the possibility of informal intersessional meetings. Such meetings have been convened in the context of the *1997 Anti-Personnel Mine Ban Convention*.[3] These intersessional meetings and the organization and functioning of the various 'Standing Committees' are not dealt with in that Convention itself, but they have been important in facilitating implementation. The *1997 Anti-Personnel Mine Ban Convention* moreover does not mention an implementation support unit, but the establishment and functioning of such a secretariat to support the Meetings of States Parties, the intersessional meetings, as well as the Review Conferences under that treaty has been instrumental in promoting its effective implementation.[4] Thus, the lack of any reference to such informal meetings or implementation support in the Convention on Cluster Munitions does not imply that similar mechanisms should not be established in the context of this Convention.

Preparatory discussions and negotiations

11.4 The Lima Discussion Text contained the basis for the article as ultimately adopted, and it was closely based on the corresponding provisions in the *1997 Anti-Personnel Mine Ban Convention*. There are, however, two especially notable differences. In the case of the *1997 Anti-Personnel Mine Ban Convention*, the Meeting of States Parties was authorized to 'consider' but not necessarily 'take decisions' on any matter concerning the application or implementation of the Convention.[5] This additional mandate was added in the Vienna Discussion Text and maintained in the Convention on Cluster Munitions as adopted. Second, the possibility of convening a Special Meeting of States Parties to consider compliance or other possible emergency issues[6] was not included in the Lima Discussion Text or any of the following texts, despite a call by one State for its inclusion.[7]

---

[3] The formal title of this treaty is the Convention on the Prohibition of the Use, Stockpiling, Production and Transfer of Anti-Personnel Mines and on their Destruction.

[4] For further details on the Implementation Support Unit (ISU), <http://www.apminebanconvention.org/implementation-support-unit/overview/> (accessed 26 March 2010).

[5] Though the lack of such a specific mandate has not prevented Meetings of States Parties to the *1997 Anti-Personnel Mine Ban Convention* from taking many such decisions.

[6] *Cp.* Articles 8 and 11 of the *1997 Anti-Personnel Mine Ban Convention*.

[7] See, e.g., Harrison, K., 'Report from the Lima Conference on Cluster Munitions, 23–25 May 2007', Women's International League for Peace and Freedom.

Paragraph 1

The States Parties shall meet regularly in order to consider and, where necessary, take decisions in respect of any matter with regard to the application or implementation of this Convention, including:

(a) The operation and status of this Convention;

(b) Matters arising from the reports submitted under the provisions of this Convention;

(c) International cooperation and assistance in accordance with Article 6 of this Convention;

(d) The development of technologies to clear cluster munition remnants;

(e) Submissions of States Parties under Articles 8 and 10 of this Convention; and

(f) Submissions of States Parties as provided for in Articles 3 and 4 of this Convention.

Commentary

The duty to meet 'regularly'

11.5 States Parties are required to meet 'regularly', which is defined, initially, as once a year until the convening of the first Review Conference of the Convention. This implies that the Review Conference may not decide not to convene any more meetings of States Parties, although 'regularly' is not capable of precise definition. It does not, though, necessarily mean 'often'.

The application or implementation of the Convention

11.6 States Parties can consider any matter with regard to the 'application or implementation' of the Convention. No role is foreseen in determining the 'interpretation' of any of the provisions, but if a dispute regarding interpretation of the Convention arises between two or more States Parties, the Meeting of States Parties can play a role in resolving such disputes.[8] It is made explicit that the list of specific matters to be considered is not exclusive. Nonetheless, paragraph 1 enumerates a list of specific issues some or all of which may be considered by the Meeting of States Parties. These are:

- matters arising from reports submitted in accordance with Article 3, paragraph 8; Article 4, paragraph 1(c); and Article 7;

---

[8] *Cp.* Article 10 of the Convention on Cluster Munitions and see, *supra,* the commentary on this provision, *esp.* §§10.6–10.7.

- the development of technologies to clear cluster munition remnants;
- a request for an extension of the deadline for stockpile destruction of cluster munitions[9] or clearance and destruction of cluster munition remnants;[10]
- the provision of international cooperation and assistance in accordance with Article 6;
- requests for clarification of compliance in accordance with Article 8;
- support for dispute settlement between two or more States Parties regarding the application of the Convention in accordance with Article 10; and, more generally,
- the operation and status of the Convention.

The operation and status of the Convention

11.7 The operation and status of the Convention potentially covers a range of issues, including universalization of adherence and the interpretation or understandings of the Convention's provisions. For example, in the context of the *1997 Anti-Personnel Mine Ban Convention*, the President-Designate of the Second Review Conference submitted a report on that treaty's operation and status in which he addressed the following main issues:

- Universalizing the Convention,
- Destroying stockpiled anti-personnel mines,
- Clearing mined areas,
- Assisting the victims,
- Cooperation and assistance,
- Transparency, and
- Implementation support.[11]

Matters arising from reports submitted under the Convention

11.8 Each State Party is required by Article 7 to provide a report to the Secretary-General of the UN 'as soon as practicable, and in any event not later than 180 days' after entry into force of the Convention for that State Party, on a number of issues, such as details of cluster munition stockpiles and progress in stockpile destruction, national implementation measures adopted, the threat

---

[9] In accordance with Article 3.   [10] In accordance with Article 4.

[11] 'Review of the Operation and Status of the Convention on the Prohibition of the Use, Stockpiling, Production and Transfer of Antipersonnel Mines and on Their Destruction: 2005–2009, Part I, Submitted by the President-Designate of the Second Review Conference', doc. APLC/CONF/2009/WP.2, 18 December 2009.

from cluster munition remnants and progress in addressing that threat, and national and international support for implementation of the Convention.[12] The Meeting of States Parties provides a formal opportunity to comment on and discuss those reports.[13]

11.9 Each State Party is also required by Article 3, paragraph 8 to report on an annual basis to the Secretary-General of the UN no later than 30 April of the following year on any cluster munitions or explosive submunitions it retains, acquires, or transfers for permitted purposes.[14] These are: development of and training in cluster munition and explosive submunition detection; clearance or destruction techniques; or for the development of cluster munition counter-measures. If cluster munitions or explosive submunitions are transferred to another State Party for these purposes, the report must include reference to the receiving party.

11.10 Each State Party that is affected by cluster munition remnants is required to make a declaration of compliance to the next Meeting of States Parties after completing clearance and destruction of cluster munition remnants located in cluster munition contaminated areas under its jurisdiction or control.[15]

11.11 The Meeting of States Parties may also discuss the development of technologies to clear cluster munition remnants. This overlaps with the obligation on each State Party 'in a position to do so' under Article 6, paragraph 4 to provide 'information concerning various means and technologies related to clearance of cluster munitions'.

11.12 The Meeting of States Parties is specifically authorized to consider and decide on a request for an extension of the deadline for stockpile destruction of cluster munitions[16] or clearance and destruction of cluster munition remnants.[17] Each State Party is required by Article 3 to destroy all stockpiles of cluster munitions under its jurisdiction and control within eight years of entry into force of the Convention for it. Should a State Party be unable to meet this deadline, it may submit a request for an extension to either a Meeting of States Parties or a Review Conference of up to four years and, 'in exceptional circumstances',[18] for further periods of up to four years at a time.[19] A

---

[12] See, *supra*, the commentary on Article 7.

[13] In the context of the *1997 Anti-Personnel Mine Ban Convention*, however, most of the substantive discussions on the reports have taken place in the intersessional Standing Committee meetings.   [14] In accordance with Article 3, paragraphs 6 and 7.

[15] See, *supra*, the commentary on Article 4, paragraph 1(c), *esp.* §4.56.

[16] In accordance with Article 3.   [17] In accordance with Article 4.

[18] Presumably, the Meeting of States Parties will determine what constitute exceptional circumstances, as they are not defined in the Convention.

[19] In accordance with Article 3, paragraphs 3–5. See, *supra*, the commentary on these provisions.

request for an extension must be submitted a minimum of nine months prior to the Meeting of States Parties (or Review Conference) at which it is to be considered.[20]

11.13 The Meeting of States Parties or the Review Conference will, taking into consideration the set of factors listed in Article 3, paragraph 4 of this Article, assess the request and decide by a majority of votes of States Parties present and voting whether to grant the request for an extension. The States Parties may decide to grant a shorter extension than that requested and may propose benchmarks for the extension, as appropriate.[21]

11.14 Each State Party is required by Article 4 to destroy all cluster munition remnants[22] located in cluster munition contaminated areas[23] within 10 years of entry into force of the Convention for it. Should a State Party be unable to meet this deadline, it may submit a request for an extension to either the Meeting of States Parties or a Review Conference of up to five years and then subsequent extension periods of up to five years at a time.[24] A request for an extension shall be submitted to a Meeting of States Parties or Review Conference prior to the expiry of the deadline for the State Party concerned. Each request must be submitted a minimum of nine months prior to the Meeting of States Parties or Review Conference at which it is to be considered.[25]

11.15 The Meeting of States Parties (or Review Conference) will, taking into consideration the set of factors listed in Article 4, paragraph 6, 'including, *inter alia*, the quantities of cluster munition remnants reported', assess the request and decide by a majority of votes of States Parties present and voting whether to grant the request for an extension. The States Parties may decide to grant a shorter extension than that requested and may propose benchmarks for the extension, 'as appropriate'.[26]

11.16 The Meeting of States Parties is authorized to discuss the provision of international cooperation and assistance in accordance with Article 6 of the Convention on Cluster Munitions. Under the *1997 Anti-Personnel Mine Ban Convention*, States Parties established an information contact group on resource mobilization to promote the effective provision of financial assistance.

11.17 The Meeting of States Parties is authorized to discuss requests for clarification of compliance in accordance with Article 8. As noted above in

---

[20] Article 3, paragraph 5.   [21] Article 3, paragraph 5.

[22] Defined in Article 2, paragraph 7 as 'failed cluster munitions, abandoned cluster munitions, unexploded submunitions, and unexploded bomblets'.

[23] Defined in Article 2, paragraph 11 as 'an area known or suspected to contain cluster munition remnants'.

[24] In accordance with Article 4, paragraph 8. See, *supra*, the commentary on this provision.

[25] Article 4, paragraph 6.   [26] Article 4, paragraph 7.

the commentary on this provision, the Convention on Cluster Munitions has streamlined the procedure for 'facilitation and clarification of compliance' foreseen under the *1997 Anti-Personnel Mine Ban Convention*. Where a compliance issue has been submitted to it pursuant to paragraph 3 of Article 8, a Meeting of States Parties must first determine whether to consider the matter further, taking into account all information submitted by the States Parties concerned.[27] If it does so determine, the relevant Meeting of States Parties 'may suggest to the States Parties concerned ways and means further to clarify or resolve the matter under consideration, including the initiation of appropriate procedures in conformity with international law'.[28]

11.18 In circumstances where the compliance issue is determined to be due to circumstances 'beyond the control of the requested State Party', the Meeting of States Parties may recommend appropriate measures, including the use of 'cooperative measures' of international cooperation and assistance referred to in Article 6 of the Convention. The Meeting of States Parties may also, however, decide 'to adopt such other general procedures or specific mechanisms for clarification of compliance, including facts, and resolution of instances of non-compliance with the provisions of this Convention as it deems appropriate'.[29]

11.19 The Meeting of States Parties is authorized to discuss ways to settle disputes between two or more States Parties regarding the interpretation or application of the Convention in accordance with Article 10. Under Article 10, paragraph 1, the States Parties concerned must 'consult together with a view to the expeditious settlement of the dispute by negotiation or by other peaceful means of their choice, including recourse to the Meeting of States Parties and referral to the International Court of Justice in conformity with the Statute of the Court'. Under paragraph 2, a Meeting of States Parties 'may contribute to the settlement of the dispute by whatever means it deems appropriate, including offering its good offices, calling upon the States Parties concerned to start the settlement procedure of their choice and recommending a time-limit for any agreed procedure'.

11.20 Finally, the Meeting of States Parties is authorized to discuss more generally the operation and status of the Convention. This 'catch-all' phrase seemingly allows the Meeting to discuss any issue affecting the Convention.

Paragraph 2

The first Meeting of States Parties shall be convened by the Secretary-General of the United Nations within one year of entry into force of

---

[27] Article 8, paragraph 5.   [28] Article 8, paragraph 5.   [29] Article 8, paragraph 6.

this Convention. The subsequent meetings shall be convened by the Secretary-General of the United Nations annually until the first Review Conference.

11.21 In accordance with paragraph 2, the Secretary-General of the United Nations is required to convene the first Meeting of States Parties within one year of entry into force of the Convention on Cluster Munitions. Subsequent meetings are to be convened until the first Review Conference. Under Article 14 of the Convention, the burden of costs related to each Meetings of States Parties is calculated in accordance with the UN scale of assessment, adjusted to take account of the fact that not all members of the UN are party to the Convention.[30] As noted in the commentary on Article 12 below, the First Review Conference of the Convention on Cluster Munitions will have the explicit task of deciding on the need for, and intervals between, future Meetings of the States Parties.

11.22 On 2 December 2009, the UN General Assembly adopted Resolution 64/36 'Convention on Cluster Munitions' without a vote, whereby the Assembly:

1. Welcomes the offer of the Government of the Lao People's Democratic Republic to host the First Meeting of States Parties to the Convention on Cluster Munitions . . . following its entry into force;

2. Requests the Secretary-General, in accordance with article 11, paragraph 2, of the Convention, to undertake the preparations necessary to convene the First Meeting of States Parties to the Convention following its entry into force.

Paragraph 3

States not party to this Convention, as well as the United Nations, other relevant international organisations or institutions, regional organisations, the International Committee of the Red Cross, the International Federation of Red Cross and Red Crescent Societies and relevant non-governmental organisations may be invited to attend these meetings as observers in accordance with the agreed rules of procedure.

---

[30] *Cf., infra*, the commentary on Article 14. In the context of Meetings of States Parties and Review Conferences of the *1997 Anti-Personnel Mine Ban Convention*, it has been consistent practice that all observer States have paid in accordance with this rule, *cf.*, <http://www.apminebanconvention.org/>.

11.23 States not party to the Convention, including signatory States, the UN, 'other relevant international organisations or institutions, regional organisations, the International Committee of the Red Cross, the International Federation of Red Cross and Red Crescent Societies and relevant non-governmental organisations' may be invited to attend the Meeting of States Parties as observers.[31] The decision on whom to invite is left to the States Parties when elaborating the rules of procedure for the Meeting. In accordance with Article 14, paragraph 1, of the Convention on Cluster Munitions any State not party to the Convention attending the Meeting of States Parties as an observer will bear costs of the relevant meeting in accordance with the United Nations scale of assessment adjusted appropriately.[32]

---

[31] Specific mention of the International Federation of Red Cross and Red Crescent Societies was added during the Dublin Diplomatic Conference.

[32] *Cf., infra*, the commentary on this provision.

Article 12. Review Conferences

Stuart Casey-Maslen

Article 12—Review Conferences

1. A Review Conference shall be convened by the Secretary-General of the United Nations five years after the entry into force of this Convention. Further Review Conferences shall be convened by the Secretary-General of the United Nations if so requested by one or more States Parties, provided that the interval between Review Conferences shall in no case be less than five years. All States Parties to this Convention shall be invited to each Review Conference.

2. The purpose of the Review Conference shall be:

(a) To review the operation and status of this Convention;

(b) To consider the need for and the interval between further Meetings of States Parties referred to in paragraph 2 of Article 11 of this Convention; and

(c) To take decisions on submissions of States Parties as provided for in Articles 3 and 4 of this Convention.

3. States not party to this Convention, as well as the United Nations, other relevant international organisations or institutions, regional organisations, the International Committee of the Red Cross, the International Federation of Red Cross and Red Crescent Societies and relevant non-governmental organisations may be invited to attend each Review Conference as observers in accordance with the agreed rules of procedure.

Overview of the Article

12.1 Article 12 on Review Conferences complements the provisions of Article 11 on Meetings of States Parties. The purpose of the Review Conference is to: review the operation and status of the Convention (a task also allocated to Meetings of States Parties);[1] consider the need for and the interval between further Meetings of States Parties after the first Review Conference;[2] and to take decisions on any request by a State Party for an extension to the deadline for stockpile destruction (Article 3) or clearance and destruction of cluster munition remnants (Article 4). Again, these are tasks also allocated to the Meeting of States Parties.[3] The Review Conferences do not have a mandate to review the Convention itself—this would be the potential task of an amendment conference.[4]

Preparatory discussions and negotiations

12.2 The provision reflects very closely the provisions laid down in the *1997 Anti-Personnel Mine Ban Convention*,[5] requiring the Secretary-General of the United Nations (UN) to convene a Review Conference five years after the entry into force of the Convention on Cluster Munitions and then allowing for possible future Review Conferences at the request of one or more States Parties as long as the interval between each such conference is at least five years. There are, however, two significant differences between the two instruments. First, the text of paragraph 2 is amended to take account of the possibility of requesting an extension to the stockpile destruction deadline laid down in Article 3 (no such extension is possible under the *1997 Anti-Personnel Mine Ban Convention*).[6] Second, in contrast to this latter treaty, a Review Conference of the Convention on Cluster Munitions is not specifically tasked to 'adopt, if necessary, in its final report conclusions related to the implementation of this Convention'.[7]

---

[1] See also *supra* the commentary on Article 11, paragraph 1.
[2] See also *supra* the commentary on Article 11, paragraph 2.
[3] See also *supra* the commentary on Article 11, paragraph 1.　　　　　[4] See Article 13.
[5] See Article 12, *1997 Anti-Personnel Mine Ban Convention*. The formal title of this treaty is the Convention on the Prohibition of the Use, Stockpiling, Production and Transfer of Anti-Personnel Mines and on their Destruction.
[6] *Cp.* Article 4, *1997 Anti-Personnel Mine Ban Convention*.
[7] *Cp.* Article 12, paragraph 2(d), *1997 Anti-Personnel Mine Ban Convention*. This deletion was already present in the Lima Discussion Text of May 2007. See Article 12, Chair's discussion text on a legally binding international instrument that will prohibit the use, production, transfer and stockpiling of cluster munitions that cause unacceptable harm to civilians, Lima, 23–25 May 2007 (see Annex 3 to this Commentary).

Paragraph 1

A Review Conference shall be convened by the Secretary-General of the United Nations five years after the entry into force of this Convention. Further Review Conferences shall be convened by the Secretary-General of the United Nations if so requested by one or more States Parties, provided that the interval between Review Conferences shall in no case be less than five years. All States Parties to this Convention shall be invited to each Review Conference.

12.3 The Secretary-General of the United Nations is obliged to convene the first Review Conference of the Convention on Cluster Munitions five years after its entry into force. Subsequently, a Review Conference shall be held at the request of one or more States Parties as long as the interval between each Review Conference is at least five years.[8] All States Parties to the Convention must be invited to each Review Conference.

Paragraph 2

The purpose of the Review Conference shall be:

(a) To review the operation and status of this Convention;

(b) To consider the need for and the interval between further Meetings of States Parties referred to in paragraph 2 of Article 11 of this Convention; and

(c) To take decisions on submissions of States Parties as provided for in Articles 3 and 4 of this Convention.

12.4 There are three specific components to the purpose stipulated for a Review Conference. In contrast, to the preceding provision dealing with Meetings of States Parties,[9] the list appears to be exhaustive rather than indicatory, although the first of these, a review of the operation and status of the Convention,[10] could seemingly cover any issue regarding interpretation, application, or implementation of its provisions. The term 'to review the operation and status of this Convention' has, in the context of the *1997 Anti-Personnel Mine Ban Convention*, been interpreted to cover a wide range

---

[8] At the Lima Conference, Mauritania asked whether, given the rapid development of military technology, five years was too long an interval between each Review Conference. Statement of Mauritania, Lima Conference, 25 May 2007. Harrison, K., 'Report from the Lima Conference on Cluster Munitions, 23–25 May 2007', *Women's International League for Peace and Freedom,* 5 June 2007.   [9] *Cp.* Article 11, paragraph 1.

[10] Paragraph 2(a).

of issues. In operationalizing this requirement, the Review Conferences have adopted, in addition to its formal report, a review document (describing the progress in implementation of the Convention in the course of the five years that have passed), an Action Plan (for enhancing implementation for the next five years), and a political declaration.[11]

12.5 Under paragraph 2(b), each Review Conference is required to 'consider the need for and the interval between further Meetings of States Parties'. Given that it is required that the States Parties meet 'regularly',[12] it does not appear possible under the text of the Convention—let alone likely—that a Review Conference will decide there is no need for further Meetings of States Parties.

Paragraph 3

> States not party to this Convention, as well as the United Nations, other relevant international organisations or institutions, regional organisations, the International Committee of the Red Cross, the International Federation of Red Cross and Red Crescent Societies and relevant non-governmental organisations may be invited to attend each Review Conference as observers in accordance with the agreed rules of procedure.

12.6 Participation in a Review Conference is potentially the same as for the Meeting of States Parties. States not party to the Convention, including signatory States, the UN, 'other relevant international organisations or institutions, regional organisations, the International Committee of the Red Cross, the International Federation of Red Cross and Red Crescent Societies and relevant non-governmental organisations' may be invited to attend the Meeting of States Parties as observers.[13] The decision on whom to invite is left to the States Parties when elaborating the rules of procedure for the meetings. In accordance with Article 14, paragraph 1, of the Convention on Cluster Munitions any State not party to the Convention attending a Review Conference as an observer will bear costs of that Review Conference in accordance with the United Nations scale of assessment adjusted appropriately.[14]

---

[11] *Cf.*, e.g., <http://www.cartagenasummit.org/decisions-and-documents/>.

[12] *Cp.* Article 11, paragraph 1 (*chapeau*): 'The States Parties shall meet regularly...'.

[13] Specific mention of the International Federation of Red Cross and Red Crescent Societies was added during the Dublin Diplomatic Conference.

[14] *Cf.*, *infra*, the commentary on this provision. In the context of Meetings of States Parties and Review Conferences of the *1997 Anti-Personnel Mine Ban Convention*, it has been consistent practice that all observer States have paid in accordance with this rule, see <http://www. apminebanconvention.org/>.

Article 13. Amendments

Stuart Casey-Maslen

Article 13—Amendments

1. At any time after its entry into force any State Party may propose amendments to this Convention. Any proposal for an amendment shall be communicated to the Secretary-General of the United Nations, who shall circulate it to all States Parties and shall seek their views on whether an Amendment Conference should be convened to consider the proposal. If a majority of the States Parties notify the Secretary-General of the United Nations no later than 90 days after its circulation that they support further consideration of the proposal, the Secretary-General of the United Nations shall convene an Amendment Conference to which all States Parties shall be invited.

2. States not party to this Convention, as well as the United Nations, other relevant international organisations or institutions, regional organisations, the International Committee of the Red Cross, the International Federation of Red Cross and Red Crescent Societies and relevant non-governmental organisations may be invited to attend each Amendment Conference as observers in accordance with the agreed rules of procedure.

3. The Amendment Conference shall be held immediately following a Meeting of States Parties or a Review Conference unless a majority of the States Parties request that it be held earlier.

4. Any amendment to this Convention shall be adopted by a majority of two-thirds of the States Parties present and voting at the Amendment Conference. The Depositary shall communicate any amendment so adopted to all States.

5. An amendment to this Convention shall enter into force for States Parties that have accepted the amendment on the date of deposit of acceptances by a majority of the States which were Parties at the date of adoption of the amendment. Thereafter it shall enter into force for any remaining State Party on the date of deposit of its instrument of acceptance.

Overview of the Article

13.1 Any State Party to the Convention on Cluster Munitions may suggest an amendment to the Convention following its entry into force. Should a majority of States Parties expressly support further consideration of the proposed amendment, the Secretary-General of the United Nations (UN) will call an Amendment Conference. At such a conference, should two-thirds of the States Parties present and voting support it the amendment will be adopted. It will then enter into force for all States Parties that have accepted the amendment on the date of deposit of acceptances by a majority of the States which were party to the Convention at the date of adoption of the amendment. Thereafter it enters into force for any remaining State Party on the date of deposit of its instrument of acceptance.

Preparatory discussions and negotiations

13.2 Article 13 on amendments to the Convention is drawn almost verbatim from the corresponding provision in the *1997 Anti-Personnel Mine Ban Convention*. The Lima Discussion Text, the Vienna Discussion Text, and the Draft Cluster Munitions Convention all maintained that text. The only textual changes made during the Diplomatic Conference were to add 'the International Federation of Red Cross and Red Crescent Societies' to those specifically entitled to attend any Amendment Conference as an observer, and to allow States Parties 90 days rather than 30 to express their initial views to the Secretary-General of the UN as to whether they desired further consideration of a proposed amendment.

Paragraph 1

At any time after its entry into force any State Party may propose amendments to this Convention. Any proposal for an amendment shall be communicated to the Secretary-General of the United Nations, who shall circulate it to all States Parties and shall seek their views on whether an Amendment Conference should be convened to consider the proposal. If a majority of the States Parties notify the Secretary-General of the United Nations no later than 90 days after its circulation that they support further consideration of the proposal, the Secretary-General of the United Nations shall convene an Amendment Conference to which all States Parties shall be invited.

13.3 Once the Convention on Cluster Munitions enters into force, any State Party may propose an amendment through the Secretary-General of the United Nations, as Depositary of the Convention.[1] Upon receipt of a proposed amendment, the Depositary will circulate it to all States Parties. If a majority indicate to the Depositary that they wish to consider further the proposal within 90 days of its circulation, the Depositary will convene an 'Amendment Conference' to which all States Parties will be invited.

13.4 In accordance with Article 14 of the Convention, the costs related to any Amendment Conference will be borne by the States Parties as well as by the States not party to the Convention participating therein. The division of costs is in accordance with the UN scale of assessment 'adjusted appropriately' (to take account of the fact that not all UN Members are also party to the Convention on Cluster Munitions or will attend its meetings as an observer).

Paragraph 2

States not party to this Convention, as well as the United Nations, other relevant international organisations or institutions, regional organisations, the International Committee of the Red Cross, the International Federation of Red Cross and Red Crescent Societies and relevant non-governmental organisations may be invited to attend each Amendment Conference as observers in accordance with the agreed rules of procedure.

13.5 Similar to the provision on participation in the Meeting of States Parties and a Review Conference, States not party to the Convention, including signatory States, the UN, 'other relevant international organisations or institutions, regional organisations, the International Committee of the Red Cross, the

---

[1] The amendment can seemingly be of any nature, substantive, technical, financial, or procedural. It is not clear, however, if additional proposals for amendments can be made by the proposing State Party or any other State Party during an Amendment Conference itself.

International Federation of Red Cross and Red Crescent Societies and relevant non-governmental organizations' may be invited to attend any Amendments Conference as observers in accordance with the agreed Rules of Procedure.[2]

Paragraph 3

The Amendment Conference shall be held immediately following a Meeting of States Parties or a Review Conference unless a majority of the States Parties request that it be held earlier.

13.6 The Amendment Conference shall be held immediately following the Meeting of States Parties or a Review Conference unless a majority of the States Parties request that it be held earlier. In contrast to certain other instruments,[3] there are no time-limits specified between the decision to hold an Amendment Conference and the convening of the Conference itself.

Paragraph 4

Any amendment to this Convention shall be adopted by a majority of two-thirds of the States Parties present and voting at the Amendment Conference. The Depositary shall communicate any amendment so adopted to all States.

13.7 At a specially convened Amendment Conference any proposed amendment will be adopted if it is supported by at least two-thirds of the States Parties present and voting.[4] The Secretary-General of the United Nations as Depositary will communicate any amendment adopted to all the States Parties.

Paragraph 5

An amendment to this Convention shall enter into force for States Parties that have accepted the amendment on the date of deposit of acceptances by a majority of the States which were Parties at the date of adoption of the amendment. Thereafter it shall enter into force for any remaining State Party on the date of deposit of its instrument of acceptance.

---

[2] Presumably the rules of procedure for any Amendment Conference would be adapted from the rules governing participating in the Meeting of States Parties or a Review Conference.

[3] *Cp.*, e.g., Article 121, paragraph 2, of the *1998 Statute of the International Criminal Court.*

[4] This margin is the same as in the *1997 Anti-Personnel Mine Ban Convention.*

13.8 Subsequent to the adoption of any amendment, States Parties notify the depositary of their consent to be bound by the amendment through the deposit of an instrument of acceptance. Once a majority of the States Parties have accepted the amendment, it will enter into force for all those who have deposited an instrument of acceptance. Subsequently, the amendment will enter into force for each remaining State Party immediately upon deposit of its instrument of acceptance. There is, however, no obligation on any State Party to accept any amendment.

13.9 It is assumed that the Secretary-General of the UN will, in accordance with established practice, inform all States Parties of instruments of acceptance and of the entry into force of any amendments.

Article 14. Costs and administrative tasks

Stuart Casey-Maslen

Article 14—Costs and administrative tasks

1. The costs of the Meetings of States Parties, the Review Conferences and the Amendment Conferences shall be borne by the States Parties and States not party to this Convention participating therein, in accordance with the United Nations scale of assessment adjusted appropriately.

2. The costs incurred by the Secretary-General of the United Nations under Articles 7 and 8 of this Convention shall be borne by the States Parties in accordance with the United Nations scale of assessment adjusted appropriately.

3. The performance by the Secretary-General of the United Nations of administrative tasks assigned to him or her under this Convention is subject to an appropriate United Nations mandate.

Overview of the Article

14.1 Article 14 deals with how the costs of organizing specific meetings[1] and conducting certain activities related to the Convention will be borne and also addresses the need of the Secretary-General of the United Nations (UN) for an 'appropriate...mandate' in order to perform the administrative tasks assigned to him or her. This latter issue was added to the draft of the Convention during the Diplomatic Conference at the request of the

---

[1] The Convention makes no provision for States Parties to finance any intersessional Standing Committee meetings nor any Implementation Support Unit (ISU) that may be established by a decision of a Meeting of States Parties, along the lines of those created by the *1997 Anti-Personnel Mine Ban Convention*. During the negotiation of the Convention States decided not to include a provision on the establishment of a secretariat to support its implementation.

UN.[2] The first two paragraphs of the Article were taken directly from the *1997 Anti-Personnel Mine Ban Convention*,[3] with the only change being to delete the specific reference to 'the costs of any fact-finding mission' as Article 8 did not ultimately include specific provision for any such mission (although the Meeting of States Parties could presumably decide to conduct one).[4]

Paragraph 1

The costs of the Meetings of States Parties, the Review Conferences and the Amendment Conferences shall be borne by the States Parties and States not party to this Convention participating therein, in accordance with the United Nations scale of assessment adjusted appropriately.

14.2 The costs of the three formal gatherings envisaged by the Convention—the Meeting of States Parties, Review Conferences, and Amendment Conferences—are to be met by States Parties, and, on the basis of their participation, States not party. The burden of costs is calculated in accordance with the UN scale of assessment adjusted to take account of the fact that not all UN members are party to the Convention on Cluster Munitions (or will attend its meetings as an observer).

Paragraph 2

The costs incurred by the Secretary-General of the United Nations under Articles 7 and 8 of this Convention shall be borne by the States Parties in accordance with the United Nations scale of assessment adjusted appropriately.

14.3 The costs incurred by the UN Secretariat in receiving and transmitting reports submitted by States Parties under Article 7 of the Convention are to be borne by the States Parties in accordance with the UN scale of assessment adjusted to take account of the fact that not all UN members are party to the

---

[2] Fax from the UN Office of Legal Affairs to the Permanent Representative of Ireland to the United Nations, 16 May 2008.

[3] See Article 14, *1997 Anti-Personnel Mine Ban Convention*. The formal title of this treaty is the Convention on the Prohibition of the Use, Stockpiling, Production and Transfer of Anti-Personnel Mines and on their Destruction.

[4] See, *supra*, the commentary on Article 8, *esp.* on paragraph 6.

Convention. A similar burden is imposed on States Parties with respect to costs incurred by the UN in facilitating compliance under Article 8.[5]

14.4 During the Diplomatic Conference, the United Kingdom (UK) proposed adding the costs incurred by the Secretary-General of the UN under Article 6 (international cooperation and assistance). However, after consulting with the UK, the President of the Conference declared that he was satisfied that their concern could be met by a small change to paragraph 10 of Article 6. The President noted that were no objections to this proposal.[6]

Paragraph 3

> The performance by the Secretary-General of the United Nations of administrative tasks assigned to him or her under this Convention is subject to an appropriate United Nations mandate.

14.5 The final paragraph of Article 14 is a statement of fact rather than a provision directed to actions by States Parties. Typically, the Secretary-General of the UN receives a UN General Assembly resolution to undertake certain actions with respect to an international treaty, particularly one that has been negotiated outside UN auspices. Accordingly, UN General Assembly Resolution 63/71, adopted without a vote on 2 December 2008:

> Requests the Secretary-General to render the necessary assistance and to provide such services as may be necessary to fulfil the tasks entrusted to him by the Convention on Cluster Munitions.[7]

---

[5] See 'Proposal by the United Kingdom for the amendment of Article 14', 19 May 2008, Diplomatic Conference doc. CCM/44; see also 'Summary Record of Fifth Session of the Committee of the Whole', Diplomatic Conference doc. CCM/CW/SR/5, 18 June 2008.

[6] See 'Summary Record of Seventh Session of the Committee of the Whole', Diplomatic Conference doc. CCM/CW/SR/7, 18 June 2008.

[7] See also 'Final Document of the Diplomatic Conference for the Adoption of a Convention on Cluster Munitions, Dublin, 19–30 May 2008', Diplomatic Conference doc. CCM/78, Part II, contained in Annex 8.

Article 15. Signature

Stuart Casey-Maslen[1]

Article 15—Signature

This Convention, done at Dublin on 30 May 2008, shall be open for signature at Oslo by all States on 3 December 2008 and thereafter at United Nations Headquarters in New York until its entry into force.

Overview of the Article

15.1 Article 15 lays down the conditions under which a State may sign the Convention on Cluster Munitions.[2] The Convention was opened for signature in Oslo, Norway, on 3 December 2008. Similar to the *1997 Anti-Personnel Mine Ban Convention*,[3] any State that did not do so could sign the Convention on Cluster Munitions at the headquarters of the United Nations (UN) but only until the Convention entered into force (i.e. until 1 August 2010).[4] Any

---

[1] The author would like to thank Christophe Lanord for his input into the commentary on this Article.

[2] Contrary to what prevails in lay language, the signature of a treaty by a State is not always tantamount to the consent of that State to be bound by that treaty: on the basis of its sovereignty, a State may decide to sign a treaty and, afterwards, not to become party to it.

[3] See Article 15, *1997 Anti-Personnel Mine Ban Convention*. The formal title of this treaty is the Convention on the Prohibition of the Use, Stockpiling, Production and Transfer of Anti-Personnel Mines and on their Destruction.

[4] Full powers are required for signature of the Convention in accordance with Article 7 of the *1969 Vienna Convention on the Law of Treaties*, unless the signatory is one of the permissible categories set out in that provision. In accordance with the Depositary practice of the Secretary-General of the UN, full powers are required for all signatories other than Heads of State, Heads of Government, and Ministers of Foreign Affairs (*cf.* UN, 'Summary of Practice of the Secretary-General of the United Nations as Depositary of Multilateral Treaties', UN doc. ST/LEG/7/Rev.l, paras. 101–119).

State wishing to adhere to the Convention that did not sign it before that date must accede directly in accordance with Article 16.[5]

The adoption of the Convention

15.2 Article 15 indicates that the Convention was 'done at Dublin on 30 May 2008'. The word 'done' should be understood as the formal adoption of the draft Convention by the Plenary of the Diplomatic Conference, on 30 May 2008. The Convention was adopted by consensus, in accordance with Rule 36 of the Rules of Procedure which encouraged adoption by 'general agreement'.[6]

The signing conference

15.3 In accordance with Article 15, the signing ceremony of the Convention on Cluster Munitions was held in Oslo on 3 December 2008.[7] A total

---

[5] A simple signature does not result in positive legal obligations under the Convention. (See Article 18 of the *1969 Vienna Convention on the Law of Treaties*, and, *infra*, §§15.5–15.7.) A definitive signature, however, common in bilateral treaty-making and in certain multilateral treaties, binds a signing State upon signature and is the legal equivalent to consenting to be bound through ratification, approval, acceptance, or accession. (See Article 12, *1969 Vienna Convention on the Law of Treaties*, which provides as follows:

1. The consent of a State to be bound by a treaty is expressed by the signature of its representative when:

(a) the treaty provides that signature shall have that effect;

(b) it is otherwise established that the negotiating States were agreed that signature should have that effect; or

(c) the intention of the State to give that effect to the signature appears from the full powers of its representative or was expressed during the negotiation.

[6] According to Rule 36 (General agreement):

1. The Conference shall make its best endeavours to ensure that the work of the Conference is accomplished by general agreement.

2. If, in the consideration of any matter of substance, all feasible efforts to reach general agreement have failed, the President of the Conference shall consult the General Committee and recommend the steps to be taken, which may include the matter being put to the vote.

See 'Draft Rules of Procedure, 21 February 2008', Diplomatic Conference doc. CCM/2, 19 May 2008. See also Article 9, *1969 Vienna Convention on the Law of Treaties*.

[7] See <http://www.clusterconvention.org/pages/pages_iv/iv_signingconference.html>.

of 94 States signed the Convention on that date,[8] with four announcing
that they were also depositing their instrument of ratification with the
Depositary.[9] The signing conference was also attended by four States that
had not participated in the Dublin Diplomatic Conference,[10] a further
14 that were in Dublin as full participants but which decided not to sign
on 3 December 2008,[11] and 10 States which had attended the Diplomatic
Conference as observers.[12]

Signature after the signing conference

15.4 Between December 2008 and 20 May 2010, a further 12 States signed
the Convention, the most recent being Mauritania, on 19 April 2010.[13]

Consequences of signature

15.5 Although signature of the Convention does not make a State a party
to it, there are nonetheless certain obligations that result. As laid down in

---

[8] Afghanistan, Albania, Angola, Australia, Austria, Belgium, Benin, Bolivia, Bosnia and
Herzegovina, Botswana, Bulgaria, Burkina Faso, Burundi, Canada, Cape Verde, Central African
Republic, Chad, Chile, Colombia, Comoros, Congo (Republic of), Cook Islands, Costa Rica, Côte
d'Ivoire, Croatia, Czech Republic, Denmark, Ecuador, El Salvador, Fiji, France, Gambia, Germany,
Ghana, Guatemala, Guinea, Guinea-Bissau, Holy See, Honduras, Hungary, Iceland, Indonesia,
Ireland, Italy, Japan, Kenya, Laos, Lebanon, Lesotho, Liberia, Liechtenstein, Lithuania, Luxembourg,
the former Yugoslav Republic of Macedonia, Madagascar, Malawi, Mali, Malta, Mexico, Moldova,
Monaco, Montenegro, Mozambique, Namibia, Nauru, The Netherlands, New Zealand, Nicaragua,
Niger, Norway, Palau, Panama, Paraguay, Peru, Philippines, Portugal, Rwanda, Samoa, San Marino,
Sao Tome and Principe, Senegal, Sierra Leone, Slovenia, Somalia, South Africa, Spain, Sweden,
Switzerland, Tanzania, Togo, Uganda, United Kingdom, Uruguay, Zambia. According to the
UN, two of these States, Côte d'Ivoire and Guinea-Bissau, signed the Convention on 4 December
2008. See the UN website, 'Convention on Cluster Munitions, Signatories and Ratifying States', at:
<http://www.unog.ch/80256EE600585943/(httpPages)/67DC5063EB530E02C12574F8002E9
E49?OpenDocument> (visited 7 November 2009). Upon signature, Belgium declared that: 'This
signature is equally binding the region of Walloon, the Flemish region and the region of the capital
of Brussels.' See <http://www.unog.ch/80256EDD006B8954/(httpAssets)/983407CD1B93E5E2
C12575160038D2A0/$file/BELGIUM.pdf> (accessed 1 March 2010).

[9] Holy See, Ireland, Norway, and Sierra Leone.

[10] Bangladesh, Brazil, Georgia, and Republic of Korea.

[11] Cambodia, Cameroon, the Democratic Republic of Congo (DRC), Estonia, Finland, Morocco,
Nigeria, Papua New Guinea, Qatar, Serbia, Slovakia, Sudan, Swaziland, and Timor-Leste.

[12] Cyprus, Eritrea, Greece, Iraq, Latvia, Poland, Thailand, Turkey, Ukraine, and Vietnam.
Cyprus subsequently signed the Convention on 23 September 2009.

[13] The other 11 were: Cameroon, Cyprus, the Dominican Republic, the DRC, Haiti, Iraq,
Jamaica, Nigeria, Saint Vincent and the Grenadines, the Seychelles, and Tunisia.

Article 18 of the *1969 Vienna Convention on the Law of Treaties*:

A State is obliged to refrain from acts which would defeat the object and purpose of a treaty when:

(a) it has signed the treaty or has exchanged instruments constituting the treaty subject to ratification, acceptance or approval, until it shall have made its intention clear not to become a party to the treaty; or

(b) it has expressed its consent to be bound by the treaty, pending the entry into force of the treaty and provided that such entry into force is not unduly delayed.

15.6 Determining the object and purpose of the Convention, therefore, is a prerequisite to defining which acts a signatory State may or may not lawfully commit. In contrast to the *1997 Anti-Personnel Mine Ban Convention* or most other treaties regulating weapons, the object and purpose of the Convention cannot be discerned from its title.[14] However, the preamble and the text of Article 1 (general obligations) leave little doubt that the object and purpose of the Convention is to prohibit cluster munitions.

15.7 Certainly, new use of cluster munitions by a signatory State would constitute an act that would defeat the object and purpose of the treaty. The second preambular paragraph of the Convention makes it clear that the States Parties are '[d]etermined to put an end for all time to the suffering and casualties caused by cluster munitions at the time of their use, when they fail to function as intended or when they are abandoned'. In addition, the first prohibition included in Article 1, paragraph 1 is the undertaking 'never under any circumstances to use cluster munitions'. Arguably, new production or transfer (other than for the purposes of destruction or for other purposes explicitly authorized by the Convention under certain circumstances) would also fall within the category of an act that would defeat the object and purpose of the Convention on Cluster Munitions. The legality of other analogous acts, such as continued stockpiling of the weapons, would be more difficult to so categorize.[15]

---

[14] See, *supra*, the commentary on the title, in §0.78.
[15] An argument against the application *in toto* of Article 1 is the provision in Article 18 whereby:

> Any State may, at the time of its ratification, acceptance, approval or accession, declare that it will apply provisionally Article 1 of this Convention pending its entry into force for that State.

This suggests that even a signatory State that had already deposited its instrument of ratification or a State that had acceded is not required to observe all of Article 1's requirements so, *a fortiori*, a signatory State that has not done so (and which never does so) could not be committed to apply all of Article 1.

Article 16. Ratification, acceptance, approval or accession

Stuart Casey-Maslen[1]

Article 16—Ratification, acceptance, approval or accession

1. This Convention is subject to ratification, acceptance or approval by the Signatories.

2. It shall be open for accession by any State that has not signed the Convention.

3. The instruments of ratification, acceptance, approval or accession shall be deposited with the Depositary.

Overview of the Article

16.1   This Article lays down the means by which a State can become party to the Convention on Cluster Munitions. As with many international treaties, there are two possibilities: ratification (or the analogous acts of acceptance or approval) by signatory States (paragraph 1) or accession for any State that has not signed it (paragraph 2). In both cases, the relevant instruments should be deposited with the Depositary of the Convention, determined by Article 22 as being the Secretary-General of the United Nations.

Preparatory discussions and negotiations

16.2   This Article was one of the few provisions that were subject to almost no discussion at the Diplomatic Conference. Its content is almost the same as

---

[1] The author would like to thank Christophe Lanord for his input into the commentary on this Article.

the corresponding provision in the *1997 Anti-Personnel Mine Ban Convention*, with two small linguistic modifications: replacing 'of the signatories' with 'by the Signatories' in paragraph 1, and replacing 'which' with 'that' in the second paragraph. The latter modification was already included in the Draft Cluster Munitions Convention submitted to the Conference;[2] the former was not. Moreover, it was neither contained in the Presidency Text transmitted to the Plenary on 21 May 2008,[3] nor in the final text approved by the Committee of the Whole and transmitted to the Plenary on 28 May.[4] The modification appears only in the text approved by the Plenary on 30 May.[5]

Paragraph 1

> This Convention is subject to ratification, acceptance or approval by the Signatories.

16.3 Paragraph 1 makes it explicit that to become party to the Convention on Cluster Munitions, a State that has signed the Convention[6] is bound by all of its provisions only[7] if and when it ratifies, accepts, or approves it.[8] This is in conformity with the *1969 Vienna Convention on the Law of Treaties*, according to which:

(t)he consent of a State to be bound by a treaty may be expressed by . . . ratification, acceptance, approval or accession, or by any other means if so agreed.[9]

---

[2] Diplomatic Conference doc. CCM/3.   [3] Diplomatic Conference doc. CCM/PT/5.
[4] Diplomatic Conference doc. CCM/PT/15. See also Diplomatic Conference doc. CCM/CW/SR/5.   [5] Diplomatic Conference doc. CCM/77.
[6] For the signature of the Convention by States, see, *supra*, the commentary on Article 15, *esp.* §§15.5–15.7.
[7] The mechanism of ratification was originally devised to guard against the dangers of a State's plenipotentiary exceeding his powers or the instructions from his capital with regard to a particular treaty. Formerly a function of the sovereign, it is now subject to the constitutional control of the Executive. See, e.g., Shaw, M. N., *International Law*, Fourth Edition (Cambridge: Cambridge University Press, 1997), pp. 639–640.
[8] There is no practical difference in the meaning of the words 'ratification', 'approval', and 'accession', although there may be differences in the national legislation of a given State. Acceptance and approval perform the same function on the international plane as ratification; the main reason for the popularity of these terms is that they enable a State to evade provisions in its own constitution requiring the consent of the legislature for ratification. Malanczuk, P., *Akehurst's Modern Introduction to International Law*, Seventh Revised Edition (London: Routledge, 1997), p. 134.
[9] Article 11, *1969 Vienna Convention on the Law of Treaties*. The Vienna Convention defines the following words: 'ratification', 'acceptance', 'approval', and 'accession' mean in each case the international act so named whereby a State establishes on the international plane its consent to be bound by a treaty. See Article 2, paragraph 1(b), *1969 Vienna Convention on the Law of Treaties*.

As of 20 May 2010, all signatories that had joined the Convention had done so by ratification, except for Japan, which had accepted the Convention on 14 July 2009.[10] The UN had also recorded that Moldova had acceded to the Convention,[11] but this proved to have been an inadvertent error, which was corrected as of the beginning of June 2010.[12]

Paragraph 2

It shall be open for accession by any State that has not signed the Convention.

16.4 Since 1 August 2010, the day of entry into force of the Convention on Cluster Munitions, it has no longer been possible to sign the Convention, in accordance with Article 15. Any non-signatory State that has since sought to adhere to the Convention is therefore obliged to accede to it. Accession is equivalent to the act of both signature and ratification.

16.5 It would also appear possible for a State that wishes to accede directly prior to entry into force of the Convention to do so. This issue was not discussed at the Dublin Diplomatic Conference.[13] As of 11 May 2010, however, no non-Signatory State had acceded to the Convention.[14]

---

[10] See UN Treaty Collection website, <http://treaties.un.org/Pages/ViewDetails. aspx?src=TREATY&mtdsg_no=XXVI-6&chapter=26&lang=en> (accessed 27 May 2010).

[11] *Ibid*. (accessed 25 May 2010).

[12] *Ibid*. (accessed 2 June 2010), and email from Sherry Holbrook, Facilitator/Legal Affairs Officer, Office of the Special Adviser to the Secretary-General on Cyprus (OSASG–Cyprus), United Nations 2 June 2010.

[13] *Cp*. discussions in the Oslo Diplomatic Conference that resulted in the adoption of the *1997 Anti-Personnel Mine Ban Convention*, and the cases of Equatorial Guinea and the former Yugoslav Republic of Macedonia, both of which acceded to the *1997 Anti-Personnel Mine Ban Convention* before its entry into force. Maslen, S., *Commentaries on Arms Control Treaties, Volume I: The Convention on the Prohibition of the Use, Stockpiling, Production, and Transfer of Anti-Personnel Mines and on their Destruction*, Second Edition, Oxford Commentaries on International Law (Oxford: Oxford University Press, 2005), §§16.6–16.7.

[14] See UN Treaty Collection website, <http://treaties.un.org/Pages/ViewDetails. aspx?src=TREATY&mtdsg_no=XXVI-6&chapter=26&lang=en> (accessed 25 May 2010). As of 27 May 2010, Moldova was still listed by the UN as having acceded to the Convention, even though as a signatory State this option was not open to it. It appears that this was an inadvertent oversight on the part of the UN Office of Legal Affairs. Moldova's internal legislation referred to ratification of the Convention and in May 2010 a representative of the Moldova Ministry of Foreign Affairs told the Norwegian non-governmental organization, Norwegian People's Aid, that it had deposited an instrument of ratification not accession. Telephone interview with Grethe Oestern, Policy Adviser, Mine Action Department, Norwegian People's Aid, 26 May 2010. Furthermore, it is standard practice for the UN as depositary to clarify with a signatory State that purports to accede to a treaty that in fact ratification is intended. See Law on Ratification of Convention on Cluster Munitions,

Paragraph 3

The instruments of ratification, acceptance, approval or accession shall be deposited with the Depositary.

16.6 Paragraph 3 requires that the instruments of ratification, acceptance, approval, or accession be deposited with the Depositary in order for a State to become party to the Convention. Article 22 of the Convention determines that the Depositary of the Convention is the Secretary-General of the United Nations.

No. 101-XVIII of 15.12.2009, Moldova Official Gazette No. 197–200/640 of 31.12.2009; and UN, 'Summary of Practice of the Secretary-General as Depositary of Multilateral Treaties prepared by the Treaty Section of the Office of Legal Affairs, UN, New York, 1999', §133, <http://treaties. un.org/doc/source/publications/practice/summary_english.pdf> (accessed 27 May 2010). In June 2010, the UN issued a notification of ratification by Moldova.

Article 17. Entry into force

Stuart Casey-Maslen and Gro Nystuen[1]

Article 17—Entry into force

1. This Convention shall enter into force on the first day of the sixth month after the month in which the thirtieth instrument of ratification, acceptance, approval or accession has been deposited.

2. For any State that deposits its instrument of ratification, acceptance, approval or accession after the date of the deposit of the thirtieth instrument of ratification, acceptance, approval or accession, this Convention shall enter into force on the first day of the sixth month after the date on which that State has deposited its instrument of ratification, acceptance, approval or accession.

Overview of the Article

17.1 This Article defines the entry into force of the Convention both as a whole and also for any State adhering to it after the Convention is in force. The threshold of ratifications or accessions needed to trigger entry into force was set at 30. This was achieved on 16 February 2010, when both Burkina Faso and the Republic of Moldova deposited their instruments of ratification with the Depositary. In accordance with the provisions of Article 17, the Convention on Cluster Munitions entered into force on 1 August 2010. Any State ratifying or acceding after the thirtieth ratification was deposited (i.e. since 16 February 2010), becomes party to the Convention on the first day of the sixth month following the date of deposit of the relevant instrument of ratification or accession.

---

[1] The authors would like to thank Christophe Lanord for his input into the commentary on this Article.

Preparatory discussions and negotiations

17.2 Aside from agreeing on the number of ratifications or accessions need-ed for entry into force, the negotiation of this provision was straightforward. Indeed, the remainder of the proposed text was unchanged from the initial draft, which was taken verbatim from the *1997 Anti-Personnel Mine Ban Convention*.[2] That Convention had—after some discussion—set the thresh-old at 40 ratifications or accessions.[3]

17.3 The Lima and Vienna discussion texts and the Draft Cluster Munitions Convention had all proposed setting the threshold at 20.[4] At the beginning of the Dublin Diplomatic Conference, the United Kingdom (UK) proposed that the figure be increased to 40.[5] This proposal was discussed in the Committee of the Whole on 21 May 2008.[6] France started the discussion, claiming that if universal adhesion was the goal, it would be 'paradoxical' to have entry into force triggered by only 20 ratifications. With support from Comoros, Fiji, Germany, Indonesia, the Netherlands, the Philippines, Slovakia, Switzerland, and the UK, France suggested the figure be revised to 40, citing the *1997 Anti-Personnel Mine Ban Convention* as an example. France further noted that other instruments required 60 ratifications before entry into force, for example, the *1993 Chemical Weapons Convention*,[7] the *Nuclear Test Ban Treaty*,[8] and the *1998 Statute of the International Criminal Court*.

17.4 A greater number of delegations, however, spoke in favour of a lower figure: New Zealand, supported by 28 States[9] and the Cluster Munition Coalition (CMC), supported retaining the existing proposal of 20. New

---

[2] The formal title of this treaty is the Convention on the Prohibition of the Use, Stockpiling, Production and Transfer of Anti-Personnel Mines and on their Destruction.

[3] See Maslen, S., *Commentaries on Arms Control Treaties, Volume I: The Convention on the Prohibition of the Use, Stockpiling, Production, and Transfer of Anti-Personnel Mines and on their Destruction*, Second Edition, Oxford Commentaries on International Law (Oxford: Oxford University Press, 2005), §§17.3–17.5.

[4] See Lima Discussion Text, Vienna Discussion Text, and the Draft Cluster Munitions Convention, contained in Annexes 3, 4, and 5, respectively.

[5] See 'Proposal by the United Kingdom for amendment of Article 17', Diplomatic Conference doc. CCM/45, 19 May 2008.

[6] See 'Summary Record of Fifth Session of the Committee of the Whole', Diplomatic Conference doc. CCM/CW/SR/5, 18 June 2008.

[7] The actual figure is 65, according to Article XXI of the *1993 Chemical Weapons Convention*.

[8] In fact, this statement was not accurate since the mechanism of entry into force for this trea-ty is more complicated, requiring the ratification of 44 specific States. See UN, 'Chapter XXVI: Disarmament, 4. Comprehensive Nuclear-Test-Ban Treaty', <http://treaties.un.org/Pages/ViewDetails.aspx?src=TREATY&mtdsg_no=XXVI-4&chapter=26&lang=en&clang=_en> (accessed 10 November 2009).

[9] Argentina, Austria, Belize, Burkina Faso, the Cook Islands, Democratic Republic of the Congo, Ghana, Guinea, Ireland, Kenya, Lesotho, Madagascar, Mali, Mauritania, Mexico, Mozambique,

Zealand drew attention to the 'contemporary trend' towards 20 as a figure of ratification for entry into force on international agreements, giving the examples of *2003 Protocol V*[10] of the *Convention on Certain Conventional Weapons*,[11] the *Convention on Protection from Enforced Disappearances* and the *Convention on the Rights of Persons with Disabilities*. Norway pointed out that only 2 ratifications were required for the Geneva Conventions to enter into force, referring to their humanitarian aim.[12] The President decided to put aside the discussion, and to settle it as part of an overall proposal from the Chair.[13] In his Presidential text of 28 May he proposed the figure of 30 ratifications or accessions as a compromise, which was accepted by all delegations.

Paragraph 1

This Convention shall enter into force on the first day of the sixth month after the month in which the thirtieth instrument of ratification, acceptance, approval or accession has been deposited.

17.5 Entry into force of a treaty means that it has full legal effects for all States Parties from that date. For the Convention on Cluster Munitions, this will occur on the first day of the sixth month following the month in which the thirtieth instrument of ratification or accession has been deposited. This delay is intended to allow States adhering to the Convention to take the necessary domestic measures to comply with its provisions, such as adopting legislation providing for penal sanctions for violations. As noted above, the requisite number of ratifications was deposited with the Depositary of the Convention, the Secretary-General of the United Nations (UN), on 16 February 2010.[14]

Niger, Nigeria, Norway, Panama, Paraguay, Qatar, Swaziland, Timor-Leste, Uganda, Uruguay, Vanuatu, and Zambia.

[10] The formal title of this instrument is the Protocol on Explosive Remnants of War (Protocol V).

[11] The figure for the Protocol actually stemmed not from the Protocol itself, but from Article 5, paragraph 3 of the *Convention on Certain Conventional Weapons* itself. The formal title of this treaty is the Convention on Prohibitions or Restrictions on the Use of Certain Conventional Weapons Which May Be Deemed to Be Excessively Injurious or to Have Indiscriminate Effects, as amended on 21 December 2001.

[12] See 'Summary Record of Fifth Session of the Committee of the Whole', Diplomatic Conference doc. CCM/CW/SR/5, 18 June 2008.

[13] See 'Summary Record of Fifth Session of the Committee of the Whole', *op. cit.*, and 'Summary Record of Ninth Session of the Committee of the Whole', Diplomatic Conference doc. CCM/CW/SR/9, 18 June 2008.

[14] These are, in chronological order: Norway (3 December 2008), Ireland (3 December 2008), Holy See (3 December 2008), Sierra Leone (3 December 2008), Lao People's Democratic Republic (18 March 2009), Austria (2 April 2009), Mexico (6 May 2009), Niger (2 June 2009), Albania

17.6 Pending entry into force, certain provisions are already applicable. As laid down by the *1969 Vienna Convention on the Law of Treaties*,

'[t]he provisions of a treaty regulating the authentication of its text, the establishment of the consent of States to be bound by the treaty, the manner or date of its entry into force, reservations, the functions of the depositary and other matters arising necessarily before the entry into force of the treaty apply from the time of the adoption of its text.[15]

This applies to Articles 15 to 20 and 22 to 23 of the Convention on Cluster Munitions.

17.7 As noted above, a Signatory State is obliged to refrain from any acts that would frustrate the object and purpose of the Convention.[16] Pending entry into force, a State may declare that it will provisionally apply Article 1 of the Convention, in accordance with Article 18.

Paragraph 2

> For any State that deposits its instrument of ratification, acceptance, approval or accession after the date of the deposit of the thirtieth instrument of ratification, acceptance, approval or accession, this Convention shall enter into force on the first day of the sixth month after the date on which that State has deposited its instrument of ratification, acceptance, approval or accession.

17.8 For any State that ratifies or accedes to the Convention after 30 States have already done so, the Convention will also enter into force on the first day of the sixth month after the date on which that State has deposited its instrument of ratification or accession. This allows time for necessary domestic measures to ensure compliance with the Convention to be put in place. Pending entry into force, a State may declare that it will provisionally apply Article 1 of the Convention, in accordance with the provisions of Article 18.

(16 June 2009), Spain (17 June 2009), Germany (8 July 2009), Luxembourg (10 July 2009), San Marino (10 July 2009), Japan (14 July 2009), Zambia (12 August 2009), Croatia (17 August 2009), Slovenia (19 August 2009), Uruguay (24 September 2009), Malta (24 September 2009), France (25 September 2009), Burundi (25 September 2009), Malawi (7 October 2009), the former Yugoslav Republic of Macedonia (8 October 2009), Nicaragua (2 November 2009), New Zealand (22 December 2009), Belgium (22 December 2009), Montenegro (25 January 2010), Denmark (12 February 2010), Burkina Faso (16 February 2010), and Moldova (16 February 2010). See, generally, UN, 'Convention on Cluster Munitions, Signatories and Ratifying States', <http://www.unog.ch/80256EE600585943/(httpPages)/67DC5063EB530E02C12574F8002E9E49?OpenDocument> (accessed 1 March 2010).

[15] Article 24, paragraph 4, *1969 Vienna Convention on the Law of Treaties*.
[16] See, *supra*, the commentary on Article 15 (§15.7) for a discussion of which acts might be thereby prohibited.

Article 18. Provisional application

Stuart Casey-Maslen and Gro Nystuen[1]

Article 18—Provisional application

Any State may, at the time of its ratification, acceptance, approval or accession, declare that it will apply provisionally Article 1 of this Convention pending its entry into force for that State.

Overview of the Article

18.1 This Article, which replicates a similar—but not identical provision from the *1997 Anti-Personnel Mine Ban Convention*,[2] allows a State to declare that it will apply Article 1 of the Convention (general obligations) pending the Convention's entry into force for that State. These obligations are, notably, never under any circumstances to use cluster munitions; to develop, produce, otherwise acquire, stockpile, retain, or transfer to anyone, directly or indirectly, cluster munitions; nor to assist, encourage, or induce anyone to engage in any activity prohibited to a State Party under this Convention.

Preparatory discussions and negotiations

18.2 This Article, like many other provisions from the Convention, finds its origin in the *1997 Anti-Personnel Mine Ban Convention*. However, there are three differences. One is of minor importance: the comma after the word

---

[1] The authors would like to thank Christophe Lanord for his input into the commentary on this Article.

[2] The formal title of this treaty is the Convention on the Prohibition of the Use, Stockpiling, Production and Transfer of Anti-Personnel Mines and on their Destruction.

'may' is a grammatical correction. The two others have more significance: the *1997 Anti-Personnel Mine Ban Convention* refers only to paragraph 1 of Article 1 and not to the full Article; and the words 'for that State' were added to clarify the scope of the obligations.[3]

18.3 In the *1997 Anti-Personnel Mine Ban Convention*, the reference to paragraph 1 of Article 1 was justified because there was a second paragraph in that Article which was as follows: 'Each State Party undertakes to destroy or ensure the destruction of all anti-personnel mines in accordance with the provisions of this Convention.' In the Diplomatic Conference that led to the adoption of that treaty, this provision was adopted as a compromise between two different views among the negotiating States:[4] those that felt that such an Article specifically permitting provisional application should apply to the full Convention, and those who were opposed to that proposal.

18.4 The Draft Cluster Munitions Convention differed in that it did not include an obligation of States in Article 1 to destroy or ensure the destruction of all cluster munitions. Instead, the second paragraph of the draft clarified that the Convention did not apply to mines. As a consequence, the text of Article 19 could be simplified, and refer to Article 1 instead of Article 1, paragraph 1.

Commentary

18.5 The possibility for a State to apply provisionally part of a Convention or the whole of it is described in the *1969 Vienna Convention on the Law of Treaties*:

A treaty or a part of a treaty is applied provisionally pending its entry into force if: (a) the treaty itself so provides; or (b) the negotiating States have in some other manner so agreed.[5]

---

[3] On 21 May, the President introduced that amendment, and explained that the purpose was 'to take into account the views of the United Nations Office of Legal Affairs'. This point was not discussed further during the Diplomatic Conference. See 'Summary Record of Fifth Session of the Committee of the Whole', Diplomatic Conference doc. CCM/CW/SR/5, 18 June 2008.

[4] See Maslen, S., *Commentaries on Arms Control Treaties, Volume I: The Convention on the Prohibition of the Use, Stockpiling, Production, and Transfer of Anti-Personnel Mines and on their Destruction*, Second Edition, Oxford Commentaries on International Law (Oxford: Oxford University Press, 2005), §18.3.

[5] Article 25, paragraph 1, *1969 Vienna Convention on the Law of Treaties*.

In the case of the Convention, the provision that can be applied according to Article 18 is Article 1 only.[6] As of 25 June 2010, only one State that had adhered to the Convention on Cluster Munitions had formally declared that it would provisionally apply Article 1 of the Convention: Norway.[7]

[6] Of course, nothing prevents a State that is not party to the Convention on Cluster Munitions to decide, at any point in time, that it will provisionally apply some or all of the provisions of the Convention.

[7] See the UN website, 'Convention on Cluster Munitions, Signatories and Ratifying States', <http://www.unog.ch/80256EDD006B8954/(httpAssets)/149F96DA53641DD8C1257516003 8C55F/$file/NORWAY.pdf>.

Article 19. Reservations

Stuart Casey-Maslen and Gro Nystuen[1]

Article 19—Reservations

The Articles of this Convention shall not be subject to reservations.

Overview of the Article

19.1 This Article is the shortest of the Convention on Cluster Munitions but is one of the most important as it unifies the legal obligations of State Parties by prohibiting any reservations to its provisions. A reservation is defined by the *1969 Vienna Convention on the Law of Treaties* as:

a unilateral statement, however phrased or named, made by a State, when signing, ratifying, accepting, approving or acceding to a treaty, whereby it purports to exclude or to modify the legal effect of certain provisions of the treaty in their application to that State.[2]

Preparatory discussions and negotiations

19.2 The text of this Article is exactly the same as the one which was included in both the *1997 Anti-Personnel Mine Ban Convention*[3] and the Draft Cluster Munitions Convention submitted to the Dublin Diplomatic Conference. However, there was pressure from some delegations during the Conference to modify the text, in order to allow reservations. On 21 May 2008, the United Kingdom (UK) requested that Article 19 be 'kept open'

---

[1] The authors would like to thank Christophe Lanord for his input into the commentary on this Article.　　　[2] Article 2, paragraph 1(d), *1969 Vienna Convention on the Law of Treaties*.
[3] The formal title of this treaty is the Convention on the Prohibition of the Use, Stockpiling, Production and Transfer of Anti-Personnel Mines and on their Destruction.

pending the resolution of the issue of interoperability.[4] In the same discussion, Slovakia, supported by the Czech Republic, stated it would be hard to join the consensus on Article 19 in the absence of agreement on Article 1. Botswana noted a general trend in humanitarian issues that States should not be allowed to enter reservations, but noted that '(t)he competing argument in favour of State sovereignty was that States might be slower to ratify a Convention that did not allow reservations'.

19.3 Speaking in support of the draft text, Norway stated that the proposal should stand as is and that no reservations should be allowed. Australia declared its view that Article 19 belonged in the bundle of Articles that had not been concluded by virtue of its connection to Article 1. The President decided to set the Article aside, pending the overall deal to be proposed to the negotiating States.[5] Therefore, Article 19 was not tabled as a separate Presidential text during the negotiations.

19.4 When the Presidential text was submitted on 28 May, the text was unchanged. The President stated that the discussion of this Article in the Committee of the Whole was inconclusive, with some delegations taking the view that they were not in a position to accept that the Articles of the Convention shall not be subject to reservations in advance of agreement being reached on all Articles. Confident that agreement on all Articles was by then not far away, the President suggested that the text of this Article follow the text as in the draft Convention.[6]

Commentary

19.5 The prohibition of reservations can be found in a number of treaties, for instance the *1998 Statute of the International Criminal Court*,[7] or the *1993 Chemical Weapons Convention*. Although it is clear that any declaration by a State that 'purports to exclude or to modify the legal effect of certain provisions

---

[4] See 'Summary Record of Fifth Session of the Committee of the Whole', Diplomatic Conference doc. CCM/CW/SR/5, 18 June 2008.

[5] *Ibid.*; see also 'Summary Record of Ninth Session of the Committee of the Whole', Diplomatic Conference doc. CCM/CW/SR/9, 18 June 2008.

[6] See 'Summary Record of Fifteenth Session of the Committee of the Whole', Diplomatic Conference doc. CCM/CW/SR/15, 18 June 2008.

[7] See Article 120, *1998 Statute of the International Criminal Court*. If such a prohibition on reservations is not expressly mentioned in a treaty, one must assume that reservations are lawful, provided always that a reservation is not 'incompatible with the object and purpose of the treaty'. See Article 19, *1969 Vienna Convention on the Law of Treaties* (contained in Annex 1).

of the treaty in their application to that State' would amount to a reservation,[8] determining in practice what constitutes a reservation (as opposed to a lawful declaration) with respect to a given treaty can sometimes be difficult.[9] In particular, the content of any declaration as to the legal consequences of Article 21, paragraphs 3 and 4, on the issue of interoperability are likely to be scrutinized carefully.

19.6 In case of dispute among States Parties as to whether a declaration is actually a reservation, there could be recourse to the procedure for the settlement of disputes set out in Article 10 of the Convention.[10]

---

[8] It is assumed that a State ratifying a treaty does so with respect to all sovereign territory. Indeed, certain provisions in the Convention on Cluster Munitions apply to territory under the jurisdiction of a State Party (*cf.*, e.g., *supra*, the commentary on Articles 3, 4, 5, and 9. Thus, the status of notifications to the Secretary-General of the United Nations by Denmark and New Zealand upon their respective ratifications of the Convention on Cluster Munitions are open to question. Denmark informed the Secretary-General that: 'Until further notice, the Convention shall not apply to the Faroe Islands.' Upon its ratification to the Convention, the Government of New Zealand notified the Secretary-General that:

> ... consistent with the constitutional status of Tokelau and taking into account the commitment of the Government of New Zealand to the development of self-government for Tokelau through an act of self-determination under the Charter of the United Nations, this ratification shall not extend to Tokelau unless and until a Declaration to this effect is lodged by the Government of New Zealand with the Depositary on the basis of appropriate consultation with that territory...

UN Treaty Collection, 'Convention on Cluster Munitions', Status as at 30 March 2010, <http://treaties.un.org/Pages/ViewDetails.aspx?src=TREATY&mtdsg_no=XXVI-6&chapter=26&lang=en>.

[9] As the Convention clearly forbids reservations, experience suggests that the Depositary would refuse to accept into deposit an instrument of ratification, acceptance, approval or accession with a statement that arguably 'purports to exclude or to modify the legal effect of certain provisions of the treaty in their application to that State'. The Depositary would call the attention of the State concerned to the difficulty and would not issue any notification concerning the instrument to any other State concerned. See 'Summary of Practice of the Secretary-General of the United Nations as Depositary of Multilateral Treaties', UN doc. ST/LEG/7/Rev.l, paragraphs 189–196.

[10] See, *supra*, the commentary on this provision.

Article 20. Duration and withdrawal

Stuart Casey-Maslen and Gro Nystuen[1]

Article 20—Duration and withdrawal

1. This Convention shall be of unlimited duration.

2. Each State Party shall, in exercising its national sovereignty, have the right to withdraw from this Convention. It shall give notice of such withdrawal to all other States Parties, to the Depositary and to the United Nations Security Council. Such instrument of withdrawal shall include a full explanation of the reasons motivating withdrawal.

3. Such withdrawal shall only take effect six months after the receipt of the instrument of withdrawal by the Depositary. If, however, on the expiry of that six-month period, the withdrawing State Party is engaged in an armed conflict, the withdrawal shall not take effect before the end of the armed conflict.

Overview of the Article

20.1 This Article focuses on two aspects, as indicated by its title. First, it defines that the duration of the Convention is unlimited in time. Second, it recalls that any State Party has the right to withdraw from the Convention, and defines under which conditions a State can lawfully do so.

[1] The authors would like to thank Christophe Lanord for his input into the commentary on this Article.

Preparatory discussions and negotiations

20.2 The first three paragraphs of this Article are exactly the same as the *1997 Anti-Personnel Mine Ban Convention*[2] and the Draft Cluster Munitions Convention submitted to the Dublin Diplomatic Conference. However, both texts also included a fourth paragraph, reading as follows:

The withdrawal of a State Party from this Convention shall not in any way affect the duty of States to continue fulfilling the obligations assumed under any relevant rules of international law.

The deletion of this paragraph was the main subject of discussion during the negotiation of Article 20.

20.3 On 21 May 2008, during the first discussion of Article 20 before the Committee of the Whole at the Diplomatic Conference, there was confusion on the precise issue being discussed. A number of delegations[3] had requested the Secretariat to circulate a proposal under the headline 'Article 20— Relationship with Other International Agreements' which read as follows:

This Convention shall be considered as complementary to any existing international agreement binding on the Parties.[4]

That confusion led the President to state that a member of his team 'would consult with interested delegations on Article 20'.[5]

20.4 The following day, a Presidential text was circulated,[6] which included the initial draft, with the fourth paragraph deleted. In the discussion that followed[7] the President underlined that this language had been taken directly from the *1997 Anti-Personnel Mine Ban Convention* and it was intended that those withdrawing from that treaty would still be bound by *1996 Amended*

---

[2] The formal title of this treaty is the Convention on the Prohibition of the Use, Stockpiling, Production and Transfer of Anti-Personnel Mines and on their Destruction.

[3] Australia, Canada, Denmark, Finland, France, Germany, Italy, Japan, the Netherlands, and the United Kingdom.

[4] 'Proposal by Australia, Denmark, Finland, France, Germany, Italy, Japan, the Netherlands and the United Kingdom for additional text', 19 May 2008, Diplomatic Conference doc. CCM/48.

[5] See 'Summary Record of Fifth Session of the Committee of the Whole', Diplomatic Conference doc. CCM/CW/SR/5, 18 June 2008.

[6] 'Presidency Text transmitted to the Plenary—Article 20', Diplomatic Conference doc. CCM/PT/11.

[7] See 'Summary Record of Seventh Session of the Committee of the Whole', Diplomatic Conference doc. CCM/CW/SR/7, 18 June 2008.

Protocol II[8] to the *Convention on Certain Conventional Weapons*[9] unless they withdrew from that Protocol as well. The President added that, as a result, a similar provision would appear to be redundant in this case. It was also clear that the *1969 Vienna Convention on the Law of Treaties* sets out the principles for the relationship between treaties concerning the same subject matter.

Paragraph 1

> This Convention shall be of unlimited duration.

20.5 This paragraph is self-explanatory. It means that the States considered that there should be no limitation in time for the Convention. This is always the case for modern international humanitarian law treaties, although that formula is not always explicit in the text.[10] The only hypothesis leading to the Convention ceasing to be applicable would be the withdrawal of all States Parties or the end of those States; some very unlikely scenarios, obviously.

Paragraph 2

> Each State Party shall, in exercising its national sovereignty, have the right to withdraw from this Convention. It shall give notice of such withdrawal to all other States Parties, to the Depositary and to the United Nations Security Council. Such instrument of withdrawal shall include a full explanation of the reasons motivating withdrawal.

20.6 Unless explicitly prohibited by a treaty, withdrawal from it by a State is always possible, as a consequence of State sovereignty.[11] When this possibility is explicitly mentioned, treaties sometimes set conditions for such a

---

[8] The formal title of this instrument is the Protocol on Prohibitions or Restrictions on the Use of Mines, Booby-Traps and Other Devices as amended on 3 May 1996 (Protocol II to the CCW as amended on 3 May 1996).

[9] The formal title of this treaty is the Convention on Prohibitions or Restrictions on the Use of Certain Conventional Weapons Which May Be Deemed to Be Excessively Injurious or to Have Indiscriminate Effects, as amended on 21 December 2001.

[10] Such a formula can be found, for instance, in Article XIII.1 of the *1972 Biological Weapons Convention*; in Article VII of the 1976 Convention on the prohibition of military or any hostile use of environmental modification techniques; in Article XVI.1 of the *1993 Chemical Weapons Convention*, and in Article 11 of the Optional Protocol to the Convention on the Rights of the Child on the involvement of children in armed conflict.

[11] This is the point made by the inclusion of the words in the article 'in exercising its national sovereignty'. See also Article 54, *1969 Vienna Convention on the Law of Treaties*.

withdrawal as in the present case. The formal condition is to provide all other States Parties, the Depositary, and the United Nations (UN) Security Council with a notice, which must include a 'full explanation' of the reasons motivating withdrawal.

20.7 This formula is based on the *1972 Biological Weapons Convention*[12] and the *1993 Chemical Weapons Convention*.[13] However, in these two treaties, the formula is stricter, as it requires the State to include, in the notice, 'a statement of the extraordinary events it regards as having jeopardised its supreme interests'.[14] The burden of evidence of 'extraordinary events' lies with the withdrawing State. In practice, however, it is rare that a State withdraws from a treaty, especially a treaty on international humanitarian law or disarmament.[15] Indeed, the very few such cases that have taken place have been related to weapons of strategic importance.[16]

Paragraph 3

> Such withdrawal shall only take effect six months after the receipt of the instrument of withdrawal by the Depositary. If, however, on the expiry of that six-month period, the withdrawing State Party is engaged in an armed conflict, the withdrawal shall not take effect before the end of the armed conflict.

---

[12] The formal title of this treaty is the Convention on the Prohibition of the Development, Production and Stockpiling of Bacteriological (Biological) and Toxin Weapons and on their Destruction.

[13] The formal title of this treaty is the Convention on the Prohibition of the Development, Production, Stockpiling and Use of Chemical Weapons and on their Destruction. Article 1, paragraph 1, reads as follows:

Each State Party to this Convention undertakes never under any circumstances:

(a) To develop, produce, otherwise acquire, stockpile or retain chemical weapons, or transfer, directly or indirectly, chemical weapons to anyone;

(b) To use chemical weapons;

(c) To engage in any military preparations to use chemical weapons;

(d) To assist, encourage or induce, in any way, anyone to engage in any activity prohibited to a State Party under this Convention.

[14] Article XIII.2 of the 1972 Convention on the Prohibition of the Development, Production and Stockpiling of Bacteriological (Biological) and Toxin Weapons and on their Destruction; and Article XVI.2 of the *1993 Chemical Weapons Convention*.

[15] See the examples mentioned by Maslen, S., *Commentaries on Arms Control Treaties, Volume I: The Convention on the Prohibition of the Use, Stockpiling, Production, and Transfer of Anti-Personnel Mines and on their Destruction*, Second Edition, Oxford Commentaries on International Law (Oxford: Oxford University Press, 2005), §20.1. [16] See, e.g., *ibid*.

20.8 A withdrawal by a State Party will only take effect at the end of the six-month notice period, unless the withdrawing State is involved in armed conflict in which case withdrawal only takes effect at the end of the conflict. The consequences of the involvement of a State in an armed conflict that seeks to withdraw during it are also set out in the four *1949 Geneva Conventions*[17] and their two *1977 Additional Protocols*,[18] as well as in a number of other international humanitarian law treaties.[19] The primary purpose of including such a provision in the Convention on Cluster Munitions is to prevent a State involved in an armed conflict—whether international or of a non-international character—from starting to use cluster munitions as soon as the six-month period elapses. There might be disagreements, however, on what constitutes an armed conflict.[20]

---

[17] See, for instance, Article 63, 1949 Geneva Convention for the Amelioration of the Condition of the Wounded and Sick in Armed Forces in the Field.

[18] See Article 99, Protocol Additional to the Geneva Conventions of 12 August 1949, and relating to the Protection of Victims of International Armed Conflicts (Protocol I); and Article 25, Protocol Additional to the Geneva Conventions of 12 August 1949, and relating to the Protection of Victims of Non International Armed Conflicts (Protocol II); see also Article 14, Protocol Additional to the Geneva Conventions of 12 August 1949, and relating to the Adoption of an Additional Distinctive Emblem (Protocol III)

[19] See, e.g., Article 37, 1954 Convention for the Protection of Cultural Property in the Event of Armed Conflict; Article 9, *Convention on Certain Conventional Weapons* (Convention on Prohibitions or Restrictions on the Use of Certain Conventional Weapons Which May be Deemed to be Excessively Injurious or to Have Indiscriminate Effects, as amended on 21 December 2001).

[20] See, e.g., 'How is the term "Armed Conflict" defined in international humanitarian law?', published in 2008 by the International Committee of the Red Cross, available at: <http://www.icrc.org/web/eng/siteeng0.nsf/html/armed-conflict-article-170308>; and the Rule of Law in Armed Conflicts (RULAC) Project, 'Qualification of Armed Conflicts', <http://www.adh-geneva.ch/RULAC/qualification_of_armed_conflict.php>.

Article 21. Relations with States not party to this Convention

Torfinn Rislaa Arntsen[1]

Article 21—Relations with States not party to this Convention

1. Each State Party shall encourage States not party to this Convention to ratify, accept, approve or accede to this Convention, with the goal of attracting the adherence of all States to this Convention.

2. Each State Party shall notify the governments of all States not party to this Convention, referred to in paragraph 3 of this Article, of its obligations under this Convention, shall promote the norms it establishes and shall make its best efforts to discourage States not party to this Convention from using cluster munitions.

3. Notwithstanding the provisions of Article 1 of this Convention and in accordance with international law, States Parties, their military personnel or nationals, may engage in military cooperation and operations with States not party to this Convention that might engage in activities prohibited to a State Party.

4. Nothing in paragraph 3 of this Article shall authorise a State Party:

(a) To develop, produce or otherwise acquire cluster munitions;

(b) To itself stockpile or transfer cluster munitions;

(c) To itself use cluster munitions; or

(d) To expressly request the use of cluster munitions in cases where the choice of munitions used is within its exclusive control.

[1] Virgil Wiebe assisted in the research and writing of the sections on Preparatory Discussions and Negotiations.

Overview of the Article

21.1 Article 21 sets out certain obligations that States Parties shall undertake in their relations with States not party to the Convention and specifies the scope of responsibility for acts prohibited by the Convention in situations of military cooperation and operations with States not party.

21.2 This Article primarily addresses the notion of interoperability, which in the present context can be explained in general terms as the ability of forces or agents of various States or international organizations to operate jointly in the performance of a task, mission, or operation.[2] Article 21 employs the term

---

[2] Thus, interoperability is not limited to questions of law. The NATO Glossary defines interoperability as:

> The ability of Alliance forces and, when appropriate, forces of Partner and other nations to train, exercise and operate effectively together in the execution of assigned missions and tasks.

Cf. NATO Glossary, 2-I-6. 'Force interoperability' is 'the ability of the forces of two or more nations' to undertake these activities together. *Cf.* NATO Glossary, 2-F-6. Interoperability is also defined as 'the ability of systems, units or forces to provide services to and accept services from other systems, units or forces and to use the services so exchanged to enable them to operate effectively together'. US Department of Defense, Joint Chiefs of Staff, *Dictionary of Military Terms*, p. 198. 'Interoperability refers to the ability of different forces to operate safely and effectively together in joint or combined operations.' Inquiry Report: Australia's Defence Relations with the United States, para. 3.26, House of Representatives, Canberra 2006, <http://www.aph.gov.au/house/committee/jfadt/usrelations/report.htm> (accessed 15 January 2010). In other contexts, interoperability refers to a technical standard, e.g. the compatibility of computer systems or the ability to exchange and use information. 'Interoperability' is also described as the 'ability of a system (as a weapons system) to work with or use the parts or equipment of another system'. *Cf.* the definition of interoperability in *Merriam-Webster Online Dictionary*, <http://www.merriam-webster.com/dictionary/interoperability> (accessed 15 January 2010). Only a French proposal originally put forward at Wellington and submitted as doc. CCM 16 to the Dublin Diplomatic Conference suggested including the term interoperability in the 'military cooperation and operations', a term referring to a range of activities not further defined in the Convention or in other instruments of international law. The concept of interoperability, which refers to certain characteristics of such activities, is not a defined legal term either. It will be used in the following commentary to describe the rationale behind the provisions of Article 21 that govern engagement in military cooperation and operations with States not party.

21.3 Two overarching concerns lay behind the desire to include provisions on military cooperation and operations in the Convention on Cluster Munitions. One concern has been the potential responsibility of a State Party for assisting in activities performed by the forces or agents of a State not party. Such activities in breach of a Convention obligation could either occur in combined operations involving the forces of a State Party and those of a State not party, or they could occur on the territory of a State Party in connection with the hosting of forces of a State not party. Another concern has been the potential criminal liability of a State Party's nationals for their involvement in such activities by agents of a State not party in military cooperation or operations.[3]

21.4 Article 21 sets out certain positive obligations on States Parties to promote adherence to the Convention and its norms while providing that they may still pursue military cooperation and operations with States not party, even if a State not party might engage in conduct contrary to the Convention. The provisions of Article 21 should be read as a whole. While paragraph 3 provides that a State Party may engage in military cooperation and operations, paragraphs 1, 2, and 4 provide a legal framework for assessing the scope of the permission to engage with States not party in interoperability situations. The wording of paragraphs 1 and 2 does not present significant problems of interpretation or application.[4] However, paragraphs 3 and 4 raise a number of questions of interpretation as to the exact limits of States Parties' obligations under the Convention in these situations. This is owing to the problem of transposing

Convention text itself: 'Nothing in this Convention shall be interpreted as in any way preventing military interoperability between States parties and non-States parties to the Convention.' All other proposals have employed different wording to express this concern.

    [3] This will be further explained below, see §§21.40–21.41, 21.52–21.53, and 21.58–21.60.

    [4] However, in no way diminishing the importance of these paragraphs in advancing the humanitarian standard of the Convention, *cf. infra*. See also Hulme, K., 'The 2008 Cluster Munitions Convention: Stepping Outside the CCW Framework (Again)', *ICLQ*, Vol. 58, January 2009, pp. 219–227 at p. 222 and 'Staying True to the Ban on Cluster Munitions', article by Human Rights Watch, 23 June 2009, available at: <http://www.hrw.org/node/83975#_ftn32> (accessed 15 January 2010).

the general principle allowing for military cooperation between States into precise treaty provisions, given the Convention's object and purpose.[5]

21.5 As a point of departure it should be observed that in any type of scenario where the forces of a State Party to the Convention operate together with the forces of a State not party, their respective international obligations in relation to cluster munitions will not be equivalent. In the event that forces of a State not party in such circumstances engage in activities prohibited to a State Party under the Convention, there is a need to assess the legal consequences of the Convention for the latter. This is particularly the case with respect to the provision in paragraph 1(c) of Article 1, which lays down general obligations concerning potential complicity by a State Party in the conduct of another State. This provision prohibits a State Party 'under any circumstances' to 'assist, encourage or induce anyone to engage in any activity prohibited to a State Party'.[6]

21.6 Thus, in principle, whenever the respective military forces of a State Party and a State not party engage in military cooperation or operations, Article 21 may be invoked. Interoperability therefore concerns the limits on lawful assistance to a State not party in situations of military cooperation and operations. The implication of one State in the conduct of another State may involve international responsibility of the former State in connection with the acts of the latter. However, it may be observed that international military operations are often conducted under a separate legal structure within an international chain of command and control, involving personnel from various troop-contributing States. Within this framework, specific categories of personnel with clearly defined but limited functions may be included in complex multinational structures. The status of such forces may well be that of an organ of an international organization or organs or personnel placed at the disposal of an international organization. It is therefore pertinent to consider the interoperability provisions in relation to the norms of attribution of conduct to participating States in international military cooperation and operations. Consequently, in the analysis of the broader context in which the provisions relating to interoperability are to be interpreted, other applicable

---

[5] This was clearly captured in the Statement of the Government of Iceland at the Dublin Diplomatic Conference, where it was said, with later reference to Article 21, that:

Many of the provisions of the Convention reflect the need to reach political compromises during the negotiations, the States concerned, having agreed on the form of a legally binding treaty, have brought the results into the realm of international law.

'Statement by the Government of Iceland upon the adoption of the Convention on Cluster Munitions, Dublin', Diplomatic Conference doc. CCM/CRP/2, 30 May 2008.

[6] See, *supra*, on this provision, §§1.62–1.80.

rules of international law are relevant legal sources.[7] They include the notion of international responsibility in peace support operations and other military cooperation, attribution of conduct and potential individual liability, both civil and criminal, for personnel concerning their involvement in activities that might be deemed to constitute assistance to others in their performance of acts prohibited to a State Party under the Convention.

21.7 By the wording 'notwithstanding the provisions of Article 1 of this Convention', paragraph 3 of Article 21 is formulated as an exception to Article 1 of the Convention, which sets out the main obligations of States Parties. Where, however, Article 1 is specific with regard to what obligations are incumbent on a State Party, paragraph 3 of Article 21 does not list any specific activities that a State Party may engage in despite its obligations under Article 1. Thus, paragraph 3 modifies the scope of Article 1 where issues of interoperability are at stake without further defining its scope beyond the words 'may engage in military cooperation and operations'. Paragraph 4 of Article 21 is in turn formulated as a limitation on the exception set out in paragraph 3, and is intended to clarify the scope of the latter provision by listing examples of activities not authorized by the provision in paragraph 3.

21.8 While Articles 1 and 9 are drafted in terms similar to those employed in preceding treaties on disarmament and humanitarian law, such as the *1993 Chemical Weapons Convention*[8] and the *1997 Anti-Personnel Mine Ban Convention*,[9] there is no provision in these treaties that is equivalent to Article 21 of the Convention on Cluster Munitions. This does not imply, however, that the issue of interoperability has not been dealt with in the negotiation and conclusion of prior instruments of international law.[10] In this context, it

---

[7] *Cf.* Article 31, paragraph 3(c), *1969 Vienna Convention on the Law of Treaties*, and *infra*, §§21.61–21.71.

[8] Article 1, paragraph 1, Convention on the Prohibition of the Development, Production, Stockpiling and Use of Chemical Weapons and on their Destruction. Other relevant provisions on assistance are included in the Treaty on the Prohibition of the Emplacement of Nuclear Weapons and Other Weapons of Mass Destruction on the Seabed and the Ocean Floor and in the Subsoil Thereof *(Seabed Arms Control Treaty)*, Article 1; the Convention on the Prohibition of the Development, Production and Stockpiling of Bacteriological (Biological) and Toxin Weapons and on their Destruction *(1972 Biological Weapons Convention)*, Article 3; the Convention on the Prohibition of Military or Any Other Hostile Use of Environmental Modification Techniques *(Environmental Modification Treaty)*, Article 1, paragraph 2; and the Comprehensive Nuclear Test-Ban Treaty, Article 1, paragraph 2.

[9] Article 1, paragraph 1(c), *1997 Anti-Personnel Mine Ban Convention*.

[10] Interoperability concerns are not limited to different legal obligations or national positions in respect of cluster munitions. For an overview of other relevant issues, see Col. M. Kelly; 'Legal Factors in Military Planning for Coalition Warfare and Military Interoperability', *Australian Army Journal*, Vol. II, No. 2, Autumn 2005, pp. 161–172 and a report from the US Center for Law and

suffices to cite the declarations made by a number of States Parties to the *1997 Anti-Personnel Mine Ban Convention* upon ratification. These include interpretative observations made by Australia,[11] Canada,[12] the Czech Republic,[13] Montenegro,[14] Serbia,[15] and the United Kingdom (UK).[16] These declarations confirm an understanding that the prohibition on a weapons system such as anti-personnel mines may have an effect on interoperability, but that the

Military Operations; *Forged in the Fire: Legal Lessons Learned During Military Operations (1994–2008)*, September 2008, pp. 350–351, available at: <http://www.loc.gov/rr/frd/Military_Law/pdf/forged-in-the-fire-2008.pdf> (accessed 15 January 2010).

[11] 'It is the understanding of Australia that, in the context of operations, exercises or other military activity authorised by the United Nations or otherwise conducted in accordance with international law, the participation by the Australian Defence Force, or individual Australian citizens or residents, in such operations, exercises or other military activity conducted in combination with the armed forces of States not party to the Convention which engage in activity prohibited under the Convention would not, by itself, be considered to be in violation of the Convention. It is the understanding of Australia that, in relation to Article 1(a), the term "use" means the actual physical emplacement of anti-personnel mines and does not include receiving an indirect or incidental benefit from anti-personnel mines laid by another State or person. In Article 1(c) Australia will interpret the word "assist" to mean the actual and direct physical participation in any activity prohibited by the Convention but does not include permissible indirect support such as the provision of security for the personnel of a State not party to the Convention engaging in such activities, "encourage" to mean the actual request for the commission of any activity prohibited by the Convention, and "induce" to mean the active engagement in the offering of threats or incentives to obtain the commission of any activity prohibited by the Convention.'

[12] 'It is the understanding of the Government of Canada that, in the context of operations, exercises or other military activity sanctioned by the United Nations or otherwise conducted in accordance with international law, the mere participation by the Canadian Forces, or individual Canadians, in operations, exercises or other military activity conducted in combination with the armed forces of States not party to the Convention which engage in activity prohibited under the Convention would not, by itself, be considered to be assistance, encouragement or inducement in accordance with the meaning of those terms in Article 1, paragraph 1 (c).'

[13] 'It is the understanding of the Government of the Czech Republic that the mere participation in the planning or execution of operations, exercises or other military activities by the Armed Forces of the Czech Republic, or individual Czech Republic nationals, conducted in combination with the armed forces of States not party to the [Convention], which engage in activities prohibited under the Convention, is not, by itself, assistance, encouragement or inducement for the purposes of Article 1, paragraph 1 (c) of the Convention.'

[14] '[I]t is the understanding of Serbia and Montenegro that the mere participation in the planning or conduct of operations, exercises or any other military activities by the armed forces of Serbia and Montenegro, or by any of its nationals, if carried out in conjunction with armed forces of the non-State Parties (to the Convention), which engage in activities prohibited under the Convention, does not in any way imply an assistance, encouragement or inducement as referred to in subparagraph 1 (c) of the Convention.'   [15] *Ibid.*

[16] 'It is the understanding of the Government of the United Kingdom that the mere participation in the planning or execution of operations, exercises or other military activity by the United Kingdom's Armed Forces, or individual United Kingdom nationals, conducted in combination with the armed forces of States not party to the [said Convention], which engage in activity prohibited under that Convention, is not, by itself, assistance, encouragement or inducement for the purposes of Article 1, paragraph (c) of the Convention.'

interpretation and application of the said Convention shall not imply liability for 'mere participation' in international military cooperation or operations in which States not party participate.

21.9 Few other States Parties to the *1997 Anti-Personnel Mine Ban Convention* have claimed that 'mere participation' *per se* in military cooperation or operations with States not party constitutes a breach of an obligation under that treaty.[17] Based on this understanding, and the interpretation of the identical provision on assistance in paragraph 1(c) of Article 1 of that treaty, there is ample *opinio juris* from State practice in dealing with practical challenges in interoperability situations. For example, there is evidence that 'mere participation' means that remote or accidental assistance to a State not party's engagement in any activity prohibited by the Anti-Personnel Mine Ban Convention does not qualify as wrongful assistance and that forces of a State Party may derive an accidental benefit in the form of protection from landmines placed by a State not party.[18] Such existing practice will also have guiding value in respect of implementing Article 21 of the Convention on Cluster Munitions.[19]

21.10 While paragraphs 1 and 2 of Article 21 express the goal of universal adherence to the norms of the Convention, paragraph 3 deals with the possible performance by a State not party of 'activities prohibited to a State Party'. The Convention on Cluster Munitions does not create legal obligations for a third State without its consent.[20] But the entry into force of the Convention for coalition partners or co-contributors to military operations will obviously also have an impact on States not party in respect

---

[17] As noted by Human Rights Watch: 'The permissibility of "mere participation" is a widely accepted principle on which states and civil society have agreed,' *supra*, fn. 4, *op. cit.* See also Maslen, S., *Commentaries on Arms Control Treaties, Volume 1: The Convention on the Prohibition of the Use, Stockpiling, Production, and Transfer of Anti-Personnel Mines and on their Destruction* (Oxford: Oxford University Press, 2005), *esp.* §§1.22 *et seq.* and 1.68–1.72 (hereinafter, this work is referred to as the *Commentary on the 1997 Anti-Personnel Mine Ban Convention*), and with regard to combined operations: Rule 164 of the *HCPR Manual on International Law Applicable to Air and Missile Warfare* (Bern: Program on Humanitarian Policy and Conflict Research at Harvard University, 15 May 2009), available at: <http://www.ihlresearch.org/amw/> (accessed 22 March 2010).

[18] State practice in relation to the *Anti-Personnel Mine Ban Convention* is described by S. Maslen, *Commentary on the 1997 Anti-Personnel Mine Ban Convention, op. cit.*

[19] As e.g. suggested by Cdr. J. Orr, 'Draft Convention for Cluster Munitions', in *NATO Legal Gazette*, 15 July 2008, at p. 20:

[I]t would appear that the combination of past state practice with regard to similar language in other treaties, and the addition of the new paragraph expressly authorizing states party the ability to cooperate in operations with non-party states, should mitigate the extent to which the convention [...] would interfere with training and operations.

[20] Article 34, *1969 Vienna Convention on the Law of Treaties.*

of interoperability. Nevertheless, the practical interoperability concerns addressed in Article 21 are expected to be of limited duration.[21] A change of circumstances might come about by a development in law or fact. First, the norms of the Convention may attract universal adherence by such endeavours as are envisaged in paragraph 1 of Article 21, or the prohibition on cluster munitions may become binding on a State not party as a customary rule of international law, recognized as such.[22] The interoperability concerns will only materialize in situations that occur prior to the universalization of the norm prohibiting cluster munitions. Secondly, the Convention's prohibition of cluster munitions may alter the assessment of the utility of such means of warfare among States not party as well, which in practical terms would make it less likely that third States engage in 'activities prohibited to a State Party'.[23] Thirdly, States not party may choose not to develop or acquire future weapons systems that would fall within the Convention's definition of cluster munitions, thus making existing stocks of such munitions obsolete in relation to any future military cooperation or operations with States Parties to the Convention.

21.11 An important feature of Article 21 is that it projects the concept of interoperability into the provisions of the treaty itself. The legal obligations on States Parties laid down in paragraphs 1 and 2 both strengthen the Convention and set legal precedent.[24] As an argument for adhering to the Convention, paragraphs 3 and 4 of this Article may also have the effect of convincing those who would otherwise be in doubt about the operational consequences of doing so. The legal effects of Article 21 largely remain to be seen, and will become clearer as State practice and national implementing legislation on the issue of interoperability evolve. The Meeting of States Parties to the Convention will no doubt be in a position to address

---

[21] This was also pointed out by the Australian delegation at the beginning of the Diplomatic Conference. *Cf.* 'Summary Record of First Session of the Committee of the Whole', Diplomatic Conference doc. CCM/CW/SR/1, 18 June 2008.

[22] Article 38, *1969 Vienna Convention on the Law of Treaties*.

[23] 'The stigma associated with further use will in itself most likely prevent countries that have not yet signed [the Convention] from using cluster munitions.' *Cf.* address by the Norwegian Deputy Minister of Defence, Mr Espen Barth Eide, at the NATO Parliamentary Assembly, Oslo, 23 May 2009, <http://www.regjeringen.no/nb/dep/fd/aktuelt/taler_artikler/politisk_ledelse/statssekretaer_espen_barth_eide/2009/cluster-munitions-and-the-oslo-process-.html?id=562973> (accessed 15 January 2010).

[24] *Cf.* Docherty, B., 'Breaking New Ground: The Convention on Cluster Munitions and the Evolution of International Humanitarian Law', *Human Rights Quarterly* 31 (2009), pp. 934–963, at p. 956.

issues of implementation and practices with regard to the interoperability provisions.[25]

21.12 At the time of writing it seems probable that in future there will not be very many situations involving the use of cluster munitions in circumstances involving a State Party to the Convention.[26] It also seems more probable than not that the practical consequences of the provisions set out in paragraphs 3 and 4 will be of limited duration. These provisions may, though, have an impact on the overall assessment of interoperability issues in international humanitarian and human rights law, including in relation to other instruments that take a 'humanitarian approach to disarmament'.[27] While military experts and representatives of civil society welcome different parts of Article 21 and for different reasons, the provisions of paragraphs 3 and 4 are somewhat ambiguous and may be open to various interpretations.[28] These provisions may also find their way into national implementing legislation and possibly give rise to similar questions of interpretation. In general there is reason to believe that as part of national law, such provisions will protect individuals against uncertainty over the extent of criminal liability that may ensue from their participation in joint operations with forces of a State not party that might engage in activities prohibited by the Convention. Many in the military community regard this as a desirable outcome. And it is perhaps not unreasonable that it is first and foremost up to the States Parties to ensure that the suffering and casualties caused by cluster munitions are brought to an end, through policy development and careful operational planning, rather than by relying on penal provisions targeting individuals serving in difficult circumstances in international operations.

Relationship to other Articles of the Convention

21.13 The legal rule on interoperability must be interpreted in conjunction with Article 1, on general obligations. In addition, Article 9 lays down the obligation to implement national legislation, including penal sanctions,

---

[25] It has been pointed out that the Convention is 'a product of in-depth cooperation by states and civil society, which is expected to continue in the implementation phase', *cf.* Marschik, M., 'The Administration of Arms Control: Ensuring Accountability and Legitimacy of Field Operations' *International Organizations Law Review* 6 (2009), pp. 627–653, at p. 648.

[26] 'NATO, for example, does not currently use cluster munitions in any of its operations.' *Cf.* report by US Center for Law and Military Operations, *op. cit.*, p. 353, note 56.

[27] *Cf.*, *supra*, §0.180.

[28] This is further discussed *infra*, in the commentaries to paragraphs 3 and 4.

to prevent and suppress those activities that are prohibited to a State Party under Article 1 (undertaken by persons or on territory under its jurisdiction or control).[29] Thus, Article 21 specifies the scope of the obligations laid down in Article 1 and Article 9 in situations of interoperability as these are defined in paragraph 3 of Article 21. Article 7 requires transparency in reporting on issues referred to in Article 9 of the Convention.[30] There is a complex relationship between Articles 21, 1, and 3. Pursuant to Article 1 a State Party undertakes never under any circumstances, *inter alia*, to stockpile or retain cluster munitions. Article 3 requires it to destroy or ensure destruction of cluster munitions under its 'jurisdiction and control' as soon as possible. Whether therefore Article 3 applies to stockpiles of cluster munitions owned or possessed by a State not party to the Convention but located on the territory of a State Party will depend on whether these munitions are understood to be under the latter's jurisdiction and control. The stockpiling of cluster munitions by a State not party to the Convention on the territory of a State Party is most likely to occur in the context of military cooperation or operations between such States, a matter regulated by Article 21.[31]

Preparatory discussions

21.14 Although the text of Article 21 of the Convention was first contemplated at the Dublin Diplomatic Conference in May 2008, as one of the main outstanding issues in the final stages, interoperability concerns had been raised throughout the Oslo Process by a large number of— mostly Western—delegations.[32] They expressed, *inter alia*, the fear that

---

[29] See, *supra*, the commentary on implementing measures in accordance with Article 9.

[30] See, *supra*, the commentary on reporting duties in Article 7, §§7.29–7.30.

[31] See, *supra*, §§3.16–3.17 for commentaries on the relationship between Article 3 and Article 21, and §§3.22–3.25 for comments on the terms 'jurisdiction' and 'control'.

[32] Some of them were inspired by the position of the US, which did not participate in the Oslo Process. According to a report by Human Rights Watch and Landmine Action, a State Department official said the US had communicated its views on the process and the draft convention to more than 100 nations. Foremost among the concerns it raised with other States about the possible impact of a future Convention that prohibits cluster munitions was the issue of 'interoperability' (joint military operations involving the US and States Parties to the Convention), with the US seeking to ensure that a new Convention would not impede its ability to employ cluster munitions in NATO and other coalition military operations. *Cf.* Human Rights Watch 'Banning Cluster Munitions, State Policy and Practice, United States,' country report published by Mines Action Canada on behalf of Landmine Monitor, <http://lm.icbl.org/index.php/publications/display?act=submit&pqs_year=2009&pqs_type=cm&pqs_report=usa#footnote-9929–20-backlink> (accessed 15 January 2010).

the proposed prohibition on assistance in paragraph 1(c) of Article 1 would jeopardize future joint military operations and potentially be at odds with existing international obligations of States hosting foreign bases or belonging to military alliances.[33] Further, it was feared that the proposed obligation to impose penal provisions (under Article 9 of the Convention) would put national service personnel at risk of being prosecuted for their involvement in joint activities with the forces of States not bound by a future Convention. Other delegations underlined that the proposed provisions in question were largely identical to the provisions of *inter alia* the *1997 Anti-Personnel Mine Ban Convention* and the *1993 Chemical Weapons Convention*, and that no insurmountable obstacles to continued interoperability had been identified in the implementation of those treaties. However, those who voiced interoperability concerns pointed out that even though there were legal similarities between the evolving discussion texts of the Convention and existing humanitarian instruments, cluster munitions could not be compared to already prohibited means of warfare due to their central role in domestic military inventories and existing national doctrines with regard to defence and security operations.

21.15 To substantiate the real difficulties involved, examples of interoperability issues were presented, covering a wide range of types of involvement and different scenarios. These included international peace operations, enforcement action, and international chains of command, from planning, exercises and training activities to fleet visits and hosting of foreign military bases. It was underlined that the wording of the proposed Convention could have significant practical effects that would be detrimental to the maintenance of international peace and security. Even though the language of international peace operations was employed, it was clear that delegations concerned about interoperability also had in mind situations involving collective self-defence structures. While some delegations favoured wording that would cater for all kinds of practical needs and cover different situations, others preferred a rewording of the proposed Article 1, amendments to Article 9 or new treaty wording in the form of a special provision setting out in more general terms that the convention should not hinder interoperability.[34]

---

[33] The UK and others warned that States would not sign up to an agreement which posed a risk to participation in UN peacekeeping operations, a position later reiterated in Dublin. *Cf.* 'Summary Record of First Session of the Committee of the Whole', Diplomatic Conference doc. CCM/CW/SR/1, 18 June 2008, p. 1. Bilateral hosting agreements were also an issue in this context.

[34] *Cf.* further, *infra*, §21.18.

21.16 In this context, the issue of interoperability was raised by a number of delegations, including Australia, Canada, Japan, Poland, and the UK[35] in relation to paragraph 1(c) of Article 1 of what was termed the Chair's discussion text at the Lima Conference on Cluster Munitions in May 2007.[36] This text included an obligation not to 'assist, encourage or induce, in any way, anyone to engage in any activity prohibited to a State Party under this convention', a phrase identical to the corresponding Articles of the *1997 Anti-Personnel Mine Ban Convention* and the *1993 Chemical Weapons Convention*, suggesting that the wording was meant to cover both direct and indirect assistance. At the Lima Conference, several delegations called for a specific provision to address the issue.[37]

21.17 Since the draft text meant that a State Party would undertake 'never under any circumstances' to assist, encourage or induce anyone to engage in any activity prohibited to a State Party under the Convention,[38] it could be questioned whether the words 'in any way' added substance to the obligations set forth in paragraph 1(c) of Article 1. (The phrase 'in any way' was omitted from paragraph 1(c) of the Vienna Discussion Text.)[39] A significant number of delegations felt that the text was far from addressing their concerns about interoperability. For example, it was stated that the wording of the chair's discussion text could pose significant legal barriers to maintaining interoperability, including for operations with a United Nations (UN) mandate and for operating multinational military bases. At the Vienna Conference, some called for clear provisions to allow for military interoperability with States not party. Others pointed out that existing interoperability concerns due to disparities with regard to international legal obligations between alliance partners had been overcome in practice without putting international peace and security at risk. It was also pointed out that States participating in international operations could still contribute to such operations and work with international partners even though not all of their partners might join a future ban on cluster munitions.

[35] Cluster Munition Coalition, 'Report on the Lima Conference on Cluster Munitions and Next Steps', undated, p. 3.

[36] Chair's discussion text on a legally binding international instrument that will prohibit the use, production, transfer and stockpiling of cluster munitions that cause unacceptable harm to civilians, Lima, 23–25 May 2007 (see Annex 3).

[37] 'Within the framework of the current phrasing on general obligations and scope, it should be noted that at the Lima meeting, some States proposed that specific provision needed to be made for military interoperability with non States Party.' Explanatory Annex, Vienna Discussion Text, 14 November 2007.

[38] *Cf.* Article 1, paragraph 1 of the discussion text and the Convention on Cluster Munitions.

[39] *Cf.*, *supra*, §1.62.

21.18 At the Wellington Conference,[40] a group of delegations presented a discussion paper detailing their concerns about interoperability as follows:

The current Article 1(c) prohibition would apply to international operations where personnel from a State party to a future cluster munitions convention [...] assist, encourage or induce [...] personnel from a non-State party to that convention [...] to use, develop, produce, acquire, stockpile, retain or transfer cluster munitions that are prohibited under that convention.

This would presumably require mental and causation elements to be satisfied. In other words, a State and its personnel would attract liability for acts which have, and are intended to have, a substantial effect in facilitating a specific act prohibited under the Draft Cluster Munitions Convention.

The current text could inhibit a range of military activities essential to the effectiveness of international operations (that involve non-State parties who may use cluster munitions). This would render participation by State parties in such operations unworkable. For instance, the prohibition could potentially affect essential interoperability functions where a State party's personnel:

- engage in headquarters, mission or other planning activities while embedded with non-State party personnel in coalition structures;
- call in close air support or artillery fire support, including for force protection, from non-State party personnel;
- relay intelligence relating to targeting to non-State party personnel;
- provide logistics (such as refuelling services, air traffic control and other support) to non-State party forces;
- conduct joint training exercises with a non-State party's forces.[41]

---

[40] Details of the Wellington Conference are provided *supra*, §§0.48–0.54.

[41] An overview of possible interoperability issues was provided in what has been referred to as the Australian Discussion paper, see 'Cluster Munitions and Inter-Operability: The Oslo-Process Discussion Text and Implications for International Operations', Discussion paper distributed at the Wellington Conference on Cluster Munitions by Australia, Canada, the Czech Republic, Denmark, Finland, France, Germany, Italy, the Netherlands, Sweden, Switzerland, and the UK, February 2008, <http://www.mfat.govt.nz/clustermunitionswellington/conference-documents/Discussion-paper-Au-et-al.pdf >(accessed 15 January 2010). See also the proposal by Germany, supported by Denmark, France, Italy, Slovakia, Spain, the Czech Republic, and the UK, for the amendment of Article 1 (reintroduced in Diplomatic Conference doc. CCM/13) and alternative suggestions by France, Canada and Germany, included in the Compendium of proposals submitted by delegations during the Wellington Conference, pp. 7–8, *cf*, *infra*, Annex 6, addressing interoperability concerns, and a proposal by Japan for the amendment of Article 1 (*cf.* Diplomatic Conference doc. CCM/10) to narrow the wording of Article 1, paragraph 1(c) to: 'assist, encourage or induce anyone to develop, produce or otherwise acquire cluster munitions'.

It was argued that cluster munitions posed more complex challenges than anti-personnel mines in joint operations: cluster munitions were more likely to be used and there were a 'wide variety of planned and unplanned scenarios in which cluster munitions may be used and the short planning lead time involved'.[42] Others disputed the claim about likelihood of use, countering that the military utility of cluster munitions was in fact declining as the nature of warfare changed.[43]

21.19 Following discussions, a large number of proposals on interoperability were put forward at the Wellington Conference. One such proposal limited the prohibition on assistance to 'acquisition, development and production' of cluster munitions, leaving out 'use, stockpiling, retention and transfer' of cluster munitions by States not party.[44] Another proposal was to retain the broad prohibitions of paragraph 1(c) of Article 1 with the caveat that:

> This provision does not preclude the mere participation in the planning or the execution of operations, exercises or other military activities by the armed forces or by an individual national of a state party to this Convention, conducted in combination with the Armed Forces of States not Parties to this Convention which engage in activity prohibited under this Convention.[45]

---

[42] *Ibid.*, p. 2. Similar questions were raised by Canada in its statement to the Wellington Conference:

> Would, for example, the simple participation in combined operations with States not party that may use cluster munitions prohibited under a new convention, be permitted? Would this preclude our forces' engagement in headquarters, missions or other planning activities while embedded with non State party personnel? Would it preclude calling in close air support or other fire support from non-State party personnel, or prevent our forces from providing logistics support to non-State party forces? Would it prevent non-State parties from having bases on our territory or their warships from using our ports?

Statement by Canada on General Obligations and Scope of Application, undated, <http://www.mfat.govt.nz/clustermunitionswellington/conference-documents/Canadian-Statement-on-General-Obligations-Scope.pdf >(accessed 15 January 2010 but no longer available).

[43] The following paper, which laid out counter-arguments for the Dublin Diplomatic Conference, explained how the military utility of cluster munitions was declining. Human Rights Watch and Harvard Law School's International Human Rights Clinic, 'Interoperability and the Prohibition on Assistance: Memorandum to Delegates of the Dublin Diplomatic Conference on Cluster Munitions', May 2008, pp. 11–13, <http://www.hrw.org/en/reports/2008/05/19/interoperability-and-prohibition-assistance> (accessed 26 March 2010).

[44] 'Alternative text for Article 1, paragraph 1(c) as proposed by Japan, and supported by Australia, the Czech Republic, Denmark, Germany, France, Italy, Turkey, and the United Kingdom': '1. Each State Party undertakes never under any circumstances to:... (c) Assist, encourage or induce anyone to develop, produce or otherwise acquire cluster munitions.' Wellington Compendium, p. 7, and *cf. infra*, Annex 6, reintroduced in Diplomatic Conference doc. CCM/10, 19 May 2008.

[45] Proposal by Germany, supported by Denmark, France, Italy, Slovakia, Spain, the Czech Republic and the United Kingdom. *Cf.* Wellington Compendium, p. 6, and *cf. infra*, Annex 6, reintroduced in Diplomatic Conference doc. CCM/13, 19 May 2008.

In a similar way, Canada, France, and Lithuania proposed a separate provision to address the interoperability issue.[46]

21.20 In these discussions in Wellington, Norway pointed out that interoperability issues had been addressed in other contexts, including joint operations involving States Parties and States not party to the *1977 Additional Protocols to the Geneva Conventions*, the *1998 Statute of the International Criminal Court*, and the *1997 Anti-Personnel Mine Ban Convention*. Differing interpretations of the *1993 Chemical Weapons Convention* or international human rights treaties were cited as other examples. The Norwegian delegate went on to state that:

All of these various sets of issues can create practical challenges in the planning and conduct of international operations. National constraints result in various caveats to, for example, [the] Rules of Engagement for each operation. While this might be a problem in itself, it will not in any way be unique for cluster munitions.[47]

Several other delegations, among them Bangladesh, Ghana, and Senegal, current contributors to UN peace operations, and the Lao People's Democratic Republic (Laos) stated their support for the wording of Article 1 of the discussion text without exceptions for fear that concepts like interoperability could open the door to continued use of cluster munitions that cause unacceptable harm to civilians.[48]

---

[46] *Cf.* alternative text as proposed by France (to be included in an additional article, for example Article 9 ter), *cf.* Diplomatic Conference doc. CCM/16, 19 May 2008:

Nothing in this Convention shall be interpreted as in any way preventing military interoperability between States parties and non-States parties to the Convention.

Cf. also alternative text as proposed by Canada (Wellington Compendium, p. 8, *cf. infra*, Annex 6):

Notwithstanding any other provision of this Convention, a State, on becoming a party to this Convention, may declare that, for a period of [xx] years after the entry into force of this Convention for the State concerned, it does not accept the application of Article I (c) with respect to its participation in combined operations and activities with non-party states. A declaration under this article may be withdrawn at any time. During this period in which the declaration under this article remains in force, the State concerned shall take steps to encourage the government of any non-party state participating in such combined operations and activities to ratify this Convention.

See also Statement of Lithuania on general obligations and scope of application, 18 February 2008, <http://www.mfat.govt.nz/clustermunitionswellington/conference-documents/Lithuania-statment-scope-obligations.pdf> (accessed 15 January 2010 but no longer available).

[47] Statement of Norway on general scope and obligations in relation to interoperability, Wellington Conference, 18 February 2008, <http://www.mfat.govt.nz/clustermunitionswellington/conference-documents/Norway-interoperability-statement.pdf> (accessed 15 January 2010).

[48] See Statement of Bangladesh, 'General obligations and scope of application', <http://www.mfat.govt.nz/clustermunitionswellington/conference-documents/Bangladesh-article-one.pdf>;

Negotiations

21.21 It was clear from these discussions that the issue of interoperability would be one of the biggest challenges to achieving consensus during the negotiating stage, which took place at the Diplomatic Conference held in Dublin from 19 to 30 May 2008. These formal negotiations were based on the Wellington Declaration,[49] in which the participants decided to forward the draft text of the 'Cluster Munitions Convention' dated 21 January 2008 as the basic proposal, together with other relevant proposals, 'including those contained in the compendium' attached to that declaration. At the outset of the Diplomatic Conference, several States, among them Albania, Australia, Canada, Costa Rica, the Czech Republic, Denmark, Finland, Germany, Guatemala, Indonesia, Italy, Japan, Lithuania, Peru, Malta, Portugal, the UK, Venezuela, and Zambia, raised the issue of interoperability and Article 1, pointing to the need to clarify the future legality of military cooperation between States Parties and States not party, including in UN peace operations.[50] Indonesia, Portugal and Zambia stressed that the treaty's core provisions should not be weakened in such discussions. Laos stated that a provision on interoperability could respect obligations to military alliances without condoning the use of cluster munitions, using the *1997 Anti-Personnel Mine Ban Convention* as guidance.

21.22 Proposals along the lines of those made at the Wellington Conference were made again on the second day of the Diplomatic Conference. The UK proposed eliminating the paragraph on assistance, encouragement, and inducement in its entirety.[51] France renewed the proposal for interoperability language it had put forward at the Wellington Conference, to be included in Article 1 or as a separate Article.[52] In addition, Germany, supported by the Czech Republic, Denmark, France, Italy,

---

Statement of Laos on Article 1 of the Draft Convention on Cluster Munitions, 18 February 2008, <http://www.mfat.govt.nz/clustermunitionswellington/conference-documents/Laos-statement.pdf>; Statement of Senegal on Article 2, <http://www.mfat.govt.nz/clustermunitionswellington/conference-documents/Senegal-statement.pdf>; and Statement of Ghana, Wellington Conference, accessed 15 January 2010 at: <http://www.mfat.govt.nz/clustermunitionswellington/conference-documents/Ghana-definitions.pdf >(all accessed 15 January 2010 but no longer available).

[49] See Annex 7 for the text of the declaration.

[50] See 'Summary Record of First Session of the Committee of the Whole', Diplomatic Conference doc. CCM/CW/SR/1, 18 June 2008.

[51] 'Proposal by the United Kingdom for the amendment of Article 1', Diplomatic Conference doc. CCM/13, 19 May 2008.

[52] 'Nothing in this Convention shall be interpreted as in any way preventing military interoperability between States parties and non-States parties to the Convention.' 'Proposal by France for the amendment of Article 1', Diplomatic Conference doc. CCM/16, 19 May 2008.

Slovakia, Spain, and the UK, renewed its proposed revision to paragraph 1(c) of Article 1:

(c) Assist, encourage or induce anyone to engage in any activity prohibited to a State Party under this Convention. *This provision does not preclude the mere participation in the planning or the execution of operations, exercises or other military activities by the Armed Forces or by an individual national of a State Party to this Convention, conducted in combination with Armed Forces of States not Parties to this Convention which engage in activity prohibited under this Convention.*[53]

A subsequent proposal by Morocco, supported by Mauritania and Senegal, sought to limit the potential exceptions to the general prohibitions by suggesting the further addition of the following text after the word 'Convention' in the quote above:

provided that the States not party explain to the States Parties participating in the planning or the execution of operations, the military necessity for engaging in such activities and taking into account the humanitarian concerns addressed by the Convention. The States Parties shall refrain from engaging in activities prohibited under this Convention in any joint military operations with States not parties.[54]

21.23 The President of the Dublin Diplomatic Conference, Ambassador Dáithí O'Ceallaigh, appointed Ambassador Christine Schraner Burgener of Switzerland as 'Friend of the President' to conduct informal consultations on Article 1 and the issue of interoperability. After a first informal session open to all delegations, these consultations were largely kept to a relatively small group of around 20 delegations and a handful of observers, as 'interoperability was arguably of key importance for only a limited number' of negotiating States.[55] From the outset, the Friend of the President listened to the concerns and arguments put forward by key proponents of treaty provisions addressing interoperability. Moreover, a small number of delegations from various regions, representing major differing views on interoperability, were invited to participate in this informal setting. A number of

---

[53] 'Proposal by Germany, supported by Denmark, France, Italy, Slovakia, Spain, the Czech Republic and the United Kingdom for the amendment of Article 1', Diplomatic Conference doc. CCM/13, 19 May 2008.

[54] 'Proposal by Morocco, supported by Senegal and Mauritania, for the amendment of the Proposal by Germany, supported by Denmark, France, Italy, Slovakia, Spain, the Czech Republic and the United Kingdom for the amendment of Article 1', Diplomatic Conference doc. CCM/69, 20 May 2008.

[55] Borrie, J., *Unacceptable Harm: A history of how the international treaty banning cluster munitions was won* (Geneva: United Nations Institute for Disarmament Research, 2009), pp. 286–287. 'The Friend was at first trying to orientate herself but later came to the view that it was no longer useful to prefer consultations limited to a smaller set of delegations', *ibid.*, p. 288.

delegations, including Austria, Jamaica, and Zambia, were opposed to any potential weakening of the general obligations in Article 1. Meanwhile, proponents of specific interoperability provisions, including Australia, Canada, Germany, and the UK, did not want to give the impression they were trying to weaken the scope of general obligations to prohibit cluster munitions.[56] The balancing act of formulating the text of the interoperability provisions should therefore, in the view of the delegations involved, preserve in sufficiently accurate terms the right of a State Party to engage in military cooperation and operations with States not party, while at the same time not undermining the humanitarian aims of the Convention by exempting States Parties from their general obligations in situations of interoperability.

21.24 During the first week of consultations with interested delegations, it emerged that the best way forward would be to draft a new, separate Article addressing interoperability concerns rather than to consider amendments to the proposed Article 1 of the Convention.[57] It was further accepted that this new Article should cover relations with States not party in a balanced way. At a later stage it was also decided to place this new Article among the miscellaneous provisions towards the end of the Convention.[58]

21.25 As the provisions of Article 21 were not included in any of what were termed the chair's discussion texts during the Lima, Vienna, and Wellington conferences, they were in fact the only provisions of the Convention that were not elaborated during the Oslo Process. Thus, the text of a new Article had to be devised rather hastily. The starting point was the legal obstacles to interoperability deemed to follow from the proposed general obligations of the Convention. In contrast to the simultaneous informal discussions conducted on other outstanding issues in Dublin, there was a certain lack of clarity as to what exactly were the legal problems that needed to be resolved. Discussions concentrated on finding ways to overcome the perceived obstacles to interoperability. This was approached through legal drafting rather than by exploring the limits of the general obligations in Article 1, and in the light of other relevant rules of international law implicitly referred to in the catalogue of interoperability problems presented. Those who were most concerned about the interoperability issues presented their wish to include separate treaty provisions on interoperability as an absolute condition for achieving consensus

---

[56] *Ibid.*, p. 289.

[57] *Cf.* 'Summary Record of Ninth Session of the Committee of the Whole', Diplomatic Conference doc. CCM/CW/SR/9, 18 June 2008, p. 1.

[58] See Borrie, J., *Unacceptable Harm, op. cit.*, p. 289.

on a draft text of the Convention.[59] Even though several delegations were initially sceptical of the idea of including a treaty provision on interoperability, among them Asian and Latin American countries, it eventually emerged that they had sufficient flexibility to consider proposals to this effect as part of a balanced final outcome.[60] At this juncture it should be recalled that there was broad sympathy for the principle that the Convention should not hinder 'mere participation' in international operations.

21.26 The Friend's drafting proposals quickly took on a four-paragraph structure. But for minor revisions, the first two paragraphs were agreed by the end of the first week.[61] Even though the provisions of paragraphs 1 and 2 were considered important and innovative expressions of obligations in respect of third parties, the main focus of the discussions was not on the content of these provisions. The first paragraph, obligating States Parties to encourage States not party to join the Convention, remained the same throughout numerous drafts and made its way unchanged into the Convention.[62] The proposed second paragraph went further, suggesting an obligation that States Parties 'notify the governments of all States not party to this Convention, referred to in paragraph 3 of this Article, i.e. those with whom it would cooperate militarily, of its obligations under this Convention', and that they 'promote the norms it establishes'. States Parties would be called upon 'to discourage States not party to this Convention from using cluster munitions as defined in Article 2 of this Convention'.[63] The only controversy concerning paragraph 2 was the level of intensity of that discouragement: should the wording be 'shall make its best

[59] 'These states presented a legally workable solution on interoperability as a prerequisite for their signing and ratifying.' *Ibid.*, p. 286.

[60] e.g., Peru stated at the outset that a clear provision on interoperability would enrich the Convention by securing the agreement of States, *cf.* 'Summary record of First Session of the Committee of the Whole', Diplomatic Conference doc. CCM/CW/SR/1, 18 June 2008, p. 2. Zambia, which coordinated the positions of the group of African States at the Dublin Diplomatic Conference, stated that it had difficulties with the concept of interoperability but considered this to be an element of compromise in the negotiations, *cf.* 'Summary Record of Tenth Session of the Committee of the Whole', Diplomatic Conference doc. CCM/CW/SR/10, 18 June 2008, pp. 5 and 8.

[61] 'There was broad consensus on paragraphs 1 and 2 of the text proposed in Ambassador Schraner's informal paper.' *Cf.* 'Summary Record of Ninth Session of the Committee of the Whole', Diplomatic Conference doc. CCM/CW/SR/9, 18 June 2008, p. 1.

[62] 'Each State Party shall encourage States not party to this Convention to ratify, accept, approve or accede to this Convention, with the goal of attracting the adherence of all States to this Convention.' Article 21, paragraph 1. *Cf.* 'Informal Proposal by the Friend of the President on Interoperability', dated 21 May 2008.

[63] *Ibid.* The modifier 'as defined in Article 2 of this Convention' was dropped from the Convention with little or no opposition even though at the outset of the Dublin Diplomatic Conference a number of proposals were submitted to this effect.

efforts to discourage'[64] or 'shall make in all circumstances its best efforts to discourage'.[65] Different proposals went back and forth until the less forceful wording won out.[66]

21.27　The more controversial wording of the proposed Article was set out in paragraphs 3 and 4. An informal proposal by the Friend of the President on 21 May 2008 had the following wording:

3. Notwithstanding the provisions of Article 1 of this Convention and for the purposes of the maintenance of international peace and security in accordance with international law, a State Party may,

a.　host States not party to this Convention which engage in activities described in Article 1.

b.　participate in the planning or execution of operations, exercises or other military and related logistic activities by that State Party, its armed forces or individual nationals, conducted in combination with armed forces of States not parties to this Convention which engage in activities described in Article 1.

4. Nothing in paragraph 3 of this Article shall, however, authorise a State Party to itself use cluster munitions as defined in Article 2 of this Convention.

21.28　To a number of delegations the concept of 'derogating' from the general obligations of the Convention by hosting military forces or installations of a State not party was perceived as creating a loophole, potentially undermining an effective ban on cluster munitions. The notion of 'hosting' was not reflected in any formal proposal submitted to the Diplomatic Conference but was thought to address particular concerns expressed to the Friend of the President by the UK and other countries that had US military bases on their soil.[67] It was understood that if a host State, for example, had territorial juris-

---

[64] *Ibid.* See also 'Informal Proposal by the Friend of the President on Interoperability (revised version)', dated 23 May 2008; and 'Proposal by the Friend of the President on Interoperability', dated 27 May 2008.

[65] 'Proposal by the Friend of the President on Interoperability for the Committee of the Whole', 23 May 2008, and 'New Proposal by the Friend of the President on Interoperability', 26 May 2008.　　　　　　　　　　　　　　　　[66] *Cf.* Article 21, paragraph 2 of the Convention.

[67] According to John Borrie (*Unacceptable Harm, op. cit.*, pp. 289–290):

While US military bases on British territory, which included places like Diego Garcia in the Indian Ocean, as well as mainland Britain, were in practice controlled by the United States, the British government was legally responsible for them. These controversial arrangements had recently been highlighted over the use of British facilities in the rendition of people deemed by the US government to be terrorist suspects from other parts of the world without due legal process. In the context of interoperability, the concern was that the US would likely have cluster munitions stockpiled in many of these hosted bases, which could put the UK in violation of the Convention on Cluster Munitions if it became a state party. Concerns about

diction but not operational control over a foreign military base, a number of legal as well as practical questions would arise in relation to the main obligations of the Convention, not least in connection with the provisions on storage and stockpile destruction. At the last moment, however, the explicit reference to 'hosting' was omitted from the text.[68]

21.29 An alternative text proposed by the Friend included the wording in paragraph 3 that a State Party 'may declare, at the deposit of its instrument of ratification, acceptance, approval or accession that, in accordance with international law, it may' host States not party or participate in operations as outlined above. A new paragraph 5 made it clear that such declarations could be withdrawn at any time.

21.30 Far from all negotiating States saw an interoperability provision as indispensable for their joining a ban on cluster munitions. In original proposals by Canada and Japan,[69] interoperability concerns were addressed by permitting States Parties to make a reservation on this point. An acceding State might thus declare that the Convention should not prevent hosting or participating in activities in combination with armed forces of a State not party which engage in activities described in Article 1, and such declarations could be withdrawn at any time. As a consequence of this proposed drafting, the phrase 'notwithstanding any other provision of the Convention' was included, a phrase that with some adjustments made its way into the final wording of the Friend's text. However, there was firm and consistent resistance against any provision allowing reservations. The idea of having to make a reservation to safeguard potential interoperability concerns was not viable.

21.31 As noted above,[70] the original proposals for interoperability provisions had suggested a clarification in, or a reference to, paragraph 1(c) of Article 1, which prohibits 'assistance'. The draft proposal from the Friend of the President widened the scope of Article 21 by referring to Article 1 as such. At the same time, the proposed paragraph 4 was intended to clarify certain limits to what a State Party could legitimately do with reference to its interoperability requirements.

---

the interoperability draft article as regards hosting of foreign bases also affected Italy, Japan and Central and East European members of NATO to varying degrees.

[68] *Ibid.* On the overall balance of interests concerning foreign military bases, it should be pointed out that the word 'and' was inserted at the last minute to replace the word 'or', as in the basic proposal, between 'jurisdiction' and 'control' in paragraph 1 of Article 3 on storage and stockpile destruction (*cf.* paragraph 2 in the basic proposal). Also, the emerging text of paragraph 4(b) of Article 21 meant that the provision would only refer to a State Party's own stockpiling or transferring of cluster munitions by the reference to a State Party 'itself'. *Cf. supra*, §§3.17 and 3.26–3.27, and *infra*, §§21.36 and 21.80–21.84.

[69] See Wellington Compendium, p. 8, *infra*, Annex 6.   [70] §21.22.

However, it was called into question whether the proposed text of paragraph 4 actually clarified the meaning of draft Article 21. Several delegations also raised concerns about the correct interpretation of the scope of the proposed Article, in particular the meaning of paragraph 4 and the legal concepts introduced therein. Some pointed out that by making a clear reference in paragraph 3 to paragraph 1(c) of Article 1, dealing with assistance, alternatively by deleting the reference to Article 1 altogether, there would no longer be a rationale for including the provisions of paragraph 4 to limit the potential scope of paragraph 3.

21.32 In this vein, alternative wording was suggested, substituting the reference 'notwithstanding the provisions of Article 1' for the words 'without prejudice to Article 1' in order to clarify that the provision in paragraph 3 was meant to facilitate military cooperation and not modify States' obligations under the Convention. Further alternative wording was put forward, suggesting that paragraph 3 should not be read as permitting the intentional assistance by a State Party in any activity contravening the obligations of the Convention by a State not party, alternatively that the authorization provided by paragraph 3 should be limited to situations where a State Party is not in a position to exercise effective control over such conduct as might contravene Article 1 of the Convention carried out by a State not party.[71]

21.33 By the end of the first week of negotiations, the Friend of the President had issued a revised proposal to the Committee of the Whole, which delegates were urged to consider:

3. While implementing the obligations of States Parties under Article 1 of this Convention, a State Party, in accordance with international law, may,

a. host States not party to this Convention which engage in activities described in Article 1.

b. take part in planning, operations, exercises or other military and related activities conducted by that State Party, its armed forces or individual nationals, in combination with armed forces of States not parties to this Convention which engage in activities described in Article 1.

4. Nothing in paragraph 3 of this Article shall, however, authorise a State Party to itself use, or expressly request the use of, cluster munitions as defined in Article 2 of this Convention.[72]

---

[71] Zambia, on behalf of the African delegations, stated that it had reservations about the concept of 'effective control' as this would require further study to avoid problems of interpretation. *Cf.* 'Summary Record of Tenth Session of the Committee of the Whole', Diplomatic Conference doc. CCM/CW/SR/10, 18 June 2008, p. 8.

[72] 'Informal Proposal by the Friend of the President on Interoperability', revised version, dated 23 May 2008.

21.34 The subsequent discussion in the Committee of the Whole on 26 May revealed a shift towards broader acceptance of an independent article on interoperability. While several Latin American delegations, including Honduras, Mexico, and Venezuela, continued to express opposition to a new article on interoperability,[73] others, including Argentina, Guatemala, and Uruguay, opposed the draft Article in principle, but indicated a willingness to engage in further negotiations on the issue.[74] Zambia, on behalf of the African delegations, emphasized that it had difficulties with the concept of interoperability but considered this to be an element of compromise in the negotiations. A significant number of delegations supported the proposed Article in principle, although some of them, including Australia, Canada, Denmark, Italy, and the former Yugoslav Republic of Macedonia, had issues with specific wording in sub-paragraph 3(b) and paragraph 4. Other delegations, including France, Germany, Indonesia, Japan, and the Netherlands, saw the text as a good basis for further progress.[75]

21.35 On 27 May, a final proposal by the Friend of the President had been put forward in an attempt to resolve outstanding differences:

3. Notwithstanding the provisions of Article 1 of this Convention and in accordance with international law, States Parties, or their military personnel or their nationals, may engage in military cooperation with States not party to this Convention which might engage in activities prohibited to a State party.

4. Nothing in paragraph 3 of this Article shall authorise a State Party

(a) to develop, produce or otherwise acquire cluster munitions as defined in Article 2 of this Convention,

(b) to itself stockpile or transfer such cluster munitions, and

(c) to itself use, or expressly request the use, of such munitions in cases where the choice of munitions used is within its exclusive control.[76]

---

[73] See 'Summary Record of Tenth Session of the Committee of the Whole', *op. cit.*, pp. 7–8. Mexico stated that 'interoperability had no place in the Convention'; Venezuela pointed out that including an additional Article 'would risk creating two orders of States Parties, those complying immediately with the Convention and those continuing to effectively have recourse to cluster munitions'; Honduras said that interoperability was 'inappropriate in a Convention seeking to eliminate cluster munitions and their use'.

[74] *Ibid.*, pp. 7–9. According to Argentina, 'several delegations shared a general reservation about including the concept of interoperability in the Convention, as it may create a window for the use of cluster munitions by military coalitions [...] Despite concerns voiced about inclusion of the concept, paragraph (c) [*sic*] of the Friend's text actually widened the scope of interoperability by referring to Article 1 as a whole and not merely Article 1(c) [i.e. assistance].'   [75] *Ibid.*

[76] 'Proposal by the Friend of the President on Interoperability', dated 27 May 2008.

21.36 Importantly, the term 'host' had been deleted from the new draft. While such a provision had been regarded as crucial for the UK if it was to adhere to the treaty,[77] the provision set out in paragraph 4(b), that no State Party shall be authorized 'to itself stockpile' cluster munitions, read in conjunction with paragraph 1 of Article 3, nevertheless implied that stockpiling by a State not party on the territory of a State Party would still be allowed. Hence, it was understood that the obligations not to stockpile and to ensure their destruction would not apply to cluster munitions stockpiled on the territory of a State Party that remained under the jurisdiction and control of a State not party to the Convention.

21.37 At this point the President of the Diplomatic Conference told his Friends that he would reassume direct responsibility for the draft Convention text and conduct bilateral consultations.[78] Concerns still persisted, particularly over the wording 'notwithstanding the provisions of Article 1', which was still perceived to give general priority to paragraph 3 of Article 21 over the general obligations laid down in Article 1 of the Convention. Several delegations pleaded with the President to consider further negotiations on draft Article 21.

21.38 The Conference President and key proponents of draft Article 21 were approached by the Cluster Munition Coalition on the afternoon of 28 May in a last bid to reconsider the wording of the proposed text of paragraph 3 of Article 21. However, as other outstanding issues had been dealt with in the meantime through extensive consultations, at that point there was an unwillingness to re-open any element of the draft text of the Convention for fear it would unravel.[79] The President's assessment was that an alternative wording of Article 21 would not command consensus in the Committee of the Whole. With minor grammatical corrections and removal of the phrase 'as defined in Article 2' from paragraph 4(a), and the consequential removal of the word 'such' from the following paragraphs, the 27 May formulation was retained in the President's text and in the final Convention as Article 21.[80] Thus, the negotiating States now had a compromise text that at least satisfied some delegations' interoperability concerns, without causing the remaining, more sceptical delegations to reject the overall result of the negotiations.[81]

---

[77] See Borrie, J., *Unacceptable Harm, op. cit.*   [78] *Ibid.*, p. 291.

[79] *Ibid.*, pp. 300–301.

[80] *Cf.* Article 21 in 'Presidency Paper, draft Convention on Cluster Munitions', Diplomatic Conference doc. CCM/PT/15, 28 May 2008.

[81] In the words of the Friend on the President, the text represented the language most likely to strike a balance between positions and stood the best chance of commanding general agreement. *Cf.*

21.39 In statements made in the Committee of the Whole on 28 May 2008, the delegates informally accepted the President's text as basis for consensus on the final wording of the treaty to be adopted by the Plenary of the Diplomatic Conference. However, the Cluster Munition Coalition, in particular, expressed disappointment with the wording of Article 21, calling on all States 'to clarify that Article 21 does not allow intentional assistance in prohibited acts, foreign stockpiling or acts that undermine fundamental obligations of the Convention in any way'.[82]

21.40 A crucial motivation behind these negotiations had been the safeguarding of national service personnel from the risk of criminal liability, for example, for accidental assistance or for complying with superior orders in situations involving international military cooperation or joint operations. Unlike the rules concerning war crimes in international humanitarian law, the Convention on Cluster Munitions does not establish as international crimes any acts contravening the prohibitions laid down in Article 1. Instead, by virtue of Article 9 of the Convention, penal sanctions as well as other implementing provisions shall be defined in national legislation.[83] Consequently, such penal provisions will vary depending on the specific requirements of the legal systems of the respective States Parties. The issues of State responsibility and individual criminal liability were not addressed separately in the negotiations of Article 21.

21.41 While there remain questions on the interpretation of Article 21 with regard to the potential limits to States' obligations in situations of interoperability, it is clear from the negotiating history that by referring to their military personnel or nationals in paragraph 3, States intended to leave sufficient room for manoeuvre in adapting their national criminal legislation to the prohibitions laid down in the Convention. This understanding of the wording of paragraph 3 was based on broad acceptance by delegations. Thus, in their implementing provisions, States Parties may take into account, for example, command structures in international operations or other military cooperation, the threshold of criminal assistance in

Diplomatic Conference doc. CCM/CW/SR/13, 27 May 2008, p. 1. This did not prevent a feeling of discomfort that was largely absent in relation to all other issues in the President's text that were settled during the negotiations in Dublin.

[82] *Cf.* 'Summary Record of Sixteenth Session of the Committee of the Whole', Diplomatic Conference doc. CCM/CW/SR/16, 18 June 2008, p. 9.

[83] While there were attempts to include a provision on universal jurisdiction in the negotiations of Article 9 of the 1997 *Anti-Personnel Mine Ban Convention, cf.* Maslen, S., *Commentary on the 1997 Anti-Personnel Mine Ban Convention, op. cit.,* §§9.2 *et seq.*, this was not an issue during the negotiations of the Convention on Cluster Munitions.

national law, and the requirement of wrongful purpose (*mens rea*) in such circumstances.[84]

Paragraph 1

Each State Party shall encourage States not party to this Convention to ratify, accept, approve or accede to this Convention, with the goal of attracting the adherence of all States to this Convention.

Commentary

21.42 Paragraph 1 of Article 21 obliges States Parties to strive for the universalization of the norm prohibiting cluster munitions by encouraging States not party to the Convention to adhere to it. Ultimately, the universalization of the prohibition on cluster munitions will solve the issue of interoperability. This particular obligation is aimed at balancing Article 21, which deals with relations with States not party, in a way that puts emphasis on the humanitarian goal to protect civilians from the adverse consequences of cluster munitions. It thereby goes further than the preamble, which in its nineteenth paragraph emphasizes 'the desirability of attracting the adherence of all States' to the Convention and 'to work strenuously towards the promotion of its universalization and its full implementation'.[85]

21.43 Unlike the corresponding preambular paragraph in the *1997 Anti-Personnel Mine Ban Convention*, paragraph 1 of Article 21 does not specify in which fora States Parties shall encourage other States to join the Convention.[86] It must therefore be up to the States Parties themselves to decide in good faith

---

[84] *Cf., infra*, §§21.55–21.56. As observed by Borrie, J. (*Unacceptable harm, op. cit.*, p. 289):

there was the strong wish of the Like-minded to safeguard their military personnel from liability in joint operations with forces of states not party... [B]y early in the second week, the Like-minded seemed reasonably comfortable with the text of draft Article 21 as it pertained to this concern.

[85] See, *supra*, §§0.178–0.179.

[86] The ninth paragraph of the preamble to the *1997 Anti-Personnel Mine Ban Convention* reads as follows:

Emphasizing the desirability of attracting the adherence of all States to this Convention, and determined to work strenuously towards the promotion of its universalization in all relevant fora including, inter alia, the United Nations, the Conference on Disarmament, regional organizations, and groupings, and review conferences of the Convention on Prohibitions or Restrictions on the Use of Certain Conventional Weapons Which May Be Deemed to Be Excessively Injurious or to Have Indiscriminate Effects.

how to carry out this obligation and whether to convey their invitation to other States to join the Convention in multilateral forums, through bilateral contacts, or both. However, the positive legal obligation on States Parties introduced by the words 'shall encourage' will not be satisfied if States remain silent on the matter in relevant contacts with representatives of States not party.

21.44 The obligation to encourage adherence to the Convention may be significant in relation to relevant international organizations concerned with military cooperation and operations that have a mixed membership of States Parties and States not party. In these circumstances a group of States Parties to the Convention may also discharge their obligation by joint action in the relevant organs of the organization, by promoting resolutions, joint statements, or otherwise.

Paragraph 2

Each State Party shall notify the governments of all States not party to this Convention, referred to in paragraph 3 of this Article, of its obligations under this Convention, shall promote the norms it establishes and shall make its best efforts to discourage States not party to this Convention from using cluster munitions.

Commentary

21.45 Paragraph 2 of Article 21 lays down specific obligations that can be viewed as a continuation of the more general obligation in paragraph 1 to strive for universalization of the ban on cluster munitions. These obligations are relevant in relation to situations of interoperability with States not party to the Convention, by reference to those States not party 'referred to in paragraph 3', which deals specifically with military cooperation and operations with States not party to the Convention. Thus, in addition to the specific obligations it sets out, paragraph 2 is also significant when interpreting the legal norms established by paragraphs 3 and 4.

21.46 States Parties are obliged to notify the governments of States not party to the Convention with which they are engaged in military cooperation or operations about their obligations under the Convention. This is a formal requirement and must in this context be interpreted as applicable to all situations of military cooperation between States involving their service personnel, equipment, or other facilities, or covering activities conducted on territory under the jurisdiction or control of a State Party. Given the unconditional wording of this paragraph, it cannot be inferred that the obligation of a State Party to provide notification of its obligations under the Convention is applicable only to situations where that State Party is actually exercising its authority or control over the operation, personnel, or facilities in question.[87] Nor can the reference in paragraph 2 to States not party that 'might engage in activities prohibited to a State Party' in paragraph 3 limit the obligation to notify based on an assessment of whether it appears foreseeable under the prevailing circumstances that the State not party in question would engage in such activities. Given that the object and purpose of this provision are to ensure that prohibited acts do not occur in interoperability situations, notifications should be submitted to relevant governments by the time the Convention enters into force for the State Party in question, and thereafter as applicable prior to the commencement of future military cooperation or operations with States not Party.

21.47 Paragraph 2 further obliges States Parties to promote the norms of the Convention. This positive expression of good faith performance of treaties, to promote its object and purpose, and to abstain from acts calculated to frustrate the object and purpose of the treaty,[88] in addition to the formal requirement of notifying at government level, is of a general nature and closely connected with the effort to achieve universalization of the humanitarian norm as laid down in paragraph 1. Even though Article 21 deals with relations with States not party to the Convention, this particular provision is not strictly linked to the concept of State and should therefore also be seen in the light of the twelfth paragraph of the Convention's preamble, which addresses non-State actors.[89] There may also be an obligation to promote the humanitarian norms of the Convention in relation to non-State armed groups that might engage in prohibited activities. In Nicaragua v. United States of America[90] the International Court of Justice considered that there is an obligation in the terms of Article 1 of the Geneva Conventions, to 'respect' the Conventions

---

[87] Within the meaning of Articles 6 and 8 of the ILC's Articles on Responsibility of States for Internationally Wrongful Acts or Articles 4 and 5 of the ILC's draft Articles on Responsibility of International Organizations. See further discussion *infra*.

[88] The obligation to abstain from acts calculated to frustrate the object and purpose of a treaty is implicit in the obligation to perform the treaty in good faith. *Yearbook of the International Law Commission*, 1966, Vol. II, p. 211.

[89] This paragraph reads: 'Resolved also that armed groups distinct from the armed forces of a State shall not, under any circumstances, be permitted to engage in any activity prohibited to a State Party to this Convention.'

[90] Military and Paramilitary Activities in and against Nicaragua, Judgment 27 June 1986, *ICJ Reports 1986*, para. 220. Common Article 1 of the *1949 Geneva Conventions* and Article 1 of *1977 Additional Protocol I* thereto oblige States Parties to 'respect and secure respect' for the norms therein.

and even 'to ensure respect' for them 'in all circumstances', since such an obligation does not derive only from the Conventions themselves, but from the general principles of humanitarian law to which the Conventions merely give specific expression. This negative obligation 'not to encourage persons or groups' engaged in conflict to act in violation of humanitarian law extends also to non-State actors.

21.48 In situations of interoperability, this provision must be understood to impose an obligation on States Parties in all relevant relations with States not party to the Convention actively to promote the norms the Convention establishes. In order to be effective in situations of military cooperation and operations, the obligation to promote the norms of the Conventions must apply to agents of States Parties at all levels, and in particular at the appropriate military level.

21.49 As noted above, the obligation to promote the norms of the Convention is also relevant in relation to international organizations. Interoperability issues frequently arise in the conduct of international operations undertaken either by a coalition of States or by an international organ. The latter situation exists when an operation constitutes an organ of an international organization, for example UN peace operations or international operations established by the African Union, the European Union, or by NATO. An international operation may also constitute a joint organ of several States and/or international organizations. An international organ will not as such become bound by the norms of the Convention unless that organ itself undertakes to respect the ban on cluster munitions or it is established that a rule of customary law has developed. A customary rule would then become binding on all subjects of international law. Thus, the obligations to seek to achieve universalization of the Convention and to promote its norms oblige a State Party that is a member of a relevant international organization to promote a ban on cluster munitions within that organization as well.

21.50 Finally, paragraph 2 imposes an obligation on States Parties to make their best efforts to discourage States not party from using cluster munitions. This provision is primarily relevant to the conduct of armed conflict or participation in international operations as there is less likelihood of a participating State not party to the Convention actually using cluster munitions in other circumstances. However, 'use' could also comprise training and exercises not covered by the limited exceptions for the purposes of detection, clearance, or destruction techniques, or for the development of counter-measures as laid down in paragraph 6 of Article 3. The obligation to discourage use is therefore general and not limited to situations of interoperability. In the event of an armed conflict or other situation that could trigger the use of military force, States Parties would be expected to promote the humanitarian norms of the Convention and request that cluster munitions not be used. In interoperability situations, the obligation to discourage the use of cluster munitions will also prohibit any request by a State Party that cluster munitions should be used by a participating State not party. As will be discussed below, this implies that paragraph 4(d) of Article 21 cannot be interpreted *a contrario*, taking into account this provision in paragraph 2.[91]

21.51 In relation to interoperability, this provision also raises questions pertaining to the joint strategic planning of international operations and establishment of standard operating procedures and Rules of Engagement (ROE) for the particular operation,[92] since it is at this stage that restraints on the use of force and safeguarding of national restrictions (*caveats*) may be established with respect to the conduct of national contingents taking part in the operation.[93] A State Party may be confronted by such operative rules

---

[91] See, *infra*, §§21.88 and 21.91.

[92] In respect of peace support operations, the United States Field Manual states that 'ROE define when and how force may be used. ROE may reflect the law of armed conflict and operational considerations but are principally concerned with restraints on the use of force. ROE are also the primary means by which commanders convey legal, political, diplomatic, and military guidance to the military force' (100–23, Peace Operations, Chapter 3). 'In coalition operations outside formal alliances, each participating state drafts and approves its own ROE. Thus, the national chain of command approves changes to the ROE. In OIF [Operation Iraqi Freedom], Coalition partner ROE were different from US ROE, reflecting each partner's law and policy. [..] Where issued NATO ROE exists, commanders and staffs will track any additional restrictions to which a contingent is subject (referred to as national *caveats*).' See report from the US Center for Law and Military Operations, above, fn. 10, *op. cit.*, pp. 344 and 347. See also definition of 'joint operation planning' in the US Department of Defense Dictionary of Military and Associated Terms, p. 288, <http://www.dtic.mil/cgi-bin/GetTRDoc?AD=ADA439918&Location=U2&doc=GetTRDoc. pdf> (accessed 15 January 2010).

[93] Within a NATO context, e.g., troop-contributing States may even agree with the commander of an international operation to deploy what is termed a 'red card holder', a national representative combining a national role with a staff function in the international peace support operation. The specific circumstances generally relate to the sensitivity of the means deployed. The red card holder has formal authority to reject specific missions assigned to the national contingent by the international commander. See further Zwanenburg, M., *Accountability of International Peace Support Operations*, International Humanitarian Law Series (Leiden: Martinus Nijhoff, 2005), pp. 47–48. The experience of 'red card' in Operation Iraqi Freedom is further assessed by M. Kelly, *supra*, fn. 10, *op. cit.*, p. 165. The potential use of cluster munitions by a participating State not party may create such national sensitivities as described above. A further example: in a note on the measures taken by Ireland to implement Article 21 of the Convention issued by the Department of Foreign Affairs on 11 March 2009, it is submitted that: 'in respect of each peacekeeping mission to which a contingent of the Irish Defence Forces has been committed, and as soon as the conditions on which it will serve (including caveats) have been settled, appropriate orders will issue to that contingent to ensure that under no circumstances does any member of it deliberately assist, encourage or induce the commission of an act prohibited by the Convention by a non-state party'.

by participating in the planning of international operations or by contributing personnel to an ongoing operation where the ROE have already been decided by others. ROE do not normally go into much detail on various types of munitions that may be employed at given levels of conflict, but they may refer to international humanitarian law provisions where these are perceived to be customary in nature by the participating States.[94] At the time of entry into force of the Convention, participating States Parties to international operations would normally be able to deal with the prohibition on cluster munitions by national caveats. As a general measure to enhance interoperability, legal advisers deployed with contingents of peace support operations are generally advised to keep a database of relevant treaties, legal codes, rules, and regulations, as well as a lessons learned manual, to ensure respect for ROE and such national caveats.[95] While it may be questioned whether the obligation to make their best efforts to discourage the use of cluster munitions can be interpreted as compatible with a State Party's subsequent participation in developing or deciding on ROE expressly permitting such use, this provision would not, in the context of Article 21 as a whole, rule out participation in any operation were the ROE silent on this point, provided that national restrictions or red lines are effectively safeguarded.[96]

Paragraph 3

Notwithstanding the provisions of Article 1 of this Convention and in accordance with international law, States Parties, their military personnel or nationals, may engage in military cooperation and operations with States not party to this Convention that might engage in activities prohibited to a State Party.

Commentary

21.52 Paragraph 3 of Article 21 addresses the issue that adherence to the Convention should not unduly restrict States Parties' continued or future

---

[94] *Cf.* Fleck, D. (ed.), *Handbook of International Humanitarian Law*, Second Edition (Oxford: Oxford University Press, 2008), p. 648, *cf.* also pp. 655–662.   [95] *Ibid.*, p. 662.

[96] This will be further commented on *infra* in relation to paragraphs 3 and 4. E.g., a member State of an international organization would not incur responsibility for assisting in the commission of a wrongful act by participating in the decision-making process of the organization. *Cf.* the ILC commentary to draft Article 57 on Responsibility of International Organizations, *cf.* UN doc. A/64/10, 2009, p. 160.

participation in international military cooperation and operations, even though other participants in such activities might not join the ban on cluster munitions. The final wording of this paragraph features a number of elements from earlier proposals to this effect; however, questions remain on how to interpret the limits of such engagement in the context of Article 21 and in the light of the object and purpose of the Convention.[97] These questions can be addressed in particular by analysing the meaning of the phrase 'notwithstanding the provisions of Article 1', the reference to international law, the inclusion of the reference to 'military personnel or nationals' of a State Party, and the words 'may engage' in military cooperation and operations.

21.53 In addition to a textual interpretation of paragraph 3, the reference to Article 1 must be interpreted in conjunction with the material scope of those general obligations prohibiting assistance, encouragement, or inducement to engage in any activity prohibited to a State Party,[98] and the provisions of paragraph 4 exemplifying actions that a State Party shall not be authorized to perform. Only insofar as Article 1 is interpreted to constitute a material obstacle to interoperability, as understood in paragraph 3 of Article 21, will States Parties have to deviate from their general obligations by invoking Article 21 as a legal basis for engaging in military cooperation or operations. The concept of assistance in wrongful conduct can best be approached by comparing the relevant provisions of the Convention to other rules of international law applicable between the parties,[99] namely the rules on State responsibility, including attribution of conduct, and the legal concepts of 'jurisdiction' and 'control'.[100] This is also the case with regard to the determination that a certain act is performed by the State 'itself', within the meaning of paragraph 4. It is therefore pertinent to add to the commentary on paragraph 3 a brief overview of the

---

[97] *Cf.* Article 31, paragraph 1, *1969 Vienna Convention on the Law of Treaties.*

[98] See, *supra*, §1.68 on the term 'assist', §§1.72 *et seq.* on assistance in the form of investment, §1.69 on the terms 'encourage' and 'induce'.

[99] *Cf.* Article 31, paragraph 3 (c), *1969 Vienna Convention on the Law of Treaties.*

[100] For an analysis of the meaning of the terms 'jurisdiction' and 'control', implied by the reference to Article 1, see, *supra*, §§3.22 *et seq.* It is arguable that the notion of 'jurisdiction or control' referred to in Article 9 of the Convention, *cf.* also Articles 4 (1), 5 (1), 6 (6) and (11) (a) and (c), and 7 (1) (h) and (j), may be interpreted in a similar way as the reference to 'jurisdiction' in certain human rights instruments, as a factual question of effective control that a State exercises over its territory, organs, nationals and over conduct in factual situations. *Cf.* Milanović, M., 'From Compromise to Principle: Clarifying the Concept of State Jurisdiction in Human Rights Treaties', 8 *Human Rights Law Review*, 2008, p. 411; *cf.* also Wilde, R., 'Triggering State Obligations Extraterritorially: The Spatial Test in Certain Human Rights Treaties', 4 *Israel Law Review*, 2007, pp. 503–526 at pp. 508 and 513–514. See also Farrant, J., 'Is the Extra-territorial Application of the Human Rights Act Really Justified?', *International Criminal Law Review 9* (2009), pp. 833–854. In this context paragraph 3 of Article 21 will be analysed applying a factual test of effective control over conduct.

concept of State responsibility in interoperability situations, bearing in mind however that the norms of attribution are implicitly referred to in several of the provisions set out in paragraph 4 of Article 21 and indeed in most of the examples of practical interoperability challenges submitted during the negotiation of Article 21.[101]

'Notwithstanding the provisions of Article 1'

21.54 A first question when interpreting the wording of paragraph 3 is to what extent it derogates from the general obligations set out in Article 1 of the Convention not to use, develop, produce, acquire, stockpile, retain, or transfer cluster munitions, or to assist, encourage or induce anyone to engage in such prohibited activity. The word 'notwithstanding' supports the interpretation that paragraph 3 indeed formulates an exception to the more general rules laid down in Article 1 or that it deviates from the legal situation that would otherwise have prevailed. The words 'notwithstanding the provisions of Article 1 of this Convention' are also employed in paragraphs 6 and 7 of Article 3 of the Convention, which in their context clearly formulate exceptions to the general obligations in Article 1 not to retain, acquire, or transfer cluster munitions for the limited development and training purposes defined. During the negotiations, it was questioned whether this wording in paragraph 3 of Article 21 was needed to obtain sufficient guarantees that interoperability concerns would be adequately addressed. The proponents of treaty provisions on interoperability responded to this in the affirmative. But the broad wording of paragraph 3 accentuated the need to clarify its limits, and provisions to that effect were later set out in paragraph 4 of Article 21. At the outset it may be concluded that paragraph 3 establishes a special rule that clarifies the general obligations laid down in Article 1.

'In accordance with international law'

21.55 Paragraph 3 of Article 21 makes it clear that the rule permitting engagement in military cooperation and operations only covers activities undertaken by a State Party in accordance with international law. Therefore, Article 21 cannot be interpreted as derogating from any other obligation under international law, including any relevant provision of international humanitarian or human rights law.[102] Thus, paragraph 3 does not govern the particular

---

[101] See, *supra*, §21.19.

[102] As cluster munitions have an indiscriminate effect, their use may constitute a serious violation of international humanitarian law, *cf.* Prosecutor *v.* Milan Martić (Judgment), IT-95–11-T,

legal consequences of activities or situations that may result in international criminal liability, nor does it engage the doctrine of command responsibility or effects of superior orders in a chain of command as governed by international criminal law.[103] As noted above,[104] the temporal scope of Article 21 would be limited by, for example, a development in law making the use of cluster munitions prohibited under customary international law. If the relevant criteria are fulfilled in future, a breach of customary law relating to cluster munitions could also entail State responsibility and international criminal liability.[105] At present, however, it is for States Parties to implement the necessary statutory provisions in their national criminal law. Consequently, it is for national authorities and courts to investigate and prosecute activities in contravention of the Convention through relevant implementing provisions and in accordance with national penal statutes and international law.[106] In this

---

International Criminal Tribunal for the former Yugoslavia (ICTY), 12 June 2007. The reference to international law also includes other norms such as *jus ad bellum* and non-intervention. *Cf., supra*, the commentary on preambular paragraph 12, *esp.* §0.136.

[103] Under international law there is a clear distinction between State responsibility and individual criminal liability. Article 58 of the ILC's Articles on Responsibility of States for Internationally Wrongful Acts affirms that: 'These articles are without prejudice to any question of the individual responsibility under international law of any person acting on behalf of a State.' See also draft Article 65, the ILC's draft articles on responsibility of international organizations with commentaries, UN doc. A/64/10, 2009, p. 38. Article 25, paragraph 4, of the Rome Statute of the International Criminal Court states that: 'No provision of this Statute relating to individual criminal responsibility shall affect the responsibility of States under international law.' The roots of individual criminal responsibility lie in the commission of an act or in conduct that has been criminalized by international law and that can be attributed to a particular individual who satisfies the relevant requirements of *actus reus* and *mens rea*. By contrast, State responsibility is triggered by the breach of obligations and responsibilities as are binding upon a State under international law and as might result from the conduct of an organ of that State, an agent or another person whose conduct may be attributed to the State, *cf.* Mettraux, G., *The Law of Command Responsibility* (Oxford: Oxford University Press, 2009), p. 71.　　　　　　　　　　　　　　　　　[104] See, *supra*, §21.10.

[105] See, e.g., Article 8(b) (xx), *1998 Statute of the International Criminal Court.*

[106] Including relevant limits to national criminal jurisdiction. Unlike the obligation to repress grave breaches of international humanitarian law laid down in Article 86, paragraph 1, *1977 Additional Protocol I* to the *1949 Geneva Conventions; cf.* also Sandoz, Y. *et al., Commentary on the Additional Protocols of 8 June 1977 to the Geneva Conventions of 12 August 1949* (Geneva: ICRC, 1987), p. 975, the Convention on Cluster Munitions does not establish universal jurisdiction over breaches of its obligations, nor does it entail an obligation on States Parties to extradite or prosecute—'*aut dedere aut judicare*'. As noted *supra* (§21.10), the conclusion of the Convention on Cluster Munitions, the adherence to it of a large number of States, and consistent practice in its application may change the status of customary law and make recourse to the universality principle possible. *Cf.* also with regard to chemical weapons, Gestri, M., 'Control By States Parties over Private Extra-Territorial Activities: Issues of Jurisdiction and International Responsibility', in Bothe, M., Ronzitti, N., and Rosas, A. (eds.), *The New Chemical Weapons Convention—Implementation and Prospects* (The Hague: Martinus Nijhoff, 1998), p. 469.

context, implementation of or reference to Article 21 in national legislation will potentially enhance interoperability.

21.56 The same would be the case in the event of national criminal proceedings against an agent of a State not party to the Convention for providing assistance in any activity prohibited to a State Party. It is also conceivable that a national of a State Party could engage in such activity, acting as a member of the military forces or other agent of a State not party. In such cases the reference in paragraph 3 to international law must be interpreted as also including a reference to relevant provisions of international law on immunities applicable to international military cooperation and operations.[107]

'Their military personnel or nationals'

21.57 In this connection it should be borne in mind that paragraph 3 refers to States Parties, their military personnel, or *nationals*. Interoperability situations are defined as military cooperation or operations between a State Party and a State not party. Nationals as referred to in this provision would therefore normally hold an official position as members of the military forces or other agents of a State Party or, exceptionally, act as agents of a State not party that might engage in activities prohibited by the Convention. In interoperability situations, nationals could also be agents of an international organization or members of its organs.[108] On the other hand, paragraph 3 cannot be interpreted as comprising private activity, so that the nationals of a State Party could

---

[107] *Cf.* for functional immunity for acts of members of the force as acts of the State to which the force belongs: Jennings, R. and Watts, R. (eds.), *Oppenheim's International Law*, Ninth Edition, Vol. 1, Part 1 (Oxford: Oxford University Press, 2008), p. 1158; *cf.* for inviolability: Brownlie, I., *Principles of Public International Law*, Sixth Edition (Oxford: Oxford University Press, 2003), p. 365. Immunity could result from provisions of particular international law, such as e.g. Status of Forces Agreements and Headquarters Agreements. *Cf.* also UN Convention on Jurisdictional Immunities of States and Their Property (not yet in force at the time of writing), Article 2, paragraph 1(b) (iv), adopted 2 December 2004 by Resolution of the UN General Assembly, *cf.* UN doc. A/59/38. For comments on immunity in relation to obligations under Article 3, *cf. supra*, §§3.20–3.21.

[108] *Cf.* Article 2(c) of the ILC's draft Articles on responsibility of international organizations: 'Agent' includes officials and other persons or entities through whom the organisation acts, *cf.* also International Court of Justice, advisory opinion on *Reparation for Injuries Suffered in the Service of the United Nations*, defining an 'agent' as '[a]ny person who, whether a paid official or not, and whether permanently employed or not, has been charged by an organ of the organization with carrying out, or helping to carry out, one of its functions—in short, any person through whom it acts', *ICJ Reports 1949*, p. 177.

'International organizations do not act only through natural persons, whether officials or not. Thus, the definition of 'agent' also covers entities through whom the organization acts.' *Cf.* commentary on the ILC's draft Article 2, UN doc. A/64/10, 2009, p. 51.

themselves engage in a private capacity in prohibited activity by entering into cooperation with the agents of a State not party.[109] State responsibility is also an issue only for acts undertaken in an official capacity. If on the other hand a national of a State Party should act contrary to the Convention's prohibitions in a private capacity, even in an interoperability situation, the State Party would not be held internationally responsible for the private acts undertaken by one of its citizens. But responsibility under the Convention would ensue if the State Party did not take the appropriate action to prevent the prohibited activity or prosecute the author of such conduct in accordance with its obligations under Article 9.

'May engage in military cooperation and operations'

21.58 The key words 'may engage' in paragraph 3 clearly set out an acknowledgement that a State Party may participate in military cooperation and operations with States not party. As described above, this principle has now been established in a humanitarian Convention itself and not by the tacit understanding among States Parties or by non-opposed declaratory statements of interpretation by States on becoming party to the agreement, as is the case with previous instruments. As the interpretative declarations to the *1997 Anti-Personnel Mine Ban Convention* and several of the initial proposals cited above[110] refer to 'participation', or indeed to 'mere participation', the question arises whether with the words 'may engage' the negotiating States have expanded the scope of the interoperability exception. As the words 'engage in' and 'participate' are synonymous[111] and nothing in the negotiating history supports the notion that a different meaning was intended, it may be asserted that it is the inherent right to participate in certain international activities under the terms and conditions laid down in the Convention that is set out in paragraph 3.[112]

---

[109] However, nationals of a State Party providing services to a visiting force may have a defence against criminal liability insofar as the activities by forces of a non-State Party are authorized by the State Party. See, e.g., Clause 8 of the United Kingdom Cluster Munitions (Prohibitions) Bill.

[110] See, *supra*, fnn. 10–15.

[111] In the French text this provision reads '... peuvent s'engager dans une coopération et des opérations militaires', and in the Spanish text: '...podrán cooperar militarmente y participar en operaciones'. All texts in the official languages of the Convention 'shall be equally authentic' according to Article 23 of the Convention. See, *infra*, §23.5.

[112] It may be asked whether the permissive language of paragraph 3 sets out a 'right' to participate in military cooperation or operations with States not party under the regime of the Convention, or if the norm simply refers to the inherent capacity of sovereign States to carry out such acts and activities within the boundaries of international law, in particular the norms of *jus ad bellum*, since

21.59 It is also important to note that paragraph 3 in general terms deals with the right to participate in military cooperation and operations with States not party. The wording of this provision does not allow for participation in any specific activities prohibited to a State Party under the Convention. This was also pointed out by several delegations when the Convention text was adopted by the Dublin Diplomatic Conference. It was specifically recorded by one negotiating State that Article 21 recognizes the need for continuing cooperation in what it is hoped will be a short transition period and that this intention is captured clearly in paragraph 3 of the Article, 'which should not be read as entitling States Parties to avoid their specific obligations under the Convention for this limited purpose'.[113] Clearly, if a State not party engages in activity which is lawful for that State, but which would not be lawful under the Convention if carried out by a State Party, paragraph 3 still permits the State Party to participate in the military cooperation or operation in which that conduct might take place. The legal effect of paragraph 3 for a State Party is therefore to clarify that participation in military cooperation and operations in which a State not party might engage in activity prohibited under the Convention shall not be regarded as assistance, encouragement, or inducement within the meaning of paragraph 1(c) of Article 1 by that State Party in the commission of an otherwise wrongful act. However, as will be discussed below in relation to paragraph 4 and to principles of attribution of conduct, a State Party may not 'itself' engage in activity that constitutes a breach of its general obligations under the Convention. Moreover, a State Party will, in situations where a State not party might engage in activities prohibited by the Convention, have to abide by its other obligations under Article 21 to promote the norms of the Convention and discourage the use of cluster munitions as described above.

21.60 At this stage it may be concluded that paragraph 3 permits military cooperation and operations between States Parties and States not party. However, paragraph 3 does not define any particular activity which shall be open to States Parties in such situations, despite their general obligations as laid down in Article 1 of the Convention. Nor does paragraph 3 clarify what would be an appropriate level of engagement or participation, or indeed any concrete action of assistance in military cooperation or operations, to define

the State possesses the totality of rights and obligations under international law. *Cf.* International Court of Justice, Advisory Opinion on *Reparation for Injuries Suffered in the Service of the United Nations, ICJ Reports 1949*, p. 180.

[113] *Cf.* 'Statement by the Government of Iceland upon the adoption of the Convention on Cluster Munitions', Diplomatic Conference doc. CCM/CRP/2, 30 May 2008.

the outer limits of permitted interoperability, except for the examples provided in paragraph 4. The interoperability provision is therefore open to various interpretations and to potential refinement through subsequent State practice. At the time of writing, the textual interpretation of paragraph 3 should be supplemented by further legal sources to fill in the gaps, in particular by other applicable provisions of international law.

Attribution of conduct in interoperability situations

21.61 In interoperability situations, the norms on assistance governed by the rules on State responsibility[114] may supplement a textual interpretation of the scope of the obligations set out in paragraph 1(c) of Article 1. In such a scenario as envisaged in paragraph 3 of Article 21, States Parties have legal capacity to engage in military cooperation or operations with a State not party that might engage in activities prohibited by the Convention. Thus, the relevant issue here is to what extent military cooperation can constitute complicity by a State Party in the performance of a prohibited act by a State not party. Depending on the degree of complicity, responsibility for the former State may ensue.[115] First, this raises the question as to how far the prohibition on assistance in Article 1 of the Convention can be extended in interoperability situations. Second, what consequences would flow from complicity in such activities performed by a State not party if analysed from the perspective of general rules on State responsibility in international law?

21.62 The general obligations laid down in the Convention, including the obligation not to assist, encourage or induce others to do any proscribed act, are expressions of primary or substantive rules of international law, i.e. they define the reach and content of those obligations. Secondary rules of international law on responsibility for wrongful acts, on the other hand, are not principally concerned with the interpretation of a primary rule. Instead they determine whether that primary obligation has been violated and what should be the consequences of the violation.[116] Hence, these rules establish the general conditions under international law for the State to be considered responsible for wrongful acts or omissions, and the legal consequences which flow therefrom. They

---

[114] *Cf.* in particular Article 16 of the ILC's Articles on Responsibility of States for Internationally Wrongful Acts. See, *supra*, §§1.65–1.66.

[115] Various examples of joint conduct that may result in accessory responsibility are detailed in the report by the ILC's Special Rapporteur on State responsibility, James Crawford, *cf.* UN doc. A/CN.4/498/Add.1, 1 April 1999, pp. 3–4.

[116] *Cf. Yearbook of the International Law Commission, 2001*, Vol. II, Part Two, see also UN doc. A/56/10, p. 31.

pertain especially to attribution of conduct. For example, certain requirements are implied by the wording of paragraph 4 of Article 21 to attribute a specific act or activity to the State 'itself'. The same is true for, for example, the obligation in Article 9 to prevent and suppress any prohibited activity undertaken by persons or on territory under the State Party's jurisdiction or 'control'. The concept of acts undertaken by the State 'itself' or performed under its 'control' cannot be fully appreciated unless it is considered in connection with the similar notion of direction and control over conduct and rules governing attribution in the law of responsibility of States and international organizations.

21.63 In interoperability situations, the primary obligation not to 'assist' in certain conduct and the rules on attribution of conduct are parallel in the sense that they both imply a legal threshold needed to hold that a particular activity amounts to internationally wrongful conduct. As observed by the International Law Commission, the idea of the implication of one State in the conduct of another is analogous to problems of attribution.[117] In relation to international operations, similar questions of attribution of conduct to international organizations may become equally relevant.

21.64 Turning to the question of what is generally understood by the term 'assistance' under international law on attribution of conduct, as a general rule, a State should not be able to do through another what it may not do itself.[118] The threshold requirement for considering an act or omission as wrongful assistance does not imply that a State Party is generally responsible, through the acts or omissions of its organs, for the conduct of another State in interoperability situations. On the other hand, there is no requirement that aid or assistance in the form of military cooperation or participation in an international operation should have been essential to the performance of an internationally wrongful act by another State. It is sufficient if it contributed significantly to that act.[119] As reported by the International Law Commission when reviewing its draft articles, for assistance to be attributed to the State, it must be given:

with the specific object of facilitating the commission of the principal internationally wrongful act in question. . . [I]t is not sufficient that aid or assistance provided without such intention could be used by the recipient State for unlawful purposes, or that the State providing aid or assistance should be aware of the eventual possibility of such use. The aid or assistance must in fact be rendered with a view to its use in committing the principal internationally wrongful act.[120]

---

[117] *Ibid.*, commentary to draft Article 16, p. 69. [118] *Ibid.* [119] *Ibid.*, p. 66.
[120] *Cf.* the ILC's commentary to the former Article 27 of the ILC's draft articles on State responsibility, cited by Crawford, *Second Report on State Responsibility, op. cit.*, p. 9.

The threshold for wrongful assistance is high. By, for example, 'knowingly providing an essential facility', a State Party may be deemed to have unlawfully assisted another State in the commission of an internationally wrongful act. On the other hand, the idea of 'mere participation' in military cooperation and operations in which other participants might perform acts contrary to the Convention would not normally satisfy this requirement for complicity under international law on State responsibility.[121] By this standard, actions that are carried out by a State Party during military cooperation and operations, and that only have a remote and indirect relationship to a State not party's use of cluster munitions, do not constitute internationally wrongful conduct.

21.65 These rules on international responsibility are generally applicable in situations governed by Article 21 of the Convention, but their function is only to supplement treaty provisions binding on States Parties. The primacy of substantive or primary norms of international law is laid down in Article 55 of the ILC's articles on State responsibility on *lex specialis*.[122] The provisions of paragraph 1(c) of Article 1 and Article 21 of the Convention are important in one particular respect: international responsibility for assisting another State or another international legal subject in the commission of any activity prohibited to a State Party would otherwise require that the conduct also constitutes an internationally wrongful act for the State being assisted in the commission of the act in question.[123] However, as a primary legal obligation on States Parties, paragraph 1(c) of Article 1, which prohibits assistance 'to anyone', prevails regardless of whether the proscribed conduct would in fact be wrongful if committed by a State not party. Conduct by a State not party contrary to the Convention would not normally constitute an internationally wrongful act on the part of the acting State since the Convention is formally binding only on States that become party to it. Therefore, assistance by a State Party in conduct prohibited under the Convention is not lawful even if provided to a State not party. That is the case even though the State not party may lawfully engage in such conduct. Thus, in interoperability situations Article 21 may prevent a

---

[121] It is recalled in this connection that attribution of wrongful conduct to the State is normally also a procedural requirement for an international court or other judicial organ to establish jurisdiction *ratione personae* to entertain an individual claim addressed to that State.

[122] Cf. Article 55 of the ILC's Articles on Responsibility of States for Internationally Wrongful Acts, which states that: 'These articles do not apply where and to the extent that the conditions for the existence of an internationally wrongful act or the content or implementation of the international responsibility of a State are governed by special rules of international law.'

[123] *Cf.* the ILC's Articles on Responsibility of States for Internationally Wrongful Acts, Article 16, *cf.* also Articles 17 and 18 and the ILC's draft Articles on Responsibility of International Organizations, Article 57, *cf.* also Articles 58 and 59.

State Party's participation in military cooperation or operations if the conduct in question exceeds the threshold of 'assistance' and is attributable to that State in accordance with general international law.

21.66 Turning then to the question of what conduct may be attributed to a particular State under international law, it should be recalled that only acts performed by organs or agents of a State representing the authority of that State or under its direction and control are attributable to that State.[124] Two different scenarios should be borne in mind when analysing the rules on attribution of conduct in interoperability situations. The first category of questions deals with the conduct of the military forces of a State Party operating outside its territory, typically in an international operation. The second category deals with the conduct of the military forces or agents of a State not party operating on the territory or in a situation that is under the jurisdiction or control of a State Party. In both scenarios questions of State responsibility for the acts or omissions of its own organs or agents may arise. In addition, Article 21 deals with questions of individual liability for conduct prohibited by national implementing provisions enacted in accordance with Article 9 of the Convention.

21.67 With regard to the question of what particular circumstances might lead to a State Party becoming responsible for activity jointly carried out in interoperability situations, the following principles shed light on the issue of attribution of conduct.

21.68 First, it should be noted that the armed forces of a State and its members[125] are organs of that State wherever they perform their functions,[126] that the sending State also exercises exclusive organic jurisdiction over its military forces when abroad,[127] and that its actions under international law are attributable to that State when performing a task in its own name, i.e. in a national capacity, in situations of military cooperation and operations, including military occupation. Therefore, a State Party is responsible only for its own

---

[124] *Cf.* the ILC's Articles on Responsibility of States for Internationally Wrongful Acts, Chapter II, and *supra*, §21.57.

[125] *Cf.* the law applicable in armed conflict in the Fourth Hague Convention respecting the Laws and Customs of War on Land of 1907, Article 3; and *1977 Additional Protocol I* to the 1949 Geneva Conventions, Article 91.

[126] *Cf.* Article 4 of the ILC's Articles on Responsibility of States for Internationally Wrongful Acts and Jennings, R. and Watts, R. (eds.), *Oppenheim's International Law*, Ninth Edition, Vol. 1, Part 1 (Oxford: Oxford University Press, 2008), pp. 1154 and 1156.

[127] *Cf.* Seyersted, F., *Common Law of International Organizations* (Leiden: Martinus Nijhoff Publishers, 2008), pp. 177–182, *cf.* also Amerasinghe, C. F., *Principles of the Institutional Law of International Organizations*, Cambridge Studies in International and Comparative Law, Volume 1 (Cambridge: Cambridge University Press, 1996), p. 403. Organic jurisdiction includes disciplinary powers and criminal jurisdiction over the members of its armed forces (*cf. infra*).

conduct; that is to say the conduct of persons acting, on whatever basis, on its behalf.[128]

21.69 Second, when an organ of a State is placed at the disposal of another State[129] or an international organization,[130] the conduct of that organ is attributable to the State or organization at whose disposal it is placed, where the latter exercises effective control over the conduct in question.[131] In the case of an international peace operation conducted under UN operational command, which in such case constitutes a subsidiary organ of the UN, the troop-contributing States retain disciplinary powers and criminal jurisdiction over the members of their military contingent. This may have specific consequences with regard to attribution of conduct to either the contributing State or the receiving UN operation.[132] However, international responsibility in these situations also lies where effective command and control is vested and actually exercised, and the fact that any wrongful act may have been performed by members of a national military contingent forming part of a peacekeeping operation does not affect the international responsibility of the international organization vis-à-vis third States or individuals.[133] Consequently, neither a

---

[128] ICJ judgment, 26 February 2007, Application of the Convention on the Prevention and Punishment of the Crime of Genocide (Bosnia and Herzegovina *v.* Serbia and Montenegro), *ICJ Reports 2007*, para. 406.

[129] *Cf.* Article 6 of the ILC's Articles on Responsibility of States for Internationally Wrongful Acts with commentary recorded in the Official Records of the General Assembly, Fifty-sixth Session, Supplement No. 10, doc. A/56/10, p. 95. See also Article 8 on direction or control of conduct of a person or group of persons.

[130] *Cf.* Article 5 of the ILC's draft Articles on Responsibility of International Organizations.

[131] The decisive question in determining in what capacity a member of an international operation had acted is in whose name and for whom (from the functional standpoint) that person was acting at the moment when the act was carried out. *Cf.* Sari, A., 'Jurisdiction and International Responsibility in Peace Support Operations: The Behrami and Saramati Cases', 8 *Human Rights Law Review* 1 (2008), pp. 151–170, at p. 161.

[132] 'Members of a UN force who have been individually enlisted will normally be officials of the organization, even if they are not considered regular officials for internal purposes. But members of national contingents, too, have been temporarily placed under the jurisdiction of the organization to the extent that their national states have not retained (disciplinary and criminal) powers over them. Their position vis-à-vis the UN is that of international personnel under the authority of the UN and subject to the instructions of the Commander, through the chain of command.'

Cf. Seyersted, F., *Common Law of International Organizations, op. cit.*, p. 269.

[133] *Cf. United Nations Juridical Yearbook 2004*, p. 355, and UN doc. A/51/389, paragraphs 17–18. See also the UN's response to questions on the attribution of conduct of peacekeeping operations posed by the ILC in doc. A/CN.4/545, 25 June 2004, pp. 17–18. As a consequence, a contributing State may not instruct its national commander who is part of a UN peacekeeping force to disobey the orders of the force commander. *Cf.* Sarooshi, D., *The United Nations and the Development of Collective Security, The Delegation of the Security Council of its Chapter VII Powers* (Oxford: Oxford University Press, 2003), p. 69. Particular questions of attribution of conduct to international organs in relation to the territorial administration of Kosovo and the international security presence

troop-contributing State nor a State in whose territory an international peace operation under UN command and control is being carried out incurs responsibility for the conduct of that operation, nor could they exercise jurisdiction or control over the operation.

21.70 Third, when an international operation is carried out by a multinational coalition of States with (or without) the authorization of the UN Security Council, under the operational command and control of the participating States, any act must be attributed to the State that exercises effective control over the conduct in question.[134]

(Kosovo Force), authorized by the Security Council, were raised before the European Court of Human Rights (ECtHR), in the case of Behrami *v.* France and Saramati *v.* France, Germany and Norway (Application Nos. 71412/01 and 78166/01), admissibility decision 2 May 2007. In its Saramati decision the ECtHR did not attribute the conduct of the Commander of the Kosovo Force, acting under unified command and control, to the troop-contributing State of which that agent was a national. However, in R (Al Jedda) *v.* Secretary of State for Defence [2007] UKHL 58, [2008] 1 AC 332, [2008] 2 WLR 31, 12 December 2007, the House of Lords distinguished the case with respect to the multinational force in Iraq operating under Security Council authorisation, *cf.* resolution 1546 (2004). In the case NK *v.* Austria, the actions of a member of an Austrian military unit serving in the UN peacekeeping force in Cyprus were not attributed to the Austrian State as the agent in question was acting as an organ of the UN and not of Austria when the damage was caused. The court, in determining which legal entity was responsible, found that the decisive factor was not whose organ (from the organizational standpoint) the person alleged to have caused the damage actually belonged to, but rather in whose name and for whom (from the functional standpoint) that person was acting at the moment when the act was carried out, *cf.* Superior Provincial Court (*Oberlandesgericht*) Vienna, 26 February 1979, 77 ILR, pp. 470–474. In its judgment of 10 September 2008 the District Court of The Hague found that the acts and omissions of the Dutch Battalion in Bosnia and Herzegovina should be assessed in the context of the UNPROFOR operation they formed part of and 'strictly attributed, as a matter of principle, to the United Nations.' The Court stated that if the Dutch Battalion had carried out instructions by the Dutch government contrary to UN orders, their conduct could have been attributed to the Netherlands, *cf.* case No. 265615/HA ZA 06–1671, H.N. *v.* The State of the Netherlands, paragraph 4.14.1. As regards the coalition forces in Iraq, the ECtHR in Hussein *v.* several States (Application no. 23276/04) dismissed a motion based on alleged (State) jurisdiction for exercising control of territory where certain conduct took place, and did not find any established principle of international law for the exercise of jurisdiction on the sole basis of a State forming part of a coalition, which in the case was under the overall command of a non-State Party, i.e. the US, being a non-State Party to the European Convention on Human Rights and Fundamental Freedoms.

[134] *Cf.* Seyersted, F., 'United Nations Forces: Some Legal Problems', 37 *BYBIL* 1961, pp. 351 and 411 *et seq.*; Seyersted, F., *UN Forces in the Law of War and Peace*, Leiden 1966, pp. 117–126; and Simma, B. (ed.), *The Charter of the United Nations—A Commentary* (Oxford: Oxford University Press, 2002), p. 542. According to the Brahimi report (Report of the Panel on United Nations Peace Operations, *cf.* doc. A/55/305 - S/2000/809), '[i]t is recognized that the United Nations does not wage war and that where enforcement action is required, it has consistently been entrusted to coalitions of willing States, with the authorisation of the Security Council, acting under Chapter VII of the Charter,' (paragraph 53), *cf.* also Schermers, H. G., and Blokker, N. M., *International Institutional Law*, Fourth Edition (Leiden: Martinus Nijhoff Publishers, 2003), paragraph 1495, p. 944.

21.71 It follows from the premises above that even when supplemented with other applicable rules of international law, the scope for derogation from Article 1 in international peace operations is rather limited. Moreover, one may run an additional risk of exacerbating the consequences for interoperability that may be caused by legal disparities between participants in international operations in respect of other applicable instruments of international law. To be sure, any *a contrario* interpretation of other instruments that do not include an interoperability exception should be avoided. Article 21 does not imply that the threshold for 'assistance' is lower, for example, with regard to anti-personnel mines than with regard to cluster munitions. For example, it was submitted during the negotiations that Article 1 of the Convention would pose a risk to those participating in UN peacekeeping operations.[135] This would normally not be the case insofar as the operation is under the command and control of the UN, or another international organization by delegation of Security Council powers. Moreover, cluster munitions are not normally associated with the mainly self-defence nature of peacekeeping missions.[136] As regards peace support operations where the Security Council authorizes Member States themselves to enforce a decision taken to maintain international peace and security, conduct in performing the operation will normally be attributed to the participating State that exercises effective control over that conduct. Consequently, in interoperability situations where a State Party participates in enforcement action authorized by the Security Council with the forces of a State not party to the Convention, paragraph 3 of Article 21 clarifies the scope of paragraph 1(c) of Article 1, proscribing acts of assistance, in accordance with international law. *How far* this exception goes in permitting a State Party to perform any act otherwise prohibited under the Convention will be further discussed in relation to paragraph 4.

---

[135] See e.g. the intervention by the UK at the Dublin Diplomatic Conference in 'Summary Record of First Session of the Committee of the Whole', Diplomatic Conference doc. CCM/CW/SR/1, 18 June 2008.

[136] The distinction between peacekeeping and enforcement has been blurred in some operations though; see Gray, C., *International Law and the Use of Force*, Third Edition (Oxford: Oxford University Press, 2008), pp. 302–326. *Cf.* also *A New Partnership Agenda, Charting a New Horizon for UN Peacekeeping*, consultation document by the Department of Peacekeeping Operations and Department of Field Support, New York, July 2009, pp. 12 and 31, <http://209.85.129.132/search?q=cache:mF3XQqWeWIsJ:www.un.org/en/peacekeeping/documents/newhorizon.pdf+DPKO+peace-keeping+mission+self+defence&cd=3&hl=no&ct=clnk&gl=no> (accessed 15 January 2010).

Paragraph 4

Nothing in paragraph 3 of this Article shall authorize a State Party:

(a) To develop, produce or otherwise acquire cluster munitions;

(b) To itself stockpile or transfer cluster munitions;

(c) To itself use cluster munitions; or

(d) To expressly request the use of cluster munitions in cases where the choice of munitions used is within its exclusive control.

Commentary

21.72 During the negotiations on Article 21 it was felt that draft paragraph 3, in the same way as existing practice such as that based on interpretative declarations on interoperability to preceding humanitarian law instruments, lacked legal clarity and that it would be difficult to predict the consequences of State practice in implementing Article 21. With a view to obtaining a better level of precision, it was therefore agreed to add a fourth paragraph to Article 21 that would clarify specific limits to the scope of the interoperability exception.

21.73 Paragraph 4 of Article 21 narrows the potential scope of paragraph 3 in interoperability situations, ensuring that States Parties may not invoke interoperability as a legal basis for engaging in a number of activities prohibited under the Convention.[137] From the wording 'nothing in paragraph 3 shall *authorise* a State Party' to engage in the activities listed in paragraph 4, it is clear that this provision rules out any deviation from the general obligations as laid down in Article 1 and referred to in paragraph 4 by engaging in such activities with a State not party.[138] However, by listing a selection of activities that should not be covered by the interoperability provision in paragraph 3, paragraph 4 seems to raise separate and difficult issues of interpretation and application. If on the other hand paragraph 3 of Article 21 is not interpreted as authorizing a State Party to deviate from its general obligations under the Convention, as indicated above, various interpretations of the wording of paragraph 4 will

---

[137] As pointed out by the UK delegation with support from other delegations, paragraph 4 should ensure that States Parties may not use the interoperability provision as an exception to their obligations under Article 1, *cf.* 'Summary Record of Tenth Session of the Committee of the Whole', Diplomatic Conference doc. CCM/CW/SR/10, 18 June 2008.

[138] *Cf.* the similar wording of Article 6 (3) of the International Covenant on Civil and Political Rights, *cf.* also the preamble to the *1998 Statute of the International Criminal Court*, which states that 'nothing in this Statute shall be taken as authorizing any State Party to intervene in an armed conflict or in the internal affairs of any State'.

not have the potential effect of undermining the comprehensive ban on cluster munitions, since the function of paragraph 4 is not to allow States Parties any specific departure from their general obligations, but to reassure other States Parties that the exception set out in paragraph 3 of Article 21 does not entail a loophole in the ban on cluster munitions in interoperability situations.

21.74 As pointed out above, paragraph 3 of Article 21 does not permit a State Party to engage in any particular activity in interoperability situations. As such, paragraph 3 does not authorize anyone to perform any specific act prohibited to a State Party in Article 1 of the Convention. Nothing in paragraph 3 authorizes a State Party to commit any of the acts listed in paragraph 4. However, as paragraph 3 is formulated as an exception to Article 1, the purpose of paragraph 4 must be to provide reassurances that paragraph 3 should not permit any of the activities listed, given the ambiguity of the latter provision. Regardless of how States Parties choose to implement the interoperability provisions in their national law, international agreements, and relevant operational manuals, the effect of paragraph 4 of Article 21 is that it sets certain absolute limitations on forms of assistance that may be lawfully provided to a State not party in situations of military cooperation and operations.

21.75 A central issue when analysing paragraph 4 is therefore whether the list of activities set out in sub-paragraphs (a) to (d) is exhaustive or indicative. It has been pointed out that reading the list in paragraph 4 as exhaustive would possibly permit a wide range of activities constituting assistance that would otherwise be prohibited under the Convention.[139] This would require a reading *a contrario* of paragraph 4, meaning that the activities listed in (a) to (d) are not authorized by paragraph 3, and therefore any other activity otherwise prohibited by Article 1 of the Convention is authorized. If this were the case, serious questions could be raised with regard to the effectiveness of the prohibition on cluster munitions and indeed the humanitarian norm of the Convention.

21.76 In itself, the wording of paragraph 4, read in the light of the ordinary meaning to be attributed to the terms applied, does not rule out an interpretation that sub-paragraphs (a) to (d) are to be taken literally as exhaustive prohibitions applicable in interoperability situations. As a general presumption, the express mention of certain prohibited activities in paragraph 4 could be taken to exclude other acts prohibited by Article 1, but not listed.[140] Even if,

---

[139] See further: Docherty, B., 'Staying True to the Ban on Cluster Munitions, Understanding the Prohibition on Assistance in the Convention on Cluster Munitions', Human Rights Watch, 23 June 2009 available at: <http://www.hrw.org/node/83975#_ftnref38> (accessed 15 January 2010).

[140] An interpretation referred to as: '*expressio unius est excluso alterius*', cf. Aust, A., *Modern Treaty Law and Practice* (Cambridge: Cambridge University Press, 2000), p. 201.

however, one accepts the proposition that the activities listed in paragraph 4 are exhaustive and should not be read as examples of prohibited conduct in interoperability situations, it does not necessarily follow that any activity not listed would have to be regarded as 'authorized' by paragraph 3 and therefore permitted. Indeed, when read in the light of the context of the Convention as a whole and in the light of its object and purpose,[141] it would be difficult to accept such an understanding of paragraph 4. As we shall see, it would be particularly difficult to reconcile the obligation to discourage States not party from using cluster munitions laid down in paragraph 2 of Article 21 with the notion that a State Party might still be permitted to assist in the use of cluster munitions by that State not party. Moreover, to be effective, the interoperability concerns underlying Article 21 do not require a reading of paragraph 4 that could set aside parts of the general obligations laid down in the Convention.

21.77 There are some indications from the negotiating history that delegations saw paragraph 4 as indicative, and that Article 21 should not permit any deviation from the general obligations in Article 1. For example, the Government of Iceland noted that 'listing some examples in paragraph 4 cannot therefore be interpreted to allow departures in other respects'.[142] The Norwegian delegation specifically stated the understanding that Article 21 'does not create loopholes'.[143] In a later statement, Ireland expressed its view that any deliberate assistance by a State Party in the commission of an act prohibited by the Convention in the context of military cooperation with a State not party will be 'inconsistent' with its obligation to make its best efforts to discourage the use of cluster munitions by the latter and that Article 21, paragraph 3 must be interpreted accordingly.[144] Further examples of State practice have been compiled by Human Rights Watch.[145] These various cited statements given by a wide range of sources after the adoption of the Convention differ in terms of content. They indicate a restrictive practice with regard to deviations from the general

---

[141] Particularly the humanitarian need 'to put an end for all time to the suffering and casualties caused by cluster munitions', *cf.* second paragraph to the preamble of the Convention. 'Article 21 should advance and not interfere much with the treaty's aim to eliminate cluster munitions.' *cf.* Docherty, B., *op. cit. supra*, fn. 22, at p. 958.

[142] *Cf.* Statement by the Government of Iceland, above, *op. cit.*, fn. 113.

[143] *Cf.* Statement by Steffen Kongstad, Ambassador of Norway, Dublin Diplomatic Conference on Cluster Munitions, 30 May 2008, at: <http://www.clustermunitionsdublin.ie/pdf/Norway.pdf> (accessed 15 January 2010).

[144] Department of Foreign Affairs of Ireland, 'Note on the Measures Taken by Ireland to Implement Article 21 of the Convention on Cluster Munitions', 11 March 2009, p. 1, attached to letter from Ambassador Dáithí O'Ceallaigh, Permanent Mission of Ireland to the United Nations in Geneva, to Thomas Nash, Coordinator, Cluster Munition Coalition, 16 March 2009.

[145] See, *supra*, fn. 139.

obligations of the Convention in interoperability situations. At this stage, one should be a bit cautious about reading too much into such statements as they should be considered in light of two different concerns:[146] on the one hand the extent of State responsibility for assisting in activities that run counter to the prohibition on cluster munitions, and on the other hand limitations on the scope of individual liability in interoperability situations with reference to a State Party's exercise of 'jurisdiction' or 'control' as laid down in Article 9 of the Convention. This caution applies particularly to statements that refer to the need to enact national legislation to implement the provisions of Article 21. Such legislative measures deal with provisions that may be executed by national authorities and domestic courts vis-à-vis individuals or entities falling within the State's enforcement jurisdiction. The four sub-paragraphs of paragraph 4 should therefore be analysed with the underlying dual purpose of Article 21 in mind.

21.78 As regards activities not authorized to a State Party, paragraph 4 does not list 'assist, encourage or induce' as laid down in paragraph 1(c) of Article 1.[147] Since paragraph 3 of Article 21 deals with consequences for States Parties of situations where a State not party may engage in prohibited activity, it is nevertheless evident, as discussed above, that Article 21 sets out limitations on the prohibition on assistance in situations involving military cooperation and operations.

21.79 Sub-paragraph (a) rules out that a State Party may be authorized to 'develop,[148] produce[149] or otherwise acquire[150] cluster munitions' as part of military cooperation or operations. This provision makes it clear that if a State Party enters into military cooperation with a State not party, the interoperability exception does not apply to such activities as defined in sub-paragraph (a). Thus, Article 1 applies to these three categories of activity, including the prohibition on assistance. It may be concluded on a general basis that the interoperability concerns governed by Article 21 do not under any circumstances apply to assistance to a State not party in the form of military industrial cooperation, trade,[151] procurements or research, and possibly

---

[146] *Cf.*, *supra*, §21.3.   [147] On the definition of 'assist', see above, §1.68.
[148] See, *supra*, §1.36.   [149] See, *supra*, §1.40.   [150] See, *supra*, §1.48.
[151] Trade could be understood as assisting in the acquisition of cluster munitions by a State not party, but would also fall under the prohibition of transfer in sub-paragraph (b). Several States have implemented new export control restrictions to prevent trade in cluster munitions, including the US and the UK. According to UK legislation, trading between two overseas countries where any part of that trading takes place within the UK, or is carried out by British nationals anywhere in the world, will be controlled, as will any act calculated to promote the supply or delivery of cluster munitions, *cf. Banning Cluster Munitions, Government Policy and Practice, op. cit.*, <http://lm.icbl.org/index.php/publications/display?act=submit&pqs_year=2009&pqs_type=cm&pqs_report=uk&pqs_section=#footnote-9978–45> (accessed 15 January 2010).

also investment[152] in any such activity, at least to the extent that paragraph 1(c) of Article 1 prohibits a State-owned or State-controlled company from investing in or facilitating activities prohibited by the Convention, or to the extent that it prohibits public funding for such purposes. Several States have enacted national legislation imposing a general prohibition on investment in the development and production of cluster munitions.[153]

21.80 Sub-paragraph (b) rules out that a State Party may be authorized to 'itself stockpile[154] or transfer[155] cluster munitions' as part of military cooperation or operations. Stockpiling and transfer of cluster munitions are activities that might occur in military cooperation with a State not party, typically when the latter State operates a military base,[156] a naval ship, or aircraft on the territory of a State Party. They might also occur during an international operation if a multinational force operates a joint logistic supply line bringing capabilities prohibited by the Convention into a theatre of operations. In such situations a State Party might inadvertently assist in the transfer or stockpiling of cluster munitions carried out by a coalition partner or allied State. Sub-paragraph (b) therefore defines the outer limits of a State Party's obligations not to assist others in the stockpiling or transfer of cluster munitions as set out in paragraph 1(c) of Article 1 in interoperability situations. The key qualifier

---

[152] See above, §§1.72–1.80. See also '*Worldwide Investment in Cluster Munitions*', report by IKV Pax Christi and Netwerk Vlaanderen, Utrecht, October 2009.

[153] *Cf.* e.g. Section 10 (2) of the New Zealand Cluster Munitions Prohibition Act 2009: 'A person commits an offence who provides or invests funds with the intention that the funds be used, or knowing that they are to be used, in the development or production of cluster munitions,' <http://www.legislation.govt.nz/act/public/2009/0068/latest/DLM2171615.html> (accessed on 15 January 2010).

[154] See, *supra*, §§1.50, 3.16–3.17 and 3.25. Sub-paragraph (b) does not include 'retain' on the list of non-authorised activities, however, if a State Party retains cluster munitions outside the limits set by Article 3 of the Convention, this would become an illegal stockpile of prohibited munitions.

[155] See, *supra*, §1.56.

[156] This provision is therefore relevant to the question of the hosting of foreign military bases. It may be recalled that Article 3 on storage and stockpile destruction requires that cluster munitions be under the jurisdiction and control of the State Party. Responding to a question about foreign stockpiling of cluster munitions on British territory in the House of Lords on 3 June 2008, the then Minister of State, Foreign and Commonwealth Office, Lord Malloch-Brown stated that, 'The short answer is that while, in the coming period, the US may if it so wishes continue to keep these weapons in its bases, there is an eight-year period during which they will need to be eliminated. The reading of the treaty indicates that there are overriding political reasons to expect that there will be no such weapons on British territory at the end of that eight-year period. That includes other people's bases situated on our territory. [..] The assumption is that at the end of that eight-year period, as the treaty reads, even a country such as the US, were it not a signatory, would no longer be able to keep such weapons on UK territory.' Available at: <http://www.publications.parliament.uk/pa/ld200708/ldhansrd/text/80603–0002.htm> (accessed 15 January 2010).

introduced in sub-paragraph (b) is the word 'itself'. A State Party may not 'itself' commit an act contrary to the prohibition on stockpiling or transfer.

21.81 While the reference to acts performed by the State 'itself' is not always clear in complex interoperability situations with potentially varying forms and levels of assistance to other States, the rules on attribution of conduct to the State provide guidance on the limits of that responsibility in interoperability situations.[157] In this connection the relevant test is whether the conduct of a person or group of persons may be attributable to a particular State as the conduct of an organ of that State or an organ exercising governmental authority on behalf of that State, or whether such person or group of persons is in fact acting under the direction or control of that State.[158] The military forces of a State are organs of that State. In coalition situations, the military forces of the respective States do not normally exercise authority on behalf of another State.[159] The conduct of forces acting as an organ of the UN or another international organization, operating under its unified command and control, is attributable to the organization as long as it exercises effective control.[160] As laid down in sub-paragraph (b), what a State Party may not do 'itself' is to commit an act contrary to the prohibition on stockpiling or transfer of cluster munitions when that State exercises effective control over the conduct or operation in question. A State Party is responsible only for such conduct as it can effectively control and is therefore in principle in a position to prevent.[161]

21.82 Although sub-paragraph (b) prohibits 'transfer' as defined in Article 2, particular attention has been paid to the concept of 'transit' of prohibited munitions through the territory of a State Party.[162] If a State Party should grant permission to transit cluster munitions through its territory, this

---

[157] See, *supra*, §§21.68–21.71 and §1.65–1.66.

[158] *Cf.* the ILC's Articles on Responsibility of States for Internationally Wrongful Acts, Chapter II, particularly Article 8, which sets out rules of customary law of international responsibility, *cf.* ICJ judgment 26 February 2007, Application of the Convention on the Prevention and Punishment of the Crime of Genocide (Bosnia and Herzegovina *v.* Serbia and Montenegro), paragraph 398.

[159] Unless these forces are placed at the disposal of another State or are acting under the direction and control of that other State, *cf.* Articles 6 and 8 of the ILC's Articles on Responsibility of States for Internationally Wrongful Acts.   [160] See, *supra*, §21.69.

[161] However, in relation to international operations, States Parties should also observe paragraph 2 of Article 21 and as appropriate avoid placing themselves in a position where they may be unable at the material time to control events that might lead to such activities by a State not party, see, *supra*, §21.51. It should also be underlined that even if the conduct of military troops exceeds their authority or contravenes instructions, it is considered an act of the State under international law, *cf.* Article 7 of the ILC's Articles on Responsibility of States for Internationally Wrongful Acts.

[162] See, *supra*, §1.61. *Cf.* also Docherty, B., 'Staying True to the Ban on Cluster Munitions, *op. cit.*, and for the discussion concerning the *1997 Anti-Personnel Mine Ban Convention*, see Maslen, S., *Commentary on the 1997 Anti-Personnel Mine Ban Convention, op. cit.*, §§1.41–1.50.

would amount to assisting others in the stockpiling of such munitions, contrary to paragraph 1(c) of Article 1 of the Convention. However, even if a State Party has notified a State not party of its obligations under the Convention and discouraged the use of cluster munitions in accordance with paragraph 2 of Article 21, it may still prove impossible for a State Party to verify assurances that cluster munitions are not being carried on board a foreign naval vessel or are not present in a foreign-operated military base. Even if such verification cannot be obtained, a State Party may continue its military cooperation with a State not party, for example. by allowing a visit by a foreign fleet or by hosting a military base.

21.83 This delimitation of responsibility for assisting in the commission of an act contrary to the Convention is also significant in relation to individual liability for any person acting in joint military operations with the forces of a State not party. Acts that are carried out during joint exercises and operations that only have a remote and indirect relationship to a State not party's stockpiling or transfer of cluster munitions are not prohibited by the Convention. The limitation of the scope of responsibility laid down in sub-paragraph (b) does not allow the forces of a State Party themselves to carry out actions prohibited by the Convention; however, this clarification is intended to facilitate an unambiguous interpretation of the Convention in such situations and thereby protect against unintended and too far-reaching criminal liability for assisting in the commission of a wrongful act. Therefore, liability for assisting in a prohibited activity does not apply to participation in international military cooperation and operations *per se*, but only to such qualified assistance that would amount to responsibility under international law for the troop-contributing State Party.[163]

---

[163] See, *supra*, §21.64. This position is maintained *inter alia* by Ireland: 'It is Ireland's view that any deliberate assistance in the commission of an act prohibited by the Convention in the context of military co-operation with a state not party will be inconsistent with this obligation' (paragraph 3), and that: 'appropriate orders will issue [...] that under no circumstances does any member of it deliberately assist, encourage or induce the commission of an act prohibited by the Convention by a non-party state' (paragraph 7), *cf. supra*, fn. 144, *op. cit.* The Norwegian implementing legislation sets out a similar standard, *cf.* the explicit reference in the parliamentary bill to the Norwegian Military Penal Code, according to which: 'The liability for aiding and abetting in the implementation Act is to be interpreted in the same way as in the Convention, so that it does not apply to participation in international military cooperation and international cooperation per se, unless Norwegian forces or service personnel conduct themselves in such a way as to incur responsibility under international law for Norway as a troop-contributing State.'

cf. Excerpts from Proposition No. 7 (2008–200) to the Odelsting on a Bill relating to the implementation of the Convention on Cluster Munitions in Norwegian law and Proposition No. 4 (2008–2009) to the Storting on consent to ratification of the Convention on Cluster Munitions. See also Section 11 (6) of the New Zealand Cluster Munitions Prohibition Act 2009:

21.84 Sub-paragraph (c) rules out that a State Party may be authorized to 'itself use cluster munitions'[164] as part of military cooperation or operations. The reference to acts performed by the State 'itself' must be understood in the same way as the corresponding reference in sub-paragraph (b) discussed above. The obligation of a State Party to make its best efforts to discourage the use of cluster munitions laid down in paragraph 2 of Article 21 is particularly relevant when interpreting the provision in sub-paragraph (c). It would be inconsistent in the context of Article 21 as a whole and in the light of the object and purpose of the Convention to require a State Party to discourage use of cluster munitions by a State not party and at the same time permit the State Party to assist that State not party in the use of cluster munitions during military cooperation or operations. To the extent that a State Party exercises effective control over the conduct in question, it may not engage in the use of cluster munitions carried out by a State not party.

21.85 Sub-paragraph (d) rules out that a State Party may be authorized to 'expressly request the use of cluster munitions in cases where the choice of munitions used is within its exclusive control' in military cooperation or operations. This particular rule addresses an operational situation where the prohibition to assist in the use of cluster munitions comes into play. What the drafters of this provision must have had in mind is situations of joint military operations where the forces of a State Party may have to request the support, for example in the form of aerial or artillery bombardment, of units belonging to a State not party in order to secure the objective of their mission or defend their perimeters. It should be borne in mind that the discussion paper on interoperability presented at the Wellington Conference specifically mentioned a situation where the forces of a future State Party may 'call in air support

> A member of the Armed Forces does not commit an offence [...] merely by engaging, in the course of his or her duties, in operations, exercises, or other military activities with the armed forces of a State that is not a party to the Convention and that has the ability to engage in conduct prohibited...

Cf. supra, fn. 153. And compare Clause 9 of the UK Cluster Munitions (Prohibitions) Bill, which details an interoperability defence when 'the person's conduct took place in the course of, or for the purposes of, an international military operation or an international military co-operation activity.' According to explanatory notes submitted to parliament on 8 February 2010:

> The interoperability defence is not available, in accordance with Article 21(4) of the Convention, if a person is charged with the offence of: using a prohibited munition; developing or producing a prohibited munition; acquiring a prohibited munition; making arrangements under which another person acquires a prohibited munition; or transferring a prohibited munition.

See: <http://www.publications.parliament.uk/pa/cm200910/cmbills/063/en/index_063.htm> (accessed 26 February 2010).

[164] See also, *supra*, §1.27.

or artillery fire support from State not party personnel'.[165] As this is not an entirely improbable scenario in interoperability situations, it raises pertinent questions both of State responsibility and of individual liability for making a request that may in turn trigger the use of cluster munitions by a State not party.

21.86 There are two main difficulties when interpreting sub-paragraph (d). The first problem is that the non-authorization to 'expressly request the use of cluster munitions' is conditioned on a requirement of 'exclusive control'. It would seem incompatible with the requirement to discourage the use of cluster munitions if a State Party were allowed thereafter to 'expressly request the use of cluster munitions' by a State not party. The second problem is the qualifier that, in order for this provision to apply, it is required that the requesting State Party should have 'exclusive control' over the means of delivery by a State not party. One would imagine that a State Party, having decided to ban cluster munitions because they cause unacceptable harm to civilians, would not in any circumstances want to be associated with a request to others to use cluster munitions. The meaning of this sub-paragraph could be simply to distance an unqualified request for fire support in interoperability situations from the scope of unlawful assistance under the Convention (even if cluster munitions are thereafter used by a State not party). But it would then appear impractical to speak of a requesting State's 'exclusive control' over the choice of munitions, and the drafters would possibly have preferred instead to clarify that a requesting State Party could in no circumstances direct or control the use of cluster munitions by a State not party.

21.87 The provision in sub-paragraph (d) could thus be construed to run counter to the obligation to discourage the use of cluster munitions laid down in paragraph 2 of Article 21. The problem in sub-paragraph (d) is the second part of the sentence, which reads: 'in cases where the choice of munitions used is within its exclusive control'. Obviously, if a State Party exercises exclusive control over the munitions used by military personnel or units belonging to another participating State, the State Party is not authorized by paragraph 3 of Article 21 to expressly request that cluster munitions be used. The question is therefore only whether sub-paragraph (d) may be interpreted *a contrario*

---

[165] See, *supra*, §21.18. In the Australian discussion paper (*op. cit.*, *supra*), and in interventions by its sponsors, the issue of 'expressly requesting' the use of cluster munitions was not raised, but the paper stated that 'it is not feasible for forces to refrain from calling in air support (in circumstances where it is the effect which is called for, *not a particular type of munition*)' and that an 'inability to undertake these tasks would undermine significantly the ability of States to operate in coalition and maintain alliance relationships' (emphasis added).

to mean that in other situations, where the requesting State Party does not exercise exclusive control over the choice of munitions used, it may expressly request that cluster munitions be used. There is reason to be cautious of any contrary interpretation of sub-paragraph (d) in the light of the obligation to discourage such use as laid down in paragraph 2.

21.88 Apart from the potential inconsistency between paragraph 2 and sub-paragraph (d) of Article 21, it does not seem that the criterion that a State Party must exercise 'exclusive control' over the 'choice of munitions used' by the forces of a State not party reflects most realistic situations of air or artillery supportive action in international operations. To be in a position to exercise 'exclusive control' over the choice of munitions used would mean that, in order to fall within the scope of this provision, the requesting State would have to be able to decide effectively whether or not cluster munitions were to be delivered by the military forces of another State on demand, and that those forces of a State not party would simply execute a decision taken by the requesting State on what munitions to employ in a supportive action. Even though this provision does not require that a State Party exercise 'exclusive control' over any other conduct of the requested non-State personnel, this test would nevertheless resemble the agency test of 'exclusive' or 'strict' control applied by the International Court of Justice in its *Nicaragua v. United States of America* and *Bosnian Genocide*[166] cases. This could then raise the question whether the actual use of cluster munitions could be attributed to the requesting State Party when it exercises such control over the conduct of a foreign military organ.

21.89 If we compare this provision with the otherwise applicable rules of attribution of conduct based on the test of effective control, it seems clear that if a State Party is in a position to exercise effective control over the delivery of cluster munitions by a State not party, then the conduct would be attributable to the requesting State Party. The State Party would in that case incur international responsibility directly for committing the wrongful act of using cluster munitions. Within the meaning of sub-paragraph (c), the State Party would be responsible for the use of cluster munitions, and sub-paragraph (d)

---

[166] Military and Paramilitary Activities in und against Nicaragua (*Nicaragua v. United States of America*), Judgment. of 27 June 1986, *ICJ Reports 1986*, paras. 109 *et seq.* and 277, and Application of the Convention on the Prevention and Punishment of the Crime of Genocide (*Bosnia and Herzegovina v. Serbia and Montenegro*), Judgment of 26 February 2007, *ICJ Reports 2007*, paragraphs 384 and 391–393. See also the ILC's commentary to Article 6 on Responsibility of States for Internationally Wrongful Acts, where it is a requisite for considering a State organ as placed at the disposal of another State, that the latter exercises exclusive direction and control over that organ, *op. cit.*, p. 44.

would seem superfluous. If that State Party exercised 'exclusive control' over the choice of munitions to be delivered, the same result would clearly apply. It is thus not a viable option to interpret the qualifier 'exclusive control' as instead referring to a test of effective control based on the rules on State responsibility. Such an interpretation would not be sufficient to amend the inconsistency between sub-paragraph (d) and paragraph 2, nor would it remedy the understanding of the scope of sub-paragraph (d) in relation to sub-paragraph (c).

21.90 Based on the obligation to perform treaty obligations in good faith and interpreting the wording of sub-paragraph (d) in the light of the context and the object and purpose of the Convention, the reference to 'exclusive control' over the 'choice of munitions used' should not be understood *a contrario* to mean that a State Party may be authorized to expressly request the use of cluster munitions in any other interoperability situation.[167] On the other hand, and in order to safeguard legitimate interoperability concerns, a mere request by a State Party to the forces of a State not party for fire support that results in cluster munitions actually being used by that State not party should not be construed as unlawful assistance in the commission of a prohibited act as long as the State Party does not exercise effective control over the conduct.

21.91 It is therefore submitted that, in keeping with the general obligations and the object and purpose of the Convention, a State Party may not expressly request the use of cluster munitions under any circumstances. Moreover, if a State Party exercises effective or 'exclusive' control over the choice of munitions to be used, then the subsequent use of cluster munitions by a State not party could constitute an internationally wrongful act attributable to the requesting State Party. What Article 21 should allow in these situations, therefore, is for a State Party and the members of its armed forces to call in a strike delivered by a State not party in an international operation even if there is no guarantee that cluster munitions will not be used. Military personnel would thus not incur penal sanctions for the use of cluster munitions by others as long as they do not exercise effective control over the tactical decisions following their request for support. This interpretation is based on the generally recognized principle

---

[167] The Permanent Court of International Justice in its Advisory Opinion No. 131 stressed that the context is not merely the Article or section of the treaty in which the term occurs, but the treaty as a whole:

> In considering the question before the Court upon the language of the Treaty, it is obvious that the Treaty must be read as a whole, and that its meaning is not to be determined merely upon particular phrases which, if detached from the context, may be interpreted in more than one sense.

Competence of the ILO to Regulate Agricultural Labour, *PCIJ* (1922), Series B, Nos. 2 and 3, p. 23.

that mere participation in international operations with the forces of a State not party that might engage in activities prohibited by the Convention (or by any other international legal instrument) is not regarded as assistance in the commission of a wrongful act on the part of the participating State Party.[168]

---

[168] A State Party may take steps to safeguard its position as described in sub-paragraph (d) by issuing appropriate national caveats to relevant ROE or joint operational plans (see, *supra,* §21.51).

Article 22. Depositary

Stuart Casey-Maslen and Gro Nystuen[1]

Article 22—Depositary

The Secretary-General of the United Nations is hereby designated as the Depositary of this Convention.

Commentary	597

Commentary

22.1 This Article designates the Secretary-General of the United Nations (UN) as the Depositary of the Convention on Cluster Munitions. This is in accord with the *1969 Vienna Convention on the Law of Treaties*, which expressly allows the Chief Administrative Officer of an international organization to be designated as the Depositary of a treaty, and for the designation to be made in the treaty itself.[2] As described below, a Depositary has to carry out a number of functions with respect to the Convention, among others to allow States to sign it, as well as to accept and record instruments of ratification, acceptance, approval, and accession.[3]

22.2 The appointment of the Secretary-General of the UN as the Depositary of the Convention is not unusual, given that the office serves as the Depositary for more than 500 treaties.[4] It is, however, noteworthy that the negotiation of the Convention took place outside the auspices of

---

[1] The authors would like to thank Christophe Lanord for his input into the commentary on this Article.

[2] Thus Article 76, paragraph 1, *1969 Vienna Convention on the Law of Treaties* provides that:

The designation of the depositary of a treaty may be made by the negotiating States, either in the treaty itself or in some other manner. The depositary may be one or more States, an international organization or the chief administrative officer of the organization.

[3] *Cp.* with the 'administrative tasks' allocated to the Secretary-General of the UN under Articles 7 and 8 of the Convention; see in this regard Article 14, paragraph 3 *supra* and the accompanying commentary.

[4] See <http://treaties.un.org/Pages/Overview.aspx?path=overview/overview/page1_en.xml&clang=_en>.

the UN.[5] A similar situation existed with respect to the *1997 Anti-Personnel Mine Ban Convention*.[6] On 30 May 2008, the Secretary-General of the UN formally indicated that he was 'honoured to accept depositary functions under the Convention',[7] confirming the opening statement delivered on his behalf 10 days before.[8] In contrast to the administrative functions entrusted to his office under Article 14, paragraph 3, no formal mandate from the UN General Assembly was required,[9] as opposed to the other functions to be carried out under the Convention. The latter are to be seen as requiring a formal acceptance from the UN General Assembly, in accordance with Article 14, paragraph 3, of the Convention.[10]

22.3 According to the *1969 Vienna Convention on the Law of Treaties*, the functions of a Depositary include the following:

(a) keeping custody of the original text of the treaty and of any full powers delivered to the Depositary;

(b) preparing certified copies of the original text and preparing any further text of the treaty in such additional languages as may be required by the treaty and transmitting them to the parties and to the States entitled to become parties to the treaty;

(c) receiving any signatures to the treaty and receiving and keeping custody of any instruments, notifications and communications relating to it;

---

[5] Although certain UN agencies were very supportive of the Oslo Process. See, e.g., Statement of Ad Melkert, UN Under-Secretary-General and Associate Administrator of the UN Development Programme, Dublin Diplomatic Conference, 19 May 2008, available at: <http://www.clustermunitionsdublin.ie/documents/general-statements/undp.pdf> (accessed 1 March 2010).

[6] See Maslen, S., *Commentaries on Arms Control Treaties, Volume I: The Convention on the Prohibition of the Use, Stockpiling, Production, and Transfer of Anti-Personnel Mines and on their Destruction*, Second Edition, Oxford Commentaries on International Law (Oxford: Oxford University Press, 2005), §21.2.

[7] <http://www.clustermunitionsdublin.ie/pdf/UNSG.pdf> (accessed 1 March 2010).

[8] See Statement of Ad Melkert, UN Under-Secretary-General and Associate Administrator of the UN Development Programme, Dublin Diplomatic Conference, 19 May 2008.

[9] A/RES/63/71, Convention on Cluster Munitions.

[10] See the remarks of the President of the Dublin Diplomatic Conference during the Fourth Session of the Plenary, when the Procedural Report was adopted:

> ...[p]aragraph 21 contained a decision that the President of the Conference would report to the next session of the UN General Assembly on the outcome of the Conference. As the Secretary-General of the United Nations would require an appropriate mandate to carry out the administrative functions assigned to him under the Convention, as distinct from his depositary functions, a General Assembly Resolution in the autumn would be necessary.

'Summary Record of Fourth Session of the Plenary and Closing Ceremony of the Conference', Diplomatic Conference doc. CCM/SR/4, 18 June 2008, p. 8.

(d) examining whether the signature or any instrument, notification or communication relating to the treaty is in due and proper form and, if need be, bringing the matter to the attention of the State in question;

(e) informing the parties and the States entitled to become parties to the treaty of acts, notifications and communications relating to the treaty;

(f) informing the States entitled to become parties to the treaty when the number of signatures or of instruments of ratification, acceptance, approval or accession required for the entry into force of the treaty has been received or deposited;

(g) registering the treaty with the Secretariat of the United Nations;

(h) performing the functions specified in other provisions of the present Convention.[11]

Given this generally accepted understanding, no further clarification of the specific functions of the Secretary-General of the UN as Depositary of the Convention on Cluster Munitions was deemed necessary.

---

[11] Article 76, paragraph 2, *1969 Vienna Convention on the Law of Treaties.*

Article 23. Authentic texts

Stuart Casey-Maslen and Gro Nystuen[1]

Article 23—Authentic texts

The Arabic, Chinese, English, French, Russian and Spanish texts of this Convention shall be equally authentic.

Commentary	600

Commentary

23.1 Article 23 defines all six official United Nations (UN) language versions of the text of the Convention as authentic: Arabic, Chinese, English, French, Russian, and Spanish. This is despite the fact that most of the negotiations took place either in English alone, or in English, French, and Spanish.

23.2 The draft of this provision as submitted to the Diplomatic Conference was exactly the same as the corresponding provision in the *1997 Anti-Personnel Mine Ban Convention*.[2] That draft, however, was mixing two aspects: the fact that the six language versions of the Convention were of equal value and that the original text of the Convention would be deposited with the Secretary-General of the UN. The latter aspect was superfluous, due to the existence of another Article on the Depositary.[3] As a consequence, the text was simplified, quite early in the Conference, and circulated as a Presidential text.[4] There was no discussion on this draft in the Committee of the Whole,[5] which maintained the text unchanged, as did the Plenary subsequently, leading to the text as it stands in the final version of the Convention.

---

[1] The authors would like to thank Christophe Lanord for his input into the commentary on this Article.

[2] Article 22. The draft text was as follows:

The original of this Convention, of which the Arabic, Chinese, English, French, Russian and Spanish texts are equally authentic, shall be deposited with the Secretary-General of the United Nations.

[3] Article 22 of the Convention; this was Article 21 in the Draft Cluster Munitions Convention.

[4] CCM/PT/7, circulated on 21 May 2008.

[5] CCM/CW/SR/5. Also see CCM/CW/SR/9 and CCM/CW/SR/15.

23.3 When introducing the new draft before the Committee of the Whole, the President indicated that the change of wording was 'in response to the suggestions of the UN Office of Legal Affairs'.[6] These comments were not made public.

23.4 The languages used during the Dublin Diplomatic Conference were English, French, and Spanish, in accordance with the Rules of Procedure.[7] All documents had to be provided in these three languages, but not in other languages.[8] Therefore, when the Convention was adopted, it only existed in these three languages, and not in the three others mentioned by the Convention itself. One delegate regretted that situation, stating that: 'Arabic-speaking delegations would have greatly benefited from having Arabic as a working language of the Conference.'[9] The task of translating the Convention in the three remaining languages was one of those that fell to the Secretary-General of the UN, on the basis of his role as Depositary of the Convention.[10] In the period leading up to the signing ceremony in Oslo on 3 December 2008, the text was therefore made available in the three remaining languages.[11]

23.5 According to Article 23, the Convention has the same value in each of the six language versions.[12] As is common with all treaties equally authentic in more than one language, difficulties of interpretation may arise, especially because some terms may not have an equivalent word in another language. In such case, the rules laid down in the *1969 Vienna Convention on the Law of Treaties* should apply.[13]

---

[6] CCM/CW/SR/5.

[7] Rule 54, see CCM/2. The responsibility of making the documents available in all languages of the Conference was with the Secretariat of the Conference (see Rule 16.b). [8] Rule 54.

[9] Statement of Bahrain, 'Summary Record of Sixteenth Session of the Committee of the Whole', Diplomatic Conference doc. CCM/CW/SR/16, 18 June 2008.

[10] See, *supra*, the commentary on Article 22; see also §19 of the Final Report of the Conference, Diplomatic Conference doc. CCM/78.

[11] For the text of the Convention in all six official languages, see UN doc. A/C.1/63/5.

[12] This being said, special attention would have to be paid to the English version, as most of the negotiations took place in English, especially at informal level.

[13] See in particular, Article 33, paragraphs 3 and 4, *1969 Vienna Convention on the Law of Treaties*, which stipulate that: '(t)he terms of the treaty are presumed to have the same meaning in each authentic text', and that '(e)xcept where a particular text prevails in accordance with paragraph 1, when a comparison of the authentic texts discloses a difference of meaning which the application of articles 31 and 32 does not remove, the meaning which best reconciles the texts, having regard to the object and purpose of the treaty, shall be adopted'.

Bibliography

Books

Amerasinghe, C. F., *Principles of the Institutional Law of International Organizations, Cambridge Studies in International and Comparative Law, Volume 1* (Cambridge: Cambridge University Press, 1996).

Aust, A., *Modern Treaty Law and Practice*, Second Edition (Cambridge: Cambridge University Press, 2007).

Bernhardt, R. (ed.), *Encyclopaedia of Public International Law*, Vol. 1 (Amsterdam: North-Holland Publishing, 1992).

—— (ed.), *Encyclopaedia of Public International Law*, Vol. 4 (Amsterdam: North-Holland, 2000).

Bolger, D. P., *Americans at War: 1975–1986, An Era of Violent Peace* (Novato, CA: Presidio Press, 1988).

Boothby, W. H., *Weapons and the Law of Armed Conflict* (Oxford: Oxford University Press, 2009).

Borrie, J., *Unacceptable Harm: A history of how the international treaty banning cluster munitions was won* (Geneva: United Nations Institute for Disarmament Research/United Nations, 2009).

Borrie, J. and Martin Randin, V. (eds.), *Thinking Outside the Box in Multilateral Disarmament and Arms Control Negotiations* (Geneva: UNIDIR, 2006).

——, *Disarmament as Humanitarian Action: From Perspective to Practice* (Geneva: UNIDIR, 2006).

Borrie, J. and Thornton, A., *The Value of Diversity in Multilateral Disarmament Work* (Geneva: UNIDIR, 2008).

Bothe, M., Ronzitti, N., and Rosas, A. (eds.), *The New Chemical Weapons Convention—Implementation and Prospects* (The Hague: Martinus Nijhoff, 1998).

Brownlie, I., *Principles of Public International Law*, Sixth Edition (Oxford: Oxford University Press, 2003).

——, *Principles of Public International Law*, Fifth Edition (Oxford: Clarendon Press, 1998).

Cameron, M. L., Lawson, R., and Tomlin, B. (eds.), *To Walk without Fear: The Global Movement to Ban Landmines* (Ottawa: Oxford University Press, 31 December 1998).

Cassese, A., *International Criminal Law* (Oxford: Oxford University Press, 2003).

Cianchi, M., *Leonardo da Vinci's Machines* (Becocci: 1988).

Clapham, A., *Human Rights Obligations of Non-State Actors* (Oxford: Oxford University Press, 2006).

Corum, J. S., *Wolfrum von Richthofen: Master of the German Air War* (Lawrence, KS: University Press of Kansas, 2008).

de la Guardia, E., *Derecho de los tratados internacionales* (Buenos Aires: Abaco de Rodolfo Depalma, 1997).

Dinstein, Y., *The Conduct of Hostilities under the Law of International Armed Conflict*, Second Edition (UK, Cambridge University Press, 2010).

Fleck, D. (ed.), *Handbook of International Humanitarian Law*, Second Edition (Oxford: Oxford University Press, 2008).

——(ed.), *The Handbook of Humanitarian Law of Armed Conflicts* (Oxford: Oxford University Press, 2004).

Gray, C., *International Law and the Use of Force*, Third Edition (Oxford: Oxford University Press, 2008).

Jappy, M. J., *Danger UXB*, (UK: Macmillan's Publisher's, 2001).

Langdon-Davies, J., *Finland: The First Total War* (London: George Routledge & Sons, 1940).

McNair, A., *Law of Treaties*, Second Edition (Oxford: Clarendon Press, 1961).

Maslen, S., *Commentaries on Arms Control Treaties, Volume I: The Convention on the Prohibition of the Use, Stockpiling, Production, and Transfer of Anti-Personnel Mines and on their Destruction*, Second Edition, Oxford Commentaries on International Law (Oxford: Oxford University Press, 2005).

Meron, T., *Human Rights and Humanitarian Norms as Customary Law* (Oxford: Clarendon Press, 1991).

Mettraux, G., *The Law of Command Responsibility* (Oxford: Oxford University Press, 2009).

Ness, L. and Williams, A. G. (eds.), *Jane's Ammunition Handbook 2006–2007* (UK: Jane's Information Group, November 2006).

Neuhold, H., Hummer, W., Schreuer, C. (eds.), *Handbuch des Völkerrechts*, Fourth Edition (Vienna: Manz Verlag, 2004).

Oppenheim's International Law, Ninth Edition, Vol. 1 (Oxford: Oxford University Press, 2008).

Prokosch, E., *Technology of Killing: A Military and Political History of Antipersonnel Weapons* (London: Zed Books, 1995).

Quoc Dinh, N., Dailler, P. and Pellet, A., *Droit International Public*, Sixth Edition (Paris: L.G.D.J, 1999).

Reuter, P., *Introduction au droit des traités*, Third Edition (Geneva: Publications de l'Institut Universitaire des Hautes Etudes Internationales—Genève, 1995).

Rodman, M. K., *A War of Their Own: Bombers over the Southwest Pacific* (Alabama: Air University Press, Maxwell Air Force Base, 2005).

Rousseau, C., *Droit International Public*, Tome I (Paris: Sirey, 1970).

Sandoz, Y. *et al.*, *Commentary on the Additional Protocols of 8 June 1977 to the Geneva Conventions of 12 August 1949* (Geneva: ICRC, 1987).

Sarooshi, D., *The United Nations and the Development of Collective Security, The Delegation of the Security Council of its Chapter VII Powers* (Oxford: Oxford University Press, 2003).

Schermers, H. G., and Blokker, N. M., *International Institutional Law*, Fourth Edition (Leiden: Martinus Nijhoff Publishers, 2003).

Scutts, J. (ed.), *B-25 Mitchell at War* (London: Ian Allan, 1983).

Seyersted, F., *Common Law of International Organizations* (Leiden: Martinus Nijhoff Publishers, 2008).

_____, *UN Forces in the Law of War and Peace* (Leiden: Martinus Nijhoff Publishers, 1966).

Shaw, M. N., *International Law*, Sixth Edition (Cambridge: Cambridge University Press, 2008).

_____, *International Law*, Fourth Edition (Cambridge: Cambridge University Press, 1997).

_____, International Law, Third Edition (Cambridge: Cambridge University Press, 1994).

Simma, B. (ed.), *The Charter of the United Nations—A Commentary* (Oxford: Oxford University Press, 2002).

Sinclair, I., *The Vienna Convention on the Law of Treaties*, Second Edition (Manchester: Manchester University Press, 1984).

Swinarski, C. (ed.), *Etudes et essais sur le droit international humanitaire et sur les principes de la Croix Rouge en l'honneur de Jean Pictet* (Dordrecht: Martinus Nijhoff, 1984).

Triffterer, O. (ed.), Commentary on the Rome Statute of the International Criminal Court: Observers' Notes, Article by Article (Baden-Baden: Nomos Verlagsgesellschaft, 1999).

Villiger, M. E., *Customary international law and treaties* (The Hague: Kluwer Law International, 1997).

Williams, J., Goose, S. D., and Wareham, M. (eds.), *Banning Landmines: Disarmament, Citizen Diplomacy, and Human Security* (US: Rowman and Littlefield, 2008).

Zwanenburg, M., *Accountability of International Peace Support Operations*, International Humanitarian Law Series (Leiden: Martinus Nijhoff, 2005).

Dictionaries

Black's Law Dictionary (Eighth Edition, 2004).

Brown, L., (ed.), *The New Shorter Oxford English Dictionary* (Oxford: Clarendon Press, 1993).

Larousse online dictionary.

Lindberg, C. A. (ed.), *The Oxford American Thesaurus of Current English* (Oxford: Oxford University Press, 1999).

Oxford English Dictionary, CD-ROM Version 3.1 (Oxford: Oxford University Press, 2004).

Oxford Reference Online (Oxford: Oxford University Press, 4 July 2009).

Articles, fact sheets, monographs, and reports

'US—Third JSOW Variant Tested Oct 18,' *Aviation Week & Space Technology*, 18 October 1999.

Benvenisti, E., 'Responsibility for the Protection of Human Rights under the Interim Israeli Palestinians Agreements', 28 *Israel Law Review* 297 (1994).

Borrie, J., 'The "long year": Emerging international efforts to address the humanitarian impacts of cluster munitions, 2006–2007', *Yearbook of International Humanitarian Law*, Vol. 10 (2007), T. M. C. Asser Press/Cambridge University Press, Cambridge, 2009.

——, 'How the cluster munition ban was won: Oslo treaty negotiations conclude in Dublin', *Disarmament Diplomacy*, No. 88 (Summer 2008).

——, 'The road from Oslo: Emerging international efforts on cluster munitions', *Disarmament Diplomacy*, No. 85 (Summer 2007).

Borrie, J. and Cave, R., 'The humanitarian effects of cluster munitions: Why should we worry?', *Disarmament Forum*, No. 4 (Geneva: United Nations Institute for Disarmament Research, 2006).

Brinkert, K., 'Lessons learned from the AP Mine Ban Convention for the destruction and retention of cluster munitions in accordance with the Convention on Cluster Munitions', Berlin Conference on the Destruction of Cluster Munitions, 25–26 June 2009.

——, 'Making sense out of the Anti-Personnel Mine Ban Convention's obligation to landmine victims', March 2006.

Bryant, K. 'Cluster munitions and submunitions – a personal view', *Disarmament Forum*, No. 4 (Geneva: United Nations Institute for Disarmament Research, 2006).

Cassese, A., 'The Martens Clause: Half of a Loaf or Simply Pie in the Sky?', *European Journal of International Law*, Vol. 11, No. 1 (2000).

——, 'Weapons causing unnecessary suffering: are they prohibited?', *Rivista di diritto internazionale*, Vol. 58, 1975.

Cdr. J. Orr, 'Draft Convention for Cluster Munitions', *NATO Legal Gazette*, 15 July 2008.

Charney, J. I., 'The persistent objector rule and the development of customary international law', *British Yearbook of International Law*, Vol. 56, 1985.

Clapham, A., 'Extending International Criminal Law beyond the Individual to Corporations and Armed Opposition Groups', *Journal of International Criminal Justice*, Vol. 6 (2008).

——, 'Human rights obligations of non-state actors in conflict situations', *International Review of the Red Cross*, Vol. 88, No. 863 (2006).

Clark, C., 'The Convention on Cluster Munitions: considering implementation from a battle area clearance perspective', *Disarmament Forum*, No. 1 (Geneva: United Nations Institute for Disarmament Research, 2010).

Cluster Munition Coalition (CMC), 'German proposal is not a basis for a new cluster munition treaty', Press release, Geneva, 27 April 2007.

——, 'Investment in Civilian Suffering to be Halted by Future Cluster Munitions Convention', CMC Policy Paper, undated.

Coupland, R. M., 'Abhorrent weapons and superfluous injury or unnecessary suffering: from field surgery to law', *British Medical Journal*, Vol. 315, 1997.

——, 'Antipersonnel Mines: Why a Ban?', *Community Eye Health Journal*, Vol. 10, 1997.

Courtney-Green, Peter, 'Technical Aspects of Cluster Munitions Stockpile Destruction', Berlin Conference on the Destruction of Cluster Munitions, 25–26 June 2009.

Department of the Navy, Naval Historical Center, 'Korean War: Chronology of U.S. Pacific Fleet Operations, September–December 1952', 21 June 2000.

Di Ruzza, T., 'The Convention on Cluster Munitions: Towards a Balance between Humanitarian and Military Considerations?', *Military Law and the Law of War Review*, Vol. 47, Nos. 3–4 (2008).

Diplomatic Conference on the Reaffirmation and Development of International Humanitarian Law Applicable in Armed Conflicts, 'Working Paper CDDH/DT/2 submitted by Egypt, Mexico, Norway, Sudan, Sweden, Switzerland and Yugoslavia', 21 February 1974.

Diskant, E. B., 'Comparative Corporate Criminal Liability: Exploring the Uniquely American Doctrine Through Comparative Criminal Procedure', 118 *Yale Law Journal* 126 (2008).

Docherty, B., 'Breaking New Ground: The Convention on Cluster Munitions and the Evolution of International Humanitarian Law', *Human Rights Quarterly*, Vol. 31 (2009).

——, 'Staying True to the Ban on Cluster Munitions: Understanding the Prohibition on Assistance in the Convention on Cluster Munitions', June 2009.

Farrant, J., 'Is the Extra-territorial Application of the Human Rights Act Really Justified?', *International Criminal Law Review* 9 (2009).

Forecast International 2005, 'Ordnance & Munitions Forecast, Kill Runway Improved Submunition – Archived 12/2006'.

Gahr Støre, Jonas, 'Special comment on cluster munitions' *Disarmament Forum*, No. 4 (Geneva: United Nations Institute for Disarmament Research, 2006).

Garraway, C., 'The International Fact-Finding Comission', *Commonwealth Law Bulletin*, Vol. 34, No. 4 (December 2008).

Geneva International Centre for Humanitarian Demining (GICHD), *Detectors and Personal Protective Equipment Catalogue 2009*, Geneva, January 2009.

_____, *A Guide to Cluster Munitions*, Second Edition, Geneva, 2009.

_____, *A Guide to Cluster Munitions*, First Edition, Geneva, November 2007.

_____, *A Guide to Mine Action and Explosive Remnants of War*, Second Edition, Geneva, 2007.

_____, *A Guide to International Mine Action Standards*, Geneva, April 2006.

_____, *A study of scrap metal collection in Lao PDR*, Geneva, 2005.

_____, *Explosive Remnants of War (ERW), Undesired Explosive Events in Ammunition Storage Areas*, Geneva, November 2002.

Goose, S. D., 'Cluster Munitions: Ban Them,' *Arms Control Today*, January/February 2008.

Government of Lebanon, 'Higher Relief Commission Daily Situation Report No. 78', 19 October 2006.

Grant, R., 'The Stuka Terror', *Air Force Magazine*, November 2008.

Handicap International, *Circle of Impact: The Fatal Footprint of Cluster Munitions on People and Communities* (Brussels: Handicap International, 2007).

_____, *Fatal Footprint: The Global Human Impact of Cluster Munitions* (Brussels: Handicap International, 2006).

_____, 'Living with UXO: Final Report National Survey on the Socio-Economic Impact of UXO in Lao PDR', Vientiane, 1997.

Harrison, K., 'Report from the Wellington Conference on Cluster Munitions, 18–22 February 2008', Women's International League for Peace and Freedom.

_____, 'Report from the Lima Conference on Cluster Munitions, 23–25 May 2007', Women's International League for Peace and Freedom.

——, 'Report of the Vienna Conference on Cluster Munitions, 5–7 December 2007', Women's International League for Peace and Freedom, January 2008.

HCPR Manual on International Law Applicable to Air and Missile Warfare (Bern: Program on Humanitarian Policy and Conflict Research at Harvard University, 15 May 2009).

Hewson, R., *Jane's Air-Launched Weapons*, Issue 53 (Coulsdon, UK: Jane's Information Group, 2009).

Hiznay, M., 'Operational and technical aspects of cluster munitions' *Disarmament Forum*, No. 4 (Geneva: United Nations Institute for Disarmament Research, 2006).

Holy See, Ratification Declaration, 3 December 2008, <http://www.unog. ch/80256EDD006B8954/(httpAssets)/42E72A73A7F63697C125756D003EA D09/$file/HolySee.pdf>.

Human Rights Watch, 'Cluster Munition Information Chart', 20 November 2009.

_____, *A Dying Practice: Use of Cluster Munitions by Russia and Georgia in August 2008*, April 2009.

_____, *Flooding South Lebanon: Israel's Use of Cluster Munitions in Lebanon in July and August 2006*, Vol. 20, No. 2(E), February 2008.

Human Rights Watch and Harvard Law School, International Human Rights Clinic, 'User State Responsibility for Cluster Munition Clearance: Memorandum to Delegates of the Wellington Conference on Cluster Munitions', 19 February 2008.

_____, *Civilians Under Assault: Hezbollah's Rocket Attacks on Israel in the 2006 War*, Vol. 19, No. 3(E), August 2007.

_____, *Off Target: The conduct of the war and civilian casualties in Iraq* (Washington, DC: Human Rights Watch, 2003).

_____, *Fatally Flawed: Cluster Bombs and Their Use by the United States in Afghanistan*, Vol. 14, No. 7(G), December 2002.

_____, *Ticking Time Bombs: NATO's use of cluster munitions in Yugoslavia*, Vol. 11, No. 6(D), June 1999.

Human Rights Watch and Landmine Action, *Banning Cluster Munitions: Government Policy and Practice* (Ottawa: Mines Action Canada, May 2009).

ICTY, Prosecutor v Milan Martić, Judgement, Case No. IT-95–11-T, 12 June 2007.

IKV Pax Christi and Netwerk Vlaanderen, 'Worldwide Investment in Cluster Munitions', Report, Utrecht, October 2009.

International Campaign to Ban Landmines (ICBL), Guiding Principles for Victim Assistance, compiled by the working group on victim assistance of the ICBL (2007).

_____, *Landmine Monitor Report 2009: Toward a Mine-Free World* (Ottawa: Mines Action Canada, 2009).

_____, *Landmine Monitor Report 2008: Toward a Mine-Free World* (Ottawa: Mines Action Canada, 2008).

_____, *Landmine Monitor Report 2004: Toward a Mine-Free World* (New York: Human Rights Watch, 2004).

_____, *Landmine Monitor Report 1999, Toward a Mine-Free World* (Washington, DC: Human Rights Watch, April 1999).

International Committee of the Red Cross, 'Physical Rehabilitation', undated, <http://www.icrc.org/web/eng/siteeng0.nsf/htmlall/section_physical_rehabilitation?opendocument>.

_____, *Humanitarian, Military, Technical and Legal Challenges of Cluster Munitions, Montreux, Switzerland, 18 to 20 April 2007* (Geneva: ICRC, 2007).

_____, *Caring for Landmine Victims* (Geneva: ICRC, June 2005).

_____, 'Fact Sheet on the Convention on Certain Conventional Weapons', Geneva, March 2004.

_____, Conference of Government Experts on the Use of Certain Conventional Weapons (Second Session – Lugano, 28 January–26 February 1976): Report (Geneva: ICRC, 1976).

_____, Conference of Government Experts on the Use of Certain Conventional Weapons (Lucerne, 24 September–18 October 1974): Report (Geneva: ICRC, 1975).

_____, Les armes de nature à causer des maux superflus ou à frapper sans discrimination, Rapport sur les travaux d'un groupe d'experts (Geneva: ICRC, 1973.

Kelly, Col. M., 'Legal Factors in Military Planning for Coalition Warfare and Military Interoperability,' *Australian Army Journal*, Vol. II, No. 2, Autumn 2005.

King, C., *Explosive Remnants of War: A Study on submunitions and Other Unexploded Ordnance: A Study* (Geneva: ICRC, August 2000).

——, Dullum, O., and Oestern, G., *M85—An Analysis of Reliability* (Oslo: Norwegian People's Aid, 2007).

Landmine Action, 'International Criminal Tribunal: Milan Martić guilty of indiscriminate use of cluster munitions in Zagreb war crime verdict', London, 12 June 2007.

Laurie, G., 'An analysis of Mine Risk Education provisions in mine action-related treaties', undated but 2008.

Livingstone Declaration on Cluster Munitions, 1 April 2008.

Mann, F. A., 'The Doctrine of International Jurisdiction Revisited After Twenty Years', *Recueil des Cours* 111 (1964-I).

——, 'The Doctrine of Jurisdiction in International Law', *Recueil des Cours* 186 (1984-III).

Maresca, L., 'A new protocol on explosive remnants of war: The history and negotiation of Protocol V to the 1980 Convention on Certain Conventional Weapons', *International Review of the Red Cross*, Vol. 86, December 2004.

——, 'Cluster munitions: Moving toward specific regulation' *Disarmament Forum*, No. 4 (Geneva: United Nations Institute for Disarmament Research, 2006).

Marschik, M., 'The Administration of Arms Control: Ensuring Accountability and Legitimacy of Field Operations' *International Organizations Law Review* 6 (2009).

Martinez Bande, J. M., *Vizcaya. Monografías de la Guerra de España, No. 6* (Madrid: Librería Editorial San Martin, 1971).

Maslen, S., *Cluster Bombs and Landmines in Kosovo: Explosive Remnants of War* (Geneva: ICRC, 2001).

——, *Explosive Remnants of War: Cluster Bombs and Landmines in Kosovo*, Revised Edition (Geneva: ICRC, June 2001).

—— and Herby, P., 'An international ban on anti-personnel mines: History and negotiation of the "Ottawa treaty"', *International Review of the Red Cross*, No. 325, 1998.

Maslen, S. and Wiebe, V., *Cluster Munitions, A Survey of Legal Responses* (London: Landmine Action, March 2008).

McCormack, T., Mtharu, P. B., and Finnin, S., Report on States Parties' Responses to the Questionnaire: International Humanitarian Law and Explosive Remnants of War, Asia Pacific Centre for Military Law, University of Melbourne Law School, March 2006.

Milanović, M., 'From Compromise to Principle: Clarifying the Concept of State Jurisdiction in Human Rights Treaties', 8 *Human Rights Law Review*, 2008.

Milanović, M., and Papic, T., 'As Bad as it Gets: The European Court of Human Rights' Behrami and Saramati Decision and General International Law', International and Comparative Law Quarterly, Vol. 57, 2008.

Mine Action Co-ordination Centre—South Lebanon, 'Civilian Cluster Bomb Victims since 14 August up to 01 January 2009' (chart in '320 Casualties as at January 01, 2009').

——, *Quarterly Report: July-September 2008*, 20 October 2008.

Mines Advisory Group, *Eliminating the legacy of conflict, Annual Review 2008*, Manchester, 2009.

Moyes, R., *Tampering: the deliberate handling and use of live ordnance in Cambodia* (Phnom Penh: Handicap International Belgium, Mines Advisory Group, Norwegian People's Aid, 2004).

——, *Cluster munitions in Kosovo: Analysis of use, contamination and casualties* (London: Landmine Action, February 2007).

Nash, T., *Foreseeable Harm, The use and impact of cluster munitions in Lebanon: 2006* (London: Landmine Action, October 2006).

——, 'Stopping cluster munitions' *Disarmament Forum*, No. 4 (Geneva: United Nations Institute for Disarmament Research, 2006).

NATO Glossary of Terms and Definitions, AAP-6 (2009), 2-S-14.

Nystuen, G., in Baillet, C. (ed.), *Security: A Multidisciplinary Normative Approach* (Leiden/Boston: Brill, 2009).

O'Dwyer, G., 'Defense Stocks and Ethics', *Defense News*, 2 March 2009.

Organization of American States, 'Demining', <http://www.oas.org/en/topics/demining.asp>.

OSCE Handbook of Best Practices on Conventional Ammunition, September 2008.

Pax Christi Netherlands, 'Conference Report: Cluster Munition Coalition International Launch Conference, 12–13 November 2003', The Hague, Netherlands.

Petrova, M. H., 'Small States and New Norms of Warfare', EUI Working Papers MWP 2007/28 (San Domenico di Fiesole: European University Institute, 2007).

Putrich, G. S., 'Cluster-Bomb Ban Exempts Some Smart Munitions', *Defense News*, 2 June 2008.

Rappert, B., and Moyes, R., 'The Prohibition of Cluster Munitions: Setting International Precedents for Defining Inhumanity', *Nonproliferation Review*, Vol. 16, No. 2 (July 2009).

Reiterer, M. A., 'Assistance to cluster munition victims: a major step towards humanitarian disarmament', in *Disarmament Forum*, No. 1 (Geneva: United Nations Institute for Disarmament Research, 2010).

Remarks of Professor John Cerone at the 31st San Remo Round Table on Current Problems of International Humanitarian Law, 'Peace operations and the complementarity of human rights law and international humanitarian law', San Remo, Italy, 14 September 2008.

Sari, A., 'Jurisdiction and International Responsibility in Peace Support Operations: The Behrami and Saramati Cases', 8 *Human Rights Law Review* 1 (2008).

Sassòli, M., 'Transnational Armed Groups and International Humanitarian Law' (Harvard University: Program on Humanitarian Policy and Conflict Research, 2006).

Scheffran, J., 'Missiles in conflict: the issue of missiles in all its complexity', *Disarmament Forum*, Vol. 1, 2007.

Seyersted, F., 'United Nations Forces: Some Legal Problems', 37 *British Yearbook of International Law* 1961.

Shane, K., 'Lao PDR', *Journal of Mine Action*, Winter 2006 (Harrisonburg, VA: Mine Action Information Center, 2006).

Sivakumaran, S., 'Binding Armed Opposition Groups', *International and Comparative Law Quarterly*, Vol. 55 (2006).

Survivor Corps: *Connecting the Dots – Victim Assistance and Human Rights: Mine Ban Treaty, Convention on Cluster Munitions, and Convention on the Rights of Persons with Disabilities* (2009).

Tice, S., 'Cluster Munitions: The Ban Process', *Journal of Mine Action*, Summer 2008.

Ticehurst, R., 'The Martens Clause and the Laws of Armed Conflict', *International Review of the Red Cross*, No. 317 (1997).

United Kingdom Glossary of Joint and Multinational Terms and Definitions, Joint Doctrine Publication 0–01.1, Seventh Edition, June 2006.

US, 'International Law—The Conduct of Armed Conflict and Air Operations', Air Force Pamphlet 110–31, US Department of the Air Force, 1976.

US Army, Marine Corps, Navy, Air Force, UXO: Multi-Service Tactics, Techniques, and Procedures for Unexploded Explosive Ordnance Operations, FM 3–100.38, MCRP 3–17.2B, NTTP 3–02.4.1, AFTTP(I) 3–2.12, August 2005.

US Center for Law and Military Operations, Forged in the Fire: Legal Lessons Learned During Military Operations (1994–2008), September 2008.

US Defense Science Board Task Force on Munitions System Reliability, Munitions System Reliability, Office of the Under Secretary of Defense for Acquisition, Technology and Logistics, Washington, DC, 20301–3140, September 2005.

US General Accounting Office, Report to the Honorable Lane Evans, House of Representatives, Military Operations: Information on U.S. Use of Land Mines in the Persian Gulf War, GAO-02–1003, Washington, DC, September 2002.

US Joint Chiefs of Staff, Joint Doctrine for Barriers, Obstacles, and Mine Warfare, Joint Pub, 3–15, 24 February 1999.

UXO Lao, *Lao National Unexploded Ordnance Programme 2008 Annual Report* (Vientiane: UXO Lao, 2009).

——, 'The Unexploded Ordnance (UXO) Problem' (Vientiane: UXO Lao, undated).

van Woudenberg, N., 'The Long and Winding Road Towards an Instrument on Cluster Munitions,' *Journal of Conflict and Security Law*, 1 November 2007.

Watch List on Children in Armed Conflict, 'UN Security Council Resolution 1612 and Beyond: Strengthening Protection for Children in Armed Conflict', New York, May 2009.

Weidacher, R., Wezeman, S., and Hollestelle, M., Cluster Munitions: Necessity or Convenience?, Pax Christi Netherlands, 2005.

Wiebe, V., 'For Whom the Little Bells Toll: Recent Judgments by International Tribunals on the Legality of Cluster Munitions', 35 *Pepperdine Law Review* 895 (2008).

Wilde, R., 'Enhancing Accountability at the International Level: The Tension between International Organization and Member State Responsibility and the Underlying Issues at Stake', *Journal of International and Comparative Law*, No. 416, 2006.

——, 'Triggering State Obligations Extraterritorially: The Spatial Test in Certain Human Rights Treaties', 4 *Israel Law Review* 2007.

UN documents, reports, and resolutions

Basic Principles and Guidelines on the Right to a Remedy and Reparation for Victims of Gross Violations of International Human Rights Law and Serious Violations of International Humanitarian Law, adopted by the UN General Assembly in its Resolution 60/147 of 16 December 2005.

Committee on Economic, Social and Cultural Rights, 'Substantive Issues Arising in the Implementation of the International Covenant on Economic, Social and Cultural Rights, General Comment No. 9, The domestic application of the Covenant', UN doc. E/C.12/1998/24, CESCR, 3 December 1998.

Declaration on Cluster Munitions, Third Review Conference of the States Parties to the CCW, Geneva, UN doc. CCW/CONF.III/WP.18, 17 November 2006.

Draft CCW Protocol on Cluster Munitions submitted by Germany, 2007 Session of the CCW Group of Governmental Experts on Cluster Munitions, UN doc. CCW/GGE/2007/WP.1, Geneva, 1 May 2007.

Draft Mandate on Explosive Remnants of War for a Group of Governmental Experts, 'Final Document of the Second Review Conference of the 1980 Convention on Certain Conventional Weapons', UN doc. CCW/CONF.II/2, 11–21 December 2001.

'ERW Framework Paper: Possible structure for an ERW instrument', UN doc. CCW/GGE/IV/WG.1/WP.1, 28 February 2003.

'Final Document of the Second Conference of the High Contracting Parties to Protocol V on Explosive Remnants of War to the CCW', UN doc. CCW/P.V/CONF/2008/12 of 23 January 2009.

'Final Document of the Third Review Conference of the High Contracting Parties to the CCW', Geneva 7–17 November 2006, UN doc. CCW/CONF.III/11 (Part II).

'Final Document of the Second Review Conference of the States Parties to the CCW, Geneva, December 11–21, 2001', UN doc. CCW/CONF.II/2.

Flanagan, J., UN Mine Action Service, 'ERW—Experience from field operations', UN doc. CCW/GGE/II/WP.13, July 2002.

Germany, 'Draft CCW Protocol on cluster munitions', UN doc. CCW/GGE/2007/WP.1, 1 May 2007.

Human Rights Committee, 'General Comment No. 31 – The Nature of the General Legal Obligation Imposed on States Parties to the Covenant', UN doc. CCPR/C/21/Rev.1/Add.13, 26 May 2004).

'Overview of Existing and Proposed Definitions, Submitted by the Geneva International Centre for Humanitarian Demining (GICHD)', UN doc. CCW/GGE/2007/WP.5, Geneva, 12 June 2007.

International Law Commission (ILC), Draft articles on Responsibility of States for Internationally Wrongful Acts, with commentaries 2001, UN, 2008.

Norway, 'National interpretation and implementation of International Humanitarian Law with regard to the risk of Explosive Remnants of War', Sixth Session of the CCW Group of Governmental Experts (GGE) on Explosive Remnants of War, Geneva, UN doc. CCW/GGE/VI/WG.1/WP.3, 24 November 2003.

'Proposal for a Mandate to Negotiate a Legally-Binding Instrument that Addresses the Humanitarian Concerns Posed by Cluster Munitions, Presented by Austria, Holy See, Ireland, Mexico, New Zealand, and Sweden', Third Review Conference of States Parties to the CCW, Geneva, 25 October 2006, UN doc. CCW/CONF.III/WP.1.

Recommendations on the transport of dangerous goods: model regulations, Twelfth Revised Edition, New York, 2001, UN doc. ST/SG/AC.10/1/Rev.12.

'Report of the Meeting of the High Contracting Parties to the Convention on Prohibitions or Restrictions on the Use of Certain Conventional Weapons Which May Be Deemed to Be Excessively Injurious or to Have Indiscriminate Effects', UN doc. CCW/MSP/2007/5, 3 December 2007, p. 9.

'Report of the Secretary-General on the follow-up to the implementation of the outcome of the World Summit for Social Development and of the twenty-fourth special session of the General Assembly', UN doc. A/63/133, 16 July 2008.

'Report of the Secretary-General on the protection of civilians in armed conflict', UN doc. S/2007/643, 28 October 2007.

'Report of the Secretary-General on the protection of civilians in armed conflict', UN doc. S/2009/277, 29 May 2009.

'Report of the Secretary-General to the Security Council on the protection of civilians in armed conflict', UN doc. S/2004/431, 28 May 2004.

'Responsibility of international organizations, Comments and observations received from international organizations', UN doc. A/CN.4/545, 25 June 2004, p. 18.

Secretary-General of the United Nations, 'Message to the third Review Conference of the Convention on Certain Conventional Weapons', UN doc. SG/SM/10720, 7 November 2006.

Secretary-General's Bulletin, Observance by United Nations forces of international humanitarian law, UN doc. ST/SGB/1999/13.

UN, 'Lauding disability convention as "dawn of a new era," UN urges speedy ratification', Press release.

UN Department of Peacekeeping Operations and Department of Field Support, 'A New Partnership Agenda, Charting a New Horizon for UN Peacekeeping', (New York: UN, July 2009).

UNICEF and Coalition to Stop the Use of Child Soldiers, Guide to the Optional Protocol on the Involvement of Children in Armed Conflict, (New York: UNICEF, 2003).

UNMAS, E-MINE (Electronic Mine Information Network), <http://www.mineaction.org/overview.asp?o=22>.

UNMAS, UNDP and UNICEF, 'Proposed definitions for cluster munitions and submunitions', UN doc. CCW/GGE/X/WG.1/WP.3, 8 March 2005.

UN Office at Geneva, 'Disarmament: Article 7 reporting forms', <http://www.unog.ch/80256EE600585943/(httpPages)/2B050F75A5100D47C12573E800670E42?OpenDocument>.

——, Article 7 reports for the *1997 Anti-Personnel Mine Ban Convention*, <http://www.unog.ch/80256EE600585943/(httpPages)/A5378B203CBE9B8CC12573E7006380FA?OpenDocument>.

——, Article 10 reports for *2003 Protocol V*, <http://www.unog.ch/80256EE600585943/(httpPages)/B84B4C205835421DC12574230039C42E?OpenDocument>.

Universal Declaration of Human Rights, adopted by the UN General Assembly in Resolution 217 A (III) of 10 December 1948.

Security Council Resolutions

1882 (1999) of 4 August 2009.

1738 (2006) of 23 December 2006.

1674 (2006) of 28 April 2006.

1539 (2004) of 22 April 2004.
1460 (2003) of 30 January 2003.
1379 (2001) of 20 November 2001.
1314 (2000) of 11 August 2000.
1296 (2000) of 19 April 2000.
1261 (1999) of 25 August 1999.
1265 (1999) of 17 September 1999.

Other resolutions

Resolution 3 (on the Reaffirmation and implementation of international humanitarian law) of the Thirtieth International Conference of the Red Cross and Red Crescent Movement (Geneva, 26–30 November 2007).

1997 Anti-Personnel Mine Ban Convention documentation

'Ending the Suffering Caused by Anti-Personnel Mines: Nairobi Action Plan 2005–2009, Final Report: First Review Conference of the States Parties to the Convention on the Prohibition of the Use, Stockpiling, Production and Transfer of Anti-Personnel Mines and on Their Destruction', 29 November—3 December 2004, doc. APLC/CONF/2004/5, 9 February 2005.

Final Report of the 1997 Anti-Personnel Mine Ban Convention, Part II: Review of the Operation and Status of the Convention on the Prohibition of the Use, Stockpiling, Production and Transfer of Antipersonnel Mines and on Their Destruction: 1999–2004, doc. APLC/CONF/2004/5, 9 February 2005.

Final Report of the Eighth Meeting of States Parties, doc. APLC/MSP.8/2007/6, 20 January 2008.

Final Report of the Seventh Meeting of States Parties, doc. APLC/MSP.7/2006/5, 17 January 2007.

Nairobi Summit on a Mine-free World, Review of the Operation and Status of the Convention on the Prohibition of the Use, Stockpiling and Production and Transfer of Anti-Personnel Mines and on their Destruction: 1999–2004, contained in doc. APLC/CONF/2004/5.

'Review of the operation and status of the Convention on the Prohibition of the Use, Stockpiling, Production and Transfer of Anti-Personnel Mines and on their Destruction 1999–2004' (Part II of the Final Report of the First Review Conference of the States Parties).

Convention on Cluster Munitions documentation

'Addressing the Humanitarian Impacts of Cluster Munitions: Key Issues', Background Paper to the Oslo Conference on Cluster Munitions, 22–23 February 2007.

Cluster Munition Coalition, 'CMC Briefing Paper on the Convention on Cluster Munitions', July 2008.

——, '(Revised) Observations by the Cluster Munition Coalition on the Draft Cluster Munitions Convention, dated 21 January 2008'.

——, 'Cluster Munitions in the Asia-Pacific Region', October 2008, prepared by Human Rights Watch.

——, 'CMC Report on the Lima Conference and Next Steps', 2007.

——, 'CMC Statement on the Agreement to Adopt the Cluster Munition Convention', delivered by Steve Goose, Human Rights Watch, CMC Co-Chair, 28 May 2008, Dublin Diplomatic Conference.

——, 'Denmark ratifies landmark convention banning cluster munitions', Press release, 12 February 2010, <http://www.stopclustermunitions.org/media/press-releases/?id=2038> (accessed 1 March 2010).

——, 'Dublin Diplomatic Conference on Cluster Munitions 2008 – Lobbying Guide' (London: CMC, 2008).

——, 'Observations by the Cluster Munition Coalition on the draft Convention on Cluster Munitions, dated 21 January 2008'.

Department of Foreign Affairs of Ireland, 'Note on the Measures Taken by Ireland to Implement Article 21 of the Convention on Cluster Munitions', 11 March 2009, attached to Letter from Ambassador Daíthí O'Ceallaigh, Permanent Mission of Ireland to the UN in Geneva, to Thomas Nash, Coordinator, CMC, 16 March 2009.

Human Rights Watch, 'Observations on the Cluster Munition Convention Discussion Text', December 2007.

International Committee of the Red Cross, 'The Convention on Cluster Munitions', Fact Sheet, Geneva, November 2008.

——, 'Comments of the International Committee of the Red Cross on the Wellington draft of a future cluster munitions convention', 8 February 2008.

——, 'Comments of the International Committee of the Red Cross to the Vienna Discussion Text', December 2007.

Permanent Mission of France to the Conference on Disarmament, 'French non-paper on Cluster munitions', 19 April 2007.

——, 'Intervention de la délégation française concernant la définition des armes à sous munitions, Conférence de Lima, Lima, 24 mai 2007'.

National legislation and preparatory materials

B 60 Forslag til folketingsbeslutning om Danmarks godkendelse af konventionen om klyngeammunition undertegnet den 4. december 2008 i Oslo, 19 November 2009.

'Bundesgesetz über das Verbot von Streumunition', (NR: GP XXIII RV 232 AB 350 S. 42. BR: AB 7873 S.751.), *Austrian Federal Law Gazette*, BGBl. I Nr. 12/2008, 7 January 2008.

Cluster Munitions and Anti-Personnel Mines Act 2008 (Ireland, 2008).

Cluster Munitions Prohibition Act 2009, 2009 No. 68, Part 1, §5 (1) (New Zealand, 17 December 2009).

Loi du 4 juin 2009 portant approbation de la Convention sur les armes à sous-munitions, ouverte à la signature à Oslo le 3 décembre 2008, Doc. parl. 5981; sess. ord. 2008–2009.

Loi interdisant le financement de la fabrication, de l'utilisation ou de la détention de mines antipersonnel et de sous-munitions, F. 2007 — 1661 [C - 2007/03169], 20 March 2007, published in Belge Moniteur, 26 April 2007.

Proposition No. 7 (2008–2009) to the Odelsting on a Bill relating to the implementation of the Convention on Cluster Munitions in Norwegian law.

Websites

Cluster Munition Coalition, <http.//www.stopclustermunitions.org>.

Government of Ireland, Dublin Diplomatic Conference website, <http.//www.clustermunitionsdublin.ie/>.

International Committee of the Red Cross, 'Cluster Munitions and International Humanitarian Law', <http.//www.icrc.org/Web/Eng/siteeng0.nsf/html/section-ihl-cluster-munition>.

International standards and guidelines

'Clearance of Cluster Munitions Based on Experience in Lebanon', TNMA [Technical Notes for Mine Action] 09.30/06, Version 1.0, January 2008.

IMAS 01.10: 'Guide for the application of International Mine Action Standards (IMAS)', Second Edition, 1 January 2003.

IMAS 02.10: Guide for the Establishment of a Mine Action Programme', First Edition, 1 January 2003.

IMAS 04.10: 'Glossary of mine action terms, definitions and abbreviations', Second Edition, 1 January 2003.

IMAS 07.11: 'Guide for the management of mine risk education', First Edition, 23 December 2003.

IMAS 08.10: 'General mine action assessment', Second Edition, 1 January 2003.

IMAS 08.20: 'Land release', First Edition, New York, 10 June 2009.

IMAS 08.21: 'Non-Technical Survey', First Edition, New York, 10 June 2009.

IMAS 08.40: 'Marking mine and UXO hazards', Second Edition, 1 January 2003.

IMAS 09.10: 'Clearance requirements', Second Edition, 1 January 2003.

IMAS 09.11: 'Battle Area Clearance (BAC)', First Edition, 1 September 2007.

IMAS 10.70: 'Safety & occupational health – Protection of the environment', First Edition, 1 October 2007.

IMAS 11.10: 'Guide for Stockpile Destruction', Second Edition, 1 January 2003.

IMAS 12.20: 'Implementation of Mine Risk Education Programmes and Projects', First Edition, 23 December 2003.

IMAS 12.10: 'Planning for mine risk education programmes and projects', First Edition, 23 December 2003.

UNICEF and GICHD, 'Emergency Mine Risk Education', IMAS Mine Risk Education Best Practice Guidebook 9, Geneva, 2005.

Media reports and press releases

10 Downing Street press briefing, 21 May 2008, 'cluster bombs', <http.//www.number-10.gov.uk/output/Page15599.asp>.

10 Downing Street, 'Breakthrough on cluster bombs draws closer', 28 May 2008, <http.//www.number10.gov.uk/output/page15608.asp>.

'Klasebomber laases ned' ('Cluster Bombs Locked Down'), *Aftenposten*, 3 November 2006.

'Netherlands imposes moratorium on cluster bombs', *Xinhua*, 26 June 2007.

'U.S. open to negotiations on cluster bombs but no ban', *Reuters*, Geneva, 18 June 2007.

BBC, 'Nato dumps bombs in Adriatic', 16 May 1999.

BBC, 'Hezbollah Denies Cluster Bomb Use', 19 October 2006.

Cluster Munition Coalition, 'Survivors and States Join Forces Against Cluster Bombs', Press release, Belgrade, 4 October 2007.

Corder, M., 'Dutch military ordered to stop using cluster bombs until further notice', *Associated Press*, 26 June 2007.

Coster, K. B., 'Boy finds lethal WWII bomb in Qormi valley', *Times of Malta.com*, 29 October 2009.

Dutch Court of Appeal, 'Mothers of Srebrenica cannot sue UN for compensatory damages', News release, The Hague, 30 March 2010.

Hundley, T., 'Kosovo War's Jetsam Leaves Italy Fishermen Trawling For Trouble', *Chicago Tribune*, 16 July 1999.

ICBL, 'Anti-Landmine Treaty Working, Lives and Limbs Saved', Press release, 12 November 2009.

IKV Pax Christi, 'Netherlands suspends use of cluster munitions, but questions remain', Press release, 27 June 2007.

Kilian, M., '"The War Has Just Started": Terrorist Vows Revenge as the U.S. Stands Firm', *Chicago Tribune*, 22 August 1998.

Letter from General Sir Hugh Beach, Field Marshal Lord Bramall, Major-General Patrick Cordingley, Lieutenant-General Sir Roderick Cordy-Simpson, Lieutenant-General Sir Jack Deverell, Major-General the Rev. Morgan Llewellyn, General Lord Ramsbotham, General Sir Michael Rose, and General Sir Rupert Smith, 'Cluster bombs don't work and must be banned', *The Times*, 19 May 2008.

Lin, J., 'Shellshocked Laos', *Hobart Mercury* (Australia), 20 December 1996.

Norton-Taylor, R., 'UK ready to scrap killer cluster bombs: Ministers overrule opposition from military over controversial weapons', *Guardian*, 28 May 2008.

——, 'Italian fishermen strike over lethal haul', *Guardian*, 15 May 1999.

Norway Ministry of Finance, 'Cluster weapons manufacturer excluded from the Government Pension Fund—Global', Press release no. 14/209, 30 January 2009.

Norway Ministry of Finance, A Further Eight Companies Excluded from the Petroleum Fund, Press Release No. 57/205, 2 September 2005.

Norwegian Ministry of Foreign Affairs, '46 Countries endorsed Oslo-declaration', Press release, February 2007.

Norwegian Ministry of Foreign Affairs, 'Cluster munitions to be banned by 2008', Press release No. 21/07, 23 February 2007.

Norwegian Ministry of Foreign Affairs, 'Norway takes the initiative for a ban on cluster munitions', Press Release No. 104/06, 17 November 2006.

Norwegian Ministry of Foreign Affairs, 'Norway to take the lead in efforts to achieve an international ban on cluster munition', Press release, 3 November 2006.

Norwegian People's Aid, 'Scale of cluster bomb problem in Serbia revealed for first time', Press Conference, Belgrade, 10 March 2009.

Owen, R., 'NATO Jets Dump Bombs Off Venice', *The Times* (London), 15 May 1999.

Ramsbotham, General Sir Michael Rose, and General Sir Rupert Smith, 'Cluster bombs don't work and must be banned', *The Times*, 19 May 2008.

Rappaport, M., 'Israeli Defence Force commander: We fired more than a million cluster bombs in Lebanon', *Haaretz*, 12 September 2006.

Trial Chamber of the ICTY, 'Summary of Judgment for Milan Martić,' Press release, The Hague, 12 June 2007.

UK Ministry of Defence, 'New precision "search and destroy" anti-armour weapon', News release, 19 November 2007.

ANNEXES

ANNEX 1: *1969 VIENNA CONVENTION ON THE LAW OF TREATIES* (EXTRACTS)

Article 7—Full powers

1. A person is considered as representing a State for the purpose of adopting or authenticating the text of a treaty or for the purpose of expressing the consent of the State to be bound by a treaty if:

(a) he produces appropriate full powers; or

(b) it appears from the practice of the States concerned or from other circumstances that their intention was to consider that person as representing the State for such purposes and to dispense with full powers.

2. In virtue of their functions and without having to produce full powers, the following are considered as representing their State:

(a) Heads of State, Heads of Government and Ministers for Foreign Affairs, for the purpose of performing all acts relating to the conclusion of a treaty;

(b) heads of diplomatic missions, for the purpose of adopting the text of a treaty between the accrediting State and the State to which they are accredited;

(c) representatives accredited by States to an international conference or to an international organization or one of its organs, for the purpose of adopting the text of a treaty in that conference, organization or organ.

Article 9—Adoption of the text

1. The adoption of the text of a treaty takes place by the consent of all the States participating in its drawing up except as provided in paragraph 2.

2. The adoption of the text of a treaty at an international conference takes place by the vote of two thirds of the States present and voting, unless by the same majority they shall decide to apply a different rule.

Article 10—Authentication of the text

The text of a treaty is established as authentic and definitive:

(a) by such procedure as may be provided for in the text or agreed upon by the States participating in its drawing up; or

(b) failing such procedure, by the signature, signature ad referendum or initialling by the representatives of those States of the text of the treaty or of the Final Act of a conference incorporating the text.

Article 11—Means of expressing consent to be bound by a treaty

The consent of a State to be bound by a treaty may be expressed by signature, exchange of instruments constituting a treaty, ratification, acceptance, approval or accession, or by any other means if so agreed.

Article 18—Obligation not to defeat the object and purpose of a treaty prior to its entry into force

A State is obliged to refrain from acts which would defeat the object and purpose of a treaty when:

(a) it has signed the treaty or has exchanged instruments constituting the treaty subject to ratification, acceptance or approval, until it shall have made its intention clear not to become a party to the treaty; or

(b) it has expressed its consent to be bound by the treaty, pending the entry into force of the treaty and provided that such entry into force is not unduly delayed.

Article 19—Formulation of reservations

A State may, when signing, ratifying, accepting, approving or acceding to a treaty, formulate a reservation unless:

(a) the reservation is prohibited by the treaty;

(b) the treaty provides that only specified reservations, which do not include the reservation in question, may be made; or

(c) in cases not falling under subparagraphs (a) and (b), the reservation is incompatible with the object and purpose of the treaty.

Article 24—Entry into force

1. A treaty enters into force in such manner and upon such date as it may provide or as the negotiating States may agree.

2. Failing any such provision or agreement, a treaty enters into force as soon as consent to be bound by the treaty has been established for all the negotiating States.

3. When the consent of a State to be bound by a treaty is established on a date after the treaty has come into force, the treaty enters into force for that State on that date, unless the treaty otherwise provides.

4. The provisions of a treaty regulating the authentication of its text, the establishment of the consent of States to be bound by the treaty, the manner or date of its entry into force, reservations, the functions of the depositary and other matters arising necessarily before the entry into force of the treaty apply from the time of the adoption of its text.

Article 25—Provisional application

1. A treaty or a part of a treaty is applied provisionally pending its entry into force if:

(a) the treaty itself so provides; or

(b) the negotiating States have in some other manner so agreed.

2. Unless the treaty otherwise provides or the negotiating States have otherwise agreed, the provisional application of a treaty or a part of a treaty with respect to a State shall be terminated if that State notifies the other States between which the treaty is being applied provisionally of its intention not to become a party to the treaty.

Article 26— 'Pacta sunt servanda'

Every treaty in force is binding upon the parties to it and must be performed by them in good faith.

Article 27—Internal law and observance of treaties

A party may not invoke the provisions of its internal law as justification for its failure to perform a treaty. This rule is without prejudice to article 46.

Article 28—Non-retroactivity of treaties

Unless a different intention appears from the treaty or is otherwise established, its provisions do not bind a party in relation to any act or fact which took place or any situation which ceased to exist before the date of the entry into force of the treaty with respect to that party.

Article 29—Territorial scope of treaties

Unless a different intention appears from the treaty or is otherwise established, a treaty is binding upon each party in respect of its entire territory.

Article 31—General rule of interpretation

1. A treaty shall be interpreted in good faith in accordance with the ordinary meaning to be given to the terms of the treaty in their context and in the light of its object and purpose.

2. The context for the purpose of the interpretation of a treaty shall comprise, in addition to the text, including its preamble and annexes:

(a) any agreement relating to the treaty which was made between all the parties in connection with the conclusion of the treaty;

(b) any instrument which was made by one or more parties in connection with the conclusion of the treaty and accepted by the other parties as an instrument related to the treaty.

3. There shall be taken into account, together with the context:

(a) any subsequent agreement between the parties regarding the interpretation of the treaty or the application of its provisions;

(b) any subsequent practice in the application of the treaty which establishes the agreement of the parties regarding its interpretation;

(c) any relevant rules of international law applicable in the relations between the parties.

4. A special meaning shall be given to a term if it is established that the parties so intended.

Article 32—Supplementary means of interpretation

Recourse may be had to supplementary means of interpretation, including the preparatory work of the treaty and the circumstances of its conclusion, in order to confirm the meaning resulting from the application of article 31, or to determine the meaning when the interpretation according to article 31:

(a) leaves the meaning ambiguous or obscure; or

(b) leads to a result which is manifestly absurd or unreasonable.

Article 33—Interpretation of treaties authenticated in two or more languages

1. When a treaty has been authenticated in two or more languages, the text is equally authoritative in each language, unless the treaty provides or the parties agree that, in case of divergence, a particular text shall prevail.

2. A version of the treaty in a language other than one of those in which the text was authenticated shall be considered an authentic text only if the treaty so provides or the parties so agree.

3. The terms of the treaty are presumed to have the same meaning in each authentic text.

4. Except where a particular text prevails in accordance with paragraph 1, when a comparison of the authentic texts discloses a difference of meaning which the application of articles 31 and 32 does not remove, the meaning which best reconciles the texts, having regard to the object and purpose of the treaty, shall be adopted.

Article 34—General rule regarding third States

A treaty does not create either obligations or rights for a third State without its consent.

Article 42—Validity and continuance in force of treaties

1. The validity of a treaty or of the consent of a State to be bound by a treaty may be impeached only through the application of the present Convention.

2. The termination of a treaty, its denunciation or the withdrawal of a party, may take place only as a result of the application of the provisions of the treaty or of the present Convention. The same rule applies to suspension of the operation of a treaty.

Article 43—Obligations imposed by international law independently of a treaty

The invalidity, termination or denunciation of a treaty, the withdrawal of a party from it, or the suspension of its operation, as a result of the application of the present Convention or of the provisions of the treaty, shall not in any way impair the duty of any State to fulfil any obligation embodied in the treaty to which it would be subject under international law independently of the treaty.

Article 46—Provisions of internal law regarding competence to conclude treaties

1. A State may not invoke the fact that its consent to be bound by a treaty has been expressed in violation of a provision of its internal law regarding competence to conclude treaties as invalidating its consent unless that violation was manifest and concerned a rule of its internal law of fundamental importance.

2. A violation is manifest if it would be objectively evident to any State conducting itself in the matter in accordance with normal practice and in good faith.

Article 54—Termination of or withdrawal from a treaty under its provisions or by consent of the parties

The termination of a treaty or the withdrawal of a party may take place:

(a) in conformity with the provisions of the treaty; or
(b) at any time by consent of all the parties after consultation with the other contracting States.

Article 76—Depositaries of treaties

1. The designation of the depositary of a treaty may be made by the negotiating States, either in the treaty itself or in some other manner. The depositary may be one or more States, an international organization or the chief administrative officer of the organization.

2. The functions of the depositary of a treaty are international in character and the depositary is under an obligation to act impartially in their performance. In particular, the fact that a treaty has not entered into force between certain of the parties or that a difference has appeared between a State and a depositary with regard to the performance of the latter's functions shall not affect that obligation.

Article 77—Functions of depositaries

1. The functions of a depositary, unless otherwise provided in the treaty or agreed by the contracting States, comprise in particular:

(a) keeping custody of the original text of the treaty and of any full powers delivered to the depositary;
(b) preparing certified copies of the original text and preparing any further text of the treaty in such additional languages as may be required by the treaty and transmitting them to the parties and to the States entitled to become parties to the treaty;
(c) receiving any signatures to the treaty and receiving and keeping custody of any instruments, notifications and communications relating to it;
(d) examining whether the signature or any instrument, notification or communication relating to the treaty is in due and proper form and, if need be, bringing the matter to the attention of the State in question;

(e) informing the parties and the States entitled to become parties to the treaty of acts, notifications and communications relating to the treaty;

(f) informing the States entitled to become parties to the treaty when the number of signatures or of instruments of ratification, acceptance, approval or accession required for the entry into force of the treaty has been received or deposited;

(g) registering the treaty with the Secretariat of the United Nations;

(h) performing the functions specified in other provisions of the present Convention.

2. In the event of any difference appearing between a State and the depositary as to the performance of the latter's functions, the depositary shall bring the question to the attention of the signatory States and the contracting States or, where appropriate, of the competent organ of the international organization concerned.

ANNEX 2: OSLO DECLARATION

Oslo Conference on Cluster Munitions

22–23 February 2007

Declaration

A group of States, United Nations Organisations, the International Committee of the Red Cross, the Cluster Munition Coalition and other humanitarian organisations met in Oslo on 22–23 February 2007 to discuss how to effectively address the humanitarian problems caused by cluster munitions.

Recognising the grave consequences caused by the use of cluster munitions and the need for immediate action, states commit themselves to:

1. Conclude by 2008 a legally binding international instrument that will:

   (i) prohibit the use, production, transfer and stockpiling of cluster munitions that cause unacceptable harm to civilians, and

   (ii) establish a framework for cooperation and assistance that ensures adequate provision of care and rehabilitation to survivors and their communities, clearance of contaminated areas, risk education and destruction of stockpiles of prohibited cluster munitions.

2. Consider taking steps at the national level to address these problems.

3. Continue to address the humanitarian challenges posed by cluster munitions within the framework of international humanitarian law and in all relevant fora.

4. Meet again to continue their work, including in Lima in May/June and Vienna in November/December 2007, and in Dublin in early 2008, and welcome the announcement of Belgium to organise a regional meeting.

Oslo, 23 February 2007

ANNEX 3: LIMA DISCUSSION TEXT

Chairs' discussion text on a *legally binding international instrument that will prohibit the use, production, transfer and stockpiling of cluster munitions that cause unacceptable harm to civilians*

Lima 23–25 May 2007

Preamble......

....

....

....

Have agreed as follows:

Article 1—General obligations and scope of application

Because of their unacceptable harm to civilians and civilian objects during and after use, each State Party undertakes never under any circumstances:

a) To use cluster munitions as defined in Article 2.

b) To develop, produce, otherwise acquire, stockpile, retain or transfer to anyone, directly or indirectly, cluster munitions as defined in Article 2.

c) To assist, encourage or induce, in any way, anyone to engage in any activity prohibited to a State Party under this convention.

Article 2—Definition

The following weapons systems shall be considered prohibited cluster munitions under this treaty:

Air carried dispersal systems or air delivered, surface or sub-surface launched containers, that are designed to disperse explosive sub-munitions intended to detonate following separation from the container or dispenser, unless they are designed to, manually or automatically, aim, detect and engage point targets, or are meant for smoke or flaring, or unless their use is regulated or prohibited under other treaties.

Article 3—Storage and stockpile destruction

1. Each State Party undertakes to separate cluster munitions as defined in Article 2 from stocks for potential use, and keep in separate stockpiles for the purpose of destruction.

2. Each State Party undertakes to destroy or ensure the destruction of all cluster munitions as defined in Article 2 under its jurisdiction or control, as soon as possible

but not later than six years after the entry into force of this Convention for that State Party.

3. If a State Party believes that it will be unable to destroy or ensure the destruction of all cluster munitions referred to in paragraph 1 within that time period, it may submit a request to a Meeting of the States Parties or a Review Conference for an extension of the deadline for completing the destruction of such cluster munitions, for a period of up to ten years.

4. Each request shall contain:

a) The duration of the proposed extension;

b) A detailed explanation of the reasons for the proposed extension, including the financial and technical means required for the destruction of all the cluster munitions referred to in paragraph 1,

c) A plan for how and when stockpile destruction will be completed.

5. The Meeting of the States Parties or the Review Conference shall, taking into consideration the factors contained in paragraph 4, assess the request and decide by a majority of votes of States Parties present and voting whether to grant the request for an extension period.

6. Such an extension may be renewed upon the submission of a new request in accordance with paragraphs 3, 4 and 5 of this Article. In requesting a further extension period a State Party shall submit relevant additional information on what has been undertaken in the previous extension period pursuant to this Article.

Article 4—Clearance of unexploded ordnance from cluster munitions

1. Each State Party undertakes to clear all unexploded ordnance from cluster munitions in areas under its jurisdiction and control, as soon as possible but not later than ten years after the entry into force of this Convention for that State Party.

2. Each State Party shall make every effort to identify all areas under its jurisdiction or control in which cluster munitions are known or suspected to be present and shall ensure as soon as possible that all cluster munitions in such areas under its jurisdiction or control are perimeter-marked, monitored and protected by fencing or other means, to ensure the effective exclusion of civilians, until all cluster munitions contained therein have been destroyed. The marking shall at least be to the standards set out in the Protocol on Prohibitions or Restrictions on the Use of Mines, Booby-Traps and Other Devices, as amended on 3 May 1996, annexed to the Convention on Prohibitions or Restrictions on the Use of Certain Conventional Weapons Which May Be Deemed to Be Excessively Injurious or to Have Indiscriminate Effects.

3. If a State Party believes that it will be unable to destroy or ensure the destruction of all cluster munitions referred to in paragraph 1 within that time period, it may submit a request to a Meeting of the States Parties or a Review Conference for an extension

of the deadline for completing the destruction of such cluster munitions, for a period of up to ten years.

4. Each request shall contain:

a) The duration of the proposed extension;

b) A detailed explanation of the reasons for the proposed extension, including:
   i) The preparation and status of work conducted under national clearing/demining programs;
   ii) The financial and technical means available to the State Party for the destruction of all the cluster munitions; and
   iii) Circumstances which impede the ability of the State Party to destroy all the cluster munitions in contaminated areas;

c) The humanitarian, social, economic, and environmental implications of the extension; and

d) Any other information relevant to the request for the proposed extension.

5. The Meeting of the States Parties or the Review Conference shall, taking into consideration the factors contained in paragraph 4, assess the request and decide by a majority of votes of States Parties present and voting whether to grant the request for an extension period.

6. Such an extension may be renewed upon the submission of a new request in accordance with paragraphs 3, 4 and 5 of this Article. In requesting a further extension period a State Party shall submit relevant additional information on what has been undertaken in the previous extension period pursuant to this Article.

Article 5—International cooperation and assistance

1. In fulfilling its obligations under this Convention each State Party has the right to seek and receive assistance, where feasible, from other States Parties to the extent possible.

2. Each State Party undertakes to facilitate and shall have the right to participate in the fullest possible exchange of equipment, material and scientific and technological information concerning the implementation of this Convention. The States Parties shall not impose undue restrictions on the provision of clearance equipment and related technological information for humanitarian purposes.

3. Each State Party in a position to do so shall provide assistance for clearance of cluster munitions and related activities. Such assistance may be provided, inter alia, through the United Nations system, international or regional organizations or institutions, non-governmental organizations or institutions, or on a bilateral basis.

4. Each State Party in a position to do so shall provide assistance for the destruction of stockpiled cluster munitions as defined in Article 2.

5. States Parties may request the United Nations, regional organizations, other States Parties or other competent intergovernmental or non-governmental fora to

assist its authorities in the elaboration of a national program to determine, inter alia:

a) The extent and scope of the contamination of unexploded ordnance from cluster munitions;

b) The financial, technological and human resources required for the implementation of the program;

c) The estimated number of years necessary to clear all unexploded ordnance in contaminated areas under the jurisdiction or control of the concerned State Party;

d) Awareness activities to reduce the incidence of injuries or deaths caused by unexploded ordnance from cluster munitions;

e) Assistance to victims from cluster munitions;

f) The relationship between the Government of the concerned State Party and the relevant governmental, inter-governmental or non-governmental entities that will work in the implementation of the program.

6. Each State Party giving and receiving assistance under the provisions of this Article shall cooperate with a view to ensuring the full and prompt implementation of agreed assistance programs.

Article 6—Victim assistance

1. Each State Party shall, in accordance with applicable international human rights standards, endeavour to take adequate steps such as providing medical care and rehabilitation as well as facilitating social and economic reintegration of victims of cluster munitions, in order to ensure the full realisation of their human rights and respect for their inherent dignity.

2. Each State Party in a position to do so shall provide assistance for the medical care and rehabilitation as well as social and economic reintegration of victims of cluster munitions and for cluster munitions awareness programs. Such assistance may be provided, inter alia, through the United Nations system, international, regional or national organizations or institutions, the International Committee of the Red Cross, national Red Cross and Red Crescent societies and their International Federation, non-governmental organizations, or on a bilateral basis.

Article 7—Transparency measures

1. Each State Party shall report to the Secretary-General of the United Nations as soon as practicable, and in any event not later than 180 days after the entry into force of this Convention for that State Party on:

a) The national implementation measures referred to in Article 9;

b) The total of all stockpiled cluster munitions as defined in Article 2 owned or possessed by it, or under its jurisdiction or control, to include a breakdown of their type, quantity and, if possible, lot numbers of each type;

c) To the extent possible, the location of all areas that contain, or are suspected to contain, unexploded ordnance from cluster munitions under its jurisdiction or control, to include as much detail as possible regarding the type and quantity of each type of cluster munitions in each affected area and when they were used;

d) The status of programs for the conversion or de-commissioning of production facilities for cluster munitions as defined in Article 2;

e) The status of programs for the destruction, in accordance with Article 3, of cluster munitions as defined in Article 2, including details of the methods which will be used in destruction, the location of all destruction sites and the applicable safety and environmental standards to be observed;

f) The types and quantities of all cluster munitions destroyed in accordance with Article 3, after the entry into force of this Convention for that State Party, to include a breakdown of the quantity of each type of cluster munition destroyed;

g) The technical characteristics of each type of cluster munition as defined in Article 2 produced, to the extent known, and those currently owned or possessed by a State Party, giving, where reasonably possible, such categories of information as may facilitate identification and clearance of cluster munitions; at a minimum, this information shall include the dimensions, fusing, explosive content, metallic content, colour photographs and other information which may facilitate the clearance of unexploded ordnance caused by these munitions; and

h) The measures taken to provide an immediate and effective warning to the population in relation to all areas identified to be contaminated by unexploded ordnance from cluster munitions.

2. The information provided in accordance with this Article shall be updated by the States Parties annually, covering the last calendar year, and reported to the Secretary-General of the United Nations not later than 30 April of each year.

3. The Secretary-General of the United Nations shall transmit all such reports received to the States Parties.

Article 8—Facilitation and clarification of compliance

1. The States Parties agree to consult and cooperate with each other regarding the implementation of the provisions of this Convention, and to work together in a spirit of cooperation to facilitate compliance by States Parties with their obligations under this Convention.

2. If one or more States Parties wish to clarify and seek to resolve questions relating to compliance with the provisions of this Convention by another State Party, it may submit, through the Secretary-General of the United Nations, a Request for Clarification of that matter to that State Party. Such a request shall be accompanied by all appropriate information. Each State Party shall refrain from unfounded Requests for Clarification, care being taken to avoid abuse. A State Party that receives

a Request for Clarification shall provide, through the Secretary-General of the United Nations, within 28 days to the requesting State Party all information which would assist in clarifying this matter.

3. If the requesting State Party does not receive a response through the Secretary-General of the United Nations within that time period, or deems the response to the Request for Clarification to be unsatisfactory, it may submit the matter through the Secretary-General of the United Nations to the next Meeting of the States Parties. The Secretary-General of the United Nations shall transmit the submission, accompanied by all appropriate information pertaining to the Request for Clarification, to all States Parties. All such information shall be presented to the requested State Party which shall have the right to respond.

4. Pending the convening of any meeting of the States Parties, any of the States Parties concerned may request the Secretary-General of the United Nations to exercise his or her good offices to facilitate the clarification requested.

5. The Meeting of States Parties may consider and approve further procedures and mechanisms for determining instances of non-compliance with the provisions of this Convention and on the steps that may be taken in such instances.

Article 9—National implementation measures

Each State shall take all appropriate legal, administrative and other measures, including the imposition of penal sanctions, to prevent and suppress any activity prohibited to a State Party under this Convention undertaken by persons or on territory under its jurisdiction or control.

Article 10—Settlement of disputes

1. The States Parties shall consult and cooperate with each other to settle any dispute that may arise with regard to the application or the interpretation of this Convention. Each State Party may bring any such dispute before the Meeting of the States Parties.

2. The Meeting of the States Parties may contribute to the settlement of the dispute by whatever means it deems appropriate, including offering its good offices, calling upon the States parties to a dispute to start the settlement procedure of their choice and recommending a time-limit for any agreed procedure.

Article 11—Meetings of States Parties

1. The States Parties shall meet regularly in order to consider any matter with regard to the application or implementation of this Convention, including:

a) The operation and status of this Convention;
b) Matters arising from the reports submitted under the provisions of this Convention;
c) International cooperation and assistance in accordance with Article 5 and 6;

d) The development of technologies to clear unexploded ordnance from cluster munitions;

e) Submissions of States Parties under Article 8 and 10;

f) Decisions on submissions of States Parties as provided for in Article 3 and 4.

2. The First Meeting of the States Parties shall be convened by the Secretary-General of the United Nations within one year after the entry into force of this Convention. The subsequent meetings shall be convened by the Secretary-General of the United Nations annually until the first Review Conference.

3. States not parties to this Convention, as well as the United Nations, other relevant international organizations or institutions, regional organizations, the International Committee of the Red Cross and relevant non-governmental organizations may be invited to attend these meetings as observers in accordance with the agreed Rules of Procedure.

Article 12—Review conferences

1. A Review Conference shall be convened by the Secretary-General of the United Nations five years after the entry into force of this Convention. Further Review Conferences shall be convened by the Secretary-General of the United Nations if so requested by one or more States Parties, provided that the interval between Review Conferences shall in no case be less than five years. All States Parties to this Convention shall be invited to each Review Conference.

2. The purpose of the Review Conference shall be:

a) To review the operation and status of this Convention;

b) To consider the need for and the interval between further meetings of the States Parties referred to in paragraph 2 of Article 11;

c) To take decisions on submissions of States Parties as provided for in Article 3 and 4.

3. States not parties to this Convention, as well as the United Nations, other relevant international organizations or institutions, regional organizations, the International Committee of the Red Cross and relevant non-governmental organizations may be invited to attend each Review Conference as observers in accordance with the agreed Rules of Procedure.

Article 13—Amendments

1. At any time after the entry into force of this Convention any State Party may propose amendments to this Convention. Any proposal for an amendment shall be communicated to the Depositary, who shall circulate it to all States Parties and shall seek their views on whether an Amendment Conference should be convened to consider the proposal. If a majority of the States Parties notify the Depositary no later than 30 days after its circulation that they support further consideration of the proposal, the Depositary shall convene an Amendment Conference to which all States Parties shall be invited.

2. States not parties to this Convention, as well as the United Nations, other relevant international organizations or institutions, regional organizations, the International Committee of the Red Cross and relevant non-governmental organizations may be invited to attend each Amendment Conference as observers in accordance with the agreed Rules of Procedure.

3. The Amendment Conference shall be held immediately following a Meeting of the States Parties or a Review Conference unless a majority of the States Parties request that it be held earlier.

4. Any amendment to this Convention shall be adopted by a majority of two-thirds of the States Parties present and voting at the Amendment Conference. The Depositary shall communicate any amendment so adopted to the States Parties.

5. An amendment to this Convention shall enter into force for all States Parties to this Convention which have accepted it, upon the deposit with the Depositary of instruments of acceptance by a majority of States Parties. Thereafter it shall enter into force for any remaining State Party on the date of deposit of its instrument of acceptance.

Article 14—Costs

1. The costs of the Meetings of the States Parties, the Review Conferences and the Amendment Conferences shall be borne by the States Parties and States not parties to this Convention participating therein, in accordance with the United Nations scale of assessment adjusted appropriately.

2. The costs incurred by the Secretary-General of the United Nations under Article 7 and 8 of this Convention shall be borne by the States Parties in accordance with the United Nations scale of assessment adjusted appropriately.

Article 15—Signature

This Convention, done at (...), on (...), shall be open for signature at (...), by all States from (...) until (...), and at the United Nations Headquarters in New York from (...) until its entry into force.

Article 16—Ratification, acceptance, approval or accession

1. This Convention is subject to ratification, acceptance or approval of the Signatories.

2. It shall be open for accession by any State which has not signed the Convention.

3. The instruments of ratification, acceptance, approval or accession shall be deposited with the Depositary.

Article 17—Entry into force

1. This Convention shall enter into force on the first day of the sixth month after the month in which the 20th instrument of ratification, acceptance, approval or accession has been deposited.

2. For any State which deposits its instrument of ratification, acceptance, approval or accession after the date of the deposit of the 20th instrument of ratification, acceptance, approval or accession, this Convention shall enter into force on the first day of the sixth month after the date on which that State has deposited its instrument of ratification, acceptance, approval or accession.

Article 18—Provisional application

Any State may at the time of its ratification, acceptance, approval or accession, declare that it will apply provisionally Article 1 of this Convention pending its entry into force.

Article 19—Reservations

The Articles of this Convention shall not be subject to reservations.

Article 20—Duration and withdrawal

1. This Convention shall be of unlimited duration.

2. Each State Party shall, in exercising its national sovereignty, have the right to withdraw from this Convention. It shall give notice of such withdrawal to all other States Parties, to the Depositary and to the United Nations Security Council. Such instrument of withdrawal shall include a full explanation of the reasons motivating this withdrawal.

3. Such withdrawal shall only take effect six months after the receipt of the instrument of withdrawal by the Depositary. If, however, on the expiry of that six- month period, the withdrawing State Party is engaged in an armed conflict, the withdrawal shall not take effect before the end of the armed conflict.

4. The withdrawal of a State Party from this Convention shall not in any way affect the duty of States to continue fulfilling the obligations assumed under any relevant rules of international law.

Article 21—Depositary

The Secretary-General of the United Nations is hereby designated as the Depositary of this Convention.

Article 22—Authentic texts

The original of this Convention, of which the Arabic, Chinese, English, French, Russian and Spanish texts are equally authentic, shall be deposited with the Secretary-General of the United Nations.

ANNEX 4: VIENNA DISCUSSION TEXT

VIENNA DISCUSSION TEXT OF 14 NOVEMBER 2007

.....

Resolved to do their utmost in providing assistance for the medical care and rehabilitation, psychological support and social and economic inclusion of victims of cluster munitions, which *inter alia* include the persons directly affected, their families and communities,

Determined to ensure the full realisation of the rights of victims of cluster munitions, and recognizing their inherent dignity;

Bearing in mind the Convention on the Rights of Persons with Disabilities which, *inter alia*, requires that States Parties to this Convention undertake to ensure and promote the full realization of all human rights and fundamental freedoms of all persons with disabilities without discrimination of any kind on the basis of disability.

Mindful of the need to adequately coordinate efforts undertaken in various fora to address the rights and needs of victims of various types of weapons

......

Article 1—General obligations and scope of application

Each State Party undertakes never under any circumstances to:

a) Use cluster munitions.
b) Develop, produce, otherwise acquire, stockpile, retain or transfer to anyone, directly or indirectly, cluster munitions.
c) Assist, encourage or induce anyone to engage in any activity prohibited to a State Party under this Convention.

Article 2—Definitions

For the purposes of this Convention,

'**Cluster munition**' means a munition that is designed to disperse or release explosive sub-munitions, and includes those explosive sub-munitions. It does not mean the following:

a) ...
b) ...
c) ...

'**Explosive sub-munitions**' means munitions that in order to perform their task separate from a parent munition and are designed to function by detonating an explosive charge prior to, on or immediately after impact.

'**Unexploded cluster munitions**' means cluster munitions that have been primed, fused, armed, or otherwise prepared for use and used. They may have been fired, dropped, launched or projected, and should have exploded but failed to do so.

'**Abandoned cluster munitions**' means cluster munitions that have not been used and that have been discarded or dumped, and that are no longer under the control of the party that discarded or dumped them. Abandoned cluster munitions may or may not have been prepared for use.

'**Cluster munition remnants**' means unexploded cluster munitions and abandoned cluster munitions.

'**Transfer**' means the physical movement of cluster munitions into or from national territory or the transfer of title to or control over cluster munitions, but does not include the transfer of territory containing cluster munition remnants.

Article 3—Storage and Stockpile Destruction

1. Each State Party undertakes to separate cluster munitions from stocks for potential use and keep them in separate stockpiles for the purpose of destruction.

2. Each State Party undertakes to destroy or ensure the destruction of all cluster munitions under its jurisdiction or control, as soon as possible but not later than six years after the entry into force of this Convention for that State Party. Each State Party undertakes to ensure that destruction methods comply with applicable international standards for protecting public health and the environment.

3. If a State Party believes that it will be unable to destroy or ensure the destruction of all cluster munitions referred to in paragraph 1 within that time period it may submit a request to a Meeting of the States Parties or a Review Conference for an extension of the deadline for completing the destruction of such cluster munitions for a period of up to ten years.

4. Each request shall contain:

a) The duration of the proposed extension;

b) A detailed explanation of the reasons for the proposed extension, including the financial and technical means available to or required by the State Party for the destruction of all cluster munitions referred to in paragraph 1 of this Article;

c) A plan for how and when stockpile destruction will be completed.

5. The Meeting of the States Parties or the Review Conference shall, taking into consideration the factors contained in paragraph 4 of this Article, assess the request and decide by a majority of votes of States Parties present and voting whether to grant the request for an extension period.

6. Notwithstanding the provisions of Article 1 the transfer of cluster munitions for the purpose of destruction is permitted.

Article 4—Clearance and Destruction of Cluster Munition Remnants

1. Each State Party undertakes to clear and destroy or ensure the clearance and destruction of cluster munition remnants existing prior to entry into force of this Convention, in areas under its jurisdiction or control, as soon as possible but not later than 5 years after the entry into force of this Convention for that State Party.

2. As soon as feasible after entry into force of this Convention, each State Party that has been affected in the past or may be affected in the future by cluster munition use shall take the following measures, taking into consideration the provisions of Article 6 of this Convention regarding international cooperation and assistance.

(a) survey and assess the threat posed by cluster munition remnants;

(b) assess and prioritise needs and practicability in terms of marking, protection of civilians and clearance and destruction and take steps to mobilise resources to carry out these activities.

(c) ensure that all cluster munition remnants in such areas under its jurisdiction or control are perimeter-marked, monitored and protected by fencing or other means, to ensure the effective exclusion of civilians. The marking shall at least be to the standards set out in the Protocol on Prohibitions or Restrictions on the Use of Mines, Booby-Traps and Other Devices, as amended on 3 May 1996, annexed to the Convention on Prohibitions or Restrictions on the Use of Certain Conventional Weapons Which May Be Deemed to Be Excessively Injurious or to Have Indiscriminate Effects.

(d) clear and destroy all cluster munition remnants within its jurisdiction.

3. In conducting the above activities State Parties shall take into account international standards, including the International Mine Action Standards.

4. Where cluster munition remnants were delivered by a State Party before entry into force of this Convention to territory now under the jurisdiction or control of another State Party to this Convention, the former State Party shall provide bilaterally, *inter alia*, technical, financial, material or human resources assistance to facilitate the marking, clearance and destruction of such cluster munition remnants.

5. If a State Party believes that it will be unable to clear and destroy or ensure the clearance and destruction of all cluster munition remnants, referred to in paragraph 1 of this Article, within that time period, it may submit a request to a Meeting of the States Parties, or a Review Conference, for an extension of the deadline for completing the clearance and destruction of such cluster munition remnants, for a period of up to 5 years.

6. Each request shall contain:

a) The duration of the proposed extension;

b) A detailed explanation of the reasons for the proposed extension, including:

    i) The preparation and status of work conducted under national clearance and demining programmes;

    ii) The financial and technical means available to, and required by, the State Party for the clearance and destruction of all cluster munition remnants; and

    iii) Circumstances which impede the ability of the State Party to destroy all the cluster munition remnants in contaminated areas;

c) The humanitarian, social, economic, and environmental implications of the extension; and

d) Any other information relevant to the request for the proposed extension.

7. The Meeting of the States Parties or the Review Conference shall, taking into consideration the factors contained in paragraph 6 of this Article, assess the request and decide by a majority of votes of States Parties present and voting whether to grant the request for an extension period.

8. Such an extension may be renewed upon the submission of a new request in accordance with paragraphs 5, 6 and 7 of this Article. In requesting a further extension period a State Party shall submit relevant additional information on what has been undertaken in the previous extension period pursuant to this Article.

Article 5—Victim Assistance

(1) Each State Party with respect to victims of cluster munitions in areas under its jurisdiction or control shall, in accordance with applicable international human rights standards, adequately provide for their medical care and rehabilitation, psychological support and social and economic inclusion. Each State Party should make every effort to collect reliable relevant data with respect to victims of cluster munitions.

(2) In fulfilling its obligation under paragraph 1 of this Article each State Party shall take into consideration relevant guidelines and good practices in the areas of medical care and rehabilitation, psychological support as well as social and economic inclusion.

Article 6—International Cooperation and Assistance

1. In fulfilling its obligations under this Convention each State Party has the right to seek and receive assistance.

2. All States Parties in a position to do so shall provide technical, material and financial assistance to States Parties affected by cluster munitions, aimed at the implementation of the obligations of this Convention. Such assistance may be provided, *inter alia*, through the United Nations system; international, regional or national organizations or institutions, non-governmental organizations or institutions, or on a bilateral basis.

3. Each State Party undertakes to facilitate and shall have the right to participate in the fullest possible exchange of equipment, and scientific and technological

information concerning the implementation of this Convention. The States Parties shall not impose undue restrictions on the provision of clearance equipment and related technological information for humanitarian purposes.

4. Each State Party in a position to do so and in particular a State Party that has used cluster munitions on the territory of another State Party, shall provide assistance for clearance of cluster munition remnants and information concerning various means and technologies related to clearance of cluster munitions, as well as lists of experts, expert agencies or national points of contact of clearance of cluster munition remnants and related activities.

5. Each State Party in a position to do so shall provide assistance for the clearance and destruction of stockpiled cluster munitions.

6. Each State Party in a position to do so shall provide assistance to State Parties affected by the use of cluster munitions to identify, assess and prioritize needs and practical measures in terms of marking, protection of civilians and clearance and destruction as provided in Article 4.

7. States Parties may, with the purpose of developing a national action programme, request the United Nations, regional organizations, other States Parties or other competent intergovernmental or non-governmental institutions to assist its authorities to determine, *inter alia*:

a) The extent and scope of the contamination of cluster munition remnants;
b) The financial, technological and human resources required for the implementation of the program;
c) The estimated number of years necessary to clear all cluster munitions remnants in contaminated areas under the jurisdiction or control of the concerned State Party;
d) Awareness activities to reduce the incidence of injuries or deaths caused by cluster munition remnants;
e) Assistance to victims from cluster munitions;
f) The coordination relationship between the Government of the concerned State Party and the relevant governmental, inter-governmental or non-governmental entities that will work in the implementation of the program.

8. Each State Party in a position to do so shall provide assistance for medical care, rehabilitation and psychological support, social and economic reintegration of victims of cluster munitions and for risk education and cluster munitions awareness activities. Such assistance may be provided, *inter alia*, through the United Nations System, international, regional or national organizations or institutions, the International Committee of the Red Cross, national Red Cross and Red Crescent societies and their International Federation, non-governmental organizations, or on a bilateral basis.

9. Each State Party in a position to do so may contribute to relevant trust funds, in order to facilitate the provision of assistance under this Article.

10. Each State Party giving and receiving assistance under the provisions of this Article shall cooperate with a view to ensuring the full and prompt implementation of agreed assistance programs.

Article 7—Transparency Measures

1. Each State Party shall report to the Secretary-General of the United Nations as soon as practicable, and in any event not later than 180 days after the entry into force of this Convention for that State Party on:

a) The national implementation measures referred to in Article 9;

b) The total of all stockpiled cluster munitions owned or possessed by it, or under its jurisdiction or control, to include a breakdown of their type, quantity and, if possible, lot numbers of each type;

c) To the extent possible, all other cluster munitions that are stockpiled on its territory;

d) The technical characteristics of each type of cluster munitions produced, to the extent known, and those currently owned or possessed by a State Party, giving, where reasonably possible, such categories of information as may facilitate identification and clearance of cluster munitions; at a minimum, this information shall include the dimensions, fusing, explosive content, metallic content, colour photographs and other information which may facilitate the clearance of cluster munition remnants;

e) To the extent possible, the location of all areas that contain, or are suspected to contain, cluster munition remnants, under its jurisdiction or control, to include as much detail as possible regarding the type and quantity of each type of cluster munitions in each affected area and when they were used;

f) The status of programs for the conversion or de-commissioning of production facilities for cluster munitions;

g) The status of programs for the destruction, in accordance with Article 3, of cluster munitions, including details of the methods which will be used in destruction, the location of all destruction sites and the applicable safety and environmental standards to be observed;

h) The types and quantities of all cluster munitions cleared and destroyed in accordance with Article 4, after the entry into force of this Convention for that State Party, to include a breakdown of the quantity of each type of cluster munitions cleared and destroyed; and

i) The measures taken to provide an immediate and effective warning to the population in relation to all areas identified to be contaminated by cluster munition remnants.

j) The measures taken in accordance with the provisions of Article 5 to adequately provide for the medical care and rehabilitation, psychological support and social and economic inclusion of victims of cluster munitions as well as to collect reliable relevant data.

k) In addition, each State Party shall provide the name and contact details of the institutions mandated to provide information as described in this Article and of the institutions mandated to carry out the measures described in this Article.

2. The information provided in accordance with this Article shall be updated by the States Parties annually, covering the previous calendar year, and reported to the Secretary-General of the United Nations not later than 30 April of each year.

3. The Secretary-General of the United Nations shall transmit all such reports received to the States Parties.

Article 8—Facilitation and Clarification of Compliance

1. The States Parties agree to consult and cooperate with each other regarding the implementation of the provisions of this Convention, and to work together in a spirit of cooperation to facilitate compliance by States Parties with their obligations under this Convention.

2. If one or more States Parties wish to clarify and seek to resolve questions relating to a matter of compliance with the provisions of this Convention by another State Party, it may submit, through the Secretary-General of the United Nations, a Request for Clarification of that matter to that State Party. Such a request shall be accompanied by all appropriate information. Each State Party shall refrain from unfounded Requests for Clarification, care being taken to avoid abuse. A State Party that receives a Request for Clarification shall provide, through the Secretary-General of the United Nations, within 28 days to the requesting State Party all information that would assist in clarifying the matter.

3. If the requesting State Party does not receive a response through the Secretary-General of the United Nations within that time period, or deems the response to the Request for Clarification to be unsatisfactory, it may submit the matter through the Secretary-General of the United Nations to the next Meeting of the States Parties. The Secretary-General of the United Nations shall transmit the submission, accompanied by all appropriate information pertaining to the Request for Clarification, to all States Parties. All such information shall be presented to the requested State Party which shall have the right to respond.

4. Pending the convening of any Meeting of the States Parties, any of the States Parties concerned may request the Secretary-General of the United Nations to exercise his or her good offices to facilitate the clarification requested.

5. Where a matter has been submitted to it pursuant to paragraph 3 the Meeting of the States Parties shall first determine whether to consider that matter further, taking into account all information submitted by the States Parties concerned. If it does so determine the Meeting of the States Parties may suggest to the States Parties

concerned ways and means further to clarify or resolve the matter under consideration, including the initiation of appropriate procedures in conformity with international law. In circumstances where the issue at hand is determined to be due to circumstances beyond the control of the requested State Party, the Meeting of the States Parties may recommend appropriate measures, including the use of cooperative measures referred to in Article 5.

6. In addition to the procedures provided for in paragraphs 2 to 5 of this Article the Meeting of States Parties may decide to adopt such other general procedures for clarification and resolution of instances of non-compliance with the provisions of this Convention as it deems appropriate.

Article 9—National Implementation Measures

Each State Party shall take all appropriate legal, administrative and other measures, including the imposition of penal sanctions, to prevent and suppress any activity prohibited to a State Party under this Convention undertaken anywhere by natural persons possessing its nationality, or by any natural or legal person anywhere on its territory or in any other place under its jurisdiction or control.

Article 10—Settlement of Disputes

1. When a dispute arises between two or more States Parties relating to the interpretation or application of this Convention, the States Parties concerned shall consult together with a view to the expeditious settlement of the dispute by negotiation or by other peaceful means of their choice, including recourse to the Meeting of the States Parties and referral to the International Court of Justice in conformity with the Statute of the Court.

2. The Meeting of the States Parties may contribute to the settlement of the dispute by whatever means it deems appropriate, including offering its good offices, calling upon the States Parties concerned to start the settlement procedure of their choice and recommending a time-limit for any agreed procedure.

Article 11—Meetings of States Parties

1. The States Parties shall meet regularly in order to consider and, where necessary, take decisions in respect of any matter with regard to the interpretation, application or implementation of this Convention, including:

a) The operation and status of this Convention;
b) Matters arising from the reports submitted under the provisions of this Convention;
c) International cooperation and assistance in accordance with Article 6;
d) The development of technologies to clear cluster munition remnants;
e) Submissions of States Parties under Articles 8 and 10;
f) Submissions of States Parties as provided for in Articles 3 and 4.

2. The First Meeting of the States Parties shall be convened by the Secretary-General of the United Nations within one year of entry into force of this Convention. The subsequent Meetings shall be convened by the Secretary-General of the United Nations annually until the first Review Conference.

3. States not parties to this Convention, as well as the United Nations, other relevant international organizations or institutions, regional organizations, the International Committee of the Red Cross and relevant non-governmental organizations may be invited to attend these Meetings as observers in accordance with the agreed Rules of Procedure.

Article 12—Review Conferences

1. A Review Conference shall be convened by the Secretary-General of the United Nations five years after the entry into force of this Convention. Further Review Conferences shall be convened by the Secretary-General of the United Nations if so requested by one or more States Parties, provided that the interval between Review Conferences shall in no case be less than five years. All States Parties to this Convention shall be invited to each Review Conference.

2. The purpose of the Review Conference shall be:

a) To review the operation and status of this Convention;
b) To consider the need for and the interval between further Meetings of the States Parties referred to in paragraph 2 of Article 11;
c) To take decisions on submissions of States Parties as provided for in Articles 3 and 4.

3. States not parties to this Convention, as well as the United Nations, other relevant international organizations or institutions, regional organizations, the International Committee of the Red Cross and relevant non-governmental organizations may be invited to attend each Review Conference as observers in accordance with the agreed Rules of Procedure.

Article 13—Amendments

1. At any time after its entry into force any State Party may propose amendments to this Convention. Any proposal for an amendment shall be communicated to the Depositary, who shall circulate it to all States Parties and shall seek their views on whether an Amendment Conference should be convened to consider the proposal. If a majority of the States Parties notifies the Depositary no later than 30 days after its circulation that they support further consideration of the proposal, the Depositary shall convene an Amendment Conference to which all States Parties shall be invited.

2. States not parties to this Convention, as well as the United Nations, other relevant international organizations or institutions, regional organizations, the International Committee of the Red Cross and relevant non-governmental organizations may be invited to attend each Amendment Conference as observers in accordance with the agreed Rules of Procedure.

3. The Amendment Conference shall be held immediately following a Meeting of the States Parties or a Review Conference unless a majority of the States Parties requests that it be held earlier.

4. Any amendment to this Convention shall be adopted by a majority of two-thirds of the States Parties present and voting at the Amendment Conference. The Depositary shall communicate any amendment so adopted to the States Parties.

5. An amendment to this Convention shall enter into force for all States Parties to this Convention that have accepted it upon deposit with the Depositary of instruments of acceptance by a majority of States Parties. Thereafter it shall enter into force for any remaining State Party on the date of deposit of its instrument of acceptance.

Article 14—Costs

1. The costs of the Meetings of the States Parties, the Review Conferences and the Amendment Conferences shall be borne by the States Parties and States not parties to this Convention participating therein, in accordance with the United Nations scale of assessment adjusted appropriately.

2. The costs incurred by the Secretary-General of the United Nations under Articles 7 and 8 of this Convention shall be borne by the States Parties in accordance with the United Nations scale of assessment adjusted appropriately.

Article 15—Signature

This Convention, done at (…), on (…), shall be open for signature at (…), by all States from (…) until (…), and at the United Nations Headquarters in New York from (…) until its entry into force.

Article 16—Ratification, Acceptance, Approval or Accession

1. This Convention is subject to ratification, acceptance or approval of the Signatories.

2. It shall be open for accession by any State that has not signed the Convention.

3. The instruments of ratification, acceptance, approval or accession shall be deposited with the Depositary.

Article 17—Entry into force

1. This Convention shall enter into force on the first day of the sixth month after the month in which the 20th instrument of ratification, acceptance, approval or accession has been deposited.

2. For any State that deposits its instrument of ratification, acceptance, approval or accession after the date of the deposit of the 20th instrument of ratification, acceptance, approval or accession, this Convention shall enter into force on the first day of the sixth month after the date on which that State has deposited its instrument of ratification, acceptance, approval or accession.

Article 18—Provisional Application

Any State may at the time of its ratification, acceptance, approval or accession, declare that it will apply provisionally Article 1 of this Convention pending its entry into force.

Article 19—Reservations

The Articles of this Convention shall not be subject to reservations.

Article 20—Duration and Withdrawal

1. This Convention shall be of unlimited duration.

2. Each State Party shall, in exercising its national sovereignty, have the right to withdraw from this Convention. It shall give notice of such withdrawal to all other States Parties, to the Depositary and to the United Nations Security Council. Such instrument of withdrawal shall include a full explanation of the reasons motivating withdrawal.

3. Such withdrawal shall only take effect six months after the receipt of the instrument of withdrawal by the Depositary. If, however, on the expiry of that six-month period, the withdrawing State Party is engaged in an armed conflict, the withdrawal shall not take effect before the end of the armed conflict.

4. The withdrawal of a State Party from this Convention shall not in any way affect the duty of States to continue fulfilling the obligations assumed under any relevant rules of international law.

Article 21—Depositary

The Secretary-General of the United Nations is hereby designated as the Depositary of this Convention.

Article 22—Authentic Texts

The original of this Convention, of which the Arabic, Chinese, English, French, Russian and Spanish texts are equally authentic, shall be deposited with the Secretary-General of the United Nations.

EXPLANATORY ANNEX

Article 1: General obligations and scope of application

Within the framework of the current phrasing on general obligations and scope, it should be noted that at the Lima meeting, some States proposed that specific provision needed to be made for military interoperability with non States Party.

Article 2: Definitions

At the Lima Meeting there appeared to be broad agreement that landmines would be excluded from the definition of 'cluster munition' since they are already covered by other treaties. Some States also proposed that one or more of the following should be excluded: flare, smoke and chaff munitions and sub-munitions that are inert post impact. There were other proposals to exclude sub-munitions that aim, detect and engage point targets, and some States proposed to exclude cluster munitions which contain fewer than a specified number of explosive sub-munitions, sub-munitions with self destruct or self deactivation or other failsafe mechanisms, explosive sub-munitions with a tested failure rate of less than a specified percentage, and that the age of the sub-munition should be relevant. Some other States opposed some or all of these elements, with some proposing a comprehensive prohibition on all cluster munitions.

Article 3: Stockpile Destruction

At the Lima Meeting some delegations raised the possibility of permitting the retention of cluster munitions (or sub-munitions) to facilitate the development of clearance and disposal capabilities. Other delegations expressed the view that such retention was neither necessary nor justified.

A range of views was expressed as to the time-frame that should be permitted for stockpile destruction.

ANNEX 5: DRAFT CLUSTER MUNITIONS CONVENTION AND EXPLANATORY NOTE

Draft Cluster Munitions Convention

21 January 2008

The States Parties to this Convention,

Deeply concerned that civilian populations and individual civilians continue to suffer most from armed conflict,

Determined to put an end for all time to the suffering and casualties caused by the use of cluster munitions that kill or maim innocent and defenceless civilians and especially children, obstruct economic development and reconstruction, delay or prevent the return of refugees and internally displaced persons, and have other severe humanitarian consequences that can persist for many years after use,

Concerned that cluster munition remnants can undermine international efforts to build peace and security, as well as implementation of human rights and fundamental freedoms,

Believing it necessary to do their utmost to contribute in an efficient and coordinated manner to resolving the challenge of removing cluster munition remnants located throughout the world, and to assure their destruction,

Deeply concerned also at the dangers presented by the large stockpiles of cluster munitions retained for operational use in national inventories, and determined to ensure the speedy destruction of these stockpiles,

Determined to ensure the full realisation of the rights of victims of cluster munitions, and recognizing their inherent dignity,

Resolved to do their utmost in providing assistance for the medical care and rehabilitation, psychological support and social and economic inclusion of victims of cluster munitions,

Bearing in mind the Convention on the Rights of Persons with Disabilities which, *inter alia*, requires that States Parties to that Convention undertake to ensure and promote the full realisation of all human rights and fundamental freedoms of all persons with disabilities without discrimination of any kind on the basis of disability,

Mindful of the need adequately to coordinate efforts undertaken in various fora to address the rights and needs of victims of various types of weapons, and resolved to avoid discrimination among victims of various types of weapons,

Welcoming the global support for the international norm prohibiting the use of anti-personnel mines, enshrined in the 1997 Convention on the Prohibition of the Use, Stockpiling, Production and Transfer of Anti-Personnel Mines and on Their Destruction,

Welcoming also the entry into force on 12 November 2006 of the Protocol on Explosive Remnants of War, annexed to the Convention on Prohibitions or Restrictions on the Use of Certain Conventional Weapons which may be Deemed to be Excessively Injurious or to have Indiscriminate Effects, and wishing to enhance the protection of civilians from the effects of cluster munition remnants in post-conflict environments,

Welcoming furthermore the steps taken in recent years, both unilaterally and multilaterally, aimed at prohibiting, restricting or suspending the use, stockpiling, production and transfer of cluster munitions,

Stressing the role of public conscience in furthering the principles of humanity as evidenced by the global call for an end to civilian suffering caused by cluster munitions and recognizing the efforts to that end undertaken by the United Nations, the International Committee of the Red Cross, the Cluster Munition Coalition and numerous other non-governmental organisations around the world,

Reaffirming the Declaration of the Oslo Conference on Cluster Munitions, by which States *inter alia* committed themselves to conclude by 2008 a legally binding instrument that would prohibit the use, production, transfer and stockpiling of cluster munitions that cause unacceptable harm to civilians, and to establish a framework for cooperation and assistance that ensures adequate provision of care and rehabilitation to survivors and their communities, clearance of contaminated areas, risk education and destruction of stockpiles,

Guided by the principle of international humanitarian law that the right of parties to an armed conflict to choose methods or means of warfare is not unlimited, and in particular on the general rule that parties to a conflict must at all times distinguish between the civilian population and combatants and between civilian objects and military objectives and accordingly direct their operations against military objectives only,

HAVE AGREED as follows:

Article 1—General obligations and scope of application

1. Each State Party undertakes never under any circumstances to:

(a) Use cluster munitions;

(b) Develop, produce, otherwise acquire, stockpile, retain or transfer to anyone, directly or indirectly, cluster munitions;

(c) Assist, encourage or induce anyone to engage in any activity prohibited to a State Party under this Convention.

2. This Convention does not apply to 'mines' as defined by the Protocol on Prohibitions or Restrictions on the Use of Mines, Booby-Traps and Other Devices, as amended on 3 May 1996, annexed to the Convention on Prohibitions or Restrictions on the Use of Certain Conventional Weapons which may be Deemed to be Excessively Injurious or to have Indiscriminate Effects.

Article 2—Definitions

For the purposes of this Convention:

'**Cluster munition victims**' means persons who have suffered physical or psychological injury, economic loss, social marginalisation or substantial impairment of the realisation of their rights caused by the use of cluster munitions. They include those persons directly impacted by cluster munitions as well as their families and communities;

'**Cluster munition**' means a munition that is designed to disperse or release explosive sub-munitions, and includes those explosive sub-munitions. It does not mean the following:

(a) a munition or sub-munition designed to dispense flares, smoke, pyrotechnics or chaff;

(b) a munition or sub-munition designed to produce electrical or electronic effects;

(c) ...

'**Explosive sub-munitions**' means munitions that in order to perform their task separate from a parent munition and are designed to function by detonating an explosive charge prior to, on or after impact;

'**Unexploded cluster munitions**' means cluster munitions that have been primed, fused, armed, or otherwise prepared for use and which have been used. They may have been fired, dropped, launched or projected, and should have exploded but failed to do so. 'Unexploded cluster munitions' includes both unexploded parent munitions and unexploded explosive sub-munitions;

'**Abandoned cluster munitions**' means cluster munitions that have not been used and that have been discarded or dumped, and that are no longer under the control of the party that discarded or dumped them. They may or may not have been prepared for use;

'**Cluster munition remnants**' means unexploded cluster munitions and abandoned cluster munitions;

'**Transfer**' means the physical movement of cluster munitions into or from national territory or the transfer of title to or control over cluster munitions, but does not include the transfer of territory containing cluster munition remnants.

Article 3—Storage and stockpile destruction

1. Each State Party undertakes to remove all cluster munitions from stockpiles of munitions retained for operational use and keep them in separate stockpiles for the purpose of destruction.

2. Each State Party undertakes to destroy or ensure the destruction of all cluster munitions under its jurisdiction or control as soon as possible but not later than six years after the entry into force of this Convention for that State Party. Each State Party undertakes to ensure that destruction methods comply with applicable international standards for protecting public health and the environment.

3. If a State Party believes that it will be unable to destroy or ensure the destruction of all cluster munitions referred to in paragraph 1 of this Article within that time period it may submit a request to a Meeting of the States Parties or a Review Conference for an extension of the deadline for completing the destruction of such cluster munitions for a period of up to ten years.

4. Each request shall contain:

(a) The duration of the proposed extension;

(b) A detailed explanation of the reasons for the proposed extension, including the financial and technical means available to or required by the State Party for the destruction of all cluster munitions referred to in paragraph 1 of this Article; and

(c) A plan for how and when stockpile destruction will be completed.

5. The meeting of the States Parties or the Review Conference shall, taking into consideration the factors contained in paragraph 4 of this Article, assess the request and decide by a majority of votes of States Parties present and voting whether to grant the request for an extension period.

6. Notwithstanding the provisions of Article 1 of this Convention the transfer of cluster munitions for the purpose of destruction is permitted.

Article 4—Clearance and destruction of cluster munition remnants

1. Each State Party undertakes to clear and destroy, or ensure the clearance and destruction, of cluster munition remnants located in areas under its jurisdiction or control, as follows:

(a) Where cluster munition remnants are located in areas under its jurisdiction or control at the date of entry into force of this Convention for that State Party, such clearance and destruction shall be completed as soon as possible but no later than 5 years from that date;

(b) Where, after entry into force of this Convention for that State Party, cluster munitions have become cluster munition remnants located in areas under its jurisdiction or control, such clearance and destruction must be completed as soon as possible but no later than 5 years after such cluster munitions became cluster munition remnants.

2. In fulfilling the obligations set out in paragraph 1 of this Article, each State Party shall as soon as possible take the following measures, taking into consideration the

provisions of Article 6 of this Convention regarding international cooperation and assistance:

(a) Survey and assess the threat posed by cluster munition remnants;

(b) Assess and prioritise needs and practicability in terms of marking, protection of civilians and clearance and destruction, take steps to mobilise resources and develop a national plan to carry out these activities;

(c) Ensure that all cluster munition remnants located in areas under its jurisdiction or control are perimeter-marked, monitored and protected by fencing or other means to ensure the effective exclusion of civilians. The marking shall at least be to the standards set out in the Protocol on Prohibitions or Restrictions on the Use of Mines, Booby-Traps and Other Devices, as amended on 3 May 1996, annexed to the Convention on Prohibitions or Restrictions on the Use of Certain Conventional Weapons which may be Deemed to be Excessively Injurious or to have Indiscriminate Effects;

(d) Clear and destroy all cluster munition remnants located in areas under its jurisdiction or control; and

(e) Conduct risk education to ensure awareness among civilians living in or around areas in which cluster munition remnants are located of the risks posed by such remnants.

3. In conducting the above activities each State Party shall take into account international standards, including the International Mine Action Standards.

4. This paragraph shall apply in cases in which cluster munitions have been used or abandoned by one State Party prior to entry into force of this Convention for it and have become cluster munition remnants located in areas under the jurisdiction or control of another State Party at the time of entry into force of this Convention for the latter. In such cases, upon entry into force of this Convention for both States Parties, the former State Party shall provide, *inter alia*, technical, financial, material or human resources assistance to the latter State Party, either bilaterally or through a mutually agreed third party, including through the UN system or other relevant organisations, to facilitate the marking, clearance and destruction of such cluster munition remnants. Such assistance shall include information on types and quantities of the cluster munitions used, precise locations of cluster munition strikes and areas in which cluster munition remnants are known to be located.

5. If a State Party believes that it will be unable to clear and destroy or ensure the clearance and destruction of all cluster munition remnants referred to in paragraph 1 of this Article within that time period it may submit a request to a Meeting of States Parties or a Review Conference for an extension of the deadline for completing the clearance and destruction of such cluster munition remnants for a period of up to 5 years.

6. A request for an extension shall be submitted to a Meeting of States Parties or a Review Conference prior to the expiry of the time period referred to in paragraph 1 of this Article for that State Party. Each request shall contain:

(a) The duration of the proposed extension;

(b) A detailed explanation of the reasons for the proposed extension, including:

 (i) The preparation and status of work conducted under national clearance and demining programmes;

 (ii) The financial and technical means available to, and required by, the State Party for the clearance and destruction of all cluster munition remnants; and

 (iii) Circumstances that impede the ability of the State Party to destroy all cluster munition remnants located in areas under its jurisdiction or control;

(c) The humanitarian, social, economic, and environmental implications of the extension; and

(d) Any other information relevant to the request for the proposed extension.

7. The Meeting of States Parties or the Review Conference shall, taking into consideration the factors contained in paragraph 6 of this Article, assess the request and decide by a majority of votes of States Parties present and voting whether to grant the request for an extension period.

8. Such an extension may be renewed upon the submission of a new request in accordance with paragraphs 5, 6 and 7 of this Article. In requesting a further extension period a State Party shall submit relevant additional information on what has been undertaken in the previous extension period pursuant to this Article.

Article 5—Victim assistance

1. Each State Party with respect to cluster munition victims in areas under its jurisdiction or control shall, in accordance with international human rights law, adequately provide for their medical care and rehabilitation, psychological support and social and economic inclusion. Each State Party shall make every effort to collect reliable relevant data with respect to cluster munition victims.

2. In fulfilling its obligation under paragraph 1 of this Article each State Party shall take into consideration relevant guidelines and good practices in the areas of medical care and rehabilitation, psychological support as well as social and economic inclusion.

Article 6 – International cooperation and assistance

1. In fulfilling its obligations under this Convention each State Party has the right to seek and receive assistance.

2. Each State Party in a position to do so shall provide technical, material and financial assistance to States Parties affected by cluster munitions, aimed at the implementation of the obligations of this Convention. Such assistance may be provided, *inter alia*, through the United Nations system, international, regional or national organisations or institutions, non-governmental organisations or institutions or on a bilateral basis.

3. Each State Party undertakes to facilitate and shall have the right to participate in the fullest possible exchange of equipment and scientific and technological information concerning the implementation of this Convention. The States Parties shall not impose undue restrictions on the provision of clearance equipment and related technological information for humanitarian purposes.

4. In addition to any obligations it may have pursuant to paragraph 4 of Article 4 of this Convention, each State Party in a position to do so shall provide assistance for clearance of cluster munition remnants and information concerning various means and technologies related to clearance of cluster munitions, as well as lists of experts, expert agencies or national points of contact on clearance of cluster munition remnants and related activities.

5. Each State Party in a position to do so shall provide assistance for the destruction of stockpiled cluster munitions, and shall also provide assistance to identify, assess and prioritize needs and practical measures in terms of marking, risk education, protection of civilians and clearance and destruction as provided in Article 4.

6. Where, after entry into force of this Convention, cluster munitions have become cluster munition remnants located in areas under the jurisdiction or control of a State Party, each State Party in a position to do so shall urgently provide emergency assistance to the affected State Party.

7. Each State Party in a position to do so shall provide assistance for medical care, rehabilitation and psychological support, social and economic inclusion of all cluster munition victims. Such assistance may be provided, *inter alia*, through the United Nations System, international, regional or national organisations or institutions, the International Committee of the Red Cross, national Red Cross and Red Crescent societies and their International Federation, non-governmental organisations or on a bilateral basis.

8. Each State Party in a position to do so shall provide assistance to contribute to the economic and social recovery needed as a result of cluster munition use in affected States Parties.

9. Each State Party in a position to do so may contribute to relevant trust funds in order to facilitate the provision of assistance under this Article.

10. Each State Party may, with the purpose of developing a national action plan, request the United Nations, regional organisations, other States Parties or other competent intergovernmental or non-governmental institutions to assist its authorities to determine, *inter alia*:

(a) The nature and extent of cluster munition remnants located in areas under its jurisdiction or control;

(b) The financial, technological and human resources required for the implementation of the plan;

(c) The time estimated as necessary to clear all cluster munition remnants located in areas under its jurisdiction or control;

(d) Risk education programmes and awareness activities to reduce the incidence of injuries or deaths caused by cluster munition remnants;

(e) Assistance to cluster munition victims; and

(f) The relationship between the Government of the State Party concerned and the relevant governmental, inter-governmental or non-governmental entities that will work in the implementation of the plan.

11. States Parties giving and receiving assistance under the provisions of this Article shall cooperate with a view to ensuring the full and prompt implementation of agreed assistance programmes.

Article 7—Transparency measures

1. Each State Party shall report to the Secretary-General of the United Nations as soon as practicable, and in any event not later than 180 days after the entry into force of this Convention for that State Party, on:

(a) The national implementation measures referred to in Article 9 of this Convention;

(b) The total of all stockpiled cluster munitions owned or possessed by it, or under its jurisdiction or control, to include a breakdown of their type, quantity and, if possible, lot numbers of each type;

(c) To the extent possible, all other cluster munitions that are stockpiled on its territory;

(d) The technical characteristics of each type of cluster munitions produced, to the extent known, and those currently owned or possessed by a State Party, giving, where reasonably possible, such categories of information as may facilitate identification and clearance of cluster munitions; at a minimum, this information shall include the dimensions, fusing, explosive content, metallic content, colour photographs and other information that may facilitate the clearance of cluster munition remnants;

(e) To the extent possible, the location of all areas that contain, or are suspected to contain, cluster munition remnants, under its jurisdiction or control, to include as much detail as possible regarding the type and quantity of each type of cluster munitions in each affected area and when they were used;

(f) The status of programmes for the conversion or de-commissioning of production facilities for cluster munitions;

(g) The status of programmes for the destruction, in accordance with Article 3 of this Convention, of cluster munitions, including details of the methods that will be used in destruction, the location of all destruction sites and the applicable safety and environmental standards to be observed;

(h) The types and quantities of cluster munitions destroyed in accordance with Article 3 of this Convention, including details of the methods of destruction used, the location of the destruction sites and the applicable safety and environmental standards observed;

(i) Stockpiles discovered after reported completion of the programme referred to in paragraph 7(h) of this Article;

(j) The types and quantities of all cluster munitions remnants cleared and destroyed in accordance with Article 4 of this Convention, to include a breakdown of the quantity of each type of cluster munitions remnants cleared and destroyed;

(k) The measures taken to provide risk education and, in particular, an immediate and effective warning to civilians living in areas under its jurisdiction or control in which cluster munition remnants are located;

(l) The measures taken in accordance with the provisions of Article 5 of this Convention adequately to provide for the medical care and rehabilitation, psychological support and social and economic inclusion of victims of cluster munitions as well as to collect reliable relevant data; and

(m) The name and contact details of the institutions mandated to provide information and to carry out the measures described in this paragraph.

2. The information provided in accordance with paragraph 1 of this Article shall be updated by the States Parties annually, covering the previous calendar year, and reported to the Secretary-General of the United Nations not later than 30 April of each year.

3. The Secretary-General of the United Nations shall transmit all such reports received to the States Parties.

Article 8—Facilitation and clarification of compliance

1. The States Parties agree to consult and cooperate with each other regarding the implementation of the provisions of this Convention, and to work together in a spirit of cooperation to facilitate compliance by States Parties with their obligations under this Convention.

2. If one or more States Parties wish to clarify and seek to resolve questions relating to a matter of compliance with the provisions of this Convention by another State Party, it may submit, through the Secretary-General of the United Nations, a Request for Clarification of that matter to that State Party. Such a request shall be accompanied by all appropriate information. Each State Party shall refrain from unfounded Requests for Clarification, care being taken to avoid abuse. A State Party that receives a Request for Clarification shall provide, through the Secretary-General of the United Nations, within 28 days to the requesting State Party all information that would assist in clarifying the matter.

3. If the requesting State Party does not receive a response through the Secretary-General of the United Nations within that time period, or deems the response to the

Request for Clarification to be unsatisfactory, it may submit the matter through the Secretary-General of the United Nations to the next Meeting of the States Parties. The Secretary-General of the United Nations shall transmit the submission, accompanied by all appropriate information pertaining to the Request for Clarification, to all States Parties. All such information shall be presented to the requested State Party which shall have the right to respond.

4. Pending the convening of any meeting of the States Parties, any of the States Parties concerned may request the Secretary-General of the United Nations to exercise his or her good offices to facilitate the clarification requested.

5. Where a matter has been submitted to it pursuant to paragraph 3 of this Article the Meeting of the States Parties shall first determine whether to consider that matter further, taking into account all information submitted by the States Parties concerned. If it does so determine the Meeting of the States Parties may suggest to the States Parties concerned ways and means further to clarify or resolve the matter under consideration, including the initiation of appropriate procedures in conformity with international law. In circumstances where the issue at hand is determined to be due to circumstances beyond the control of the requested State Party, the Meeting of the States Parties may recommend appropriate measures, including the use of cooperative measures referred to in Article 5 of this Convention.

6. In addition to the procedures provided for in paragraphs 2 to 5 of this Article the Meeting of States Parties may decide to adopt such other general procedures for clarification and resolution of instances of non-compliance with the provisions of this Convention as it deems appropriate.

Article 9—National implementation measures

Each State Party shall take all appropriate legal, administrative and other measures, including the imposition of penal sanctions, to prevent and suppress any activity prohibited to a State Party under this Convention undertaken by persons or on territory under its jurisdiction or control.

Article 10—Settlement of disputes

1. When a dispute arises between two or more States Parties relating to the interpretation or application of this Convention, the States Parties concerned shall consult together with a view to the expeditious settlement of the dispute by negotiation or by other peaceful means of their choice, including recourse to the Meeting of the States Parties and referral to the International Court of Justice in conformity with the Statute of the Court.

2. The Meeting of the States Parties may contribute to the settlement of the dispute by whatever means it deems appropriate, including offering its good offices, calling upon the States Parties concerned to start the settlement procedure of their choice and recommending a time-limit for any agreed procedure.

Article 11—Meetings of States Parties

1. The States Parties shall meet regularly in order to consider and, where necessary, take decisions in respect of any matter with regard to the interpretation, application or implementation of this Convention, including:

a) The operation and status of this Convention;

b) Matters arising from the reports submitted under the provisions of this Convention;

c) International cooperation and assistance in accordance with Article 6 of this Convention;

d) The development of technologies to clear cluster munition remnants;

e) Submissions of States Parties under Articles 8 and 10 of this Convention; and

f) Submissions of States Parties as provided for in Articles 3 and 4 of this Convention.

2. The First Meeting of the States Parties shall be convened by the Secretary-General of the United Nations within one year of entry into force of this Convention. The subsequent meetings shall be convened by the Secretary-General of the United Nations annually until the first Review Conference.

3. States not parties to this Convention, as well as the United Nations, other relevant international organisations or institutions, regional organisations, the International Committee of the Red Cross and relevant non-governmental organisations may be invited to attend these meetings as observers in accordance with the agreed Rules of Procedure.

Article 12—Review conferences

1. A Review Conference shall be convened by the Secretary-General of the United Nations five years after the entry into force of this Convention. Further Review Conferences shall be convened by the Secretary-General of the United Nations if so requested by one or more States Parties, provided that the interval between Review Conferences shall in no case be less than five years. All States Parties to this Convention shall be invited to each Review Conference.

2. The purpose of the Review Conference shall be:

a) To review the operation and status of this Convention;

b) To consider the need for and the interval between further Meetings of the States Parties referred to in paragraph 2 of Article 11 of this Convention; and

c) To take decisions on submissions of States Parties as provided for in Articles 3 and 4 of this Convention.

3. States not parties to this Convention, as well as the United Nations, other relevant international organisations or institutions, regional organisations, the International Committee of the Red Cross and relevant non-governmental

organisations may be invited to attend each Review Conference as observers in accordance with the agreed Rules of Procedure.

Article 13—Amendments

1. At any time after its entry into force any State Party may propose amendments to this Convention. Any proposal for an amendment shall be communicated to the Depositary, who shall circulate it to all States Parties and shall seek their views on whether an Amendment Conference should be convened to consider the proposal. If a majority of the States Parties notifies the Depositary no later than 30 days after its circulation that they support further consideration of the proposal, the Depositary shall convene an Amendment Conference to which all States Parties shall be invited.

2. States not parties to this Convention, as well as the United Nations, other relevant international organisations or institutions, regional organisations, the International Committee of the Red Cross and relevant non-governmental organisations may be invited to attend each Amendment Conference as observers in accordance with the agreed Rules of Procedure.

3. The Amendment Conference shall be held immediately following a Meeting of the States Parties or a Review Conference unless a majority of the States Parties requests that it be held earlier.

4. Any amendment to this Convention shall be adopted by a majority of two-thirds of the States Parties present and voting at the Amendment Conference. The Depositary shall communicate any amendment so adopted to the States Parties.

5. An amendment to this Convention shall enter into force for all States Parties to this Convention that have accepted it upon deposit with the Depositary of instruments of acceptance by a majority of States Parties. Thereafter it shall enter into force for any remaining State Party on the date of deposit of its instrument of acceptance.

Article 14—Costs

1. The costs of the Meetings of the States Parties, the Review Conferences and the Amendment Conferences shall be borne by the States Parties and States not parties to this Convention participating therein, in accordance with the United Nations scale of assessment adjusted appropriately.

2. The costs incurred by the Secretary-General of the United Nations under Articles 7 and 8 of this Convention shall be borne by the States Parties in accordance with the United Nations scale of assessment adjusted appropriately.

Article 15—Signature

This Convention, done at (…), on (…), shall be open for signature at (…), by all States from (…) until (…), and at the United Nations Headquarters in New York from (…) until its entry into force.

Article 16—Ratification, acceptance, approval or accession

1. This Convention is subject to ratification, acceptance or approval of the Signatories.

2. It shall be open for accession by any State that has not signed the Convention.

3. The instruments of ratification, acceptance, approval or accession shall be deposited with the Depositary.

Article 17—Entry into force

1. This Convention shall enter into force on the first day of the sixth month after the month in which the 20th instrument of ratification, acceptance, approval or accession has been deposited.

2. For any State that deposits its instrument of ratification, acceptance, approval or accession after the date of the deposit of the 20th instrument of ratification, acceptance, approval or accession, this Convention shall enter into force on the first day of the sixth month after the date on which that State has deposited its instrument of ratification, acceptance, approval or accession.

Article 18—Provisional application

Any State may at the time of its ratification, acceptance, approval or accession, declare that it will apply provisionally Article 1 of this Convention pending its entry into force.

Article 19—Reservations

The Articles of this Convention shall not be subject to reservations.

Article 20—Duration and withdrawal

1. This Convention shall be of unlimited duration.

2. Each State Party shall, in exercising its national sovereignty, have the right to withdraw from this Convention. It shall give notice of such withdrawal to all other States Parties, to the Depositary and to the United Nations Security Council. Such instrument of withdrawal shall include a full explanation of the reasons motivating withdrawal.

3. Such withdrawal shall only take effect six months after the receipt of the instrument of withdrawal by the Depositary. If, however, on the expiry of that six-month period, the withdrawing State Party is engaged in an armed conflict, the withdrawal shall not take effect before the end of the armed conflict.

4. The withdrawal of a State Party from this Convention shall not in any way affect the duty of States to continue fulfilling the obligations assumed under any relevant rules of international law.

Article 21—Depositary

The Secretary-General of the United Nations is hereby designated as the Depositary of this Convention.

Article 22—Authentic texts

The original of this Convention, of which the Arabic, Chinese, English, French, Russian and Spanish texts are equally authentic, shall be deposited with the Secretary-General of the United Nations.

DRAFT CLUSTER MUNITIONS CONVENTION
EXPLANATORY NOTES

Preamble

The Oslo Process is premised on concern about the humanitarian impact of cluster munitions and the need to end the suffering and casualties they cause among civilians. A Preamble setting out the context and background supporting international efforts to address the humanitarian concerns posed by cluster munitions has been incorporated into the text.

Several delegations at the Vienna Conference expressed a preference for the objectives of the process, as set out in the Oslo Declaration, to be highlighted within the text. A reference reaffirming the Oslo Declaration has been incorporated into the Preamble accordingly.

Article 1: General obligations and scope of application

The first part of this Article lays down the obligations of States Parties not to use, develop, produce, acquire, stockpile, retain or transfer cluster munitions as defined in Article 2. The scope of application of the treaty is 'never under any circumstances', meaning that application of the treaty does not require qualification of the level of armed conflict. The provision thus is largely similar to corresponding provisions in the Biological Weapons Convention, the Chemical Weapons Convention and the Anti-Personnel Mine Ban Treaty.

The second part of this Article specifies that the present Convention does not regulate mines as defined in Article 2 (1) of Amended Protocol II to the CCW, reflecting the discussion at the Lima and Vienna Conferences. This means that neither anti-vehicle mines nor anti-personnel mines fall under the scope of application of this Convention.

At the Vienna Conference, a number of delegations again expressed the need for detailed work on the issue of military interoperability with States not Party to the

Convention with regard to Article 1 c) on assistance. In particular, a need for dedicated consideration of this issue at the Wellington Conference was identified.

Article 2: Definitions

This article identifies and describes key terms used in the Convention.

Cluster munition victims: The definition comprehensively details the elements necessary for defining cluster munition victims, clarifying (as was done in the preambular part of the Vienna Discussion Text) that the term encompasses the directly affected person, and also his/her family and community.

Cluster munition: The definition specifies that the term includes both the 'parent' munition and the explosive sub-munitions contained therein. Reflecting the discussion at Vienna, there is an exception from the term 'cluster munition' for some sub-munitions which may be categorised as explosive, but which are not considered to be cluster munitions for the purposes of the Convention, such as pyrotechnical or electronic units.

Explosive sub-munition: This is a part of the definition of cluster munitions. Explosive sub-munitions falling within the definition are designed to function by detonating an explosive charge. The term 'function' indicates that this definition will not cover sub-munitions that are inert, such as kinetic rods, which are not meant to function through an explosion. Explosive sub-munitions covered by the convention are designed to detonate prior to, on, or after impact. This means that the timing of the detonation does not have any bearing on whether or not an explosive sub-munition falls within the prohibition.

At the Vienna Conference, a range of views were expressed on what might constitute a cluster munition causing unacceptable harm to civilians. Some States suggested that exemptions to the definition of 'cluster munition' should be based on the concepts of reliability and accuracy, although there were no specific proposals on how such an approach could be implemented, nor on how concepts of reliability or accuracy could be objectively quantified. There were, however, a number of proposals made relating to specific exemptions in addition to those referred to above. Building on work done at the Lima Conference, the list of exemptions proposed by various delegations includes: explosive sub-munitions that aim, detect and engage point targets; cluster munitions which contain fewer than a specified number of explosive sub-munitions; explosive sub-munitions with self-destruct and self-deactivation or other failsafe mechanisms, explosive sub-munitions with a tested failure rate of less than a specified percentage, explosive sub-munitions of a non-conventional nature, explosive sub-munitions above a minimum threshold for volume and mass. Other suggestions have been that the age of the sub-munitions should be relevant, and that combinations of some proposed exclusion criteria merited further consideration. Some other states opposed any possible exemptions to the definition of 'cluster munitions', expressing support for a total prohibition on all cluster munitions. It is envisaged that there will be detailed discussion of these issues at the Wellington Conference.

Unexploded cluster munitions: This definition now specifically states that both unexploded parent munitions and unexploded explosive sub-munitions are included within its scope.

Article 3: Stockpile Destruction

This Article lays down an obligation to separate cluster munitions from ordinary stockpiles while awaiting destruction. Stockpiles shall be destroyed within six years, but there is a possibility to get an extension of that deadline. The Article contains proposed procedures for applications for extensions.

There is broad agreement that safe and secure destruction of cluster munitions is a technical and logistical challenge, and that this must be reflected in the relevant time frames. A range of views have been expressed as to what the actual deadlines for stockpile destruction should be. These views have ranged on both sides of the deadlines suggested in the discussion text.

During the consultations some delegations have raised the possibility of permitting the retention of cluster munitions and/or sub-munitions to facilitate the development of clearance and disposal capabilities. Other delegations expressed the view that such retention was neither necessary nor justified.

Article 4: Clearance and destruction of cluster munition remnants

In the light of discussions in Vienna, some revisions were made to Article 4. Paragraph 1 has been reworded to address the two different sets of circumstances in which clearance of cluster munition remnants may be required; that is clearance of cluster munitions remnants existing at entry into force of the Convention and clearance of cluster munition remnants that may be created after entry into force.

A new sub-paragraph (e) has been added to paragraph 2 to address the need for risk education. The requirement for a national plan has been included in paragraph 2(b) to reflect recent experience in clearance programmes and to be consistent with Article 6.

Paragraph 4 has been reworded in order to define more precisely the circumstances in which a State Party, whose past use of cluster munitions has created cluster munition remnants on the territory of another State Party, should provide bilateral assistance to the affected State Party. Language from CCW Protocol V has been used to describe the methodology of providing such assistance. A new sentence has been added prescribing certain elements of information that should be provided as part of such bilateral assistance.

At the beginning of paragraph 6 a new sentence has been inserted requiring that any request for an extension should be submitted to a Meeting of States Parties or a Review Conference prior to the expiry of the five year period for clearance.

There has also been some redrafting in order to ensure consistency of language throughout the Article but this has not altered the substance of the Article.

Article 5: Victim Assistance

Discussions held on assistance to cluster munitions victims throughout the consultation process in Vienna, Brussels, Belgrade, Lima and Oslo have shown unequivocal support for clear and comprehensive provisions on victim assistance to be contained in the future Convention and that a broad concept of the term victim should be employed. Provisions on victim assistance are now contained in various places throughout the text: the Preamble (paragraphs 6 to 8), Article 2, Article 5, Article 6 (paragraph 7), and Article 7 (paragraph 1, sub-paragraph l).

In response to points raised in Vienna, paragraph 9 of the Preamble now also expresses the resolve to avoid discrimination among victims of various types of weapons.

An explanation of the definition of 'cluster munition victims' is covered in the notes on Article 2 (see above).

The slightly amended version of Article 5 now clarifies that the provision of medical care, rehabilitation, psychological support, and social and economic inclusion shall be done in accordance with international human rights law. The obligation to collect data has been slightly strengthened.

Future discussions on the issue of victim assistance might also concentrate on the importance to include victims in decision making as well as on formulating in a more concrete manner a provision on how national implementation should or could be framed including through the determination of national focal points and the elaboration of national action plans.

Article 6: International cooperation and assistance

Many delegations have highlighted the central role of this Article for the implementation of the Convention and especially supported the language regarding the assistance that shall be provided by each State Party in a position to do so, as well as the State Party that has used cluster munitions on the territory of another State Party. This obligation on the latter is already explicit in Article 4, paragraph 4, and is also referred to in paragraph 4 of Article 6.

A paragraph regarding the need for provision of emergency assistance to State Parties that may be affected by cluster munitions use has been included.

In response to several interventions made in Vienna, risk education and awareness-raising activities were included as areas for which assistance should also be provided by States in a position to do so.

Another concern expressed in Vienna, addressed in paragraph 8, is the request for assistance from States Parties in a position to do so, to contribute to the economic and social recovery needed as a result of cluster munitions use in affected States Parties.

Article 7: Transparency Measures

During the discussions held in Vienna, a growing support for transparency measures was evident. Significant differences were established between the type and quantity of cluster munitions destroyed and the type and quantity of cluster munitions remnants cleared and destroyed. The reporting requirements relating to these separate categories have been clarified.

The reports should include information regarding the status of destruction programmes, the types and quantities of cluster munitions destroyed, and the discovery of any stockpiles after the reported completion of destruction programmes.

A requirement to report on measures taken to provide risk education has also been incorporated.

Article 9: National Implementation Measures

At the Vienna Conference, several delegations expressed concern regarding potential incompatibilities with existing national legal systems. This concern also related to the scope of jurisdiction based on nationality envisaged in the text. This Article has now been amended to replicate the equivalent provision in the Anti-Personnel Mine Ban Treaty, to clarify that national implementation measures shall be undertaken in accordance with a State Party's existing national legislative framework.

Article 10: Settlement of disputes

Several States noted at the Vienna Conference that reference of a dispute to the International Court of Justice would require mutual consent of the Parties. This is already reflected in paragraph 1, which refers to other peaceful means 'of their choice', and also says 'in conformity with the Statute of the Court'.

ANNEX 6: WELLINGTON COMPENDIUM

NB: Proposals by States included in the Wellington Compendium, which were subsequently introduced as formal documents at the Dublin Diplomatic Conference, are included in Annex 8 and are not repeated here.

Preamble
ICRC

[pp2] Determined to put an end for all time to the civilian suffering and casualties caused by cluster munitions at the time of their use, when they fail to function as intended or when they are abandoned,

[pp3] Concerned that cluster munition remnants kill or maim civilians, especially children, obstruct economic development and reconstruction, delay or prevent the return of refugees and internally displaced persons, can undermine international peace building and humanitarian assistance efforts and have other severe consequences that can persist for many years after use,

[pp15] Basing themselves on the rules of international humanitarian law that the right of parties to an armed conflict to choose methods or means of warfare is not unlimited, that the parties to a conflict shall at all times distinguish between the civilian population and combatants and between civilian objects and military objectives and accordingly direct their operations only against military objectives, that in the conduct of military operations constant care shall be taken to spare the civilian population, civilians and civilian objects and that the civilian population and individual civilians enjoy general protection against dangers arising from military operations,

UN MINE ACTION TEAM

pp 9 Mindful of the need adequately to coordinate efforts undertaken in various fora to address the rights and needs of victims of various types of weapons, and resolved to avoid discrimination among victims of various types of weapons **or from any source of disability,**

Article 2
ICRC

For the purposes of this Convention:

'Cluster munition' means a munition that is designed to disperse or release explosive submunitions.

It does not mean the following:

a) a munition or sub-munition designed to dispense flares, smoke, pyrotechnics or chaff;

b) a munition or sub-munition designed to produce electrical or electronic effects;

c) ...

'Explosive sub-munitions' means munitions that in order to perform their task are dispersed or released from a cluster munition and are designed to function by detonating an explosive charge prior to, on or after impact;

'Failed cluster munitions' means cluster munitions that have been fired, dropped, launched, projected or otherwise delivered and which should have dispersed or released their explosive submunitions but failed to do so;

'Unexploded explosive submunitions' means explosive submunitions which have been released dispersed or otherwise separated from a cluster munition and have failed to explode as intended;

'Cluster munition remnants' means failed cluster munitions, abandoned cluster munitions and unexploded explosive submunitions;

[The definitions of cluster munition victims, abandoned cluster munitions and transfer would remain unchanged.]

Article 4

UN MINE ACTION TEAM

Article 4 – Clearance and Destruction of Cluster Munition Remnants **and Risk Reduction Education**

Conduct risk reduction education among at-risk civilian populations living in or around areas in which cluster munition remnants are located, to prevent and reduce the number of casualties, in parallel with marking, fencing, warnings, clearance and stockpile destruction.

Article 5

ICRC

2. In fulfilling its obligations under paragraph 1 of this Article each State Party shall make no distinction with respect to other victims of armed conflict on any grounds other than medical ones or the rehabilitative, psychological or social-economic needs of the victim. States Parties shall also endeavour to implement the relevant professional guidelines and best practices in the care, treatment, support and socio-economic inclusion of victims.

Article 6

CMC

Article 6(2): Add the phrase 'and particularly user states' after 'each State Party'

UN MINE ACTION TEAM

1. Each State Party with respect to **all** victims of cluster munitions in areas under its jurisdiction or control shall, in accordance with applicable international human rights standards, adequately provide **age- and gender-appropriate** medical care and rehabilitation, psychological support, **personal mobility** and social and economic inclusion. Each State Party should make every effort to collect reliable relevant data with respect to victims of cluster munitions.

2. In fulfilling its obligation under paragraph 1 of this Article, each State Party shall endeavour to implement the relevant professional guidelines and best practices in the **provision** of **age- and gender-appropriate** medical care and rehabilitation, psychological support, **personal mobility,** as well as social and economic inclusion.

ANNEX 7: WELLINGTON DECLARATION

Declaration of the Wellington Conference on Cluster Munitions

The following States met in Wellington from February 18 to 22, 2008, to pursue an enduring solution to the grave humanitarian consequences caused by the use of cluster munitions. They are convinced that this solution must include the conclusion in 2008 of a legally binding international instrument prohibiting cluster munitions that cause unacceptable harm to civilians.

In that spirit they affirm that the essential elements of such an instrument should include:

- A prohibition on the use, stockpiling, production and transfer of cluster munitions that cause unacceptable harm to civilians,
- A framework for cooperation and assistance that ensures adequate provision of care and rehabilitation to survivors and their communities, clearance of contaminated areas, risk education, and destruction of stockpiles.

The following States:

encouraged by the work of the Wellington Conference, and previous Conferences in Vienna, Lima and Oslo;

encouraged further by numerous national and regional initiatives, including meetings in Costa Rica, Belgrade and Brussels, and measures taken to address the humanitarian impact of cluster munitions;

encouraged by the active support given to this subject by the United Nations, and in other fora;

encouraged, finally, by the active support of the International Committee of the Red Cross, the Cluster Munition Coalition and numerous other Non-Governmental Organisations;

welcome the convening of a Diplomatic Conference by the Government of Ireland in Dublin on 19 May 2008 to negotiate and adopt such an instrument;

also welcome the important work done by participants engaged in the cluster munitions process on the text of a draft Convention, dated xxx, which contains the essential elements identified above and decide to forward it as the basic proposal for consideration at the Dublin Diplomatic Conference together with other relevant proposals which may be put forward there;

affirm their objective of concluding the negotiation of such an instrument prohibiting cluster munitions that cause unacceptable harm to civilians in Dublin in May 2008;

invite all other States to join them in their efforts towards concluding such an instrument.

ANNEX 8: DOCUMENTATION FROM THE DUBLIN DIPLOMATIC CONFERENCE

DIPLOMATIC CONFERENCE FOR THE ADOPTION OF A CONVENTION ON CLUSTER MUNITIONS

DUBLIN 19–30 MAY 2008

CCM/1: DRAFT AGENDA

1. Opening of the Conference by the Secretary-General
2. Election of the President
3. Adoption of the Agenda
4. Adoption of the Rules of Procedure
5. Election of Vice-Presidents
6. Organisation of work
7. Convention on Cluster Munitions
8. Closure of Conference

CCM/2: DRAFT RULES OF PROCEDURE

21 February 2008

CHAPTER I

Participation

Rule 1

Participation

1. States that have subscribed to the Wellington Declaration of 22 February 2008, on that date or subsequently, shall be invited to participate in the Conference. Other States that have been invited by the Government of Ireland may attend the Conference as observers.

2. The Secretary-General of the United Nations, the International Committee of the Red Cross, the United Nations Development Programme and other relevant United Nations programmes and agencies, the International Federation of Red Cross and Red Crescent Societies, regional intergovernmental organisations and the Cluster Munition Coalition may attend the Conference as observers.

3. Other organisations that have been invited by the Government of Ireland may attend the Conference as observers.

CHAPTER II
Representation and credentials

Rule 2
Composition of delegations

The delegation of each State participating in the Conference shall consist of a head of delegation and such other accredited representatives, alternate representatives and advisers as may be required.

Rule 3
Alternates and advisers

The head of delegation may designate an alternate representative or an adviser to act as a representative.

Rule 4
Submission of credentials

The credentials of representatives and the names of alternate representatives and advisers shall be submitted early to the Executive Secretary of the Conference and, if possible, not later than 24 hours after the opening of the Conference. Any later change in the composition of delegations shall also be submitted to the Executive Secretary. The credentials shall be issued either by the Head of State or Government or by the Minister for Foreign Affairs. The Executive Secretary shall report to the Conference on the submission of credentials if it so requests.

Rule 5

If an objection is raised against the participation of a delegation, such objection shall be considered by the General Committee, whose report thereon shall be submitted to the Conference.

Rule 6

Pending a decision of the Conference regarding an objection against the participation of a delegation, the latter shall be entitled to participate provisionally in the Conference with the same rights as other participating delegations.

CHAPTER III
Officers

Rule 7
Elections

The Conference shall elect a President and eight Vice-Presidents. The Conference may also elect such other officers as it deems necessary for the performance of its functions.

Rule 8

General powers of the President

1. In addition to exercising the powers conferred upon him or her elsewhere by these rules, the President shall preside at the plenary meetings of the Conference, declare the opening and closing of each such meeting, direct the discussion, ensure observance of these rules, accord the right to speak, promote the achievement of general agreement, put questions to the vote and announce decisions. The President shall rule on points of order and, subject to these rules, shall have complete control of the proceedings and over the maintenance of order thereat. The President may propose to the Conference the closure of the list of speakers, a limitation on the time to be allowed to speakers and on the number of times each representative may speak on a question, the adjournment or the closure of the debate and the suspension or the adjournment of a meeting.

2. The President, in the exercise of his or her functions, remains under the authority of the Conference.

Rule 9

Acting President

1. If the President finds it necessary to be absent from a meeting or any part thereof he or she shall designate a Vice-President to take his or her place.

2. A Vice-President acting as President shall have the powers and duties of the President.

Rule 10

Replacement of the President

If the President is unable to perform his or her functions a new President shall be elected.

Rule 11

Voting rights of the President

The President, or a Vice-President acting as President, shall not vote in the Conference, but shall appoint another member of his or her delegation to vote in his or her place.

CHAPTER IV

General Committee

Rule 12

Composition

There shall be a General Committee consisting of the President and Vice-Presidents of the Conference. The President, or in his or her absence one of the Vice-Presidents designated by him or her, shall serve as Chairman of the General Committee.

Rule 13

Substitute members

If the President or a Vice-President finds it necessary to be absent during a meeting of the General Committee, he or she may designate a member of his or her delegation to sit and vote in the Committee.

Rule 14

Functions

The General Committee shall assist the President in the general conduct of the business of the Conference and, subject to the decisions of the Conference, shall ensure the coordination of its work. It shall also exercise the powers conferred upon it by rule 36.

CHAPTER V

Secretariat

Rule 15

Duties of the Secretary-General

1. The Secretary-General, designated by the Government of Ireland, shall act in that capacity in all meetings of the Conference and its subsidiary bodies.

2. The Secretary-General may designate a member of the Secretariat to act in his or her place at these meetings.

3. The Secretary-General shall appoint an Executive Secretary of the Conference and shall provide and direct the staff required by the Conference and its subsidiary bodies.

Rule 16

Duties of the secretariat

The secretariat of the Conference shall, in accordance with these rules:

(a) Interpret speeches made at meetings;
(b) Receive, translate, reproduce and distribute the documents of the Conference;
(c) Publish and circulate the official documents of the Conference;
(d) Prepare and circulate records of public meetings;
(e) Make and arrange for the keeping of sound recordings of meetings;
(f) Arrange for the custody and preservation of the documents of the Conference in the archives of the Government of Ireland; and
(g) Generally perform all other work that the Conference may require.

Rule 17

Statements by the secretariat

The Secretary-General or any other member of the staff of the secretariat who may be designated for that purpose may, at any time, make either oral or written statements concerning any question under consideration.

CHAPTER VI
Opening of the Conference

Rule 18

Temporary President

The Secretary-General shall open the first meeting of the Conference and preside until the Conference has elected its President.

Rule 19

Decisions concerning organisation

At its first meeting the Conference shall move to:

(a) Elect its President;
(b) Adopt its agenda, the draft of which shall, until such adoption, be the provisional agenda of the Conference;
(c) Adopt its rules of procedure, the draft of which shall, until such adoption, be the provisional rules of procedure of the Conference;
(d) Elect its other officers; and
(e) Decide on the organisation of its work.

CHAPTER VII
Conduct of business

Rule 20

Quorum

The presence of representatives of twenty five participating States shall be required for any decision to be taken.

Rule 21

Speeches

No one may address the Conference without having previously obtained the permission of the President. Subject to rules 22, 23 and 26 to 28, the President shall call upon speakers in the order in which they signify their desire to speak. The secretariat shall be in charge of drawing up a list of speakers. The President may call a speaker to order if his or her remarks are not relevant to the subject under discussion.

Rule 22

Precedence

The chairman or an officer of a committee or the representative of a working group may be accorded precedence for the purpose of explaining the conclusions arrived at by that committee or working group.

Rule 23

Points of order

During the discussion of any matter, a representative may at any time raise a point of order which shall be decided immediately by the President in accordance with these rules. A representative may appeal against the ruling of the President. The appeal shall be put to the vote immediately and the President's ruling shall stand unless overruled by a majority of the representatives present and voting. A representative may not, in raising a point of order, speak on the substance of the matter under discussion.

Rule 24

Closing of the list of speakers

During the course of a debate, the President may announce the list of speakers and, with the consent of the Conference, declare the list closed.

Rule 25

Right of reply

Notwithstanding rule 24, the President may accord the right of reply to any representative who requests it.

Rule 26

Adjournment of debate

A representative may at any time move the adjournment of the debate on the question under discussion. In addition to the proposer of the motion, two representatives may speak in favour of, and two against, the adjournment, after which the motion shall, subject to rule 29, be put immediately to the vote.

Rule 27

Closure of debate

A representative may at any time move the closure of the debate on the question under discussion, whether or not any other representative has signified his or her wish to speak. Permission to speak on the motion shall be accorded only to two speakers opposing the closure, after which the motion shall, subject to rule 29, be put immediately to the vote.

Rule 28

Suspension or adjournment of the meeting

Subject to rule 40, a representative may at any time move the suspension or the adjournment of the meeting. Such motions shall not be debated, but shall, subject to rule 29, be put immediately to the vote.

Rule 29

Order of motions

Subject to rule 23, the motions indicated below shall have precedence in the following order over all proposals or other motions before the meeting:

(a) To suspend the meeting;
(b) To adjourn the meeting;
(c) To adjourn the debate on the question under discussion;
(d) To close the debate on the question under discussion.

Rule 30

Basic proposal

The draft Cluster Munitions Convention, dated 21 January 2008, shall constitute the basic proposal for consideration by the Conference.

Rule 31

Other proposals

Other proposals shall normally be submitted in writing to the Executive Secretary, who shall circulate copies to all delegations. As a general rule, no proposal shall be considered at any meeting of the Conference unless copies of it have been circulated to all delegations not later than the day preceding the meeting. The President may, however, permit the consideration of amendments, even though these amendments have not been circulated or have only been circulated on the same day.

Rule 32

Withdrawal of proposals and motions

A proposal or a motion may be withdrawn by its proposer at any time before a decision on it has been taken, provided that it has not been amended. A proposal or a motion that has thus been withdrawn may be reintroduced by any representative.

Rule 33

Decisions on competence

Subject to rules 23 and 29, any motion calling for a decision on the competence of the Conference to discuss any matter or to adopt a proposal submitted to it shall be put to the vote before the matter is discussed or a decision is taken on the proposal in question.

Rule 34

Reconsideration of proposals

When a proposal has been adopted or rejected it may not be reconsidered unless the Conference, by a two-thirds majority of the representatives present and voting, so decides. Permission to speak on a motion to reconsider shall be accorded only to two speakers opposing the motion, after which it shall be put immediately to the vote.

Rule 35

Invitation to Technical Advisers

The Conference may invite to one or more of its meetings any person whose technical advice it considers useful for its work.

CHAPTER VIII

Decision-Making

Rule 36

General agreement

1. The Conference shall make its best endeavours to ensure that the work of the Conference is accomplished by general agreement.

2. If, in the consideration of any matter of substance, all feasible efforts to reach general agreement have failed, the President of the Conference shall consult the General Committee and recommend the steps to be taken, which may include the matter being put to the vote.

Rule 37

Voting rights

Each State participating in the Conference shall have one vote.

Rule 38

Majority required

1. Subject to rule 36, decisions of the Conference on all matters of substance shall be taken by a two-thirds majority of the representatives present and voting.

2. Decisions of the Conference on matters of procedure shall be taken by a majority of the representatives present and voting.

3. If the question arises whether a matter is one of procedure or of substance, the President shall rule on the question. An appeal against this ruling shall be put to the vote immediately and the President's ruling shall stand unless overruled by a majority of the representatives present and voting.

4. If a vote is equally divided, the proposal or motion shall be regarded as rejected.

Rule 39

Meaning of the expression 'representatives present and voting'

For the purpose of these rules, the phrase 'representatives present and voting' means representatives present and casting an affirmative or negative vote. Representatives who abstain from voting shall be considered as not voting.

Rule 40

Method of voting

Except as provided in rule 47, the Conference shall normally vote by show of hands or by standing, but any representative may request a roll-call. The roll-call shall be taken in the English alphabetical order of the names of the States participating in the Conference, beginning with the delegation whose name is drawn by lot by the President. The name of each State shall be called in all roll-calls and its representative shall reply 'yes', 'no' or 'abstention'.

Rule 41

Conduct during voting

The President shall announce the commencement of voting, after which no representative shall be permitted to intervene until the result of the vote has been announced, except on a point of order in connection with the process of voting.

Rule 42

Explanation of vote

Representatives may make brief statements, consisting solely of explanations of their votes, before the voting has commenced or after the voting has been completed. The President may limit the time to be allowed for such explanations. The representative of a State sponsoring a proposal or motion shall not speak in explanation of vote thereon, except if it has been amended.

Rule 43

Division of proposals

A representative may move that parts of a proposal be decided on separately. If a representative objects, a decision shall be taken on the motion for division. Permission to speak on the motion shall be accorded only to two representatives in favour of and to two opposing the division. If the motion is carried, those parts of the proposal that are subsequently approved shall be put to the Conference for decision as a whole. If all operative parts of the proposal have been rejected, the proposal shall be considered to have been rejected as a whole.

Rule 44

Amendments

1. A proposal is considered an amendment to another proposal if it merely adds to, deletes from or revises part of that proposal.

2. Unless specified otherwise, the word 'proposal' in these rules shall be considered as including amendments.

Rule 45

Decisions on amendments

When an amendment is moved to a proposal, the amendment shall be decided on first. When two or more amendments are moved to a proposal, the Conference shall first decide on the amendment furthest removed in substance from the original proposal and then on the amendment next furthest removed therefrom and so on until all the amendments have been decided on. Where, however, the adoption of one amendment necessarily implies the rejection of another amendment, the latter amendment shall not be put to a decision. If one or more amendments are adopted, a decision shall then be taken on the amended proposal.

Rule 46

Decisions on proposals

1. If two or more proposals relate to the same question, the Conference shall, unless it decides otherwise, decide on the proposals in the order in which they were submitted. The Conference may, after each decision on a proposal, decide whether to take a decision on the next proposal.

2. Revised proposals shall be decided on in the order in which the original proposals were submitted, unless the revision substantially departs from the original proposal. In that case, the original proposal shall be considered as withdrawn and the revised proposal shall be treated as a new proposal.

3. A motion requiring that no decision be taken on a proposal shall be put to a decision before a decision is taken on the proposal in question.

Rule 47

Elections

All elections shall be held by secret ballot unless otherwise decided by the Conference.

Rule 48

Elections—one elective place to be filled

1. If, when one person or one delegation is to be elected, no candidate obtains in the first ballot a majority of the representatives present and voting, a second ballot restricted to the two candidates obtaining the largest number of votes shall be taken. If in the second ballot the votes are equally divided, the President shall decide between the candidates by drawing lots.

2. In the case of a tie in the first ballot among three or more candidates obtaining the largest number of votes, a second ballot shall be held. If a tie results among more than two candidates, the number shall be reduced to two by lot and the balloting, restricted to them, shall continue in accordance with the preceding paragraph.

Rule 49

Elections—two or more elective places to be filled

1. When two or more elective places are to be filled at one time under the same conditions, those candidates, in a number not exceeding the number of such places, obtaining in the first ballot a majority of the votes of the representatives present and voting and the largest number of votes shall be elected.

2. If the number of candidates obtaining such majority is less than the number of places to be filled, additional ballots shall be held to fill the remaining places, the voting being restricted to the candidates obtaining the greatest number of votes in the previous ballot, to a number not more than twice the places remaining to be filled, provided that, after the third inconclusive ballot, votes may be cast for any eligible person or delegation. If three such unrestricted ballots are inconclusive, the next three ballots shall be restricted to candidates who obtained the greatest number of votes in the third unrestricted ballot, to a number not more than twice the places remaining to be filled, and the following three ballots thereafter shall be unrestricted, and so on until all the places have been filled.

CHAPTER IX

Subsidiary Bodies

Rule 50

Committee of the Whole

The Conference shall establish a Committee of the Whole, the Chairman of which shall be the President of the Conference. If the Chairman finds it necessary to be absent from a meeting of the Committee or any part thereof he shall designate a Vice-President of the Conference to take his or her place.

Rule 51

Other Subsidiary Bodies

The Conference may establish such other committees and working groups as it considers necessary.

Rule 52

Officers

Except as otherwise provided in rule 7, each subsidiary body shall elect its own officers.

Rule 53

Officers, conduct of business and voting

The rules contained in chapters III, VII and VIII (except rule 36) above shall be applicable, *mutatis mutandis*, to the proceedings of subsidiary bodies, except that:

(a) The Chairman of the General Committee may exercise the right to vote; and

(b) Decisions shall be taken by a majority of the representatives present and voting, except that the reconsideration of a proposal shall require the majority established by rule 34.

CHAPTER X
Languages and records

Rule 54
Languages of the Conference

English, French and Spanish shall be the languages of the Conference.

Rule 55
Interpretation

1. Speeches made in a language of the Conference at meetings of the Conference or of the Committee of the Whole shall be interpreted into the other such languages.

2. A representative may speak in a language other than a language of the Conference if the delegation concerned provides for interpretation into one such language.

Rule 56
Languages of official documents

Official documents of the Conference shall be made available in the languages of the Conference.

Rule 57
Sound recordings of meetings

The secretariat shall make sound recordings of meetings of the Conference and the Committee of the Whole. Such recordings shall be made of meetings of other committees when the committee concerned so decides.

CHAPTER XI
Public and private meetings

Rule 58
Plenary meetings and meetings of the Committee of the Whole

The plenary meetings of the Conference and the meetings of the Committee of the Whole shall be held in public unless the body concerned decides otherwise. All decisions taken by the plenary of the Conference at a private meeting shall be announced at an early public meeting of the plenary.

Rule 59

Meetings of other subsidiary bodies

As a general rule, meetings of other subsidiary bodies shall be held in private.

CHAPTER XII
Amendments to the Rules of Procedure

Rule 60

Method of amendment

These Rules of Procedure may be amended by a decision of the Conference taken by a two-thirds majority of the representatives present and voting.

CCM/3: DRAFT CONVENTION ON CLUSTER MUNITIONS

[*See Annex 5 above*]

CCM/4: PROPOSAL BY IRELAND FOR THE AMENDMENT OF THE PREAMBLE

The States Parties to this Convention,

Deeply concerned that civilian populations and individual civilians continue to suffer most from armed conflict,

Determined to put an end for all time to the suffering and casualties caused by the use of cluster munitions that kill or maim innocent and defenceless civilians and especially children, obstruct economic development and reconstruction, delay or prevent the return of refugees and internally displaced persons, and have other severe humanitarian consequences that can persist for many years after use,

Concerned that cluster munition remnants can undermine international efforts to build peace and security, as well as implementation of human rights and fundamental freedoms,

Believing it necessary to do their utmost to contribute in an efficient and coordinated manner to resolving the challenge of removing cluster munition remnants located throughout the world, and to assure their destruction,

Deeply concerned also at the dangers presented by the large stockpiles of cluster munitions retained for operational use in national inventories, and determined to ensure the speedy destruction of these stockpiles,

Determined to ensure the full realisation of the rights of victims of cluster munitions, and recognizing their inherent dignity,

Resolved to do their utmost in providing assistance for the medical care and rehabilitation, psychological support and social and economic inclusion of victims of cluster munitions,

Bearing in mind the Convention on the Rights of Persons with Disabilities which, *inter alia*, requires that States Parties to that Convention undertake to ensure and promote the full realisation of all human rights and fundamental freedoms of all persons with disabilities without discrimination of any kind on the basis of disability,

Mindful of the need adequately to coordinate efforts undertaken in various fora to address the rights and needs of victims of various types of weapons, and resolved to avoid discrimination among victims of various types of weapons,

Welcoming the global support for the international norm prohibiting the use of anti-personnel mines, enshrined in the 1997 Convention on the Prohibition of the Use, Stockpiling, Production and Transfer of Anti-Personnel Mines and on Their Destruction,

Welcoming also the entry into force on 12 November 2006 of the Protocol on Explosive Remnants of War, annexed to the Convention on Prohibitions or Restrictions on the Use of Certain Conventional Weapons which may be Deemed to be Excessively Injurious or to have Indiscriminate Effects, and wishing to enhance the protection of civilians from the effects of cluster munition remnants in post-conflict environments,

Welcoming furthermore the steps taken in recent years, both unilaterally and multilaterally, aimed at prohibiting, restricting or suspending the use, stockpiling, production and transfer of cluster munitions,

Stressing the role of public conscience in furthering the principles of humanity as evidenced by the global call for an end to civilian suffering caused by cluster munitions and recognizing the efforts to that end undertaken by the United Nations, the International Committee of the Red Cross, the Cluster Munition Coalition and numerous other non-governmental organisations around the world,

Reaffirming the Declaration of the Oslo Conference on Cluster Munitions, by which States *inter alia* committed themselves to conclude by 2008 a legally binding instrument that would prohibit the use, production, transfer and stockpiling of cluster munitions that cause unacceptable harm to civilians, and to establish a framework for cooperation and assistance that ensures adequate provision of care and rehabilitation to survivors and their communities, clearance of contaminated areas, risk education and destruction of stockpiles,

Emphasising **the desirability of attracting the adherence of all States to this Convention, and determined to work strenuously towards the promotion of its universalisation,**

Basing themselves **on the rules of international humanitarian law that the right of** parties to an armed conflict to choose methods or means of warfare is not unlimited, that the parties to a conflict shall at all times distinguish between the civilian population and combatants and between civilian objects and military objectives and accordingly direct their operations only against military objectives, **that in the**

conduct of military operations constant care shall be taken to spare the civilian population, civilians and civilian objects and that the civilian population and individual civilians enjoy general protection against dangers arising from military operations,

HAVE AGREED as follows:

CCM/5: Proposal by France for the Amendment of the Preamble

Reaffirming **the purpose of the Convention as defined by** the Declaration of the Oslo Conference on Cluster Munitions.....

CCM/6: Proposal by the United Kingdom for the Amendment of the Preamble

The States Parties,

Deeply concerned that civilian populations and individual civilians continue to suffer ~~most~~ from armed conflict,

Determined to put an end for all time to the suffering and casualties caused by the use of **those** cluster munitions that kill or maim innocent and defenceless civilians and especially children, obstruct economic development and reconstruction, delay or prevent the return of refugees and internally displaced persons, and have other severe humanitarian consequences that can persist for many years after use,

Concerned that cluster munition remnants **might impact negatively on** international efforts to build peace and security, as well as implementation of human rights and fundamental freedoms,

Concerned **also that large stockpiles of prohibited cluster munitions earmarked** for destruction are stored carefully and destroyed in a timely manner to prevent them from causing humanitarian suffering,

Believing it necessary ~~to do their utmost~~ to contribute in an efficient and coordinated manner to resolving the challenge of removing cluster munition remnants ~~located throughout the world,~~ and to ensure their destruction,

Deeply concerned also at the dangers presented by the large stockpiles of cluster munitions retained for operational use in national inventories, and determined to ensure the speedy destruction of these stockpiles,

Determined to ensure the full realisation of the rights of victims of cluster munitions, and recognising their inherent dignity,

Resolved to ~~do their utmost in~~ providing assistance for the medical care and rehabilitation, psychological support and social and economic inclusion of victims of cluster munitions,

Bearing in mind the Convention on the Rights of Persons with Disabilities which, inter-alia, requires that States Parties to that Convention undertake to ensure and promote the full realisation of all human rights and fundamental freedoms of all persons with disabilities without discrimination of any kind on the basis of disability,

~~*Mindful of the need adequately to coordinate efforts undertaken in various fora to address the rights and needs of victims of various types of weapons, and resolved to avoid discrimination among victims of various types of weapons,*~~

Welcoming the **broad international** support for the international norm prohibiting the use of anti-personnel mines enshrined in the 1997 Convention on the Prohibition of the Use of Stockpiling, Production and Transfer of Anti-personnel mines and on their Destruction,

Welcoming also the entry into force on 12 November 2006 of the Protocol on Explosive Remnants of War, annexed to the Convention on Prohibitions, Restrictions on the Use of Certain Conventional Weapons which may be Deemed to be Excessively Injurious or to have Indiscriminate Effects, and wishing to enhance the protection of civilians from the effects of cluster munition remnants in post-conflict environments.

Welcoming furthermore the steps taken in recent years, both unilaterally and multilaterally aimed at prohibiting, restricting or suspending the use, stockpiling, production and transfer of **certain** cluster munitions,

Stressing the role of public conscience in furthering the principles of humanity as evidenced by the ~~global~~ call for an end to civilian suffering caused by cluster munitions and recognising the efforts to that end undertaken by the United Nations, the International Committee of the Red Cross, the cluster munition coalition and numerous other non-governmental organisations around the world,

Reaffirming the declaration of the Oslo Conference on cluster munitions, by which States inter-alia committed themselves to conclude by 2008 a legally binding instrument that would prohibit the use, production, transfer and stockpiling of cluster munitions that cause unacceptable harm to civilians, and to establish a framework for cooperation and assistance that ensures adequate provision of care and rehabilitation to survivors ~~and their communities~~, clearance of contaminated areas, risk education and destruction of stockpiles,

Guided by the principle of international humanitarian law that the right of parties to an armed conflict to choose methods or means of warfare is not unlimited, and in particular on the general rule that parties to a conflict must at all times distinguish between the civilian population and combatants and between civilian objects and military objectives and accordingly direct their operations against the military objectives only,

HAVE AGREED as follows:

CCM/7: Proposal by Lesotho for the amendment of the Preamble

pp 2 *Determined* to put an end for all time to the suffering and casualties caused by the use of cluster munitions,

new pp3 *Aware/cognizant of* **other irreparable harm caused by the use of** cluster munitions including to kill or maim innocent and defenceless civilians [and] especially women and children; obstruct economic development and reconstruction; delay or prevent the return of refugees and internally displaced persons and have other severe humanitarian consequences that can persist for many years after use,

CCM/8: Proposal by Indonesia for the amendment of the Preamble

new pp 'Emphasizing the desirability of attracting the adherence of all States to the Convention, and determined to work strenuously towards the promotion of its universalisation in all relevant fora including, inter alia, the United Nations, the Conference on Disarmament, regional organisations, and groupings'

CCM/9: Proposal by Mozambique for the amendment of the Preamble

Determined to put an end for all time to the suffering and casualties caused by the use of cluster munitions that kill or maim innocent and defenceless civilians and especially children, obstruct economic development and **post-war** reconstruction, delay or prevent the return of refugees and internally displaced persons, and have other severe humanitarian consequences that can persist for many years after use,

(new pp) *Wishing* **to enhance the protection of civilians from the effects of cluster munition remnants in post-conflict environments,**

Concerned that cluster munition remnants can undermine **national and international** efforts to build peace and security, as well as implementation of human rights and fundamental freedoms,

CCM/10: Proposal by Japan for the amendment of Article 1

1. Each State Party undertakes never under any circumstances to:

(a) Use cluster munitions;

(b) Develop, produce, otherwise acquire, stockpile, ~~retain,~~ **own, possess** or transfer to anyone, directly or indirectly, cluster munitions; or

(c) Assist, encourage or induce anyone to ~~engage in any activity prohibited to a State Party under this Convention~~ develop, produce or otherwise acquire cluster munitions.

2. Any State Party may declare at the time of the deposit of its instruments of ratification, acceptance, approval or accession that, while implementing paragraph 1 of this Article, it will continue to use, only when strictly necessary, cluster munitions for a limited period of time not exceeding [x] years from the entry into force of this Convention for that State Party.

2. In the event that a State Party determines that it cannot immediately comply with paragraph 1 (a) of this Article, it may declare at the time of the deposit of its instruments of ratification, acceptance, approval or accession that it will defer compliance with paragraph 1 (a) of this Article for a period not to exceed [X] years from the entry into force of this Convention for that State Party. During this period, a State Party may use cluster munitions only when strictly necessary.

3. This Convention does not apply to 'mines' as defined by the Protocol on Prohibitions or Restrictions on the Use of Mines, Booby-Traps and Other Devices, as amended on 3 May 1996, annexed to the Convention on Prohibitions or Restrictions on the Use of Certain Conventional Weapons which may be Deemed to be Excessively Injurious or to have Indiscriminate Effects.

CCM/11: Proposal by France for the amendment of Article 1

1. Each State Party undertakes never under any circumstances to:

a) Use cluster munitions **as defined in Article 2**;
b) Develop, produce, otherwise acquire, stockpile, retain or transfer to anyone, directly or indirectly, cluster munitions **as defined in Article 2**;
c) ...

CCM/12: Proposal by Switzerland for the amendment of Article 1

1. Each State Party undertakes never under any circumstances to:

a) Use cluster munitions **as defined in Article 2**;
b) Develop, produce, otherwise acquire, stockpile, retain or transfer to anyone, directly or indirectly, cluster munitions **as defined in Article 2**;
c) ...

CCM/13: Proposal by Germany, supported by Denmark, France, Italy, Slovakia, Spain, the Czech Republic and the United Kingdom for the amendment of Article 1

1. Each State Party undertakes never under any circumstances to:

(a) Use cluster munitions;

(b) Develop, produce, otherwise acquire, stockpile, retain or transfer to anyone, directly or indirectly, cluster munitions;

(c) Assist, encourage or induce anyone to engage in any activity prohibited to a State Party under this Convention. **This provision does not preclude the mere participation in the planning or the execution of operations, exercises or other military activities by the Armed Forces or by an individual national of a State Party to this Convention, conducted in combination with Armed Forces of States not Parties to this Convention which engage in activity prohibited under this Convention.**

CCM/14: Proposal by the United Kingdom for the amendment of Article 1

1. Each State Party undertakes never under any circumstances to:

a) **Use sub-munitions as defined in Article 2b;**

b) Develop, produce, otherwise acquire, stockpile, retain or transfer to anyone, directly or indirectly, **sub-munitions as defined in Article 2b;**

c) Assist, encourage or induce anyone to engage in any activity prohibited to a State Party under this Convention. **For the purposes of this Convention, Article 1 does not come in to force until [x] years after entry in to force of the Convention.**

2. This Convention does not apply to 'mines' as defined in the Protocol on Prohibitions or Restrictions on the Use of Mines, Booby-Traps and Other Devices, as amended on 3 May 1996, annexed to the Convention on Prohibitions or Restrictions on the Use of Certain Conventional Weapons Which May Be Deemed to Be Excessively Injurious or to Have Indiscriminate Effects

CCM/15: Proposal by Ireland for the amendment of Article 1

1. Each State Party undertakes never under any circumstances to:

a) Use cluster munitions;

b) Develop, produce, otherwise acquire, stockpile, retain or transfer to anyone, directly or indirectly, cluster munitions;

c) Assist, encourage or induce anyone to engage in any activity prohibited to a State Party under this Convention.

2. Dispensers, affixed to an aerial platform and designed to disperse or release explosive bomblets, are subject to the same provisions as cluster munitions

3. This Convention does not apply to mines as defined in the Protocol on Prohibitions or Restrictions on the Use of Mines, Booby-Traps and Other Devices, as amended on 3 May 1996, annexed to the Convention on Prohibitions or Restrictions on the Use of

Certain Conventional Weapons Which May Be Deemed to Be Excessively Injurious or to Have Indiscriminate Effects.

CCM/16: Proposal by France for the amendment of Article 1

(or to be included in an additional Article, for example Article 9 *ter*)

Nothing in this Convention shall be interpreted as in any way preventing military interoperability between States parties and non-States parties to the Convention.

CCM/17: Comments by Australia, Canada, Denmark, Finland, France, Germany, Italy, Japan, the Netherlands and the United Kingdom concerning elements for Definitions

Definitions—alternative elements

The following weapon reliability and accuracy characteristics, either individually or in some combination, were posed by several States as being potential descriptors of those cluster munitions which do not cause unacceptable harm to civilians:

1. sensor fuzing (multiple or single) (point target discrimination) (deliver effects within a defined area);
2. fail-safe systems (self-destruct and self-neutralisation) (and self-deactivation) (mechanical and/or electronic based systems);
3. restrictions on the numbers of sub-munitions per cluster munition;
4. delivery by direct fire;
5. failure rates; and
6. accuracy (in terms of delivery of the cluster munition to the target area).

Several States also posed further consideration of:

1. other general reliability and accuracy considerations;

2. transition periods (for commencement of the primary prohibitions in Article 1); and

3. transition periods (for those munitions with a reliability of <1% and which possess failsafe systems.)

CCM/18: Proposal by Japan for the amendment of Article 2

For the purposes of this Convention:

...

'Cluster munition' means a munition that is designed to disperse or release **more than 10** explosive sub-munitions, and includes those explosive sub-munitions. It does not mean the following:

(a) a munition or sub-munition designed to dispense flares, smoke, pyrotechnics or chaff;

(b) a munition or sub-munition designed to produce electrical or electronic effects; or

(c) **reliable cluster munitions or accurate cluster munitions.**

'Reliable' cluster munitions are those cluster munitions which contain explosive sub-munitions which are equipped either with self-destruction mechanism, self-neutralization mechanism or self-deactivating mechanism or those cluster munitions which cause cluster munition remnants at the rate of not more than one percent.

'Accurate' cluster munitions are those cluster munitions which are equipped with guidance system or otherwise effective only within a pre-defined area.

...

CCM/19: Proposal by Germany for the amendment of Article 2

For the purposes of this Convention:

....

'**Cluster munition**' means a munition that is designed to disperse or release explosive sub-munitions, and includes those explosive sub-munitions. It does not mean the following:

(a) a munition or sub-munition designed to dispense flares, smoke, pyrotechnics or chaff;

(b) a munition or sub-munition designed to produce electrical or electronic effects;

(c) **a munition containing less than [x] explosive sub-munitions each designed to engage a point target within a pre-defined area and equipped with a self-destruct and self-deactivation mechanism; (new text)**
    (Note: 'Point Target' is a target, which requires the accurate placement of bombs or fire. 'Area Target' is a target, consisting of an area rather than a single point).

(d) ....

'**Explosive sub-munitions**' means munitions that in order to perform their task separate from a parent munition and are designed to function by detonating an explosive charge prior to, on or after impact;

'Reliable' cluster munitions mean cluster munitions which contain explosive sub munitions of a dud rate below one percent. (new text)

'Accurate' cluster munitions or explosive sub munitions are munitions which are effective only within a pre-defined target area. (new text)

CCM/20: Proposal by France for the amendment of Article 2

For the purposes of this Convention,

(…)

'**Cluster Munition**' means a carrier/container which contains conventional explosive sub-munition: and is designed to eject, disperse or release conventional explosive sub-munitions.

It does not mean:

(a) A munition or sub munition designed to dispense flares, smoke, pyrotechnics or chaff;

(b) A munition or sub munition designed to produce electrical, electronic or illuminating effects;

(c) A munition containing less than [X] explosive sub munitions

(d) Option 1: A munition designed to engage targets within a pre defined area in a reliable and accurate manner. (new text);

Option 2: A munition that fulfils a combination of precise criteria regarding its reliability and its accuracy;

'Carrier-container' means:

(a) a conventional munition that may be artillery shell, air bomb, guided or unguided missile or,

(b) a dispenser, affixed to an aircraft, which is not designed to dispense direct-fire munitions,

'**Explosive sub-munitions**' means a conventional explosive munition which is designed to separate from a cluster munition and is designed to detonate on, prior to or after impact.

'**Reliable**' cluster munitions means cluster munitions which contain explosive sub munitions of a dud rate below one percent and/or equipped with a self safe mechanism.

'**Accurate**' cluster munitions or explosive sub munitions are munitions which are effective only within a pre-defined target area.

CCM/21: Proposal by Switzerland for the amendment of Article 2

For the purposes of this Convention,

(…)

'Cluster Munition' means a carrier/container which contains explosive sub-munitions and is designed to disperse or release or eject these explosive sub-munitions.

It does not mean:

(a) A munition or sub-munition designed to dispense flares, smoke, pyrotechnics or chaff;

(b) A munition or sub-munition designed to produce electrical, electronic or illuminating effects;

(c) A munition or sub-munition designed to engage a point target within a pre-defined area and contains a self-destruct, self-neutralization or self-deactivation mechanism;

'Carrier-container' means:

(a) a conventional munition that may be artillery shell, air bomb, guided or un-guided missile or,

(b) [OPTION 1] a dispenser, affixed, to an aircraft, which is designed to dispense multiple sub-munitions in a single act.

(b) [OPTION 2] a dispenser, affixed to an aircraft, which is not designed to dispense direct-fire munitions.

'Explosive sub-munition' means a conventional explosive munition which is designed to separate from a cluster munition and is designed to detonate on, prior to or after impact.

~~"Cluster munition victims" means persons who have suffered physical or psychological injury, economic loss, social marginalisation or substantial impairment of the realisation of their rights caused by the use of cluster munitions. They include those persons directly impacted by cluster munitions as well as their families and communities;~~

CCM/22: Proposal by France and Germany for the amendment of Article 2

Alternative or additional definitions proposed for 'cluster-munition remnants':

'Unexploded sub-munition'1 means explosive sub-munition that has been primed, fused, armed, or otherwise prepared for use and used in an armed conflict. It may have been fired, dropped, launched or projected and should have exploded but failed to do so.

'Abandoned explosive cluster-munition'2 means explosive cluster-munition that has not been used during an armed conflict, that has been left behind or dumped by a party to an armed conflict and which is no longer under control of the party that left it behind. Abandoned explosive cluster-munitions may or may not have been primed, fused, armed or otherwise prepared for use.

'Explosive remnants of cluster munitions'3 means unexploded sub-munitions and abandoned explosive cluster-munitions.

'Existing explosive remnants of sub-munitions'4 means unexploded submunitions and abandoned explosive cluster-munitions that existed prior to the entry into force of this Convention for the State party on whose territory exists.

CCM/23: Proposal by the United Kingdom for the amendment of Article 2

2.1. For the purposes of this Convention:

a. 'Cluster munition' means a carrier-container which contains more than [x] conventional explosive sub-munitions and is designed to dispense conventional explosive sub-munitions over targets in a pre-defined area.

b. 'Conventional Explosive Sub-munition' means a conventional explosive munition which is designed to separate from a cluster munition and which is designed to detonate on, prior to or after impact on a target.

2.2. For the purposes of this convention, we need to consider the elements and characteristics that should exempt a submunition from a prohibition within specified reliability and accuracy benchmarks, including:

a. Munitions which incorporate a failsafe system.

b. Munitions which are direct fire weapons or which incorporate systems designed to deliver effects within a pre-defined area or on point targets.

2.3. We continue to support the following types of munitions remaining as exemptions: those designed to dispense flares, smoke, pyrotechnics or chaff Smoke, flare, chaff or pyrotechnic munitions and those designed to produce electrical or electronic effects.

'Cluster Munition Victims' means any persons who have suffered physical or psychological injury or economic loss, caused by the use of cluster munitions; cluster munition victims include such persons directly impacted by cluster munitions.

CCM/24: Proposal by Peru for the amendment of Article 2

For the purposes of this Convention:

'**Cluster munition**' means a munition that is designed to disperse or release explosive sub-munitions, and includes those explosive sub-munitions. It does not mean the following:

(a) a munition or sub-munition designed to dispense flares, smoke, pyrotechnics or chaff;

(b) a munition or sub-munition designed to produce electrical or electronic effects;

(c) **a munition or sub-munition which has the technical characteristics that allow to limit the area affected and reduce the risk of UXO contamination;**

CCM/25: Proposal by Ireland for the amendment of Article 2

For the purposes of this Convention,

'**Cluster munition victims**' means persons who have suffered physical or psychological injury, economic loss, social marginalisation or substantial impairment of the realisation of their rights caused by the use of cluster munitions; cluster munition victims include those persons directly impacted by cluster munitions as well as their families and communities.

'**Cluster munition**' means a munition that is designed to disperse or release explosive sub-munitions, and includes those explosive sub-munitions. It does not mean the following:

a) a munition or sub-munition designed to dispense flares, smoke, pyrotechnics or chaff;

b) a munition or sub-munition designed to produce electrical or electronic effects;

c) ...

'Explosive sub-munition' means a munition that in order to perform its task separates from a **cluster** munition and is designed to function by detonating an explosive charge prior to, on or after impact.

'Explosive bomblet' means a munition which in order to perform its task is dispersed or separated from a dispenser, affixed to an aerial platform, and is designed to function by detonating an explosive charge prior to, on or after impact.

'**Failed cluster munition**' means a cluster munition that has been fired, dropped, launched, projected or otherwise delivered and which should have dispersed or released its explosive submunitions but failed to do so;

'**Unexploded explosive submunition**' means an explosive submunition which has been released dispersed or otherwise separated from a cluster munition and has failed to explode as intended;

'**Unexploded explosive bomblet**' means an explosive bomblet which has been released, dispersed or otherwise separated from a dispenser, affixed to an aerial platform, and has failed to explode as intended;

'Cluster munition remnants' means <u>failed cluster munitions</u>, abandoned cluster munitions, <u>unexploded explosive submunitions and unexploded explosive bomblets</u>;

'Transfer' means the physical movement of cluster munitions into or from national territory or the transfer of title to or control over cluster munitions, but does not include the transfer of territory containing cluster munition remnants.

CCM/26: Proposal by Sweden for the amendment of Article 2

A. Among the criteria to apply in order to exclude cluster munitions from the scope of the future convention one <u>essential feature</u>, in considering current and future munitions, is the existence of an electrical fail safe system which must embrace <u>both</u> self destruct (SD) **and** self-deactivation (SDA) mechanisms.

The rationale for electrical systems is that batteries always discharge and render the munitions inoperable in the self-deactivating phase.

B. <u>In addition</u>, we propose that cluster munitions with an internal guidance system - including sensors – to <u>aid accuracy</u> should be a prominent feature.

A and B shall also be cumulative criteria.

CCM/27: Proposal by Indonesia for the amendment of Article 2

<u>'Cluster munitions areas' mean areas which are dangerous due to the presence or suspected presence of cluster munitions</u>

CCM/28: Proposal by Australia, Denmark, Finland, France, Germany, Italy, Japan, Slovakia, Sweden, Switzerland and the United Kingdom for the amendment of Article 3

Exceptions (new text):

6. <u>Notwithstanding the general obligations under Article 1, the retention, acquisition or transfer of a limited number of cluster munitions and sub munitions for the development of and training in cluster munitions and sub munitions detection, cluster munitions and sub munitions clearance, or cluster munitions and sub munitions destruction techniques, or for the development of cluster munition countermeasures is permitted. The amount of these cluster munitions shall not exceed the minimum number absolutely necessary for the above-mentioned purposes.</u>

Transfer (ex para 6. rev.)

7. Notwithstanding the provisions of Article 1 (**1**), the transfer of cluster munitions for the purpose of destruction **as well as for the purposes referred to in paragraph 6 of this Article** is permitted[1].

---

[1] Text on testing, exercises and training is new.

CCM/29: Proposal by United Kingdom for the amendment of Article 3

1. Each State Party undertakes to remove all cluster munitions from stockpiles of munitions retained **for potential use**.

2. Each State Party undertakes to destroy or ensure the destruction of all cluster munitions under its jurisdiction or control, as soon as possible but not later than 10 years after the entry into force of this Convention for that State Party. Each State Party undertakes to ensure that destruction methods **protect public health and the environment**.

3. If a State Party believes that it will be unable to destroy or ensure the destruction of all cluster munitions referred to in paragraph 1 within that time period it may submit a request to a Meeting of the States Parties or a Review Conference for an extension of the deadline for completing the destruction of such cluster munitions for a **further** period of up to ten years.

4. Each request shall contain:

a) The duration of the proposed extension;

b) A detailed explanation of the reasons for the proposed extension, including the financial and technical means available to or required by the State Party for the destruction of all cluster munitions referred to in paragraph 1 of this Article; and

c) A plan for how and when stockpile destruction will be completed.

5. The meeting of the States Parties or the Review Conference shall, taking into consideration the factors contained in paragraph 4 of this Article, assess the request and decide by a majority of votes of States Parties present and voting whether to grant the request for an extension period.

6. **Notwithstanding the provisions of Article 1, the retention, acquisition or transfer of a limited number of cluster munitions and sub-munitions for the development of and training in cluster munitions and sub-munitions detection, clearance or destruction techniques, or for the development of cluster munition counter-measures is permitted. The amount of cluster munitions and sub-munitions shall not exceed the minimum number absolutely necessary for the above mentioned purposes.**

7. Notwithstanding the provisions of Article 1 the transfer of cluster munitions for the purpose of destruction **as well as for testing, exercises and training in detection, cluster munitions and sub-munitions clearance or destruction techniques** is permitted.

CCM/30: Proposal by Peru for the amendment of Article 3

2. Each State Party undertakes to destroy or ensure the destruction of all cluster munitions under its jurisdiction or control as soon as possible but not later than **10** years after the entry into force of this Convention for that State Party. Each State Party undertakes to ensure that destruction methods comply with applicable international standards for protecting public health and the environment.

CCM/31: Proposal by Ireland for the amendment of Article 4

Article 4

Clearance and destruction of cluster munition remnants

1. Each State Party undertakes to clear and destroy, or ensure the clearance and destruction of, cluster munition remnants located in areas under its jurisdiction or control, as follows:

(a) Where cluster munition remnants are located in areas under its jurisdiction or control at the date of entry into force of this Convention for that State Party, such clearance and destruction shall be completed as soon as possible but no later than 5 years from that date;

(b) Where, after entry into force of this Convention for that State Party, cluster munitions have become cluster munition remnants **that are** located in areas under its jurisdiction or control, such clearance and destruction must be completed as soon as possible, but no later than 5 years after **the end of the active hostilities during which** such cluster munitions became cluster munition remnants.

(c) **Upon fulfilling either of the obligations set out in sub-paragraphs (a) and (b) of this paragraph, the relevant State Party shall make a declaration of compliance to the next Meeting of States Parties.**

2. In fulfilling the obligations set out in paragraph 1 of this Article, each State Party shall as soon as possible take the following measures, taking into consideration the provisions of Article 6 of this Convention regarding international cooperation and assistance:

(a) Survey, assess and **record** the threat posed by cluster munition remnants, **making every effort to identify all areas under its jurisdiction or control in which cluster munitions remnants are known or suspected to be located**;

(b) Assess and prioritise needs ~~and practicability~~ in terms of marking, protection of civilians and clearance and destruction, take steps to mobilise resources and develop a national plan to carry out these activities, **building, where appropriate, upon existing structures, experiences and methodologies**;

(c) **Take all feasible steps to** ensure that all cluster munition remnants located in areas under its jurisdiction or control are perimeter-marked, monitored and protected by fencing or other means to ensure the effective exclusion of civilians. ~~The marking shall at least be to the standards set out in the Protocol on Prohibitions or Restrictions on the Use of Mines, Booby-Traps and Other Devices, as amended on 3 May 1996, annexed to the Convention on Prohibitions or Restrictions on the Use of Certain Conventional Weapons which may be Deemed to be Excessively Injurious or to have Indiscriminate Effects.~~ **Warning signs based on methods of marking recognised by the affected community should be utilised in the marking of suspected hazardous areas. Signs and other hazardous area boundary markers should as far as possible be visible, legible, durable and resistant to environmental effects and should clearly identify which side of the marked boundary is considered to be within the area affected by cluster munition remnants and which side is considered to be safe;**

(d) Clear and destroy all cluster munition remnants located in areas under its jurisdiction or control; and

(e) Conduct risk-**reduction** education to ensure awareness among civilians living in or around areas in which cluster munition remnants are located of the risks posed by such remnants.

3. In conducting the above activities each State Party shall take into account international standards, including the International Mine Action Standards.

4. This paragraph shall apply in cases in which cluster munitions have been used or abandoned by one State Party prior to entry into force of this Convention for it and have become cluster munition remnants **that are** located in areas under the jurisdiction or control of another State Party at the time of entry into force of this Convention for the latter.

(a) In such cases, upon entry into force of this Convention for both States Parties, the former State Party shall provide, inter alia, technical, financial, material or human resources assistance to the latter State Party, either bilaterally or through a mutually agreed third party, including through the UN system or other relevant organisations, to facilitate the marking, clearance and destruction of such cluster munition remnants.

(b) Such assistance shall include, **where available**, information on types and quantities of the cluster munitions used, precise locations of cluster munition strikes and areas in which cluster munition remnants are known to be located.

5. If a State Party believes that it will be unable to clear and destroy or ensure the clearance and destruction of all cluster munition remnants referred to in paragraph 1 of this Article within that time period it may submit a request to a Meeting of States Parties or a Review Conference for an extension of the deadline for completing the clearance and destruction of such cluster munition remnants for a period of up to 5 years. **The requested period shall not exceed the minimum number of years strictly necessary to fulfil the obligations under paragraph 1 of this Article.**

6. A request for an extension shall be submitted to a Meeting of States Parties or a Review Conference prior to the expiry of the time period referred to in paragraph 1 of this Article for that State Party. Each request shall contain:

(a) The duration of the ~~proposed~~ **requested** extension;

(b) A detailed explanation of the reasons for the proposed extension, including:

   i) The preparation and status of work conducted under national clearance and demining programmes **during the initial five year period**;

   ii) The financial and technical means available to, and required by, the State Party for the clearance and destruction of all cluster munition remnants **during the requested extension period**; and

   iii) Circumstances that have impeded the ability of the State Party to destroy all cluster munition remnants located in areas under its jurisdiction or control **during the initial five year period, and those that may impede this ability during the requested extension period**;

(c) The humanitarian, social, economic, and environmental implications of the extension; and

(d) Any other information relevant to the request for the proposed extension.

7. The Meeting of the States Parties or the Review Conference shall, taking into consideration the factors contained in paragraph 6 of this Article, assess the request and decide by a majority of votes of States Parties present and voting whether to grant the request for an extension period. **The States Parties may decide to grant a shorter extension period than that requested and may propose benchmarks for the extension period as appropriate.**

8. Such an extension may be renewed **for a period of up to 5 years** upon the submission of a new request in accordance with paragraphs 5, 6 and 7 of this Article. In requesting a further extension period a State Party shall submit relevant additional information on what has been undertaken in the previous extension period pursuant to this Article.

CCM/32: Proposal by France and Germany for the amendment of Article 4

Article 4

Clearance, **removal** *and destruction of* **explosive remnants of cluster munitions (ERCM)**[1]

1. [2]**Each State party and party to an armed conflict shall bear the responsibilities set out in this Article with respect to all explosive remnants of cluster munitions**

---

[1] It is proposed to change the title in accordance with a methodology more consistent with Protocol V.

[2] It is proposed to add this paragraph, based on Article 3(1) of CCW Protocol V, with the understanding that, as with Protocol V, it only applies to <u>future</u> ERCM. It clearly spells out the

in territory under its control. In cases where a user of cluster munitions which have become explosive remnants of cluster munitions, does not exercise control of the territory, the user shall, after the cessation of active hostilities, provide where feasible, inter alia, technical, financial, material or human resources assistance, bilaterally or through a mutually agreed third party, including inter alia through the United Nations system or other relevant organizations, to facilitate the marking and clearance, removal or destruction of such explosive remnants of cluster munitions.

2. Each State Party undertakes to **Option I (Wellington text unchanged)**: clear and destroy, or ensure the clearance and destruction of / **Option 2[3]: mark and clear, remove or destroy/ Explosive** Remnants **of** Cluster Munitions located in areas under its control, as follows:

a) [4]Where, after entry into force of this Convention for that State Party, cluster munitions **used during an armed conflict**[5] have become **explosive** remnants **of** cluster munitions located in areas under its jurisdiction **or/** control, such clearance, **removal or** ~~and~~ destruction must be completed as soon as possible but no later than [x] years **after cessation of active hostilities**[6] ~~after such cluster munitions became cluster munitions remnants.~~

b) Where **explosive** remnants **of** cluster munitions are located in areas under its [jurisdiction or] control at the date of entry into force of this Convention for that State Party, ~~such clearance and destruction shall be completed as soon as possible but no later than 5 years from that date~~ provisions of Paragraph/Article [xl][7] shall apply to the clearance, removal or destruction of such explosive remnants of cluster munitions[8];

3. In fulfilling the obligations set out in paragraph ~~1~~ 2a), each State Party shall as soon as possible take the following measures, taking into consideration the

responsibilities of States (affected and users) and, while referring to 'all' explosive remnants of cluster munitions (ERCM) it does not link this reference directly and specifically to clearance obligations. The term 'Explosive Remnants of Cluster Munitions', which should include both 'unexploded sub-munitions' and 'abandoned explosive cluster munitions', will have to be defined in Article 2 of the Draft Convention (see CCM/22).

  [3] Option 2 is based on Protocol V, Article 3.

  [4] Reversing the order of the two sub-paragraphs is suggested: it seems more logical to start with the situation which will be given a clear priority, i.e. future ERCM, and not existing ones.

  [5] This is meant to clarify the fact that clearance of cluster munitions used e.g. for training will be out of the scope of this Convention.

  [6] It is proposed that the time line for counting down the time limit be the same as in Protocol V, Article 3.

  [7] See CCM/47.

  [8] Reference proposed to an additional paragraph/article, which should be mainly based on Article 7 of Protocol V applicable to existing ERW and would exclude retrospective obligations.

provisions of Article 6 of this Convention regarding international cooperation and assistance:

a) Survey and assess the threat posed by **explosive** remnants **of** cluster munitions;

b) Assess and prioritise needs and practicability in terms of marking, protection of civilians and clearance, **removal or** ~~and~~ destruction, take steps to mobilise resources and develop a national plan to carry out these activities;

c) Ensure that ~~all~~ **explosive** remnants **of** cluster munitions located in areas under its [jurisdiction on] control are perimeter-marked, monitored and protected by fencing or other means, to ensure the effective exclusion of civilians. The marking shall at least be to the standards set out in the Protocol on **Explosive Remnants of War (Technical Annex)** ~~Prohibitions or Restrictions on the Use of Mines, Booby Traps and Other Devices, as amended on 3 May 1996~~, annexed to the Convention on Prohibitions or Restrictions on the Use of Certain Conventional Weapons Which May Be Deemed to Be Excessively Injurious or to Have Indiscriminate Effects;

d) Clear, **remove or** ~~and~~ **destroy** ~~all~~ **explosive** remnants **of** cluster munitions located in areas under its **[jurisdiction or]** control; and

e) Conduct risk education to ensure awareness among civilians living in or around areas in which **explosive** remnants **of** cluster munitions are located of the risks posed by such remnants.

4. In conducting the above activities each State Party shall take into account international standards, including the International Mine Action Standards.

(cf. CCM/47) ~~4. This paragraph shall apply in cases in which cluster munitions have been used or abandoned by one State Party prior to entry into force of this Convention for it and have become cluster munition remnants located in areas under the jurisdiction or control of another State Party at the time of entry into force of this Convention for the latter. In such cases, upon entry into force of this Convention for both States Parties, the former State Party shall provide, inter alia, technical, financial, material or human resources assistance to the latter State Party, either bilaterally or through a mutually agreed third party, including through the UN system or other relevant organisations, to facilitate the marking, clearance and destruction of such cluster munition remnants. Such assistance shall include information on types and quantities of the cluster munitions used, precise locations of cluster munition strikes and areas in which cluster munition remnants are known to be located.~~

5. If a State Party believes that it will be unable to clear, **remove or** ~~and~~ destroy or ensure the clearance, **removal or** ~~and~~ destruction of all **explosive** remnants **of** cluster munitions referred to in paragraph **2a)** of this Article, within that time period, it may submit a request to a Meeting of the States Parties, or a Review Conference, for an extension of the deadline for completing the clearance, **removal or** ~~and~~ destruction of such **explosive** remnants **of** cluster munitions, for a period of up to *[x]* years.

6. A request for an extension shall be submitted to a Meeting of States Parties or a Review Conference prior to the expiry of the time period referred to in paragraph ~~1~~ **2a**) of this Article for that State Party. Each request shall contain:

a) The duration of the proposed extension;

b) A detailed explanation of the reasons for the proposed extension, including:

    (i) The preparation and status of work conducted under national clearance ~~and demining~~ programmes;

    (ii) The financial and technical means available to, and required by, the State Party for the clearance, **removal or** ~~and~~ destruction of all **explosive** remnants **of** cluster munitions; and

    (iii) Circumstances that impede the ability of the State Party to **clear, remove or** destroy ~~all~~ **explosive** remnants **of** cluster munitions located in areas under its [**jurisdiction or**] control;

c) The humanitarian, social, economic, and environmental implications of the extension; and

d) Any other information relevant to the request for the proposed extension.

7. The Meeting of the States Parties or the Review Conference shall, taking into consideration the factors contained in paragraph 6 of this Article, assess the request and decide by a majority of States Parties present and voting whether to grant the request for an extension period.

8. Such an extension may be renewed upon the submission of a new request in accordance with paragraphs 5, 6 and 7 of this Article. In requesting a further extension period a State Party shall submit relevant additional information on what has been undertaken in the previous extension period pursuant to this Article.

CCM/33: Proposal by the United Kingdom for the amendment of Article 4

1. **After the cessation of active hostilities and as soon as feasible**, each State Party undertakes to clear and destroy, or ensure the clearance and destruction of cluster munition remnants **that pose a humanitarian threat** located in areas under its jurisdiction or control, and **shall complete such clearance no later than 10 years from the date of entry in to force of this Convention for that State Party**.

2. In fulfilling the obligations set out in paragraph 1, each State Party shall as soon as possible take the following measures, taking into consideration the provisions of Article 6 of this Convention regarding international cooperation and assistance:

(a) Survey and assess the threat posed by cluster munition remnants;

(b) Assess and prioritise needs and practicability in terms of marking, protection of civilians and clearance and destruction, take steps to mobilise resources and develop a national plan to carry out these activities;

(c) Ensure to the maximum extent possible that all cluster munition remnants located in areas under its jurisdiction or control are perimeter-marked, monitored and protected by fencing or other means to ensure the effective exclusion of civilians. The marking shall at least be to the standards set out in the Protocol on Prohibitions or Restrictions on the Use of Mines, Booby-Traps and Other Devices, as amended on 3 May 1996, annexed to the Convention on Prohibitions or Restrictions on the Use of Certain Conventional Weapons Which May Be Deemed to Be Excessively Injurious or to Have Indiscriminate Effects;

(d) **To the extent possible** clear and destroy **sub-munition remnants that pose a humanitarian threat** located in areas under its jurisdiction or control; and (e) Conduct risk education to ensure awareness among civilians living in or around areas in which cluster munition remnants are located of the risks posed by such remnants.

3. In conducting the above activities each State Party shall take into account international standards, including the International Mine Action Standards.

4. If a State Party believes that it will be unable to clear and destroy or ensure the clearance and destruction of all cluster munition remnants referred to in paragraph 1 of this Article within that time period it may submit a request to a Meeting of States Parties, or a Review Conference, for an extension of the deadline for completing the clearance and destruction of such cluster munition remnants, for a period of up to **10** years.

5. A request for an extension shall be submitted to a Meeting of States Parties or a Review Conference prior to the expiry of the time period referred to in paragraph 1 of this Article for that State Party. Each request shall contain:

(a) The duration of the proposed extension;
(b) A detailed explanation of the reasons for the proposed extension, including:
  i) The preparation and status of work conducted under national clearance and demining programmes;
  ii) The financial and technical means available to, and required by, the State Party for the clearance and destruction of all cluster munition remnants; and
  iii) Circumstances which impede the ability of the State Party to destroy all cluster munition remnants located in areas under its jurisdiction or control;
(c) The humanitarian, social, economic, and environmental implications of the extension; and
(d) Any other information relevant to the request for the proposed extension.

6. The Meeting of the States Parties or the Review Conference shall, taking into consideration the factors contained in paragraph 6 of this Article, assess the request and decide by a majority of votes of States Parties present and voting whether to grant the request for an extension period.

7. Such an extension may be renewed upon the submission and assessment of a new request in accordance with paragraphs **4, 5 and 6** of this Article. In requesting a further extension period a State Party shall submit relevant additional information on what has been undertaken in the previous extension period pursuant to this Article.

CCM/34: Proposal by Italy for the amendment of Article 4

Delete Article 4 (4)

CCM/35: Proposal by Switzerland for the amendment of Article 5

1. Each States Party with respect to ~~cluster munition~~ victims in areas under its jurisdiction or control shall, in accordance with **applicable** international human rights ~~law~~ **standards**, adequately provide for **the access and quality of** their medical care and rehabilitation, psychological support and social and economic ~~inclusion~~ **reintegration as well as a participatory inclusion**. Each State Party shall make every effort to collect reliable relevant data with respect to ~~cluster munition victims~~ **all victims in global and already existing data collection system if available**.

2. In fulfilling its obligation under paragraph 1 of this Article each State Party shall take into consideration relevant guidelines and good practices in the areas of medical care and rehabilitation, psychological support as well as social and economic inclusion **and the practices and frameworks developed to assist the victims in the context of other multilateral disarmament/arms control instruments**.

3. **In fulfilling its obligations under paragraph 1, each State Party shall** endeavour to enhance in the most efficient and effective way existing State responses to the medical care and rehabilitation, psychological support and social and economic inclusion needs of its population, including cluster munition **victims and other persons with disabilities**.

4. **In fulfilling its obligations under paragraph 1, each State Party shall** ensure that there is no discrimination between cluster munition victims and those who have suffered injuries or who live with disabilities resulting from other circumstances.

CCM/36: Proposal by the United Kingdom for the amendment of Article 5

1. Each State Party with respect to cluster munitions victims **injured in its own territory** shall, **in accordance with national laws and practices,** provide for their medical care **and treatment**. Each State Party shall make every effort to collect reliable relevant data with respect to victims of cluster munitions.

2. In fulfilling its obligation under paragraph 1 of this Article each State Party shall **ensure that the measures adopted are in accordance with fundamental human rights principles, including non-discrimination**, and shall take into consideration relevant guidelines and good practices in the areas of medical care **and treatment**.

CCM/37: Proposal by Denmark, France, Germany and Sweden for the amendment of Article 6

9. *bis* **Each State Party that receives assistance shall take all appropriate** measures in order to facilitate the timely and effective implementation thereof, including by collecting and releasing all relevant data and information, by granting favourable entry and visa regimes for international personnel involved in assistance programmes, and by ensuring the unimpeded import of relevant material and equipment free of financial and administrative burdens.

CCM/38: Proposal by the United Kingdom for the amendment of Article 6

1. In fulfilling its obligations under this Convention each State Party has the right to seek and receive assistance, **where feasible, from other States Parties to the extent possible**.

2. Each State Party in a position to do so shall provide technical, material and financial assistance to States Parties affected by cluster munitions, aimed at the implementation of the obligations of this Convention. Such assistance may be provided, *inter alia*, through the United Nations system; international, regional or national organisations or institutions, non-governmental organisations or institutions, or on a bilateral basis.

3. Each State Party undertakes to facilitate and shall have the right to participate in the fullest possible exchange of equipment, and scientific and technological information concerning the implementation of this Convention. The States Parties shall not impose undue restrictions on the provision of clearance equipment and related technological information for humanitarian purposes.

4. In addition to any obligations it may have pursuant to Article 4, paragraph 4, each State Party in a position to do so shall provide assistance for clearance of cluster munition remnants and information concerning various means and technologies related to clearance of cluster munitions, as well as lists of experts, expert agencies or national points of contact of clearance of cluster munition remnants and related activities.

5. Each State Party in a position to do so shall provide assistance for the destruction of stockpiled cluster munitions, and shall also provide assistance to identify, assess and prioritise needs and practical measures in terms of marking, risk education, protection of civilians and clearance and destruction as provided in Article 4.

6. Where, after entry into force of this Convention, cluster munitions have become cluster munition remnants located in areas under the jurisdiction or control of a State Party, each State party in a position to do so, shall urgently provide emergency assistance to the affected State Party.

7. Each State Party in a position to do so shall provide assistance for medical care, rehabilitation and psychological support, social and economic inclusion of all **victims of cluster munitions**. Such assistance may be provided, *inter alia*, through the United Nations System, international, regional or national organisations or institutions, the International Committee of the Red Cross, national Red Cross and Red Crescent societies and their International Federation, non-governmental organisations, or on a bilateral basis.

8. Each State Party in a position to do so may contribute to relevant trust funds, in order to facilitate the provision of assistance under this Article.

9. Each State Party may, with the purpose of developing a national action plan, request the United Nations, regional organizations, other States Parties or other competent intergovernmental or non-governmental institutions to assist its authorities to determine, *inter alia*:

(a) The nature and extent of cluster munition remnants located in areas under its jurisdiction or control;

(b) The financial, technological and human resources required for the implementation of the plan;

(c) The time estimated as necessary to clear all cluster munition remnants located in areas under its jurisdiction or control;

(d) Risk education programmes and awareness activities to reduce the incidence of injuries or deaths caused by cluster munition remnants;

(e) Assistance to **victims from cluster munitions**; and

(f) The **coordination** relationship between the Government of the **concerned State Party** and the relevant governmental, inter-governmental or non-governmental entities that will work in the implementation of the plan.

10. States Parties giving and receiving assistance under the provisions of this Article shall cooperate with a view to ensuring the full and prompt implementation of agreed assistance programmes.

CCM/39: Proposal by Italy for the amendment of Article 6

4. ~~In addition to any obligations it may have pursuant to paragraph 4 of Article 4 of this Convention, each~~ Each State Party in a position to do so shall provide assistance for clearance of cluster munition remnants and information concerning various means and technologies related to clearance of cluster munitions, as well as lists of

experts, expert agencies or national points of contact on clearance of cluster munition remnants and related activities.

CCM/40: Proposal by Australia, Denmark, France, Germany, Italy, Sweden, Switzerland and the United Kingdom for the amendment of Article 7

1. Each State Party shall report to the Secretary-General of the United Nations as soon as practicable, and in any event not later than 180 days after the entry into force of this Convention for that State Party, on:

a)–m) ....

n) **the total number, types and locations of cluster munitions kept under the provisions of paragraph 6 of Article 3.**

CCM/41: Proposal by the United Kingdom for the amendment of Article 7

1. Each State Party shall report to the Secretary-General of the United Nations as soon as practicable, and in any event not later than 180 days after the entry into force of this Convention for that State Party, on:

a) The national implementation measures referred to in Article 9;
b) The total of all stockpiled cluster munitions owned or possessed by it, or under its jurisdiction or control, to include a breakdown of their type, quantity and, if possible, lot numbers of each type;
c) To the extent possible, all other cluster munitions that are stockpiled on its territory;
d) The technical characteristics of each type of cluster munitions produced, to the extent known, and those currently owned or possessed by a State Party, giving, where reasonably possible, such categories of information as may facilitate identification and clearance of cluster munitions; at a minimum, this information shall include the dimensions, fusing, explosive content, metallic content, colour photographs and other information which may facilitate the clearance of cluster munition remnants;
e) To the extent possible, the location of all areas that contain, or are suspected to contain, cluster munition remnants, under its jurisdiction or control, to include as much detail as possible regarding the type and quantity of each type of cluster munitions in each affected area and when they were used;
f) The status of programmes for the conversion or de-commissioning of production facilities for cluster munitions;

g) The status of programmes for the destruction, in accordance with Article 3, of cluster munitions, including details of the methods which will be used in destruction, the location of all destruction sites and the applicable safety and environmental standards to be observed;

h) The types and quantities of cluster munitions destroyed in accordance with Article 3, including details of the methods of destruction used, the location of the destruction sites and the applicable safety and environmental standards observed;

i) Stockpiles discovered after reported completion of the programme referred to in paragraph 7h;

j) The types and quantities of all cluster munitions remnants cleared and destroyed in accordance with Article 4, **after the entry into force of this Convention for that State Party**, to include a breakdown of the quantity of each type of cluster munitions remnants cleared and destroyed;

k) The measures taken to provide risk education and, in particular, an immediate and effective warning to civilians living in areas under its jurisdiction or control in which cluster munition remnants are located; and

l) The measures taken in accordance with the provisions of Article 5 to adequately provide for the medical care and rehabilitation, psychological support and social and economic inclusion of victims of cluster munitions as well as to collect reliable relevant data.

m) **In addition, each State Party shall provide** the name and contact details of the institutions mandated to provide information as described in this Article and of the institutions mandated to carry out the measures described in this **Article**.

n) **The total number, types and locations of cluster munitions kept under the provisions of Article 3, paragraph 6**.

2. The information provided in accordance with this Article shall be updated by the States Parties annually, covering the previous calendar year, and reported to the Secretary-General of the United Nations not later than 30 April of each year.

3. The Secretary-General of the United Nations shall transmit all such reports received to the States Parties.

CCM/42: PROPOSAL BY THE UNITED KINGDOM FOR THE AMENDMENT OF ARTICLE 8

1. The States Parties agree to consult and cooperate with each other regarding the implementation of the provisions of this Convention, and to work together in a spirit of cooperation to facilitate compliance by States Parties with their obligations under this Convention.

2. If one or more States Parties wish to clarify and seek to resolve questions relating to a matter of compliance with the provisions of this Convention by another State

Party, it may submit, through the Secretary-General of the United Nations, a Request for Clarification of that matter to that State Party. Such a request shall be accompanied by all appropriate information. Each State Party shall refrain from unfounded Requests for Clarification, care being taken to avoid abuse. A State Party that receives a Request for Clarification shall provide, through the Secretary-General of the United Nations, within 28 days to the requesting State Party all information that would assist in clarifying the matter.

3. If the requesting State Party does not receive a response through the Secretary-General of the United Nations within that time period, or deems the response to the Request for Clarification to be unsatisfactory, it may submit the matter through the Secretary-General of the United Nations to the next Meeting of the States Parties. The Secretary-General of the United Nations shall transmit the submission, accompanied by all appropriate information pertaining to the Request for Clarification, to all States Parties. All such information shall be presented to the requested State Party which shall have the right to respond.

4. Pending the convening of any meeting of the States Parties, any of the States Parties concerned may request the Secretary-General of the United Nations to exercise his or her good offices to facilitate the clarification requested.

5. Where a matter has been submitted to it pursuant to paragraph 3 the Meeting of the States Parties shall first determine whether to consider that matter further, taking into account all information submitted by the States Parties concerned. If it does so determine the Meeting of the States Parties may suggest to the States Parties concerned ways and means further to clarify or resolve the matter under consideration, including the initiation of appropriate procedures in conformity with international law. In circumstances where the issue at hand is determined to be due to circumstances beyond the control of the requested State Party, the Meeting of the States Parties may recommend appropriate measures, including the use of cooperative measures referred to in Article 5. *[Add references from Ottawa Convention Articles* 8(6) and 8(19) with regard to special meetings, fact finding missions and the *mechanism for reaching decisions at States Parties meetings.]*

CCM/43: Proposal by the United Kingdom for the amendment of Article 10

1. When a dispute arises between two or more States Parties relating to the interpretation or application of this Convention, the States Parties concerned shall consult together with a view to the expeditious settlement of the dispute by negotiation or by other peaceful means of their choice, including recourse to the Meeting of the States Parties and referral, **by mutual consent,** to the International Court of Justice in conformity with the Statute of the Court.

2. The Meeting of the States Parties may contribute to the settlement of the dispute by whatever means it deems appropriate, including offering its good offices, calling upon the States Parties concerned to start the settlement procedure of their choice and recommending a time-limit for any agreed procedure.

CCM/44: PROPOSAL BY THE UNITED KINGDOM FOR THE AMENDMENT OF ARTICLE 14

1. The costs of the Meetings of the States Parties, the Review Conferences and the Amendment Conferences shall be borne by the States Parties and States not parties to this Convention participating therein, in accordance with the United Nations scale of assessment adjusted appropriately.

2. The costs incurred by the Secretary-General of the United Nations under Articles 6, 7 and 8 of this Convention shall be borne by the States Parties in accordance with the United Nations scale of assessment adjusted appropriately.

CCM/45: PROPOSAL BY THE UNITED KINGDOM FOR THE AMENDMENT OF ARTICLE 17

1. This Convention shall enter into force on the first day of the sixth month after the month in which the **40th** instrument of ratification, acceptance, approval or accession has been deposited.

2. For any State that deposits its instrument of ratification, acceptance, approval or accession after the date of the deposit of the **40th** instrument of ratification, acceptance, approval or accession, this Convention shall enter into force on the first day of the sixth month after the date on which that State has deposited its instrument of ratification, acceptance, approval or accession.

CCM/46: PROPOSAL BY GERMANY FOR THE AMENDMENT OF ARTICLE 18

1. Any State may at the time of its ratification, acceptance, approval or accession declare that, while implementing the prohibitions on cluster munitions prohibited under Article 1, it will continue to use no more than [x] types of cluster munitions for a limited period of time not exceeding [y] years from the entry into force of this Convention; such munitions must be reliable and accurate as defined in Article 2, and they must be equipped with a self-destruct, self-neutralization or self-deactivation system.

2. Any use of cluster munitions pursuant to Paragraph 1 shall be in compliance with the provisions of International Humanitarian Law. In particular, it is prohibited in all circumstances to make the civilian population as such, individual civilians or civilian objects the object of attack by cluster munitions.

3. <u>During the transition period pursuant to Paragraph 1, the State Party concerned shall not, under any circumstances, transfer to anyone, directly or indirectly, any cluster munitions.</u>

4. <u>The provisions under Paragraph 1 are subject to the following transparency measures by the State Party concerned:</u>

(a) <u>The declaration under Paragraph 1 shall be notified to the Secretary General of the United Nations at the time of ratification, acceptance, approval or accession by the State Party concerned. It shall include details of the type of cluster munitions including on its reliability and accuracy as well as its self-destruct/self-neutralisation/self-deactivation features, the quantity, the deadline for removal from service, the beginning of the phasing out of operational stocks and the completion of the destruction process.</u>

(b) <u>The provisions on Transparency Measures under Article 7, including on annual reporting, shall also apply to the issues contained in the declaration under Paragraphs 1 and 4 (a) of this Article.</u>

CCM/47: Proposal by France and Germany for additional text

Additional provisions on assistance with respect to Explosive Remnants of cluster-munitions existing prior to the entry into force of the Convention[1]

Such a provision could be included in Article 4 or preferably in Article 6 with the other provisions dealing with international assistance

This paragraph/**Article** shall apply in cases in which cluster munitions have been used or abandoned by ~~one~~ a State Party **or non-party** prior to entry into force of this Convention [*for* it] and have become **explosive** remnants **of** cluster munitions located in areas under the [**jurisdiction or**] control of ~~another~~ a State Party at the time of entry into force of this Convention for the latter. In such cases, upon entry into force of this Convention for **each affected State party**:

1. Each State party has the right to seek and receive assistance, where appropriate, from other States parties, from states non-party and relevant international organizations and institutions in dealing with the problems posed by existing **explosive remnants of cluster-munitions**.

2. Each State party in a position to do so shall provide assistance in dealing with the problems posed by existing **explosive remnants of cluster-munitions**, as necessary and feasible.

3. <u>States parties in a position to do so and which, during an armed conflict, have used or abandoned Cluster Munitions on the territory of another State party which may have become explosive remnants of cluster munitions are invited to make</u>

available, without delay after the cessation of active hostilities and as far as practicable, subject to these parties' legitimate security interests, such information to the party or parties in control of the affected area, bilaterally or through a mutually agreed third party including inter alia the United Nations or, upon request, to other relevant organizations which the party providing the information is satisfied that they are or will be undertaking risk education and marking and clearance, removal or destruction of explosive remnants of cluster munitions in the affected area.[2]

4. **In so doing, States parties shall also take into account the humanitarian objectives of this Convention, as well as international standards including the International Mine Action Standards.**

[1] It is proposed that the issue of Explosive Remnants of Cluster Munitions existing before the entry into force of the Convention be dealt with either by adding a paragraph to Article 4 or a separate Article, as in Protocol V (Article 7). In the additional paragraph/Article proposed above the chapeau is based on the first part of Article 4, paragraph 4 of the Wellington text (with amendments): the first 2 sub-paragraphs (1 and 2) are based on Article 7(1) and 7(2) of CCW Protocol V: sub-paragraph 3 is based on Article 4(2) of Protocol V; and sub-paragraph 4 is added for the sake of coherence with Article 4(4) above.

[2] It should be noted that the addition of this sub-paragraph would be – even with 'should' or 'are invited to' instead of 'shall'– a meaningful step forward compared to obligations under Protocol V, since Article 4 of Protocol V only applies to 'ERW other than existing ERW...'

CCM/48: Proposal by Australia, Denmark, Finland, France, Germany, Italy, Japan, the Netherlands and the United Kingdom for additional text

Article 20
Relationship with Other International Agreements

This Convention shall be considered as complementary to any existing international agreement binding on the Parties.

CCM/48/Corr.: Proposal by Australia, Denmark, Finland, France, Germany, Italy, Japan, the Netherlands and the United Kingdom for additional text

New Article
Relationship with Other International Agreements

This Convention shall be considered as complementary to any existing international agreement binding on the Parties.

CCM/49: Proposal by Canada (withdrawn)

CCM/50: Proposal by Switzerland for additional text

New Article

Transition period

(a) At the time of its notification of consent to be bound by this treaty, a High Contracting Party may opt for a transition period not exceeding [X] years to progressively replace the munitions described under Article 2 of this treaty but that are equipped with a self-destruct, self-neutralization or self-deactivation system, by another type of weapon/munitions in conformity with this treaty and the principles of international humanitarian law.

(b) Transition periods are not allowed for munitions described under Article 2 of this treaty which are not equipped with a self-destruct, self-neutralization or self-deactivation system.

(c) During this transition period, the High Contracting Party shall not, under any circumstances, transfer to anyone, directly or indirectly, those prohibited munitions mentioned in paragraph (a).

(d) During this transition period, the High Contracting Party is allowed for training purposes, as last resort or in the case of self-defence to use those prohibited munitions mentioned in paragraph (a) if those have not been replaced yet and in conformity with the principles of international humanitarian law.

Note: a further provision prohibiting the use of the munitions mentioned in paragraph (a) against military objectives located in or near populated areas could be added. In this respect, inspiration could be drawn from Protocol III to the CCW on the Use of Incendiary Weapons.

CCM/51: Agenda

1. Opening of the Conference by the Secretary-General

2. Election of the President

3. Adoption of the Agenda

4. Adoption of the Rules of Procedure

5. Election of Vice-Presidents

6. Organisation of work

7. Convention on Cluster Munitions

8. Closure of Conference

CCM/52: RULES OF PROCEDURE

19 May 2008

DIPLOMATIC CONFERENCE FOR THE ADOPTION OF
A CLUSTER MUNITIONS CONVENTION
DUBLIN MAY 2008
RULES OF PROCEDURE
CHAPTER I
Participation

Rule 1

Participation

1. States that have subscribed to the Wellington Declaration of 22 February 2008, on that date or subsequently, shall be invited to participate in the Conference. Other States that have been invited by the Government of Ireland may attend the Conference as observers.

2. The Secretary-General of the United Nations, the International Committee of the Red Cross, the United Nations Development Programme and other relevant United Nations programmes and agencies, the International Federation of Red Cross and Red Crescent Societies, regional intergovernmental organisations and the Cluster Munition Coalition may attend the Conference as observers.

3. Other organisations that have been invited by the Government of Ireland may attend the Conference as observers.

CHAPTER II

Representation and credentials

Rule 2

Composition of delegations

The delegation of each State participating in the Conference shall consist of a head of delegation and such other accredited representatives, alternate representatives and advisers as may be required.

Rule 3

Alternates and advisers

The head of delegation may designate an alternate representative or an adviser to act as a representative.

Rule 4

Submission of credentials

The credentials of representatives and the names of alternate representatives and advisers shall be submitted early to the Executive Secretary of the Conference and, if possible, not later than 24 hours after the opening of the Conference. Any later change in the composition of delegations shall also be submitted to the Executive Secretary. The credentials shall be issued either by the Head of State or Government or by the Minister for Foreign Affairs. The Executive Secretary shall report to the Conference on the submission of credentials if it so requests.

Rule 5

If an objection is raised against the participation of a delegation, such objection shall be considered by the General Committee, whose report thereon shall be submitted to the Conference.

Rule 6

Pending a decision of the Conference regarding an objection against the participation of a delegation, the latter shall be entitled to participate provisionally in the Conference with the same rights as other participating delegations.

CHAPTER III
Officers

Rule 7
Elections

The Conference shall elect a President and eight Vice-Presidents. The Conference may also elect such other officers as it deems necessary for the performance of its functions.

Rule 8
General powers of the President

1. In addition to exercising the powers conferred upon him or her elsewhere by these rules, the President shall preside at the plenary meetings of the Conference, declare the opening and closing of each such meeting, direct the discussion, ensure observance of these rules, accord the right to speak, promote the achievement of general agreement, put questions to the vote and announce decisions. The President shall rule on points of order and, subject to these rules, shall have complete control of the proceedings and over the maintenance of order thereat. The President may propose to the Conference the closure of the list of speakers, a limitation on the time to be allowed to speakers and on the number of times each representative may speak on a question, the adjournment or the closure of the debate and the suspension or the adjournment of a meeting.

2. The President, in the exercise of his or her functions, remains under the authority of the Conference.

Rule 9

Acting President

1. If the President finds it necessary to be absent from a meeting or any part thereof he or she shall designate a Vice-President to take his or her place.

2. A Vice-President acting as President shall have the powers and duties of the President.

Rule 10

Replacement of the President

If the President is unable to perform his or her functions a new President shall be elected.

Rule 11

Voting rights of the President

The President, or a Vice-President acting as President, shall not vote in the Conference, but shall appoint another member of his or her delegation to vote in his or her place.

CHAPTER IV

General Committee

Rule 12

Composition

There shall be a General Committee consisting of the President and Vice-Presidents of the Conference. The President, or in his or her absence one of the Vice-Presidents designated by him or her, shall serve as Chairman of the General Committee.

Rule 13

Substitute members

If the President or a Vice-President finds it necessary to be absent during a meeting of the General Committee, he or she may designate a member of his or her delegation to sit and vote in the Committee.

Rule 14

Functions

The General Committee shall assist the President in the general conduct of the business of the Conference and, subject to the decisions of the Conference, shall ensure the coordination of its work. It shall also exercise the powers conferred upon it by rule 36.

CHAPTER V
Secretariat

Rule 15

Duties of the Secretary-General

1. The Secretary-General, designated by the Government of Ireland, shall act in that capacity in all meetings of the Conference and its subsidiary bodies.

2. The Secretary-General may designate a member of the Secretariat to act in his or her place at these meetings.

3. The Secretary-General shall appoint an Executive Secretary of the Conference and shall provide and direct the staff required by the Conference and its subsidiary bodies.

Rule 16

Duties of the secretariat

The secretariat of the Conference shall, in accordance with these rules:

(a) Interpret speeches made at meetings;
(b) Receive, translate, reproduce and distribute the documents of the Conference;
(c) Publish and circulate the official documents of the Conference;
(d) Prepare and circulate records of public meetings;
(e) Make and arrange for the keeping of sound recordings of meetings;
(f) Arrange for the custody and preservation of the documents of the Conference in the archives of the Government of Ireland; and
(g) Generally perform all other work that the Conference may require.

Rule 17

Statements by the secretariat

The Secretary-General or any other member of the staff of the secretariat who may be designated for that purpose may, at any time, make either oral or written statements concerning any question under consideration.

CHAPTER VI
Opening of the Conference

Rule 18

Temporary President

The Secretary-General shall open the first meeting of the Conference and preside until the Conference has elected its President.

Rule 19

Decisions concerning organisation

At its first meeting the Conference shall move to:

(a) Elect its President;

(b) Adopt its agenda, the draft of which shall, until such adoption, be the provisional agenda of the Conference;

(c) Adopt its rules of procedure, the draft of which shall, until such adoption, be the provisional rules of procedure of the Conference;

(d) Elect its other officers; and

(e) Decide on the organisation of its work.

CHAPTER VII
Conduct of business

Rule 20

Quorum

The presence of representatives of twenty five participating States shall be required for any decision to be taken.

Rule 21

Speeches

No one may address the Conference without having previously obtained the permission of the President. Subject to rules 22, 23 and 26 to 28, the President shall call upon speakers in the order in which they signify their desire to speak. The secretariat shall be in charge of drawing up a list of speakers. The President may call a speaker to order if his or her remarks are not relevant to the subject under discussion.

Rule 22

Precedence

The chairman or an officer of a committee or the representative of a working group may be accorded precedence for the purpose of explaining the conclusions arrived at by that committee or working group.

Rule 23

Points of order

During the discussion of any matter, a representative may at any time raise a point of order which shall be decided immediately by the President in accordance with these rules. A representative may appeal against the ruling of the President. The appeal shall be put to the vote immediately and the President's ruling shall stand unless overruled by a majority of the representatives present and voting. A representative may not, in raising a point of order, speak on the substance of the matter under discussion.

Rule 24

Closing of the list of speakers

During the course of a debate, the President may announce the list of speakers and, with the consent of the Conference, declare the list closed.

Rule 25

Right of reply

Notwithstanding rule 24, the President may accord the right of reply to any representative who requests it.

Rule 26

Adjournment of debate

A representative may at any time move the adjournment of the debate on the question under discussion. In addition to the proposer of the motion, two representatives may speak in favour of, and two against, the adjournment, after which the motion shall, subject to rule 29, be put immediately to the vote.

Rule 27

Closure of debate

A representative may at any time move the closure of the debate on the question under discussion, whether or not any other representative has signified his or her wish to speak. Permission to speak on the motion shall be accorded only to two speakers opposing the closure, after which the motion shall, subject to rule 29, be put immediately to the vote.

Rule 28

Suspension or adjournment of the meeting

Subject to rule 40, a representative may at any time move the suspension or the adjournment of the meeting. Such motions shall not be debated, but shall, subject to rule 29, be put immediately to the vote.

Rule 29

Order of motions

Subject to rule 23, the motions indicated below shall have precedence in the following order over all proposals or other motions before the meeting:

(a) To suspend the meeting;

(b) To adjourn the meeting;

(c) To adjourn the debate on the question under discussion;

(d) To close the debate on the question under discussion.

Rule 30

Basic proposal

The draft Cluster Munitions Convention, dated 21 January 2008, shall constitute the basic proposal for consideration by the Conference.

Rule 31

Other proposals

Other proposals shall normally be submitted in writing to the Executive Secretary, who shall circulate copies to all delegations. As a general rule, no proposal shall be considered at any meeting of the Conference unless copies of it have been circulated to all delegations not later than the day preceding the meeting. The President may, however, permit the consideration of amendments, even though these amendments have not been circulated or have only been circulated on the same day.

Rule 32

Withdrawal of proposals and motions

A proposal or a motion may be withdrawn by its proposer at any time before a decision on it has been taken, provided that it has not been amended. A proposal or a motion that has thus been withdrawn may be reintroduced by any representative.

Rule 33

Decisions on competence

Subject to rules 23 and 29, any motion calling for a decision on the competence of the Conference to discuss any matter or to adopt a proposal submitted to it shall be put to the vote before the matter is discussed or a decision is taken on the proposal in question.

Rule 34

Reconsideration of proposals

When a proposal has been adopted or rejected it may not be reconsidered unless the Conference, by a two-thirds majority of the representatives present and voting, so decides. Permission to speak on a motion to reconsider shall be accorded only to two speakers opposing the motion, after which it shall be put immediately to the vote.

Rule 35

Invitation to Technical Advisers

The Conference may invite to one or more of its meetings any person whose technical advice it considers useful for its work.

CHAPTER VIII
Decision-Making

Rule 36
General agreement

1. The Conference shall make its best endeavours to ensure that the work of the conference is accomplished by general agreement.

2. If, in the consideration of any matter of substance, all feasible efforts to reach general agreement have failed, the President of the Conference shall consult the General Committee and recommend the steps to be taken, which may include the matter being put to the vote.

Rule 37
Voting rights

Each State participating in the Conference shall have one vote.

Rule 38
Majority required

1. Subject to rule 36, decisions of the Conference on all matters of substance shall be taken by a two-thirds majority of the representatives present and voting.

2. Decisions of the Conference on matters of procedure shall be taken by a majority of the representatives present and voting.

3. If the question arises whether a matter is one of procedure or of substance, the President shall rule on the question. An appeal against this ruling shall be put to the vote immediately and the President's ruling shall stand unless overruled by a majority of the representatives present and voting.

4. If a vote is equally divided, the proposal or motion shall be regarded as rejected.

Rule 39
Meaning of the expression 'representatives present and voting'

For the purpose of these rules, the phrase 'representatives present and voting' means representatives present and casting an affirmative or negative vote. Representatives who abstain from voting shall be considered as not voting.

Rule 40
Method of voting

Except as provided in rule 47, the Conference shall normally vote by show of hands or by standing, but any representative may request a roll-call. The roll-call shall be taken in the English alphabetical order of the names of the States participating in the Conference, beginning with the delegation whose name is drawn by lot by the

President. The name of each State shall be called in all roll-calls and its representative shall reply 'yes', 'no' or 'abstention'.

Rule 41

Conduct during voting

The President shall announce the commencement of voting, after which no representative shall be permitted to intervene until the result of the vote has been announced, except on a point of order in connection with the process of voting.

Rule 42

Explanation of vote

Representatives may make brief statements, consisting solely of explanations of their votes, before the voting has commenced or after the voting has been completed. The President may limit the time to be allowed for such explanations. The representative of a State sponsoring a proposal or motion shall not speak in explanation of vote thereon, except if it has been amended.

Rule 43

Division of proposals

A representative may move that parts of a proposal be decided on separately. If a representative objects, a decision shall be taken on the motion for division. Permission to speak on the motion shall be accorded only to two representatives in favour of and to two opposing the division. If the motion is carried, those parts of the proposal that are subsequently approved shall be put to the Conference for decision as a whole. If all operative parts of the proposal have been rejected, the proposal shall be considered to have been rejected as a whole.

Rule 44

Amendments

1. A proposal is considered an amendment to another proposal if it merely adds to, deletes from or revises part of that proposal.

2. Unless specified otherwise, the word 'proposal' in these rules shall be considered as including amendments.

Rule 45

Decisions on amendments

When an amendment is moved to a proposal, the amendment shall be decided on first. When two or more amendments are moved to a proposal, the Conference shall first decide on the amendment furthest removed in substance from the original proposal and then on the amendment next furthest removed therefrom and so on until all the amendments have been decided on. Where, however, the adoption of one amendment necessarily implies the rejection of another amendment, the latter amendment shall not be put to a decision. If one or more amendments are adopted, a decision shall then be taken on the amended proposal.

Rule 46

Decisions on proposals

1. If two or more proposals relate to the same question, the Conference shall, unless it decides otherwise, decide on the proposals in the order in which they were submitted. The Conference may, after each decision on a proposal, decide whether to take a decision on the next proposal.

2. Revised proposals shall be decided on in the order in which the original proposals were submitted, unless the revision substantially departs from the original proposal. In that case, the original proposal shall be considered as withdrawn and the revised proposal shall be treated as a new proposal.

3. A motion requiring that no decision be taken on a proposal shall be put to a decision before a decision is taken on the proposal in question.

Rule 47

Elections

All elections shall be held by secret ballot unless otherwise decided by the Conference.

Rule 48

Elections—one elective place to be filled

1. If, when one person or one delegation is to be elected, no candidate obtains in the first ballot a majority of the representatives present and voting, a second ballot restricted to the two candidates obtaining the largest number of votes shall be taken. If in the second ballot the votes are equally divided, the President shall decide between the candidates by drawing lots.

2. In the case of a tie in the first ballot among three or more candidates obtaining the largest number of votes, a second ballot shall be held. If a tie results among more than two candidates, the number shall be reduced to two by lot and the balloting, restricted to them, shall continue in accordance with the preceding paragraph.

Rule 49

Elections—two or more elective places to be filled

1. When two or more elective places are to be filled at one time under the same conditions, those candidates, in a number not exceeding the number of such places, obtaining in the first ballot a majority of the votes of the representatives present and voting and the largest number of votes shall be elected.

2. If the number of candidates obtaining such majority is less than the number of places to be filled, additional ballots shall be held to fill the remaining places, the voting being restricted to the candidates obtaining the greatest number of votes in the previous ballot, to a number not more than twice the places remaining to be filled, provided that, after the third inconclusive ballot, votes may be cast for any eligible person or delegation. If three such unrestricted ballots are inconclusive, the next three ballots shall be restricted to candidates who obtained the greatest number of votes in the third unrestricted ballot, to a number not more than twice the places remaining to be filled, and the following three ballots thereafter shall be unrestricted, and so on until all the places have been filled.

CHAPTER IX
Subsidiary Bodies

Rule 50
Committee of the Whole

The Conference shall establish a Committee of the Whole, the Chairman of which shall be the President of the Conference. If the Chairman finds it necessary to be absent from a meeting of the Committee or any part thereof he shall designate a Vice-President of the Conference to take his or her place.

Rule 51
Other Subsidiary Bodies

The Conference may establish such other committees and working groups as it considers necessary.

Rule 52
Officers

Except as otherwise provided in rule 7, each subsidiary body shall elect its own officers.

Rule 53
Officers, conduct of business and voting

The rules contained in chapters III, VII and VIII (except rule 36) above shall be applicable, *mutatis mutandis*, to the proceedings of subsidiary bodies, except that:

(a) The Chairman of the General Committee may exercise the right to vote; and

(b) Decisions shall be taken by a majority of the representatives present and voting, except that the reconsideration of a proposal shall require the majority established by rule 34.

CHAPTER X
Languages and records

Rule 54

Languages of the Conference

English, French and Spanish shall be the languages of the Conference.

Rule 55

Interpretation

1. Speeches made in a language of the Conference at meetings of the Conference or of the Committee of the Whole shall be interpreted into the other such languages.

2. A representative may speak in a language other than a language of the Conference if the delegation concerned provides for interpretation into one such language.

Rule 56

Languages of official documents

Official documents of the Conference shall be made available in the languages of the Conference.

Rule 57

Sound recordings of meetings

The secretariat shall make sound recordings of meetings of the Conference and the Committee of the Whole. Such recordings shall be made of meetings of other committees when the committee concerned so decides.

CHAPTER XI
Public and private meetings

Rule 58

Plenary meetings and meetings of the Committee of the Whole

The plenary meetings of the Conference and the meetings of the Committee of the Whole shall be held in public unless the body concerned decides otherwise. All decisions taken by the plenary of the Conference at a private meeting shall be announced at an early public meeting of the plenary.

Rule 59

Meetings of other subsidiary bodies

As a general rule, meetings of other subsidiary bodies shall be held in private.

CHAPTER XII
Amendments to the Rules of Procedure

Rule 60

Method of amendment

These Rules of Procedure may be amended by a decision of the Conference taken by a two-thirds majority of the representatives present and voting.

CCM/53: PROPOSAL BY INDONESIA FOR THE AMENDMENT OF THE PREAMBLE

New pp '*Recognizing* the grave consequences by the use of cluster munitions and the need for immediate action to prohibit the use, production, transfer and stockpiling of cluster munitions that cause unacceptable harm to civilians'

New pp '*Emphasizing* the desirability of attracting the adherence of all States to the Convention, and determined to work strenuously towards the promotion of its universalisation in all relevant *fora* including, *inter alia*, the United Nations, the Conference on Disarmament, regional organisations, and groupings'[1]

---

[1] See CCM/8

CCM/54: PROPOSAL BY INDONESIA FOR THE AMENDMENT OF ARTICLE 1

To replace paragraph 2 with the following:

'Each State Party undertakes to destroy or ensure the destruction of all cluster munitions in accordance with the provisions of this Convention'.

CCM/55: PROPOSAL BY LAO PDR FOR THE AMENDMENT OF ARTICLE 4, PARAGRAPH 7

7. The Meeting of States Parties or the Review Conference shall, taking into consideration the factors contained in paragraph 6 of this Article, assess the request, **particularly the request from most affected States Parties,** and decide by a majority of votes of States Parties present and voting whether to grant the request for an extension period. **Special consideration shall be granted to the request from most affected States Parties.**

CCM/56: PROPOSAL BY PHILIPPINES FOR ADDITIONAL TEXT TO ARTICLE 1

3. **This Convention shall also apply to situations resulting from conflicts referred to in Art. 1, paragraphs 1 to 6, of the Convention on Prohibitions or Restrictions**

on the Use of Certain Conventional Weapons Which May be Deemed to be Excessively Injurious or to have Indiscriminate Effects, as amended on 21 December 2001.[1]

4. <u>Armed groups that are distinct from the armed forces of a State shall not, under any circumstances, engage in any activity prohibited to a State Party under this Convention.</u>[2]

[1] Reference model: Article 1(3) of the 2003 Protocol V on Explosive Remnants of War annexed to the CCW.
[2] Reference model: Article 4(1) of the 2000 Optional Protocol to the Convention on the Rights of the Child on the Involvement of Children in Armed Conflict.

CCM/57: Proposal by Philippines for the amendment of Article 2

'**Cluster munition victims**' means persons who have suffered <u>death,</u> physical or psychological injury, economic loss, social marginalization or substantial impairment of the realization of their rights caused by the use of cluster munitions. They include those persons directly impacted by cluster munitions as well as their families and communities and also <u>migrants under the jurisdiction and control of an affected State</u>.

CCM/58: Proposal by Philippines for the amendment of Article 5

1. Each State Party with respect to cluster munitions victims in areas under its jurisdiction or control shall, in accordance with international human rights law <u>and international humanitarian law</u>, adequately provide for their medical care and rehabilitation, psychological support and social and economic inclusion. Each State Party shall make every effort to collect reliable relevant data with respect to cluster munition victims.

2. In fulfilling its obligation under paragraph 1 of this Article each State Party shall take into consideration relevant guidelines and good practices in the areas of medical care and rehabilitation, psychological support as well as social and economic inclusion.

<u>New para</u>: <u>When a State Party, before entry into force of the Convention for it, has used or abandoned cluster munitions in areas under the jurisdiction or control of another State Party, the former State Party shall have the responsibility to help the latter State Party in addressing the requirements of victim assistance as delineated in Article 5(1)</u>.

CCM/59: Proposal by Philippines for the amendment of Article 6

7. Each State Party in a position to do so shall provide assistance for medical care, rehabilitation and psychological support, social and economic inclusion of *all* cluster munition victims **including migrants**. Such assistance may be provided, *inter alia*, through the United Nations System, international, regional or national organisations or institutions, the International Committee of the Red Cross, national Red Cross and Red Crescent societies and their International Federation, **the International Organization for Migration**, non-governmental organisations or on a bilateral basis.

New para: **The States Parties to this Convention shall explore its interface with other relevant treaty regimes, such as but not limited to the Convention on Prohibitions or Restrictions on the Use of Certain Conventional Weapons Which May be Deemed to be Excessively Injurious or to have Indiscriminate Effects, and shall develop mechanisms for this purpose**.

CCM/60: Proposal by Philippines for the amendment of Article 9

Each State Party shall take all appropriate legal, administrative and other measures **to implement this Convention**, including the imposition of penal sanctions, to prevent and suppress any activity prohibited to a State Party under this Convention undertaken by persons or on territory under its jurisdiction or control.

CCM/61: Proposal by Philippines for the amendment of Article 13

1. At any time after its entry into force any State Party may propose amendments to this Convention. Any proposal for an amendment shall be communicated to the Depositary, who shall circulate it to all States Parties and shall seek their views on whether an Amendment Conference should be convened to consider the proposal. If a majority of the States Parties notifies the Depositary no later than ~~30 days~~ **90 days or three months** after its circulation that they support further consideration of the proposal, the Depositary shall convene an Amendment Conference to which all States Parties shall be invited.

CCM/62: Proposal by Hungary for the amendment of the Title of the Convention

To replace the title with the following:

Convention on the Prohibition of Cluster Munitions that Cause Unacceptable Harm to Civilians.

CCM/63: PROPOSAL BY SLOVAKIA FOR THE AMENDMENT OF ARTICLE 1

1. Each State Party undertakes never under any circumstances to:

(a) Use cluster munitions **as defined in Article 2**;

(b) Develop, produce, otherwise acquire, stockpile, retain or transfer to anyone, directly or indirectly, cluster munitions **as defined in Article 2**;

(c) Assist, encourage or induce anyone to engage in any activity prohibited to a State Party under this Convention.

2. This Convention does not apply to 'mines' as defined by the Protocol on Prohibitions or Restrictions on the Use of Mines, Booby-Traps and Other Devices, as amended on 3 May 1996, annexed to the Convention on Prohibitions or Restrictions on the Use of Certain Conventional Weapons which may be Deemed to be Excessively Injurious or to have Indiscriminate Effects.

3. **This Convention does not apply to cluster munitions, which contain explosive sub-munitions of a failure rate of not more than one percent, equipped with self-destruction, self-neutralization or self-deactivating feature.**

CCM/64: PROPOSAL BY SLOVAKIA FOR THE AMENDMENT OF ARTICLE 2

'Cluster munition' means a munition that is designed to disperse or release explosive sub-munitions, and includes those explosive sub-munitions. It does not mean the following:

(a) a munition or sub-munition designed to dispense flares, smoke, pyrotechnics or chaff;

(b) a munition or sub-munition designed to produce electrical or electronic effects;

(c) **cluster munitions, which contain explosive sub-munitions of a failure rate of not more than one percent, equipped with self-destruction, self-deactivation or self-neutralization feature.**

(…)

CCM/65: PROPOSAL BY SLOVAKIA FOR THE AMENDMENT OF ARTICLE 3

1. ~~Each State Party undertakes to remove all cluster munitions from stockpiles of munitions retained for operational use and keep them in separate stockpiles for the purpose of destruction.~~

1. **Each State Party undertakes to clearly designate all cluster munitions in its stockpiles for the purpose of its destruction.**

(…)

CCM/66: Proposal by Slovakia for additional text (Article 18 bis)

New Article (18 *bis*)

Any State Party may at the time of its ratification, acceptance, approval or accession declare that, while implementing Article 1 of this Convention, it will continue to use, only when strictly necessary, cluster munitions for a limited period of time not exceeding twelve years from the entry into force of this Convention for that State Party.

CCM/67: Proposal by Spain for the amendment of Article 2

For the purposes of this Convention:

...

'**Cluster munition**' means a carrier-container which contains and is designed to dispense explosive sub-munitions. It does not mean the following:

(a) a munition or sub-munition designed to dispense flares, smoke, pyrotechnics or chaff;

(b) a munition or sub-munition designed to produced electrical or electronic effects;

(c) A munition or sub-munition equipped with a self-safe mechanism, that, combined with the normal functioning mechanism, guarantees that the number of remaining dangerous duds that can cause unacceptable harm to non-combatants is in practice equal to zero. In addition that munition or explosive sub-munition is painted and marked in order to distinguish it from the terrain and to warn about their dangerousness.

'Carrier-container' means:

(a) a conventional munition that may be artillery shell, air bomb, guided or unguided missile or,

(b) a dispenser, affixed to an aircraft, which is not designed to dispense direct-fire munitions.

'Explosive sub-munition' means a conventional explosive munition, which is designed to separate from a cluster munition and to detonate on, prior to or after impact on a target.

'Self-safe mechanism' means a combined self-destruction and self-deactivation mechanism, or other type of mechanism with a similar effect, that guarantees that a cluster munition remnant will become an inert explosive remnant in any case and will not detonate accidentally. [new definition]

'Self-destruction mechanism' means an incorporated or externally attached auto-matically-functioning mechanism which secures the destruction of the munition into which it is incorporated or to which it is attached.[1]

'Self-deactivating' means automatically rendering a munition inoperable by means of the irreversible exhaustion of a component, for example a battery, that is essen-tial to the operation of the munition.[2]

[1] from Amended Protocol II.
[2] from Amended Protocol II.

CCM/68: PROPOSAL BY THE CZECH REPUBLIC FOR THE AMENDMENT OF ARTICLE 2

For the purposes of this Convention:

. . .

'**Cluster munition**' means a munition that is designed to disperse or release explosive sub-munitions, and includes those explosive sub-munitions. It does not mean the following:

(a) a munition or sub-munition designed to dispense flares, smoke, pyrotechnics, or chaff;

(b) a munition or sub-munition designed to produce electrical or electronic effects;

(c) a munition containing landmines;

(d) a munition containing less than 10 explosive sub-munitions, equipped with a self-destruction and/or self-deactivation mechanism.

'**Explosive sub-munitions**' means munitions that in order to perform their task sepa-rate from a parent munition and are designed to function by detonating an explosive charge prior to or **immediately** after impact;

CCM/69: PROPOSAL BY MOROCCO, SUPPORTED BY SENEGAL AND MAURITANIA, FOR THE AMENDMENT OF THE PROPOSAL BY GERMANY, SUPPORTED BY DENMARK, FRANCE, ITALY, SLOVAKIA, SPAIN, THE CZECH REPUBLIC AND THE UNITED KINGDOM FOR THE AMENDMENT OF ARTICLE 1

1. Each State Party undertakes never under any circumstances to:

(a) Use cluster munitions;

(b) Develop, produce, otherwise acquire, stockpile, retain or transfer to anyone, directly or indirectly, cluster munitions;

(c) Assist, encourage or induce anyone to engage in any activity prohibited to a State Party under this Convention. <u>This provision does not preclude the mere participation in the planning or the execution of operations, exercises or other military activities by the Armed Forces or by an individual national of a State Party to this Convention, conducted in combination with Armed Forces of States not Parties to this Convention which engage in activity prohibited under this Convention,</u>[1] **provided that the States not party explain to the States Parties participating in the planning or the execution of operations, the military necessity for engaging in such activities and taking into account the humanitarian concerns addressed by the Convention. The States Parties shall refrain from engaging in activities prohibited under this Convention in any joint military operations with States not parties.**

[1] For the German proposal for the amendment of Article 1 see CCM13.

CCM/70: Proposal by Argentina, Ecuador, Guatemala, Uruguay, Dominican Republic, Mexico, Nicaragua, Panama, Peru, Costa Rica, Chile, Honduras, Zambia and Guinea for the amendment of Article 5

1. Each State Party with respect to cluster munition victims in areas under its jurisdiction or control shall, in accordance with international human rights law **and principles, including non-discrimination, full and effective participation, and inclusion in society,** adequately provide **assistance, including** ~~for their~~ medical care and rehabilitation, psychological support and social and economic inclusion. Each State Party shall **develop, implement and enforce relevant laws and policies, and** make every effort to collect reliable relevant data with respect to cluster munition victims.

2. In fulfilling its obligations under paragraph 1 of this Article each State Party shall:

(a) **assess the needs of victims, take steps to mobilise national and international resources and develop a national plan**[1] <u>including the time estimated to carry out these activities,</u>[2] <u>with a view to incorporating it within existing disability, development and human rights frameworks and mechanisms;</u>

(b) **closely consult with and actively involve victims and their representative organisations;**[3]

(c) **designate a focal point within the government to coordinate activities undertaken in different sectors and at different levels;**[4]

[1] Based almost word-by-word on Article 4(2)(b) of the current draft treaty.
[2] See Article 6(10)(c).
[3] Based on CRPD Article 4(3).
[4] Based on CRPD Article 33(1).

(d) take into consideration relevant guidelines and good practices in the areas of medical care and rehabilitation, psychological support as well as social and economic inclusion.

CCM/71: Proposal by Argentina, Costa Rica, Ecuador, Guatemala, Lebanon, Mexico, Palau and Uruguay for the amendment of Article 2

For the purposes of this Convention:

'**Cluster munition victims**' means persons who have suffered physical or psychological injury, economic loss, social marginalisation or substantial impairment of the realisation of their rights caused by the use of cluster munitions. They include those persons directly impacted by cluster munitions as well as their families and communities;

'**Cluster munition**' means a munition that is designed to disperse or release explosive sub-munitions, and includes those explosive sub-munitions. It does not mean the following:

(a) a munition or sub-munition designed to dispense flares, smoke, pyrotechnics or chaff;

(b) a munition or sub-munition designed to produce electrical or electronic effects; .

~~(c)...~~

CCM/72: Proposal by Norway for the amendment of Article 2

Add the following definitions:

'<u>Self-destruct mechanism' means a mechanism that physically destroys the warhead in the event that it does not function as intended and thus leaving no unexploded objects behind;</u>

'<u>Self-deactivation mechanism' means a mechanism that drains the sub-munition of the energy required to bring it to detonation and thus rendering the remaining unexploded object safe to handle and safe in any incidental contact;</u>

CCM/73: Proposal by Norway for the amendment of Article 2

For the purposes of this Convention:

(...)

'**Transfer**' means, <u>in addition to</u> the physical movement of cluster munitions into or from national territory, or the transfer of title to or control over the cluster munitions, but does not include the transfer of territory containing cluster munitions remnants.

CCM/74: Proposal by Canada for the amendment of Article 2

For the purposes of this Convention:

(...)

'**Cluster munition**' means a munition that is designed to disperse or release explosive sub-munitions, and includes those explosive sub-munitions. It does not mean the following:

(a) a munition or sub-munition designed to dispense flares, smoke, pyrotechnics, or chaff;

(b) a munition or sub-munition designed to produce electrical or electronic effects;

(c) <u>a munition that has all the following characteristics that ensure greater accuracy and reduce the risk of unexploded ordnance contamination from its use:</u>

    (i) <u>each sub-munition is designed to locate and engage a point target within a pre-defined area;</u>

    (ii) <u>each sub-munition is equipped with an electronic self-destruct mechanism;</u>

    (iii) <u>each sub-munition is equipped with an electronic self-deactivation mechanism.</u>

CCM/75: Proposal by the United Kingdom for the amendment of Article 2

Addressing the humanitarian concerns:

- Numbers. Need to address the issue of preventing an area from being contaminated with ERW. This can be done by either limiting the number of submunitions within a cluster munition or by ensuring that each submunition has a fail safe system, including self-destruct systems.
- Accuracy. Need to enhance compliance with distinction and proportionality to reduce civilian casualties and minimize the area of effect. This can be done by a point target capability, which locates and engages a target in a pre-defined area, or by direct fire, which ensures direct human control over the effects as the operator has sight of the target at the time of attack and can make a higher quality assessment of compliance with distinction and proportionality rules.
- Reliability. Need to increase reliability in order to minimize the incidence of ERW. This can be achieved by the inclusion of fail safe systems, including self-destruct systems.

Effects: Effects can be controlled:

- At time of attack: low numbers, point target capabilities or direct fire control minimize the effects at the time of attack. They ensure greater definition of and adherence to the distinction and proportionality IHL rules.

- Post attack: fail safe systems minimize the effects post attack.

Approach: Building on the Friend of the Chair's proposals contained in a number of criteria in Models C, F and G and proposals submitted by the UK in the Wellington Compendium would address the humanitarian concerns.

Definition:

For the purposes of this Convention:

(...)

'**Cluster Munition**' means a munition **which contains more than 10 conventional sub-munitions and which** that is designed to disperse or release **conventional** explosive sub-munitions, and includes those explosive sub-munitions. **over targets in a pre-defined area.** It does not mean the following:

(a) a ~~munition or~~ sub-munition designed to dispense flares, smoke, pyrotechnics or chaff; **or a munition designed to be an air defence system;**

(b) a ~~munition or~~ sub-munition designed to produce electrical or electronic effects;

(c) **a sub-munition designed to be fired directly into a pre-defined area or to locate and engage a point target within a pre-defined area or which is equipped with a self-destruct system.**

CCM/76: PROPOSAL BY SPAIN FOR THE AMENDMENT OF ARTICLE 2

For the purposes of this Convention:

(...)

'**Cluster munition**' means a munition that is designed to disperse or release explosive sub-munitions, and includes those explosive sub-munitions. It does not mean the following:

(a) a munition or sub-munition designed to dispense flares, smoke, pyrotechnics or chaff;

(b) a munition or sub-munition designed to produce electrical or electronic effects;

(c) **a munition that does not cause unacceptable harm to civilians and has all the following characteristics which minimise its area effect and the risk of unexploded ordnance contamination from its use:**

(i) **a munition which contains sub-munitions which only address the area encompassed by the intended military objective;**

(ii) **each sub-munition is equipped with an electronic self-destruction mechanism;**

(iii) **each sub-munition is equipped with an electronic self-deactivation mechanism;**

'Explosive sub-munitions' means ~~munitions that in order to perform their task separate from a parent munition and are designed to function by detonating an explosive charge prior to, on or after impact;~~ a conventional explosive munition, which is designed to separate from a cluster munition and to detonate on, prior to or after impact on a target;

'Military objective' means, so far as objects are concerned, any object which by its nature, location, purpose or use makes an effective contribution to military action and whose total or partial destruction, capture or neutralisation, in the circumstances ruling at the time, offers a definite military advantage; [from Protocol III on Prohibitions or Restrictions on the Use of Incendiary Weapons, and also from Protocol II on Prohibitions or Restrictions on the Use of Mines, Booby-Traps and other Devices].

'Self-destruction mechanism' means an incorporated or externally attached automatically-functioning mechanism which secures the destruction of the munition into which it is incorporated or to which it is attached; [from Amended Protocol II]

'Self-deactivating' means automatically rendering a munition inoperable by means of the irreversible exhaustion of a component, for example a battery, that is essential to the operation of the munition; [from Amended Protocol II]

(. . .)

Rationale for the proposed Article 2(c)(i):

Concerning the proposed definition: the intention is to establish a relationship between accuracy and the final effects, irrespective of the specific means of delivery used (GPS direct observation of the military objective, guided weapons, sensor fuzed weapons, . . .).

Concerning the use of the concept 'military objective', it is proposed to employ the agreed and consolidated concept in international law.

Further explanation on the use of cluster munitions for the protection of civilians and civilian objects (adapted from Protocol III on Prohibitions or Restrictions on the Use of Incendiary Weapons):

a) It is prohibited in all circumstances to make the civilian population as such, individual civilians or civilian objects the object of attack by cluster munitions.

b) It is prohibited in all circumstances to make any military objective located within a concentration of civilians the object of attack by cluster munitions.

c) It is further prohibited to make any military objective located within a concentration of civilians the object of attack by means of cluster munitions except when such military objective is clearly separated from the concentration of civilians and all feasible precautions are taken with a view to limiting the cluster munitions effects to the military objective and to avoiding, and in any event to minimizing, incidental loss of civilian life, injury to civilians and damage to civilian objects.

CCM/77: Convention on Cluster Munitions

[Text contained in Annex 9.]

CCM/78: Final Document

CONTENTS

Part I. PROCEDURAL REPORT OF THE DIPLOMATIC CONFERENCE

I. Introduction

II. Organisation and work of the Conference

Annex I Agenda

Annex II Rules of Procedure

Annex III List of Documents of the Diplomatic Conference

Annex IV Documents of the Diplomatic Conference

Annex V List of Delegates

Part II CONVENTION ON CLUSTER MUNITIONS

Part III SUMMARY RECORDS OF THE PUBLIC MEETINGS OF THE DIPLOMATIC CONFERENCE

PART I PROCEDURAL REPORT OF THE DIPLOMATIC CONFERENCE

I. Introduction

1. At the Oslo Conference on Cluster Munitions (Oslo, 22–23 February 2007), a group of States, the United Nations, the International Committee of the Red Cross, the Cluster Munition Coalition and other humanitarian organisations recognised the grave consequences caused by the use of cluster munitions and the need for immediate action. States participating in the Oslo Conference committed themselves in the Oslo Declaration to:

'1. Conclude by 2008 a legally binding international instrument that will:

i. prohibit the use, production, transfer and stockpiling of cluster munitions that cause unacceptable harm to civilians, and

ii. establish a framework for cooperation and assistance that ensures adequate provision of care and rehabilitation to survivors and their communities, clearance of contaminated areas, risk education and destruction of stockpiles of prohibited cluster munitions.

2. Consider taking steps at the national level to address these problems.

3. Continue to address the humanitarian challenges posed by cluster munitions within the framework of international humanitarian law and in all relevant fora.'

2. Pursuant to the Oslo Declaration, further conferences were held in Peru (Lima, 23–25 May 2007), Austria (Vienna, 5–7 December 2007), and New Zealand (Wellington, 18–22 February 2008) with the objective of addressing effectively the humanitarian problems caused by cluster munitions and to prepare for negotiations at the Dublin Diplomatic Conference.

3. The Declaration adopted at the Wellington Conference on Cluster Munitions, *inter alia*:

'welcome[d] the convening of a Diplomatic Conference by the Government of Ireland in Dublin on 19 May 2008 to negotiate and adopt a legally binding instrument prohibiting cluster munitions that cause unacceptable harm to civilians;

also welcome[d] the important work done by participants engaged in the cluster munitions process on the text of a draft Cluster Munitions Convention, dated January 21 2008, which contains the essential elements identified above and decide[d] to forward it as the basic proposal for consideration at the Dublin Diplomatic Conference, together with other relevant proposals including those contained in the compendium attached to this Declaration and those which may be put forward there;

affirme[d] their objective of concluding the negotiation of such an instrument prohibiting cluster munitions that cause unacceptable harm to civilians in Dublin in May 2008 ...'

4. Conferences in support of the Oslo Process on Cluster Munitions were also held as follows:

- Regional Forum in Southeast Asia (Phnom Penh, Cambodia, 15 March 2007);
- Regional Conference (San José, Costa Rica, 4–5 September 2007);
- Belgrade Conference of the States Affected by Cluster Munitions (Belgrade, Serbia, 3–4 October 2007);
- European Regional Conference on Cluster Munitions (Brussels, Belgium, 20 October 2007);
- Livingstone Conference on Cluster Munitions (Livingstone, Zambia, 31 March – 1 April 2008);
- Latin American and Caribbean Conference on Cluster Munitions (Mexico City, Mexico, 16–17 April 2008).

II. Organisation and work of
the Dublin Diplomatic Conference

5. The Dublin Diplomatic Conference for the Adoption of a Convention on Cluster Munitions was held at Dublin from 19 to 30 May 2008.

6. On 19 May 2008, the Conference was opened by Mr. Colm Ó Floinn, who was designated by the Government of Ireland to serve as Secretary-General of the Diplomatic Conference. The Secretary-General of the Conference was assisted by Mr. Damien Cole as Executive Secretary of the Conference.

7. At the opening ceremony, the Conference was addressed by Mr. Micheál Martin, T.D., Minister for Foreign Affairs of Ireland; Mr. Ad Melkert, United Nations Under-Secretary-General and Associate Administrator of the United Nations Development Programme; Dr. Jakob Kellenberger, President of the International Committee of the Red Cross; and Mr. Branislav Kapetanovic, Cluster Munition Coalition.

8. In addition, Mr. Ban Ki-moon, Secretary-General of the United Nations, addressed the Conference by video message.

9. At its first plenary meeting, on 19 May 2008, the Conference elected by acclamation Ambassador Dáithí O'Ceallaigh, Permanent Representative of Ireland to the United Nations Office at Geneva, as President of the Conference.

10. At the same plenary meeting, the Conference adopted its Agenda (attached at Annex I to this Report) and the Rules of Procedure (attached at Annex II).

11. At the same plenary meeting, on the proposal of the President and pursuant to Rule 7 of the Rules of Procedure, the Conference unanimously elected the following eight Vice-Presidents:

Ambassador Najla Riachi Assaker Lebanon
Ambassador Jean-François Dobelle France
Ambassador Juan Eduardo Eguiguren Chile
Ambassador Mohamed Yaha Ould Sidi Haiba Mauritania
Ambassador Steffen Kongstad Norway
Ambassador Pablo Macedo Mexico
Ms. Sheila Mweemba Zambia
Ambassador Sándor Rácz Hungary

12. The following 107 States participated in the Conference: Albania, Argentina, Australia, Austria, Bahrain, Belgium, Belize, Benin, Bolivia, Bosnia and Herzegovina, Botswana, Brunei Darussalam, Bulgaria, Burkina Faso, Burundi, Cambodia, Cameroon, Canada, Chad, Chile, Comoros, Republic of the Congo, Cook Islands, Costa Rica, Côte d'Ivoire, Croatia, Czech Republic, Democratic Republic of the Congo, Denmark, Dominican Republic, Ecuador, El Salvador, Estonia, Fiji, Finland, France, Germany, Ghana, Guatemala, Guinea, Guinea-Bissau, Holy See, Honduras, Hungary, Iceland, Indonesia, Ireland, Italy, Jamaica, Japan, Kenya, Kyrgyzstan, Lao People's Democratic Republic, Lebanon, Lesotho, Lithuania,

Luxembourg, Madagascar, Malawi, Malaysia, Mali, Malta, Mauritania, Mexico, Moldova, Montenegro, Morocco, Mozambique, The Netherlands, New Zealand, Nicaragua, Niger, Nigeria, Norway, Palau, Panama, Papua New Guinea, Paraguay, Peru, Philippines, Portugal, Qatar, Samoa, San Marino, Sao Tome and Principe, Senegal, Serbia, Seychelles, Sierra Leone, Slovakia, Slovenia, South Africa, Spain, Sudan, Swaziland, Sweden, Switzerland, Tanzania, The former Yugoslav Republic of Macedonia, Timor-Leste, Togo, Uganda, United Kingdom of Great Britain and Northern Ireland, Uruguay, Vanuatu, Venezuela and Zambia.

13. The following 20 States attended the Conference as observers: Colombia, Cyprus, Egypt, Eritrea, Ethiopia, Greece, Iraq, Kazakhstan, Kuwait, Latvia, Libyan Arab Jamahiriya, Oman, Poland, Romania, Saudi Arabia, Singapore, Thailand, Turkey, Ukraine and Viet Nam.

14. The representatives of the United Nations Children Fund (UNICEF), United Nations Development Programme (UNDP), United Nations High Commissioner for Refugees (UNHCR), United Nations Institute for Disarmament Research (UNIDIR), United Nations Mine Action Service (UNMAS), United Nations Office for the Coordination of Humanitarian Affairs (OCHA), United Nations Office for Disarmament Affairs (UNODA), United Nations Office of Legal Affairs (UNOLA), the International Committee of the Red Cross (ICRC), the International Federation of Red Cross and Red Crescent Societies (IFRC), the European Commission, the Cluster Munition Coalition and the Geneva International Centre for Humanitarian Demining (GICHD) also attended the Conference as observers.

15. The Conference held plenary meetings and meetings of the Committee of the Whole and considered the draft Convention on Cluster Munitions (document CCM/3), as well as other documents listed in Annex III and attached at Annex IV.

16. The Conference met in plenary on Wednesday 28 May and agreed to adopt the text.

17. The Conference met in plenary again on Friday 30 May at 10.00 am and adopted the text of the Convention on Cluster Munitions as set out in document CCM/77 (attached at Part II of the Final Document).

18. The Conference expressed deep gratitude to the chairpersons and co-chairs of all the conferences that have constituted the Oslo Process, the United Nations, the ICRC and the Cluster Munition Coalition for their efforts that led to the adoption of the Convention on Cluster Munitions.

19. The Conference invited the Secretary-General of the United Nations to prepare authentic Arabic, Chinese and Russian texts of the Convention on Cluster Munitions, as adopted at Dublin on 30 May 2008. Once the authentic Arabic, Chinese and Russian texts are prepared, the Conference agreed that they should be circulated to all States. The original Convention, in the six authentic languages, will be established by the Secretary-General of the United Nations, and the Secretary-General or his

representative shall be invited by the Government of Norway to open the Convention for signature in Oslo on 3 December 2008. All costs related to the preparation of the authentic Arabic, Chinese and Russian texts shall be covered by the Government of Ireland.

20. The Conference invited all States to consider their adherence to the Convention on Cluster Munitions as a matter of priority.

21. The Conference adopted this Procedural Report and decided that the President shall report to the next session of the General Assembly of the United Nations on the outcome of the Conference.

[Annexes to the Final Document omitted.]

CRP/1: Perspectives and Considered Position of the Government of the Federal Democratic Republic of Ethiopia on the Global Process to Conclude a Legally Binding International Treaty aimed at Banning Cluster Munitions

1. The Government of the Federal Democratic Republic of Ethiopia (FDRE) has been keenly following the many encouraging developments witnessed in the course of the past sixteen months since the launch of the Oslo Process, in February 2007, towards the eventual achievement of a comprehensive global ban on Cluster Munitions by means of a legally binding international treaty now being concluded to this effect. The fundamental reasons underlying such a keen interest, certainly shared by others in a similar situation, are closely linked to some well-placed concerns which may be explained by the fact that:

- Ethiopia knows the indiscriminate and unacceptable harmful effects of these destructive weapons from its own tragic experience in recent history;
- These lethal devices are still a commonplace rampantly circulating in huge abundance through both licit and illicit channels in the day-to-day reality of its own turbulent sub-region (the Horn of Africa), which is a damping ground for various external sources that heedlessly supply assorted explosives of this type to belligerent parties to a conflict, including non-state actors and even terrorist organizations;
- Any global endeavour geared towards the conclusion of an international legal instrument aimed at curbing the hitherto uncontrolled use, production, transfer and stockpiling of cluster munitions essentially requires the full and unwavering conviction, support participation and practical commitment of all concerned states (big and small; developed and developing) for want of its unfettered implementation, as desired;
- The particular dimension and significance that such a global endeavour assumes from a regional perspective, in which it requires the indiscriminate allegiance of

all concerned, should be critically considered: it cannot afford to be elected by some while being rejected/ignored by others in as much as they are fated to affect one another through proximate inter-state actions and interactions, hence the imperative to ensure collective responsibility in such a setting, fortiori; and,

• Given empirical experiences drawn from the implementation of other previously adopted international instruments of a similar nature, the question of affording sufficient and reliable treaty-based guarantees to protect and vindicate those state parties strictly amenable to their legally committed obligations in face of possible contraventions by others, be it through individual defiance, outside intervention/instigation or an act of conspiracy threatening the interest/existence of the law-abiding party, remains to be crucial.

2. Each major turn taken since the onset of the whole Oslo Process, particularly the understandings reached, the different perspectives registered, the milestone declarations issued and the draft convention developed through the successive international conferences (held in Lima, Vienna, and Willington, respectively after Oslo) as well as the corresponding regional consultations (convened in Brussels, Belgrade, San José, Livingstone) that deliberated on this very subject have therefore been carefully studied in light of the aforementioned critical concerns, and from the viewpoint of the overall stated policy being pursued by the Government of the FDRE in this particular area. It should also be noted that Ethiopia was one of the 22 countries, 8 of them being African including itself, which attended the Belgrade Conference in October 2007 that brought together those most affected states from various parts of the world to confer around the initiative for the first time.

Thus, taken together, what has been accomplished so far in promoting the ideal objectives of the Oslo Process, along the direction charted out more than a year ago, can be summed up as truly remarkable with scores of considerable positive achievements. This being said, however, there remains still much to be desired in adequately addressing the kinds of concerns reflected above within the framework of the draft convention that has now been brought before the Dublin Diplomatic Conference.

3. As it stands in its current content and form, the draft Convention for the Prohibition of the Use, Production, Transfer and Stockpiling of Cluster Munitions can serve as a bulwark that can be used to accommodate the interests, concerns and apprehensions of all state parties and stakeholders that may be directly or indirectly negotiating this landmark international instrument. For its part, Ethiopia remains anxious to see an improved text of the draft convention for which it is determined to play a constructive role and to make a positive contribution in its present capacity as an observer at the Dublin Diplomatic Conference. The fact that Ethiopia has, for the time being, opted to take an observer seat at this Conference should not, however, cast any doubt on its acceptance of, and commitment to the Oslo Process, which it principally and, to a large extent, substantively supports, as demonstrated by its participation at the Vienna and the Belgrade Conferences.

4. In this regard, one may need to recall Ethiopia's strong track record in scrupulously implementing the purpose, objectives and obligations stipulated in the Convention on Conventional Weapons (CCW) on its own part as a party to the latter. More importantly, it is known that Ethiopia was one of those few the forerunning state parties which advocated, negotiated and endorsed the Ottawa Mine Ban Convention, whose membership has now reached 156 countries, as well as the United Nations resolution and plan of action for the prohibition of illicit trafficking in Small Arms and Light Weapons (SALW), including its regional platform of cooperation based in Nairobi, Kenya.

Nevertheless, due to the long-known turbulence and conflict-ridden nature of the particular sub-region where Ethiopia belongs, and the negative intervention of various external actors that use the region as a dumping ground as well as a conduit for countless assorted mines and munitions, the otherwise desired implementation of these instruments has largely remained in vain for lack of equal commitment, at least in respect of that sub-region. Such a precarious situation leaves some faithfully treaty-bound states unduly disadvantaged and jeopardised by the manipulative acts of others. This is what Ethiopia does not wish to see happening with the new Cluster Munitions Convention, yet again; and that's why it prefers to act cautiously, lest the realization of the new convention's lofty ideals would not be similarly frustrated for lack of shared foresight and precaution.

5. Thus, the Government of the FDRE desires to draw the above-mentioned serious concerns upon the Diplomatic Conference being held in Dublin to negotiate on the substantive and legal details of the draft Convention banning Cluster Munitions. On a more particular note, the Government wishes to state its firm position that:

- As far as countries belonging to a specific region or sub-region (like the Horn of Africa) are concerned, the draft Convention should not be merely confined to the securing of a wider headcount of individual nations membership, and to the ensuring of their commitment on an isolated basis as a party to the Convention. It should rather be made to seek the simultaneous membership, and count on the evenly balanced commitment of all states in that particular region/sub-region by taking them as a group, and addressing them collectively. This would consequently create the necessary legal ground for the enforcement of individual and collective responsibility of all concerned; hence ensure an evenly distributed and scrupulous implementation of the contemplated Convention.
- The draft Convention should, concurrently with the above, contain distinct provisions catering for the effective and timely protection of those treaty-bound states which may find themselves threatened by the acts or omissions of others. Alternatively put, this is to mean that the Convention should be able to offer solid legal guarantees that could be invoked in the event of its possible contravention by a state party, as well as through the manipulative manoeuvrings

of third/external parties, including even non-state actors, as a reliable recourse mechanism readily available for those rightful victims who may have to be adequately redressed/vindicated.

- The United Nations, more pertinently the Security Council - as a vanguard of international peace and security – should, in close collaboration with the relevant regional organizations, be called upon to assume their deserved role and responsibility in ensuring the unfettered implementation of the contemplated Convention by enabling the strict enforcement of its critical provisions, like the ones suggested above, including though the application of Chapter VII measures under the United Nations Charter, so as to properly discipline the wrongdoing party, where deemed necessary.

- In the interest of producing a meticulously prepared international legal instrument agreeable to all, and to responsively address the kinds of concerns outlined above, it remains imperative to ensure that the draft Convention under negotiation is made to be firmly anchored on the findings of an objective, sober and comprehensive assessment of the practical implementation of the Convention on Conventional Weapons (CCW), as well as those treaties and resolutions adopted under the CCW regime, with a particular focus on the major challenges and shortcomings encountered, lest similar problems would not recur to frustrate the new Convention.

Contingent upon the above, Ethiopia would wholeheartedly support the on-going treaty-making process, along with a solemn pledge to ensure the realization of its lofty ideals through global/regional collaboration and the discharging of individual treaty obligations.

CRP/2: Statement by the Government of Iceland upon the adoption of the Convention on Cluster Munitions, Dublin

The Government of Iceland fully supports the Convention on Cluster Munitions adopted in Dublin today and expresses its appreciation for the cooperation which has led to this result.

Although many of the provisions of the Convention reflect the need to reach political compromises during the negotiations, the States concerned, having agreed on the form of a legally binding treaty, have brought the results into the realm of international law. States Parties will thus be guided in their interpretation and application of the Convention by the rules of international law, in particular, International Humanitarian Law and the Law of Treaties, including the overarching principle of good faith performance (1969 Vienna Convention on the Law of Treaties, article 26), with the concomitant rules on State Responsibility, including on attributability (e.g. International Law Commission Articles on State Responsibility, Chapter II).

Specifically, the language in Article 21 on relations between States Parties and States not parties to the Convention was drafted to deal with particular concerns on the operability of the Convention in cases where a State Party engages in military cooperation with a State not a party to the Convention. While the article sets out an appeal to States which are not parties to join the regime of the Convention, it recognizes the need for continuing cooperation in what is hoped will be a short transition period. This intention is captured clearly in paragraph 3 of the Article which should not be read as entitling States Parties to avoid their specific obligations under the Convention for this limited purpose. The decision to reinforce this position by listing some examples in paragraph 4 cannot therefore be interpreted to allow departures in other respects.

ANNEX 9: CONVENTION ON CLUSTER MUNITIONS

Convention on Cluster Munitions

The States Parties to this Convention,

Deeply concerned that civilian populations and individual civilians continue to bear the brunt of armed conflict,

Determined to put an end for all time to the suffering and casualties caused by cluster munitions at the time of their use, when they fail to function as intended or when they are abandoned,

Concerned that cluster munition remnants kill or maim civilians, including women and children, obstruct economic and social development, including through the loss of livelihood, impede post-conflict rehabilitation and reconstruction, delay or prevent the return of refugees and internally displaced persons, can negatively impact on national and international peace-building and humanitarian assistance efforts, and have other severe consequences that can persist for many years after use,

Deeply concerned also at the dangers presented by the large national stockpiles of cluster munitions retained for operational use and *determined* to ensure their rapid destruction,

Believing it necessary to contribute effectively in an efficient, coordinated manner to resolving the challenge of removing cluster munition remnants located throughout the world, and to ensure their destruction,

Determined also to ensure the full realisation of the rights of all cluster munition victims and *recognising* their inherent dignity,

Resolved to do their utmost in providing assistance to cluster munition victims, including medical care, rehabilitation and psychological support, as well as providing for their social and economic inclusion,

Recognising the need to provide age- and gender-sensitive assistance to cluster munition victims and to address the special needs of vulnerable groups,

Bearing in mind the Convention on the Rights of Persons with Disabilities which, *inter alia*, requires that States Parties to that Convention undertake to ensure and promote the full realisation of all human rights and fundamental freedoms of all persons with disabilities without discrimination of any kind on the basis of disability,

Mindful of the need to coordinate adequately efforts undertaken in various fora to address the rights and needs of victims of various types of weapons, and *resolved* to avoid discrimination among victims of various types of weapons,

Reaffirming that in cases not covered by this Convention or by other international agreements, civilians and combatants remain under the protection and authority of the principles of international law, derived from established custom, from the principles of humanity and from the dictates of public conscience,

Resolved also that armed groups distinct from the armed forces of a State shall not, under any circumstances, be permitted to engage in any activity prohibited to a State Party to this Convention,

Welcoming the very broad international support for the international norm prohibiting anti-personnel mines, enshrined in the 1997 Convention on the Prohibition of the Use, Stockpiling, Production and Transfer of Anti-Personnel Mines and on Their Destruction,

Welcoming also the adoption of the Protocol on Explosive Remnants of War, annexed to the Convention on Prohibitions or Restrictions on the Use of Certain Conventional Weapons Which May be Deemed to be Excessively Injurious or to Have Indiscriminate Effects, and its entry into force on 12 November 2006, and *wishing* to enhance the protection of civilians from the effects of cluster munition remnants in post-conflict environments,

Bearing in mind also United Nations Security Council Resolution 1325 on women, peace and security and United Nations Security Council Resolution 1612 on children in armed conflict,

Welcoming further the steps taken nationally, regionally and globally in recent years aimed at prohibiting, restricting or suspending the use, stockpiling, production and transfer of cluster munitions,

Stressing the role of public conscience in furthering the principles of humanity as evidenced by the global call for an end to civilian suffering caused by cluster munitions and *recognising* the efforts to that end undertaken by the United Nations, the International Committee of the Red Cross, the Cluster Munition Coalition and numerous other non-governmental organisations around the world,

Reaffirming the Declaration of the Oslo Conference on Cluster Munitions, by which, *inter alia*, States recognised the grave consequences caused by the use of cluster munitions and committed themselves to conclude by 2008 a legally binding instrument that would prohibit the use, production, transfer and stockpiling of cluster munitions that cause unacceptable harm to civilians, and would establish a framework for cooperation and assistance that ensures adequate provision of care and rehabilitation for victims, clearance of contaminated areas, risk reduction education and destruction of stockpiles,

Emphasising the desirability of attracting the adherence of all States to this Convention, and *determined* to work strenuously towards the promotion of its universalisation and its full implementation,

Basing themselves on the principles and rules of international humanitarian law, in particular the principle that the right of parties to an armed conflict to choose methods or means of warfare is not unlimited, and the rules that the parties to a conflict shall at all times distinguish between the civilian population and combatants and between civilian objects and military objectives and accordingly direct their operations against military objectives only, that in the conduct of military operations constant care shall be taken to spare the civilian population, civilians and civilian objects and that the civilian population and individual civilians enjoy general protection against dangers arising from military operations,

HAVE AGREED as follows:

Article 1

General obligations and scope of application

1. Each State Party undertakes never under any circumstances to:

(a) Use cluster munitions;

(b) Develop, produce, otherwise acquire, stockpile, retain or transfer to anyone, directly or indirectly, cluster munitions;

(c) Assist, encourage or induce anyone to engage in any activity prohibited to a State Party under this Convention.

2. Paragraph 1 of this Article applies, *mutatis mutandis,* to explosive bomblets that are specifically designed to be dispersed or released from dispensers affixed to aircraft.

3. This Convention does not apply to mines.

Article 2

Definitions

For the purposes of this Convention:

1. **'Cluster munition victims'** means all persons who have been killed or suffered physical or psychological injury, economic loss, social marginalisation or substantial impairment of the realisation of their rights caused by the use of cluster munitions. They include those persons directly impacted by cluster munitions as well as their affected families and communities;

2. **'Cluster munition'** means a conventional munition that is designed to disperse or release explosive submunitions each weighing less than 20 kilograms, and includes those explosive submunitions. It does not mean the following:

(a) A munition or submunition designed to dispense flares, smoke, pyrotechnics or chaff; or a munition designed exclusively for an air defence role;

(b) A munition or submunition designed to produce electrical or electronic effects;

(c) A munition that, in order to avoid indiscriminate area effects and the risks posed by unexploded submunitions, has all of the following characteristics:

  (i) Each munition contains fewer than ten explosive submunitions;

  (ii) Each explosive submunition weighs more than four kilograms;

(iii) Each explosive submunition is designed to detect and engage a single target object;

(iv) Each explosive submunition is equipped with an electronic self-destruction mechanism;

(v) Each explosive submunition is equipped with an electronic self-deactivating feature;

3. '**Explosive submunition**' means a conventional munition that in order to perform its task is dispersed or released by a cluster munition and is designed to function by detonating an explosive charge prior to, on or after impact;

4. '**Failed cluster munition**' means a cluster munition that has been fired, dropped, launched, projected or otherwise delivered and which should have dispersed or released its explosive submunitions but failed to do so;

5. '**Unexploded submunition**' means an explosive submunition that has been dispersed or released by, or otherwise separated from, a cluster munition and has failed to explode as intended;

6. '**Abandoned cluster munitions**' means cluster munitions or explosive submunitions that have not been used and that have been left behind or dumped, and that are no longer under the control of the party that left them behind or dumped them. They may or may not have been prepared for use;

7. '**Cluster munition remnants**' means failed cluster munitions, abandoned cluster munitions, unexploded submunitions and unexploded bomblets;

8. '**Transfer**' involves, in addition to the physical movement of cluster munitions into or from national territory, the transfer of title to and control over cluster munitions, but does not involve the transfer of territory containing cluster munition remnants;

9. '**Self-destruction mechanism**' means an incorporated automatically-functioning mechanism which is in addition to the primary initiating mechanism of the munition and which secures the destruction of the munition into which it is incorporated;

10. '**Self-deactivating**' means automatically rendering a munition inoperable by means of the irreversible exhaustion of a component, for example a battery, that is essential to the operation of the munition;

11. '**Cluster munition contaminated area**' means an area known or suspected to contain cluster munition remnants;

12. '**Mine**' means a munition designed to be placed under, on or near the ground or other surface area and to be exploded by the presence, proximity or contact of a person or a vehicle;

13. '**Explosive bomblet**' means a conventional munition, weighing less than 20 kilograms, which is not self-propelled and which, in order to perform its task, is dispersed or released by a dispenser, and is designed to function by detonating an explosive charge prior to, on or after impact;

14. 'Dispenser' means a container that is designed to disperse or release explosive bomblets and which is affixed to an aircraft at the time of dispersal or release;

15. 'Unexploded bomblet' means an explosive bomblet that has been dispersed, released or otherwise separated from a dispenser and has failed to explode as intended.

Article 3

Storage and stockpile destruction

1. Each State Party shall, in accordance with national regulations, separate all cluster munitions under its jurisdiction and control from munitions retained for operational use and mark them for the purpose of destruction.

2. Each State Party undertakes to destroy or ensure the destruction of all cluster munitions referred to in paragraph 1 of this Article as soon as possible but not later than eight years after the entry into force of this Convention for that State Party. Each State Party undertakes to ensure that destruction methods comply with applicable international standards for protecting public health and the environment.

3. If a State Party believes that it will be unable to destroy or ensure the destruction of all cluster munitions referred to in paragraph 1 of this Article within eight years of entry into force of this Convention for that State Party it may submit a request to a Meeting of States Parties or a Review Conference for an extension of the deadline for completing the destruction of such cluster munitions by a period of up to four years. A State Party may, in exceptional circumstances, request additional extensions of up to four years. The requested extensions shall not exceed the number of years strictly necessary for that State Party to complete its obligations under paragraph 2 of this Article.

4. Each request for an extension shall set out:

(a) The duration of the proposed extension;

(b) A detailed explanation of the proposed extension, including the financial and technical means available to or required by the State Party for the destruction of all cluster munitions referred to in paragraph 1 of this Article and, where applicable, the exceptional circumstances justifying it;

(c) A plan for how and when stockpile destruction will be completed;

(d) The quantity and type of cluster munitions and explosive submunitions held at the entry into force of this Convention for that State Party and any additional cluster munitions or explosive submunitions discovered after such entry into force;

(e) The quantity and type of cluster munitions and explosive submunitions destroyed during the period referred to in paragraph 2 of this Article; and

(f) The quantity and type of cluster munitions and explosive submunitions remaining to be destroyed during the proposed extension and the annual destruction rate expected to be achieved.

5. The Meeting of States Parties or the Review Conference shall, taking into consideration the factors referred to in paragraph 4 of this Article, assess the request and decide by a majority of votes of States Parties present and voting whether to grant the request for an extension. The States Parties may decide to grant a shorter extension than that requested and may propose benchmarks for the extension, as appropriate. A request for an extension shall be submitted a minimum of nine months prior to the Meeting of States Parties or the Review Conference at which it is to be considered.

6. Notwithstanding the provisions of Article 1 of this Convention, the retention or acquisition of a limited number of cluster munitions and explosive submunitions for the development of and training in cluster munition and explosive submunition detection, clearance or destruction techniques, or for the development of cluster munition counter-measures, is permitted. The amount of explosive submunitions retained or acquired shall not exceed the minimum number absolutely necessary for these purposes.

7. Notwithstanding the provisions of Article 1 of this Convention, the transfer of cluster munitions to another State Party for the purpose of destruction, as well as for the purposes described in paragraph 6 of this Article, is permitted.

8. States Parties retaining, acquiring or transferring cluster munitions or explosive submunitions for the purposes described in paragraphs 6 and 7 of this Article shall submit a detailed report on the planned and actual use of these cluster munitions and explosive submunitions and their type, quantity and lot numbers. If cluster munitions or explosive submunitions are transferred to another State Party for these purposes, the report shall include reference to the receiving party. Such a report shall be prepared for each year during which a State Party retained, acquired or transferred cluster munitions or explosive submunitions and shall be submitted to the Secretary-General of the United Nations no later than 30 April of the following year.

Article 4

Clearance and destruction of cluster munition remnants and risk reduction education

1. Each State Party undertakes to clear and destroy, or ensure the clearance and destruction of, cluster munition remnants located in cluster munition contaminated areas under its jurisdiction or control, as follows:

(a) Where cluster munition remnants are located in areas under its jurisdiction or control at the date of entry into force of this Convention for that State Party, such clearance and destruction shall be completed as soon as possible but not later than ten years from that date;

(b) Where, after entry into force of this Convention for that State Party, cluster munitions have become cluster munition remnants located in areas under its jurisdiction or control, such clearance and destruction must be completed as soon as possible but not later than ten years after the end of the active hostilities during which such cluster munitions became cluster munition remnants; and

(c) Upon fulfilling either of its obligations set out in sub-paragraphs (a) and (b) of this paragraph, that State Party shall make a declaration of compliance to the next Meeting of States Parties.

2. In fulfilling its obligations under paragraph 1 of this Article, each State Party shall take the following measures as soon as possible, taking into consideration the provisions of Article 6 of this Convention regarding international cooperation and assistance:

(a) Survey, assess and record the threat posed by cluster munition remnants, making every effort to identify all cluster munition contaminated areas under its jurisdiction or control;

(b) Assess and prioritise needs in terms of marking, protection of civilians, clearance and destruction, and take steps to mobilise resources and develop a national plan to carry out these activities, building, where appropriate, upon existing structures, experiences and methodologies;

(c) Take all feasible steps to ensure that all cluster munition contaminated areas under its jurisdiction or control are perimeter-marked, monitored and protected by fencing or other means to ensure the effective exclusion of civilians. Warning signs based on methods of marking readily recognisable by the affected community should be utilised in the marking of suspected hazardous areas. Signs and other hazardous area boundary markers should, as far as possible, be visible, legible, durable and resistant to environmental effects and should clearly identify which side of the marked boundary is considered to be within the cluster munition contaminated areas and which side is considered to be safe;

(d) Clear and destroy all cluster munition remnants located in areas under its jurisdiction or control; and

(e) Conduct risk reduction education to ensure awareness among civilians living in or around cluster munition contaminated areas of the risks posed by such remnants.

3. In conducting the activities referred to in paragraph 2 of this Article, each State Party shall take into account international standards, including the International Mine Action Standards (IMAS).

4. This paragraph shall apply in cases in which cluster munitions have been used or abandoned by one State Party prior to entry into force of this Convention for that State Party and have become cluster munition remnants that are located in areas under the jurisdiction or control of another State Party at the time of entry into force of this Convention for the latter.

(a) In such cases, upon entry into force of this Convention for both States Parties, the former State Party is strongly encouraged to provide, *inter alia*, technical, financial, material or human resources assistance to the latter State Party, either bilaterally or through a mutually agreed third party, including through the United Nations system or other relevant organisations, to facilitate the marking, clearance and destruction of such cluster munition remnants.

(b) Such assistance shall include, where available, information on types and quantities of the cluster munitions used, precise locations of cluster munition strikes and areas in which cluster munition remnants are known to be located.

5. If a State Party believes that it will be unable to clear and destroy or ensure the clearance and destruction of all cluster munition remnants referred to in paragraph 1 of this Article within ten years of the entry into force of this Convention for that State Party, it may submit a request to a Meeting of States Parties or a Review Conference for an extension of the deadline for completing the clearance and destruction of such cluster munition remnants by a period of up to five years. The requested extension shall not exceed the number of years strictly necessary for that State Party to complete its obligations under paragraph 1 of this Article.

6. A request for an extension shall be submitted to a Meeting of States Parties or a Review Conference prior to the expiry of the time period referred to in paragraph 1 of this Article for that State Party. Each request shall be submitted a minimum of nine months prior to the Meeting of States Parties or Review Conference at which it is to be considered. Each request shall set out:

(a) The duration of the proposed extension;

(b) A detailed explanation of the reasons for the proposed extension, including the financial and technical means available to and required by the State Party for the clearance and destruction of all cluster munition remnants during the proposed extension;

(c) The preparation of future work and the status of work already conducted under national clearance and demining programmes during the initial ten year period referred to in paragraph 1 of this Article and any subsequent extensions;

(d) The total area containing cluster munition remnants at the time of entry into force of this Convention for that State Party and any additional areas containing cluster munition remnants discovered after such entry into force;

(e) The total area containing cluster munition remnants cleared since entry into force of this Convention;

(f) The total area containing cluster munition remnants remaining to be cleared during the proposed extension;

(g) The circumstances that have impeded the ability of the State Party to destroy all cluster munition remnants located in areas under its jurisdiction or control during the initial ten year period referred to in paragraph 1 of this Article, and those that may impede this ability during the proposed extension;

(h) The humanitarian, social, economic and environmental implications of the proposed extension; and

(i) Any other information relevant to the request for the proposed extension.

7. The Meeting of States Parties or the Review Conference shall, taking into consideration the factors referred to in paragraph 6 of this Article, including, *inter alia,* the quantities of cluster munition remnants reported, assess the request and decide by a

majority of votes of States Parties present and voting whether to grant the request for an extension. The States Parties may decide to grant a shorter extension than that requested and may propose benchmarks for the extension, as appropriate.

8. Such an extension may be renewed by a period of up to five years upon the submission of a new request, in accordance with paragraphs 5, 6 and 7 of this Article. In requesting a further extension a State Party shall submit relevant additional information on what has been undertaken during the previous extension granted pursuant to this Article.

Article 5

Victim assistance

1. Each State Party with respect to cluster munition victims in areas under its jurisdiction or control shall, in accordance with applicable international humanitarian and human rights law, adequately provide age- and gender-sensitive assistance, including medical care, rehabilitation and psychological support, as well as provide for their social and economic inclusion. Each State Party shall make every effort to collect reliable relevant data with respect to cluster munition victims.

2. In fulfilling its obligations under paragraph 1 of this Article each State Party shall:

(a) Assess the needs of cluster munition victims;

(b) Develop, implement and enforce any necessary national laws and policies;

(c) Develop a national plan and budget, including timeframes to carry out these activities, with a view to incorporating them within the existing national disability, development and human rights frameworks and mechanisms, while respecting the specific role and contribution of relevant actors;

(d) Take steps to mobilise national and international resources;

(e) Not discriminate against or among cluster munition victims, or between cluster munition victims and those who have suffered injuries or disabilities from other causes; differences in treatment should be based only on medical, rehabilitative, psychological or socio-economic needs;

(f) Closely consult with and actively involve cluster munition victims and their representative organisations;

(g) Designate a focal point within the government for coordination of matters relating to the implementation of this Article; and

(h) Strive to incorporate relevant guidelines and good practices including in the areas of medical care, rehabilitation and psychological support, as well as social and economic inclusion.

Article 6

International cooperation and assistance

1. In fulfilling its obligations under this Convention each State Party has the right to seek and receive assistance.

2. Each State Party in a position to do so shall provide technical, material and financial assistance to States Parties affected by cluster munitions, aimed at the implementation of the obligations of this Convention. Such assistance may be provided, *inter alia*, through the United Nations system, international, regional or national organisations or institutions, non-governmental organisations or institutions, or on a bilateral basis.

3. Each State Party undertakes to facilitate and shall have the right to participate in the fullest possible exchange of equipment and scientific and technological information concerning the implementation of this Convention. The States Parties shall not impose undue restrictions on the provision and receipt of clearance and other such equipment and related technological information for humanitarian purposes.

4. In addition to any obligations it may have pursuant to paragraph 4 of Article 4 of this Convention, each State Party in a position to do so shall provide assistance for clearance and destruction of cluster munition remnants and information concerning various means and technologies related to clearance of cluster munitions, as well as lists of experts, expert agencies or national points of contact on clearance and destruction of cluster munition remnants and related activities.

5. Each State Party in a position to do so shall provide assistance for the destruction of stockpiled cluster munitions, and shall also provide assistance to identify, assess and prioritise needs and practical measures in terms of marking, risk reduction education, protection of civilians and clearance and destruction as provided in Article 4 of this Convention.

6. Where, after entry into force of this Convention, cluster munitions have become cluster munition remnants located in areas under the jurisdiction or control of a State Party, each State Party in a position to do so shall urgently provide emergency assistance to the affected State Party.

7. Each State Party in a position to do so shall provide assistance for the implementation of the obligations referred to in Article 5 of this Convention to adequately provide age- and gender-sensitive assistance, including medical care, rehabilitation and psychological support, as well as provide for social and economic inclusion of cluster munition victims. Such assistance may be provided, *inter alia*, through the United Nations system, international, regional or national organisations or institutions, the International Committee of the Red Cross, national Red Cross and Red Crescent Societies and their International Federation, non-governmental organisations or on a bilateral basis.

8. Each State Party in a position to do so shall provide assistance to contribute to the economic and social recovery needed as a result of cluster munition use in affected States Parties.

9. Each State Party in a position to do so may contribute to relevant trust funds in order to facilitate the provision of assistance under this Article.

10. Each State Party that seeks and receives assistance shall take all appropriate measures in order to facilitate the timely and effective implementation of this Convention, including facilitation of the entry and exit of personnel, materiel and equipment, in a manner consistent with national laws and regulations, taking into consideration international best practices.

11. Each State Party may, with the purpose of developing a national action plan, request the United Nations system, regional organisations, other States Parties or other competent intergovernmental or non-governmental institutions to assist its authorities to determine, *inter alia*:

(a) The nature and extent of cluster munition remnants located in areas under its jurisdiction or control;

(b) The financial, technological and human resources required for the implementation of the plan;

(c) The time estimated as necessary to clear and destroy all cluster munition remnants located in areas under its jurisdiction or control;

(d) Risk reduction education programmes and awareness activities to reduce the incidence of injuries or deaths caused by cluster munition remnants;

(e) Assistance to cluster munition victims; and

(f) The coordination relationship between the government of the State Party concerned and the relevant governmental, intergovernmental or non-governmental entities that will work in the implementation of the plan.

12. States Parties giving and receiving assistance under the provisions of this Article shall cooperate with a view to ensuring the full and prompt implementation of agreed assistance programmes.

Article 7

Transparency measures

1. Each State Party shall report to the Secretary-General of the United Nations as soon as practicable, and in any event not later than 180 days after the entry into force of this Convention for that State Party, on:

(a) The national implementation measures referred to in Article 9 of this Convention;

(b) The total of all cluster munitions, including explosive submunitions, referred to in paragraph 1 of Article 3 of this Convention, to include a breakdown of their type, quantity and, if possible, lot numbers of each type;

(c) The technical characteristics of each type of cluster munition produced by that State Party prior to entry into force of this Convention for it, to the extent known, and those currently owned or possessed by it, giving, where reasonably possible, such categories of information as may facilitate identification and clearance of cluster munitions; at a minimum, this information shall include the dimensions, fusing, explosive content, metallic content, colour photographs and other information that may facilitate the clearance of cluster munition remnants;

(d) The status and progress of programmes for the conversion or decommissioning of production facilities for cluster munitions;

(e) The status and progress of programmes for the destruction, in accordance with Article 3 of this Convention, of cluster munitions, including explosive submunitions, with details of the methods that will be used in destruction, the location of all destruction sites and the applicable safety and environmental standards to be observed;

(f) The types and quantities of cluster munitions, including explosive submunitions, destroyed in accordance with Article 3 of this Convention, including details of the methods of destruction used, the location of the destruction sites and the applicable safety and environmental standards observed;

(g) Stockpiles of cluster munitions, including explosive submunitions, discovered after reported completion of the programme referred to in sub-paragraph (e) of this paragraph, and plans for their destruction in accordance with Article 3 of this Convention;

(h) To the extent possible, the size and location of all cluster munition contaminated areas under its jurisdiction or control, to include as much detail as possible regarding the type and quantity of each type of cluster munition remnant in each such area and when they were used;

(i) The status and progress of programmes for the clearance and destruction of all types and quantities of cluster munition remnants cleared and destroyed in accordance with Article 4 of this Convention, to include the size and location of the cluster munition contaminated area cleared and a breakdown of the quantity of each type of cluster munition remnant cleared and destroyed;

(j) The measures taken to provide risk reduction education and, in particular, an immediate and effective warning to civilians living in cluster munition contaminated areas under its jurisdiction or control;

(k) The status and progress of implementation of its obligations under Article 5 of this Convention to adequately provide age- and gender-sensitive assistance, including medical care, rehabilitation and psychological support, as well as provide for social and economic inclusion of cluster munition victims and to collect reliable relevant data with respect to cluster munition victims;

(l) The name and contact details of the institutions mandated to provide information and to carry out the measures described in this paragraph;

(m) The amount of national resources, including financial, material or in kind, allocated to the implementation of Articles 3, 4 and 5 of this Convention; and

(n) The amounts, types and destinations of international cooperation and assistance provided under Article 6 of this Convention.

2. The information provided in accordance with paragraph 1 of this Article shall be updated by the States Parties annually, covering the previous calendar year, and reported to the Secretary-General of the United Nations not later than 30 April of each year.

3. The Secretary-General of the United Nations shall transmit all such reports received to the States Parties.

Article 8

Facilitation and clarification of compliance

1. The States Parties agree to consult and cooperate with each other regarding the implementation of the provisions of this Convention and to work together in a spirit of cooperation to facilitate compliance by States Parties with their obligations under this Convention.

2. If one or more States Parties wish to clarify and seek to resolve questions relating to a matter of compliance with the provisions of this Convention by another State Party, it may submit, through the Secretary-General of the United Nations, a Request for Clarification of that matter to that State Party. Such a request shall be accompanied by all appropriate information. Each State Party shall refrain from unfounded Requests for Clarification, care being taken to avoid abuse. A State Party that receives a Request for Clarification shall provide, through the Secretary-General of the United Nations, within 28 days to the requesting State Party all information that would assist in clarifying the matter.

3. If the requesting State Party does not receive a response through the Secretary-General of the United Nations within that time period, or deems the response to the Request for Clarification to be unsatisfactory, it may submit the matter through the Secretary-General of the United Nations to the next Meeting of States Parties. The Secretary-General of the United Nations shall transmit the submission, accompanied by all appropriate information pertaining to the Request for Clarification, to all States Parties. All such information shall be presented to the requested State Party which shall have the right to respond.

4. Pending the convening of any Meeting of States Parties, any of the States Parties concerned may request the Secretary-General of the United Nations to exercise his or her good offices to facilitate the clarification requested.

5. Where a matter has been submitted to it pursuant to paragraph 3 of this Article, the Meeting of States Parties shall first determine whether to consider that matter further, taking into account all information submitted by the States Parties concerned. If it does so determine, the Meeting of States Parties may suggest to the States Parties concerned ways and means further to clarify or resolve the matter under consideration, including the initiation of appropriate procedures in conformity with international law. In circumstances where the issue at hand is determined to be due to circumstances beyond the control of the requested State Party, the Meeting of States Parties may recommend appropriate measures, including the use of cooperative measures referred to in Article 6 of this Convention.

6. In addition to the procedures provided for in paragraphs 2 to 5 of this Article, the Meeting of States Parties may decide to adopt such other general procedures or

specific mechanisms for clarification of compliance, including facts, and resolution of instances of non-compliance with the provisions of this Convention as it deems appropriate.

Article 9
National implementation measures

Each State Party shall take all appropriate legal, administrative and other measures to implement this Convention, including the imposition of penal sanctions to prevent and suppress any activity prohibited to a State Party under this Convention undertaken by persons or on territory under its jurisdiction or control.

Article 10
Settlement of disputes

1. When a dispute arises between two or more States Parties relating to the interpretation or application of this Convention, the States Parties concerned shall consult together with a view to the expeditious settlement of the dispute by negotiation or by other peaceful means of their choice, including recourse to the Meeting of States Parties and referral to the International Court of Justice in conformity with the Statute of the Court.

2. The Meeting of States Parties may contribute to the settlement of the dispute by whatever means it deems appropriate, including offering its good offices, calling upon the States Parties concerned to start the settlement procedure of their choice and recommending a time-limit for any agreed procedure.

Article 11
Meetings of States Parties

1. The States Parties shall meet regularly in order to consider and, where necessary, take decisions in respect of any matter with regard to the application or implementation of this Convention, including:

(a) The operation and status of this Convention;
(b) Matters arising from the reports submitted under the provisions of this Convention;
(c) International cooperation and assistance in accordance with Article 6 of this Convention;
(d) The development of technologies to clear cluster munition remnants;
(e) Submissions of States Parties under Articles 8 and 10 of this Convention; and
(f) Submissions of States Parties as provided for in Articles 3 and 4 of this Convention.

2. The first Meeting of States Parties shall be convened by the Secretary-General of the United Nations within one year of entry into force of this Convention. The subsequent meetings shall be convened by the Secretary-General of the United Nations annually until the first Review Conference.

3. States not party to this Convention, as well as the United Nations, other relevant international organisations or institutions, regional organisations, the International Committee of the Red Cross, the International Federation of Red Cross and Red Crescent Societies and relevant non-governmental organisations may be invited to attend these meetings as observers in accordance with the agreed rules of procedure.

Article 12

Review Conferences

1. A Review Conference shall be convened by the Secretary-General of the United Nations five years after the entry into force of this Convention. Further Review Conferences shall be convened by the Secretary-General of the United Nations if so requested by one or more States Parties, provided that the interval between Review Conferences shall in no case be less than five years. All States Parties to this Convention shall be invited to each Review Conference.

2. The purpose of the Review Conference shall be:

(a) To review the operation and status of this Convention;

(b) To consider the need for and the interval between further Meetings of States Parties referred to in paragraph 2 of Article 11 of this Convention; and

(c) To take decisions on submissions of States Parties as provided for in Articles 3 and 4 of this Convention.

3. States not party to this Convention, as well as the United Nations, other relevant international organisations or institutions, regional organisations, the International Committee of the Red Cross, the International Federation of Red Cross and Red Crescent Societies and relevant non-governmental organisations may be invited to attend each Review Conference as observers in accordance with the agreed rules of procedure.

Article 13

Amendments

1. At any time after its entry into force any State Party may propose amendments to this Convention. Any proposal for an amendment shall be communicated to the Secretary-General of the United Nations, who shall circulate it to all States Parties and shall seek their views on whether an Amendment Conference should be convened to consider the proposal. If a majority of the States Parties notify the Secretary-General of the United Nations no later than 90 days after its circulation that they support further consideration of the proposal, the Secretary-General of the United Nations shall convene an Amendment Conference to which all States Parties shall be invited.

2. States not party to this Convention, as well as the United Nations, other relevant international organisations or institutions, regional organisations, the International Committee of the Red Cross, the International Federation of Red Cross and Red Crescent Societies and relevant non-governmental organisations may be invited to

attend each Amendment Conference as observers in accordance with the agreed rules of procedure.

3. The Amendment Conference shall be held immediately following a Meeting of States Parties or a Review Conference unless a majority of the States Parties request that it be held earlier.

4. Any amendment to this Convention shall be adopted by a majority of two-thirds of the States Parties present and voting at the Amendment Conference. The Depositary shall communicate any amendment so adopted to all States.

5. An amendment to this Convention shall enter into force for States Parties that have accepted the amendment on the date of deposit of acceptances by a majority of the States which were Parties at the date of adoption of the amendment. Thereafter it shall enter into force for any remaining State Party on the date of deposit of its instrument of acceptance.

Article 14

Costs and administrative tasks

1. The costs of the Meetings of States Parties, the Review Conferences and the Amendment Conferences shall be borne by the States Parties and States not party to this Convention participating therein, in accordance with the United Nations scale of assessment adjusted appropriately.

2. The costs incurred by the Secretary-General of the United Nations under Articles 7 and 8 of this Convention shall be borne by the States Parties in accordance with the United Nations scale of assessment adjusted appropriately.

3. The performance by the Secretary-General of the United Nations of administrative tasks assigned to him or her under this Convention is subject to an appropriate United Nations mandate.

Article 15

Signature

This Convention, done at Dublin on 30 May 2008, shall be open for signature at Oslo by all States on 3 December 2008 and thereafter at United Nations Headquarters in New York until its entry into force.

Article 16

Ratification, acceptance, approval or accession

1. This Convention is subject to ratification, acceptance or approval by the Signatories.

2. It shall be open for accession by any State that has not signed the Convention.

3. The instruments of ratification, acceptance, approval or accession shall be deposited with the Depositary.

Article 17

Entry into force

1. This Convention shall enter into force on the first day of the sixth month after the month in which the thirtieth instrument of ratification, acceptance, approval or accession has been deposited.

2. For any State that deposits its instrument of ratification, acceptance, approval or accession after the date of the deposit of the thirtieth instrument of ratification, acceptance, approval or accession, this Convention shall enter into force on the first day of the sixth month after the date on which that State has deposited its instrument of ratification, acceptance, approval or accession.

Article 18

Provisional application

Any State may, at the time of its ratification, acceptance, approval or accession, declare that it will apply provisionally Article 1 of this Convention pending its entry into force for that State.

Article 19

Reservations

The Articles of this Convention shall not be subject to reservations.

Article 20

Duration and withdrawal

1. This Convention shall be of unlimited duration.

2. Each State Party shall, in exercising its national sovereignty, have the right to withdraw from this Convention. It shall give notice of such withdrawal to all other States Parties, to the Depositary and to the United Nations Security Council. Such instrument of withdrawal shall include a full explanation of the reasons motivating withdrawal.

3. Such withdrawal shall only take effect six months after the receipt of the instrument of withdrawal by the Depositary. If, however, on the expiry of that six-month period, the withdrawing State Party is engaged in an armed conflict, the withdrawal shall not take effect before the end of the armed conflict.

Article 21

Relations with States not party to this Convention

1. Each State Party shall encourage States not party to this Convention to ratify, accept, approve or accede to this Convention, with the goal of attracting the adherence of all States to this Convention.

2. Each State Party shall notify the governments of all States not party to this Convention, referred to in paragraph 3 of this Article, of its obligations under this

Convention, shall promote the norms it establishes and shall make its best efforts to discourage States not party to this Convention from using cluster munitions.

3. Notwithstanding the provisions of Article 1 of this Convention and in accordance with international law, States Parties, their military personnel or nationals, may engage in military cooperation and operations with States not party to this Convention that might engage in activities prohibited to a State Party.

4. Nothing in paragraph 3 of this Article shall authorise a State Party:

(a) To develop, produce or otherwise acquire cluster munitions;
(b) To itself stockpile or transfer cluster munitions;
(c) To itself use cluster munitions; or
(d) To expressly request the use of cluster munitions in cases where the choice of munitions used is within its exclusive control.

Article 22

Depositary

The Secretary-General of the United Nations is hereby designated as the Depositary of this Convention.

Article 23

Authentic texts

The Arabic, Chinese, English, French, Russian and Spanish texts of this Convention shall be equally authentic.

ANNEX 10: STATES PARTIES AND SIGNATORY STATES OF THE CONVENTION ON CLUSTER MUNITIONS[1]

STATES PARTIES[2]

Albania	Malta
Austria	Mexico
Belgium	Moldova
Burkina Faso	Montenegro
Burundi	New Zealand
Croatia	Nicaragua
Denmark	Niger
France	Norway
Germany	San Marino
Holy See	Sierra Leone
Ireland	Slovenia
Japan	Spain
Lao People's Democratic Republic	The former Yugoslav Republic of Macedonia
Luxembourg	Uruguay
Malawi	Zambia

SIGNATORY STATES

Afghanistan, Angola, Australia, Benin, Bolivia, Bosnia and Herzegovina, Botswana, Bulgaria, Cameroon, Canada, Cape Verde, Central African Republic, Chad, Chile, Colombia, Comoros, Republic of Congo, Cook Islands, Costa Rica, Côte d'Ivoire, Cyprus, Czech Republic, the Democratic Republic of Congo, the Dominican Republic, Ecuador, El Salvador, Fiji, Gambia, Ghana, Guatemala, Guinea, Guinea-Bissau,

---

[1] As of 1 August 2010.

[2] Samoa ratified on 28 April 2010, becoming a State Party on 1 October 2010, while the United Kingdom ratified on 4 May 2010, Ecuador ratified on 11 May 2010, the Seychelles ratified on 20 May 2010 and Fiji and Lesotho ratified on 28 May 2010, all six becoming States Parties on 1 November 2010.

Haiti, Honduras, Hungary, Iceland, Indonesia, Iraq, Italy, Jamaica, Kenya, Lebanon, Lesotho, Liberia, Liechtenstein, Lithuania, Madagascar, Mauritania, Mali, Monaco, Mozambique, Namibia, Nauru, The Netherlands, Nigeria, Palau, Panama, Paraguay, Peru, Philippines, Portugal, Rwanda, Saint Vincent and the Grenadines, Samoa, Sao Tome and Principe, Senegal, the Seychelles, Somalia, South Africa, Sweden, Switzerland, Tanzania, Togo, Tunisia, Uganda, the United Kingdom of Great Britain and Northern Ireland.

ANNEX 11: DECLARATIONS UPON SIGNATURE OR RATIFICATION OF THE CONVENTION ON CLUSTER MUNITIONS

BELGIUM

Declaration made upon signature:

'This signature is equally binding the region of Walloon, the Flemish region and the region of the capital of Brussels.'

DENMARK

Upon its ratification to the Convention, the Government of Denmark notified the Secretary-General of the following:

'Until further notice, the Convention shall not apply to the Faroe Islands.'

HOLY SEE

Declarations made upon ratification:

'In ratifying the Convention on Cluster Munitions the Holy See desires to encourage the entire International Community to be resolute in promoting effective disarmament and arms control negotiations and in strengthening international humanitarian law by reaffirming the preeminent and inherent value of human dignity, the centrality of the human person, and the "elementary considerations of humanity", all of which are elements that constitute the basis of international humanitarian law.

The Holy See considers the Convention on Cluster Munitions an important step in the protection of civilians during and after conflicts from the indiscriminate effects of this inhumane type of weapons. The new Convention is a remarkable achievement for multilateralism in disarmament, based on constructive cooperation between governmental and non governmental actors, and on the link between humanitarian law and human rights.

The Holy See would like to underline the following points:

1. The Convention adopts a broad definition of cluster munitions victims, including persons directly impacted, their families and communities, and requests States Parties to provide them with assistance. The Holy See is mindful that this broader assistance must be respectful of the right to life from the moment of conception to natural death, in order to conform to the fundamental principles of respect for human life, and ensure the recognition of human dignity. Preserving life and creating

the conditions of an existence worthy of the human person should be at the core of humanitarian assistance.

2. States Parties, in designating a focal point within government (art.5.2(g)), will have to guarantee that the coordination of national disability, development and human rights frameworks and mechanisms ensures effective assistance to all victims. In this regard, the Holy See also wishes to restate its understanding and interpretation of article 5.2 (c), where the Convention recognizes "the specific role and contribution of relevant actors": when a State Party develops a national plan and budget to carry out assistance activities according to the Convention "with a view to incorporating them within the existing national disability, development and human rights frameworks and mechanisms", it shall guarantee the pluralism that is inherent in any democratic society and the diversity of relevant non governmental actors. This respectful form of coordination of the various activities of governmental and non governmental actors is in line with the Preamble (PP 10) (see also Dublin Diplomatic Conference for the adoption of a Convention on Cluster Munitions, Summary Record, CCM/SR/4, 18 June 2008).

3. The Holy See, by ratifying the Convention on Cluster Munitions, understands the term "gender", used in the Preamble (PP 8) and in articles 5.1, 6.7 and 7.1 (k) of the Convention, in accordance with its Interpretative Statement to the Beijing Declaration and Platform for Action, made in Beijing at the Fourth World Conference on Women.

4. Article 4.4 highlights moral responsibility in cases where cluster munitions have been used or abandoned and have became cluster munitions remnants prior to the entry into force of the Convention. State responsibility should be given effective expression in the area of cooperation and assistance.

5. In relation to Article 21, joint military operations do not imply, in any way, a suspension of the obligations under the Convention. "States Parties, their military personnel or nationals" shall never engage in activities prohibited by the Convention. On the contrary, joint military operations should be opportunities for States Parties to promote the standards introduced by the new instrument with the objective to protect civilians during and after armed conflicts.

The Holy See recognizes the spirit of partnership between States, United Nations bodies, International Organizations, the international Committee of the Red Cross and civil society which, through collective action, has sustained the process which has led to the adoption of the Convention. The Holy See considers the implementation of the Convention as a legal and humanitarian challenge for the near future. An effective implementation should be based on constructive cooperation of all governmental and non governmental actors and should reinforce the link between disarmament and development. This can be done by directing human and material resources towards development, justice and peace, which are the most effective means to promote inter-national security and a peaceful international order.

In conformity with its proper nature, with its particular mission, and with the particular condition of Vatican City State, and according to its international practice, the Holy See, by means of the solemn act of ratification, expresses its pledge to work towards a peaceful international order in which human dignity and fundamental rights are fully respected.'

NEW ZEALAND

Upon its ratification to the Convention, the Government of New Zealand notified the Secretary-General of the following:

'... consistent with the constitutional status of Tokelau and taking into account the commitment of the Government of New Zealand to the development of self-government for Tokelau through an act of self-determination under the Charter of the United Nations, this ratification shall not extend to Tokelau unless and until a Declaration to this effect is lodged by the Government of New Zealand with the Depositary on the basis of appropriate consultation with that territory...'

NORWAY

In its notification of provisional application, Norway notified the Secretary-General that:

'Pursuant to Article 18 of the Convention, the Government of the Kingdom of Norway declares that it will apply provisionally Article I of this Convention pending its entry into force for Norway.'

Index